"I did not think it was possible for David Lewis to surpass what he had accomplished in the first volume of his Du Bois biography, but he has. . . . He confirms the view of many of us who believe that he is the finest American historian plying his craft today."
—John Hope Franklin,
James B. Duke Professor of History Emeritus at Duke University

"A masterpiece of the biographer's craft. With this volume, David Levering Lewis has brought to magnificent completion his definitive biography of W. E. B. Du Bois. Lewis writes with consistent empathy, balance, and grace about one of the twentieth century's most complicated and controversial figures. A must-read for anyone seeking to understand the tortured history of race relations in the modern world."
—David M. Kennedy,
Donald J. McLachlan Professor of History at Stanford University and author of
Freedom from Fear: The American People in Depression and War, 1929–1945,
winner of the 1999 Pulitzer Prize

"His superb command of the complexity of his subject and time make this a major work of American biography and history . . . a must-read."
—*Publishers Weekly,* starred review

"Monumental . . . A joy to read. A work of keen scholarship that will appeal to the general reader responsive to graceful, lucid prose."
—John Patrick Diggins, *Los Angeles Times*

"A stirring yet subtle portrait . . . brings Du Bois to life with startling detail and judicious frankness."
—Jack E. White, *Time*

"Succeeds not only because of its meticulous scholarship but because unlike the average American history book, it places African Amer important events of the twentieth century."

"[Du Bois's] life was driven by a hunger for justice, and with clarity and passion."

"Lewis writes fluently and has the ability to make historica vibrant immediacy."
—Lorenzo Thoma

"Resonates with beautiful imagery, graceful prose and rive
—Loren Schweninger, *Raleig*

W.E.B.
DU BOIS

DAVID LEVERING LEWIS

W.E.B.
DU BOIS

THE FIGHT FOR EQUALITY

AND THE

AMERICAN CENTURY

· 1919-1963 ·

A JOHN MACRAE / OWL BOOK

HENRY HOLT AND COMPANY   ·   NEW YORK

Henry Holt and Company, LLC
Publishers since 1866
115 West 18th Street
New York, New York 10011

Henry Holt® is a registered trademark of
Henry Holt and Company, LLC.

Library of Congress Cataloging-in-Publication Data

Lewis, David L.
    W.E.B. Du Bois—biography of a race,
    1868–1919 / David Levering Lewis.—1st ed.
        p.   cm.
    Includes bibliographical references and index.
    ISBN 0-8050-6813-9
        1. Du Bois, W.E.B. (William Edward Burghardt), 1868–1963.
    2. Afro-Americans—Biography.   3. Afro-Americans—Civil
    rights.   4. Afro-Americans—History—1877–1964.   5. Civil
    rights movements—United States—History.   I. Title.
E185.97.D73L48   1993   93-16617
973'.0496073'0092—dc20   CIP
[B]

Henry Holt books are available for special promotions
and premiums. For details contact: Director, Special Markets.

First published in hardcover in 2000 by Henry Holt and Company.

First Owl Books Edition 2001

A John Macrae / Owl Book

Designed by Victoria Hartman

Printed in the United States of America

1   3   5   7   9   10   8   6   4   2

Ad Ruth vitae salvatorem

Had it not been for the race problem early thrust upon me and enveloping me, I should have probably been an unquestioning worshipper at the shrine of the established social order into which I was born. But just that part of this order which seemed to most of my fellows nearest perfection seemed to me most inequitable and wrong; and starting from that critique, I gradually, as the years went by, found other things to question in my environment.

—W.E.B. Du Bois, *The Autobiography:*
A Soliloquy on Viewing My Life from
the Last Decade of Its First Century

ACKNOWLEDGMENTS

Fifteen years ago, I began the reading, researching, interviewing, and writing that produced in the winter of 1993–94 a biography of fifty-one years in the life of William Edward Burghardt Du Bois. The assistance of several hundred people on four continents and the cooperation of a dozen institutions in this country and abroad have enabled me to complete the remaining extraordinary forty-four years from 1919 to 1963. Few twentieth-century Americans' lives were as productive, multiple, controversial, and emblematic as Du Bois's — and almost none as long. Volume one — 1868 to 1919 — was rather ambitiously subtitled *Biography of a Race*. Ultimately, prudence dictated that I not call volume two the biography of a century, although that desire still resonates in the chosen subtitle. Moreover, because of the generosity of many, the insightfulness of some, and the labors of more than a few, this final effort is, in a real sense, a biography by committee. But I have spoken to and corresponded with so many people in so many places over so many years that, inescapably, there will be omissions from the following list of names. My remorse in failing to thank them is as profound as is my gratitude to those who are acknowledged (posthumously in several cases) below.

To one person above all others — except my wife — I owe an incommensurable debt: Herbert Aptheker. Although his views of my subject differ in significant ways from my own, without Professor Aptheker's editions of the selected correspondence, periodical literature, *Crisis* editorials, newspaper columns, and invaluable introductions to the complete run of the published monographs of W.E.B. Du Bois, any attempt to write a comprehensive life and times would have required richer resources and greater endurance than this biographer cares to contemplate.

Others in the United States to whom a prioritized debt of gratitude is owed are those who read portions of the manuscript, shared their own particularly pertinent scholarship, or called attention to significant persons, matters, or sources I might otherwise not have discovered.

At Rutgers University, my colleagues Paul Clemens, William Gillette, and Donald Roden read and critiqued chapters; as did John Hope Franklin at Duke University, Irwin Gellman at Chapman University, Paula Giddings at Duke (who indulged endless therapeutic telephone calls), Robert Hill at UCLA, Kenneth Janken at University of North Carolina–Chapel Hill, August Meier (emeritus) Kent State University, Wilson J. Moses at Pennsylvania State University, Arnold Rampersad at Stanford University, and Claudia Tate at Princeton University.

Those who volunteered information and responded to pleas were Rae Alexander-Minter at Rutgers, David Anthony III at UC Santa Cruz, Edward Beliaev at the Harriman Institute (Columbia), Esme Bhan at Howard University, Leonard Bethel at Rutgers, Faith Berry at UC Santa Barbara, John Bracey at University of Massachusetts–Amherst, Marcus Bruce at Bates College, A'Lelia Bundles at NBC, Jack Cargill at Rutgers, Johnnetta Cole at Spelman College, Leslie Collins at Fisk University, Maceo Dailey at University of Texas–El Paso, Martin Duberman at CUNY, Gabrielle Edgecomb (deceased) of Washington, D.C., Vanessa Gamble at University of Wisconsin-Madison, Marvin Gettleman (emeritus) Polytechnic University, Justin Hart at Rutgers, Walter Hill at the National Archives, Allen Howard at Rutgers, Spencer Jourdain at MetaStar, Inc., Kiyofumi Tsubaki at Tuda College (Japan), Peter Lau at Rutgers, Wilson J. Moses at Pennsylvania State University, Kathy Nicastro at the National Archives, Richard Newman at Harvard, Brenda Gayle Plummer at University of Wisconsin–Madison, Paul Robeson, Jr., of Brooklyn, Barbara Savage at University of Pennsylvania, Arthur Schlesinger, Jr. (emeritus), CUNY, Victor Schuster at Einstein College of Medicine, Ann Shockley at Fisk, William Strickland at University of Massachusetts-Amherst, Jerry Thornberry at the Gilman School, Richard Thornell at Howard University Law School, Ernestein Walker (emerita), Morgan State University, Carolyn Wedin at University of Wisconsin–Whitewater, Deborah Gray White at Rutgers, Sondra K. Wilson of New York City, Du Bois Williams at Xavier University, C. Vann Woodward (deceased) at Yale.

I wish to thank those who especially facilitated the progress of this biography in Western Europe. Berlin (former German Democratic Republic): Ollie Harrington (deceased); Kay Panke (deceased); and Irene Runge. Brussels: Robin and Simon Hinson-Jones, Victor and Mady Loewenstein. London: Paul Bremen; Cameron Duodu; Heywot (Gretta) and Yawand-Wossen Mangasha. Paris: Barbara Chase-Riboud, Ruth Lazarus.

I extend the same appreciation to those who were of assistance in the former Union of Soviet Socialist Republics. Kiev: Igor Semida. Moscow: Alexei

Andreyev, Carl Bloice, Lili Golden, Ovid and Alla Bobricheva Gorchakov, Alia and Alexei Grechurkin, Rhobert Ivanov, Elena Kanga, Tatiana Kudriavtseva, Frieda Lurie; Yuri Surovtsev; and Afanasy Vesilitsky. St. Petersburg: Ina Smirnova. Tashkent: Ulugbek Eshtaev.

In Accra, Ghana, Du Bois's final resting place, the following individuals were exceptionally cooperative: Adu Boahen; Robert and Sara (deceased) Lee; Owusu of Hertz; Efua Sutherland (deceased); J. O. Vanderpuye.

Of my excellent research assistants, Charles Cooney, Kimn Carlton-Smith, Florice Kovan, and Betty Gubert, it could be said that they performed the difficult on the appointed day, then took an extra day to do the impossible. The death of two computers might have spelled the death of the Du Bois biography along with its author, but for the wizardry of Robert De Mariano. For the efficient, timely transcription of some 150 taped interviews, some in poor quality and several in Russian, I thank Carol Grant of Pro-Typist. I thank Robert Arons for his fascinating limousine-service lectures.

In the final phase of preparation, six persons labored indefatigably as a team for three weeks of eight-hour days decoding, checking, and supplementing where necessary an ocean of end notes in order to make it possible for the author to deliver the manuscript in time to appear before the end of the twentieth century. My gratitude to Matthew Guterl, my former graduate student and now fellow author (who provided close reading of several chapters); Khalil Muhammad and William Jelani Cobb, my graduate students and authors to be; David Brighouse, my model honors student now a graduate scholar; and Betty Gubert and Alice Adamczyk, librarians extraordinaire, formerly of the Schomburg Center for Research in Black Culture, is everlasting.

Edward Gordon arranged a stimulating year at the City University of New York's Graduate Center during the academic year 1994–95 with an obligation to deliver several public lectures, but no teaching. Kenneth Wheeler, former senior vice president for academic affairs, and Richard Foley, former arts and sciences dean of Rutgers, good and true friends, encouraged this project through the years with sage advice, good conversation, and the provision of generous resources. I was extremely fortunate to receive a five-year fellowship from the John D. and Catherine T. MacArthur Foundation in June 1999. It could not have come at a more propitious moment.

The papers of W.E.B. Du Bois are housed at the W.E.B. Du Bois Library, University of Massachusetts–Amherst. I am profoundly grateful to Linda Seidman, head of special collections, and her predecessor, John Kendall, for their unstinting assistance through the years. The following libraries and repositories were also indispensable for volume two; their staffs were superb: American Academy and Institute of Arts and Letters; Special Collections, Robert W. Woodruff Library, Clark Atlanta University; Du Sable Museum, Chicago;

Special Collections, Fisk University Library; Houghton Library, Harvard University; Records Management Division, Federal Bureau of Investigation, U.S. Department of Justice; The Lenin Library, Moscow; Manuscript Division, Library of Congress; Marcus Garvey Papers, African Studies Center, UCLA; Moorland-Spingarn Research Center, Howard University; Rare Books and Manuscripts Division, New York Public Library; Rockefeller Archive Center, Pocantico Hills, North Tarrytown, New York; Special Collections and University Archives, Archibald S. Alexander Library, Rutgers, The State University of New Jersey; The Schomburg Center for Research in Black Culture, NYPL; Tamiment Library, New York University; Harry S. Truman Library, Independence, Missouri; Special Collections, Walter P. Reuther Library, Wayne State University; State Historical Society of Wisconsin;

But for the companionship and generosity of friends and acquaintances sensitive to the pressures of writing, the ordeal of completing this biography would have been far greater than it was. Ruth and I offer affectionate thanks to Mary Belfrage and Sophie Lerman, Jean-Claude Boffard and Marie Laure, Lisle Carter and Jane Livingston, Paula Cooper, Pat Ellis, Lois and Alan Fern, Sheila Goldberg-Astori, Francine Du Plessix and Cleve Gray, Amanda and Lawrence Hobart, Jacqueline Hoefer, Dolores Lewis, Joan and Roderick Nordell, Eloise and John Norton, Alida O'Loughlin and Washington Ledesma, Susan and Fred Plum, Morris Polan, Carol Ann Preece, Helen Quigless, Victor Schuster and Sandra Masur, Kaye and Ronald Springwater, Isabel and Donald Stewart, Judy and Gordon Street, Carolyn and Richard Thornell, Lee and Stewart Udall, Ann and Gordon Winchester.

My editor, Jack Macrae, who was there with steady cheer from the beginning, cajoled and excised, suggested and objected, and, until the last chapter, was the soul of patience. Thanks also to Carl Brandt, my agent, the very voice of reason. The other editor of this biography, my wife, Ruth Ann Stewart, has improved *W.E.B. Du Bois* by endless rereadings and suggestions, and she has also continually improved the biographer. I thank her as well for saving the quality of our lives. Allison, Jason, and Allegra, thank you for the grown-up patience required of you as all of you and this book were growing up.

DAVID LEVERING LEWIS
New York, May 25, 2000

CONTENTS

W.E.B.
DU BOIS

· 1 ·

THE REASON WHY

Sitting at his large, uncluttered desk at *The Crisis* on a damp October morning in 1919, W.E.B. Du Bois must have wondered if he would ever see the last of such images as the one before him. The editor was examining a photograph grisly enough to cause the stomach of someone less inured to retch. It had been taken by the *Chicago Tribune* reporter so soon after the final agony in Omaha, Nebraska, that the body still sizzled. The blackened, naked remains, twisted and scabious like a badly burnt pretzel, sank into a pyre heaped up by the grinning white mob at a downtown intersection. The victim, a young male, was one of the last black Americans to die in the more than twenty-five race riots during what had become known as the Red Summer of 1919. "The picture is a splendid one and we will bill you at the usual [two-dollar] rate for this type of photo," the *Tribune*'s picture editor advised Du Bois, if he wanted to run it in the NAACP's monthly magazine. By the time the Omaha atrocity appeared in the December 1919 *Crisis*, seventy-six black men and women had been lynched—eighteen more than in the previous year—these mainly in the rural South. Some two hundred fifty more were slaughtered in urban riots in the North and during a pogrom in the Arkansas Delta.

The Red Summer's long powder train had ignited on May 10, a Saturday night, in Charleston, South Carolina, less than six weeks after Du Bois's boat docked from France at New York Harbor. The grandly symbolic Pan-African Congress successfully concluded and documents revealing the mistreatment of Negro troops in France packed in a steamer trunk, W.E.B. Du Bois had returned to New York to resume his post at the National Association for the Advancement of Colored People (NAACP) resolved to do his considerable part in the service of racial democracy in America. Whatever their skepticism about the near-term, tens of thousands of *Crisis* readers applauded the brave assurances of "Returning Soldiers," his ringing May editorial. "Make way for Democracy,"

Du Bois had proclaimed. "We saved it in France, and by the Great Jehovah, we will save it in the United States, or know the reason why." Such sentiments resonated deeply with a thousand or more commissioned officers and 367,000 doughboys of African descent whose attitudes about race and rights in America had been forever changed by their war experience. His words were like marching orders for the bellhops, Pullman porters, and Post Office employees now swelling the ranks of the older, smaller group of professional men and women — teachers, preachers, doctors, and undertakers — who had been the backbone of what Du Bois himself famously baptised the Talented Tenth. To the smartest and the boldest of the migrants shaking off the red clay of Georgia in Manhattan or the loam of Mississippi in the Windy City, Du Bois's elevated language, if accessible only when mediated through the palaver of barbershop and beauty parlor, began, nevertheless, to register powerfully. "Returning Soldiers" spoke to all of them in their new, self-proclaimed, exhilarating incarnation: The New Negro.

Fifty-two on his next birthday, Du Bois was the founding editor of one of the most remarkable journals of opinion and propaganda in America. Its monthly circulation of 100,000 and better exceeded that of Herbert Croly's four-year-old *New Republic* and Oswald Villard's just reorganized *Nation*, and was four times larger than Max Eastman's *Liberator*, the successor to the banned *Masses*. The September *Crisis* promised an additional sixteen pages in the redesigned number debuting in November — all for a mere five-cent increase in price. Sounding like any successful businessman, Du Bois announced "this year the [gross] income will probably reach $72,000" and boasted to readers of twelve full-time employees in the association's headquarters at 70 Fifth Avenue and twelve hundred subscription agents across the country. A children's magazine would appear in January 1920, to be called *The Brownie's Book*, prompting a precocious seven-year-old to send a dollar for a year's subscription because it was the "propper [sic] time for me to begin to learn something about my own race." Officially, *The Crisis: A Record of the Darker Races* was the almost ten-year-old organ of the NAACP. In reality, it was the expression, in monthly installments, of its editor's intellectual and moral personality. Often enough, the association's board of directors endured this arrangement with exasperation, alarm, and fruitless attempts at editorial supervision.

To know Du Bois was to become acquainted with the problem of the twentieth century — the problem of the color line — in one of its most intensely complex embodiments, and the experience of knowing Du Bois was frequently a searing one. The author of *The Souls of Black Folk* comported himself as the avatar of a race whose troubled fate he was predestined to interpret and to direct. For that very reason, most American Negroes who read seriously or listened carefully, who were increasingly alienated from the educational philosophy of

Booker Washington, or who raged against a fraudulent national doctrine of separate racial equality, looked to the editor for inspiration. Although many of the large and growing number of white Americans who subscribed to *The Crisis* must have frequently been discomforted by its militancy, and not a few of them infuriated by Du Bois's periodic defense of racial intermarriage, they regarded the magazine as an indispensable source of information about black America. If some whites were distressed, many working-class black people were indifferent or hostile to both the magazine and the association, as Du Bois's good friend, Colonel Charles Young, found in his travels on behalf of the NAACP. "They regard the NAACP as a Negro snob affair," the retired army officer wrote the editor, "and I have been trying from Philadelphia to Topeka in the West to disabuse their minds of such a preposterous idea."

Despite Young's alarming discovery, his letter came at the very moment Du Bois sent the board of directors a glowing publications report: For August — "usually our worst month of the year"—*Crisis* circulation figures reached 103,000 copies. "The general condition of *The Crisis* is excellent." Whatever their numbers, indifferent black and irritated white readers receded, at least during this spectacular period, into relative unimportance. Du Bois allowed the magazine's proper and precise business manager, Augustus Granville Dill, whose years of service since leaving Atlanta University were a model of uncomplaining dedication, to take a vacation "for the first time in two years." Du Bois added Jessie Fauset to the masthead as literary editor, a well-deserved reward for running the magazine during his European sojourn. Fully salaried, she was finally able to leave her teaching position at the District of Columbia's elite Dunbar High School and escape a murky sexual scandal involving a dubious Dutch anthropologist whose research entailed photographs of nude female public school teachers. As far as the editor was concerned, the nude photography affair was a scientific venture scuttled by bureaucratic bungling and hysteria. The annual July "Education Number" and October "Children's Number" had achieved a popularity that now made them staple reading even in circles where *The Crisis* was otherwise seldom available. After the three issues covering his investigations of army racial policies and the performance of Negro troops in France (March, May, and June 1919), *The Crisis* mail room was flooded with letters, documents, and even diaries from officers and enlisted men responding to Du Bois's appeal for information and money to help prepare a three-volume history of the Great War, optimistically projected to appear in October.

In the beginning, far more African Americans had known the name Jack Johnson, ex–world heavyweight boxing champion, than they had that of W.E.B. Du Bois, civil rights militant. But by 1919, the editor's influence and renown began to give every indication of attaining household familiarity even among unskilled factory workers and trapped tenant farmers. The issues of the magazine during summer 1919 powerfully stoked the fires of New Negro rage and discontent, and the accents of Du Bois's "Returning Soldiers" were to be clearly heard in the Jamaican poet Claude McKay's ardent "If We Must Die":

> And for their thousand blows deal one deathblow!
> What though before us lies the open grave?
> Like men we'll face the murderous, cowardly pack,
> Pressed to the wall, dying, but fighting back!

But Du Bois and the NAACP were civil rights militants, not social revolutionaries—defenders of the Constitution, not exponents of class war—and like the association he sometimes unpredictably represented, the editor occasionally could appear exceedingly sensitive, if not squeamish, about charges of espousing political subversion and social unrest. There had been the April editorial that ran during his absence in France, probably authored by Fauset, that seemed to write off the beleaguered Industrial Workers of the World (the "Wobblies" of the IWW) because of the union's opposition to the war. Immediately upon returning, the editor set the record straight, praising the IWW as one of the few movements that "draws no color line" in its membership; but though admirable in their objectives, he was compelled to doubt that the "*methods* of the IWW are today feasible or advisable." The editor made it clear, repeatedly, that the Bolshevik Revolution was not in his eyes what it was in Asa Philip Randolph's—"the greatest achievement of the twentieth century." Du Bois would stick pretty much to the argument advanced in the July 1921 "The Negro and Radical Thought"—essentially one of militant petit bourgeois opportunism—throughout the decade.

Seeing little relevancy in the Bolshevik triumph in Russia to the United States, and abhorring the politics of violence, Du Bois would insist in a June 1921 editorial, "The Class Struggle," that "we do not believe in revolution. We expect revolutionary changes to come mainly through reason, human sympathy and the education of children, and not by murder." The Hamiltonian progressivism of Harvard classmate Herbert Croly's *The Promise of American Life* had greater appeal than did the hard-edged gospel of Lenin's *What's to Be Done?*. Still, *The Crisis* sprang to the defense of the *Messenger* in late 1919, when federal authorities appeared ready to suppress it again. The editor held no brief for the *Messenger, Negro World*, "and other periodicals, but they have a right to speak." He didn't "believe in Revolution," but he did believe profoundly "in free speech and freedom to think, and it is the duty of every Negro to see that the right of black men to think and write and criticize shall not be abridged and taken away under the guise of curbing revolution." A lengthy report, forwarded in late September 1919 to Attorney General A. Mitchell Palmer by a twenty-four-year-old graduate of George Washington University Law School, aimed to accomplish that very objective. "Radicalism and Sedition Among Negroes as Reflected in Their Publications" was signed by John Edgar Hoover, the darkly ambitious head of the Justice Department's new General Intelligence Division (GID), created in emergency response to a terrifying monsoon of anarchist bombings raining on Washington, D.C., Cleveland, Paterson (New Jersey), Boston, Pittburgh, and Philadelphia. With assassination attempts against the attorney general of the United States, a justice of the Supreme Court, members of the United States Senate, the secretary of labor, and prominent public officials barely foiled or failing through luck, and a final blast in September 1920 ripping through the heart of Wall Street itself, killing thirty people, many Americans believed the country was experiencing the terminal chaos before Armageddon.

Bomb-throwing anarchists, antiwar Socialists, levelling Wobblies, and conspiring Communists seemed bent on recasting America in shapes as alien as many of their foreign-sounding names. In Seattle, the shipyard upheaval in January sent temblors rolling across the country over Judge Elbert Gary's U.S. Steel mills and Boston's police force by September, then shaking the coal mines of West Virginia in November, until four million workers had gone out on strike. What became known as the Red Scare of 1919 unfolded against a backdrop of revolutionary consolidation in Russia, establishment of the Third International, rapid advance of soviets in Germany and Hungary, and the formation of two feuding blocs of North American Communists (Charles Ruthenberg's Communist Party and John Reed's Communist Labor Party). The U.S. House of Representatives expelled Socialist Victor Berger, and the New York state legislature promptly kicked out its five Socialist members. Disabled by a stroke suffered in his manic campaign to drum up public support for the League of Nations, Woodrow Wilson languished bedridden through the remaining months of his presidency. Law and order was in the hands of Attorney General Palmer, the ambitious "Fighting Quaker," whose uncomplicated solution to the national crisis was to terrorize those who couldn't be deported and deport those who, because they were aliens, were ipso facto terrorists or subversives. "Not for at least a half century, perhaps at no time in our history," declared one historian of the period, "had there been such wholesale violation of civil liberties."

Du Bois's *Crisis* provided Palmer's Department of Justice with abundant and unambiguous evidence of sedition and conspiracy, or so it would claim. Unintimidated by the Post Office delay of the controversial May issue containing the exposé of military documents and the defiant editorials "Returning Soldiers" and "The League of Nations," Du Bois had continued to write and speak about the new militancy of the race. Negroes would not be passively butchered nor would they allow themselves to be indiscriminately barred or ousted from their wartime labor gains. Addressing the association's spirited tenth-anniversary national conference in Cleveland that June, but clearly speaking beyond the NAACP to white America, the editor called racism the handmaiden of Bolshevism: a sentiment overwhelmingly endorsed by the 265 delegates from thirty-four states. South Carolina congressman James F. Byrnes, whose political ambitions were as broad as his racial ideas were narrow, heard the message. Anarchists and Wobblies were far less vexatious to Byrnes than was a Harvard-educated Negro editor whose inflammatory writings were being read and talked about by thousands of black people in his part of the country. Future secretary of state, presidential aspirant, and Supreme Court justice Jimmy Byrnes demanded that the Justice Department do something about Du Bois. Byrnes charged the editor with causing race riots in Washington and Chicago and with posing the gravest threat to race relations and order in America. For good measure he read a *Crisis* editorial into the *Congressional Record*. Cordially thanking Byrnes for providing him a readership of "some seventy-five million of our fellow citizens," a sardonic Du Bois countered the politician with his own indictment in the October *Crisis*, making Byrnes and his kind responsible not only for the urban race riots of the Red Summer, "but also of encouraging for fifty years the lynching of 4,000 Negroes, the disfranchisement of a million and a half voters, the enforced ignorance of three million human beings and the theft of hundreds of millions of dollars in wages."

Nor did he stop with a blast in the magazine. In an unprecedented feature article in the New York *Sun* for October 12, "Causes of Discontent," Du Bois wondered, ironically, whether Americans had "lost their sense of humor?" Could they really seriously believe that Negroes were increasingly discontented because they were being "unduly excited by the Russian Bolsheviki?" Learning that the Justice Department intended to investigate the causes of racial discontent was even more reason to laugh in order not to cry, Du Bois groaned. "We black folk have for some years been trying to get the United States Department of Justice to look into several matters that touch us." The danger facing the nation came not from Communist revolution but from the consequences of its own moral and humanitarian failure. "Negroes are in a fighting mood," he asserted, and mainstream America would have to learn to live without the class of race leaders who told whites that "Negroes wanted nothing but the right to work at such wages as the white people wished to give them." Du Bois and Hoover were never to meet in person, but their encounter in print during the late summer and fall of 1919 imbued both with prejudices that would fester in the years ahead with fateful consequences.

"Radicalism and Sedition Among Negroes as Reflected in Their Publications," his 1919 report to Palmer, won young J. Edgar Hoover (as he now signed himself) a starring role in the Red Scare capers. The head of the new General Intelligence Division had saved his severest censure for Randolph's *Messenger*—"the most able and the most dangerous of all negro publications"— but there was no doubt that he and his superiors regarded Du Bois's *Crisis* as a major menace to the status quo. The report made him invaluable to the attorney general and commenced his unique role as purveyor to congressional bodies of confidences about the actions, ideas, and morals of American citizens. Palmer incorporated Hoover's report into the Justice Department's comprehensive report forwarded to the Senate in mid-November. A curious coincidence unnoticed until now was that "Radicalism and Sedition Among Negroes" was remarkably similar in analytical power and scope of detail (covering the NAACP, the UNIA, the *Messenger*, Hubert Harrison's Liberty League, and Cyril Briggs's West Indian Marxists in the African Blood Brotherhood) to a document submitted to the director of military intelligence by Major Walter Loving, a man of impressive culture and one of the army's most effective wartime Negro undercover agents. Loving's report weighing the pros and cons of Du Bois's officer's commission two years earlier had been a major factor in Colonel Marlborough Churchill's decision to withdraw the army's offer. Loving's fifteen-page essay, "Final Report on Negro Subversion," had been handed in to military intelligence on August 6, just in time for young Hoover to acquire his expertise in this area.

Congressman Byrnes had taken a more accurate measure of Du Bois's significance as a leader of his people than had the inexperienced Hoover. The editor's power to inspire returning soldiers, ambitious migrants, and determined college men and women to stand up for their basic citizenship rights was far more dangerous in his eyes than any prospect of Negro Americans being converted in significant numbers to communism, as Byrnes (and even Hoover) knew, whatever was stated in official documents or barked into the *Congressional Report*. And never was inspiration more needed as 1919 flamed out. The riot in Charleston had been contained fairly quickly by the authorities, but there were two black fatalities. The three-day convulsion in the nation's capital, triggered partly by *The Washington Post*'s incendiary journalism at the end of July and extinguished as much by heavy rains as by two thousand infantry ordered up by Secretary of War Newton Baker, injured more than a hundred people and killed six. In Washington, as was the case in the Chicago riot beginning on July 27, people of color defended themselves with guns, bricks, and other makeshift weapons. Reporting on the situation in the capital, NAACP field secretary James Weldon Johnson was positively euphoric: "The Negroes saved themselves and saved Washington by their determination not to run, but to fight." In Chicago, black and white workers and demobilized soldiers and sailors skirmished for twelve days back and forth along Wentworth Avenue, the line dividing the white, blue-collar stockyard neighborhoods from those in what Chicagoans called the Black Belt. Fifteen white people joined twenty-three black people in death, while more than five hundred Chicagoans were treated for their wounds and another thousand emerged stunned and homeless from the Windy City's mimicry of a battle in the just-ended European war. Knoxville came at the beginning of September; then, at the end of September, the riot in Omaha, suppressed only by the intercession of the U.S. Army.

Race relations seemed to reach a nadir in the Arkansas outback that October. Gunfire from black sharecroppers meeting in a church near Elaine, a town in the Arkansas Delta, had left a deputy sheriff dead and several white citizens wounded in the early morning of October. Having provoked the Wednesday shootout, enraged white planters and farmers chased down black men and women in the high cotton of Phillips County in a frenzy lasting seven days, until the count of the dead approached two hundred. The fact that Elaine's whites had paid for their jamboree with five of their own dead made the "legal" aftermath notably outrageous even for the Deep South of that time. U.S. infantry, arriving from Camp Pike, took the side of the frenzied whites. A thousand or so black men were rounded up by soldiers and vigilantes and packed into a stockade where the sheriff and the big planters selected seventy-nine of them for rapid grand jury indictment. Six of these were sentenced to hang on November 18 and another six on the following day after five-minute deliberations, while the rest were convicted in batches and given prison terms of from five to twenty-five years. Their alleged crime, as *The New York Times* reported in all seriousness, was conspiracy to seize control of the county by armed force.

Furious about distortions in the press concerning the Arkansas bloodlettings, Du Bois sent a three-page letter to the editor of the New York *World* that served as a powerful corrective when it appeared in the November 28 edition. The real crime of the Phillips County sharecroppers, he said, was to have the gall to hire a maverick white Arkansas lawyer to help organize and incorporate a farmer's protective association in order to compel landlords to open their books on prices and profits of supplies and cotton revenues. The normal practice in that part of Arkansas, Du Bois explained to the *World*'s readers, was for a farmer to sell to the planter and wait a full year to be told "how much his crop was worth, and what is the balance due" for the supplies bought on credit from the company store. It was slavery by another name, but to dispute such an arrangement was, "in Arkansas custom, to dispute 'white supremacy.'" "There is not a civilized country in the world that would for a moment allow this kind of justice to stand." The editor and officers of the NAACP had inside information about the Arkansas pogrom, thanks to Walter Francis White, the twenty-six-year-old new assistant secretary. White's sensational expose in *The Nation* of a six-person lynching in two Georgia counties in May 1918 had already caught the attention of northern progressives. A small, trim man of seemingly bottomless, nervous energy and enormous self-confidence, White was the light-skinned, blond, blue-eyed son of an austere postal employee and his civic-minded wife, both of whom were highly respected members of Atlanta's colored community. Du Bois knew the White family well from his years spent at Atlanta University; he regarded young Walter, who played football and graduated from "AU" with high marks, as a model representative of the Talented Tenth.

Because Walter White looked so white, his services to the NAACP were invaluable, but they also placed him in situations of awful danger. Aboard a train leaving a Deep South lynching bee, the assistant secretary was once challenged by a suspicious white passenger who boasted that he could always spot a "yaller nigger" by the absence of half moons on the fingernails. White's half moons saved him. Hurrying back to NAACP headquarters from Arkansas undercover work as a white reporter (the governor gave him a reference and Phillips County vigilantes took him into their confidence), White handed in a detailed report of surreal barbarity. When White's revised report appeared in *The Nation* under the startling title " 'Massacring Whites in Arkansas,' " ten days after Du Bois's letter in the *World*, public opinion outside the Deep South began to shift to the association. The Arkansas cases became known as *Moore v. Dempsey*, and as court costs rose in regular five-thousand-dollar increments over the next year, and two years beyond that, Du Bois made contributions to the legal defense fund the litmus test of racial loyalty. *The Crisis* published a list of delinquent NAACP branches, with Texas and Georgia having the largest number, but the critical state of Illinois had, surprisingly, as many as five. "If the officers of these branches will take no action," the editor admonished, then the members themselves ought to take matters into their own hands and appeal directly to the national headquarters. Meanwhile, the legal battle on behalf of the twelve condemned defendants proceeded like a grim game of volleyball back and forth between the federal courts and Arkansas courts, with *The Crisis* continuing to play its decisive role in mobilizing public opinion and raising funds for the NAACP's defense treasury.

The situation demanded a voluntary of prose, an editorial reveille crackling over those of limp resolve and shaken courage. Du Bois's response was predictable. "Progress," the lead essay in the November 1920 *Crisis*—the tenth-anniversary issue—sought to wrench inspiration from the jaws of desperation. "But above all comes the New Spirit," the editor wrote. "From a bewildered, almost listless, creeping sense of impotence and despair have come a new vigor, hopefulness and feeling of power." The bugle call ended on a confident note: "We are no longer depending on our friends. We are depending on ourselves." Impressive evidence of this new self-dependence came with the latest twist of the Arkansas saga. *The Crisis* ran an exciting replay in the December issue of a roller-coaster extradition contest between the Arkansas attorney general and lawyers hired by the NAACP in the case of Robert Hill, alleged ringleader of the Phillips County insurgents, who had fled to Topeka, Kansas. With NAACP board member and Kansas U.S. senator Arthur Capper interceding with the governor, and a Shawnee County attorney acting as Hill's lawyer, the sympathetic Kansas authorities refused to honor the extradition writ on the certain grounds that Hill's return to Arkansas would prove fatal. The dismissal of federal charges against the Arkansas farmer in early October 1920 enormously enhanced the NAACP's creditability, making it possible to raise another five thousand dollars above the eight thousand already expended in legal fees. "Thus ends one of the most dramatic legal fights the Association has ever undertaken," Du Bois wrote, rightly predicting that it would have "a most far-reaching effect."

The "far-reaching effect" would finally come in January 1923 when the U.S. Supreme Court delivered an opinion, revolutionary in its civil rights implications, that the twelve sharecroppers had been denied a fair trial, thereby reversing the federal appeals court's September 1921 decision against them and remanding the case for reconsideration of the facts. Only eight years had elapsed since the high court's decision upholding the infamous rape conviction of Atlanta Jewish businessman Leo Frank on grounds that the mere observance of judicial formalities was sufficient to preclude reversal of state court decisions involving capital crimes. Given the seven-to-two decision in *Frank v. Mangum*, Moorfield Storey, the NAACP's honorific and aged president, still highly respected and enormously capable, had confessed serious doubts about winning the justices to his argument that the Phillips County trials had been judicial farces. But when the day came for arguments, Storey had exquisitely refined the brief handed over by Scipio Africanus Jones, the portentously named black Little Rock attorney retained earlier by the NAACP. Attorney Jones's race made an appearance in person before nine glowering justices tactically unwise, but without his meticulous lawyering no victory could have been sustained. Writing for the majority in *Moore v. Dempsey*, Oliver Wendell Holmes noted such circumstantial peculiarities in the case as the all-white Phillips County juries in a population two-thirds black, the hysteria surrounding the trials, the absence of basic procedural guarantees of counsel, speed of conviction, and other matters, which led the leonine senior jurist to sneer that the trials had been nothing more than a charade in which "the whole proceeding is a mask." *The Crisis* would record the last Gothic act in the drama in the issue for April 1925 when, after fifty thousand dollars in legal fees and six years of propaganda, all the original defendants—the twelve sentenced to die along with the seventy-six clapped in prison—were finally released. It was "a complete victory for the NAACP," Du Bois wrote, even though he, above all others, must have realized how remote was the time when even minimal due process standards would be found in real-world trials of colored people in the south.

DARKWATER: VOICES FROM Within the Veil was released by the new firm of Harcourt, Brace & Howe in February 1920. It was Du Bois's sixth book since the 1896 publication of *The Suppression of the African Slave Trade to the United States, 1638–1870,* his Harvard dissertation. The attraction for Du Bois of Alfred Harcourt's firm was Joel Spingarn, recent former chairman of the NAACP board of directors and one of the principal partners in the year-old publishing house. Du Bois and Spingarn, despite greatly differing origins of race and class, were curiously attuned to each other. Neither man suffered fools lightly, and both gave the impression, frequently, that they were the only ones dedicated to the work of the association who were not fools themselves. In aristocratic bent and demanding intellectual temperament they were spiritual siblings and, oftentimes, rivals. *The Negro,* Du Bois's last nonfiction work, had been published five years earlier by the venerable New York firm of Henry Holt, with whom his dealings had been quite satisfactory, but when Alfred Harcourt and Donald Brace left Holt to form their company in partnership with Spingarn, Du Bois's allegiance went with them. There was a certain appropriateness of moment in claiming that *Darkwater* was finished on February 23, 1918 — "my fiftieth birthday," as he wrote in "The Shadow of Years," the collection's opening essay — but Du Bois actually continued to retouch the manuscript over the next eighteen months, between *Crisis* deadlines and European travel. Many years later, he wrote of having intended for *Darkwater* to serve as his apologia — "a sort of semi-biography" — since he believed, at the time, that the largest part of his life "had passed." The finished work arrived at Harcourt, Brace and Howe in September 1919. Its 270-odd pages consisted of an autobiographical sketch and nine major pieces of social commentary and fiction, half of which had appeared in somewhat shorter versions in publications such as *The Atlantic Monthly, The Crisis,* and *The Independent.* Each of these was followed by eleven shorter entries of poetry and symbolic vignettes.

Du Bois dedicated the book to Nina, his wife of twenty-four years. Among *Darkwater's* ten substantial essays and fictional pieces was "The Damnation of Women," a paean to the rights of women in general and to the grandeur of black women in particular — a document of such radiance as to place it among the worthiest feminist texts. His imprecations against antebellum concubinage and contemporary rape figuratively scorched the pages as the author served notice to the Anglo-Saxon South that it could be forgiven slavery, secession, bogus aristocracy, and "the passion of its hot blood," but one thing never to be forgiven — "neither in this world nor the world to come," proclaimed Du Bois — was the South's "wanton and continued and persistent insulting of the black womanhood." He was an uncompromising advocate of female suffrage who had burnished some of his most memorable prose in the service of the National American Women's Suffrage Association (NAWSA) and for the full empower-ment of the other half of humanity. Now that the enfranchisement of women was at least a formal reality with the ratification, at that very moment, of the Nineteenth Amendment, Du Bois spoke through "The Damnation of Women" not only for full economic rights for women, but for equal rights in the highly controversial sphere of procreation. The future woman must have "a life work and economic independence," he declared. She must have knowledge and the right of motherhood "at her own discretion. The present mincing horror at free womanhood must pass." The essay put him solidly on the side of the Washing-ton feminist Anna Julia Cooper, sole female member of the American Negro Academy, whose volume of uncompromising essays, A Voice from the South, Du Bois had read avidly upon its appearance in 1892. "Damnation" also paid a debt to Charlotte Perkins Gilman, whose 1898 classic Women in Economics the author knew well, as well as to Alice Paul's National Women's Party and Mar-garet Sanger's soon-to-be-established American Birth Control League. Yet even as he postulated that the uplift of women was "our greatest modern cause," to his thinking it remained subordinate to the problem of the color line and "the peace movement." Du Bois wrote as one of the most enlightened men of his time, one whose failure to see the inseparable parity of these issues many fem-inists even today might be able to forgive—all the more so since it was incon-ceivable to Du Bois, unlike Gilman and Paul and so many of the white feminists of his time, that equal rights for white women should ever take precedence over civil rights for black people.

In dedicating Darkwater to Nina, however, there was a sense in which Du Bois's tribute of affection and esteem was somewhat incongruous with his lib-erating essay on women's rights. Indeed, his dedication may have been less an act of tribute than of atonement for the subordinate role imposed upon Nina Du Bois, whose world—governed by the demands of her driven husband and their teenage daughter—ended at the borders of W.E.B. Du Bois's cosmic con-cerns. Her condition, and that of millions of other wives, he summed up con-summately: "Only at the sacrifice of intelligence and the chance to do their best work can the majority of modern women bear children. This is the dam-nation of women." But Du Bois went on to reveal that black women—more valued by their race than women of any other "modern race"—were, neverthe-less, doubly damned. The racial history of its institutions and the economics of color-coded work operated at cross purposes in contemporary society. For Amer-ican Negroes above all others, the family group was the "ideal of the culture with which these folk have been born," posited Du Bois. But this was a concept that rejected the idea "of an economically independent working mother." Yet black working women outnumbered black men in the labor force. And the inevitable result of what Du Bois called the "clash of such ideals and such facts" was the broken family and the female-headed household. What Du Bois failed to observe, however, was that the other inevitable consequence of the "clash of ideals" was the rigidly patriarchal household, such as the one in which Nina Du Bois lived. To tap into Nina's correspondence during the early twenties is to catch a thinning stream of ideas and emotions, to scan a sad record of psychosomatic debility and shriveling superego. "I am some rested," is one such typical sigh written to Will during another of his lengthy absences. "The neck still aches badly," and Yolande was complaining of an abscessed tooth. "The first two Sundays you were away, I spent most of the days in bed," reads another. What thoughts about the plight of women may have come to her in their small house in Brooklyn's Johnson Street if, indeed, she ever read Will's essay, have gone unrecorded.

By the time he arranged and polished the *Darkwater* essays for final submission, there had been four months of Red Summer bloodlettings, and Du Bois's already grim state of mind verged on apocalyptic bitterness. Could his readers imagine the hypocrisy of the United States protesting Turkish atrocities in Armenia? he challenged. What was Armenia or Louvain, Belgium, razed by the Hun, "compared with Memphis, Waco, Washington," places where American citizens of African descent had been brutally dispatched? In several of these pieces — exceptionally so in "The Souls of White Folk," the retouched essay originally appearing in an August 1910 issue of *The Independent* — Du Bois once again showed himself to be the incomparable mediator of the wounded souls of black people. In its original form, his earlier essay hissed with the fury of a tightly clamped pressure cooker over a building flame, as Du Bois, "high in the tower" above "the loud complaining of the human sea," mocked the arrogance that caused his and his people's historic troubles — this modern European discovery of "personal whiteness" as the supreme virtue. A two-hundred-year-old dogma of stupendous fraudulence was well on the way to supplanting Christianity, humanity, and democracy, said Du Bois, as he and other colored men and women had it drummed into their heads that "whiteness is the ownership of the earth forever and ever, Amen!"

His consternation had been especially fueled by the great popularity of pseudoscience works such as *The Passing of the Great Race, or, the Racial Basis of European History*, the 1916 potboiler (reissued in 1920) by Madison Grant. In prose as grave and portentous as any used by Du Bois himself, this Manhattan lawyer and eugenics enthusiast caught the attention of much of middlebrow America with the warning, "Ours is a solemn moment. We stand at a crisis — the supreme crisis of the ages." Teeming millions were rising out of Asia and Africa, imperiling the West from without by sheer numbers and from within by intermixings of "blood." "If white civilization goes down," lamented Grant, "it will be swamped by the triumphant colored races, who will obliterate the white man by elimination or absorption." In a coincidence of inescapable significance, Du Bois would see his 1915 essay "The African Roots of the War" singled out for rebuke in Lothrop Stoddard's *The Rising Tide of Color Against White World-Supremacy*, another acclaimed defense of white supremacy, released by Scribner's in 1921 but copyrighted just as *Darkwater* went on sale. Du Bois would meet and defeat Stoddard in a highly publicized public debate in Chicago at the end of the decade when the racial thinking of genteel white America was somewhat less hysterical, but, then as in the spring of 1920, the Grants and the Stoddards spoke to cherished prejudices that the author and hardly more than a handful of American intellectuals resolved to disprove and denounce. Because he was "in the world, but not of it," Du Bois proclaimed himself endowed with a wisdom of "inner torment," and from this "inner torment of souls the human scene without" had interpreted itself "in unusual and even illuminating ways." With that, he threw down his collection of essays and poetry as a gauntlet to racism in its vast manifestations.

The revised "Souls of White Folk" now belched fire in *Darkwater* as Du Bois seemed almost to scream ("Merciful God! in these wild days and in the name of Civilization, Justice, and Motherhood") at what had been done to men and women of Negro descent in the United States through "orgy, cruelty, barbarism, and murder." Sounding like Frederick Douglass, Bishop Henry McNeal Turner, and other Aframericans forming a long column of unforgiving reproach, Du Bois wrote that, instead of standing as a great example of the success of democracy "and the possibility of human brotherhood," his country was an awful example of its pitfalls and failures, "as far as black and brown and yellow people are concerned." As this pulsating essay made clear, he construed the failure of American racial democracy to be integral to the evolving European world order in which — "and leave no room for mistaken meaning" — the Great War was primarily "the jealous and avaricious struggle for the largest share in exploiting darker races." The rape of Belgium (mild in comparison to Belgian atrocities in the Congo, he observed), the killing fields of Flanders, and the sausage grinding of armies on the eastern front were not aberrations, as most Europeans wanted to believe, but inherent in the history, culture, and institutions of the West. The Great War was not aberration nor insanity, he wrote: "This is Europe; this seeming Terrible is the real soul of white culture — back of all culture — stripped and visible today."

Here Du Bois scared thousands of white readers with a prediction. Terrible as the Great War had been, it was nothing compared to the impending holocaust of the races — "that fight for freedom which black and brown and yellow men must and will make unless their oppression and humiliation and insult at the hands of the White World cease. The Dark World is going to submit to its present treatment just as long as it must and not one moment longer."

Du Bois incorporated much of "The African Roots of the War" (his remarkably prescient 1915 *Atlantic Monthly* thinkpiece about global competition for markets) into the new essay "The Hands of Ethiopia," as well as into "The Souls of White Folk." The result was a greatly enhanced critique of global capitalism. The internal contradictions of capitalism—aggregating extremes of wealth and poverty—had generated such influential treatises as those of English economist John Hobson and French politician Jules Ferry, decades before Lenin's just-published thesis arguing that capitalism continued to thrive by exporting the exploitation of labor to Asia and Africa. What distinguished Du Bois's analysis in "The Hands of Ethiopia" and "The Souls of White Folk" was not the somewhat derivative economic interpretation, but its cogency in exposing the paramount factor of racism in selling imperial expansion to the white working classes. It was plain as day to modern white civilization that the "white working classes cannot much longer be maintained," he contended. "But there is a loophole." In places beyond the Suez Canal where "no labor unions or votes or questioning onlookers or inconvenient consciences" existed—"where 'niggers' are cheap and the earth is rich"—Europe and America could rack up profits sufficient "not simply to the very rich, but to the middle class and to the laborers." But the justification for injustice, the rationale for rapacity that made the collusion of classes politically and intellectually viable was, Du Bois insisted, the dichotomy of color—the ideology of white supremacy: "There must come the necessary despisings and hatreds of these savage half-men, this unclean *canaille* of the world—these dogs of men. All through the world this gospel is preaching. It has its literature, it has its priests, it has its secret propaganda and above all—it pays!"

Conceding the superiority of European cultural achievements to "any culture that arose in Asia or Africa," Du Bois discounted Europeans as the reason for these achievements. "Europe has never produced and never will in our day bring forth a single human soul who cannot be matched or over-matched in every line of human endeavor by Asia and Africa." His roster of non-European world-beaters—Nefertari, Jesus, Muhammed, Askia, Confucius, and Buddha—sufficed to prove the point. The real reasons for Europe's hegemony lay "quite outside and beyond Europe—back in the universal struggles of all mankind," in Negroid Egypt of the Pharaohs, Semitic Phoenicia, and multiracial Islam. But alas, education meant European education for subject peoples of color—"deliberately educated ignorance," Du Bois scolded, "by which they remember Napoleon and forget Sonni Ali," the fifteenth-century ruler of the Songhai Empire. Because "most men today cannot conceive of a freedom that does not involve somebody's slavery." More than half of humanity—people of color, women, workers—had no active role in constructing the education of the masses of people. "Lions have no historians," he noted at one point, "and therefore lion hunts are thrilling and satisfactory human reading." In Du Bois's scheme of democratic learning, the matching of Sonni Ali with Napoleon would be complemented by the pairing of Mary Shadd and Harriet Beecher Stowe, Samuel Coleridge-Taylor and Antonín Dvořák. "The Souls of White Folk," "The Damnation of Women," and "The Immortal Child," along with much else in *Darkwater*, made the argument for the broadest public education, for expansion of the canon of general culture to include the lives and works of the excluded and oppressed. The objective was "to make all intelligent" by exposing them to what a generation in the last decades of the twentieth century would know as multiculturalism, the better, Du Bois said, "to discover special talents and genius."

If *The Souls of Black Folk* achieved its singular impact through Du Bois's masterly interweaving of the personal and the universal in such a way that each appropriated something of the illustrative and symbolic value of the other, much of *Darkwater* was a cri de coeur in which the author's personal bitterness and anger crackled through the text like electric jolts with the power to scorch, illumine, or stun. In one of several entries serving to bridge the main essays in the collection, "The Riddle of the Sphinx" (originally published in *The Crisis* for November 1914 as "The Burden of Black Women"), Du Bois was carried away by his wrath against white racism into excoriation bordering on the homicidal. A similar anguish animated those whiplash sentences inserted in the final version of "The Souls of White Folk" and spoke to his own fate as an intellectual and a black man. Few knew better from long experience the efficaciousness with which American Negroes of conscience and courage were stigmatized and marginalized in a nation as guilt-ridden about race relations as it was ill-disposed to face up to them—inevitably, the message was buried with the punished messenger. Foreseeing accurately the reception of *Darkwater* in much of mainstream America, Du Bois observed acridly, "my word is to them mere bitterness and my soul, pessimism. They deny my right to live and be and call me misbirth!" Imitating his detractors, he sneered, "My poor, un-white thing! Weep not nor rage. I know, too well, that the curse of God lies heavy upon you. Why? That is not for me to say, but be brave!" But his white readers knew in their hearts that he and others living behind the veil of race possessed special powers of insight. Du Bois boasted that he possessed knowledge of whites far superior to that "which servants have of masters, or mass of class, or capitalist of artisan." Rather, he knew them from "the back and side." He saw the "working of their entrails." He knew the thoughts of whites as well as they did—"and they know that I know"—and this, he noted with supreme contempt, made them lurch from fury to chagrin.

The collection of essays, fiction, and poetry was somewhat more varied and occasionally less assaultive than the angry reactions of many white reviewers and readers suggested. In "The Shadow of Years," Du Bois told his saga of the Black Burghardts of the Berkshires and of growing up "by a golden river" in Great Barrington, of the lordly Du Boises and his austere paternal grandfather, and finally, of the "age of miracles" at Fisk, Harvard, and Berlin. It was here that Du Bois shared what was, for him, a decidedly personal confession, musing that in those ten years of "great spiritual upturning" in Atlanta he had "found" himself. He had grown "more broadly human," he wrote, developing those few "holy friendships" that would sustain him in the trials ahead. Then he pondered, rhetorically, what a different run of luck might have meant: "*Suppose* that pompous old village judge" had sent him to reform school for stealing apples? "*Suppose* Principal [Frank] Hosmer had been born with no faith in 'darkies.' . . . *Suppose* I had missed a Harvard scholarship?" These were suppositions that cultural historians of the future would read as critical markers of opportunity in the general phase of early twentieth-century racial, religious, and ethnic confrontation, negotiation, and assimilation in America. Two trenchant personal documents that were synecdoches of upper-class Jewish experience appeared within two years of *Darkwater*: Edward Bok's *The Americanization of Edward Bok*, followed by Ludwig Lewisohn's *Up Stream*. The incommensurable difference between Du Bois's personal drama and theirs, however, was that in a figurative sense Bok and Lewisohn were able to write themselves out of the capriciousness and strictures of bigotry while Du Bois could only write himself ever more profoundly into his.

The author celebrated his own genius with affecting immodesty in this rhapsodic memoir in order to underscore to his white reading public the wasted lives of countless other gifted boys and girls of color who found the escape hatch of education nailed shut. Du Bois's evangelical faith in the transformative power of education was at open throttle in "The Immortal Child," a sometimes lyrical evocation of the short, extraordinary career of his friend, the Afro-English composer Samuel Coleridge-Taylor, and a plea for progressive education of the young along the instrumentalist lines traced by John and Alice Dewey. The aim of education was to identify talent, nurture curiosity, and promote social democracy, and to do so early and generously, he insisted. Du Bois aphorized splendidly, "In the treatment of the child the world foreshadows its own future and faith."

Two of the longer creative pieces, the allegorical "Jesus Christ in Texas" (originally published in 1911 as "Jesus Christ in Georgia") and the satirical "Comet" were lively written short stories whose ethical and social messages the reader could readily interpret. When Du Bois tried his hand at fiction, the usual result was history or sociology dressed up with dialogue and female protagonists, but "Jesus" (despite its ornate prose) blended gallows humor, irony, and Gothic absurdity to make a parable in which a Texas town becomes Gethsemane and a swarthy Jesus figure is narrowly spared a lynch mob's noose. In "The Comet," a valued black bank messenger emerges from a vault deep beneath the city to discover that he and the beautiful daughter of a white millionaire are the only people alive after poisonous gases from a comet's tail have exterminated the population of Manhattan, Harlem included. Written in what was for Du Bois middlebrow prose, the story's ending brings these two handsome people almost together as man and woman: "Silently, immovably, they saw each other face to face—eye to eye. Their souls lay naked to the night." The story toyed tantalizingly with sex across the color line—the great American fictional taboo. Suddenly, rapture is pierced by the honk of an automobile horn as millionaire father and Galahad fiancée arrive from the uncontaminated suburbs. "I've always liked your people. If you ever want a job, call on me," says the father as he hurries his daughter away from desecration and into safety.

Moving from fiction to social commentary in "The Servant in the House," Du Bois recapitulated the dogged struggle out of slavery by black labor, taking as departure point his own experience waiting tables at a Minnesota resort on Lake Minnetonka the summer after graduating from Fisk University. There had been no possibility for black men and women to move up significantly in the world of work—to advance beyond service occupations and to escape menial service and the mudsill of unskilled labor. The mark of Canaan and the stigmata of the auction block made servitude and color synonymous in America: "*Negroes are servants; servants are Negroes.*" Barring intervention by a poisonous comet, Du Bois seemed to be saying, organized labor would hold the door shut "to factory and trade in their fellows' faces and [batten] down the hatches" to keep 300,000 dark-skinned citizens from ever earning equal pay with whites. But if the white unions decided on this as their strategy, they were likely to find the ultimate cost higher than they could afford, Du Bois prophesied in the related essay "Of Work and Wealth," as he had in a key editorial in *The Crisis* for September 1919. He warned that black labor possessed the negative power either to force itself into the unions or, if necessary, to wreck them through its willingness to play the scab and underbid white labor. It was to be a favorite Du Bois threat, one which the American Federation of Labor would placidly ignore for almost two decades.

Du Bois accumulated virtually every review here and abroad of *Darkwater*. He pasted them onto the pages of an old 1909 annual report of the New Jersey Board of Assessors that remained in his personal library until he died. Unfriendly reviews would run the gamut from dyspeptic to penetrating, yet almost without exception none of the critics panned the literary quality of any of the entries. The best of *Darkwater*—"The Shadow of Years," "The Damnation of Women,"

"Of Beauty and Death," "Credo"—ranged from outstanding to superlative, while the recurrence of "genius" as defining noun or adjective applied to the author even by hostile reviewers is striking. Thus, since the best of the collection was so good and the intellectual caliber of the author was uncontested (a genius, but also, inescapably, a "Negro genius"), the weaker, flawed pieces escaped serious literary criticism. Some of the pieces reworked for the collection were surcharged with symbolism to the point of opacity or encrusted with prose of such deep purple as to render them increasingly inaccessible to many modern readers. If none of it was literary dross, some of the pieces suffered either from being time-bound by their Late Victorian matrix or from melodramatic compulsions of their author—or from both. "The Princess of the Hither Isles," taken from the October 1913 Crisis, was an allegorical exuberance that delivered a timely message smothered in fustian. Here, Du Bois fused the thesis of his forthcoming book The Gift of Black Folk (a folk possessed of intuition, compassion, artistic prowess, and grace) with his reiterated condemnation of a social order in which people of color and women of whatever color were ruled by a class of white men whose authority derived mainly from the accident of color and gender.

What Darkwater revealed to black and white readers alike far more vividly than The Souls of Black Folk or the general run of Crisis writings was the temperament of its intellectual author, for whom language was as much an aphrodisiac as a weapon in the service of rights. The riot of imagery and emotional inflation in the short feminist allegory "The Call," in the long poem "The Children of the Moon," or in the blazing threnody "A Litany at Atlanta" suggest trances, Gnostic visions, dark nights of the soul, and, as one perceptive biographer observes, other intensely religious moments that are surprising at first to see in an agnostic and publicly restrained Du Bois." In these and other pieces, the problem of race was mediated, with sometimes excessive symbolism, through themes of aesthetics, gender, mortality, the family, childhood, and religion. Often, Du Bois's exaltation of the beauty, goodness, and superiority of blackness bordered on cultural chauvinism. "The Call," first published in the May 1911 Crisis as "The Woman," combined the courage of black womanhood with the nobility of blackness in such a way as to suggest that both were incomparably splendid. Even more: that God himself was black—"the King spake not, but swept the veiling of his face aside and lifted up the light of his countenance upon her and lo! it was black," as was that of God's son in "Jesus Christ in Texas" and "The Second Coming."

On March 22, three weeks after publication, Du Bois received a royalty check for $280. Darkwater had already sold fourteen hundred copies, a robust number for such a book. Harcourt, Brace and Howe would run off a second printing in August 1920, and an edition from Constable was already selling well in Great Britain. *Darkwater* was meant to be drunk deeply by whites. Having seen the human drama "from a veiled corner," Du Bois had set about trying to lift the veil of race enough for white people to see—and even to feel—through the medium of arresting language and moral signposts what it was like to be a second-class citizen in America, a virtual caste whose pariah status inhered in the inescapability of skin color. In doing so, he also meant to show much more: how the veil fell over African savannahs and Asian rice fields. Obscured and distorted by the veil, real and relative differences between peoples based on geography, natural resources, and history became moral and genetic manifestations of inferiority justifying dominion and debasement by those who reduced technological advantage ultimately to color. It must have pleased the author when *The Socialist Review* proclaimed the book's universal significance, praised pieces on the manipulation of women and children, and touted its nutshell observations of the "circumscribed Jew, of the Hindu, of the dark peoples whom imperialism holds in subjection."

The collection raised a firestorm of reviews abroad as well as in the United States. It was one of the most controversial English-language nonfiction works published that year. In London, the *Athenaeum* superciliously dismissed *Darkwater* as pathetic, while the Paris edition of the New York *Herald* alerted readers to Du Bois's "Bolshevist madness." *The Times Literary Supplement* much preferred Moton's conciliatory *Finding a Way Out* to the dark, "fanatical" mind of Du Bois. The *New Statesman* showed more tolerance for this "born artist with words," but counseled him and his sympathizers to forgo fixation with color and to give whites the benefit of the doubt. Even the London School of Economics's Harold Laski, the voice of academic socialism, found *Darkwater* "a very brilliant, but hateful book—rather like," he wrote Supreme Court Justice Holmes, "what the southerner would write if he turned negro." In many of the mainstream American newspapers and periodicals the standard reproach was similar: *Darkwater* was tragically infected with its author's bitterness. It was hardly surprising that the book was dismissed as a madman's "hymn of racial hate" by the Greensboro, North Carolina, *Daily News*, that Nashville's *Southern Agriculturist* denounced it as "full of bitterness against white people," or that the Kansas City *Star* saw it as full of "threat, foreboding and intimidation" (although, interestingly, the Montgomery *Advertiser* conceded it had "undeniable charm of style"). Similar handwringing over Du Bois's alleged intemperance, resentfulness, "inferiority complex," and "extreme bitterness" also went on in *The Bookman, The Christian Science Monitor, The Outlook, The New York Times,* and even in *The Nation* where, on May 29, 1920, Villard, conceding that "no other colored American has ever written like this and few white," went on to deplore the author's "note of bitterness, tinctured with hate, and the teaching of violence which often defeats his own purpose."

As much of the serious white readership in America and Britain debated his book, Du Bois must have been conscious of two relatively recent developments in what was, overall, an intensely proud and grateful Negro reception: it was both more broadly based than ever and more critical. As he had the good sense seldom to comment on bad reviews (the contretemps with Villard over *John Brown* being a notable exception), whatever irritation or anger he may have felt is unknowable. But he could well have taken some satisfaction from the fact that he, the widely acknowledged "leader of his people," was being criticized by other activists and intellectuals of his race: satisfaction in seeing it as a measure of how much liberation and sophistication had come about in black America since the era of Booker Washington when he, Du Bois, and a handful of others had defied the Tuskegee Machine and dissent had usually been professionally fatal. Some of the criticism was razor sharp; some of it acidly personal. Fellow Harvard man Carter Godwin Woodson, as intellectually self-confident as Du Bois and by his own lights the better historian, was downright patronizing in the *Journal of Negro History,* describing the author as a "poet" whose mind was not yet adequate to the task of "scientific treatment" of the race problem. Du Bois could hardly have been offended when Yale and Harvard man William Ferris brushed aside his publishers' hyperbole that he, Du Bois, was chief spokesman for "two hundred million men and women of African blood." Nor was he completely astonished to read that Ferris believed the book to be circumscribed by temperament and class—an amazing revelation of the "soul of a cultured, refined Negro of mixed blood," Ferris called it in the influential *Negro World.* But Ferris, who was very dark-skinned, unattractive to women, and notoriously unkempt, went for the jugular, and Du Bois may have winced at the assertion that his "agony" was only his white blood "crying for its own." In closing, the pugnacious new editor of *The Negro World* pronounced a severe judgment that many who thought they knew Du Bois fully shared, and one that would pursue him until he drew his last breath—that the editor of *The Crisis* looked down upon the masses and their infirmities "from the heights of his own greatness." But it was the *Messenger's* William N. Colson, recently demobilized as a lieutenant from the 367th Infantry, whose essay may have given Du Bois the greatest pause for thought. Extolling him as a "poet rather than a thinker" whose sweeping grasp somehow floated above the needs of "the man farthest down," Colson thought that there was too much Hegel and not enough Debs in *Darkwater.* For all its marvelous learning and championing of democracy, the young socialist reviewer saw it as the testament of a "moralist and a mystic." Paraphrasing Du Bois's famous dictum, Colson declared that "the distribution of wealth and knowledge is the problem of the twentieth century."

The culture of criticism of the New Negro, then, was becoming more robust, with Du Bois serving both as its preeminent model and victim. And even in the role of victim, there could be no doubt that the overwhelming response to him and his work was summed up by the Washington *Bee*, which pronounced *Darkwater* as nothing less than "a milestone in the history of the Negro race." *The Souls of Black Folk* had stirred many thousands of humble black men and women who heard of it through the church, barbershop, streetcorner seminar, or read about it in the black press; and a great many of them actually came to own a copy of the book. Total sales for *Darkwater* probably ran to between eight and ten thousand by the end of the decade, figures about matching sales for *Souls* during its first ten years. What surprised Harcourt, Brace and Howe, amazed *The Literary Digest*, and earned a column in the New York *Morning Telegram* was the unprecedented interest of southern farmers, sharecroppers, northern domestics, and janitors in buying *Darkwater*—a veritable groundswell of common folk. "Negro workmen all over the country and some abroad have sent in letters" along with the two-dollar purchase price, revealed *The Literary Digest* for June 2, 1920. "Misspelled and almost illegible letters from colored men and women in the Black Belt of Alabama, Mississippi, Louisiana, Georgia, Arkansas and other states have been pouring in," gasped the *Telegram*. Some were unsigned and gave only post office box numbers, a wise precaution, the newspaper noted, given a recent three-month jail sentence imposed in one Deep South state on a Negro citizen who tried to subscribe to *The Crisis*. Many of them even gave "the life-history of the writer," such as that from a carpenter orphaned into a pitiless coming-of-age by his West Indian parents. "I am but a child. I need that book," his repetitious letter pleaded.

That a collection of essays of encyclopedic scope, most of which made scant concession to ordinary spoken English, could have such remarkable resonance with working-class black folk was indisputable evidence of its author's singular endowments of insight and inspiration. To read, or to hear read, certain passages from "Of Beauty and Death," for instance, describing the emotional purgatory of riding the Jim Crow car "up next to the baggage car and engine," or those disclosing the perpetual, debilitating predicament of being tightly coiled against impending insult and assault, was to open oneself to a catharsis transcending the particular reader or listener's class background. For all its hieratic language, *Darkwater*, in its many sections of complete verisimilitude, could sound the emotional depths of a whole people, as in the imagined dialogue about racial paranoia between two educated acquaintances, one black the other white, again, in "Of Beauty and Death." " 'This is my life. It makes me idiotic. It gives me artificial problems,' " the man of color confesses. " 'Do you mean to sit there and tell me that this is what happens to you each day?' 'Certainly not, I answer low.' " Then, after the man of color qualifies his denial, an exchange ensues that could as easily have taken place during the Civil Rights era of the sixties:

"But you just said—"

"They do happen. Not all each day—surely not. But now and then—now seldom, now sudden; now after a week, now in a chain of awful minutes; not everywhere, but anywhere—in Boston, in Atlanta. That's the hell of it. Imagine spending your life looking for insults or for hiding places from them—shrinking (instinctively and despite desperate bolsterings of courage) from blows that are not always but ever; not each day, but each week, each month, each year."

It was poignant verisimilitude such as this that brought one *Crisis* subscriber to write Du Bois that he had sat up until two o'clock in the morning "trying to break the spell" of *Darkwater*. It was so much easier to grasp the complexities of the race problem, "as pointed out by our own people," he added. "One awakes to a fuller realization of life." To say that *Darkwater* summoned a new ethos into being among the most oppressed and disadvantaged American Negroes would be extravagant even as a figure of speech. Rather, it was the new ethos fostered by literacy and town living, tremendously stimulated by the so-called Great War, and the emergence of a generation more than half a century out of slavery, that primed the popular response to the book. The achievement of *Darkwater* was that it provided the New Negro with a textbook uncannily suited to his/her new needs, a manual in which past, present, and future experiences of the group seemed to be invested with luminous meaning and shrewd prescription, even as the author, in his role as seer, was still groping for a formula of progress and empowerment that combined in the right proportions unity based on color with economic democracy based on class.

THE ELEVENTH ANNUAL conference of the NAACP met on the campus of Atlanta University at the beginning of June 1920. The choice of venue was auspicious. A national conclave had never before been held in the Deep South. Moreover, the association's Atlanta branch had only been organized the previous year. In choosing to meet in Atlanta, symbol both of the region's rebirth and of the doctrine of separate racial equality, the leadership meant to serve notice of the NAACP's growing numbers and determination to force change in the status quo in the Jim Crow South. It was the sort of gesture Du Bois could have been expected to propose, and he weighed in to carry the vote in the board of directors for the site. The editorial in the May issue of *The Crisis*, "Atlanta," threw down the gauntlet, declaring, with characteristic brio, that Negro citizens insisted on their "full rights in the South and everywhere else." But the editor and the association also graciously acknowledged the sporting invitation received from the mayor and Chamber of Commerce of Atlanta. No doubt wanting to atone in part for the 1906 riot but also to demonstrate how well segregation and civil rights could coexist, the capital of the New South executed an adroit maneuver in wasting little time before sending the NAACP its positive response.

With a recent gun battle in Lexington, Kentucky, taking the lives of five black men and the lynching of another on the way to trial, as well as the furious legal skirmishing to save the Arkansas sharecroppers in the news, and much else North and South to underscore the deteriorating state of race relations, going to Atlanta was a case of offense being the best defense. Mississippi had banned the circulation of materials "favoring social equality" and Texas was trying to outlaw the association. John Shillady, the NAACP's third executive secretary and the third white to hold that position, had tendered his resignation on the eve of the annual conference, still badly shaken many months after a white mob including a judge and a constable were reported to have savagely beaten him in August 1910 when he went to Austin, Texas, to reason with officials who claimed that the NAACP was a business operating without a state charter. Under subpoena from the Texas attorney general to make its records available, the Austin branch had appealed for help from New York. Shillady's battering, shocking to a broad segment of northern public opinion, gave the NAACP something of a cause célèbre, with the board demanding that President Wilson appoint an investigatory commission and branches throughout the country mounting protest rallies. Du Bois's *Crisis*, several issues of which had given especial offense to the Texas authorities, thundered against brutish cowards and demanded a moral reckoning when the executive secretary returned to testify before a grand jury. Shillady, a veteran social worker once noted for his cheerfulness, now confessed that he had become deeply pessimistic about the prospects for better times between the races, or that the NAACP could even hope to possess "within a reasonable period . . . the means and methods" sufficient to combat the opposition. He wouldn't be returning to Austin. *The Crisis* thundered again: "The haters of black folk beat him and maltreated him and scarred him like a dog because he tried to talk quiet reason to Texas."

When Bishop John Hurst, chairman of the selection committee, looped the sash and bronze pendant of the Spingarn Medal around Du Bois's starched collar on the opening day of the Atlanta convention, the NAACP merely formalized in ceremony the reality that the editor and his magazine were the association's most valuable assets. The bestowal of its highest honor symbolized, as well, the widely held belief among American Negroes everywhere that in W.E.B. Du Bois the race found a tribune of peerless audacity, intellect, and principles. Twenty-seven years ago, on the night of his lonely twenty-fifth birthday, tipsy and exalted in his Berlin student quarters, he had vowed that he would raise his race by becoming renowned in social science and in literature, "or perhaps to raise a visible empire in Africa." He had turned fifty-two on his last birthday, a little more than three months earlier. Trim, erect, in superb physical condition, goateed and with mustaches pointed up, and a dark, well-tailored suit making him seem taller than his five feet six inches, he graciously acknowledged the delegates' applause with a brief address. As he stepped from the platform that June day in 1920—his medal glinting in the brilliant sun—Du Bois had not only trumped the scholarly and literary portion of his twenty-fifth birthday wager, he had contributed mightily to the laying of the foundations for an empire of the mind among people of color, a realm in which culture and history offered a degraded race possibilities of enoblement and empowerment against ignominy and impotence.

His personality and pen defined the NAACP in the public's mind, black and white. In Europe he was regarded as the most important thinker of his race. One series of letters from a French aristocrat living in England and asking for a reading list and general guidance through the morass of American racial theories was especially illustrative of Du Bois's international stature. The Comte de Voilemont was writing "some articles on the color question in the United States" for a French periodical. The American attitude toward the Negro was deeply puzzling, the Frenchman insisted, and he found one popular book, *America's Greatest Problem: The Negro*, an example of "manifest bad faith." He proposed to "contradict" such racism, and would be "very much obliged indeed" for Du Bois's help. De Voilemont received letters of advice, a bibliography, and three parcels of articles—all forwarded by Nina to a post office box in the village of Harpenden. Less than a month before leaving for Europe, Du Bois sent a final letter and a copy of his article in *The Nation* to show the Frenchman "our attitude toward the next election." There are more than a few surprising and bizarre letters in Du Bois's enormous correspondence. But Voilemont's Harpenden letters were unique. Du Bois never realized that his French correspondent was Ferdinand-Walsin Esterhazy, the officer whose treason in 1894 had sent Captain Alfred Dreyfus to Devil's Island, France into a decade of paroxysm in one of the greatest judicial and political scandals of the twentieth century, and Europe into the maw of "scientific" anti-Semitism. It was the very period during which Nina was mailing parcels to their incognito aristocrat that Du Bois joined with more than a hundred other prominent Americans in signing a protest against the circulation by Henry Ford of the insidious forgery *The Protocols of the Elders of Zion*. The exchange between Du Bois and Esterhazy was an irony of breathtaking implausibility.

Even as the editor fulfilled his unique role as propagandist and prophet, there were changes under way both in the NAACP and the colored community, as well as in the nation at large that would alter imperceptibly, at first, and then with increasing tensions his relationship to the organization. The changes occurring at the 70 Fifth Avenue headquarters made the civil rights organization racially more representative and more aggressive, which would have the double-edged effect of enhancing the work of the editor and, as time passed, of creating agendas that increasingly competed with it. James Weldon Johnson, after an earlier stint as acting secretary and a highly successful tenure as secretary for branches, replaced the shell-shocked Shillady in August. Doubts about Johnson's Bookerite past and some white board members' fears about social and professional handicaps to be encountered by a Negro executive secretary had largely dissipated. Board chairperson Ovington admitted that she had been too suspicious of Johnson, whom she now positively admired nearly as much as the always difficult Du Bois. At long last, the time had arrived for the NAACP to hire a black permanent executive secretary. Mr. Johnson would do quite nicely, Ovington, Storey, Villard, and Spingarn agreed, easily overcoming whatever resistance remained, especially as Du Bois, Archibald Grimké, George Crawford, and the other Negroes on the board believed the decision was long overdue. Final confirmation of Johnson awaited the board's December 1920 meeting, but the new regime had already begun functioning even before the Atlanta convention, with Walter White assuming the duties of associate secretary. Although they shared an Atlanta University education, Johnson and White were a study in temperamental and intellectual contrasts as striking as their physical differences. Johnson, forty-nine, brown-skinned, fairly tall, and graceful as a panther, calculated the possibilities of a situation with the mind of a chess master; whereas the blue-eyed and blond White, twenty-seven, short and terrier-like, seldom met a civil rights impulse he could resist.

As a team, however, Johnson and White complemented each other admirably, imbuing the NAACP's undertakings with energy, efficiency, boldness, and design. During August and September 1920, *The Nation* ran four articles on Haiti by Johnson that caught the attention of the American public and the approval of the Republican National Committee. Occupied and run by the U.S. Marine Corps (Franklin Roosevelt, Wilson's secretary of the navy, boasted that he had drafted the island's constitution in a few hours), Haiti's people lived under political and economic conditions reminiscent of the Belgian Congo during the reign of Leopold II. The National City Bank of New York controlled the Banque Nationale d'Haiti, an arrangement facilitating the transfer of the country's revenues to the United States. The Haitian president took his orders from the American military authorities and without benefit of the National Assembly, dissolved five years earlier at bayonet point. The people lived in terror of the largely southern white troops who policed the country. Johnson came back from a two-week investigation in Haiti to report that, despite the Wilson administration's propaganda of uplift, the United States had done nothing to improve public education, that three thousand men, women, and children had been shot down in a so-called pacification campaign, and that the building of the modern highway from Port au Prince to Cap Haitien had reduced much of the population to slavery. In the name of progress, the Marine Corps had transformed the relatively benign and inefficient Haitian labor system requiring a few days a year of work for the state (the *corvée*) into a national labor dragnet of long-term, imbruting service. Readers of *The Nation* learned that the recent, bloody "pacification" campaign — "caco hunting," the Marines called it — was ordered by Washington in response to the guerrilla movement led by an educated Haitian, the charismatic Charlemagne Peralte, after he escaped a five-year sentence on the *corvée*. The Republican Party used "Self-Determining Haiti" in the 1920 national elections to influence the Negro vote, and after Warren Harding's victory the State Department and the Senate indulged in a charade of inspections and hearings on the occupation scandal. The Marines would stay in Haiti, nevertheless, until 1934.

Meanwhile, White's undercover reporting in *The Crisis* in early 1921 on Florida's homicidal election chicanery added another chapter to the Gothic South — wholesale murder, dispossession, and exile of Negroes as the reborn Ku Klux Klan rampaged across the state. Data on the Florida elections had been presented to Congress that December when Johnson and White, along with Grimké and two other NAACP officers, testified before the House Committee on the Census about Fourteenth Amendment violations in the South. After much debate, the association leadership had concluded that the only way to restore the colored vote in the South was to petition Congress to apply the sanction in Section II of the Fourteenth Amendment which called for reduction of the number of representatives in proportion to the percentage of people unlawfully excluded from the franchise — notwithstanding the risk that some southern states might claim that reduction of congressional representation would make their disfranchisement legal under the Constitution. Du Bois's contribution to the strategy was a forceful editorial exposing the objections of Tuskegee's Robert Moton and other conservative race leaders as specious. Privately, he wrote exasperatedly to a college administrator ally about Moton, "I am continually astonished by his lack of courage." Despite Du Bois's assurance that the Fifteenth Amendment would nullify claims of legal disfranchisement, unease about the Fourteenth Amendment ploy remained strong among many, perhaps even a majority, of Negroes, and the power of the white South through the seniority system soon made it obvious that Congress would never act on the NAACP's petition.

But even as the trial balloon of the Section II sanction was about to be launched, Du Bois wrote an important conjectural piece for *The Nation*, "The Republicans and the Black Voter," which seems to have contained the first outlines of the balance-of-power concept that would become a staple of American Negro politics after World War II and lead to the hard-fought recovery of the ballot in the South. Let the GOP take the Negro for granted and let the Democrats race bait, he challenged with bravado, "neither attitude will disturb the new Negro voter." In four major electoral states—Illinois, Michigan, Indiana, and Kentucky—the Negro voter "holds the balance of power," Du Bois crowed, and the eventual consequences of the Great Migration would increase the leverage of the race on national politics. The day would come when the GOP would stop taking the Negro for granted and even the Democrats would have to seek the black vote. If the short-term prospects for a national realignment of political parties were little short of dismal, Du Bois still thought that smart bargaining on a case-by-case basis could win more clout for the race in congressional, gubernatorial, and local politics down to the level of alderman and sheriff. The *Nation* article enumerated a seven-point NAACP questionnaire submitted to all presidential candidates calling for support of federal antilynching legislation, enforcement of Section II of the Fourteenth Amendment, abolition of Jim Crow cars in interstate travel, termination of racial segregation in the federal civil service; withdrawal of American forces from Haiti; federal aid to elementary education equally apportioned; and the enrollment of Negro officers and soldiers in the armed forces in proportion to their numbers in the population. Modifying the disastrous 1912 electoral ploy in which he had championed Woodrow Wilson, Du Bois opted for a flexible partisanship, a testing of candidates with the questionnaire. It was still quite possible, he argued, for state and local Democratic candidates "to attract a considerable number of Negro votes." Du Bois was not surprised that the presidential candidates declined to commit themselves to the NAACP's seven points.

Uncertainty was out of character, and yet the months following the award of the Spingarn Medal were somewhat unfocused for Du Bois. The ambitious history of the Negro's participation in the Great War was still not much more than an outline at the close of 1920. *Crisis* deadlines, articles for mainstream publications, *Darkwater*, speaking commitments, delay in launching his new children's magazine (there was a printers' strike)—all this and more would certainly have been enough to retard work on the war history. He would hardly have permitted himself to feel scooped when Emmett Scott's informative *Official History of the American Negro in the World War* came out, handsomely illustrated, at the end of 1919, any more than Kelly Miller's *Authentic History of the Negro in World War*, advertised in *The Crisis* for February 1921, would have fazed him. After all, his call for materials had produced a considerable quantity of written recollections and leads to explore that had the potential to make his own study a unique revelation. There was the firsthand account by one Wellington Willard describing how white officers had covered up their own cowardice and incompetence during the disastrous Argonne offensive. There was Elmer A. Carter's sharp analysis of the army's covert policy on discrediting the

Negro fighting man. One S. D. Redmond passed along the bitter feelings of his Georgia-born friend Eugene Bullard, the American Negro air ace who flew with the Lafayette Escadrille and bagged at least one German triplane, but was turned away when he offered his services to his own country's air force. E. C. Williams, librarian of Howard University, had set himself the task of obtaining statistical data on the American Expeditionary Force as soon as the boxes arrived from France and were put in some kind of order by the War Department. Du Bois was still holding on to the remarkable manuscript sent by a Washington insider and Talented Tenth notable, Major Adam E. Patterson, in summer 1919, some ten of a projected twenty-five chapters of a war history that Du Bois thought were "excellent and informing." The editor had been so pleased with these materials he wrote Patterson that he planned (after "very careful editing") to make it the first volume in a three-volume history of the war to be advertised in *The Crisis*. Presumably, Du Bois had intended to write volumes two and three himself.

As the year ended, he circulated a memorandum to the board asking for advice about his next major project. Should it be the research and writing of the war history, financed by the association, or the mounting of another Pan-African Congress, this one also to be subventioned by the association? At its December meeting, the board agreed to underwrite a portion of the expenses for the second Pan-African Congress. There is little doubt that the congress option held a powerful appeal for Du Bois, but the board was divided, with most directors, Ovington included, of the opinion that there were far more urgent domestic calls on the organization's limited resources. The NAACP was gearing up for a major campaign to build national support for a federal anti-lynching act. The lynching of three colored men in Duluth, Minnesota, of all places, less than a month after the December meeting made a favorable vote on H.R. 13 in the House Judiciary Committee a grim priority. The editor's vague announcement in the January 1921 *Crisis* that the congress would meet in early fall of that year revealed a general lack of enthusiasm on the part not merely of board members but a broad spectrum of the national membership. The NAACP wanted it to be made clear that it was bowing out: "Its official connection will thereupon cease and the Pan-African Congress will," Du Bois hoped, "become thereafter a permanent, self-supporting body." Once again, vision was hostage to the practical and the circumscribed, he felt, explaining later that "the older liberalism among the white people did not envisage Africa and the colored peoples of the world. . . . It seemed quixotic to undertake anything of the sort." As for Africans in America, "they felt themselves Americans, not Africans. They resented and feared any coupling with Africa."

It was up to him to push the international agenda of Aframericans, to cast the predicament of darker peoples in a global context, if only symbolically and despite the drain on his organization's resources. As a founder and the most visible officer of the nation's paramount civil rights organization, Du Bois believed it was both his obligation and privilege to rise above the NAACP's immediate, tactical, and parochial concerns. With Jessie Fauset translating into French, he busied himself doing so, beginning a decidedly one-sided correspondence with Blaise Diagne, the powerful Senegalese deputy who had chaired the first congress and, Du Bois hoped, would keep his promise to chair the second. Two Belgian influentials, Paul Otlet and Paul Panda, a European and an African, respectively, sent immediate replies offering to host a session in the Palais Mondial in Brussels. Du Bois wrote the cautious head of the British Anti-Slavery and Aborigines Protection Society to propose cosponsorship of a London venue for the congress. Hoping to make it possible for John Langalibalele Dube, the South African educator and founder of the African National Congress, to remain in Britain with his delegation long enough to attend the Pan-African Congress, Du Bois fired off requests for contributions in order to help defray their expenses. Too late to take advantage of the offer, Du Bois expressed regretful appreciation to the League of Nations senior official who volunteered to arrange for a Geneva session. Another response from Geneva seemed to hold great potential. The distinguished French Socialist Albert Thomas, who now headed the League's International Labor Organization, wrote that he endorsed Du Bois's proposal for a section within the ILO to investigate the needs of African labor. Thomas suggested a meeting immediately after the Pan-African Congress to make plans for such an arrangement. Meanwhile, Du Bois's point man in Paris, Rayford Logan, reported that Diagne and Gratien Candace, representing Senegal and Guadeloupe, respectively, in the Chamber of Deputies, were dragging their feet. A Williams College Phi Beta Kappa, who made a living by speculating in currencies, Lieutenant Logan had been so soured by race prejudice in the American army that he insisted on being demobilized in France. The editor's connection to Logan came through Fauset, Logan's French teacher at Washington's elite M Street High School. "You will find [Messieurs] Diagne and Candace a bit slow, but do not get discouraged," Du Bois wrote. It was a busy time.

He hoped to leave for France in early August. Fauset and White were expected to sail together for England at about the same time. But meantime, he was finding himself in a thicket of family concerns and professional troubles. Nina was not going to Europe. He would have had to pay for her travel out of personal funds. On a declared net income of $4,382.25 they might have been able to afford the expense, had Will, as Nina always called him, wanted her along, but they agreed that she should get Yolande ready and off again to her second year of college in early September. Yolande was self-indulgent, underachieving, uncertain, chronically overweight, and often ill. She appears to have craved her father's approval in almost exactly the proportions she sensed that her inadequacies would preclude her winning it. Not that her father ever neglected her material needs or failed to intervene when she needed encouragement or protection. When it was suggested that Yolande and three other girls of color attending Brooklyn's Girls' High School might prefer not to attend the senior class prom at a swank Brooklyn hotel, Papa had roared like an offended mastodon at the principal: class funds to pay for a function that "arbitrarily exclude[s] from that entertainment members of the class in good standing!" Outrageous! In the ensuing exchange of letters, an increasingly feckless Principal William Felter denied racism, hid behind the senior-class vote of 43 to 11 to restrict the prom to white girls, protested that the function was private, and hoped that Dr. Du Bois would be pleased to learn that Miss Gwendolyn Bennett, "one of the very able [excluded] colored girls," had written the words to the class song. "Are you voting to see if the Jewish girls shall be invited to their own class promenade or the Irish girls, or the red-headed girls?" Yolande's father demanded. "This is not democracy; it is sheer tyranny."

Yolande would be returning for her sophomore year at Fisk University after her 1920 graduation from Girls' High School. At Fisk, her father's college, there were no more racial exclusions, and there was release, at least for four years, from the soul-weariness of living always under a white microscope—although her fears about good grades were only too well founded. During her first year, Yolande had spent part of February in the college hospital suffering from a serious inflammation of the gums. "Much pain, couldn't sleep; I just cried continually," she wrote Nina. "Honestly, I've *never* been hurt so badly before." Somewhat better the following month, she had reported a 95 in history and 83 on her French exam. "I don't know what my other marks are, but I think I passed," a relieved Du Bois read. He had sent money to a faculty member to arrange drawing-room accommodations to avoid segregation aboard the express for her return home that June. It was "very expensive," she noted gratefully, thanking Papa in the same breath for the checks that had come "some time ago." In the coming academic year, 1922–23, she would take a required chemistry course, for which she had already been given stern advice, with more to follow from her father. Nina, whose own health was always delicate, not only carried the burden of their troubled daughter's affairs but singlehandedly executed the liquidation of the Brooklyn homestead at 94 Johnson Street when Nail and Parker, the Harlem real estate brokerage firm, finally located suitable housing in Manhattan. She would write Will about another flare-up of Yolande's abscessed tooth a few days after he reached Paris, adding that her own neck still ached badly. Though Nina complained of aches, hers and Yolande's, she rarely faltered in the management of family affairs. With a better head for practical details than Will's and a sense of duty in its own way as compelling as his, she was tireless in her quiet devotion to the well-being of their family. Hers was the private sphere of housekeeping, children, bills, and church, indispensable to her famous husband's unhindered attention to world-important concerns and increasingly underappreciated by him, his edifying, feminist professions notwithstanding.

Very likely, Du Bois found the mentoring of his daughter a steeper challenge than providing guidance to young people in general, but nineteen years of dealing with Yolande was undoubtedly a valuable experience in producing the magazine for young people, *The Brownies' Book*, which finally made its delayed appearance in January 1920. The idea for a magazine devoted to what Du Bois called "the children of the sun" was his own. "Heretofore the education of the Negro child has been too much in terms of white people," he had announced in the October 1919 *Crisis*. "All through school life his text-books contain much about white people and little or nothing about his own race." This theme of what a much later generation would call multicultural education (evolving from the Black Studies in the 1960s) was a constant preoccupation of Du Bois's, as evidenced by some of the most intense passages in *Darkwater*. Only after being subjected to a regime of nurturing in which there was neither "shielding and indulgence" against the color line nor too much "race consciousness prematurely," he insisted in "The Immortal Child," would colored parents be blessed with resilient and proud youngsters. Many parents, not quite knowing which course was better, left their children to sink or swim in a "sea of race prejudice," he noted. Some children emerged strengthened and self-reliant; others, as he had good reason to know, experienced "bewilderment, cringing deception, and self-distrust." He and Nina must have thought they had tried to avoid extremes in educating Yolande; she had certainly benefited from some of the wisest aphorisms and admonitions of almost any child in America. Yet Du Bois had chosen to send his daughter to an experimental boarding school in Great Britain, entrusting the shaping of her impressionable mind and spirit not merely to white teachers in an insular and exclusively white environment but to teachers who, though more enlightened than those at the great public schools, thought it self-evident that the British Empire was ordained by God working through history to be global custodian of the white man's burden. The Bedales School experience in Great Britain had left its mark. It had pretty nearly crushed whatever self-confidence might have survived the burden of being her father's daughter. As bewildered Yolande entered college, her father may well have felt that his children's magazine afforded another opportunity for paternal advice—advice that now had the painful, chastening, compensatory benefit of hindsight.

Published by the new firm of Du Bois and Dill, *The Brownies' Book* would run through twenty-four issues until December 1921 when, as Du Bois wistfully announced, "unless we got at least one in every hundred to read our pages . . . we knew we must cease to be." The hands-on search for talent and editing fell to the competent Fauset and dutiful Dill. The magazine was beautifully illustrated (principally by Laura Wheeler, whose drawings appeared regularly in *The Crisis*), with Du Bois's "As the Crow Flies" column emphasizing past and present achievements of people of color. There was a section for letters from young readers ("The Jury") and another for adult opinion ("The Judge," written by Fauset), with poetry, plays, short stories, and biographical profiles by such talented unknowns as Langston Hughes, Willis Richardson, and Nella Larsen, along with contributions from Georgia Douglas Johnson, Arthur Huff Fauset, Eulalie Spence, Colonel Young, and other well-recognized members of the Talented Tenth. Captioned "Some Little Friends of Ours," photographs of scrubbed, bright-eyed boys and girls, hair parted and pigtailed, beamed from its pages both in innocence and in defiance of the realities the magazine's editors were fighting gamely to ameliorate.

If not enough parents chose or could afford to pay the $1.50 annual subscription fee to sustain it longer, judging by letters from the jury, those young people who read *The Brownies' Book* loved it. A boy in Toronto, who dreamed of going to Africa after finishing school, read the magazine because he "ought to know a great deal about our people and all the places where they live, all over the world, don't you think so?" Alice Martin in Philadelphia hated her geography lessons sometimes: "when we read about the different people who live in the world, all the pictures are pretty, nice-looking men and women, except the Africans. . . . I see lots of ugly white people, too; [but] . . . they are not the ones they put in the geography. . . . Mother said for me to write you about it." In "The Grown-Ups' Corner," Mrs. Bella Seymour of Manhattan reported that her little girl was studying Betsy Ross, George Washington, "and the others, and she says: 'Mamma, didn't colored folks do anything?' " Mrs. Seymour's prayers were answered by a stream of vivid profiles — "A Pioneer Suffragette" (Sojourner Truth), "America's First Martyr" (Crispus Attucks), "Toussaint L'Ouverture"; " 'Saint' Gandhi"; "Story of Harriet Tubman." Pocahontas Foster from Orange, New Jersey, thought they were the best history she'd ever read, because she had always felt that history "wasn't much good." Then she read the story about Paul Cuffee, the early nineteenth-century shipowner, to her eight-year-old friend, who said, " 'Now that's the kind of history I like. Won't you ask *The Brownies' Book* to tell some more stories like that?' " Fauset's dedicatory poem in the January 1920 issue had pledged:

> To Children, who with eager look
> Scanned vainly library shelf and nook,
> For History or Song or Story

That told of Colored Peoples' glory—
We dedicate *The Brownies' Book.*

With her help and special touch, and the reliable Dill's business sense, Du Bois could feel satisfaction in having launched a unique venture. There was much talk among preachers and teachers and leaders about the emotional and intellectual care and feeding of black children ("immortality is the present child," proclaimed Du Bois), but not until *The Brownies' Book* had emotional care and feeding been packaged in monthly installments for the hope of the race.

Du Bois had anticipated the problematic life span of his children's magazine. The sharp downturn in *Crisis* subscribers—from the August 1919 high of more than 100,000—was another, far more serious, development. By April 1921, their number had declined to 53,000. The cost of paper had necessitated an increase in the price of the magazine just before the depression of 1921 began to bite, and, although Du Bois's reports to the board contained no racial breakdown of subscribers, the lost readers would almost certainly have been disproportionately black. "Our agents everywhere are feeling the industrial depression," he lamented. Not even the July issue recounting the details of the Tulsa riot, a Gehenna of arson and murder in which some forty-four blocks of the Oklahoma city's thriving Negro quarter were laid waste, was able to lift circulation. Tulsa had erupted on May 31, after a local newspaper, *The Tribune*, excited mob fury over an elevator incident involving a female operator and a young colored shoeshine employee. Pharmacies, barbershops, grocery stores, cinemas, a bank, rows of neat homes—the incarnation in wood and brick of a generation of black people's faith in hard work and respectability—were incinerated in a twenty-four-hour invasion by hundreds of white Tulsans armed with rifles, machine guns, and a strafing airplane. *The Crisis* reproduced a stark aerial photo showing a gridiron of devastation receding into the horizon, and it claimed that scores of Tulsa refugees had arrived in New York, "possessing practically nothing except the clothes on their backs."

The dropoff of revenues coming to *The Crisis* worried the board's executive committee, which now began regularly to vex the editor. Reverend John Haynes Holmes, a founding member and conscientious officer, tactfully floated a proposal to consolidate the staffs of the association and the magazine. In addition to Dill, Fauset, and Madeline Allison, a stylish, recently hired assistant literary editor, Du Bois was responsible for a half dozen salaries, a number that Haynes suggested could be reduced significantly. Failing that, the NAACP would be drawn into a burgeoning subsidy of the magazine. Holmes's proposal was met with a categorical negative, the problems of merger having been "so fully proven in the past," the annoyed editor responded, as to merit no further consideration. Not only was a reduction in staff out of the question, but he refused, as in the past, to share with the NAACP fees generated on his regular speaking tours. Du Bois, who was still the sole employee who sat on the board of directors, reminded his fellow officers that, as director of publications and research, whatever he did was uniquely beneficial to the NAACP, while they countered that—however valuable his unique role—the growing number of branches, national campaigns, refinement of staff roles, bureaucratic economies, and employee morale nevertheless imposed new exigencies to which even he should be expected to accede. Meanwhile, to the mounting ire of Chairperson Ovington and the executive committee, the editor insisted on researching and writing books and accepting commissions from outside magazines with little regard for the priorities of the association. There was also the thorny bookkeeping problem of monthly remittals of membership fees and subscription revenues, a percentage of each to be divided between the association and *The Crisis*.

The hostile atmosphere worsened during Ovington's California vacation to the point that the diplomatic James Weldon Johnson complained his own effectiveness was being impaired by internecine conflict. By the time she returned in mid-July, Ovington found herself confronted with accusations about the editor's morals as well as the chronic oversight and financial disputes. A potentially bankrupting libel suit against *The Crisis* had been settled out of court by the association's attorney, Arthur Spingarn. But now there was scandal. Du Bois was said to have compromised himself so egregiously, Holmes and several others believed, as to be "unfit" to serve as editor. A real tug of war had gotten under way at the beginning of 1921, with the normally unflappable President Storey telling the greatly agitated Holmes to "give him *The Crisis* and let him go," if the editor refused to mend his ways. Memoranda were shuttled among board members; caucuses were formed, attitudes hardened; and Du Bois, unfazed by the hubbub, was reported to evidence no "appeal to mercy." The trail of speculation about the cause of certain board members' outrage led to a curious arrangement between *The Crisis* and Madeline Allison, the assistant literary editor. The February 1921 issue was the first of several to carry a full page advertising the "Allison Shopper," a service providing a range of specialty household items. Interested readers were invited to write Miss Allison at 70 Fifth Avenue. "Let me explain prices and descriptions, qualities, etc.," urged the caption accompanying the photograph showing her to be a comely young woman of Levantine appearance.

Whatever Du Bois had done, and with whom, Ovington, although apparently deeply shocked, was unwilling to countenance an NAACP without him. Her warm feelings for Du Bois had endured over a quarter of a century, dating from that evening in the Atlanta University dining hall when she first gazed upon his "noble head" and delighted in his brilliant badinage. But the present embarrassment made her positively wrathful. If the Negro board members were given the complete facts, "the decision would be less lenient than the one I have agreed to," she admitted to Arthur Spingarn. She had worked with him and she knew he was "a slippery customer," she confided. He would take advantage of "any false step the other side would make." He counted on his power "over white people"; "his career has been made by the whites; first Dr. Bumstead, next various members of the NAACP." Well, this time, he would be brought to account. She and Spingarn set about crafting a three-part take-it-or-leave-it statement that Holmes was asked to submit to the editor on July 29. "All special privileges will cease," supervision of *The Crisis* would be imposed; the editor would be accountable in the same way as all other executives. Board minutes reveal nothing and Du Bois is silent about this curious dustup, yet it seems obvious that he found himself too much on the defensive to deflect the executive committee's anger. He signed the agreement Holmes presented him on July 29, and sailed for France two weeks later.

· 2 ·

DU BOIS AND GARVEY:

TWO "PAN-AFRICAS"

Rayford Whittingham Logan met the Boulogne boat train bringing Du Bois to Paris on August 16, 1921. Logan, a fluent French-speaker making a colorful living speculating in European currencies, was twenty-four. Fifty-three years later, he remembered their first meeting at the Gare St. Lazare as if it were yesterday. His French teacher at M Street High School, Jessie Fauset, had sent Logan careful instructions about Du Bois and his epic European mission. He would be able to recognize Dr. Du Bois immediately by his distinctive visage and carriage, Fauset wrote. "What I remember particularly was her reference to his noble head," recalled Logan. Unable to imagine Du Bois arriving "in any other way except first class," Logan nearly decided to leave the station after waiting in vain to spot a noble head even among the second-class boat train passengers. Knowing how much Miss Fauset would disapprove of any shortcoming in the discharge of his assignment, however, he waited for the last boat train, bringing third-class passengers. Suddenly, he recognized a well-dressed man with a cane walking "very nonchalantly down the platform." Although he knew it must be Du Bois, Logan was rather surprised that he was not as tall as the famous personality's towering reputation had led him to expect. Introductions made, they proceeded to the pension run by Madame Loulouse Chapoteau at 9 rue Jasmin in the Sixteenth Arrondissement where Du Bois hoped to find a communique from the elusive Blaise Diagne, president of the Pan-African Congress.

Du Bois's determination to follow through on the formal pledge of 1919 to convene yet another congress two years later had clearly surprised the Francophone Africans. As the editor prodded them in letters translated into French by Fauset, surprise soured into resentment and finally into passive resistance. Gratien Candace and Isaac Beton, men of exemplary culture and Gallic manners who perpetually represented the *département* of Guadeloupe in the Chamber of Deputies, had only minimal enthusiasm for the enterprise by the time Du Bois reached Paris. Part of the difficulty was Du Bois's almost innocent imperiousness as he forced the planning into high gear. Meeting sites had had to be negotiated, agendas drafted, funds raised in record time. Inevitably, egoes were bruised as Du Bois ignored or overrode the advice of his European organizing committees. A case in point was Brussels, selected by him as the venue for the most important of the three sessions. When secretary Robert Broadhurst objected in the name of the London-based African Progress Union to meeting in the Belgian capital, with all that Brussels evoked of extreme African exploitation, Du Bois brushed him aside. Senator La Fontaine and Monsieur Otlet were "personal friends" who were doing everything "to promote the Congress," and, far more significantly, he explained impatiently, Belgium was the only European nation offering semiofficial recognition of the Pan-African Congress by allowing it to convene in the grandiose Palais Mondial.

In a hurried attempt at mollification, Du Bois sent the unavailable Diagne an urgent note stating his readiness to bring an interpreter for his "bad French" in order to have "a long conference" about the business of the congress, that he would gladly consult with him at a place of his choosing. The exact date of their meeting remains uncertain (probably on the twenty-fourth or twenty-fifth), but what was said between the two men Logan never forgot. Although Du Bois sometimes boasted that he could be silent in six languages, Logan discovered that French was not one of them. Nor was Diagne able to converse in English. The Frenchman claimed to be distressed about the Garveyite agitation in Africa and almost as alarmed about the Pan-African Congress being charged with Bolshevism. Calming Diagne with expressions of his own distaste for Garvey and his movement, Du Bois could make no headway at all when it came to self-government in Africa and the Caribbean. Africans living under the tricolor wanted to become *more* French, not less so—they wanted assimilation not independence, Diagne explained haughtily. As the politician and the editor grew more agitated in their native tongues, Logan ceased translating faithfully in order to preclude an irreparable breach. A word here, a shade of meaning there, several complete omissions along the way, and the ex-lieutenant managed to navigate Du Bois and Diagne to a working agreement in principle, what the politician called "*une formule transactionelle,*" final details of which Logan was charged to work up as soon as possible in a second meeting. Accompanying Du Bois to the Gare du Nord for the channel train, Logan was told to do whatever was necessary to keep the Frenchman from dumping the Congress.

In Du Bois the Pan-African idea found an intellectual temperament and organizational audacity enabling it to advance beyond the evangelical and literary to become an embryonic movement whose cultural, political, and economic potential would assume, in the long term, worldwide significance. No other person of color then living, with the significant and calamitous exception of Marcus Garvey, was more capable of articulating the idea and mobilizing others in its service. "Seven hundred and fifty years before Christ the Negroes were rulers of Ethiopia and conquerors of Egypt," the editor had reminded his readers in the March issue, but "supremacy brought no continental unity." Then came the rise and fall of kingdoms in the Sudan, followed by the confusion of the slave trade. For the first time in history, conditions were propitious for the construction of a global movement to advance the common cultural and political objectives of people of color, Du Bois proclaimed. Pan-Africanists had nothing to fear but fear of their own audacity, he might have written — and racial parochialism. With that visionary passion for justice nurtured in Great Barrington and present in every book from *The Suppression of the African Slave Trade* onward, Du Bois rose above particularisms to deliver the same solution to Arkansas pogroms and Gompers's American Federation of Labor, as to South African land acts and systematic brutality of cartels in the Belgian Congo: "The absolute equality of races — physical, political and social — is the founding stone of world peace and human advancement." There was, he would later claim with hollow modesty, "nothing spectacular nor revolutionary" about his plans. Perhaps in time — "in decades or a century" — they would bring about a "world organization" of black people in order to present a united front to European aggression. But he knew "the power and guns of Europe and America"; for the present, then, in the face of this power, it would be splendid enough achievement "to sit down hand in hand with colored groups and across the council table to learn of each other, our condition, our aspirations."

The men and women of color attending the three sessions (Du Bois listed about thirty from the United States) came, in large part, because they needed to believe in Du Bois's vision, to make some commitment of time and money to an undertaking that, by virtue of its pure symbolism and undeniable incongruity with quotidien concerns, invested the predicament of living in a dark skin with ecumenical purpose. Undoubtedly, too, some came to London, Brussels, and Paris because they wanted to boast about their travels when they returned home. But it is very likely that the famous tenor Roland Hayes, the research librarian Ruth Anna Fisher, the young sociologist on fellowship in Denmark E. Franklin Frazier, Morehouse College president John Hope, the educator and Philadelphia banker Richard R. Wright, Sr., along with YMCA secretary Channing Tobias, war hero Captain Napoleon Bonaparte Marshall and Mrs. Marshall, and the spellbinding Chicago prelate Bishop Archibald Carey, Sr., and Mrs. Carey, were part of a genuinely interested American contingent attending the London meeting. Also attending were Hastings Banda, the East African physician, John L. Dube, the South African educator, and Albert Marryshaw, the Grenadian trade unionist, all of whom were to play similar senior-statesmen roles in their respective countries, as would Ibidunni Obadende of Nigeria. The wealthy mulatto planter from São Tomé, Nicola de Santos-Pinto, represented the Liga Africana, an organization of highly assimilated Portuguese Africans. Mrs. Helen Curtis, the able consul general at Brussels, represented Liberia. The evidence is circumstantially strong that a peripatetic young Annamese nationalist named Nguyen That Tan, who became much better known as Ho Chi Minh, attended the Paris session.

Thanks to the energetic efficiency of Walter White, who had sailed with Du Bois on the Dutch steamer *Ryndam*, the opening of the London meeting on the twenty-seventh was assured, whatever the francophone Africans decided. White had disembarked at Plymouth with instructions to contact Norman Angell and Harold Laski in London and "get things started at once," while Du Bois had proceeded to Boulogne. On the day before the conference, Du Bois and White spent an hour or so with Sidney Webb and Norman Angell of the Labour Party's executive committee in cordial but ultimately meaningless discussion of British abuses in the African colonies. "We received only vague evasions," White would record in his autobiography of Du Bois's earnest attempt to convince colleagues of his old acquaintance Ramsay MacDonald of the rightness of a formal Labour Party pledge to rectify the most extreme conditions when it came to power. White was even disposed to credit the Colonial Office's almost comic overreaction to Marcus Garvey and his "Back to Africa Movement" as a factor in the decision to accord Du Bois the high-level Labour parley. In fact, Du Bois found himself on a number of occasions having to conceal his annoyance as he drew careful distinctions for the British press between his movement and Garvey's. In one interview, Du Bois explained that, although sharing the Jamaican's "main aspirations," he believed Garvey's methods lacked "plain sense" and that his finances were unsound.

The well-attended proceedings in Central Hall opposite Westminster Abbey moved apace over two intense days. "We were all one family in London," Fauset enthused. "What small divergences of opinion, slight suspicions, doubtful glances there may have been at first were all quickly dissipated." With Du Bois in the chair as secretary on the twenty-ninth, the Congress voted unanimous approval of eight general motions that became known as the London resolutions. Several speakers had gone out of their way to reassure watching European officialdom of their patient and realistic understanding of the burdens of empire. Dr. John Alcindor, a London physician of Trinidadian origin, was reported to have deflected criticism of colonial regimes with the admonition that the Africans' worst enemies were "very often the Africans themselves, who lacked character, education, and cohesion." The combining of conservative convictions with boilerplate diplomacy imbued the manifesto of the second Pan-African Congress, *To the World*, with a placatory, even unctuous, tone here and there.

Even though Belgium showed no disposition to allow Africans under her dominion "any voice in their own government," or even to grant them ownership of land or any say in negotiating labor conditions, the manifesto expressed satisfaction that Brussels was now "considering a liberal program of reform for the future." The verdict on French imperialism was virtually an endorsement: "France alone . . . has sought to place her cultured black citizens on a plane of absolute legal and social equality with her white [citizens] and given them representation in her highest legislature." Much more remained to be done in order to perfect *la mission civilisatrice*, but the authors of the manifesto (primarily secretary Du Bois) were well pleased with the Third Republic. Still, in the context of the times, when the end of white supremacy was inconceivable even to the great majority of its victims, the manifesto's arraignment of two of the most powerful exploiters showed that conservatism and conciliation had definite limits. *To the World* ventured to excoriate Britain and the United States for falling far short of their own professed ideals of stewardship and civil rights, reproaching the vaunted Pax Britannica for fostering systematic ignorance and enslavement "among the natives" and indicting America for "throwing the freed men upon the world penniless and landless."

Du Bois's role in drafting *To the World* was unmistakable in the paragraph asserting that the great modern problem was to "correct maladjustment in the distribution of wealth, . . . the outrageously unjust distribution of world income between the dominant and the suppressed peoples." Calling on European regimes to recognize "civilized men as civilized despite their race or color," the manifesto enunciated three demands—resolutions—whose implications for the new world order of European hegemony under the League of Nations would have been, if ever taken seriously, extremely destabilizing. Resolution II, calling for "local self-government for backward groups," was the most radical in its demand that local self-government must grow "as experience and knowledge grow" until formerly subject territories achieved complete self-determination "under the limitations of a self-governing world." After the Paris session, Du Bois planned to spend several days in Geneva lobbying to implement Resolution VIII: establishment of an international section in the Labor Bureau of the League of Nations, "charged with the protection of native labor."

"The world must face two eventualities," Du Bois intoned as he reached the conclusion of *To the World*. Africa must either be assimilated completely by Europe on the basis of absolutely equal political, civil, and social privileges for its black and white citizens or Europe must allow the rise of an autonomous "great African state" based on popular education, industry, and freedom of trade. It would have been needlessly provocative and given ammunition to the enemy had he alluded to a third alternative, the one in *Darkwater* predicting a global war of the races if peoples of color were everlastingly held back and exploited.

Instead, Du Bois ended solemnly in the hushed Central Hall on a note of supplication and mysticism. "Out of the depths we have cried unto the deaf and dumb masters of the world. Out of the depths we cry our own sleeping souls. The answer is written in the stars."

Taking the measure of Du Bois, the London *Challenge* concluded that he was more than a "personal force"; he symbolized the New Negro. "He does not tower as an isolated figure above his fellows," the paper observed; he was simply first among equals among the many men and women of eminence attending the Congress. Even though the supercilious British press revealed that most of the visitors to Central Hall came out of amusement or curiosity, the dignified proceedings and the import of the London resolutions evoked an at least momentary thoughtfulness in some quarters. *Punch* reported the headline in the London *Times* — "No Eternally Inferior Races" — with the pun, "No, but in the opinion of our colored brothers, some infernally superior ones." A pleased Du Bois observed that the attention received by the Congress "was astonishing." Du Bois, Fauset, White, and most of the delegates from the London meeting reached Brussels on Tuesday, August 30. With its outsized public squares, monumental government palaces, and florid architecture, the capital had served as the unnamed city in *Heart of Darkness* that always reminded Conrad's hero of a "whited sepulcher." In the novel and in reality, Brussels was headquarters to one of imperialism's most malefic cartels, a rapacious entity using quasi–slave labor to strip an area half the size of Europe of its seemingly bottomless wealth in copper, rubber, and ivory. As Du Bois and the others had to know, the construction of King Leopold II's new Brussels — the city within the hexagonal belt of sweeping, broad boulevards beyond the ancient center — depended upon the grinding exploitation of the people and minerals of the Congo. The better to promote and obscure the practices at the foundation of the little country's enormous wealth, the Belgian government colluded with the cartel to seal off the Congo from the outside world. Du Bois and Fauset were made more aware of well-mannered unease on the part of their hosts about a roving symposium on Africa and imperialism. "After all, who were these dark strangers speaking another language and introducing heaven knew what ideas to be carried into the Congo?" asked Fauset rhetorically in her *Crisis* report of the Congress. The Union Congolaise, comprised of pliant Africans led by young Mfumu Paul Panda and an elegant personage identified as Madame Sorolea, attested to the satisfactory state of affairs in what had not so long ago been acknowledged as the nadir of Europe in Africa.

Belgian officials appear to have regarded Panda, among the very few Congolese with advanced academic training, as one of their most able African mascots. Bouncy and articulate, he was assigned to guide the delegates on a tour of the cavernous Musée du Congo at Tervuren (today's Musée Royal de l'Afrique centrale), a few miles outside the capital. The Museum of the Congo was in a literal and figurative sense a mausoleum *for* the Congo, its twenty exhibition halls radiating like spokes in a giant wheel from a towering central court. Du Bois admitted to being simply "astounded." "It was marvelous," he gasped—"the visible, riotous wealth of the Congo . . . the infinite, intriguing, exquisite beauty of art." At his side, Fauset was equally ecstatic over what she saw. "Such treasures! Such illimitable riches!" After visiting the hall of musical instruments, she exclaimed that there wasn't a single instrument anywhere in the world for which the Congo "cannot furnish a prototype." Enthusiasm led her to suggest to Panda that American Negroes and Africans would be mutually enriched by a select number of teachers visiting the Congo, which caused the unnerved educator, according to Fauset, to recoil in horror, spluttering, "Oh, no, no, no! Belgium would never permit that, the colored Americans are too clever."

The second session of the Congress opened in an enormous Beaux-Arts structure in the sprawling Parc du Cinquantenaire east of the city. The park had been laid out in 1880 to commemorate the fiftieth anniversary of Belgium's founding as an independent state. Dominated by three triumphal arches, the ninety-acre park of tree-lined allées decorated by ornate fountains provided the Congress with an ostentatiously European theater in which to contemplate the future of Africa. "We could not have asked for a better setting," wrote Fauset with no thought of irony. It was a setting Du Bois described as "palpitating with curiosity." The press tables were crowded. Two generals sat on either side of Blaise Diagne. A white French deputy sat with them, along with an Ethiopian and an American woman of color. In the audience were several hundred Europeans and dozens of Congolese. In Diagne, who presided over the Brussels meeting in his capacity of president of the Pan-African Congress, the Belgians had a steadfast supporter. His tall frame superbly tailored, the regal, frock-coated high commissioner conducted the meetings uniquely in French and with imperious disregard for Du Bois and his Americans who found themselves, as Du Bois put it, "linguistically stranded." The London resolutions had not been well received in the principal colonial ministries, and Diagne's handlers intended to scuttle them before they reached Paris.

Du Bois wrote later in *The New Republic* that he had risen "in no spirit of trouble-making" to read the London resolutions on the last afternoon. Fauset thought the Congress was about to end in a rather disgraceful affair after Diagne's implacable opposition completely polarized the delegates. Du Bois claimed that he didn't dream of the consternation he had caused. "His French was almost too swift for my ears," he said of Diagne's furious reaction. The relatively mild sentence in *To the World* about Belgium's reluctance to allow the Congolese any participation in government, followed by the charge that "her colonial policy is still mainly dominated by the banks and great corporations" stunned the assembly. Resolution VI calling for the restoration of the "ancient common ownership" of African lands plunged the hall into pandemonium. There were cries of "Bolshevist!" and *absolument inadmissible!*" Diagne behaved as though he might have personal investments at risk in Central Africa. The perplexed Panda was swallowed up in a huddle of several philanthropists, a general, and his Belgian foster mother. A Belgian diplomat hurried forward with a compromise resolution that Diagne put to a vote without discussion, and declared approved even though Du Bois complained that "guests and visitors" had voted.

With much of the European press beginning to follow its deliberations, Du Bois was determined to maneuver the Congress into issuing a ringing challenge to white world supremacy. Commanding the podium, from which he didactically exposed iniquities under colonial rule, yet also generously acknowledged the bright spots, Du Bois invoked the ideals of the Enlightenment and the covenant of the League of Nations in defense of universal rights that he posited as inviolable, regardless of a society's cultural or technological level of evolution. "That in the vast range of time, one group should in its industrial technique, or social organization, or spiritual vision, lag a few hundred years behind another, or forge fitfully ahead, or come to differ decidedly in thought, deed and ideal, is proof of the essential richness and variety of human nature, rather than proof of the coexistence of demi-gods and apes in human form. The doctrine of racial equality does not interfere with human liberty," Du Bois ended to loud applause, "rather, it fulfils it." Fauset was enormously proud of him: under his leadership the Americans "showed themselves to be real masters of the situation." In an eleventh-hour compromise on Friday, September 2, 1921, the Congress accepted Diagne's watered-down motion and voted to submit the London resolutions for definitive approval, amendment, or rejection at the last round of meetings in Paris.

"Whether or not you like Mr. Burghardt Du Bois, whether or not you agree with his program," the newspaper, *Echo de la Bourse*, sportingly conceded, "you have to bow to his brilliant intellect and his devotion to the black race." Recounting the roller-coaster proceedings in Brussels to her *Crisis* readers, Fauset wrote that the delegates left Belgium "in a thoughtful and puzzled mood." The contest with Diagne, Panda, and the other European ultras among the Africans was essentially a replay of the leadership contest of the decade before World War I between Booker Washington's machine and Du Bois's Talented Tenth. Yet, if conservative francophones were performing the same dutiful function of legitimizing European overlordship in Africa that the Bookerites had discharged on behalf of racial segregation in the United States, that reality was somewhat obscured for Du Bois and many other American Negroes by the admiration they felt for the assimilationist ideals opportunistically preached by some French and Portuguese imperialists. There was much talk at the time of the "humane" Portuguese "native code" and of "*la France Outre-Mer*" ("Overseas France") and the "France with 100 million inhabitants." "How fine a thing to be a black Frenchman in 1919," Du Bois had limned in an editorial bitterly contrasting the Third Republic's gratitude to her African troops with the treatment meted out to black soldiers by America. Africans sat in legislative assemblies in Paris and Lisbon; they held teaching posts at universities; they advanced in the army and civil service; intermarriage of Africans and Europeans occasioned little if any public controversy; France's highest literary distinction, the Prix Goncourt, would go in 1921 to René Maran, a novelist from Martinique. Paris had been synonymous with sanctuary to a generation or more of American Negro expatriates. Small wonder, then, that when they compared the mystique of French civilization to the reality of Jim Crow America, American men and women of color — even those as cosmopolitan as Du Bois and his fellow delegates — sometimes displayed considerable gullibility.

Unlike the ambitious congregations of the past in which he had played a commanding role — the Pan-African Conference of 1900, convened in London by the visionary Henry Sylvester Williams, the Universal Races Congress of 1911, where "fifty races look[ed] each other in the eye," and even the Pan-African Congress of 1919 — this latest Paris conclave could be described as fairly representative of Du Bois's Darker World. Among the 120-odd men and women assembling on a clear Sunday morning in the narrow rue Blanche not far from place de l'Opera were delegates from Indochina, India, Madagascar, the Philippines, the British and French Antilles, the independent nations of Haiti, Liberia, and Ethiopia, more than thirty from the United States (including Florence Kelly and the Arthur Spingarns), and at least two or three persons (amounting to a third of the Congress) from every region of sub-Saharan Africa. As Fauset had noted in London, there were no delegates in Paris from the French, Spanish, and Italian portions of North Africa. The British Government kept interested Egyptians away. The scene in the meeting hall, the Salle des Ingénieurs, moved Fauset to rapture, and she probably expressed Du Bois's own elation. Looking at that "dark sea of faces," her heart palpitated. "On that platform was, I suppose, the intellectual efflorescence of the Negro race." To her friend and employer, she gave complete credit for the achievement, "for he had first envisaged this moment."

In the short time before deliberations had resumed on September 4, however, the Francophone Africans warned that any criticism of French colonial policies or practices was unacceptable. "We are willing to help in an evolution which we ourselves have prepared," the influential daily *Le Matin* warned, "but we do not hold with being the victims of a revolution." A courtesy call to Diagne (who occupied, according to White, "as large and imposing an office and was as carefully protected by as many secretaries and flunkies" as the prime minister) brought an explicit threat of public denunciation of the Congress and an implicit one of possible expulsion from France if Du Bois and the Americans offended their hosts. After opening remarks in which Diagne denounced Garveyism as a mad idea (*"une idée insensée"*) and communism as an insidious temptation, the day was taken up with pledges of loyalty to France. "It seemed absurd to have the floor given repeatedly to speakers who dwelt on the glories of France and the honor of being a black Frenchman," an exasperated Fauset complained. Henry Ossawa Tanner, the American Negro painter who was a permanent Paris resident and a Du Bois enthusiast, may have been similarly disconcerted. As the speeches droned on with Diagne and fellow *assimilé* Gratien Candace presiding, while Logan and the Haitian diplomat Dantes Bellegarde tirelessly translated back and forth, the bomb defused in Brussels began to tick again loudly. Even Isaac Beton drew away from his fellow *assimilés*, confiding his distress to Fauset and passing along useful intelligence.

Walter White recalled a dramatic turning point when a Frenchman belonging to an organization for "native protection" gained the dais to tear into his own government's policies in so-called Overseas France with telling illustrations and hard figures. As the Congress drew to its close on Monday, the transparent Francophone attempt to focus discussion on lynching and civil rights abuses in the United States ran up against solid opposition. Once again, Du Bois worked to impose his agenda on the proceedings, ably assisted by White, Logan, Fauset, and Hunt, along with Yale divinity student William Stuart Nelson, George Jackson, E. Franklin Frazier, and others in the feisty American delegation. The Paris edition of the New York *Herald* captured Du Bois's appeal with canny fidelity. "The question of the status of the Negro in modern society," it reported, "is no longer a domestic problem of the United States, or a parochial problem of Jamaica, or a colonial problem. It is rather a great world-wide problem to be viewed and considered as a whole." Du Bois would brook no compromise of the principles of absolute racial equality and eventual rule of Africa *by* Africans (and not Africa ruled *with* the consent of Africans, as the 1919 Congress had demanded). He insisted on retaining the general criticisms of European colonial regimes and on keeping the mandate to present grievances to the League of Nations. A clear majority shifted behind Du Bois, finally forcing the Francophones to accept the London resolutions as the platform of the Congress and of the new, permanent Pan-African Association to be headquartered in Paris. But Diagne, refusing to cede the entire contest to Du Bois, succeeded in excluding from the final document a paragraph about capitalism deemed to be noxiously socialist. "But the rest [of the demands] that yearning, groping audience accepted with their souls," Fauset rejoiced in distinctly Du Boisian accents.

Exhilarated, Du Bois left for Geneva almost immediately with Fauset at his side. He carried news clippings in his briefcase that went a long way toward rebutting the skepticism of much of the NAACP leadership and disinterest among the rank and file. The organ of the French Communist Party drew precisely the conclusion Du Bois would have wanted. Expressing incredulity at the nonproletarian character of the meeting in the rue Blanche, *L'Humanité* acknowledged that the Pan-African Congress, nevertheless, "showed us by its very existence that the black race is not naturally or essentially an inferior race, and that it is not destined to remain so forever." Just before taking leave of Madame Chapoteau and the Young family in the rue Jasmin, Du Bois composed a document eloquently embodying the determination of the men and women meeting at London, Brussels, and Paris to see their concerns registered as dramatically and broadly as possible. *Manifesto to the League of Nations* contained the three requests to the world body approved by the Congress: that a special section be set aside in the International Labor Bureau (known later as the International Labor Organization) to deal "with the conditions and needs of native Negro labor"; that a man of Negro descent ("properly fitted in character and training") be appointed to the League's Mandates Commission at the first vacancy; and, even though its power to intervene in the affairs of sovereign members was virtually nil, that the League use its "vast moral power" to affirm "the absolute equality of races." To facilitate this third request, the *Manifesto* urged the creation of an "International Institute for the Study of the Negro Problems," an eminently worthwhile proposal that Du Bois himself would have been outstandingly capable of implementing. It was a fine document, as any struck off by him invariably was, but as their train approached Geneva, the confidence the secretary of the Pan-African Congress evinced to his companion that the *Manifesto* would be officially received may have been somewhat feigned. Fauset wondered how on earth they would pull it off, and she continued to fret as they checked into their modest bed-and-breakfast. But within two hours of his arrival, invitations and requests for interviews "poured in." Whatever his misgivings, the gamble paid off, to Fauset's impressed relief—"Dr. Du Bois's name and reputation proved the open sesame."

In keeping with his importance, then, Du Bois was able to arrange an invitation to use the sedate Hotel des Familles as his headquarters. Lady Cecilia Roberts, whose distinguished spouse held an important post at the League, was pleased to preside at table while Du Bois loftily pressed his agenda for recognition and action as titled personages came for lunch or high tea and earnest discussions. Bellegarde, representing Haiti at the League as well as at Paris, had rooms at the Hotel des Familles, and so was able to play the role in Geneva of interpreter and lobbyist that Logan had played in Paris. An old acquaintance from the heady days of the Universal Races Congress, Gustave Spiller, had

Du Bois and Fauset to dinner. The secretaries of the Anti-Slavery and Aborigines Protection Society and the Société Internationale pour la Protection des Indigènes paid calls and promised unofficial support for the principles stated in the *Manifesto*. By week's end Du Bois had gained the sympathetic though noncommited attention of the noted classicist Gilbert Murray, on leave from his regius professorship at Oxford to represent South Africa, and from Albert Thomas himself the promise to study seriously the request for a special section on "native affairs" in the ILO. On the evening of the twelfth, a Monday, Du Bois addressed a well-attended gathering at the English Club of Geneva. With the official acceptance of the *Manifesto* a few days later by the League's secretary, Sir Eric Drummond, the mission appeared to be virtually accomplished. William Rappard, head of the Mandates Commission, endorsed the recommendation for appointment of a person of African descent.

Formal action on the *Manifesto to the League of Nations* would take place after Bellegarde's address to the world body several months later. Despite the support he believed his mission had garnered, and the large significance of its precedent, the League would take only minimal action on Du Bois's appeal. The ILO would maintain a native affairs research section for a few years, Du Bois wrote, but it eventually disappeared due to inattention. The Mandates Commission continued to be staffed exclusively by Europeans, nor would there ever be any institute for the "study of the Negro problems." As for the exercise of "vast moral power" to promote the equality of races, the League would cede the pursuit of that ideal entirely to member states. Disappointing in practical terms, the London Resolutions and *Manifesto to the League* comprised one of the earliest displays by educated men and women of African descent of the dramatic art of racial protest and liberation acted out before a global audience — an early dress rehearsal of a production whose plot surprised, disquieted, and bemused those Europeans alert to its subversive meaning, but a drama still much too far ahead of its time really to educate or even alarm the critics. It was stagecraft eliciting little more than the equivalent of a few curious reviews. For Du Bois and his allies, the play was the thing; performance was meant to be everything, for by acting as though they spoke for hundreds of millions of the darker world, by reading their provocative lines across the footlights of Europe, they intended to propitiate audiences for the new cultural and political roles that black people were determined to adopt in what he and they hoped would be their liberated, triumphant future. Even though Du Bois soon admitted to himself that it had been unrealistic to expect meaningful institutional modifications or broad policy shifts in the status quo founded at Geneva, his certainty that the germinal impact of the second Pan-African Congress would ultimately transform global power relations never wavered.

Now that he had been on the go without a moment's relaxation since arriving in France on August 16, Du Bois headed for Chamonix-Mont-Blanc, the fashionable resort town in the French Alps. Two letters from Nina were awaiting his return to Paris at Madame Chapoteau's. The first had arrived soon after the Paris session ended on September 5. In that letter, dated August 30, Nina acknowledged the letters Du Bois had written on board the *Ryndam*, wrote of Yolande and preparations for the fall semester at Fisk, and sent greetings from a recent visitor to their new Edgecombe Avenue house. As usual, she hadn't been feeling well, but Nina said she "owe[d] it to you and Yolande not to give out entirely." She had been "going rather slowly now." The second letter waiting for him in Paris was more cheerful. She was "trying not to get too given out," and Yolande was being bustled off to Nashville. Dear Miss Pingree had spent part of the week with them. "You will be coming home pretty soon, won't you?" she wondered. He would, but first there was the balm of the Alpine mountain resort.

Du Bois and Fauset are silent after Geneva about their movements as a team. With the official business of the Congress over, they may have been concerned about the propriety of a week of companionship whose obvious motive of mutual enjoyment, if reported to 70 Fifth Avenue, might distress some of the more prudish NAACP board members. That they had been lovers for some time now, there could be little doubt. Typically, he revealed nothing in writing, but Fauset was barely able to screen her feelings of amorous worship from the readers of "Impressions of the Second Pan-African Congress," her vivid account in *The Crisis* of how Dr. Du Bois spent the summer attempting, as she would have it, to overhaul the world order. Her discreet poem about their relationship, which would appear in the July 1922 *Crisis*, probably hadn't yet been written, but the emotions informing it must have been given a large boost during this Pan-African summer abroad. Yet if there is a strong probability that he and she were together in Chamonix, proof is now part of the entropy of the past. Fauset's whereabouts are missing, and, as for Du Bois, his stay in the Alps is recorded with great emotional inflation, but with himself as the solitary focus.

Hiking, resting, and writing, and no doubt managing his per diem with considerable care (prices had quadrupled after the war), Du Bois reveled in the outsized beauty of the locale, the play of light and the bracing climate, and gave way to an afflatus whose periodic recurrence had become a personality trait since his Berlin student days. He fancied himself praying to Mont Blanc, "throwing [his] hands in ecstasy, screaming [his] tears," if he were to stay long in Chamonix. He sat, he told his *Crisis* readers, scribbling, scribbling, and then returning again to admire the great mountain from his window. "The marvel of it, the sheer inhuman perfectness of it all," he rhapsodized, "the almost pain of its beauty and hurt of its joy!" Du Bois's agitated state was the understandable condition of a mind that had conceived, organized, and largely dominated a strenuous undertaking whose magnitude of importance he would have believed at that moment to be incalculable. At the foot of Mont Blanc, he was close to being literally on top of the world. Jessie Fauset's presence would have been a perfect complement to his mood.

DU BOIS SAILED HOME in triumph in late September 1921. A few weeks later, he found himself embroiled in the second great controversy of his life, a confrontation in which not only his ideas and standing as the leading intellectual of his people, but also his very birthright, were to be bitterly assailed by Marcus Garvey, one of the most gifted mobilizers of the mass discontent and ambition of black people during the first quarter of the twentieth century. On Tuesday, April 25, 1916, the day Garvey had bounded into the offices at 70 Fifth Avenue, neither man yet thought of the other as a traitorous lunatic or a half-breed, libels Du Bois and Garvey would hurl at each other seven years later. The young Jamaican had been in New York for only about a month, the departure point for a speaking tour of the country that would take him to thirty-eight states. His plan was to raise money to establish a vocational institute in Jamaica based on the Tuskegee model. Booker Washington had replied encouragingly to Garvey's letters, invited him to Tuskegee, and had even indicated that he would appear at certain fundraisers on Garvey's behalf. Washington's death in 1915 deprived Garvey's undertaking of invaluable support, and the new head of Tuskegee, Robert Russa Moton, manifested considerably less enthusiasm. Moton had merely replied by cordial formula to the cryptic letter in which Garvey announced that he had "many large schemes on [his] mind" but could say nothing about them because his numerous enemies were "ever anxious to misrepresent [him]." Du Bois, however, whose influence and renown now exceeded that of the recently deceased Wizard, had shaken the Jamaican's hand and briefly heard something about his schemes during a visit to the island the previous May. Garvey thought he had good reason to anticipate a sympathetic reception from Du Bois.

Unfortunately, the editor was away from his desk when Garvey visited the association's headquarters. Du Bois returned to find a friendly and rather flattering calling-card message expressing the hope that he, Du Bois, "could be so good as to take the 'chair' at my first public lecture" in the United States. The lecture — "Jamaica" — was to be given at St. Mark's Church on West 138th Street. Du Bois politely declined Garvey's invitation, and so spared himself witnessing what one reliable source described as a fiasco — "one of the most amusing that I have ever seen." Wilfred Adolphus Domingo, a militant black nationalist who was an old friend of Garvey's from Jamaica, was present. Garvey fainted, crashing from the stage amid a crescendo of booing and guffaws. Domingo described this scene some time after he had become as fierce an enemy of Garvey as Du Bois, spicing it with a tasteless description of his former friend's physical features that was curiously reminiscent of Monroe Trotter's notorious lampoon of Booker Washington. If the short, round, dark man with flashing eyes and brilliant teeth was hardly the grotesque of Domingo's calumny, it was also true that there was probably no standard of physical attractiveness by which Garvey could ever have been deemed handsome. Had Du Bois joined him on the St. Mark's rostrum, they would have presented a contrast of extremes, the one compact, understatedly tailored, and precise, the other squat, badly clad, and explosive. But if Du Bois declined to join in the American debut, he did at least cooperate by announcing in the May *Crisis* that "Mr. Marcus Garvey, founder and president of the Universal Negro Improvement Association of Jamaica, BWI, is now on a visit to America. He will deliver a series of lectures on Jamaica in an effort to raise funds for the establishment of an industrial and educational institution for Negroes in Jamaica."

Du Bois and Garvey's initial interaction in the spring of 1916 appears, therefore, to have been correct, deferential on the latter's part, and entirely free of animus, a far cry from what it would become in a few years. The point is important in light of Garvey's famous version of his first impression of the scene at 70 Fifth Avenue as one that sent him hurrying away in distressed puzzlement, "unable to tell whether he was in a white office or that of the NAACP." Whatever his true reactions that day to encountering the mix of white and black officers and staff at NAACP headquarters (a sizable proportion of them light-complexioned persons of color), several years were to elapse before Garvey's consternation erupted into print. Until the battle of editorials led to all-out war during 1923, Du Bois proceeded cautiously in his dealings with Garvey. As Garvey himself had not been altogether sure what his long-term plans were, whether to return to Jamaica or attempt to build a racial-uplift organization in the United States, Du Bois, curious and somewhat perplexed, waited and watched. But neither he nor anyone else at the NAACP really paid the visitor from Jamaica much attention.

Left to his own devices and surviving a bout of pneumonia, Garvey had finally managed to save enough money working as a printer in New York to begin traveling and speaking in summer 1916. His cross-country lecture tour opened his eyes as never before to the relative vitality of American Negroes and to the potential for a mass-based race movement. Whereas his own West Indians had been asleep for the last eighty years, "and are still under the spell of Rip Van Winkle," Garvey "unhesitatingly and unreservedly" praised people of color in the United States as the "most progressive and the foremost unit in the expansive chain of scattered Ethiopia." What American Negroes had going for them, Garvey decided, was white racism — what he saw as the "honest prejudices of the [white] South" which forced black people to build their own segregated institutions and to develop a race consciousness that could in time command respect from their oppressors. This was to be a fundamental construct of what became Garveyism—the postulate that racial liberation and empowerment were inherent in racial opposition and alienation.

This proud, black-skinned son of an even prouder father had received a solid primary education in the Anglican Church School in St. Ann's Bay, the small seaport town where he was born on August 17, 1887. Garvey's cantankerous father, who doggedly impoverished his own family in court battles over grudges and picayune wrongs, was a stonemason and small landowner. Many years later, a claim would be fabricated (probably by the son's second wife) that Garvey *père* was descended from the Maroons, the escaped African slaves whose ferocity in the Jamaican highlands had forced the British to grant them a measure of autonomy. Although Garvey's father had little formal schooling, his respect for knowledge became so consuming that he spent hours by himself reading, solitude that Mrs. Garvey and their children learned never to intrude upon. Captivation by books and ideas, as well as a decidedly patriarchal view of women and the world, were legacies from an autocratic and monastic father to a driven and somewhat paranoid son. There was another legacy from St. Ann's Bay— that of a psychic affront astonishingly (even suspiciously) similar to that recounted in *The Souls of Black Folk* of an adolescent wound inflicted by a callous white female classmate upon a young, innocent Du Bois· in Great Barrington. Writing in *Current History* in September 1923, Garvey would disclose how, at age fourteen, he, also, had been devastated when a white playmate's parents forbade her ever to speak to him again, "for I was a 'nigger.' " It was then that he had understood for the first time, supposedly, "that there was some difference in humanity, and that there were different races, each having its own separate and distinct social life."

Garvey learned the trade of printer in St. Ann's Bay, and later in the larger town of Port Maria, before going to Kingston in 1906 to work as a compositor in a commercial printing establishment. Four years on a fast learning curve in the capital propelled him into politics, unionism, and serious trouble with his employer. First, there was Dr. Robert Love, a septuagenarian of considerable learning and legendary political acumen, one of the first black men elected to the Legislative Council of the colony. Love, a committed Pan-Africanist and admirer of fellow physician and Trinidadian Henry Sylvester Williams, organized the Pan-African Association of Jamaica in April 1901, not quite a year after the London Pan-African conference at which Du Bois had proclaimed the color line to be the problem of the twentieth century. A Garvey biographer would characterize the physician as, "in a very real sense, a Du Bois–type intellectual." Garvey revered Love and swore by the *Jamaica Advocate*, Love's newspaper which, asserted the young printer, "one cannot read . . . without getting race consciousness." Finally, there was Garvey's apparently peripheral connection to

Kingston's National Club, organized in 1909 by a mulatto barrister named S.A.G. Cox. Garvey may well have been introduced to Sinn Fein and the struggle for Irish independence at the club.

Serious trouble occurred in November 1908. By that time, Garvey had risen to the position of vice-president of the Jamaican branch of the Typographical Union of America. He either led or, it seems more probable, followed his union out on strike against the island's printing establishments. Blacklisted by the private sector, he was able to secure an appointment as a government printer, a position he held while putting out a periodical during 1910 called *Garvey's Watchman*. His growing reputation as an activist almost surely influenced the twenty-three-year-old compositor's decision to take a job on a Costa Rican plantation less than two years later. Garvey soon moved on to Bocas del Toro, Panama, where he saw Jamaican laborers being horribly exploited by the banana and coffee cartels. His protests to the British consulate on behalf of these abused subjects of the empire were unavailing. Then he wrote editorials about their conditions in a Panamanian newspaper called *La Prensa*. By late 1911, on his way back to Jamaica, Garvey had seen firsthand how Africans and Indians were allowed a bare living in Guatemala and Panama.

Garvey had a burning desire to know what life was like for Africans in Europe, what they thought and hoped for, and how they were treated by supposedly civil and cosmopolitan white people. How he was actually treated while in Great Britain and on the Continent depends on which of his myriad accounts is cited. The leading Garvey expert has insisted that Garvey was generally well received wherever he went, citing the sojourner's own words in evidence. But other words of Garvey's relate dismay and rage, and protest that in Great Britain and on the Continent, as in Jamaica and throughout Central America, he found himself banging his head against the Caucasian ceiling, "found the same stumbling block—'You are black.' " Sailing home in June 1914 from a two-year stay in England where he had written at least one piece in Duse Muhammad Ali's *African Times and Orient Review*, probably taken classes at the University of London, made contacts with African and Asian students and merchant seamen, and visited Scotland, France, Spain, Germany, and Italy, this dejected man of destiny claimed to have had a blinding vision. Badly shaken by what a Guyanese passenger, returning from missionary service in Basutoland, told him about "horrible and pitiable" abuse of the Africans there, Garvey had retreated to his cabin:

> I asked, "Where is the black man's Government?" "Where is his King and his kingdom?" "Where is his President, his country, and his ambassador, his army, his navy, his men of big affairs?" I could not find them. . . . My brain was afire. There was a world of thought to conquer. . . . All day and the following night I pondered over the subject matter of that conversation,

and at midnight, lying flat on my back, the vision and thought came to me that I should name the organization the Universal Negro Improvement Association and African Communities (Imperial) League. Such a name I thought would embrace the purpose of all black humanity.

Five days after returning home, on July 20 he had established his new organization in Kingston. But embracing the "purpose of all black humanity" was more than a notion. By late April 1915, when Du Bois visited Jamaica and met Garvey for an instant at the garden party hosted by the royal governor, Sir Sidney Olivier, the young idealist and his Universal Negro Improvement association (UNIA) had made almost no impact. Writing that he "never really knew there was so much color prejudice in Jamaica, in my native home," the dark-skinned Garvey had discovered that the island's mulatto population was generally indifferent if not hostile to his mission. It was then that he had sought the help of Booker Washington and resolved to go the United States.

When he came back to New York exhilarated from his continental speaking tour in summer of 1917, Marcus Mosiah Garvey felt that the years of weary searching and wandering were about over. Thirty years old and world-traveled, he now believed that he had found a place on which to stand and move the earth, a race that he could lead, a chosen people to whom he could be Moses and who would thrill to his gospel of a black Zion. An invitation to address the inaugural meeting of the Liberty League of Colored Americans, a racial-uplift movement founded by Hubert Henry Harrison, gave Garvey his opportunity. Bellhop, telephone operator, evening school prodigy, Virgin Islander Harrison was already a fixture in Harlem. The "speakers' corner" at 135th Street and Lenox Avenue owed much of its reputation for pungent oratory to the dark-skinned agitator with the potato-shaped face framed by horn-rimmed glasses. He had pledged himself to the Socialist party, served as assistant editor of the *Masses*, and ventured to criticize the Tuskegee Machine, which had cost him a secure position in the Post Office in 1911. Two years later, Harrison had marched with "Big" Bill Haywood, Elizabeth Gurley Flynn, and John Reed in the Paterson, New Jersey, silk workers strike. Self-improved to the point that his broad learning would gain him the monicker "Black Socrates" and a position as staff lecturer with the New York City Board of Education, Harrison's collected wisdom would appear in 1920 as *When Africa Awakes: The Inside Story of the Stirrings and Strivings of the New Negro and the Nation*, a black nationalist classic. On Tuesday, June 12, 1917, Harrison introduced Garvey to some two thousand Harlemites filling Bethel AME Church. There was no pratfall that night. Experienced and confident, he was a hit. From that success Garvey had gone on to hold weekly Sunday afternoon meetings in Lafayette Hall on 131st Street in Harlem. His byline appeared regularly in *The Voice*, official organ of the Liberty League.

Those who began showing up at Garvey's increasingly charged Sunday meetings tended to be younger, angrier, poorer, and darker than the typical card-carrying members of the NAACP or the National Urban League. That the majority of them, at least in the early years, were overwhelmingly from the West Indies was a powerful asset that would become, with help from Garvey, a liability exploited by enemies. West Indians poured into the United States between 1911 and 1924, the year in which the new immigration act would severely reduce their influx. Almost thirty thousand would settle in Harlem during the period roughly corresponding to Garvey's rise and fall. Being a West Indian in Harlem was to belong to a double minority — discriminated against by whites because of the color of their skins and resented by native blacks because of differences perceived under the same skin color. Still, it happened often enough to rankle the native-born Negroes that West Indians were better treated by some white Americans than they were, as when an astonished Claude McKay, his documents missing, was ordered released from vagrancy charges after a smiling judge in Pittsburgh heard his Jamaican lilt. Virgin Islander G. James Fleming, small, smart, and as articulate as a British extra in Hollywood, had been in New York less than twenty-four hours when someone shouted, "Oh, you're a monkey chaser!" Fleming observed the scene at Liberty Hall, fascinated, but never joined the UNIA; instead, he earned degrees in journalism and political science, and, later, even aspired to edit *The Crisis*. "Some said West Indians were smarter than anybody else," Fleming recalled in his retirement from college teaching — "a double-edged compliment like saying, 'Jews are smart.' " "There was a great deal of antagonism," George Schuyler confirmed more than fifty years after Garvey had disappeared from Harlem, and he blamed it on organizations such as the UNIA.

Nominally, Garvey remained a soldier in Harrison's militant organization; in reality the older man increasingly deferred to his spellbinding collaborator. Liberty League rallies became UNIA rallies and their popularity so great that they had to be held at the Palace Casino, one of Harlem's largest entertainment centers. Du Bois stayed away from the Palace Casino, but he began to pay more attention to the cresting excitement engendered by a man he soon described as "a little difficult to characterize." John Edward Bruce, a famous Aframerican correspondent better known as "Bruce Grit," cast a cynical professional eye on the Palace Casino theatrics in the *Home News* and called Garvey a "glib phrase maker and a dreamer with a tolerably florid imagination." In a poor imitation of a West Indian accent, Bruce mocked, "you won't do, Mr. Garvey. Too *mu-chee talkee*." Three years later, however, the veteran journalist would place his pen at Garvey's service until his death in 1923. But while Bruce scoffed for the moment, no less a personage than Mary Church Terrell, an erstwhile Du Bois ally and a Talented Tenth *grande dame*, addressed a meeting in the Palace casino in early October 1917. Terrell's appearance was followed by news of a statewide elocution contest sponsored by the UNIA in December. Du Bois may have really been surprised to learn that a justice of the state Supreme Court, another from the Court of Special Session, distinguished divines, and Columbia University's Nicholas Murray Butler, arguably the country's most august university president, presided over the competition. Writing Garvey that the Palace Casino evening inspired him with "a new feeling of pride and satisfaction at what the members of the Association and their friends are accomplishing," President Butler found himself, after another Palace casino appearance, ducking serial invitations to UNIA meetings.

Whatever his long-term plans were, Garvey finally made it unmistakably clear that he intended to pursue them from Manhattan. On July 31, 1918, a certificate of incorporation for the Universal Negro Improvement Association and African Communities League was recorded by the commissioner of deeds for the city of New York. To be headed by a "Potentate" "of Negro blood and race," the actual "working head" of the UNIA was invested in the "President-General and Administrator" (later, "Provisional President-General of Africa"), an office reserved by Garvey for Garvey. Article V of the Constitution and Book of Laws stipulated that "he shall be responsible to the Potentate for the entire working and carrying out of all commands." Two years later, Du Bois would be dumbstruck to find himself summoned by Garvey to run for the honorific position of "Supreme Potentate." As the new UNIA took shape over the summer and fall of 1918, it became a magnet for discontented and radical elements now especially alienated by the NAACP's policy on American entry into the war. "Close Ranks," Du Bois's editorial temblor in the July 1918 *Crisis*, sundered black leadership into jagged antagonisms. For some, such as Robert Abbot, publisher of the Chicago *Defender*, and John Hope, president of Morehouse College, the appeal to "forget our special grievances and close our ranks shoulder to shoulder with our white fellow citizens and the allied nations" made perfect sense. Deferring goals for full rights of citizenship until the War for Democracy was won, they signed off on a Jim Crow army officer corps and rallied to the flag, if not to the NAACP itself. Others, such as Trotter, Archibald Grimké, and Ida Wells-Barnett broke ranks with their Talented Tenth peers and savaged Du Bois as a betrayer, but had little use as yet for the UNIA.

To Caribbean newcomers, as well as to some of the newcomers from the Deep South, Du Bois, Joel Spingarn, James Weldon Johnson, and the rest of the NAACP cadre were outdated racial militants, well-meaning fuddy-duddies at best. Du Bois was astonished to find his Sunday appearance at something called the People's Educational Forum repaid with insolence. The forum's organizer, the young West Indian Socialist Richard B. Moore, challenged the editor's opinion that black labor should keep its distance from both white labor and white capital. "As for that young man who waves his hands and froths at the mouth," Du Bois harrumphed (in Moore's account), "I didn't come here to engage in this sort of exchange. I thought you wanted to learn something, but you know everything." They might not know everything, but the young radicals were certain that their elders no longer merited the presumption of wisdom. The roiling controversy over Du Bois's hankering for a captaincy in military intelligence (splitting the association's national headquarters and almost causing the Washington branch to secede) seemed only to prove them right. They applauded when Garvey's new weekly newspaper, *The Negro World*, castigated "Close Ranks" with the jeremiad, "They enslave their children's children who make compromise with sin." A. Philip Randolph and Chandler Owen, having praised the October Revolution in Russia as the defining event of the century, welcomed the UNIA as a companion movement after *The Negro World* cheered the Bolsheviks. Garvey's friend Domingo, a contributing editor to Randolph's *Messenger* and editor of *The Emancipator*, his own periodical, found nothing to laugh about now and much to praise in the President-General and Administrator.

Among the organizations eventually affiliating in some fashion with the UNIA, none would sound more revolutionary than the Hamitic League of the World and its ideological cousin, the African Blood Brotherhood (ABB), each formed sometime between 1917 and 1919 by a small band of young West Indian intellectuals in Harlem who synthesized black nationalism and communism into a unique doctrine. Two men were the engines of the group: George Wells Parker, founder of the Hamitic League, and his thirty-one-year-old disciple, Cyril Valentine Briggs, a black nationalist so Caucasian in appearance that the New York *News* once called him an "angry blond Negro." Although the Hamitic league prated its Afrocentric nationalism while the Blood Brotherhood served up a stew of communistic nationalism, the ideological distinctions tended greatly to blur as the two groups increasingly collaborated. The Hamitic League published a remarkable little monthly, *The Crusader*. The first ten-cent *Crusader* appeared in September 1918, along with the inaugural *Negro World*. In mocking tribute to Du Bois, it reproduced Robert Browning's poem "The Lost Leader." "Just for a handful of silver he left us./ Just for a riband to stick in his coat—/ Found the one gift of which fortune bereft us,/ Lost all the others she lets us devote." Parker served up the group's Afrocentric cosmology in a *Crusader* series reminiscent of Du Bois's columns in *The Horizon*: Parker's "The Children of the Sun" anointed the African race as "the real founder of human civilization"; white people were pale derivatives of a once great black race. Briggs supplied the political economy with its blend of working-class unity across racial lines in America, on the one hand, but nation-building in Africa based on racial exclusivity, on the other. By *The Crusader*'s logic, there was nothing inconsistent about backing Randolph's Socialist party candidacy for state comptroller while approving Garvey's race purity and "back to Africa" platform. As the Hamitic League enlarged and its ABB persona became preponderant, apparatchiks of the soon-to-be-established American Communist Party such as Otto Huiswoud, Lovett Fort-Whiteman, Grace Campbell, Harry Haywood, and Richard Moore joined it. The ABB persuaded itself that it was a revolutionary conspiracy with paramilitary potential, an Aframerican version of the reorganized Sinn Fein. Briggs had been profoundly impressed by the Irish Easter Rebellion and thought it held valuable lessons for black nationalists. On that score, he and Garvey saw eye to eye.

As far as Du Bois was concerned, reproaches from a few uncredentialed and immigrant intellectuals were minor nuisances. Randolph's prestige would become as impressive as his resonant voice in a few years, but in the editor's estimation Randolph spoke only for a tiny circle of mutual admirers. The irruption of self-proclaimed "New Negro" publications — The Voice, The Messenger, The Emancipator, The Challenge, The Crusader, The Negro World — Du Bois saw as encouraging signs of an emergent complex of diverse American Negro opinions, useful, certainly, but subordinate if not marginal factors in the formulation of racial policy. He would thoughtfully downplay their relevancy in "The Class Struggle," an essay in the June 1921 issue of The Crisis. Still, he couldn't ignore that Garvey's appeal was widening. The editor had risked his reputation appealing to his people to fight in a foreign war on the dubious proposition that they would win their long-denied civil rights when peace came. Garvey had bellowed from the stage of the Palace Casino that Wilson's war was a white man's calamity having nothing to do with black people. The War for Democracy over, Du Bois had commanded America to honor the claims of its African citizens in the defiant Crisis editorial "We Return Fighting." Garvey's Negro World, its circulation already at ten thousand, chronicled the seamless postwar perfidy of the White House, the War Department, and most of white America; and the President-General and Administrator was said to have wept salt tears as he watched the black troops march home to Harlem. Du Bois acclaimed the League of Nations "as absolutely necessary to the salvation of the Negro race." Garvey reserved judgment, but drew inspiration from Briggs's belligerent black nationalism and would soon pronounce the League "null and void as far as the Negro is concerned."

Du Bois would have sensed a definite rise in Garvey's credibility as he monitored the procession of dignitaries in and out of the Casino. Ida B. Wells-Barnett, a founder of the NAACP, tenacious civil libertarian, and archetypal feminist, made common cause with the UNIA, as did Reverends George Frazier Miller of Brooklyn and Adam Clayton Powell, Sr., of the powerful Abyssinian Baptist Church, now about to relocate to Harlem. Madame C. J. Walker, the immensely wealthy manufacturer of hair and beauty products, helped finance the start-up of *The Negro World* as well as the purchase of the UNIA's permanent meeting hall in 1919. Three weeks after the signing of the armistice on November 11, 1918, the Bureau of Investigation's special agent reported a dramatic Palace Casino meeting whose agenda was the structure of the postwar world. The audience of nearly five thousand roared approval as the President-General nominated Wells-Barnett and Randolph to represent the UNIA at the Versailles Peace Conference. Wells-Barnett, exuding her trademark ebullience, rose to say that she was ready to go to Paris, but she suggested that the UNIA proceed cautiously with its back-to-Africa agenda. Their delegates' specific demands were less fixed than the heated rhetoric in Liberty Hall suggested, but the slogan "Africa for the Africans," was obviously intended to embrace an unprecedented role for American and Antillean blacks in administering Germany's forfeited colonial possessions. Garvey spoke as though he fully expected the Allied Powers to transfer the Cameroons and Tanganyika to the UNIA. A twenty-two-year old Haitian named Eliezer Cadet was designated UNIA commissioner to Paris and was to act as interpreter for Randolph and Wells-Barnett. With emotions at fever pitch, Garvey prophesied that the next war would be fought between blacks and whites, unless the former achieved political and social justice — and he boasted that "with the aid of Japan on the side of the Negroes they will be able to win such a war."

Sailing to the Versailles Peace Conference from New York aboard the *Orizaba* on December 1, with the cream of the press corps, Du Bois would be on the high seas as Garvey, Randolph, Trotter, Wells-Barnett, and the other dissenters held meetings and passed resolutions. Trotter's rival organization, the National Equal Rights League (NERL), had drawn Garvey and 250 prominent Negroes to Washington, D.C., a few days before Du Bois left for France. Too busy with visa red tape and last-minute affairs in New York to be present, Du Bois informed himself, nevertheless, about Trotter's Washington conference. The NERL meeting voted to send eleven representatives (Randolph and Wells-Barnett among them) to the peace conference carrying a Fifteenth Point to add to Wilson's Fourteen — "elimination of civil, political, and judicial distinctions based on race or color in all nations for the new era of freedom everywhere." By the time the *Orizaba* docked at Brest, the President-General had accompanied Wells-Barnett, Randolph, Powell, and Miller to a meeting with America's first self-made distaff millionaire. Sarah Breedlove had risen by grit and aptitude from Louisiana Delta poverty to become the fabled Madame C. J. Walker, whose hair and beauty-culture empire was to early twentieth-century Negro Americans what Revlon or Vidal Sassoon became to generations of white Americans after World War II. "I got myself a start by giving myself a start," Madame Walker liked to say of the mail-order business in hot combs and relaxing agents she and her second husband had operated in Pittsburgh and Indianapolis. Mr. Walker was now a memory. Devoting herself to good works and racial uplift, Madame held court at Villa Lewaro, her stately Hudson River mansion a stone's throw from robber baron Jay Gould's estate. It was there that she received Garvey and the other guests, ardently embraced their proposal for an International League of Darker Peoples, and agreed to help defray the costs of the delegates to Paris.

While upwards of a hundred thousand *Crisis* readers followed Du Bois across the battlefields of France into the bivouacs of Negro troops and into the portentous deliberations of the first Pan-African Congress, the visa applications of Garvey's and Trotter's would-be emissaries were summarily rejected, their letters and petitions ignored ("never heard one syllable from the lips of Woodrow Wilson," Garvey complained). Cadet, Garvey's young "High Commissioner" had managed to reach Paris on his Haitian passport before Du Bois headed home in late March 1919. Trotter himself had sailed much later as a cook on the old Canadian ship *Yarmouth*, perhaps even passing Du Bois's returning ship on the high seas. These were bound to have been fools' errands, as neither Cadet or Trotter possessed even the fiction of importance extended to Du Bois by Clemenceau, Diagne, Colonel House, George Beer, Walter Lippmann, and the international press. Disheveled and friendless, the valiant Trotter was taken in by a compassionate family of color that must have observed with perplexity his fruitless efforts to make contracts with high officials at the conference. Cadet's dispatches to Harlem, alluding to significant meetings and imminent breakthroughs, were mostly fabrications that had the direct consequence of provoking Garvey's first public attack on Du Bois. On March 29, 1919, at Mother Zion AME Church, after Randolph spoke and the regal Amy Ashwood, Garvey's future first wife, recited a poem, the President-General called on the capacity audience to show its "complete repudiation of Dr. Du Bois" for interfering with Cadet's "already difficult duties." "The reactionary leader" was denounced in "the most spirited and patriotic manner," reported *The Negro World*. A substantial offering filled the collection plate to enable Cadet to "combat Dr. Du Bois" and to press the peacemakers to place Germany's African colonies under the stewardship of educated persons of color.

Rumors spread from Harlem to the country at large of the editor's alleged sabotage. Because he alone had been visaed of the score of public figures wishing to bring a message to the peace conference, a certain amount of suspicion about Du Bois's anti-imperialist militancy was hardly surprising. But the UNIA indictment considerably aggravated the credibility problems of a leader whose articles exposing officially sanctioned racism in the military could now be construed as proof of his own previous myopia, if not worse. A few weeks after his return from France, Du Bois was heckled in St. Philip's Episcopal Church,

Harlem's toniest place of worship. Some demanded to know why only he and Moton had been allowed to sail. Others asked if Du Bois favored the Egyptians and Indians rebelling against their British rulers. There was much booing when he replied no. Whether or not he fully grasped yet what was happening, Du Bois, the NAACP, and the leadership class they represented were about to undergo an unprecedented challenge of authority in comparison to which the Bookerite contest during the first decade of the century would appear to have been a mild misunderstanding. Unlike the previous internecine dispute, which had often been more about the uses and abuses of powerful white philanthropists than about mobilizing the hoi polloi, the emergent Du Bois–Garvey struggle would shake the race from bottom to top. "For thousands of years, the Negro has been the outcast of the world," but no longer, the President-General trumpeted from the pages of *The Negro World* as he announced the convening of a "great convention" for the month of August. Today the Negro was determined to play his part in the "reorganization of world affairs." "All Negroes who are interested in themselves, in their race, and in future generations will wend their way to New York City to form a part of this great convention assembled." As the summer of 1919 closed, the institutional stakes became much clearer and the personal vulnerabilities far greater.

Garvey incorporated the Black Star Line (BSL) in Delaware on July 27, 1919, announcing that the UNIA would operate ships "to trade to all parts of the world. The corporation will offer employment to thousands of our men and women." A week later, he presided over the dedication of the UNIA's permanent assembly place, Liberty Hall, a Baptist church whose congregation had given up on its construction after being able to complete only the basement. Like *The Negro World*, which took its inspiration from *The Irish World*, this unfinished structure at 120–140 West 138th Street took its name from Liberty Hall in Dublin, reflections of Garvey's fascination with the struggle for Irish independence. Du Bois, too, praised Irish resistance. Unlike Garvey, however, the editor characteristically reminded readers of the irony that no people had more willingly " 'kill[ed] niggers' from Kingston to Delhi and from Kumasi to Fuji" than the Irish, who had provided the backbone for the AFL's policies excluding Negro workers. "In this world it is the Oppressed who have continually been used to cow and kill . . . in the interest of the Universal Oppressor," Du Bois sighed. Garvey was not much given to qualified endorsements, and less so now that his popularity took a quantum leap with the acquisition by the Black Star Line of its first ship. Skepticism surrounding the UNIA leader vanished overnight from the streets of Harlem, Boston, Philadelphia, Baltimore, Chicago, and New Orleans; nor was it any longer quite so fashionable to mock the President-General and Administrator in the parlors of the Talented Tenth. The anchoring of the old Canadian ship *Yarmouth* at 135th Street pier on September 14, 1919, was received by five thousand jostling, cheering Harlemites as one of the greatest events in the modern history of the Negro race.

Du Bois frankly had no idea what to make of it yet. Nearly a full year was to pass before he inquired of the United States Shipping Board about the particulars of age, construction, and ownership of Garvey's ships. Moving cautiously, one of the first things he did was warn Uncle James Burghardt in Great Barrington not to invest any money in the Black Star Line: "The District Attorney of New York County has pronounced its methods as fraudulent." An enquiry of a prominent Jamaican, C. Dodd, brought the much-delayed reply that Garvey's standing in the island was negligible. Du Bois wrote another prospective source for advice about how best to proceed in obtaining information about the *Yarmouth*'s "ownership, liens, etc." The situation called for diplomacy, Du Bois decided, moderation that was in striking contrast to the shrill denunciations of Garvey in the Chicago *Defender*, black America's leading newspaper. A raucous UNIA meeting at Carnegie Hall in late August 1919 had driven *The Defender* to declare that the race ought to sever any ties to "a man like Garvey," who was not even an American citizen. The newspaper's aspersion that the Black Star Line was a fraudulent operation resulted in a court verdict in Garvey's favor, which showed that he was as ready to sue detractors as his father had been. Still moving cautiously, however, the September 1920 *Crisis* acknowledged for the first time, in "The Rise of the West Indian," this "new ally in the fight for black democracy." Rising up against the historic hegemony of Europeans and mulattoes, the peasant masses of the Caribbean were becoming a force throughout the Western Hemisphere, noted the article, and underscored the electric impact of the "new cry of 'Africa for the Africans.' "

The editor's off-the-record comments, however, were far from civil when he was interviewed in late August 1920 by a representative from the National Civic Federation (a coalition of conservative white businessmen). Garvey was not sincere, Du Bois was reported to have said to Charles Mowbray White. He was a demagogue whose movement would collapse "in a short time . . . and his followers are the lowest type of Negroes, mostly from the West Indies." Barring some not readily discernible motive for misrepresentation, White's report (whose authorship was identified by one source as a white lecturer on socialism) captured the editor in a particularly supercilious and reactionary frame of mind. Garvey's followers were allies of Bolsheviks and of the post–Easter Rebellion Sinn Feiners, he charged. These people were not representative "in any sense of the word." But given the "boiling point" hatred that black Americans now felt for white Americans as a result of their war experiences and the upsurge of violence against them, Du Bois speculated that Garvey's movement just might succeed. "I shan't raise a hand to stop it," he declared somewhat imperiously. Four days earlier, Garvey had told White exactly what he thought of the editor of *The Crisis*. Du Bois represented the antebellum Negro whose time was fast running out. He had obligated himself to the white folks, Garvey charged, "and is in no sense or way free to break with them now."

Meanwhile, the editor's apprehensions were shared by some of the early collaborators of the UNIA. Briggs and the African Blood Brotherhood were in a much less positive frame of mind by then, not only because of Garvey's decided cooling over socialism but also because of the state of the Black Star Line's finances. When Charles Mowbray White interviewed Randolph and Owen on August 20, 1920, they were as dismissive as Du Bois had been. Owen called Garvey an ignoramus and a "fool or a rogue." The solidarity of the *Messenger* group with the UNIA had crumbled in recent months, largely due to Garvey's equivocation about socialism. Although Garvey had predicted in his newspaper in late March 1919 that Bolshevism would continue to spread among the oppressed of the world until it produced "a universal rule of the masses," six months later he had expelled his boyhood friend and earliest New York collaborator, Domingo, from his post as *The Negro World*'s first editor. The Red Scare and the Red Summer of 1919 caused Garvey to regret praise for the Russian Revolution and collaboration with its American enthusiasts, especially after incriminating documents written by Domingo turned up in a Lusk Committee raid on the Rand School of Social Science. Domingo was charged with insinuating Bolshevism into the movement and driven out of the UNIA. With Booker Washington, Garvey believed that wealth and the power that came with it were the results of sweat, savings, and risk-taking. With the Palmer raids and their local imitations sweeping the country, to abandon his left-leaning allies cost Garvey little in the way of conscience and nothing more than the appearance of ideological consistency.

The watchword for Garveyites was now "race first," which meant building the New Jerusalem on the model of the National Negro Business League rather than the New Economic Policy. Barely out of Assistant District Attorney Edwin P. Kilroe's office, where he had been grilled about Wobblies, anarchists, and Reds, Garvey made a hard turn to the political right, telling his followers, "we are not going to waste time over the white man's politics. All the time we have to waste is with pro-Negro politics." Dictatorship *over* the proletariat was as close as he ever came to an understanding of dialectical materialism. International socialists need no longer apply, said Garvey, who soon wondered why a leader as gifted and determined as Lenin had ever wanted to experiment with communism. That message was communicated in no uncertain terms to a deeply disappointed Claude McKay, the dazzling young Jamaican poet serving as associate editor of *The Liberator*. The poet had corralled Harrison, Briggs, Grace Campbell, and one or two others for weekly political discussions in Greenwich Village. McKay said he wanted to use nationalism as a bridge to communism by winning over the UNIA, "this great army of awakened workers . . . to the finer system of Socialism." Yale man William Ferris, tiny author of the big book *The African Abroad*, and Domingo's successor at *The Negro World*, rebuffed McKay's overtures after attending a meeting or two. A saddened McKay decided that, although his fellow Jamaican possessed a revolutionary spirit, Garvey failed to understand "the significance of modern revolutionary developments. Maybe he chose not to understand," the poet added perceptively.

The growing number of followers certainly understood Garvey's appeal to ethnic pride better than they would have the economics of Marx and Lenin. Many of them—Port of Spain shopkeepers, Panamanian stevedores, New Orleans cooks, and Harlem bellhops—were as conservative in their economic outlook as they were hopeful of righting ancient racial wrongs. Industrious, frugal, and commonsensical—petit bourgeois to the core—they were, nonetheless, far from immune to utopian aspirations. When the President-General spoke to them of past glories and imminent triumphs, as he did to a black American crowd in Norfolk, Virginia, in October 1919, they were electrified. "The Negro gave [the white man] science and art and literature and everything that is dear to him today," they heard him shout, "and the white man has kept them for thousands of years, and he has taken advantage of the world." With greater intellectual tidiness, Du Bois had advanced similar claims in *Darkwater* and other writings, but Garvey made them come alive for the little people as never before. Ovington saw how he affected them and wrote about the phenomenon some years later with sensitivity: "Garvey was the first Negro in the United States to capture the imagination of the masses. . . . The sweeper in the subway, the elevator boy, eternally carrying fat office men and perky girls up and down a shaft, knew that when night came he might march with the Africa army and bear a wonderful banner to be raised some day in a distant, beautiful land." They wore uniforms and marched under banners, as she said, but they also sent money and bought issue after issue of BSL stock—$200,000 in less than four summer months in 1919. From September 1920 to August 1921, they bought $55,000 worth of stock in the teeth of the economic downturn, and when Garvey launched the Liberian Construction Loan in October 1920 in order to raise $2 million for the UNIA's Liberian beachhead and a sizable loan to the Liberian government, the faithful bought $137,500 worth of bonds virtually overnight.

The drama of the first International Convention of the Negro Peoples of the World opened on Sunday, August 1, 1920, under angry Harlem clouds, with rainfall intermittent throughout the day. For one month, from August 1 through September 1, thousands of delegates would file through Harlem and Liberty Hall. The weather on Sunday was in stark contrast to the mood of the elated thousands streaming into Liberty Hall that morning. The hall had been enlarged for the occasion to seventeen thousand square feet (three times its original dimensions) and to a seating capacity of 12,000. The Red, Black, and Green hung alongside the Stars and Stripes in alternating arrangements, with pride of place given to a gigantic American flag draping a dais seating fully two hundred notables. Two bands rendered spirited versions of the national anthem and "Onward Christian Soldiers." When the curtain rose on Tuesday afternoon, a pageant the likes of which had never been seen before in America unfolded. That Tuesday night, August 3, 1920, 25,000 people of color would pack the old Madison Square Garden between 12th and 14th streets. In the afternoon hours before that legendary event happened, the legions of the UNIA marched 25,000-strong in gorgeous weather through Harlem in a display of civic, commercial, martial, and pan-African prowess.

The parade stepped off promptly at 2 P.M. from UNIA headquarters in 138th Street, headed by four mounted policemen. Behind them came the first vice-president of the Black Star Line, Jeremiah Certain, and the secretary of the Negro Factories Corporation, Arden "Socrates" Bryan, on horseback. Next came the convertible automobile in which the Honorable Gabriel Johnson, mayor of Monrovia, Liberia, resplendent in his robes of office, sat with Provisional President-General Garvey, his rotund frame in black attire, the feathers of his regal bicornate headress waving. Harlem, at full turnout, bordered on delirium as hundred-member bands played and choirs sang, followed, in order of march as reported in the *Negro World Convention Bulletin*, by the men of the African Rifles Corps, immaculate in their black uniforms as they quickstepped down Lenox Avenue, "the Philadelphia contingent with banners showing they represent the 9,500 members of that division . . . ; the Norfolk, Va., Band; the Black Cross nurses of Philadelphia, who with their fellow sisters of the New York division, made a truly inspiring spectacle," clad in white costumes and flowing white caps. There were contingents from Jamaica, Panama, St. Lucia, Bermuda, and Nigeria. Five hundred automobiles brought up the rear, trailed by two mounted policemen. Forty years later, Hugh Mulzac of the Black Star navy and first mate of the *Frederick Douglass*, recalled that day as "the greatest demonstration of colored solidarity in American history, before or since."

And the spectacular of the day was yet to come. Twenty-five thousand wildly cheering people rose from every filled seat in Madison Square Garden as Garvey in cape and regalia led the UNIA nobility to the speakers' platform at precisely 8:45 that night. "Onward Christian Soldiers" resounded as the band of the Black Star Line gamely complemented Harlem's regimental band of the fabled Fifteenth Infantry. "The Universal Ethiopian Anthem" had not yet been adopted. Reverend George Alexander McGuire, a regal Episcopal priest from Antigua soon to comport himself as religious patriarch of the UNIA, delivered the invocation. McGuire would feud bitterly with Garvey the following year, only to return three years later bringing his African Orthodox Church with its catechism of black divinities to the UNIA faithful. After a stirring musical program, Garvey was introduced by presiding officer Henrietta Vinton Davis, the stylish, vibrant Baltimore elocutionist. At that moment, as the crowd hushed, his boasts that he spoke for tens of millions of people of color no longer seemed a mad conceit. "I have in my hand two telegrams," Garvey announced dramatically, one received from a Jew, the other to be sent to an Irishman. Reading the message from Louis Michel, a California Zionist—"there is no justice and no peace in this world until the Jew and the Negro both control side by side Palestine and Africa"—he waited for applause to die down before reading the second message, his own, to President Eamon de Valera: "We believe Ireland should be free even as Africa shall be free for the Negroes of the world. Keep up the fight for a free Ireland."

The young historian Charles Harris Wesley, like Du Bois a product of Fisk and Harvard, may not have been in the Garden on that historic night, but he did hear Garvey speak in public more than once during the early twenties and was impressed. "I hadn't heard anybody dramatize Africa in the way that Garvey had done it," he recalled fifty-five years later. "It would have appealed to Du Bois, if he'd heard it," Wesley thought. There is even a slight probability that Du Bois may have been in the audience that night. Ferris, who had known Du Bois for years, claimed he saw the editor in the Garden, inconspicuous yet unmistakable among the thousands. Du Bois was already gathering information about Garvey, making enquiries in Jamaica, probing his business affairs, seeking data from maritime organizations, even sending Garvey a questionnaire in late July in order, the editor explained, "to present to our readers a critical estimate" of UNIA objectives. When he finally decided to present Garvey and his organization to the NAACP readership in the December–January issue of the magazine, Du Bois wrote about his subject with all the keenness of the investigative journalist. "Garvey is an extraordinary leader of men. Thousands of people believe in him," the editor advised his readers. "He is able to stir them with singular eloquence and the general run of his thoughts is of a high plane." The two-part essay bristled with balance-sheet numbers, contained much material on the inner workings of the UNIA, and presented its subject's personality with a sure touch. The trail of money Du Bois followed into and out of the Garvey's various enterprises—the Black Star Line, the Negro Factories Corporation, the Liberian Loan Fund—plunged, twisted, and detoured as crazily as the path through a circus chamber of horrors.

Of even greater destructive potential than these data-filled observations, however, was Du Bois's highlighting of what he saw as the Garvey movement's alien and invidious elements. The West Indian antagonism between blacks and mulattoes had no place in the United States, Du Bois warned. Pigmentocracy was "absolutely repudiated by every thinking Negro." The greatest mistake Garvey could make was to attempt to perpetrate the politics of color conflict here in America. "American Negroes recognize no color line in or out of the race, and they will in the end punish the man who attempts to establish it," he stated as a simple, fatal fact. The reason Du Bois's threat was likely to be fulfilled, however, was not because Garvey's exploitation of the in-group color line was nothing more than an inflammatory libel but precisely because it violated one of the most sensitive taboos of the native leadership class. The explosive reality was that one of the best-known secrets in the United States was the persisting correspondence between light skins and influence and position in black America. Color reigned even at Tuskegee Institute in the Black Belt, as the farmer wanting to send his son there lamented in Charles S. Johnson's 1934 classic, *The Shadow of the Plantation*: "I suppose if I'd gone to Tuskegee and had schooling I'd a married a yellow woman too. . . . So many colored folks only want to be with white folks. All of them Tuskegee people is like that." Sentiments such as these, usually ignored or humorously discounted, contained less truth than Garveyites claimed, but still more than enough to cause Du Bois and his peers to wince whenever they were insisted upon. There was an almost plaintive dismay in Du Bois's distress over the UNIA leader's insolent ingratitude, his profoundly reckless roiling of the waters of civil rights power relations. "Why then does he sneer at the work of the powerful group of his race in the United States where he finds asylum and sympathy?"

Attempting to make sense of the UNIA's July 1920 financial report (the only one available to the public), indicating neither profit nor loss, Du Bois calculated, now that the first cycle of enthusiastic giving was over, that the UNIA would be able to collect no more than $150,000 annually from some 300,000 devoted UNIA members (Du Bois dismissed the figure of three million) in order to finance its leader's grandiose schemes—more ships, a grocery chain, a restaurant, laundries, real estate investments, a publishing house, an autonomous community in Liberia. By the close of 1920, Du Bois also knew the real story behind the rechristened *Yarmouth*'s implausible voyage to Cuba and the West Indies, the first of three trips to the Caribbean. On a cold, clear October 31, 1919, six thousand members of the UNIA, the red, green, and black official colors streaming above their heads, had marched, bursting with pride, to 135th Street pier for the *Yarmouth*'s rechristening as the S. S. *Frederick Douglass*. Ignoring Captain Joshua Cockburn's protests of mechanical unreadiness, Garvey had signed a full-liability contract with the Green River Distillery Company to transport liquor on the eve of the January 1920 federal enforcement of the prohibition amendment. Its boilers wheezing and the hull listing dangerously due to the hasty, lopsided loading of the $4.8 million whiskey cargo, the *Frederick Douglass* had been towed under Coast Guard protection back to port for repairs soon after weighing anchor from New York. A portion of the cargo had been thrown overboard in order to steady the ship. Boilers patched and the black star standard flapping from its mast, the *Douglass* had finally limped into Havana harbor on March 3 with much of the whiskey stolen by gangsters and the crew while in port, the line's paltry eleven-thousand-dollar transportation fee wiped out many times over by the contract's indemnification clause. A gasp might have been heard coming from Talented Tenth parlors across America. Less than two months after the International Convention closed, the Black Star Line had acquired two more boats: the *Kanawha*, a tired yacht priced at $65,000 ("$55,000 more than she was worth," said Mulzac later); and the *Shadyside*, a rickety excursion boat sold for an inflated $35,000.

"The great difficulty with him," Du Bois sadly observed of Garvey, "is that he has absolutely no business sense, no *flair* for real organization and his general objects are so shot through with bombast and exaggeration that it is difficult to pin them down for examination." Briggs's *Crusader* soon disclosed, however, that, contrary to Garvey's boast, the *Yarmouth* had yet to be registered as the property of the Black Star Line, that it still belonged to the North American Shipping Corporation, Ltd., and that there was an $83,500 balance due on the aged ship's ludicrous sale price of $168,000. No answer was forthcoming from Garvey about the nearly $200,000 taken in during the four months since the first Black Star Line stock issue in June 1919. Du Bois sensed a racial catastrophe in the making, another knockout blow to group self-confidence comparable in magnitude to the collapse of the Freedmen's Bank in the early 1870s. "He can have all the power and money that he can efficiently and honestly use," Du Bois wrote anxiously, "and if in addition he wants to prance down Broadway in a green shirt, let him—but do not let him overwhelm with bankruptcy and disaster one of the most interesting spiritual movements of the modern Negro world."

Among those who had roared approval of the President-General in Madison Square Garden on the night of August 3, 1920, were two Negroes in the employ of the Bureau of Investigation, special agents P-138 and 800, the first and, for another forty years, the last Hoover would allow to serve under him. Their dutiful, detailed reports monitored the UNIA's leader's racial boldness, which seemed to increase in proportion to his declining economic radicalism, infuriating the bureau's director and fully convincing him that the Jamaican immigrant was a danger to the republic. According to Agent P-138's report, Garvey had enjoined his followers on the last night of the international convention to be ready to face death in the cause of Negro solidarity. The white races were their "natural foe, irrespective whether they were American, English, French or Germans." There was also the alarming phenomenon of large UNIA affiliates springing up across the country, with the New Orleans branch even surpassing in size those in Philadelphia and Chicago. Not a full year had elapsed since the general counsel of the powerful United Fruit Company had written to warn the secretary of state that, unless actions were taken, Garvey's activities in Latin America "might repeat the French experience in Haiti." In Cuba, the UNIA had become significant enough for that country's president to entertain the officers of the *Frederick Douglass*. Lord Curzon of Kedleston, secretary of state for the colonies, received a warning from the secretary of the West Indian Protective Society, a New York–based organization, that the Garvey movement was plotting to foment racial discord among whites and coloreds in the British Empire. The 1921 Report of the South African Department of Native Affairs expressed similar concern about the seven UNIA branches that had sprung up across the country, especially the increasingly robust ones in Cape Town and Johannesburg. *The Negro World* was suppressed throughout British Africa, a policy that would be enforced by the colonial ministries in Paris and Lisbon when the newspaper appeared with French and Spanish-language sections after 1922.

If Lord Curzon and the American secretary of state were mildly dismayed by the phenomenon, the leadership class of American blacks began to feel seriously threatened by the Provisional President-General of Africa and his UNIA. From Boston, Reverend Elmer Thompson, influential pastor of the Massachusetts Avenue Baptist Church, had written in alarm to *The Crisis* about the "increasing number of our own people" joining that city's new UNIA. "You owe it to the race to give words of warning," Reverend Thompson implored Du Bois. Plainly alarmed about his own organization being tainted by Garveyite excess, Du Bois had drafted and sent a careful disclaimer to Secretary of State Charles Evans Hughes on the eve of the second Pan-African Congress, explaining that, despite "some public misapprehension," his Congress had "nothing to do with the so called Garvey movement and contemplates neither force nor revolution in its program." But there was also the important, competing consideration of maintaining a common front against white racism. The two organizations were still officially pledged to collaboration, with the UNIA permitting joint membership in the NAACP and supporting passage of the Dyer antilynching bill. After first denouncing the congressional bill to grant Liberia a desperately needed $5 million loan as a plot to control the black republic, Garvey reversed himself and joined Du Bois and the NAACP in supporting its passage. Their personal animosity aside, when he wasn't fiercely attacking Du Bois, Garvey continued to invite the editor's participation in UNIA activities, sending complementary tickets to UNIA events, and even approaching him in early November to contribute a special essay on the "higher development of our Race" for the Christmas issue of *The Negro World*. Moreover, in their deep concern for the welfare of the continent of Africa, Du Bois and Garvey could even find themselves excoriating the same persons and policies whose malice they saw as posing an even more egregious threat than each thought of the other as constituting. Smuts of South Africa was one such threat. "He stands now not only for a white South Africa, but for a white world," Garvey declared. Thomas Jesse Jones was another.

The Welshman Jones had parlayed his Hampton Institute affiliation and self-professed understanding of the Negro Problem into a role with the great foundations as a global expert on race relations. *Negro Education,* Jones's two-volume study that had caused Du Bois's pen to run red in *The Crisis* in 1917, was followed in 1922 by *Education in Africa,* a detailed report funded by the Phelps-Stokes Commission on Africa. Whether or not his Pan-African Congress acquaintance Norman Leys, whose own Fabian socialist writings about African education were markedly advanced for his day, actually revealed to Du Bois what Jones had stated as a fact—that it wasn't "sensible to teach a Negro child what European children are taught"—the editor would already have divined as much about the direction of the Phelps-Stokes study. A Jones-run commission could only mean that the Hampton-Tuskegee model of low-order vocational training would be foisted on black Africa, and South Africa in particular, Du Bois believed. "The English associations got the idea that Mr. Jones represented expert scientific opinion in America," he regretted, "and are placing great faith in his decisions." Garvey was equally alarmed, and as he and Du Bois anxiously monitored the involvement of Moton and the able but somewhat pliable young West African educator J.E.K. Aggrey with the commission, they sounded a simultaneous alarm in October 1921. No member of the race should pay any attention to what Moton says about Africa's needs, Garvey admonished in *The Negro World.* "Now that the Negro has started to think for himself, the white Christian leaders and philanthropists realize that it will be very hard . . . to convince us to accept their 'friendly protection.'"

The real-world consequences of Garvey's heightened emphasis upon racial exclusivism very soon became evident. In a passionately argued, controversial November 1920 essay, "The Social Equality of Whites and Blacks," Du Bois had defended intermarriage of races (but without advocating such unions) as neither "physically criminal or deleterious," unequivocally asserting the "moral, mental and physical fitness to associate with one's fellowmen." Declaring that it was time for *The Crisis* "to take a public stand on this question," Du Bois and the NAACP were to find this forthright stand on social equality denounced not only by Garvey but also by the president of the United States in an Alabama address that shamelessly pandered to the prejudices of the white South. It seemed that Harding was offering explicit rebuttal of Du Bois's *Crisis* editorial when he spoke to whooping Birmingham whites a year later. Shouting a rhetorical answer to his own rhetorical question, the president proclaimed, "racial amalgamation there cannot be," and went on to say, after the rebel yells died down, that "men of both races may well stand uncompromisingly against every suggestion of Social Equality." Harding's October 1921 Birmingham speech came seventeen years after Teddy Roosevelt's similar endorsement of white supremacy in a swing through Dixie. This time, though, black Americans were a good deal more outraged because of the role the NAACP was perceived to have played in supplying the genial, slow-witted Republican with presidential campaign ammunition about the scandalous occupation of Haiti by U.S. Marines. In return, there had been White House commitments to pull the marines out of Haiti, to form an interracial commission to study domestic race relations, to back the passage of the Dyer antilynching bill, and to assign the Justice Department to investigate the resurgent Ku Klux Klan.

Upon reflection, Du Bois decided, President Harding ought to be thanked for unblocking a public debate over a fifty-year-old evasion by "throwing caution to the winds" in Alabama. It was the arrogant policy *not* to discriminate between classes of men and women if their skins were dark; it was the fatal power to nullify merit *even* as the creed of advancement through education, work, and civicism was solemnly promulgated; it was, in a word, the chronic collusion, federal, regional, religious, and bipartisan, with the white South to maintain the *real*, ulterior agenda of *Plessy v. Ferguson* that made Harding's October 1921 speech so pernicious. But what the editor espoused as a founding democratic principle, Garvey reviled as racial treason. More than a month before *The Crisis* chastised Harding, rolling applause and loud amens had filled Liberty Hall as Garvey praised the Birmingham message. Who could dissent from Harding's injunction that the black man should be the best possible black man, rather than the "best possible imitation of the white man," he asked? Garvey speculated, even as the president's speechwriter conceivably may have intended, that the Birmingham speech was a "direct slap or hit at Dr. Du Bois. That is the unkindest cut of all," he added, as Liberty Hall roared with laughter. A signal that the NAACP was about to harden its public antipathy to Garvey came that September with James Weldon Johnson waving a reproving finger at Garvey in the New York *Age*. "Does Mr. Garvey realize the full implications of his statement?" he wondered. Responsible black people never knowingly gave white racists ammunition through public statements validating second-class citizenship. Johnson closed with a ringing affirmation of the NAACP's creed: "The only possible end of the race problem in the United States to which we can now look without despair is one which embraces the fullest cooperation between white and black in all the phases of national activity."

As 1921 ended, Du Bois and the Talented Tenth leadership found themselves repeatedly ridiculed and denounced. Having managed to reenter the country just in time for a stupendous second international conclave after a running battle with U.S. immigration authorities, Garvey began the steady assault upon the editor's reputation and character that would rapidly escalate into unconditional warfare. Missing no occasion now to proclaim that the only authentic value shared by blacks and whites was their determination to remain apart and in parallel and mutually indifferent cultural and political commonwealths, Garvey's real message was an ulterior one aimed at assuaging and propitiating the American white power structure. The African Zion was to be built by "Negro capitalism," the economic system that was not only "necessary to the progress of the world," but had no place in it for labor unions. The black worker, in order to "keep the good will of the white employer and live a little longer under the present scheme of things," ought to be willing to work for less than the white worker, advised Garvey. He adopted with a clear conscience the survival calculus of a messiah willing to play the mountebank if that was the price of his people's deliverance. And if the gambit flattered his innate conservatism and megalomania, it was equally obedient to values forming the vital core of Garvey's racial credo: that all politics was racial and that duplicity in the service of racial solidarity was a virtue. This flawed strategy depended upon guile and cynicism, one in which white enemies were to be bought off by a UNIA, performing the service of undermining those blacks who mounted the most troublesome opposition to the racial status quo in America.

It was for this reason, then, that he now hastened to reassure the United States Government that racial chauvinism was fully compatible with patriotism, proclaiming that "the Negro must be loyal to all flags under which he lives." If Hoover's agents no longer reported hearing threats of race wars in Liberty Hall and postal authorities lightened their scrutiny of BSL stock issues, Garvey counted on being able to buy enough time and space to build an empire powerful enough, eventually, to bargain its way to toleration in the United States while steadily expanding his influence in Africa and the Caribbean. Whether it was the integrationism of the NAACP, the socialism of the *Messenger* group, or the communism of the *Crusader* circle, he indulged his full showmanship powers to broadcast the chasm dividing his own ideology from theirs. In his determination to present a conservative face to mainstream America, Garvey fought with and finally expelled Briggs's *Crusader* group, one of the most able, articulate supporters of the UNIA, at the close of the 1921 international convention. The timing of these expulsions seems very likely to have been accelerated by the aggressiveness of the *Crusader* group and the Blood Brotherhood who made a bid for UNIA support of the new Communist Worker Party. Briggs, Harrison, and Moore, Campbell, Huiswood, and Hall, and perhaps a score more had succeeded in winning a place on the program for Rose Pastor Stokes at the second convention. Stokes, playwright, journalist, and wealthy white revolutionary, was a member of the Communist party's central committee who, some amused observers claimed, regularly darted into the Waldorf Astoria to shake her federal surveillance. A gracious Garvey presented Stokes after putting the press on notice that no one should misinterpret the UNIA as "being Soviets. . . . The press I wish to understand us as not being ultra-radical, because we are not radicals," he reiterated. Stokes came to Liberty Hall on the night of August 19 with Robert Minor, the gifted cartoonist from Texas who became the party's principal proselytiser among American Negroes, in tow. With members of the Brotherhood cheering from strategic locations in the hall, Stokes gave a stirring speech from the platform, declaiming that "wherever the workers want the land, there they shall have it." A week later, Garvey expelled the African Blood Brotherhood, shouting that these agents of "Sovietism" were the hirelings of "certain destructive white elements which aimed at exploiting Negroes for their own subservient ends."

Yet Garvey must have sensed that he was running out of time. Du Bois was certain of it; consequently, the tone of *The Crisis* turned sharper, even minatory. "Let the followers of Mr. Garvey insist that he get down to bed-rock business," *The Crisis* had challenged many months earlier. It was high time for severe economies, published audits, and the gagging of this inspired wild man in order to "preserve his wide powers and influence," the journal pleaded. Salary checks had begun bouncing like tennis balls at the hugely overstaffed UNIA head-quarters in 135th Street, an embarrassment serious enough to persuade the entire executive council to vote a unanimous 40 to 50 percent reduction in their own salaries in early January 1921. By the beginning of 1922, the denounced civil rights leaders had become extremely concerned about the domino effect of Garvey's collapse. Whenever Du Bois wrote or spoke of Garvey there was always the unmistakable hint of a tolerant, well-bred preceptor's exasperation when forced to deal with a gifted, unruly, somewhat gauche *parvenu* — someone woe-fully uninstructed in the vicarious and solemn symbolism of responsible black leadership. What possible value could there be in talk of pride of race without responsible, efficient racial conduct, he would have had the Jamaican answer? Garvey's charge was so much nonsense that he, Du Bois, and other American Negro leaders were jealous of his success. They were simply afraid of Garvey's failure, "for his failure would be theirs." No doubt it was the expectation of that failure that explained why "Pan-Africa," a *tour d'horizon* in the March *Crisis*, had omitted all mention of the Provisional President-General and his organi-zation.

The exodus of well-known West Indian radicals from the UNIA, their in-formed and somewhat principled denunciations, and the willingness of Briggs and Domingo to assist the mail-fraud probe of federal examiners, were serious blows to Garvey's movement. "Figures Never Lie, But Liars Do Figure," Domingo's coruscating piece on Garvey in the October 1921 *Crusader*, reproached his former friend's dictatorial methods, detailed the profligate mismanagement of tens of thousands of dollars, and defended the pan-African efforts of Du Bois. Derided by Garvey as a "Negro for convenience" because of his European appearance, Briggs hauled his fellow West Indian into court for libel and won such a crushing settlement that the *Yarmouth* had to be sold as scrap (for a mere $6,000) at the end of 1921 to satisfy it. One of Garvey's most trusted American associates and a member of the executive council, Reverend J. D. Brooks, had been arrested on charges of grand larceny at the end of November 1921. Months earlier, the crew of the expired *Kanawha* had been brought home courtesy of the United States Government. The excursion boat, *Shadyside*, after a few trips up the Hudson in summer 1920, now lay capsized on the beach near 175th Street. On December 20, 1921, special agent 800 reported to Hoover that postal inspectors had questioned UNIA personnel and been seen leaving 135th Street with circulars, correspondence, and copies of *The Negro World*. In Washington, Hoover fretted as he followed the eleventh-hour maneuverings of Garvey's attorney, Henry Lincoln Johnson, who apparently hoped to persuade Postmaster General Hays to drop mail-fraud charges for a $20,000 consideration. There was to be no deal. Garvey was arrested on January 12, 1922, and released on $2,500 bail. Always choosing the bold stroke over retrenchment and repair, three weeks before his arrest, Garvey had instructed his agents to place a downpayment (but only $10,000 of the expected $25,000) with the U.S. Shipping Board to buy the largest Black Star Line ship yet, the S. S. *Orion* (to be rechristened the *Phyllis Wheatley*) for the projected UNIA trade with Africa and Liberian resettlement. On February 15, the sanction that Du Bois had predicted, that Briggs, by providing the authorities with evidence, had greatly facilitated, and that Hoover had patiently supervised, struck the UNIA broadside. Garvey and three officials of the Black Star Line, Elie Garcia, George Tobias, and Orlando Thompson, were indicted on twelve counts of fraudulent use of the mails. Released on bail, their trials were postponed until the government's investigation was completed. The Shipping Board now cancelled the *Orion* contract and returned the Black Star Line's money. By now, Du Bois knew enough about the shaky finances of Garvey's multiple operations to be certain that the UNIA edifice was bound to collapse in noisy, humiliating failure.

Meanwhile, Du Bois had done a good deal more than continue to accumulate evidence of the unworthiness of the Provisional President-General. He had taken steps to hamper the UNIA's most ambitious undertaking—the Liberian construction and resettlement scheme. Who but he, Du Bois—mind and voice of his race—could have a greater categorical imperative to act with quiet, principled resolve to mitigate the terrible damage wrought by these fiascoes of a reckless and fraudulent Moses? It was his vision of Africa as a continent evolving from underdevelopment and exploitation by way of education and civic experience into prosperous self-rule that had animated the pan-African ideology for more than twenty years. His was the synoptic strategy of presenting the progressive forces of Europe and America with a prudent program for the gradual empowerment of the darker world. It was a program that would lead these forces, gradually, then ever more rapidly, to concert their skills, high purposes, and resources to bring an end to imperialism and racism not only because it was the right thing to do, but, in the end, the only sane thing to be done. Garvey threatened the continuity of these efforts with an opera bouffe act that amounted to little more, really, than pageantry and incantation—"Africa for the Africans," a heady slogan in place of a sober program. Du Bois had written and spoken of Africa for the Africans, but he had never meant by this that Africa "should be administered by West Indians or American Negroes," he reiterated, highly annoyed.

DU BOIS WOULD CLAIM that, at first, even he had been genuinely intrigued by Garvey's electrifying vision of ships steaming to Liberia manned by black technicians and teachers from the United States and the Caribbean, of an advance guard of canny organizers cautiously implementing a master plan to accelerate the decolonization of Africa. But "instead of keeping this plan hidden," Du Bois, shaking his head sadly, had watched as Garvey "yelled and shouted and telegraphed it all over the world," leaving the frightened Liberians no other choice than to distance themselves. The dual purpose of Garvey's Liberian Construction Loan, inaugurated in October 1920, had been to raise money for a $2 million loan to the government of Liberia and to buy land for the resettlement of a small number of skilled Negroes. The prospect of UNIA money for Liberia had come at the lowest point in the republic's undistinguished history since the scissoring off by Britain and France of large portions of its territory at the turn of the century. Liberian coffee had been displaced in the world market by Brazilian. Liberian revenues were virtually nonexistent and compound interest on foreign indebtedness amounted to a death sentence for its sovereignty. Unless the United States Government could be persuaded to lend the orphaned republic $5 million, Liberia's disappearance as an independent nation was unavoidable. President C.D.B. King and the ranking officers of his government were already planning an extended sojourn in Washington and New York in order to press their case with the U.S. Senate. Having been constrained to lay on a charade of government reform in order to win the $5 million American loan, the tight-knit, spendthrift Americo-Liberian clans salivated at the promise of an unexpected, alternative source of millions. Given assurances by the secretary of the Black Star Line, the impressive Elie Garcia, that the UNIA stood ready to "raise subscriptions all over the world" to help Liberia retire its foreign debt, the Liberian political elite responded with all the enthusiasm consonant with its dignity. The gladhanding mayor of Monrovia, Gabriel Johnson, agreed to serve as the UNIA's munificently compensated Supreme Potentate. The nation's Machiavellian secretary of state, Edwin Barclay, assured the UNIA Executive Council that his government stood ready to "afford the Association every facility legally possible in effectuating in Liberia industry, agriculture, and business prospects."

Three months after launching the Liberian Construction Loan, a delegation of UNIA officials headed by the resident commissioner for Liberia, Cyril Crichlow, sailed for Monrovia with His Highness, Supreme Potentate and Monrovia Mayor Johnson. President King and a considerable entourage departed for the United States to lobby for passage of the loan to Liberia not long after the UNIA delegation had reached Monrovia to begin negotiations for a land concession. Some weeks later, when Crichlow, now unpaid and beleaguered by his fellow commissioners, reported from Monrovia that the UNIA might be able to develop some five thousand square miles in the Grand Cape Mount region near Sierra Leone, President King and his officers were making their antipathy to Garvey's Liberia scheme unequivocally clear to official Washington. France and England were likely to become "anxious with regard to the position of Liberia in connection with this movement," a State Department official reported them to have stated when he paid the visiting dignitaries a courtesy call in early April 1921. In the Liberian capital, Secretary of State Barclay, serving as acting president, struck the perfect note of Americo-Liberian cunning. Despite British and French disquiet about Liberia's dealings with the UNIA, Barclay offered Garvey's representatives assurances that a suitable allocation of territory was forthcoming, provided publicity was kept to a minimum: "But it is not always advisable nor politic to openly expose our secret intentions — our secret thoughts. That is the way we do — or rather don't do — in Liberia. We don't tell them what we think; we only tell them what we like them to hear — what, in fact, they like to hear."

While Garvey's mission languished in Monrovia, Du Bois communicated with President King during early April 1921 to discuss the republic's participation in the forthcoming second Pan-African Congress. At some point, they discussed Garvey. The editor was well aware that the UNIA connection had become a source of friction in the inner councils of the True Whig Party, the country's ruling oligarchy, a development made all the more irritating in light of the UNIA's incapacity to provide sufficient funds to lubricate the republic's political machinery. Du Bois thought that this was an opportune moment for Liberia to issue a public statement, offering *The Crisis* as an ideal vehicle. "Your suggestion that a statement be published over my signature setting forth the position of Liberia with respect to Mr. Garvey's movements" was timely, King decided a few days later. The June 1921 issue of *The Crisis* featured President King's declaration. The declaration stopped short of writing off the UNIA, but guaranteed that "under no circumstances will [Liberia] allow her territory to be made a center of aggression or conspiracy against other sovereign states."

Du Bois would have felt doubly justified in hobbling Garvey's West African initiative when he learned that same June that an exasperated Cyril Crichlow, contraried at every turn by his fellow commissioners, disgusted by endless Liberian cabals, and seriously ill, had tendered his resignation and sailed for New York shortly after publication of the King statement. To protect his reputation against charges from Johnson and Marke, Crichlow had handed over to the American ambassador confidential UNIA documents, including a damning appraisal of the country's rulers, which would be published in the December 1922 edition of *The African World* in London with fatal consequences for Garvey's future Liberian plans. Most of the readers of *The Crisis* were readily persuaded that Garvey and his movement spelled shame and catastrophe. Still, Ida May Reynolds, a faithful subscriber, posed a large question about group loyalty that Du Bois, in his reply to her, chose to sidestep. It was her impression, as well as that of "quite a large number of the readers," she wrote in early July 1923, that it would have been far better if *The Crisis* had spent as much time arousing interest among the NAACP membership in the UNIA and in helping it, "as has been given by you and your organization [to] sending Mr. Garvey to jail and trying to wreck" the UNIA.

Du Bois emphatically saw things differently, having decided that the moment was finally right to inform his readers of the danger posed by the Garvey movement. "The Demagog" had run in the April 1922 *Crisis*. Its prose bore the inflections readers had come to recognize whenever the editor was about to speak, as it were, *ex cathedra*. The race was reaching a new plateau of maturity, one on which there were dangers of a new kind for a New Negro. "From now on in our new awakening, our self-criticism, or impatience and passion," Du Bois admonished, "we must expect the Demagog among Negroes more and more. He will come to lead, inflame, lie and steal. He will gather large followings and then burst and disappear." For all the half measures and heartbreak of the past, the Negro experience had been characterized by a solidarity bred of "common social oppression and serfdom." Thanks to their long oppression by whites, blacks had survived and struggled in a democracy of deprivation—"a surging group of low intelligence and poverty," wrote Du Bois—where class formation had been retarded and deformed. Racism had saved people of color from internal class conflict by leaving them "with smaller inequalities in wealth and education than most groups of twelve millions." But this mixed blessing was ending as, slowly, inevitably, people of color in America became differentiated by education and affluence.

Here was the gravest of dangers—the setting of one class against another. Although Du Bois made no reference to Booker Washington, his readers would have sensed how different, unprecedented, the current controversy was from the one that ensued from *Plessy v. Ferguson.* The war with the Tuskegee Machine, for all its divisive and enduring legacies, had been fought primarily over ideas and personalities, with only the most muted class dissonances audible. Class had not been irrelevant, certainly. Du Bois spoke for and mobilized those whose socioeconomic profile was mainly northern, urban, college-educated, professional, and light-skinned. Washington spoke for farmers, domestics, and tradespeople located principally in the South, but fairly broadly dispersed geographically; although his real priorities centered on the urban, college-educated, well-connected, and business-engaged wherever he found them. In simplest terms, Washington and Du Bois had competed for and split the allegiances of the same class formation. Since the climax of the Du Bois–Washington controversy, however, the sounds of class conflict had begun to be heard. "The ties between our privileged and our exploited, our educated and ignorant, our rich and poor, our light and dark, are not what they should be," Du Bois acknowledged. The Demagog finds "the cleft between our incipient social classes," and with Garvey unmistakably accused, Du Bois underscored how the Demagog exploits the "kernel of truth" about class in order to destabilize legitimate leadership. "It is here that the New Negro Demagog thrives and yells and steals. 'They are ashamed of their race'; 'They are exploiting us'; 'They are copying the white man's color line'—he shrieks, as he dexterously fills his own pockets and waters the pennies of the poor." Du Bois had warned in the two-part "Marcus Garvey" appearing in December–January 1921 that the native leadership class of Negroes would punish anyone who attempted to play off one group of colored people against another, by which he clearly meant, without saying so explicitly, that any challenge from outsiders to the paramount authority of the Talented Tenth would be fiercely repelled—and ruthlessly repelled if the aggressor were reckless enough to use skin color as a weapon.

If Garvey could claim that mulattoes and Ivy Leaguers were overrepresented in the top tier of civil rights leadership, he and his circle could find themselves at least as vulnerable to being vilified as aliens who understood little about American history, culture, and race relations, and who misunderstood almost everything about black people of achievement in the United States. As Garvey knew from the slurring references in the Baltimore *Afro-American*, the Chicago *Defender*, the *Messenger*, and much of the domestic black press, his being a West Indian subject of the British Empire had become a convenient substitute for reasoned criticism of himself and his movement. Du Bois's complicity in the anti–West Indian counterattack gathering momentum in the spring of 1923 was somewhat masked and ambiguous. When a deeply hurt Domingo, one of Garvey's bitterest critics, asked his view of the xenophobic turn taken by *The Messenger*, Du Bois replied that the only issue was the "opinion of the man and not the man himself or his birthplace," adding that American Negroes were under a deep obligation to such West Indian contributions as the Haitian revolution. "I, myself, am of West Indian descent and am proud of the fact." James Weldon Johnson could have made the same lineal claim. In print, Du Bois still maintained an air of pained objectivity. Still, his disclaimer was not entirely accurate. The issue may not have been one of West Indian origins, but it certainly came down increasingly to knocking West Indians who were Garveyites.

In September 1922 and January of the following year, *The Crisis* carried, respectively, "The Black Star Line" and "The U.N.I.A." The first article, based on a broad canvas of materials, including Briggs's evidence, described a serio-comic financial disaster drawn in Garvey's own words from various trial transcripts. The *Crisis* piece piled on examples of fantastical bookkeeping (the full purchase price of the *Yarmouth* was listed as an asset), of quixotic sailing schedules causing paying passengers to be stranded and cargoes abandoned at dockside, of multiple boiler repairs running into the tens of thousands, of the *Kanawha* and the *Shadyside* beached and expiring like an iron and wooden whale, and of Garvey's own surreal disclaimers of responsibility—"what could Jesus do dealing with a dishonest man but to wait to punish him at His judgment?" He was no sailor, "not a navigator; he is not a marine engineer," Garvey was quoted as saying in syllogistic self-defense. "Therefore, the individual who would criticize Marcus Garvey for a ship of the Black Star Line not making a success at sea is a fool." Or as Garvey would later conclude in his darkest hour, "The Negro has no method or system to his dishonesty." The follow-up stroke in January, "The U.N.I.A.," reproduced the organization's financial report for 1922, from which Du Bois calculated, on the basis of the UNIA's per capita ten-cent, annual "death tax" (burial insurance), that Garvey could count on a paid UNIA membership of 17,784, rather than the claimed hundreds of thousands. The text of Du Bois's article was uncharacteristically spare, columns of figures unaccompanied by the usual prophecy, jeremiad, exhortation, or indictment— an accountant's audit of a failure.

The New York Times had reported an angry mass rally at Harlem's Douglass Hall in late August of the previous year, the first of the "Marcus Garvey Must Go" protests organized by the Friends of Negro Freedom. With Randolph in the chair, the meeting had taken a sharp nativist turn as two thousand people cheered Bagnall, the normally equable NAACP field secretary, who skewered the UNIA head and called for his deportation to Jamaica. Had Du Bois not stayed away he would surely have overheard scurrilous commonplaces about West Indians that evening — that troublemakers and revolutionaries were bound to be overeducated and out-of-work West Indians; that UNIA stood for "ugliest Negroes in America", "monkey-chasers," and so forth. The editor refrained from unseemly public attacks, but his patience had already thinned to the point that he described Garvey as a scheming "West Indian agitator" in a letter to the Department of State seeking specific information in order to discredit Garvey in the eyes of "the Negro public." On the other hand, it is impossible not to suspect that Du Bois may have known about Bagnall's savage piece written for the March 1923 issue of the *Messenger*. "The Madness of Marcus Garvey" viciously caricatured its subject's physical attributes and character. Garvey was reviled as a "Jamaican Negro of unmixed stock, squat, stocky, fat and sleek, with protruding jaws, and heavy jowls, small bright pig-like eyes and rather bull-dog-like face. Boastful, egotistical, tyrannical, intolerant, cunning, shifty, smooth and suave, avaricious," and on and on in a stream of distemper devoid of intellectual argument.

Machinations with white racists became more and more dismaying as news and rumor spread that Garvey had gone from a Ku Klux Klan rendezvous to meetings with archracist Theodore Bilbo, Mississippi's senior senator, and courtly John Powell, head of the Anglo-Saxon League of America; that he spoke at a rally of racists in North Carolina. Garvey had explained himself, typically, with twisted logic wrapped in hyperbole. "Between the Ku Klux Klan and the Moorfield Storey National Association for the Advancement of 'Certain' People, give me the Klan for their honesty of purpose toward the Negro," he boomed. He was fed up with integrationist hypocrisy and black dependence on feckless whites and the whole Dyer antilynching campaign of the civil rights establishment. Taking the UNIA out of the civil rights collaboration, he claimed that while on a speaking tour of Missouri he had been unable to get a soda "served even by a dirty Greek who kept his so-called white soda fountain in a Negro section" of Congressman Dyer's St. Louis district. Speaking in Youngstown, Ohio, in the fall of 1923 Garvey appealed to "the soul of White America" to help him achieve the only feasible solution to the race problem — which was "to provide an outlet for Negro energy, ambition, and passion, away from the attraction of white opportunity and [to] surround the race with opportunities of its own." If it took an understanding with the Klan to help make it possible for black people to survive and thrive separately, equally, and totally apart from white people in the Americas and on the African continent, then Garvey was up to the challenge. The days of "subtle and underhand propaganda fostered by a few men of color in America, the West Indies, and Africa to destroy the pride of the Negro race by building up what is commonly known as a 'blue vein' aristocracy" were finished.

But it was Garvey himself who was just about finished. The concert with the Klan had the effect of binding his opponents into a solid, raucous, and unforgiving mass. Hoover's agents reported holding covert interviews with Chandler Owen, Bagnall, Pickens, and others who wanted to see Garvey prosecuted. "Mr. Garvey apparently does not know," James Weldon Johnson declared solemnly some months later, "that the American Negro considers himself, and is, as much an American as any one." Johnson, Du Bois, and Randolph chose not to sign the fateful open letter sent on January 12, 1923, to the U.S. attorney general asking the Justice Department to use "full influences completely to disband and extirpate this vicious movement," a signal that Hoover's agents had almost certainly suggested as useful to speed up the start of Garvey's trial for mail fraud. But there could be no question that the eight signatories of the open letter represented the spectrum of Talented Tenth leadership—Owen; Abbott, publisher of *The Defender*; Bagnall and Pickens of the NAACP; John Nail, Harlem's leading realtor and James Weldon Johnson's brother-in-law; Julia P. Coleman, civic leader; George Harris, alderman; and Harry Pace, venturesome businessman and Du Bois protégé. On February 16, Carl Murphy, influential and highly respected publisher of the Baltimore *Afro-American*, followed up with an editorial asking Attorney General Harry M. Daugherty to explain the government's delay.

By the time "Back to Africa," Du Bois's liquidating retrospective of the Garvey Movement, appeared in the February 1923 issue of *Century* magazine, the Provisional President-General of Africa had wrecked the UNIA hierarchy, expelled most of his closest associates except elocutionist Henrietta Vinton Davis, dissolved the Black Star Line, declared his admiration (as would Winston Churchill, John Foster Dulles, and Bernard Shaw) for Italy's new dictator, Benito Mussolini, and conspired in Eason's assassination to prevent his appearing as a witness in the upcoming fraud trial. Eason, who was scheduled to leave New Orleans the next morning to be deposed by government attorneys in New York, had been fatally shot in the back twice as he left church on the night of January 1. Taking careful, well-rehearsed aim, Du Bois's *Century* essay centered Garvey in the lethal crosshairs of history, analysis, Du Boisian judgment, and satirical contempt at the most vulnerable, desperate period in the UNIA chief's public career. The opening sentence—"It was upon the tenth of August, in High Harlem of Manhattan Island, where a hundred thousand Negroes live"— primed the readers (overwhelmingly white) for storytelling at its best about hilarious doings. There in a church basement, "low and unfinished," Du Bois presented Marcus Mosiah Garvey to highbrow America as a character bound to evoke fresh memories of Eugene O'Neill's Emperor Jones or vaudeville's Bert Williams: "A little, fat black man, ugly, but with intelligent eyes and big head, was seated on a plank platform beside a 'throne,' dressed in a military uniform of the gayest mid-Victorian type." Amid the epaulettes, plumage, and swirling capes, and "in the presence of a thousand or more applauding dark spectators," the elite of the UNIA "were duly 'knighted' and raised to the 'peerage' as knight-commanders and dukes of Uganda and the Niger. . . . What did it all mean?"

Du Bois positioned the article's final coffin nail. In Garvey's pandering to the Klan, the author saw another variation of the Great Accommodator's Faustian bargain with the white supremacist South. Two grave temptations had challenged the present generation of Negroes. First had come Washington's—"the greater one"—which said, " 'Let politics alone, keep your place, work hard, and do not complain,' " and which meant, insisted Du Bois, "perpetual color caste for colored folk by their own cooperation and consent." The present challenge of the race was to survive Garvey's lesser temptation, which said, "Give up! Surrender! The struggle is useless; go back to Africa and fight the white world." The hope of the future lay in disciplined work and unflagging courage, exhorted the editor, in owning property and earning education, in the well-kept homes of families living on 138th Street in Harlem's swank Strivers' Row. This was the future in which all members of the Wizard's National Negro Business League would have taken out life memberships in the NAACP—a future in which Garvey would be remembered as no more than an exotic, diverting parenthesis.

The fabled chance meeting of Du Bois and Garvey may well have happened soon after the February *Century* magazine went on sale. Asked half a century later about some vivid instance that captured these two dissimilar titans, their contemporaries invariably recalled seeing or hearing about the editor and the UNIA president rushing to a public dinner affair and arriving at the same time before an elevator. Compelled to ride up in eerie silence together with a group, Garvey was said to tremble violently while Du Bois's nostrils were observed to flare. Charles Wesley, George Schuyler, Arthur Davis, and several others claimed that, when asked about the behavior of his nose, Du Bois icily attributed the flaring to odors emanating from the kitchen. But whatever violent urges were suppressed in the Harlem elevator, there was no restraint in the editorial letter published in *The Negro World* on February 17. Unnerved and seething, Garvey lowered the bar on vilification yet another notch. Du Bois was an "unfortunate mulatto who bewails every day the drop of Negro blood in his veins." Garvey charged that Du Bois arrogated the privilege of condemning and criticizing other people, but held himself up as "the social 'unapproachable' and the great 'I am' of the Negro race." Hating himself and loathing other blacks, the founder of the NAACP preferred the company of white people. "That is why he likes to dance with white people and dine with them and sometimes sleep with them," Garvey lashed out, "because from his way of seeing things all that is black is ugly, and all that is white is beautiful."

Garvey's rage against Du Bois and his kind ("a group that hates the Negro blood in their veins") became even more scurrilous in the months ahead. His interminable trial, running through four sweltering weeks from May 18 to June 21, he saw as persecution engineered by the NAACP. U.S. Circuit Court of Appeals judge Julian Mack, one of the most incisive minds ever to edit the *Harvard Law Review* and second only to Louis Brandeis in the American Zionist movement, was widely reputed to be both a cofounder and active member of the NAACP. The jurist's official connection to the association remains somewhat cloudy, although Du Bois, when asked about it later by the Virginia newspaper publisher P. B. Young, replied that Mack was probably a contributor or supporter. In any case, Judge Mack refused to step down, a decision he may have regretted after Garvey, smoldering under his breath about Jews and near-white Negroes, dismissed his first attorney after the second day and assumed his own voluble, hair-splitting defense. "If Garvey conducted his business as he did his trial," opined the Pittsburgh *Courier*, "there is little wonder it failed." "The result is that he can talk big, but cannot do big," a disillusioned Ferris, observing the trial day after day, wrote Pickens in its final week. The price of failure in Mack's court was a verdict of guilty and a sentence of five years in federal prison and a thousand-dollar fine. A more baleful consequence of the trial was Garvey's embrace of anti-Semitism. Until then, what he had had to say about Jews, although gauche and misinformed, was usually meant to be complimentary, as when he marveled at their power both to start and end World War I. Behind Mack's NAACP membership and presidency of the American Jewish Congress Garvey divined sinister, clandestine forces bent upon destroying black people's best hope of advancement. From this curious moment onward into the late twentieth century, black Zionism would carry a distinct malodor of ideological anti-Semitism.

For Du Bois, Garvey's conviction was a self-inflicted tragedy. But even with that miscalculation and the mail fraud conviction, Du Bois fully expected Garvey to display his finest acting and propaganda skills while his appeal worked its way through the courts. There was still something "attractive and understandable in his personality and his program," Du Bois conceded. The trial and denial of bail, as well as fears of insurgency within the leadership, forced Garvey to cancel the third International Convention scheduled for August–September, but he sacked Ferris, Davis, Marke, and the rest of his inner circle a few days after his trial ended to dispel any misapprehensions about his authority. Confined in the Tombs Prison until September 10, when the court finally approved his petition for bail, he put the time to excellent use by writing a short, self-absolving autobiography blaming his troubles on "very light colored negroes [sic] in America and the West Indies," as well as thieves and incompetents in his organizations. If Du Bois had ever had a second's doubt about his role in toppling Garvey, it must have vanished as he read the autobiographical "The

Negro's Greatest Enemy" in the New York *World* for August 5, 1923. Reiterating a belief "in the purity of both races," the essay predicted a "terrible clash" and race war in another fifty or one hundred years. Unless—and here it struck at the very core of the established civil rights agenda—black people were encouraged to leave white people's countries and were responsibly discouraged from hoping to participate in political life by holding elective office in America. Washington's exhortation to leave politics alone had been tragedy; coming from Garvey, Du Bois must have deplored the advice as deadly farce.

ON BEING CRAZY
AND SOMEWHAT DEVIOUS

O n Being Crazy" ran in the July 1923 issue of *The Crisis*. A short piece of fiction, it was a model satire on the zany, demoralizing state of race relations imposed upon black Americans by white Americans. Du Bois imagined himself a traveler seeking food and entertainment in almost any northern city. Entering a restaurant, his presence evoked astonished protest from a white diner. " 'Are you aware, Sir, that this is social equality?' 'Nothing of the sort, Sir, it is hunger—and I ate,' " was the editor's retort. Later, taking a seat in a concert hall, he noticed that the woman beside him "shrank and squirmed." " 'Do you enjoy being where you are not wanted?' she asked coldly. 'Oh no,' I said. 'Well you are not wanted here.' I was surprised. 'I fear you are mistaken,' I said. 'I certainly want the music and I like to think the music wants me to listen to it.' 'Usher,' said the lady, 'this is social equality.' 'No, madame,' said the usher, 'it is the second movement of Beethoven's Fifth Symphony.' " The hotel near the end of the traveler's obstacle course features a scowling desk clerk. " 'We don't keep niggers,' he said. 'We don't want social equality.' 'Neither do I.' I replied gently, 'I want a bed.' " Tired and disgusted, Du Bois quits the unfamiliar city, intending to purchase a "sleeper" aboard an express train to Texas. No social equality allowed aboard Pullmans heading south, he's told. The allegory ends on a note of demented hilarity, with a screaming white ragamuffin demanding to know why Du Bois *doesn't* want to marry his daughter.

"On Being Crazy" struck readers' nerve endings. Today, it may seem a cliché, a contrivance whose situational dilemmas have lost much of their saliency since the enormous transformation in race relations that began in the sixties. But in 1923, most cultured whites who read *The Crisis* were either shamed or angered, or both, while Aframericans, virtually without exception, found themselves vividly reliving a welter of large and small hurts as they measured their own bitter experiences against those of Du Bois's sarcastic traveler. The special resonance of "On Being Crazy" came from the fact that it was written against the unique psychic backdrop of the early twenties when hundreds of thousands of men and women of color were still being propped up and recharged by a one-time-only optimism and earnestness. Life in the North was one of rising expectations. One out of every two Negro males in New York had been employed in domestic service in 1910; ten years later the percentage was down to 37.4. More than 20 percent of the city's male manufacturing workforce was now colored, up from 13.9 percent in 1910, 90 percent of it unskilled. Men had made steady, if undramatic, gains in the city's trade and transportation sectors, from 30.3 percent to 35.1 in a decade. Advancement was steeply uphill, yet enough men made it into the professions between 1910 and 1920 to augment their percentages from 4.7 to 5.9. Because colored men's wages rose during this period, the much higher number of colored women than white seeking work outside the home declined somewhat. Numbers varied, whether in Philadelphia, Chicago, or Pittsburgh, but overall the picture was one of upward movement in wages for the Negro workingman, notwithstanding his near total exclusion from skilled labor by Samuel Gompers's American Federation of Labor (AFL). More of a flux than a rising tide, perhaps, but the better jobs in the North for the masses of Negroes decidedly buoyed the professional opportunities of their better-educated cousins, the graduates of Atlanta, Fisk, Howard, and a select number of mainstream universities. Dentists, physicians, and morticians, preachers, lawyers, and pharmacists serviced the Great Migration in increasing numbers, with a sizable percentage of them enrolling as active members of the Talented Tenth.

As a "record of the darker races," *The Crisis* kept track of the things that were crazy, and becoming even crazier. "A University Course in Lynching," in the issue for June 1923, reported the fate of James T. Scott, a janitor at the University of Missouri accused of raping a white teenager. Thus far, no American university had actually offered a comprehensive course in lynching, the editor wrote, discounting a nighttime hanging near the campus of the University of Georgia because female students "did not have a fair chance to see it." Lynching 101 was perfected at Missouri, however, with a demonstration in broad daylight, ample notice given, and a "comparatively orderly" audience of five hundred men and boys along with some fifty women students. "We are very much in favor of this method of teaching 100 per cent Americanism," Du Bois observed sarcastically. So long as mob execution was a nationally approved institution, university students should have firsthand instruction so as to understand "exactly what lynching is." But far more realistic than the danger of college credits for lynching was the reshaping of the national memory through film. *The Birth of a Nation*, in the judgment of more than one historian of the period, was uniquely responsible for encoding the white South's version of Reconstruction on the DNA of several generations of Americans. Rerelease of the 1915 film in the spring of 1923 inspired an eloquent editorial denouncing its inflammatory power and "perversion of historic truths." Once again, in full support of the NAACP's petition to suppress the film under New York's motion picture censorship law, Du Bois unhesitatingly chose a restrictive reading of the First Amendment in the interests of racial justice as he perceived them.

In May and August, *The Crisis* reminded Americans just how everlastingly unpredictable racial justice for Negro Americans was. After well over fifty thousand NAACP dollars in legal costs, roller-coaster appeals in state and federal courts, and heroic feats of lawyering by attorney Scipio Jones, six of the twelve men sentenced to death in the 1919 Elaine, Arkansas, conspiracy trials were freed after their case, *Moore v. Dempsey*, was remanded for rehearing before the high court of the state. With a scrupulosity both tardy and rare in such cases, the Supreme Court of the United States accepted the argument of Moorfield Storey (strategically replacing attorney Jones) that the mere formality of a trial was an insufficient guarantee of due process *The Crisis* predicted that the remaining six would soon be released, a prediction that was to be realized six years after their conveyor-belt trials by a kangaroo court of white landowners had convicted them of the capital crime of organizing a farmers' cooperative in the Arkansas Black Belt. The May 1923 issue reported that Representative Dyer had agreed to barnstorm the Midwest to breathe new life into his federal anti-lynching bill, his expenses underwritten by the NAACP. The filibustered death of the Dyer bill in the Senate had come—not unexpectedly but no less mortifyingly—despite petitions and telegrams from a broad array of religious and civic groups, NAACP-sponsored parades and public addresses in major cities, tireless lobbying in the Capitol by Johnson and White, full-throttle editorials by Du Bois, and hard-won passage in the House. Putting a brave face on defeat in the immediate aftermath of Senate "lynching," the editor issued standby orders to the association's faithful and praised the potential power Negroes had demonstrated, now that they had mastered "the mere rudiments of using it." "What a trumpet blast, what a call to hope and courage, are your editorials!" Joel Spingarn fairly shouted.

In issues published just before and immediately after "On Being Crazy" appeared, *The Crisis* had disclosed three appalling institutional developments of major consequence to educated colored people: racial discrimination at Harvard; southern white control of the new Veterans Administration Hospital at Tuskegee; and the denial of scholarship assistance by the Fontainebleau School of the Fine Arts to colored American artists. Individually, each amounted to a brutal uppercut; taken together, they seemed to deliver an immobilizing body blow to the aspirations of the Talented Tenth. First came the news of Harvard's decision in the fall of 1921 to bar men of color from the freshmen dormitories. Opening his orientation and registration packet, William J. Knox of New Bedford, Massachusetts, class of 1925, had been nonplussed to find his room assignment in Standish Hall canceled. He was instructed to report to Weld Hall along with five other entering colored students, each of whom was the son of an affluent, professionally accomplished family, and two, Edward Wilson and Roscoe Conkling Bruce, Jr., who were second-generation Harvard. Bruce, Jr.'s father had graduated in the class of 1902, and his grandfather, Blanche K. Bruce, had represented Mississippi in the United States as its second senator during Reconstruction. Pritchett Klugh was the son of a distinguished Boston clergyman. Bertram Bland's family was old New England. Cecil Blue's father was a prosperous Washington, D.C., physician. When the new residence halls, Standish, Smith, and Gore, were built along the Charles River in 1912–13, much had been made of them as molders of "class identity." These halls were conceived as performance venues in which the distinguishing qualities of manner and mind that made Harvard men special would be preliminarily learned, rehearsed, and commonly reinforced. If the few Negroes admitted each year insisted on residing on campus, Weld Hall in the Yard, with its mix of graduate students and presumably already molded upperclassmen, was deemed appropriate by the administration.

A science major who would earn a doctorate in chemistry from the Massachusetts Institute of Technology, Knox was to cap his career as a member of the exclusive band of scientists working on the Manhattan Project to build the atomic bomb. In September 1921, however, Bill Knox, whose racial identity the admissions office had only recently discovered, was a depressed young man whose privileged New England background left him poorly equipped to deal with the stigma of ostracism. Harvard admission was prized by select Talented Tenth families as though it were the Holy Grail. But it was equally true, even for the many thousands of ambitious families whose children had almost no prospects for an Ivy League education, that "Fair Harvard" was upheld as a precious symbol of what was finest in New England values—a color-blind meritocracy in a democracy corrupted by racial subordination. A distraught Knox had turned to his friend and hometown mentor, Edwin Jourdain, and decided on Harvard partly due to Jourdain's urging. Handsome, self-confident Jourdain, class of 1921, holder at that moment of the world's broad jump record, had stayed on for a year of graduate studies in the business school. Stunned by his friend's news, he did what was expected of a son whose father had joined Du Bois at Niagara: Jourdain confronted the patrician President Abbott Lawrence Lowell at his home and politely demanded an explanation. Offering the sophistry that the policy amounted to segregation without denigration, Lowell implored him to understand Harvard's dilemma as more southerners enrolled yearly. He understood the position, Jourdain was supposed to have said, respectfully accepting the president's insistent hand-clasp. "It's just that I don't respect it."

By late summer 1922, the sweeping cultural agenda driving President Lowell and his supporters had become clear, as he worried in the *Literary Digest* about the recent slippage of the Harvard persona. Lowell wished the nation to under-stand that Harvard's "flavor can be imparted successfully to men of any race or religion," but the flavor was "most easily imparted to men of the old New England stock." Writing to a distinguished Negro alumnus, Lowell explained (in a letter published in the New York *Tribune*) that, while the university owed the colored man and white man the same educational opportunities, "we do not owe it to him to force him and the white into social relations that are not, or may not be, mutually congenial." But it was Jewish students for whom the imparting of special flavors was deemed most problematic. While men of color were to be made to feel out of place by a residence hall bar, the more urgent matter was to curtail the much larger influx of Jews. In this context, Harvard's discrimination against Negroes was merely a sidebar, a sop to sons and daughters of southern whites whose attendance it and other elite schools wished to en-courage in order to serve as WASP counterweights to the new ethnics pressing at the gates. But, ultimately and most significantly, discrimination against Ne-groes was the logical as well as symbolic requirement in a broad policy of strategic "whitening" of the hubs of culture and power.

Believing themselves called to action in a fateful time of crisis, then, Lowell and a majority of the Harvard board of overseers committed the nation's oldest university to the hallowed task of preserving what remained of the genteel in gentile America.

The New Republic served up Lowell's rationale in delicious satire: "Five Jews to the hundred will necessarily undergo prompt assimilation. Ten Jews to the hundred might assimilate. But twenty or thirty—no . . . What they got out of Harvard might be worth their time and effort, but it would not be the price-less Harvard flavor. . . . Better one true Jewish Harvard man than ten mere Jew-ish scholars." As one of the leading students of the subject, Leonard Dinnerstein, wrote of this dark and shameful period, "throughout the United States there was near universal concern about Jews infiltrating cherished organ-izations and abodes." Lewis Gannett, a *Nation* journalist who was intensely en-gaged in the Harvard crisis, supplied Villard with hard statistics (undoubtedly passed along to Du Bois) concerning the elite universities' response to what was being called the Jewish "saturation point." In one year, Columbia had reduced its enrollment of Jewish students from 40 percent to 10; New York University from 80 to 16 percent; Princeton reportedly kept the entering number fixed at forty students.

Spearheaded by large, increasingly vocal numbers of Anglo-Saxon Protestants who were distressed by pullulating slums where no English was spoken, who grew fearful of violence supposedly spawned by alien political ideas, felt threatened by high birthrates among people whose complexions, religions, and diets were different, and who saw corrupt, big-city machines fueled by white immigrants and Negro migrants, old-stock Americans demanded federal action in order to preserve "Nordic" civilization. The immigration act of 1917 (passed over Wilson's veto) had barely made a dent, despite its imposition of a literacy test. Throughout 1920 and 1921, the national press reported that millions more Slavs, Italians, and Russian Jews intended to book passage for Ellis Island now that the war was over. When it became clear that the AFL found its best economic interests served by ending the flow of cheap labor from Europe, the 1921 and 1924 restriction acts became inevitable. Du Bois had deplored the collusion of nativists and labor unionists in the January 1920 *Crisis* as a "despicable and indefensible drive against all foreigners [to shut] the gates of opportunity to the outcasts and victims of Europe." He would have no truck with those Negro leaders who cynically applauded immigration restriction as a boon to black labor.

Du Bois had been so shocked by the dormitory exclusion that he had agreed with Harvard men Storey and Villard to work quietly with other alumni to reverse the policy, even though his old rival, Trotter, had blasted it immediately in the *Guardian*. *The Crisis* maintained discreet, uncharacteristic silence until August of the following year, when it had become clear that Lowell was adamant about maintaining the ban. When Du Bois finally broke silence, he unleashed a double-barreled charge in the August 1922 *Crisis* with "Americanization" and "Fair (!) Harvard." He knew that there was a certain ambivalence not only among the authors of the dormitory protest petition, but even within the NAACP hierarchy and its membership, about combining the issues of residence hall exclusion of Aframericans and admittance quotas for Jews. As Gannett wrote to Storey, after assuming responsibility for circulating the petition, the question of discriminating against a class of students "after their admission seems to have a much more certain answer than the question of limitation of enrollment." Talented Tenth objections to Lowell's policies were inclined to reflect a bias stressing class and breeding—an aristocratic exceptionalism that found discrimination painful *because* it failed to be sufficiently discriminating, because it was arbitrary rather than selective, as novelist Charles Chesnutt and educator Roscoe Bruce, Sr., saw the injustice. "No half dozen men picked at random among the Harvard freshman class could present any better family history or training," Harvard man Raymond Pace Alexander would note in *Opportunity*, the Urban League's new magazine. Such was the reasoning animating the circulating petition authored by seven alumni, including Storey (1866) and novelist Robert Benchley (1912). Nor was the attitude of prominent Jews free of ambiguity about linking quotas to residence rights, as the battling newspaperman, Ernest Gruening, a Harvard graduate and now a driving force at *The Nation*, clearly sensed when he expressed the hope to Villard that "some of our prominent Jews" would see the wisdom of weighing in against anti-Negro discrimination. In fact, the forces opposing the Aframerican segregation and Jewish exclusion would persevere on two parallel tracks, almost never converging except for Du Bois's editorial on the subject.

"Americanization" put the Harvard controversy in the larger political and cultural context of, as Du Bois wrote, the latest "renewal of the Anglo-Saxon cult; the worship of the Nordic totem, the disfranchisement of Negro, Jew, Irishman, Italian, Hungarian, Asiatic and South Sea Islander—the world rule of Nordic white through brute force." By that time, the dire cultural and political implications of the new policy had driven Du Bois into a rage that few other Negro public figures seemed to share. A growing majority of his countrymen envisaged Americanization as a democratic challenge of breathtaking scope and unprecedented idealism, he declared. It meant an America striving to become "one great homogeneous whole" out of its teeming disparateness. But there were those other Americans, quavering and resentful, for whom Americanization meant dominion of the past over the present—narrow forces in Brahmin New England and the Bourbon South who were mobilizing against modern America and its ethnics. It was this "dry rot of aristocracy . . . entering New England and Harvard that has ruined in other days the aristocracies of the world." Even if it were true that "neither side in this vast developing controversy loves Jew or Negro or Irishman as such," Du Bois predicted in a surcharge of optimism that political logic was bound to bring advantaged and disadvantaged Americans together to oppose Anglo-Saxon privilege. The forces that wanted to proscribe Negroes and Jews were the same forces "south and east that are fighting democracy in the United States." Readers would never have suspected that Du Bois knew that neither Storey nor Julian Mack was optimistic about the Harvard outcome. Gannett and Greuning had told Villard that both jurists believed they had "nobody on the board of overseers." The attitude was much changed since the war, Mack sighed.

While the overseers awaited the report of the faculty committee appointed to review Lowell's dual policies, expected in early spring of 1923, the editor championed another cause of equal symbolism and even greater political significance: the racial composition of the staff at Tuskegee's Veterans Administration Hospital. "The last place on God's green earth to put a segregated Negro hospital was in the lynching belt," *The Crisis* roared after Principal Moton had been given two days' advance notice that the new federal facility would be run by a white director and all-white medical and nursing staff. The U.S. Government's premier medical center for Negro veterans, the hospital was to be located at Tuskegee, Alabama, only after Veterans Administration authorities had been rebuffed by prominent white citizens in one southern community after another. But once the huge, T-shaped structure on landscaped grounds adjacent to the Tuskegee Institute campus was ready, southern white politicians orchestrated a takeover. Conflict had been virtually assured from the beginning when the Treasury Department, responsible for the hospital's construction, had promised Tuskegee's white citizens control of the facility and the major portion of its $65,000 payroll, while the Veterans Administration had promised the timorous Moton that Negroes would eventually staff the hospital under a northern white director. Instead, Colonel Robert Stanley, a churlish Alabamian, and his staff of white medical officers had arrived in early February 1923. A grim, New England–born nurse accompanied them at the head of a cadre of white women of remarkably sour mien. To comply with state law governing racial separation, as well as to avoid "contamination" from the patients, each white nurse would command a Negro "nurse-maid."

Fearing himself in danger of irrevocable compromise, Moton appealed to Washington and resisted demands from scores of "eminent white citizens" that he state publicly that Negro physicians were too inexperienced to serve in the hospital. At the same time, however, he declined to back publicly the demands of the colored National Medical Association for total control by Negroes of the facility. Principal Moton's office figuratively sat just below the mouth of a smouldering volcano, with each rumble sending him ducking for cover beneath his imposing oak desk. Although he once described the principal as the most distinguished living graduate of Hampton Institute, Du Bois now smirked that Moton was "a much simpler and more straightforward type" than Booker Washington. Negro America, as Du Bois well knew, had never forgotten the incident in which Mrs. Moton had been ejected from a Pullman car in Alabama. A white trustee of Tuskegee who volunteered to handle the humiliating situation had spoken in Moton's name to say that Moton firmly disapproved of Negroes riding Pullman cars. For the sake of his own position and that of the larger cause of peaceful accommodation in the *Plessy v. Ferguson* South, Moton had kept silent, as he had wished to do in the hospital controversy. But the stakes were such that now he no longer could risk not taking a public position. Du Bois declared his sympathy for the educator "in his undoubted danger and humiliation," although he still rapped Moton's knuckles for his compliant past. "Here was a great government duty to take care of the black soldiers wounded in soul and body," Du Bois asserted. But Moton's earlier collusion had made it possible for the Veterans Administration to duck caring for them "without discrimination in the same hospitals and under the same circumstances as white soldiers."

After a February Oval Office conference with Moton, President Harding had instructed the Civil Service Commission to find qualified Negroes to staff the hospital, although the authority of Colonel Stanley remained unchallenged. The NAACP leadership, backed by the influential National Medical Association and the National Negro Press Association, had made it clear to the White House that it regarded the staffing issue of sufficient importance to influence the Negro vote in the upcoming three-way presidential contest among the Republican, Democratic, and La Follette Farmer-Labor parties. "We had understood that Southern white people simply could not be asked to nurse and heal black folk," the editor wrote in "The Fear of Efficiency." Yet here were Deep South congressmen and the Alabama governor salivating to grab physicians' and nurses' salaries reserved for Negroes. "Nothing more astonishing has happened in this astonishing generation." On a Tuesday night in July, Moton's "undoubted danger" seemed real enough. With a debauched sense of occasion, some seven hundred Klansmen paraded through the town of Tuskegee and across the hospital grounds on the night before the Fourth of July. The parade took on an even more macabre aspect when a reliable informant wrote Du Bois that the head nurse had supplied the Ku Klux Klan with new sheets from the hospital storeroom. Tuskegee was "no place for such a hospital," Du Bois snapped; furthermore, despite Moton's nervously correct response, it had been evident from the beginning that Tuskegee had been induced to accept the facility as part of a deal that had been struck by federal officials sympathetic to the white South. The editor growled throughout the summer of 1923 over the foot-dragging by the Civil Service Commission. What galled him more than the blatant intimidation at Tuskegee was the white South's convincing propaganda campaign in the North. Despite a nine-point refutation of misinformation about the hospital in the July Crisis, he knew that the gently skeptical letter his "Tuskegee Hospital" evoked from Mrs. John K. Howe reflected a bias broadly shared among many well-meaning whites. A subscriber who gave her copy each month to the apartment house janitor, Mrs. Howe wondered if sometimes "something that excites you" mightn't have a less ulterior cause. Reminding the editor that white people "suffer just as much when unjustly accused as colored people do," she enclosed a clipping from the current Outlook informing its well-bred readers that the Veterans Hospital was originally intended to be run and staffed by whites, that the government had been unable to find a large enough pool of available Negro physicians; that the NAACP and other militant organizations had demanded that the Civil Service Commission adjust standards in favor of unqualified applicants; finally, that the racial friction in Tuskegee was due to agitation by the NAACP.

If he betrayed an almost harsh impatience in replying to Mrs. Howe and the Outlook's willful disregard for the facts, it was partly due to the fact that Du Bois had become bitterly distraught after the failure of the Justice Department to intervene. At first, he'd been cautiously encouraged by White's report to the board of his breakthrough meeting with Justice Department officials, claiming that the Bureau of Investigation was entering the case. Dashing to the sweltering capital on June 6, the NAACP secretary had eventually reached Colonel Theodore Roosevelt, Jr., who enabled him to meet with the assistant chief of the Bureau of Investigation, apparently about the only Justice Department official in town at the time. "Cordially received" by this official he identified as "Mr. John E. Hoover," White had insisted that the Klan was plotting to intimidate the local Negro community, only to have the assistant chief explain that he lacked authority to act without specific instructions from the attorney general. Ascertaining the name of the official empowered to speak for the absent attorney general, White promptly telephoned from Hoover's office and not only received assurance from Attorney General Harry Daugherty's deputy, "a Mr. Crim," of the Harding administration's concern, but listened over the telephone extension while the deputy dictated instructions to Hoover to investigate "any situation where Government property or government interests were involved." The July outrage of the Klan parade at Tuskegee, the refusal by the town's white merchants to sell to black customers, the expulsion of the only black doctor, and the summary dismissal of black nursemaids from the hospital had followed hard on the heels of White's Justice Department discussions. Yet Washington had done nothing prior to Harding's sudden death at the beginning of August—not even the removal of Colonel Stanley. Before the matter came to Calvin Coolidge's attention, the white South was very likely to have settled it on the ground while the Civil Service Commission vacillated. "Human hatred, meanness and cupidity gone stark mad!" Du Bois expostulated.

Du Bois saw yet more evidence of madness in the treatment meted out to Augusta Savage during spring 1923 by the directors of the Fontainebleau School of the Fine Arts, a recently established, American-sponsored academy outside Paris. Ernestine Rose, the white head librarian of the 135th Street branch of the New York Public Library who hovered over her patrons like a mother hen, had written the chairman of the school's sculpture department for an explanation; could there have been a mistake, she wondered? Miss Savage had done outstanding work in sculpture at Cooper Union. From a poor Florida family, thirty-one and patchily educated in the public schools of the state, Savage had been in New York less than three years, yet her talent had already won enthusiastic support among a small circle that would eventually see its faith in her outstandingly rewarded. Savage's commissioned sculpture, *The Harp*, would be the central attraction in the Contemporary Arts Building at the 1939 New York World's Fair. That she was destined for an exceptional future was already evident from the evaluation of her work sent to the Fontainebleau School by the Cooper Union: "excellent and her conduct irreproachable." But she was never going to be white, and "to be perfectly frank . . . we did learn that Miss Savage was of the colored race," Miss Rose was told by Ernest Peixotto, director of painting and sculpture at Fontainebleau and a distinguished American painter. Back at his desk after a month's speaking tour in the West, Du Bois fired off his own inquiry to each of the school's eight prominent American directors as soon as the Rose correspondence reached him. "In the next issue of *The Crisis*, we hope to have their answers and to comment on them," he announced in his June catalogue of horrors, "The Fear of Efficiency."

WHEN THE EXPATRIATE writer Malcolm Cowley recalled in his *Exile's Return*, many years after the Harlem Renaissance had become a gorgeous memory, that "one heard it said that the Negroes had retained a direct virility that the whites had lost through being overeducated," he could have very appropriately cited *The Gift of Black Folk* as his source. Du Bois had begun writing this influential book, whose contributions to the aesthetic, literary, and dramatic conceptions of his people were to be permanent, sometime during 1922. The Negro was "primarily an artist," the author pronounced canonically, and possessed of a special sense of beauty—"particularly for sound and color, which characterizes the race." Probing further, Du Bois exposed the racial essence as being "a certain spiritual joyousness; a sensuous, tropical love of life, in vivid contrast to the cool and cautious New England reason." "Finally the Negro has played a peculiar spiritual role in America," Du Bois's foreword trumpeted, a "living, breathing test of our ideals and an example of the faith, hope and tolerance of our religion." In one sense, however, Du Bois's stipulations that black people had contributed "a sense of meekness and humility which America never has recognized and perhaps never will," or that they possessed "a slow and dreamful conception of the universe; a drawling and slurring of speech, an intense sensitiveness to spiritual values," could as easily have been stigmatized by hostile racialists as esteemed by admiring racialists. *The Gift of Black Folk* was an outstanding example of the complexity of unintended consequences, a work whose copious evidence and emphatic thesis cut both ways across the plane of racial typologies, an argument that could be construed to have exactly opposite meanings.

The book was commissioned by the Knights of Columbus Historical Commission just as the alliance of the northeastern Protestant establishment, Middle America, the Klan-ridden South, and much of organized skilled labor was heading for victory in a frenzied campaign to revise the nation's immigration laws. The redoubtable Dr. Edward McSweeney, the Historical Commission's chair and former deputy immigration commissioner at Ellis Island, hoped that a thoughtful book by the foremost intellectual of color might help to blunt the runaway momentum of Anglo-Saxon racism and religious bigotry. The Historical Commission's series on the making of America underwrote two other studies dealing with distinctive populations—*The Germans in the Making of America* and *The Jews in the Making of America*. McSweeney's "Introduction" to *Gift* fully complemented Du Bois's perspicacity in the Harvard dormitory controversy about the preeminent national values at stake in the nativistic irruption of the twenties. "To attempt, in this country, to set up a 'caste' control based on the accident of birth, wealth, or privilege, is a travesty of Democracy," McSweeney protested. Yesterday, the bigoted slogan was "No Irish need apply," he recalled. Today, the cry was to turn back the Jews and the Italians, slogans with strong appeal to the pocketbooks of white working men and women (and, he might well have added, to those of most black Americans). What McSweeney and Du Bois gamely tried to do was to oppose conservative Gentile elites, Ku Klux Klan loyalists, hardshell Baptists, gentrified eugenicists, and Henry Ford's *Dearborn Independent* readership with the counterweight vision of an American pluralism or multiculturalism that had only just begun to be conceptualized at the beginning of the century. Harvard philosopher Josiah Royce and Du Bois's approximate Harvard contemporaries Horace Kallen and Hutchins Hapgood, along with Greenwich Village's Randolph Bourne and Waldo Frank, offered a vision of a democracy that celebrated differences rather than reviled and suppressed them, a vision, said Du Bois, that might never have materialized but for the unique role the Negro American had been forced to play in the nation's history. After all, the so-called democracy of the Founding Fathers was never a "democracy of the masses of men," but an Athenian democracy in which slavery along with class and gender hegemony formed the natural order of things.

By selecting *The Negro in the Making of America* as the subtitle for his contribution to the Knights of Columbus series, Du Bois intended to suggest that more than labor, duty, and loyalty were involved in the African contribution. The gift of black folk (a noun resonating with the German *Volk*) was uniquely more moral and spiritual than that exemplified by any of the other groups. It was the gift of soul. Black folk had an unfailing faith in the world, "an unfaltering hope for betterment and a wide and patient tolerance for opposition and hatred." With insight that would find converts among revisionist historians only half a century later, Du Bois contended that it was black people who forced the consideration "of this incongruity, who made emancipation inevitable and made the modern world at least consider if not wholly accept the idea of a democracy including men of all races and colors." In reality, what *Gift* represented in the no-holds-barred fight by a large number of Anglo-Saxon Americans to maintain political and cultural primacy after World War I was an almost quixotic attempt to deflate the modern age's most pernicious invention: what Du Bois in *Darkwater* denounced as the "discovery of personal whiteness among the world's people"—the conquering ideology of "whiteness."

As Du Bois foresaw, the subtly intimidating dogma of privilege by pigment would not merely succeed in exalting whiteness as a condition of general beatitude in America, it would erect hierarchies of whiteness in which "Nordic" whiteness would be the glorified ideal — Jack London's Blond Beast matched with Mary Pickford's alabaster perfection. It portended a dismal reconfiguration of the national identities, one in which the inviolable "one drop rule" of the white South prevailed everywhere and "mulatto" was extruded from the U.S. Census (implemented in 1920); a binary society in which blackness and whiteness were indissolubly calcified in the popular mind by minstrelsy and where swarthy complexions, too much expressiveness, and pronounced facial features of a certain type were stigmatized in magazine advertisements and Hollywood films.

In its hard and soft varieties, this upsurge of nativism clamored for ethnic cleansing. The softer variety, of which Theodore Roosevelt and Woodrow Wilson had been leading exponents, was committed to melting-pot metamorphosis. Italians, Jews, Poles, and Hungarians were destined to melt in the national cauldron until, whiter and blander, they were ready to be poured into WASP molds. The process of Nordic whitening, as names and noses and religious affiliations were altered, demanded that people of color serve as reverse examples of the national ideals, mudsill populations below a rising tide of generally optimistic white immigrants. "We push below this mudsill the derelicts and half-men, whom we hate and despise, and seek to build above it — Democracy!" Du Bois had sneered in *Darkwater*. Among antiassimilationist hardliners, however, such as Charles Davenport, Harry Laughlin, Lothrop Stoddard, Alexander Graham Bell, David Starr Jordan, and numerous influentials of the American Eugenics Association (generously funded by Mrs. Mary Harriman and the Carnegie Institution of Washington), the policy of making one out of many was reviled as genetic folly. The hardliners demanded an end to liberal immigration policies that had already badly undermined the Republic with hordes of unassimilables.

The Gift of Black Folk was as well a written history lesson ranging over art, music, education, women's rights, and political theory. The book would supply an important charge that helped jump-start the so-called renascent arts phenomenon. On the other hand, the gifts of black folk vaunted by Du Bois had neglible appeal to white ethnics made unsure whether or not they were sufficiently white in pigment and culture to meet the demanding binary standards of old stock Protestants of English and German descent, seemingly unassailably positioned atop the mythic City on a Hill. No two controversies highlighted with more heat the lockstep march of American ethnics into the mythic purity of whiteness than the Rhinelander and Ossian Sweet cases exploding across newspaper front pages in the closing weeks of 1925.

Leonard Rhinelander, wealthy scion of an old Westchester County German family, had married Alice Jones for love and across class lines. But the initial newspaper depiction of a Cinderella match ("Society Youth Marries Cabman's Daughter") abruptly switched to one of high-drama scandal ("Alleges Race Deceit") when the Rhinelander family apparently compelled the hapless heir to sue for annulment on grounds that Miss Jones had concealed her true racial identity. "This man begged to marry her and did," Du Bois reminded New York. "And what then? Did he care because she had black blood? Not a rap. But his family did not want other white folk to know." In the ensuing one-month trial, during which she was actually compelled to disrobe to the waist before the all-male jury, Alice Jones was made to embody the racial (and gender) pollution that only scrupulous social segregation reinforced by laws that honored the spirit, if not the letter, of the one-drop rule could guard against. The Rhinelander family lost the case because the jury decided there was no intent to deceive on the part of Alice Jones, but the one-drop rule would be ratified in the nation's consciousness and confirmed in a number of pivotal state court cases.

Neighborhoods were believed to be as susceptible to racial contamination as bedrooms, and in the affluent family of pediatrican Ossian Sweet, white Detroit saw a threat to property values as well as a terrible affront to residential purity. When the mob came for the Sweet family on the night of September 8, it was met by a hail of gunfire, killing one ringleader and wounding another. The arrest, indictment for first-degree murder, and monthlong imprisonment of Ossian and Gladys Sweet and nine family members and friends brought a howl from *The Crisis*. "Dear God! Must we not live? And if we live may we not live somewhere?" The Sweet case epitomized the values of the New Negro for Du Bois and for tens of thousands of others, the values of culture and courage, of the upstanding professional man and woman ready for self-defense if and when reason and exemplary conduct failed their purpose. In December 1925, *The Crisis* ran "Now or Never," a veritable order from on high to ten million people of color after the first Sweet trial had ended in a mistrial on Thanksgiving Day. This was the moment, Black Folk of America. "No listless foolishness, no carping criticism," the editor commanded, "but to work! Pay! Sacrifice! Be men and women! Be free!" "The cost of freedom to the Negro today is $50,000." Six months and a $71,000 NAACP Defense Fund later, Ossian Sweet walked out of court a free man on the arm of Clarence Darrow.

In "Americanization," the August 1922 *Crisis* opinion piece, the editor had wanted to believe that a great alliance between the darker peoples the world over with "disadvantaged groups like the Irish and the Jew and between the working classes everywhere is the one alliance that is going to keep down privilege." But as McSweeney had feared in his introduction to *Gift*, multiethnic, multicultural America was already a doomed cause, one in which Du Bois's special pleading encouraged his people even as it convinced many white Americans that, for the sake of a unifying whiteness, they needed to believe that there was an incommensurable gulf separating them from black Americans—and, many thought, *vive la différence*! It was hardly surprising, then, that the 1920 U.S. census revealed (inferentially) that almost half a million of the mulattoes counted in the 1910 census had "passed" over into the white race during the intervening decade.

White supremacy had already fixed athletic competition, making it virtually impossible for Negroes to tackle, pitch, or hit with other Americans on equal terms, the editor had reminded readers a few issues back. Jack Johnson's genius in the ring had nearly incited a race war and finally driven congressional racists to outlaw the interstate sale of prizefighting films. With Rhodes scholarship competition eliminated, appointment to West Point and Annapolis no longer possible, and premier mainstream colleges and universities becoming more unreceptive, the escape hatches for colored ambitions were sealed fast. Yet the ground rules governing artistic expression were supposed to be relatively insulated from racial handicapping, Du Bois noted, the myth being that "eagerness for ability unstained by discrimination of any sort was eagerly desired." "The Technique of Race Prejudice," appearing that August, categorically laid such fictions to rest. One by one, the distinguished trustees of the new American school at Fontainebleau squirmed, bluffed, cited technicalities, or succumbed to amnesia as *The Crisis* reproduced their replies. One had to be mindful of the school's financial backers and of the students from the South. Two southern white female students had refused to sail on the same ship with Savage. The nub of it, wrote J. Monroe Hewlett of the admissions committee to Du Bois, was that Savage's rejection "was due quite as much to consideration for her as to any other thought or feeling." His editorial lip curled, Du Bois wrote disdainfully that it was silly "to talk of race prejudice as simply a child of ignorance and poverty. . . . The real deep and the basic race hatred in the United States is a matter of the educated and the distinguished leaders of white civilization." *The Crisis* gave Daisy King, a successful white sculptor, the last, devastatingly personal word. Wasn't it unbelievable, she had asked a colleague, that Thomas Hastings, designer of the Forty-second Street Library and America's foremost architect since Stanford White, could "stoop to place a stone in the path of a little colored girl who has won distinctive honor, against odds?"

The Crisis underscored a great many issues in which there was a decided class-driven interest, yet the editor's race relations caveat—"those who are wise have noticed some curious changes in the attitude of the white world recently"—contained the broadest ramifications. To those Negroes who followed the unfolding controversies with deepening distress, Harvard, Tuskegee, and Fontainebleau signaled a new willingness by the white ruling class to stigmatize, marginalize, and reject people of color. These three injustices could be seen as tantamount to semiofficial declarations that mainstream America recognized no amount of merit, conceded not even the most minimal authority, and esteemed no expression of creativity, however rarely talented, insofar as Negro citizens were concerned. To be sure, several million men and women of color were either ignorant of or sullenly indifferent to stipendiary reverses suffered by gifted artists or humiliating dormitory restrictions imposed upon student aristocrats of color. Many of them had never even heard of the Dyer bill, as the editor of the AME Church's *Christian Recorder* told Du Bois, after he conducted an informal poll of "a large number of colored people standing on a corner one Sunday afternoon." But whatever their divergent priorities, *The Crisis* managed to cut through the overlapping layers of class and to strike racial bedrock more often than not. In those infrequent pieces in which the editor permitted his personal emotions to show, as in "Charles Young," appearing in the same July issue as "On Being Crazy," this was especially true.

Du Bois had written about Young in February 1922, as soon as news of the colonel's death, expected but still deeply saddening, arrived from West Africa. After John Hope, Charles Young was probably his closest friend, although Wendell Dabney of Cincinnati, whose salty personality Du Bois sketched in a rippling April profile that year, may have shared equal billing. In the deflating period immediately following Young's forced retirement from active duty on the eve of World War I, Du Bois had become his steadying counselor, gaining Young a place on the association's board, involving him in fact-finding missions, and trying, as the powerful nostalgia for command pressed upon Young, to restore perspective to his friend's options and obligations. Young's options were not great. "Africa calls, Haiti makes a bid; and the War Camp Community People have made an offer," Young had written in the spring of 1919. "I have promised none." Du Bois had fought against Young's admirable sense of obligation. "Believe that if you refuse Liberia New York position would open," he advised by telegram at the close of 1919. But, in the end, when the army he loved more than his life, and which had cut him off from a star and inevitable command of the 92nd Division in France, recalled him to service, Young had sailed away to Liberia as military attaché and, stoically, to an almost certain death from nephritis in that brutal climate. Ada Young, whom the Du Boises hosted after her return from France ("we had a lovely time"), had barely unpacked her trunk in Wilberforce when the news came of her husband's death on January 2 in a British military hospital in Lagos, Nigeria.

"Colonel Young" in the February 1922 *Crisis* was restrained, stately, above bitterness. Du Bois had written it in a tone sufficiently lofty to mute the bite of several severe charges it contained, declaring there that his friend's life "was a triumph of tragedy." He added that "no one ever knew the truth about the Hell he went through at West Point. He seldom ever mentioned it." Du Bois knew, noting sardonically that Young had been sent to Africa "because the Army considered his blood pressure too high to let him go to *Europe!*" Still, he had kept the emphasis upon Young's triumphal humanity, his uncompromising patriotism, and his Homeric sense of duty—"and Duty to him, as to few modern men, was spelled in capitals." But when the second "Charles Young" appeared in the July 1923 *Crisis*, Du Bois injected an emotional charge into it that was remarkable, even for him. Young had suffered a fatal stroke while on an inspection tour in Nigeria and been buried with full military honors by the British. In death, he became a useful racial symbol to the Harding administration and the disingenuous War Department for whom his exceptional career had long been an embarrassment. Before his remains were brought home, an impressive memorial ceremony was conducted in the great hall of New York's City College, where Du Bois, Joel Spingarn, Brigadier General Fred W. Sladen, and Theodore Roosevelt, Jr., payed tribute, on May 27, 1922. Both the *Amsterdam News* and the *World* carried page-one accounts of the fireworks set off by Du Bois— "possibly one of the greatest [speeches] he has ever made in his public career," the *Amsterdam News* reporter thought. Charging that his friend had died of a "broken heart" because the War Department had unjustly denied him a field command on the western front, the editor reviewed the grinding years of institutional racism assailing Young. General Sladen, West Point commandant and classmate of Young's there, was reported to have laid aside his notes in order to deliver a pointed rebuttal. Theodore Roosevelt undoubtedly summed up the feelings of the audience when he declared that "by sheer force of character, [Young] overcame prejudices which would have discouraged many a lesser man."

What it had really cost Young to overcome in those last months in Africa, not even Du Bois then knew the full, debilitating details. More than a quarter century later, Rayford Logan would share the bitter confidences Young had entrusted to Dr. Emery Ross, a white American Methodist missionary. Ross recounted an evening when Young, "who swore like a trooper and drank like a gentleman," had asked from the depths of a misery close to tears, "Lad, how would you like to be a nigger?" But Du Bois already knew more than enough about Young's calvary to feel a solemn obligation to mock the official hypocrisy surrounding his burial in Arlington Cemetery on June 1, 1923, the better to exalt the meaning of his death. "Charles Young" was both a luminous apostrophe and a condign indictment. A full-dress funeral processional accompanied the remains through the capital to Arlington, where the catafalque reposed in the grand marble amphitheater during the interment ceremony, only the fourth warrior so honored after two Confederate veterans and the Unknown Soldier. The colored public schools of the District of Columbia were closed, and thousands of young faces looked with wonderment as the colonel's black stallion cantered past with his reversed cavalry boots and saber. Civilian and military notables of both races orated, and the Howard University choir sang. In life, the people Young served loyally had thrown him to the wolves, Du Bois asserted. "They simply got out of the way and left him to his fate. And today, when it is all over and the man has lived and conquered and suffered and died," he remonstrated, "then his successful class-mates and fellow officers come forward and say, 'Young? We knew Young. He was a splendid fellow! Insulted! We never insulted him; we never saw him insulted. He was a favorite at West Point." That lie must not stand, Du Bois lectured. "Children will grow up and believe that merit is recognized at West Point whether clothed in black or white; and that Charles Young, [Johnson] Whittaker, [Henry] Flipper and the rest had no unusual difficulties." Du Bois bore on, to charge again that the United States Government had first defrauded Young and colored America of a great wartime servant, then "murdered him" by sending him to Africa. "God rest his sickened soul, but give our own souls no rest if we let the truth concerning him droop, overlaid with lies."

Even though *The Crisis* had continued its slide from the monthly circulation high of 100,000 to less than 60,000, it remained the premier organ of civil rights opinion among colored people and a significant one among progressive whites — the better class of white folks, as the editor would say. If it had become predictable and even somewhat prickly about the political opinions of many of the younger radicals coming into prominence in Harlem (and haughtily hostile to Garvey and the UNIA), even its detractors conceded the excellence of the journal's production and the towering courage of the editor. Moreover, *The Crisis* was beginning to change under Fauset's literary impulsions. The issue for June 1923 announced the results of the first Prize Story Competition. Fauset and Dill were somewhat disappointed, however; of nineteen entrants, only seven undertood the meaning of a plot. "Are they ever shown the prose of Shaw, Galsworthy, Mrs. Wharton, Du Bois or Conrad?" Fauset sighed. "Bread and Wine," a poem by the precocious Countee Leroy Cullen appearing in the same issue, was a considerable compensation, nonetheless, for which Fauset could take full credit. Two poems published in May 1922, "To a Dead Friend" and "My Loves" by another Harlem prodigy, had marked the reappearance of Langston Hughes, whose *Crisis* debut Fauset arranged a year earlier with "The Negro Speaks of Rivers," one of his signature verses. In April 1922, she had introduced readers to the gifted Washington writer Eugene Nathan Toomer, with the haunting prose-poem "Song of the Son." In "Art for Nothing," published the following month, Du Bois had unbraided people of color for their widespread artistic insouciance. The Meta Warrick Fullers, May Howard Jacksons, and William

A. Scotts—rarely gifted sculptors and painters—stumbled and perished, he claimed, because "we are united with singular unity to starve colored artists."

What would shortly be dubbed the Harlem Renaissance was beginning. Still, Fauset's input notwithstanding, *The Crisis* remained firmly focused on politics, civil rights, and racial propaganda. What most readers found engrossing during the summer and fall of 1923 was hardly the short-story competition and poetry but coverage of the Dyer antilynching bill, the Sterling-Towner education bill providing federal funds to the southern states, the release of the Arkansas Six, and the unfolding dramas in Cambridge, Tuskegee, and France. And whether or not they subscribed to the monthly, nearly 14,000 Americans heard the editor between mid-February and the beginning of April as he traveled more than eight thousand miles, addressing NAACP branches, lecturing in colleges and universities, speaking in Ys and in numerous churches. Circuit-riding into and out of the purlieus of the Talented Tenth, his route passed through Toledo, Zanesville, and Chicago; Indianapolis, Denver, and Portland; Eugene, Sacramento, and San Francisco; Oakland, Los Angeles, and San Diego. He had left New York a week before his fifty-fifth birthday, a decision that may have saddened Nina and affected her delicate health. Wishing Will "many happy returns of the day" on the eve of his birthday, her letters from 108 Edgecombe Avenue seem one long sigh as she described cold, dark, wintry days and her various ailments, telling him in early March, "The first two Sundays you were away I spent most of the day in bed." He shouldn't worry, she added, because she was "taking good care of [her] neck."

MILDRED BRYANT, THE petite, playfully disrespectful music teacher Du Bois had first met a decade ago in Louisville, Kentucky, devotedly welcomed him to Chicago, as she was to do many times again. At Berkeley, his campus visit resulted in another of those life-changing impacts that were becoming a Du Bois stock and trade. Louise Thompson's parents were the whitest people of color in Oakland, and about the poorest. They had an abundance of what people called native intelligence, and raven-haired Louise, twenty-one years old and endowed with a will of iron, was one of the smartest seniors at the university. Sixty-odd years after first laying eyes on him in an auditorium, Louise Thompson Patterson, the notorious "Madame Moscow" of Harlem Renaissance legend, still felt the moment. Once, as a child, she had heard Booker Washington tell "darky jokes" in Walla Walla, Washington, the only important black person she'd ever seen. But Du Bois was something marvelous: "But there he stood and talked without notes and without paper, and I had never seen such a black man in my life." Louise walked out of that room "for the first time in my life, proud to be black." She began dreaming from that moment how she could go to New York and work for *The Crisis*. It would take Louise what seemed an eternity to reach Manhattan—almost four years—but their friendship was to be an asset after she joined the Hampton faculty and Du Bois began an investigation into the paternalism of the school's white administrators in 1926.

In Los Angeles, Du Bois's sophistication and avuncular charm shook the earth beneath another talented, attractive young woman. By pure coincidence, she was also named Thompson—Anita Thompson—the aspiring daughter of Mrs. Beatrice Thompson, a *grande dame* of imposing carriage and towering social authority in the city's Negro community. The editor had already introduced Anita to his readers that January when she appeared on the cover of *The Crisis* in profile, turbaned and sultry, her left shoulder bared, a bit of drapery pressed to her right shoulder and the tilt of her head emphasizing her aquiline features. Du Bois had yet to meet her in person. She was known to him only as the daughter of a prominent family active in the Los Angeles branch of the association. By the time the June 1923 issue featured a group photograph of Anita, her mother, Du Bois, and two others on a visit to the child actor Ernest Morrison ("Sunshine Sammy") at the Hal Roach Studios, the editor and the lovely ingenue had developed an intimate rapport. More uncloaked in his correspondence than usual, he thanked her for a carton of cigarettes (probably Benson and Hedges) and expressed delight at the prospect of her arrival in New York. He told her that deep emotions could take one only so far—"I hate to say it, but still one cannot exist indefinitely on that sort of thing, and marriage is a serious and more or less hum drum matter," he added. Anita floated on memory's ether, writing that his visit was like a lovely dream "from which it has been rather difficult for me to awaken (I haven't known since if you were really here and 'adopted' me or if the Chinaman gave me a six-months pipe o' rap. Perhaps? ha ha)."

She savored his letters, telling him they were "part of the dream." The "At Hollywood" photo with a benevolent Du Bois looking down at Sunshine Sammy was a delightful "eye-opener." She could actually hear him "chuckling over it." Thanks to Du Bois, she now wanted to spend the next fifteen years studying philosophy, French, Latin, Greek, psychology, and painting, and to live in New York. She hadn't finished college and had no professional skills or enough money for tuition at Columbia or Harvard (she feared that at Howard University she'd be "out of tune at a colored school"). "Tell me what to do this fall," she pleaded. "I'll love you forever for it." Anita was sure they would see each other at the the NAACP annual convention that July in Kansas City, Kansas, and afterward in New York, where her mother might leave her—"if she thinks I'm being 'properly watched,' ha ha." But then, at the last minute, there had been a misunderstanding with Ovington and Johnson about travel expenses, and the editor would surprise everyone by withdrawing his name from the 1923 convention program. They must have met again late that summer when Anita and her mother came to New York, but the last letter from this period is an undated one written from Philadelphia where Anita, traveling by then with an acting troupe, confessed that she's been thinking of Du Bois "night and noon for two days. Is it because you're wondering why I haven't written?"

While he traveled that spring, Nina, as usual, coped with their private affairs in usual faltering health. His being on the road probably couldn't have come at a worse time for her. At the beginning of January 1923 they had paid $2,000 down on a five-story apartment building at 606 St. Nicholas Avenue. It sold for $22,000 and came with three mortgages. Nina had felt tired during the early part of March ("resting and resting some more"), but she began packing in preparation for the move from the 108 Edgecombe Avenue apartment. Plans called for repairs to be finished by the end of April, the renting of the upper-floor apartments, and the transport of their household belongings to St. Nicholas to take place in early May. Three and a half months of annoyed correspondence with Harlem's leading realtor, John Nail, had ensued. On January 15, the tenants had refused to let Du Bois inspect their apartments. A week later, Nail was instructed to serve the third-floor tenants notice that the editor wished to take possession "as soon as possible" — and no later than April 1. Jack Nail was James Weldon Johnson's brother-in-law, as polished as ivory and, as the former owner of the Tenderloin's infamous Marshall's Hotel, schooled in emergencies and irregularities. Delays and defects at 606 St. Nicholas he explained away with aplomb. On March 5, he was pleased to inform the Du Boises that they could occupy the building, but two days later Nina, somewhat distressed, wrote Will that the apartment they intended to move into was in "pretty bad shape." Off to consult with Nail about repairs, she wondered, with perhaps just a hint of reproach, if Will had any suggestions to offer "from such a distance?" Closer scrutiny of their new property prompted a mid-April stream of letters after Du Bois's return from his speaking tour. There was fourth-floor rot, basement subsidence, Nina's demand of a new bathtub in their apartment, and, to Nail's professed bewilderment, a question about missing fire escape ladders. But these housing worries paled into insignificance when, at the worst possible moment, Yolande was hospitalized at Fisk at the end of April with deadly complications resulting from an appendectomy performed in early September 1922 by Louis T. Wright, Harlem's leading surgeon.

Yolande's health had caused them much concern since the beginning of her junior year. Dr. Wright had operated not a moment too soon, as he reported to the Nashville physician in whose charge Du Bois had placed their daughter. Although Wright anticipated a complete recovery, he must have advised the Du Boises that Yolande's health remained delicate, subject to disorders caused by intestinal adhesions. She needed to follow a sensible dietary regime. But her appetite was voracious, and she seems to have spent most of her allowance for food, and much of that on sweets. Her father's long letter in mid-February had been filled with desperate advice about the perils of indifferent health care and especially about the dangers of allowing herself to become "chronically consti-pated." He proffered detailed, exasperated, instructions about elimination: "Your bowels must move daily at a regular hour. Let nothing interfere—meals, classes, engagements, study or prayers. Every day at that hour be at your toilet." He upbraided her about money too. Yolande had given lavish Christmas gifts to classmates, then borrowed from them to pay for her own indulgences. At one point, her bill for books at the college bookstore ($47.93—"an extraordinary sum") had amazed her bibliophile father. Increasing Yolande's weekly allow-ance, he put her on notice that his "income was limited," reminding her of his "heavy extra expense for you and your mother." Qualms about food and health remained uppermost, however, as Du Bois alternated warnings of "pain, sick-ness, and suicide" with paternal admonitions about her love life. When news came of Yolande's collapse at Fisk, he and Nina were greatly concerned but hardly surprised.

They hurried to Nashville, where the editor's brief appearance focused as much keen attention from the Fisk administration upon himself as upon his gravely ill daughter at McMillan Hospital. He was back at his desk on Wednes-day, May 2, while Nina remained parked by Yolande's hospital bedside for what would stretch into a three-week stay, leaving Du Bois to handle the move into St. Nicholas Avenue. "I am just in from the hospital," she wrote Will on Sun-day, May 6. Although there was "some pain still," Yolande was getting along all right from what was probably a laperotomy for adhesions and bowel obstruc-tion. The doctors told Nina that the surgical wound would be tender for some time with the "least pressure of food or gas" causing discomfort.

"Be sure to empty all the closets and drawers at 108," she penned as an important afterthought. While Nina waited in the home of Nashville friends for Yolande to be well enough to return to New York, Du Bois, as usual, readied the next issue of *The Crisis* and occupied himself with the move from Edge-combe to St. Nicholas Avenue. He consulted Nail about the new building, and even boasted a bit to Nina about how well he was managing their affairs "pro-vided you don't rush in on me too soon." Their friends the Alexanders had taken him to dinner in the park. The Bouttés, another prominent Harlem fam-ily, had given him dinner, and Fauset and her sister, Helen Lanning, had laid on Sunday breakfast. The movers came to take their belongings to 606 St. Nicholas on Monday, May 14. Du Bois sent precise instructions for Nina and Yolande's return by train a week later: a full supper before starting; thermos bottle for hot or cold drink "according to the weather"; avoidance of Jim Crow indignities by remaining in their sleeping compartment "until the train has stopped in the Cincinnati depot."

It would have been too modern and much too Freudian (and, therefore, too threatening to the serene proprieties of their value system) for Will and Nina to have drawn any connection between their daughter's improvident shopping, huge bookstore bills, feeding frenzies, manic extracurricular involvement, dauntingly excessive course loads and mediocre grades, and her chronic illnesses — psychosomatic and real — as manifestations of a capricious, hostile, frightened young girl reaching out to them. Not to mention — in this transparent strategy for her father's attention and for Yolande's own minimal self-validation — their divining the significance of Yolande's choice of a seemingly unprepossessing, music-major antithesis of her father as prospective fiancé. The whirlwind of activities reported in letters home had seemed to reach gale force in the weeks before her intestines failed. Hard on the heels of the costume ball of the college's annual George Washington Social that February ("you should have seen your daughter with white hair") came news of frenetic duties as president of the campus's exclusive distaff Decagynian Society. The March *Crisis* carried a photograph of its members, a score of refined young woman clad in gauzy white, Yolande seated, front center, on the grass. The Decagynians were to present a pageant in mid-March, and club president Yolande, whose task was to keep everything on schedule, wrote home jauntily, "You should see me presiding. . . . Dignity is getting to be my middle name. I get right tickled with myself." And with all this, there was a romance with James Melvin Lunceford, not quite twenty-one, a junior music major at Fisk from Fulton, Missouri.

Jimmie Lunceford, dark-skinned with laughing eyes, perfect teeth, and a jaunty mustache shaped like two check marks, would become one of the most accomplished jazz band conductors of the thirties. Writing in the international music review *Le Jazz Hot*, the doyen critic Hugues Panassié enthused in 1937 that "aside from Duke [Ellington], Jimmie Lunceford's orchestra is the only one capable of exciting us as much by its arrangements as by its soloists." Lunceford's arrangements (much indebted to trumpeter Melvin "Sy" Oliver) always had *"quelque chose à dire,"* said Panassie. By all accounts, Lunceford was Yolande's enduring passion, the man about whom she would spend much of her life dreaming, wondering how different things could have been if they had married. Ten years before this volume of biography was published, Yolande's only daughter, Du Bois Williams, remembered being taken backstage at about age eleven to meet Lunceford at Baltimore's Royal Theatre. "Tears came down his face like you wouldn't believe," she recalled, "and he said to my mother," looking at little daughter Du Bois, "She should have been mine." She fingered the keys of Lunceford's saxophone and never saw him again. That Du Bois's maiden name was to be Williams and not Lunceford was due mainly to her august namesake, who was adamantly opposed to having a jazz musician with an un-distinguished family background for a son-in-law. "I am not taking Jimmie very seriously," her father had written a month before her collapse. Lunceford might develop into "a fine man but that is yet to be learned." In any case, such a union was unthinkable. "Nothing," she was told, was more "disheartening and idiotic than to see two human beings without cultivated tastes, without trained abilities and without power to earn a living locking themselves together and trying to live on love."

Papa had spoken *ex cathedra*. The kind of man he would find suitable for his daughter had already begun to make a name for himself as a poet prodigy.

By the time Du Bois sailed for the third Pan-African Congress during the third week in October 1923, the situation at Harvard and the crisis at Tuskegee had taken encouraging turns. The board of overseers had voted unanimously on April 9 to comply with the faculty committee's report recommending the abandonment of Harvard's exclusionary policies. A victory in principle for Du Bois, the NAACP, and progressive alumni; nevertheless, Harvard and other elite universities would persevere in maintaining their WASP character, that "flavor" Lowell had so haughtily cherished. The presence of men of color in the college's freshmen dormitories would continue to be exceedingly meager, while the gradual increase in the number of Jewish students remained subject to covert admissions criteria that still smacked of religious discrimination. Although the actual occupation of the Veterans Hospital by Negro doctors and nurses was still several months in the future, Du Bois was now confident that Calvin Coolidge would sustain his predecessor's decision to place the facility completely under the control of the Tuskegee administration. The right of black people to run their own federally segregated hospital in the Alabama Black Belt was hardly the race-relations victory he would have wished for, but in a far-from-ideal world there was some consolation in seeing even the doctrine of separate but equal vindicated for once.

Augusta Savage's misfortunes were to be long-term and only occasionally relieved. The directors of the Fontainebleau School of the Fine Arts comfortably weathered the squall over her rejection, leaving Du Bois temporarily stymied but determined somehow to advance her career. Three years would elapse before he was able to tap the influence of a well-connected acquaintance, the Countess Irene de Robilant of the Italian-American Society based in New York. Readily agreeing to interview the sculptor, the countess confirmed Du Bois's understanding that students recommended by her organization were able to enroll tuition-free in Italian institutions. "I think she was a trifle disappointed to find that I am a realist instead of a modernist, however we got on famously," Savage wrote Du Bois delightedly early in May 1926. Admission to the Royal Academy of Fine Arts in Rome was granted, but Savage's laundry earnings had to support the now paralyzed father who had done his violent best during her Florida youth to keep her from sculpture. In the end, there would not be enough money for travel and living expenses. Finally, six years after the Fontainebleau rejection, Savage reached Paris in 1929 on a two-year fellowship from the Julius Rosenwald Fund. By then, at thirty-seven, her once steep artistic learning curve would have begun to flatten after so much time wasted waiting and deprived of expert mentoring.

ABOUT SIX WEEKS before sailing for Europe on October 24, 1923, Du Bois had sent a less than reassuring circular to persons likely to come to the third Pan-African Congress. The choice of London as the venue for the main meeting had been "rather suddenly thrust upon us because of unexpected developments in the Pan-African movement," it announced. This circular, and several others purporting to explain the sudden confusion surrounding the meeting that had originally been called for Lisbon, concealed much more than it revealed. Behind the scenes, from March 1922 until August 1923, the planning for the Congress had been compromised by honest misunderstandings and growing acrimony at the outset and sabotaged by elaborate deceit on Du Bois's part and desperate, last-minute improvisation in the final stage. In the Du Boisian version, the fault lay squarely with those in Paris responsible for organizing the Congress. As he confided by letter to Miss Ira Aldridge, descendant of the great expatriate Aframerican tragedian, the Francophone Africans had practically scuttled the enterprise. "the whole work of six years seemed about to fail." The loyal Rayford Logan, still in Paris, was told that failure was not permitted. Even though the secretary of the Pan-African Association and others "have fallen down on us," Americans did not propose to be stopped "by any little difficulties like that," the editor commanded. "The holding of the Congress . . . is obligatory and not optional . . . The secretary cannot of his own motion postpone a congress." The collapse and reconstitution of the third Pan-African Congress in late summer and fall of 1923 was a story Du Bois was no longer either interested in or honestly capable of reconstructing accurately.

Isaac Beton, editor of the *Revue coloniale française* and the Pan-African Association's earnest secretary, was a highly cultured man of somewhat delicate sensibilities and a penchant for gossip. He was genuinely committed to the cause of Talented Tenth Pan-Africanism. Du Bois had judged Béton to be the best of the Francophones during the 1921 proceedings. Rayford Logan thought highly of him, and the editor knew he could count on Fauset's special influence over the finicky secretary. When dealing with Fauset, Béton could be positively purry and pliant. Begging her not to think of him as "*a man who makes gossip,*" he had written to Fauset at the beginning of 1922 "as [he] would a close confidant," denigrating the imperious Gratien Candace, who had succeeded Diagne as president of the Pan-African Association and who seemed bent on applying brakes to the movement. Du Bois had finally decided that Candace was "virulently French" and devoid of any conception of "Negro uplift, as apart from French development." Béton took credit for inveigling the first of Candace's resignations in the fall of 1922 ("*Je vous apprends la bonne nouvelle*"), for which Du Bois and Fauset had at first been grateful. How he had come to believe that he might hope for more than gratitude from Fauset is unclear, but clearly Monsieur Béton's Gallic soul harbored amorous desires. Fauset had become "the apple of [his] eye, a part of [his] soul," he had sighed in a letter in which he renewed a proposal of marriage. Declaring his *"amour indéfectible,"* he protested Fauset's reasons for refusing him: *"C'est l'amour seul qui doit décider"* (love alone ought decide their fate). Dutifully, if somewhat fussily, while hoping for a change of Fauset's heart, he had set about planning for the third meeting. He leapt at the invitation from the learned president of Portugal's Liga Aficana (a society of Creole men of letters), to hold the congress in Lisbon in early September 1923. Observing the secretary at firsthand at 8 avenue du Maine, the Pan-African Association's headquarters, Logan believed that Béton had been "untiring in his efforts and lavish in his expenditures" to make the Congress a success.

Logan felt particularly aggrieved by his idol's conduct, going so far as to remind Du Bois in early September 1923 that Béton hadn't "received from you the support that he deserved." As for Du Bois's request that he publicly disavow the secretary, Logan icily replied that he was forbidden to do so by his conscience. "M. Béton deserves unlimited praise rather than the blame implied in your letter," Logan countered. The faithful Ida Hunt sided with Du Bois, but she may have betrayed more than a little sympathy for the secretary when she added, by way of explaining Béton's bitter disappointment, that he "doesn't understand your brief and American business-like way of writing him." Whatever Du Bois's real motives for wanting to scuttle Béton's plans (procolonial sentiments among the Paris and Brussels members, upstaging Garvey in his own backyard, fear of a diminished role for himself), one of them must have been financial. The large expenditures for the new apartment building, combined with Yolande's surgery and Nina's support during almost a month in Nashville, left him without funds to finance a trip to Portugal, even had he been willing to spend his own money. Such an inference can readily be drawn from his correspondence with the Grenadian barrister T. A. Marryshaw. The Caribbean as a venue for the Congress he could afford. But when his West Indian contacts, almost surely discouraged by British authorities, failed to follow through, Du Bois had been compelled to throw himself into a frantic letter-writing campaign in order to save face.

Regretting that it was now much too late to mount a full-dress Pan-African

Congress that included the league's colonial branches ("two months is the minimum time for a response from Mozambique or Angola"), the courtly Creole José de Magalhaes, a member of the Portuguese Assembly, generously offered to sponsor a small conference in late November "with you and your friends." Logan was dispatched to Lisbon to jump-start the Portuguese Creoles. As for Du Bois's own travel to Portugal, his appeal for funds had just been answered by the National Association of Colored Women (NACW), whose Foreign Relations Committee voted him a special appropriation. Knowing that the meeting in Portugal could now hardly amount to more than a formality and that the French had opted out of participating, Du Bois improvised boldly. "Now that I am running it," a letter dashed off to one of his supporters explained, "I'm adding London to Lisbon." Agreeing to serve as cochair of the London session, Ida Hunt joined a fund-raising marathon in Paris with a somewhat out-of-sorts Logan, just back from Lisbon. They had some success in persuading the Francophones that, as Logan wrote Fauset, "inasmuch as Dr. Du Bois is going ahead with the Congress in spite of all the difficulties," they might all just as well pitch in to avoid a miserable outcome. Logan managed to extract 500 francs from hard-pressed African-American jazz musicians in Montmartre, to which Hunt donated 300 out of her own pocket.

Meanwhile, Du Bois fired off long shots to East and West Africa. Did the head of the British and Foreign Bible Society in Khartoum "know of anybody in London of Negro descent who could represent Egypt and the Sudan?" Perhaps Mrs. Casely-Hayford of Sierra Leone could send him names of Sierra Leone nationals residing in London? Norman Leys answered Du Bois's eleventh-hour plea by suggesting the Fabian Society's auditorium as the conference site and forwarded a blue-ribbon roster of prospective Fabian participants that included Gilbert Murray, Ramsay MacDonald, Harold Laski, and Sir Sydney Olivier, the former governor of Jamaica. MacDonald hoped to be able to attend if he returned in time from Istanbul. Du Bois had assured MacDonald, who would become Britain's prime minister in a few months, that the Pan-African conclave was entirely unrelated to the "wild but unimportant Garvey movement in the United States." H. G. Wells, writing that he'd long wanted to meet Du Bois, promised to look in one of the sessions, although declining to speak because he didn't "quite know your drift." With something approximating a Pan-African Congress back on track, Du Bois sailed for London on Wednesday morning, October 24, not only relieved but already savoring triumphs that would enhance the ambitious cause of which he was the preeminent leader. He dashed off regrets to Carter Woodson that he couldn't address the annual meeting of the Association for the Study of Negro Life and History (ASNLH) in Atlanta. "I sail for Europe to attend the Third Pan-African Congress."

Rather surprisingly, Du Bois made no mention of the fact that he was finally going to Africa. "If I do not succeed in getting to Liberia," he had promised President King that August, "it will not be from any want of eagerness on my part, as a visit to Africa has long been my dream." In a letter in late September to William H. Lewis, Harvard football great and the first Negro assistant U.S. attorney general who now sat in the highest councils of the Republican Party, Du Bois had planted the idea of a special appointment as diplomatic representative at King's inauguration that December. Three weeks before sailing, the editor had Lewis's encouraging reply. Bascon Slemp, President Coolidge's secretary, "seemed to think very favorably of it," Lewis wrote, and both Emmett Scott and Perry Howard, an unscrupulous fixture of black GOP cloakroom politics, were on board. Du Bois's September 20 memorandum to Johnson and White also suggested that the NAACP urge the White House to consider his appointment as minister plenipotentiary to Liberia a capital idea. "Great and Good Friend, I have made choice of Doctor W.E.B. Du Bois as my special representative, with the rank of Envoy Extraordinary and Minister Plenipotentiary." President Coolidge would write President-elect King on the day after Christmas, 1923, in language that seemed to owe something to Indian treaties of the previous century.

Meanwhile, the London session had unfolded at Denison House in two rather chummy meetings on a cold and wet Wednesday and Thursday, with here and there, as Du Bois recalled, "the white sunshine of promise." The timing of the Pan-African Congress could hardly have been worse. The rulers of much of the planet had only just adjourned their own conclave in the capital, and Du Bois heard newsboys shouting grand pronouncements about stewardship and civilization by viceroys and prime ministers in attendance at the Imperial Conference of the British Empire. A token presence of maharajas was allowed, but not a single black person preened himself among the imperial fauna of overlords. Once again the brilliant Jan Smuts, whom Du Bois both detested and respected more than any other hierophant of white nationalism, had spoken in the name of fifty million black Africans. "In this atmosphere, Pan Africa sat and whispered," Du Bois wrote. "But some few listened." The tone of his own meetings on November 7 and 8 was decidedly British. Distinguished Fabians filled the benches on both days, with only a handful of delegates coming from across the Channel. (Logan and cochairperson Ida Hunt were listed on the program as representing France, along with Madame Chapoteau, the Paris landlady; Martha Gruening became a German for two days. Du Bois's upbeat telegram to Fauset the day after the London session ended mentioned delegates from thirteen nations and from six of the United States, as well as one "African chief present" (Amoah III of the Gold Coast), but *Punch* might suitably have featured a cartoon with the caption, "Dr. Du Bois presides over a meeting of the Bloomsbury Socialist club."

Rayford Logan had given lively responses that morning to Du Bois's address, "History of the Pan African Movement." Ramsay MacDonald, after all, had not been able to join his remarks to those of Du Bois on "The Black World at Present," scheduled for 7:00 on the first evening. At the end of the evening, Ida Hunt responded to yet another Du Bois speech, "The Colored Races and the League of Nations," with prepared remarks whose implications were to receive attention the following evening. Thursday's proceedings were livelier, with Du Bois and Harold Laski, the brilliant young London School of Economics professor, taking as their topic in the morning session "The American Negro." The reporter from the Manchester *Guardian* was obviously intrigued that Du Bois's talk moved from voting rights and lynching to mentioning schemes by large American phonograph record corporations to bankrupt Pace and Handy, the sole Negro-owned record company providing records for the Aframerican population. The sole representative of the Liga Africana, Kamba Simango of Portuguese East Africa, with whom Du Bois would stay in Lisbon, followed with a discourse on the situation in Portuguese Angola. When the Congress resumed after dinner, Du Bois took the rostrum again to present a ranging talk on the future of pan-Africanism. He was joined on the rostrum by Sir Sidney Olivier. Praising the independence and culture of African workers as an example to the modern capitalist world, Olivier stressed the great importance of the pan-African movement as an agent for conserving "African genius and power for the black man's freedom."

In the closing meeting there were remarks by Leys, Gilbert Murray, H. G. Wells, the reformation historian R. H. Tawney, and Laski. The Union of South Africa's Natives Land Act came in for searing criticism, as did the master-race abuses of British settlers in Kenya and Uganda after the delegates heard John Alcindor, the Afro-British physician and veteran pan-Africanist, read the appeal of Ugandan Africans. With what was coming to be recognized as his trademark concision and self-assurance, Laski rose to offer a more ambitious reformulation of Du Bois's own earlier recommendations to the League of Nations. It was "the striking suggestion," Du Bois wrote soon thereafter in *The New Republic*, that accredited representatives of ministerial rank, trained in anthropology and empowered with full investigative powers, should be sent to all the mandated territories in order to present regular reports to the League. Except for the significant addition of the right to armed self-defense by subject peoples, the Congress let stand the eight-point *Declaration to the World* of 1921 as the expression of what Du Bois called the "irreducible needs of our people." The orderly and well-behaved delegates also readily subscribed to a "Charter of Rights" drawn up by Du Bois at the end of the meeting. It demanded, among other things, the suppression of slavery in Mozambique, an end to brutal exploitation in the Belgian Congo, land rights for "natives" in Kenya, Rhodesia, and South Africa, appointment of people of African descent to the League's Mandates Commission, and "restoration of the Egyptian Sudan to an independent Egypt."

But if the tone of the document was somewhat more confrontational than the pronouncements of past Congresses, it remained essentially melioristic and trickle-down in its expectations. Whereas the UNIA and the loose affiliation of groups in Madame C. J. Walker's short-lived International League of Darker Peoples had demanded independence for African colonies, prompt handing over of German colonies to be administered by qualified Africans of the Diaspora, international acceptance of the equality of races, and "proportional representation in any scheme of the world government," Du Boisian pan-Africanism continued to shun such immediatism as both impractical and too provocative. In much the same way that the editor and his Talented Tenth loyalists tended to harbor doubts about the civic maturity of the mass of poor, undereducated black people in the United States, so he and they were inclined to concede European arguments that not only were all Africans not equal but that few of them would be ready to rule themselves in the near future. "Local self-government for backward groups . . . in the measure that their development permits" was the pitch in the *Declaration to the World*—more than a difference in tone. It would take several decades of shifting social perspectives before Du Bois and much of his class began to modify their deeply embedded presumptions of ethical and cultural hierarchies. Upper-class in structure and piecemeal in agenda, Du Boisian pan-Africanism nevertheless professed its fidelity to the spirit of liberal democracy and, therefore, in contrast to its UNIA rival, disdain for Caesarism and racial chauvinism. The British publication *African World* quoted Du Bois's careful distinction between such "militant movements of hate against the world" as pan-Germanism, pan-Slavism, and pan-Islamism. Partly from determination to fix in the mind of respectable Europe that there was no connection to Garveyism, as well as from purer motives of principle, he limned his movement's quest for peace and world democracy "through the inclusion of all in opposition to the idea of aristocracy of races where the backward are to be *permanently* ruled by the forward."

"Successful congress," Du Bois wired Fauset as he left for Lisbon by way of St. Etienne, Marseilles, Carcassonne, and Madrid. At St. Etienne, he stopped with Ida Hunt and her husband, William, one of the few persons of color to survive the State Department purge under Woodrow Wilson. William Henry Hunt was now a class-eight U.S. consul in his mid-fifties, one of the very few Negro foreign service officers ever assigned to Europe. Competent, gracious, and gregarious, he and his wife had established themselves at the center of elegant St. Etienne society since their arrival there from Madagascar in 1906. "The State Department is worried over Hunt," Du Bois wrote in *The Crisis*. "He deserves promotion and they dare not promote him." A few years later, the

State Department would abolish the St. Etienne consulate and reassign Hunt to the Azores. A warm *au revoir* to the Hunts, and Du Bois was off to Valence and Avignon, scattering mostly canned descriptions of these and several other cities that were second-rate Baedeker, and usually florid: "From a hill to the right the ghost of the twelfth century stares stonily down upon us. Valence, town to the Gauls, which knew Romans, Visigoth, Lombard, and Moor." Avignon was "shadow and dying day," which must have meant that he arrived too late and left too early to explore "the Palace of the shadow of the Popes somewhere down between me and the bridge." He stayed in Marseilles for a day, roamed the old port city as water came down in sheets, and ate mediocre bouillabaisse in a pricy cafe that was on the must-do list for tourists in the gamy Canebière quarter. Heading north from Provence and then in a westerly direction by train he took more notebook snapshots from his window of half a dozen cities at high speed to show readers of *The Crisis*. In Carcassonne, instead of going to sleep after checking into his hotel, he patrolled the moonlit, narrow streets until daybreak, alternately absorbed and appalled by the musty dignity and medieval filth encircled by its walls. Muttering something about its "crumpled beauty," Du Bois left for Spain with the dissonant image in his memory of telephone wires hanging over Carcassonne's ancient tournament field.

Whenever he traveled outside the United States, Du Bois was invariably seized by an almost giddy feeling of liberation, an exhilaration that often billowed into magniloquent opinionatedness and archly inflected prose. To be free of America's enveloping racism and New Negro sniping was intoxicating. On this trip, he spoke and wrote, as he had on past reprieves from his condition, in the manner of a man whose cosmopolitan, upper-class Edwardian birthright had been certified for the duration of his visa. "My brown face attacts no attention," he almost sang in the streets of Barcelona. "I am darker than my neighbors, but they are dark. I become, quite to my own surprise, simply a man." As he informed readers of *The Nation* that winter, "Going south from London, as the world darkens it gets happier." Sowing more judgments left and right like barley seeds, he decided that Madrid was a disappointment. "It is artificial." The soul of the city had been cut away leaving "the empty Prado, the wide and ghostly park, the ranging avenues and the empty countryside." Yet he conceded that a day's sojourn may have been too brief to form a valid opinion, that no one who saw Goya "writhing in oil" could regret coming to Madrid. Du Bois reached Lisbon on the weekend of November 30, 1923, where he lodged with the Kamba Simangos, who gave him a beautifully carved walking stick that he would leave on a streetcar his first day back in New York.

The two-day Lisbon session of the Pan-African Congress began on December 1, a Saturday evening, in the small, frescoed hall of the Liga Africana. There may not have been fifty participants among the doctors, engineers, lawyers, professors, and merchants, but Du Bois was particularly impressed by the well-dressed and courteous manner of the university students from the Portuguese colonies of Angola, Mozambique São Tomé, Guinea, Goa, and Cape Verde. The courtly Creole, José de Magalhães (or Magellan, in the Anglicized form Du Bois gave it), a man of about fifty who was not only professor of medicine in the National School of Tropical Medicine but also sat in the Portuguese Assembly representing São Tomé, one of nine Creole deputies, presided at the meeting. Largely due to his influence, the Congress was graced by the attendance of the incumbent minister of colonies and his predecessor, both of whom addressed the gathering. But Logan had done more than anyone to pull off the conclave. Despite his own financial difficulties ("short of money myself as the result of an unfortunate investment"), Logan had rushed to Lisbon on September 20 to finalize arrangements with officers of the Liga Africana, returning to Paris slightly embarrassed after having to give his Pan-African Association IOU in exchange for 350 escudos borrowed from de Magalhães.

The format at Lisbon approximated London's with two days of presentations covering the history of the pan-African movement, conditions in Portugal's most advanced colony, São Tomé, the past and contemporary state of Africans in the United States, and the future of pan-Africanism. Du Bois's lecture in English on the imperative need of a pan-African movement was translated by a former colonial office official. "We had general conversation in French," Du Bois wrote Arthur Spingarn. Between meetings, there were tours of the city, time to watch a corrida, a visit with de Magalhães to the Assembly, and a Sunday afternoon supper for twenty at the home of a wealthy Afro-Portuguese businessman. A catered affair of several courses, white wine, port, and champagne, capped off by violin and piano in the parlor, Du Bois thought it was "one of the simplest and most pleasing meetings, in perfect taste and good will, that I have ever seen." The editor was invited to pay a courtesy call by the American ambassador, which he did as one senior official representing the United States to another. Du Bois relished the society of Lisbon and Madeira, took vicarious pride in the accomplishments of men and women of color such as the diminutive, expressive de Magalhães, and lost no opportunity to contrast the easy interaction of whites, near-whites, and blacks in Lisbon's public places with American Jim Crow in its legal and informal varieties. "There is so much ancient black blood in this peninsula," he enthused. But his investigative eye and innate good judgment never entirely failed him, and in "Worlds of Color," a continental evaluation of Europe in Africa appearing in Foreign Affairs, Du Bois would detail the widespread use of slave labor on São Tomé plantations and the chasm between Portugal's high-minded new colonial code and the endemic illiteracy and poverty that made a mockery of that nation's paper reforms.

On balance, what Du Bois had accomplished in forcing his own time and venues on the Pan-African Association was more personal than collective, a tour de force of inspired obstinacy and ego rather than a significant promotion of an ambitious ideology and program. By even the most liberal head count, no more than two dozen men and women of color with any intrinsic connection to the movement had attended the proceedings at Denison House, while the Lisbon affair hardly qualified even as a rump assembly of pan-Africanists, comprised as it was of Du Bois and the members of the Liga Africana resident in the Portuguese capital. Whenever Du Bois, Logan, and Hunt (who did much of the talking) surrendered the podium, they had been followed center stage at Denison House by the likes of Laski, Olivier, Tawney, and Wells. The meetings in London and Lisbon garnered little of the European newspaper attention that had been accorded the 1921 sessions in London, Brussel, and Paris. An aggrieved Béton accepted the claims for the Lisbon meeting at face value, but, in generously congratulating Du Bois on his success, Béton reminded the movement's secretary that nothing had yet been done to "provide their national associations with strong financial means." Except for Béton, however, Paris passed over the third Congress in stoney silence. Partly, Du Bois blamed Garvey for causing confusion about his objectives in the minds of respectable world opinion. "Marcus Garvey walked into the scene"—his scene, Du Bois might well have said. Partly, he explained the lackluster results as due to too much optimism on his part about the speed of Europe's postwar recovery. The continent's political and social revolutions and economic upheaval made a setting for "any such movement as [he] envisaged . . . probably at the time impossible."

But mostly, during and immediately afterward, Du Bois proclaimed the undertaking a success. His American critics would have to measure their pens against his, a contest he was supremely confident of winning as his version of history began to run in *The Nation, The New Republic, Foreign Affairs,* and other journals of mainstream opinion, as well as in *The Crisis.* Kelly Miller, the Howard University philosopher and dean who had so maddeningly straddled the fence during the height of the Booker Washington controversy, could announce a preference for Garvey's pan-Africanism over Du Bois's. In a witheringly sardonic *Messenger* editorial, Randolph and Owen could picture Du Bois in London representing twelve million American Negroes "without their consent, and Mr. H.G. Wells together with some other white English liberals, doubtless, constituted the voice of the African section of Great Britain." *The Negro World* could gleefully report a Manchester *Guardian* item about the apparent indifference to the London meeting on the part of Africans residing in the United Kingdom. Let them denigrate, but while they splashed about in banal and parochial carping, he was off to Africa, taking pan-Africanism there with him.

REARRANGING ETHIOPIA
ABROAD AND AT HOME

A nd now as a sort of ambassador of Pan Africa I turn my face toward Africa," Du Bois informed his readers in the February 1924 *Crisis*. He had sailed from Tenerife in the Canary Islands on Sunday, December 16, aboard the German freighter *Henner*. Describing his companions aboard the *Henner*, the editor announced, "We are six Germans in this little floating Germany." He downed the Bremen beer, smoked cigarettes, and joined in telling tall tales in fluent German. By Friday afternoon, he was practically overwhelmed by excitement and impatience. Still no sight of land, but the heat was remorseless. That night he thought of that "little black Bantu" ancestor who crooned the untranslatable West African tune at the fireside of his Great Barrington childhood: "*Do bana coba, gene me, gene me!/Do bana coba, gene me, gene me!/Ben d'nuli, ben d'le.*"

On Saturday morning, December 22, Du Bois packed his trunk and large travel bag, photographed the officers, and fidgeted as he tried to read. At precisely 3:22 P.M., he saw Africa. "So my great great grandfather saw it two centuries ago," he reflected. It was Cape Mount, pale against the far horizon. The moment was historic for him, a solemn experience few American men and women of color in his generation, or even in the next, would ever savor. William Edward Burghardt Du Bois, the sixth of his line in America, had returned to the ancestral continent. Five hours more elapsed before the *Henner* arrived within range of the longboats. Finally at 9:00 P.M., the distinguished visitor clambered down the ladder into a longboat escorted by President-designate King's aide-de-camp, "a brown major in brown khaki." Chanting oarsmen rowed him ashore, their lean torsos bending and muscles rippling to the beat as he sat ecstatically in the bow of the longboat knifing through the moonlit surf. "And lo!" the minister plenipotentiary was in Africa. He slept that night in the United

States legation as the guest of Solomon Porter Hood, Lincoln University graduate and Harding's appointee as minister resident.

Accompanied on his rounds by the commander of the Frontier Force that Charles Young had brought to near spit-and-polish perfection, the special envoy roamed the capital's unpaved streets, the waterfront with its jumble of wharves and crazily leaning houses, then chugged up the St. Paul River past polychrome vegetation and dilapidated homesteads whose sheet-iron roofs glinted in the sunlight until the "broad, black, murmuring" waterway reached villa country. Sprawling coffee plantations along the river produced much of Liberia's modest wealth. Du Bois disembarked with his retinue at a plantation about twenty miles above Monrovia. The host was an Americo-Liberian senator whose family had lived on its estate for five generations, a descendant of American slaves resettled before the Civil War.

It was Christmas Day and there were cakes and champagne, and a regiment of smiling servants happy to be commanded. The senator's daughters were comely, and Du Bois observed with particular pleasure the chains of pale Liberian gold delicately encircling "the beautiful black skin of their necks." The exuberant dinner of chicken, beef, and duck, rice, plantains, and collard greens was washed down with Madeira. "Then we went and looked at the heavens, the uptwisted sky—Orion and Cassiopeia at zenith," he beamed. There was "sun for snow at Christmas, and happiness and cheer." "I have walked three hours in the African bush," the editor exulted, describing a minisafari in mid-January in *Jungle Book* clichés as one of "whine of monkeys, scramble of timid unseen life, glide of dark snake." There were more passages of surpassing Dark Continent Gothic: "The spell of Africa is upon me. The ancient witchery of her medicines is burning my dreamy, drowsy blood. This is not a country, it is a world—a universe of itself and for itself, a thing Different, Immense, menacing, Alluring." (*The Crisis* for June 1924 featured the editor doffing his pith helmet to the camera as three villagers struck dignified poses.) Du Bois of Liberia relished each day of his symbolic sojourn in an Africa whose perception was almost as much the product of his eight-year-old book, *The Negro*, as it was the result of firsthand observation. That book's opening sentence set the tone for much of what he would see and feel in the winter of 1923–24: "Africa is at once the most romantic and the most tragic of continents," a realm of "mystery and wide-ranging influence."

A seventy-five-year remove from these African effusions invites a certain amount of amusement at Du Bois's expense, and, perhaps, for some, even disappointment bordering on reproach. Pan-Africanism's orgins in the Black Diaspora elite were never more evident than during his performance in Liberia and Sierra Leone, where a tone of unconscious cultural superiority permeated

Du Bois's carefully crafted statements proclaiming the solidarity of darker peoples. Too many gestures and phrases bore the stamp of the classic European in Africa, as though Cecil Rhodes and Kipling were shaking hands with Delany and Alexander Crummell. Whether or not Howard University professor Alain Locke had his Harvard elder in mind when he wrote "Apropos of Africa," appearing in *Opportunity* shortly after Du Bois left Liberia, the cultural conceits Locke deplored in this brilliant thinkpiece as much too prevalent among his peers also applied to Du Bois. "We need to be the first of all Westerners to rid ourselves of the . . . insufferable bias of the attitude of 'civilizing Africa,' " Locke admonished. Exhilarated as seldom before in life by what he saw as the significance of being in Africa, puffed up by Ethiopianist presumptions and conceits embedded in his uplift ideology, Du Bois came perilously close to imagining himself a pan-African proconsul empowered to redirect the political course of the continent. No longer the result of a cynical White House favor arranged at his own request by a powerful GOP stalwart, the mission to Monrovia took on unprecedented historic and political valence as Du Bois moved among the Liberians. Burdened by foreign debt and threatened by Britain and France on its borders, the tiny republic had been left high and dry by its mentor without even an official expression of regret after the insurgent U.S. Senate scuttled the $5 million development loan. "It was then that the United States made a gesture of courtesy," Du Bois explained—"a little thing, merely a gesture, but one so fine and so unusual that it was epochal." It appointed him, a Negro, as special envoy, "the highest rank ever given by any country to a diplomatic agent in black Africa," as a means of mollifying a proud, poor people for the insult. There was nothing personal. "Another appointee would have been equally significant," Du Bois observed generously, but it held enormous meaning to the Liberians.

In the opinion of the State Department, their special envoy had gone overboard in conveying enormous meanings when he presented his credentials to the president of the Republic of Liberia. The occasion was a heady one. Resplendent in top hat and tails, he and Minister Hood were met at the entrance to the presidential mansion by Secretary of State Barclay. The honor guard saluted as the band struck up the Liberian anthem and the envoy extraordinary and minister plenipotentiary ascended a grand staircase leading to a room that stretched the width of the old, two-story frame residence. There he joined the other ministers of the diplomatic corps—ministers of Britain, France, Germany, Spain, Belgium, and Panama—arrayed in semicircle with the cabinet secretaries awaiting President King. Had there ever been a comparable moment in his life, Du Bois asked himself (and readers of *The Crisis*), a finer hour, than this one unfolding on the first day of 1924 in one of the world's oldest republics? His 1890 commencement address at Harvard had been a news item. Standing in for the indisposed Sir Harry Johnston, he had spoken to the "assembled races of the world" at the 1911 Universal Races Congress. These were high points, yes, but "not greater than the day when I was presented to the President of the Negro Republic of Liberia," he decided. His message was tailored to the occasion's significance. He informed President King that in designating him, Du Bois, as his personal representative, President Coolidge had wished to express two thoughts: "publicly and unmistakably . . . the interest and solicitude" of a hundred million Americans in the fate of Liberia, America's "sister Republic." Indeed, warned the minister plenipotentiary, his government would view any obstacle or misfortune imposed upon Liberia "with sorrow and alarm," remarks the British and French ministers absorbed with some surprise. Du Bois's interpretation of "Silent Cal's" second thought would be news to the Foreign Affairs Committee of the U.S. Senate. To the redoubled delight of President King, he informed the assembled diplomatic corps that his appointment signaled the Coolidge administration's acknowledgment of the great importance that black rule in Africa held for the struggle against color caste in the United States.

While versions of Du Bois's singular address circulated throughout Monrovia society and its European community, another unusual message was on its way to President King. On December 5, 1923, President General Garvey had entrusted a letter to three emissaries to be delivered in person when they reached Liberia. Costly mistakes had been made during the first UNIA mission to Liberia, Garvey admitted: a bad choice of emissaries and poor planning. But now people understood much better after false starts and false friends what was at stake. The Liberian president no doubt knew of the bitter struggles rending the diaspora. "In America and the West Indies we have had a tremendous fight of the lighter element against the darker ones," an allusion to the battle royal with Du Bois and the Talented Tenth, which Garvey was certain that King would interpret correctly. Garvey assured King that "large numbers of them who are fairly independent are desirous of permanent home settlement." If only the Liberian Government were to send the right signal, there was no reason King and his government "could not become in a few years the Saviour of our wandering people." If there was a hint of the desperation that failed to conceal a crumbling empire and prospect of prison, the letter also conveyed the author's characteristic vision and resilience: Liberia and the UNIA were being summoned to change history. On December 11, the UNIA mission under the direction of the three special emissaries sailed from New York to Europe aboard a Cunard boat inauspiciously called the S. S. *Britannia*. UNIA secretary general "Sir" Robert L. Poston, a thirty-four-year-old black journalist who had actually attended Princeton during Woodrow Wilson's tenure, headed the mission. Henrietta Vinton Davis, perhaps Garvey's most capable adviser and one whose loyalty outlasted all but two or three others, was now the fourth assistant president general. Milton Van Lowe, West Indian–born and educated in California and at the University of Pennsylvania, practiced law in Detroit. Stopping in Lisbon on the final stage of its journey in late January, Garvey's mission was received by de Magalhães and the Liga Africana with ceremony and cordiality matching that accorded to Du Bois.

What Du Bois could have known about the advent of Poston, Davis, Lowe, and the half dozen accompanying technical experts is largely speculative. Gossip being one of the liveliest activities in the languorous Liberian capital, he would almost certainly have heard about any cablegrams the mission might have sent to UNIA sympathizers in Monrovia. Not only was he on excellent terms with Solomon Porter Hood, but, as a resident guest of the legation, Du Bois had also cultivated a warm relationship with consular clerk Lillie Mae Hubbard. Miss Hubbard was delighted to serve not only as an impeccable source of wide-ranging information (official as well as casual) for the envoy extraordinary, she served as the hands-on member of what appears to have been a silent partnership in an export business involving Du Bois and Hood. Back at his desk in New York months later, the editor would puzzle over coded cables from Hubbard about coffee and gold consignments in connection with a venture referred to as "The Bopopoti"—more often than not, as on May 1, throwing up his hands with a, "My dear Lillie May, your last cablegram was quite indecipherable." Had Du Bois actually been aware while in Monrovia of the Lisbon reception of the UNIA delegation and of its almost imminent arrival in Liberia, it hardly stretches conjecture to suppose that he would have used his considerable influence with President King and his cabinet to put an end once and for all to Garvey's African settlement schemes. What is clear, however, is that the detailed recommendations Du Bois submitted to King shortly before sailing home by way of Sierra Leone were incompatible with UNIA participation in the future development of Liberia. This January document was similar in scope to the letter Du Bois had sent a year earlier to Secretary of State Hughes broaching the possibility of the U.S. Government somehow facilitating the restructuring of Garvey's defunct Black Star Line.

Du Bois would also provide Hughes with an expanded version of his January 1924 recommendations to the Liberian president. "Certain considerations of [his] as to the economic development of Liberia" called for the construction of fifty to a hundred miles of railroad track from Monrovia to St. Paul, the incorporation of a large bank under Negro control, large amounts of capital raised from American Negro sources, and the recruitment of "colored technical experts to help . . . in the development of agriculture, industry, and commerce." What needed doing, Du Bois explained to King, and Hughes, was for Liberia to adopt a twenty-year plan. A national bank and trust company to finance development should be chartered in New York by an interracial group of bankers. In lieu of visionary, unpredictable Garveyites pouring into Liberia, Du Bois proposed that politically astute men and women knowledgeable about Africa (with his pan-African cadre clearly in mind) would choose qualified black farmers, mechanics, and merchants, as well as educators and engineers, for stipulated periods of service in the West African republic. When Du Bois sent the Liberians a copy of his official State Department report at the end of March, President King was deeply impressed by its "sympathy and friendly character," so much so that he wrote his recent visitor that he had read that portion of the report to his cabinet in which Secretary of State Hughes was urged to adopt a policy fostering Liberian development through a "system of advice." Such a system of advice, entreated Du Bois, "should not be a more or less concealed attempt to take the functions of Government out of the hands of the Liberians, but it should be real advice of the highest order . . . offered to Liberia with the idea that America wishes her progress and is pointing out the way." But Liberia's critical need was money—immediately, with or without sympathy. There was a real danger to the republic's sovereignty if some means were not soon found to retire the large debts owed to foreign banking interests.

In 1922, British possessions produced 75 percent of the world's rubber, 70 percent of which was consumed mainly on roads in the United States. When the British Parliament suddenly restricted the output of its Asian plantations, Firestone rubber hunters desperately combed their atlases for new sources of supply. The prospect of a Liberian economy much improved through American investment finally seemed no longer merely hypothetical when a representative of the rubber company turned up in Monrovia shortly before Du Bois sailed home. The special envoy described his trek into the rubber-producing upcountry with Hood and Donald Ross of Firestone in suitably momentous accents. "I stood in an Enchanted Forest at Christmas," he told the readers of The New Republic. Rows of trees planted by a failed British venture stretched before him. "On one side was a black man, United States Minister to Liberia. On the other hand was a white man. . . . We all saw thick, straight, gray trees stretching endlessly about us, and we all saw more than this." Both he and Hood appear to have been susceptible to a certain amount of understandable self-delusion as they excitedly discussed the Firestone possibilities. In a lengthy, self-congratulatory narrative he would send to Du Bois almost two years later, Hood boastfully claimed that the Firestone concession proposal and subsequent $5 million loan had had their origins in the diplomat's letter to Harvey Firestone, and in Hood's own State Department reports, copies of which were subsequently provided to the Firestone officers. But Du Bois had believed that he saw more than either Hood or Ross. He soon convinced himself that by gaining the ear of company president Harvey Firestone himself he would be able to safeguard the interests of both Liberia and the Pan-African Congress movement. Du Bois's letter to Firestone, written just a few weeks before Hood's letter claiming all the credit, would betray similar naïveté. Commending a more humane colonial experiment in Liberia than those pursued by the French, British, or Portuguese throughout Africa, the editor cautioned Firestone that "usually Americans send whites used to 'handling' colored labor. These get results by cruelty and browbeating alternating with pandering to drunkenness, gambling, and prostitution." Far better results could be gotten, Du Bois's three-page, single-spaced, typewritten letter insisted, if Firestone employed sophisticated whites, educated Liberians, and experienced colored Americans. Firestone's spokesman responded with a cordial invitation to Du Bois to share "any further ideas or suggestions."

The breach between ideal and reality—between illusion and cynicism in the Firestone rubber concession in Liberia—would widen to form a veritable abyss of exploitation on a continent already notorious for merciless plunder by powerful European interests. The engines of American economic imperialism consistently lived down to the standards of regimented abuse set by such European precursors as Belgium's Union Minière, Great Britain's De Beers Consolidated Mines, Ltd., and France's Compagnie Française de l'Afrique Outre-mer (CFAO). Objectively, there was scant reason to suppose that Firestone in Africa would behave differently from United Fruit and Standard Oil in Latin America or Dole in Hawaii. Yet Du Bois, who would write about Portuguese depredations in Angola and British machinations in Sierra Leone with tough-minded perspicacity after his return from Africa, faltered when it came to Firestone in Liberia. Liberia was to the League of Nations what Atlanta or Fisk universities meant to black higher education for Du Bois: solitary African promise in a mocking European universe of independent states. Haiti, occupied by the U.S. Marines in 1915, was not much better than a eunuch among the polities at Geneva. Ethiopia still remained a mysterious mountain kingdom, inspiring for its defiance of conquering Europeans, yet somehow almost too culturally exotic. But Liberia, with all its comic mimicry of American political institutions, and despite the virtual enslavement of its original peoples, was still envisaged by Du Bois as the lodestar of Africa's struggle for independence. The African republic's problems were not of her own making; they came from her colonial neighbors who coveted her natural resources and despised her people. This experiment in black self-government had produced "for size an unusual number of exceptional men," Du Bois reminded readers of The New Republic, providing some salient examples of balance-of-power diplomacy worthy of Talleyrand and Bismarck. The editor's psychic need for a plausible Negro state among the world's nations was a pan-African imperative so exigent that it distorted his keen judgment and even corrupted his humanitarianism. Time and again he excused the republic's unscrupulous rulers and the barbarous treatment of its citizens, even going so far as to tell a white American in Monrovia that the scorched-earth incursions of the Frontier Force trained by his soulmate Young were no worse than "brutalities practiced by soldiers everywhere—Americans in the Philippines, the English in Ireland, the French everywhere." Government-authorized attacks upon the Kpelle, Gola, Mano, and Kissi peoples were "absolutely necessary . . . in order to assure them that it really was a government; otherwise the tribal chiefs would take matters into their own hands."

Judgment and Liberia were like oil and water in Du Bois's optic. When King wrote him at the end of June 1924 about the potential dividends from the rubber concession under negotiation, the editor posited a theorem about American investment overseas so sanguine that it could have been valid only if the NAACP had already achieved the major civil rights goals that would take it at least another two decades to begin to win. American investments were a much safer bet, he told King, because if white businessmen failed to "treat Liberia fairly and they try and get the United States Government to back up their demands, the Negroes of America have enough political power to make the government go slowly." Then, too, there was the not-irrelevant factor of his own influence with Firestone directors—or so Du Bois seemed to believe. After all, hadn't Harvey Firestone's spokesman given assurances that the company had felt "all along that this enterprise is much greater than a purely commercial project"? But did Du Bois really think that Negro Americans had the political clout to affect government policy vis-à-vis a corporation whose own clout could modify the State Department's policies when its vital interests were at stake? As he himself would acknowledge in "Liberia and Rubber" in *The New Republic* for November 1925, "everything really depends upon the attitude of white capital in America." It seems unlikely that even his sometimes astonishing capacity for self-deception and racial romanticism could have misled Du Bois so badly. Yet he must have felt obliged not to focus on the bleakest scenario possible for Firestone in Liberia, given his earlier cautious sharing of Hood's enthusiasm and now the Liberian government's determination to proceed to closure. The preliminary agreement negotiated in June 1924 even seemed to have justified his optimism: a ninety-nine-year lease of one million acres, no less than 20,000 of which must be under cultivation in five years with Firestone paying six cents per acre annually on land actually under cultivation. The agreement projected a company investment of millions of dollars and the hiring of tens of thousands of Liberians. Neither side broached the subject of a loan at that time.

Before the signing of the final accord in November 1926, however, Harvey Firestone would come to the conclusion that the best way to protect his investment was to make the republic an offer it couldn't refuse—a $5 million loan, in order to hamstring the republic with long-term indebtedness. Secretary of State Barclay and others immediately saw the unsolicited arrangement as a snare and a threat to Liberian autonomy. Indeed, President King had earlier insisted to Du Bois that their unhappy experiences had convinced Liberians to forgo the fools' gold of foreign loans for a policy of frugal domestic savings and prudent investments from overseas. Such squeamishness soon began to evaporate in the face of power politics and surgical bribes, especially after the loan project became a priority of Liberia's Customs Receivership bureaucracy. This multinational agency had been established during World War I by the United States, in collaboration with Britain and France, to handle the payment of the interest on the republic's 1912 foreign loans. The prospect of a sizable percentage of the Firestone millions underwriting generous salaries for an enlarged Customs Receivership of white American mediocrities strongly appealed to General Receiver Sidney de la Rue, an aggressive American, who paid a personal call on Harvey Firestone in July 1924 in order to coordinate strategy. The gambit required liens to be placed on all Liberian revenues and a financial adviser designated by the president of the United States to oversee repayment of the projected Firestone loan. When the Liberian legislature finally balked before the trap of perpetual indebtedness and dared to insert twenty-four amendments, a furious Firestone wired the State Department, "They must accept agreement without a single change if we go into Liberia." The Firestone five millions, at 7 percent and with twenty-six years to pay, would bring virtually no improvement to Liberia, as most of the money went to liquidate the 1912 indebtedness. As details of these negotiations reached him in New York, Du Bois must have begun to harbor an undeclared understanding that his Liberian friends were being compelled to accept an offer they wanted to refuse. "Thus Liberia becomes a pawn in the duel between England and America for control of the rubber production," he wrote to *New Republic* editor Bruce Bliven.

Just as the Garvey mission was tacking down the West African coast, Du Bois, red sash and Star of Ethiopia draped across a starched dickey, was addressing the Sierra Leone branch of the National Congress of British West Africa (NCBWA), an organization whose goals roughly paralleled those of his own Pan-African Congress. The meeting in Freetown, the British colony's neat, picturesque capital, was the NCBWA's second conclave, the first one having met in Accra, capital of the old Gold Coast, in March 1920, under the founding chairmanship of J. E. Casely Hayford, the West African barrister every bit as visionary as Du Bois. Like Du Bois's Pan-African Congress movement, Casely Hayford's National Congress would lose momentum after holding a fourth and final meeting in Lagos, Nigeria, in 1930. By then, however, it would have served as a critical catalyst in the emergent nationalisms south of the Sahara. The founder of the NCBWA and the cofounder of the NAACP were mutual admirers. Casely Hayford's 1911 classic, *Ethiopia Unbound*, owed a transparent debt to *The Souls of Black Folk* for its opening paragraph, which paraphrased Du Bois's famous question about the problem of the twentieth century. But

Casely Hayford had also been critical of Du Bois for what he took to be the editor's racial assimilationism, and he was a genuine admirer of Garvey.

It was not surprising, then, that Bruce Grit, Garvey's venerable ally, had cabled a warning about Du Bois from New York shortly before Casely Hayford and twenty-five others headed for Freetown. "Watch him. . . . Make no committals," the fatally ill journalist gasped, adding spuriously that Joel Spingarn, "a Jew, and other interests (white) inimical to African independence" had underwritten Du Bois's trip. Whether Bruce's cable had any impact is unknown. In any case, Adelaide Casely Hayford, the founder's activist second wife and a Sierra Leonean herself, brought warm official greetings on behalf of the NCBWA at the meeting on January 27 in Wilberforce Memorial Hall. Speaking from the text he had carefully prepared before sailing from Monrovia, a deeply bronzed Du Bois traversed the history of black people in the United States with a brilliant combination of generalization and detail. "This is all the more necessary," Du Bois lectured his rapt audience, "because all over the world colored people have great difficulty in understanding each other because they learn from each other through the words of those who despise them." This was the raison d'être of the Pan-African Congress movement, to inform, to plan, and, ultimately, to mobilize the darker world. "Whatever we do," he said in closing, "there should be common action"; and he added, for the enlightenment of this African assembly, that American Negroes had learned that the brains of women were as good as those of men, "and we are using them." His visit prominently noted in the Sierra Leone *Weekly News*, Du Bois headed for Senegal, whose capital city, Dakar, he would find more courteous than New York, London, and Paris. "The primitive black man is courteous and dignified" throughout Africa, he declared sweepingly, adding that he never saw even "one respectable quarrel."

President Coolidge's special envoy had left Monrovia on January 22, with West African ports of call along the way. If his Liberian stay had actually overlapped the arrival of the UNIA mission in the first week of February 1924 (as might be mistakenly assumed due to Du Bois's own inaccuracy), it would demand the faith of the gullible to credit Du Bois's repeated denials that he never even discussed Garvey with his hosts. But if his denials benefit from the fact of his absence from Monrovia, there is an overwhelming probability, nevertheless, that understandings about preventing a UNIA beachhead in the republic would already have been reached between Du Bois and the Liberians by the time the Poston group disembarked. Certainly, Du Bois played no direct part in the duplicity of the politicians and government officials, many of whom professed allegiance to Garvey, reached agreements in principle about the establishment of a UNIA commune, and (as in the case of King's stepson) gladly leased a large warehouse to the UNIA delegation at a handsome rate. The Liberian liaison committee was not only blessed by the president but numbered among its distinguished members the vice-president, the chief justice of the Supreme Court, and two former presidents of the republic. When Poston and his associates spooned themselves into the longboats taking them to their U.S.-bound steamer, they had good reason to believe that day in early March that they would soon return leading some twenty thousand Garveyites to a Liberian Zion.

DU BOIS CAME HOME in late March 1924, in what seemed a shimmering corona of international feats. Serious problems in the operation of *The Crisis* awaited him, as did another ruckus about attending the NAACP convention that June. And there had been criticisms—some of them sharp and mocking— poked at the third Pan-African Congress. These were false notes that had little resonance, however, in a symphony of articles conducted by Du Bois in *The Crisis, Current History, Foreign Affairs, The Nation,* and *The New Republic.* Moorfield Storey spoke for much of that well-disposed white opinion the editor had targeted. The NAACP's venerable president wrote to Du Bois, after reading about Africa in *The Crisis,* that he felt more strongly than ever that "we are gradually gaining ground everywhere, that the colored people are showing that they are the equals of other men, and that they have, moreover, certain qualities and abilities of their own which are sources of power." The overwhelming impression among interested Aframericans was that the editor's recent odyssey was an epic success. "When is that 'Envoy Extraordinary and Minister Plenipotentiary' coming to Chicago?" Mildred Jones, the schoolteacher who was now a part of his intimate life, cooed a few days after his return.

Fitting recognition of what had been accomplished not only in London, Lisbon, and West Africa, but of a lifetime of learning and overcoming, came on the evening of April 13 at the Cafe Savarin in Manhattan, seven weeks after his fifty-sixth birthday. Nearly five hundred prominent men and women of letters and other distinctions came to honor Du Bois that Sunday evening. Storey, Joel Spingarn, Albert Bushnell Hart, Zona Gale, Witter Bynner, Eugene O'Neill, Channing Tobias, and others kept away by health, commitments, or georgraphy sent regrets and eloquent testimonials. "Fundamentally, Mr. Du Bois is one of the great teachers of Democracy in America," said Wisconsin novelist Gale through James Weldon Johnson's melodious voice. One generation removed from a proud Irish peasant heritage, Eugene O'Neill spoke through Jessie Fauset of his feeling of kinship with Du Bois in the struggle "against intolerance and prejudice." The young playwright permitted himself the "selfish" regret that, in giving himself unsparingly to the cause of humanity instead of devoting himself to that "fine and moving prose which distinguishes his books," Du Bois had deprived American letters of the full benefit of his muse.

Ridgely Torrence read Bynner's poem "To Du Bois and His People." The

Negro spirituals "Go Down Moses" and "Nobody Knows the Trouble I've Seen" cast their spell. New York's Lieutenant Governor was followed by the far more formidable Mary McLeod Bethune, who gave only a "set speech," according to Arthur Spingarn. But Arthur thought that, while "the music was fine, the poetry fair," the speeches were "all execrable," as he wrote his ailing brother at Troutbeck. One of the speakers, the aged Mary Austin, mistaking the occasion for a tribute to Sitting Bull, prattled on about the influence of Indian art and music. Near the end came the bubbly prodigy Countee Cullen, reciting all seven stanzas of his "The Fledglings to the Eagle":

> Men raised a mountain in your path,
> Steep, perilous with slime,
> Then smouldered in their own hot wrath
> To see you climb and climb
>
> . . .
>
> Strong eagle, we, the fledglings, try
> Our wings, though thinly spun,
> Because we know you watch, and cry
> Us, "Courage!" from the sun.

After the half broiled chicken, chiffonade salad, and ice cream had been consumed, the guest of honor rose, resplendent in his new Liberian decoration and formal attire. "The crowd was quite ready to be carried off its feet," Arthur declared, but instead (and in his opinion missing "a great chance"), Du Bois gave "one of his cold, statistical and historical argumentation talks on Liberia." More likely, the speech was somewhat better received than Spingarn reported. The honoree certainly thought his address was a great success. "Really an astonishing occasion," Du Bois wrote the master of Troutbeck, one that made it possible to spotlight his work for all races and "not simply for one," and to plead his cause "with artistry."

At fifty-six, Du Bois was remarkably fit. There had been no complications from the removal of his left kidney at the end of 1916, major surgery the patient rather dramatically advertised as going "down into the valley of the shadow of death." He was fond of walking, paid attention to his diet, drank alcohol in moderation, took his beloved Benson and Hedges cigarettes only with meals, and scrupulously went to bed at ten. It was at about this period that head-to-toe health reports began arriving annually from the Life Extension Institute, Inc., of New York City, a private health clinic. Du Bois's enrollment would lapse once or twice over the next two decades, but he was able to benefit from the 20 percent discount the institute extended to former members. The Life Extension staff learned to keep on its toes when dealing with this particular client, who regularly forwarded critiques of examination results and occasionally up-braided the director for work deemed to be below par, as in the case of some dental X-rays in summer 1923: "May I call your attention to the superior excellence of these photographs as compared with the work done in your laboratory." There was no sign yet of vitiligo, a chronic skin condition that would slowly affect his hands and arms, splotchily turning much of the skin alabaster white. But some of the editor's friends may have begun to detect a greater irritabilty, a heightened testiness in matters small or routine, and even lapses in his phe-nomenal memory.

The spat with James Weldon Johnson over attendance at the association's annual convention that June in Philadelphia was a case in point. He had ab-sented himself from the 1923 NAACP convention in Kansas City after being "surprised and hurt" when Johnson, Ovington, and White readily accepted his pro forma offer to save money by remaining in New York. "No amount of argument" could make him believe that his services would be needed at Phil-adelphia, "if [his] services were unnecessary at Kansas," he pouted. Festering suspicions of the last two years deepened into a feeling that he was "no longer needed in this capacity and that my gradual elimination as a speaker on the platform of the NAACP was desirable." No, he would not go to Philadelphia. Although he had attended every national conference from 1909 to 1922, self-respect now required nonparticipation. Working up to a considerable lather, he declared that, if a man is kicked once, he may not be at fault, "but to offer himself for repeated kicking is spiritual suicide." On the other hand, Johnson and White might have been pardoned had they suspected that an offer to un-derwrite convention expenses on the association's budget, with no contribution from The Crisis, would have considerably mollified the editor.

Johnson's reply, a mixture of flabbergast and sensitive concern, meticulously rehearsed the background facts of the two conferences. Rather than trying to eliminate Du Bois, the effort of his fellow officers had been one of balancing the editor's demanding multiple activities with the work of the conferences. Johnson reminded Du Bois that, at the first hint of what he assumed to be a scheduling conflict, he had pleaded in person with Du Bois to find a way to come to Philadelphia. Closing the skillful rejoinder on his own note of self-respect, the executive secretary wondered if he oughtn't resent Du Bois's in-sulting implication of conspiring "against your prestige in the Association." Ten years before, Joel Spingarn had written a long letter to the editor, similarly combining reasoned rebuke with conciliatory esteem. The NAACP was then in its infancy, and Spingarn had admonished his friend to wear his indispensability more lightly. A telling measure of the organization's growth and diversification since then was that Johnson informed Du Bois that, valuable as they were to the association, he didn't believe "the services of any single individual are now indispensable to the NAACP." Less than indispensable, Du Bois would finally decide, nevertheless, to go to the Philadelphia conference.

But he would evince no such reasonableness about another touchy subject, "The Black Man and the Wounded World," his long-awaited study of American Negro participation in the Great War, bearing the subtitle, "A History of the Negro Race in the World War and After." "On account of its length and pro-Negro attitude," the monograph would probably have to be published by subscription, readers had learned from the January 1924 issue of *The Crisis*. "Sign and return the appended blank or one similar to it." The issue contained a preliminary version of a first chapter, entitled "Interpretations," in which the editor blamed all the participants equally and contended that the ideology of white supremacy had begun to lose its grip over the white working classes in the aftermath of the Great War. Readers were given the definite impression that "The Black Man and the Wounded World" was nearly finished. When, therefore, Adam E. Patterson, a prominent black Chicago Democrat and former infantry major in the 92nd Division, requested the return of the manuscript he had loaned to Du Bois almost four years earlier, he was plainly miffed to be told that it was impossible. Outraged by aspersions recently cast on the 92nd by General Robert Bullard, wartime commander of the American 2nd Army, ex-Major Patterson wanted his material back in order to prepare a series of corrective articles for the *Chicago Tribune*. He was one of several veterans whose diaries, memoirs, and other writings had been entrusted to the editor to help compile a true record of Negro participation in the war. Patterson had also forwarded to Du Bois a large quantity of photographs of black troops in action and in bivouac, an invaluable source that Du Bois had flatly refused to return a year earlier, even though the Chicagoan protested that the men who loaned them were "clamoring for their return."

Patterson's history, Du Bois explained peremptorily, was now an inextricable part of his own twenty-one-chapter manuscript—"I find it quite impossible to restore or copy your manuscript." Morever, Du Bois claimed untruthfully, sixteen chapters of "The Wounded World" were already finished. The rest could be done in another two or three months, and "the whole of the matter can be rewritten and condensed and put in final form for the printer" by January 1926. Du Bois suggested that Patterson and his organization of black veterans, the Committee of One Hundred, would be better served by making a contribution toward the $2,500 needed to publish "The Wounded World." Patterson refused to be put off, however, and arranged a meeting with Du Bois at which he secured the editor's agreement to accept the services of the former's clerk for one week's work disentangling the mess. But Du Bois would have the last word, writing Patterson in late July 1925 that he had decided that it was "impossible for any one to go through [the material] without disturbing my work of years."

The truth was that "The Wounded World" was far from ready for publication, and that Du Bois repaid Patterson's generosity with a selfish ruse in order to keep his manuscript until he, Du Bois, got around to finishing the history of the war.

In years to come, he would periodically approach foundations and sound out publishers about the book, but (although it seems implausible), as he would never get much beyond the outline stage and a trunk full of sources, Du Bois's contribution to the history of World War I went the way of his missing University of Berlin thesis. Surprisingly, in light of their testy exchange of letters in 1919 about competing war histories, Carter Woodson offered to publish the monograph through his Association Press in April 1924. Woodson would have to see the manuscript, of course, but he assumed that it was much more than "merely a history of the Negro in the World War" because that was a subject about as dead, he said, "as the League of Nations. The Negroes themselves have lost interest in their own record during that upheaval." A work of broader scope and grand interpretation, however, had definite possibilities. That Du Bois intended to make it much more than a narrative in the genre of Emmett Scott's competent *Official History of the American Negro in the World War* is evident from the preliminary first chapter. Part of what he had in mind was derived from the paradigm worked up in "The African Roots of the War," the brilliant 1915 essay published in *The Atlantic Monthly* that anticipated Lenin's thesis on the unanticipated resiliency of capitalism. Perhaps the flagging public interest Woodson detected in the topic caused Du Bois to have increasing doubts about following through with the time and concentration required in order to overcome conventional assumptions about what would have been an unconventional book.

As Du Bois aged, impatience and principles came together in more extreme concentrations, as in the case of his dealings with his undergraduate college. Neither Fisk University nor much of higher education in black America would ever be the same again. The month-old invitation to address the Fisk alumni on June 2 was on his desk when he returned from Africa. Recalling the "everlasting impression" made upon the students the previous year when Du Bois had rushed to the campus to be with Yolande, the alumni association president left open the choice of subject. As Du Bois fully intended to be present for Yolande's graduation on June 1, the alumni invitation seemed almost an obligation. He and Nina were relieved and proud that the final year had been their daughter's best ever at Fisk, but, as Du Bois wrote Yolande, Nina was too ill to consider making the trip to Nashville. The "memory of her last trip makes her a little nervous." His acceptance of the alumni association's invitation was motivated by more than parental duty, however. By 1924, Fisk, with its well-regarded interracial faculty, its six hundred students largely recruited from the Talented

Tenth, and its successful million-dollar capital campaign, had become the pre-eminent liberal arts college catering to Negroes. Hampton and Tuskegee institutes had larger endowments (Hampton's exceeded that of the University of Virginia and dwarfed William and Mary's), but Fisk's endowment drive for the magic number of one million dollars was the first to be mounted by an institution committed to superior liberal arts education. In the eyes of the great majority of informed Americans, Fisk University, under the leadership of white president Fayette A. McKenzie, was a glorious success. To Du Bois, Fisk was fast becoming an insult to black people.

McKenzie had begun his career in Wyoming as a teacher of the Shoshone Indians. He had brought something of the Native American drillmaster to Fisk, imposing a demeaning surveillance of social activities and even going so far as to forbid the establishment of fraternities and sororities, lest fornication and alcohol sweep the campus. He abolished the student government along with the *Herald*, the oldest student literary magazine among Negro colleges and universities. Expulsion without due process, and for the most trivial offenses, was routine. The hated Fisk Code of Discipline regulated hours of sleep, eating, study, and obligatory religious services. It banned smoking, dancing between the sexes, dating, and even forbade men and women walking together about campus. Fisk women were required to wear high-necked, gingham dresses with long sleeves; silk or satin clothing was outlawed. Across town at white Peabody College, coeds wore the latest flapper fashions and men inhaled their favorite brands in public. McKenzie applied the rod just as sternly to faculty. Stool pigeons abounded. Hires and promotions were based on loyalty to the president. White college undergraduates were hired to teach Fisk undergraduates. In Du Bois's eyes, McKenzie's rigid fidelity to an autocratic, outmoded model of superintendency was yet another case study in a game plan of social subordination by powerful white reactionaries North and South—that new North-South *entente cordiale* of malevolent Nordics, repeatedly assailed by him in print, that was dedicated to the retardation of aspiring ethnic and racial groups.

An initial $500,000 toward the Fisk capital campaign had come from the Rockefeller family's General Education Board (GEB), followed by another $250,000 from the Carnegie Corporation. Raising the final quarter million among friends and alumni before the deadline had tested not only McKenzie's considerable powers of persuasion, but had placed a terrible strain upon his commitment to the quality education of black collegians. In mounting disbelief, the alumni saw their president striking an accommodationist bargain with the white South in general and with its Nashville representatives in particular. In a mix of concurrence and acquiescence, the trustee board's northern white majority supported the bargain. The rationale of the McKenzie administration was that Fisk served itself best by serving the interests of the white South. There would be no college chapter of the NAACP or inflammatory literature in the library, the president decreed. "Anyone who does not like the way things are being done here may get out," McKenzie told the faculty.

Courting Nashville's white community, the president agreed to a city concert to launch the European tour by the men's glee club at which even the faculty was divided racially into separate sections and tickets were sold at "white" and "Negro" windows. Paul Cravath, senior partner in the august New York law firm of Cravath, Henderson & deGersdorff and chairman of the university's trustee board, had proclaimed at a fund-raiser in Cleveland, to which no alumni were invited, that "complete [racial] separation" was the "only solution to the Negro problem." Paul Cravath was the son of Erastus, the great president of Du Bois's undergraduate years. L. Hollingsworth Wood, grandee financier as tall as his name and vice-president of the board, shared Cravath's point of view, although more discreetly. Delighted with the deeper understanding of the South's racial problems as signified by policies urged upon the country's most prestigious Negro college, the influential Nashville *Banner* gave the capital campaign its blessings: "We believe that every consideration demands that Nashville meet its challenge in full. . . . It owes it to the splendid institution, Fisk University, the most noted and notable college for Negroes in the world." The contribution of fifty thousand dollars to a black college by Nashville's wealthy white citizens was a southern breakthrough, reported in the national press and widely applauded as the earnest of a new day in race relations below the Mason-Dixon Line.

Months before McKenzie's formal announcement, forthcoming that July, of the successful conclusion of the capital campaign, Du Bois had decided that Fisk's million dollars was tainted money. Cravath Memorial Chapel provided an imposing setting in which to register a complaint that was meant to rattle teacups in the headquarters of the General Education Board and the Carnegie Corporation. The original Jubilee Singers observed Du Bois from the life-sized oil painting above the bank of organ pipes as he placed his text on the lectern, sunlight cascading through the stained-glass windows. On the stage behind him, President McKenzie, senior faculty members, and several trustees awaited his address without the slightest notion of what Du Bois was going to say. He had resolved to do an "unpleasant duty, and to do it thoroughly," he wote later. He chose as the Latin title of his alumni address *"Diuturni Silenti,"* words taken from an oration in which Cicero, gravely addressing the Roman senate, broke a long silence. Du Bois reminded those whose Latin was a bit rusty of the Roman senator's words: "To my long continued silence, Conscript Fathers, . . . this day brings an end and also a beginning." Striking a Ciceronian tone straightaway, he told the surprised assembly, "frankly, I have come to criticize." Twenty years after departing Fisk, he had come to give the 1908 commencement address, and the administration of that time had winced under his criticism of the school's embrace of vocational education. The speaking invitation from the alumni association was the first extended to him in sixteen years.

Fisk University was "choking freedom," Du Bois charged. The ultimate source of authority must be the alumni, and that alumni had been ignored and insulted as the administration deliberately embraced a propaganda that discredited "all of the hard work which the forward looking fighters for Negro freedom have been doing." Margaret Murray Washington, the Great Accommodator's widow, who now sat with the trustees, must have wondered if her famous classmate had lost his moorings when he declared, "Of all the essentials that make an institution of learning, money is the least"—even though Du Bois made clear that he knew the needs of a college required much more than a proverbial boy and a teacher on opposite ends of a log. Material resources, emphatically yes. But Du Bois prayed that the day would never come when it would be said of Fisk, as once was said of Brown, " 'Yesterday Brown University had a president; today it has a million dollars.' " What Fisk needed were the upper-case virtues of its illustrious past—Freedom of Spirit, Self-Knowledge, and the Truth. Instead, his few days on campus had revealed a garrison state whose marching orders commanded its captives to accept the white South's ascendency, catechizing "that the only thing required of the black man is acquiescence and submission."

But it was what was being required of black women that prompted the bitterest words from Victorian feminist Du Bois. Standing on its head the white South's patriachal fixation on white female honor and purity, Du Bois implacably condemned the president's alleged exploitation of black female students in rolling cadences. There were to be several versions of the scandal involving McKenzie, the women's Glee Club, the Shriners of Al Menah Temple, and a local white rathskeller—that the alley had been well lighted or that the entrance was on a side street—but the variant details were irrelevant to the moral veracity of the charge. McKenzie had insulted Black Ladyship, and Du Bois, the public feminist and private patriarch, intended to personify wrath itself. "I am told the President of Fisk University took the fifteen or twenty girls from the Glee Club, girls from some of the best Negro families in the United States, carried them down town at night to a white men's club, took them down an alley and admitted them through the servants' entrance and had them sing in a basement to southern white men while these men smoked and laughed." Du Bois's voice rolled off the walls of the chapel as he thundered, "If Erastus Cravath . . . knew a thing like that had happened at Fisk University, he would, if it were in any way possible, rise from the grave and protest against this disgrace and sacrilege." Shaken and angered by the flood of applause, McKenzie vindictively noticed a coed furiously clapping from a seat near the front of the chapel. She would soon be charged with cheating on an examination and suspended. "No president can stand against such attacks and such intrigue unless he has militant and unreserved support," McKenzie immediately warned his trustees.

The following month, the success of the million-dollar endowment was announced, an epic achievement praised by the Urban League's *Opportunity* as bringing a "national university for colored people" within imminent reach. But if the president and the trustees thought that the news would lance the boil, they were wrong. "Unless McKenzie is removed from Fisk," the editor thundered in the second issue of the new *Herald* (resurrected and published in New York by Du Bois and several activist alumni), "I intend to publish every word of evidence I hold to prove he is unfit and a detriment to the cause of higher education for our race." Describing Fisk as a "place of sorrow, of infinite regret; a place where the dreams of great souls lay dusty and forgotten," the September *Crisis* promised to give full coverage to the situation. Du Bois delivered on that promise the following month with "The Dilemma of the Negro" in *The American Mercury* and "Gifts and Education" in the February 1925 issue of *The Crisis*, a one-two body blow that figuratively rattled the General Education Board windows at 61 Broadway. These *American Mercury* and *Crisis* missiles (one aimed at the mainstream, the other targeted for the minority stream) were like mortars bursting above a festive gathering, timed to arrive just as the self-congratulatory celebrants were leaving.

"Gifts and Education" acknowleged that "the only hope for Negro education lies in the gift of the [white] rich." What else could the Negro do, he challenged, when southern white laborers prevented state legislatures from voting appropriations for "decent common schools and high schools for Negroes?" Whether or not Du Bois really believed that the South's poor whites bore the major responsibility for the region's miserable expenditures for black public education, there was no disputing his passionate depiction of the consequences—a race compelled, he wrote, "to go begging up and down the land, hat in hand, crawling to the door steps of the rich and powerful for the dole of knowledge." In the North, organized labor played an analogous role, "sneer[ing] and yell[ing] and curs[ing] at black labor because it is not intelligent and underbids them." Caught between the Scylla of white working-class hostility north and south and the Charybdis of tainted philanthropy, the predictable results were the triumph of the pusillanimous, making "free and self-respecting manhood and frank open and honest criticism increasingly difficult among us." Like dominoes falling, the editor saw the handful of quality liberal arts colleges collapsing into intellectual obsequiousness and vocational irrelevance: Atlanta badly wounded; Talladega and Shaw increasingly marginalized; Lincoln hanging on; Howard's federal appropriation hostage to Dixiecrat congressmen. "If someone starts to tell the truth or disclose incompetency or rebel at injustice," the editor scolded, "a chorus of 'Sh!' arises from the whole black race. 'Sh!' You're opposing the General Education Board! 'Hush!' You're making enemies in the Rockefeller Foundation! 'Keep still!' or the Phelps-Stokes Fund will get you." The flow of funds to Fisk or Talladega or a hospital might stop.

Du Bois had made many of the same charges in *The American Mercury*, whose readers, unlike most of the *Crisis* subscribers, were hardly to be thought of as ready-made converts to his scolding message. Driving home the "recognized rule of philanthropy that no Negro higher school can survive unless it pleases the white South," "The Dilemma of the Negro" contrasted the impoverishment of Atlanta University with the opulence of Hampton. At Atlanta, the faculty was interracial, students and faculty took meals in common, and the alumni exercised real power on the board of trustees. The result? "Atlanta University is starving today." Hampton, "the pet of philanthropy and of the white South," had everything a school could want, except racial integrity. *American Mercury* readers had no need to be reminded that Booker Washington was Hampton's most illustrious graduate, nor would most have found the institute's inculcation of Puritan industry, Christian patience, and racial circumspection inappropriate. According to Du Bois, though, Hampton's white masters had long since crossed the line dividing circumspection from abasement, and he cited the recent campus visit of the school's second most illustrious son in graphic evidence. Moton had taken a seat simply to chat with a staff member in Hampton's whites-only faculty dining room when a female teacher "arose and ostentatiously left the table and the dining room. She is still teaching in Hampton," Du Bois noted sardonically. A single bright light glowed at Morehouse (the former Atlanta Baptist College), where his able and principled friend John Hope had replaced a white president and soldiered on with modest boosts from the American Baptist Home Missionary Society. Hope at Morehouse was proof that black-run institutions were no longer ipso facto synonymous with retrogression.

Yet it was precisely here that Du Bois underscored the dilemma in the title for his *American Mercury* readers, for he foresaw another kind of defeat if "illiberal and insulting policies" were to convince Negroes that the trustees, administrations, faculties, and students of their colleges and universities should become racially exclusive. Voicing an integrationist rationale worthy of Frederick Douglass, he insisted that the cultural contact of white and black teachers "with each other and of students with a mixed faculty has undoubtedly been one of the greatest sources of racial peace in the United States"—to lose it "would be calamitous." Devoid of the cultural and racial romanticism that had already begun to vex some of his other pronouncements on segregation, "The Dilemma of the Negro" was an admirable combination of prediction and admonition. The ideal American society was one that would draw strength from the interaction and interdependence of its heterogeneous groups, a *civitas* of which Fisk and Atlanta were fragile microcosms. The chance for that ideal in higher education was being squandered by the white supremacist cabal, on the one hand, and the embittered recoil into militant black separatism of upwardly mobile men and women of color, on the other. What Du Bois seemed to be saying, with a sagacity that would inform Gunnar Myrdal's *An American Dilemma*, twenty years in the future, was that if the nation did a better job of encouraging its liberal democratic ideals, racial separatism would gradually diminish yet also, simultaneously (and somewhat paradoxically), acquire a degree of naturalness and nonbellicose legitimacy as the stigma of enforced segregation was lost. "The Dilemma of the Negro" contained an embryonic vision of the multiculturalism that would continue to elude the United States into the twenty-first century.

By the time "Gifts and Education" ran in the February *Crisis*, the situation at the college was speeding to a climax. The editor had begun to mobilize allies in order to force the results his writings called for soon after leaving campus for New York with a diplomaed Yolande at his side. Charles Wesley, class of 1911, pledged his support in the campaign to save Fisk. Wesley, on the faculty at Howard University, was a few months away from becoming the third Negro, after Du Bois and Woodson, to earn a Ph.D. in history from Harvard. "There is need for action," Wesley wrote to Du Bois at about the same time that Abram Harris, a graduate of Virginia Union University, rallied to the cause. Harris, just finishing his master's in economics at the University of Pittsburgh, was another brilliant scholar who would become one of the small group of Howard professors known as the Young Turks. In a letter-writing campaign worthy of a candidate for national office, Du Bois had gained the backing of much of the alumni and a number of prominent educators and leaders by the end of 1924. Writing on Slater Fund stationery, John Hardy Dillard, a philanthropoid and perhaps the white South's most influential liberal, frankly stated that the time had come "when Fisk should have a colored man as head of the institution." Under Du Bois's prodding, the large Fisk Club of Chicago petitioned the trustees to reform the presidency, lamenting that the "old confidence and trust that formerly existed between President, Faculty, and student body seems to have passed." More than one hundred and fifty Fisk Club delegates were summoned by Du Bois to an early January meeting in order to form a federated Fisk Club organization. The resurrected *Herald*, its first number carrying "*Diuturni Silenti*," announced that it would be "published occasionally at 2339 Seventh Avenue," headquarters of the New York Fisk Club.

Du Bois's determination to mold important segments of Aframerican opinion was manifest in the letter sent to the Associated Negro Press. "I want the

Press Association to get into this Fisk fight on the right side," he commanded its president and promised to send the ANP "inside information for the accuracy of which" he vowed to take personal resonsibility. His "inside information" came from several sources. A professor provided Du Bois with an insider's lengthy, revealing "Analysis of Fisk University," and student informants were indispensable. None proved more valuable than George Streator, a precocious twenty-one-year-old senior from Nashville with a natural aptitude for organizing. Du Bois had met Streator during the June visit to the campus, and had instantly taken the measure of the young man's abilities. Streator's devotion to Du Bois was instantaneous. He would spend much of the next ten years more or less in service to the editor, as indispensable *Crisis* staffer and the New York eyes and ears of Du Bois during and after the editor's phased return to Atlanta University. An excellent essayist with strong political views that would eventually cause him to lecture his idol, he would be the first Negro journalist to land a position with *The New York Times*.

Streator's intelligence gathering was impressive. Running narratives of the machinations of pro-McKenzie faculty and staff arrived at *The Crisis* almost weekly when the college was in session. Streator's crucial service was to organize a corps of students soon after the start of the fall semester to bring the McKenzie administration to its knees through demonstrations. Meanwhile, the editor devoted his fall lecture tour to the Fisk situation, speaking to dozens of Fisk clubs in the Northeast and Midwest. "Fisk" appeared in the October *Crisis*. It was his college, "the shrine of [his] young years of high idealism and infinite faith," the editorial remonstrated, but it was failing every test of higher education for Negroes. When the trustees convened for their annual meeting on campus that November, the stage had been set for confrontation. To save money, the administration had discontinued intercollegiate baseball and trimmed the football budget. That season, the Fisk Bulldogs suffered the ignominy of a 67 to 0 defeat by Tuskegee—the galling symbolism of which was too much to bear. With faculty support for McKenzie badly eroded, more than a hundred students greeted the stunned board with shouts of "Away with the Czar!" "Down with the Tyrant!" Later in the day, groups of male students began to chant, "Hey Boys! Who Boys! Du Bois! Down with McKenzie!" Streator, along with six other student activists, forced a meeting with the badly disconcerted board. They left an hour later believing that their demands were going to be looked into in good faith. "Impressed and pleased with the fair and manly way in which the students conducted their case," Cravath had accepted a proposal for a faculty-student arbitration committee.

The trustees were surprised and deeply concerned by the November disturbances. They continued to be genuinely puzzled by Du Bois's thunderous writings, alumni rumblings, and mounting student unrest. In the imperfect world ordained by *Plessy v. Ferguson*, men such as Paul Cravath, L. Hollingsworth Wood, William H. Baldwin, and, certainly, Thomas Jesse Jones honestly believed that their philanthropic labors greatly encouraged developments that would make the separated races less unequal in the long term. The fact that the national black leadership was by no means united behind Du Bois greatly reassured Fisk's white trustees of the rectitude of their policies. They would have known of the substance of Mrs. Booker T. Washington's irritated response to Du Bois's request for support in her new capacity as an alumni representative on the board. McKenzie's stewardship of their college might not be unflawed, replied Margaret Washington, but she did wonder "if a man who is able to secure a million dollars; if a man who is able to secure $50,000 from a southern white citizenship; who is able to have every room in his buildings filled with students . . . ought not have their entire support until we are absolutely sure that he in no way deserves it." These were precisely the sentiments of the Grand Grammateus of Sigma Pi Phi, the elected head of the puissant, quasi-hereditary society informally known as the "Boulé" and comprised of some of the country's most accomplished black professional men. Du Bois's fraternity, Alpha Phi Alpha, oldest of the Negro Greek letter societies, founded at Cornell in 1907, also ducked his request for an endorsement of the Streator-authored resolution sent to it on behalf of the student leadership. There was also a fair number of conservative parents like the physician who praised McKenzie's disciplinary code as the best thing for daughters who should be educated "as pure Christian young women."

Even though John Hope hinted that his friend's campaign risked destroying more than it reformed, Du Bois showed no inclination to lower his battering ram. Hope, who wrote to thank him for the *American Mercury* compliments, spoke as an experienced college administrator who knew just about everything there was to know about clashing ideals and agendas in higher education. Fisk was a delicate organism. It was almost human. "It *is* human," he wrote. Ovington gave Du Bois another reason (had he wanted one) to reflect upon the acerbity with which he castigated the McKenzie regime's rigid discipline. She reminded her noble friend "how [he] stood by discipline then" when the Atlanta students had complained to her during a visit to the campus years ago. Ovington thought the Fisk problem might have more to do with institutional conservatism than it had to do with racism. Claiming that "no one stands for proper discipline of youth stronger than I," Du Bois turned a deaf ear to pleas for moderation. With wealthy white Nashville watching over his shoulder with mounting disapproval, McKenzie was equally inflexible. As soon as the semester had ended the president sped off to New York in January to confer with the executive committee of the trustees. Successfully defending his regime and the racial stakes at risk, he returned to Nashville to promulgate a diktat: "a complete ignoring of the charges made against the administration will be the policy of the Board of Trustees of Fisk University."

It was a bad policy. On Wednesday evening, February 4, 1925, the men in Livingtone Hall kept their lights on past the ten o'clock curfew. Until that night, for all his editorializing and public speaking about the troubles at Fisk, Du Bois had failed to bring about a broad-based mobilization against the McKenzie administration. All that was to change shortly after midnight on Thursday morning when fifty white Nashville policemen charged into Livingstone Hall and forced the men out of their beds, pistols drawn and clubs poking into rib cages, herding them to McKenzie's office. The students were given the choice either of signing a statement denouncing the protest or leaving the college. Seven "ringleaders" (the seven who had met with the trustees in November) were placed under arrest on the president's orders, although released immediately after the embarrassed president failed to substantiate charges of property damage and incitement to riot. No life had been lost and the police officers had been relatively restrained, but the violation of the Talented Tenth's flagship campus by the city's notoriously bigoted police force at the invitation of the Fisk president was a surpassing outrage. The following day, nearly three thousand of the city's black citizens poured into St. John's AME Church in a show of solidarity and indignation. Du Bois had been given a *cause célèbre* that would blast into the presidential offices and trustee meeting rooms of one historically black institution of learning after another. As for the fourth president of Fisk University, the Chicago *Defender* accurately forecast his fate—"McKenzie, You're Through."

Eight weeks of boycotted classes ensued. The trustees released a ringing statement "squarely and unanimously" backing McKenzie at the end of the first week. White Nashville cheered him. The Chamber of Commerce voted unanimous commendation, and the Kiwanis Club entertained him. The city's two newspapers, the *Banner* and *Tennesseean*, railed against the students and those Bolshevistic and antiwhite forces who were plotting, according to McKenzie, to turn Fisk black from top to bottom. "*Equality of rights* in all respects" was a goal these students "can never attain," huffed the *Banner*. Many students went home at their parents' insistence or withdrew outright from Fisk, with dozens of them transferring to Howard. But the majority kept up the momentum, guided by a general staff receiving orders from the editor of *The Crisis* and sustained by the local community's remarkable support. Black Nashville opened its homes, with the Negro Board of Trade sponsoring fund-raising meetings and offering credit to students ousted from dorms and denied dining hall meals. Citizens Savings Bank & Trust Company, black-owned, cashed money orders refused by the Fisk post office. The boycott uniform for coeds was flapper dresses, silk stockings, and high heels. They even smoked in public. No more cotton stockings and gingham dresses, one young woman wrote Du Bois—"it was too much." One alumnus McKenzie supporter fled in confusion from campus after seeing students in skirts "split almost to their waists exposing their nakedness." To the relief of the board's white moderates and the consternation of Thomas Jesse Jones, Fayette McKenzie finally threw in the towel, his resignation effective April 16, 1925. Du Bois congratulated Streator on the "excellent work which you and the students have done at Fisk University." His statement, that "of course I knew nothing of your plans," was a prudent fabrication. Even so, he couldn't restrain himself from admitting to having worried that the students would fail to carry through to the finish, "but you did." It was a job well done.

In August of that year, Du Bois sent a memorandum to the trustees announcing that the time had come "when the claims of colored men for the presidency of our Negro schools should be considered and considered on the same terms as the claims of white men." That the editor may have had himself in mind for the position is more than a remote possibility, although John Hope could have told him that it was about as likely as McKenzie being elected to the NAACP's board of directors. In any event, Fisk's white-dominated board appears to have given no thought whatsoever to a Du Bois candidature nor to any serious contemplation of a break with the tradition of selecting white males. On the other hand, virtually all of the demands of the students were conceded. Elected student government returned to the campus along with the suppressed *Herald*. Proscriptions on dating and dancing were modernized. The dress code disappeared and, for better and worse, Greek letter organizations appeared. Expelled students were readmitted, and the transcripts of those who preferred to transfer to Howard released. When academic year 1926 commenced, numbered among the new Fisk faculty members were Bertram Doyle, E. Franklin Frazier, and Paul Radin in sociology, Alrutheus Taylor in history, St. Elmo Brady in chemistry, Elmer Imes in physics, Warner Lawson and John Work in music, and Lorenzo Dow Turner in literature and linguistics. Under its new coach, the Fisk Bulldogs came roaring back to dominate the black gridiron as the "Fastest Team in Colored America."

Less than a month after McKenzie's capitulation, Howard University students struck against the iron-fisted regime of their white president, J. Stanley Durkee, a New England–trained Congregationalist minister. Lincoln University would erupt the following year. Hampton's turn would come in 1927 as the tidal effect of "*Diuturni Silenti*" rolled across the campuses. From promising beginnings as an enlightened reformer who honored the tradition of white presidents collaborating with Howard's triumvirate of black deans, Durkee had begun to rule by decree as he set about implementing his own master plan for the university's restructuring. As he merged departments, forced long-serving administrators into retirement, and fired faculty, the president's autocratic policies embroiled him in disputes whose racial resonances (virtually unavoidable in any case) were greatly amplified. To his credit, however, Durkee had won federal funds for new buildings and operating capital from congressional committees dominated by white southerners, some of whom came occasionally to enjoy spirituals in the university chapel.

The troubles at Howard reached the critical point on a Thursday morning in early May 1925, when a disturbance in dignified Rankin Memorial Chapel quickly escalated into a campuswide strike lasting for eight days. Since the advent of Durkee, compulsory chapel services had come to consist of little else than the singing of spirituals, with the president commanding the audience to rise in song while his great bulk swayed to the music, his moods on the platform alternating between joy and tears. "Fifteen minutes in Chapel every Monday is devoted to the singing of familiar popular songs, plantation melodies, army songs, and so forth," reported the *Howard University Record*. Tiny Mae Miller, the accomplished, playwriting daughter of Kelly Miller, ventilated the frustrations of her comrades in a chapel assembly convened by the astonished trustees, even though family friend Carter Woodson had warned Miller that her father's current position as chairman of the sociology department was bound to be jeopardized once the overweight, and too often overwrought, eleventh president felt secure enough again to act. Miller, a 1920 honor graduate of Howard who taught high school dramatics in nearby Baltimore, told the trustees that the men and women of Howard loved all types of music, but they resented "being relegated only to the singing of spirituals." They were modern Americans who wanted it understood that slavery was no longer the most salient experience in their lives.

It quickly became obvious that dissatisfaction with the current regime entailed much more than musical repertory. Another former Howard student, always notoriously unpredictable in her partisanship, hurried into print in the *Messenger* to cast doubt on the incessant singing of spirituals as the real cause of the demonstrations. From her days at the university before transferring to study anthropology at Barnard College, Zora Neale Hurston recalled the chapel services and the psalm-reading president with affection. " 'Negro music began where "white" music left off,' " Hurston quoted Durkee as fond of saying. "We used to respond cheerfully." The administration's decision that year to enforce the regularly ignored requirement of four years of compulsory ROTC for men and mandatory physical education for both sexes significantly dampened the cheerful responses and was a major reason the singing of spirituals ignited the long-simmering discontent.

As had been done with Fisk, *The Crisis* commenced a fateful tattoo of editorials during the summer of 1925 sharply critical of the Howard situation. The August number reported the dismissal of Kelly Miller, perhaps the most distinguished alumnus, from the university after thirty-five years of devoted tenure. (The same editorial disclosed that Miller's sacking had been rescinded almost immediately, which was "exceedingly lucky" for Durkee, "but it does not end the matter.") The September *Crisis* revealed that the president had hastily reversed the enforced retirement of another Howard institution, George William Cook, the dean of the faculty, after much disquiet in Washington. Meanwhile, Locke himself had been fired along with three other professors who had argued the case for improved faculty salaries and more secure terms of employment. What did Howard alumni intend to do about the disgrace of Durkee? *The Crisis* wanted to know.

Key faculty and administrators were put on notice that the editor urgently needed deep background information about persistent rumors of presidential high-handedness. Was it true, he demanded to know from Locke, that the president had become so enraged during an office conference that he had called Kelly Miller a "black dog" and then physically manhandled the smaller, much older man as he showed him the door? What of the other fracas involving a biology professor also reported to have been physically accosted by the president in a dispute about new equipment for his laboratory? Locke's "confidential" response, running to three single-spaced, typed pages, was a motherlode. Miller, described as shaken and deeply depressed by his momentary dismissal, had "vanished in South Carolina" while the canine obscenity, now softened to "contemptible puppy," was traced to an earlier demotion as dean of arts and sciences. Meanwhile, in lieu of filing assault charges, biology professor Thomas Turner was said to have extracted a glowing recommendation from an embarrassed Durkee and taken a post at Hampton. Locke's surmise that Miller had also entered into a gentleman's agreement was corroborated when Miller sent Du Bois an off-the-record reply in which he pleaded the restrictions of an "honorable settlement of an angry issue." What the aged dean declined to validate formally, the editor would document from other sources, publishing "Contemptible Puppy" in the October number for 1925 in order to expose Durkee as flagrantly unworthy of any further trust on the part of black people.

Du Bois's insistent editorials had already played a major part in shaping the reactions of Howard alumni. The distinguished prelate and executive officer of the General Alumni Association, George Frazier Miller, informed him that he had woven the "trenchant" August editorial into a speech given to the Howard Welfare League. Reverend Miller had wanted Du Bois to address the meeting of the General Alumni Association in Atlantic City at the end of August, an invitation the editor much regretted being unable to accept. In another instance of their uncommon cooperation, an unemployed Locke (he would join the Fisk faculty the following year with Du Bois's approval) convinced editor Freda Kirchwey to invite Du Bois to write an essay for *The Nation* about the Howard situation "as openly and vigorously as the facts warrant."

"Negroes in College," appearing in the March 1926 issue of *The Nation*, began with a recitation of infamies inflicted upon Howard: the forced resignation of Carter Woodson, wholesale faculty firings, racial epithets and rumbles in the president's office, and the "almost total lack of social contact" between the white president and the black faculty and students. Du Bois thought it scarcely conceivable that such a deplorable record would have survived a vote at Yale or Harvard, yet Howard's trustees had reaffirmed their "confidence in President Durkee's character and purpose" in a special meeting at the close of 1924. Moving on to the various predicaments at Atlanta, Hampton, Lincoln, and Wilberforce, "Negroes in College" introduced the magazine's *bien pensant* readers to a history of betrayed idealism, bigotry, and incompetence. Atlanta "was starving to death," Du Bois lamented. Hampton had instituted a "system of racial segregation upon its own campus." Lincoln remained without a single black professor on its bucolic Pennsylvania campus and "never had a colored member on its board of trustees." Wilberforce, where Du Bois had begun his teaching career, was provincial, narrow, "vindictive, and without discipline or ideal."

Du Bois's stark narration of exclusion from "white" institutions flickered past like frames in a newsreel: Georgia (a typical southern example) spending $655,135 a year on the higher education of whites and $10,000 for its black citizens; Bryn Mawr, Radcliffe, Wellesley, and Smith excluding virtually all women of color except those admitted accidentally; Princeton barring black men from its undergraduate college; Yale and Harvard discouraging applications; and Johns Hopkins going so far as to Jim Crow extension courses for teachers offered in Washington and Delaware where no laws required its imposition. Among Catholic schools only Fordham and Detroit accepted blacks. The nation faced a simple choice. "Do we want Negroes educated according to their ability" in order to become independent, "self-directing, modern men," Du Bois demanded, or did white people intend for them to be educated only "as a subordinate caste?" The editor would have heard a qualified yes to the training of "self-directing, modern men [and women]" in the news of Stanley Durkee's resignation a few days after the appearance of his essay in *The Nation*. Mordecai Wyatt Johnson, a tall, thirty-five-year-old Baptist preacher with a complexion as white as his predecessor's and a speaking voice like that of the Archangel Gabriel, became Howard's twelfth president and its first Negro. Alain Locke would regain his professorship in the fall of 1927.

Much had changed in the structure of the leadership class and in the relations of power in black America since the time, hardly twenty years earlier, when a signal from Tuskegee had been sufficient to cower and crush all but the most obdurate or imprudent critics. The message *The Crisis* had sought to inculcate, in enlightened contrast to the ethos of the Atlanta Compromise, was one of political and cultural emancipation—of deference accorded only to those who were genuinely worthy, irrespective of race or class. Du Bois's decisive role in undermining the authority of Washington and the association's displacement of the Tuskegee Machine contributed enormously to the diffusion of power and with it the growth of independence, opposition, and opportunism. In fall of 1927, independence, opposition, and opportunism came to Hampton Institute when the student body erupted in protest that October against the policies of the white adminstration. Spied upon by their white teachers and engirdled by a code of conduct two parts Puritan strictures and three parts plantation discipline, hundreds of angry students burst out of Ogden Hall on a Saturday evening when lights were turned up during a movie to discourage necking. "We students have been wronged, wronged. Yesterday we struck. No inspection, no church, no grace at dinner," one of the strike leaders wrote Du Bois anonymously. "At chapel we refused to show off before some Governor from Europe." By midweek Hampton Institute had become engulfed in the wave of revolts that had rolled from Fisk to Howard and onward over Lincoln (Missouri), Shaw, Johnson C. Smith, and several other black institutions. "It was long overdue," Du Bois cheered. The anonymous strike leader ("a loyal Hamptonian") described the whites as "bewildered at the sudden action of these 'Southern Negroes.'" The strikers needed Du Bois's help. "Please let our mothers, fathers and our race know," he begged. "The future of the Negro youth depends upon the results of this serious uprising."

One of the best-endowed schools in the country, Hampton symbolized for the editor and his supporters the choke hold of white conservatism, North and South, on the higher education of young men and women of color. If Du Bois regarded Tuskegee Institute as falling far short of a modern learning experience, Washington's legacy had at least the virtue of being administered by black people. Hampton, on the other hand, was a showcase for white paternalism, little more than a technical high school whose autocratic white principal and condescending faculty segregated themselves from the students and segregated the students from visiting whites. Three hundred students had left the campus, pledging not to return unless the administration met their demands for improved meals, increased social privileges between the sexes, improved curriculum, and replacement of white teachers equipped with only high school diplomas. Principal James Gregg had rejected their demands out of hand and countered with the diktat that all returning students must sign a pledge of "loyalty and obedience."

According to a vivid, blow-by-blow account Du Bois received from one of the few Negro teachers, the principal had conceded that the strike leaders were the "foremost men on the campus," even though statements released to the public maligned them as "disobedient boys and girls who were led on to do what they did." This teacher had become bitterly disillusioned by the school's hypocrisy, racism, and "general backwardness." The teacher was none other than Louise Thompson, the young Berkeley graduate Du Bois had met and fatefully impressed four years ago, now finishing her first semester at Hampton. In the personal message to Du Bois accompanying her detailed history of the troubles, Thompson feared that Hampton had "warped" her and made her so "bitter" that she doubted whether she had any capacity left for objectivity. She even doubted now that it was possible for whites and blacks to work together harmoniously. She begged the editor to summon the Negro world "to see the justice in the students' stand." He obliged her immediately, although Thompson had hardly expected Du Bois to publish much of her confidential history of the Hampton troubles unaltered except for her identity (but her authorship unmistakable to the Hampton authorities).

Breaking into print in *The Nation*, Du Bois acidly characterized the institute's paternalist history and defended the striking students as the finest representatives of a new generation. "Hampton was no longer dealing with docile and half-grown elementary students, regimented to strict military discipline." Quoting the anonymous Thompson, "The Hampton Strike" admonished the enlightened of both races that the outcome depended "very much on public opinion in this affair." But by the time Thompson's appeal ran in the early November *Nation*, the strike had been defeated, five students expelled, twenty-nine suspended, and thirty classified as "temporarily ineligible." Many of the black colleges had refused to consider admitting those who were expelled. Their actions deplored at home and disparaged in their communities as disrespectful, immature, and prankish, all but a handful of the leaders had folded into demoralization. "Slowly the students are drifting back," Du Bois noted sadly in *The Nation.* In the December issue of his own magazine, he castigated the race for undermining the fundamental qualities expected of educated young people. "Students are not sent to school to learn to obey," Du Bois snapped, sounding like an angry John Dewey. "They are sent there to learn to do, to think, to execute, to be men and women." Expressing consternation at the betrayal of a cause whose symbolism went to the core of New Negro values, Du Bois lamented that "the most disconcerting thing in the Hampton strike is the way in which graduates and parents repudiated their own children." The impact of modernism, undermining traditional authority throughout American society in the late twenties, a cultural force conditionally espoused by Du Bois, embraced with mounting enthusiasm by college students, and manifest in the sexual mores of certain classes of urban Americans, had little or no resonance as yet among

most black and many white parents. Conservative, deeply religious, and conditioned to behave as though fully satisfied with their place in the southern
scheme of things, Hampton parents had reacted with horrified anger to a strike
that jeopardized their children's problematic chances to have better, freer lives
than themselves. Paternalism and parochialism had triumphed in tidewater Virginia over collegiate reform and its heady successes at Fisk and Howard in which
the editor took intense, proprietary pride.

MARCUS GARVEY SPOKE in Madison Square Garden on the night of March
16, 1924, shortly after his emissaries to Liberia had sailed for the United States.
It was his most publicized appearance in New York since his release from jail,
pending appeal of his five-year prison sentence. Robert Lincoln Poston's sudden
death from lobar pneumonia, just as the S.S. *President Grant* sailed into New
York Harbor on the eve of this large, ebullient UNIA rally, might have been
read as a bad omen by the superstitious, but the crowd roared and thundered
as the President-General spun visions of the Africa they were destined to build.
"The sweep of the 'Hallelujah Chorus,' the clank of sabres and the rhythmical
military tread of his legion, his Black Cross nurses, his motor corps and his
juvenile soldiers-to-be ushered in the public reappearance of Marcus Garvey,"
the New York *World* reported in a style worthy of Garvey's own rodomontade.
The Belgian ambassador to the United States noted in his despatch to Brussels
that once again Garvey had proclaimed that worrisome catchphrase, "Africa for
the Africans."

Since his release, the leader had spent much of his time speaking in urban
centers and at educational institutions in the Midwest and as far south as Tuskegee, and his ideas had become more shocking to many native colored people
and his language more bombastic as the weeks passed. He reiterated his love
for the "straightforward, honest white man," and stressed that that was why he
had "great respect for the members of the Ku Klux Klan." Under the heading
"An Appeal to the Soul of White America" (and to the horror of *The Crisis*,
Messenger, and *The Daily Worker*), he invited prominent whites to participate
in a national debate about the necessity for black emigration. Lenin, whose
ideological epigones he had chased from the ranks of the UNIA two years earlier, he now apostrophized upon news of the revolutionary's death. Sounding
more like Domingo or Richard Moore than himself, Garvey exhorted 400 million Negroes to mourn the founder of the Soviet state, "because Russia promised
great hope not only to Negroes but to the weaker peoples of the world." Once
again, though, it was Lenin the modernizing molder of disparate millions who
caught Garvey's imagination—Lenin as nationalist—rather than Lenin the ruthless enforcer of Soviet communism. But Garvey's obsession was, above all, the

fecklessness he saw in his own race, upon which he expended supreme, repetitious contempt. He shouted that the world despises the Negro "because the world knows that the Negro has made absolutely no independent contribution to the civilization of the world." He sneered, "Let Edison turn off his electric light and we are in darkness in Liberty Hall in two minutes." The sole and sane course of action for his people, he bellowed to the faculty and students of Howard University in mid-January 1924, was emigration: "If Asia is good for the Asiatics, if Europe is good for the Europeans, and America for the Americans, we are going to have ours in Africa, and we are going to fight and die for it, if you please."

Du Bois had observed Garvey's resiliency with supreme annoyance. While the editor had been away nurturing the ideology of Pan-Africanism in Europe and Africa, his Jamaican nemesis had not only rebounded from the disgrace of foreclosures and a prison sentence, Garvey, that unique blend of the incendiary and the visionary, even appeared to be on the verge of successes that would confound his detractors and dazzle millions. The hawking of an expanded *Negro World* in Harlem's major thoroughfares and the proliferation of posted leaflets ("Let's Put It Over") announcing one-way fares to West Africa aboard an ocean-going vessel assailed Du Bois after his return from Liberia. Until now, he believed that he had succeeded in keeping his criticisms of Garvey in a dignified pitch. The eight leaders who signed the January 1923 letter to Attorney General Harry Daugherty had insisted that Garvey be prosecuted and steps taken to "disband and extirpate this vicious movement." Field Secretary Bagnall had reviled the UNIA head a few weeks later in the *Messenger* as a "squat, stocky, fat and sleek" Jamaican. Du Bois had declined to associate himself with such tactics and ad hominem remarks. But as he sat to compose his first published words about Garvey since returning from Africa, he decided that the time had come for a memorable editorial.

Marcus Garvey was the "most dangerous enemy of the Negro race in America and in the world," without a doubt. He was "either a lunatic or a traitor." The literature being sent out in his name to all parts of the country appealing to politicians, businessmen, philanthropists, and educators to endorse the forcible separation of the races and African emigration of black people was perfidy beyond belief, Du Bois fumed. "Not even Tom Dixon or Ben Tillman or the hatefulest enemies of the Negro ever stooped to a more vicious campaign than Marcus Garvey, sane or insane, is carrying on." Garvey was not attacking white prejudice, "he is grovelling before it and applauding it; his only attack is on men of his own race who are striving for freedom; his only contempt is for Negroes; his only threats are for black blood." Du Bois alluded to Garvey's alleged role in the assassination of Eason. "Everybody, including the writer, who dared to make the slightest criticism of Garvey has been intimidated by threats and threatened with libel suits." But enough. Speaking in his *ex cathedra* voice, the editor declared that American Negroes had "endured this wretch all too long with fine restraint and every effort at cooperation and understanding."

The Liberians now acted according to plan. Leo Weinthal, editor of the London-based *African World*, congratulated Du Bois on the "bold stand" against Garvey and his "criminal gang," and assured him that President King was "very pleased about it." On July 10, 1924, Consul General Ernest Lyons wrote from Baltimore to inform Du Bois of his government's decision. Lyons had been instructed to say that "no person or persons leaving the United States, under auspicies of the Garvey Movement in the United States, will be allowed to land in the Republic of Liberia." Two weeks after the date of Lyons's letter, a UNIA advance party arrived in Monrovia and was immediately placed under arrest and deported on a German ship. Secretary of State Barclay's notification to international shipping companies that no UNIA personnel would be admitted to his country had been given just after Garvey's emissaries sailed. By the time the cargo ship entered Liberian waters, the U.S. Shipping Board had wired that it should be returned because Garvey's check to the shipping agent had bounced the day after the ship left port. In the ensuing confusion of claims (the UNIA made good its check but there were various fees in Monrovia), the cargo would remain locked away in a warehouse until it was sold to cover storage costs several years later. When *The Daily Worker* printed Robert Minor's suspicions about Du Bois's collusion with Liberia against Garvey, the editor denounced the story as an "unmitigated lie." But it was understandable that the Communist daily thought it had good circumstantial evidence for its claim.

The last UNIA International Convention of the Negro Peoples of the World that Garvey would preside over in the United States opened in Madison Square Garden on August 1, 1924, against a backdrop of intraracial rancor. Garvey made no mention of Du Bois in his keynote address to the convention. He had much more important issues to confront. He knew that his days at liberty might be numbered and that the last opportunity to pull off his grand scheme of selective migration depended upon the enthusiasm, numbers, and money generated by the monthlong conclave. After the strains of the anthem "O Africa, Awaken" subsided, and the gorgeous and seemingly endless procession of the nobility, the Africa Legion, and the Black Cross Nurses finally concluded, after Archbishop McGuire of the African Orthodox Church exhorted and persauded the convention to canonize Jesus as the Black Man of Sorrows and Mary as the Black Virgin (a major deviation from UNIA theology), a solemn Garvey spoke as though possessed of preternatural foresight. "The Negro is dying out, and he is going to die faster and more rapidly in the next fifty years than he has in the past three hundred," he intoned. The sole hope of the race depended on the immediate shouldering of its resonsibilities, but Garvey told the assembly that that might never happen. "Unfortunately, we are the most careless and indifferent people in the world," he suddenly shouted. In the 1880s and some years afterward, white southerners of a sociological bent had predicted the dying out of Negroes as the "blessings" of "white" culture receded. But Garvey's chilling prescience was informed by an opposite peril—the enervating consequences of too much whiteness. According to him, black people might soon be "as completely and complacently dead as the North American Indian or the Australian Bushman" if they failed to "face the world with a program of African nationalism." That program seemed to acquire fabulous prospects in the middle of August when Garvey announced to the screaming convention that the Black Cross Navigation and Trading Company had finally acquired its first ship, the five-thousand-ton, hundred-thousand-dollar S.S. *General Goethals*, to be renamed the *Booker T. Washington*—only an additional $70,000 was needed "to come into complete possession of same."

With this accomplishment, he and his movement reached their apogee. The thousands of participating delegates, legionnaires, and nurses made the fourth international convention the largest and the most spectacular, its parades and receptions captured for posterity through the lens of James Van Der Zee's remarkable camera. If Supreme Potentate Gabriel Johnson found himself facing serious charges by his fellow Liberians and UNIA advance teams were being forced to reembark from Monrovia even as his people were challenged to pay up and sail for Zion, the President-General seemed unconfounded as he presented to the convention another representative of Africa, the Dahomeyan prince Kojo Tovalou-Houénou, whose pedigree and presence were vital assets to the UNIA. Du Bois was greatly upset by the prince's acceptance of UNIA hospitality, writing to another member of the Ligue pour la Défense de la Race Noire, the acclaimed Francophone novelist, René Maran, that it was unconscionable for the organization's president to endorse a "scoundrel and a thief." When Tovalou-Houénou calmly replied that he refused to be forced "to choose between two adversary brothers," Du Bois huffily withdrew from the committee sponsoring the prince's American lecture tour. Six months later, the U.S. Circuit Court of Apeals, Second Circuit, upheld Garvey's mail-fraud conviction. He was transported to the federal penitentiary in Atlanta to serve out his sentence.

In his righteous determination to destroy Garvey as a leader, Du Bois seems never to have honestly considered the possibility that personal loathing for Garvey prevented him from taking even the most minimal steps toward finding an accommodation. With the probable exception of the historic night in Madison Square Garden, the editor kept an icy, suspicious distance from the very beginning. Given Garvey's inferiority complex and volatile ego, it is unlikely that he would have welcomed for long Du Bois's critical and constructive advice in any case. But it is also true that Du Bois was incapable of making any effort to extend to him the slightest convincing display of personal respect that might have solaced the headstrong younger man's obvious intellectual insecurity. It was just not Du Bois's way, but it may well be, as Wesley still believed years later, that Du Bois's animus was greatly intensified by the meteoric rise of an untrained, uncouth foreigner whose success at corralling the masses was simply phenomenal. After the smoke of battle cleared and Garvey, defeated but unbowed, was shunted into exile, Du Bois would come to admit publicly that there was much about the UNIA founder's program that was sound. The call for unity based on race and culture and for race-based commerce and industry in order to promote the liberation of Africa were concepts fully in accord with those Du Bois promulgated at the second Pan-African Congress. Despite his histrionics, Garvey was too intelligent not to see the limits of color in politics. He understood that the real problem in racial relations existed, as he said once, "not because there is a difference between us in religion or in color, but because there is a difference between us in power." From his perspective, the tragic miscalculation of leaders such as Du Bois was that they criticized American society only to the degree and duration of their exclusion from it. It was their reflex to defend and preserve the system by which they were exploited that dismayed and enraged the UNIA leader.

The self-styled Provisional President-General of Africa may have been far too prone to crude hyperbole and garish costumes for the tastes of the editor of *The Crisis*, but most of Garvey's ideas (unlike those of the Wizard of Tuskegee) could have been made compatible with his own. What was at stake in the Du Bois–Garvey conflict were not so much ideas, however, but the national origins and social class of those aiming for a near monopoly in the leadership of black people in the United States: whether that class would continue to be recruited from the homegrown bourgeoisie (the Talented Tenth) generally loyal to aristocratic Du Bois, or whether it was to be supplanted by parvenu West Indians marching behind charismatic Garvey. Whether, in a word, it would be the NAACP and the National Urban League raising money from and issuing marching orders to twelve million second-class American citizens, or the UNIA and its affiliates. Finally, it came down to the threat posed by the messenger, rather than to the crux of the message.

· 5 ·

CIVIL RIGHTS BY COPYRIGHT

On a Friday evening in late March 1924, an exclusive interracial gathering had filled the Civic Club on Twelfth Street just off Fifth Avenue to participate in *Opportunity*'s presentation of what amounted to the first act of the Harlem Renaissance. Five days earlier, Garvey's immaculately uniformed legions had marched once again into Madison Square Garden to cheer his defiant orations in the largest and most theatrically orchestrated UNIA convention yet assembled. It would be the last such occasion in the United States over which Garvey would preside, the final scene in one of the century's most inspirational yet unluckiest of folk dramas. The collective forces of the Talented Tenth would need less than two years from the turning-point month of March 1924 before they succeeded in formulating an alternative belief system, institutionally supported and enveloped in enough mystique, to begin to fill the vacuum created by Garvey's defeat. It remained to be seen whether the Talented Tenth in its new manifestation as the New Negro, operating principally through the NAACP and the National Urban League (NUL), could really succeed over the long haul in capturing for its new, elitist racial agenda the excitement and loyalty that large numbers of ordinary men and women had felt for Black Zionism.

The Civic Club affair on March 21 was the sort of venture Du Bois himself might well have been expected to have conceived, or, at the very least, to have been involved in its planning and shaping, had not the Pan-African Congress and trip to West Africa intervened. Hadn't he warned in "Art for Nothing," a scolding *Crisis* editorial written two years earlier, that unless colored people were willing to support their artists with money and organization, they would get just what they failed to pay for—little or nothing in the way of broad cultural recognition? Whatever its literary shortcomings, his thirteen-year-old *The Quest of the Silver Fleece* likely inspired the first wave of Talented Tenth writers by the robustness of the effort and the suggestiveness of its themes. His encouragement had helped Fauset, the evening's guest of honor, "discover" Langston Hughes and Jean Toomer. She had published their works in the association's monthly when they were still completely unknown to the Negro public and only just beginning to appear in the little reviews run by white writers and poets. She had captured Hughes for *The Brownies' Book* as early as 1921, even persuading him to dedicate "The Negro Speaks of Rivers," one of his most enduringly popular poems, to Du Bois. She reeled in Toomer in early 1923, offering the self-educated marvel advice about overripe prose and the value of mastering foreign languages.

When the first tide of white novels about people of color arrived at the top of the decade bringing in T. S. Stribling's *Birthright* and Clement Woods's *Nigger*, Fauset had been among the very first to propose testing the waters for colored talent. *Birthright*, appearing in spring of 1922, was the first major novel by a white writer since *Uncle Tom's Cabin* to feature a sympathetic black protagonist, a naive Harvard graduate returning to a tragic fate in the South. Stribling represented a welcome advance over Thomas Nelson Page and Thomas Dixon, or the demeaning, popular short stories of Octavus Roy Cohen, but the literary editor of *The Crisis*, with the editor's full backing, proposed to write her own novel for the benefit of the New Negro. "We reasoned, 'Here is an audience waiting to hear the truth about us,'" Fauset elucidated. "'Let us who are better qualified to present that truth than any white writer, try to do so.'" *There Is Confusion* appeared from Boni & Liveright in early spring of 1924, portions of which had run earlier in the magazine. Widely and positively reviewed in mainstream publications, it received enthusiastic appraisals by Locke in *The Crisis*, Schuyler in the *Messenger*, and in the black press generally (although one astute Negro critic later remarked that the novel was nothing if not well titled). Du Bois decreed that Fauset's large novel about color, class, and manners among Philadelphia's colored shabby genteel "mark[ed] an epoch. . . . Spread the glad tidings."

But lately, the care and feeding of artists and writers had been pushed to the sidelines of Du Bois's urgent concerns. Uppermost in those concerns had been eleventh-hour anxieties about the third Pan-African Congress, the mission to Liberia, the two months of related traveling to and from Europe and West Africa, and—before, during, and after—the unremitting Garvey menace. Several association board members, Ovington and Joel Spingarn in particular, had begun to worry that the declining circulation of *The Crisis* was due to Du Bois's pan-African pursuits, book contracts, and outside lecturing and writing. Clearly, the editor was paying less attention to the daily operation of the magazine. But the larger problem of *The Crisis* was one of sameness, of a slow slide into a deep groove, Spingarn would warn at the end of April 1924. Sales were down to about forty thousand. "Something should be done." The magazine needed "a fundamental overhauling." But how, asked the editor? He had the same feeling, but he was not at all certain what improvements to make. Did Spingarn have "specific suggestions of improvement?" "The State of *The Crisis*," Ovington's lengthy report, landed on Du Bois's desk in early May like a large rock thrown through the office transom. Its findings were severe: "The magazine had . . . fallen off somewhat in its illustrations." It lacked an index. The covers and the photographs were "wretched." The staff was top heavy and too expensive. There had never been "a good piece of research" in it. The editor had turned the magazine into a "business success" that supported him while he devoted himself to "personal lecturing, his personal writing, his voluminous correspondence." Then came Ovington's coup de grace: "The magazine now in the ascendant is *Opportunity*, published by the Urban League." Indeed, in the opinion of Chairperson Ovington, the last *Opportunity*, containing Albert Barnes and Locke's essays on modern art, was the best number "of any colored magazine that has been printed since we have existed as an Association." There is little doubt that Spingarn and Ovington had colluded in order to presure Du Bois into livening up *The Crisis*. But the editor of the premier civil rights publication cannot have been pleased to find himself unfavorably compared to upstarts Johnson and Locke.

Charles Spurgeon Johnson was the son of a gutsy Virginia Baptist preacher who had once stared down a lynch mob. The younger Johnson had graduated with honors from Virginia Union University, an historically black collegiate institution in Richmond that would boast an alumni roster stretching from J. Max Barber, comrade-in-arms with Du Bois against Booker Washington, to Douglas Wilder, the state's first African-American governor. After seeing action as a sergeant major in the Meuse-Argonne, Johnson resumed course work at the University of Chicago, concentrating in sociology under Robert Park, the Wizard of Tuskegee's former ghostwriter now well on his way to legendary leadership of the discipline. Johnson was on his way to becoming something of a legend himself in a career that would be gilded by numerous honorary degrees, multiple consultancies and directorships with educational philanthropies such as the General Education Board, Rosenwald Fund, Carnegie Corporation, Ford Foundation, the United Negro College Fund, and the presidency of Fisk University. As author and editor of *The Negro in American Civilization* (1930), *Shadow of the Plantation* (1934), *Growing Up in the Black Belt* (1941), and *Patterns of Negro Segregation* (1943) — classics whose titles encapsulated twentieth-century American race relations — Johnson would earn distinction as one of the foremost sociologists of his generation.

Unlike Du Bois, who always regarded Johnson's scholarship and statesmanship skeptically, Charles Spurgeon Johnson was a consummate diplomat and a sage optimist whose tranquil writings tracked the "vectors of social change" he interpreted as evidence of the steady racial meliorism guiding American society. The two sociologists could not have been temperamentally and ideologically more dissimilar. Johnson had come to the Urban League in 1921 to serve as editor of *Opportunity* and director of research after writing most of *The Negro in Chicago: A Study of Race Relations and a Race Riot*, the massive monograph produced by the municipal riot commission primarily financed by Julius Rosenwald of Sears and Roebuck. A blend of fastidious calculation, courtesy, and professionalism, Johnson had thus far discharged his duties at the magazine with unexceptionable orthodoxy. In keeping with the legend on its masthead, "Not Alms, but Opportunity," the monthly Johnson was hired to edit had devoted itself to subjects compatible with the social-science objectives articulated in the start-up issue of January 1923.

After the appearance of "The Debut of the Younger School of Negro Writers" in the May issue of *The Crisis*, however, a sudden change occurred. *Opportunity* switched within a couple of issues from being a forum for the cutting-edge articles of distinguished social scientists and educators to become the premier review for the literary and artistic effusions of the so-called New Negro. It was the rare man and woman of color who would have envisaged the promotion of poetry, novels, plays, and painting as viable means for improving relations between the races. Johnson was one such a rarity, however, and he would be the principal architect of a plan to persuade others to join him in building a civil rights arts movement. After the Red Summer of 1919 with its backwash of southern lynchings, Klan klaverns spreading into the American heartland and as far west as California, and patterns of residential and job discrimination in the North increasingly mimicking the Deep South, such a strategy could only strike most Americans, whatever their color, as a thoroughgoing implausibility. But Johnson was ready to gamble, as were a few other privileged Negroes (nearly all second-generation college graduates), that, although the roads to the ballot box, the union hall, the decent neighborhood, and the white-collar position were becoming blocked almost everywhere by racism, the two paths of arts and letters remained relatively unbarred. Probably because of their very unlikelihood, as well as their irrelevancy to most Americans, he had become certain that these cultural avenues offered a way around the obstacles. He and Locke and James Weldon Johnson, Fauset, White, and, above all, the indispensable Du Bois, espied small cracks in the wall of racism that could, over time, be widened through the production of exemplary racial images in collaboration with liberal white philanthropy, the culture industry centered in Manhattan, and artists from white bohemia. It was intended to be a generation-skipping display of artistic talent and discipline calculated to make it increasingly harder for influential whites to deny full social and civil rights to blacks.

The more than one hundred men and women of both races who filled the Civic Club on the evening of March 21 were attending what Charles S. Johnson called a writers and poets "coming out party." Nothing quite like the Civic Club evening had ever happened before in America; and it was to be a spectacular success. More than a dozen men and women of color with varying degrees of literary talent, proven and prospective, attended the affair in response to the *Opportunity* editor's invitation promising an evening spent in the company of Eugene O'Neill, H. L. Mencken, Oswald Villard, Mary Johnston, Zona Gale, Robert Morss Lovett, Carl Van Doren, Ridgely Torrence, "and about twenty more of this type." The white grandees of editing and publishing beamed from Civic Club tables at which sat a fair representation of the city's progressive establishment: Devere Allen of *The World Tomorrow*, Freda Kirchwey of *The Nation*, Mr. and Mrs. Horace Liveright, Louis Weitzenkorn of the *World*, Paul Kellogg of the *Survey*, the Arthur Spingarns, Ovington, Fisk trustee and Urban League chairman L. Hollingsworth Wood, Mr. and Mrs. Graham Taylor, and Roger Baldwin of the American Civil Liberties Union.

The luster of the whites was complemented by a distinguished roster of the Talented Tenth that included the economist George Edmund Haynes and his wife, the bibliophile Arthur Schomburg, the Eugene Kinckle Joneses, the YMCA executive Jesse Moorland and Mrs. Moorland, along with Crystal Bird and Eunice Hunton, two YWCA powerhouses. Not just a couple of singular black people two generations removed from plantation slavery and adept at prose and verse (exceptions like Dunbar or Chesnutt or Frances Leroy Harper who proved no rule at all) were being hailed, but a veritable vanguard with dozens more to come, according to what Du Bois, Locke, and both Johnsons would tell the assembled whites. Although Hughes, Toomer, and McKay, three of the brightest stars in what was already being called the New Negro Arts Movement, were out of the country, their creative presence was almost palpable during the evening as repeated references were made to their work. Up from Washington, Du Bois's close friend and frequent hostess Georgia Douglas Johnson glowed in the presence of fellow poets Gwendolyn Bennett and Cullen and in the dream-come-true applause from this glittering audience when *The Heart of a Woman* and *Bronze*, her two books of poetry, were mentioned.

Ostensibly, the gathering had assembled to celebrate the publication of Fauset's *There Is Confusion*, although in the hands of master of ceremonies Locke the focus of the evening was allowed to veer somewhat away from her. At least Fauset thought so, and years later she would let Locke know how much she had been infuriated when he told her brother, Arthur, "that the dinner given at the Civic Club . . . wasn't for me." That night, however, bristling under good manners, she remained a picture of demure geniality, her nerves probably much soothed by the presence of Du Bois, who was making his first public appearance since returning from West Africa. She would call him her "best friend and severest critic" when it came time for her to say a few words. Mischievously introduced as a representative of the "older school" of letters by Locke, the editor spoke briefly of earlier Negro writers and of his own generation whose styles had been distorted and choice of subjects blocked by racial conventions.

Du Bois proceeded to tick off some of the names in the burgeoning crop of literary comers. There was Langston Hughes, Countee Cullen, Claude McKay, Georgia Douglas Johnson, Gwendolyn Bennett, and Eric Walrond. And he had just learned of Walter White's success in bagging a book contract with Alfred A. Knopf for *The Fire in the Flint*. The appearance of *There Is Confusion* marked "an epoch"—the end of the literature of apology—he proclaimed proudly, as did *Cane*, the year-old book of haunting vignettes by the young Washington, D.C., writer Jean Toomer. "Here then is promise sufficient to attract us," Du Bois said, yielding the lectern to James Weldon Johnson, who rose to be praised by Locke for having given "invaluable encouragement to the work of this younger group." The normally buttoned-up Charles Johnson was positively exhilarated by the attendance of the prominent whites that evening, a response that had been greatly assisted by Urban League board member William H. Baldwin III and Frederick Lewis Allen, a Harper & Brothers editor whose *Only Yesterday: An Informal History of the 1920's* would become a staple for students of American culture.

Having already bet on the Civic Club gambit by signing up first Toomer, then Fauset, Horace Liveright came to offer advice about books that would sell well with the general public (Negroes should rein in their inferiority complexes and avoid " 'impossibly good' fiction types"). But as *Cane* showed, he conceded, even fine books often sold poorly. Albert Barnes, the Philadelphia pharmaceutical tycoon and notoriously cantankerous art collector, shared with the audience his long-held belief that America's most vital source of creative energies lay in its African citizens. Not a man or woman there had been unimpressed by the cultural and commercial potentialities implicit in Carl Van Doren's talk, the most salient of the evening. The story of any aspiring black man or woman told with simplicity by a Negro novelist would have the force of a bugle, the respected poet and literary critic asserted, calling "all just persons, white or black, to listen to him." But the American Negro was also uniquely endowed to be a powerful cultural catalyst. "What American literature decidedly needs at the moment is color, music, gusto, the free expression of gay or desperate moods," Van Doren sermonized. "If the Negroes are not in a position to contribute these items, I do not know what Americans are." As Du Bois joined in applauding Van Doren, it is possible that he may even at this early moment have entertained a flash of disquiet about white prescriptions of "color, music, gusto" for black people, but he could not have anticipated then the degree to which Van Doren's cry for "free expression of gay or desperate moods" would be answered.

As the grandly successful night drew to a close, twenty-year-old Countee Cullen, a junior at New York University and widely regarded as Harlem's literary *Wunderkind*, sent a charge snapping through the air with several poems written for the occasion. Johnson reported in *Opportunity* that they were received with a "tremendous ovation," but whether the applause may have been for "Yet Do I Marvel"—whose trenchant lines ran, "Yet do I marvel at this curious thing:/ To make a poet black and bid him sing!"—the editor neglected to mention. One of those who would certainly have clapped enthusiastically for Cullen was Du Bois himself. He had become increasingly fond of the tiny poet with the high voice, fine mind, and good manners. He had not been altogether pleased by a recent interview in the Brooklyn *Eagle* quoting Cullen as saying that if he were going to be a poet, then he would be "a POET and not a NEGRO POET," but Du Bois felt as proud as most Harlemites to see the young genius being so widely and positively noticed.

There was probably already more to his interest in Cullen than literary and racial pride. Ever since their meeting the previous summer, Fauset had kept her "best friend and severest critic" informed of Countee and Yolande's tentative relationship. Harold Jackman, whose handsome features would shortly grace a full page in the special Negro issue of the *Survey Graphic*, had made the introductions. He followed up with advice to Yolande about recreational reading, especially poems by Edna St. Vincent Millay, of which Countee was particularly fond. Dutifully sampling them, Yolande had reported back that she liked "all of them." As for Countee, she liked him, too. He seemed "so young," and she liked "to hear him talk."

Ten years earlier, in a suggestive paper written for the American Academy of Political and Social Science, Du Bois had candidly regretted that, as he judged, the time had not yet come "for the great development of American Negro literature." The hardships of earning a living and the scourge of racial discrimination simply precluded the necessary "leisure and poise." But like his Talented Tenth peers, Du Bois had left the Civic Club elated by what the Urban League's Johnson, Locke, Fauset, White, and the others saw as the potential of the arts to transform the negative images of people of color in the minds of the great majority of white Americans. Encouraging its writers, poets, and painters would be one of the most efficacious means of establishing the right of the black race to "universal recognition," he had exhorted in "Art for Nothing." James Weldon Johnson professed the same ideal at the identical moment, declaring in the preface to his 1922 anthology, *The Book of American*

Negro Poetry, the first of its kind, that "the final measure of the greatness of all peoples is in the amount and standard of the literature and art they have produced."

Thirteen months after Jessie Fauset's night at the Civic Club, the level of literary and artistic momentum by and about people of color would encourage Du Bois to write an article for the *Los Angeles Times* (June 14, 1925) captioned "A Negro Art Renaissance." According to him, the "vast hiatus in Negro development" was over and done with. Only five weeks earlier, the New York *Herald Tribune* had actually been the first to call what was happening a "Negro renaissance." The editor's new mind-set had come about mainly in response to Ovington's critical report the previous May almost amounting to a vote of no confidence. The wrist slap about the "good piece of research" prompted Du Bois's successful application to the American Fund for Public Research (the Garland Fund). There would be a notice in November 1925 that *The Crisis* had been awarded five thousand dollars to undertake research "in the social condition of American Negroes." The young scholar Horace Mann Bond had already been hired as the project's research assistant.

Meanwhile, Joel and Amy Spingarn had played the second card in the scheme hatched with Ovington to maneuver their prickly friend into recasting the magazine. Joel's unpredictable health kept them from attending the coming-out party, but both had been keen observers of the rising fascination with Negroes among sophisticated whites for some time. Expressing great faith in the potential of Negro art and letters, Amy enclosed a check for three hundred dollars in mid-July 1924 with a suggestion that *The Crisis* establish a "series of prizes for literary and possibly also artistic prizes."

On August 22, the NAACP released a brief press statement announcing the intention to underwrite several prizes for fiction and nonfiction; definite details would follow shortly. James Weldon Johnson received an additional three hundred dollars for the *Crisis* awards a week later along with Joel Spingarn's query about the Urban League's unexpected announcement earlier that month of plans for its own prize competition. "I shall be glad to hear any further news you may learn in regard to the way our thunder was stolen," wrote the association's dumbfounded treasurer. Although Charles Johnson rather generously explained away the *Opportunity* press release as a "singular coincidence," Du Bois thought he saw an unscrupulous end run by his fellow editor. "Neither I nor you had any idea that they were offering prizes until after your offer was made," he wrote the Spingarns. Anxious to preclude another public relations triumph by the Urban League editor, the board of directors authorized Du Bois in late September to offer *Crisis* prizes in five categories: short stories, drama, illustrations, poetry, and essays.

Looking back, it seems evident that any astute observer who monitored the psychological repackaging of people of color in the fiction of writers such as Theodore Dreiser, e. e. cummings, and Gertrude Stein, and in the cultural pronouncements of Greenwich Village intellectuals such as Randolph Bourne, Van Wyck Brooks, Waldo Frank, and Hart Crane could have predicted the seemingly sudden emergence during the early twenties of the black presence at the center of white Americans' cultural consciousness. Some of the Lost Generation had actually read Freud and Marx, Henri Bergson and Max Weber. Most of the others equipped themselves with ideas and vocabulary through osmosis. As a group, these artists and intellectuals subscribed to new ways of thinking and feeling about society that tended to subvert the rigid separation of public and private spheres, the total disconnect of civilized and savage, and the moral certainties of the Victorian order. They were the avatars of what a later generation would call Modernism, the belief system that would come to define most of the twentieth century.

A "new race, differently endowed," would bring back the joy that was dying "so rapidly in the Great Caucasian Race," novelist Edna Worthley Underwood exulted as she accepted Charles Johnson's invitation to judge the first *Opportunity* contest. She, like Van Doren and so many others of her Lost Generation, was ready to be saved by the "unspoiled," "intuitive," "sensual" Negro American—the only American supposedly still ruled by his id, a modern primitive wearing a loose-fitting superego, as in cummings's Jean Le Negre in *The Enormous Room* and O'Neill's Brutus Jones in *The Emperor Jones*. As 1926 unfolded, Du Bois and the principal officers of the NAACP agreed with Johnson at the Urban League that they were standing on the threshhold of a civil rights breakthrough by way of artistic, literary, dramatic, and musical achievement.

The double success of the first *Opportunity* Awards banquet in May 1925 and of the first *Crisis* Prizes presentation that August Du Bois saw as an earnest of the superior artistic and literary future he and the civil rights leadership were nurturing. The challenge to Talented Tenth custodians of culture, then, was to raise up the masses and lead them away from extreme separatism and dangerous radicalism. Locke's *The New Negro* would serve as the template of the arts-and-letters movement, "an extraordinary book [that] in many ways marks an epoch," Du Bois wrote in *The Crisis*. Published by Albert and Charles Boni at the end of 1925, the anthology had its origins in the collection of essays, short stories, letters, and poetry appearing in the March issue of the *Survey Graphic* that editor Paul Kellogg had excitedly proposed after the Civic Club gala. Assembled by Locke and entitled "Harlem: Mecca of the New Negro," this special number sold 42,000 copies, more than twice the magazine's regular circulation, and, by showcasing a variety of ideas and themes largely unsuspected by its upper-middle-class readership, it had primed the mainstream pump of expectations for more writings from this source. With contributions by Charles Johnson on the

Great Migration, James Weldon Johnson on "The Making of Harlem," Domingo on West Indians in Harlem, Herskovits on assimilation, Arthur Schomburg on the African past, Elise Johnson McDougald on sexual, racial, and economic emancipation of women, interspersed with lively Winold Reiss drawings of Roland Hayes, Paul Robeson, and Jackman, poems by Hughes, Cullen, McKay, Toomer, Anne Spencer, and Angelina Grimké, the *Survey Graphic* had featured much of the Renaissance talent pool. Du Bois's delightful "The Black Man Brings His Gifts" was commissioned for the issue, as was Rudolph Fisher's ironic "The South Lingers On."

Curiously, though, Du Bois was on a slow boil over Locke during this period. Of no small importance was the fact that the normally *politique* philosophy professor had failed to invite the wounded Fauset, who had been passed over in the *Survey Graphic*, to contribute to his *New Negro* anthology until Du Bois had sternly advised, "The more I think the matter over, the more I am convinced that something by Miss Fauset should appear in the book." Nor would he himself "feel at all like contributing" to the anthology without her presence there. Although Locke now dutifully took Fauset's "The Gift of Laughter," a kaleidoscope review of Negro dramatic comedy, Du Bois was not entirely appeased, and Locke was clearly disappointed with "The Negro Mind Reaches Out," a rehash of Du Bois's African travels that the Howard professor claimed had been casually tossed his way. Still smoldering, Du Bois then icily rejected the new Phillis Wheatley Publishing Company's proposal for a biography of himself as part of the series *Who's Who in Colored America* with Locke as the principal author. In strictest confidence, Du Bois told Roscoe Conkling Bruce, director of the publishing house and bearer of one of the race's most illustrious family names, that he wanted nothing more to do with Locke. "Recently he has shown repeatedly a nasty attitude toward *The Crisis,* and I am through." Locke's quicksilver mastery of ideas and fluency of expression (qualities that should have appealed) appear to have grated increasingly on Du Bois's intellectual temperament after the fussily self-assured Rhodes scholar revealed both a disinclination to defer to the editor and a greater compatibility with Johnson and the *Opportunity* group. The unsettling part that Locke and Johnson had come near playing in Du Bois's pan-African dispute with Beton in 1923 still rankled, and the professor's condescension to Fauset angered Du Bois further. There is also the warranted speculation that Alain Locke's brand of homosexuality, circumspect yet evident, was a factor in Du Bois's distate for the man.

Endowed with an exquisitely refined temperament, one infused with snobbery, decadence, and misogyny in about equal parts, Locke's aesthetic and social values were molded to the high-culture contours of Matthew Arnold and Walter Pater. Generations of Howard undergraduates could recall the classroom iteration that the "highest intellectual duty is the duty to be cultured." But many of the young men also became intimately acquainted with the cultured philosophy professor's epicene creed of the "superiority of the third sex," and, as the legendary Will Marion Cook's son, Mercer, revealed with mellow disapproval years after Locke's death, many a yokel freshman's head was turned in the beautiful apartment just off campus on R Street Northwest. Whatever he knew or cared about the unconventional details of Locke's private life (he still claimed to know almost nothing about homosexuality), Du Bois did care about a preciosity that could cast a mauve glow over politics and protest, making them flaccid and secondary to art and belles lettres. He had begun to fear that too much Locke could "turn the Negro renaissance into decadence" with young artists and writers doing "pretty things . . . to catch the passing fancy of the really unimportant critics and publishers." His careful reading of *The New Negro* discerned a disturbing intellectual temperament operating between the lines. Locke's explicit renunciation of propaganda and emphasis on beauty as the measure and object of literature and art were to be guarded against. In fact, *The New Negro* was "filled and bursting with propaganda," Du Bois countered, but it was precisely the kind of propaganda that was needed but that Locke was averse to. Du Bois wanted propaganda—masculinist propaganda infused by art and literature with social purpose and political efficacy. Locke, on the other hand, simply failed to grasp that there had never been a renaissance that wasn't a "passionate effort . . . made holy by the vision of eternal beauty," Du Bois insisted. To paraphrase a venerable French premier speaking about generals and the seriousness of war, Du Bois was cautioning that the purpose of art was too serious a business to be left to artists, a dictum whose exigency would soon compel him to break openly with the stalwarts of the Renaissance.

The facts were that Harlem's cultural explosion was not caused by *The Crisis* or *Opportunity*, though the mobilizing role of Du Bois and Johnson and their respective cadres was indispensable. Nor was the arts-and-letters movement brought into being solely through the nurturing fascination of Village bohemians and civil rights sympathies of wealthy and well-connected whites, even though white capital and influence were both crucial and constraining, at least in the early bohemian and Talented Tenth phases of the Renaissance. But for the decisive agency of the Great Migration, as Locke saw, none of these contributing elements could have amounted to much. "In the very process of being transplanted," he wrote, "the Negro is becoming transformed." Describing the massive relocation under way since the middle of the second decade as a part of a global quickening of peoples, Locke made the startling claim that, until the shaping of feelings, mores, grievances, aspirations, and ideas in the twin force vortexes of industrialization and nationalism, American Negroes had been a race "more in name than in fact, or to be exact, more in sentiment than in experience." Echoing Du Bois's "The Conservation of Races," the anthologist postulated that a great race was now in the making, stirring and moving. But would this stirring end in alienation and sedition, or was it a portent of participation and civic maturity? "The answer," Locke noted solemnly, "is in the migrating peasant."

Locke heard the early sounds of the migrating peasants' answer as they streamed into the large cities of the East and Midwest, and above all into Harlem in order to seize upon their first chances "for group self-expression and self-determination." When readers of the New Negro anthology turned to "The City of Refuge," Fisher's paragon short story about a Harlem migrant born to buy the Brooklyn Bridge twice, they met King Solomon Gillis, the epigone of Locke's stirring, restless mass man as he stumbled out of the Lenox Avenue subway at 135th Street for the first time, exclaiming, "Done died an' woke up in Heaven." The sight of a black cop bawling out a white driver was too much for Gillis: "Black might be white" in Harlem, "but it couldn't be that white." In Charles Johnson's "The New Frontage on Negro Life," readers could ponder migrant letters whose drab sincerity conveyed that self-determination alluded to by Locke. "I haven't heard a white man call a colored a nigger you know how — since I been here. I can ride the street or steam car anywhere I get a seat. . . . I am not crazy about being with white folks, but if I have to pay the same fare I have to learn to want the same acomidation [*sic*] and if you are first in place here shopping you don't have to wait till all the white folks get thro."

By no means was Locke the first to explain the new Negro arts movement in the context of the Great Migration bringing more than three hundred thousand Negroes out of the South in less than a decade. Emmett Scott, now serving as treasurer of Howard University, had made the first attempt at a comprehensive treatment with *Negro Migration During the War*, published in 1920. Woodson's *Negro in Our History* had followed two years later with a thoughtful chapter entitled "The Migration of the Talented Tenth." James Weldon Johnson and Du Bois had written prescient articles in the early twenties about the seismic consequences in store for the race and the nation from the surging exodus out of the South: power through the ballot, prosperity through decent jobs, due process in the courts, decent public education. Moreover, just as *The New Negro* arrived in bookstores, V. F. Calverton's two-year-old *Modern Quarterly* carried Du Bois's "The Social Origins of American Negro Art," a typically cogent overview of the subject that was an excellent companion piece. However individualistic the artistic and literary production of its Tanners, Braithwaites, and Chesnutts, or exceptional the promise of its Cullens, Hugheses, Fausets, and Hayeses, the arcing Aframerican creativity was propelled by "a certain group compulsion," Du Bois explained, "meaning that the wishes and thoughts and experiences of thousands of individuals influence consciously and unconsciously the message of the one who speaks for all." With greater economic freedom, people of color were going to deliver a more sophisticated, focused message, he insisted, adding, however (and with Locke no doubt in mind), that the method of expression would preclude for generations "the mere stylist and dilettante."

But it was still Locke's seminal *New Negro* essay that excelled in vivid, vitalist linkage of the migration to the urban crucible, the urban crucible to the Renaissance, the Renaissance to cultural awakenings worldwide, and, finally, the worldwide cultural awakenings to the construction of a modern group personality for people of color in the United States. Locke described the race as on the march into history, its movements increasingly governed by the collective mind. Like the persecuted Jews, Africans in America were acquiring an international sense of connectedness, he asserted. "A transformed and transforming psychology permeates the mass," the anthologist trumpeted. "The tide of Negro migration, northward and city-ward" was not "a blind flood started by the demands of war industry coupled with the shutting off of foreign migration." Crop failures and lynchings failed to explain the Great Migration. "The boll-weevil nor the Ku Klux Klan is a basic factor," he theorized in virtual disregard of socioeconomic data readily available and well known to him. It was not the "push" and "pull" of segregation and jobs that unleashed the migration, but a dramatic new stage in the psychology of the racial group — "a new dynamic phase, the buoyancy from within compensating for whatever pressure there may be of conditions from without." Readers were assured that what the New Negro had set about to accomplish was a "unique social experiment" whose ultimate objective was to become more American by becoming more Negro — "to build his Americanism on race values."

Those readers who reflected on Du Bois's famous passage in *The Souls of Black Folk* about the divided self may well have sensed that Locke's essay glossed over a paradox at this point, one that presaged trouble ahead for the consistency of Talented Tenth artistic and cultural ideals: "One ever feels his two-ness — An American, a Negro; two souls, two thoughts, two unreconciled strivings; two warring ideals in one dark body." Although *The New Negro* endowed "migrating peasants" with almost mystical powers of motion and growth, Locke actually revealed an even greater commitment than Du Bois now did to the agency of the Talented Tenth. In the final analysis, it must be the elites who would issue marching orders and set destinations for the masses, who would guide the organic mass bursting out of the South and reconstituting itself in cities across the nation. Class trumped mass. It would be in the achievements of "our talented groups" that the greatest gains for the greatest number of black people would come, Locke maintained with all the faith held by some of the Village bohemians in the power of cultural movements to alter political realities. Indeed, Locke invested the cultural recognition that was being won by intellectuals, artists, and writers with a revolutionary potency that bordered on the fabulous, postulating that such recognition "should in turn prove the key to that revaluation of the Negro which must precede or accompany any considerable further betterment of race relationships."

In a hallmark sentence in *The New Negro*, Locke promoted Harlem as the "race capital" and predicted that, "without pretense to their political signficance, Harlem has the same role to play for the New Negro as Dublin has had for the New Ireland or Prague for the New Czechoslovakia." All in all, Locke's introduction to *The New Negro* was a brilliant encapsulation of the social ambitions of a minuscule class of educated professionals, primarily located in the urban North, almost all of whom had imbibed Du Bois's notions of racial identity and civil rights militancy with their mothers' milk or on their fathers' knees. The "New Negro" essay was a manifesto as potentially meaningful for the emergence of a distinct, expanding, and vital Negro American artistic and literary production no longer subservient to "white" models as Emerson's "The American Scholar" had been for the promotion of American cultural independence from Great Britain almost a hundred years earlier.

AS DU BOIS and Charles Johnson entered into a competitive collaboration to promote (in Benjamin Brawley's words) "anything that calls attention to our development along the higher lines," both editors drew on the considerable resources of their organizations in order to accelerate the recruitment of able young men and women throughout 1925 and into the next year. In addition to the pool of five hundred or more entrants in *The Crisis* and *Opportunity* prizes and the much smaller number of actors and playwrights signing up for what Du Bois called his Krigwa productions, solicitations were sent to Negro newspaper editors in New York and across the country, as well as to literary clubs in Boston, Philadelphia, Washington, D.C., and Chicago, all with the aim of building an impressive cadre for the Renaissance as quickly as possible.* Secretaries in Du Bois's and Charles Johnson's offices, along with those on the staffs of James Weldon Johnson and Walter White, were told to comb the newspapers and college literary magazines and to clip and file any mention of aspiring writers, poets, musicians, and artists. Charles Johnson's new secretary, Ethel Ray, a brilliant, beautiful woman from Minnesota whose life would become deeply entangled with Du Bois's, kept meticulous, updated files. Many years later, she looked back on Johnson's management style and decided that "he could be quite ruthless, and maybe, as some people say, . . . he maneuvered people like chess on a board." Fauset and Dill could have said similar things about Du Bois. But the goal of inventing an arts-and-letters movement among people two generations out of slavery, the overwhelming majority of whom could scarcely

---

*Krigwa: Crisis Guild of Writers and Artists.

have regarded painting, poetry, and novels as anything other than a bewildering conceit and luxury, was a priority that consumed huge amounts of time and application in the NAACP and the Urban League.

In faraway Kansas, for example, Aaron Douglas, fed up with teaching art to high school students and wondering if he would ever see Paris, received what was tantamount to a Renaissance induction notice in the summer of 1925. At Johnson's behest, Ray, who had met Douglas while serving as secretary of the Kansas City Urban League, sent the twenty-six-year-old painter an ultimatum: "Better to be a dishwasher in New York than to be head of a high school in Kansas City." Taking the bait, Douglas closed his bank account and presented himself for duty at the *Opportunity* office in the fall of 1925, whence Ray and the fine short-story writer and business manager, Eric Walrond, led him to Harlem's Sugar Hill and the apartment Ray shared with librarian Regina Anderson and Louella Tucker at 580 St. Nicholas Avenue. One historian of the period called the apartment at 580 "a sort of Renaissance USO, offering a couch, a meal, [and] sympathy." Not long afterward, Du Bois advised Douglas of an "unexpected vacancy" in the *Crisis* stockroom. His credentials vouched for by Du Bois and Charles Johnson, Reiss, the German-American magazine illustrator who had done the art work for the *Survey Graphic* special, took Douglas on as an apprentice. He could "follow right into [Reiss's] own footsteps," said Douglas. "I had hardly reached the city before I was called upon to prepare cover designs and drawings and sketches" for *Opportunity* and *The Crisis*. Some of what he drew in a frenzy of learning, he later feared may have been "monstrous." Even so, his patrons "ate this sort of thing up," Douglas chuckled, and the Harlem Renaissance acquired its "official" illustrator, painter, and muralist.

Arna Bontemps, Zora Neale Hurston, and Wallace Thurman were already in Harlem when Douglas arrived. Bontemps and Thurman were the same age (twenty-three), worked as mail clerks in the same Los Angeles post office, and aspired to become famous as writers (Thurman aimed for the Great American Negro Novel), but they couldn't have been more unalike physically and temperamentally. Suave and politely taciturn, Bontemps was a double for the poet who would become his best friend, Langston Hughes, though somewhat handsomer, with chiseled features and a burnished roseate complexion that made him look young always. Wally Thurman was small, thin, hyperkinetic, and so dark-skinned that, when the extravagant Richard Bruce Nugent met him, Nugent cried that anyone so brilliant should have to be so black. Bontemps's origins were Louisiana Creole, Thurman's a mysterious and improbable genesis in Salt Lake City, Utah. Dissimilar yet yoked together by literary aspirations, both men had followed the Harlem scene avidly ever since the appearance of McKay's *Harlem Shadows*. In mid-August 1924, *The Crisis* arrived with Bontemps's first published poem. He quit the Los Angeles central post office, "packed [his] suitcase and bought a ticket for New York City." It took Thurman a few months more to arrange his affairs before he could enroll in the Renaissance and become its most probing iconoclast.

Hurston showed up at the *Opportunity* offices in early January 1925 with less than two dollars in her purse, but with an excess of what a later generation would recognize as attitude. She was older by ten years than her declared 1901 birthdate. She had come a long way from Eatonville, the all-black Florida town run by her preacher father, a larger-than-life patriarch who lost interest in Zora and her siblings after the death of their mother. "Jump at sun, chile," her doting mother had told her repeatedly. Working her way through Howard University as a manicurist, Hurston had so impressed the mysogynist Locke with her writing ability that he called her to Charles Johnson's attention. "Drenched in Light" had run in the magazine the year before, and "Spunk," a second beautifully crafted short story with a peasant focus and written in luscious vernacular, was already a top contender in the first *Opportunity* awards. With an I.Q. off the charts and a "bodaciousness" to match (Hurston was the neologist of the Renaissance, coining the pungent nouns "Niggerati" and "Negrotarian"), she moved quickly from 580 St. Nicholas to the position of secretary to novelist Fannie Hurst and, with Johnson's intercession, a full scholarship to Barnard. She would be one of the strongest novelists of the movement, its sole avowed feminist, and, as was already manifest through "Drenched in Light," the writer most in touch with the souls of those black folk who were yet to migrate to the cities, or had only just gotten there.

A reflective essay on the significance of Eugene O'Neill by one of the movement's prize recruits, Paul Robeson, ran in the December 1924 *Opportunity*. The well-established New York law firm headed by Rutgers trustee William Louis Stotesbury had seen the last of Columbia Law School graduate Robeson more than two years earlier. More than likely, after his unflattering notices in a 1922 Freudian pastiche called *Taboo* on Broadway and *Voodoo* in London, Robeson had prudently retired whatever acting aspirations he may have had in favor of the law. But white secretaries disliked taking dictation from "nigger" lawyers and the Stotesbury firm's clients cringed at the prospect of rulings handed down by judges unaccustomed to black attorneys appearing before them. Out of the blue came an urgent invitation from Provincetown Players director Kenneth MacGowan for the lead in *All God's Chillun Got Wings*. The rest, as they say, was history—history and Walter White, who claimed, with a good deal of plausibility, that he had convinced a still unsure Robeson to give up law for acting and for the greater glory of the Renaissance. Robeson's *Opportunity* essay, "Reflections on O'Neill's Plays," read like copy from Charles Johnson's desk—"I am sure that there will come Negro playwrights of great power and I trust that I shall have some part in interpreting that most interesting and much needed addition to the drama of America"—and may have been.

Du Bois was guardedly pleased by the way the Talented Tenth Renaissance was taking shape. *Appearances*, a play by an elementary school dropout and San Francisco bellhop, was a case in point. The play opened on Broadway in mid-October 1925 at the Frolic Theatre and survived for twenty-three nights, the first full-length production written by a Negro. The plot involved rape and exoneration due to the sheer force of the accused's character. Al Jolson had lobbied Manhattan theatrical backers on behalf of the author, Garland Anderson, and President Coolidge had said a good word for *Appearances* after a White House meeting with the playwright. Noting that "everybody who saw it was enthusiastic"—white as well as black—Du Bois praised *Appearances* as "an excellent play" in *The Crisis*. Considering the fact that the artistically more sensitive James Weldon Johnson also thought *Appearances* was farily good, perhaps, after all, the play did offer more than uplifting racial propaganda. The editor noted with particular pride in June 1925 that *Vanity Fair* was publishing five poems by Cullen and Harper & Brothers was about to release *Color*, the young man's first volume of poetry. To read but "a few stanzas of Countee Cullen's great poem, 'The Shroud of Color,' " was enough to show all Americans the depth and power of the new movement, Du Bois promised. Cullen's long, somber mediations on the burden of race and the divided self began in an agony of shame and irresolution and ended, after a dozen stanzas, on a note of clearheaded affirmation: "And somehow it was borne upon my brain/How being dark, and living through the pain/Of it, is courage more than angels have."

When Knopf released *The Weary Blues* in spring 1926, Du Bois lavished praise on Hughes's first volume of poetry, as he would *Fine Clothes to the Jew*, Hughes's second volume, the following year. The editor had grown increasingly fond of the twenty-three-year-old ever since their first encounter, a Civic Club luncheon arranged by Fauset for the somewhat shy poet and his loquacious mother during Hughes's first and only semester at Columbia in the fall of 1921. Hoping to avoid appearing "as dumb as I felt myself to be," the poet had been a bundle of nerves that day about meeting the austere legend, who, as it turned out, was almost affectionate. Wanderlust and boredom with studies had caused Hughes to sail away from America soon after meeting Du Bois, dumping his college books into the ocean along with any ambitions for a conventional middle-class life. He had actually been to West Africa, a distinction the poet and editor alone shared among the New Negroes. An excellent brain and an impressive Talented Tenth family pedigree (one ancestor had fought beside John Brown at Harper's Ferry; another, John Mercer Langston, had gone to the U.S. House of Representatives from Virginia) endeared the young man who was only three years older than Du Bois's son, Burghardt, would have been.

The second *Opportunity* awards banquet took place in early May 1926, with Du Bois once more on the road and Charles Johnson masterminding what appeared to be another upward turn of the race relations spiral. Some of the winners would fall into obscurity rather quickly. Lee Wallace, who took third prize in the short-story competition, can hardly have impressed judges Zona Gale, Jean Toomer, and Carl Van Doren, any more than Ford Kramer of Lincoln University and Ariel Williams of Fisk University, who shared first prize for poetry, gave Witter Bynner, Vachel Lindsay, or Robert Frost much reason to want to see them return the following year. The gifted Louisville poet Joseph Cotter and the determined academic playwright John Matheus would be back. Somewhat surprisingly, though, Hurston's "Muttsy," a charming story about venial backsliding in the wicked city, was pushed to second place by Arthur Fauset, who went on to win first prize in the essay competition. Arna Bontemps rose to receive the one-hundred-dollar Alexander Pushkin Prize for the poem "Golgotha Is a Mountain," a splendid vindication for Bontemps's having had the pluck to leave the Los Angeles post office. Of the many Renaissance prizes, the Pushkin was unique in being endowed by a single Negro donor, Caspar Holstein, the numbers king of Harlem.

As the pell-mell release by major publishing houses of works by and about people of color continued, the editor's enthusiasm for the arts-and-letters gambit grew. *Tropic Death*, the marvelous collection of well-spun, macabre short stories by Trinidadian Eric Walrond, appeared from Boni & Liveright at the end of 1926. Studding his approving review with qualifiers such as "impish," "somber," "fatal," Du Bois confessed that the book's impressionism and heavy use of Caribbean dialect made it "hard reading and difficult to understand in parts," but a work, nevertheless, of "deep significance and great promise." *The Crisis* also carefully tracked the appearance in the South of more sympathetic literature about the race. Two aristocratic South Carolina writers, Julia Peterkin and DuBose Heyward, had rediscovered the descendants of their ancestors' slaves with an empathy scarcely seen in the Deep South since the novels of George Washington Cable.

The new Negro arts-and-letters movement had begun to take on an animation every bit as kinetic as that to be seen nightly on the ballroom floor of the cavernous new Savoy. The movement energized people of color in the large metropoli as well as in hundreds of good-sized towns where earnest literary and dramatics groups (usually run by prim, light-skinned wives of doctors, lawyers, preachers, and teachers) discussed novels, plays, poetry, and nonfiction, a few of these groups even tithing themselves to support a publication. Philadelphians published *Black Opals*, one of the best of the little reviews. Bostonians launched the *Saturday Evening Quill*. In Washington, Georgia Johnson regularly attracted such stellar out-of-towners to read, talk, and drink with her coterie of "Saturday

Nighters" as Du Bois, James Welson Johnson, Fauset, and Hughes. A tell-all Harlem newspaper with a national readership that placed the private lives of public figures under a powerful magnifying glass, *The Inter-State Tattler* had begun its weekly run in 1925. The *Tattler* excelled as a well-written gossip sheet with a racial conscience, and was even capable of serious literary commentary. It paused to note the significance of Walter White's 1926 Guggenheim Fellowship, the first of a half dozen to be awarded by the new foundation to persons of color. The NAACP associate secretary's second novel, *Flight* (the pros and con's of passing), had been in bookstores for several months and *The Fire in the Flint*, his first novel, was being translated into French and Japanese.

From Du Bois's perspective, what was truly of serious significance was the second wave of monetary encouragement of New Negro potential. In January 1926, the William E. Harmon Foundation decided to shift its philanthropy from loans to students and aid to the blind to awards to Negro Americans. The Harmon Foundation announced the striking of seven annual gold and bronze medals for prizes in literature, music, fine arts, industry, science, education, and race relations, with an eighth prize of five hundred dollars reserved for a distinguished American of any race. Boni & Liveright announced a one-thousand-dollar prize that March for the "best novel on Negro life" by a writer of "Negro descent." For the musically gifted, there were prizes in the Louis Rodman Wanamaker Musical Competition. Rosenwald Fellowships for deserving southerners of both races would come in 1928. Qualitatively comparable to Guggenheim Fellowships, the Rosenwald grants to individual scholars, writers, and artists were to finance a major portion of the professional training of the second generation of the Talented Tenth. Numbers king Holstein's endowment of the *Opportunity* Pushkin Prize, Van Vechten's contribution to the *Opportunity* treasury, and Amy Spingarn's six hundred dollars in support of the *Crisis* awards were broadcast by the NUL and the NAACP as proof that the New Negro Arts and Letters Movement had come of age. The Talented Tenth phase of the Renaissance appeared to be so institutionally anchored and economically solid that the production of books, plays, paintings, and sculpture would be fostered and controlled for many years to come by the elite of the civil rights leadership. James Weldon Johnson, the most adroit race diplomat on the scene and one of the most cosmopolitan men in the country, also came to the conclusion that the old approaches— "religious, educational, political, industrial, ethical, economic, sociological"—had been superseded, he wrote, by what "may be called the art approach to the Negro problem." Here was the agenda affording the least friction and, Johnson would claim as late as 1928 in *Harper's*, "great and rapid progress . . . and a common platform upon which most people are willing to stand."

But the "art approach" was no longer a platform on which Du Bois was willing to stand. The magic of the movement had pretty well worn off for him by summer of 1926. There was a profound difference in how most white and colored artists, writers, and intellectuals conceived the ultimate ends to which they pledged their talent and genius. The Lost Generation *révoltés* were lost in the sense that they professed to have no wish to find themselves in a mammon-mad, homogenizing, materialistic American society. The New Negroes of the arts and letters movement wanted full acceptance in mainstream America, even if some, like Du Bois and McKay, might exercise sooner rather than later the privilege of rejecting it. For the modernist whites, art was the means to change society before they would embrace it fully. For the Late Victorian Negroes, art was the means to change society in order to be partly accepted into it. For this reason, although Du Bois and George Schuyler and many of those who were driving forces in the Renaissance found the Negro vogue by whites to be problematic at best, they gritted their teeth over white insensitivity, voyeurism, calumny, and burlesquing as long as they could believe that the civil rights benefits of the culture strategy were potentially greater than the liabilities. As literary critic Benjamin Brawley put the issue bluntly to James Weldon Johnson at the start of the Renaissance: "We have a tremendous opportunity to boost the NAACP, letters, and art, and anything else that calls attention to our development along the higher lines." "Development along the higher lines" was in the eye of the beholder, however, and Brawley and Du Bois would experience, like many custodians of culture, alternating elation and despair as they monitored what the vogue in blackness produced.

The 1921 Broadway hit *Shuffle Along*, with music and lyrics by the magical Negro team of Flournoy Miller, Aubrey Lyle, and Eubie Blake, had shaped the Broadway musical, popularized the Charleston, and given the Jazz Age two of its classic songs, "I'm Just Wild About Harry" and "Love Will Find a Way." Du Bois had heartily approved of *Shuffle Along*, less so of *Blackbirds*, a raging Broadway success starring Florence Mills; and not at all of Mills in the coarse *Dixie to Broadway* running in December 1924, or of *Chocolate Dandies* by Miller and Lyle that same year (introducing a bandy-legged Josephine Baker). The even more demeaning box-office breakthroughs *Liza* and *Runnin' Wild* he found disheartening. But the brilliant, flawed Charles Gilpin as Brutus Jones in *The Emperor Jones* pleased Du Bois enormously, as had Paul Robeson's debut in the spring of 1923 as a serious actor in *All God's Chillun*. The editor and his Talented Tenth associates were positively enchanted by tenor Roland Hayes, whose Town Hall concert in December 1923 of lieder and spirituals was a triumph comparable to that of the Fisk Jubilee Singers fifty years earlier. "There will never be another concert like that first one at Town Hall," Ovington enthused. The NAACP awarded Hayes the Spingarn Medal, its highest honor. Exactly one year later, 1924, baritone Jules Bledsoe, still a Columbia University medical student, sang a program of Handel, Bach, Purcell, and Brahms at Aeolian Hall to the unalloyed delight of the editor. Bledsoe was a large, gay, very black man with a razor wit and an infectious laugh who would soon be a feature of the landscape in a Packard landau that careened dangerously through the Harlem streets. Then came *Lulu Belle*, a musical melodrama, and Du Bois may have had to fight an urge to cancel the Renaissance, although he wrote an equivocal review that the popular David Belasco, the show's producer, found to his liking. Opening on Broadway in February 1926 and starring white Lenore Ulric in blackface, *Lulu Belle* was a racially exploitative farce that pretended to depict Harlem street life. It virtually jump-started the rush of sightseeing Caucasians to those parts of Harlem where people of color were predominant.

Until the spring of 1926, the influx of outside Caucasians had been largely confined to parlor socialists and progressives on civil rights business and to venturesome artists, writers, and musicians, mostly from Greenwich Village and often guided by caustic McKay and, later, Eric Walrond, smooth as long-staple cotton. After *Lulu Belle*, the white influx was democratized, and almost anybody with a hip flask and taxi fare became a candidate for a night at the Cotton Club, Connie's Inn, or Small's Paradise. In March 1926, the cavernous, block-long Savoy opened its doors in Harlem. With its marble staircase, cut-glass chandeliers, and 250-foot, burnished maple dance floor anchored by two band-stands at either end, the Savoy offered Aframericans and Caucasians a temple in which to stomp through the Jazz Age. Out of the guide business and now on the staff of *Opportunity*, Walrond wrote frankly that Harlem was becoming "a white man's house of assignation." The situation distressed Du Bois and Charles Johnson even more than it did the Trinidadian writer. By the following summer, neither would be amused by Rudolph Fisher's witty piece in *The American Mercury*, "The Caucasian Storms Harlem," in which a long-absent denizen exclaims, as he roams old haunts, "What a lot of fays [whites]!" "The best of Harlem's black cabarets have changed their names and turned white," he laments. Jack Johnson's Club Deluxe (the old Douglass Club) had become the Cotton Club in 1923, owned now by Owney Madden and the Chicago mob who banned Negroes as patrons (Jules Bledsoe was among the occasional exceptions) but hired them, "tall, tan, and terrific," by the dozens as performers. In another year, the drawing power of the quarter would have reached far beyond the five boroughs of New York City, pulling into the whirring force field between 130th and 145th streets legions of gawking, bibulous whites in frenzied nightly flight from prohibition, as well as swarms of untested singers, dancers, and musicians hoping to spend enough time in the presence of an Ethel Waters, Bojangles Robinson, or a Fletcher Henderson to be able to divine the secrets of professional success and celebrity.

By 1927, Harlem had become the Jazz Age's address of choice. One Hundred Thirty-third Street was the "Jungle," location of Brown's, Dicky Wells's, Connor's, Mexico's, and the Clam House where the huge, sexually ambiguous Glady's Bentley ("pianist and torrid warbler") held court. The Nest Club was there, the Jungle nightspot favored by some of Harlem's own society folk such as Rudolph Fisher's sister Pearl and his future wife. Two blocks north was "P & J's" (the Catagonia Club) where Willie "the Lion" Smith performed. P & J's was favored by Al Smith, Beatrice Lillie, Jimmy Walker, Tallulah Bankhead and her Harlem beau George, and other downtown swells. The place gave the tortured musical prodigy Artie Shaw a "temporary haven," and drew in Bix Beiderbecke, Hoagy Carmichael, Benny Goodman, the Dorsey Brothers, and Paul Whiteman, all of whom took away impressions that made their own music more special, yet not too black. With a little persistence, contacts, and money, the likes of Phil Harris, Mae West, and Van Vechten could gain entry to the transvestite floor shows, sex circuses, and marijuana parlors along 140th Street. As far as can be determined, Du Bois and Jimmy Durante never met, but if they had Du Bois would have been greatly pained by what the comedian had to say about white people on safari above Central Park. "You go sort of primitive up here," the comedian warned, "with the bands moaning blues like nobody's business, slim, bare-thighed brown-skin gals tossing their torsos, and the Negro melody artists bearing down something terrible on the minor notes." When producer Lew Leslie underwrote the tempestuous *Blackbirds of 1928*, with Bojangles dancing on Broadway for the first time and "I Can't Give You Anything But Love" mesmerizing audiences for five hundred curtains, Harlem, "Mecca of the New Negro," had become, it seemed, equally as much the mecca of the new whites.

WHEN LOCKE COINED the expression "Mecca of the New Negro" in the spring of 1925, the skid into what the custodians of culture would deplore as demeaning parody and vulgar exhibitionism—the period from *Lulu Belle* to *Blackbirds*—had not quite begun. The Harlem Renaissance as arts and letters calculated to impress the best whites and make the best blacks proud had seemed securely under way. Although his disenchantment appeared to come on in a rush, in reality Du Bois had been wrestling with doubts about the Renaissance that only grew the more he tried to ignore them. He had always worried about what he saw as the inherent susceptibility of an artistic and literary enterprise to go off track, spinning in its own momentum away from what he deemed to be the central purpose. By temperament and politics, he was always inclined to take *The Crisis* in a different direction, one that Fauset, Johnson, and White found increasingly less appealing. He had gravely informed his readers in May 1925 that the magazine would soon begin to focus on issues such as economic development, political independence, educational policy, and international peace, as well as the arts; and he warned that *The Crisis* would become "more frankly critical of the Negro group." Du Bois continued to be nagged by misgivings. Locke's denigration of propaganda, the ubiquity and persiflage of the decadent Van Vechten, the growing resistence of the younger writers and poets to advice from their seniors, whirligig cocktail parties downtown and nightclubbing uptown that substituted for the integration of Manhattan restaurants and hotels, motorcades and Hudson River excursions to A'Lelia Walker's Villa Lewaro, sex in three genders, and demeaning voyeurism—it all began to grate on the editor's civil rights nerves.

When the association met for its annual convention in Chicago in late June 1926, Du Bois took the podium, his dry voice rising, to insist that "all art is propaganda and ever must be, despite the wailing of the purists." Storytelling, versifying, painting, and the rest had value only to the extent that society stood to gain something positive from them, and Du Bois was appalled when artists arrogated the right to express themselves without due, circumspect regard for racial sensibilities or just plain good manners. As for art for art's sake, this was a concept as close to blasphemy as an agnostic Du Bois could conceive. The civic function of the arts was what mattered above all else. "I do not care a damn for any art that is not used for propaganda," he fairly shouted from the platform in Chicago. Universality, catholicity, transcendent beauty—these were noble ideals, commendable goals, he went on to say. The day would ultimately come when there would be artists and writers whom white America would praise simply as the finest practitioners of their craft. "And then do you know what will be said?" Du Bois asked rhetorically. "Just as soon as true art emerges; just as soon as the black artist appears, someone touches the race on the shoulder and says, 'He did that because he was an American, not because he was a Negro. . . . He is just human; it is the kind of thing you ought to expect.' " Human beings belong to races, though, and the Negro race had to determine for itself what kind of art and literature it wanted to promote.

A. Philip Randolph had held the convention delegates spellbound with his liquid bass voice when he spoke the night before of the Brotherhood of Sleeping Car Porters' struggles to be recognized by the Pullman Corporation. Clarence Darrow, the hero of Detroit, evoked the fighting legacy of John Brown while two thousand spectators had to be turned away from the auditorium. Du Bois's delivery was no match for theirs, but, message for message, his speech addressed concerns no less vital. He insisted that his audience understand that the Renaissance and its offshoots involved the whole question of group identity. "What do we want? What is the thing we are after?" Was it simply to be "full-fledged

Americans?" But surely, people of color were more than just Americans, he urged. "The ultimate judge has got to be you," he commanded in this extraordinary lecture he called "Criteria of Negro Art." It was their universality, catholicity, humanity that mattered above all else. "We who are dark can see America in a way that white Americans can not." There was a growing danger of the Renaissance being coopted, of "handing everything over to a white jury." As in *Souls*, where Du Bois described the state of racial being "of always looking at one's self through the eyes of others," so the dilemma of second sightedness animated his words to the NAACP convention: "If a colored man wants to publish a book, he has got to get a white publisher and a white newspaper to say it is great; and then you and I say so."

The full implications of "Criteria of Negro Art" would be delayed until the end of the year when it appeared as the punctuating document in the seven-month *Crisis* series "The Negro in Art." This series (symposium, Du Bois called it) had already been announced in February, more than five months before the Chicago convention, in an issue that carried a seven-part questionnaire sent out by the editor to authors and publishers. There was something slapdash and repetitive about it, however. Clearly, Fauset hadn't been asked to give the document the benefit of her punctilious scrutiny. Corrected for overlap, the seven questions boiled down to five: whether an artist was "under any obligations or limitations as to the sort of character" he or she should portray; the social obligations of publishers; countermeasures for racist literature; the class perspective appropriate to black fiction; and the vulnerabilities of young black and white writers. Questions four and seven went to the heart of Du Bois's concerns— didn't the "pathos, humiliation, and tragedy" of America's "educated Negroes" deserve as much sincere sympathy as DuBose Heyward had lavished on illiterates in *Porgy*? Or to put the same matter another way—wouldn't the stream of novels about the "debauched tenth" (as Du Bois wrote elsewhere) discourage the new crop of Negro talents from writing truthfully about themselves and their own social class? Responses to the questionnaire were already in hand from Van Vechten, Sinclair Lewis, and the now forgotten Major Haldane McFall, noted the February *Crisis*. Each month thereafter, until the symposium ended that October, the magazine would publish the replies.

If the arts symposium was intended to draw the attention of white writers and publishers to what Du Bois saw as an almost unrelieved portrayal of denigrated black life in fiction, the responses of Alfred Knopf and John Farrar could have been only partially reassuring. There had been an almost palpable ire and pain in Du Bois's fourth question about people of color being "continually painted at their worst and judged by the public as they are painted." Knopf dismissed the question about the social obligations of publishers as "senseless" and doubted that good writers were handicapped or seduced by popular fascination with squalid subject matter. Farrar called for Negroes to display "as little self-consciousness as possible," took delight in what Du Bois had deplored as the "monstrosities" of Octavus Roy Cohen's coon stories, felt that *The Fire in the Flint* was "a trifle one-sided," and agreed with Knopf that Du Bois's social and ethical concerns about the "creative spirit" were misplaced. In any case, the fundamental problem was twofold, most of the whites counseled: too much racial sensitivity and not enough artistic quality (yet). What Negroes had to complain about any more than whites when it came to caricature and mockery was a mystery to Sherwood Anderson. The Irish had survived *Mr. Jiggs* and the Jews *Mr. Potash*, as Farrar and Julia Peterkin recalled. Ovington, chairperson of the NAACP, even denied that Du Bois's claim of negative portrayals held any truth, at least "within the past few years." Hooting at bad white depictions of blacks, Mencken wanted to know why the Renaissance novelists didn't turn the tables and ridicule the whites — "What a chance!" Meantime, as Van Vechten admonished in *Vanity Fair* and on his *Crisis* questionnaire, Negroes were "moanin' wid' a sword in ma han' " while white writers were running away with a "wealth of novel, exotic, picturesque material." Nobody was interested in Du Bois and his Talented Tenth peers as literary subjects for the very good reason that they were, indeed, just like white folks "of the same class," Van Vechten twittered. On the other hand, the squalor of Negro life — "the vice of Negro life" — was irresistible! Among the white respondents, only Vachel Lindsay agreed that major publishing houses deserved censure for showing a distinct aversion to manuscripts dealing with educated and accomplished people of color. Yet even the puritanical Benjamin Brawley found that proposition unacceptable; after all, publishing was a business like any other.

It was curious that, of some twenty symposium respondents, it was neither Joel Spingarn, founder of the school of New Criticism, nor Sinclair Lewis, the future Nobel laureate, who provided the most perceptive set of answers, but the novice man of letters Walter White instead. White had no doubt that the literary tradition of denigration decried by Du Bois was patently harmful and not to be finessed by a simpleminded sense of humor. But racist denigration was also "bad art" that good publishers ought to be capable of weaning themselves from. As for artistic freedom to write about black life at the bottom or from the Striver's Row top, White insisted that the only imperative was that it be genuine and well done. Regretting that, at the very moment when they were beginning to be read, "there should arise a division of opinion as to what or what not" should be written, the associate secretary sighed philosophically that it was only to be expected. Even as Du Bois's symposium published the first responses from Van Vechten, Mencken, and Heyward, the Talented Tenth phase of the New Negro

Arts Movement was about to end in a riot of controversy. Phase three of the Renaissance — the Negro Renaissance — made its appearance that spring with all the decorum of a Harlem rent party. It would last almost a decade, although its vitality would have been spent by the time the New Deal was organized. The division of opinion that was about to renounce Du Bois's custodial authority and radically diminish the canon of artistic civicism expressed itself in the same April issue that had carried White's lengthy response. "I think like this," was all Langston Hughes had to say in a few pithy sentences. "What's the use of saying anything — the true literary artist is going to write about what he chooses anyway regardless of outside opinion." Du Bois wrote about intelligent Negroes, Rudolph Fisher about the unintelligent ones. "Both of you are right," declared the young poet.

When his symposium turn came, Countee Cullen spoke out eloquently in the name of the younger generation against the freewheeling brand of artistic license espoused by Hughes and some of the others. Du Bois could not have wished for a better statement of Late Victorian principles than his future son-in-law's symposium contribution. His would be the last vote, Cullen stated primly, "for any infringement of artistic freedom," but, alas, the poet prodigy knew that all was not so simple. Negroes had not quite yet a sufficient corpus of "sound, healthy race literature" to justify writing about aberrant subjects that other people were "all too prone to accept as truly legitimate." He would never turn away from true art, Cullen insisted, but what the race needed urgently were fictional types that were "truly representative of us as a people." Anyone audacious enough to point to statements in Du Bois's own writings eloquently defending the opposite position on art and culture would have been immobilized by a piercing stare in the spring and summer of 1926. How many times had Du Bois censured the religious parochialism of the race, its constricting peasant morality that made sexual intercourse a crude sine qua non of procreation? Delighted by the women in Toomer's *Cane*, had he not written almost maliciously of frank portrayals that would cause black readers to "shrink and criticize"? At the Chicago NAACP convention had he not sensitively examined the historic reasons black folk had learned to look nervously over their shoulders whenever they enjoyed themselves or confided their deepest truths — why they had been so long ashamed and apologetic for a past they had only just begun to value? "Our worst side has been so shamelessly emphasized that we are denying that we have or ever had a worst side," he lectured. Again and again, Du Bois had inveighed against the cultural taboos of sex, color, and class that hobbled the creative spirit of the race. He relished British novelist Ronald Firbank's *Prancing Nigger* at least partly from a desire to challenge his readers to surmount a visceral repugnance for the title of a book whose fabulous Antillean tale they should certainly read. Yet now that the Talented Tenth Renaissance had begun to attract young artists unfettered by racial taboos—men and women who saw art not only as antithetical to propaganda but as the expression of their own individualism—Du Bois's own deep antimodernist taboos surfaced.

When the editor read Hughes's "The Negro Artist and the Racial Mountain" in *The Nation*, at the end of June, he saw his worst fears confirmed about the direction the movement was taking. If he harbored reservations about Cullen's high-culture objections to *The Weary Blues* and took exception to Schuyler's deriding Renaissance writers as nothing less than "lamp-blacked Anglo-Saxons," Du Bois could only look upon Hughes's sassy essay as a deeply disturbing manifestation of anarchy, rather than the declaration of artistic independence intended by its author. Schuyler's "The Negro Art Hokum" had run in *The Nation* the week before Hughes's "The Negro Artist and the Racial Mountain." Writing at his ribald best there, Schuyler dismissed the racialism of the Renaissance as sheer nonsense and "no more 'expressive of the Negro soul'—as the gushers put it—than are the scriblings of Octavus Cohen or Hugh Wiley." Metaphorically speaking, Hughes turned his backside to the editor of *The Crisis*, Schuyler, Brawley, Cullen, Fauset, and every custodian of culture north and south—and mooned them. There was poor, misguided Cullen (indentified only as "one of the most promising of the young Negro poets"), who simply wanted to be " 'a poet—not a Negro poet,' meaning subconsciously, . . . 'I want to write like a white poet'; meaning behind that . . . 'I would like to be white.' " But great poets are never afraid to be themselves, said Hughes—never willing to let the mountain of racial denial get in their way. Poets and novelists from bourgeois families where the catechism ran "don't be like niggers" were only capable of producing bourgeois poems and novels. The mountain of Nordic manners, "Nordic faces, Nordic hair, Nordic art (if any), and an Episcopal heaven" was too high a mountain to climb. Better to plant one's feet solidly on the plain, with regular excursions into the deep gorges where the low-down folks, "the so-called common element," abounded. Here was "a great field of unused material" that was alien to the "Nordicized Negro intelligentsia." Hughes's essay roared to its now famous finish as it summoned the blare of Negro jazz bands "and the bellowing voice of Bessie Smith singing Blues" to ring in the ears of the "colored near-intellectual[s]. . . .

> We younger Negro artists who create now intend to express our individual dark-skinned selves without fear or shame. If white people are pleased we are glad. If they are not, it doesn't matter. We know we are beautiful. And ugly too. The tom-tom cries and the tom-tom laughs. If colored people

are pleased we are glad. If not, their displeasure doesn't matter either. We build our temples for tomorrow, strong as we know how, and we stand on top of the mountain, free within ourselves.

Van Vechten's novel *Nigger Heaven*, and Wallace Thurman's magazine, *Fire!!*, were like one-two punches to the solar plexus for Du Bois. Knopf released *Nigger Heaven* in August 1926. *Fire!!* appeared in November. Van Vechten's gamy novel enraged Harlemites to the point that the gangling author became persona non grata above Central Park, banished from A'Lelia Walker's "Dark Tower" mansion at 136th Street. True enough, James Weldon Johnson thought Van Vechten's tragic love story of frustration, seduction, betrayal, homicide, the capers of the low-down and the pretentions of the snobs was a marvelous breakthrough. But even his loyal secretary, Richetta Randolph, adamantly demurred. "I am serious when I say," she entreated her employer, "that I think only you can redeem Mr. Van Vechten by writing something to counteract what he has done." For Du Bois, *Nigger Heaven* was a "blow in the face," an affront to the hospitality of black folk and to the intelligence of white. The best-selling novel, containing an epigraph poem by Hughes, reeked of precisely the kind of decadence, debauchery, and squalor that its author had commended in "The Negro in Art" symposium. That it was the first novel by a white author to cover the Harlem Renaissance scene only made Van Vechten's alleged voyeurism that much more sinister. Under Thurman's editorship, *Fire!!*, "Devoted to the Younger Negro Artists," assembled the Young Turks of the movement — Nugent, Douglas, Hurston, Bennett, Edward Silvera, Waring Cuney, Arthur Huff Fauset, and John Preston Davis. Hughes and Thurman jointly authored the free-form verse giving the goal of what was to be a one-issue quarterly: ". . . Beauty/ . . . flesh on fire — on fire in the furnace of life blazing. . . . /'Fy-ah,/Fy-ah, Lawd,/ Fy-ah gonna burn ma soul!' " The magazine's editors acknowledged Van Vechten's patronage and admired influence by calling for a statue in his honor at the corner of 135th Street and Seventh Avenue, where he had been hanged in effigy. To compound the insurgency, *Fire!!* published Nugent's "Smoke, Lilies and Jade," a paean to pederasty and androgyny in which Hughes, Harold Jackman, and the cartoonist Miguel Covarrubias appeared in transparent disguise. Refusing to be provoked, the editor of *The Crisis* sportingly confined himself to a one-line notice of the magazine's appearance. Theophilous Lewis, the *Messenger*'s literary and theater critic, snapped that he had thrown his copy of *Fire!!* into the fire.

By the time Thurman's iconoclastic "Negro Artists and the Negro" ran in *The New Republic* in late August 1927, Du Bois had withdrawn *The Crisis* from the Renaissance. Although the awards ceremony on October 25, 1926, had been an elegant evening enlivened by choral music and the playing of the Negro

String Quartet, Du Bois had seemed somewhat preoccupied and even perfunctory in his role as master of ceremonies at International House. Indeed, while the "Negro in Art" symposium proceeded on autopilot, the editor had left the main arrangements for the Krigwa, or *Crisis*, awards in Dill's faithful hands, along with those of young Bates graduate John P. Davis, while he sailed aboard the steamship *Pennland* on the first leg of his trip to the Soviet Union, to return only a few days before the International House ceremony. A notice at the beginning of 1927 would inform prospective entrants that much of the $2,035 prize money was earmarked for topics dealing with business and education — $725 in business prizes, to be exact. In addition to Amy Spingarn's six-hundred-dollar contribution, eight black banks, five insurance companies, and the Empire State Federated Women's Clubs provided an additional $860. Another $350 was subscribed by seven anonymous donors to fund an honorarium named for Charles Chesnutt. Amy Spingarn expressed a twinge of surprise at the new emphasis, an emphasis that would hardly have been congenial to Jessie Fauset had she still been closely associated with the magazine. But she had relinquished the position of literary editor in May of the previous year and was now merely an occasional presence as contributing editor.

The editor was on the high seas, returning to New York, when the October 1926 number of *The Crisis*, carrying the full text of his NAACP convention address, reached subscribers. The "Criteria of Negro Art" closed the seven-month symposium. Du Bois's address had opened with a fateful question: "How is it that an organization like this, a group of radicals trying to bring new things into the world, a fighting organization of this kind can turn aside to talk about art?" There were many good reasons to do so. There were many more talented young men and women of color to give voice to the rich cultural life of the race, and those who left themselves to be interpreted by others, however well-intentioned, ran the risk of distortion and exploitation. But Du Bois suspected that there were invidious motives behind the vogue of the Negro arts-and-letters movement. "One comforting thing is occurring to both black and white," he revealed. Too many were whispering, 'Here is a way out. Here is the real solution to the color problem.' " The acclaim accorded Cullen, Hughes, Fauset, White, and the others was cited as proof that the color line was rapidly fading. " 'Keep quiet! Don't complain! Work! All will be well!' " Du Bois had stopped just short of seeing a white conspiracy behind the Renaissance, but he underscored what he took to be the obvious truth that there was "a surprising number of white people who are getting great satisfaction out of these younger Negro writers because they think it is going to stop agitation of the Negro question." Here was a grave danger to which the NAACP must call attention. The efflorescence of novels and painting and poetry did not mean that black people had gained firm control of their creative energies. The NAACP had to wage a new fight in which it broadcast that "the Beauty of Truth and Freedom which shall some day be our heritage and the heritage of all civilized men is not in our hands yet and that we ourselves must not fail to realize." He had not yet said a final farewell to the Harlem Renaissance, however. Before he did so, Du Bois would present the movement with a bildungsroman of a propaganda novel— *The Dark Princess*—the kind of novel that he believed the younger generation ought to be writing.

BOLSHEVIKS AND
DARK PRINCESSES

I t can be imagined that Georgia Douglas Johnson read Du Bois's letter from Moscow with a feeling of exquisite pleasure. At the top of the letter, written on *Crisis* stationery in barely legible scrawl and dated September 17, 1926, Du Bois had traced his travel itinerary in lines running from city to city. Since sailing from New York in mid-August, the lines arrowed from Antwerp to Odessa by way of Frankfurt, Berlin, Leningrad, Moscow, Nizhni Novgorod, and Kiev. That nothing was said to her about the line passing through Thuringia, the locale of Du Bois's first summer of German seasoning more than thirty years ago, is hardly surprising. More surprising, however, is that whatever Thuringian memories came to him of the Marbach family and their golden-haired daughter, Dora, appear not to have been recorded at a later time elsewhere. As her eyes followed the lines descending into the text, Georgia Johnson learned that Du Bois would return home on October 15, after stops in Constantinople, Athens, and Italy. The motive behind the letter was distinctly salacious. "Dear Georgia, I'm thinking of you. I'd like to have you here," she read. "Write me. I['m] coming to see you at midnight. Please come down half-dressed with pretty stockings. I shall kiss you." He had kissed her before — many times, probably — because their intimate relationship antedated by a few years the recent demise of her husband, Henry Lincoln ("Link") Johnson, former recorder of deeds for the District of Columbia and frustrated counsel to a willful Marcus Garvey. "Grandly isolate as the God of day," Johnson had eulogized in "A Sonnet to Dr. W.E.B. Du Bois," on the occasion of the great man's fiftieth birthday. She and the editor were as close as Du Bois was to Fauset, although it seems clear that, unlike the increasingly dispirited Fauset, Johnson never deceived herself about the prospect of becoming the second Mrs. Du Bois.

It was not surprising that Du Bois thought of Johnson thousands of miles away in the American capital as he set off from Moscow on the next leg of his trip. Vulnerable, sensitive, her once willowy frame now fuller and more matronly from childbearing, this handsome, well-born woman had reached out to him for encouragement as she turned from the music of her Oberlin training to pour her soul into romantic verse. Hers was the feeling poetry of woman's condition — gendered, cosmopolitan, and, probably because of her multiracial, advantaged background, only secondarily inclined to dwell on racial protest. Johnson's Cherokee ancestry was visible in facial features inherited from her mother, as were the lineaments of her English paternal grandfather, a wealthy and cultured north Georgia planter. *The Heart of a Woman*, her first book of poetry, appeared in 1918, two years after *The Crisis* published three of her earliest poems. William Stanley Braithwaite, the dean of Aframerican belles-lettres, praised the collection in his introduction for its lyrical evocation of the genteel dignity and duress of a certain class of women of color. Much of her life with "Link" Johnson, a conniving patronage seeker indifferent to her literary aspirations, can be read into the collection's title poem, "The Heart of a Woman" although what she had to say transcended the plight of a black woman married to a minor professional in a philistine capital city. As with Du Bois's passionate "The Damnation of Women," Johnson's poetry inveighed against the patriarchal restraints and blatant sexism confronting gifted women of all colors everywhere. "The heart of a woman falls back with the night," Johnson sighed, "And enters some alien cage in its plight,/ And tries to forget it has dreamed of the stars/ While it breaks, breaks, breaks on the sheltering bars." Yet even as fatalism seemed to overtake her, Johnson broke free to assert that her dream would not be lost: "Let me not lose the vision, gird me, Powers that toss/ the worlds, I pray!/ Hold me, and guard, lest anguish tear my dreams/ away!"

By the time she and Du Bois had become intimate enough for a spicy note from Russia to be a matter of course, her reputation as the first female Negro American poet of the twentieth century was well established. *Bronze: A Book of Verse* had been touted by Du Bois and Fauset and others on the eve of the Harlem Renaissance. Like Mabel Dodge a few years earlier, though with more literary talent, Johnson came to exert a radiating influence upon the Negro artists of the twenties through the famous salon she ran in her Washington home at 1461 S Street NW: "Halfway House," its familiars called it. On a corner lot bordered by roses in season, the house was comfortably furnished in a style that seems to have blended the flea market and the bordello. On late, liquescent, and often memorably animated Saturday nights, Jazz Age muses gathered around Georgia Johnson's concert piano or paired off in lively huddles, their talk flowing back and forth between tangy gossip and serious debate as indiscretions were revealed and old and new poetry, drama, fiction, and art were critiqued. Toomer, Locke, Fauset, and the playwrights Angelina Grimké and Mae Miller were regulars; as were Bruce Nugent, Fisher, the underappreciated sculptor May Howard Jackson and short-story writer Alice Dunbar-Nelson. The wandering Hughes came often and Countee Cullen came occasionally. Zona Gale, Waldo Frank, and H. G. Wells joined the Saturday Nighters at least once. Du Bois had begun to drop in frequently, almost never missing the opportunity when speaking engagements and other *Crisis* business routed him through Washington. "Please invite me to spend Easter Sunday with you," read a typical presumption sent to her more than two years before Link made his definitive exit from their moribund marriage. "I simply must arrange for Sunday dinner." Johnson was always more than glad to accommodate the affectionate autocrat. Promising him her best blackberry jam when he came to town to tell her about Africa and Paris, she offered to invite "a friend or two if you say so."

Johnson found that her husband's modest bequest, combined with the salary from her new patronage position as commissioner of conciliation in the U.S. Department of Labor, enabled her just barely to support her family. Her two bright sons, Henry, Jr., and Peter, were finally about to complete their law and medical studies at Howard after solid educations at Bowdoin and Dartmouth, respectively. Her bureaucracy's treadmill seldom slackened, however, and after-hours attempts at poetry left Johnson drained and demoralized. The friendship of one of the nation's leading intellectuals meant a great deal, therefore. Du Bois had been a consistent champion in the court of letters, "blazing an orbit through the dark and gloom" as much for her, she hoped, as for the race at large. No word had come from him for weeks after sailing for Russia, and she had been at a loss to explain a silence that had never before occurred during his travels. "To lose friends one has come to appreciate and hold dear is something akin to the touch of death," she wrote after getting his wicked Moscow letter. And now he was on his way to her from the other side of the world, arriving on December 11, to stay four days, Du Bois wrote after returning to New York. As she had often done during past visits, Johnson may have made his few days with her even more pleasurable by the company of other attractive women of a modern bent. According to Mae Miller, it was a poorly kept secret in Washington's upper-class community of color that Johnson regularly invited women Du Bois wanted to meet to her home.

By the mid-twenties, the emotional core below the Du Boisian layers of public virtue and personal rigor implicated him in an evolving state of affective being in which he seemed ever more driven to exploit the enormous fascination he exercised over many women, a fascination intensified in the eyes of some by Du Bois's advanced ideas about women's rights. Many liberated women were strongly predisposed to admire a liberated man whose writings espoused not only equal political rights for women but equal pay for equal work in all the professions, as well as the radical right to control their own bodies. "He was well aware of the fact that he cut a path for himself that was a little different," and that impressed the independent-minded Anne Cooke (dramatist and future spouse of sociologist Ira DeA. Reid), who would always be grateful for the experience of having known him. More than that, he seems to have possessed the knack of making gifted women believe that their existence became more complete through the transgressive relationships he made possible. It was not so much ideology—feminist politics—that fascinated and commanded as it was the exhilarating sense he gave these women of entering the realm of culture, ideas, and vast happenings he inhabited on terms of genuine respect. "He never made me feel inferior," said Anne Cooke, a sentiment many women would express. For many more, however, the attraction they felt for Du Bois was more basic. "He was very well hung," a distinguished scholar-diplomat remembered as she mused in retirement about her mentor. "And I always had an impression that when sex was concerned, he was well endowed and was interested [in women] and his wife certainly was never around."

In all probability, Du Bois ranked these women, with some coming as close as his publicly correct marriage and complex egocentrism allowed to being treated as uniquely important, cherished equally for their minds as for their bodies. Others were grouped in a more transient category, pleasant, amoral diversions more than willing to go along for the romp, as was often true, apparently, of the "prettiest girls" Arthur Spingarn noticed working for the magazine over the years. Alluding to what was called by those in the know the "casting couch" in the inner office of The Crisis, Spingarn would share an off-the-record observation after Du Bois's death that the editor had "plenty of trouble, not all of it limited to the male race [sic]." Frequently enough, Du Bois overreached himself, abusing the trust of young women who placed themselves in his hands out of innocent admiration. Marvel Jackson came from Minneapolis at the beginning of 1927 to work as his secretary. Then in her early twenties, she had grown up hearing her mother speak adoringly of the Willie Du Bois whom she had dated one summer while employed as a serving girl in Great Barrington. When Du Bois assembled Darkwater, he paid Marvel's mother the tribute of special mention in "The Servant in the House," a new essay composed expressly for the collection. Sometime during 1922 or 1923, Marvel Jackson had finally met the illustrious editor on a trip to New York. She was "just immobilized. I couldn't say a word," she sighed, still under the spell of that moment more than sixty years later. As Marvel Jackson Cook (always profanely grateful for the collapse of her engagement to Roy Wilkins), she married and matured over time to become a pugnacious journalist and a valued member of the Communist Party. But in 1927 she was an inexperienced, ambitious, vulnerable young woman in awe of the new employer in whose service she was to remain almost three years. The editor took her to her first Broadway play and, in contrast to his reputation, she found him to be one of the warmest persons she'd ever known. But she also quickly discovered that he was "pretty much a ladies' man," and that led to intimacies she wished she could have evaded. "You know, when we were working up at the magazine," she remembered, her voice trailing away at the end, "he'd put his hand on my leg, and I was so in awe of him—his intellect—that I really didn't know [what to do]."

Marvel Jackson's experience was not unusual, and James Weldon Johnson's goddaughter, Wilhelmina Adams, reported her straitlaced mother tut-tutting that she no longer thought "that old man was a gentleman." Mrs. Adams, it seems, had been especially discountenanced to learn of the editor's triangular affair with the young wife of a New Jersey physician who was also involved with Paul Robeson. Had the two Adamses known of the affair involving Du Bois in a triangle with another lively, modern woman and none other than James Weldon Johnson, these two proper Harlemites might have wondered what was left of the moral code of the Talented Tenth. On the other hand, if black life at the upper end of the social scale was more Victorian in its moral protestations than white life, there was at least as much, if not more, duplicity in its sexual conduct. Regardless of what people like the Adamses thought of them, such extramarital caperings were considered by many to be the privileges and prerogatives enjoyed by men of influence and affairs, considerations of ethical leadership notwithstanding. Victorian men of color behaved as all men sometimes did in their relations with women. As the loosening up of sexual mores accelerated after World War I, women also began to participate as free agents and even as initiators of recreational sex. Life imitated art with such fidelity during the Harlem Renaissance for the simple, evident reason that much of the fiction, ardent and torrid, submitted to *The Crisis* and *Opportunity* contests accurately reflected the new eroticism of the Modernist Age in which Du Bois and other putative guardians of the old values were, in reality, zealous underground participants. As an objective fact of the era, the gap between principles and practice was a statistical male commonplace. Yet in Du Bois's case it was also a disjunction that would open him to severe reproach by a much later generation because, in his fervent advocacy of feminist ideals, he had seemed to tower above his contemporaries. "I don't think he was too straitlaced about the ladies," chuckled the economist and Du Bois disciple Robert Weaver, very much to the point, adding sternly, "but he was very straitlaced about most other things."

As much as they said he loved the ladies, the inevitable day came when he left them. The women who loved Du Bois would come to understand, as their grief grew weightier through the years, that Nina would remain the official and everlasting Mrs. Du Bois until her death released him. She had become practically invisible by the late twenties, a frail, grey creature, always well attired, if uninterestingly so, to be escorted to benefit functions, annual NAACP balls, and increasingly elaborate celebrations of her husband's birthday. It can be inferred from what the correspondence says, as well as from its silences, that Will had come to regard Nina as both a burden and a shield, much as his crippled, undereducated mother had been. A burden that some would say explained his wanderings, but a shield that precluded his becoming permanently entangled. Marvel Cook, sighing in characteristic ellipsis, was like so many others who thought they understood his domestic situation ". . . because I don't think his wife. . . . It must have been difficult for him." But as Fauset had painfully come to realize after returning from Europe in the spring of 1925, it was difficult for the women, too. Nineteen twenty-six had proved to be a particularly hard period for the associate editor, whose health appeared to be as precarious as her finances. Her difficulty with the editor must be money, Fauset thought. Fauset felt compelled to write at length to Joel Spingarn about an even more humiliating misunderstanding involving Du Bois, with whom she was now becoming more estranged with each dismaying month. She and her sister, Helen Lanning, had loaned altogether $2,500 to help Du Bois carry the notes and mounting repairs on his ever more costly venture into Harlem real estate. Having endured three years of straitened economies, the sisters needed desperately to be repaid, but, sighed Fauset, because Du Bois was unable to manage his investment, he was "behaving badly." By the beginning of 1926, the apartment building at 606 St. Nicholas had become an albatross dragging its owner into indebtednesses survived only through lecture revenues, loans from associates, and borrowing against his life insurance policy.

Sifting through Du Bois's accounts for this period is a bewildering exercise; some figures add up, others don't. What is clear, though, is that after deducting triple mortgage payments, property taxes, coal, electricity, janitor's wages, and serial repairs, the five units renting at sixty to seventy dollars a month never yielded a profit. Based on his own figures of five thousand dollars in salary, combined with lecture fees of about eight hundred dollars and writing revenues of more than four hundred, Du Bois's gross income for 1925–26 should have been easily in excess of $6,200 at a time when average American family earnings were $1,500. But as he explained in a plea for another loan from Joel Spingarn (only two weeks after Fauset had sent her letter), his seemingly robust resources paled before an outstanding property debt of $7,764.75, to make no mention of Yolande and Nina's educational and medical expenses as well as his own rather high level of personal expenditures separate and apart from St. Nicholas Avenue. The apartment building, like the neighborhood, cried out for more resources than either Du Bois could provide or the city cared to supply. His pleas for better policing and trash removal had never made much difference. Construction of the Eighth Avenue subway (the route of the famous A train) in front of the property imposed a nuisance and made the block temporarily less desirable. Nina complained, "It seems that all the machinery they have is just in front of our house." Then there was the problem of mulish Mrs. Turner, the second-floor tenant whose gross behavior and rent-party visitors grated on the landlord. "The men urinate out of the windows," Du Bois protested without effect, "and the women sit with their feet out of the front windows." By the fall of 1928, with prostitutes and bootleggers filling up the block and real estate broker Nail virtually writing off Harlem as a place for his and Du Bois's "kind of people," Du Bois would be ready to walk away from 606 St. Nicholas and move to a large apartment building.

Meanwhile, despite knowing that Fauset faced the prospect of major surgery, Du Bois had apparently brushed off the sisters' debt with such callousness at the beginning of 1926 that Fauset confided to Spingarn that she felt not only angry "but disturbed and frightened." She was certain that this "ordinarily . . . very generous and kind man" could regain his composure and The Crisis be rejuvenated once his property woes were alleviated. Fauset's perturbation revealed itself in an uncharacteristically awkward proposal (assented to by Nina) that the Spingarns and a few other wealthy friends give Du Bois a sixtieth-birthday monetary present two years early on some honorific pretext. If he learned of her appeal to Joel and Amy Spingarn (as is highly likely), a haughtily irritated Du Bois would surely have considered Fauset's conduct to be a breach of their relationship, a disloyal act that demeaned his business acumen and even his competency as a family provider. Deeming the unrepaid-loan business to be an intrusion upon weightier concerns such as planning the fourth Pan-African Congress, completing an education research project underwritten by the Garland Fund, or persuading Pennsylvania to include The Star of Ethiopia in its Sesquicentennial Exposition, he now treated his helpmate of many years with cold correctness. He turned his attention to Rachel Davis DuBois, a young white Pennsylvania widow whose career in interracial education was just starting, and to Ethel May Ray (Ethel Ray Nance), the adoring Minnesotan whose Talented Tenth parents had weaned her on The Crisis and Trotter's Guardian. They had met in 1920 when her father invited the great man to Duluth to speak to the NAACP's new branch. Both Rachel DuBois's and Ethel Ray's emotional and professional lives would remain commingled with the editor's until he died.

On February 1, the editor wrote Joel Spingarn, detailing his finances to the penny and asking for another loan. Four days later, he headed West on a lecture tour, leaving instructions that Ray receive his addresses en route. "I hope I may run across you," he prompted. In effect, Du Bois had also walked out of Jessie Fauset's life. When he returned to The Crisis, he was able to repay the sisters in full out of a three-thousand-dollar loan subscribed to in equal amounts by Amy and Joel Spingarn and Mrs. Jacob Schiff, "payable at your convenience." He thanked Fauset for her "patience in awaiting the repayment." She could only have been immensely relieved. The Harlem physician she had consulted had sentenced her to a costly, perilous gastroenterostomy. Another month would pass before the specialist consulted on the recommendation of the Spingarns told an ecstatic Fauset that no operation was needed. As she regained her emotional balance, Fauset came to realize that the special relationship with Du Bois had about run its course. A psychic and intellectual bond that once had been so vital for Fauset that she had often imagined herself Du Bois's alter ego was now merely a business partnership with memories. "La Vie c'est la Vie," the poem in which she poured out her feelings, spoke of "a man whose lightest word" set her afire: "Fulfillment of his least behest/Defines my life's desire." The May 1926 issue of the magazine announced her graceful retreat from center stage. Henceforth, Miss Jessie Fauset would be the contributing editor of *The Crisis*. She composed "Noblesse Oblige" not long afterward, the stiff-upper-lip poem Cullen published in *Opportunity*. "That I dance and sing and spar,/Juggling words and making quips/To hide the trembling of my lips" was the goodbye that preceded engagement and marriage to a New Jersey businessman with whom she would be demurely miserable. "Love is lost, and — bitter ruth — /Pride is with me yet." By the time Du Bois sailed for Russia in late summer, the redesign of the magazine had been all but completed without Fauset's input, an omission that would have been unthinkable a year before.

Meanwhile, during the short period between Fauset's withdrawal and Davis Du Bois's apprenticeship, Du Bois engaged in several controversies that epitomized the contemporary state of race relations in the United States as well as the British empire. Release of the second and final volume that spring of the Phelps-Stokes Fund's *Education in Africa: Recommendations of the African Education Committee* confirmed his worst expectations. This massive, three-year survey of educational conditions below the Sahara, undertaken in cooperation with the International Missionary Council of England, was intended to serve as the template for the instruction of Africans for decades to come. Norman Leys had alerted Du Bois to the deeply conservative prejudices of most of the members of the African Education Committee at the time of the second Pan-African Congress. The fact that Thomas Jesse Jones had chaired the committee's roving investigations from Monrovia to Nairobi was, for Du Bois, prima facie evidence of the study's ulterior design. Secretary of the influential Phelps-Stokes Fund, adviser to the General Education Board, executive trustee of Fisk University and Hampton Institute, Jones had risen from humble Welsh immigrant to world expert on the educational needs of black people. *Negro Education: A Study of the Private and Higher Schools for Colored People in the United States*, Jones's 1917, two-volume study had drawn rigid boundaries and fixed low ceilings for the majority of aspiring black men and women. Du Bois had meticulously dissected *Negro Education* in the February 1918 *Crisis* with cold fury.

Seeing history now being repeated on the African continent drove him nearly into apoplexy in his detailed review of *Education in Africa* in the issue for June 1926. Castigating the committee for its casual devaluation of college preparatory schools in Liberia, Sierra Leone, Nigeria, and South Africa, the editor called attention to such typical Jones recommendations as less time being devoted to "conventional requirements of university preparation," to observations that higher education was responsible for unrest in India, and to his prescriptions for the "right type" of education for Africans. By the "right type," Jones's document explained that Africa must avoid the mistake "generally made by New England in dealing with the Negro in the Southern States of America immediately after emancipation." The models suited to the continent were Hampton and Tuskegee, "where education was adapted directly to a people's needs. Here was real education," the study decreed. "Small wonder that British officialdom is rhapsodic over Jones," Du Bois wrote sarcastically; small wonder, with the Phelps-Stokes Fund "making Africa safe for white folks," that American mission boards were refusing to send more able men of color like Max Yergan to serve among the Africans. Du Bois repeated the widely circulated charge that Jones had tried to sabotage Yergan's YMCA appointment to South Africa.

The editor had good reason to know from the troubles afflicting Carter Woodson that attacking Jones could be costly. Woodson's unease over Jones's ascendancy had impelled him to criticize Jones in his *History of the Negro*, then to write a formal protest to the Phelps-Stokes trustees in 1924 followed by an angry letter printed in the Indianapolis *Freeman*. Unburdening himself in the letter, the normally restrained historian declared that Jones had "neither the economic nor the moral worth" to serve the disadvantaged. If he was truly " 'a friend of the Negro,' " Woodson added caustically, then it was "rather strange that the race is daily praying to God that the curse of his friendship may be speedily removed." In a letter praising Woodson's forthrightness at the time, Du Bois had expressed identical indignation to Anson Phelps Stokes and professed incomprehension that "the chairman and trustees of the fund could permit this sort of imposition upon the colored race." Whatever connection there may have been to the Carnegie Corporation's refusal two years later to continue funding Woodson's historical association or to the Laura Spelman Rockefeller Memorial Fund's reduced appropriation, the message Jones sent Woodson through an intermediary threatened the historian with precisely such consequences for his temerity. "I honestly believe that you have injured yourself and your cause," wrote Jones's dutiful subaltern, "and that for sometime to come you will have to work hard to regain the confidence of many important persons, both black and white."

Du Bois's lack of success in securing foundation support for research projects had always been handicapped by foundation censorship of the oblique kind that resembled Woodson's after his confrontation with Jones. An old favorite project, his languishing history of Negro Americans in the Great War, was a case in point. He had put off demands year after year from veterans for return of documents generously loaned him at the end of the war. One of them, now an attorney in New York, would complain once again in the spring of 1927, as so many others had repeatedly: "In February 1920, you stated that you hoped to be through with my material in a few months and thanked me for letting you keep it for that time." A few weeks after attorney James Johnson's plea, Du Bois approached James Hardy Dillard, dean emeritus of Tulane University and now benign president of the Jeanes Fund, about a grant enabling him to finish the multivolume "The Black Man and the Wounded World." Dillard thought the project inappropriate for any of the foundations, but offered to sound out General Education Board director Raymond Fosdick and Colonel Arthur Woods of the Laura Spelman Fund about a direct approach to the junior Rockefeller.

Du Bois gratefully accepted Dillard's offer. Four months of silence passed. Then Du Bois heard from Dillard, who wrote in a long-winded surprise that a chance enconter with one Trevor Arnett, a GEB philanthropoid, revealed that the powers at 61 Broadway knew "nothing of my letter." Arnett had promised to look into the matter, asking Dillard in parting, though, whether Du Bois intended his monograph to be "plain records and history, or whether there might be controversial matter." Dillard wrote that he replied that it was the former, but urged Du Bois to write to Fosdick himself. From its frank and almost impassioned contents, it may be inferred that Du Bois's request for Rockefeller's personal funding of the war history would have struck the notables at 61 Broadway as a project only slightly less appealing than underwriting Ida Tarbell's *History of the Standard Oil Company*. "It goes without saying that anything I write is pro-Negro," Du Bois declared. "Naturally, it is going to defend the poor black and ignorant against prejudice and power." Still, he reminded Fosdick and Rockefeller, his scholarship in history and social science had always "stood up well under severe criticism." Du Bois would get his answer at the end of November 1927 after Fosdick transmitted his letter to John D. Rockefeller, Jr. Speaking through his personal secretary, Mr. Rockefeller regretted that he was disinclined to assist for reasons of "principles which experience has shown him to be wise." Du Bois was assured "of no lack of sympathy for the objects which [he had] in mind." Desperate, he applied for a Guggenheim in order to complete the work "it is my duty to conclude," he explained, but was turned down because of his age. A decade later, the loaned documents still in his possession and his great war history still begging for subvention, the Penrose Fund would reject Du Bois's application for a grant.

Uncompromising month after month in his editorials and exposés, Du Bois's courage was a reminder of the insurmountable odds faced by dark-skinned people in their native country. As recently as November 1925, *The New York*

Times had once again rejected his plea to capitalize Negro. Denial of upper-case existence in the newspaper of record merely affirmed symbolically the literal denial of the humanity of an entire race—token diminution that both reflected and sustained the cruelest beliefs and actions in the real world. The policy of the *Times* suited an era in which thirty-four "negroes" were to be lynched in 1926. William Edgar Borah, Idaho's perpetual senator and chairman of the Foreign Relations Committee, gave no thought to capitalizing Negro when he wrote a three-page letter to Du Bois in mid-July 1926. In opposing the constitutionality of the Dyer antilynching bill in the Senate, Borah, one of the upper chamber's most influential members, had surprised the editor by publicly questioning the wisdom of the Fifteenth Amendment. How, Du Bois wondered, could a man of the senator's "breadth and knowledge of world events" exempt black Americans from his "sympathy with struggling classes?" Very simply, Borah replied—blanket enfranchisement of a people subjected to a thousand years of barbarism and three hundred years of slavery had been a terrible mistake. "No race in the history of the world has ever been equal to such a thing." Exceptions could have been made for "the very intelligent and those who served as soldiers," but Borah insisted that the South's handling of its complex Negro problem deserved the "highest credit" and entitled it to the "confidence and cooperation of the North." In an amicable follow-up consenting to have his letter published in *The Crisis*, Borah urged Du Bois to find time for a chat when next in Washington. Borah promised he would share with him the real history of the Dyer bill's progress through the Senate Judiciary Committee. "It is one of the finest illustrations of how we played politics with the negro that I know of," he confided.

Even with sympathizers like Borah in politics or Lowell in higher education, the level of racial violence tolerated in the white South periodically embarrassed and strained the entente cordiale between the two regions. A lynching of three family members who were dragged away from their cells and slaughtered by an Aiken, South Carolina, mob would appall northern public opinion and even a considerable portion of southern. Once again Walter White would assume his practiced role as a southern white man in order to compile a full report on the complicity of law officers and citizens in the triple butchery of the Lowmans, one of whom was a woman. The assistant secretary's account would induce several major newspapers to cover the story, with the New York *World* sending a reporter whose regular dispatches from Aiken became increasingly interrogative and revealing. The South Carolina lynchings took place shortly before Du Bois's return from Russia in mid October; his part in them would be confined mainly to editorials as the grand jury abided by the fraudulent script written by the state's attorney general in collaboration with the new governor. Du Bois had already anticipated South Carolina's lawlessness in a trenchant essay appearing in the June issue of the *North American Review*. "The Shape of Fear" described the national chrysalis out of which southern violence and northern malevolence unmysteriously emerged. Drawing lines between the red spots on the racial map, the editor connected them to the new Ku Klux Klan, whose octopusal spread across the nation he detailed in the article out of his own extensive travels. As a sort of National Association for the Advancement of Anglo-Saxon People, the Klan was the last best hope of genteel racists—educated folk too "ashamed to do and say" what the KKK says and does.

LINCOLN STEFFEN'S 1919 effusion about the future at work had done a great deal to make it almost mandatory by the mid-twenties for intellectuals to visit the Soviet Union. Convoys of British Fabians had followed hard on the tracks of Steffens, an enthusiastic H. G. Wells and a repelled Bertrand Russell among them. Granted an hour's interview alone with Lenin in May 1920, Russell had been impressed by the Bolshevik leader's self-assurance but he found the regime loathsome, writing his good friend, the writer Colette, that there was "less liberty in modern Russia than ever existed anywhere before." Uncritical readers of his quick book, *The Practice and Theory of Bolshevism*, would have been inclined to abandon all travel plans to see Bolshevism being practiced. Two years after Russell's visit, *The Liberator*'s Max Eastman had come to St. Petersburg to attend the Fourth Congress of the Communist International, accompanied by a temporarily exhilarated Claude McKay. Eastman, who had bitterly assailed Russell as a gullible catspaw of Menshevik propaganda, became an impassioned champion of Leon Trotsky and fell in love with the sister of the minister of justice, whom he married. McKay, who enjoyed the special distinction of addressing the world body of communism on the unique racial circumstances confronting the American Communist Party, wrote *Negry v. Amerike*, a small book on the subject that would become required reading among the Soviet hierarchy. The poet recalled being feted like a "black ikon in the flesh," much to the surprise of the African Blood Brotherhood's light-complexioned Otto Huiswood, who had been cast by the American Communist Party delegates as the black embodiment of class solidarity. But both McKay and Eastman, like the indomitable Emma Goldman, had soon become disillusioned with the Soviet system, Eastman's explosive *Since Lenin Died* appearing two years after Goldman's *My Disillusionment in Russia* and only a year before Du Bois embarked to see the future for himself. The editor was familiar with the literature inspired by the Soviet Union's growing stream of political tourists, and it is clear from his writings during the early twenties that he resolved not to prejudge the Russian experiment. He refused to be moved either by the "superficial omniscience of Wells [or] the reports in the New York *Times*."

When *The Liberator* charged in summer of 1921 that he "sneered" at the

Revolution, Du Bois had responded to McKay, then an enthusiastic partisan of the Bolsheviks, with the equipoised "Negro and Radical Thought," a *Crisis* thinkpiece denying scorn but asserting a right to skepticism. How could one dismiss a movement whose paramount duty was not only to unite the European working class, but, as the Comintern now proclaimed, to achieve the unity "of all colors: white, yellow, and black—the toilers of the world"? he asked. The "marvelous set of phenomena" known as the Russian Revolution might well be all that McKay, Asa Randolph, Hubert Harrison, Cyril Briggs, and others prophesied—"the greatest achievement of the twentieth century," in Randolph's words—but Du Bois had urged an inquiring patience. "Russia is incredibly vast, and the happenings there in the last five years have been intricate to a degree that must make any student pause." Even though he had sanctioned the blood-soaked antislavery crusade of John Brown in the biography, Du Bois made it clear that he was deeply disturbed by the violent transfer of power in Russia. "We do not believe in revolution," he had announced dogmatically in "The Class Struggle," another provocative *Crisis* editorial in summer 1921. There may have been rare circumstances in history where "organized murder" was the sole option, but those occasions belonged in the past. Revolutionary changes must come "mainly through reason, human sympathy and the education of children, and not by murder," Du Bois moralized.

Morality aside, however, Du Bois also concluded that the application of Marxist class analysis to people of color had limited validity. Black Americans might look and act like proletarians. Theoretically they were indeed "part of the world proletariat," he conceded in one of the earliest of what were to become significant Du Boisian revisions of scientific socialism, but, as a practical reality, they were not only unrecognized and excluded from the white world proletariat, they were victimized by the "physical oppression, social ostracism, economic exclusion, and personal hatred" of the white working class. European workers, after all, had discriminated against Asians: why, therefore, assume on the part of "unlettered and suppressed" white masses "a clearness of thought, a sense of human brotherhood, sadly lacking in the most educated classes?" However appealing the communist ideal, the Briggses, McKays, and Randolphs were mistaken to assume that we have only to embrace "the [white] working class program to have the working class embrace ours," Du Bois admonished. It would be foolish, he thought, to abandon the practical program for Negro emancipation "laid down and thought out" by the NAACP "by seeking to join a revolution which we do not at present understand." The life-and-death question was this: "How far can the colored people of the world, and particularly the Negroes of the United States, trust the [white] working classes?" Those who skimmed the essays in *Darkwater* could easily find Du Bois's not very encouraging answers.

This cautious approach to the new order in Russia, which contrasted so markedly with his frequently audacious embrace of the radical and the unpopular, only had the effect of redoubling the attacks upon the editor. Indulging in a bit of sneering itself, the *Messenger* derided Du Bois's "criminal ignorance of the trend of the modern working world." According to McKay, who had sought to enlighten the aging editor prior to his own disillusionment, the problem of the twentieth century was far less one of race than of class. The black American was "ostracized only technically" because of his color, McKay explained in a lengthy letter. "In reality," black workers were discriminated against because they were "the lowest type of worker"—because they allowed themselves to be manipulated against the white working class by the capitalists. Du Bois would have heard the theme of class over race being stridently sounded in the *Messenger* shortly before sailing for Russia. Speaking on behalf of the recently organized Brotherhood of Sleeping Car Porters (BSCP), now the principal support for Randolph and Owen's magazine, the magnetic young Negro socialist, Frank W. Crosswaith, predicted the imminent founding of the Worker State soon after the BSCP and "all the workers of the nation" realized that the fate of the whole working class was "inextricably bound up with that of every section of the working class." In revealing contrast to the indignant response the previous year when a subscriber had repeatedly needled the editor for ignoring Crosswaith and Randolph, whom *The Nation* and *The New Republic* found worthwhile, *The Crisis* lost no time announcing its full backing of Randolph and Owen's courageous venture into organized labor politics and its looming battle with the gargantuan Pullman Railroad Corporation. When the Communist Party operative, Lovett Fort-Whitman, sent an invitation to participate in something called the American Negro Labor Congress (ANLC), Du Bois admitted not knowing "anything about you personally," but subsequently praised the Party's effort to mobilize black workers, although he declined to attend the ANLC's founding in Chicago in October 1925. "The Black Man and Labor," appearing in the December *Crisis*, marked a significant advance in thinking about the USSR, with Du Bois enjoining readers to "stand before the astounding effort of Soviet Russia to organize the industrial world with open and mind and listening ears."

While not quite a revolving-door socialist, Du Bois had shown not a little inconsistency by decisions such as choosing Wilson over Debs in 1912 and by supporting the United States' entry into the war. Yet, because he was sincere in his determined profession of Socialist ideals, he found himself intellectually and temperamentally predisposed to condone the economic critique and social vision of Marx and Engels while reserving a troubled judgment on the tactics of Lenin, Trotsky, and Josef Stalin. The puissant *Darkwater* essay "Of Work and Wealth" had seemed almost to verge on revising the epic pronouncement about the color line being the problem of the century. Perhaps with the French nineteenth-century philosophical anarchist Charles Fourier in mind, Du Bois had come close to suggesting that the greater cause of human misery was due to the theft of property as the primordial act generating the market economy, proclaiming, "Today, therefore, we are challenging this ownership. We are rapidly approaching the day when we shall repudiate all private property in raw materials and tools." In Russia, repudiation of private ownership of the major means of production was already a fact that cheered Du Bois. Although far from ready to "dogmatize with Marx and Lenin," as he put it, by the end of 1925 he had progressed from curiosity to guarded approval of the Soviet experiment. When the International Committee for Political Prisoners published the book *Letters from Russian Prisons*, Du Bois was sufficiently troubled by the irate protests of Tass and the CPUSA that he asked Roger Baldwin and Elizabeth Gurley Flynn to remove his name from the organization's list of supporters. He was not a Communist and he deplored violence, he explained to Flynn, but he was "especially sensitive" with regard to Russia. Having heard all kinds of stories that had proven to be lies about the USSR, he was reluctant to "believe anything under ordinary circumstances." Indeed, he now believed that Russia was "trying to do a great and wonderful thing for the economic organization of industry." Russia hadn't yet succeeded, of course, but he hoped for her success.

Many readers would have found it ideologically pertinent that the young Marxist economist Abram Harris was beginning to write for *The Crisis*. Du Bois had been impressed by the unsolicited advice during the Fisk controversy from the then twenty-three-year-old undergraduate at Virginia Union University. One of the most brilliant minds of the younger Talented Tenth generation (the second Negro professor to be hired by the University of Chicago), Harris had no confidence in the NAACP's program of legal redress and incremental integration. He, too, was convinced that the problem of the century was essentially one of class exploitation, of which racism was merely the most virulent manifestation.

Bolshevik Russia strongly enticed Du Bois now. Intellectuals of his stature were expected to possess informed opinions about what he would soon describe as the greatest event in history since the French Revolution. The editor thought of himself with good reason as someone who helped to set the trends of his time, yet he surely recognized that his hesitations and qualifications about the Russian Revolution and the white workers of the world had diminished his standing among many of the so-called New Negroes. At fifty-eight, he was thought of as the peerless embodiment of Negro civil rights and intellectual culture, an iconic figure after whom high schools were named in West Virginia and Illinois and whose birthday brought interracial tributes from many of America's most distinguished men and women. Yet, also and increasingly, Du Bois had come to be regarded by young militants as the superannuated representative of a magnificent past. The mocking tone *Messenger* regularly employed when reporting some accomplishment of the editor's (especially after the Rabelaisian George Schuyler joined its staff) was symptomatic: "The sixth award of the Spingarn Medal . . . [went] to the King of Kings, William E. Burghardt Du Bois, noted author, famed editor of *The Crisis*, intellectual Grand Lama of Aframerica and coiner of that militant wartime slogan: 'Close Ranks Let Us Forget our Grievances.' " Despite the barbs of the young insurgents, astute observers on the left had closely monitored the shift in Du Bois's thinking. One of them, George Goetz, editor of the new *Modern Quarterly*, a brilliant fusion of Socialist and Communist theorizing, made overtures through Abram Harris at the close of 1924. Goetz, a recent graduate of Johns Hopkins who used the nom de plume V. F. Calverton, appears to have failed to gain an audience until Harris made a special plea. Sympathetic to the Soviet experiment but probingly critical, Goetz soon earned the editor's regard for his lively mind and mission to bring advanced ideas to the common man and woman.

Not surprisingly, then, as Du Bois would recall in *Dusk of Dawn*, with his usual inaccuracy for vital autobiographical details, "sometime in 1927 [sic]," three visitors from the Soviet Union presented themselves at the offices of *The Crisis*. "They were probably clandestine agents of the Communist dictatorship," he suspected. One, "a blond German and active revolutionist," was too ideologically aggressive for Du Bois's taste, but the married couple were "persons of education and culture," unlike the impatient German, who wanted to organize blacks into revolutionary cell groups immediately. "He gradually faded out of the picture," Du Bois noted. The husband and wife, however, became social acquaintances from whom he learned much as he "sat at their feet to hear what was taking place" in Russia. Their offer to finance a trip to the USSR, which Du Bois seems to have accepted without delay, cannot have been unexpected. It probably came sometime in June 1926, just as Du Bois was making final arrangements for a junket to Switzerland and Germany. Russia seems to have been added to the itinerary at the very last moment. Du Bois insisted on a written stipulation that he was under no obligation or agreement of any kind. "I was to go on a journey of free inquiry to see the most momentous changes in modern human history." That his departure would come immediately after the association's annual convention in Chicago, taking him away from the work of selecting winners from hundreds of *Crisis* literary contest entrants, as well as from arranging the gala dinner at International House and planning for the fourth Pan-African Congress—all without Fauset's dutiful efficiency—were suddenly concerns of secondary importance.

Honorable mention in the 1925 *Opportunity* contest had prompted twenty-one-year-old John P. Davis to write Du Bois early the following year asking about "vacancies in July in the editorial department at *The Crisis.*" Davis had grown up in a home where *The Crisis* was required reading and attendance at the District of Columbia's elite Dunbar High School an obligation of class. Always with something of the charming confidence man about him, Davis would achieve the distinction in 1932 of special appointment to the Republican National Committee and, four years later, that of cofounding the Popular Front's National Negro Congress. Georgia Johnson had brought this charming, self-confident Saturday Nighter to Du Bois's attention and first mention in the magazine, soon after which Davis had attracted wide coverage in the black press as the powerhouse member of the traveling Bates College debating team. Several weeks after graduating with honors, Davis rushed to New York in response to an unexpected summons from Du Bois. Three days after arriving, amazed and swamped with deadlines, he found himself appointed de facto editor of the magazine. His passport issued on July 14 and valises packed, Du Bois dropped Oswald Garrison Villard a note offering *The Nation* articles about Russia "from my point of view." Identified on the ship's passenger manifest as "Col. W.E.B. Du Bois" (the racial notation "colored" had somehow morphed into military ranking), he departed for the unknown.

Nineteen twenty-six was the first summer of the Locarno Pact, the multilateral agreements about national borders signed by the foreign ministers of France, Germany, Belgium, Poland, and Czechoslovakia, with Britain and Italy serving as guarantors. Proclaimed by florid gentlemen in frock coats as the beginning of a new order based on collective security, Locarno—a European illusion as doomed as the Wilsonian idealism it imitated—did in fact foster a long moment of euphoria. *"Nous avons parlé européen"* ("we've spoken European"), France's suave foreign minister, Aristide Briand, quipped. As Du Bois's train carried him along the familiar route from Antwerp via Frankfurt to Berlin, the hot, dry summer weather making for the outstanding wine harvests that year perfectly complemented the sanguine mood that seemed to envelop the continent. He arrived in Berlin, mistakenly anticipating only a brief stay before heading northeast by rail to Stettin (today, the Polish port city Szczecin), then across the Baltic Sea to Leningrad. The account of his transit through Germany is astonishingly brief. Where he stayed, persons he saw, sites he visited are unrecorded, despite the singular fact that this was his first visit in more than thirty years. Perhaps impatience with the delay, distress by things seen, and excitement about the unknown ahead explain Du Bois's unusual taciturnity—the formulaic sentences somehow devoid of depth.

He writes of seeing poverty "struggling on the ruins of the empire," of much oppression and disorganization that left an "unforgettable impression." It cannot be known how keenly he may have sensed the lift being given the people by the Dawes Plan which had just regularized Germany's reparations debt and provided for a massive infusion of American and British bank loans to help stabilize the mark. The Locarno Pact had ended the French army's humiliating occupation of the Ruhr, authorized the Allied evacuation of Cologne, and enabled Germany to enter the League of Nations just as Du Bois arrived. But the scene in Berlin was still one of widespread, gnawing hardship for the working classes and deepening political disaffection on the part of the middle classes. Cabaret life had begun to sizzle with an athletic decadence, but the shabby street crowds had the look of outpatients, hollow-eyed victims recovering from the disastrous inflation of 1923–24 when people bought food with wheelbarrows filled with marks.

To enter the Soviet Union in late summer of 1926 was to catch up with history, or so Du Bois believed. He had finally been able to sail from Stettin on August 14, disembarking at Kronshtadt, the fortified naval port in the Gulf of Finland. The history of the great naval base stretched back to the first fortifications raised by Peter the Great in 1703. The Bolshevik revolution had stumbled badly there five years earlier after the Kronshtadt sailors mutinied against the regime they had helped to make possible. Kronshtadt marked the real beginnings of an ideological pilgrimage that would lead Du Bois "mentally . . . to know Karl Marx and Lenin." Never before in life had he been as stirred as he would be by two months in Russia. Everywhere there still existed the ravages of the civil war and xenophobic memories of the American, British, French, and Japanese invasions. Petrograd, recently renamed after Lenin, had easily as many shabby crowds and as much dilapidation as Berlin, yet Du Bois reacted differently to what he saw there. As he strolled the Nevsky Prospekt, following its grand course to the Neva and its monumental Alexander Nevsky bridge, Du Bois began almost immediately to feel a special relationship to the Soviet experiment. Walking in the Palace Square at twilight, he meditated on the misspent glory of the fallen tsarist regime as he stared at the massive Winter Palace. It "loomed red-brown, and the statues and chimneys above it were as ghosts," he recorded in his notebook." No ghosts inhabited the regime born in the Smolny Institute a little farther along the Neva.

"Russia is at work," the notebook exclaimed. "God how these officials work!" A hardworking Du Bois marveled at the pace kept up by these servants of the people who spent six hours in their offices and "six to eight hours in inspections and lectures." Traveling by rail to Moscow on an itinerary that would take him afterward to Nizhni Novogorod (Gorki, today), a cradle of Russian civilization, Kiev, capital of the Ukraine, then south to Odessa, he would observe legions of ragged, hungry peasants and scores of ruined towns. In the Soviet capital, where not even a dozen automobiles circulated, he watched masses of "truculent and over-assertive" Muscovites fight for places in packed streetcars. He described seeing the "wild waifs of the sewers." Yet even though the "red weal of war-suffering and of famine still lay across the land," Du Bois caught the spirit of sacrifice and onward movement animating the people. The evening of his Moscow arrival, the twenty-eighth, he was disgusted by a story in *The New York Times* dated the very day he had landed at Kronshtadt claiming, Du Bois recalled, " 'Revolution has broken out in Cronstadt. Streets are flowing with blood!' " He patrolled new museums and toured some of the new factories, listening attentively. He wrote of gathering some documents and figures, and of plying "officials and teachers with questions." All these things were "physical," however, he said. What touched him at his core was the spirit of the new Soviet Man and Woman. "Here was a people seeking a new way of life through learning and truth." There was little prostitution or crime to be seen, some drunkenness, yes, and, although priests were everywhere, the state had taken religion out of the schools. Watching 200,000 young people marching through Red Square on Youth Day moved him. Not everyone was happy, but Du Bois was certain that most Russians "saw a bitter past being succeeded by a great future, not swiftly, but surely."

Yet, despite these enthusiasms, there is a curious solitariness to his reporting as he roamed about from his hotel in Red Square, no mention of people he could have been expected to meet in the fields of education, the arts, or government. August was not the best month in which to find them, probably, as many of the *nomenklatura* would have been away from Moscow on vacation, nor had the rushed decision to come to Russia allowed him time to write ahead. "Russia, in 1926," in the November *Crisis*, grandly and vaguely relates conversations with "peasants and laborers, Commissars of the Republic, teachers and children," but no names and titles are given. Du Bois might have been expected to request an interview with Maxim Gorky, inspirer of the Soviet regime's official cultural doctrine of Socialist Realism, or with Anatoly Lunacharsky, the commissar of education whose reforms were moderately influenced by American ideas of progressive education. In fact, he does seem to have met Karl Radek and Lunacharsky's assistant. The young director Sergei Eisenstein, whose *Battleship Potemkin* had catapulted him into the front ranks of world filmmaking early that year, was on location. Given Du Bois's writings on the subject of women's rights, should he not also have tried to see Alexandra Kollontai, whose *New Morality and the Working Class* pushed the envelope of the new morality of the sexes ("free love") further than Lenin felt he could permit? These and other architects of the much professed, and soon suppressed, proletarian culture movement ("Proletkult") such as Vladimir Mayakovski, Vsevolod Meyerhold, and above all Alexander Bogdanov, were the nurturers of the new Soviet Man and Woman who so much impressed Du Bois—citizens unfettered by religious superstition, able to divorce on grounds of incompatibility, afforded the option of abortion, and provided free child day care. These new men and women were being liberated from avarice and the class enmities it bred, he thought, and were learning to live unselfishly for the good of the collective. After less than three weeks in the country, zeal for the regime impelled him to write James Weldon Johnson one of the most ebulliently friendly letters preserved in the immense Du Bois correspondence. The place was "a revelation—a tremendous eye-opener," he cheered. Russia was pointing the way, "and we've got to get in the line. . . . Regards to White, Bagnall, and all the gang. Tell Seligman that Moscow has the greatest collection of modern art in the world—Monet, Degas, Gauguin, Matisse, Derain, Picasso, Van Gogh—marvellous. Yours truly."

Du Bois's travels in Russia, "alone and unaccompanied," coincided with the last months of the "High NEP," the three relatively prosperous years of 1924, 1925, and 1926 that came after the Tenth Party Congress had adopted Lenin and Nikolai Bukharin's New Economic Policy (NEP) in 1921. In order to gen-erate capital for the economy's state-run sectors of heavy industry, public utili-ties, transportation, and natural resources, the NEP allowed peasant proprietors to hire up to twelve workers and to profit from the private sale of produce; small private businesses were legalized and a robust market economy encouraged within limits. As a result, Russia enjoyed a level of prosperity in 1926 not seen since 1913. Du Bois would not have known that the modest signs of economic abundance he saw that summer had fueled a deadly political crisis within the Communist party leadership that had only just been temporarily contained a month before he disembarked at Kronshtadt. Stalin's uninspired, autocratic, and increasingly sinister performance as general secretary of the Party had finally convinced the ablest intellectual (with the worst sense of timing) among the Bolsheviks, Leon Trotsky, that he should join the "United Opposition" led by Grigori Zinoviev, the Party boss of Leningrad and head of the Comintern, Lev Kamenev, former chairman of the Moscow Soviet, and a large number of other dissidents. Nearly two years of polemics—from early 1926 until December 1927—would ensue from Trotsky's fateful decision in which the so-called United Opposition dressed up a largely raw power struggle in ideological purity, ac-cusing the general secretary of favoring rich peasants over industrial workers and of failing to advance world revolution. Stalin had trumped them ideologically with his defense of "socialism in one country" and, more importantly, politically with the loyalty of Bukharin and enough votes at the mid-July Plenary Session of the Central Committee to strip Trotsky, Kamenev, Zinoviev, and their allies of Politburo membership and Party titles. The United Opposition would regroup and persevere, but had Du Bois been extended the privilege of meeting any of its members, it would have been a rendezvous with the doomed. The Fifteenth Party Congress convened by Stalin in December 1927 would expel the entire opposition group, sending Trotsky into internal exile at Alma-Ata and replacing the New Economic Policy with the First Five Year Plan.

Solitary (although he does mention "one Russian speaking friend"), communicating in German when he could, Du Bois could have been at best only dimly aware of the momentous political tragedy unfolding in the Kremlin. A month in Moscow was enough anyway, he decided. "Moscow is bureaucracy. Real Russia lies outside." He pressed on to Nizhni Novogorod and Kiev, finding everywhere in the more than two thousand miles of travel signs of a new egalitarian social order that until then he had only dreamt might be possible. Many times, he was moved simply to sit still and gaze at Russia so that "the spirit of its life and people might enter" his veins. Rejoicing in finding that the Soviet regime was determined to make working men and women "the center of modern power and culture," the editor predicted, much as would the young Sidney Hook on a visit two years later, that the Russian Revolution would "sweep the world" if it succeeded in harnessing wealth and knowledge for the benefit of the majority. The teleology of global class revolution now began to vie powerfully with the concept of the superordinate power of race in Du Bois's thinking. If race was the problem of the twentieth century, after this first encounter with the Soviet Union he also began to regard class as a dilemma of comparable magnitude. A more thorough reading of the works of Marx, Engels, and Lenin would have to be deferred several years, but Du Bois had seen enough in two months of the theory of scientific socialism being put into practice to venture an informed opinion in "Russia, 1926." In pregnant language reminiscent of a Protestant Reformation divine, Du Bois told of standing "in astonishment and wonder at the revelation of Russia" that had come to him. He might be "partially deceived and half-informed," but if what he had seen and heard with his eyes and ears in Russia was Bolshevism, "I am a Bolshevik." He would write later that when he left Russia he saw more clearly than ever before the limitations inherent in the belief of people of color that achieving full voting rights and "letting a few of our capitalists share with whites in the exploitation of our masses would never be the solution of our problem."

He returned by way of Italy and Greece in first-class comfort to the United States in October breathing anticapitalist fire and very probably writing the first pages of what would become *Dark Princess*, his second novel. American and Western European capital were using "every modern weapon to crush Russia," and the editor would discourse gravely in *The Crisis* on the spread of monopoly capital in the United States. "Poverty and Wealth will gird themselves for a new battle in this land during the 21st Century," he predicted with what may prove to be awful accuracy. The redesigned magazine, appearing in December 1927 and bearing a strong resemblance to *Opportunity*, took on a more aggressive tone. The March issue permanently deleted contributing editor Fauset from the masthead and substituted "The Wide Wide World" for the editor's longstanding, pugnacious "Opinion" department. Much to one original board member's regret, Du Bois's particular opinions were now lodged in a section called "Postscripts." The format was different but the animating voice was, as always, pure Du Bois. "My Recent Journey" appeared in the December issue along with a lamentation for Eugene Debs, the one national political figure Du Bois admired above all others for many years. The loss of "so great a mind and so brave a heart" was a national calamity. Debs had bowed to shortsighted expediency in his 1912 presidential campaign when he declined to make a special appeal to black voters, but Du Bois insisted that the broken old Socialist leader had gone to his grave in the full knowledge that organized labor must embrace Negroes, that "unless white labor recognizes the brotherhood of man it becomes the helpless tool of modern industrial imperialism." "Judging Russia" appeared that February. "The Wide Wide World" in the March issue focused on the growing repression of Italian fascism and the struggle for power in Germany between the right and left. United States investments in Latin America were also likely to supply rationales for widespread interventions on the Nicaragua model, warned Du Bois. Nevertheless, some of his sharpest critics would have noted the editor's lame interpretation of the Liberian Firestone concession as a "cause for concern" that could readily be minimized by the influence of vigilant black American voters.

THE SOVIET UNION had a greater impact on Du Bois than it had on the magazine. Circulation figures for *The Crisis* continued to slide, whether because of or in spite of the editor's Bolshevism. At the beginning of the year, 1927, they ran at about 30,000 a month. Dill searched diligently for advertisements, squeezed out savings, and fretted terribly over the monthly fumbles. A swastika design on page 66 of the December issue had escaped detection. He hoped "our Jewish friends . . . will forgive us," and he could only pray that Walter White's distressing grammar on page 74 ("whom") wouldn't "give us a bad name." Taken on by Du Bois as a special research assistant during 1926, recent University of Chicago graduate Horace Mann Bond recalled the scene at *The Crisis*. "It was something out of Dickens," Bond said. The "gnome-like" business manager sat in the outer office guarding his employer's inner sanctum where "every inch of wall space [was] covered with books that were also liberally distributed on every possible repository." For sixteen dedicated years, the forty-six-year-old, bachelor business manager had had no other life than *The Crisis* and its master. Du Bois took their interdependence, his and Dill's, for granted; whereas it sustained Dill's very identity. But Du Bois noticed that Dill was running down. He had encouraged him to attend a family reunion, his first in twenty-five years, and Dill returned to work claiming to be refreshed, though obviously still tired. Shortly afterward, this cultured, fastidious man's life fell apart in a homosexual encounter and arrest in a public lavatory. Du Bois's reaction was one of formal Victorian displeasure masked by genuine compassion. Never for a moment had he "contemplated continuing my life work without you by my side," his letter terminating their relationship began. But the work of *The Crisis* was more important than individuals. "For ten years we have been losing ground," and the magazine could not "longer afford [Dill's] salary." Urging Dill to "forget the little incident that has so worried you out of all proportion to its significance," Du Bois closed with the assurance that the "little incident" had no bearing at all upon his painful decision. More than thirty years later, however, the editor made a self-reproachful admission in *The Autobiography*, writing of a "new and undreamed aspect of sex" bursting upon him, of having "never understood the tragedy of Oscar Wilde," and of dismissing a "coworker forthwith" and spending "heavy days regretting my act."

In fact, the unhinged business manager would remain at his desk until February 1928, while *The Crisis* continued its decline. Du Bois had already begun to think that Dill would have to go even before the "little incident." Afterward, however, he heaped more than a fair share of blame on Dill for the falling circulation, confiding to Dill's sister that, "although he has tried hard to stem the tide," the business manager simply was not "fit for the work." Only Ovington or Joel Spingarn would have dared to ask if the editor himself continued to be as deeply interested in the work as in earlier years. The widening span of interests and information Du Bois brought to the magazine—Africa, imperialism, Soviet communism, labor, literary criticism, social science research—remained exceptional. Annual special issues on higher education and children were still eagerly awaited and provided valuable data on the social progress of the upper tiers of colored America. Even so, signs of a grip less steady and of hurried experimentation were unmistakable. "The Wide Wide World" department, which had replaced "Opinion" in March 1927, was replaced three months later by "As the Crow Flies." A plethora of photographs of cute, neat children, prospering citizens, Greek letter and club activities, accompanied by a feast of advertisements altered somewhat the publication's activist texture. Without Fauset and now that Dill was underperforming, worrisome mixups in attribution continued. Georgia Johnson was astonished to see one of her poems credited to Frank Home in the April number. Young John Davis, having done a masterful job with Dill's help of putting out *The Crisis* and winnowing finalists for the Krigwa awards, had been given barely enough time to make his first literature classes in Harvard's graduate school that September. Marvel Jackson had arrived from Minneapolis at the beginning of the year to serve as capable secretary to the editor, but the publication functioned throughout 1927 increasingly on autopilot.

Du Bois was overcommitted, overworked, distracted, and occasionally even disinterested. He had hurried from the docks almost immediately to preside over the *Crisis*/Krigwa awards ceremony at International House on the evening of October 25. The field reports he expected to find on his desk pertaining to Negro common schools had not been sent by one of his assistants. This was the research project Du Bois had persuaded the new American Fund for Public Service (the Garland Fund, established by a young millionaire who declined his father's million-dollar legacy) to underwrite for five thousand dollars in May of 1925. Garland Fund chairman Roger Baldwin's esteem for the editor and James Weldon Johnson's election to the board of directors had assured the project a fair hearing. A broad, careful study of Negro elementary school education was of the highest priority for Du Bois. In effect, it was intended to update the 1911 Atlanta University Study. The growing racial disparities in per capita expenditures in the southern states were devastating the minds of almost an entire generation of young people of color. In another twenty-five years or more, he knew that the educational and cultural consequences would have become irreversible. Du Bois had turned immediately for research assistance to two of the best young minds in the pool of Talented Tenth scholarship, E. Franklin Frazier and Horace Mann Bond. Frazier's performance during the summer of 1925, as he filed reports and expenses for research conducted in Alabama and South Carolina, had been fully satisfactory, so much so that in January 1927 Du Bois and Dill hoped to obtain Rosenwald money in order to offer Frazier the position of managing editor of *The Crisis*. But Bond's Oklahoma materials were still undelivered when Du Bois returned from Europe. Reading between the apologetic lines, the annoying upshot of correspondence between Chicago, where Bond had resumed graduate studies at the university, and Fifth Avenue was that the Oklahoma common school investigation had been a casualty of time constraints and competing agendas. The never-to-be-completed report on southern elementary school conditions would shortly involve Du Bois and Johnson in a libel suit.

Meanwhile, Du Bois managed more activities and balanced more commitments than a professional juggler. He sped away to a California lecture tour in mid-January after his friends the Somervilles of Los Angeles assured him the trip was worthwhile. "As to the number of lectures, use your own judgment," he wrote. Barely back at his desk, he found an S.O.S. from Frazier, who was being forced out of the directorship of Morehouse College's new Atlanta School of Social Work. Assertive and often blunt-spoken, Frazier's dismissive review of *The Basis of Racial Adjustment* was a case in point. The author of the book, T. J. Woofter, was one of the white South's foremost self-proclaimed liberals. Frazier's criticism of the study as a "rationalization of the southern position" was deemed recklessly cheeky. When he violated southern racial etiquette by

The burning of William Brown, Omaha, Nebraska, September 28, 1919. *Prints and Images, The Library of Congress.*

Nina Yolande Du Bois.
*Special Collections,
The W.E.B. Du Bois Library,
University of Massachusetts
at Amherst.*

(Right to left) Marcus Garvey, Prince Tovalou Houenou of Dahomey, and a Garvey associate, ca. 1924. *Courtesy of Mrs. Donna Mussenden VanDerZee.*

"And So the Girl Marries." The wedding of Yolande Du Bois and Countee Cullen, 1928. *Special Collections, The W.E.B. Du Bois Library, University of Massachusetts at Amherst.*

Langston Hughes, Charles S. Johnson, E. Franklin Frazier, Rudolph Fisher, and Hubert Delaney. Photographed by Regina Andrews, ca. 1926. *Moorland-Spingarn Research Center, Howard University.*

ABOVE RIGHT: Jackson Davis, associate director of the General Education Board, ca. late 1930s. *Courtesy of the Rockefeller Archive Center.*

LEFT: James Weldon Johnson and W.E.B. Du Bois at ease at Johnson's summer home in Great Barrington, Massachusetts, ca. early 1930s. *Courtesy of Dr. Sondra K. Wilson.*

Meeting of the board of advisers of the *Encyclopedia of the Negro*, May 1936. (Left to right, back row) Arthur Schomburg (second), Joel Spingarn (third), Florence Read (eighth), Mordecai Johnson. (Front row) Otelia Cromwell, Monroe Work, Charles H. Wesley, Benjamin P. Brawley, James Weldon Johnson (center), W.E.B. Du Bois, and second from right, Alain Locke, May 1936. *Special Collections, The W.E.B. Du Bois Library, University of Massachusetts at Amherst.*

Second Amenia conference participants. (Last row, third from left) Roy Wilkins. (Left to right, third row) Ralph Bunche, W.E.B. Du Bois (second), E. Franklin Frazier (fifth), Mary White Ovington (seventh), and last, standing on the right, Walter White. (Second row, seated) Joel Spingarn in center, August 18–21, 1933. *Courtesy of Dr. Sondra K. Wilson.*

W.E.B. Du Bois, Richard B. Harrison ("De Lawd" in Marc Connelly's musical play, *The Green Pastures*), John Hope, president of Atlanta University, and Will W. Alexander, director of the Commission on Interracial Cooperation, standing in front of President Hope's home, ca. 1934. *Special Collections, Robert Woodruff Library, Clark Atlanta University.*

W.E.B. Du Bois in Sisters Chapel, Spelman College, on the occasion of his seventieth birthday convocation, February 1938. *Special Collections, The W.E.B. Du Bois Library, University of Massachusetts at Amherst.*

James E. Jackson, as an Eagle Scout, age sixteen, before joining the Communist Party, 1930. *Courtesy of Esther and James Jackson.*

Fiftieth Harvard class reunion (1890), June 1940. W.E.B. Du Bois, center rear. *Special Collections, The W.E.B. Du Bois Library, University of Massachusetts at Amherst.*

Walter Francis White, executive
director, NAACP, ca. 1940s.
*Portrait Collection, Schomburg
Center for Research in Black
Culture, New York Public Library.*

W.E.B. Du Bois, E. Franklin Frazier, and Horace Mann Bond and children, Julian and
Jane. Fort Valley State College, Fort Valley, Georgia, 1924. *Courtesy of Hon. Julian Bond.*

The Du Boises on a visit to the Thomas Bells in Newark, New Jersey. Du Bois Williams, W.E.B. Du Bois, Yolande, Nina, Mrs. Bell, ca. 1939. *Courtesy of Mrs. Katherine Bell Banks.*

Virginia Alexander, ca. 1935. *Special Collections, The W.E.B. Du Bois Library, University of Massachusetts at Amherst.*

Edwin Embree, director, Julius Rosenwald Fund, and George Streator, first black *New York Times* reporter, in Fisk University Chapel, 1947. *Fisk University Archives.*

W.E.B. Du Bois with Henry A. Wallace, 1948. Donated in the memory of Dr. W.E.B. Du Bois and Henry Wallace by Julius Lazarus.

Paul Robeson, W.E.B. Du Bois, and Vito Marcantonio, 1950. *Special Collections, Moorland-Spingarn Research Center, Howard University.*

The Peace Information Center defendants and Shirley Graham Du Bois. (Left to right) Kyrle Elkin, Sylvia Soloff, W.E.B. Du Bois, Abbott Simon, February 1951. *Special Collections, The W.E.B. Du Bois Library, University of Massachusetts at Amherst.*

(Left to right) Alphaeus Hunton, Dorothy Hunton, Paul Robeson, W.E.B. Du Bois, on the occasion of Alphaeus Hunton's release from federal prison, 1955. *Courtesy of Mrs. Dorothy Hunton.*

(Left to right) Shirley Graham Du Bois, W.E.B. Du Bois, Ruth Lazarus, Paul Strand, and Elizabeth Moos, Orgeval, France, 1958. *Courtesy of Madame Ruth Lazarus.*

W.E.B. Du Bois with Mao Tse-tung at Mao's villa in south central China, April 1959. *Special Collections, The W.E.B. Du Bois Library, University of Massachusetts at Amherst.*

(Left to right) Alla Bobricheva, W.E.B. Du Bois, Nikita Khruschev, and Shirley Graham Du Bois. Meeting in the Kremlin on November 7, 1958, after the October Day parade in Red Square. *Special Collections, The W.E.B. Du Bois Library, University of Massachussetts at Amherst.*

Cutting the ninety-fifth-birthday cake at the Du Boises, with the Kwame Nkrumahs, Accra, Ghana, February 23, 1963. *Special Collections, The W.E.B. Du Bois Library, University of Massachusetts at Amherst.*

The last photo taken of W.E.B. Du Bois at home in Accra, Ghana, 1963. *Special Collections, The W.E.B. Du Bois Library, University of Massachusetts at Amherst.*

refusing to kowtow to a white female associate, however, his fate was sealed by the school's white trustees. For a brief few weeks, Fisk had looked like an ideal forum for Frazier's stellar abilities. But Frazier's Fisk sources reported that the new white president, Thomas Elsa Jones, had been advised by influential whites, in the manner of the instructions that would accompany the protagonist of *Invisible Man*, to "keep this nigger running." At thirty-two, with a wife to support, the able sociologist was desperate. The Fisk president had already written to explain to Du Bois why, even though Frazier had impressed him, he was "not certain that Mr. Frazier is just the man we need . . . because of local conditions here." Du Bois's second letter in the matter advised Jones not to make a mistake on Frazier: "one of the classic ways of getting rid of well-educated and efficient colored men . . . is the more or less vague accusation that they cannot get on with the white South." Jones wrangled. Frazier's professors confided "peculiarities about his personality." But rather than risk the fury of a *Crisis* thunderbolt, Fisk finally decided to gamble on an outstanding scholar. Frazier joined its faculty in academic year 1927–28.

The penultimate round of Krigwa awards required attention. Setting the deadline for June 15, a significant portion of the prize money was earmarked for entries dealing with business, although a purse of six hundred dollars was set aside in Chesnutt's honor. Du Bois's expressed reservations about the literary thrust of the Renaissance had been well received by several of the race's most successful capitalists. Maggie Lena Walker, president of Richmond, Virginia's St. Luke's Penny Savings Bank and *grande dame* of rags-to-riches success after the demise of Madame Walker in 1919; Charles Clinton Spaulding, president of Durham's powerful North Carolina Mutual Life Insurance Company; and Harry Pace, a Du Bois protégé who now headed Cleveland's Northeastern Life Insurance Company, sent checks for business prizes. This time, the editor would have to read nearly four hundred Krigwa entries without experienced helpers. Entrants probably would have received gentler rejections from Fauset than such typical Du Bois responses as one to a Mrs. Butler—"My dear Madame, your poetry . . . is rather too trite for our use." His disappointment with the quality of the submissions for the business prizes (only 13 out of 375) would cause Du Bois to cancel awards in that category for 1927. "The young Negro writers do not realize the tremendous development and paramount importance of business," he lamented to Maggie Walker after extending the business deadline to July 1928. As much as he had recently come to admire communism in Russia, Du Bois continued to praise the virtues of private enterprise in the United States and to exhort Negroes to acquire habits of industry and frugality that he deemed to be in all too short supply among them. "I have long been a socialist," he would reiterate in the summer of 1928, yet he had no illusions about the practical application of Socialist solutions to problems of labor and wealth under the prevailing economic system. As was often the case, however, even as he pushed one set of ideas or policies of Du Bois was already beginning to think of formulating very different approaches to the accumulation of minority wealth. He was still a year away from the grim conclusions of "Our Economic Future," an editorial that skewered the creed of bootstrap group advancement that exercised such a powerful hold on the followers of Washington and Garvey.

Preparations for the fourth Pan-African Congress, another Du Bois venture, had not gone smoothly. Toward the end of 1925, he had finally had to abandon plans for a venue in the West Indies. Once again, the clubwomen whose treasury had helped make possible the third Pan-African Congress came to his assistance with a proposal to underwrite an August 1927 meeting in New York City. Although Du Bois's lack of enthusiasm for the New York venture is evident from the correspondence, the dedicated women of the NACW and of the Women's International Circle (League) for Peace and Foreign Relations, led by Mrs. Annie Dingle and the redoubtable Addie Waits Hunton, plunged into preparations for the congress. The sixty-year-old Hunton was a legend among feminists and civil rights leaders. A founding member of the NACW, she had been one of only three women of color commissioned by the YWCA to serve black troops in France during the war. As president of the International Council of Women of the Darker Races, Hunton volunteered the womanpower and considerable resources of the interlinked women's organizations. Du Bois supplied names of distinguished sponsors and potential delegates, alerting Dingle and Hunton to pitfalls of colonial censors and subservient Francophones — men, such as Diagne and Candace, who were "both conservative and reactionary and afraid of American Negro radicalism."

The officers of the Women's International Circle for Peace and Foreign Relations immediately ran into pitfalls much closer to home. Their plan to have the congress endorsed by the Democratic governor of the state and New York's mayor was temporarily shelved when the city's powerful black commissioner of civil service, Harvard-educated Ferdinand Q. Morton ("the boss of Black Tammany"), judged the proposal impolitic and advised the editor and his collaborators that most black people believed their destiny would be "determined by our national origins rather than our ethnic origins." More misunderstandings arose during the final weeks. Hunton had supposed that the NAACP would handle publicity for the congress, whereas Du Bois had agreed only to advertise the meeting in The Crisis. At the end of July, the astonished officers of the Circle for Peace and Foreign Relations learned that they, not Du Bois, were responsible for the speakers and topics for the congress. "We have taken no thought of the above, thinking our duty lay in getting money and delegates," Hunton wrote plaintively. Another major oversight would result in no stenographic report being made of the fourth Pan-African Congress. "She is incompetent, though has splendid ideas," Du Bois would say later of the energetic Hunton. Even so, the clubwomen succeeded in raising three thousand indispensable dollars and a fine editorial tribute from the *Amsterdam News*, Harlem's newspaper of record. Still, it would probably have been wiser from the point of view of publicity and attendance not to have scheduled the congress to run simultaneously with the national convention of the Elks, fifty thousand of whom paraded through Harlem on opening day.

The lengthy article running in the Sunday *New York Times* a week before the congress opened was almost certainly written by Du Bois himself. The declaratory sentences were unmistakable trademarks. "The question of the status of the negro [sic] in modern society" was no longer a domestic problem of the United States, the unsigned writer lectured. Nor was it a parochial West Indian or a colonial policy problem. "It is rather a great world-wide problem to be viewed and considered as a whole." Above all, emphasized the *Times* article, the problem of the Negro had nothing to do with Garvey's "now defunct 'Back to Africa Movement.' " With Du Bois presiding and Logan serving as secretary, the first of the four days of sessions opened in Harlem's St. Mark's Methodist Episcopal Church on Sunday afternoon, August 21, with the singing of the Negro National Anthem. Once again, Ida Gibbs Hunt and Jessie Fauset, joined by sister Helen, had attended to critical organizational details that might have escaped the flustered Hunton and held no interest for a preoccupied Du Bois. When the final session closed at Abyssinian Baptist Church on Wednesday night the congress would have drawn some five thousand participants, among whom 280 were paid delegates representing twenty-two states and the District of Columbia, as well as Haiti, the Virgin Islands, the Bahamas, and Barbados; the Gold Coast, Sierra Leone, Nigeria, and Liberia; Germany; and India. Governor Alfred E. Smith's and Mayor James Walker's noncommittal greetings were read to Sunday's opening session, followed by Hunton, who spoke movingly of the "vision of brotherhood of the darker races," according to the *Amsterdam News*. Du Bois crisply rehearsed the history of the pan-African movement, delighting the capacity audience with a procession of young women carrying the flags of countries with significant African populations along with a census for each country.

The editor had after all taken on the job of coralling an impressive roster of eleventh-hour speakers. The Gold Coast's Chief Nana Amoah III, over from London to replay his role in the third congress, brought greetings in full regalia and was reported to have caused the assembly "almost to gasp" by his British English as he praised the work of women in Africa and America. Haiti's internationally respected Dantes Bellegarde aroused similar Harlem wonderment when he followed Amoah at the podium to deliver a spirited discourse in purest French with Logan giving a running translation. Leslie Pinckney Hill, principal of Pennsylvania's Institute for Colored Youth and one of Du Bois's close friends, discussed impediments to providing quality education. The address by the NAACP's Pickens, who reported on his participation in the Brussels Conference for Oppressed Races, outmatched the attention paid by the press to all others on opening day. Due to sail for Russia soon, Pickens managed to sound like a schooled convert to Marxism. "Urges Proletarian Unity," the *Herald Tribune* captioned its article on the congress and Pickens's speech. The congress moved to Grace Congregational Church for Monday's and Tuesday's proceedings, which were well attended by audiences the *Amsterdam News* described as "seemingly unmindful of the [Elks] parade taking place as they considered soberly the future of Africa."

The closing session at Abyssinian Baptist Church was presided over by Du Bois's old Harvard classmate Clement Morgan. The assembly was particularly engrossed by two relatively young scholars whose anthropological knowledge of Africa was probably unexcelled in the United States: Northwestern University's Melville Herskovits and Howard University's William Leo Hansberry. Virtually unknown to the public for most of his professional life, Hansberry, drawn to his field by reading Du Bois's *The Negro* as an undergraduate, had offered the first courses in an American university on Negro civilizations in the ancient world. Hansberry's Howard colleague and contemporary, the historian Charles Wesley, summarized the principal findings of his *Negro Labor in the United States, 1850–1925*, a new monograph destined to become a classic. Writer John W. Vandercook, whose *Black Majesty*, a popular history of Haiti's Henri Christophe, was scheduled for imminent release by Harper & Brothers, presented a fascinating account of the island's early nineteenth-century political history. The delegates restated the demand that Africa be developed for the Africans "and not merely for the profit of Europeans." The attitude of all imperial powers was "fundamentally wrong," declared the Congress in a resolution that reflected less worldliness than might have been expected. "They are seeking profit, not men; they want trade and industry more than civilization and spiritual uplift." Narrow focusing of concerns was deplored. The race in America was exhorted to fix its eyes "upon the international problems of the color line." The voice of Du Bois in the text was unmistakable: "We desire to see freedom and real national independence in Egypt, in China, in India. We demand the cessation of the interference of the United States in the affairs of Central and South America."

Despite notice by the New York press, *The Christian Science Monitor,* and even the *Daily Worker,* Du Bois was clearly disappointed with the results of the congress. Less than three hundred delegates from the United States and a handful representing the Antilles, West Africa, Europe, and India fell far short of the parliament of the darker races he had once envisaged. In comparison with the second congress, whose sessions in London, Brussels, and Paris were well-attended, the Harlem convocation was distinctly a mediocre affair. Recuperating in the Catskills, an exhausted and depressed Ida Hunt came to the conclusion that the Pan-African Congress movement was too nonexclusive and publicity-conscious for its own good. Imperial powers would never permit it to succeed while it conducted its business so openly. At the very least, the name should be changed to the Human Rights Association or the Free Government Association, she urged Hunton. "Ask Du Bois what he thinks about this." For Du Bois, however, the movement's ailments went deeper than its name or than the refusal of the French government to permit the convening of the next Pan-African Congress in Algiers, Tunis, or even Marseilles, as voted by the delegates. He had resolved some time ago, he wrote Bellegarde, that "until we black folk developed international interests, that I would not undertake to push the Pan African Congress." He was "willing to do anything that the race is willing to do." Clearly the race was more inclined to share the view of civil service commissioner Morton that its most pressing concerns stopped at the water's edge. Yet to peruse any issue of *The Crisis* was to be reassured that its editor possessed the keenest understanding of the importance of those national concerns. Eighteen years would elapse before the fifth Pan-African Congress was convened in Manchester, England.

DU BOIS'S VARIOUS activities during the summer and fall of 1927 were remarkable even for him, partly because Hunton and her associates spared him considerable toil by taking on the fund-raising and paperwork involved in mounting the congress. There were pressing family matters. Yolande wished to spend the summer studying in France. Madame Calman-Levy obliged his request to find good, inexpensive lodgings in Paris, while he wrote to the University of Grenoble in order to arrange accommodations in the Foyer de l'Etudiante during Yolande's three-month study abroad. Their daughter's accommodations secured, Will and Nina turned anxiously to solving their own. St. Nicholas Avenue had become untenable. The lodgers were more obstreperous than ever, and the former janitor, now living elsewhere, had begun to harass them. That September they decided to move to the Dunbar and have Nail sell 606. The Paul Laurence Dunbar Apartments, a cooperative complex under construction at 149th–150th streets, was financed by the Rockefellers. An oblong block wide and deep between Seventh and Eighth Avenues, the Dunbar, its cocoa brown brick facade incised by archways giving it the appearance of a Florentine palazzo, was to be the ne plus ultra in Harlem housing.

The announced intent of the Rockefellers had been to provide affordable, well-built housing for black working-class families. In short order, however, the

Dunbar would become the preserve of the Talented Tenth. It was also home for flashy, prospering families, such as the Enrique Cachemailles and the Lewis H. Faircloughs and such stylish singles as Sadella Ten Eyck and Ollie Capdeville, their apartment soirees and country retreat weekends reported breathlessly in the *Dunbar News* bulletin. In applying for membership in the coop, Du Bois paid lip service to the Rockefeller pledge that it was meant to serve "the working class of people and that their demands should prevail." That said, however, he expressed the hope that resident manager Roscoe Conkling Bruce (fellow Harvard man and son of a Mississippi Negro Reconstruction senator) might persuade the Dunbar's board to permit the purchase of a seven-room apartment, the six-room unit being "really too small for us." In the final negotiations in November 1927, the Du Boises were permitted to buy two combined apartments (5G and J), into which they would move at the end of January.

Yolande's summer abroad and the acquisition of a new bundle of mortgages challenged Du Bois's messy financial virtuosity. The raucous dispute running throughout 1927 with Robert Lee Vann, the pugnacious publisher-editor of the Pittsburgh *Courier*, was a deadly serious challenge to his integrity. Vann was a model self-made man, a believer in Booker Washington's precepts who had risen from poverty in rural North Carolina to earn a law degree and achieve high municipal office in Pittsburgh. Unlike the Great Accommodator, however, Vann was as courageous as he was pragmatic. Opinionated, brilliant, fiercely independent, the forty-seven-year-old businessman hated Jim Crow with a passion that suffused his newspaper. His detestation of GOP racial hypocrisy was equally deep, but, in contrast to most black leaders who fumed in impotent loyalty, Vann would deserve considerable credit for leading black voters out of the party of Lincoln. The rival Chicago *Defender*, along with much of the black press, had withheld support from Randolph's BSCP after it demanded union recognition by the Pullman Corporation. The *Courier* championed the Brotherhood's cause. There was speculation that Vann sometimes applied his principles where they would do the most good for the *Courier*'s circulation. If true, then he had the right principles. By 1927, sixteen years after taking control, Vann had transformed a small, local newspaper into a sixteen-page weekly with a circulation of 60,000 and status as the most respected in black America, featuring bylines by Schuyler, White, and amateur historian Joel A. Rogers and reports from syndicated Washington correspondent Louis Lautier.

Relations between the *Courier*, *The Crisis*, and the NAACP collapsed in late 1926 with the unexpected suddenness of a highway accident. Breaking the news on October 9 with the headline "NAACP SLUSH FUND AIRED," the *Courier* uncovered what it predicted would be "the biggest scandal of the New Year." The brunt of Vann's attack was directed at the association's secretary. Johnson had exploited his membership on the Garland Fund's board of directors in order to steer more than thirty thousand dollars to the NAACP—dollars being misused, according to Vann, for rent, salaries, expenses, and to pay for "expensive and palatial offices on Fifth Avenue." Meanwhile, the Garland Fund had seen fit to award the BSCP, fighting for its life against the Pullman juggernaut, a mere $11,200. Vann compared that amount to the $26,552 granted to the Sweet Fund, which everybody knew was simply the NAACP's legal defense budget under another name. The *Courier* story compounded its charges with an aspersion on the validity of the $5,000 research award to Du Bois, insinuating that the editor's education study was a boondoggle. Both NAACP men always claimed to have no explanation for the newsman's motives other than some unintended slight of Vann. Until the October accusations, Du Bois and Vann had found themselves in general agreement. Both supported the BSCP and both were infuriated by Van Vechten's *Nigger Heaven*, Vann refusing to advertise the novel until White telegraphed an urgent appeal to reconsider. The editor reacted to Vann's accusations furiously, signing a press release with Johnson demanding an immediate retraction, followed by the threat of a lawsuit when Vann refused.

As the controversy raged throughout 1927, one of the Talented Tenth's most influential bodies, Sigma Pi Phi (the exclusive society of professional men called the Boulé), declined to take sides, despite Du Bois's repeated insistence. The editor didn't at all "like being called a thief," he seethed in a letter to the Grand Grammateus of Sigma Pi Phi, serving notice of protests sent to all the constituent chapters, or boulés. If the Boulé were truly a society of gentlemen with all members "pledged to uphold [its] 'honor,'" then Vann was a flagrant transgressor. But Du Bois received the distinct impression that The Grand Grammateus missed the gravity of Vann's offense. "Every American is entitled to a trial, but do we want a trial?" Dr. Allen Wesley wondered, rather too genially inviting Du Bois to help him "adjust this matter without much ado." After all, "people do not as a rule get to calling one another names without there is [sic] something back of it," he speculated in a follow-up letter. That some of the officers may have suspected that Vann's wounding allegations contained a grain of truth (especially as only portions of the education study materialized) made the Boulé's adoption of a nonpartisan stance all the more reasonable. Nearly a year after the initial *Courier* attack, Du Bois and Johnson were still awaiting a response to their two draft statements that were to have been presented to Vann by a special Boulé committee. "I have waited patiently for more than a month," Du Bois snapped at the end of September 1927. The Boulé's last word about "the unfortunate incident" came the following month when Du Bois received word of the special committee's decision that "both parties had erred and that the matter be closed without further action." Du Bois and Johnson would skirmish continually with Vann for three years, until the publisher-editor finally signed a retraction appearing simultaneously in the newspaper and the monthly. That Du Bois and Johnson failed to rally the Boulé to their side in a controversy impugning their professional integrity was a telling measure of the limitations of personal and organizational influence as the maturity and diversity of power and opinion began to shape a much different racial landscape. Much had changed in the structure of the leadership class and in the relations of power in black America since the time, hardly twenty years earlier, when a signal from Tuskegee had been sufficient to silence all but the most determined critics.

DU BOIS'S PRIDE in the Harlem Renaissance had always been ambivalent. In the fall of 1927, he figuratively held his nose as he reviewed McKay's *Home to Harlem,* sniffing that for the most part the novel "nauseated" him and made him feel "distinctly like taking a bath." Having been dealt a "blow in the face" a year earlier by Van Vechten's *Nigger Heaven,* Du Bois's distaste for the subject matter being featured by the young Renaissance artists and writers had become acutely painful by the beginning of 1928. More than a year had elapsed since "The Criteria of Negro Art," his revealing symposium in *The Crisis.* He knew now that a unique opportunity for art and letters, and therefore civil rights, was about to be forfeited by people of color, as he wrote Amy Spingarn in a long, late January letter. The opening was "greater than ever before and the number who are writing is growing," but they were still handicapped by cruel racial paradox. If they wrote honestly about their own inner lives and environments, white publishers claimed there was no market for the material. But if they caricatured their experiences, spicing them up with low comedy, sex, and violence ("follow[ing] the lead of Carl Van Vechten and Knopf and Boni and Liveright"), then publishers were only too happy to give white America "what it thinks that it wants to hear from Negroes." He was determined to "build up a counterpoise" to the Van Vechtens and the McKays. A black book-of-the-month club, perhaps, or prize monies distributed on a monthly rather than on an annual basis, he conjectured, inviting Spingarn's suggestions. Du Bois chose not to mention that a few weeks earlier he had sent his publisher the final manuscript for a novel written with the intention of putting the Harlem Renaissance back on the right track of art, virtue, and politics. "All art is propaganda, and ever will be" he had declared at the NAACP convention, and he was determined to put the axiom to the test.

Dark Princess: A Romance, Du Bois's three-hundred-page novel, was released by Harcourt, Brace and Company in April 1928. It was Du Bois's first large work of fiction since *The Quest of the Silver Fleece* seventeen years before, and he conceived of it as volume one in a series of novels encompassing the Aframerican experience — "a sort of black *Comédie Humaine*" in the manner of Balzac, he promised Alfred Harcourt. Strong women, intelligent and decisive (*virile* may not be inappropriate), and sensitive, educated males—well intentioned but underwhelming—were the signatures of Du Boisian fiction, along with a plenitude of history acted out across multiple time zones. *The Silver Fleece,* a spacious-enough drama unfolding in the red sunlight of Jim Crow, moves from African mystery in the rural South to sophisticated purlieus in Washington and New York and then returns to its climax in the New South of Henry Grady. *Dark Princess,* set in the 1920s, encompasses a great portion of the planet stretching "from Benares to Chicago," Du Bois wrote, "and from Berlin to Atlanta." As in the first novel, whose dark-skinned protagonist, Zora, energizes her unfocused lover Bles Alwyn, the main character in the second, "H.R.H. the Princess Kautilya of Bwodpur, India," stiffens the moral-fiber resolve and expands the world vision of an uprooted Matthew Towns, the Hampton-educated hero surnamed for George Towns, Du Bois's ally and friend from Atlanta University days.

Ovington believed she had seen the model for the princess on Du Bois's arm descending a ballroom staircase during the 1911 Universal Races Congress in London ("I thought her the loveliest person there, except perhaps for the darker daughter of the Haitian President"). Kautilya of Bwodpur was not a single woman, of course, but an amalgam of Du Boisian memories and current interests. Matthew Towns's astonished description upon first seeing her mimics Du Bois's own teenage bedazzlement at first seeing Lena Horne's great-aunt in the Fisk dining hall: "No human being could possibly have been as beautiful as she seemed to my young eyes in that far-off September night of 1885." Sensitive and sensual, Du Bois's protagonist may have been borrowed in some measure from Georgia Johnson. Toward the end of the novel, the princess sounds like Mildred Bryant, the author's Chicago lover, when she writes Towns from Virginia, "Dearest Matthew, my man." But then, Kautilya's regal bearing and cosmopolitan culture more often evoke Fauset. The model for Matthew Towns is Du Bois himself (as Bles Alwyn was in *The Silver Fleece*), a man of feminine sensibilities who defers to women and finds himself alternately manipulated and wonderfully improved by them—a man very different from the Du Bois the world knew.

Heroine and hero become acquainted over tea in Berlin's Tiergarten after Towns flattens an impudent white American whose unwanted attentions have distressed the princess. The southern-born Towns had abandoned the United States after Manhattan University annulled his medical school admission on racial grounds. "I was firm in my Hampton training," the bewildered valedictorian tells the princess. "Prejudice was [to be] a miasma that character burned away." "A radiantly beautiful woman, and she was colored," Kautilya is first and foremost of royal blood, serene in her centuries' old pedigree and only spottily informed about the descendants of American slaves. Intrigued, she reveals her membership in a secret international: "We represent—indeed I may say frankly, we are—part of a great committee of the darker peoples; of those who suffer under the arrogance and tyranny of the white world." Taking leave, she invites Towns to dinner to meet the committee. At dinner the following evening, the question of American Negro admission to the Great Council of the Darker Races caroms off the members, Arab, Chinese, Egyptian, Japanese, Hindu, like a billiard ball, until the Japanese, although professing "every human sympathy," cuts to the quick. "But for us here and for the larger company we represent," Du Bois has him explain, "there is the deeper question—that of the ability, qualifications, and real possibilities of the black race in Africa or elsewhere." This extraordinary question posed one of the central issues of Du Bois's novel, a question the princess seeks to answer for herself north and south of the Mason-Dixon Line, as she reappears at climactic moments in Towns's tumultuous odyssey.

His sense of purpose rekindled, Du Bois's hero returns to America, stopping in Harlem to deliver a message from the secret committee to a colorful personality wickedly modeled on Garvey: "Matthew had at first thought him an egotistic fool. But Perigua was no fool. He next put him down as an ignorant fanatic—but he was not ignorant." Overwhelming Towns with nonstop rhetoric, the fictional Garvey discloses a plan to mine the South's "lynching belt" with dynamite—"dynamite for every lynching mob," he shouts. Perplexed yet curious, Towns sets off to discover how much of Perigua's rantings about a national underground of black terrorists can be believed. The large chapter entitled "The Pullman Porter," an overload of melodrama and propaganda, converts Du Bois's *Crisis* endorsements of Randolph's BSCP into vivid fiction, capturing through Towns's ordeal aboard the Atlanta–Chicago express the brutal hours and demeaning treatment of "George," the typically courteous and efficient porter who brings "cup after cup of ice water to people too lazy to take a dozen steps." In a passage described with what was for Du Bois startling concupiscence, Towns, exhausted and lonely ("slipp[ing] his clothes off, and clasping his arms around her curving form"), spends the night with a Chicago prostitute. The chapter roars on to an encounter with Perigua, the princess, and a plot to bomb Klansmen heading to a convention in Chicago. Warned of the scheme by Kautilya, Towns stops the express within yards of the trestle where Perigua's body lies mangled by his own explosive device. Suspected of complicity, unwilling to compromise the global mission of the princess, Towns is convicted and incarcerated in Joliet prison after a highly publicized trial in Chicago.

As in *The Silver Fleece*, the sinewy designs of a beautiful, cold, sophisticated woman of color intervene in the hero's fate. Towns's command of language and dignified manner during the trial had impressed the calculating Sara Andrews, private secretary to Sammy Scott, Chicago's most powerful Negro boss, who controls the Second Ward through graft, patronage, and legerdemain from his office at the corner of 33rd and State Street. The gears of the city machine shift quietly and the hero is pardoned, marries Sara, and finds himself in quick sequence ward politician, member of the state legislature, and on the verge of being nominated to Congress just as the princess reappears to remind him of their great obligations. As the author had explained to his publisher, "when the Indian Princess with her great dream of world unity for the darker races dramatically reappears in his life, he surrenders all to become a common laborer on the new Chicago subway." Jettisoned by Sara, Towns comes to identify with the proletariat. Finally, he leaves the city in answer to Kautilya's summons to rural Virginia, where she has toiled as a domestic and common laborer. Many months pregnant from their last meeting, she too has found clarifying simplicity under the tutelage of Towns's aged, wise, unlettered mother. Towns's gnarled mother, whom the princess addresses as "Kali" (the black one), utters temporal and otherworldly profundities signifying that, like Shiva's wife, she is a primordial force anterior to color and caste, one that sustains perpetual renewal, order and disorder. Her spiritual resemblance to Du Bois's own mother is unmistakable. The birth of a son, the new maharaja of Bwodpur, removes the final obstacle to permanent union between Kautilya and Matthew, for, as Kautilya explains to Towns, "had it been a girl child, I must have left both babe and you. Bwodpur needs not a princess, but a King."

As the loquacious story line runs out in a wedding scene whose sylvan solitude is suddenly filled with a votive crowd reminiscent of both adoring magi and the final act of *Star of Ethiopia* ("and then out of the gloom of the wood moved a pageant"), many readers must have found themselves agreeing with one of the South's keenest literary critics: reviewing the novel for the Nashville *Tennesseean*, Donald Davidson declared it to be "by turns impressive and preposterous." Lifting Madhu (" 'Matthew' in our softer tongue"), their newborn, to the heavens, the princess proclaims the unity of the darker peoples in an apostrophe that was, nevertheless, decidedly skewed to her own Hindu destiny:

> Slowly Kautilya stepped forward and turned her face eastward. She raised her son toward heaven and cried: "Brahma, Vishnu, and Siva! Lords of Sky and Light and Love! Receive from me, daughter of my fathers back to the hundredth name, his Majesty, Madhu Chandragupta Singh, by the will of God, Maharaja of Bwodpur and Maharajahdhirajah of Sindrabad." Then the forest, with faint and silver applause of trumpets: "King of the Snows of Guarisankar!" "Protector of Ganga the Holy!" "Incarnate Son of the Buddha!" "Grand Mughal of Utter India!" "Messenger and Messiah to all the Darker Worlds!"

Although *Dark Princess* had taken little more than a year to write, the novel was meticulously researched. Wendell Dabney provided details about Cincinnati's railroad stations and special train schedules from Atlanta. Family physician Louis Wright vetted segments of the novel dealing with medical particulars. An Illinois state senator was quizzed on hotel and restaurant policies in the state capital: "Can a colored member of the legislature get accommodations?" "Could he go there for meals?" Although he appears never to have gotten a reply to questions about regulations governing the issuance of municipal bonds, Du Bois's letters to a cagey Chicago official were typical of the scholarship informing the novel. For all its grandiosity of plot, walking antitheses, and deus ex machina devices, *Dark Princess* not only managed to capture the flavor of ward politics in Chicago, but to anticipate a major real-world political development with uncanny accuracy. When white Congressman Doolittle, representing the burgeoning black population in the Second Ward, suddenly dies after serving serial terms as the Republican machine's cipher, the Hamlet-like Towns is primed to become the first northern member of his race to go to Washington. The real Congressman Doolittle was one Martin B. Madden who died in 1928 shortly after another routine GOP primary victory, having served twenty-three undistinguished years in the House of Representatives. The real Matthew Towns was to be Oscar DePriest, catapulted overnight by Mayor William ("Big Bill") Thompson's machine into Madden's seat as the first Negro congressman in almost a generation.

Du Bois's research for the Indian background was to invest the novel with a prefigurative power of greater significance than its astute reading of Chicago politics. Curiously, and largely because he must have come to feel that the novel's racialist romanticism was unworthy of the scientific socialism of his final decades, Du Bois himself would fail to capitalize on the prophetic pertinence of his ambitious experiment. Had it enjoyed greater commercial success at the time, however, *Dark Princess* might well have become required reading twenty-seven years later when international excitement over Third World solidarity reached an apex with the Bandung Conference of twenty-nine Afro-Asian nations representing more than half the world's population. Kautilya's prediction to Towns misses the Bandung Conference by a mere three years: "In 1952, the Dark World goes free—whether in Peace and fostering friendship with all men, or in Blood and Storm—it is for them—the Pale Masters of today—to say." No American of note writing in the years following the Great War (and no Negro writer without exception) had incorporated Hindu themes into his or her fiction other than Du Bois. Few American Negroes had ever been well disposed to a society cemented by rigid castes erected on the historic subjugation of dark-skinned peoples by lighter-skinned ones. But as one of his biographers has insisted, Du Bois "could not have become educated without some sense of the intellectual connections between his native land and the Indian subcontinent." The Indian-tinctured writings of Emerson, Thoreau, and especially Whitman in the poem "Passage to India," were part of the cultural weather of his Berkshire, Fisk, and Cambridge environments. But the New England transcendental link (such as it was) connecting Du Bois to India must have been far weaker than that he forged with that nation's culture and politics through one of the subcontinent's most captivating personalities, Lala Lajpat Rai, an aristocratic writer, militant nationalist, and Congress party theoretician. Du Bois and Lajpat Rai had become friends when the fiery Brahmin lived in the United States during World War I. Lajpat Rai's impressions about this country, published as a book in 1916, profited from discussions with Du Bois in his home and at the Civic Club, much as the editor's growing knowledge of India benefitted from correspondence with Lajpat Rai, who spent the early 1920s jailed by the British. Lajpat Rai took time to read and annotate passages from the *Dark Princess* manuscript even as he plunged at sixty-three into another round of boycott agitation against British rule that would cause his death six months after the publication of the novel. Du Bois sent a fine letter of indignation to the Lahore *People* and then reviewed *Unhappy India,* Lajpat Rai's posthumous reflections, in *The Crisis.*

Du Bois called *Dark Princess* a "romance with a message" and liked it so well that it remained his "favorite book" until his Marxist phase after World War II. Locke would call it the "skyscraper problem novel of the Negro intellectual and the world radical" in the Sunday *Herald Tribune.* Although it fell somewhat short of the mark, Locke felt that *Dark Princess* "offer[ed] the framework of a truly great novel," which complemented the view of the anonymous *New York Times Book Review* critic who thought there was enough material for several novels. The acerbic Schuyler broke off halfway through reading his review copy to write Du Bois that the novel had gripped him "as no other book . . . since Knut Hamsun's *Hunger.*" *Dark Princess* was fine literature, but he thought it was even greater "as a portrayal of the soul of our people." Du Bois's novel was essentially an old-fashioned narrative that reinforced a slender tradition of Negro fiction that began with Sutton Elbert Griggs, a shadowy Baptist preacher in Memphis, Tennessee, who wrote five novels by 1908. *Imperium in Imperto,* a rambling story about a conspiracy to overthrow white power, published by Griggs himself in 1899, was probably the first political novel written by a Negro. Du Bois himself had been the thinly disguised hero of one political novel, *Of One Blood: Or the Hidden Self,* a 1902–3 serial by the editor of the *Colored American,* Pauline Hopkins, featuring an underground African city ruled by a king and queen destined to resolve the race problem. Widely and, for the most part, respectfully reviewed, *Dark Princess* would disappear from most bookstores after a decent sale of almost three thousand copies in the first year. If *Opportunity*'s verdict that the author had "undertaken too heavy a load even for his real talents" was sound enough, it was also true that any large, complicated propaganda novel—even one unencumbered by Du Bois's Victorian glaze—ran fatally against the genres of a period made notable by Fitzgerald's *The Great Gatsby* (1925), Hemingway's *The Sun Also Rises* (1926), Lewis's *Elmer Gantry* (1927), and Forster's *A Passage to India*, appearing four years before *Dark Princess*. As a literary experiment and an antidote to Renaissance excesses, then, the novel was a failure—a failure, nevertheless, whose sociological imagination and heavily eroticized symbolism achieve a meaningfulness that seems to mitigate failure in a peculiarly Du Boisian way.

Still, if the literary neglect awaiting *Dark Princess* was not undeserved, the novel was remarkable for its time and place as a meditation on the use and abuse of race. Du Bois expected readers to go beyond the adventure story to the "second and deeper aim of the book." They were supposed to comprehend the "difficulties and realities of race prejudice on many sorts of people—ambitious black American youth, educated Asiatics, selfish colored politicians, ambitious self-seekers of all races." More than that, though, by centering the novel in an ancient nonwhite civilization (Egypt might have been an even better choice), Du Bois was able to undercut the hubris of whites with a gospel of derivative human experience. The Machine Age was Europe's achievement, but the knowledge that made triumphant industrialism possible came from people who had counted their past in millennia before Europeans acquired table manners. In the Upanishads and the Ramayana, the great texts of Hinduism, reposed the truths of being, understanding, and nonbeing. India's achievements in politics, sciences, and the arts under the Moghuls were incomparable. Kautilya's soliloquy frames the novel's postulate: "India! India! Out of black India the world was born. Into the womb of India the world shall creep to die. All that the world has done, India did, and that more marvelously, more magnificently. . . . Man is there in every shape and kind and hue." Implicit in all this was the message of ineluctability expressed as racial truth. The great wheel of being would turn for Europe and America as surely as it had for Nineveh, Babylon, Egypt, and India. *Dark Princess* prophesied that Africa bonded to Asia was the next cycle, a prediction all the more conceivable, the author must have hoped, if the racial politics of this "skyscraper problem novel" were taken seriously by the dark world's vanguard.

INVITATIONS TO YOLANDE'S wedding were being received just as her father's second novel reached the public. Any chance of putting brakes on the spectacular scale of the marriage had soon given way to the imperious enthusiasms of his own dark princess. Yolande required a large wedding attended by sixteen bridesmaids, presided over by both her future father-in-law, Frederick Asbury Cullen of Salem Methodist in Harlem, and family intimate George Frazier Miller of St. Augustine Episcopal in Brooklyn, followed by a large reception at the Madame Walker Studio on 136th Street. Her preference for a four o'clock ceremony troubled her father, who confided his punctiliousness in matters of correct dress to the increasingly helpless groom. Preferring the hour of six, notwithstanding its requirement of cutaway coats with white vests and striped trousers, Du Bois sighed, "I should imagine they would be about as easy to provide as clawhammers." He and Mrs. Du Bois had decided "that the proper thing would be a large church wedding and a small reception," Countee Cullen was informed in a detailed letter at the end of January. Two weeks later over lunch at the Civic Club, future father- and son-in-law set 6:00 P.M., April 9, as the fateful date and resolved to try to rein in Yolande. "We must be careful not to be too ostentatious and showy as to be vulgar," she was reminded. Couldn't they settle on between six and eight bridesmaids? "Fifteen is beyond all possibility," Du Bois pleaded, putting his foot down on inviting more than two hundred to the reception—an "awful mob" that the mere thought of feeding made him "feel weak." Yolande held fast to fifteen, not counting her maid of honor, the sloe-eyed Margaret Welmon of classic Talented Tenth pedigree. The final list of wedding invitees would nearly treble the five hundred contemplated in mid-February, hardly a surprising number given the prominence of the Cullen and Du Bois clans, the one headed by a pastor with twenty-five years of service in one church and the other by a man "who knows good people in forty-five states and three continents," Du Bois wrote later in *The Crisis*.

The Du Bois–Cullen nuptial was the Harlem social event of the decade. The *Inter-State Tattler* and the *Amsterdam News*, along with much of the national black press, accorded the ceremony the attention commensurate with its racial and social significance, although not even the daughter of W.E.B. Du Bois was excused from the ban excluding people of color from the wedding and society pages of mainstream newspapers. Leading families in places as far away as Washington, D.C., and Chicago agonized over alibis in the terrible event that no invitation came, while those receiving the coveted request were widely regarded as possessing the surest certification of social prominence. Like so many others of their class, bridesmaids Mae Miller of Washington and Chita McCard of Baltimore, invites Wilhelmina Adams of Harlem and Katherine Bell of Newark, retained memories of the wedding they would delight in recapturing long years afterward with virtually no loss of gossipy detail. As the music of Harlem's premier organist, the primly dignified Melville Charlton of Union Theological Seminary, trembled lightly against the walls, a thousand spectators watched fifteen hundred participants, dressed to the nines, file into Salem

Methodist Church on a cloudy, somewhat chilly Easter Monday evening. It was possible to imagine that not since the convening of the Estates-General at Versailles on the eve of the French Revolution had such a rainbow of hats, bonnets, feathers, and gowns, waistcoats, jewelry, and gleaming footwear been seen. The groomsmen were the handsomest, most polished of men—ten peers of the Renaissance, Bell thought: suave Arna Bontemps, winner of the 1926 *Opportunity* Pushkin Prize; tall Robert Weaver, destined to become the first Negro federal cabinet officer; William Alphaeus Hunton, Addie's equally tall, scholarly son and a future victim of the Cold War; Edward Perry; Albert Walker; Alex Miller; Embrey Bonner; and bohemian Langston Hughes, who had carped about Cullen's "parade" yet somehow managed to look comfortable in rented formal attire.

Whether or not it was true that Du Bois had wanted two thousand white doves released after the *Lohengrin* bridal march, the symbolism with which he meant to invest the occasion was unmistakable in the grandiloquent "So the Girl Marries," running with two pages of wedding photoes in the June *Crisis*. Recycling prose from *The Gift of Black Folk* and the closing pages of *Dark Princess*, Du Bois proclaimed, "The symbolism of that procession was tremendous." The march of young black America was set in motion by the union of a maiden and a fine young poet. "America, because there was Harvard, Columbia, Smith, Brown, Howard, Chicago, Syracuse, Penn, and Cornell. . . . There were poets and teachers, actors, artists, and students. But it was not simply conventional America," he limned. "It was a new race; a new thought; a new thing rejoicing in a ceremony as old as the world." But was so much "of pomp and ceremony—flowers and carriages and silk hats; wedding cake and wedding music"—really called for (five hundred had been invited to the select reception originally planned for the Walker Studio but now less expensively mounted in the church rectory). It was only a marriage. "Quite," and were he "merely white," Du Bois revealed, there would have been much less pageantry. But he had done far more than give his daughter to a prodigy of letters whose star he believed was destined to rise far above the plebeian promise of musician Jimmie Lunceford. He had in a sense made a gift of Yolande to the Negro race in a lavish ceremony designed to celebrate family values and cultural refinement in a manner that resonated with black people. He felt that he, Du Bois, above all, owed something "extra to an Idea, a Tradition"—to the unremarkable institution of matrimony. "We who are black and panting up hurried hills of hate and hindrance" needed to establish "new footholds on the slipping by-paths through which we have come." Alienated as blacks often were by what seemed the dessicating conventions of whiteness but also repelled by the irrational frenzy of black religion, Du Bois exhorted them, nevertheless, to cherish the ceremonializing of "Birth, Death, Pain, Mating, Children, Age. Ever and anon we must point to these truths," he insisted. An exalted Du Bois was convinced that, "with music and ceremony" at Salem Methodist, he had marked an evolutionary moment in the progress of black people. "It must be as this soul wills. The Girl wills this," his tribute to Yolande concluded. "So the Girl marries."

The Volksgeistian nuptial had unfolded with perfection, and from the confluence of two phenomenal bloodlines (Cullen's adoptive status was ignored) a uniquely endowed life force was supposed to issue. Life, imitating art, was expected to produce its version of Matthew and Kautilya's maharaja of Bwodpur—a wonderful dark prince genetically enhanced by the union across generations of two geniuses, Du Bois and Cullen. Although he had steadfastly denounced the Nordic eugenics movement launched from Cold Spring Harbor, Long Island, as racist and an insult to democracy, Du Bois's views about family eugenics were a quite different matter. As far as his own flesh and blood were concerned, he believed that genes were destiny. Probably no one present at Salem Methodist who knew Yolande thought her possessed of more than average intelligence, yet her father, who shared that opinion, believed that he had engineered the almost certain outcome that his grandchildren would be brilliant and well formed. As he stood beside his daughter, she radiant in her white gown and he immaculate in swallow tails and wearing the Star of Ethiopia, it can also be inferred that Du Bois harbored another deep-seated family wish. It was a subconscious yearning (and not at all concordant with his public feminism) to find in and through his son-in-law some repair of his life's incommensurable disappointment—the "passing of the first-born," the loss of the infant son, the golden-haired Burghardt. The florid passage in *Dark Princess* describing Madhu's veneration echoes the rococo messianism of the twenty-five-year-old "Of the Passing of the First-Born" in *The Souls of Black Folk*: "The world loved him; the women kissed his curls, the men looked gravely into his wonderful eyes, and the children hovered and fluttered about him." Whenever the subject is Yolande, however, the air seeps out of the prose, didactically deflating the writing until it seems more dutiful than genuinely affectionate. The words the author chooses for Kautilya to express her relief at delivering a boy cannot but be construed as expressive in an almost cruel way of Du Bois's feelings about Yolande: "had it been a girl child, I must have left both babe and you. Bwodpur needs not a princess, but a King."

Four days after the wedding, Du Bois wrote Mildred Bryant Jones in Chicago. He was fifteen hundred dollars poorer but sounded satisfied and relieved. He told Mildred he was "home and free at last." Mrs. Countee Cullen was now no longer his responsibility. Bride and groom were off to an auspicious start. The splendid news of Cullen's Guggenheim Fellowship had come just two weeks before the marriage, "due to no small degree to your endorsement of my application," the bubbly poet wrote his prospective father-in-law. The couple's honeymoon had not gone smoothly, however, but the difficulties, whatever their exact nature, were thought to be minor, temperamental, and transient. Du Bois was in any case much too busy preparing for the meeting of the annual NAACP convention in Los Angeles and a southern lecture circuit that would cover four thousand miles to take much notice of aborning problems. He finished the major piece on the need for a national black cooperative movement, "Our Economic Future," for the May *Crisis*. Roger Baldwin successfully pressed him, as chair of the association's resolutions committee, to consider incorporating some of the ACLU's broader civil liberties concerns for presentation at the convention. But while the editor was preoccupied with national questions involving the race, Harlemites, along with a significant portion of the Talented Tenth elsewhere, were roiled by gossip and innuendo. There were strong suspicions that Countee Cullen was gay. Indeed, many of the groom's friends had no doubt that he was. Young Charles Cullen, a gay, white illustrator and intimate, unrelated despite his name, disconsolately sent word of having been "too ill the night of the wedding to attend." A female friend at Hampton, still struggling to accept the arrangement, wrote the groom a month after the marriage, "My! how strange. 'Tis true!!!" William Brown, one of Cullen's ushers, had been relieved to learn that his friend appeared to have "no overromantic illusions" about the union. "There was a whole crowd of rather nice gay blacks around Countee Cullen," an aged French artist, himself gay, would tell a cultural historian specializing in the world of gay American males.

Formal disapproval of overt homosexuality was arguably more rigorous among middle-class blacks than among comparable whites during this period. Incensed by white stereotypes denigrating black morals and partial to biblical condemnations of unconventional behavior, well-bred blacks were given to extreme execrations of what they perceived as deviant sexual practices. It was also true, to a degree insusceptible of precise determination, that, even among urban, middle and upper-middle-class colored Americans, there was not only considerable informal tolerance of homosexuality's discreet manifestations but even of such glorious expressions as the annual Hamilton Lodge drag ball and of the torrid gay speakeasies along 133rd Street. When one of the mightiest voices thundered against sodomy from Abyssinian Baptist Church in the winter of 1929, it was because the senior reverend Powell believed the times had never been more urgent for a policing of Harlem's loosening morals. Discomfort alternating with fascination, nervous hypocrisy with unfazed socializing, yielded unpredictable consequences. Neither A'Lelia Walker, whose romantic partiality to accomplished women was an open secret in Harlem, nor Locke, whose meanderings among college football players were the subject of clubhouse ribaldry, ever found themselves excluded from the best heterosexual company because of their sexual preferences. Then there was Richard Bruce Nugent, whose homoeroticism was so flamboyant that it won an amused, sometimes admiring indulgence—an occasional dispensation accorded "artistic types." When Harlem learned that the Negro race's latest Guggenheim recipient intended to sail with his best man, Harold Jackman, for a study year abroad, his wife to follow a month later, suspicion and rumor degenerated into hilarity, followed quickly by sympathy for the recent bride.

Jackman, judged by Caucasian standards, may have been the handsomest man in Harlem. Tall and trim with acquiline features and a personality as light and smooth as the complexion of his skin, Jackman had sat for Winold Reiss's "A College Lad," a drawing featured in the famous March 1925 issue of Survey Graphic. Thirty years later, still trim and matinee-idol handsome, he would model for a popular Rhinelander beer ad. Twenty-eight years old at the time of the Du Bois–Cullen wedding, Jackman had come as a youngster from London to Harlem, a brilliant, bisexual product of his Barbadian mother's liaison with an influential Englishman. A rare copy of Fire!! found in the Atlanta University Library contains Cullen's dedicatory signature to Harold beneath the poem "Timid Lover": "I who adore exotic things,/Would shape a sound/To be your name, a word that sings/Until the head goes round." "We always knew that there was [Countee's] little interest in Harold," Geraldyn Dismond Major, who wrote for the Tattler as Lady Nicotine, would confide fifty years later, an opinion shared by an aged but keen Mae Miller. Marvel Jackson, Du Bois's affectionate secretary, thought the match between Yolande and Countee was "absurd."

Du Bois accepted at face value the explanation Cullen had given him a few weeks after the marriage for traveling without his wife. Yolande had said that she had too much to do to be able to leave before early August, Cullen wrote. Because his father had arranged to sail for the Middle East and Europe on June 30, however, Cullen explained that by accompanying his parent his own travel expenses would be partly underwritten. Another advantage to this arrangement was that he would be able to see "a few places of importance in the plan of one of [his] narrative poems." Besides, the money saved on his fare could be applied to a first-class ticket for Yolande in August, instead of the third-class fare if they had traveled together. It was to be inferred from the letter that the underwriting of Jackman's passage was explained by Reverend Cullen's frail health and need of a strong arm on the return trip to the United States. Departing for a speech in Chicago at the end of June and a warm reunion with Mildred Bryant Jones, after which he would go to the NAACP convention in Los Angeles, Du Bois sent a short letter regretting their failure to have a good talk before Cullen sailed. He asked Cullen to write him regularly and with much warmth assured him that he would do everything to make his year abroad successful. In the weeks ahead after Jackman had returned to New York and

Yolande had taken his place in Paris, Du Bois's commitment to his son-in-law's career remained the absolute priority.

Robert Weaver had found it hard to believe that the distinguished editor "knew what was going on. I really don't," he still thought not long before his death. William Montague Cobb, Howard University Medical School's legendary professor of anatomy, thought differently. Du Bois knew Cullen was gay, the patrician old Amherst man contended, but Du Bois thought Cullen "might make it one time" for the sake of producing brilliant children. Cobb was much more likely to have been right than Weaver. Having dismissed the once indispensable Dill the previous year, even as he consoled the shattered *Crisis* business manager over his public lavatory humiliation, Du Bois's conscience had had to wrestle with the social touchiness of a homosexually compromised friendship. There was a sense in which Weaver's disbelief may have been entirely correct, however. Given his own robust and impressively varied heterosexual relationships, it would have been entirely possible for Du Bois not to understand that there were intelligent males, equipped with the requisite physiology, whose disinclination for coitus with a woman could be so intense as to preclude impregnation of their spouses. Aversions as deep as that Du Bois really never did understand.

As disastrous letters from the couple poured into the Dunbar from 4 rue du Parc Montsouris during autumn of 1928, Du Bois consoled his son-in-law and excoriated his daughter. Her job, he had written less than a week before the first devastating news arrived, was to help "a great poet to become greater." And that meant that Yolande ought not distract him "or make him spend too much time catering to [her] entertainment. For once in your life and in your own thought, get out of the center of the picture." His September 11 letter to Cullen expressed such distress that Du Bois would call it "incoherent and unsatisfactory" when next he wrote Cullen. "More grieved and overcome" than he could say, he moaned that he would never have permitted the marriage had he dreamt that Yolande hadn't "loved and respected" Cullen. But nothing could excuse Yolande's conduct (presumably, her rejection of her husband's overtures), Du Bois was forced to conclude. She simply couldn't "realize what she has done. She meant no evil." "Try for the sake of the great love you gave her," he pleaded — "try to make this crisis of her broken life as easy as you can." But above all, Du Bois wished Cullen to know that he was deeply concerned about his son-in-law's studies and writing. Cullen's career had always been "very dear" to him, and he had "dreamed fine things from this marriage." Yes, he knew their honeymoon had been "trying," but at the time he had thought — he still did — that "the main trouble is physical and psychological," leaving unspecified what other possible troubles he may have had in mind.

The couple had clashed frenziedly, Yolande rejecting Countee's presumably uninstructed mating maneuvers. Yolande's admission to the American Hospital ensued for an expensive condition whose precise nature is presently unknown. Before going, she locked the lid to their phonograph and took the key with her, sending Cullen into a fierce tizzy and eliciting an admonitory letter from Jackman about "not standing for all that foolishness." Du Bois prayed that if his son-in-law "could just bear with her and try again perhaps, all would be well." Perhaps he thought he asked too much, though. "At any rate keep her til Christmas if any way possible and then—god show us all the way." A week later, Du Bois had steadied himself. He proposed a face-saving strategy "to keep down unkind gossip and enable the break to come after a decent interval." The silent Nina would come to Paris just before Christmas to take Yolande in hand (the wedding indebtedness precluded an earlier departure); they would find an inexpensive apartment together and remain until summer.

When Countee and Yolande appeared to have reconciled in early October—a false prospect, as it soon turned out—the overjoyed paterfamilias proffered the most quaintly misplaced advice to Cullen. "The whole problem comes because we are not frank over sex and do not teach the young," he philosophized, probably knowingly echoing Freud's thirty-year-old remonstrance that in matters of sexuality "we are all of us, the healthy as much as the sick, hypocrites nowadays." Nina had shielded Yolande so completely in accordance with the mores of middle-classness that their "spoiled and often silly" daughter was bound to have found her sexual initiation "unpleasant and disconcerting." In complete conformity with Victorian manuals asserting that few females enjoyed sexual intercourse, and that civilized men and women approved of sex in marriage mainly for procreation, Du Bois counseled his son-in-law that the act that "gives her husband pleasure may be exquisite torture physically" for a new wife. Never have sexual intercourse "except with a willing wife," he added. He shared with Cullen a salient memory of his own sexual imprudence, an unforgettable moment of consternation when Nina refused "what I thought [. . .] was my *right* to demand. Of course, no man *owns* a woman's body," Du Bois continued. In any case, sex wasn't "the main thing about marriage." Unfortunately, in Yolande's eyes, sex was likely to be the last thing about her marriage. By January, the union in the name of genius was over. "Well, well, well," the delighted Jackman chuckled to Cullen in a letter from Harlem, "I didn't think it would be so soon, really." Du Bois assured Cullen of his unflagging affection and promised him a permanent welcome in *The Crisis*.

Patriarch that he was when it concerned his immediate family, Du Bois had written too much about the rights due modern women to fall back altogether into the "father-family" ideology of the previous century. The strength of that troglodyte ideology in the first decade of the twentieth century and a good many years beyond (the decade in which so much of Du Bois's intellectual thought matured) was exemplified in *War and Other Essays*, the 1909 collection of essays summing up the postulates of the founder of American sociology, William Graham Sumner. Woman's role, Sumner reminded gentlemen in their clubs and taverns, was that "of an inferior whose status and destiny came from her position as an adjunct." The author of "The Damnation of Women" and of an essay on birth control for Margaret Sanger's journal, not to mention numerous appropriate *Crisis* editorials, Du Bois would have protested any linkage to the misogynist Sumner. Insofar as abstract rights were to be advanced and defended for women, Du Bois's voting record was, as has been shown, one of the best. Nevertheless, when abstract gender rights, racial dignity, exemplary class conduct, and the fermentation of a twenty-nine-year-old bereavement fused in an egocentric eruption uncontained and uncontainable by an intimidated Nina, the consequences were spectacularly wrongheaded. For an intellectual whose profound understanding of the human condition was often matchless, Du Bois serenely arrogated the right to decide the fate of two young people whose intrinsic emotional needs he willfully, myopically resolved not to understand. In so doing, he succumbed to a tyranny that resulted in the symbolic and literal immolation of his own flesh and blood in the service of genetic, gendered, classist, and racial fantasies.

THE POSSIBILITY OF
DEMOCRACY IN AMERICA

As Du Bois approached his next birthday he began to think that his active years were coming to an end. *The Crisis*, resting at what now appeared to be a natural monthly circulation of less than 25,000, thundered along in more or less predictable grooves requiring only a small portion of his fabulous reserves of discipline and moral outrage—although still a source of fierce proprietary pride to him. On February 28, 1929, he would reach his sixty-first year, an age that placed him near the edge of the actuarial life span of the average American male, and well beyond the longevity allotted to most black men. Looking back many years later, he would marvel that his misjudgment of the full agenda in the years ahead had been so wide of the mark. He had more than three decades remaining, thirty-four charged years in which there would be time for teaching, writing, ideological controversy, remarriage, federal prosecution, and expatriation. Editor of the most significant Aframerican journal of opinion in 1929, Du Bois would attain the incommensurable status in 1959 of both political pariah in his native land and venerated elder savant among the leaders of postcolonial Africa and the Communist rulers of Eastern Europe, Russia, and China. In the winter of 1928–29, however, as he and Nina recovered from the financial and emotional toll of their daughter's marriage, Du Bois's attention turned to Great Barrington and to thoughts of eventual retirement. A testimonial fund organized by the Spingarn brothers, including among its fifty-odd donors Mary Bethune, Clarence Darrow, Jane Addams, Mrs. Jacob Schiff, and Charles Chesnutt, had purchased the old family homestead—"the house of the Black Burghardts"—on Egremont Plain as a sixtieth-birthday present to the editor. Du Bois had made plans with a local contractor in the spring of 1928 to begin restoring his grandfather's house "at moderate cost, doing it little by little" as funds became available.

Clement Morgan, Du Bois's Harvard classmate, and Charles Bentley, the

Chicago physician who had been a stalwart of the Niagara Movement, were to pass from the scene in 1929. Moorfield Storey followed in December, preceding Louis Marshall by several weeks. That same year, James Weldon Johnson, worn down by the burdens of association secretary, would take a year's leave in mid-July to attend the Conference on Pacific Relations in Japan, after which he was to begin writing a history of Harlem, subsidized by the first of the new fellowships inaugurated that year by the Rosenwald Fund. Johnson had confided in Mencken six years before that " 'uplifting' any portion of the human race beyond the size of a family" demanded more time and energy than the average man possessed. Johnson and Du Bois were not average men, but the toll of unremitting advocacy mounted up. A sense of mortality, of entropy foreclosing important options, accompanied by peevish impatience and a martyr complex, can be detected just below the editor's elegant, austere surface. He composed a revealing letter to the Bouttés, as unusual for its length as for its introspection, during this period. Prominent Harlem alumni who rendered valuable help during the Fisk crisis, the Bouttés (anticipating by several weeks the creation of the Spingarn testimonial committee) had expressed the wish to organize a national birthday observance of Du Bois's diamond jubilee, to be capped off with a suitable gift. Fisk men and women, the NAACP membership, progressive whites, and the great majority of the Talented Tenth would welcome the opportunity to pay tribute, the Bouttés thought. "But you do not realize, my friend — no one realizes as I do — how unlikely, how impossible any such manifestation of approval" could be, Du Bois riposted. It was possible that "in some far off day" much praise would come to his memory, he conceded, but in the fickleness of an ungrateful present he had only the succor of a "few fine and loyal friends" and of a small audience that approved and applauded his work, even though it did not "like [him] personally." But then there were the many black people who were "entirely ignorant of [his] work and quite indifferent to it," Du Bois reminded the Bouttés. Worse still were the legions of "the envious and jealous," an appalling number of whom "actively dislike[d] and hate[d]" him. An historical novel published in 1928, John Vandercook's *Black Majesty*, a favorite of his for many years, contained the following passage underscored in Du Bois's hand: "To be great, Duncan, is to be lonely. To be magnificent is to have men hate you."

A walking institution, Du Bois was increasingly aware that he was the target of public and private criticism. J. Max Barber, an old newspaper friend from fighting days in Atlanta when Booker Washington had menaced their livelihoods, hovered alienated and petty in the editor's shadow, claiming that the great man barely noticed him except "occasionally when he wants something." He was still willing to consider helping Du Bois, Barber wrote waspishly to Pickens, but only when it didn't entail "too much violence to [his] contempt" for the editor. In the larger scheme of things, the injured feelings of the scores of families left off Yolande's wedding invitation list should have been of passing importance. Nevertheless, as an apologetic exchange with a distinguished Mr. and Mrs. James Thomas suggests, several weeks elapsed after the ceremony before the editor was able to walk about the streets of Harlem untroubled by wounded or furious stares. "Then came the uncomfortable feeling . . . every time I meet any friend nowadays," he wrote Mr. Thomas. Checking his card catalogue of invited guests "as soon as [he] came into the office Monday," the editor was chagrined not to "find your name." The wedding comments of another Thomas were a much more serious matter. Neval Thomas, vice principal of the District of Columbia's elite Dunbar High School, was one of the association's most aggressive branch presidents. From the days of Wilsonian apartheid to the lily white Republicanism of Hoover, Thomas had led the fight against segregation in the nation's capital with such clamorous singlemindedness as to make him a national legend in civil rights circles. But the former history teacher had also been one of Du Bois's most acerbic critics as far back as the "Close Ranks" editorial and the abortive captaincy in Military Intelligence. Instead of being "a record of the darker races," *The Crisis* was one man's soliloquy, according to Thomas. Nothing got printed "about any person or any work that he does not like," he snarled in a letter to the board of directors. In the midst of a fight to save the jobs of the Negro clerks in Washington's General Land Office ("when publicity was our greatest need"), Thomas made the exaggerated but hardly frivolous charge that Du Bois had given "seven pages . . . to his daughter's wedding, a beautiful social event, but one that has no place in the organ that is supposed to voice people's woes."

If the carping, calumny, and genuine misunderstandings were sometimes very painful, it would still be misleading to emphasize unduly the emotional stress they may have caused Du Bois. The rare outburst triggered by the Bouttes' proposal was authentic, as were his more typical, quiet averrals about often feeling shy, socially inadequate, and usually quite incapable of being gregarious. All this was true enough, but the lonely, insecure boy growing up in the Berkshires had long ago come into possession of an aggrandized sense of self that was, and would always be, proof against the disregard or vilification of others, whatever their race or class. For the most part, the wordsmith whose imagery of the veil etched itself into the American consciousness deflected abuse not by confessional revelations but by screening his vulnerabilities with an imperturbable dignity, catholicity, and principled destiny. Beleaguered and feeling increasingly frustrated in his editorial role at sixty-one, Du Bois comported himself like the colossus his public self had become. The result was stiff formality even with colleagues and an off-putting *froideur* to most strangers, coupled with spring-loaded vigilance against the slightest hint of racial put-down. It was only after Joel Spingarn had ventured a 1927 holiday-season suggestion that, after a twelve-year friendship, they cease addressing each other by title, that Du Bois adjusted his salutation to "My dear Spingarn."

An unsigned profile of Du Bois in the August 1929 *World Tomorrow* captured, if somewhat effusively, the substance and symbol of what its author described as "this dreamer, this dynamo, this finest expression of the inner meaning of American democracy." The author thought it was an incalculably good thing for the race that Du Bois existed. "In a group given too much to humility and depreciation," she judged that the career "of this proud and fearless fighter" was heaven-sent. Jessie Fauset ended her profile on a perfect note, writing of the man who still meant so much to her: "He is so indubitably somebody."

That sense of indubitable somebodiness Du Bois conveyed in a letter to an idealistic Harvard instructor who, drawn increasingly from teaching chemistry into journalism and human rights advocacy, had sought career advice. He wished to devote himself "wholly to writing, speaking and working for . . . liberalism, truth, and justice." This young southerner had given *Dark Princess* a warm review in a marginal Boston monthly called *The Lantern* whose editors had also been persuaded to reproduce portions of "The Possibility of Democracy in America," Du Bois's excellent article on disfranchisement running in the September–October *Crisis*. Leonard Cartwright's embrace of socialism and civil rights had cost him dearly. Friends shunned him, and his "Nordic, 100% American" family ostracised him. In Du Bois's response to Cartwright are to be heard accents of the Calvinist stoicism that formed the bedrock of his character: lonely obedience come what may to indwelling precepts carved from New England granite. There was one thing Cartwright must remember: "The world will not give a decent living to the persons who are out to reform it." He had to face this reality: "How long can you get the necessary bread and butter by speaking out frankly and plainly? When you can no longer do this, what compromises can you make in unessentials that will allow you to save your soul? Beyond that, is oblivion. The oblivion of complete surrender or of complete silence. The object of life is to avoid either of these." Cartwright had received in succinct summation the credo of the "indubitable somebody."

The dilemma of surrender or silence came home to Du Bois in the spring of 1929 with all the vengeance of the cliche. He had sent in "The Negro in the United States" in May of the previous year, the lengthy essay under contract to the *Encyclopaedia Britannica* for its fourteenth edition. From the moment of first contact, Du Bois moved to parlay his unprecedented *Britannica* commission into a group of discrete studies. Mrs. Worth T. Hedden, former assistant to Norman Thomas and influential staff member of the encyclopedia, had responded with enthusiasm to his proposal to commission several Negro entries in addition to his own comprehensive treatment of the subject. On Du Bois's advice, four colored experts were invited to write about music, religion, economics, and education; contracts were quickly negotiated with Locke, James Weldon Johnson, George E. Haynes, and William Albert Robinson, a relative unknown employed by the North Carolina State Department of Education. In light of the distortions and even grotesqueries written about people of color in standard reference works of the period, it was not so surprising that even among many sophisticated people of color access to the *Encyclopaedia Britannica* was greeted with an almost pitiable hopefulness—so much was theirs in mainstream America to so little allow. Ecstatic at the prospect of his education article appearing in the distinguished reference, thirty-eight-year-old Robinson told the editors that they could have no idea "how much [their] new attitude on this matter cheered and heartened Negroes all over the country," adding that the Negro teaching profession regarded it as a watershed development "that a Negro had been asked to write the article." The contributors' heady expectations had survived the phase of preliminary review, with Du Bois reaching amicable agreement about several suggested editorial changes and the paring down of his entry to the regulation five thousand words within two weeks after submission.

By the time galley proofs for "The Negro in the United States" reached Du Bois's desk in mid-February 1929, however, the *Britannica* had undergone a recent corporate upheaval. Worth Hedden was a memory, and Du Bois found himself dealing no longer with congenial editor Walter Pitkin but with a bilious Franklin Henry Hooper, who blue-penciled whole paragraphs, altered the emphases of phrases, and nitpicked over words. The two men unleashed a train of letters that serves as an extraordinary illustration of the separate and unequal status of knowledge dividing the races between the world wars—an exchange exemplifying perfectly how color-coded cognitive dissonance impelled most educated white people, in the name of "objective" history and social science, to discount the beliefs of most educated colored people as propaganda or fiction. Writing Hooper immediately that he was "very much dissatisfied," Du Bois cursorily reviewed his deliberations with Hedden and the *Britannica* staff, noted that the article's present length was within the stipulated limit, and insisted that a small number of "additions and restorations" were indispensable to the integrity of the entry. He saw no reason why the number of Negroes lynched "should not be plainly stated" or why the role of Negro explorers should go unmentioned, any more than dropping an explanation for the causes of the Atlantic slave trade made sense. Nor did he like the dilution of intent on page two where, in reference to the South's Black Codes, the sentence, "showed a determination to reestablish Negro slavery in everything but name" was altered to "seemed to show an inclination." As for the rendering of "Negro" in lower case, Du Bois reprovingly informed Hooper that that would never do, as he, Du Bois, regarded "the use of a small letter for the name of twelve million Americans and two hundred million human beings as a personal insult." But above all, there was the virtual lobotomy performed on Du Bois's Reconstruction paragraph, trepanned by Hooper to read: "Negroes were gradually forced from the ballot box by one means or another."

Hooper's stuffy response conceded the capitalization of Negro, opposed factual objections to data relating to the slave trade together with several other "excessive" statements that "contradicted information given in other articles," and he insisted on deleting passages written, in his judgment, "in vindication of the colored people," and therefore, "quite unnecessary." Informing Du Bois that most of the material he wished to incorporate did not seem "essential to the article," Hooper underlined what he took to be the entry's most egregious error — Du Bois's interpretation of Reconstruction. "No statement as broad as this and as questionable" could survive any conscientious editorial pen, Hooper declared, for Du Bois had stated as a fact that, "after the Civil War it was Negro loyalty and the Negro vote alone that restored the South to the Union, established a new democracy, both for white people and black.'"

But surely the point to bear in mind was that he, Du Bois, was "the author of the article," Du Bois volleyed. Hooper had no right to demand that he "subscribe to a wording which I deem false or misleading." And so it went throughout February until the first week in March, one courteously adamant letter batting another. Nor was Du Bois's entry alone in encountering difficulties. Although Johnson had received his *Britannica* galley proofs with only a "few insignificant changes," Robinson's article on Negro education also ran into complications of content and length, if less problematic than Du Bois's. Hedden commiserated over what Du Bois described as "having some queer experiences with the editors." "I'm afraid that everybody had 'had some queer experiences,'" she said.

By March 2, their dispute was stalemated, with Hooper insisting that Du Bois's "most fundamental" demands had been met and that his otherwise "excellent" entry would have to be dropped from the edition if Du Bois insisted on retaining the revisionist statement on Reconstruction. Two days later, Du Bois wrote to propose on take-it-or-leave-it terms what seemed to him a reasonable compromise, a solution suggested by Joel Spingarn: "White historians have ascribed the faults and failures of Reconstruction to Negro ignorance and corruption. But the Negro insists that it was Negro loyalty and the Negro vote alone that restored the South to the Union; established the new Democracy, both for white and black, and instituted the public schools." Franklin Hooper replied regretfully on March 8, 1929, that the new paragraph was unacceptable and that he was compelled to delete Du Bois's article from the fourteenth edition of the *Encyclopaedia Britannica*. Economics, education, and art, drama, music, and poetry, folklore, and Harlem as presented by Johnson, Locke, Haynes, and Robinson were judged to be unproblematic, and, but for a stubborn insistence upon black people's agency in Reconstruction, the Negro entries would have had the benefit of Du Bois's shaping, lively, and authoritative essay. With the legal assistance of Arthur Spingarn, Du Bois was soon to overcome the encyclopedia's initial disinclination to remit full payment for his unpublished article. The large space that had been set aside for the rejected essay was filled by Rosenwald Fund director Edwin Embree.

A week to the day after receiving the *Britannica*'s definitive refusal to publish "The Negro in the United States," Du Bois met the archpriest of Nordic supremacy, Theodore Lothrop Stoddard, in public debate at Chicago's cavernous Coliseum. The question before the house could not have failed to hold a surfeit of irony for the editor: "Shall the Negro Be Encouraged to Seek Cultural Equality?" A lively radio debate between Du Bois and Stoddard in September 1927 had sparked the curiosity of whites throughout much of the North. Described as a "corker" by one experienced white publicist, it had been broadcast on Friday, September 23, from New York City. Among colored people, news of the radio debate had spread by word of mouth well beyond Talented Tenth parlors into the homes, barbershops, and beauty salons of many working-class folk. Whether or not more than a few had heard of Stoddard's most recent affront, *Re-forging America: The Story of Our Nationhood* (1927), and even if most Negroes had never actually read his masterpiece, *The Rising Tide of Color,* there were not many among the literate who failed to recognize this well-born Harvard man, in the words of a leading historian of the subject, as "one of the most active propagandists for racism this country has ever produced." Interest in the match was so lively that, as the Open Forum Speakers Bureau anticipated, hundreds had to be turned away after more than four thousand Chicagoans (three quarters of them Negro) packed the auditorium.

Speaking first, Du Bois cut straight to the premise at the explosive center of the resolution—racial intermarriage, the perennial question, "Would you want your daughter . . . ?" Even though some might think it did violence to the meaning of culture and civilization, no one would deny Nordics who believe in their own superiority the choice of working voluntarily "by themselves and for the development and encouragement of their own gifts." No one was going to deny Anglo-Saxon Protestants the right "not to mingle their blood with other races, or contaminate their culture with foreign strains." "Nobody is going to make Nordics marry outside of their group unless they want to marry outside," Du Bois stated with polite sarcasm. But this has never been the "Nordic program." It was the Nordics whose conduct had produced the mixing of races. They had overrun the earth and brought not simply "modern civilization and technique, but with it exploitation, slavery and degradation to the majority of men." His debater's voice throbbing with passion, Du Bois denounced Stoddard's Nordics for having "broken down native family life, desecrated the homes of weaker peoples and spread their bastards to every corner of land and sea." Inflicting this miscegenation on helpless, unwilling slaves by force, fraud, and insult, they had had the impudent hypocrisy to cry, " 'You shall not marry our daughters!' " As applause rocked the auditorium, Du Bois shouted the reply, " 'Who in Hell asked to marry your daughters?' "

What did it truly mean to seek cultural equality, he asked rhetorically? It meant nothing less than the right of the world's peoples of color to be men and women, to have the artificial barriers torn down, to invest the rights of formal citizenship with vital meaning in the United States. "They demand a voice in their own government; the organization of industry for the benefit of colored workers and not merely for white owners and masters; they demand education on the broadest and highest lines and they demand as human beings social contact with other human beings on a basis of perfect equality." Not too many decades ago, he reminded the audience, the possibility had existed that the rise of Americans from slavery to freedom, "from squalor, poverty and ignorance to thrift and intelligence and the beginnings of wealth, would bring unstinted applause. Negroes themselves expected this," Du Bois pressed on in what sounded like a passage from a letter to Hooper. "They looked eagerly forward to this day when you cannot write a history or statement of American civilization and leave the black man out, as proof of their equality and manhood and they expected their advance, incomplete and imperfect though it remains, nevertheless, to be greeted with applause."

Taking the negative, Stoddard professed to share in the applause for Negro advancement; he insisted only that it proceed on another track from that guiding white folk. The highest duty of both races was that of maintaining racial purity; otherwise there would be deadly race conflict, Stoddard insisted. Praising the situation in the South, he described its "full fledged Negro society . . . with grades of all kinds, and as a result of that social differentiation . . . careers and social stratification for talented Negroes on their own side of the color line." It was an ideal arrangement disparaged only by a small minority of northern intellectuals unable to find social status commensurate with their professional aspirations. Obviously lacking the callousness of his convictions on this occasion, Du Bois's opponent chose not to make the claim that whites were culturally superior to brown, black, and yellow peoples but, rather, that all these "races" were "different"—"it is not fundamentally a matter of superiority or inferiority *per se*," Stoddard equivocated; it was a matter of "racial difference." Reaching for a new euphemism, he described "in one word" the South's arrangement of "bi-racialism" as both beneficent and inescapable. "Bi-racialism is not discrimination; it is separation," Stoddard declared in the same breath that invoked the separatist wisdom of Washington and Moton, the great leaders of "American Negrodom." George White reported to younger brother Walter that a patently ill-at-ease Stoddard had been outclassed by his adversary. "Du Bois had him licked before he opened his mouth," George gloated, as Stoddard sank into what he described as a "sea of irresistible logic." "DU BOIS SHATTERS STODDARD'S CULTURAL THEORIES," the *Defender* banner headline cheered.

The editor would have fully seconded George White's debate assessment. The young associate secretary of the American Missionary Association had been especially impressed by the compelling personal reference Du Bois had made to his own struggles in order to illustrate the absurd arbitrariness of racism. Stating that it was "almost impossible in America to think logically," Du Bois had reminded the audience that he was not only "gladly . . . the representative of the Negro race," but was also "equally" capable of being "a representative of the Nordic race." Pure races were pure fictions, and he might have added that Stoddard's Anglo-Saxon bloodlines were as much a genetic composite as Du Bois's own hybrid descent from Dutch, French, and African forebears. Yet, whenever white America denied him his humanity, Du Bois was told that it was because he was black. But whenever Du Bois did anything that was worth doing, he became "suddenly . . . preponderatcly white." White relished Du Bois's spelling out the foolproof, white-supremacist formula that reduced entire generations of able, industrious American citizens to invisibility. Summing up its significance for *Crisis* readers, the editor claimed that Stoddard himself knew that his arguments were already fatally undermined by modern social science data. Read between the lines, the sense of the May "Postscript" column was that Stoddard had lost the whites in the Coliseum not so much because they exulted in the editor's vision of integration as because many flinched when confronted by the social and political implications, as nakedly unmasked by Du Bois, of Stoddard's antidemocratic prejudices. "The whole Nordic theory of the Superman assumes that civilization and culture is a gift of the few from above and never arises from the great masses of men, the masses of ordinary people," Du Bois had said in concluding his rebuttal. The lesson of the Chicago debate was that white Americans could be made to feel guilty about racism (and not only in the North); the challenge was to make them do something substantive about their guilt.

Socialists were stunned in the fall of 1929 when Du Bois wrote *The Nation* to protest his name being listed among those endorsing Norman Thomas for mayor of New York. In spite of his "great respect for" the Socialist leader, the editor of *The Crisis* intended to vote for the incumbent, James J. "Jimmy" Walker, the Tammany Machine's uproariously popular, songwriting fashion plate.

Du Bois had "so stated publicly," pleading the "peculiar circumstances of the Negro in New York," and propagandizing not for the noble Thomas or the colorful reformer Fiorella LaGuardia, but for the candidate whose dapper insouciance would bring grief to the city's finances and a resounding negative to the question posed by his favorite song, "Will You Love Me in December as You Do in May?" Harry Laidler, executive director of the League for Industrial Democracy, rapped Du Bois across his own high principles. The opportunist line of reasoning was "utterly inconsistent with your whole life," Laidler contended, an opportunism worthy of Booker Washington.

The rationale of Negro votes for Walker and DePriest was a textbook illustration of the inherent fragility of a political morality erected on the ineludible fault line of color. In a candid reply excusing the politics of race—*his* own race—Du Bois proffered the rationale that "no 100% American will vote for a Negro candidate under ordinary circumstances," and that elective office for his group was obtainable, therefore, only through cooperation with a "corrupt political machine." Oscar DePriest might be an unscrupulous character strutting out of *Dark Princess*, Du Bois readily averred, but the Illinois congressman would condemn lynching, discrimination, disfranchisement, and demand the enforcement of the Thirteenth, Fourteenth, and Fifteenth Amendments. Du Bois maintained that he knew "very few white congressmen who will stand for any of these things." Behind this editorial, "The Negro Politician," could be detected a state of mind no longer patient with the niceties of a controversy.

With lynch law tolerated by the federal government as a regional anomaly, with 98 percent of the Deep South's Negro adults barred from the polls and all of them from Democratic primaries, with a line drawn across the map of the United States below which a third of the population was told daily where it could *not* eat, sleep, study, travel, and go to the lavatory and the movies, while all forms of color discrimination were multiplying outside the South, and black workers in agriculture and industry were being laid off in droves—with all these vectors before him, Du Bois shuddered at the options and then embraced the crooks in prose inflected by defiance and despair. "We do not have a chance to vote on the real merits of the questions presented," he declared:

> We cannot consider the tariff, farm, relief, war, peace, municipal ownership, superpower, and a dozen other pressing political questions. No, we have got to ask: Does Herbert Hoover believe that Negroes are men or sub-men? What is the attitude of Al Smith toward the Negro problem? Does Reed of Missouri believe in education for Negroes or is he part of the conspiracy that deprives Lincoln University of decent buildings? Can any man born south of the Mason and Dixon Line be for a moment considered as a man or must he always be put down as a raging beast,

in alliance with lynching, disfranchisement, "Jim Crow" cars and public insult?

Still so loyal to the Republican party on the national level as to be taken for granted, Harlemites were in the growing vanguard of those who were willing to risk the Democrats on the state and local levels. Throughout the twenties, Ferdinand Q. Morton held the power of patronage as chairman of the Municipal Civil Service Commission, a powerful reward for the 74 percent mayoral vote Harlem's Negroes had given John F. Hylan, the Democratic winner in 1921. Morton, known as the boss of "Black Tammany," was a Harvard man, almost as stylish as Jimmy Walker and haughtier, it was said, than Du Bois. Morton's staying power at the Civil Service Commission was to prove remarkable — from 1921 to 1944, as occupants of Gracie Mansion came and went. When Fiorella La Guardia's GOP-Fusion reform ticket swept into office in 1932, the snappy "F.Q." would skip right along as a born-again reformer. Some in Harlem were of the opinion that Morton did a much better job of looking out for himself than for most of his constituents, and that his United Colored Democracy (UCD) was shortsightedly class-bound. His major patronage achievement had been four Negro physicians appointed to the staff of Harlem Hospital.

In the case of Tammany Hall, the general rationale favoring big-city machines was informed and complicated by personal relationships too discreet to be disclosed to Du Bois's Socialist comrades. The professional predicament facing Jessie Fauset and so many others of her class persuaded the editor that Morton's influence made an especially good argument for keeping Walker in Gracie Mansion. Harlem's Negro population had risen like a thermometer in August during and after World War I, cresting at about 170,000 by 1930. Yet middle-class city jobs for middle-class Negroes barely existed, and, for Du Bois, the appalling exclusionary policies governing the public libraries and the schools had long ago assumed a special, enraging urgency. However impressive their credentials and competent their service records, persons of color were barely ever hired and rarely promoted either in the New York public school system or in the New York Public Library's three-borough system. A few dozen people of color taught in New York's primary and secondary schools; a literal handful dispensed books from lending-library counters. Manhattan's awesomely capable William L. Bulkley, Ph.D in ancient languages and literature from Syracuse University and a founder of both the NAACP and National Urban League, had become the first Negro high school principal in the consolidated school system in 1899. Almost thirty years later, his achievement was still unique.

Well-meaning whites wanted to make the world better, while well-educated Negroes found themselves straining merely to have a place in it. Du Bois saw the faces of the strainers frequently at the Civic Club, or daily on the bus, or chatted with them in the gardens of the Dunbar Apartments. Fauset's had been particularly strained in the spring of 1929 as she watched the list of high school teaching appointments dwindle with little prospect that she would be hired. "Thank you for writing Mr. Morton," the new Mrs. Harris wrote Du Bois. "Do ask him to step on it." Du Bois received a grateful note in June: "I am very sure now if it hadn't been for you and Mr. Morton, I'd have been squeezed out completely." The fate of Brooklyn schoolteacher Dorothy Peterson, a Du Bois acquaintance possessing an exceptionally broad educational background and a minor light of the Renaissance, who remained wedged for years in the position of elementary night school principal (the promotion limbo reserved to Negroes), was yet another case where a Faustian political bargain brought at least some prospect of fair professional treatment for a dozen or more qualified individuals of color.

The public library situation, with its apparent pigeonholing of talent at the 135th Street branch, was especially galling to Du Bois. Regina Andrews (soon to become Mrs. William T. Anderson) and her roommate Ethel Ray (Nance) had given indispensable service to Du Bois and Charles Johnson in the start-up years of the Renaissance. Anderson, as Ernestine Rose's first assistant, arranged literary evenings and Krigwa drama productions in the basement of the 135th Street library. But Anderson, like her somewhat older colleague Catherine Latimer, though filling the duties of first assistant librarian, was denied the position's title and pay, as well as the opportunity for a lateral move outside Harlem that would have positioned her for advancement. Nor was there much prospect that the 135th Street head librarian might apply for a transfer, as Miss Rose confronted her own professional barrier—the public library's unofficial quota on Jewish head librarians. The fact that the thirty-five-year-old Latimer, the system's first Negro trained professional, was repeatedly passed over would lead Du Bois to bombard Morton and the library directorate with letters of protest and incriminating documents in the fall of 1931, followed up by protests from such prominent community spokespersons as Adam Powell, Sr., Reverend William Lloyd Imes, newspaper publisher Fred Moore, and columnist George Schuyler.

When spun out in Du Boisian prose, Faustian political bargains could be made to seem viable. The dismal actuality, however, was that they invariably failed to yield more than minimal material benefits to large numbers of Aframericans. Though hardly devoid of all intrinsic significance and possessing important psychic value to the group, machine politics in Philadelphia, St. Louis, and New York generally delivered little more than token appointments and symbolic gestures whose paltry gains usually redounded to middle-class supporters of the NAACP and the Urban League. In Chicago, where the Thompson machine delivered jobs in large volume to all its supporters, a white ceiling kept Negroes from rising above positions as janitors and laborers.

The national elections of 1924 and 1928 had been calamities for black people. At the 1924 Republican National Convention, the party's black delegates were greeted in Cleveland by chicken wire strung across the section assigned to them. Coolidge promised nothing to the million Negroes who voted the GOP ticket. Six months after being returned to the White House, the president observed in wonted silence as his onomatopoeically named special secretary, Bascom C. Slemp, former Virginia congressman, all but completed the racial segregation of the federal bureaucracy officially begun under Woodrow Wilson. Trotter's alarmed White House audience ended with a blank expression and a cordial dismissal by Coolidge. The president's silence on the pending Dyer antilynching bill would be audible. The power of the reincarnated Klan, spreading from the South and like wildfire out of Indiana across the Southwest into Oklahoma and Colorado, had been only too manifest at the raucous 1924 Democratic National Convention in New York City. By a one-vote margin the delegates elected to say nothing about the anti-Catholic, anti-Semitic, and anti-Negro agenda of the Invisible Empire. Badly divided by region, religion, class, and dynastic antagonisms, the party staggered through 103 ballots to nominate John W. Davis, a colorless Wall Street lawyer from West Virginia.

Speaking for himself in the fall of 1924, Du Bois had blazoned that his ballot would go to third-party candidates Robert La Follette and Burton K. Wheeler, "unusually honest and straight-forward men. I believe in them," he vowed. Senator La Follette, the Wisconsin dynast, and his Montana running mate said no more than Coolidge about racial discrimination and disfranchisement, but the editor underscored that (in response to the NAACP's urging) there had been "a clear cut condemnation of the Klan and [a] promise to free Haiti." The Progressive-Farmer Labor party platform of 1924 appealed as strongly to Debs, Laidler, and Thomas's Socialist party as it did to Gompers' AFL, along with an amalgam of reformers under the umbrella Conference for Progressive Political Action (CPPA). Until Moscow corrected its premature popular front enthusiasm, the Workers (Communist) party (not yet the CPUSA) endorsed the La Follette movement. Warming to its ambitious program, Du Bois exhorted Negroes to look beyond the Progressive party's racial evasions. "But what are our problems," the editor asked rhetorically in "La Follette"? Black people's problems were the world's problems "and something more"—color prejudice. But back of color there was class—"an imperative as tremendous for us as for any working people," he lectured. La Follette's fourteen-point platform calling for "the crushing of monopoly by Federal power," taxation of wealth, collective bargaining for farmers and laborers, public ownership of railroads, the outlawing of war, and the other splendid goals was, Du Bois proclaimed, "one of the best programs ever laid down by a political party in America." Of the 4.8 million Americans who agreed with Du Bois, the editor estimated that almost 500,000 were colored, helping to give "Fighting Bob's" Progressives the largest third-party ballot in American history. Still, *The Crisis* recorded a million Negro votes going to swell Coolidge's 15.7 million crushing majority—"a last pathetic appeal for justice in the face of unparalleled flouting of black men by this administration," he hoped. The business of America was not economic fair play, to say nothing of racial justice, but what Coolidge had proclaimed it to be—business, generally regarded as the exclusive province of white men.

Irrelevant in 1924, American Negroes were sacrificial goats four years later, drawn and quartered on the butcher's block of the white South's 136 electoral college votes. At the outset, Du Bois had done his best to give an optimistic spin to the prospective power of black votes, predicting, "all things considered," that the 1928 elections afforded the greatest chance for "intelligent and purposeful independence" in a generation. Now, as the 1928 presidential campaign roared out of the late summer, *The Crisis* vacuumed the census data, extrapolated liberally from them, and spun creative electoral outcomes in which the empty glass was depicted as half full. The transformation of the race from a debt-locked, voteless peasantry into the most urban people in America, as tens of thousands poured steadily northward and westward as if on a conveyor belt, was already beginning to alter the two-party dynamic. Du Bois's "Negro Voter" essay may have struck large numbers of readers as a well-researched excursion driven by a desperate need to find an at least hypothetical deliverance from the straitjacket of irrelevancy. In a maximum-voting scenario, *The Crisis* tabulated black-to-white voting ratios state by state outside the former Confederacy in order to instruct readers in the crucial exercise of balance-of-power politics. Subtracting the 2.7 million men and women disfranchised in the six hard-line white supremacist states of Georgia, South Carolina, Florida, Alabama, Mississippi, and Louisiana, subtracting another 1.5 million illiterates, the number of eligible Negro voters still came to an impressive 3 million. Distributed disproportionately in the largest cities—Chicago, Philadelphia, Detroit, Pittsburgh, St. Louis, New York, and Baltimore—registered in greater percentages than whites (77 percent to 68), Negroes, who were slightly less than 10 percent of the total population of 110 million, had the capacity, Du Bois emphasized, to muster decisive turnouts in the large industrial states. In predicting that the race's political destiny was tied to its demographics, "The Negro Voter" presented a Du Bois whose political-science understanding would become received wisdom a decade or more in the future in the writings of Ralph Bunche and Henry Lee Moon.

The problem, however, was that both political parties insisted, for the time being, on drawing conclusions diametrically opposed to Du Bois's. The Coolidge presidency unfolded as a racial disaster compounded by one of the greatest national disasters of the twentieth century—the Great Mississippi flood of 1927.

When the lower Mississippi exploded out of the gigantic earthwork levees built by the Army Corps of Engineers to corset its 1,100 mile run from Cairo, Illinois, to the Gulf of Mexico, a million and a half people were displaced. Perhaps a billion dollars in property, crops, livestock, and public works were swept away, killing several hundreds as land on either side of the river was flooded for distances as great as 150 miles. On Saturday night, April 16, swollen by months of biblical rains, the river gave the back of its swollen hand to the great federal levee thirty miles below Cairo, roiling over 175,000 acres and roaring on for hundreds of miles at the redoubling force of three million cubic feet of water per second through Missouri into Mississippi and Louisiana. Five nights later, the levee broke at the prosperous town of Greenville, Mississippi, the economic and political epicenter of the Delta and satrapy of Leroy and William Alexander Percy. Leroy and William, leonine father and inadequate son, represented the flower of the southern plantocracy. Leroy Percy, former U.S. senator and a Federal Reserve Board governor, sat on the board of the Carnegie Institution for Peace, and inspired genuine respect from Secretary of Commerce Herbert Hoover, charged by Coolidge to macromanage the flood crisis. Leroy Percy sincerely believed in the feudal obligations of his class toward the black people who worked the incredibly rich black soil of his cotton kingdom. Son William was a tortured spirit whom the crisis would woefully outmatch.

Hoover's reputation as brilliant engineer and humanitarian had been justly earned during World War I when, as chief Allied relief administrator and then U.S. national food administrator, he masterminded the production and distribution of 18.5 million tons of food and $100 million in aid to more than thirty European countries. Inspecting the vast dislocation and misery along the river's course from his Pullman car as chairman of the Special Mississippi Flood Committee, the commerce secretary soon learned that Europe had been an easier challenge than Mississippi. Speaking for his fellow planters as well as for the sugar and banking interests downriver in New Orleans, Leroy Percy convinced Hoover, the officials of the American Red Cross, and the National Guard command to sanction a plan to make the town of Greenville the receiving center for redistribution throughout the county of Red Cross and other relief shipments for more than fifty thousand flood victims. Several thousand Negroes would be accommodated in a refugee camp at Greenville to provide labor for the levee and the transhipment of food and supplies. Percy *père* turned over the formidable task of levee maintenance and repair to Will Percy, who played his part with the cruelty of an incompetent Simon Legree. By the end of the first week in May, Hoover knew that his own reputation and that of the Flood Committee were in serious danger. From Claude Barnett, owner of the Associated Negro Press (ANP) and a stalwart Republican, came the warning that thousands of Negro laborers were being held against their will in virtual concentration camps ringed by National Guardsmen and local law officers. Thousands of dislocated Negro men and women were being forced at bayonet point into peonage because they were unable to repay "charges" for relief supplies the Red Cross had entrusted to Delta planters for distribution. Conditions at Greenville, where the Negro laborers were being driven without rest by an hysterical Will Percy, were nightmarish. Senator Arthur Capper of Kansas, an NAACP board member, forwarded Hoover a copy of *The Defender*'s headline story, "Use Troops in Flood Area to Imprison Farm Hands," with the advice that the report be taken seriously. Vann's *Courier* repeated the charges. Jane Addams urged the appointment of a special "colored committee" to investigate.

At 70 Fifth Avenue, Du Bois and the officers of the association were in possession of conclusive information that prompted a telegram to Washington from Secretary Johnson demanding an immediate inquiry. White had hurried back to New York from the Delta at the end of May after another of his in-depth investigations as a white man with grisly details of malnourishment, concentration camps, and boxcar prisons for black Mississippians caught attempting to head north. On the twenty-seventh, the *Times* and *Herald Tribune* reported the assistant secretary's allegations. Hoover, flustered and furiously denying the association's accusations, reached for Moton, whose reliability he knew firsthand from having been involved in the Hampton-Tuskegee endowment campaign. Moton quickly assembled a nonwhite investigating committee consisting of the Urban League's Eugene Kinckle Jones, Negro Business League secretary Albon Holsey, the YMCA's Eva Bowles, Claude Barnett, and a dozen others who were *not* affiliated with the NAACP. If the Special Mississippi Flood Committee and the Red Cross anticipated absolution from Moton, White's chilling "The Negro and the Flood" in the June 24 issue of *The Nation*, followed by Du Bois's *Crisis* editorial the following month, encouraged the Moton committee to probe aggressively and report accurately. "Flood," starkly titled, recalled the electric discharges of Du Bois's earlier years. With the authority of a diplomaed Moses, the editor called the black people of Mississippi and Arkansas out of peonage and hopelessness. "Let them ride, run and crawl out of this hell. There is no hope for the black man there today," he roared. Let them risk death to escape, for they could expect no relief from the president or the secretary of commerce. "Mr. Hoover is too busy having his picture taken and Mr. Coolidge, when an Arkansas mob burns the body of an imbecile, feeding the bonfire with lumber torn from a Negro church, while the mayor of the city keeps the Negro leaders imprisoned in their own business block — Mr. Coolidge tells the world of the privileges of American civilization." The Moton committee's report corroborated more of the NAACP's allegations of collusion, corruption, and cruelty than the Red Cross establishment would permit to be published. Even so, when the

Moton report was finally released after considerable delay, airbrushed and toned down, the performance of the Special Mississippi Flood Committee along with Will Alexander Percy's conduct were sufficiently exposed to serve as the basis for correcting the most egregious abuses. To ensure that end, from January through March 1928, Du Bois ran a three-part exposé in the magazine, "The Flood, the Red Cross, and the National Guard," which provided much of the unexpurgated and as yet unreleased Moton report.

If Hoover's flood relief came close to being a calamity, the southern strategy he devised in order to win the 1928 presidential election was an uncanny harbinger of the regional GOP gambit that was to be tentatively tested by Dwight Eisenhower twenty-four years later and unambiguously exploited by Barry Goldwater in 1964. The nomination of Al Smith, a spunky Irish Catholic from New York in favor of repealing the Eighteenth Amendment, was an act of Democratic self-mutilation almost certain to deliver parts of the solid South to the GOP. Building on Coolidge, Hoover accelerated the policy of whitening the GOP below the Mason-Dixon Line in order to bring about a major political realignment. Supreme Court Chief Justice Taft privately described the electoral calculus as coldly designed "to break up the solid South and to drive the Negroes out of Republican politics." "Herbert Hoover has started something," Du Bois would signal. "We very much doubt if he understands the ramifications of his late declaration." What Hoover did understand fully was that he needed the votes of southern white delegates in order to carry the GOP nomination against Robert La Follette, Jr., son of the deceased standard bearer of progressivism. Teddy Roosevelt, facing a similar threat within the party in 1903, had assured himself of Negro delegates' votes at the GOP convention by inviting Booker Washington to dine at the White House. Hoover reversed Roosevelt's strategy, inviting southern Negro loyalists to surrender their titles and perks so as to allow the GOP to become lily white. Using the pretext of restoring high standards of office and cleaning up "rotten boroughs," candidate, and later president, Hoover authorized the removal of Negroes serving on the Republican National Committee and as state chairmen in the South.

Benjamin Davis, Sr., of Georgia, Perry Howard of Mississippi, and William McDonald of Texas were dismissed. The assault on the GOP "black and tans"—the leaders of the rump party in the Deep South—and the elimination of all but three Negro delegates to the national convention was unprecedented. The lone exception to the purge was the party leader of Tennessee. Mary Church Terrell's worldly brother, Robert Reed Church, Jr., a major force on the Republican National Committee whose Memphis family bank enabled him to contribute significantly to party coffers, escaped the purge with his prestige fully intact. Davis, a powerfully built man in his late fifties who masked his ruthlessness with geniality, was a successful Atlanta businessman, newspaper publisher, and fraternal order chieftain, deserving of Du Bois's qualified respect. His control of federal patronage in the Deep South almost placed him above the canons of Jim Crow, or so it had seemed to teenaged Ben Junior, the future Communist party politician. Davis, Sr., spent a week in Washington during the summer of 1928 defending himself against charges of misappropriation of federal funds before a Senate committee. The fifty-year-old Perry Howard may have been as unsavory as Mabel Walker Williebrandt, the Justice Department's assistant attorney general, believed, but her investigation and eventual indictment of the Mississippi State Republican Committee chairman seemed personal to the point of obsession. Howard's patronage power not only matched that of Davis's, but the light-skinned, blue-eyed Republican National Committeeman cut a dashing social figure in the segregated nation's capital, where he served as special assistant to the attorney general of the United States. Poised, articulate, he must have been a presence even more troubling to the grim Mabel Williebrandt than to Herbert Hoover. The high opinion in which Du Bois once held Howard had nosedived when the politician ("the lickspittle politician") toadied to conservative opponents of the Dyer bill. The editor let Howard's acquittal on federal felony charges by two white Mississippi juries pass unremarked. Mississippi whites preferred a Republican party structure headed by a colored man than one rejuvenated "lily white" by President Hoover and Assistant Attorney General Williebrandt. "All this is singularly contradictory," Du Bois insisted. Hoover had chosen to condemn only the leaders of Mississippi and Georgia, two of the three states where Negroes had managed to hang on to power.

Thoroughly disgusted by Republican tactics as they calculated the outside chances of the Democratic presidential nominee, the influential owners of Norfolk's *Journal and Guide*, Baltimore's *Afro-American*, and Boston's *Guardian* shifted their support to Al Smith. The Democratic presidential nominee ultimately disappointed the Negro political class even more than Hoover. The early expectations, however, ran from optimistic to exuberant. White had interrupted his Guggenheim Fellowship year in the south of France to meet in New York with Smith's campaign manager, Belle Moscowitz, widow of one of the founders of the NAACP. The initiative for the meeting had been Smith's, on the advice of Moscowitz and the association's pro bono counsel and famous party-giver, Charles Studin. For a brief, heady week, a skeptical Du Bois, remembering his own disastrous experience with Wilson, watched as White attempted to pin Smith to a mutually profitable agreement that could be the beginning of the end of the "chronic Republicanism" of black people. "Mr. Smith is posing as a liberal," Du Bois would finally scoff in *The Nation*. But he kept his suspicions about Smith's inevitable capitulation to the white South to himself for the time being. There had never been a more propitious time for an alliance between the Democratic leadership and the Negroes, White argued with infectious enthusiasm. Smith's enemies were "the Negro's enemies." The Spingarns agreed, as did Moorfield Storey. In return for White's taking leave of the NAACP to run a separate campaign organization on Smith's behalf, Smith was to declare publicly and unequivocally that he would be president of *all* the people, and that he opposed racism. White informed influential Methodist bishop and board member John Hurst that Smith was prepared privately to give "more specific pledges." Awaiting Moscowitz's confirmation of their accord, the assistant secretary overreached himself. The election of Hoover would make Moton "practically to him what Booker T. Washington was to Roosevelt," but a victory for Smith would make the NAACP "the power behind the throne." But the deal, as Du Bois, formally announcing for Norman Thomas, had predicted, proved too radical for Smith and utterly unacceptable to his ticket-balancing running mate, Arkansas senator Joseph Taylor Robinson. Smith sent word that he hadn't changed his heart, only the promises he could make, and Moscowitz urged White to take the Democratic candidate on faith.

Secretary Johnson now sided with Du Bois, Bishop Hurst, and Clarence Darrow and instructed White to resume his duties at 70 Fifth Avenue. Smith not only lost the election and every state above the Mason-Dixon Line except Massachusetts and Rhode Island, but, as Hoover and his strategists had hoped, seven southern states, among them Tennessee, North Carolina, Florida, and Texas. White was bitter to the point of disillusionment, writing Storey that, frankly, he saw "no solution of the dilemmas which the Negro voter faces." Sparing himself the disillusionment, Du Bois presented readers with the carefully reasoned essays that he wrote in response to the 1924–28 brick wall of elective politics. In "The Possibility of Democracy in America," and two reflections on third parties, he calmly faced the reality that Negro Americans appeared to have exhausted their political options. Caught between the hostility of the Democrats and the indifference of the Republicans, 10 percent of the people was effectively all but excluded from the American social contract. "It might be assumed that the practical disfranchisement of the great majority of Negroes. . . . had no effect upon the state and nation, but simply upon them," but Du Bois hammered home the broad, corrosive consequences of democracy for white people only. As he contended in a paper presented that year to the American Academy of Political and Social Science, "on account of the 'Negro problem' we are making democratic government increasingly impossible in the United States."

The assertion that racial disfranchisement made a mockery of the Fourteenth and Fifteenth Amendments had seldom been better documented as

Du Bois statistically tracked the elimination after the late 1880s of Negro voters and the collateral impact upon white men and, later (under the Nineteenth Amendment), white women in the South. Under white supremacy, the wealthy and their satellites voted regularly—poor men and most women demonstrably didn't. In Alabama, Georgia, Mississippi, Louisiana, and South Carolina, Du Bois gave the stark figure of 635,512 votes cast in the 1920 elections, a mere 19,000 of which were by Negroes. He calculated the number of eligible non-voting whites at 2,297,799. Du Bois demonstrated a similar dwindling in the franchise for white women in these five states, noting that 150,000 white women out of some 2 million had gone to the polls in 1920. Four years later, 50,000 fewer white women voted in spite of 1 million increase in the female population. The exceptional 19,000 colored men and women who voted in 1920 had exercised a right denied to some 2.2 million other Negroes aged twenty-one and older. The percentages for all nonvoters in the Deep South must have shocked readers: 79 percent in both Alabama and Arkansas; 86 and 89 percent in Louisiana and Georgia, respectively; above 90 percent in Mississippi and South Carolina. The goal of the argument was not so much to document Mencken's famous quip that the Deep South was civilization's Sahara, as it was to vivify the deadly impact upon history's most noble experiment—"here in the United States, here where we have essayed the greatest experiment in democracy." But where, Du Bois feared, "we have perhaps the greatest failure." For "The Possibility of Democracy in America" disclosed a trend that has become an integral civic dysfunction afflicting Americans, ongoing and worsening over time. Nonvoting, Du Bois could have said of 1920, was as American as apple pie—well over 40 percent in Michigan, Massachusetts, Maryland, New Jersey, New York, and Connecticut; falling to a tolerable 30 percent only in Delaware, Indiana, Utah, and North Dakota.

Du Bois of course knew that a combination of factors—regional, demographic, economic, historic—explained the national voting decline, but he chose to blame the oligarchic, racist South as the underlying cause. People voted less because they had less from which to choose. They lacked viable third-party alternatives. They understood that no reasonable hope existed that shopworn political structures could be made to yield to new ones. "The Populists failed. The Socialists failed. The Progressives failed. The farmer-Labor movement failed." Du Bois offered a novel explanation for these failures ("the real effective reason . . . seldom discussed") that is now conventional wisdom. With its control of 124 Electoral College votes, its disfranchisement of masses of blacks and whites, its election of "forty-five congressmen to Washington while a million voters on the Pacific Coast send but twelve," its seniority over the key committees in the Senate and House, its exercise of fatal filibusters, the Bourbon South, Du Bois claimed, exercised through the Democratic party a veto over the nation's future. "The political power of this rump electorate is astonishing," he warned in *The Nation*. So long as the South was the Republicans' to win, and the Democrats' to lose, Negroes would remain disfranchised and discriminated against and the forces of reform and progress decisively stymied. Al Smith's debacle Du Bois took to be a perfect illustration of the straitjacket in which the eastern, urban, prolabor, so-called liberal wing of the Democratic party would remain imprisoned. Before the staid Academy of Political and Social Science in Philadelphia, Du Bois scored the cause behind the deformation of America's national life, raising his refined voice to deplore the constitutional lapses allowing the Democratic party "to establish itself in perpetuity by permitting it to use the political power of the black men and white men which it has illegally disfranchised."

Du Bois was not always consistent, nor was he inclined to be especially distressed by any such accusation. In "The Negro Politician" (May 1928), he defended collusion with corrupt urban political machines as an expediency forced upon mostly poor black people by conservative political elites pledged equally to government renewal and black removal. On the other hand, in "The Negro Voter" (August 1928), a prescient analysis of demographic redistribution and balance-of-power openings, the editor exhorted the race to exercise the ballot "for intelligent and purposeful independence." Yet, in "Thomas" (November 1928), Du Bois backed the third-party candidate who had no chance of making even an impressive showing and denounced Smith, for whose core coalition many Negroes should have felt an affinity. Yet the third-party alternative, although offering the important moral and psychological lift of decrying lynch law and disfranchisement, was, as Du Bois conceded, an exercise in futility. These different emphases, if not outright contradictions, were certainly not caused by slipshod reasoning. They were the result of the Hobson's choices open to colored men and women, their citizenship dilemmas that seemed to Du Bois (and with less cogitation to Walter White) to defy any prospect of solution in the near future. In truth, Du Bois loathed machine politics and he inveighed against vulgar Negro opportunism, just as he called attention to callous white evasions and decried the invidious one-drop rule of inferiority and exclusion unique to North America and which skewed insanely its race relations. As the decade drew to a close, his Calvinist anguish over race and injustice boiled over repeatedly, as in "Race Relations in the United States," his paper for the political and social-science academy, in which he cried out, "What is going to become of a country which allows itself to fall into such an astonishing intellectual and ethical paradox? Nothing but disaster," he foresaw. "Intellectual and ethical disaster in some form must result unless immediately we compel the thought and conscience of America to face the facts in this so-called racial problem."

His mood was somber and reflective as Christmas season 1928 approached. *The Crisis* proclaimed Hoover's victory the "Victory of Wall Street and the KKK." It grumbled at the favorable treatment much of the American press gave to Mussolini, in distressing contrast to the coverage it had given to Lenin. In the same December number, Du Bois returned to the Sacco and Vanzetti Case to condemn the executioners of the two confessed anarchists as "murderers." Curiously, it was only the second time that the editor had addressed himself in print to this grand moral and legal drama, one of the twentieth century's most impassioned, in which two immigrant Italians, a shoemaker and fishmonger, had been sentenced to death in 1920 for a payroll robbery and murder in South Braintree, Massachusetts. Nicola Sacco and Bartolomeo Vanzetti protested their innocence in steadily improving and eloquent English as the years passed and the global demonstrations swelled, until the specially appointed "Lowell Committee" (Harvard's A. Lawrence Lowell presiding) ratified their convictions seven years later as, "on the whole," just. "We who are black can sympathize with Sacco and Vanzetti and their friends more than other Americans," the editor had written soon after their execution in "The Terrible Truth," an editorial about a little-known Tennessee miscarriage of justice almost as grotesque as the one millions accused Massachusetts of perpetrating. "We are used to being convicted because of our race and opinions regardless of our proven guilt," Du Bois hammered away. "We are used to seeing judge, jury and public opinion lay down the rule: 'Better ten innocent Negroes lynched, than one guilty one go free.'"

As in politics where the checkmate was decisive, the exclusion of Negroes from organized labor was broad and sustained. Hardly a year passed in which Du Bois had failed to plead against the anti-black policies of Gompers and now William Green's AFL. Early in 1927, in a upbeat editorial on the organizing success of the BSCP in its fight with the Pullman Corporation, he had pretended to be encouraged by reports of modest increases here and there in the number of unionized Negroes. But the "old AFofL [sic] spirit" was hard to kill, and he cited the white musicians who were at that moment striking against the admission of Negroes to their union. Three years earlier, in a direct editorial appeal to the AFL, Du Bois had warned labor leaders of an industrial Faustian bargain replicating the political alliance of big-city bosses and Negro voters. "The Negro is entering the ranks of semi-skilled and skilled labor and he is entering mainly as a 'scab,' " and the editor had predicted that a Negro worker would soon be able "to break any strike when he can gain economic advantage for himself." Wasn't it time, then, Du Bois had hoped almost desperately, "for white unions to stop bluffing and for Negro laborers to stop cutting off their noses to spite their faces?" To that end, as has been seen, speaking for the NAACP, Du Bois proposed the establishment of an Interracial Labor Commission comprised of the AFL, NAACP, BSCP, and "any other bodies agreed upon."

His appeal had not been deemed worthy of the courtesy of an answer, but by the end of 1928 the exclusionary policies of organized labor spoke for themselves. Within a few months, the editor would have in hand the careful occupational tabulations compiled by the National Urban League's Department of Industrial Relations. Of 2.5 million Negroes engaged in nonagricultural work, the league's T. Arnold Hill calculated that 81,658 belonged to unions. More than three thousand of these were members of Randolph's BSCP and another 12,585 belonged to independent Negro unions. The NUL study gave black membership in predominantly white labor unions as a mere 66,000. The vision of a society in which workers controlled the means of production had begun to exercise a strong ideological appeal after his Russian visit, yet Du Bois was compelled to view Marxist nostrums with qualified skepticism as he took the full measure of working-class racism in America, as revealed by statistics as bleak as those compiled by Hill. The complexities of a distant triumph of the proletariat aside, the editor assailed the ongoing, quotidian apartheid imposed upon the universe of work by the dominant workers themselves as a greater iniquity than the exploitation perpetrated by the capitalists. Furthermore, the political power exercised by organized labor gave Negroes another major reason to mistrust the Democratic Party.

Yet because the logic of working-class solidarity was a self-evident imperative to Du Bois, he was always ready to extol the slightest hint of interracial collaboration as the beginning of what might become a powerful trend. Reaction to Hoover's nomination in April 1930 of a supposedly moderate southerner to the Supreme Court was to result in just such a collaboration. Republican John J. Parker had run for governor of North Carolina and then been elevated by Harding to the Court of Appeals for the Fourth Circuit. North Carolina had been one of the breakaway states that had made Hoover's southern strategy successful. Parker was the better sort of white southerner, courtly, professionally dutiful, whose Senate confirmation should have been little more than a formality. When information reached NAACP national headquarters that the nominee had voiced impeccably racist opinions during his 1920 gubernatorial campaign, White sent a telegram with a three-day deadline demanding to know if Judge Parker's views had become less unenlightened. It appeared to be a matter of record that the North Carolinian had declared that Negro participation in politics was "a source of evil and danger to both races." He was even alleged to have promised that he would resign the governorship if he found that his election "was due to one Negro vote." NAACP branches were mobilized and mass meetings held across the country with greater resolve than at any time since the *Birth of a Nation* campaign. The Negro press depicted Hoover's nominee as the most serious judicial threat to racial rights since Justice Taney of *Dred Scott* infamy. Du Bois denounced Parker in scores of churches and schools throughout the northwest soon after taking leave of Stoddard in Chicago. Meanwhile, Parker's worries deepened when protests began to pour in from the United Mine Workers and the AFL about a 1927 decision upholding "yellow dog" contracts impeding union organizing in West Virginia coal mines. William Green and Walter White appeared before the Senate Judiciary Committee on the same day to testify against the nominee (although the AFL chief ostentatiously avoided being photographed with the association's acting secretary). "The Defeat of Judge Parker" in the July *Crisis* reproduced much of the press coverage North and South (some of it, like the Montgomery, Alabama, *Advertiser*, crediting the jurists's rejection to the NAACP) and cheerfully divined in the surprising outcome "a union of forces between the Liberals and the Labor unions on one side, and the Negroes, on the other." Du Bois knew better; organized labor and civil rights had traveled in the same direction to the same goal, but on parallel tracks. Six years remained before a real "union of forces" would begin.

There were others who shared Du Bois's highly intellectualized yet volcanic disquiet about America — others who believed that the potential for much fuller participation of the people in the political and economic life of the nation was being squandered. On a Saturday evening, two weeks before the close of 1929, the editor joined fifty like-minded academics, writers, publishers, organizers, and citizen-activists at International House on Manhattan's Upper West Side to launch the League for Independent Political Action (LIPA). The animating spirit behind the league was Columbia University's John Dewey, America's premier philosopher and educator. Dewey and Du Bois were well known to each other, though hardly social acquaintances. Their earliest encounter probably occurred at the historic National Negro Conference, the chrysalis of the NAACP, held at the end of May 1909 in New York's Charity Organization Hall. Close friendship with the collector Albert Barnes gave Dewey more than a nodding awareness of the writers and writings of the Harlem Renaissance, and on more than one occasion, the philosopher had been a speaker at the Harlem YMCA, not far from Morningside Heights. The philosopher's rather tenuous involvement in some of the NAACP's broad policy considerations during the early thirties was due to the editor's encouragement. Dewey agreed to serve as national chair of the LIPA at the urging of Benjamin Marsh, a labor union lobbyist. Approached by Devere Allen, editor of the Christian socialist magazine, *The World Tomorrow*, Du Bois had attended a preliminary meeting called in the fall of 1929 to formulate third-party solutions to the stasis created by the two major political parties. Agreeing to serve as one of the vice-presidents, he immediately forwarded to Allen precise recommendations for the LIPA platform.

After departing the December 15 International House meeting as one of the three vice-chairpersons of the league, along with the novelist Zona Gale, the Socialist James Maurer, and a young academic economist from Chicago, Paul Douglas, a future U.S. senator. Among the other prominent men and women present were Debs's successor, Norman Thomas, sometime Du Bois antagonist Villard, League for Industrial Democracy director Laidler, and radical theologian Reinhold Niebuhr. A Dewey biographer describes these men and women as "veterans of a decade of frustration and failure in popular politics."

The life span of the league was to run about four years, its final agony coming in the fall of 1933 with the Democratic congressional landslide. Its vital signs had begun to oscillate alarmingly before the end of its first year in existence, however. Having agreed unequivocally on the imperative of a third party, the LIPA's membership disagreed about the pedigree of the third party. The Thomas Socialists had signed on with the assumption that their party would be the chosen vehicle. The LIPA's liberals and progressives resisted cooptation by the Socialists in the belief that only a new third party unencumbered by old labels and dogmas could attract a wide following among both working and middle-class Americans. But it was the determination of Du Bois and Dewey to have their special agendas ratified by LIPA that soon tested the inherently fragile structure of the loose coalition of middle-class reformers and intellectuals. Not only were the LIPA Socialists disaffected by the Columbia professor's unanticipated appeal in December 1930 to an independent and reform-minded Republican senator to head the third-party movement, but even many of the progressives were incredulous that Dewey could seriously propose Nebraska's George W. Norris to lead them. To LIPA fellow travelers such as Christian socialist A. J. Muste, Dewey's antisocialist and distinctly middle-class biases were risibly off the mark as pragmatic gambits. Muste, a radical pacifist who would inspire the creation of the Congress of Racial Equality (CORE) three years later, seems to have been one of the few in the LIPA who made the same connection as Du Bois between racial discrimination and a viable reform politics. He reached out to Du Bois immediately, proposing a meeting of a small group during the Christmas holidays "to talk about the problem of worker's education among Negro workers in which we are mutually interested." Nothing of a practical nature seems to have come from Muste's *démarche*, however.

Du Bois had been ready to give the liberals, progressives, and socialists at the core of the LIPA the benefit of the doubt because of professed convictions such as Devere Allen's about Negro disfranchisement. As Allen drafted a preliminary statement of principles, the *World Tomorrow* editor had reassured Du Bois that the organization had to make its position "in this issue absolutely clear. If we have to compromise on that for the sake of [southern] votes," he stressed, "we might as well go out of business before we start." These distinguished authors, columnists, professors, Fabian-type socialists, and Rauschenbusch Christians were very much Du Bois's crowd—people such as Gale and publisher Kirby Page, with whom he sometimes dined at the Civic Club. Gale had served as a judge in the first *Opportunity* contest. Page had commissioned Fauset's recent, glowing profile of Du Bois in the August 1929 issue of *The World Tomorrow*. Fourteen months later, in response to a symposium inquiry to be published in the October 1930 number of *The World Tomorrow*, Du Bois gave Page an extraordinarily penitent answer concerning responsibility for World War I. The author of "Close Ranks," who had coveted an army captaincy in 1918, had changed his mind about the rights and wrongs of that cataclysm. He knew German militarism firsthand and had "greatly feared it," he told Page. Only later had he come to understand how the French and the British had intrigued and manipulated international developments. With millions of others he had been swept off his feet "by the emotional response of America to what seemed to be a great call to duty. The thing that I did not understand is how easy and inevitable it is for an appeal to blood and force to smash to utter negation any ideal for which it is used," Du Bois admitted. "Instead of a war to end war, or a war to save democracy, we found ourselves during and after the war descending to the meanest and most sordid of selfish actions, and we find ourselves today nearer moral bankruptcy than we were in 1914."

Such cultural and political affinities associated with the League for Independent Political Action prompted Du Bois's August *Crisis* editorial, "A New Party," a tribute to the men and women who were "committed personally and as a group" to building a party like the Labour Party of Great Britain. If it was and, indeed, would continue to be true, as a late-twentieth-century student of the American left observed, that even though Du Bois encountered difficulty in finding a "clear role for himself in the ranks of the Left," the editor obviously did experience a degree of guarded optimism during the start-up period of the political action league. The program of the LIPA as spelled out in *The Crisis* was strikingly similar to La Follette's 1924 platform: tax policies on wealth designed to underwrite government health insurance, public education, augmented unemployment benefits, a minimum wage, and low tariffs. The editorial emphasized that the LIPA aimed "to restore political rights to Negroes and to foreign-born citizens where they are now disfranchised." Pan-Africanist resonances were to be heard in the LIPA's desire to "stop imperial domination of backward countries." Yet Du Bois's enthusiasm already had begun to cool six months or more before Dewey's divisive overture to Norris. As the editor reiterated in a fairly sharp letter to Paul Douglas in February 1930, he had expected his views about Negro disfranchisement to be evident in the LIPA's final statement of concerns. The South's unconstitutional elimination of a third of its voters was a non-negotiable issue that the LIPA executive committee was supposed to have accepted months ago at his behest. But with *Why a Political Realignment*, the LIPA pamphlet drafted by Douglas, on his desk, Du Bois demanded to know what had happened to the voting issue. "Nowhere in this pamphlet, and more particularly for the program for the new party, is any mention made of the political rights for Negroes or for any other disfranchised classes," Du Bois objected. When an earlier draft had been flagged because of this omission, Douglas had explained that the matter "had simply been forgotten." Du Bois wondered "what the difficulty is now, [since] in the alignment of parties" he found absolutely no reference to the South. This would not do, he upbraided Douglas. The South was the center of new industry being grafted on to its "rotten borough vote system." He simply couldn't see "how this situation can be ignored." How about that, Douglas answered somewhat sheepishly, remarking that he hadn't "realized that we had omitted the Negro from our program." Of course, the LIPA's "tentative leaflet issued in November" had broached the subject, and Du Bois must certainly know that absence of "explicit recognition" in Douglas's final document did not mean "that we do not have the issue at heart. It is not necessary to stress every issue all the time," he offered lamely.

Nothing could have been more painfully obvious to Du Bois as the decade of the twenties wound down than that the task of making race an integral part of reform was close to being impossible in America. He was more and more prone to bitter eruptions, to rhetorical excoriations — "What has the United States to contribute to this world problem [of color]? Darkness rather than light — paradox rather than logic." Almost devoid of political leverage, marginalized at best when they were not rendered completely invisible, he saw his people as a perdurable presence whose 310 years of adversity had made them the paradox of American exceptionalism — ciphers who could be blamed, nevertheless, for their own condition as well as the imperfections of most everything else. Whether it concerned the aims of organized labor, the emerging liberal wing of the Democratic party, the Socialists, Progressives, and their Christian and good-government collaborators, or the urban political machines and the southern-strategizing GOP, people of color struggled, usually without success, to avoid being reduced to pawns, patronized into impotence.

Among the possible options involving collaboration with Euro-Americans, there was one significant, but as yet unexplored, alternative: the Workers (Communist) Party, renamed in 1929 the Communist Party of the United States of America (CPUSA). Du Bois had taken cautious, approving note in 1925 when the Communists, meeting in Chicago that October, had founded the American Negro Labor Congress (ANLC). Responding to Talented Tenth concerns that Communists were "boring" into colored organizations, he suggested that there was an effective antidote readily at hand in the elimination of racism. But the Communists were only beginning to formulate an approach to American Negroes, the Sixth World Congress of the Comintern having only determined in 1928, under Stalin's orders, the paradoxically useful doctrine of Negro Soviets in the Deep South. It was hardly coincidence that Lovett Fort-Whiteman, his Garveyite and African Blood Brotherhood days long behind him, asked for an appointment with the editor in mid-April of the same year. Fort-Whiteman was the national organizer for the ANLC and the ranking Negro in the American party's hierarchy. The nucleus of the CPUSA's organizational and theoretical talent upon which it would shortly depend in order to attract colored members—Harry Haywood, Otto Hall, William Patterson, Maude White, James Ford—was still undergoing training in Russia at Far East University and the Lenin School. The Great Depression, Scottsboro, the Popular Front, and all that that was to mean to the radicalizing of Du Bois and Negro Americans lay just ahead.

SCOTTSBORO SHOULD HAVE been the NAACP's Dreyfus Affair instead of a capital embarrassment it was never able to live down. The essential details of the case, even with the passing of nearly seventy years, are still generally familiar. A rumble between black and white hoboes on a freight train heading southwest out of Chattanooga for Memphis ended badly for the whites on the morning of March 25, 1931. Ousted from the train as it picked up speed after a stop in Stevenson, Alabama, the whites shuffled, somewhat bruised, into the presence of the local sheriff to complain of being attacked and ejected by a "bunch of niggers." They demanded to "press charges against 'em." The right of white hoboes to be secure in their persons from assaults by Negro hoboes was a serious southern consideration. A telegram to the next station halted the train at Paint Rock, where local law officers and a posse removed and arrested nine Negro males ranging in age from thirteen to nineteen. Two whites in overalls and caps sharing the boxcar with the Negroes surprised the sheriff when they revealed that they were females. Ruby Bates and Victoria Price, young prostitutes from Huntsville, Alabama, claimed that they had been raped by the nine black men. None of the "boys" (their almost instantaneous label) had better than a sixth-grade education. One of them, Willie Roberson, was so cankered by syphilis and gonorrhea that he was sexually dysfunctional. Incarceration in Scottsboro, the Jackson County seat, dispatch of one hundred Alabama National Guardsmen by the governor to cure the town's lynch fever, and four jury trials in four days resulted in death sentences for all but one of the convicted, thirteen-year-old Eugene Williams. Petrified and even more incoherent than was his normal state, one of the accused, Clarence Norris, had testified on cross-examination that all of his fellow defendants had ravished Bates and Price. From the day of the last batch of convictions, on April 9, onward over the next twenty years until the last Scottsboro defendant was finally paroled from prison, Alabama's public officials would insist that the trials had reflected credit on the state's capacity to guarantee due process against mob law. A majority of white southerners concurred. To the rest of the world, Scottsboro was a human rights cynosure.

The reactions at NAACP headquarters were conflicted from the beginning. Decisions in the case had been hampered in New York by the necessity of relying on information and legal talent available through the association's inefficient Chattanooga branch. The white Chattanooga attorney retained by the NAACP at the last minute to represent the defendants, Stephen Roddy, had generously fortified himself with liquor and arrived just as the Scottsboro proceedings began. He was unable to discuss the case with the local court-appointed white attorney or even to meet with the accused. Even so, Roddy had been able to enter into the trial record an objection of jury contamination that would be the basis for the appeal that the NAACP, tardily alert to the enormous public-relations value of the Scottsboro Boys, would commit itself to pursuing. But the CPUSA had already taken the measure of the case as a *cause célèbre*— another Sacco and Vanzetti, one of its observers at the trial had cabled Party headquarters—and was determined to exploit its political significance with as little collaboration as possible with the NAACP. The Party's legal arm—the International Labor Defense (ILD)—sped its chief attorney, Joseph Brodsky, to Birmingham's Kilby Prison to obtain exclusive rights to represent the boys on April 20.

Du Bois's response to Scottsboro was astonishingly conventional. It might have seemed to be an injustice perfectly suited to the editor's temperament, a legal travesty in search of a Negro American Emile Zola. Yet he, Walter White, and the board of directors had already squandered crucial weeks and committed several missteps in the handling of the Scottsboro case. Defending nine unlettered black males, whose questionable character seemed self-evident, against a charge of gang-raping two white women in the Deep South was hardly an inviting prospect. White, officially appointed as James Weldon Johnson's successor only two weeks before the trials, regarded the Scottsboro Boys as more of a risk than an opportunity. In spite of their indicting bluntness, then, Du Bois's first written words about the case in the July *Crisis* conveyed the impression of a delayed response. A train ride shared with two prostitutes was "no crime, except in the slave belt. . . . The unwritten penalty for that sort of social equality in Alabama is death," he observed with dry disgust. He avowed that the NAACP was determined to see that the boys' lives were spared. Returning to the case sixth months later, there was still an odd remoteness, an uncustomary philosophical fatalism, to his editorializing, as he wrote in "Blunders" of "men and women all over stand[ing] ready to pull these wretched things from the grip of what we call Law." Criticizing both the NAACP and ILD by implication, Du Bois spoke of "organizations rush[ing] up and down the land and fume[ing] and yell[ing]. And yet little is done. The [two white] girls will be set free to go on to hell. The boys will either be murdered swiftly in cold blood; or else murdered slowly in an Alabama jail; or else be murdered a bit less quickly in the slums and streets and brothels of the South."

Meanwhile, four weeks after the last trial and still uncertain of his next move, White had cockily assured inquiring board member Clarence Darrow and the editor of *The Nation* that the NAACP had the situation well in hand. America's preeminent trial lawyer was advised to refuse the ILD's request to enter the case. In an attempt to rescue his organization from a fabrication, the executive secretary authorized the hiring of a well-connected white Alabama attorney to take over the case from the ineffective Roddy. Telephone calls overwhelmed the switchboard, and cablegrams from a half dozen branches and from scores of members poured into the national office in such volume that the executive secretary realized the need to sprint in order to place the NAACP at the head of its following. The Pickens bombshell on April 24 figuratively rattled the windows in the directors' boardroom. A letter from the field secretary effusively endorsing the ILD's Scottsboro involvement in the case appeared on the front page of the *Daily Worker*. The impulsive Pickens praised the Communists for moving "more speedily and effectively than all other agencies put together," and went on to urge "every Negro who has intelligence" to send contributions to the *Worker* and the ILD. The very next day, the party brought the Scottsboro Boys to Lenox Avenue in the person of Mrs. Janie Patterson, mother of Haywood and a surprisingly effective public speaker. The fracas that ensued after ILD organizers led the inflating crowd, incendiary banners streaming, into the blue wall of the NYPD garnered the desired headlines. Mrs. Patterson's Harlem appearance marked the debut of a six-month Communist roadshow in which Scottsboro parents would appear in the major cities outside the South and before two hundred mass rallies in sixteen European countries by September 1932.

Even as Pickens shriveled apologetically in the hot blast of chairman Ovington's reprimand (he denied knowing that his employers intended to enter the case), *The Defender*, Baltimore *Afro-American*, *Amsterdam News*, Oklahoma City *Black Dispatch*, and a growing number of other black newspapers applauded the vigor of the Communists throughout the spring and summer of 1931. *The New Masses* offered yet another derisory variation on N-A-A-C-P with *Opportunity* prize contestant Eugene Gordon's article suggesting the name change to the *Nicest* Association for the Advancement of Certain People. May Day banners in New York and Chicago parades proclaimed the innocence of the Scottsboro Boys, the perfidy of southern justice, and the bourgeois treason of the NAACP.

Robert Minor, editor of the *Daily Worker* and devastating cartoonist, racheted up the pressure with "The Negro and His Judases," a blistering piece in which the NAACP was lumped with the Norman Thomas Socialists and other "social-fascist" conspirators. "The masses cannot be led by the NAACP towards anything but slavery," Minor sneered. While Langston Hughes was fond of White and admiring of Du Bois, he increasingly distanced himself from the association's handling of the case, publishing a poem and a one-act play about the case in *The New Masses*. Vann's *Courier* called on readers to give the association its due for two decades of prudent and effective civil rights leadership, but the private alarums sent to White by the young editor of the Kansas City *Call*, Roy Wilkins, were a far better indication of the rising mood of public skepticism verging on contempt.

More than two months after the last of the boys had been sentenced, the association's chief officer journeyed to Birmingham to confer with the prestigious white law firm of Fort, Beddow, and Ray, whose junior partner, Roderick Beddow, had provisionally consented to take an appeal to the Alabama Supreme Court, but no further—provided the ILD was excluded from the case. White finally spoke with the prisoners on May 14 at Kilby Prison, where he promised them the full backing of the NAACP in return for their signed agreements to discharge the ILD and entrust their fates to Fort, Beddow, and Ray. The next day, White issued a full statement of the association's position. In attempting to explain the shifting cast of lawyers, he offered the patronizing observation that the boys and their parents were "humble folk and have had few opportunities for knowledge. They have been confused by the conflicting statements made to them." Plainly, they were still confused, because the boys withdrew their co-operation in less than twenty-four hours. Two weeks later, after a now fiercely anti-Communist Pickens tongue-lashed them in their cells, the Scottsboro nine reaffirmed their trust in the association—only to repudiate their commitment again after a visit from ILD officials with their parents in tow. The revolving-door struggle at Kilby Prison for exclusive possession of the Scottsboro Boys would continue until the first week of January 1932, when the NAACP officially renounced its objective. But five months before the board of directors voted to cede the case to the ILD, the mother of Eugene Williams had spoken her mind in public about White's assessment of the parents' understanding of the issues. "Well," she said, in a consummate reproach, "we are not too ignorant to know a bunch of liars and fakers when we meet up with them and are not too ignorant to know that if we let the NAACP look after our boys, that they will die." Mrs. Williams spoke for a growing number of ordinary Negro men and women to whom the aggressive, public tactics of the Communists held far greater meaning than the Margold litigation master plan or the Supreme Court's agreeing to hear arguments in the Texas white primary case, *Nixon v. Condon*. If there were a possibility for democracy in America, these men and women had every reason to hope that Communists could help them build it.

As Du Bois watched the CPUSA outmaneuver his organization and propel the fate of nine juveniles onto the stage of international attention, his distress was unrelenting. Although he had been as surprised as White by the tactics of the Communists, the editor was much quicker to gauge the profound implications of the case not only to the association but also to the prospective course of the national civil rights struggle. Neither he nor Johnson felt much confidence in White's management of the controversy. When the new secretary wrote the former secretary that, if the Communists "lose, they lose, and if they win, they lose" because everyone would understand that an ILD victory had been made possible because of the 1919 U.S. Supreme Court ruling on fair trials won by the NAACP, Johnson had been genuinely disappointed and alarmed. "Not one person in a thousand would either hear or understand the basis on which the victory might be won," he shot back. White's penchant for glib pronouncements and facile solutions was already well known. But this was no time for sophistry, an alarmed Du Bois realized, as there could be no doubt that the Communists were bent on supplanting the Negro leadership class in a time of maximum vulnerability. They proposed to "build on this case an appeal to the American Negro to join the Communist movement as the only solution of their problem," he cautioned. Du Bois had made it his business to monitor the Comintern's rapidly evolving position on the "Negro question," which had been given doctrinal firmness in the Communist International's October 1930 resolution "Equal Rights and Self Determination."

The American Negro, whose special significance had remained under consideration from the time of Claude McKay's 1923 Russian sojourn, had by 1928 become the subject of intense Kremlin discussions and resolutions. As formulated personally by Stalin at the Sixth Congress of the Communist International, the American Negro was defined as a special case—a "peculiarity . . . not only in view of the prominent *racial distinctions*" but as an "oppressed nation" whose eventual self-determination in the Black Belt would be followed by integration into the working class and final liberation as a constituent of the triumphant proletariat. To sophisticated people of color, all this seemed to amount to little more than a preposterous inspection of the American South through the lens of Uzbekistan or Soviet Mongolia. Even so, and despite the fact that the CPUSA generally preferred to downplay the doctrine as the years passed, "Self-Determination for Negroes in the Black Belt" carved out an extremely useful exception for racial and cultural nationalism in the otherwise hostile doctrine of the class struggle. As a matter of practical politics, the doctrine gave the Communists a potential advantage in recruitment of Negro Americans. However misconceived the curious concept of Black Belt self-determination—which both racially separated blacks from whites yet also incorporated them in the class struggle—it had the consequence of embedding the Negro in the national program of the Party. As a troubled Du Bois conceded, neither the Democratic or Republican parties had made as concerted an effort to enroll Negroes as the CPUSA or to place them in prominent administrative and elective positions.

In the wake of Wall Street's collapse, the Comintern had ordered the national Communist parties to accelerate and intensify their recruitment and confrontation in Western Europe and the United States as part of Stalin's "Third Phase"—the supposedly penultimate period leading to the triumph of the proletariat. The American Communist Party's monopolizing of the Scottsboro Boys was a breakthrough into black America that followed hard on several propaganda successes. The staged public trial of August Yokinen, the Finnish immigrant who barely spoke English, on the charge of "white chauvinism" had yielded the Party a lode of goodwill among colored people. Two thousand spectators in the Harlem Casino had witnessed the conviction and expulsion of the bewildered janitor only eight days before the arrest of the Scottsboro Boys. Coverage of the Yokinen trial in *The New York Times* and wide attention in the Negro press had been followed by sensational developments five days later when the CPUSA launched the first large-scale, nationwide protests against worsening economic conditions on March 6, "International Unemployment Day." With more than 5 million Americans out of work, thousands of unemployed Negroes marched together with white workers in New York's Union Square and fought pitched battles with the police who blocked the way to City Hall. Newspapers took excited notice of an unprecedented interracial solidarity that party organizer Cyril Briggs trumpeted as a "successful breaking down of the wall of prejudice between white and Negro workers fostered by the employers."

Gunfire at Camp Hill, Alabama, on the evenings of July 15 and 16, 1931, sounded like the opening shots in the class war in the Deep South to some alarmists. Spreading the gospel of self-determination through its new organ, the Chattanooga-based *Southern Worker*, and audaciously putting it to the test in grindingly poor Tallapoosa County, Alabama, Party organizers had enrolled more than eight hundred Negro farmers in a sharecroppers' union, the Croppers and Farm Workers Union (CFWU), in order to force wage negotiations with the local planters. To believe James Allen's *Southern Worker*, the Third Phase was alive and thriving as Negro sawmill workers and farmers in Tallapoosa County "enthusiastically welcomed Communist leadership." Ignition of this highly inflammatory situation came when more than 150 croppers assembled in a vacant house to hear about the Scottsboro case. The final shootout on the sixteenth with a posse of enraged planters and poor whites cost the lives of four CFWU members, seriously wounded the sheriff, and led to the incarceration of thirty-five or more croppers. Headlines in the Birmingham *Age-Herald* reflected the hysteria engulfing many Alabama whites—"Negro Reds Reported Advancing."

All this proved too much for Du Bois, as it did for Pickens, who was as quick to call the Alabama farmers "innocent dupes" of the Communists as he had earlier been to praise the Party. Camp Hill Du Bois saw as another cynical example of Communist irresponsibility—"too despicable for words." He felt nothing but compassion for the half-starved, destitute peons of Tallapoosa County living under the heel of merciless oppression. Their plight "shriek[ed] for remedy," but to organize a union and then to hold a public meeting to denounce the Scottsboro sentences in rural Alabama amounted to nothing less, Du Bois castigated, than "drawing a red herring across the trail of eight innocent children." That *Opportunity* and even Vann's conservative *Courier* showed more sympathy than Du Bois for the Party's conduct in the Camp Hill gun battle only underscored Du Bois's distemper. Camp Hill was a classic illustration of the Communists' techniques, their arrogant, uninformed exploitation of humble folk in order to advance improbable political and social objectives, he charged. Part of the reason for what Du Bois regarded as tactics of provocation and exploitation derived from the Communists' ignorance of southern racial conditions. The Party's understanding was as nothing when measured against the cumulative experience of the NAACP in negotiating the shoals of Jim Crow justice, he insisted. How could an organization largely comprised of newcomers to the cities of the East and Midwest—men and women of Russian and Eastern European backgrounds—presume to preempt a civil rights agenda reaching back to the Niagara Movement? He and the association "deserve[d] from Russia something better than a kick in the back from the young jackasses who are leading Communism in America today," he protested.

Du Bois answered his rhetorical question and much else with a good deal of heat in "The Negro and Communism," a long, score-settling editorial in the September 1931 *Crisis*, followed by a combative narrative of events in the December issue of *Harper's* under White's signature but unmistakably indebted to the editor. He discerned, rather fearfully as the crisis around Scottsboro peaked, another twentieth-century problem impending, one that would seriously complicate and muddle the problem of the color line—that of the relationship of civil rights to communism. The die was cast, he noted. Scottsboro had brought squarely before the American Negro "the question of his attitude toward Communism," by which he also meant his own attitude toward the ideology and the political movement. An economic system and a race were confronted with a momentous decision: "If socialism as a form of government and industry" was on trial in Russia, capitalism was "just as surely on trial throughout the world and [was] more and more clearly recognizing the fact."

Having decided to undertake both a thorough immersion in the theory of Marxism and a methodical assessment of real-world implications of communism in the United States, Du Bois would soon boast of assembling one of the most comprehensive private libraries on scientific socialism in the country. With the help of Abram Harris, Du Bois broadened his circle of leftist associates, and developed a close relationship with Will Herberg and Benjamin Stolberg, two apt young theoreticians. Stolberg was never a member of the CPUSA and would write exposés in the late thirties of the "Stalinist" threat posed by the Party to the new Congress of Industrial Organizations (CIO). The twenty-two-year-old Herberg was a disciple of Jay Lovestone, former CPUSA leader recently expelled by the Comintern after he misjudged the staying power of Stalin's critic Nikolai Bukharin. Du Bois found Herberg's brand of Marxism congenial enough to feature in *The Crisis* for July 1931, telling Rachel Davis DuBois that he believed it was incumbent upon him to give communism a hearing when it was expressed "as temperately as this is." In opposition to Albon Holsey's *Crisis* essay, "Business Points the Way," Herberg hoisted the banner of worker solidarity and extolled "a course of united struggle against the white capitalist members of the country whose rule of ruthless exploitation rests upon the racial subjection of the Negro as well as upon the class subjection of the worker."

Herberg's was decidedly a new note whose reverberations were still in the air when "The Negro and Communism" appeared. Du Bois began the essay appreciatively. He could be fair, he wished to emphasize, even if the Communist Party failed the test. Concisely reviewing the dreary civil rights history of the two major parties, along with the feckless record of the Socialists and the Progressives, Du Bois complimented the exceptional interracialism of a political party that was to choose a Negro as its candidate for vice-president of the United States in the 1932 election. "They have insisted in their strikes and agitation to let Negroes fight with them and that the object of their fighting is for black workers as well as white workers," he wrote of the CPUSA. As for the Socialists, the editor ironized that the only time that "so fine a man and so logical a reasoner as Norman Thomas becomes vague and incoherent is when he touches the black man, and consequently he touches him as seldom as possible." But Du Bois reproached the Communists for two fatal errors: 1) the savaging of the NAACP; and 2) their myopia about racism. In addition to Robert Minor and James Allen, the CPUSA now had such able Negro organizers and journalists as Briggs, James Ford, Eugene Gordon, and William Patterson, who kept up a barrage of "social-fascist" charges against the NAACP in *The Liberator*, *Daily Worker*, and *Southern Worker*.

Not since the heyday of Garvey had Du Bois felt so affronted as he heard himself called a "class enemy," a "Judas," a lickspittle of the capitalists—vituperation applauded by Dreiser, Dos Passos, Steffens, Lola Ridge, and other literary lions of the left. The founder of the Talented Tenth bridled at the very notion of a "Negro bourgeoisie" disconnected from and unresponsive to the common folk, and he fumed that it had been the grossest of libels to charge the association with indifference in the defense of the Scottsboro Boys and its leadership with toadying to the capitalists. Differences in wealth and distinctions in culture did exist within the race, but he dismissed the phenomena of deracination and alienation as no more than Marxist caricatures. The editorial soared into an aria as Du Bois praised a group like no other "group of leaders on earth who have so largely made common cause with the lowest of their race as educated American Negroes, and it is their foresight and sacrifice and theirs alone that has saved the American freedman from annihilation and degradation." He foresaw annihilation as precisely the fate awaiting the Scottsboro Boys, as well, if the NAACP was forced to withdraw and leave the case solely to the ILD. It was a contention Darrow would also shortly make in public. Had the CPUSA leadership been broad-minded and farsighted, the editor insisted, it could never have gainsaid the "honesty, earnestness and intelligence of the NAACP during twenty years of desperate struggle." His organization was the sole organization and "its methods the only methods available" capable of saving the boys, and the NAACP would have done so in collaboration with "capitalists and laborers north and south, black and white."

A decade later, after two Fourteenth Amendment decisions by the Supreme Court reversing the Scottsboro convictions (*Powell v. Alabama* in 1932 and *Norris v. Alabama* in 1935), Du Bois still maintained that the Communists had bungled the boys' appeals. "Had it not been for their senseless interference, these poor victims of southern injustice would today be free." Indeed, in *Dusk of Dawn* he would contend that "they would have been freed in a couple of years without fanfare or much publicity." The wanton Communist propaganda assault on the association had been motivated by the Comintern's calculation that Scottsboro was an opportunity "to foment revolution in the United States" — "the actual fate of the victims was a minor matter." Here, the editor pressed on to the crux of his dispute with American Communists — race relations in America. "Threatening judges and yelling for mass action on the part of white southern workers" were fatally flawed tactics based on the same ideological evasion that Du Bois had repeatedly reproached in the Socialists: the supposed identity of interests of white and black labor.

For the CPUSA, it was axiomatic that the empowerment of the white working class meant the civil emancipation of the Negro people, that the resolution of the class struggle resolved the race problem. But that kind of talk to Negroes was "like a red flag to a bull," declared Du Bois, for he and they knew that if and when the CPUSA began to exercise significant national appeal it must come at the expense of genuine interracialism. Immigrant Communists — however dedicated and color-blind — were doomed to bang their heads against the granite wall of race in America. Du Bois would postulate repeatedly that the race split in the American working class was yet another manifestation of this nation's much vaunted exceptionalism. He was passionate in believing that the exploitation of black workers by white workers was preordained, inscribed, as it were, on the DNA of the white American proletariat. White Alabama and Arkansas workers would prevent black workers from rising out of the mudsill by mob action and apartheid laws, Du Bois claimed in "The Negro and Marxism," just as their northern counterparts had historically done through urban riots and exclusionary union rules. When Herberg protested, the editor replied with what he saw as a crucial revision of the class-struggle doctrine, one to which he would devote considerable theoretical elaboration in the coming months. Curiously, Herberg, like Bertram Wolfe, his coadjutor, spoke for a small but influential Marxisant cadre that strove to tailor world communism to the very exceptionalism that Du Bois indicted as being inimical to the experiment. The difference between us, Du Bois told the precocious editor of the Lovestoneite *Revolutionary Age*, was that Herberg sincerely believed that the attainment by white workers of their class interests would "make them rise above racial antipathy" whereas he, Du Bois, was certain that race hatred would persist in the United States "even when the lines of the class struggle are closely defined and the Russian experience is so definite that it does not disprove but rather strengthens my belief."

As he faced the decade of the Great Depression affronted by the Party's Scottsboro behavior and dogmatically convinced of the perfidiousness of America's white working class, Du Bois set himself the challenge of formulating a grand design for the redress and resurgence of the race, a theory of political economy to serve African America that turned away from an expended capitalism but spurned the panacea of proletarian dictatorship. "American Negroes do not propose to be the shock troops of the Communist Revolution, driven out in front to death, cruelty, and humiliation in order to win victories for white workers," he had almost seemed to bellow in the fall of 1931. His was to be a new race-centered political economy that could be said to combine cultural nationalism, Scandinavian cooperativism, Booker Washington, and Marx in about equal parts. No other alternative had been left to him and his people. "From Brook Farm down to the LIPA," he concluded with embittered clarity, "the face of reform has been set to lift the white producer and consumer, leaving the black man and his peculiar problems severely alone, with the fond hope that better white men will hate Negroes less and better white conditions make race contact more human and respectable." Du Bois was not at all optimistic.

HOLDING ON,

AMOROUSLY AND ANGRILY

Du Bois's finances seemed to have no explanation other than alchemy. In addition to the monthly mortgage on the double apartments in the Dunbar coop, sales prospects for the heavily mortgaged, deteriorioating St. Nicholas Avenue apartment building were dismal. Payments on his car would run until June 1929. He was now supporting both wife and daughter in Paris, Nina having gone to France in December 1928 to help Yolande recover from the broken marriage. His plan called for them to remain abroad until the fall of 1930, almost two years. Maître Jean Beauvais, the attorney retained by Du Bois to prepare and file Yolande's divorce papers, gave reasonable assurance that the matter would be resolved no later than the first months of 1930, a timetable that would prove to be more or less accurate. Meanwhile, the editor was obliged to ask his momentary son-in-law to advance Maître Beauvais's retainer, which Cullen had appeared only too happy to do by dipping into his Guggenheim funds. Yet Du Bois was somehow able to cable 3,500 francs to the Hotel Trianon in the avenue du Maine in the spring of 1929, ordering Nina "*not* [to] try to save too much. Make yourself comfortable and do not worry." He followed up with several chatty letters, one of them describing a musical evening in High Harlem at which the Bonaparte Princess Violette Murat accompanied one of Nina's friends on the piano. Another letter recounted Jessie Fauset's "very pretty" marriage, attended by about seventy-five special guests. Few letters came after May, however, mainly, he wrote, because of unsettled affairs at *The Crisis*.

His social life was emotionally so much more rewarding with Nina and Yolande parked in the Fifteenth Arrondissement that Du Bois felt the arrangement to be worth the heavy drain on his finances. The correspondence with accomplished women friends quickened, most of it dealing with the successes or worries of their professional lives, but some of it was unmistakably amorous.

It was at this point—the absence abroad of his wife and daughter—that his relationships with women, always vigorous and varied, became sexually ever more exuberant to such a degree that they resembled the compulsiveness of a Casanova. The episodic dalliances, the star-crossed love affair with Fauset, the comfortable arrangements with Georgia Johnson and Mildred Jones began to be replicated with a seeming insatiety that yielded nothing to advancing years, and may, perhaps, have been a spectacular version of the generalized male late-life crisis. Whether with wounded reluctance or compliant relief, Nina outwardly accommodated herself to Will's extramarital pursuits, to the extent, even, of allowing herself to be befriended by several of the women and, occasionally, playing hostess to them for short periods. By all accounts, Nina Yolande Du Bois had become a timid, pleasantly uninteresting phantom by the end of the 1920s, an indispensable but largely invisible fixture in her husband's concept of public marital propriety. "When he had to save face for the organization, she would appear," the *Inter-State Tattler* columnist, Geraldyn Major (a.k.a. "Lady Nicotine"), confided in an interview almost fifty years later. Katherine Bell Banks, the daughter of a close family friend, thought of Nina as "retiring, sweet, very . . . I wouldn't say aristocratic, because she wasn't haughty." Nina was simply "a real lady."

Du Bois's serial affairs, several of which were the equivalent of parallel marriages, seem to imply some deep-seated emotional incompleteness that had probably remained unresolved since the death of his mother. That the moralist of the Harlem Renaissance and author of impeccably feminist essays in *The Crisis* and of "The Damnation of Women" in *Darkwater* was a priapic adulterer compels appropriate disclosure, even though it inescapably smacks of the report of a private eye. Nor can the biographer always know with sufficient certainty whether a friendship with a particular woman was anything more than that— an abiding, supportive rapport between two worldly people. Du Bois's correspondence yields an abundance of vivid exchanges with women precisely because he found their company more interesting, egotistically sustaining, and less threatening than male companionship—and women responded, almost gratefully, to his apparent appreciation of them as fully complete beings.

He had introduced Mildred Bryant Jones in a half-length photo in the November 1928 *Crisis*, although her romantic significance would have escaped his readers. A graduate of Fisk and the New England Conservatory with study summers in Europe to her credit, Jones had just been awarded the degree of doctor of music from Chicago's National University of Music. The photo showed a pert woman in her early forties, small, light-skinned, with warm eyes and hair pulled back into a fashionable bun. She headed the music department at Wendell Phillips, Chicago's leading Negro high school. Du Bois usually spent time with her, often staying in her South Side home, when he came to Chicago;

and those times he found himself unable to do so, Jones received an explanation. Mildred Jones, if anyone could, brought out whatever folksiness Du Bois possessed behind a veil of dignity. He would tell her she was zany, that she was "never . . . going to have real good sense," and write with affectionate concern about her run-down health. She called him her "dear Mr. Man," and seeded her plaintive letters in between meetings with slightly inaccurate French protests of her aching love. "*Vous êtes mon âme,*" she said, "*ma [sic] très cher—le plus cher ami de ma vie. Oh, oh!*" "I miss seeing you, Mr. Man. It seems an awfully long time until January."

Because it was the language that certified romance and sophistication, Ethel Ray (she was two husbands away from becoming Mrs. Clarence Nance) liked to flavor her letters with French also, addressing him as André and signing herself Marielle. When her secretarial position ended with Charles Johnson's resignation from *Opportunity*, she had headed back to Minnesota at the end of 1926. She and Du Bois had an almost playful intimacy, one that would deepen after World War II and endure until his death. She delighted in those social quirks that so many others found off-putting or arrogant: his refusal to see people during his workaholic Sundays; his response when asked if he remembered a person—"Du Bois would say, 'Should I?' "; his habit of embarrassing hostesses "by just kind of leaving a party." Sometimes Ray would ask bluntly, " 'Why are you so sharp with so and so—why do you do that?' and he'd say, 'Well . . . there must be brains somewhere.' " As a short, irritated summer 1929 note suggests, Du Bois missed Ray: "My dear Ethel, I have been waiting a year to hear about you and your summer plans. Please write me." In her room in Phyllis Wheatley House in Duluth, musing on those times spent with "André" in the "City of Refuge" that had seemed wonderful, "Marielle" finally got around to writing in the fall of 1929. She closed by sending her André "thoughts of the sea and a fall a few years ago." Marielle and André continued to write each other, and they may have been reunited at least once when Du Bois traveled to the northwest. Eight years were to elapse before Marielle's dream of returning to New York became a reality, however, and by then Du Bois would have relocated to Atlanta.

Beyond an occasional *adieu*, Elizabeth Prophet made little use of French in her letters, although she had lived in Paris since 1922, first as a student at the Ecole Nationale des Beaux-Arts, then, while the gatekeepers of the art world slowly recognized her sculpting abilities, in the penury that was virtually a professional obligation. Although the time and place seems uncertain, her friendship with Du Bois must have developed a year or so before her departure for France, and probably became much more intimate during his Paris sojourns in connection with the third and fourth Pan-African Congresses. Prophet's life of adversity was inspiring proof of the overcoming powers of talent and determination, but it was hardly a life that any person who was not an artist would pursue. When she wrote Du Bois in early 1931 that she "would come through or go under, that is all, and if no one else cares why should I," Prophet's pathos was not greatly exaggerated. She had been born in 1890 to poor parents in Providence, and had shown such strong abilities in public school that she won a scholarship to the Rhode Island School of Design. Afterward, she worked as a cleaning woman in New York City until her situation was brought to the attention of Mrs. Gertrude Vanderbilt Whitney, who financed three years at the Beaux-Arts. Five years of perilous economies followed, as the fiercely dedicated Prophet worked with chisel and hammer shut away in her attic apartment in the rue Broca literally from morning to nightfall. Her diet was meager and her health suffered badly, especially during the wet, penetratingly cold Paris winters. She was in bed with a bad back when Du Bois telegraphed in September 1929 asking that she look after Augusta Savage, whose Rosenwald Fellowship had finally provided the means to study sculpture in Paris. Prophet answered him in English written as if translated from French that she would "try to undertake this which you ask of me," but begged him not to make a habit of such requests, for she had "neither friends nor money to aid me," and she was "very weary." Many months later, she wrote Du Bois that she had been too weak to work for weeks. She accused Otto Kahn, the department store tycoon and arts maven, of devaluing her work, complained of Louise Brook's insufferable vanity, and ranted that she could "no longer believe in any of them." Her one good fortune was Henry Tanner's influential sponsorship. The expatriate dean of Negro artists nominated her for the Harmon Foundation sculpture prize, which Prophet won in 1930. The Harmon money arrived just in time to enable her to continue working.

While Prophet persevered, Du Bois wrote consolatory letters. In May 1931, he would send what was for him an unusually long personal letter. Personal letters from Du Bois were seldom very personal, but to the lonely sculptor his encouraging words of artistic and racial destiny were like unguents from Cupid. He was disturbed that she had somehow been hurt by his own actions "and by the attitude of colored and white America." "No one, either in France or America, appreciates you more than I do," he vowed, but, as France was still relatively untouched, Prophet undoubtedly failed to appreciate the depth of the depression in the United States: "all philanthropy has been cut down; all business has been curtailed, breadlines have appeared everywhere, and the situation gets no better." Even in the best of times, the rich and the powerful were inimical to his "frank and unpopular writing and talking"; he was powerless to help her. Nor should Prophet expect great generosity. "As you yourself realize, this is the fate of genius," he lectured her with tough love. "It does not make you any less great, but it is the price that people like you have to pay all too often." He would do all in his power to spread news of her genius so as "to give people of colored blood here a part of the glory" that Prophet was destined to achieve. She forgave. "I am no longer angry with you, dear," Prophet had already written even before Du Bois composed the didactic May love letter. "How nice it would be if we could pass a few moments together"—but would it be, after all, she wondered? "Perhaps you would find me too thoughtful, too sad, too serious." By November, she was in better health and frame of mind as she imagined their happiness together should he find a way to come to Paris—"beautiful Paris! wonderful France!" Her mood became ecstatic: "I can never forget you, and see you often ever courageously at your work, admire and love you, but I have been through many phases since we parted. You have known it perhaps by the character of some of my letters, up and down." When Prophet decided to return to America after the exhibition at the Salon d'Automne of her prizewinning *Head of a Negro* in 1931, the Du Boises would generously house her in their apartment at the Dunbar. She and Nina had struck up a pleasant friendship during Nina's Paris stay.

Du Bois enjoyed the impishness of mentioning that there was another Mrs. Du Bois in his life, although this one was white. She was Rachel Davis Du-Bois, a Bucknell University graduate and New Jersey high school instructor whose innovative presentations of racial and ethnic instructional materials were to make her a major, recognized precursor of multiculturalism. Rachel Davis's Quaker background predisposed her to social activism, and her marriage to the affluent accountant Nathan DuBois enabled her to attend women's conferences where the topics were peace, social justice, and women's rights. As she was incapable of having children by her husband, the couple eventually decided to separate, living apart until Nathan DuBois's death. Rachel Davis DuBois's earnest white life had been changed forever by a speech delivered in the summer of 1920 by Hollingsworth Wood to the First International Conference of Friends in London. "Movingly he described the terrible race riot in Chicago in 1919," and Davis DuBois was overcome with shame at knowing nothing about race relations in her own country. Two years later, she traveled on a fact-finding mission for the Pennsylvania Committee on the Abolition of Slavery (still in business) to Aiken, South Carolina, where, at the black Voorhees Normal and Industrial School, she encountered for the first time people of color who were indistinguishable in appearance from white people. Channing Tobias, visiting the school on YMCA business, took Davis DuBois aside for a quick lesson in the one-drop peculiarities of the region. "He must have seen ignorance coming out of the cells of my skin," she wrote in her autobiography. Deeply influenced by pamphlets such as the popular *Americanizing Our Foreign-Born* and disturbed by Du Bois's "The Dilemma of the Negro" in the October 1924 *American Mercury*, one of the most penetrating magazine articles on so-called melting-pot America she had ever read, Rachel Davis Du-Bois embarked on a program of ethnic and racial self-education. She had known few if any Jews in her southern New Jersey experience; Negroes had been equally as rare; most of the immigrants were a complete mystery.

Davis DuBois knew something of the work of the NAACP through Jane Addams, with whom she had attended the Women's International League (WIL) conference at the Hague in 1922. She learned much more about Du Bois at the 1924 summer conference of the League for Industrial Democracy, where she met and quickly endeared herself to Pickens and A. Philip Randolph. She had perfected by that time her Woodbury Plan, the multicultural high school curriculum incorporating song, dance, dress, and foods together with the history and culture of America's myriad ethnic populations. Pickens, who spoke to one of her classes, urged her to attend the NAACP annual convention in Denver on her way to visit a college friend in Los Angeles the following summer, a perfect opportunity to meet the formidable editor of *The Crisis*. Rachel Davis DuBois, tall, handsomely built, with wide, lively brown eyes, was thirty-three when she finally met Du Bois in 1925. He speculated straightaway that he and she might be related by marriage, which was remotely likely. She was taken in immediately by his "subtle use of humor," impressed by his gallantry, and possibly sensed then that theirs was to be an enduring companionship. Du Bois sent her off with an introduction to one of his Los Angeles associates who could continue Davis DuBois's education in multiculturalism. She reintroduced herself later that year as the other Mrs. Du Bois and asked his help in putting together a proposal for a high school lesson on Egyptian life.

They had become friendly enough by the fall of 1928 for "W.E.B.," as she now called the editor, to introduce her playfully as Mrs. Du Bois at an interracial affair in Harlem. "Then he laughed at the look of surprise on their faces," she recorded. Davis DuBois came to know a side of the editor that not many others ever did. "He could be very, very informal, very, very loving, you know," she recalled long after his death. Du Bois saw a good deal more of her after she took early retirement from Woodbury High School in 1930 in order to devote herself completely to interracial and intercultural educational experiments. Rachel Davis DuBois's work with Quaker and other progressive organizations in New York and Washington, her peripatetic organizing of Woodbury Plan experiments in Manhattan, Englewood, New Jersey, and Boston, and her Columbia University course work for the master's in education brought her to the city frequently. The editor came to value her opinions as much as her friendship, successfully pushing her candidacy for the editorial board of *The Crisis* in the spring of 1931 and then relying on her vote to help counter the policies of White. Whenever the gap in their meetings went on overly long, he informed her of his availability or wrote her slightly annoyed letters. "My dear Rachel: I am home again. Drop in and see me," she read in late March 1931, after he returned from a lecture circuit. On that occasion, there was news that she planned to be in New York "about Wednesday of this week for the remainder of the week." He betrayed anxiety by the middle of July: "I had been hoping to hear from you for some time, but no word has come. I presume that you are having such a lovely rest or that you are so busy that you cannot write, but at any rate, try it, but better still drop up to New York." The wait for Davis DuBois was never idle time, however. Her friend Nora Waring was sometimes available when circumstances or inclination kept Davis DuBois away from W.E.B. Often enough, however, it was the editor's obligations that played havoc with his recreation. He dashed off a note to Waring: "This week is impossible. I am tied up." But he had hopes for the following week; he would write her.

As the list of parallel relationships is scrolled, Virginia Margaret Alexander appeared for the first time in the spring of 1931. Du Bois requested that she be sent an invitation to a conference sponsored by the Liberal Club of Bryn Mawr on the economic status of Negroes, at which he and White were to speak in late April. She became the true successor to Jessie Fauset in his life, the woman who might become the second Mrs. Du Bois and for whom he felt a special passion and admiration that would be memorialized in the dedication of his great book *Black Reconstruction in America*. Virginia Alexander was then thirty-two and in her fourth year of practice as an obstetrician in North Philadelphia, a quadrant of the city mainly inhabited by Negro Americans of every economic condition. She came from a background of character-building adversity. Raised by her father's relatives since the age of four, when her mother died not long after bearing her fifth child, Virginia was the second girl and fourth sibling in a Philadelphia family that had once enjoyed relative comfort. Hilliard Alexander, uneducated but enterprising, had moved from Virginia to open a profitable livery stable patronised by some of the city's wealthiest white families until the turn-of-the-century deterioration in race relations, captured *in media res* by Du Bois's *Philadelphia Negro*, caused the business to fail. Genteel poverty motivated Virginia and her brother Raymond Pace Alexander, older by a year and ruggedly handsome, to fulfill the motto of the Talented Tenth, which was to try twice as hard to become twice as good as the whites with whom they competed. Their superior high school records earned both admission to the University of Pennsylvania, where Raymond worked his way as a Pullman porter to graduation with honors followed by a law degree from Harvard in 1923. He had waded into the thick of the controversy over the exclusion of Negroes from the undergraduate dormitories, rebuking President Lowell in an *Opportunity* piece for March 1923. Virginia blazed through Pennsylvania on scholarship, graduating with a bachelor of science degree in three years.

Hers was a world of exceptions. At Penn, Virginia introduced Raymond to Sadie Tanner Mossell, her best friend and member of what Locke called the "O.P.'s," Philadelphia's oldest colored families of accomplishment. Benjamin Tucker Tanner, Mossell's grandfather, had been the premier bishop of the African Methodist Episcopal Church; Henry Ossawa Tanner, the dean of Aframerican painters, was her uncle. Four years after marrying Raymond Pace Alexander, Sadie Mossell became the first woman of color to earn a University of Pennsylvania law degree, having already earned a Ph.D. in economics from Penn, the first such degree earned by a colored American woman and only the second doctorate ever earned by a black woman in the United States. Meanwhile, Virginia had emerged from her ordeal at the Woman's Medical College of Pennsylvania, one of two Negroes in her class. She had faltered in her first year because of a failed love affair, but the Woman's Medical College had allowed her to repeat the courses. Alexander performed with distinction from then on despite the racism of some of her classmates and professors. *The Crisis* would profile Alexander's career in a caressing feature entitled, "Can a Colored Woman be a Physician?" An answer in the affirmative was clearly the exception rather than the rule, as the story revealed that her application for an internship at Philadelphia General Hospital had been rejected by the director of health, who told Alexander that he would never consent to her appointment even if she were "first in a thousand applicants." Of the 3,900 Negroes practicing medicine in the United States when Alexander had entered medical school, only sixty-five were females. A woman, a black woman, a black professional woman in the sciences, Dr. Virginia Alexander was regarded as a serious threat to the social order of male dominion white and black, as well as a reproach to women who resented the gendered significance of her ambition. Little wonder that the director of a Quaker settlement house in Philadelphia, after listening to her experiences a few years after Alexander had returned from Missouri, where she had won reluctant internship and residency at Kansas City General Hospital Number 2 (the "colored hospital"), would lose her peace of mind. "That any creature—let alone so gifted—should suffer so made me deeply angry," was her understandable comment.

Alexander was impatient with ignorance and injustice and devoted to finding the best means for combating both. The knot of Negro ignorance and conservatism tied by poverty and blessed by preachers caused the four-bed birth-control clinic she ran in conjunction with her practice to be widely regarded with suspicion and revilement, so that it was the rare husband who sent his wife to avail herself of the Aspiranto Health Home's procedures. A veteran exponent himself of birth control who had been present at the recent housewarming for Margaret Sanger's Harlem clinic, Du Bois took an almost proprietary pride in Alexander's mission. In his *Crisis* profile of her, Du Bois had written lovingly that Alexander was "the joke of her friends" when it came to business sense, "forgetting to collect her fees, handing them back to the poor, furnishing medicine for nothing." She was a passionate joiner in any philosophy or group effort whose goal was unity and betterment: international peace; developing an international language; Christian socialism; enlarging women's role in society; the Society of Friends (at the beginning of 1931, she became the only colored Quaker in Philadelphia). No one who knew her even casually failed to sense a quality of warmth, a thoughtful selflessness that made her seem at once vulnerable and indomitable. Unlike Du Bois, Alexander was able to forgive the unremitting meanness of white people because of her deep belief in the ultimate irrelevancy of race.

As Du Bois knew she would, Alexander accepted the invitation to the April 1931 Liberal Club conference on the economic status of the Negro. Paul Laurence Dunbar's sharp-eyed widow, who, a decade earlier, had been involved with a very married Emmett Scott, Howard University's self-important treasurer, observed in her garrulously spicy diary, "Virginia Alexander parked next to Du Bois and the two were inseparable and horribly obvious all day." Alexander's special relationship to Du Bois was a secret also known to many of the civil rights influentials (as had been Fauset's and would be Prophet's) that does not appear ever to have become a subject of malicious or even censorious gossip. In an era when well-bred colored people were inclined to be extremely protective of their reputations, the inviolability of Du Bois's image as dutiful husband and custodian of proper middle-class values must have been regarded as a priority of race and class. His adulterous private life was publicly concealed and privately tolerated by the Talented Tenth as a special case of a transgression more commonplace among distinguished men than acknowledged by the fiction of faithfulness. Recalling visits from Du Bois when she and her husband, Horace, occupied the president's home on the campus of Georgia's Fort Valley State College, Julia Bond could only primly shrug and say, "Everybody accepted it. [Du Bois] had always been like that. It was just sort of his personality, and people knew that he liked young women, and" — she smiled — "he always liked to be in their company." Nina's growing invisibility combined with the general knowledge that she accepted Alexander as a friend and family pediatrician may have excused for many what proved to be one of Du Bois's deepest and most enduring liaisons.

WITH HIS WIFE and daughter in Paris, Du Bois was spared some of the distractions that might also have hobbled his efforts to restore the health of *The Crisis*. The magazine's problems were fearsome, with myriad difficulties cropping up almost daily at the office. Much overdue was the registration with the U.S. Department of Commerce of the *Crisis* trademark at the beginning of

1929. More pressing, however, was the need to secure a broader base for paid advertising. Paul Kennaday, one of the association's founding board members, offered to sound out the editors of *Survey Graphic* and *Asia Magazine* about ways to attract mainstream advertisements. Kellogg of the *Survey* was frankly pessimistic, but Kennaday reported that *Asia*'s editor thought it possible that some of the large national advertisers might be responsive, but certainly not until the magazine divided the job of editor from that of advertising manager and hired a person "of equal capacity to the editor." Du Bois was willing to follow the advice, but had no money to make it a reality.

Suddenly, humiliatingly, there was not even money enough to survive the month of May. Du Bois was appalled to learn that he would have to suspend publication of *The Crisis* unless the board allowed him to petition the Garland Fund for an emergency loan of three thousand dollars. He insisted that the "suddenness of this necessity was as much a surprise to me as to the Board." The cause, he stated, was "due immediately to faulty business management." After Dill's enforced departure, the office of business manager had been filled first on an ad hoc basis and then, permanently, by a young man whose résumé turned out to be superior to his well-intentioned abilities. His character, earnestness, devotion, and hard work did him credit, the editor told the young man, but life was "crassly cruel, and . . . for the larger end we must carry on" without his services. Pierce M. Thompson had somehow allowed two months' of printer's debts to pile up, and the collection of money owed for ads had slipped badly. The next few weeks were grueling for Du Bois as he wore the hat of editor, business manager, and advertising manager while writing his usual, substantial amount of copy for the magazine. Forced to miss a Sunday affair for Johnson, he dashed a breathless note to the secretary, "We have been having a Hell of a time with the *Crisis* in the last week or so." He hadn't been able to "think about much else." He managed to scrape by on the Garland Fund reprieve, but the price exacted by the board — reasonable enough in principle — put the control of his magazine, at least from his point of view, on the slippery slope to decision-making by vote. Henceforth, there would be a four-person *Crisis* finance committee consisting of the increasingly self-important White, Joel Spingarn, Lillian Alexander, another good friend and prominent Harlemite, and Du Bois family physician and new board member, Louis Wright.

Du Bois would secure Thompson's reluctant resignation at the end of May 1929, after persuading retired federal employee and Washington realtor Thomas Junius Calloway to take the position of business manager. "T. J." Calloway was an old Fisk classmate with whom Du Bois had waitered at a resort hotel on Lake Minnetonka forty-one years earlier. Fully apprised of the steady decline in subscriptions, of mounting complaints by long-term subscribers about delayed and missed issues, and of arrears in advertising fees uncollected for many months, Calloway would devise an ambitious, aggressive battle plan. He recommended subscription drives spearheaded by historically black private and state-supported colleges and universities, and he promptly set off on visits to businesses and professional organizations across much of the country. The results were encouraging. By mid-October, Calloway could report to the new *Crisis* finance committee of having "met encouragement at all points." The Delaware State Teachers Association committed to a *Crisis* subscription campaign. Howard University agreed to a profitable renegotiation of its monthly ad. The Capitol News Company ordered three hundred copies for November. The Boston *Chronicle* and the Murphys of the Baltimore *Afro-American* were discussing distribution details. The Chicago branch of the YWCA and that city's Binga Bank (the largest Negro bank) were going to purchase advertising.

The editor's report to the finance committee for October 1929 would carry the relatively upbeat news of forthcoming ads from Tuskegee Institute and the National Negro Business League, and even of a small budget surplus. Just as these strenuous efforts were beginning to stabilize the magazine's decline, Thomas Calloway had fallen seriously ill and would expire of colon cancer within the year. His place was taken by Irene Malvan, a youngish woman whose devoted service would end two years later in bitterness. The chilling effect upon subscriptions of an ominous downturn in the economy during the summer of 1929, coupled with the death of his enterprising friend, made Du Bois almost desperate to find someone with broad professional experience in managing and marketing magazines. October 29, "Black Tuesday," must have put the editor in a deeply apprehensive frame of mind, despite the appearance of the market's full recovery after the beginning of the year. The editor began to explore hiring a young Kansas City newspaperman to whom Marvel Jackson, still assembling "The Browsing Reader" column, had once been engaged in Minnesota. Although Jackson had transferred her affections to Eric Walrond soon after she came to New York, and the tall, brown former fiancé with a low voice and thoughtful eyes had recently married a woman from St. Louis, Du Bois had remained impressed by the Roy Ottoway Wilkins described by Jackson.

Wilkins's family traced back to the Mississippi Delta, to a dusty dip in the road south of the town of Holly Springs, birthplace of Ida Wells-Barnett. Senatobia was a nether place in which Roy Wilkins would have spent his formative years deferring to mean white farmers and learning to duck ambition had not his father Willie's combustible temper necessitated a dawn escape aboard the Illinois Central Railroad direct to St. Louis with a wife of only a few months. St. Louis, where Roy was born the following year, on August 30, 1901, was much better for his life chances, but unlucky for his parents. "Sweetie" Mayfield Wilkins died of consumption when her firstborn was five years old. Roy, his younger brother Earl, and sister, Armeda, were taken to live in St. Paul by "Auntie

Elizabeth," their mother's sister. Willie Wilkins, angry and jobless, disappeared, not to come back into his children's life until Roy was nine, and then only for a frightening few days until Aunt Elizabeth and Uncle Sam retained a lawyer to draw up adoption papers for the trio. Samuel Williams, who became the children's surrogate father, was all that Willie Wilkins was not, an upstanding, civic-minded provider who owned his house on Galtier Street free and clear and was chief steward to no less a worthy than the president of the Great Northern Pacific Railroad. He was a charter member of the St. Paul branch of the NAACP and a *Crisis* subscriber who swelled with pride over Du Bois's castigations of Woodrow Wilson.

"My family and the NAACP were entwined practically from its creation," Wilkins liked to say, and Du Bois had reinforced that bond in an indelibly special way in the teenager's junior year in high school. Delighted to learn of his election to the editorship of the school's literary magazine, Wilkins savored the victory on a "wonderful day" in 1918 amid the congratulations of faculty and students. A "great surprise" awaited him when *The Crisis* arrived a month later. A short item in the magazine noted: "Roy Wilkins has been elected president of the Mechanical Arts High School Literary Society of St. Paul, Minnesota, over two white candidates." It was goodbye to the science curriculum. "After that paragraph," Wilkins decided, "it no longer occurred to me to be an engineer." In his first year at the University of Minnesota, Wilkins, like countless black men and women before and after, had experienced the psychic volcano of lynching when five thousand white citizens of nearby Duluth, driven temporarily insane by a charge of rape, hanged three innocent Negro members of a visiting carnival show from light poles. The anger and humiliation of that atrocity still festered just below his self-control when Wilkins attended the NAACP's Midwestern Race Relations Conference in summer 1923. He got to see Du Bois in action, along with Bagnall, Pickens, and White, in the Kansas City Convention Hall. But it was Johnson who swept him off his feet along with ten thousand others in the hall with a defiant platform rebuke after listening to the governor's emissary caution Negroes against pushing too hard for their rights. Pounding the dais, Johnson had shouted in Kansas City, "We are here to serve notice that we are in a fight to death for the rights guaranteed us as American citizens by the Constitution." Wilkins wrote in his autobiography, *Standing Fast*, that he knew he "had seen a great leader—and found my own cause." Desperate for an experienced business manager, however, it would be Du Bois who played a crucial role in bringing Wilkins to the cause.

Managing editor of the Kansas City *Call* since 1928, one of the best of the 200-odd Negro weeklies, the twenty-eight-year-old University of Minnesota journalism graduate had played an energizing role in the Kansas City NAACP branch. In a brief meeting during Wilkins's first visit to New York in the spring

of 1929, Du Bois had found his expectation of exceptional competency confirmed. He liked the young man and wanted to bring him to New York, he told
Jackson, who would regret many years later that she hadn't shared her misgivings
with Du Bois about what she saw as Wilkins's conservative, opportunist bent.
Suspecting nothing of Jackson's forebodings, Du Bois campaigned for a new
business manager with even less regard than usual for the competing priorities
within the association. Like *The Crisis*, the NAACP was fighting merely to keep
its revenues constant. The worst of the Depression was only just beginning, but
chairperson Ovington and especially White, as acting secretary during Johnson's
leave of absence, had begun to enforce a policy of economic triage in which
the role of *The Crisis* along with the importance of the association's field officers,
Bagnall and Pickens, were being reevaluated. Without question, the organization's quest for operating revenues would have failed catastrophically over the
next four or five years but for the "special connection"—the sustained generosity
of Jewish philanthropy. The three-year, thousand-dollar matching gift of Julius
Rosenwald's youngest son, William, leveraged an equal sum from Herbert Lehman, the future New York governor, Harold Guinzberg, the publisher of Viking
Press, Samuel Fels, the department store merchant, and Felix and Frieda Schiff
Warburg. Edsel Ford was the outstanding gentile contributor in the three-year
campaign that would yield $26,250, nearly half the association's contributions
by 1933. Given the shortfall confronting the organization, then, it was understandable that Ovington refused Du Bois's request at the beginning of 1930 for
help in making a competitive salary offer to Wilkins. She sought to assuage the
editor, however, by acknowledging a willingness to help subsidize the magazine
in principle, but not simply in response to every S.O.S., and without any previous basis for discussion and projection.

In the rigorously top-down leadership style rapidly emerging under White,
bureaucracy repeatedly trumped inspiration at 70 Fifth Avenue. The courtly
office culture of delegated authority existing under Johnson gave way to micromanagement so intrusive that Richetta Randolph, Johnson's longtime secretary
and now White's, complained that the acting secretary insisted on opening and
reading every piece of correspondence himself. The minutes of the board, once
reflective of clubby affairs in which ample time was taken to ventilate a variety
of opinions, acquired a streamlined brevity. Prim, dutiful Ovington complained
quietly to Arthur Spingarn that she was being sidelined by the new regime. "But
I am not much use except as a cheerer on," she sighed. The acting secretary
not only seemed to confound the axiom barring simultaneous appearance in
two places, he seemed literally everywhere at once in New York or Washington,
buttonholing, lobbying, nightclubbing, and name-dropping. Whatever Du Bois
actually thought of this frenetic activity, he was sufficiently concerned to write
Johnson about the acting secretary's "perfectly terrific rate" that showed no sign

of letup. The editor was going to try, however, "to get him to go a bit slower, if possible." Jackman, whose letters to Cullen in Paris read like a live transcription from the period, observed a captive audience at swank 409 Edgecombe Avenue listening to Walter White "still talking about Walter, and how he can talk about himself, and Carl and Heywood and Res and Clarence and Bernard and all the other big lights."

However much diplomacy might have lubricated organizational friction, the harried editor felt he had no time to apply it. A major office blowup had narrowly been averted a few weeks earlier when Du Bois supported Pickens and Bagnall's protest of the board's award of a much greater salary increase to White than to them, a dispute that would recur over the next two years. Du Bois's testiness was an early reaction to the shift in the balance of power within the NAACP, of which White's $1,200 salary increment was another clear sign. The formal announcement in June 1930 that the American Fund for Public Service had voted one hundred thousand of Charles Garland's inheritance dollars to establish a permanently staffed legal defense department within the NAACP greatly enhanced White's authority. The deaths in late 1929 of Storey, the venerable Boston Brahmin, and Louis Marshall, one of the nation's leading jurists and a founder of the American Jewish Committee, suddenly deprived the association of the pro bono services of its two most valuable constitutional lawyers. Du Bois paid warm tribute to Marshall as an indispensable partner in the common effort to end racism, underscoring that, in this struggle. "American Jews have been especially prominent." The president of Temple Emanu-el had not only joined Storey in successfully arguing *Nixon v. Herndon* before the Supreme Court in 1927, the major voting-rights case thus far won by the NAACP, but Marshall had endeared himself to the membership by the ardent address he delivered in Harlem's St. Mark's M. E. Church a few months before dying. Membership of the board of directors of the association was among his most cherished honors, said Marshall. "I belong to an ancient race which has had an even longer experience of oppression than you have. We came out of human bondage nearly thirty centuries ago, and we have had trouble ever since," he reminded the amused audience. Now that Marshall and Storey had departed, White saw the substantial budget awarded by the Garland Fund as providing the wherewithal to hire talent to plot a determined litigation strategy against the southern states.

Meanwhile, Du Bois's enthusiasm for Wilkins had spread by early spring of 1930 to Spingarn and Lillian Alexander of the *Crisis* finance committee, Spingarn urging that every effort be made to bring Wilkins to New York and to "share whole-heartedly the responsibility of running *The Crisis* with [Du Bois]." Encouraging long-distance telephone discussions and an exchange of letters ensued in which the journalist's keen assessment of the magazine's deficits and potentialities captivated Ovington along with most of the rest of the board. Even a sizable increase over what *The Call* paid him, however, would have left the Wilkinses barely able to survive New York City living costs. Still, as Du Bois assumed the young professional fully appreciated, to be associated with the high purpose of *The Crisis* could bring compensations well beyond monetary. His best offer was a respectable starting salary of $2,500 and a pledge to let Wilkins do anything that was "reasonable and not antagonistic to our main object . . . to make the magazine popular." Du Bois emphasized "knowledge and courage to branch out . . . consecration and high ideal" over sizable income. His business manager would be able to draw upon his, Du Bois's, "long experience over a considerable part of the world," upon his "wide acquaintanceship with influential persons of both and all races." Wilkins was clearly tempted, even though he thought that his true abilities lay with editing rather than in the business department. The confidential advice given by White strongly urged acceptance. But Wilkins finally informed Du Bois in early July 1930 that salary and family considerations, combined with the editorial freedom enjoyed at *The Call*, constrained him to remain in Kansas for the time being.

In the tone of Wilkins's letter there was just the merest presentiment of Du Bois's fading suzerainty over the younger Talented Tenth generation. There were hard times just ahead for black people, and Wilkins was typical of many young professionals who intended to combine racial idealism with hard business sense. Fresh out of UCLA in May 1927 and on his way to graduate work in political science at Harvard, Ralph Bunche had thought it *de rigueur* to present himself to Du Bois and inquire how he might be "of service to [his] race this coming summer, either in the East or in the South." Three years later, many ambitious men and women wanting to "serve the race" still considered recognition in *The Crisis* as the highest seal of approval. The future governor general of Nigeria, Nnamdi Azikiwe, then a student at Lincoln University in Pennsylvania, sent Du Bois an article about British suppression, "Murdering Women in Nigeria," his first publication. In that same year, St. Clair Drake, about to graduate from Hampton, offered Du Bois an insightful reflection on the checkered academic performance of many of his peers, also his first publication. For Roy Wilkins, the imprimatur of Du Bois was more or less an optional consideration. The editor was told by Wilkins that, with luck, he might find a young man "already established, who is not now commanding a good income," willing to extend himself to help "keep the old ship afloat." "To be brief, Doctor," the letter of refusal stated flatly, "the problem is simply to decide which activity . . . offers the best chance for larger growth and larger remuneration."

The stark reality was that the magazine was victim of the global downturn in magazine circulation—a victim considerably weaker than *The New Republic* or *The Nation*, certainly, due both to its editor's inability to build an endowment

during the Roaring Twenties and to the economic fragility of most of its subscribers. It seems doubtful that Wilkins as *Crisis* business manager would have
been much more successful in implementing his own meticulous marketing
recommendations than were Du Bois and Malvan. Many years later, Wilkins
described his final letter as "a bit impertinent" and claimed that his wife had
played a decisive part in his decision. Tiny, pert Minnie Badeau, who would
earn a reputation as fierce protector of her husband's interests, seems to have
found it easy to dislike Du Bois from the start. Had Roy forgotten that the editor
was "a notoriously prickly fellow," she scolded? She told him the story, repeated
somewhere by someone every year of Du Bois's long life, of his regally snubbing
guests invited to meet him by some awed hostess in heartland America. The
promise of partnership with such a self-important personality might mean very
little, Minnie Wilkins warned. Deciding to follow his wife's advice, Wilkins
imputed a state of mind to Du Bois that revealed much more about his own,
writing in his autobiography that in Du Bois's "weaker moments he managed
to give the impression that racial discrimination had been invented solely to
make *his* life miserable."

As the Great Depression bit deep into the summer of 1930, the editor and
Malvan struggled to retain the magazine's advertising base, to work out payment
schedules for delinquent advertisers, and, with striking successes such as Hampton and Tuskegee, even to increase the educational publicity. In March, Du
Bois had persuaded the Rosenwald Fund to make a life-saving annual grant of
$2,500 for three years to the NAACP, with the understanding that half that
amount would be credited to *The Crisis*. Once again, Mrs. Jacob Schiff provided
a crucial gift of five hundred dollars toward the magazine's reserve fund. To
board member George Crawford, who remained one of Du Bois's most loyal
yet critical allies, the Wilkins negotiations and shrinking support for the magazine were evidence of disturbing shortsightedness. Asking that his letter be read
in his absence at the July board meeting, the New Haven attorney warned that
the new "efficient and well managed executive routine" had led his colleagues
"to underestimate the extent to which the backing and prestige of the Association [were] also due to *The Crisis* and to the work of the field secretaries."

Yet never before had his authority and his explanations been subjected to
such ungenerous scrutiny, Du Bois felt; even less tolerable was the growing
unresponsiveness to his concerns in board meetings. Finally, in what appeared
to be a throwing of the dice against his magazine's future, he challenged the
board to consider terminating, suspending, or replacing *The Crisis* if it were
unwilling to vote the resources to enable the magazine to recover lost ground.
After intense deliberations, his colleagues had voted in the July meeting against
replacing *The Crisis* with a less-expensive monthly bulletin. As once before
during the early 1920s, however, the board had also decided to subject Du Bois's

monthly to management by an editorial board in order to effect, in Joel Spingarn's words, much greater correlation with "the executive organization of the
Association," this one to consist of the editor, the executive secretary, assistant
secretary, and a fourth person "to be designated by the board of directors."
Henceforth, shortfalls in the editor's salary from *The Crisis* were to be paid "from
the general funds of the Association." Although Du Bois succeeded in having
Spingarn's resolution modified when the board reconvened after the summer
recess so as to add the NAACP's well-disposed director of publicity, Herbert
Seligmann, to his editorial board, he had few illusions about the dismal forces
arrayed against the magazine — the national economy, the declining readership,
and, above all, as it seemed to him, Walter White.

Ovington had idolized Du Bois during the founding years of the association,
consistently explaining him to others and occasionally succeeding in moderating
some divisive course of action down which he was dogmatically charging. She
still admired him, but when she finished her biographical history of the NAACP
after World War II, *The Walls Came Tumbling Down*, it would be apparent
that she had long ago come to see Du Bois as a great man whose flaws counted
heavily against him. After twenty-five years of friendship, she decided a few days
before the Christmas holidays that, as his friend and chairman of the board, she
owed the editor some brutally frank advice in strictest confidence. Recalling the
old times when they had had "many a bout" around the role of *The Crisis* (most
of them won by Du Bois), Ovington acknowledged that the magazine had once
"amounted to more than the organization." But with the passage of time (and
she might have added, due also to the militancy of the magazine), the association had become "increasingly important, and *The Crisis* less important." What
Du Bois and his monthly were doing was "useful, interesting work," she believed, but work no longer "as essential to Negro progress and to radical Negro
thought as it once was." No matter who succeeded Johnson (and both knew
that it was likely to be the gregarious little blond man with the large pipe), the
next secretary would gradually reduce the importance and independence enjoyed by Du Bois in past years. Unless some unforeseen largesse befell the
magazine, "such capital as a white weekly would have," she was convinced that
he would lose control of *The Crisis*. "It cannot belong to you as it has in the
past," she warned, perceptively noting, "you won't enjoy it in the way you have."
Why not anticipate the inevitable, Ovington counseled? He might consider
taking a somewhat reduced salary as a part-time staff person, writing occasional
pieces for *The Crisis*, and lecturing to the branches.

On Christmas Eve, 1930, the editor penned an exasperated, terse reply.
Vibrating with indignation, he informed Ovington that not "for a moment"
would he consider her proposition, nor would he "work with the NAACP under

any other conditions." Slamming the door hard against all such demotions, Du Bois decreed, "Either *The Crisis* is necessary to the work of the NAACP or it is not." If not, then he should be allowed to make it an independent publication. A less-ruffled Du Bois would have appreciated that Ovington's motives were genuine and that her understanding of his predicament was only too accurate. But his remarkable self-control had tended to falter during the last half of that year. Ovington's rocket, streaming into his office while the Harlem sky was figuratively still glowing from a shimmering interracial success for which White got the lion's share of the credit, was about as welcome as an electric shock. First, there had been a downtown benefit for the NAACP at the Forrest Theatre that was unprecedented. "Downtown—think of it—downtown," Jackman crowed. He hadn't actually been there, he wrote Cullen—"couldn't afford it"— but he had mixed with some of the high-society folk afterward at the Dark Tower. Second, James Weldon Johnson's formal resignation as executive secretary, coming one week later on December 17, 1930, Du Bois regarded as the penultimate act after which the fate of the association and of the magazine now hung by a thread. The sixty-year-old poet–diplomat–civil libertarian had come back from the sojourn in Japan so well recharged that *Black Manhattan*, a history of Negro cultural life in New York that became an instant classic, was finished before his Rosenwald Fellowship expired. "I gave my best in what I knew to be a great cause," Johnson would say at the close of the emotional evening in celebration of his retirement. On that May evening in 1931, Du Bois would deliver a moving tribute at a farewell banquet where more than three hundred of the nation's distinguished men and women of letters, philanthropists, educators, public officials, and reformers gathered in Johnson's honor at the Pennsylvania Hotel. In a stab at affectionate humor, Du Bois noted that Johnson was one of the few people who could invade the office of *The Crisis* "at eleven o'clock in the morning and receive a welcoming smile." After fourteen years in its service, Johnson accepted the honorary title of vice-president of the NAACP as he prepared to join Charles Johnson at Fisk as the Adam K. Spence Professor of Creative Literature.

DU BOIS WOULD have chafed under Walter Francis White's leadership in the best of circumstances. The mismatch of age and temperament boded poorly from the start. The editor was senior to the secretary by a quarter century and, in his own mind, possessed of an incommensurably superior intellect. Although he had not been one of White's professors at Atlanta University, as was often reported, Du Bois knew White's prominent Atlanta family well and seems never to have entirely accepted the reality that the bright, competitive teenager, "Fuzzy," had grown into a formidable administrator, publicist, speaker, writer, organizer, and popular fixture in New York's literary and social circles. The very qualities that had favored White's advancement and would make his twenty-five-year stewardship of the NAACP renowned for its meld of bureaucracy and charisma, Du Bois disparaged in the beginning as flaws in the secretary's education and, finally, as defects of character. But if White was a virtuoso of the instant study and a class-A schmoozer, he was also incredibly hardworking and as uncompromising in his civil liberties convictions as Du Bois. White was "a light weight," according to one board member of many years' service, but Robert Weaver gave him most of the credit for transforming the NAACP into a powerful lobby. If Du Bois was a visionary with a contempt for minutiae, White was a CEO with a policy. If the devil is in the details, White was the devil himself. Reduced to essentials, White's policy for the NAACP was to be top-down, legalistic, and legislative — in other words, litigation and lobbying. The draft of the plan for an ambitious assault on racial segregation through the courts had been presented to the board by the new legal department underwritten by the Garland Fund. The long, costly quest for congressional votes to enact a federal law against lynching would commence in late 1933.

The combustible Du Bois–White mixture of age and ego probably could have been contained had it not been for the implosion of the national economy. As the prices of grain and cotton had dropped steadily due to domestic overproduction piling up against rising European tariffs, the American farm economy staggered under a mountain of indebtedness that was replicated in large and small towns across the country where "a dollar down and a dollar forever" had become a way of life. Industrial production slowed and unemployment climbed even as the bull market lifted Wall Street into its fatal apogee. For hundreds of thousands of black people trapped in the cycle of the last hired and first fired, it was a case of black misery finding white company when the market economy shuddered on its foundations in the winter of 1929. *The Defender* had sounded a warning months before the crash, noting that "hardly a day has ended that there has not been a report of another firm discharging its employees, many of whom have been faithful workers at these places for years." What seemed to be an overnight cataclysm to most other Americans was already a chronic state of being for Negro Americans by the end of 1928. But the chronic would become rapidly acute. The Urban League's broad 1931 survey of Aframerican economic conditions in more than a hundred cities would find unemployment rates of 31 percent in Baltimore, where Negroes were 17 percent of the total population, and 16 percent in Chicago, where they were only 4 percent of the city's population. In Harlem, unemployment ranged between 40 and 50 percent; in Philadelphia, it reached 56 percent; in Detroit, 40. "No Jobs for niggers until every white man has a job" was a Deep South slogan that nonetheless reflected the national mind. "Negro jobs" — serving in homes and hotels, cleaning streets, and collecting garbage—became white people's work. The Urban League's T. Arnold Hill declared with dismal accuracy that "at no time in the history of the Negro since slavery has his economic and social outlook seemed so discouraging."

Because Negroes suffered the ravages of the Great Depression earlier, deeper, and longer than most white Americans, the consequences were devastating for the NAACP. The organization's membership plunged to 20,000 by the end of 1930. Its ambitious legal strategy was soon in shreds. The drop in the value of the Garland Fund stock by two thirds meant that the 218-page Margold report drafted that year could now be implemented by the NAACP's legal division only slowly over time, if at all, and in piecemeal fashion. As the scramble for diminishing funds became increasingly fierce throughout 1931 and 1932, the result was that virtually any difference of opinion between Du Bois and his sympathizers and those loyal to White tended to be inflated into a dispute over high policy or character or both. Without wishing to trivialize what were, in fact, several major controversies of policy and values, it seems certain that the real source of friction between them was the inability of the association's budget to keep pace with the egos of its two principals. Money frustrations would exacerbate intrinsic philosophical disagreements between the editor and the secretary to the extreme degree that, finally, one or the other had to exit the NAACP.

White proceeded cautiously at first in attempting to trim the costs of *The Crisis*, seeking advice from founding board member Charles Russell about ways to improve the magazine's appeal. Had White shared Russell's opinion, Du Bois would have dismissed it as racially patronizing, for Russell gave precisely the sort of counsel that the editor had come to expect from aging, white parlor socialists. It was foolish to continue the magazine's diet of serious political and social commentary. Negroes needed humor, color, gossip to help them through hard times, Russell thought, and he warned that Du Bois's blunt criticisms of American democracy were "exactly what your enemies most wish you to say." Coming at roughly the same time as Ovington's friendly warning at the end of 1930, White's sharing of concerns with Russell and others greatly distressed the editor. Seeking to put an end to the secretary's meddling by erecting a firewall between the front office and the editorial bureau, Du Bois sent marching orders to Abram Harris, now on the faculty of Howard University. Harris was needed as a final member of the newly created *Crisis* editorial board in order to serve as a ballast against White. Seligmann, the director of publicity, was "quite all right, but after all White is his superior officer, and White is impossible." Unless some "radical blood" was injected into the NAACP, Du Bois warned Harris darkly, "we are done for." Harris was willing to serve but had not the train fare to pay for frequent committee meetings, but Du Bois had already decided to place Davis DuBois in the position instead, as her Teachers College studies brought her to New York weekly.

As grim as conditions were for Negro Americans, the magazine could report considerable improvement in the higher education policies of the federal government and the foundations. The Interior Department's massive *Survey of Negro Colleges and Universities* was far more objective than the 1917 document largely compiled by Du Bois's nemesis, Thomas Jesse Jones. The 1917 report had tended to discount the value of liberal arts in favor of more and better industrial and vocational training at the college level for Negroes, whereas Du Bois was pleased to quote the new study's injunction: "The immediate need is for more education, better education, and higher education." And now, as the issue for July 1930 disclosed, the GEB had decided, however belatedly, to assume the major costs of more and better higher education. From 1902 to 1919, the GEB's sole allocation for endowment at a historically black institution was a $25,000 grant to Hampton. The officers of the GEB had "sneered at Latin and Greek," *The Crisis* reminded influential whites who seemed ever prone to historical amnesia. They accused educated Negroes of being " 'ashamed of their race,' and proposed to fill the South with nonunion black artisans warranted never to vote nor strike and always to be happy." But as Negroes moved from farm to town in the South and then pell mell to the urban North, bringing their numbers above the Mason-Dixon Line to more than 2 million by 1930, the GEB had recognized the academic aspirations of the New Negro, nearly 21,000 of whom were enrolled in college—more than a tenfold increase over 1919. Of the $20,986,576.62 disbursed to the historically black colleges and universities by the GEB between 1915 and 1930, three fourths had been remitted only within the last three years. That this philanthropic *volte-face* had made possible the new Atlanta University graduate center, headed by John Hope, afforded Du Bois a special reason for rejoicing.

Whatever Russell and other board members may have thought about too much gravitas, Du Bois was incapable by temperament and conviction of altering the magazine's serious emphasis. Grim times demanded solutions, not comic relief. A "record of the darker races," *The Crisis* continued to monitor, expose, pass judgment, and exhort as the effects of the Depression worsened month after month, falling upon Negroes with redoubled intensity. Although conceding for the sake of argument that the magazine's content would benefit from experimentation, the editor was far more prone to think that what was actually needed was more of the same—only much better. The remarkable document entitled "Memorandum on the Present and Future Editorial Program of *The Crisis*," drafted at some point in mid to late 1931, presented Du Bois's best agenda to the board of directors. He made it clear that he would "carry on

The Crisis as it has been carried on before," but he proposed to give greater emphasis to new writers by establishing a fixed pay scale for work published in the magazine and the creation of a literary bureau to "advise and guide young writers." Color photographs and color reproductions of ancient, medieval, and modern masterpieces were necessary, however costly (and unaffordable, White must have muttered). The importance of the pan-African movement was to be reinforced. Above all, *The Crisis* needed to "push a program of economic development for the American Negro." For Du Bois this entailed promoting consumer cooperatives and finding ways to increase black membership in mainstream labor unions. Finally, there would be much greater self-criticism, a need that many readers might have thought the magazine had long attempted to meet. "An oppressed race is afraid to acknowledge its defects," the document stated. Negroes were strong enough now to criticize their churches, the family, social ideals, "and a hundred other matters of their group life," he insisted. Who could deny, with its track record of commitment and accomplishment, that his magazine hadn't earned the "sympathy of nine-tenths of the educated and thinking Negroes of the country"? If sold at the reduced price of ten cents an issue, the editor was confident of being able to increase circulation, appeal to general advertisers, and, despite the Depression, "make American business realize that there are twelve million black buyers in the United States." *The Crisis* needed only money—"an investment made on business principles for a great philanthropic end"—to carry on.

Even as his "Present and Future Editorial Program" was under consideration by the board, Du Bois was writing about business and bank failures within Negro America that made it almost a certainty that the era of underwriting great philanthropic ends was over. The imposing Binga State Bank collapsed in December 1930, wiping out thousands of depositors and ruining Jesse Binga, its autocratic, self-made millionaire owner who had carved out ("gouged," said some) a real estate empire on Chicago's South Side. *The Crisis* said it was "a great calamity," but it blamed the big white banks in the Loop: "They could have saved the bank and saved it easily without loss or the prospect of loss." Somewhat more than a year later, Spingarn medalist Anthony Overton's Douglass National Bank became another falling Chicago domino that collapsed its owner's Victory Life Insurance Company, but left Overton still in control of his newspaper and cosmetics factory. "Onto the door of this last of the great Negro financial enterprises in Chicago was nailed a sign—closed," the magazine lamented. *The Crisis* had carried earlier business obituaries, several much closer to home. Villa Lewaro, Madame Walker's white palladian mansion on the Hudson, was sold at auction for fifty thousand dollars, "representing practically the amount of the indebtedness" laid on it by the recently deceased A'Lelia,

Du Bois disclosed. Nail & Parker, Jack Nail's Harlem real estate engine, was virtually bankrupt, although James Weldon Johnson still hoped John D. Rockefeller III could be persuaded to advance a loan to his brother-in-law.

One case of acute financial distress *The Crisis* did not mention was that of its founding editor. Du Bois had been compelled to defer repeatedly repayment of Yolande's portion of the French divorce to his former son-in-law. He was terribly sorry, he wrote Cullen in Paris, but the effects of the Depression were so severe at the magazine that he had not "drawn [his] salary for several months in order to make things go." Dill, whose affairs had gone to deep ruin, was given a similar alibi. The $125 balance due from the former business manager's salary had to stand "until we clear away some other things," the editor explained, tacking on a reminder that "the debts that we are paying now were accumulated while you had full charge of our business." Poor Dill was mortified that it had ever been necessary to ask for the balance. It would be unpardonable if a mere business matter were to undermine a twenty-five-year bond between the Du Bois family and the " 'one-man' Dill family," he wrote affectionately. The record is unclear as to whether the salary balance was ever paid, but by the end of 1930 Du Bois learned that Dill was living on money borrowed from prominent whites. "There is no reason in the world why he shouldn't go to work and support himself," the editor upbraided the broken man's sister. Privately, though, Du Bois knew that there was a reason for Dill's indigence. "His mind is giving way," he told Arthur Spingarn. A year later, he received a distressing note from the Civic Club secretary that Dill was sleeping in the lounge, which triggered the sternest of reproaches to an associate who was becoming a discredit to the race: "Your actions are distressing and humiliating to all of your friends beyond endurance."

While Dill decomposed, his mentor tried desperately to stave off his own financial disintegration with a plea to the Spingarns to save his Harlem property. Relying on information provided by Du Bois, Joel Spingarn asked his lawyer sibling if one of his firm's clients might not agree to assume the second mortgage on the St. Nicholas Avenue apartment building. The $11,000 first mortgage had nearly another year to run, but the second mortgage of $6,409.07 with Nail & Parker was months overdue. Although its assessed value was $18,000, Du Bois had given assurances that the property was worth "conservatively $25,000." Arthur Spingarn found no mortgage rabbits in his hat for Du Bois, however. Relations with Nail & Parker began to sour, as Du Bois, admitting that "pressures of *Crisis* work" had prevented him in years past from carefully examining statements and vouchers sent him, now set himself to the task of self-appointed accountant. Where were copies of his four fire insurance policies? he wanted to know from Nail & Parker. What precisely were the repairs undertaken by

Mr. Smith? There was great distress to find that Mr. Parker had failed to supervise first-floor plumbing work at 606. His increasing testiness was undoubtedly aggravated by symptoms that led to a tonsillectomy in the summer of 1931,
a period in which Du Bois was particularly anxious again about his daughter.
Yolande had come home from Paris divorced and overweight to begin teaching
art in the fall of 1930 at Frederick Douglass High School in Baltimore.

With Du Bois's encouragement, Nina had decided that she should continue
their daughter's chaperonage, which meant that the family became entangled
in yet another housing outlay—this one at 1301 Madison Avenue in Baltimore.
During the last weeks of the school year, Yolande had felt so fatigued that her
father asked the principal to release her from commencement activities in June
1931. One source of her weariness may have been a muscular Lincoln University
dropout who was a night student in the city's teachers' college housed in the
Douglass High School basement. Arnette Franklin Williams, a football player
who could take or leave poetry, was a bit of a rogue and the antithesis of
Countee Cullen. He and Yolande were married on Wednesday, September 2,
1931, in a simple ceremony in Baltimore with a philosophical Will and Nina
present. Prophet sent felicitations and the canny observation that the newlyweds
would "give Mrs. Du Bois also another interest." The "aristocrat [sic] of the
breakfast table" (the nervous groom's description of his father-in-law) had imposed only one prenuptial condition: Williams must finish his college education. Two weeks after the wedding, the groom returned to Lincoln. "Have him
write me about his studies and credits as soon as he gets settled," Du Bois
instructed Yolande. Williams's college tuition was added to the overloaded family budget.

From his estate overlooking the Housatonic, Joel Spingarn kept abreast of
the organization's internecine anxieties and, like Ovington, he foresaw the un-
palatable changes the Depression would inescapably impose on the editor. Spingarn and the departed Johnson were among the few men of accomplishment
capable of mollifying an enraged Du Bois. A day or so before Ovington posted
her unacceptable advice on December 20, the NAACP president had urged Du
Bois to see that he had no enemies on the board, but simply men and women
"anxious to find ways of meeting the financial crisis which faces the Association." Yet it is not unduly speculative to suppose that Spingarn must have been
deeply concerned by the tone and implications of Du Bois's memorandum on
the present and future *Crisis* editorial program. As the competition for diminishing organizational resources became a desperate scramble, the NAACP president understood that *The Crisis* as conceived by its creator was at risk of being
discounted as a luxury, and even an albatross. There was not a scintilla of
recognition of these dangers in "The Present and Future Editorial Program,"

however. If the NAACP had evolved into a national force for progress in the two decades since 1910, Du Bois informed his fellow board members that it was in large measure due to his journal of opinion and protest—the *Crisis was* the NAACP, in a word. "During this period, *The Crisis* has led in an endeavor to make American Negroes stand up for their rights," the memorandum asserted. In these twenty years, his people had learned to "talk frankly and insistently about their wrongs, and use every lawful method of fighting race prejudice." "As compared with twenty years ago, the peak of the crisis has passed," lynching was abating and would soon disappear. Black higher education was building endowments; literature and the arts were gaining recognition. "Negroes are going to vote and hold office in larger numbers." If the racial future Du Bois projected was even more glowing than the balance sheet he tallied up for the recent past, it was because he intended his memorandum to wrap the magazine in a rationale of compelling contemporaneousness. Guided by *The Crisis*, the association and the people it served could "reasonably look forward to advance in the next twenty years similar to that of the past twenty."

The thesis was well argued, but less than successful in winning the board's undivided attention. The editor's tense relations with the chairperson were set on a hair trigger throughout most of the year, 1931. A board meeting that May had gone badly for both, and Ovington had apologized for "irritating" Du Bois. "But we do seem to have a good many bouts these days," her note confessed, adding rather naughtily that, after two decades of disputes, her capacity "for hero worship has left me." Du Bois fired back that she was too inclined to "monopolize the speechmaking," and he added sternly that Ovington had a very poor conception of her duties as chair. Finding himself badly in need of allies, then, Du Bois had good reason to make common cause with one of the race's most distinguished physicians, who was also a member of the board. Louis Wright, one of the newest Negro members, introduced a professional concern that temporarily absorbed much of the NAACP's energies during the summer of 1931 and pushed Du Bois into an unequivocal defense of a principle that he must have thought, in actuality, to be much more complicated. The Georgia-born Wright had finished fourth in the 1911 Harvard Medical School class. Brilliant, imperious, with Latin good looks to match his self-assurance, Wright had welcomed controversy in medical school in order to thwart racism. He refused to attend classes in order to picket the showing of *The Birth of a Nation* in Cambridge. He forced the authorities of the Boston Lying-In Hospital to honor their own regulations against barring his internship on racial grounds. His lungs damaged from a phosgene gas attack in World War I, Wright had returned from the Western Front with captain's bars and the Purple Heart to enter practice in New York City. After ten years as a private physician (the Du Bois family among his patients), he had received appointments as both the city's first Negro public surgeon and chief of surgery at Harlem Hospital, thanks to the influence of civil service commissioner Morton.

At its meeting in early February 1931, Wright raised the issue of the Rosenwald Fund's plan to underwrite medical centers in the North for the training exclusively of Negro physicians and nurses. The Rosenwald Fund had appropriated $250,000 a few months earlier to modernize Provident Hospital in Chicago, a Negro facility problematically affiliated with the University of Chicago Medical School. A well-endowed Negro hospital for New York was on the philanthropy's drawing board, an offer that some prominent Harlemites pragmatically welcomed, given the virtual exclusion of physicians of color from the municipal hospital system. Wright expressed grave anxiety about what he described as "the growing control of Negro thought and education by certain foundations" and he was adamant about the NAACP preventing such a precedent in the medical field in the North. Wright was "a special favorite of mine . . . gifted and thoroughly unselfish," Du Bois wrote later. Out of motives of friendship mixed with principles and politics, the editor readily consented to craft the association's position. The statement drafted and read on March at the meeting of the board was adopted as official NAACP policy on the Rosenwald hospital plan. It faithfully reflected the views of the influential surgeon whose board candidature and membership in the *Crisis* finance committee Du Bois had seconded with avidity. "Negroes in the North should be admitted without discrimination to the public hospitals," the Jewish philanthropy was informed. Much of the Negro press joined the NAACP in opposing the hospital plan, reiterating the observation made by a group of Negro physicians that Mr. Rosenwald "has not, as far as we know, advocated the segregation of Jewish students at the University of Chicago and the sending of Jewish students to Jewish hospitals for their clinical clerkships and internships." Opposition to the segregated New York medical facility soon caused the fund to beat an embarrassed retreat.

It needs to be recalled that nine years prior to his seemingly unqualified support of Wright's hospital position, however, Du Bois had found it necessary to rebut prosegregationist remarks attributed to him by the Negro Philadelphia *Tribune* as "an unpardonable misinterpretation." What Du Bois had actually said to a Philadelphia audience (and written in *The Crisis*) was that, as segregation in education was a fact of life, dedicated colored teachers deserved every support in order to make segregated education successful. But in a curious anticipation of Du Boisian ambiguities to come, Johnson had been so distressed by what might further be published in the magazine on the subject that he sent a long, carefully reasoned memorandum discouraging the editor from further public pronouncements. There was a "very fine line between what . . . [w]as voluntary segregation, such as we have in our churches, for example, and segregation enforced by custom or public opinion," the secretary had warned. Less than three years after the Rosenwald hospital controversy, *The Crisis* would carry an editorial unusually susceptible of being misunderstood as an endorsement of racial separatism: a plea for the best institutions possible under the fixed reality of apartheid. "Segregation" would be one of the most explosive editorials ever written by Du Bois. Bookended, as it were, by two rationalizations of racial segregation roughly a decade apart, it seems reasonable to wonder whether Du Bois's denunciation of the Rosenwald hospital plan for Harlem may not have been so strongly motivated by the stakes in the internecine NAACP politics that he subordinated certain pragmatic misgivings to them. Indeed, Du Bois himself should be given the last word, as he was to confess frankly in his autobiography, *Dusk of Dawn*, that he saw "clearly the argument on both sides to this controversy," being "heart and soul with Louis Wright . . . and yet I knew that for a hundred years in this America of ours it was going to be at least partially in vain. I was heart and soul with the Rosenwald Fund; what Negroes need is hospital treatment now."

The prospects for radical overhaul of the NAACP deterioriated badly, along with much else, as questions of merit and principle became inextricably entangled with personalities throughout 1931. In March, for better and worse, the board permanently ratified the secretary's authority. For want of an adequate salary offer, Roy Wilkins, who was never to serve as *Crisis* business manager, would accept White's offer to become assistant secretary of the NAACP, the position being vacated by White as Johnson's successor. Du Bois himself would offer the motion, voted on April 13, 1931, to hire the able newspaperman, whose abilities were now so well known to the board, at the generous salary of $3,300. The editor must have been confident that he could inspire Wilkins's allegiance in the coming test of strength with White. What Du Bois may not yet have appreciated, however, was the apparent warmth struck up between White and Wilkins several years earlier when the former had come to speak about lynching to a white congregation in Kansas City, an affinity strengthened during 1930 by *The Call*'s aggressive editorializing against Judge Parker, Hoover's Supreme Court nominee. Wilkins's reflection much later that "as a plotter . . . , Dr. Du Bois was hopelessly inept" seems to have applied with special force to his first months as assistant secretary at 69 Fifth Avenue.* Taking up his duties in September, Wilkins found himself in a "pall of office politics and intrigue thicker than smog in Los Angeles," he recalled. According to Wilkins, Du Bois had yoked Bagnall and Pickens into a cabal to put an end to White's secretariat, each of them convinced that he would make a superior replacement. A deeply offended Minnie Wilkins had wanted to cut short their first Du Bois social visit when the editor excused himself to speak conspiratorially into the telephone

---

*The NAACP moved to 69 Fifth Avenue in September 1930.

about association business in French, a language she understood. If the Wilkinses were off the mark about any ambition on Du Bois's part to become
NAACP secretary, they were accurate about the intensity of Du Bois's offensive — or counteroffensive, as he saw matters.

"White's assumption of office was to set off an explosion within a year," Du
Bois recalled three decades later. "His attitude and actions were unbearable."
Specifically unbearable was White's expenditure of the magazine's half of the
restricted Rosenwald subsidy that Du Bois had negotiated the year before. "We
must have this money," the memorandum he sent Ovington in early October
could almost be heard to shout. "*The Crisis* must have January 1, $1,540 to
balance its accounts properly." The monthly had been kept barely afloat during
September in large part because business manager Malvan (apparently as yet
untroubled) had persuaded the president of Harlem's Dunbar Bank to extend a
one-thousand-dollar short-term loan. *The Crisis* needed a monthly minimum of
$1,200 to survive. The shocking discovery that the expected Rosenwald subsidy
no longer existed convinced Du Bois that White had to be removed, especially
after the board's tepid response to the May restructuring proposal presented by
Du Bois indicated that relief was unlikely to come through any divesting of the
secretary's power. White had almost reached the same conclusion about Du
Bois, however. In the war of memoranda, the secretary's November 15 missive
nearly destroyed Du Bois's defenses. "At the present time," Du Bois read with
stupefaction, White saw "no possibility of the Association being able to give any
further help to *The Crisis* this year." With more than nine thousand dollars in
obligations to foundations and banks falling due on January 1, 1932, the secretary
stated it as a virtual certainty that "we ourselves shall end the year with a sizable
deficit." The days were long gone when the fate of the magazine was tantamount
to the fate of the civil rights organization, and White would deliver a devastating
follow-up punch a few weeks later.

Nineteen thirty-one ended with a Du Bois counteroffensive involving most
of the senior staff. "The whole staff appealed to me as the senior executive
officer to lead a protest" against White, he asserted. It was probably true that
White's imperious managerial style galvanized officers and employees who were
already distressed by economies that loomed ever more threateningly. Ovington,
dividing her exasperation equally between the editor and the secretary, was
heard to sigh that White was not always "just to others." But it was the actions
of the board's budget committee at its December 14 meeting that stampeded
field secretaries Bagnall and Pickens, along with publicity director Seligmann,
and even the cagey Wilkins, three months into his position as assistant secretary,
into staging an open revolt. Painful retrenchments had been approved: salary
reductions ranging from 5 to 10 percent; dismissal of a clerk, a special legal
assistant, and Pickens's secretary; and sharp reductions in postage, printing, and

mimeographing. The committee had also debated the tenure of Bagnall and Pickens. Finally, with the "connivance of the chairman of the board and the secretary," Du Bois fumed, the new budget committee had recommended that White be given control of the business department of *The Crisis*, an action effectively nullifying Malvan's position. The "strong and biting arraignment" Du Bois handed the board at the emergency meeting convened the following week alleged that a budget committee had been hastily appointed for the sole purpose of devaluing certain staff members—Bagnall in particular. Where was the acknowledgment of special undertakings such as Pickens's activities in connection with the Scottsboro defendants? Why had the figures submitted to the budget committee covered only the leanest two months of some $39,000 in income generated by the field secretaries? Such facts "illustrate the utter viciousness of the present method of appointing the Budget Committee and laying facts before it," the group document declared. "It is our solemn and carefully considered opinion," Du Bois intoned before the unsettled directors, "that unless the power of the Chairman of the Board over the appointment of committees is curtailed and unless Mr. White is going to be more honest and straightforward with his colleagues . . . , the chief question before this organization is how long he can remain in his present position and keep the NAACP from utter disaster?"

The Du Bois–led protest came during a period in which White seemed especially vulnerable because of growing public criticism of the association's handling of the Scottsboro case. If, as has been seen, Du Bois was as antipathetic to the ILD as White, he was careful to defend the NAACP rather than the secretary in the controversy. But it was White who received the brunt of the criticism for his hands-on responsibility in the case. He scurried about like a terrified terrier, panting, promising, negotiating, and, according to Du Bois, abasing himself before the board and showing himself "pleasant and approachable" to the staff. The stress of maneuvering between Du Bois and White finally proved too much for Ovington, whose resignation as chairperson became effective in a matter of days. Stepping down to assume the vacant post of treasurer, the sixty-six-year-old feminist and socialist handed the chair to Joel Spingarn, who now held the dual position of president of the NAACP and chairman of the board of directors. Although his motion to have the finances of both the secretariat and *The Crisis* investigated by an independent body had purchased a cooling-off period, Spingarn made it known that he found White's management of the association's accounts to be irresponsible. Having challenged the board with mutiny and finding that the directors were "deeply moved" by their complaints, Du Bois must have believed that the radical restructuring of the civil rights organization might be within his grasp. But as often transpires in the dynamic of protests, the conceding of legitimate grievance imposed the risk of premature armistice. Spingarn's appeal to the signatories to withdraw their protest in exchange for a thorough investigation of the charges by the board proved persuasive to all but one. No, the editor wouldn't do what Spingarn called "the manly thing, and make a complete retraction." He refused to "retract or change a single word," Du Bois growled. "I did not trust Walter White," who promptly changed his tact, "worked hard and went underground."

BY TEMPERAMENT AND intellect this romantic Calvinist bridled at the very thought of moderation and retrenchment in time of crisis. For Du Bois, the Great Depression was to be comprehended as a redemption enveloped in a catastrophe. The more potent the challenge, the greater must be the response, he believed with the passion of logic. The NAACP and the race at large needed another new program — or certainly one drastically revamped — suited to the next quarter century. But Du Bois was becoming convinced by the month that even he might not succeed in jolting his associates at 70 Fifth Avenue out of their institutional security. As his influence at NAACP headquarters waned, then, his response was to take what he saw as a struggle for the soul of the association to the membership, the race at large, and, finally, to much of mainstream America. As if to wash his hands of the national office, he left on another speaking tour, this one to last, intermittently, several months. Distance from New York combined with sudden, brief returns to the office in no way altered the control he exercised over the magazine, however, and some of the liveliest and most challenging material would appear in *The Crisis* during this final phase of his editorship.

The hard-hitting editorial criticizing Will Alexander, the South's most distinguished white liberal, for assuming the acting presidency of the Rosenwald-endowed new Dillard University in New Orleans was another instance of the editor ventilating an opinion many influential Negroes preferred to hold in private. The white-maned "Dr. Will," rumpled and courtly, was a walking institution, a founder of the Commission on Interracial Cooperation (CIC), affiliated under a variety of titles with all the great national foundations, senior officer of the Rosenwald Fund, and soon to become a pivotal administrator in the New Deal. But Dillard was a Negro school and Alexander was a white patriarch confronted by an inescapable dilemma, Du Bois thought: "if he becomes a companion and host and intimate social friend of black folk," Alexander wouldn't be able to "keep his southern white constituency." The college presidency would be a misfortune for the black students and a major loss for white moderates. If "Dillard University" must have seemed a somewhat gratuitous criticism of a man broadly respected by blacks and whites alike, the editorial's real significance was as a prolegomenon of the more fully developed cultural nationalism Du Bois would espouse in "The Negro College" a year later. In ways subtle and more evident, Du Bois's thinking about the American race perennial had begun to embrace separatist solutions increasingly at variance with the integrationist ideology of the NAACP. Writing in the August 1933 *Crisis,* he would insist that "there can be no college for Negroes which is not a Negro College," that while an American Negro university, "just like a German or Swiss university may rightly aspire to a universal culture unhampered by limitations of race and culture, yet . . . a Negro university in the United States of America begins with Negroes." Criticism of a southern philanthropoid was complemented by an edifying obituary of a public-spirited northern white conservative in the issue for February 1932. Notwithstanding the recent opposition to the Negro hospitals policy, *The Crisis* observed the passing of Julius Rosenwald with a genuine, if ironic, tribute to a Jewish philanthropist whose prodigious benefactions to Negro America had been a splendid reproach to the niggard charity of gentile hypocrites.

Du Bois wrote a ghastly, eyewitness account in March of the protracted coal miners' strike in Kentucky's Bell and Harlan counties. Reduced hours and reduced wages paid in scrip redeemable only at company stores had finally driven more than eleven thousand miners to lay down their tools and face the mine owners' sheriffs and armed vigilantes in a twelve-month combat of such one-sided violence that the strike had been abandoned by the United Mine Workers as hopeless. Reports of abductions, murders, and a pitched battle with machine guns eventually mobilized a small number of eastern writers, led by Theodore Dreiser, John Dos Passos, and Waldo Frank, to brave two highly publicized visits to Kentucky coal country, the first one having taken place in November 1931. Du Bois joined the February 1932 sortie, driving his reconditioned automobile to the edge of Harlan Country. Never had he seen "so much persecution, so much constant repression, ruthlessness, brutality, and utter disregard of human life and property" as perpetrated by the owners' hirelings. An investigative reporter was fatally ambushed. Bombs shattered the night, blowing up relief organization soup kitchens and cars driven by investigators from the National Student League. An ACLU representative was jailed after an arbitrary roundup, and Du Bois stressed that he had been able to circulate in Harlan County only in the company of a prominent local attorney—a wise decision, as Frank had taken a bloody beating. "Read this report from an observer on the ground at Pineville, Kentucky," the editor exhorted, crying out for universal sympathy to help these black and white workingmen obtain a living wage, overthrow feudalism, and win the right to free speech.

The issues for February and March 1932 also carried the ghastly specifics of the life under Jim Crow. Seven Negroes were recorded as being lynched in 1929, a comparatively low figure that had occasioned cautious optimism in some civil rights quarters about the slow advancement of law and order in America. But twenty-one were lynched the next year, followed by a less than encouraging drop to thirteen in 1931—"thirteen 'or more,' " Du Bois wrote. "It may have been fifteen or eighteen," but, whatever the exact count, at least one black person had been hanged by a mob somewhere in the United States every month of the year. His facts came from *Lynchings and What They Mean*, the investigative report issued by the Southern Commission on the Study of Lynching, an interracial body of eight white and five black men. Another significant fact was that the commissioners had corroborated other evidence that, during the last twenty-five years, "only one in every six persons lynched had been even accused of rape," the crime that white men of the South most often claimed as justification for insensate lawlessness. These hoisted victims seldom emerged from the horror of their statistical anonymity in the minds of readers. Indeed, sudden, random brutality hovered as an omnipresence in the lives of all classes of colored people, numbing their indignation and mocking due process at the hands of justice. The death of Fisk University's dean of women students offered a case study of such lugubrious senselessness, however, that it expelled a cry of desperation and rage from the Talented Tenth and sent a shudder through several million men and women, whatever their class or racial background.

Thirty-four-year-old Juliette Derricotte possessed the class of her name. She was well bred, as they said in those days, a graduate of Talladega who held a master's degree from Columbia's Teachers College. After a well-traveled career as secretary of the YMCA's National Student Council, she had taken the Fisk position in 1927. Her firmness, tact, and accessibility had made her popular with students and esteemed by faculty. Driving to Athens, Georgia, on family business, Derricotte had left Nashville accompanied by three Fisk students, along for a free ride to their homes in Atlanta and Athens. In circumstances that were never to be satisfactorily explained, Derricotte's car collided with another vehicle, driven by a white man, a mile or so outside the prosperous town of Dalton, Georgia, in the late afternoon of Friday, November 6, 1931. Three colored Fisk professors—physicists St. Elmo Brady and Elmer Imes and musicologist Warner Lawson—sped off by car immediately for Dalton. It was Ethel Bedient Gilbert, a white Fisk official and friend of Derricotte's from their YWCA years together, whose eleven-page, typescript chronicle was to comprise the core of "Dalton, Georgia," Du Bois's wrenching narrative five months later describing the tragedy. Believing that there would be little expert treatment of Derricotte and Johnson, the one student who was badly injured, if the attending physicians failed to appreciate their patients' social standing, Gilbert frantically called Dalton. After much confusion, she learned that no hospital ambulance had been dispatched for the Fisk group, but rather a hearse from the establishment of a prominent colored Chattanooga undertaker was on its way.

Events in Dalton, even after the investigations conducted by Fisk and the CIC, were never pinned down. Gilbert's version of them had little to say about the role of the three faculty members, but it revealed enough to surmise that it was Brady, Lawson, and Imes who eventually managed to pierce the inertia in which Derricotte's and Johnson's lives were ebbing away in the north Georgia township. The accident had occurred shortly before 4 P.M. after which at least a vital hour passed before the two badly hurt and the dazed victims were driven by a local white woman to the town, where white physicians decided that Johnson was beyond saving and that Derricotte might be able to save herself if she lived through the night. As a horrified Gilbert was to learn, the injured women had then been carted off by the "local [Dalton] Negro undertaker" to the unkempt house of a Negro woman, where, as the much later CIC report delicately stated, "physicians of Dalton have been taking patients . . . for a number of years, and major operations have been successfully performed there." As an afterthought, the CIC investigator observed that Mrs. Wilson, who was described by one of the Fisk professors as an "ugly, barefooted woman," was "without formal training or professional standing." Derricotte and Johnson had lain unattended from around 7:30 P.M. until midnight, November 6, on a sofa and bed at the overwhelmed Mrs. Wilson's. "It was sickening and heartbreaking to us to think of Miss Derricotte and Miss Johnson having been allowed to lie there and suffer for five long hours," Lawson reported later.

Confused information about ambulances leaving Dalton with and without patients for misidentified Chattanooga hospitals had wreaked havoc with the injureds' chances. Attended by colored physicians from Chattanooga, along with two from Atlanta, and a white specialist from the city hospital (Louis Wright stood by for a telephone consultation in New York), the Fisk dean opened her eyes in the Walden Hospital to the welcome sight of Brady, Imes, Lawson, and Ethel Gilbert at her beside. But Derricotte's heart and thyroid condition seriously complicated treatment of her injuries. Although the group of doctors present in Chattanooga was highly competent, Walden Hospital possessed only the most rudimentary equipment. How the choice of Walden Hospital had been made, neither Gilbert nor, curiously, anyone else ever appears to have addressed, although Gilbert later learned that "two excellent Chattanooga hospitals admit[ted] Negro patients, having not only wards but private rooms."

Derricotte never regained consciousness and died in the early morning of November 7. Derricotte's was not, unfortunately, an isolated fatality involving automotive misadventure and medical sins of omission. Black people were known to die on southern roads as they waited for ambulances that never appeared or came only to take them past the nearest "white" hospital to another Mrs. Wilson's or to some understaffed clinic miles beyond. Through the firestorm of press coverage and subsequent investigations it caused, Juliette Derricotte's obscene death would become the nightmare archetype of all such deaths, of which Bessie Smith's and Charles Drew's highway deaths would be widely interpreted as equally tragic replays. Du Bois gave Gilbert the last word in The Crisis:

I shall always have to compare in my mind all of the things that were done that would not have been done to me if I had been injured. I shall always have to remember that within one half hour after the accident, I would have been in a modern hospital. I shall always have to think of Juliette dying in a place that should not be dignified by the name of a hospital. . . . All of the people in that little [Walden] place were kindness and courtesy itself but that does not take the place of the clean walls, the soft-footed, sure-fingered nurses, the well-equipped operating room, the comfortable bed, the shaded lights, the efficient doctors, that I had when I was taken into a hospital for an emergency operation.

Evidence of the restiveness spreading across Negro America was strikingly manifest in the *Crisis* symposium Du Bois conducted in the April–May issue, "Negro Editors on Communism." His duty as senior intellectual of the race had seldom been better served than in stimulating a discourse about the potential relevance of Marxism to people of color in the United States. "The world is ill," Du Bois announced with due solemnity. "It has desperate economic problems intertwined with its problems of racial prejudice." The question to answer, then, was this: "is communism as illustrated in Russia and America, a theory good for the world and for the American Negro?" His invitation brought a range of responses from seventeen editors and publishers from all points of the compass who were reputed to speak weekly "to at least five hundred thousand subscribers and several million readers." That several of these fairly conservative businessmen—Murphy of the Baltimore *Afro-American*, Eugene Rhodes of the Philadelphia *Tribune*, and Roscoe Dunjee of the Oklahoma *Black Dispatch*—were willing to speculate on the positive aspects of communism was a measure of the political disaffection created by the economic and racial consequences of the Depression. "No white group is openly advocating the economic, political, and social equality of Negroes, except Communists," Murphy asserted, voicing the minority position. None of these men espoused the abolition of the market economy or had made, as Du Bois observed, "any study of classic Marxian socialism." They were saluting not an ideology, but possible relief from a catastrophe; their qualified indulgence of communism was motivated more by racial than by ideological considerations.

As Du Bois intended, many of the delegates to the twenty-third annual NAACP conference in late May 1932 arrived with the Negro editors' symposium fresh in their minds. Many of them not only understood that the historic alliance of the Negro and the GOP had outlived whatever minimal value it once held, but that the failure of capitalism raised profound questions about the priorities and tactics of the civil rights establishment. Wright's feeling of drift and lack of imagination was shared by many, and Du Bois came to the conference fully prepared to mobilize the membership behind a new agenda—one in which the association's secretary would play a greatly reduced part. At the historic five days in Washington and Harpers Ferry, highlighted by President Hoover's greetings, Moton's receipt of the Spingarn Medal, and set-piece addresses by Senator Arthur Capper of Kansas and the indomitable clubwoman Addie Hunton, there were rousing speeches by Lillian Wald and John Dewey. At sixty-five, Wald was one of the younger survivors of that band of progressives and settlement house workers who sang "The Battle Hymn of the Republic" as they assembled in the Great Hall of Cooper Union twenty-three years before to found the association. They were dying away. Ida Wells-Barnett had died the previous year, and the editor wrote a correct farewell to a great pioneer who "began the awakening of the conscience of the nation." Florence Kelley, on the other hand, received an almost effusive obituary less than a year later for her superlative "insight" and "daring" in race relations. Wald spoke movingly on the eighteenth of the association's two-decade journey and of its great unfinished business. Dewey's speech on behalf of the LIPA the next day was undoubtedly courtesy of fellow league officer Du Bois, whose name was still on the masthead of the organization's stationery. Calling on the delegates to take the message home that neither party deserved their support until they "face[d] the issues which have to do with employment and security of jobs," the philosopher showed how well he understood this relatively privileged audience. It was silly "to allow yourselves to be swayed by the fact that a few have received recognition and the emoluments of office," Dewey remonstrated.

Du Bois placed his four-point reorganization program before the delegates on the third day, the eighteenth. The NAACP as a mass-based organization could never become a reality so long as the attitude was to work "for the black masses but not with them," he expounded. Decentralization was a sine qua non. The association must adopt a "positive program rather than mere negative attempt to avoid segregation and discrimination," and this positive program had to concentrate on "economic guidance" and upon linking the world problems of color and race to "our problem here in America." And finally, the organization must make itself more "welcoming of youth." The ovation was thunderous as Du Bois wound up by declaring that "the interests of the masses are the interests of this Association, and . . . the masses have got to voice themselves through it." The positive response in Washington and at Harpers Ferry inspired Joel Spingarn, whose attention span like Du Bois's had begun to stray, to propose a second Amenia conference, this one, like the 1916 conclave, to convene as soon as possible at Troutbeck in order to conduct an open-ended discussion of the future course of the association. The first Amenia gathering had confirmed the Talented Tenth in its leadership position in Negro America; the imperative now was to formulate a new, revalidating position for the leadership. With

Du Bois's encouragement, Joel Spingarn asked White to oversee arrangements for a second Amenia before the end of the summer. Away from NAACP head-quarters much of the time, the editor expected to be asked by the secretary or his assistant, Wilkins, to confer about the meeting's agenda as well as to provide a list of prospective invitees. When still no word had come from the secretary's office about Amenia in early July, Du Bois inquired, only to learn that nothing had been done to prepare for the conference. The opportunity for a late summer meeting slipped away in a simulacrum of organizational interest. He always expected as much, Du Bois told Lillian Alexander.

By October, the *in extremis* situation of the magazine forced Du Bois to apply a portion of his salary to keep the publication afloat. Embree informed him that next year's Rosenwald grant omitted the previous years' stipulation that the association and the magazine were to have equal shares. A few days before the report was due, Joel Spingarn wrote a confidential letter to John Hope at Atlanta University in which he anticipated the worst outcome from the budget committee's deliberations on November 17. The association might have to "sus-pend the paper entirely," he feared, and in any case "some reorganization of our work will certainly be made." The letter disclosed, however, that the two men had discussed a mutually satisfactory solution to what had now come to seem the inescapable fate of the magazine. If Hope could wire him in advance of the Thursday budget committee meeting, Spingarn was confident of being able to delay the inevitable. Could he know "by that time whether there [was] any likelihood of your acting favorably in the matter?" the president and chair-man pleaded. A professorship for Du Bois at the new Atlanta University would save face for the association and the editor. Spingarn closed by stating what was only too obvious to Hope, who understood perfectly the elements of *amour-propre* at risk, that it was "of the greatest importance to our friend to have it go out to the world that he is leaving New York to accept an important post rather than because the paper is forced to suspend." Hope's telegram confirming his intention to invite Du Bois to be guest professor during the spring semester of 1933 reached New York on the day of the fateful meeting.

A NEW RACIAL PHILOSOPHY

The editor was deeply moved. On the evening of November 17, 1931, Helen Bryan, field secretary of the Committee on Race Relations of the Society of Friends, had organized a celebratory dinner on the occasion of the twenty-first anniversary of *The Crisis*. "Really, it was gorgeous!" Du Bois wrote her. It had lifted him out of his "Heebie Jeebies (which had dug in for the winter). . . . Even good friends and well wishers quite forget *The Crisis*," he said, "and in a sense they think of it as independent and prosperous and needing no aid or comfort." But his uneasiness would return with full force the following year. Clearly, November 1932 was a disaster. The business manager was gone. One or two clerks were slated to go, and only by adopting a cheaper grade of paper and dropping more laggard advertisers could Du Bois reassure the Spingarn brothers at the end of the month that he might just be able to keep the magazine afloat on a monthly budget of a thousand dollars and in a circulation range of about thirteen thousand copies. The arrival of Hope's telegram offering a guest professorship at Atlanta University in the midst of *Crisis* worries presented a live option that was the culmination of nearly two years of episodic deliberations. Du Bois would write in *The Autobiography* that he had "already for some years begun to canvass the possibility of a change of work."

An earlier visiting professorship arrangement had come within a hair's breadth of a signature in January 1931 when Du Bois agreed to give a two-month seminar in sociology at Atlanta University beginning in February of the following year. Although the plan had lapsed fairly quickly, Du Bois spent two weeks in March 1932 delivering ten lectures on topics such as "Imperialism in the Sudan, 1400 to 1700" and "The Economic Future of Black America" on the three Atlanta University Center campuses. He returned to New York seriously contemplating Hope's appeal to return as a permanent member of the new

Atlanta University faculty: "We could do so much together." With Joel Spingarn's confidential November 1932 letter in hand pleading that the editor be
afforded a distinguished exit from a sinking enterprise, Hope had decided that
it was the right time to deploy a bridge for Du Bois's transition from 70 Fifth
Avenue to Atlanta University's magnolia-shaded campus. A proposition of two
thousand dollars for five months of teaching made the president's suasions all
the more enticing in a period of extreme financial distress for the editor as well
as for the country.

Du Bois left for Atlanta at the beginning of January 1933 angry, disgusted,
and still fighting to keep *The Crisis* alive and out of the hands of White and
Wilkins, whom he now regarded as flawed in intellect and character. Unless he
were permitted to counter what he saw as White's malign influence with a
candidate of his own choosing to run the magazine during his absence, Du
Bois had informed Arthur Spingarn in the closing days of December that he
would refuse to withdraw his resignation from the NAACP. The managing editor
must be a person "in whom I have confidence," he snapped. "Mr. Wilkins does
not have my confidence. . . . He is lazy and unreliable." The editor could rely
on Hazel Branch and Lulu Burton to follow the precise instructions he would
forward from Atlanta in matters pertaining to copyediting, bookkeeping, and
routine *Crisis* correspondence. His New York eyes and ears, these resourceful
women would discharge a range of responsibilities with such selfless, adoring
proficiency that they evoked gratitude bordering on the sentimental from Du
Bois. Still, dedicated and dutiful as the women were, what was needed was a
competent, loyal business manager/managing editor such as Du Bois had once
believed he had found in Wilkins.

Leaving nonnegotiable demands sizzling at national headquarters like a
damp firecracker, the editor had headed south. Another "of our periodical
fights"—this one lasting more than six hours—he wrote Davis DuBois as he
left. He was almost giddy to have gotten away from NAACP headquarters, exhilarated as he steered his impeccably maintained Willis sedan away from the
snows, southwesterly across the Mason-Dixon Line into the nation's capital. Poor
Georgia Johnson told him her federal job was slated for extinction and that her
kidneys had stones, but she seemed even more disconsolate that no publishers
were interested in her latest offerings of poetry. Injoining her to have courage
and persevere, Du Bois then drove across the Upper South into the Smoky
Mountains between Tennessee and Georgia and on to Atlanta, humming lieder
and chasing in his mind loose ends from his large Reconstruction manuscript.
He reached the city on January 26, parking his car on the Spelman College
campus, where he would live during the semester.

Spelman College's white president, Florence Matilda Read, a prim, fortyish

Mount Holyoke alumna and former staffer of the Rockefeller Foundation, had arranged for a large, pleasant room in Rockefeller Hall overlooking the college's manicured quad. During a brief December visit to Atlanta five years earlier, Du Bois had been introduced to the Spelman president by Hope soon after her appointment. The editor and the Spelman president exchanged cordial, even somewhat playful, letters in the wake of their first encounter, a courtesy nourished by a second convivial interracial breakfast hosted by Read at the close of Du Bois's lecture series in spring of 1932. As visiting professor Du Bois took up the pace of the 1933 spring academic and social calendar, there was no imitation of the institution-shaking disputes that lay a few years ahead with Florence Read, a compact brunette who was as prone to infallibility as was the balding charter officer of the NAACP.

From Rockefeller Hall came contented letters to Nina, who had at last bade *au revoir* to houseguest Elisabeth Prophet. It felt good to be back in familiar surroundings, and Will recalled for Nina the brightness of February mornings in Atlanta. "The breakfast here is still the impossible time, 6:45," he complained. He solved the problem by having bread, butter, cream, and two eggs sent over daily from the Spelman dining hall; he cooked these in his room at eight. Nina's replies, with minimal mention of personal infirmities, were almost lively as they relayed news of Yolande and four-month-old "Baby Du Bois," their new granddaughter. Nina missed Will, but there was no thought at this time of her joining him, even though he would eventually begin to worry about wife, daughter, and granddaughter remaining in the Harlem apartment during the summer. The visiting professor was more concerned about teaching and lecturing than family matters, although he continued to write dutiful advice to Nina and Yolande. He plunged into his two courses, Karl Marx and the Negro and the Economic History of the Negro, incorporating data from the seminal, two-part article "The Possibility of Democracy in America" into a weekly seminar on the History and Sociology of the Black Voter. He wrote Arthur Spingarn and old friend Boutté that teaching was rejuvenating. Yes, "the South is still the South," but it was inspiring to be "again among intelligent and enthusiastic young folk," twelve graduate degree candidates and top-flight seniors who stimulated his own thinking and did valuable library legwork for the manuscript on the Reconstruction period. He was "reading and learning with the class," he would recall.

One of the intelligent and enthusiastic students whose master's degree Du Bois agreed to supervise, Louie Davis Shivery, was about twenty-five years older than the average graduate student, having received her bachelor's degree from Atlanta University in 1903. She headed the English department at Atlanta's Booker T. Washington High School, was brilliant, attractive, and endowed with a temperament as colorful as the clashing outfits she wore. Mrs. Shivery's abusive husband, George, Sr., a troubled dentist whose rages occasionally ricocheted up quiet Chestnut Street just off the Morehouse campus, had mysteriously faded, unlamented, from his family's life more than a dozen years earlier, leaving her to finish raising a son and daughter alone. George, Jr., a commercial artist in New York, had received commissions from *The Crisis*, and Du Bois was godfather to Shivery's daughter, Henrietta ("Dimples"), a graduate of Talladega College. Du Bois and Shivery would lose no time in ripening the warm friendship begun more than twenty years earlier. He had visited her in Atlanta while Nina lived in London during Yolande's matriculation at Bedales. When he moved into the extensive new Georgian complex housing graduate students and unmarried or unaccompanied faculty the following year, Shivery's small corner house, attached garage, and covered porch across the street would offer him pleasant retreat and shelter for the Willis sedan and later the Buick.

Louie Shivery would have rivals in the community for Du Bois's affections—several, in fact. One of them, a much younger, hardworking newcomer to the city, was also beginning graduate studies in the new department of sociology. Among the growing retinue of interesting and accomplished women in Du Bois's life, Ellen Irene Diggs, brilliant, trim, and stunningly black, was to grow in Du Bois's esteem and affection over the years until those who knew the depth of their relationship thought that Diggs might become the second Mrs. Du Bois. Irene Diggs certainly came to define her being in terms of that inestimable status. "She's never gotten over it," G. James Fleming, Diggs's longtime faculty colleague at Morgan State University, would reminisce a half century later. In the fall of 1933, she was twenty-seven, with a University of Minnesota bachelor's in economics and anthropology and headed for the first AU master's degree awarded for work in Professor Du Bois's sociology department. Du Bois found her energy and intellectual sophistication enormous assets as he pressed ahead on the first draft of the book he intended to call "Black Reconstruction of Democracy in America."

As the Depression groaned on and the plight of Negro Americans went largely unaddressed by the New Deal, Du Bois resolved to work out a social and economic program to fill the void into which the race's enervated political class had stumbled. Boasting that the personal library he assembled at Atlanta University contained the most comprehensive holdings on socialism and communism in the South, he set himself the formidable task of comprehensive assimilation of Marx's writings. It was to be Marx in months, not years, a mastery that would be uniquely Du Boisian. The stakes were historic, Du Bois believed. He saw the "fantastic industrial structure of America [. . .] threatened with ruin." Skilled labor was "double-tongued and helpless," and "common white labor [was] too frightened at Negro competition to attempt united action" and only begged a government handout. The NAACP was in full disarray, though it could be salvaged, possibly, if one final attempt at genuine, top-down overhaul and radical recasting of the association's policies could succeed. Who better, then, to mount a Marxisant rescue operation of the race than himself? To this imperative end, he undertook to package Marx appealingly for an introduction to black America.

Even as he motored south from New York in January, *Crisis* subscribers were reading "Toward a New Racial Philosophy," the first of two editorials bearing this significant title in which Du Bois began to lower the curtain on nearly a quarter century of NAACP history of middle-class struggle and advancement for civil rights. Because the situation had "changed enormously in its trend, objects and details," everything about what was called the "Negro problem" must be examined from "the point of view of the middle of the 20th Century." The Soviet Union was an example to be envied, Du Bois thought. *A Contribution to the Critique of Political Economy*, the basic text of Marxism, he had already seen validated in stone, steel, and flesh during the 1926 trip to Russia, and that led him to embrace fully the dictum that "the economic foundation of a nation is widely decisive for its politics, its art and its culture." What he found to be powerfully appealing were not the political parties and trade union organizations deployed in dozens of nations to further the objectives of the Comintern, rather it was the extraordinary acuity attained by Marx in decoding the life cycles of economic systems. Like so many intellectuals in the thirties who broadcast Marxism as a verifiable science of society, the Atlanta professor was mesmerized by dialectical materialism. Calling Marx the "greatest figure in the science of modern industry," Du Bois seemed to rediscover with the avidity of a gifted graduate student the thinker who Frank Taussing, his Harvard economics professor, had smugly ignored. Marx made history make sense — or more sense, Du Bois came to believe, than all other analytical systems.

Marxism also appealed to his anticlericalism. As a person of immense learning and sophistication, Du Bois's distaste for the vibrant evangelism of black religious observance was so palpable that he might well have invented the tag line about religion being the opiate of the people had not Marx supplied it. Notwithstanding those soaring passages in *Souls* and *Gift of Black Folk*, or, later, in *Black Reconstruction*, celebrating Negroes' "peculiar spiritual quality" and the "Negro Church today . . . [as] sole surviving social institution of the African fatherland," an informed reading of Du Bois's *oeuvre* discloses virtually no modern role assigned to the Negro church. Well-placed blacks and whites alike were often scandalized by the editor's castigations of what he viewed as the general mediocrity of the Negro clergy. But the screen of class standing between the worldly editor and millions of exuberant congregants was reinforced by much more than prejudices of a secular nature. Unlike a majority of Americans who, irrespective of race, spoke of "godless communism" with genuine religious aversion, Du Bois had long since weaned himself from any belief in the Almighty that could prompt such misgivings. Although he called himself an agnostic, it was an agnosticism professing such complete indifference to the hypothesis of an interactive supreme being as to be indistinguishable from atheism. No, he would write an inquiring Catholic priest some years later, no, he could see "no proof to sustain such a belief, neither in History nor in [his] personal experience," of an intelligent deity.

In "Karl Marx and the Negro," the slender piece in the March *Crisis*, Du Bois proceeded to apply this knowledge to the condition of black people. Marx's writings about the uplift of the European working classes must be qualified in their application to people of color, observed Du Bois. The great political philosopher had, unfortunately, not "studied at first hand their peculiar race problem here in America." Will Herberg's letter reacting to the large implications of such a statement betrayed a degree of astonishment at Du Bois's interpretive temerity. Did the editor intend to amend Marxist theory in its application to racism in America? Herberg, for one, "would be greatly interested in learning your views on the subject." Du Bois's matter-of-fact reply—"this is exactly what I am going to undertake in my next article"—was entirely in character. In "Marxism and the Negro Problem," therefore, Du Bois presumed both to define the racial limitations of the political philosophy as well as its considerable relevance to Negroes living in a capitalist democracy founded on white supremacy. Significantly, the essay appeared in the same month as Sidney Hook's *Towards the Understanding of Karl Marx: A Revolutionary Interpretation*, by most accounts the definitive work by an American on the subject for at least two decades. Key portions of the thirty-year-old New York University professor's book had appeared in the *Journal of Philosophy* and Calverton's *Modern Quarterly*, publications that Du Bois read regularly. Hook, advantaged by fourteen weeks of Russian residency and superlative training in philosophy, would end his distinguished career celebrated on the political right as an antisocialist socialist *par excellence* who even refused to allow the reprinting of his brilliant book.

"Marxism and the Negro Problem"—the gospel of Marx according to Du Bois—ran in the May issue of *The Crisis*, a venturesome topic the author introduced with a trace of levity. Alluding to a dinner reception for Einstein at which the story was told of a professor having "no sense of humor" because he attempted to explain the theory of relativity in a few simple words, Professor Du Bois undertook, "with all modesty," to accomplish a similar task. "Marxism and the Negro Problem" followed by two months "Karl Marx and the Negro." Leading his readers on a brisk tour of scientific socialism, starting with the labor theory of value and cantering past the seductive dialectic at breakneck speed through the war of the classes to the triumph of the proletariat, Du Bois validated the main tenets of Marxism. While conceding that the theory of surplus value imported into Marxism from Manchester economics had been refuted and that the proletarian revolution was widely dismissed as the materialist's version of faith, Du Bois confessed his own version of that faith. Du Bois had always been a socialist in his bones, a proponent, long before Lenin coined the phrase, of "controlling the commanding heights" of national economies, even though he had deserted Debs and entered into a flawed bargain to back Wilson in 1912. Indeed, the romantic authoritarianism that underlay his irrepressible, often grating, elitism was in a curious way indissolubly linked to his socialist propensities, to a deep antipathy for a market economy in which everything had its price but values were at a discount.

The framer of the Talented Tenth concept now wished it to be clearly understood in "Marxism and the Negro Problem" that the existence of a few hundred thousand educated and prosperous people out of a total Negro population of twelve million was of negligible significance. More to the point, this black petit bourgeoisie was a false class, of "peculiar position" and too recent in origin and too remote from the real exploiters of wages and labor for its existence to correspond to the authentic conquering bourgeoisie. Color prejudice would preclude these classes from making common cause with capital, with the new class of engineers and technocrats, or with the most advantaged white workers, he stipulated. Still, Du Bois warned readers, the emergence of these phantom classes in the United States, Africa, and the West Indies posed a threat to proletarian vigor by draining off "skill and intelligence into the white group, and leav[ing] the black labor poor, ignorant and leaderless save for an occasional demagog." As a socioeconomic phenomenon, then, Du Bois preferred to see the evolving Talented Tenth tethered hard and fast to the mass of black folk, to the abused and powerless toilers whose misery derived from the "fundamental iniquities of the whole capitalistic system."

Yet it was here, midstream in this watershed of a meditation, that Du Bois deployed an extraordinary conceptual disclaimer—a plangent "nevertheless"— that would evoke varying degrees of stupefaction, consternation, and revisionism among the American Old Left. "Nevertheless," he demurred, "this black proletariat is not part of the white proletariat." Despite their similar grievances against capital, the two proletariats were separate, unequal, and antagonistic, a reality only partially due to the divide-and-conquer strategies of the capitalists, he asserted. Russian *mujiks* or much of the poor white detritus of the South might be mired in visceral hatreds and too unschooled in the workings of labor manipulation to realize their employers' endgame, but not the labor aristocracy led by Mathew Woll and William Green of the AFL. These leaders of organized labor had long been his bête noires, as had Gompers before them; and the editor had repeatedly decried the racial exclusivity of their affiliated unions. But now he lobbed the incendiary accusation that the class enemy of black workers was the upper tier of white workers: "Colored labor has no common ground with white labor." Because the long memory of white working-class racism in America was soldered to his cortex with such fixity as to mock the dogma of proletarian solidarity, Du Bois expended some of his bitterest published prose on this essay. In the ironic comfort of Rockefeller Hall, he fairly ranted about white labor—"white labor that deprives the Negro of his right to vote, denies him education, denies him affiliation with trade unions, expels him from decent houses, and neighborhoods, and heaps upon him the public insults of open color discrimination." Let there be no ambiguity about the source of the black workers' misery, his screed continued. "The lowest and most fatal degree of [their] suffering comes not from capitalists but from fellow white workers."

How then did Marx's philosophy apply to the black proletariat in the twentieth century, asked Du Bois—to American Negroes, specifically? Only to a limited, modified extent, he ventured. Describing much of the American labor movement as a "post-Marxian phenomenon" evolving through rising wages and installment-plan consumerism into a "working-class aristocracy," Du Bois proceeded to such a curious blurring of the distinction between the proletariat and the bourgeoisie as to cause heartburn among scrupulous Marxist students like Abram Harris. Despite a vexing imprecision about the character and functions of the new classes wedging themselves between the proletariat and the capitalists, "Marxism and the Negro Problem" made a persuasive case for the formation of a *Herrenvolk* proletariat coexisting in such commingled collusion with capital as to force a revision of classical Marxism. Substituting a class analysis that anticipated by a generation that of Herbert Marcuse's analysis of Marx, Du Bois underscored the investment of American workers in the success ideology of capitalism. However eschatological the coming of the worker-state was, he declared, American exceptionalism would be victorious in the short term. Call them aristocrats of labor or petits-bourgeois, wrote Du Bois in effect, ordinary Americans believed they were standing on history's up escalator; and those who fell off due to hard luck or poor initiative were written off not as soldiers joining the swelling international of struggle, but simply as losers. European immigrant workers, he noted, had succumbed to a similar pattern of cooptation as they enrolled in the new global order of finance capital as clerks and constables "used to keep 'darkies' in their 'places.'"

"Marxism and the Negro Problem," Du Bois's seminal article, was still being shaped when Harris, disconcerted by what he read in "Karl Marx and the Negro," had begged Du Bois to rethink his contention that the race problem in the United States had been inadequately addressed by Marx. Quoting from Marx's constant iteration that "'labor in a white skin cannot emancipate itself without emancipating labor in a black skin,'" Harris wondered what more needed to be said. The Howard economics professor thought his mentor might do well to bone up on Hook's new book to get a better understanding of value theory, and noted in the margin of his letter that Marx's son-in-law, Paul Lafargue, was "a colored man." But it was precisely this Marxist postulate that the emancipation of the working classes would eliminate the causes of racism that Du Bois categorically rejected in the second *Crisis* essay, writing acidly that "no [American] Soviet of technocrats would do more than exploit colored labor in order to raise the status of whites." Whatever the validity of the class struggle for Europe during the Industrial Revolution, race trumped class in North America, he asserted. When the class struggle figuratively marched out of Ellis Island, it had invariably taken a detour into racism as "layer after layer" of European ethnics—Irish, German, Italians, Jews, Slavs—scrambled over generations of excluded, exploited Negro men and women in order to "escape into the wealthy class and becom[e] managers and employers of labor."

Because he saw an indissoluble linkage between democracy and racism in America, much as historians of the 1970s and beyond (Edmund Morgan, John Cell, Alexander Saxton, and David Roediger, among others) would see, Du Bois concluded that the hope of a socialist revolution in the United States based on a "united class-conscious proletariat" was a mirage. Instead, he postulated an iron law of whiteness in which citizenship and status have been defined and measured by white yeomanry and succeeding waves of ethnics in terms of their political and socioeconomic elevation above black people. Working-class divisions based on color would endure, Du Bois sadly predicted, until crisis or catastrophe awakened white workers to their true historic destiny. He was on the cusp of proposing here the radical critique of Marxism that he would make seven years later in *Dusk of Dawn*, where he wrote that the philosophy "did not envisage a situation where, instead of a horizontal division of classes, there was a vertical fissure, a complete separation of classes by race, cutting square across the economic layers." It was a split "grounded on centuries of instinct, habit and thought," he would theorize, "and implemented by the conditioned reflex of visible color. This flat and incontrovertible fact, imported Russian Communism ignored, would not discuss." Racism, then, was not for Du Bois the epiphenomenon described by Marx, a fixation existing in the penumbra above and around the reality of class antagonisms. Racism had to be understood as an integral component of the dynamic of class, possessing a life of its own, and equal in the power of its agency to class.

Despite his admiration for the Russian experiment, then, Du Bois continued to dismiss communism as a political solution for the United States and to discount its usefulness to "a minority group like the Negroes." Still smarting from the association's Scottsboro donnybrook, he remained emphatically disdainful of the American Communist Party. Unimpressed by the CPUSA vice-presidential candidacy of black James Ford, Du Bois voted against FDR and for Norman Thomas and the Socialist party in the pivotal 1932 elections. Given the deliberations expended by the Comintern on devising a coherent policy on black Americans and the high priority assigned to their recruitment, it was hardly surprising that Communist party ideologues such as Harry Haywood were distinctly ungrateful for Du Bois's admonitions and, with the editor in mind, warned of the need for "systematic but persistent struggle against the ideology and influence of petty bourgeois nationalists among the Negro toilers."

On Saturday morning, May 13, 1933, Du Bois gave the penultimate address to the Conference on the Economic Status of the Negro, a two-day Washington symposium in the Department of Interior auditorium, sponsored and underwritten by the Rosenwald Fund. With Moton presiding and Eugene Kinckle Jones and Embree seated on the stage, Du Bois peered over rows of serious brown, pink, and black faces in the vast, marbled room as he spoke to the topic "The Next Steps." Without doubt, he anticipated the ensuing ruckus. The Baltimore *Afro-American* exaggerated the message when it headlined, "U.S. WILL COME TO COMMUNISM, DU BOIS TELLS CONFERENCE." Production for private profit was immoral, inefficient, and, ultimately, destined to give way to the collective ownership of the means of production, the editor announced. Communism was still years in the future, nevertheless, and black people could best prepare in the interim for the coming economic order by creating various forms of cooperative and collective economies. *The New York Times* quoted him as saying that since all efforts by Negroes to become an integral part of American civilization had failed—having tried song and laughter "and rare good humor," having given the world "hard, backbreaking labor"—it was now the duty of the race "to give the world an example of intelligent cooperation so that when the new industrial commonwealth comes we can go into it as experienced people and not again be left on the outside as mere beggars." His people had to save themselves in the present chaos, and in doing so they could accelerate the end of the profit economy. A Professor Herman Feldman of Dartmouth College's School of Administration and Finance congratulated Du Bois on his "magnificent address," but little of that enthusiasm found its way to 69 Fifth Avenue.

University and college campuses had always been a venue for significant Du Boisian pronouncements, so much so that his presence was unwelcome at conservative institutions such as Hampton and Wilberforce and a source of administrative nervousness at schools such as Fisk and Howard. Fisk beckoned him again a few weeks after the Washington symposium. Du Bois had been invited to deliver the college alumni address, and he drove to Nashville from Atlanta in a buoyant frame of mind. President and Mrs. Thomas Elsa Jones threw a party the evening following his arrival, with Jim and Grace Johnson and Charles and Marie Johnson, along with select faculty and distinguished locals, paying court to him and to Max Yergan, the commencement speaker of South African fame. Du Bois had come to Fisk again, forty-five years after his graduation, to propound an ethnocentric ideal of service in higher education. In its own way, the oration he would give in Cravath Memorial Chapel was more explosive in its implications than "*Diuturni Silenti*," delivered nine years earlier from the same podium. "The Negro College" was a solemn farewell to a shimmering ideal, a radical revision by Du Bois of a race-relations doctrine upon which institutions such as Fisk, the NAACP, the New Negro Arts Movement, the best of white liberalism and the identity of the Talented Tenth were founded. A valedictory to the exuberant gospel of assimilationist integration, the alumni discourse spoke to epistemological and ethical tensions between the ideal and the real, the abstract and the essential, permanently lodged in the Du Boisian core, that split in black and white whose parts had gone to war in *The Conservation of Races* and then metamorphosed as the enervated "two-ness" of a divided self in *Souls*.

The current generation of Fisk students was the wealthiest yet to attend the elite institution, as it was now selected almost as much by the economies of the Depression as through the screening of the admissions office. Not for them the malaise of the split persona: an American, a Negro. Graduates of Fisk, like those of Morehouse, Howard, and Lincoln, were determined to become simply Negro Americans. These students' sentiments had been voiced recently by the august Abraham Flexner, founding director of Princeton's Institute for Advanced Study and chairman of Howard University's board of trustees, which Du Bois paraphrased. Flexner had said that he was "seeking to build not a Negro university, but a University." Du Bois knew that the alumni audience listening to "The Negro College" that June morning of 1933 fully shared Flexner's credo, his ideal of "a great institution of learning which becomes a center of universal culture." Du Bois's own writings had often enough commended the kingdom of universal truth as not only superior to that of heaven, but as begetting a state of grace in which parochialisms of race faded away. In such a state of grace, racial identity was trumped first by class and then by membership in the human race where impurities and distortions were purified in the flame of knowledge.

"With all goodwill toward them that say such words," admonished Du Bois, he had come to insist "that there can be no college for Negroes which is not a Negro college." An American university, like a German or Swiss university, could aspire to "universal culture unhampered by limitations of race and culture, yet it must start on the earth where we sit and not," Du Bois continued, "in the skies whither we aspire." Boring in on some hard truths "here in

America, in the year 1933," he called for an end to the fiction that the best attack of the Negro problem "[was] by ignoring its most unpleasant features." Du Bois described a current condition of black social ostracism "so deadening and so discouraging that we are compelled either to lie about it or to turn our faces to the red flag of revolution." The education of his people was becoming yearly not only racially more segregated but substandard by design. The chimera of universality obscured a primordial educational reality from black people, he insisted. The Spanish university was "founded and grounded in Spain, just as surely as the French university is French." And what was the focus and function of these great institutions? "A French university . . . uses the French language and assumes a knowledge of French history. The present problems of the French people are its major problems and it becomes universal only in so far as other peoples of the world comprehend and are at one with France and its mighty and beautiful history." The same syllogism applied to African-American higher education. "A Negro university in the United States begins with Negroes," he postulated in an era where few if any of them offered a course in black history. "It uses that variety of the English idiom which they understand; and above all, it is founded . . . on a knowledge of the history of their people in Africa and in the United States, and their present condition." At their most pernicious, illusions about knowledge and race could and occasionally did have pathetic consequences for impressionable black minds. In an astonishing display of disesteem at Lincoln University—the "black Princeton"—students in the class of '29, Thurgood Marshall's class, had voted overwhelmingly against the hiring of African American professors in a poll administered by the sociology department. Langston Hughes, then in his third year at the school, had been as appalled as Du Bois, who roared against this act of "racial masochism as the most astonishing blow which the higher education of Negroes has received for many a year."

Although Du Bois denied that he meant to abjure "older ideals" of university education and that he was mainly shifting emphases and largely propounding "some change of thought and modification of method," his Fisk address was truly remarkable for its anticipation and commendation of the Afrocentric and diasporic agendas that were to contend for pride of place half a century later in America. As he had stressed in "Education and Work," his commencement address at Howard University three years earlier, the primacy of technical education versus liberal arts was an exhausted debate. The essential was no longer the form of instruction, but the degree to which it was informed by and promoted racial authenticity—the frankness with which both liberal and technical education acknowledged the real-world particularity of the black experience in America. "In no other way can the American Negro college function," he underscored. "It cannot begin with history and lead to Negro history. It cannot start with sociology and lead to Negro sociology." The fragility of the arts-and-letters movement of the twenties was a perfect illustration of this contention, he added. Why had it "never taken real and lasting root?" Because it was an exotic transplant, Du Bois answered, explicitly rejecting the Lockian premise of the Harlem Renaissance. "It was literature written for the benefit of white people and at the behest of white readers, and starting out privately from the white point of view." "The Negro College" ended, as Du Bois's pivotal declarations typically did, at the gates of Armageddon, "on the threshold of a new era." Imperatives followed admonitions:

> Unless the American Negro today, led by trained university men of broad vision, sits down to work out by economics and mathematics, by physics and chemistry, by history and sociology, exactly how and where he is to learn a living and how he is to establish a reasonable Life in the United States or elsewhere—unless this is done, the university has missed its field and function and the American Negro is doomed to be a suppressed and inferior caste in the United States for incalculable time.

As usual, in reconceptualizing higher education in the life of the race, Du Bois served as the point man for a paradigm whose influence would grow powerfully in the distant future. Nor was he alone in advancing university training anchored to the cultural and economic needs of the African in America. He had been preceeded at Fisk by Woodson, whose 1931 commencement address (published in the August *Crisis* and expanded two years later into *The Mis-Education of the Negro*) was a remorseless critique of the elitism and Eurocentrism he deemed much too prevalent in the colleges and universities. Du Bois's "The Negro College" was simply the most eloquent and intellectually nuanced formulation of an evolving reassessment of racial objectives.

MEANWHILE, MEDICAL BULLETINS from the *Crisis* staff had grown more alarming during the spring semester at Atlanta. In late March, the faithful Branch reported that receipts were "pulling up little by little." A few days later, Branch's guarded optimism was punctured. "Yesterday, we had a financial feast. Today, a famine is on," she sighed as she reported a mere $8.45 as the tally for March 30, 1933. Du Bois knew that the lifeblood was ebbing from his beloved creation, an eventuality he had shared with Nina a few weeks earlier. *The Crisis* limped along only because the Atlanta University stipend enabled the NAACP to apply a portion of his unpaid salary to the magazine. His life insurance (heavily borrowed against) had been wiped out by the collapse of the two insurance companies. If Hope invited him to stay on permanently (as he assumed

Hope would), he told Nina it might be "wiser . . . to accept regularly [sic] work at least part of the year at Atlanta University, hereafter."

Nina's seismic news that Joel Spingarn had resigned in mid-March as president of the association and chairman of the board only bolstered Will's decision to arrange a chacteristically memorable exit. He was simply stunned by Spingarn's resignation, as nothing had been said about it during their "long and frank talk" in New York. "What on earth is this I hear through Mrs. Du Bois?" he now demanded to know. Although he and Spingarn had privately discussed the possibility four months earlier of the latter's leaving the presidency in favor of a colored successor, Du Bois had counseled against doing so on the persuasive grounds that "a time of stress, retrenchment, and criticism [was] not the time to make a change."

He was relieved when Spingarn wrote by return mail that, contrary to some reports, he had only left the presidency but hadn't resigned from the NAACP nor had he surrendered chairmanship of the board. Du Bois was promised a full briefing when he came to New York in a few weeks. In the meantime, Du Bois almost certainly learned the substance of two long, confidential letters in which the president stated his innermost feelings in a mournful explanation to the equally surprised Johnson and Ovington. Spingarn declared that he no longer approved of the spirit motivating the association:

> and I do not feel like allowing my name to be used to represent that spirit. If I were a lawyer like my brother, I should find some difficult and inter esting question involved in every one of our successive "cases," and I should hardly miss the cement of a programme. But as it is, I am not interested in a succession of cases. When I joined the Association we had what was a thrilling programme, revolutionary for its time, and one that gave us a little hope of solving the whole problem. Now we have only cases, no programme, and no hope. Every effort I have made to try to put this hope into our work by framing a programme has been ignored or thwarted by the Secretary or by the Board.

By coincidence, Du Bois's preliminary list of sixty-eight participants for Amenia had arrived at 69 Fifth Avenue at the very moment Spingarn announced his departure from the presidency. Neither the secretary nor his assistant had shown an interest in discussing these materials until the resignation backlash brought them to confer sheepishly with Joel Spingarn in his brother's law office on the afternoon of April 7. The mass of biographical data worked up by Du Bois in his capacity as chairman of the organizing committee seems to have overwhelmed White and Wilkins and given "new enthusiasm about the conference," a delighted Spingarn reported to Atlanta. "Both White and Wilkins were simply amazed at the mass of names so quickly assembled." The names Du Bois proposed were the flower of Negro leadership. To visualize many of them fatally injured in a train accident was to imagine the decapitation of a race. As he and Wilkins comprised the three-person organizing committee chaired by Du Bois, White now made a convincing show of busy cooperation, and a whirr of preparations for the conference filled association headquarters. As conference host, it was Spingarn's privilege to decide the final number of participants. He settled on thirty-two, but left the selection of names to Du Bois. Forwarding the thirty-two names by return mail, Du Bois suggested that Spingarn could drop Wilkins from the list "without the slightest hurt to intelligent discussion."

The correspondence for this transitional period strongly suggests that Du Bois had decided to leave the NAACP soon after taking up the guest appointment at Atlanta University. The opportunity to resume his Atlanta professorship exercised a powerful appeal, but Du Bois's decision had not yet been set in concrete for the good reason that Hope was temporarily barred from converting the visiting professorship into a permanent position. Until the directors of the General Education Board approved, two of whom, Trevor Arnett and Dean Sage, were trustees of Atlanta University, the appointment languished. Arnett, president of the GEB and chairman of the Atlanta University trustee board, had suggested to Sage during one of their frequent informal discussions a month or so after Du Bois arrived on campus, "It might be well to consider an appointment for a special period, say for a year, so that it might be seen how the matter progressed before [making] a definite commitment." Tenure for Du Bois hung in the balance of good behavior, then, even as his skepticism about crafting an effective role for the NAACP deepened. Pending the outcome of the Atlanta position, he decided to spend the second weekend in April in New York conferring with Joel Spingarn on a plan for the reorganization of the NAACP.

It was a period of high-stakes options during which the editor allowed himself to think that the civil rights organization could be overhauled almost with the stroke of a pen. Distressed to learn that business worries forced New Haven attorney Crawford, one of his closest and ablest friends, to resign from the board, Du Bois begged him to delay. "Before you take final action, wait until you see the plan," he wrote. "An Appeal to the Loyal Friends of the NAACP," the plan circulated by Du Bois in late April 1933, lived up to its billing. "Tinkering with our present organization" was pointless, Du Bois insisted. If the NAACP was to do more than "simply to survive," if it was to perform during the next quarter century "as effectively as it has in the last," then a new start from a blank page was imperative. The radical plan was unusually complicated: all salaried officers of the association were to resign in two cycles (July 1 and December 31, 1933), with himself, White, Wilkins, and the field secretaries placed on half salary and spared until the second cycle; the annual June conference, slated to meet in

Chicago, was to be postponed until December 1933; review of policies and drafting of recommendations would take place in August at the Amenia Conference; a three-day plenary board meeting in September would finalize the association's new structure, reexamine the constitution, adopt the budget, and elect new officers and staff along with a new editor for *The Crisis*. White, Wilkins, and Pickens, being immediately relieved of all organizational duties, were expected to "use the time in securing other employment" before the December resignation deadline. However complicated the particulars, the plan's real objective was instantly clear—an association purged of Walter White and Roy Wilkins.

The editor may not have been terribly surprised when Joel Spingarn wrote that he and Arthur found the reorganization plan "neither feasible nor advisable," a verdict fully shared by Harry Davis. The brothers agreed that the association's present course led to a dead end, but as the most prominent white custodians of the civil rights organization they recoiled from the stark choices imposed by a scheme they feared was too radical to "enlist the support of the colored people of the country." Crawford understandably objected that the rationale for destroying the present structure would elude the membership and the nation at large, and Wright was adamant that the association needed the services of both the editor and the secretary. Du Bois felt compelled to throw in the towel. In mid-May he told Lillian Alexander, the plan's sole booster, that he intended to do nothing further for the remainder of the year. Plainly, Du Bois was adrift, his base of support within the association indecisive and dwindling. The note of resignation in a letter to Davis DuBois was uncharacteristic. "None of us can plan for next year, for the Lord knows what it's going to bring about. Possibly, we can all get a job with President Roosevelt's reforestation gang," he joked weakly. A mixup in train schedules had denied him the pleasure of her company in New York after the Washington conference on Negro economics. Davis DuBois had gone off alone to join the crowd protesting the decision to obliterate the Diego Rivera murals at Rockefeller Center. Still, however frustrating and disheartening the times were, Du Bois sustained a remarkable level of productivity. The final draft of his book on the Reconstruction period was only months away. He leapt at an invitation from the editor of *Foreign Affairs* to write a blistering account, appearing in July, of the collusion of the State Department and the Firestone Corporation in Liberia.

Leaving the front office to wrestle with Chicago convention arrangements as well as Amenia Conference logistics, the editor returned to Atlanta and focused again on the long-simmering issue of finding a business manager for the magazine. As part of the early January compromise lifting Du Bois's resignation threat, the association had made a commitment to hire someone who could perform the dual role ("under the general direction of the editor") of business manager and managing editor, a position that was to be coequal with that of Wilkins. The candidate Du Bois had in mind was George Streator, whose excellent credentials impelled Joel Spingarn to ask whether he wasn't "too smart and literary to be business manager?" The Fisk undergraduate who had played an invaluable role in overthrowing President McKenzie was now thirty-one, equipped with a master's degree from Western Reserve University, and a popular if restive teacher of mathematics and physics at Bennett College, an exclusive black women's institution in Greensboro, North Carolina. Du Bois's appreciation of this self-assured southerner had grown stronger in the seven years since they had conspired together to liberate Fisk. Tall, heavyset, the intellectually aggressive Streator was as devoted to Du Bois as he was capable of dissent whenever issues of political principle came between them. He would also reveal a proneness for divining dark conspiracies and a capacity for personalizing honest dissent that would soon tire a remarkably patient Du Bois; but these were traits not in evidence in the spring of 1933.

Sounding more like Du Bois than even Du Bois had lately, Streator prescribed "a bit of daring, a change of tactics, less emphasis on what ought to be, and more on what is" to get sales up. If they made the magazine the "organ of the Negro masses," he was sure that the masses would buy it, "even if they did not read it." Streator's enthusiasm was infectious. Yet even as Du Bois proposed his protégé to the board at the end of May, *The Crisis* was so close to being terminal that he began to contemplate administering last rites. He was going to make a "rather desperate effort to finish this year," he confided to Ovington; prospects for 1934 verged on the "impossible," however. Signals from the board along with reports from Branch and Burton reinforced the editor's pessimism. Promising no better than a three-month trial arrangement with a monthly salary of one hundred dollars, then, Du Bois warned Streator that *The Crisis* would either "stop publication or get another editor, or change in form" if the NAACP fell short of a promised seven-thousand-dollar subsidy. In marked contrast to Wilkins, Streator brushed salary aside as secondary ("I am willing to sacrifice"). His enthusiasm decided the issue for Du Bois. The new business manager/ managing editor would finally take up his post at the beginning of September 1933.

ALTHOUGH JOEL SPINGARN'S invitation to Du Bois to put their friendship on a first-name basis had never taken, cooperation between these two imperious, principled intellectuals attained a new level of cordiality as they planned and presided over the second Amenia Conference, held in August 1933. The conference was a high-stakes ploy to infuse new life into the NAACP by bringing together the best and brightest of the Talented Tenth for four days of sharply focused review and revision of the national civil rights agenda. The premise was one that held that it was still possible in the third decade of the twentieth century to convene the small and relatively homogeneous Negro leadership class in executive session in order to inaugurate broad-gauge policies for the entire race. If the model for the gathering was avowedly elitist and even a touch paternalistic, Amenia's objectives were intended to be socially progressive at the least and even economically radical, if Du Bois had his way. He would bring to Amenia his characteristic worldview in which absolutes declared war on half measures. Nonsense was no longer an affordable luxury. "It was just as nonsensical for us to assume that the program which we had espoused in 1910 was going to work in 1950. We had got to prepare ourselves for a reorganization of society especially and fundamentally in industry," he intoned.

Du Bois would claim after the fact that one of his regrets was the sharp skew to younger professionals at the conference. "Outside of four of the Elder Statesmen, the median age was thirty," he recalled—"persons just out of college; their life work begun but not settled." Yet the decision to corral the cadets of the Talented Tenth had been as much Du Bois's as Spingarn's or White's, and probably more so. He was counting on the irreverence for tradition and readiness for experimentation of younger men and women in order to lift the NAACP out of its rut. Locke, Eugene Jones, and Channing Tobias—all of them born in the 1880s—were passed over as too senior to blend well with the youthful majority. If elder statespersons were limited by quota (Du Bois, James Weldon Johnson, Spingarn, and Pickens), another leadership group was equally restricted. Despite their authority in the community, the small number of invitations sent to ministers of the gospel guaranteed, as Du Bois much preferred, that they would be conspicuously underrepresented at Amenia. No response came from the new dean of the Howard University Chapel, Howard Thurman, a theological prodigy whose gospel of the "common ground" was to inspire over time A. Philip Randolph, Mary Bethune, and Martin Luther King, Jr. Benjamin Mays, another Howard professor whose religious scholarship and radiating influence as future president of Morehouse College would match Thurman's, pleaded the demands in connection with *The Negro's Church*, his bedrock survey published that year. The colorful, twenty-five-year-old assistant pastor of Harlem's Abyssinian Baptist Church, Adam Clayton Powell, somehow failed to survive the final invitational cut. There were other surprising or significant omissions and absences. John P. Davis, the Bates College graduate who had ably managed *The Crisis* during Du Bois's 1926 absence in Russia, appears not to have been proposed, possibly because of Davis's frenetic efforts at that time to protest the New Deal's racial indifference by organizing his Joint Committee on National Recovery. As for Cullen and Schuyler, Du Bois may have regarded his former son-in-law's attendance as problematic and that of the caustic Schuyler, a friend of White and Wilkins, as quite dispensable. Hughes sent regrets from California. He had recently returned to the United States by way of Japan after a weird sojourn in the Soviet Union. A wealthy San Francisco patron loaned the poet a beach house in Carmel in which to rest and write. The lawyer and future judge William Hastie had hoped to attend until the last week before the conference, as had Logan, who wrote that his doctor's orders to rest would now prevent it.

Accommodated in four army cots each to ten tents, the attendees began to arrive at the Spingarn estate on the morning of August 18, a rainy, unseasonably cool Friday. The conferees were uniformly exceptional. "All except one were college graduates," Du Bois's summary press report stated. "A number had advanced degrees and three had degrees of doctors of philosophy." Several (such as Frazier, described to Spingarn by Du Bois as the race's "best expert on social studies") were already acknowledged paragons. Sterling Brown would come to Troutbeck at the last moment, after several weeks of hesitation due, probably, to finances. Bunche, Harris, Charlie Houston, and Ira Reid gave firm commitments from the outset. "Thelma Taylor, Juanita Jackson, Hazel Brown, Bunch[e], Houston, Sterling Brown, Ab[e] Harris . . . worth crossing a continent to know," YWCA staffer Frances Williams would gush afterward in a summing-up letter to White. Bunche, Harris, Brown, and Houston, radicals on the Howard University faculty, were attempting to shift the Negro intelligentsia's focus on race to an analysis of the economics of class. Frazier, still at Fisk, would leave for Howard in the fall of 1934 and sign on immediately with the Young Turks, or what he called the "thinkers and drinkers" faculty group. The consistency and duration of the Young Turks' Marxism varied greatly, but they were unanimously critical of what they saw as the incorrigible, petit-bourgeois parochialisms of the black leadership class, the Horatio Alger creed of collective betterment, on the one hand, and the prescriptions for separatist nostrums, on the other. By education, lifestyles, and, in several cases, second-generation affluence, they fit the mold of Talented Tenth exemplars. Yet these same advantages tended to alienate them from the narrow class-consciousness they believed afflicted too many of their seniors. Charlie Houston's position as vice-dean of Howard's law school and imminent appointment as the NAACP's first salaried special counsel tended to muffle any public expressions of disaffection, but the reforming law dean would become a loyal dissenter within White's regime of bureaucratic legalism. Like Charlie Houston, Los Angeles–born Ralph Bunche possessed the athletic good looks on which a Talented Tenth *Crisis* cover could have been modeled. His economic analysis of the race problem had impressed Du Bois two years earlier when the editor participated in an institute on "Political Status and Condition of the Negro Race" sponsored by Bunche's political science department. In the years following Amenia, Bunche's growing antipathy for "race leaders" was to find devastating expression in "The Programs, Ideologies, Tactics and Achievements of Negro Betterment Interracial Organizations," an essay lodged in the footnotes of Myrdal's *An American Dilemma*. Bunche's controversial 1940 essay would boil over from the same distress he brought to Amenia—"that in the thinking of the Negro elite there is a tremendous gap between it and the black mass." Frazier's Marxist inclinations were less robust than the Jacobin prejudices he would pour into *The Black Bourgeoisie*, a book that incarnated the Negro elite in exquisite and perdurable caricature. Writing to a friend a year before Amenia II, Frazier had complained that "all shades of articulate Negro thought are conservative," a judgment Du Bois and Bunche would have applauded. Thirty-two-year-old Sterling Brown came to Amenia in the wake of a brilliant literary success, *Southern Road*, his first volume of poetry having achieved a folk authenticity realized by no other Renaissance poet except Hughes. Brown's Marxism, such as it was, was the most casual of the Howard group, but the success of his poetry in bridging the gap between the creative artist and common black people was a form of radical political statement in itself. With Harris and Bunche alternately assuming the role of maestro, these Young Turks performed the role of an exhorting chorus at Amenia.

In accordance with Du Bois and Spingarn's plan for the four-day event, the participants ranged the grounds of Troutbeck estate in spirited discussion, aggregated in small, freewheeling talking groups, and met at scripted intervals for plenary deliberations under a tent large enough for an audience of seventy-five. To promote the freest exchange between them, "the deliberations were voted as a private matter," noted Du Bois. He insisted that the organizers took great care that "no attempt was made to lay down a concrete program" to be implemented by any organization or group. Their goals were open discussions with optional consideration of any and all questions pertinent to race relations and the national economy. Beyond a summary narrative, therefore, no record was made of the discussions at Amenia II. In keeping with the spirit of egalitarian candor, Du Bois and elder statesmen Spingarn, Johnson, and Pickens maintained a low profile of avuncular accessibility. Distinguished whites from the neighborhood motored over to observe, mingle, and, in several instances, to sit in on sessions inconspicuously. Spingarn's friend and neighbor, U.S. Treasury Secretary Henry Morgenthau, Jr., visited on the last day of the conference and promptly fell into deep conversation with Du Bois. Ovington came for a day from her summer home in Great Barrington. The camera caught her in the group standing between Pickens and Johnson, a Progressive relic with white hair accentuated against a smiling dark background. Johnson stood beside her, fedora at the jaunty angle befitting "Gentleman Jim." He was increasingly unpopular with some of the young militants, who thought him too conservative and schmoozy in the company of powerful whites. A popular libel claimed that

Johnson could whisper in a white man's ear so quietly that not even Johnson himself could hear what he was saying. A latecomer from Wilmington, Delaware, attorney Louis Redding, sensed an aura of "deep momentousness" pervading the first plenary session. Conferees swarmed from the large tent as from a hive, forming clusters buzzing with debate well into the night.

Saturday morning belonged to the radicals, Redding observed, and "rather insistent were the pronouncements . . . of the imminence of basic change in the political, economic, and social structure of our country." If none of them is reported as actually having said that the problem of the twentieth century was not the color line but the class line, that was the unmistakable import of the Young Turks' argument: end economic exploitation through the power of organized labor and state planning and the race problem would fade away. But White and Wilkins came to Troutbeck from the Chicago convention determined to hold the line against far-reaching departures from the association's economic and political programs. For his part, elder statesman Du Bois looked on indulgently as Harris and Bunche appealed for a broad coalition with labor as part of a plan to bring about a social democratic revolution in the United States. The bespectacled, moon-faced Harris wore his scholarly activism with little of Bunche's gregarious charm. Harris possessed the considerable distinction, however, of having authored a classic at age thirty-two — the indispensable *The Black Worker: The Negro and the Labor Movement.* Du Bois's fondness for Harris in no way softened a conviction that the primacy given by Harris and others to class solutions was symptomatic of a dangerous myopia that discounted the institutional utility of racism. "Most of the younger trained college group were convinced that the economic pattern of any civilization determined its development along all cultural lines," he sighed.

Vigorous objections to the position advanced by Bunche and Harris at the conference materialized before long from a cluster of opinions forming, somewhat surprisingly, around Frazier that attempted to fuse socialism with racial solidarity. It seems inferentially apparent that Du Bois spoke through Frazier as much as Frazier spoke for himself at Amenia when the sociologist commended a course of action that combined nationalism and socialism. In any case, writing in *Dusk of Dawn* of his disappointment in the conference, Du Bois spoke of having held designs strikingly similar to Frazier's. "I had hoped for such insistence upon the compelling importance of the economic factor," he remembered, "that this would lead to a project for a planned program for using the racial segregation, which was at present inevitable, in order that the laboring masses might be able to have built beneath them a strong foundation for self-support and social uplift." Wenonah Bond and Delaware attorney Redding recorded a growing recoil from the economic radicalism of the opening session. It seemed obvious to Louis Redding, though, that the class of people attending the conference had "so subtly become infused with middle-class American 'success philosophy'" as to have trouble remembering the great mass of "poor, ignorant, uncounseled and exploited" black people.

Given Amenia's sylvan setting, good food, recreational diversions, and plenitude of credentials, perhaps it was understandable that the plight of the masses remained an abstraction for some of the conferees. After all, as Bond chirped, "it was a grand crowd—nice people with whom to swim and row and walk and play baseball, and exchange jokes; people who do successful jobs, yet have time to follow hobbies and avocations with enthusiasm." The dominant point of view held that capitalism was down but definitely not out, and that the value of Amenia was to offer pragmatic recommendations to ensure that the best and brightest Negroes rode out the Depression. Du Bois noted wryly Spingarn's frosty reaction to a clumsy attempt at Communist humor when one of the less-polished Young Turks was invited to the mansion with the other conferees. Du Bois called the young radical "Jones." "Jones stood in the parlor and grinned; and said aloud to the visitors: 'Comes the revolution and Commissar Jones will live here!' Spingarn did not appreciate the joke." Edward Spingarn, who remembers trailing along with his mother as she took moving pictures of the proceedings with an electric camera, believed his father was deeply concerned about the Communist tendencies of the younger intellectuals. "My father felt that this was a tragic mistake," he claimed.

To many, if not the majority of those who attended, the consensus for change that emerged from Amenia II—despite the incompatibilities and ambiguities—was exciting in its promise of ongoing momentum. "Four threads of thought entered into our conference," Du Bois recounted. First came recommitment to the fight against all forms of racial segregation and color discrimination. The second thread was the thin but strong one of Marxism and economic determinism. The third thread coiled around the entire group. According to Du Bois, no one dissented from the criticism that "we had been thinking of the exceptional folk, the Talented Tenth, the well-to-do; that we must now turn our attention toward the welfare and social uplift of the masses." Out of the seeming catharsis of the Sunday-night session filled with disquisitions and applause, then, came the selection of what Du Bois described as "a continuation committee," temporarily chaired by Houston and composed of Bunche, Frazier, Harris, Reid, Wilkins, and one woman, Mabel Byrd, an economist whose diligence in investigating discrimination under the NRA codes would earn notice in the black community. This was the committee, to be formally established a year later as the Committee on the Future Plan and Program, that the aggressive Harris would attempt to transform into an engine for the reinvention of the NAACP and redefinition of the civil rights struggle. If a transformation of the association was possible, Du Bois must have hoped that the brilliant economist might have a chance to achieve what Sisyphus, confounded by no less a task, had failed to accomplish. The editor revealed his cautious optimism about democratizing the association to Spingarn immediately, writing that "the results may not seem to be tremendous, yet it may well be that they will prove as epoch-making as the first Amenia Conference." Probably, though, Du Bois was already as disappointed as his verdict in *Dusk of Dawn* disclosed much later. "The end of it all was inconclusive resolutions and no agreement," he would write.

The editor had now all but decided not to return to the NAACP. Two weeks before the Amenia Conference, his ambiguous situation at Atlanta University had been resolved when he and Hope agreed over dinner in Manhattan on terms for a permanent appointment. What doubts remained about his decision can only have been strengthened the following day, August 4, when White pleaded that pressing legal bills made it impossible to honor a commitment to the magazine of several hundred dollars. In early September, Du Bois forwarded a dire memorandum to the board declaring his intention to resign "not later than January 1, 1934," unless the association guaranteed the seven-thousand-dollar subvention for the year. A second memorandum at the end of the month informed the directors of the Crisis Publishing Company not only that he was off to Atlanta immediately (returning, possibly, in November "and certainly in December") and that George Streator would run the magazine as business manager, but also that Lulu Burton and Daisy Wilson, Du Bois's secretary, were leaving with him. Hope and Florence Read approved the transfer of Wilson's salary to Atlanta University's budget and a scholarship award to the graduate school for Burton, an arrangement permitting the editor to apply these salary savings to the new business manager.

Will's plans for Nina, however, were not to her liking. Shouldn't she come to Atlanta, "at any rate for the coming year, or at least part of it"? she almost beseeched. Even though her willingness to be with him in the city of Burghardt's death was a touching proof of Nina's long-suffering desire to share in his life, her husband strongly recommended against it. Things were not definitely settled about the AU appointment, he wrote her in late May, but even were he to return the following year he saw almost insurmountable complications about being together. On the other hand, he recognized that Nina's responsibility for Yolande and their granddaughter must take its toll. More space in quieter surroundings away from the deteriorating Dunbar Apartments would be best, he thought. She might look around "somewhere," he suggested, "either in Harlem or the Bronx, or Brooklyn . . . [for] an apartment that would be suitable and near the ground with a yard." Of the four possibilities Will listed for Nina, including "a year in France with Miss Prophet," the fourth—living together in Atlanta—was least viable. His quarters next year in the new faculty dormitory would be spacious enough for the two of them, but children would not be allowed. "It would not be possible to get accommodations for Yolande and the baby. I'm afraid it would be practically impossible," Will repeated. The letter moved away from domestic complications that would resolve themselves in time to tell Nina of the recent drive to Fisk and the nervous white president's reception for him. "My love to the whole family."

Prospects for a permanent niche at AU were enhanced after a summer of teaching there. The editor informed the association of his definite intentions in late fall of 1933. Presented with a fait accompli, the board ratified a year's leave of absence for Du Bois at the reduced pay of $1,200, on November 3, "with no duties except the writing of such editorials and articles as he may wish to contribute to *The Crisis*." Streator, assisted by Wilkins, was to run the magazine on a six-month trial basis, after which time the board would decide the publication's fate. The solution allowed the editor to retain the best options. Through Streator, he would be able to maintain control of his creation as long as it remained viable; thanks to Hope, he would now be able to return to academic life at little or no cost to his level of income or his social life.

MEANWHILE, THE MOMENTUM from Amenia continued to run for several months. An astonishing hypothetical was disclosed within days after the conference adjourned. Henry Morgenthau's interest in the proceedings at Troutbeck had been motivated by more than general curiosity, Spingarn revealed to Du Bois. The U.S. secretary of the treasury was searching for a "Negro advisor," someone who knew the race problem "from the ground up." Spingarn continued with uncustomary excitement. "It seems (and I am telling you this in strict confidence) that he has found his ideal advisor in—YOU." Was it conceivable— Du Bois in service to the New Deal as special assistant on Negro Affairs to a cabinet officer? Spingarn became almost dizzy from the implications of his great, good friend offering uniquely informed advice and designing substantive federal relief policies. But, on second thought, "wouldn't your appointment frighten the South," he wondered, and even risk the plan being scuttled altogether than if a "more neutral name" were proposed? Still, on balance, Spingarn thought Du Bois should accept the risk, although he wondered "if FDR would dare to appoint you." However pleased by the unsolicited esteem, Du Bois would have known that Morgenthau's was a momentary enthusiasm doomed to expire in the first hours of the secretary's return to Washington. A gentleman farmer and Hyde Park neighbor of FDR's, Morgenthau was a thin-skinned public servant whose lack of humor was exceeded only by his ignorance of race relations. Meeting Du Bois had been a revelation, an exhilarating encounter that flattered the treasury secretary's considerable intellectual vanity and affirmed a tradition of Jewish uplift. With a bow to Spingarn's second thought, therefore, the editor recommended that Morgenthau choose the principal of Fort Valley High and Industrial School, sixty-seven-year-old Henry Alexander Hunt, a quiet, capable educator whose southwest Georgia institution maintained solid academic standards without unduly offending the local whites. Expressing his appreciation for Du Bois's "confidence and interest," Hunt, whose qualities of perseverance and prudent courage had won the 1926 Spingarn Medal, accepted the position of assistant to the governor of the treasury department's Farm Credit Administration (FCA).

That Du Bois would have been badly miscast in the role of a token New Deal bureaucrat (the first of the derided "Porkbarrelensis Africanus") seems patently obvious from the vantage of hindsight. In the months immediately prior to the Amenia Conference, Du Bois had concluded that his people would have to look out for themselves while the federal government repaired and restructured the broken national economy for the benefit of white Americans. Few students of politics possessed his detailed grasp of the intractable power of the southern oligarchy, its chokehold through the congressional seniority system on New Deal legislation. As they watched act one from offstage, the editor and the black leadership class saw their people all but excluded from playing parts in the alphabetized drama of recovery. The Agricultural Adjustment Administration (AAA) sent millions of dollars south to all-white county committees to pay for farmland retired from cultivation in order to reverse the free fall in prices due to overproduction. A study conducted by the CIC's Woofter would soon tally the dismal consequences of AAA subsidy checks that never reached a sizable percentage of black farm owners, black sharecroppers, or black field hands, leaving those who stayed with the land eking out mean annual earnings of $295 and $175 for sharecroppers and field hands, respectively, as compared to $417 and $232 for whites. The Civilian Conservation Corps (CCC), whose military-style encampments eventually housed three million men earning $30 a month for roadbuilding, irrigation, and reforestation projects, would remain 95 percent white in the first two years of operation. The Federal Relief Administration (FERA) reserved relief overwhelmingly for whites. The Tennessee Valley Authority (TVA), a lacework of dams and hydroelectric generating stations across seven southern states, was as white in its massive labor force as a Southern Baptist congregation, with less than 1 percent of its workers recruited among blacks.

Even as the young professionals had debated the future of the race with their elders at Amenia, fateful hearings were under way in Washington to set up "blanket" codes under the National Recovery Administration (NRA) to regulate production, prices, wages, hours, and collective bargaining for the major sectors of the national economy. NRA stood for "Negroes Ruined Again," the frantically resourceful John Davis charged, as he and Robert Weaver puffed themselves up that September into an ambitious paper entity they called the Joint Committee on Negro Recovery (JCNR). The Quixotic duo of Davis and Harvard-trained economist Weaver begged, borrowed, and liberated sensitive federal documents and brazened themselves into hearings where they protested the Labor Advisory Board's plan to exclude predominantly black occupations of waiters, bellhops, porters, barbers, and domestics from the NRA codes. Exclusion from federal relief was only half the story, however. Skilled and semiskilled occupations covered by the codes varied by region and race, with southern pay scales generally lower than northern, and minimum wages for black people in the South still lower. Yet if Negro leaders were to demand parity under the codes, the consequences would be terrible. To insist upon equal wages would inevitably lead to the mass displacement of blacks by whites, NRA officials gravely informed Mordecai Johnson, John Hope, Eugene Jones, T. Arnold Hill, William Hastie, and fifteen others when they assembled in a blue-ribbon gathering in mid-December. The occasion was a meeting in Howard University's Carnegie Library, requested by U.S. Commissioner of Labor Statistics Isadore Lubin, special adviser on "Negro economic status" Clark Foreman (about whom, more later), Labor Board member Rose Schneiderman, and twenty-seven white NRA administrators to ratify the separate and unequal wages policy. The meeting's awkward silence was dramatically broken by Davis, arriving fifteen minutes late, who proceeded to read the verbatim transcript of the Industrial Recovery Board's September meeting. Peppered with supercilious, demeaning remarks (made by several present at Carnegie Library) about "clamorous Negroes" and nuisance demands by people only wanting "to be appointed to something or other," the government transcript had the impact of a tear gas cannister. The Howard meeting ended too hurriedly even to be adjourned. Davis's single-handed exposure of the NRA's two-tier wage scales ricocheted off the marble hallways in Federal Triangle buildings and brought a pile of newspaper distress to the hospital room where Secretary of the Interior Harold Ickes was recovering from a broken rib.

Making no mention of Davis's JCNR, Du Bois lashed out with similar fury in *The Crisis* against the NRA's bias toward the large employers and the racially exclusive AFL, predicting that, whether the New Deal's corporatist experiment ended in socialism or fascism, his people would continue to comprise the great bulk of the American social and economic mudsill. Sympathetic signals emanating from the Department of the Interior, headed by former Chicago NAACP chapter president Ickes, or those from the Department of Labor, presided over by social reformer Frances Perkins, the first woman appointed to cabinet rank, Du Bois tended to dismiss as chimerical. Instead, they disillusioned him all the more as the kind of white-liberal goodwill that made its victims complicit in their own oppression. When Ickes persuaded FDR to agree to the appointment of a special assistant on the economic status of Negroes (a scheme proposed by Embree and Will Alexander and privately financed by the Rosenwald Fund), Du Bois exploded. The new special assistant was Clark Foreman, white, wealthy, and, by the race-relations standards of his native Georgia, a charming liberal. *The Crisis* for October 1933 roared that it was an outrage "that we again, through the efforts of some of our best friends, should be compelled to have our wants and aspirations interpreted by one who does not know them."

The democratic rhetoric with which Interior Secretary Harold Ickes, urban reformer and a past president of the Chicago NAACP, launched the Works Progress Administration (WPA)—"no discrimination exercised against any person because of color or religious affiliation"—rang hollow in Du Bois's ears. He knew in a general way of NAACP files brimming with case histories of acts of piteous discrimination against qualified applicants for federal assistance. One in particular, an anguished victim's letter to Charles Houston, was emblematic of the unfair workings of the color-coded safety net being woven by the New Deal. Nelson H. Nichols, Jr., a young Washington, D.C., attorney, had been a volunteer in the government's campaign to explain the National Recovery Act (NRA). Called for an interview at the Department of Commerce for a legal position with NRA, Nichols waited three hours until no other candidates remained and even the clerk had left. "I'll just cut the Gordian knot with you and be frank," said the annoyed assistant director of personnel, unable to leave his office without passing Nichols. "Your qualifications are good and all in order," but no one had suspected that the young attorney was black and the NRA office positions were exclusively for white people. Within days, Nichols received a letter from the NRA administrator, General Hugh S. Johnson, thanking him for his "fine services" as a volunteer but pleading the unassailable wisdom of racial segregation: "You know as well as I do that there are some situations in which the races can be mixed and some where they can't." Nichols's NAACP file closed on a bitter note that Du Bois himself had sounded a thousand times: "No nation can prosper which improperly denies recognition of the elementary civil rights of citizenship to the humblest of its loyal citizens who have labored to support it." Whether or not Nelson Nichols faced the prospect of selling apples and pencils in the vicinity of Union Station, Du Bois saw the hardship fate of the mass of African Americans as a condition that could be attenuated only by the embrace of a new racial philosophy.

Yet, even as his magazine thundered against what it saw as fecklessness and tokenism, much of the black press began to cheer the formation of the "Black Cabinet" (or "Kitchen Cabinet"). Fort Valley's Hunt at FCA was joined before the end of the year by self-reliant Vann as special adviser in the Justice Department along with Hastie and Weaver as assistant solicitor and special assistant, respectively, at Interior, to be followed by Harris and Mabel Byrd on special assignment with the NRA and Eugene Jones at Commerce. The editor persisted in seeing little or nothing by which to be encouraged. "American Negroes will be beaten into submission and degradation if they merely wait unorganized to find some place voluntarily given them in the new reconstruction of the economic world," he warned as too many influential Negroes mistook two dozen federal appointments for political leverage. Talented Tenth hopefulness would turn into euphoria after a jaunty White escorted seven leaders into the White House on January 26 for four hours of what amounted to nothing less than a warm and soulful race relations symposium for the instruction of Eleanor Roosevelt. Knowing less about Negroes than Eskimos and, according to her biographers, given to enjoying polite "darkey" stories, after this initial of many meetings to come, the First Lady became the NAACP's most valuable white ally. Stephen Early (confederate general Jubal Early's grandson) and the southern palace guard had shown their determination to keep the president from hearing from or speaking directly to 10 percent of the American population whose suffering under the Depression was greatest by banning colored reporters permanently from White House press conferences. Whatever *should* be done for citizens of color—lifting the poll tax, banning labor union discrimination, enacting federal sanctions against lynching—FDR's advisers told him he couldn't do. And what FDR *could* do—greeting the annual NAACP convention, moral suasion—Early, Louis Howe, Thomas ("Tommy the Cork") Corcoran, and other intimates told FDR he shouldn't. Remember "our [white] southern brethren," the wiley Howe counseled, and let the future take care of "our anxious colored brethren." Besides, the colored brethren had voted overwhelmingly for Hoover.

More than a year would pass until Eleanor Roosevelt found an opportunity to slip the NAACP secretary past Early, Marvin McIntyre, and other vigilant palace guardsmen onto the White House's southern portico on a warm spring Sunday where an amused FDR, pressured by his wife and mother, finally agreed to talk with White about pending antilynching legislation. White reported the president's definitive words on the subject of civil rights, spoken with as much regret as realpolitik allowed: "'I did not choose the tools with which I must work,' he told me. 'Had I been permitted to choose them I would have selected quite different ones. But I've got to get legislation passed by Congress to save America.'" It was a bravura FDR performance, leonine head aloft and cigarette holder angled, whose candor both impressed and depressed White. The Man himself said in effect that New Deal benefits would come to Negroes slowly and collaterally—after providing public relief and jobs for whites and with great care taken not to rile the white South. Had Monroe Trotter somehow been in White's place on the White House portico, Eleanor and Sara Delano Roosevelt might well have been surprised to hear the president of the United States gravely reproached for writing off millions of desperate citizens. Walter White was no Trotter, however; and Trotter himself was no more. Out of the loop of civil rights leadership and a shadow of his once fiery, uncompromising self, the old newspaperman who pulled Du Bois into the Bookerite fray and debated segregation in Wilson's Oval Office had committed suicide twelve months earlier. The era of the organization man—of White and Wilkins—had ushered this brave New England maverick from the scene. In penning his tribute, Du Bois's insightfulness came close to committing an uncomfortable truth about himself: Trotter, he wrote, "was a free lance; too intense and sturdy to loan himself to that compromise which is the basis of all real organization. . . . The mailed fist has got to be clenched. The united effort of twelve millions has got to be made to mean more than the individual effort of those who think aright."

Du Bois had done his best to prepare the race not only for the political realities governing FDR but also for the grim consequences of the descent of people of color into a pariah caste, a category all but ostracized from the social contract. "On Being Ashamed" flamed with the consternation of old in the September *Crisis*, 1933, but its thesis was new, or, rather, a novel recycling of an earlier one long since filed away by Du Bois. He restated the ideals of a once optimistic people. Committed to self-improvement and color-blind citizenship, the generation of Aframericans after slavery had worked wonders from pitifully little to become educated, industrious, and civically exemplary. "In the years between emancipation and 1900, the theory of escape was dominant," he claimed with only mild exaggeration. "We were, by birth, law and training, American citizens. We were going to escape into the mass of Americans in the same way that the Irish and Scandinavians and even the Italians were beginning to disappear. He described it as the time of "Our Country Tis of Thee" when "race" was expected to disappear from the vocabulary of the "Inter-Nation" and educated folk dispensed with watermelon, rejected spirituals, and held their noses in the presence of their less-evolved cousins "of whom this upper class of colored Americans [were] ashamed." Negro Americans faced lean times. In the national rebuilding under way, he predicted that the large state and corporate entities controlling the economy would increasingly dispense with black people. "Even trained Negroes have increasing difficulty in making a living," the editor observed, and the virtual shutout by the unions of Negroes drove him to conclude that there was "little or no chance of advancement for the Negro worker, the educated artisan, and the educated leader." Yet more dismally, in agriculture, where their numbers were greatest and their experience unmatched, blacks were being simultaneously ground into the dirt by white landowners, on the one hand, and forced off the land by federal farm policies, on the other. The historic disabilities of poverty, ignorance, and prejudice had finally acquired a phenomenology unique to no other racial or religious group in the United

States. "He is of Negro descent [was] all that is necessary for any Christian American gentleman" to explain today in withholding courtesy, quality education, a job, or merited promotion from another person, declared Du Bois. Assimilation had been reduced to a mirage as the record of biracial politics in the post–Civil War South was airbrushed from history, as the sweat, loyalty, and ambition of millions of ordinary folk neither protected them from lynch law down South nor entitled them to union cards or housing loans up North, and, the essay bemoaned, as the achievements of remarkable men and women were angrily resented or cynically contested.

Integration, the endgame of Talented Tenth advancement, was leading the race pell mell to crushing defeat, and so Du Bois broadcast the reasons for resigning his commission on the general staff of integration. "There seems no hope that America in our day will yield in its color or race hatred any substantial ground," he foresaw fatalistically, "and we have no physical nor economic power, nor any alliance with other social or economic classes that will force compliance with decent civilized ideals in Church, State, industry or art." Twenty-five years of NAACP effort amounted only to valiant futility. All that remained was the solidarity forced upon a people whose greatest ambition had once been only to be allowed to merge with and blend into the American mainstream, for "more and more largely in the last twenty-five years, colored America has discovered itself; has discovered groups of people, association with whom is a poignant joy." Pigment, family culture, superior education, and professional distinction would continue to matter behind the veil of color, Du Bois had no doubt, but, for better and worse, segregation's one-drop rule applied to the entire country had forced a black nation into being. Here was a revolutionary opportunity for his race to redefine a reversal as a breakthrough. What are we really aiming at?" he entreated. "The building of a new nation or the integration of a new group into an old nation?" With all its terrible risks, Du Bois now decreed that it must be the former. But not what he despised as the "mere rhodomontade and fatuous propaganda on which Garveyism was based." It had to be precisely and farsightedly planned and would entail increased segregation "and [even] perhaps migration." He added sagely that this conception of group advancement would be "pounced upon and aided and encouraged by every 'nigger-hater' in the land." "On Being Ashamed of Oneself" ended on a Du Boisian imperative: *The next step, then, . . . involves the organization of intelligent and earnest people of Negro descent for their preservation and advancement in America, in the West Indies and in Africa; and no sentimental distaste for racial or national unity can be allowed to hold them back from a step which sheer necessity demands.*" The rest, he might have said, was easy.

Du Bois's housecleaning designs for the association now seemed to have Joel Spingarn's full support in the afterglow of Amenia. Although the chairman had confidentially prodded Hope to take Du Bois on at Atlanta, the excitement of the conference and their years of mutual affection built on high-minded disputes and shared intellectual superiority induced a change of heart and persuaded Spingarn that without Du Bois the NAACP was not worth the candle. The controversies swirling around White made Spingarn all the more loath to see Du Bois retire from the scene. The Chicago branch of the association had come close to open mutiny during the summer of 1933 after White had ordered it to stand down from a call to boycott Sears and Roebuck. The old Chicago NAACP crowd had shrugged off years' of complaints about policies that demeaned black customers of Marshall Fields, Wieboldt's, Sears, and the other large department stores in the Loop. Women found it especially galling that they were not allowed to try on shoes in the Sears shoe department, an exclusion Sears enforced in other northern cities. The old ways ended abruptly with new NAACP leadership. In response to the local branch's letter demanding that the practice be abandoned, Sears replied with an unsigned denial of discrimination, and the Chicago branch issued an appeal for a nationwide boycott of the department chain. White's initial response was to back the Chicago branch, a decision taken immediately by the powerful National Association of Colored Women (NACW), whose annual convention was also to be held in the city that summer. In an unrelated development, however, White had recently asked for a subsidy from the Rosenwald family in order to compensate for the imminent reduction of Wilkins's salary (an action motivated in part by Spingarn's intention to unload the assistant secretary). William Rosenwald's letter to White brought a quick turnaround. He felt certain that White would want to take the appropriate steps "to uphold the reputation of your organization," to make no mention of safeguarding Wilkins's salary.

Then there was the Crawford Case, a near disaster from which the NAACP had been spared a humiliating loss of credibility largely because of Houston's juristic sangfroid. The most highly publicized case taken on by the association since Clarence Darrow's defense of Ossian Sweet, George Crawford had seemed at first to be the answer to Scottsboro, a clean-cut, passably literate victim of southern injustice accused of committing a double homicide in Loudoun County, Virginia. Martha Gruening, a seasoned investigator whose experience dated from her collaboration with the editor in uncovering the facts behind the 1917 East St. Louis race riot, had certified the alibi placing the young man in Massachusetts at the time of the murder of a Middleburg, Virginia, socialite and her maid. Riding a wave of broad sympathy outside the South, the NAACP retained the services of a former Massachusetts attorney general to defend Crawford while White fed the press background information about Virginia's culture of violence. Newspapers reported that a posse of local squires headed by fabled General "Billy" Mitchell, the father of the U.S. Air Corps, had set off to hunt and hang any black man the hounds flushed out of the woods on the night of the double murder. The battle to prevent Crawford's extradition reached the U.S. Circuit Court of Appeals after the Massachusetts District Court ruled against Virginia on grounds that the accused would be denied a fair trial, a decision that brought southern calls for Judge James A. Lowell's impeachment in Congress. Lowell was reversed by the Circuit Court and Crawford was remanded for trial in Loudoun County, his defense entirely, and unprecedentedly, in the hands of a team of Negro attorneys headed by Houston. White, galloping ahead of the learning curve that had made him one of the most successful Harlem Renaissance novelists, became an instant legal expert, joining Houston's team in late-night research sessions in Howard's law library, where a slangy, smart law student named Thurgood Marshall did gopher's duty.

The case was closely followed by major white and black newspapers, South and North, as trial preliminaries commenced in December 1933. Houston and company challenged the state's case on grounds of the historic exclusion of people of color from grand and petit jury rolls. Dismissal and exclusion motions, unheard of in trials involving a black defendant, rattled the Leesburg prosecutors. Then, in a shattering confidence to Houston from the prosecutor, the Crawford bubble burst with the discovery that the defendant had, after all, returned to Virginia to see his wife at the time of the murders and fallen in with bad company. A bungled burglary and panic had cost the lives of the two white women. Ironically, the fear of backing a guilty party in an interracial crime, the fear that kept White from intervening in Scottsboro ahead of the ILD, now came disastrously true with the association's once ideal defendant. Shifting gears seamlessly, Houston turned the Crawford trial not into a plea for a guilty man but an opportunity for the state of Virginia to rise above judicial vindictiveness. Against every precedent and all expectations, the Loudoun County jurors declined to recommend the death penalty. White's portrayal of the outcome as a southern milestone in the affirmation of due process was more persuasive, however, than his attempt to deflect sharp criticism about his management of the case. Among the most wounding would have been the editorial on the case slated for the May issue of *The Crisis*, which provoked an extremely angry letter in which White expressed utter amazement at Du Bois's imputations and ignorance of the facts. "We gladly would have supplied you with information which was right here in the files," he would complain. Streator wisely decided to withdraw the original editorial.

It was in this squallish climate that Joel Spingarn took a hard look at new barometric readings for the association's future and decided on a change of course. On October 9, 1933, a Monday, the chairman was empowered to appoint a nominating committee to reconstitute the board of directors, news of which Spingarn immediately sent to Atlanta, where his conspiring friend awaited an invitation to serve with the new committee. Spingarn was elated. "Whatever happens, I want you to feel that the Association is *yours*, something you helped to create, something you have helped to keep alive," he crooned. "Don't fail me or the Association now." The other nominating committee members were Ovington and Lillian Alexander, chairperson, a composition virtually assuring the editor a free hand. Once again, national headquarters was roiled by Du Bois's foundation-shaking redesigns. He called for more vice-presidents—an indefinite enlargement of the number of these honorary officers into a "body of Elder Statesmen" that was to include James Weldon Johnson and Arthur Spingarn. He proposed twelve additional seats on the board, three allotted to whites (Martha Gruening and two others), and two to remain temporarily vacant. The slate of eight candidates Du Bois sent to the nominating committee was clearly intended to engineer the early retirement of White and Wilkins. Sterling Brown, Frazier, and Houston personally liked White, with whom they enjoyed an occasional game of poker; nor were they susceptible to knee-jerk deference to Du Bois, whose interest in cards was minimal. On the other hand, the Howard professors were increasingly dissatisfied with an NAACP leadership style and organizational direction mainly propelled by egotism, boundless energy, and high-wire opportunism. Mabel Byrd, educated at the University of Oregon in economics and now employed by the NRA after serving with the League of Nations, had impressed Du Bois at Amenia almost as much by her Levantine beauty as her acute intelligence. Rachel Davis DuBois was a preordained vote for the editor, as was Virginia Alexander. Gruening, too, was inclined to favor greater stress on bread-and-butter issues. Harris was known for his independent intellect, but Du Bois had good reason to expect that the two of them would agree on major questions.

Winter of 1933–34 was explosive. If Du Bois had been at all inclined to any optimism about transforming the NAACP in the final weeks of the year, the contents of Harris's long, lucid despairing letter told him that time had run out. His short tenure on the board dealing with the likes of the Spingarns and distinguished Negro leaders convinced Harris that "you can't rely upon the James Weldon Johnsons and the Walter Whites for any new programs." These people stood in the way "of clear thinking on the present relation of the Negro to world forces." Lillian Alexander had suffered a mild heart attack in November. Herbert Seligmann, never a forceful personality but competent enough as publicity director and generally sympathetic to *The Crisis*, had resigned at the beginning of 1933. As a contributing editor to the *Messenger* and author of the ribald *Black No More*, Schuyler's qualifications for the job might have seemed impressive. Mencken called him the most gifted writer of the Renaissance. The editor still smoldered over the book and article on Liberia, however, and when White moved to replace Seligmann with Schuyler, Du Bois expressed his displeasure in such categorical terms that Joel Spingarn decided not to approve the secretary's recommendation. Reminding readers that he had devoted the year to making a "restatement of the Negro problem" through systematic discussion in the magazine of demography, Marxism, and employment, the vote, the "class struggle within the race," and education and religion, Du Bois ran up the warning flag of heresy in "Pan-Africa and New Racial Philosophy" that November.

If Garvey read the November *Crisis*, he must have felt some degree of sour vindication. "There are still large numbers of American Negroes who in all essential particulars conceive themselves as belonging to the white race," Du Bois admonished. The thought surely suggested Garvey, if not the prose, as the editorial deplored those who, whether "yellow, brown or black," mistook the true meaning of their history and social surroundings. They numbered in the hundreds of thousands and dominated the upper tier of the race, these Negroes for whom nationality was paramount and racial identity a secondary characteristic or even a badge of shame. They were the people who were ever ready "to flock to white America before they would flock to the brown West Indies or to black Africa or yellow Asia," people who failed to see that assimilationist options that once seemed attainable in the trial-and-error race relations before *Plessy* were now only cruel fictions, Du Bois reiterated — chimeras whose wrongheadedness in the economic warp of the present might well prove fatal. "Colored peoples of the world, and first of all those of Negro descent, should begin to concentrate upon this problem of their economic survival." Du Bois spelled out the meaning of self-sufficiency with salutes to utopian socialists Charles Fourier and Robert Owen: "What can we do? We can work for ourselves. We can consume mainly what we ourselves produce, and produce as large a proportion as possible of that which we consume."

In the past, Du Bois's periodic indulgence of black nationalist nostrums had never caused alarm; few Americans, black or white, familiar with his outsized career doubted his ardent commitment to the NAACP's dogma of integration. But in the winter of 1933–34, separatist ideas from the pen of the country's leading civil rights advocate risked political consequences that rivaled the memorable controversy ignited by "Close Ranks." A southern official of the Department of the Interior, Clarence Pickett, had invoked the authority of Du Bois before the Joint Committee on National Recovery in defense of the Homestead Subsistence Bureau's decision to fund segregated resettlement communities. White's telegram to Atlanta at the end of November conveyed understandable alarm. "Very real danger from use of your name. Please wire us collect," implored White. Although Du Bois was almost past caring about White's concerns, the secretary might have expected cooperation in countering claims in Washington that the editor condoned racially parallel relief efforts by the federal government. Instead, Du Bois responded by lobbing a concussion grenade from

The Crisis. "Segregation" appeared in the January 1934 issue. It minced no words. "The thinking colored people of the United States must stop being stampeded by the word segregation," Du Bois ordained. Racial segregation in the United States had almost always been tantamount to racial discrimination. "But the two things do not necessarily go together," he explained to his overwhelmingly surprised readers, "and there should never be an opposition to segregation pure and simple unless that segregation does involve discrimination."

The editorial hit 69 Fifth Avenue in the backdraft of weeks of machinations and recriminations that had left the national office in a state of near chaos. The shotgun wedding of Wilkins and Streator at *The Crisis* had been a disaster from the beginning. To make matters worse, the board reconstituted the magazine's publication committee, gave it veto power over all advances from the association, and reinforced White's position on it by appointing Wilkins to serve with Wright and Arthur Spingarn—all without consulting the editor-in-chief. Holding his breath, Joel Spingarn informed Atlanta University's new professor of sociology on December 12, "Yesterday, the Board took some radical steps." Could his friend please withhold judgment until they could meet? Sheepishly, Spingarn noted that somehow his brother had been "inadvertently put on [the publication committee] instead of Mrs. Alexander"—quickly adding, however, that Arthur intended to resign (presumably in Alexander's favor). There was contained anger from Atlanta at first. His own authority could not be questioned; he, Du Bois, "must either be Editor or not Editor"—"a real Editor-in-Chief" with ultimate decisions over what goes into the magazine. If not, then, he was ready to step aside and assume the honorific of contributing editor (the balance of his salary promptly to be paid), but solely on condition that the new editor "is a man whom I know and trust," he wrote both Spingarns. Streator's editorial authority and $1,200 salary must be honored. Committees were acceptable in principle, but no committee with more than purely advisory authority was acceptable to him if Walter White was a member.

But after two days of stewing, Du Bois's state of mind became almost feral. "The more I think it over, the more angry I get," he growled at Arthur Spingarn. Hazel Branch's frantic letter had just come about the printer's bill for five hundred dollars and the publication committee's immediate embargo on advances: "Please do your worst, I beg you Doctor." He was tired of being humiliated, tired of "having continually to threaten severance of all connection with *The Crisis* and the NAACP.*" As for any *Crisis* committee or board with Roy Wilkins on it, Du Bois found the idea absurd. Wilkins had "neither the brains nor guts to be a member of any board," he raved, and demanded that the assistant secretary be replaced by Lillian Alexander. Du Bois refused to be mollified. Joel Spingarn conceded that his objections were "reasonable enough," pleaded the wisdom of putting disputes on hold until a face-to-face meeting, then wearily closed his letter by confessing uncertainty as to his feelings "about the whole matter." But not only was Du Bois unmollified, Streator, his surrogate, addressed the chairman in an admonitory tone that the courtly Dutchess County squire was quite unaccustomed to receive from association employees. The young managing editor wanted Spingarn to understand that he was no impressionable idealist but a man of considerable professional experience whose office economizings, magazine redesign, and enrollment of new agents had begun to pay off in more subscribers and increased income. He had come to *The Crisis* because of Du Bois, because he "believed in the quality of his mind," said Streator. But he would never work for people he had come "cordially to distrust." Three months at the NAACP had been enough to show that White was a liability and Wilkins was a "liar and a coward." Streator predicted that "the whole movement might as well fold up" if White got control of the magazine. So much for Joel Spingarn's hope of a fortnight of peace until the conference with Du Bois over the Christmas holidays. In the end (but only for the time being), he and the board were to be spared Du Bois's December 27 resignation letter angrily imputing "the intention of the Board by two successive votes [November and December] . . . to terminate my services as active Editor-in-Chief of *The Crisis*." "Segregation" had come instead.

Segregation could be positive, and opposition to it was not "or should not be [from] any distaste or unwillingness of colored people to work with each other, to cooperate with each other, to live with each other." Segregated schools, churches, neighborhoods, public facilties were anathema only because, with rare exceptions, the resources available to them were inferior. It was, therefore, not segregation as a prescription for group life but, rather, Du Bois philosophized, the actual conditions of segregated life under white supremacy that were an abomination in the eyes of morality and the Constitution of the United States. Racial integration was also a desirable objective, of course. "Doubtless, and in the long run," as Du Bois well knew he could hardly avoid affirming, "the greatest human development is going to take place under the widest individual contact"; but in the present state of race relations the true community of all men and women was but a distant ideal. The logic of Du Boisian segregation, then, was inescapable: "It is impossible . . . to wait for the millennium of free and normal intercourse before we unite." Just as the "class-conscious working man" was destined to bring about the global liberation of labor, so, predicted Du Bois, it would be the "race-conscious black man cooperating together in his own institutions and movements" who would eventually emancipate the black race. Two sentences in "Segregation" stood out from the heretical others, leaving White and much of the Talented Tenth leadership almost as heartsick as had Garvey's overture to the Klan. With federal subsidies available to impoverished farming and mining communities in mind, Du Bois urged that blacks "should come forward, should organize and conduct enterprises" in farms and communities voluntarily inhabited by themselves. "It must be remembered," he stressed, "that in the last quarter of a century, the advance of the colored people has been mainly in the lines where they themselves working by and for themselves, have accomplished the greatest advance."

Twelve thousand *Crisis* subscribers, fifty thousand NAACP members, and hundreds of thousands of readers of *The Defender, Courier, Afro-American, Amsterdam News*, and scores of other black newspapers assimilated Du Bois's new racial philosophy in reactions varying from bafflement to apoplexy. Resented and resisted in the Department of the Interior, assaulted each day by corridor expressions that could only be read as asking, "Boy, why are you here?," Assistant Solicitor Hastie told the Washington *Afro-American* that he refused to believe the editorial was possible "until my own eyes had convinced me. Du Bois, William Edward Burghardt Du Bois, himself—or not himself—making a puny defense of segregation and hair splitting about the difference between segregation and discrimination! Oh, Mr. Du Bois! How could you?!" Hastie's was an entirely predictable reaction. With Clark Foreman, the New Deal's white specialist on Negro affairs citing Du Bois as one of the "outstanding Negro leaders who advocated cooperation *within* the race to develop leadership," White expected the editor to appreciate the discriminatory mischief to be made from his pronouncements. Surely Du Bois must know that twenty black families were currently petitioning the Federal Home Subsistence Bureau for admission to the model settlement at Arthurdale, West Virginia. Direct pressure from Eleanor Roosevelt, in response to protests from the NAACP's Charleston, West Virginia, branch and the national office, had forced the Home Subsistence Bureau to review its initial decision to limit the Arthurdale colony to whites. "We are informed that just as this was about to be done," White's urgent telegraph and letter informed Du Bois, "the editorial was published and that it has been used to hold up admission of these Negro families."

The secretary wanted clarification. Mrs. Roosevelt wanted clarification. Possibly, the editor was unaware that the secretary, together with Moton, Mordecai Johnson, Charles S. Johnson, John Hope, and several others, would be conferring with Mrs. Roosevelt at the White House in little more than a week? What was the meaning of Du Bois's refusal to publish White's own statement on the "official" NAACP position on segregation in the February *Crisis*, he asked—an assertion plain and simple that the association had never "officially budged in its opposition to segregation"? Du Bois had curtly dismissed White's statement as "untrue and unfair," instructing the dumbfounded secretary that, as a historical fact, the NAACP had never actually taken a formal position on segregation. To that end, Du Bois continued professorially, "the matter of segregation has got to be threshed out very carefully by the Association in the columns of *The Crisis.*" He returned White's letter with errors "marked" and invited him to contribute to the "Free Forum" whose announced objective would be "to seek not dogma but enlightenment." Throughout the year, the magazine would devote itself to the "subject of segregation." He was "getting terribly tired fooling away time and energy on Walter White," he wrote Lillian Alexander. "He's neither straight nor honest." As for Joel Spingarn, the bond of respect between them was still strong, but the editor understood only too well the chairman's dilemma. Although genuinely troubled by the NAACP's narrow, legalistic bent and its middle-class stodginess, Spingarn was by temperament and social position unreceptive to the radical social and economic solutions favored by Du Bois and some of his young disciples. As custodian of the nation's oldest civil rights organization, his was the difficult duty of both encouraging innovative ideas and policies yet of safeguarding cohesion through sensitive, vigilant mediation. As much due to the Talented Tenth strategy of combating white prejudice with influential whites as to his abiding diplomacy and generous philanthropy, Spingarn's race and religion had seldom been an issue publicly discussed among colored Americans. They lay just below the civil surface of interracial comity, nevertheless, as evidenced by the concern Vann had shared three years earlier with Du Bois that Spingarn's presidency was not only tantamount to a negative statement—"We are not able to lead ourselves"—but a potential source of Gentile rejection. Personally, he liked the man, but Vann had reminded Du Bois that the Christian world "as we know it does not react too favorably to non-Christian leadership." As white men who were Jews, then, Joel and Arthur Spingarn knew that they must exercise great care—whatever their feelings for Du Bois—never to appear to run against the grain of prevailing Negro opinion.

Du Bois told readers what they knew only too well, "the vast majority of the Negroes in the United States are born in colored homes, educated in separate colored schools, attend separate colored churches, marry colored mates, and find their amusements in colored YMCA's and YWCA's." Segregation was a fact of American life, he was saying. His race must learn to make a virtue of a necessity. He had decided to exit with a bang. There would be no fulsome tributes on the occasion of his retirement from *The Crisis*—no graceful fading away for him. He was disgusted personally and discouraged philosophically. Yet it was not what he said, but much more how Du Bois chose to express it that occasioned a tsunami of reproach. The Aframerican tradition justifying separate racial development on grounds of realism or chauvinism, or both, was already an old one when Booker Washington perfected it. Even as shock waves from *The Crisis* reverberated, Kelley Miller and Woodson expressed ideas similar to

Du Bois's. Support for the man rather than for his thesis was far from lacking. The January 5 "Open Letter to Carl Murphy" was typical. Black people "would as soon think of the United States without the Mississippi River as they would think of [the NAACP and *The Crisis*] without Dr. Du Bois," it claimed. Signed by a nub of Du Boisians that included Reverend George Frazier Miller, the socialist preacher, Helen Curtis, the New Jersey clubwoman, Boutee, the Harlem pharmacist, and Martha Gruening, it was addressed to the powerful board member who made no secret of his exasperation with the editor.

"Segregation—A Symposium," like the watershed "Criteria of Negro Art" eight years earlier, was designed to motivate informed controversy. It was the first of several proposed installments of the segregation controversy, appearing in March. Joel Spingarn, still prompted by philosophical integrity, expressed appreciation for Du Bois's broaching of the implications of segregation, then went on to underscore that the NAACP had "always regarded segregation as an evil." Nor was that Du Bois's intention, Spingarn astutely observed, but a "transvaluing of segregation, rather, into a *good*"—something like the cultural nationalism of the Zionists who insist that a people or a race "can achieve its true development only when it creates its own spiritual 'centre' and disregards the centres of other races or peoples." Finally allowed an opinion in *The Crisis*, White told readers that Du Bois's opinion was "merely a personal expression on his part." The historic position of the NAACP "from the date of its founding" called for unyielding opposition to segregation, "a grim struggle," said White, that the Negro must conduct for his own "physical, moral, and spiritual well-being and for that of America and of the world at large." Letters to *The Crisis* would rise like a flood from February to July until they burst onto the pages of the August number. The major black newspapers had gone on record about segregation weeks, and in the case of the Philadelphia *Tribune* months, before the second installment of symposium opinions that August, however. Lamenting that Du Bois was "slipping," the *Tribune* wagged an editorial finger about the duty of an official to "agree with the policies of his organization." Parting company with the "Race Champion," *The Defender* declared the "path of least resistance" unacceptable. The debate was still DuBois's to lose in a climate of opinion that accorded his unwelcome thesis grudging appreciation for intellectual and institutional shock value. There must have been a good number of college students like the one who wrote *The Defender* that, "for the intelligent Negro student, Dr. Du Bois is still a champion. . . . A wise general, he has seen that the point of attack can be made from a more advantageous point."

"Segregation in the North" recalled the distemper of "A Lunatic or a Traitor," the infamous 1924 editorial that consolidated the opposition and irrevocably personalized the dispute with Marcus Garvey. Accentuating an hauteur excessive even for himself, Du Bois passed in review the contributions to the symposium, imperiously grading each one. Pierce of Cleveland was unconvincing. Miller and Schuyler were "quite beside the point" and labored under an amiable misconception that the North was different, when in truth the difference between North and South "in the matter of segregation [was] largely a difference of degree." As for the chairman, "if, as Spingarn asserts, the NAACP has conducted a quarter-century campaign against segregation," then Du Bois found nothing more to say than that "the net result has been a little less than nothing. . . . We have not made the slightest impress on the determination of the overwhelming mass of white Americans to treat Negroes as men." He was unimpressed by charges of doctrinal inconsistency. "What worries me is the Truth," Du Bois announced grandly—the truth of 1934, not 1910. As for the secretary of the association, Du Bois declared him to be as irrelevant as Garvey had once asserted that Du Bois himself was—and from the same shameful *argumentum ad hominem:* "Walter White is white. He has more white companions and friends than colored. He goes where he will in New York City and naturally meets no Color Line, for the simple and sufficient reason that he isn't 'colored.'" Eight years had passed since an evening in late November when White had allowed himself to be drawn into an extraordinary conversation about racial aptitude in the chairman's Manhattan residence. Asked by Spingarn whether "frankly . . . he thought men of unmixed Negro blood capable of the highest achievement and character," the secretary had at first hedged by citing the singer Roland Hayes and a respected Methodist bishop. "[He] gave all the other arguments that I as well as he and the rest of the NAACP have given for years," Spingarn wrote his wife, but when pressed harder ("this is very confidential"), White had conceded that "unmixed" Negroes were inferior—"infinitely inferior now," Spingarn quoted him as saying, "whatever they might possibly become in the future." Even if Du Bois had come to know what an aristocratic Jew and an assimilated octoroon knew about each other's covert prejudices, the personal attack on the secretary was an egregious lapse of couth and, from a tactical point of view, a serious mistake.

The die was cast. "The debate is one of W.E.B. Du Bois versus Walter White," several newspapers concluded. Deeply pained, Joel Spingarn wrote Du Bois of his great disappointment that his friend had stooped to "hitting below the belt" to settle an honest difference of opinion. Schuyler, embittered by Du Bois's withering disapproval of his coverage of Liberia, placed his acid Pittsburgh *Courier* pen at the service of White and Wilkins. "Imagine the Top Sergeant of the Talented Tenth fouling like a punch drunk pugilist despairing of victory," was Schuyler's apt judgment. By the time the board met again on April 23, it confronted a mass of mail demanding an end to divided leadership and confusing objectives. With the avalanche of letters came Du Bois's demand for a vote on his segregation position. Deploring racial segregation in principle,

Du Bois had sent an awkwardly drafted statement on divergent development that the administration committee redrew and (with the chairman's help) considerably improved before submission to the board. "It is true that we have always recognized and encouraged the Negro church, the Negro college, the Negro school, and Negro business and industrial enterprises . . . as proofs of Negro efficiency, ability, and discipline," the modified Du Bois statement conceded. But the conditions creating such separation constituted an evil to be "combated to the greatest extent possible."

Faced with hard choices between principles and practices, then, the committee proposed a formula of prudent flexibility: "We reserve to ourselves complete liberty of action in any specific case that may arise, since such liberty is essential to the statesmanship necessary to carry out any ideal; but we give assurance to the white and colored peoples of the world that this organization stands where it has always stood, as the chief champion of equal rights for black and white, and as unalterably opposed to the basic principle of racial segregation." The board's acceptance of this improved statement would have represented not only a victory for Du Bois but, far more consequentially, it would have been an ideological revision of civil rights whose epic implications would likely have altered the arrival time of *Brown v. Board of Education* on the calendar of the U.S. Supreme Court. In the end, the board categorically rejected Du Boisian segregation, however formulated, and opted for an indivisible conception of citizenship in which full equality and parallel rights were mutually exclusive. Its final statement of position declared, "Enforced segregation by its very existence carries with it the implication of a superior and inferior group and invariably results in the imposition of a lower status on the group deemed inferior. Thus both principle and practice necessitate unyielding opposition to any and every form of *enforced* segregation."

By eliding the question of "voluntary" segregation, the NAACP not only avoided grappling with thorny issues posed by venerated black institutions and the nascent cultural nationalism but, as Du Bois interpreted the outcome, its leadership of "younger and more prosperous Negro professional men, merchants, and investors [was] clinging to the older ideas of property, ownership and profits even more firmly than the whites." He saw class privilege and its corollary of eventual mainstream incorporation as the fundamental reasons for rejection of his plan for group solidarity based on economic cooperation. "The upper class colored world did not anticipate nor understand it." Who better to reprove the socioeconomic parochialism of the Talented Tenth than Du Bois who had summoned it into being? That his was but another reinforcement of widely held assumptions about the failure of capitalism and the coming of new social orders—whether socialist or fascist—made his indictment seem all the more urgently appropriate. His ear cupped to the rail of history, Du Bois was certain he could hear the locomotive of world changes approaching. In this scheme of colossal decay and renewal, the integration of a model community in West Virginia was an irrelevancy when compared with what he saw as the unique opportunity to transform the masses of black people into an internal nation and potent economic force. Speaking for the integrationist upper tier of the race, the NAACP board chose what Du Bois deplored as a parochial position in large part from an absolute certainty that any nuanced statement of its civil rights creed—however carefully reasoned its clauses—was bound to be misconstrued and exploited in a real world whose disingenuousness intellectuals such as Du Bois fatally minimized.

Insofar as Streator and his skeleton staff were still buoyed by hopes of increasing the magazine's circulation, they must have been encouraged by the materials going into the May issue. In "Parallel Between Hitlerism and the Persecution of Negroes in America," the leading Reform Rabbi, Stephen Wise, contributed a thoughtful reflection on Nazism and Jim Crow. Anna Louise Strong, the self-taught Marxist from Nebraska whose remarkable autobiography, *I Change Worlds*, was about to appear, provided a full translation of foreign affairs commissar Maxim Litvinov's address to the Central Committee, "The End of Pacifism." Nothing in the May *Crisis* generated as much interest, however, as Du Bois's "Postscript" editorial. "Segregation"—a title as disquieting as *Nigger Heaven*—was another red flag unfurled in the midst of the confusion spreading among hundreds of thousands of colored Americans. He had said in the past that segregation was wrong. "I am still saying it," he wrote. But if compromise meant "taking less than you want, but not wanting less," then he pled guilty to the common sense of fighting for what was possible. A few blocks from his Atlanta University office was Beaver Slide, a dark, fetid slum he had seen "now and again for thirty years." In its place, a model community "for poor colored people, with all modern conveniences" was rising, funded by two million federal dollars. "This is Segregation," he thundered in a peroration that defied his critics. Heaping coals on the fire, the same May number carried the text of the segregation statement the board had rejected when offered for approval by Du Bois. The final lines of the piece, "The Board of Directors on Segregation," were a direct challenge to the board's credibility. Did it believe in Negro history, Negro literature and art, in business or in Negro spirituals," he asked? "*And if it does not believe in these things is the Board of Directors of the NAACP afraid to say so?*" With both Spingarns present, Ovington down from Great Barrington, Studin making a rare appearance, and Lillian Alexander and Davis DuBois ready for a fight on behalf of the absent editor, the board voted by a decisive majority to muzzle Du Bois at its meeting on May 14. On motions by Louis Wright and one of its newest members, the rising young lawyer-politician Hubert Delany, all communiqués to the press were censored henceforth and no salaried officer of the association was permitted to "criticize the policy, work, or officers of the Association in the pages of *The Crisis.*" The motion stipulated that *The Crisis* was the "organ of the Association."

His letter to the board, dated May 21, regretted that he was "unable to comply with this vote." He had not always been right, but he had "always been sincere," Du Bois wrote, and he was certainly not willing "at this late day to be limited in the expression of my honest opinions in the way the Board proposes." He enclosed his immediate resignation. The month-old committee on segregation, chaired by Harris, was directed to do whatever it could to mollify the editor. Du Bois agreed to stay pending the board's desperate maneuvering to find some face-saving formula. "Counsels of Despair," appearing in June, rang down the curtain on twenty-five years. At turns caustic, condescending, and edifying, Du Bois lamented the misconceptions of the antisegregation campaign. "This is not our fault, but it is our misfortune." Black America, having exhausted the means to reach a dead end, was in a citizenship limbo. "We lose our manners. We swallow our pride, and beg for things. We agitate and get angry. And with all that, we face the blank fact: Negroes are not wanted; neither as scholars nor as business men; neither as clerks nor as artisans; neither as artists nor as writers. What can we do about it? We cannot use force. We cannot enforce law, even if we get it on the statute books. . . . We are segregated. We are cast back upon ourselves, to an Island Within: 'To your tents, Oh Israel!' " Du Bois recalled the address delivered nearly forty years ago in Washington before the now defunct American Negro Academy, "The Conservation of Races." That address now spoke to him across decades of varied, forceful pronouncements with all the brilliance of a nova, recapturing him in the powerful force field of the Divided Self—the bipolar predicament soon thereafter immortalized in *The Souls of Black Folk.* "Counsels of Despair" quoted the epiphanic paragraph in "Conservation":

> Here, then, is the dilemma, and it is a puzzling one, I admit. No Negro who has given earnest thought to the situation of his people in America has failed, at some time in life, to find himself at these cross-roads; has failed to ask himself at some time: what, after all, am I? Am I an American or am I a Negro? Can I be both? If I strive as a Negro, am I not perpetuating the very cleft that threatens and separates Black and White in America? . . . Does my black blood place upon me any more obligation to assert my nationality than German, or Irish or Italian blood would? . . . Have we in America a distinct mission as a race—a distinct sphere of action and

opportunity for race development, or is self-obliteration the highest end to which Negro blood dare aspire?

Here was the paradox, he was saying: sometimes our actions are dictated by and suited to the potentialities inherent in our "Americanness"; at other times, we fall back upon and exult in our sense of uniqueness. It was a dynamic both reactive and assertive, that had produced, as its ultimate contradiction, outsiders whose historic existence placed them at the epicenter of the national experience. Yet in the dilemma was to be found a unique advantage, or so Du Bois perceived: a permanent possibility for transvaluing a predicament of race into an eschatology of civil rights. Connecting the dots in a history lesson packed with Greek letter fraternities, venerable Methodist churches, segregated officer training camps, the JCNR's fight for full inclusion in the NRA, and a good deal more, Du Bois diagrammed the zigzag struggle for civil rights across three twentieth-century decades. "Use segregation," he reiterated. "Use every bit that comes your way and transmute it into power." But by asserting in the next breath that it was a transmuted power "that someday will smash all race separation," Du Bois, in effect, gave away the Socratic game he was playing. He had already done so in a Chicago address when members of the audience, impressed by his separate-development thesis, had invited him to embrace the CPUSA's "49th State" idea. His firm response had been "naturally, that Negroes should *not* seek a separate culture in the United States," that segregation "was an evil and should be systematically fought." Neither *The Defender*, which covered the exchange between the editor and the Chicago black Communists, nor, with a few significant exceptions, the most prominent race leaders were inclined to muster the patience or acuity sufficient to interpret a new racial philosophy whose expositor chose to present it with calculating complexity and provocation. The intellectual smugness reflected in "Counsels of Despair" may well have grated on the convictions of tens of thousands when Du Bois pronounced, "On the whole, I am rather pleased to find myself still so much in sympathy with myself."

From January to June 1934, the literate class of Negroes had felt itself assailed by the editor's heuristic exercise: "Segregation" in January; "Segregation and Self-Respect" in March; "Segregation in the North" in April; "Segregation," again, in May along with "The Board of Directors on Segregation"; "Counsels of Despair" in June. Owen Reed Lovejoy, secretary of the Childrens Aid Society of New York City and a racial progressive, commiserated with the editor in a fine letter. Lovejoy grasped that the new philosophy was, as he wrote, "in no sense a reversing of the principles you have held for years but only an attempt to discriminate between principle and strategy." Lovejoy, however, was white.

The last installment of the symposium, appearing in the August number of *The Crisis*, carried anguished reflections by prominent Negroes. Ferdinand Morton, the New York civil service commissioner, confessed to being quite "unable clearly to distinguish" Du Bois's proposals from certain of those put forward by Booker Washington. Moreover, Morton was certain that Du Bois's scheme was of a magnitude that would require capital "far in excess of that which we control or could reasonably hope to control." Francis Grimké's statement—"The Battle Must Go On"—rejected unequivocally the new racial philosophy as countenancing evil. Robert Weaver pondered the baleful consequences of wage differentials based on race. There were minority voices. J. B. Watson, president of the Agricultural, Mechanical & Normal Institute of Pine Bluff, Arkansas, praised the editor for finally "seeing the following stubborn facts" after a quarter century of scorning strategy and compromise. The Pine Bluff educator claimed to concur with Du Bois that the black man was "better off by himself" and not trying to compete "with people who have a thousand years jump on him." Jews accept their fate, Watson wrote, let black people do the same. Watson, a confirmed Bookerite, was hardly an ally of choice, however.

In any case, Du Bois knew that nothing remained to be said. He had reinstated his resignation declaration on June 11. On June 26, he informed the board that he was allowing his nominal connection with *The Crisis* to extend until July 1 in deference to its request for an eleventh-hour mediation. White was now so determined to prevent further public airing of the controversy that he put his career on the line. In a blitz of letter-writing and speaking engagements, he had won wide support across the country and softened up the editor's remaining supporters. Sounding like his nemesis, the secretary informed the chairman that he was "thoroughly nauseated at the lack of moral courage on the part of some members of the present Board." Further temporizing at the July meeting would leave him no other choice than to resign. An exasperated Carl Murphy telegraphed White that he regarded Du Bois's leaving "as the solution to present intolerable situation." A prominent Chicago attorney, Irvin Mollison, complained that Du Bois's resignation threats over the board's gag rule were just a cover for the bankruptcy of the segregation issue. The disgusted Mollison accused him of attempting to sandbag the NAACP with the burden of "failing to rescue Negro workers and tenant farmers from their plight." A typescript letter from Franklin Frazier, running on for three single-spaced pages, was one of the most remarkable sent to White. Condescending in the manner of brilliant young academics passing judgment on their distinguished seniors, Frazier explained that Du Bois had nothing original to say about segregation "as a natural social phenomenon." Frazier would expect as much "from a student who has taken my introductory course in sociology." What the Howard

University professor thought he divined as especially revealing about the separate-development thesis, however, was its masking of Du Bois's ideological bent and professional opportunism. "Du Bois seems to me to be simply engaging in intellectual play," Frazier speculated. "It seems to be a confession, on his part, of the failure of his entire philosophy, and that since he is too old or is afraid to risk his livelihood in coming out in favor of communism or the destruction of competitive capitalist society as the only solution to the Negro's problem, he has sought refuge in a tame and harmless racialism." Expressing profound gratitude for the "clearest and ablest analysis" yet, White entered the meeting of the board on July 9 fully confident of victory.

Two weeks earlier, newspapers had reproduced the text of Du Bois's second resignation letter stating his refusal to accept censorship. His decision to release it presented the board with a fait accompli. His departure was accepted with a motion of appropriate regret. Privately, Ovington breathed a sigh of relief to Oswald Garrison Villard, writing the crusty, former board member, "Now we are rid of our octopus, for of late he has been draining our strength." Whether his role in the association in recent years had been as octopus or avatar, Du Bois knew how to frame his exit as one of selfless, principled commitment balked by timorousness and mediocrity. "To the very best of my ability, and every ounce of my strength," he proclaimed upon resigning,

> I have since the beginning of the Great Depression, tried to work inside the organization for its realignment and readjustment to new duties. I have been almost absolutely unsuccessful. My program for economic readjustment has been totally ignored. My demand for a change in personnel has been considered as mere petty jealousy, and my protest against our mistakes and blunders has been considered as mere petty jealousy.

The debate over segregation had been so fierce and distracting that, with the notable exception of Frazier, almost no one attacked Du Bois's plan for a cooperative economy as anticapitalist and Marxist-inspired, which was just as well if its author hoped to secure an appointment from the trustees of Atlanta University. Indeed, trustees Trevor Arnett, Dean Sage, and their fellow Euro-Americans comprising the majority of the university's board were as favorably impressed by Du Bois's segregation essays and editorials as White, Johnson, Murphy, Wright, and most Negro notables were disconcerted by them. It is more than reasonable to suspect that Du Bois fully intended his writings to be capable of diametrically opposite interpretations. His savings, along with his life insurance, wiped out by the Depression, assailed by bewildering debts (a test for Arthur Spingarn's legal skills) associated with the old St. Nicholas Avenue house and the Dunbar co-op apartment, the editor had pressing practical reasons to find work elsewhere. Du Bois certainly did not see his manufactured controversy as motivated by Jesuitical opportunism, of course. He was simply taking the Negro race to another place, more congenial and better salaried, from which to continue to the battle for civil rights. "All is not yet vanity, and there is plenty to fight for and to do," he wrote comfortingly to a distraught supporter. "I am simply changing because I had to."

ATLANTA: *BLACK RECONSTRUCTION*

AND CASANOVA UNBOUND

H e was sorely missed, Lillian Alexander wrote Du Bois at the beginning of 1934. She longed for his "jolly presence," his influence, and most of all "the rows!" The dramatic exit from the NAACP would come six months later. "So little to fight about because so little is being done," Alexander sighed. He shared her low opinion of the association under its current leadership, all the more so in light of White's recent decision to commit to an open-throttle campaign for a federal antilynching statute. The liberal wing of the Democratic party, anticipating massive gains among northern black voters in the 1934 midterm elections, welcomed the association's input in crafting the Costigan-Wagner Bill, whose authorization of Justice Department investigations of mob action and imposition of heavy fines upon delinquent state and local officials the NAACP secretary defended in late February in a bravura appearance before the Senate Judiciary Committee. When the Judiciary Committee voted a favorable report of the bill to the Senate two months later, Du Bois would still remain unpersuaded of the priority given to antilynching legislation at the cost of economic redress, especially, as he predicted, only too accurately, that Costigan-Wagner was doomed by the seniority prerogatives of southern congressmen. The departed editor's misgivings were shared increasingly by Charlie Houston, the NAACP's legal muse, who would try to wean White from this single-track strategy, telling the secretary less than a year later, "Lots of us feel that a fight for anti-lynching legislation without just as vigorous a battle for economic independence is to fight the manifestation of the evil and ignore its cause." Du Bois would have found little to add to Houston's caveat. In any case, as he prepared spring-semester lectures in the first days of 1934, the new sociology professor had already all but decided to end this chapter of his life, the quarter century at the NAACP editing its official monthly.

Even he might not have been able to say precisely when the intellectual's impatience with quotidian stopgaps and piecemeal solutions became intolerable, the exact point during the early thirties at which personal ambition and organizational stasis had intersected antithetically. The record of his doings after Johnson's retirement and the last gasp at Amenia discloses an impressive range of career options, however. There were serious rumors of an appointment as university librarian at Howard, preliminary negotiations to become editor of an ambitious race project conceived by the Phelps-Stokes Fund, an invitation to organize the sociology department at the new Atlanta University graduate center, and vague feelers concerning a special mission to Liberia. He had opted for Atlanta University for a number of reasons—the ordinariness of some offers and the tentativeness of others—but above all because the well-salaried professorship tendered by Hope afforded time and resources essential to writing a history of the Reconstruction and World War I, projects Du Bois intended to turn into his most significant works of scholarship. Informed once again by the Guggenheim Foundation that he was too senior to be eligible for a fellowship, he had petitioned the Rosenwald Fund at the beginning of 1931 for a five-year grant of $32,500 in support of the two histories. Digging in his heels at recommending such a large award from funds primarily reserved for "younger men," old admirer Embree, the Rosenwald executive officer, had haggled Du Bois down to two years and a still generous, Depression-era stipend of $6,000. Embree also permitted himself a bit of free, if futile, advice, having long felt, his note accompanying the award stated, that Du Bois's exceptional literary gift "might well express itself occasionally in general beauty rather than in advocating special aspects of truth as you see them." The final installment of the grant had come in June 1933, a full year to the month before the editor resigned from the association for the last time.

The Reconstruction challenge had consumed Du Bois from the outset, even as he managed *The Crisis* through Streator, lectured widely, conducted seminars at Atlanta, and maneuvered untiringly to oust the NAACP secretary. Learning of the intended scope of the Rosenwald project, Alfred Harcourt had offered the services of his firm in early September 1931. Responding fairly promptly, Du Bois confirmed that Harcourt's "spies" were correct. The thesis of the book, he explained, was to be "that the real hero and center of human interest in the period is the slave who is being emancipated." Du Bois's four-page outline of the book excited Harcourt, and after a meeting between the two in late October, the Harcourt, Brace and Company contract, offering a five-hundred-dollar advance, was signed within a few days. Even more than the history of black men fighting in the Great War, the story of the struggle of black people to become full citizens after the Civil War represented unconsummated scholarship that Du Bois was singularly endowed to complete. As his Rosenwald fellowship proposal reminded Embree, the Reconstruction saga had been told with learning and "intense feeling" exclusively from the point of view of the white South. With the exception of the solid scholarship of a single Negro historian whose two recent books had been virtually ignored, Du Bois observed that little of note had been written from the black point of view since "Reconstruction and Its Benefits," his own paper "read long ago" before the American Historical Association. In the twenty-odd years since Du Bois's extraordinary conference presentation, eliciting a compliment from William Archibald Dunning, eponymous maestro of Reconstruction historiography, the dozen years after Appomattox had been the jealous historical preserve of white men, assisted by two or three white women.

The impact of Du Bois's paper upon mainstream Reconstruction scholarship was as if it had never been written, even though "Reconstruction and Its Benefits" appeared in the July 1910 number of *The American Historical Review*, the standard of the discipline. For white historians and the public opinion instructed by them, the regime imposed upon the South in the wake of the Emancipation Proclamation and the Thirteenth Amendment had been a political aberration and a cultural travesty, a military dictatorship the work of conspiring fanatics whose criminal designs had inflicted at bayonet point the rule of unlettered, untamed black people over a glorious white race, proud in defeat. Avoidable tragedy had engulfed the South and the nation, a dystopian detour to be retraced over and again by mainstream historians. The humane, expedited reintegration of the Confederate states that Abraham Lincoln had prudently begun to implement was not to be. Nor was Andrew Johnson, Lincoln's well-intentioned but disastrous successor, any more capable of mastering the radicals in Congress, determined as they were to control the Republican party and the country through an obedient southern black electorate, than he was able to tame the Bourbons of the South who, like their French spiritual ancestors, neither learned nor forgot. The mainstream historians were disposed to concede the provocation to the victorious North of electing the vice-president, six cabinet officers, four generals, five colonels, and fifty-eight congressmen of the former Confederate states of America (CSA) to seats in the Thirty-ninth Congress, set to convene in December 1865. Some white historians such as John Bach McMaster also expressed dismay at Andrew Johnson's unanticipated and deeply infuriating veto of the 1866 Civil Rights Bill and even some occasional regret that the president saw fit to veto the first Freedmen's Bureau Bill providing federal relief to the former slaves. In his eight-volume epic (*From the Compromise of 1850 to the McKinley-Bryan Campaign of 1896*), James Ford Rhodes, the Ohio businessman turned historian, offered a condign judgment of the seventeenth president that would survive the coming revisionists of the discipline: "Of all men in public life it is difficult to conceive of one so ill-fitted for this delicate work as was Andrew Johnson."

Still and yet notwithstanding a chief executive well in over his head and a South teeming with impenitents, it was the consensus of the profession that, but for the insensate racial egalitarianism of a wholly unpresentative knot of Republican lawmakers in Washington and the eleventh-hour collusion of dominant financial and partisan interests in the North and East, the interlude of good-faith reconciliation between the blue and the grey would have continued until harmony reunited the regions and racial accommodation prevailed throughout the South. Professors at Columbia and Johns Hopkins universities mainly blamed the Republican radicals in Congress for the serial policy disasters that were alleged to have foreclosed a sane solution. First had come, they wrote, the invidious propaganda of fact-finding federal officials (above all the vivid report of southern horrors drafted by the revolutionary German immigrant Carl Schurz) and the terrorizing ascendancy in the Senate and House of the likes of Massachusetts's Charles Sumner and Ohio's Benjamin Wade, of Pennsylvania's Thaddeus Stevens and Illinois's George Julian. Then came subjugation of the white South under the special interest of a proposed Fourteenth Amendment to the Constitution, the object of whose second, third, and fourth sections was the neutering of the South's natural leaders and the entrenching of black rule so as to perpetuate Republican control of the national government; to be followed a year later, historians shuddered as they wrote, by the First, Second, and Third Reconstruction Acts of 1867 nullifying the new state governments and dividing all but one (Tennessee) of the eleven states of the former Confederacy into five military districts. Readmission to the Union then came at the fearful price of biracial constitutional conventions, extension of the franchise to all adult black males, and approval of the Fourteenth Amendment making people of color full citizens of the United States, with the terse Fifteenth, decreeing that no citizens shall be denied the vote "on account of race, color, or previous condition of servitude" (but not sex), soon to come. With Sumner, the uncompromsing Brahmin, discoursing in rolling periods in the Senate on the inalienable rights of black people and Stevens, a cadaverous Robespierre, snarling retribution and preaching land confiscation in the House, the impeachment of Johnson was but the prelude to the upending of civilization, according to the prevailing interpretation.

Of Radical Reconstruction—the Manichaean calamity of "nigger rule" said to have debased the South in the decade from 1867—armies of Euro-American historians (replenished across two score years) were to write with greater passion and partiality than upon any other controversy in the national experience. "No language has been spared to describe the results of Negro suffrage as the worst imaginable," a voice from the historical wilderness had cried out fifteen years after the publication of "Reconstruction and Its Benefits." The voice was Du Bois's, writing in "The Reconstruction of Freedom," a large chapter in *The Gift of Black Folk* that propounded, among others, the heterodoxy that the enfranchisement of the slaves was the "greatest and most important step toward world democracy of all men of all races ever taken in the modern world." It was, of course, a contention going against the grain of contemporary historiography, a losing proposition after ten years in which *The Birth of a Nation* had inscribed indelible images of black and white libertinage, rapine, and corruption on the national cornea. The flickering archetypes of David Griffith's technical masterpiece were shaped from *The Clansman*, Thomas Dixon's powerful propaganda novel, but both the film and the novel owed their tone, form, and content to James S. Pike's *The Prostrate State, South Carolina under Negro Government* (1873), a virulently racist tract masquerading as eyewitness journalism. Published as Reconstruction reached high noon in the Palmetto State, Pike's influential book depicted tragedy relieved only by farce in prose as vivid as it was unfair. The plight of white South Carolinians was rendered in piteous terms calculated to alienate and enrage northern white readers: "War, emancipation, and grinding taxation have conquered them. Their struggle now is against complete confiscation. They endure, and wait for the night." Describing the scene in the State House as one of disorganized, shuffling Negro legislators arriving to occupy their seats, Pike provided generations of Reconstruction detractors with an irresistable quip, writing that "seven years ago these men were raising corn and cotton under the whip of an overseer. Today they are raising points of order and questions of privilege." While "sambo" (Pike's favorite insult) orated, South Carolina burned.

Writing thirty years after *The Prostrate State*, William Archibald Dunning's principal professor at Columbia, John W. Burgess, founding grandfather of the regnant historical school, stipulated in *Reconstruction and the Constitution, 1866–1876* that "a black skin means membership in a race of men which has never of itself succeeded in subjecting passion to reason." After wrestling with the evidence and also praising the genius of his former student, diminished "only by a shadow of color," Du Bois's principal Harvard history professor, Albert Hart, felt compelled to conclude in *The Southern South* (1910) that "race measured by race, the Negro is inferior, and his past history in Africa and in America leads to the belief that he will remain inferior." That same year, Woodrow Wilson produced *Division and Reunion, 1829–1909*, an immensely influential book in the spirit of Pike, that interpreted the purging of Negroes from office-holding and the voting rolls of the South as merely the belated result of the natural, "inevitable ascendancy of the whites." Yet as hostile as was Pike to the mixed and messy blessings of South Carolina's experiment in interracial governance, even he allowed that lawmakers such as Senator Beverly Nash, "a man wholly black" and self-taught, possessed character and ability. "It is not all sham, nor all burlesque," Pike admitted. These elected ex-slaves and free persons of color managed somehow to exhibit "an earnest purpose born of a conviction that their position and condition are not fully assured, which lends a sort of dignity to their proceedings." In a similar vein, Rhodes was capable of controlling his disdain for the governments established under the Reconstruction Acts to write that "the constitutions which they adopted were on the whole moderate, excepting . . . the reaffirmation of universal negro [sic] suffrage." The occasional, and invariably begrudged, compliments historians and political scientists might pay black people tended to disappear, however, in an ocean of derision and victim-blaming. Overall, said Burgess, Negroes had been "trifling and corrupt politicians."

Burgess was a slaveholder and Rhodes a businessman of "no broad formal education," noted Du Bois, though even Rhodes found himself attacked by Wilson for antislavery sentiments. But it was Burgess's student, Dunning, whose name became synonymous with southern historiography after the Civil War. A brilliant doctoral student at Columbia with the cachet of having studied under the venerable Heinrich von Treitschke at Berlin, Dunning returned to Morningside Heights to become Francis Lieber Professor of Political Philosophy and seminar drillmaster to scores of graduate students from both sections of the country. History departments north and south were seeded with Dunning Ph.D.s who rose through tenured ranks to full professorships, heads of departments, and holders of endowed chairs. Dunning's ascendancy was such that before his death in 1922 he had achieved the rare distinction of election to the presidency of both the American Political Science Association (APSA) and the American Historical Association (AHA). Dunning himself, as Du Bois took pains to emphasize, wrote his books in a style of "scientific" scrupulosity that was the hallmark of German training. He was more often than not "judicious," the Atlanta professor observed, and "usually silent so far as the Negro is concerned"; although Du Bois remembered to quote Dunning's less than judicious contention that "all the forces [in the South] that made for civilization were dominated by a mass of barbarous freedmen." Dunning's writings and those guided by him hewed to a three-part thesis, according to Du Bois: "first, endless sympathy with the white South; second ridicule, contempt or silence for the Negro; third, a judicial attitude towards the North, which concludes that the North under great misapprehension did a grievous wrong, but eventually saw its mistake and retreated."

The Dunningite drumbeat rolled steadily on for more than three decades after 1900, some sixteen published monographs along with, perhaps, a half dozen others bearing his influence. The earliest, James W. Garner's *Reconstruction in Mississippi* (1901), was, as Du Bois judged, strikingly balanced in its discussion of the Negro. Nor were the Reconstruction studies of Michigan by Harriette M.

Dilla (1912) and Massachusetts by Edith E. Ware (1916) preoccupied with discrediting the Negro, whose presence, in any case, was minimal in the populations of their states. C. Mildred Thompson's *Reconstruction in Georgia* (1915) was characterized by a racial condescension that was moderate for the period. T. S. Staples's 1923 Arkansas study was more tendentious. Two of Dunning's best students, C. William Ramsdell and James G. de Roulhac Hamilton, simply ignored the record of black people in Reconstruction Texas (1910) and North Carolina (1914), respectively, their relative silence on the subject fully confirming "the white Southerners' view," as the noted historian David Herbert Donald has written, "that the Negro was innately inferior." There was no silence about racial inferiority in Walter Lynwood Fleming's rabidly white supremacist *Civil War and Reconstruction in Alabama* (1905), the second Dunning School monograph, or in E. Merton Coulter's *Civil War and Readjustment in Kentucky* (1933), one of the last, which became widely regarded as templates of the series. Extremism in the service of history was no vice in the mind of these southerners whose sway over the profession was long and often decisive from professorial perches at Vanderbilt and the University of North Carolina.

In Fleming's history, the Negroes who had the temerity to overreach themselves by assuming elected office (those "spoiled" through contact with carpetbaggers) are the source and cause of the mischief, malfeasance, and malevolence of the times—mindless perpetrators and deserved victims of the calamity that is Reconstruction. Negroes had comprised a majority only in the constitutional convention and founding legislature in South Carolina; they were 50 percent in the Louisiana convention. But in none of the former Confederate states were they ever a significant presence in the upper chambers. In Alabama, the object of Fleming's scholarship, they numbered only twenty-six to eighty-four whites in the first Reconstruction legislature, and, unlike South Carolina, Louisiana, and even Mississippi, where there were lieutenant governors, senators, secretaries of state, and assembly speakers, Alabama Negroes held no important state offices. Yet the legislature depicted by Fleming is a theater of the slightly absurd, evocative of *The Prostrate State*, where Negroes mimic the business of state and propose fantastic social and ruinous economic bills while responsible whites scramble to mitigate the folly of their ex-bondsmen. There was nothing inherently wrong with the Negro that stern yet fair-minded white management couldn't correct, asserted Fleming in discussing what he saw as the tragically misconceived educational policies of the Freedmen's Bureau and the American Missionary Association. The start-up of public education in the South had been one of the principal achievements of the Reconstruction governments, as Du Bois's forgotten AHA paper had trumpeted. With an illogic about race that runs throughout *Reconstruction in Alabama*, Fleming claimed that the drastic curtailment of tax monies for Negro public schools after the overthrow of Reconstruction was justified because black children "were poorly supplied with books [by northern relief agencies]; and what few they did have they promptly lost or tore up to get the pictures." "One of the results of the war was the freedom of the black race," Fleming quotes a local eminence as saying with implicit endorsement. "We deplore the result as injurious to the country and fatal to the negroes [sic], but we are in honor bound to observe the laws which acknowledge their freedom."

The Anglo-Saxon bonding between the elites of the North and South formed an ideal substrate for the Dunning School's supremacy. Its contents would have come as no surprise to Du Bois had he been shown the invitation sent by the American Historical Association's 1910 program committee to a leading northern historian. Admitting frankly that the historical deck was already stacked, the committee chairman desired, nevertheless, that "the northern position should find some expression on the programme." "There is rather a disposition in the North at the present time to allow the southern view to go without any statement on the other side," Chicago's Andrew C. McLaughlin was informed. The new orthodoxy grew with the new "understanding" among northern upper classes that the South's race problem was but an earlier version of their own problematic of immigrant "races" and migrating Negroes who were saturating Boston, New York, Pittsburgh, and Chicago. The southernization of Reconstruction historiography complemented the biases of the contemporaneous school of northern historians that, otherwise, had scant tolerance for the "Lost Cause" nostalgia and hierarchical predilections of most of the Dunningites. The Progressive Historians or the "New Historians"—Frederick Jackson Turner, James Harvey Robinson, Carl Lotus Becker, Vernon Lane Parrington—celebrated discontinuity and democratic breakthrough, while blending criticism with optimism in their study of the economic and institutional main currents in American history. But black people were either altogether excluded from the national narrative of the Progressive Historians or, when included, cursorily blamed for their own lowly and often desperate circumstances. Thus the dean of the Progressives seriously wondered why Negroes had not been more enterprising in slavery. Writing in their magnum opus, *The Rise of American Civilization*, Charles and Mary Beard determined that the slaves had not "essentially improved their status through the years of bondage; at any rate," concluded the puzzled couple, "they had made no striking developments in intelligence; nor had they succeeded in acquiring property to any extent." Like Turner and the others, the Beards dismissed the Negro as a factor in the sectional conflict and saw the cause of the Civil War in the machinations of northern capital to destroy the South's veto power over national economic policy. In a real sense, the Progressives made common cause with the Dunningites.

Little wonder that Du Bois would lament in the final pages of *Black Reconstruction* that he was writing "in a field devastated by passion and belief." His pen dipped in acid, he would rage that most of the record of the Reconstruction period was based on the "unsupported evidence of men who hated and despised Negroes and regarded it as loyalty to blood, patriotism to country, and filial tribute to the fathers to lie, steal or kill in order to discredit these black folk." A small number of Negro authors and scholars, equally ignored or dismissed by white academics and the mainstream public, had begun to join Du Bois in the seemingly futile venture at rehabilitating the post–Civil War history of their people. The Crisis Publishing Company had printed a useful 1913 memoir by Maud Cuney Hare about her father, Norris Wright Cuney, the Texas businessman-politician and Republican state national committeeman from 1885 to 1893. In that same year, the remarkable John R. Lynch, elected speaker of the Mississippi House of Representatives at age twenty-four and U.S. congressman two years later, published *Facts of Reconstruction*, a valuable reminiscence taken seriously by no more than a handful of scholars (mainly those who subscribed to Woodson's then new *Journal of Negro History*). Literature professor Benjamin Brawley's pioneering *A Short History of the American Negro*, however inadequate to the task of refuting the Dunningites, also appeared that year; the book would serve an invaluable function for more than a decade as the unique textbook suitable for Negro history courses at Fisk, Morehouse, Howard, and other historically black colleges. We have seen Du Bois returning to the Reconstruction charge in his 1924 volume, *The Gift of Black Folk*, appearing two years after Woodson published his immensely popular *The Negro in Our History*, a more dense treatment of the subject than Brawley's. Inspired by these books and the history courses promoted or taught by Brawley at Morehouse, Locke and Kelly Miller at Howard, and the economist George Edmund Haynes at Fisk, a minuscule group of scholars went on to earn doctorates at Chicago and Harvard in order to form around Du Bois and Woodson a dedicated cohort of Davids to challenge the Goliaths of white history. James Hugo Johnston, Luther Porter Jackson, and Charles Wesley, along with several others from historically black colleges, were joined by Rayford Logan and the wonderfully named Alrutheus Ambush Taylor, both graduates of mainstream northern schools.

"Dramatically, the Negro is the central thread of American history," proclaimed *The Gift of Black Folk* with hyperbole calculated to provoke revisionist thinking. There were even many Negroes who might have thought the claim was little more than Du Boisian chauvinism. Yet the overstatement contained the essential truth that the American narrative had become a monstrous binary distortion, an exercise in cultural sadism that would defy remedy so long as the part played by black people in history continued to be written as separate, unequal, and irrelevant. It was as though mainstream American history had embraced a paraphrase of Judge Taney's *Dred Scott* dictum that black historians had no interpretations that white historians were obliged to respect. There was now not the slightest ambiguity in the response of the historical profession to the fateful question Du Bois had posed in *Darkwater*: "Are we not coming more and more, day by day, to making the statement 'I am white,' the one fundamental tenet of our practical morality?"—and of our scholarship, he might have added. Du Bois had only to dip into volume one of Ellis Oberholtzer's United States history to gauge how what he called a theory of human culture had "worked itself through warp and woof of our daily thought with a throughness that few realize." Northerners had little comprehension of the southern race problem, Oberholtzer observed there, because they "had never seen a nigger except Fred Douglass"; this from the friendly historian who had proposed the subject of Du Bois's only biography, the blazing *John Brown*. Rare exceptions to the intellectual discourtesy only served to prove the immutableness of the professional rule. The invitation to Du Bois to review Ulrich B. Phillips's problematic masterpiece, *American Negro Slavery*, in the March 1918 number of the *American Political Science Review* had been one such exception in a remarkable policy departure also extended in that year for the same purpose to Woodson by the *Mississippi Valley Historical Review*.

Du Bois, as did Woodson, found it more than curious that Phillips's gracefully written book, long awaited as the definitive study of America's peculiar institution, reserved merely a supporting role to the slaves—to "darkies," "niggers," and lower-case negroes, in the usages of the plantation-born University of Michigan professor. *American Negro Slavery* was mostly about American slaveholders, those "supermen," in Du Bois's ironic words, who created a special realm based on aristocratic leadership, land, crops, and, Phillips insisted, humanely managed "conscript labor." "Less a business than a life," according to the author, slavery had made "fewer fortunes than it made men." Whatever harshness and infrequent cruelty the regime inflicted upon the "conscripts" were necessitated by the reluctant splitting up of families for sale or the sanctions enforced by troublesome "truancy." The slaves' time on the cross had been, if not pleasant, at least comfortable, Phillips assured his readers, as slavery involved ordinary human labor problems little different from those of modern factory labor—and no more, and probably less, onerous. The inference to be drawn from the book—indeed, wrote Du Bois, its "unstated major premise"—was that Negroes "were not ordinary slaves nor indeed ordinary human beings" but subhumans whose pliant, childish, inborn natures made them perfect chattel. For Du Bois, the Phillips book represented all that was deplorable about the southernization of history, its monumental accumulation of evidence in the service of conscientious obfuscation of the record and promulgation of a pernicious dogma. A model of criticism and reproach that even obliged Phillips's biographer to commend it seventy years later, Du Bois's review anticipated "The Propaganda of History," his jeremiad at the end of *Black Reconstruction in America: American Negro Slavery* was a shameful apology for slavery, Du Bois wrote sorrowfully, a defense of an institution that was "at best a mistake and at worst a crime—made in a day when we need sharp and implacable judgment against collective wrongdoing by cultured and courteous men.... The mere fact that [slavery] left to the world today a heritage of ignorance, crime, lynching, lawlessness and economic injustice, to be struggled with by this and succeeding generations, is a condemnation unanswered by Mr. Phillips and unanswerable." But far too few mainstream historians considered the objections raised by Du Bois worthy of answering.

Finally, the Rosenwald fellowship and the Harcourt, Brace book contract presented the opportunity to put black people into the national narrative at the poignant moment of their assumption of constitutional citizenship. Had the powerful philanthropies and his own restiveness in the face of scarlet racial tensions allowed Du Bois to remain at Atlanta University twenty-five years before, he most likely would have already written the Reconstruction monograph. His response to a letter from a Niagara Movement collaborator the year before resigning his Atlanta professorship to join the NAACP indicated Du Bois's strong desire to do so. "The educated Negro owes the world a history of Reconstruction," James Diggs of Lynchburg, Virginia, urged. "No subject has been treated in a way more harmful to our race than this one subject," and Diggs proposed a series of state histories to counter the Dunningite studies. Clearly, he believed that no one was more capable of carrying out such a plan than Du Bois; and, replying that Diggs's idea was "excellent," so did Du Bois in summer of 1909. Even in the thick of the UNIA controversy, the mission to Liberia, and management of *The Crisis*, the saliency of the project was to be evident again in 1924 when Du Bois included a chapter on the Reconstruction Era in *The Gift of Black Folk*. Five years later had come the *Encyclopedia Britannica* affront when he withdrew his article on the Negro in the United States rather than delete a paragraph on the positive Reconstruction role of black people. "I remember hearing some time ago that you first began to write *Black Reconstruction* because of the article . . . turned down by the [Britannica] editors," Charles Pearce at Harcourt would write in anticipation of receiving a finished manuscript in July 1933.

But the more immediate goad had been Claude G. Bowers's *The Tragic Era: The Revolution after Lincoln*, a 1930 Literary Guild selection that was the literary equivalent of *The Birth of a Nation* in Cinemascope. Author of a fine biography of Thomas Jefferson, Bowers was the editor of the *New York Post* and a fiercely partisan Democrat who believed in states' rights and raged against a recrudescent southern GOP. Alarmed by the cracks in the solid South caused by Catholic Al Smith's 1928 run for the presidency, Bowers, FDR's future ambassador to Spain, had pledged to turn his book into a potboiler about the Republican Party in the post–Civil War South that would be "the most tremendous indictment of that party ever penned in history." *The Tragic Era* was certainly the "most tremendous indictment" of black people during Reconstruction. "That the Southern people literally were put to the torture is vaguely understood," the preface intoned, "but even historians have shrunk from the unhappy task of showing us the torture chambers." No longer. In Bowers's chamber of horrors, heroic Andrew Johnson loses to Sumner and the "bitter," "abnormal" Stevens. Carpetbaggers and scalawags rile up the Negro against "those who understood him best." "The negroes would not work, the plantations could not produce. . . . The economic status of the races is to be reversed through the distribution of the land among them." Civilization crumbles as the aberrant Fourteenth and Fifteenth Amendments unleash black power. Compared to Bowers's, Fleming's text was almost insipid. While discomforting to some mainstream historians, the book was judged representative of the consensus in the field by Harvard's Arthur Schlesinger, Sr., in *The New Republic*.

Educated people of color considered the book to be the last Dunningite straw. They thought of it as tantamount to a lynching in prose, and its enduring popularity in high schools and colleges was long to be a source of angry humiliation. James Diggs's twenty-year-old appeal was taken up now by educators such as the remarkable feminist Anna Julia Cooper, by the reviewer of Bowers for *The Crisis*, and by James Weldon Johnson and others who believed in Du Bois's unique ability to mount a credible counterattack. "It seems to me that the *Tragic Era* should be answered—adequately, fully, ably, finally & again it seems to me Thou art the Man!" Cooper wrote him. And who but the editor could *The Crisis* reviewer have had in mind in asking, "who will write the Negro's side of the story written by Mr. Bowers from the viewpoint of the Negro's despisers?" That it was his duty to write such a book must have been a significant, compensating factor in Du Bois's waning interest in the affairs of the association. The plunge into research and writing began in earnest immediately after he received Embree's notification in February 1931 of the Rosenwald grant, then accelerated after signing with Harcourt, Brace that November. The next three years were devoted to what was to be one of the superlative achievements in the writing of American history. That even he was able to write this massive study while skirmishing with White and Wilkins, and all in the course of orchestrating the Amenia Conference, performing magic tricks with the magazine's debts, supplying feisty editorials, polishing lectures, and undertaking cross-country speaking engagements, is a tribute to Du Bois's disciplined genius.

On the other hand, wearing several occupational hats precluded Du Bois from conducting the kind of extensive primary research expected of a professional historian. That he chose instead to concentrate on government reports, proceedings of state constitutional conventions, dissertations, and virtually every relevant published monograph, but made only occasional use of newspapers and none of unpublished archival records at historical societies, state repositories, and courthouses would disturb scholars, several of whom would note dyspeptically the author's generous foundation support. Not only were such reproaches to be of little concern to him, for whom the book's rationale was preeminently one of aggressive reinterpretation rather than of original research, but they conveniently ignored the almost insurmountable handicaps confronting Negro scholars wishing to gain access to southern repositories. Before the Civil Rights era it was rarely possible for them to gain admission to historical societies and state archives, as the American Historical Association's first African-American president, John Hope Franklin, relates in his vivid reminiscences. It is hard to imagine Du Bois motoring from "white" courthouse to campus entreating entry of red-faced custodians or even, should he have have been admitted, agreeing to remain out of sight in a small, windowless back room poring over records provided by resentful white employees.

On May 4, 1933, Du Bois's delighted editor at Harcourt, Brace received the first draft of chapter one. The editor's sole reservation was the title Du Bois proposed for the book. Pearce thought that "Black Reconstruction of Democracy in America" would be much improved if rendered simply as "Black Reconstruction in America," to which the author readily assented. Several of his letters during this period mention intense concentration and almost monastic withdrawal from social intercourse. Mildred Jones, who'd not seen him for many months, wrote Du Bois anxiously in the spring of 1933, "where are you — and are you well?" She was alarmed. Too busy to explain. Will write more later, he promised her. A letter from Atlanta in late March shared a few details with Davis DuBois. He and his graduate students were reading *Das Kapital*. "I've got them now each working on a state study of Reconstruction in the South," he revealed to her. Still, the self-imposed timetable he had promised Pearce in March — "[not] the slightest doubt but what the manuscript will be finished and entirely rewritten by July 1" — had gone the way of most unrealistic schedules. On July 10, Du Bois wrote Pearce from Atlanta that he was still struggling to shape the book after two rewritings. He was dealing with a manuscript "more than twice as long as a book of this sort can afford to be," he complained. And there was, for the stylist Du Bois, another embarrassment: *Black Reconstruction in America* was not yet "a piece of literature. It still resembles . . . a Ph.D. thesis," Pearce was told, "well documented and with far too many figures." As he would explain to Harcourt somewhat later, there was a special reason for the manuscript's great length. From Pike to Bowers, the denigrating of Negro legislators had been remorseless, yet many were men of exceptional ability. Yet to confine himself to complimentary statements, such as, "for instance . . . that some of the Negro members of the legislatures made excellent speeches," would fail to convince, Du Bois wrote. "There was nothing for me to do but quote the [entire] speeches."

Returning to New York at the end of Atlanta's summer session, Du Bois wrote Hope in mid-September 1933 (with the Amenia Conference now behind him) that he had been working on the book "practically every day, including Saturdays and Sundays all this summer and have had no vacation, and yet the thing hangs on." He simply wouldn't be able to leave for Atlanta until just before the first week of classes. It was no one's business but his, but it seems Du Bois did allow himself a pleasurable week's respite at the end of August to entertain a Miss Sarella Shook, an adventuresome young woman on her first visit to the Big Apple from Nashville. "It was nice of you to give me so much time while I was there," she enthused, what with his book project and all. Earlier in the summer, an adoring Shook had accepted his invitation to motor as far as Chattanooga after Du Bois gave his seminal "The Negro College" address to the Fisk alumni. Back in Atlanta in early October, he bore down hard to meet the new deadline, writing furiously in his spacious living quarters in Ware Hall, AU's new graduate dormitory facility. He was sure to be quite comfortable there, he remembered to write Nina, with a parlor "nearly as large as our living room, [and] a fireplace . . . and a bedroom twice as large as my bedroom."

Finally, the first draft was ready. He wrote a delighted Mildred Jones, who hoped to see more of him now, that he had been working his "head off on that book and finished it on December 1 [1933]." To Alfred Harcourt, Du Bois wrote with considerable understatement, "It was really a very difficult job." It was also only the end of the first phase of the difficult job, however, for Du Bois informed the publisher a day or so later that another five hundred dollars above the original advance was needed in order to make the book sufficiently error-proof to withstand "a great deal of criticism." "Every lapse or mistake as to fact and every date" must be caught and corrected, Du Bois insisted. He would need to hire help. The professional reader consulted by the publishing house corroborated the general opinion that Du Bois had produced a masterpiece; she also confirmed the author's estimate of the work yet to be done. Harcourt, Brace, pleading the asperity of the times, eventually provided half Du Bois's requested amount and suggested another appeal to the Rosenwald Fund or, alternatively, the Carnegie Corporation. In light of its future dealings with Du Bois, the Carnegie Corporation's generous response to his petition was notable. On March 16, 1934, after a two-month review interval, president Frederick P. Keppel notified Du Bois that the Carnegie Corporation had awarded a one-thousand-dollar grant for the completion of *Black Reconstruction*. By then, Du Bois had yoked a half dozen persons to the project: sociologist Frazier and political scientist Emmett Dorsey, both at Howard, and historian Logan, now conveniently at Atlanta, for documentary research; poet and literary critic Sterling Brown for stylistic advice; Trotskyite journalist Benjamin Stolberg for Marxist theory; the wife of a Morehouse English professor for proofreading at thirty cents a page; and graduate student Ellen Irene Diggs for typing. Stolberg's eleventh-hour reservations, hurriedly mailed to Du Bois on October 3, as galleys were shuttlecocking between New York and Atlanta, proved invaluable. The young Marxist had become an intimate confidant and respected sounding board for ideas in the relatively short time Du Bois had known him.

Turning to the theoretical superstructure Du Bois had imposed on parts of *Black Reconstruction in America*, Stolberg expressed the view that it would get Du Bois "into critical difficulties." Originally, Du Bois had intended to call chapter ten "The Dictatorship of the Black Proletariat" and another "The Dictatorship of the White Proletariat," contending that the evidence showed "a conscious ideal" on the part of black laborers to "tax and administer the state primarily for the benefit of labor" after 1867. But Stolberg insisted that a proletarian dictatorship was a historical impossibility in the age of pre-Marxian politics — that even the Paris Commune of 1870 had foundered in petty bourgeois ideology — and that, particularly in post–Civil War America, "socialist conceptions did not exist." He observed that "our working class then — if now — was not ready for them." As Du Bois had heard similar objections from Harris, Bunche, and Dorsey, he decided to delete "dictatorship" from these chapter headings as well to elide the "scientific" connotation of "proletariat" in the text. In his invaluable introduction to the 1976 reissue of *Black Reconstruction in America*, the Marxist historian Herbert Aptheker underscored Du Bois's use of the term *proletariat* as being more classical than Marxian. "It meant the lower classes," says he, "and from the Latin *proletarius*, [meaning] a citizen of the lowest class." Unwilling to adopt Aptheker's more generous interpretation, both Marxist and anti-Marxist critics would spend a generation deploring to excess the book's overlay of unorthodox Marxism.

He was into the final stretch, allowing nothing and no one to stand in the way of the book. He annulled his commitment to teach in the workers' school sponsored by AU, and upbraided patient John Hope, who was told in no uncertain terms that teaching summer school was not covered by the contract. As Du Bois interpreted its terms, his four-thousand-dollar annual salary was to be based on nine months work. Not only did he expect additional compensation for the summer classes he was teaching as he completed the book, Du Bois virtually demanded that Hope immediately reduce his course load from fifteen to ten semester hours. He dealt with Ira Reid, his junior sociology colleague, even more peremptorily, informing him that he was withdrawing the departmental secretary from general duties in order to work on the manuscript. "Miss Diggs, from her work last year, knows more about it than anyone else," he explained to Reid, who kept his considerable annoyance to himself. Du Bois and Irene Diggs worked together in a nearly perfect master-servant bond without rest. November came as the checking of references, fine tuning of prose, sharpening of emphases, and taking of several major last-minute decisions accelerated. Pearce had been immensely relieved to get the first 160 pages of corrected proof with "comparatively few changes" at the end of October. But chapter ten (large enough for a book), covering the black proletariat in South Carolina, Mississippi, and Louisiana, had to be restructured.

After two postponements of the publishing date and ongoing revisions of and insertions in the proof, Alfred Harcourt was finally constrained to call Du Bois's attention to the contractual stipulation that the cost of all changes in the proof above 25 percent must be borne by the author. It was clear that several hundred dollars had to be spent to make the book ready, as well as that another delay in the release of the book was unavoidable. Du Bois's personal check for $250 was gratefully acknowledged by the firm, but it insisted that a perfected book would need an additional $600 in editing and typesetting. Money must be no object; no corrections must be omitted, Du Bois assured Harcourt in a letter that was almost a cri de coeur. "My method of writing is a method of 'after-thoughts.' I mean that after all the details of commas, periods, spelling and commas, there comes the final and to me the most important work of polishing and resetting and even re-stating. This is the crowning achievement of my creative process." Pondering the delays, the advance, investment in plates, and the hefty $4.50 sales price, Harcourt was moved to quip to the author, "I must say that I wish you had had your afterthoughts first." At Harcourt's suggestion, Du Bois appealed once again to the Carnegie Corporation, explaining in detail to Keppel how such large overruns had come about but why they must not further delay publication of the work. He had a book "of unusual importance," it must be said. "Of course, it will not sell widely; it will not pay, but in the long run, it can never be ignored." Answering Du Bois on November 28, Keppel said that the cupboard was pretty bare, but he could find a supplementary $250 if that would "see the job through." Recalculating the book's costs, Harcourt thought the amount, together with Du Bois's check, sufficient to proceed. On April 17, 1935, the author forwarded the last proofs. He had succeeded in trimming the text to 729 pages. *Black Reconstruction in America* reached bookstores in early June in a first printing of 2,150 copies. The dedicatory inscription to Virginia Alexander read, *"Ad Virginiam Vitae Salvatorem"*—"To Virginia, savior of my life."

A certain lore has surrounded the book. Because it was ignored by the *American Historical Review* and disparaged by some of the mainstream historians during the era of McCarthyism, the impression persisted well into the 1970s that *Black Reconstruction* received scant notice at the time of publication or, to the extent it did, that it was widely dismissed as serious scholarship. It is devoutly to be wished that readers in the twenty-first century will contemplate with astonishment that the state of race relations was such that Du Bois believed that it was imperative to stipulate to readers in the early twentieth century that he had written his history "as though Negroes were ordinary human beings, realizing that this attitude will from the first seriously curtail [his] audience." Yet, as Du Bois well knew, the book faced the code of snide denigration prevailing in upper-middle-brow publications such as *The New Yorker,* which observed that the author took the "odd view, in distinction to most previous writers, that the Negro is a human being." *Time* magazine's dismissal of Du Bois as an "ax-grinder" whose Reconstruction history was a "wonderland in which all familiar scenes and landmarks have been changed or swept away" hardly came as a surprise. The unwritten racial rules of the period precluded book-club adoption of a serious book about people of color by a colored author. Even so, there was gratifying notice by the *Book of the Month Club News,* where Jonathan Daniels, a white newspaperman of impeccable southern credentials, was moved to welcome *Black Reconstruction* as a correction "for much white history about a period in which the Negro played a great part." Daniels went so far as to applaud the book's philosophical interpretation of Reconstruction as a conflict within the labor movement "to set not only Negroes but the white proletariat free." As pleased as he must have been by such well-placed appreciation, Du Bois may have been rather surprised by the critical enthusiasm with which the Hearst dailies in New York, the *American* and *Daily Mirror,* welcomed the book. For the *Daily Mirror* reviewer, *Black Reconstruction* was a "long-burning torch on humanity's highroad," while the *American* savored it as a "bristling piece of scholarship that should disturb complacent historians."

Could it be that, with the exception of *Time,* Du Bois's extraordinary work had been hailed by the mainstream press of the North, an incredulous reader asked in a letter to the Pittsburgh *Courier*? To his elation and that of a great number of other American Negroes, the critical response to *Black Reconstruction* was generally quite positive outside the South, although even below the Mason-Dixon Line the book caused exceptional breaks in the ranks of Lost Cause historians. Lewis Gannett, friend, Harvard man, and fellow association board member, wrote an ecstatic review for the daily New York *Herald Tribune,* declaring that "if anything finer has been written in English in recent years," he was unaware of it. When a scholar such as Henry Steele Commager could justify the black codes enacted by white southerners immediately after the Civil War, Du Bois's rehabilitation of Stevens and Sumner and "impassioned attack upon slave-minded historians" was all the more welcome, Gannett believed. The reviewer for the New York *Sun* seconded Gannett, saluting the book for demolishing the "self-satisfied distortions of the period which have passed without challenge for the last thirty years." Oswald Garrison Villard, who always blamed Du Bois for driving him out of the NAACP, filled three pages of *The Saturday Review of Literature* with critical praise of the "remarkable book." The nation had taken a wrong turn into evil ways with the 1876 Hayes-Tilden Compromise, Villard wrote, and historians from Burgess to Bowers had distorted a record of Negro achievement that Du Bois's history had splendidly recaptured. William MacDonald of Yale's history department was both captivated and skeptical in his well-grounded review in the Sunday edition of *The New York Times*. Although he wondered why a scholar subventioned by the Rosenwald Fund and the Carnegie Corporation had not made fuller use of primary sources and was disturbed by interpretations "shot through with Marxian economics," MacDonald believed that Du Bois was "absolutely justified in his rancorous onslaught on American historians of the Civil War period." He found the global context of proletarian exploitation in which Du Bois situated the emancipatory struggle of black people to be as suggestive as it was suspect. But MacDonald saw *Black Reconstruction*'s "calmer" sections on the maligned Reconstruction governments to be substantial refutations of scandalous white historiography. The *Times* review offered a summation that was both severe and generous:

> One puts down this extraordinary book with mixed feelings. . . . There is no need to accept the author's views about racial equality in order to recognize the imposing contribution which he has made to a critical period in American history, nor need one be a Marxian to perceive that, in treating the Negro experience as part of the American labor movement in general, he has given that movement an orientation very different from what it has commonly had. Yet there runs through the book a note of challenge which seems to point, in the author's mind at least, to the imminence of an inescapable and deadly racial struggle.

Du Bois had done a grand piece of work, "and no one else could have done it," a tremendously proud James Weldon Johnson saluted the author in the name of the Talented Tenth. Walter White sent word that Eleanor Roosevelt promised to read the book immediately and quoted her as saying that she would " 'also try to get the President to read it.' " Another significant marker in the slow healing of the rift between Bookerites and Du Boisians was the generous salute from Emmett Scott, a man with whom Du Bois had often clashed in print and recently even in court:

> The Negro people of the United States—in fact, the colored peoples of the world, owe you a sincere debt of gratitude for your monumental work, "Black Reconstruction." We have long needed a virile pen such as yours to set forth the true facts of Reconstruction. It must be most gratifying to you to read the approving criticisms which are appearing in the Metropolitan newspapers. It will not be easy in the future for so-called historians to smear the Negroes' part in that lamentable period.

If Scott's prediction about the staying power of the Dunningite dogma was much too optimistic, his assessment of the intrinsic, transformative value of *Black Reconstruction* was to prove wholly accurate in time. The book represented one of those genuine paradigm shifts periodically experienced in a field of knowledge, one that sunders regnant interpretations into the before-and-after of its sudden, disorienting emergence. Had he ventured to paraphrase Marx, who both inspires and deforms the book, Du Bois might well have observed that he had set reconstruction historiography upright after finding it standing on its head. *Black Reconstruction*, as adumbrated by its subtitle, "the Attempt to Reconstruct Democracy," heralded a reconstruction of democracy in the writing of the history of the American South that none of the volume's seemingly considerable flaws would diminish.

As novel in thesis as it was and the result of much personal reflection and writing, Du Bois's book was nevertheless not sui generis, but the particular beneficiary of new scholarship produced by three younger academics, one of them black. Alrutheus Taylor's *The Negro in South Carolina During Reconstruction* (1924) and *The Negro in the Reconstruction of Virginia* (1926) were distinguished by meticulous primary research, clean writing, and such restrained subversive interpretation as to compel muted commendation from the few mainstream historians who deigned to read monographs published by Woodson's ASNLH press. His work exposed the inflated claims in these states of carnivalesque inefficiency, confiscatory taxation, and of vaunted superior integrity supposedly evinced afterward by the so-called "redeemers." Corruption in the post–Civil War South was color-blind and no respecter of partisan affiliation, with carpetbaggers and redeemers evenly matched in the potlatch of state contracts and railroad bonds. Furthermore, as Taylor documented, Negro legislators never controlled the key committees for graft, not even in South Carolina where they held a majority in the lower house. Francis Butler Simkins and Robert Hillard Woody, two unusually liberal White southern historians who did pay close

attention to the small, shy Fisk professor, incorporated Taylor's revisionist findings in their jointly authored and racially nuanced *South Carolina During Reconstruction*, published just as Du Bois was gearing up to write. But while Taylor
quietly concluded that Negro legislators "gave Virginia the only democratic
instrument of government it has ever had" and Simkins and Woody noted almost in afterthought that South Carolina's whites had "no disposition to keep
[Governor Wade] Hampton's promise that he would protect the political rights
of the Negroes," Du Bois scored such revelations for full orchestra. What Du
Bois borrowed, he invariably transformed and enlarged.

By far, *Black Reconstruction*'s greatest achievement was to weave a credible
historical narrative in which black people, suddenly admitted to citizenship in
an environment of feral hostility, displayed admirable volition and intelligence
as well as the indolence and ignorance inherent in three centuries of bondage.
It invested these former slaves—four million men and women whose numbers
comprised a majority in two southern states and a sizable portion in the remainder—with what a later generation of historians would gravely call agency.
Du Bois returns them to the center of the Reconstruction epic as they steal
away to freedom, a great many clueless in the early days but quickly setting
their minds to getting a plot of land, some little book learning, and soon enough
voting their own kind into office. The treatment of these first days of manu-
mission summons the author's awesome gift of lyricism to full throttle in "The
Coming of the Lord," a chapter drawn in mesmeric purple. In a passage that a
Dunningite historian might have envied, the author observes: "It was all foolish,
bizarre, and tawdry. Gangs of dirty Negroes howling and dancing; poverty-
stricken ignorant laborers mistaking war, destruction and revolution for the mystery of the free human soul." A few lines more, and the frenzy becomes majestic
in upper case: "All that was Beauty, all that was Love, all that was Truth, stood
on the top of these mad mornings and sang with the stars. A great human sob
shrieked in the wind, and tossed its tears upon the sea—free, free, free."

Writing as the scribe of his race, then, Du Bois offers the quintessence of
what he knows has been and long will continue to be the dilemma of race in
America: "Of all that most Americans wanted, this freeing of slaves was the last.
Everything black was hideous. Everything Negroes did was wrong. If they fought
for freedom, they were beasts; if they did not fight, they were born slaves. If they
cowered on the plantations, they loved slavery; if they ran away, they were lazy
loafers. If they sang, they were silly; if they scowled, they were impudent." The
tone poem celebrates its special folk in a euphony of sound clearly intended to
transport the auditor-reader into the gnosis of Jubilee. "There was joy in the
South. It rose like a perfume—like a prayer," Du Bois limns. "Men stood quivering. Slim dark girls, wild and beautiful with wrinkled hair, wept silently; young
women, black, tawny, white and golden, lifted shivering hands, and old and

broken mothers, black and gray, raised great voices and shouted to God across the fields. . . . a great song arose, the loveliest thing born on this side of the seas." The sonata builds, recapitulating the chords registered unforgettably in *Souls*:

> It did not come from Africa, though the dark throb and beat of that Ancient of Days was in it and through it. It did not come from white America — never from so pale and hard and thin a thing, however deep these vulgar and surrounding tones had driven. Not the Indies nor the hot South, the cold East or heavy West made this music. It was a new song and its deep and plaintive beauty, its great cadences and wild appeal wailed, throbbed and thundered on the world's ears with a message seldom voiced by man.

Guardians of southern history, sensing the book's potential for great mischief to their cause, were instantly on the qui vive. "There is a feeling of ripeness in the writing . . . and an occasional passage of almost Old Testament grandeur. 'Provocative' is a mild adjective for *Black Reconstruction*," warned John R. Selby in a Nashville *Tennesseean* review (syndicated to several major southern newspapers) alerting the region to a bombshell.

Volition, intelligence, and agency Du Bois applied in bountiful (and some critics would insist in overripe and excessive) portions to Afro-Americans in the Reconstruction drama. But it was in his interpretation of the generative function of black labor in the formation of industrial wealth that Du Bois posited the first of several original conceptions of profound impact. Writing in "The Black Worker," the book's opening chapter, that black labor "became the foundation stone not only of the Southern social structure, but of Northern manufacture and commerce, of the English factory system, of European commerce, of buying and selling on a world-wide scale," Du Bois cast the slave from Africa as the fulcrum of the Industrial Revolution. It had been the Treaty of Utrecht of 1713 that marked the historic moment when a small island won the means to become a global powerhouse, a significance underscored by Du Bois's inclusion of the treaty's text in the appendices to *The Suppression of the African Slave Trade to the United States*, his prizewinning Harvard dissertation. By the terms of the treaty, the victorious British acquired exclusive license ("*Assiento de Negros*") to import slaves into Spain's colonial empire, by virtue of which Georgian England became the eighteenth century's chief supplier of human flesh at twenty pounds a head times ten million. That eighteenth-century profits from the Atlantic slave trade had financed the steel production and textile manufacture of the British and French maritime bourgeoisies was a proposition that must have come as a matter of logic to the author of *The Suppression of the African Slave Trade*, now steeped in Marx. The author's embryonic thesis was to be brought to full term a decade later by a West Indian admirer whose analytical sophistication matched

Du Bois's. The scholar-politician Eric Williams's controversial classic, *Capitalism and Slavery*, argued that the profits pouring into Bristol and Liverpool from the triangular trade in slaves, sugar, rum, cotton, and finished goods underwrote to a controversial degree Great Britain's remarkable industrial takeoff.

Many of the critics who saluted the brilliance of the book tended to feel uncomfortable or become suspicious when dealing with its sweep and depth. Nor is it unexpected that much of what troubled, exercised, and alienated Du Bois's critics now seems less significant, six decades after publication, to contemporary students of society who have divined insights in *Black Reconstruction* that the former either ignored or completely overlooked. Thus, there was more than met the eye in Du Bois's vivid correction of Phillips, whose influential *American Negro Slavery* perfected the apathetic fallacy by substituting depersonalized "conscripts" and "truants" for the black men, women, and children who toiled under the overseer's lash. Du Bois wished it clearly understood that Thomas Carlyle's witticism about the cause of the Civil War—people "cutting each other's throats because one half of them prefer hiring their servants for life, and the other half by the hour"—was a deadly absurdity. For in 1935 it was still imperative to remind progressive historians and curious readers only four years before the release of *Gone With the Wind* that American slavery had not been simply another permutation in labor management but a travesty of uniquely inhuman dimensions. "Once accustomed to poverty, to the sight of toil and degradation," wrote Du Bois, "it easily seems normal and natural; once it is hidden beneath a different color of skin, a different stature or a different habit of action and speech, and all consciousness of inflicting ill disappears." Physical abuse, cultural impoverishment, economic and civil nullity were only part of the dismal condition of color-coded abasement, however.

Black Reconstruction disclosed as brilliantly as "The Souls of White Folk," written a quarter century earlier, the interlocked perniciousness of democracy and race in America, what it might well have called the metaphysics of class and skin color. Even as the racial basis of American slavery hardened over the decades, masters and slaves endured in a codependency based on coercion, manipulation, antagonism, and consanguinity that required of the millions of excluded poor whites little more than political passivity and police work. The South under slavery was not yet Brazil, but with at least 350,000 people of mixed racial heritage in 1850, a majority of them free, the trend toward hybridization showed no sign of slowing. We now know that before 1850, as one extremely knowledgeable historian maintains, "race relations in the lower South partook of the character of race relations among its Latin American and especially its West Indian neighbors." Du Bois emphasized that the planters only began to appeal across class lines to the poor whites on the basis of color with the onset of the Civil War, telling the poor, disfranchised white man that "after all he was white and that he and the planters had a common object in keeping the white man superior." (Du Bois ignored the pre–Civil War role of poor whites as citizen police authorized to challenge any black person they encountered.) Consider the consequences to social democracy of this appeal to whiteness, insisted the author in the chapter titled "The White Proletariat in Alabama, Georgia, and Florida": "So long as the southern white laborers could be induced to prefer poverty to equality with the Negro, just so long was a labor movement in the South made impossible." Leftist reviewers deplored as flagrantly un-Marxist, of course, any contention that white workers would choose compensation "by a sort of public and psychological wage." But for Du Bois, and for revisionist scholars of a later time, the "wages of whiteness" would serve as an exceptionally potent tool of social analysis in a settler nation where successive waves of dark and different Europeans were inducted into a white republic from which people of color were excluded by an almost hysterical one-drop rule.

The exclusion of black people from the white republic was an inevitability for which the victims themselves have, with a fine illogic, been blamed. Du Bois used *Black Reconstruction* to expose the homeric contradiction of an entire people being forced into the pariah status of second-class citizenship in order to justify, in policy and law, their unfitness for full citizenship. Set free without preparation, denied ownership of land, and deserted by the national political party to which they had rendered such strategic, vital service, these people were uniquely vulnerable to being scapegoated and marginalized. The reality was that whatever they did in slavery and freedom had to be discounted and denatured simply because to do otherwise was to complicate enormously the ideals, politics, and economics of the American creed of laissez-faire. There was one libel that *Black Reconstruction* would rebut that Negroes had long resented as a fabrication of surpassing historical license — the libel of the willing support of the Confederate war machine by the slaves. The lore of the Lost Cause depicted the peculiar institution as having been so benign that the slaves had been proud and happy to serve as the mainstay of the fighting South. "Many a bullet was sent into the northern lines by slaves secretly using the white soldiers' guns," Fleming maintained in his colorful history of Alabama. That the reviewer for *The Nation* offered the southern loyalties of 4 million slaves in categorical repudiation of *Black Reconstruction* was a telling instance of the libel's tenacity, its reinforcement among northerners of black unsuitability for the burdens of citizenship.

In the problematic fourth chapter of the book, therefore, Du Bois propounded a controversial "general strike" of the slaves as the second most important factor in the defeat of the South. He certainly knew that the phrase itself, with all of its anarcho-syndicalist and anti-Leninist karma, was a provocation inviting heated discussion, misconstruction, and even derision. *General strike* evoked images of millions of workers in the great capitals of Europe acting in disciplined concert to paralyze reactionary governments, men and women versed in the notions of Fernand Pelloutier and Georges Sorel and steeped in the martial ethos of the labor union. The proposition that illiterate black men and women had been capable of intelligent, collective action decisive enough to affect the course of history was as much anathema to racist historians as it was theoretically vexatious to many of socialist persuasions. Stripped of its over-lay of political theory and associations with France's Confederation du Travail or Great Britain's Trades Union Congress, Du Bois's general strike amounted to little more than the common sense of self-preservation exhibited on a massive scale. As formulated in *Black Reconstruction*, the general strike entailed whole-sale evacuation of the plantations by the slaves, and involved "directly in the end perhaps a half million people. They wanted to stop the economy of the plan-tation system," the author explained, "and to do that they left the plantation." Some 145,000 of the 180,000 Negro troops in the Union armies were slaves who had either escaped to the Union lines or signed up when the Yankees marched through the neighborhood. "What the Negro did was to wait, look and listen and try to see where his interest lay," Du Bois wrote of the slaves' mind-set with verisimilitude. "As it became clear that the Union armies would not or could not return fugitive slaves, and that the masters with all their fume and fury were uncertain of victory, the slaves entered upon a general strike against slavery by the same methods that they had used during the period of the fugitive slave." The postwar lament of one Georgia slaveholder—that "in too numerous in-stances those we esteemed the most have been the first to desert us"—was iterated on a great many plantations in the closing months of the war. By the mid-1960s, leading authorities on Reconstruction would begin to embrace the concept of a general strike in all but name, so that, first, John Hope Franklin, then Kenneth Stampp, and, in the final decade of the twentieth century, Eric Foner (an avowed Du Boisian in what was once Dunning's history department) adduced the slaves' determination to break away from the plantation system as a crucial component in the North's victory.

In "Looking Forward," a chapter brimming with fecund ideas and ending with a poem by Jessie Fauset, Du Bois deployed the concept of the "American Assumption" to explain the failure of Reconstruction. This assumption, that wealth was "mainly the result of its owner's effort and that any average worker can by thrift become a capitalist," had ceased to be valid after the Civil War, he claimed, "but its tradition lasted down to the day of the Great Depression," at which point, Du Bois announced, it had "died with a great wail of despair." In his American Assumption, Du Bois formulated a version of the creed of exceptionalism that scholars have come to regard as uniquely American: escape from the rise and fall of history into universal opportunity for individuals and endless progress for the nation. Yet, for a split historical second in the heat of Radical Reconstruction, Du Bois maintained that the American Assumption had been temporarily counterbalanced. Alarmed by the return to Congress in 1866 of unreconstructed southerners who might repudiate the Civil War debt and almost certainly reduce the tariff, Du Bois characterized "Northern industry" as frightened and moving "towards the stand which abolition-democracy had already taken: namely, temporary dictatorship, endowed Negro education, legal civil rights, and eventually even votes for Negroes to offset the Southern threat of economic attack." The American Assumption Du Bois described as a sort of trapdoor underneath the political and economic projects of Radical Reconstruction: whether it was General Sherman's Special Order Number 15 giving emancipated slaves "possessory titles" to forty acres of land in Georgia and South Carolina; whether it was the Freedmen's Bureau's success in feeding, clothing, negotiating work contracts, and educating 247,333 new citizens in 4,329 elementary schools (the first federal antipoverty program); or protecting black voters and officeholders under the Civil Rights Act of 1875. Much sooner than later, in Du Bois's version of events, the "dictatorship of labor" imposed upon the South by the alliance of northern industry and the "abolition-democracy" collapsed and dropped away through the American Assumption.

Analytical yet intuitive, densely researched but impressionistic, judicious and sweeping, *Black Reconstruction* pushed the figurative beyond the bounds of the historically permissible in its determination to integrate black labor into a Marxian schematic of proletarian overcoming. Generously interpreted, a general strike of the slaves was a valuable insight capable of factual corroboration. A dictatorship of labor, however, was, as Stolberg and others had warned, analytically much too fanciful. It was an interpretive riff that completely dismayed economic historian Sterling Spero in his *Nation* review. Quoting one of the book's most provocative passages claiming for Radical Reconstruction "one of the most extraordinary experiments in Marxism that the world, before the Russian Revolution, had seen," Spero erupted incredulously—"a proletarian dictatorship resting on the military forces of victorious industrial capital!" Not only were the fiercest congressional radicals economic liberals whose divergent interests were bound together by a "civic ideology" embracing the sanctity of property and the primacy of capital, but, as Foner, one of Du Bois's most judicious interpreters, would emphasize in his synoptic *Reconstruction: America's Unfinished Revolution*, most southern Negro officeholders were conservative to silent on the make-or-break issue of land redistribution (the "American Blindspot," in Du Bois's words), as well as moderate about sharing political power with white men of affairs. In chapter nine, "The Price of Disaster," when he reinvoked the American Assumption in explanation of the freed slaves' deceived expectation of federally distributed land—"most Americans used the Negro to defend their own economic interests, and, refusing him adequate land and real education, and even common justice, deserted him shamelessly as soon as their interests were safe" — Du Bois was somehow able to ignore the contradiction.

And so it was to be "Back Toward Slavery," the title of the throbbing, penultimate chapter with the wages of whiteness destroying any possibility of the solidarity of labor across color lines. The dilemma of divided destiny — imposed by white America on black America far more intensely than upon other people of color pressing up against the white republic — crackled again in the high-voltage prose of *Souls*. What other racial group in any advanced nation had been as widely inhibited and mentally confined as the American Negro, Du Bois implored? "Within the colored race the philosophy of salvation has been curiously twisted and distorted." From the defeat of Reconstruction to the despair of the Great Depression where had history taken them, he asked, what signposts pointed to a way out of the three-hundred-year-old box?

> Shall they use the torch and dynamite? Shall they go North, or fight it out in the South? Shall they segregate themselves even more than they are now, in states, in towns, cities or sections? Shall they leave the country? Are they Americans or foreigners? Shall they stand and sing, "My Country Tis of Thee"? Shall they marry and rear children and save and buy homes, or deliberately commit race suicide?

Long ago in the flush of a Harvard doctorate and of precocious sociological studies, Du Bois had been certain, as he would write in *The Autobiography*, that the cure for the race problem was "knowledge based on scientific investigation." The lynching of Sam Hose, policies of the General Education Board, and bloody race riots in Atlanta and Springfield, Illinois, had disabused him of an ideal far more suited to Europe in the Enlightenment than to Georgia in the reign of Tom Watson. His faith in the ameliorating power of knowledge had never dissipated, of course, but had only sought what had promised to be the more effective strategy of militant journalism informed by uncompromising principles and vital social science.

That conviction was never to be more intensely manifested than in "The Propaganda of History," the solemnly magnificent coda to *Black Reconstruction* in which the strictures of Calvin and Crummell thundered. Du Bois proclaimed that history as truth could empower true democracy, if only historians chose to lie less. He was writing in a field devastated by lies told by Rhodes and Dunning, Fleming and Bowers, and a library of others. There would never be a science of history "until we have in our colleges men who regard the truth as more important than the defense of the white race," he remonstrated, "and men who will not deliberately encourage students to gather thesis material in order to prejudice or buttress a lie." Du Bois's last chapter soared beyond an appeal to honest history into a realm where moral philosophy fused with the symbolism of the Creation. But if it was special pleading as biased in its own way as any white supremacist's, he saw it as partisanship in the cause of justice and democracy, as he proclaimed "the most magnificent drama in the last thousand years of human history." It was "the transportation of ten million human beings out of the dark beauty of their mother continent into the new-found Eldorado of the West."

> They descended into Hell; and in the third century they arose from the dead, in the finest effort to achieve democracy for the working millions which this world had ever seen. It was a tragedy that beggared the Greek; it was an upheaval of humanity like the Reformation and the French Revolution. Yet we are blind and led by the blind. We discern in it no part of our labor movement; no part of our industrial triumph; no part of our religious experience.... And why? Because in a day when the human mind aspired to a science of human action, a history and psychology of the mighty effort of the mightiest century, we fell under the leadership of those who would compromise with truth in the past in order to make peace in the present and guide policy in the future.

The writing of distorted history was but part of the encompassing sin against humanity as one reads "the truer deeper facts of Reconstruction with a great despair," Du Bois concluded. The triumph of the white South had been a phase in the global exploitation of the darker world. The last images in *Black Reconstruction* were truly horrific: "Immediately in Africa, a black back runs red with the blood of the lash; in India, a brown girl is raped; in China, a coolie starves; in Alabama, seven darkies are more than lynched; while in London, the white limbs of a prostitute are hung with jewels and silk. Flames of jealous murder sweep the earth, while brains of little children smear the hills."

It was a measure of the growing diversity and self-confidence within the Talented Tenth that two of its prodigies, Bunche and Harris, were to be found among the severest critics of *Black Reconstruction*. That both men genuinely admired Du Bois is plainly evident from correspondence. Du Bois had participated at Bunche's invitation in a conference on the Negro and the national economic crisis, jointly sponsored by Howard University's Social Science Division and Davis's Joint Committee on National Recovery, less than a month before the release of the book. Harris had continued to seek Du Bois's advice in connection with his task as chair of the NAACP's Committee on the Future Plan and Program until his resignation in frustration at the end of 1934. But if Du Bois was the person for whom Harris felt "greater affection and admiration" than any other, no holds were barred when it was a matter of a young Howard professor's opportunity for a showpiece critique in the prestigious *New Republic*. Harris graded *Black Reconstruction* as the most "completely fantastic attempt at applying Marxian dogma to history" conceivable. Both strikingly similar in tone, Harris and Bunche professed superior socialist understanding tinged with consideration for the author's advanced years, the latter opining in the *Journal of Negro Education* that Du Bois's "racialism appears . . . a much too virulent breed to permit successful crossing with Marxism," that the general strike proposition was "untenable," that Reconstruction state governments were petit-bourgeois creations, that southern white labor had been maligned, and warning, finally, that the "serious student of contemporary social forces and events must read [the book] with due caution." The Young Turk's grievance was given nutshell statement in *The New Masses* by Loren Miller, a multitalented Talented Tenth renegade. Du Bois was a romantic, a racialist, and an old man given to dreams of "a shopkeeper's paradise" as a solution to the Depression. "At a time when the masses of Negroes need more than ever to throw their support behind movements for real labor governments and genuine dictatorships of the proletariat," Miller, age thirty-two, condescended, "Du Bois can only yearn for a limited bourgeois democracy that will give him and his beloved Talented Tenth a place in the sun."

In years to come, white historians would alternate between pretended indifference to and grudging recognition of the significance of *Black Reconstruction*, until the book was rediscovered by liberal arts majors and graduate students in the 1960s — and, consequently, by publishing houses happy to cash in on the new vogue in "Black Studies." Its continuing appeal to those few historians who pushed the envelope of scholarship, however, would be reflected in the quality of letters to Du Bois from two of the profession's arbitral figures, Howard K. Beale and C. Vann Woodward. Pursuing studies at Columbia for his master's in 1932, Woodward had made it a priority to become acquainted with Du Bois, interviewing the editor at *The Crisis* before heading for a summer sojourn in Moscow. Working under Beale for the doctorate at the University of North Carolina in the mid-1930s, Woodward had gritted his teeth as he sat through the Dunningite lectures of Beale's senior colleague, J. G. de Roulhac Hamilton. Taking up his first teaching position in Atlanta, Woodward's brief flirtation with the left had caused his dismissal from Georgia Institute of Technology after he publicly defended the cause of Angelo Herndon, the black Communist labor organizer. Contemplating a visit to Atlanta from his new appointment at the University of Florida, the twenty-seven-year-old assistant professor would write Du Bois in the spring of 1938 to ask for a meeting to discuss a plan of research Woodward had in mind. The research plan in question concerned revision for publication of Woodward's doctoral dissertation, a small portion of which had just appeared in the *Journal of Southern History* as "Tom Watson and the Negro in Agrarian Politics," a copy of which Woodward proudly enclosed. Reminding Du Bois that he had followed his career for a number of years "with interest and profit," Woodson pledged that his Tom Watson article had been written "in a spirit that I hope you will approve, whether you can agree with my conclusions or not." The letter closed by especially acknowledging Woodward's "indebtedness for the insight which your admirable book, *Black Reconstruction,* has provided me." Beale had expressed his appreciation for Du Bois from the early 1930s, seeking advice in preparation for a major work on the freedom of instruction in public education. A progressive southerner who had awaited eagerly the appearance of the Reconstruction book, Beale would decide to make a professional declaration of his esteem by writing the 1940 turning-point essay in the august *American Historical Review,* "On Rewriting Reconstruction History," in which he acknowledged the catalytic scholarship not only of Du Bois but of Horace Mann Bond's *Negro Education in Alabama: A Study in Cotton and Steel.* In his endlessly rich history of the American historical profession, Peter Novick appropriately cited Beale's essay as marking the symbolic "collapse of the consensus on this highly charged issue" of Reconstruction.

Du Bois had made his disdain for Charles S. Johnson's scholarship clear enough when, instead of reviewing *The Negro in American Civilization* himself, he ran Stolberg's dismissive *Herald Tribune* assessment in *The Crisis.* It was this scrupulously neutral 1930 monograph—described by Stolberg as a "competent example of a certain type of very bad book"—that promoted Johnson to the rank of senior Negro sociologist of the day. Johnson, to his credit, resisted any temptation to repay the slight in a *Survey Graphic* appreciation that was a model of judiciousness. Dubious of what he saw as Marxist reductionism and alert to its narrative obfuscations, Johnson's review engaged the mind of the book masterfully, writing that its major thesis was simply that the result of the Civil War had been an enfranchisement of labor, black and white, "but that the entrenched bigotries of the 'landed oligarchy' and the ignorant racial prejudices of white labor so weakened the strength of labor as to render it helpless before the forces of industrialism and capitalism." When placed alongside the sportsmanlike critique of Professor Benjamin Kendrick in the *Southern Review,* concerned readers and students of history had, perhaps, the soundest temporary last words in a debate that had now been irreversibly transformed. Kendrick, a University of North Carolina historian, understood that, as he wrote, "the debate between us cannot be decided by an 'appeal to the sources.' We can both find support there for our respective contentions." Even had the white South made its archives available to a patiently petitioning Du Bois, Kendrick assured readers that the issue would still have been less one of historiography than of ideology, would remain everlasting by one of sources placed in the service of social ideals.

How meaningful *Black Reconstruction* would become for the fostering of social ideals was reflected in a letter to the author from a file clerk in the Illinois Department of Labor, Bernice Hereford: "Is it asking too much for you to autograph one [book] for me to keep and to use as a symbol to my boys[?] To give them courage to fight on."

"IT WAS NICE to see you for a moment, and we will look forward to your next visit," lonely Nina wrote Will in the second week of the year, 1936. Much had happened, and yet little had changed in her life, since Will's relocation to Atlanta. "It was nice to see you and the baby, even for a moment," he replied in the rush of his public and private activities. He had returned from New York to preoccupations with departmental and university business, as well as to plans for a short midwestern lecture circuit and a stop at "Hotel Jones," as Mildred Jones invited him to think of her Indiana Avenue home. Plans for a six-month research stay in Germany and Austria were still three or more months from completion, but they entailed a mountain of preparatory correspondence. Busy as he was, though, the family concerns of New York that had caused much worry throughout the previous year continued to tug at him, requiring numerous long-distance phone calls and a stream of didactic dispatches. The St. Nicholas Avenue property, which Du Bois had deeded to Nail in the mistaken belief that he was satisfying a mortgage indebtedness, had come near bringing financial ruin in spring of 1933 — until Arthur Spingarn came to the Du Boises' rescue once again. In a torturous, three-sided negotiation involving an uncomprehending Du Bois, a now bankrupt, vague Jack Nail, and the exigent special deputy superintendent of banks in charge of the defunct Mercantile Bank and Trust Company of New York, Spingarn managed to have the Du Boises' liability reduced. The eventual remittal of five hundred Depression-era dollars to the mortgage bank in early 1935 had sent Nina into such a deep funk that Virginia Alexander conveyed her concerns to Du Bois.

There had been much on Nina's mind at the time. All in all, Will thought she failed to realize "how little we have suffered from the Depression." Nail was finished. Their friends the Bouttés, who had enjoyed an annual income in 1929 of about ten thousand dollars, were barely solvent. "The Alexanders have lost money and felt the pinch severely." The secretary of the Harlem YMCA staggered along on 60 percent of his salary. Du Bois could have added that ordinary black people were suffering the trials of Job squared, although the 1934 midterm elections, in which Negroes dramatically switched to the Democrats, had resulted in a greater enrollment in the CCC and more attention to extending relief to them. The America of Hoovervilles under bridges and of caravans of overloaded Tin Lizzies outrunning dust bowl vortices was the stuff of

Crisis copy, mercifully remote from this Talented Tenth family. But they were by no means immune. The St. Nicholas calamity had been averted finally only when the NAACP made good on half the thousand-dollar salary debt still owed to the editor.

The solution to their predicament at the Dunbar co-op had been more complicated. Soon after the collapse of the stock market, Du Bois had converted from an apartment purchase agreement with the Dunbar co-op to a rental plan, with the understanding that deductions for that purpose were to be drawn periodically against an equity reserve of thirteen hundred dollars: a costly interim solution. The birth of Yolande's daughter, "Baby Du Bois," in October 1932 had very soon trebled the occupants of 5G and J, as mother and daughter came to live with Nina while Yolande pursued studies for her master's at Columbia University's Teachers College. It was Nina and Virginia Alexander, commuting from Philadelphia for a special course at NYU the following year, who assumed the hands-on care of the lively baby. Virginia, who had delivered Baby Du Bois, swore by cow's milk, syrup, and water for the infant. The strict feeding and bathing schedule enforced by grandmother and pediatrician contrasted markedly to the slipshod care the baby might have received given Yolande's limited capabilities.

Monitoring the stressful circumstances from Atlanta, Du Bois had preferred, ideally, some quieter, less unsettled locale for the family in Brooklyn or the Bronx, a nicely ventilated place with a garden. He had fretted over Nina's "perfectly ridiculous" Sunday washings by hand of Baby Du Bois's clothing, making the day "even less a day of rest than it can be." Futile scoldings, however, as Nina could not help herself repeating the compulsive hygienic regimen she had imposed on Yolande in her infancy. Subconsciously, perhaps, she still wished desperately to obliterate the Jim Crow microbes that had robbed her of their beloved firstborn, Burghardt, thirty-four years before, snuffing out the flame of Will's passion for her. Apostrophized in *Souls* as the "dream of . . . black fathers stagger[ing] a step onward in the wild phantasm of the world," recovered allegorically in *Dark Princess* as "Messenger and Messiah to all the Darker Worlds," Burghardt lived on in their primordial desires, a succubus on the Du Boises' affections for each other, a ghost who inhabited books and even troubled his niece's gender—Yolande's daughter, handicapped with the name Du Bois Williams.

Family economics had finally prevailed in the summer of 1935. Du Bois yielded to the inevitability of Nina's move from 226 West 150th Street to a smaller Dunbar apartment located at 210 West 150th in the complex. Although at first she had hoped to escape Harlem where, as Nina complained, "living conditions here seem to be more and more difficult," money and racial considerations had prevented her doing so. Nina had found New Rochelle, Yonkers, and other locations so disappointing. "The main trouble"—even for Mrs. William Edward Burghardt Du Bois—was that colored people were unwelcome in these communities. "The places you can get are old and worn out," she reported. It had had to be Harlem, after all. At the last minute, however, the Du Boises were required to spend money in order to save more of it. As a sine qua non to relocating, the Dunbar management stipulated that the combined apartments had to be returned to their original condition at a charge of almost five hundred dollars. A volley of letters between management and a choleric Du Bois in Atlanta had ensued after a bill arrived apparently minus an expected hundred-dollar reduction. Stating that he knew "perfectly well that there is no use of a poor man attempting to go to law against such a corporation as you represent" (the Rockefellers), Du Bois grumblingly accepted the Dunbar tally.

Relocation had finally come in mid-October 1935, an undertaking the exhausted Nina managed alone as Will was deep in the throes of galley revisions for *Black Reconstruction*. He had sympathized, writing that Nina sounded "awfully tired over the telephone." He thought it time that she realized that "as one grows older one must do less work and more and more put the burden on others." Moving to a two-bedroom apartment on a lower floor had saved money and spared Nina the difficulties of a building with no elevators. The move had also necessitated sacrificing her dining room set in order to make room for the living room furniture. "These apartment rooms really are small," Nina had sighed. Downsizing of living space had also obliged Yolande to return to her teaching position and seriously troubled marriage in Baltimore, leaving Baby Du Bois with grandmother.

Yolande's marriage had spiraled downward into alcoholism and abuse from a rocky start almost four years earlier. In almost every respect but one, his acumen at cards, young Arnette Williams was the polar opposite of Yolande's bubbly, delicate first husband. They had become lovers after Williams returned from an unsuccessful stint at Lincoln University in Pennsylvania to take night classes in the teachers' college housed at Douglass. His tuition guaranteed and his goals high-mindedly redefined by his new father-in-law, Arnett Williams had returned to undistinguished but dogged studies at Lincoln. Yolande, pregnant, had finished another year of teaching, then come to live in Harlem with Nina in the fall of 1932, where Virginia Alexander delivered Du Bois Williams in early October.

A husband's visits to his wife in his in-laws' home during holidays and semester breaks had had an inherent potential for awkwardness that Yolande seems to have done little to mitigate. Writing his father-in-law with a twinge of hurt four months after his daughter's birth, Arnett had hoped to be "hearing from home soon." He got "about one letter a month from Yolande." The drought of letters from New York had continued (Arnett thought it due to stamps being "so high"), adding to unhappiness caused by poor grades. Encouragement had come from Atlanta: "Do not be discouraged at marks. They are more or less artificial." Still, Arnett would do well to improve his English. Admonishments from Atlanta to Yolande to write and be more sensitive—"Remember, he does feel in a little awkward position and is rather alone"—had been unavailing. At the end of August 1933, Du Bois had expressed sharp exasperation. "You know you are naturally exceedingly selfish," he upbraided Yolande, "especially when it comes to your own people.... Arnett must be made to feel welcome at home."

Her parents had been bitterly deceived in their hope that Yolande's return to Baltimore in the summer of 1935 would encourage the couple to start a life on their own together. Arnett Williams had graduated Lincoln, and, more fortunate than many Americans, had even found work in the middle of the Great Depression. But Du Bois soon heard of incidents of vicious physical abuse and drunkenness, in one case, reported by Nina, of a male friend knocking Arnett down in order to stop him from mauling Yolande. "I wonder Yolande did not send him on his way long ago," her mother snapped. Du Bois heard with mounting concern, then grief, in January 1936, news of utterly unbearable marital conditions. Virginia Alexander and her sister, Sadie, the first woman of color admitted to the Pennsylvania bar and the incumbent city solicitor for Philadelphia, barreled down to Baltimore on a mission of discovery in early January. Aghast by what they found, the Alexander sisters ordered Yolande to move at once. The police were to be summoned if Arnett objected. "Sadie said that because of his belligerent tendencies I must divorce him at once... and get support for the child," Yolande bleated.

Interrupting work on the index to the Reconstruction monograph, Du Bois addressed Yolande's husband in the accents of a *Crisis* editorial, then made a lightning visit to Balimore. Despite efforts and such personal encouragement as could be given Arnett "through talks and correspondence," he concluded that it was "quite evident that the marriage is a failure." The diagnosis of the problem was plain to see, decreed this early feminist and father-in-law: "You seem to think that [marriage] involves complete physical ownership of the woman, and her utter subjection to your wishes at all times; and secondly, there seems to be no doubt but that you are drinking to excess and have been seen drunk at various times." He fully expected Williams to grant Yolande an uncontested divorce. If he did so, Du Bois would agree to cancel his son-in-law's tuition debt; if not, then Williams was expected to repay the loan immediately on pain, Du Bois warned, of bringing the indebtedness "to the attention of your employers." "It was a messy thing. I'll never forget it," Arnett Williams would recall of the protracted divorce proceedings, as he mused in comfortable retirement from government service not long before his death in the early 1990s. He bore his former father-in-law, "the aristocrat of the breakfast table" no ill will, nor Yolande, for that matter. It had just been a question of incompatibility.

Dutiful observance of the proprieties was a Talented Tenth commandment, and Du Bois must have considered his public conduct in regard to family matters to be above reproach in Atlanta. He visited during holidays and, however briefly, on other occasions. Perhaps he might have written more frequently, but his letters were seldom uninteresting and almost always intended to be helpful. Nor had he ever failed to provide adequately for the material needs of Nina and Yolande. That he failed to meet their emotional needs as the years had passed, and would do so with greater consistency in the future, Du Bois self-absolvingly regarded as the inevitable, regrettable consequence of a sacrosanct misalliance. In a sense, he came to see himself as the true victim of his marriage and of its disappointing issue, a man of outward stoicism whose private pain and passion impelled him to seek relief in serial companions, each of whom exemplified some quality he no longer discerned in his spouse. Yet Du Bois remained famously married (even if few who knew him ever laid eyes on Nina), and so, of course, at liberty to compromise his vows without the expectation of compromising his freedom. Intimate friends such as Lillian Alexander, Wendell Dabney, and John Hope might have said, in light of the array of remarkable women to whom he made himself available, that, overall, Du Bois attended to his family's needs with considerate competence.

Serial companionship ruled in Atlanta to such an extent that gossip was almost as rife as book reviews in the months following the appearance of *Black Reconstruction.* A much-whispered-about confrontation had occurred between Joel Spingarn and Streator, after the latter had complained that the NAACP president had gossiped about Du Bois's Atlanta liaisons. Ann Rucker, granddaughter of Reconstruction congressman Jefferson Long and one of colored Atlanta's social arbiters, reported to Arthur Schomburg that Du Bois was "rather quiet" and seen "now and then with a rather insignificant widow," but others described him as romantically very busy, although discreet. The "insignificant widow" in question was Louie Shivery, whose estranged husband, George, had lingered before dying of self-inflicted wounds in the fall of 1934. "A trying experience," Du Bois reported to Nina, although sparing her details of his own widely observed, ongoing solace of his prize graduate student.

Students passing along narrow Chestnut Street grew accustomed to seeing "Dr. Du Bois" sitting with book and cane in lap on Shivery's front porch patiently awaiting her return. They knew never to greet the great man. Shivery was the companion of choice for "ladies night" at the Boulé and his steady at the movies, one of his passions. "Let's go to the movies tonight and then drink wine," beckons a typical note of the period. Sometimes, the lure was ice cream and champagne. They argued a good deal, or rather Shivery argued, at breakfast in his Ware Hall suite or out riding in the Buick he garaged with her—presumably about their relationship. Sometimes she rebuffed him, and he reacted anxiously: "I phoned 3 times last night. Twice you were not there and the 3rd time you did not answer." Once he prescribed that she try holding her breath when angry until she reached the count of ten in German. A typical Du Boisian formula for harmony was one he penned in apparent dismay on an undated Saturday night in 1935. Her quarrels and tantrums were not normal, he stated, but "evidence of nervous sickness" for which there were three antidotes: "1. Stop scolding and quarrelling. *Stop* it. It is simply nerves. 2. Do not talk so much. Listen to others. Let others talk *some times*. 3. Go to bed normally at 10. *Never* work after midnight."

Theirs was an affair of the mind as well as of the heart, however. Self-improvement was expected of the women in Du Bois's life. At about the same time that Shivery was being firmly reminded in spring of 1935 to finish a seminar report on "Karl Marx and Fascism," a proud Mildred Jones wrote Du Bois about the graduate history courses she had taken that year "to justify your faith in me." Sailing to Bermuda that April, Davis DuBois committed her deck-chair reveries to paper, imagining Du Bois beside her aboard the S.S. *Volenden*. Because he was "such an artist with all senses," Davis DuBois sighed, she, too, had become "very discriminating since knowing you—rare food, drinks, etc, etc." Older than Jones and Davis DuBois, Louie Shivery played a feisty Galatea to Du Bois's Pygmalion, brilliant, temperamental, and sure of her own mind. Brief notes, admonitory memoranda, and detailed guidelines for Shivery's master's thesis ("writing up of this data is going to take all of your available time for several months") abound in the correspondence. Her thesis, "History of Organized Social Work Among Atlanta Negroes, 1890–1935," a huge study based primarily on documents drawn from Lugenia Hope's Atlanta Neighborhood Union, would only be completed with his help literally days before Du Bois was due to sail for Europe. Depositing in her mailbox the final, frenzied revisions that he and Diggs had worked over "all day," Du Bois would speed away aboard the Pullman express in order to sail from New York to Southampton on June 5, 1936. The Shivery master's thesis was a worthy exemplar of the pioneering scholarship in community studies inaugurated by Du Bois almost forty years earlier at the old Atlanta University.

Louie Shivery would wait for him to return to Chestnut Street, but two women who were also deeply involved in his emotional life in Atlanta would follow Du Bois to Europe. Irene Diggs and Elizabeth Prophet drove north together in late June, intending to sail from New York for France within a week or so, and visiting Nina in the interim. Diggs had worked as research assistant to Du Bois while completing her graduate course work in sociology at AU, a relationship that was formalized as salaried special research assistant to Du Bois after an unhappy secretarial experience with President Read of Spelman. She had been invaluable on the Reconstruction project. As the years passed, she was to be found jealously at his side in Atlanta and then in New York, until faculty responsibilities with Morgan State College's sociology department confined her to Baltimore. That Diggs would become the second Mrs. Du Bois, once the ailing Nina went to a well-deserved rest, came to be widely regarded as a certainty, at least until the end of the 1940s. Prophet's arrival from Paris in the fall of 1934 must have been something of a jolt to Diggs. Du Bois had proposed a year's residency at the University Center with studio and modest salary, a suggestion Hope, already impressed by Prophet's sculpture, had warmly endorsed. The tall, turbaned figure striding to and fro between her studio in an old power plant and the Spelman campus, head angled haughtily and long cape swirling, evoked, depending on the observer, awe, diffidence, or amusement. Prophet's majestic affectations and Du Bois's own august demeanor would occasion long-lived hilarity when faculty members re-created the memorable night Du Bois had been obliged to exit the sculptor's Spelman quarters through the window.

One deep friendship ended in 1936 as Du Bois planned his world trip, and another began. John Hope died, and Shirley Graham appeared. Hope died of cardiac arrest on February 20, the day after his wife's birthday. Magnanimous to a fault, he had fended off the inevitable coma for a dozen hours, hoarsely protesting, "I can't die today. I can't." Hope had suffered a massive heart attack three years earlier, lingering between life and death in Spelman's infirmary under the fiercely protective eye of an adoring Florence Read. Du Bois had written to Moton in alarm at the time, almost despairing of Hope's refusal to spare himself. "He does not know how to get rid of details and is, therefore, always up to his neck in worries," Du Bois had fretted. Thanks to Moton's intercession, Lugenia had maneuvered her husband into a month's stay and abdominal surgery at the Mayo Clinic in summer of 1929, only to see him undermine full recovery by insisting on chairing a YMCA World Committee meeting in Geneva. Knowing that he would die sooner than later at his present pace, Hope had clearly decided to gamble on achieving a great deal more in a shorter amount of time. The constellation of AU graduate faculty was filling up with stars worthy of its Du Bois centerpiece: Spingarn medalist William Stanley Braithwaite in literature; Logan in history; Reid in sociology; Hale Woodruff and Prophet in art; Samuel Nabrit in biology; Kemper Harreld in music; and Jesse B. Blayton in business. The merger with the University Center of two Methodist-affiliated colleges—Clark and Morris Brown—lay within the president's grasp.

Du Bois was away from campus on a western lecture trip when Hope died. He expressed as much outward emotion as he was capable of to Virginia Alexander. "It is a very terrible loss which I cannot yet realize," he wrote her.

They had been friends for almost forty years. Hope was first among equals in that pantheon of Du Bois soul mates that numbered, among its few other males, Charles Young, Joel Spingarn, James Weldon Johnson, George Crawford, Thomas Bell of Newark, and Dabney. He was "without doubt my closest friend," Du Bois would write not long before his own death. It remained to be seen if what they had dreamed of achieving together—" build[ing] in the lower South a university equal to if not superior to anything which this former seat of Negro slavery ever saw"—would be possible without Hope's quiet inspiration and accomplished foundation influence. Counselor, benefactor, and icon of the leadership class in which Du Bois still reposed his trust, John Hope had expired, alert and impatient, eight days before his friend's sixty-eighth birthday. Du Bois was outliving his generation. Morgan of Harvard College days had been dead six years. Wells-Barnett, the virago of civil rights, had passed from the struggle in 1931. Chesnutt, a great, balked talent of American letters, had succumbed in 1932, followed a year later, in May, by Henry Hugh Proctor, Du Bois's Fisk classmate and former pastor of Atlanta's first Congregational Church. Trotter, militant and bitter to the end, removed himself in 1934. Hope's memorial service in early December would be a much grander affair than required by his modest instructions for the occasion. As devastated by his death as Lugenia (and, rumor insisted, from grief that was even more affectionate), Florence Read orchestrated a statesman's farewell from Sisters Chapel, the imposing Doric temple on the Spelman campus donated by the Rockefeller family. Diggs was there to make a stenographic record for Du Bois, absent in Asia.

Du Bois's impending research trip around the world was news. To Shirley Graham, twenty-nine, and one year out of Oberlin College, it meant a splendid opportunity. "You will need a secretary. Take me along, I beg," she pleaded from Nashville. She was not a sociologist, but she did have a trained mind, knew "a little German," and was willing "to work endlessly." And she had to escape her teaching position at Tennessee Agricultural and Industrial College. "Take me out into the air," she implored. "I'm dying here." Taking her along was, of course, impossible, Du Bois replied. He proposed an assignation instead, an automobile ride with him from Tennessee to Kentucky and back on the pretext of attending a conference. As he was scheduled to speak on April 15, to a teachers' association meeting in Louisville, Du Bois informed her that he would drive from Atlanta to Nashville to collect her from some strategic locale. Clearly, though, he had no desire to drive to the remote Tennessee "A&I" campus, and his presence at Fisk would draw attention. She should "please find a place" to meet, he instructed. Graham approached the Caytons, a young couple who, she assured her idol, were "thrilled with the importance of keeping your coming a secret." Horace R. Cayton, who would coauthor *Black*

Metropolis, the finest study of urban blacks since *The Philadelphia Negro,* was then a thirty-three-year-old instructor in economics at Fisk and the maverick grandson of Hiram Revels, U.S. senator from Reconstruction Mississippi. The Grahams and the Caytons had had a nodding acquaintance in the state of Washington, where Reverend David Graham had pastored a church in Spokane and Shirley had finished Lewis and Clark High School. The plan was flawlessly executed: a pleasant dinner, animated conversation, a nightcap followed by re-tirement to separate bedrooms, an early-morning departure from the Caytons' for the teachers' conference—all superficially proper yet deliciously wicked. Du Bois was exactly as Graham remembered him, "trim, precise, quietly elegant and twinkling." The drive to Louisville, leisurely under a warm April sky, a roadside picnic finished off with the famous Du Bois coffee and two Benson and Hedges from the dented, filigree cigarette case, much talk of racial destiny in the well-received speech and afterward on the drive back—two days in par-adise for Graham. Waving goodbye from the entrance to her faculty apartment, she hurried to unwrap his gift. It was an inscribed copy of *Darkwater.*

Thirty-five years later, when Shirley Graham Du Bois re-created the Nash-ville rendezvous in *His Day Is Marching On,* a vivid, somewhat accurate mem-oir, she implied that it was their first meeting in the Tennessee capital—which it was not. To be sure, their first meeting had occurred many years earlier, when Du Bois was a guest in the family parsonage in Colorado Springs, Colorado. The Grahams had followed the Lord's commands from Indianapolis, where Shirley was born as Lola Graham in 1906, through the Southwest to Washing-ton, and, eventually, on mission for the African Methodist Church to Liberia. Lorenz Graham, one of four sons, fixed the time of Du Bois's visit as 1920, and never forgot the commotion caused by the great man's advent and the surrender of his fourteen-year-old sister's bed for two nights. If in every life there comes an unforgettable encounter, Shirley Graham represented the conversation with Du Bois on the family porch in Colorado Springs as such an experience. Of that Thursday afternoon epiphany, her memoir recalls Du Bois chiding her much later, " 'You were such a *nosy* little thing. Wanted to know everything!' " After high school, Lola morphed into Shirley Graham McCants, wife of a Se-attle newspaper publisher and mother of two boys, Robert and David. The phase as Mrs. Shadrach McCants ended quickly in divorce, followed by several years of music studies in France, further study at Howard University, and an instruc-torship at Morgan State College.

Meanwhile, Du Bois "loomed over me through all my schooling," she wrote. He noticed her again when the Jelliffes produced Graham's *Tom-Tom* in Cleveland's Municipal Stadium in the summer of 1932, with Charlotte Murray and Hazel Walker supporting lead baritone Jules Bledsoe, and composer-arranger Harry T. Burleigh on the organ. *Tom-Tom,* a somewhat unformed opera, was an imaginative composition intended to illustrate the survival of Africanisms in modern music. Du Bois introduced the Oberlin graduate student to readers of *The Crisis* the following year as a rare artistic talent, and published Graham's essay "Black Man's Music" in the August issue. She thanked him in the irrepressible style that would characterize all future letters, averring her optimism for the future of the race "when we do have such leaders" as he. His letters counseled her about professional options, and consoled her about the mediocrity in which she claimed to be drowning at A&I. Graham's outpouring on June 23, 1934, was a remarkable epistle, paragraphs tumbling over one another for pages in bitter reaction to Du Bois's resignation from the NAACP. "All great men have lived ahead of their time," she reminded him—" Socrates, Plato, Galileo, John Locke, Descartes. They have all lived surrounded by that consuming fire of loneliness." Both conspired to lessen the great man's loneliness when Du Bois came to Nashville to attend a meeting on New Year's Day of Alpha Phi Alpha, his college fraternity Du Bois and Graham slept together for the first time on the second night in January 1936, more than three months before the rendezvous at the Caytons' in mid April. The rapture of her letter, written only an hour or so after his early-morning departure, augured well for Shirley Graham's ambition to marry the man who had disappointed Jessie Fauset and Georgia Johnson, and who remained spousally unavailable to Virginia Alexander, Mildred Bryant Jones, and Louie Shivery, among several others. "My dear Dr. Du Bois," she began at 6 A.M.:

> "To part is to die a little." . . . I even smiled quite gayly as I looked back at you standing in the middle of the room with the light shining above your head. But this morning when I awoke knowing that right now you are leaving, when I see you climbing into the car and turning your back upon Nashville as you set out on the highway—I realize truly that "To part is to die a little." I send you my grateful love.

A week before Du Bois sailed, Virginia Alexander wrote to hasten his return and to tell him that she wondered how she would be able to bear a seven-month absence. "I am just not going to think about it."

DICTATORSHIPS COMPARED
GERMANY, RUSSIA, CHINA, JAPAN

The four-year-old Oberlaender Trust, a Philadelphia institution for the promotion of cultural relations between the United States and German-speaking countries, had awarded Du Bois a travel fellowship in June 1935. The purpose of the fellowship was to compare industrial education in Germany and Austria with the educational philosophy of Booker Washington and its institutional achievements in America. Despite the trust's disinterest in his proposal to study the treatment of Africans in the German colonial possessions four years earlier, Du Bois had succeeded through correspondence and an interview with its secretary in prying loose a sixteen-hundred-dollar stipend for a revised topic just as the first reviews of *Black Reconstruction* appeared. The decision of this German-American philanthropy (a component of the Carl Schurz Foundation) to provide subvention for Du Bois's research topic in the second year of Adolf Hitler's chancellorship was fully in line with the other awards it would make annually until 1938. The symbolic value of the leading Negro American intellectual on extended sojourn in the Third Reich must also surely have been contemplated by the trust's officers. In a thoughtful endorsement, the trust's outside referee, historian Frank Tannenbaum, then with the Brookings Institution, noted, significantly, that "an application from Du Bois to any foundation honors it."

Perhaps more to the point, a degree of skepticism may be in order in evaluating the primacy given by Du Bois to his Oberlaender Trust proposal. His research agenda for the half year abroad had nearly as many heads as the mythological Hydra, which suggests that, after a ten-year stretch at his editorial desk with no Pan-African Congress to justify foreign travel, followed by the research and writing demands of *Black Reconstruction*, Du Bois's unstated objective was to catch up with world developments—and to enjoy himself while doing so. He was also firing off letters to European scholars he hoped to meet and recruit for the "Encyclopedia of the Negro," a four-volume project he proposed to edit under the sponsorship of the Phelps-Stokes Fund.

Industrial education in Germany and the American South was one of several objectives of his travels, and it would have been in character for Du Bois's agile and ranging mind to seek to reconceptualize Hampton and Tuskegee from Berlin and Vienna. From the thrust of "Education and Work" and several other revisings, it could be seen that the Depression had caused him to cede a larger importance to technical education than in the past. Indeed, he envisaged the superior education of the future as a fusion of liberal arts and technical instruction. Yet Du Bois was by no means as ready as Woodson in the *Mis-Education of the Negro* to denounce the past emphasis on the liberal arts. Rather, he insisted on imputing blame in equal portions: neither the old Atlanta University with its high-minded classical orientation nor Tuskegee with its simplistic vocationalism had proven adequate to the stresses of modernization upon a race starting from the bottom of the labor heap. As he took a new, more sympathetic look at Booker Washington's educational ideas, the Oberlaender fellowship provided Du Bois with impressive cover from which to put his special stamp on the new "Negro college and technical school" in which a new Talented Tenth generation was to be formed.

Finally, Du Bois intended to extend his stay abroad after the Austro-German phase by another two months in Russia, China, and Japan, plans for which were virtually completed before leaving the United States. As if this agenda were not sufficiently charged, he planned to incorporate his observations of the political regimes on his itinerary into a book for Harcourt, Brace — "A Search for Democracy," in which he explored the differences and similarities of fascism, communism, and democracy. Unusual for his correspondence, the record is blank as to why Du Bois was not offered a contract by the publishing house when he returned to the United States with more than a third of the manuscript written. Much of this material for "A Search for Democracy" would have been drawn from weekly dispatches written in Europe and Asia for Vann's Pittsburgh *Courier*. Vann, who had not been particularly exercised by Du Bois's segregation stance, welcomed the offer of a column. "The Negro will never get any wealth from the white man," Vann replied immediately, still smoldering from dismissive treatment in FDR's administration. Storming out of his special Justice Department appointment and eventually back to the Republican party, he fumed that he was as "dedicated to the idea that the Negro must derive his wealth from himself" as he inferred Du Bois to be. They signed a contract at the beginning of 1936 for a weekly column, headed "A Forum of Fact and Opinion." Vann had vetoed "As the Crow Flies" as smacking "too much of *The Crisis*" and having, moreover, an unhappy connotation—Jim Crow, Two Black Crows, etc., he humphed. Du Bois agreed to the hundred-dollar monthly salary with alacrity.

To make his second visit to the Soviet Union possible, he had been advised by an American acquaintance in Moscow to contact Karl Radek for assistance, spelling out his plans for a book on the expansion of socialism. Du Bois would only discover his mistake in addressing this master propagandist and dictator of Soviet culture as he was winding up his industrial-education investigations. In June 1936, Radek was four months away from arrest and trial in the first wave of Stalin's purges. The Asian leg of the trip was being facilitated by one of Imperial Japan's most effective agents in the United States. Hikida Yasuichi was also something of a phantom who had sailed into Seattle harbor at age thirty, in April 1920.* What can be known at this remove about this slight figure tells us little more than biographical essentials. Enough can be gleaned from the spotty record of correspondence and Justice Department files, however, to deduce that Hikida was the point man for Japan's low-budget operation to influence black American public opinion.

In his unpublished book "Russia and America," Du Bois describes Hikida Yasuichi as a "young Japanese student" he recalls having met around 1930. Hikida may have had "official connections with his government," Du Bois acknowledges, "although this I never knew," he writes. Although he did work as a clerk in the Japanese Consulate in New York, Hikida's principal employment from 1921 to 1938 was as a cook in the employ of Colonel and Mrs. Hampton Anderson, a prominent white family of Bedford Hills, New York. Endorsed by Colonel Anderson, Hikida had worked during the 1930s as a summer cook at Camp Smith, the New York National Guard encampment at Peekskill. When Depression stringencies compelled the Andersons to part with his services in 1938, Hikida moved to a Manhattan rooming house on East 85th Street, leaving behind a four-hundred-volume library carefully packed in Bedford Hills. To Caucasians, Hikida was merely a trusted servant; to Negroes he was something vaguely more significant. Hearsay in Harlem described him as a Japanese nobleman who was supposed to have pursued graduate studies in sociology at Yale (where, although he obtained library privileges, he had never enrolled). He had, in fact, polished his English in a high school in Michigan immediately after entering the United States and then proceeded to study sociology for one year (1922) at Columbia University in order to gain a working familiarity with race-relations literature. When they became acquainted at some point during the late 1920s, Arthur Schomburg presumed that the politely serious Hikida, who manifested a genuine desire to learn about the American race problem and who

---

*Japanese names are rendered, as in Japan, surname first.

had already acquired considerable knowledge of it, was a foreign scholar and kindred book collector of apparently independent means.

The Harlem bibliophile's sponsorship was invaluable. The former instructor of literature at Osaka's Kansai University quickly established himself in the inner circles of the Talented Tenth as an interesting, well-intentioned — if rather enigmatic — sojourner whose amateur interests in the culture and struggles of the American Negro they considered it their pleasant obligation to facilitate. Supplied with impeccable references, Hikida had ranged widely within the segregated world of color, speaking about Japan to student groups at Howard, Fisk, Morehouse, and Tuskegee, as well as to church assemblies in Atlanta, New Orleans, and the District of Columbia, where he was also often warmly welcomed into the homes of the leading citizens. As his ingenuous report to Du Bois and James Weldon Johnson revealed, however, Hikida had found much goodwill, but only mild interest in Japanese affairs, and woeful ignorance. Repeatedly, he had been asked while traveling in the South "how Negroes were treated in Japan!" If he was not sadly mistaken, Hikida complained to Johnson (a participant in the 1929 Conference on Pacific Relations in Tokyo), "speaking as a whole, today, the Negro student has not much interest in the field of international affairs in the Orient." Hikida's concerns were fully appreciated by Du Bois, Johnson, Walter White, Pickens, and key personalities in the news business, including editor Percival Prattis of the *Courier* and Claude Barnett, founding director of the Associated Negro Press (ANP), a subscription service numbering some two hundred newspapers. Men and women of color who possessed a worldview of the race problem had tended to uncritical admiration of Japan after its destruction of two Russian armies in Korea and Manchuria, feats the Japanese capped off by sinking two Russian fleets in the Sea of Japan and the Gulf of Chihli in the 1904–5 Russo-Japanese War. "Triumphant Japan in a class by itself," Du Bois had crowed in the *New York Post*, notching her victory on the handle of colored pride. For only the second time in modern history a European power had been defeated by a non-European nation (Italy's defeat at Adwa by Ethiopia eight years earlier being the first). By the 1930s, when the Imperial Army manufactured the infamous Mukden Incident to justify occupation and annexation of southern Manchuria, American Negroes who paid attention had rushed to defend Japan and largely continued doing so even after, formally branded an aggressor, she self-righteously withdrew from the League of Nations.

Articulating a rationale that was two parts misunderstanding and one part cynicism, Du Bois had explained to readers of the Philadelphia *Tribune* and *The Crisis* the necessity for Japanese aggression. His rhetorical question — "could China have been saved from exploitation if Japan had not made Manchuria Asiatic by force?" — of course answered itself in the negative. The diplomatic

James Weldon Johnson had ventured a similar, but more diplomatic, opinion a decade earlier, also writing in Philadelphia's black weekly that the "rights of the western powers in the Orient are artificial and questionable while those of Japan are natural and moral." Typically, Du Bois would shave the edges of responsible opinion repeatedly when writing about the Japanese, all but welcoming explicitly what the Kaiser and Teddy Roosevelt had called the "Yellow Peril," and virtually anointing the Empire of the Rising Sun as the lodestar of all the "darker races."

Du Bois was the outspoken representative of a group mind-set ideally made for Hikida's purposes. Expansionist elements in Japan had begun to monitor the Negro press at the time of the Versailles Peace Conference after noticing the positive response to Japan's rejected proposal of a racial equality amendment to the League of Nations covenant. That Hikida arrived in the United States at about the same time certain circles in Japan were reading a retired army general's novel about the American race problem was more than coincidence. General Sato Kojiro's 1921 potboiler, *Japanese-American War Fantasy*, imagined the surprise destruction of the U.S. Pacific Fleet, occupation of Hawaii, and an invasion by Japanese forces of the U.S. mainland supported by 10 million Negroes led by Marcus Garvey. There had been more about Garvey and black unrest in the 1924 nonfiction book *The Negro Problem*, by one Mitsukawa Kametaro, the founder of an ultranationalist society. By the mid-1930s, with the pleasant cook of Bedford Hills at its center, Imperial Japan's symbolic overtures to Americans of color had become highly profiled. The *Dunbar News* reported visits by Japanese army and navy delegations to the complex, one of which brought cherry trees to be planted in the inner courtyard not many weeks before Du Bois was to sail for Europe. Led by members of the Murphy clan, prominent Baltimoreans boarded the naval training ships *Iwate* and *Yakumo*, where they exchanged sake toasts with the officers, who made a special point of professing Japan's concern for the rights of dark-skinned peoples. Little wonder that Cyril Briggs, founder of the African Blood Brotherhood and now editor of the CPUSA's newspaper *The Negro Champion*, was provoked to attack prominent Japanese sympathizers Pickens (who appears to have expected a trip to Japan at any moment) and Schuyler as colluding with Japan in her search for more Negro friends "to serve imperialist purposes."

The "Prince," as the *Courier*'s Prattis called Hikida, had been extraordinarily effective in cultivating his Talented Tenth targets. Johnson delightedly acknowledged receipt of the Japanese edition of "Lift Ev'ry Voice and Sing," whose translation and Tokyo publication were made possible by Hikida. In return, Johnson wrote an instructive critique of the amateur sociologist's manuscript on Japanese-Negro relations, "The Canary Looks at the Crow" ("a splendid piece of work"), which (under a less awkward title) Johnson passed along to Eugene

Saxton at Harper's for consideration. At the same time, a jubilant White forwarded Alfred Knopf a complimentary copy of *The Fire in the Flint* in Japanese. White's novel, translated with a preface by Hikida (under the nom de plume Yoneza Hiramara), was to be fairly widely read, although Knopf regretted that the Japanese were not obliged to remit royalties. Du Bois's turn came next. A copy of *The Souls of Black Folk* had been under consideration for translation in Tokyo for several months when he received Hikida's letter in April 1935 expressing "great pleasure" at the Oberlaender fellowship announcement and particular interest in the statement that Du Bois hoped to return to America via "Russia, China, Japan, and Hawaii." As the Japanese ambassador had brushed off Du Bois's enquiry about sponsoring organizations, Hikida's interest in his trip was a welcome straw. Along with news that his manuscript (revised during his New Haven stay) was now tentatively called "A Japanese Sees the American Negro" ("I had to kill the bird together with the Canary," he joked), Hikida proposed an early meeting to discuss details of a visit to Japan. "This idea came to my mind, and I thought it better to write you now—calling serious attention to . . . the spade work," Du Bois read. To introduce his insular compatriots to Du Bois months in advance of his projected arrival, Hikida volunteered to pay the international postage for regular shipments of the *Courier* to Japan. There was more encouraging news from Bedford Hills at the beginning of November. *Black Reconstruction* was under consideration in Tokyo and, although his contacts were doubtful about funds to cover travel expenses, the word from Tokyo was encouraging. Du Bois would sail before Hikida could relay final details of his itinerary for Manchuria and Japan, but Du Bois left the United States with a supply of his Japanese friend's embossed cards and with the confident expectation that matters were well in hand in Tokyo.

The S.S. *St. Louis* docked at Southampton on Monday morning, June 15, 1936.* Waiting for Du Bois at the end of customs formalities was Ruth Anna Fisher and an English friend, Marian Tooley. Tooley, an instructor at the University of London, he was meeting for the first time. Fisher he had known since her attendance at the third Pan-African Congress in 1923. She was a 1906 graduate of Oberlin College, a former scholarship student at the London School of Economics, current foreign manuscripts archivist for the Library of Congress, and, she was proud to claim, "the first woman [and, most likely, the first person of African descent] ever to be given a key to the British Museum." Fisher combined confidence and competence in such abundant measure that the standoffish J. Franklin Jameson, dean of the American history profession, had hired her as the London researcher for the Carnegie Institution of Washington, after

---

*S.S. *St. Louis* was the "Ship of Fools" whose Jewish passengers were denied entry into Cuba in June 1939.

observing Fisher's summer performance in London's Public Record Office. Jameson's reserve "did nothing to prevent him from having an eye for a pretty girl," Fisher would write of the man she always called her "beloved chief." Two years later, in 1928, when Jameson became chief of the manuscripts division of the Library of Congress, Fisher was appointed the library's foreign archivist, a post she would temporarily relinquish only after the British capital came under bombardment from the Luftwaffe.

In Du Bois, Fisher had another reserved admirer. The joint research project she had suggested at the end of 1934—a history of the Royal African Company—had excited her "Dear Burghardt." Nothing was to come of the venture, but, in the stimulated reply to Fisher's proposal, Du Bois supplied the embryonic, perspicacious thesis that would have underpinned their book—viz., the stock market as the progeny of the slave auction block. "I think that the international relations built up through the slave trade and based on the great crops of tobacco, cotton, sugar, and rice rebuilt and reoriented the modern world," he postulated. He was to be Fisher's guest at her comfortable flat in St. John's Wood during ten busy London days of teas and dinners with scholars Du Bois sought to interest in the *Encyclopedia of the Negro*. A call to the Far & Near Press Bureau was intended to further plans for lecturing in China and Japan. His Friday dinner in Fisher's flat with one of the world's leading anthropologists, Bronislaw Malinowski of the University of London, went exceedingly well. Malinowski readily agreed to lend his name to the encyclopedia project and suggested several ethnographers Du Bois ought to contact. On Sunday, he lunched with the H. G. Wellses. Two years Du Bois's senior, Wells had devoted himself to matching his fabulous contributions to science fiction, universal history, Fabian propaganda, and opinionated sociology with a passionate, troubled advocacy of peace brought about through world government. Much as their early afternoon together may have been a congress of mutual admiration between two believers in world democracy, a biographer naturally regrets the extreme economy of Du Bois's reference to a meeting of two intellectual giants of the twentieth century. On Thursday, twenty-fifth, after a busy round of social engagements and an evening performance of Chekhov's *Seagull*, starring John Gielgud, he crossed the Channel against a mild wind to Belgium.

Du Bois dined well and cheaply in Brussels, visited the postcard-Gothic Hotel de Ville, idled in the Grand-Place, probably Europe's most congenial public square, and indulged his fondness for movies. He was drawn repeatedly to the great park and palace at Tervuren, southeast of Brussels. Leopold II, the despoiler of the Congo, had thought to compensate his kingdom's small size by endowing Brussels with such outsized replicas of other European capitals' signature monuments such as the Versailles chateau and the Brandenburg Gate. He was vividly reminded that Tervuren was Leopold's conception of Versailles as a museum, twenty cavernous hallways gorged with mineral, fauna, and flora his agents had scooped up, shot down, and cut out of the heart of Africa at the probable cost of ten million black lives. Du Bois knew the museum well, having meditated in Brussels during the second Pan-African Congress on Tervuren's grotesque significance as an example of European rapacity on a scale almost defying comprehension.

He took pains to educate readers of his "A Forum of Fact and Opinion" to the verity that the problem of the twentieth century existed not only in white, black, and yellow but, as little Belgium exemplified, in white and white. In what must have seemed to *Courier* readers as something bizarrely similar—if immeasurably more humane—to the southern United States, Du Bois explained that French and Dutch ethnocentrism dictated that "laws must be published in two tongues; schools must be held for two races in two languages," a Belgian divide that he implied would soon "overshadow[/] all other problems but those of work and wage." (He could not have predicted, however, that issues of work and wages were destined to be overshadowed in Belgium by language and religion.) Critical of Belgium's colonialism and perceptive about its culture and politics, Du Bois was, as always when in Europe, on the alert for telling acts of racial civility, often investing them with a significance motivated as much by genuine gratitude as by the satisfaction of reproaching his own country. The distinguished professor who rushed from Antwerp to find Du Bois at the Hotel Cecil in order to discuss the encyclopedia was one such example, "at once so natural and yet unexpected that it seems hardly worth recording Yet it is there." Had Professor Natal De Cleene been an American scholar, Du Bois knew that, upon discovering his race, their encounter would have resulted in "anything from hesitation to open insult."

Although his thoughts are unrecorded as his express train rolled across Hitler's Germany to Berlin on the night of June 30, no exercise in biographical license need be invoked to state that Du Bois would have been intensely mindful that he was entering the eye of one of the deadliest political storms in modern times. But a few days shy of four months earlier, the Wehrmacht had invaded the demilitarized zone of the Rhineland in flagrant violation of the Treaty of Versailles. The breathtaking gamble of an incomparable thug, Hitler's Rhineland reoccupation had defied the superior French army, undermined the interlocking alliances by which France had enveloped Germany, neutered Locarno, and put the League of Nations on life support. Little more than eight weeks before Du Bois disembarked at Berlin's Lehrter Bahnhof, Mussolini's legions had finally occupied the Ethiopian capital, Addis Ababa, on May 2, after months of poison gas attacks and indiscriminate aerial bombing that had brought forth sanctions from the League on arms, which the Ethiopians desperately needed to defend themselves, but none on oil, which would have punished the aggressor Italians. Italy's invasion of Haile Selassie's kingdom had aroused American Negroes to international consciousness as never before. As if to accentuate the woes befalling the darker races, eleven days prior to Du Bois's Berlin advent, Joe Louis, the "Brown Bomber," had been decked in Madison Square Garden to the knockout count of twelve by Max Schmeling, the Great Aryan Hope of the Third Reich. To make matters worse, the overwhelmingly white audience in the Garden had switched allegiance in an hysterical few seconds from black American to white foreigner as Schmeling's blows staggered Louis. Many Negroes would have clung to their memories of the thrashing Louis had given Primo Carnera, Fascist Italy's heavyweight hope.

Du Bois had had much to reflect upon, consequently, before his train halted in the capital of the Third Reich at forty minutes past midnight on July 1, 1936. If more than a few *Courier* subscribers may have thought his research venue an odd choice, Jewish Americans had generally been dismayed to learn of the German project. Invited by Franz Boas in the spring of 1935 to join other intellectuals in founding the American Committee for Anti-Nazi Literature, Du Bois had explained why he could not do so. He declared that the terms of the Oberlaender grant, as well as his own unarticulated objectives, temporarily precluded a public political gesture before visiting Germany. He assured the eminent anthropologist that he was appalled by the "terrible outburst of race prejudice in Germany" and argued that his contribution as a member of the anti-Nazi committee would be greatly enhanced by "much useful accumulated knowledge" after his return. Unconvinced of the value of the sojourn, Boas had expressed the fear that German officials would be "particularly courteous" to Du Bois and "show [him] Potemkin villages." He promised to send names of Germans who should be contacted in order to avoid deceptive Nazi tactics. There was just the hint of a ruffled feather in Du Bois's correct reply to Boas that he had had "a good deal of experience in seeing beyond surface indications." Victor Lindeman, a prominent Jewish businessman active in Newark civic affairs who professed to being "highly amused" to learn of the Oberlaender fellowship, had received a curt rationale — "Sixty-six million people are always worth studying." Du Bois understandably believed himself well empowered to evaluate the new German order by virtue of education, command of the language, and his Weimar visit ten years earlier.

In the summer of 1936, the plight of Germany's 525,000 Jews (less than 1 percent of the total German population) could still be characterized as serious but not hopeless — desperate but not yet deadly. As Goebbels's Ministry of Propaganda was then about to implement a policy suspending all public manifestations of anti-Semitism for the duration of the Olympic Games in August, it was even plausible to think that the worst might be over. The Nazi worst was unprecedentedly repressive for the twentieth century. Stripped of citizenship, forbidden to marry or engage in sexual relations with gentiles, ousted from the universities and the civil service, excluded from the film, entertainment, and newspaper industries, Jews had been reduced to a form of social death by the Nuremberg Laws of September and November 1935. Nevertheless, for reasons of realpolitik, anti-Semitism, naïveté, and anticommunism, it would remain true that in the grim space between Nuremberg and Kristallnacht—three years of systematic, incremental dehumanization—few who observed the Third Reich's dress reheasal for genocide were to prove capable of grasping the ultimate logic inherent in the mephitic design being worked out in the clouds above Berchtesgaden. Kristallnacht, the night in November 1938 of shattering glass and sadistic beatings in which German Christians would descend into a moral nadir from which there was no return—a pogrom wiping out the last public vestiges of the Jewish presence—was more than two years away as an Oberlaender Trust emissary escorted Du Bois to a comfortable, modern flat in the capital's Grunewald suburb in the early hours of Wednesday, July 1, 1936. The abolition of Jewish cultural, community, and relief organizations, the prohibiting of the practice of medicine, the compulsory yellow star on clothing, and the Zyklon B experiments at Auschwitz were refinements in persecution to be perfected by the regime from 1938 onward.

It must have been immediately evident to Du Bois, after a visit to the Oberlaender Trust offices on the morning after his arrival, that posing as a neutral scholar would become increasingly distasteful. "Don't use that name—it sounds Jewish," the tall, efficient secretary assigned to the half dozen Oberlaender Fellows courteously advised when Du Bois mentioned Gustav Schmoller, his old economics professor. Yet, from that July morning until his November exit for Russia, Du Bois would be received with an exceptional courtesy everywhere in Germany, a dispensation that contrasted almost bewilderingly with the treatment accorded to Jews. He would never hear of a Jewish intellectual who might have served as an ideal informant, Victor Klemperer, a retiring, former professor of Romance languages at Dresden's Technical University. A decorated veteran of the Great War and, like Du Bois, a devout believer in the elevated humanism of the German cultural tradition, Klemperer would maintain at terrible risk to himself and his Lutheran wife a diary of a Jew living in Germany until the apocalyptic end of the Third Reich. Du Bois may well have been nearby conducting interviews and visiting technical schools when a despondent Klemperer admitted in his inestimable *I Will Bear Witness* that his dream, "the Jewish dream of being German has been a dream after all." But Klemperer's lament about the deceptions of full acceptance Du Bois would have heard a thousand times among his own people. Had he been aware of the Dresden professor's predicament, Du Bois would have been reminded of so many splendidly educated and consummately assimilated men and women of color whose lives had also been as viciously shortchanged by a racist majority population. The parallel and its lessons would have seemed conspicuous to him had he been able to know that, although dismissed from his post, Victor Klemperer would receive his pension and eke out a shabby-genteel and largely unmolested existence that appeared to enjoy a reasonable prospect of continuing at the time of Du Bois's departure from Germany.

Withholding his pained impressions from the *Courier* until after his departure, he would characterize the anti-Semitic campaign as "surpass[ing] in vindictive cruelty and public insult anything" he had ever seen—and Du Bois underscored that he had "seen much." And he would strain mightily to make sense of what he had seen, to distinguish between the German people and the totalitarian regime, to separate what many American intellectuals would insist were "good Germans" from "bad Germans." He still found the individual Germans he encountered to be among the warmest, most civilized of Europeans, and he claimed that, although the official ideology of Aryan supremacy had been grafted on to older cultural beliefs, prejudices about nonwhites were neither virulent nor the result "of long belief, backed by child teaching." If the new National Socialist race laws proscribed marriage between Aryans and non-Europeans and if the presence of a Negro in a dance hall would attract the attention of the Gestapo, the Oberlaender observer took pains, nevertheless, to emphasize that he could go to any hotel he could afford, that he dined where he pleased "and [had] the head-waiter bow [him] welcome," or that when he attended the theater "the strange lady next to [him] bow[ed] pleasantly or pass[ed] a conventional word." Racial aversions notwithstanding, it seemed to him that most Germans behaved far more correctly in public when encountering well-bred gentlemen of a different color than white Americans. He shared with readers his rendezvous with a noted professor, unnamed in an unnamed city, who rushed to Du Bois's hotel to insist that he dine with the family; after dinner, followed by port and cigarettes, there was candid academic and political talk in the library punctuated by—"Of course, you won't quote us." It was a bad time for social science in Germany, certainly, but the point to press, Du Bois thumped, "is not science—it is human fellowship: where in America could this have happened? At Chicago? At Columbia? At Harvard?"

Intellectually, Du Bois had no need to be reminded of the problematic and limited significance of his being treated as an honorary Aryan, even if some of his dispatches bespoke a disappointing degree of self-important delusion in praising German civility. The loss of perspective was more calculating than authentic, however. To be able to stipulate unequivocally that he could not "record a single instance" under German fascism of racial effrontery presented an irresistible opportunity to reproach compatriots pledged to uphold the Constitution of the United States. With far more German history in his memory banks than all but a handful of Americans streaming into the country for the 1936 Olympics, Du Bois understood perfectly well that the cordial, untrammeled public movement of a dark-skinned intellectual was a privilege of an American passport and, to a lesser degree, of personal distinction. Only the historic absence of nonwhites among the Germans made the presence of an exemplary few Africans or American Negroes exceptions to be tolerated even under the Third Reich for a short time. *Mein Kampf* on the Negro made depressing reading, as did the Negrophobic rantings in *Grundlagen des Neunzehnten Jahrhunderts* (Foundations of the Nineteenth Century), the best-selling fount of proto-Nazi ideology by Houston Stewart Chamberlain, expatriate Englishman and one of Hitler's intellectual mentors. But to theorists of European racism, Negroes and jazz music could never pose a threat to white civilization in its Nordic, Teutonic, or Aryan incarnations comparable to that of the Jews. Hitler's extraordinary aside, made extemporaneously in a speech while still an obscure Munich rabble-rouser, was probably unknown to Du Bois, but it spoke volumes for Nazism's pecking order of obsessions. Responding to meeting-hall shouts as to who, besides Jews, was unwelcome, the future Führer received a laughing ovation for his rejoinder, "I would rather have one hundred Negroes in the hall than one Jew."

In Nazi Germany, the Jew was the Negro, Du Bois explained to *Courier* readers. Indeed, he believed that anti-Semitism was embedded in the group psychology of Germans, that it was a centuries' old aversion grounded in self-fulfilling religious and economic enmities so visceral that Du Bois (with astonishing looseness for a sociologist) characterized it as a prejudice that was "nearer [to] being *instinctive*." The subjugation of Africans in America had a history quite different from the persecution of Jews, a Calvary in which medieval superstition had bonded to modern isms that Du Bois would outline in a December issue of the *Courier*; yet, in the final analysis, anti-Semitism was the German analogue of American color prejudice. But the National Socialist variant went far beyond the scourges of the past. From the widow in one of his hotels Du Bois saw a huge red poster enjoining the German people to contribute to winter relief in order to avoid the fate of " 'Jewish-Bolshevist countries of the rest of the world.' " In Munich, he would screen an issue of *Der Stürmer*, Julius Streicher's toxic weekly whose racist obscenities beggared the feral vocabularies of the South's hard-shell "nigger haters"—"not excluding Florida." Later, reading the Führer's harangues at Nuremberg and the amplifications of Goebbels, he would find his long-held belief in German intellectual seriousness profoundly shaken. "Every misfortune in the world is in whole or in part blamed on Jews— the Spanish rebellion, the obstruction of world trade, etc." The rationale of the distinguished columnist Walter Lippmann, and of several major American publications such as *The Christian Science Monitor* and the *Christian Century*, insinuating that German Jews were somehow partly responsible for their own misery had no relevance, Du Bois insisted, to the official repression unleashed by the Hitler regime.

Given what Du Bois knew of Nazi discrimination against Jews and when he knew it, it was entirely reasonable for him to equate German anti-Semitism with American Jim Crow—with the denial of the franchise to Negro Americans, the restriction by law and practice upon access to public accommodations and places of entertainment, the rigid application of a one-drop rule of racial classification, confinement to ghettoes in the North, de facto exclusion from universities and professions, the ban on intermarriage, and vulnerability to personal insult and assault. As early as September 1933, the use and abuse of companionate misery had rather nastily informed one of the earliest *Crisis* editorials on German persecution of Jews. "When the only 'inferior' peoples were 'niggers' it was hard to get the attention of the *New York Times*," he gloated. "But now that the damned include the owner of the *Times*, moral indignation is perking up." In a similar vein, another *Crisis* editorial suggested that Hitler ought to be invited to lecture at a few southern white universities. "They might not understand his German but his race nonsense would fit beautifully," Du Bois jibed.

None of this could he write while still a guest in Germany. His views of the Nazi persecution of Jews would be disclosed to *Courier* readers only after he left for Russia in early November. But once out of the country, Du Bois would vent his bottled-up consternation. "There has been no tragedy in modern times equal in its awful effects to the fight on the Jews in Germany," he warned poorly informed Americans of all races. "It is an attack on civilization, comparable only to such horrors as the Spanish Inquisition and the African slave trade. It has set civilization back a hundred years." On his last night in Berlin, Du Bois would invite an acquaintance, a cultured young civil servant who had served in World War I, to his flat for cake, drinks, wide-ranging conversation, and Reemstma, "the best cigaret [sic] I ever tasted." " 'The treatment of the Jews was shameful,' " the German averred. " 'Much has been done of which we are ashamed. But the worst is over.' " Du Bois's guest was convinced that "betterment will slowly follow in time." Tragically, until Kristallnacht, much of the American press would echo the optimism of Du Bois's sincerely misguided guest.

Long before he was ready to leave, Du Bois would have gauged from extensive travel and considerable time spent in scientific, industrial, and technical institutions that the mass of Germans had little inclination to concern themselves with the persecution of Jews, Communists, or of those the regime deemed "unfit"—Gypsies, homosexuals, and the mentally handicapped. As for the loss of their own rights of speech, assembly, voluntary association, and political affiliation, he found them to be overwhelmingly committed to the Reich. The blanket aparatus of state surveillance, the nonstop engine of hypnotic propaganda, the satanic charisma of the dark-skinned leader were explanations for their embrace of totalitarian conformity. But the fundamental reason for the broad and genuine popularity of the government was, as International News Service (INS) correspondent William Shirer conceded, that fascism appeared to be a stupendous success. "By the autumn of 1936 the problem of unemployment had largely been licked," Shirer, posted to Germany two summers before Du Bois came, would write. As Du Bois perceived, nine out of ten Germans backed Hitler because more than nine out of ten had jobs. "The whole nation is dotted with new homes for the common people, new roads, new public buildings and new public works of all kinds," Du Bois would write soon after leaving the country, and added, "public order is perfect." In comparison, the level of economic recovery he described for *Courier* readers was still far from being realized under the New Deal. Punctual trains, high-speed roadways, modern athletic facilities demanded to be admired. Pristine and outwardly prosperous under a canopy of red and black bunting centered with swastikas, Berlin exuded the self-confidence of a born-again world capital as hotels and restaurants overflowed with foreign visitors to the summer Olympics. On tramways and in beer halls and parks, Du Bois experienced the old-fashioned gemütlichkeit of ordinary people and the overbearing manners of the splendidly uniformed specimens of a new "master race."

In a desire to be objective, as well as from awe, some of Du Bois's readings of National Socialism ran from equivocal to complimentary. If he resisted praising Hitler, in contrast to Britain's Lloyd George after a recent audience with the Führer, or kept more critical balance than Charles Lindbergh had after being courted by Goering's Luftwaffe in early August, Du Bois was not entirely immune. Dictatorship had been unavoidable, had been "absolutely necessary to put the state in order," he allowed, after the implosion of the Weimar economy. He possessed an acute sense of the people's suffering since the war. Standing before the stark Denkmal in Hamburg, that city's shaft of grey granite honoring its war dead, he had been deeply moved. The "most eloquent and ghastly memory" he had even seen, the inscription stated simply, "40,000 sons of this city gave their lives for you in 1914–18." No longer convinced of Germany's guilt in starting the Great War and fully sharing, as many of his compatriots now did, the German outrage at the draconian indemnity imposed by the Allied Powers, Du Bois had not been surprised by the political turn of events in 1933. He understood how Hitler's credentials for the job of chancellor had appealed to the German majority—all that was needed was a plausible philosophy, and propaganda." As for that plausible philosophy—fascism—Du Bois expressed both indulgence and disgust. He abominated its anti-Semitism and deplored its reactionary attitude toward women. Its scurrilous propaganda and purging of the universities offended the core beliefs of his life. Still and yet, he would write that he found National Socialism to be neither "wholly illogical" nor hypocritical, but to be a still "growing and developing body of thought" in which he divined an "extraordinary straddle" between capitalism and communism, a paradoxical fostering by Hitler of emergent world socialism. Reading Hitlerian fascism as the "most astonishing sight in modern history" of state regulation of market forces, Du Bois wagered an armchair theorist's prediction that Germany was destined to become "a second Russia, and National Socialism will lose all excuse for being"—either that fate, he postulated, or economic underperformance and failure at the hands of the business cartels.

Where better to take the pulse of the new Germany than at the Olympics? *Courier* subscribers surely must have expected their distinguished columnist to serve as their eyes and ears at the eleventh Olympiad. There was tremendous interest in the games among all classes of Negroes because of the record-breaking performances by Ohio State University's James Cleveland ("J. C.") Owens, and the presence of twelve other black men on the 383-contender United States team. Seldom had symbolism and drama served to more exhilarating ends than in the contests played out before 110,000 spectators in the gigantic, grey stone stadium on Berlin's western edge. The games had begun on the morning of August 1, a Saturday, under a grey sky that soon brightened. Aloft, trailing a huge Olympic streamer was the airship *Hindenburg*, while a great bronze bell bearing the legend *"Ich rufe die Jugend der Welt,"** pealed in thirty-second intervals atop a 234-foot pylon, rolling waves of sound far beyond the Olympic Village. Forty thousand SS troops, booted and immaculate in black, lined the specially constructed "Via Triumphalis," a ten-mile stretch running from the Alexanderplatz along the Unter den Linden and down the Charlottenburger Chaussee to the largest Olympic structure yet erected, and down which Nazidom's peerage strode in peacock sumptousness. Once the Führer, ostentatiously garbed in a plain brown uniform, seated himself, the aged Richard Strauss raised his baton to conduct a monster orchestra and 3,000-voice chorus in "Deutschland über alles" and the Nazi hymn, the "Horst Wessellied."

On Sunday, the first day of the competition, German and Finnish winners had been invited to Hitler's box to be congratulated, but the Führer left the stadium under threatening evening rain before Cornelius Johnson and David Albritton, both American Negroes, won a gold and silver medal, respectively, in the high jump. Distressed by the appearance of favoritism, Count Henri Balliet-Latour, president of the International Olympic Committee, informed the German leader that, in the future, he must either congratulate all or none of the winners. On Monday, August 3, Jesse Owens avenged Joe Louis under the

---

*"I summon the youth of the world."

gaze of the flustered Führer by winning the 100-meter dash. A perfect combination of muscle to mass, the incomparable Owens brought the spectators to their feet virtually every other day, winning four gold medals, in the 100- and 200-meter dash, the broad jump, and the 400-meter relay. From American ambassador William E. Dodd's loge, where he was a guest, the southern writer Thomas Wolfe pierced a thunderous ovation made by Germans and foreigners alike with the shattering rebel yell of the Confederate infantry. No further public congratulations were extended to Olympic medalists. In a vivid narration of these exciting developments, a historian of the eleventh Olympiad framed a varsity contest of epic significance. "Hitler and Owens," Richard Mandell decided, "were rivals for popularity in Berlin during the . . . competitions of August 2 through August 9."

But Du Bois was absent from Berlin during much of the month, returning two or three weeks after the close of the games on August 16, a costly decision for sports historians and biographers. Although he did report that Owens, the star of the games, was "unable to take a step without being begged for his 'autogramme'" and cited the achievements of Johnson, James Lu Valle, and one or two others, and confirmed that the astonished German people (with Goebbels's permission) raved over the black atheletes, Du Bois's two Olympics pieces seemed decidedly more dutiful than interested. He wrote nothing in the *Courier* about Hitler's putative snub of Owens, rumors of which were soon rife in the United States and universally credited among Negroes. A possible inference is that Du Bois regarded the games as a Nazi variation of the bread-and-circus diversions favored by dictatorships since ancient days. Clearly, he thought the decrescendo of nationalistic propaganda and removal of anti-Semitic signs and grafitti were merely staged, and that, as he wrote, the insights of average non-German-speaking tourists were "worse than valueless in any direction." "They would have seen no overt oppression of Jews," he underscored. "Just as northern visitors to Mississippi see no Negro oppression." And perhaps a tinge of Du Boisian intellectual elitism was to be detected in his insistence that, although Olympic victories were harbingers of future laurels, the race "must be represented, not only in sports, but in science, in literature, and in art." One suspects that he shared the sentiments of that other intellectual, Victor Klemperer, whose troubled German lucidity he would not have the good fortune to explore, and who found the Olympics "an absurd overestimation of sport [in which] the honor of a nation depends on whether a fellow citizen can jump four inches higher than all the rest."

In any case, Du Bois was in Paris. He may have spoken with a couple of authorities there on Africa in connection with the encyclopedia; others were left calling cards and messages. Late July and August were most unlikely months for finding Parisians at their posts. *Courier* readers were invited to savor the unremarkable image of a colored soldier crossing the square by the Comédie Française, of a black bus conductor on the Boulevard Raspail, or of African students in a cafe on the boulevard St. Michel. In wonderfully civilized Europe, above all in Paris, then, one saw "black men as Frenchmen," Du Bois rejoiced. The relief at being able simply to be oneself, dark-skinned and cultured in a sea of white people, to be able to step from behind the veil almost without a care was intoxicating. After a week in Paris, Du Bois returned to Germany to treat himself to a lavish dose of culture in Bavaria. The conference held at the beginning of July with Diedrich Westermann, the world's premier student of African languages and director of Berlin's Institut fur Afrikanische Sprachen und Kulturen, had gone extremely well, he felt. Westermann's blessings on the "Encyclopedia of the Negro" had been a high priority, particularly after Du Bois was shown the manuscript in press of Westermann's seminal book *Der Afrikaner heute und morgen* (The African Today and Tomorrow). The most serious aspects of his Oberlaender Fellowship project were scheduled for the end of August when he would visit the technical high school at Siemens City, the vast complex run by the industrial giant, and the duplicate institution maintained by A.E.G., the rival industrial combine. In the meantime, though, he headed for the entertainment and Gasthauses of Munich, a city of theater, of music, "of marvelous old buildings, and," he sighed, "of beer."

Ever the preceptor of the race, Du Bois wished to impart something of the cultural exaltation aroused in him by a week in Bayreuth. Installed in a pension on Franz Liszt Street but a block from the Wagner family villa, "Wahnfried,"* Du Bois passed twice daily the house-and-walled-garden mausoleum holding the composer's remains, as he walked the two miles to the theater. "Men need places where they can renew their strength," he exulted in the *Courier*, places "where they can catch again faith in themselves and in their fellow men." Such a place was Bayreuth, he found, a shrine for incomparable creativity; and for five nights uninterrupted he bathed himself in Wagner: *Parsifal*; *Lohengrin*; and *The Ring of the Niebelungs* ending in *Die Götterdämmerung* (The Twilight of the Gods). "What for?" Du Bois asked rhetorically. "To add to my imperfect education in Life," was his lesson for the week—and life "is emotion and feeling, love and hate." Somehow he managed to mistake the *Ring* tetralogy for a "great Trilogy," but he boasted of singing to himself phrases from the familiar *Lohengrin*—"*Freudig gefuert, ziehet dahin.*"† He thought of this opera as a hymn of faith, a paean to the joy of commitment, but was unaware that *Lohengrin*'s affirmation of the will and its romantic conception of kings as the first democrats of the land had given way in the major

---

*Meaning "retreat from life's illusions."
†Literally: "Happily guided, go there." Or, more loosely: "Go there, happily led."

operas of Wagner's later years to mythological themes of blood-soaked transfiguration and fiery annihilation, of barely sublimated anti-Semitism and the nihilism of Arthur Schopenhauer.

It is highly likely that Du Bois was ignorant of Hitler's famous off-the-cuff remark that "whoever wants to understand National Socialist Germany must understand Wagner," nor could other than preternatural powers of intuition have enabled Du Bois to sense the eerie prefiguration in *The Ring of the Niebelungs* of the war, genocide, and Götterdämmerung finale of Hitler's Reich. It is difficult, however, to imagine another venue he could have chosen to venerate that was more suffused with pure evil and sheer beauty than Wagner's living monument. On July 22, one month to the night before Du Bois had been engulfed by the gorgeous sonority of *Die Walküre* at Bayreuth, Hitler had conferred with his inner circle after the performance of the same opera in the festival theater hall and decided to send the Luftwaffe to help the Nationalists in Spain.

DU BOIS RETURNED to Berlin from Vienna expecting to find authorization to spend a week or more in Moscow. The plan he had forwarded to VOKS, the Society for Cultural Relations with Russia, asked for opportunity to confer with authorities and members of the national minorities. The Austrian sojourn had been a welcome relief after four months in the Third Reich. Vienna had still seemed to retain something of its *avant-guerre* charm and vitality. "Its Parisian flavor still lives," he wrote, and he was heartened to see that not all the reforms set in motion by the Social Democrats had disappeared with the destruction of the first Austrian Republic. The workers were still determined to assert themselves despite the rising tide of Nazism in Austria that would make the Anschluss possible in less than two years. Approaching the German frontier, Du Bois struck a portentous note in "Forum of Fact and Opinion" as his Alpine route brought him near Hitler's mountain fastness at Berchtesgaden "in the gathering darkness" of mid-October. The Führer awaited the arrival on the twenty-fourth of Count Galeazzo Ciano, the Italian foreign minister and son-in-law of the Duce, to discuss things "that may be big with the fate of Africa and Europe." When Du Bois's Vienna dispatch appeared in early January 1937, the Anti-Comintern Pact between Germany and Italy, the forerunner of the Axis, would be six weeks old, and *Courier* readers would learn that their eyes on the world had already pivoted, momentously, north and east—"to Russia, to Manchukuo, to China, to Japan," where he would see again "the Towers of the Kremlin and the black waters of the Volga, the plains of Genghis Khan, the great Wall of China and all of dream and fairyland of youth done into the prose of the twentieth century."

But the news from Russia was disappointing. Awaiting Du Bois at Hegel Haus was an October 18 reply to his urgent radiogram explaining that visas were no longer as readily obtained as in the past. The sole concession was a brief stop in Moscow and permission to transit the Soviet Union. "It will be quite impossible to change this decision," regretted William Burroughs, an American Negro expatriate attached to the Moscow *Daily News*. It was now too late to undo Du Bois's miscalculation of having written the doomed, sad-eyed Karl Radek, a serious mistake made on the advice of Burroughs. Abandoning the scheme for a quick study of Russian minorities, then, Du Bois packed his bags for Moscow and the Trans-Siberian express. Thanks to Hikida Yasuichi's connections and meticulous planning, the itineraries for Manchukuo (Japanese-occupied Manchuria) and Japan were scripted in the minutest details. A letter containing timetables and points of interest had reached Du Bois in Berlin in early September from one Y. Kumazawa, an official of Manchukuo State Railways. His arrival set for November 19, Du Bois was informed that a railway pass across Manchukuo would be provided and that other arrangements were being orchestrated by Hikida. Further instructions would be posted to the Berlin office of the Japanese Ministry of Railways, Kumazawa disclosed. Nina's letter came almost simultaneously, reporting that Will's "Japanese friend" had dropped by the Dunbar to ask her to write Berlin that "everything was all right for you to go according to your plans."

Hikida's four pages of single-spaced typescript, a model of explicitness, had arrived at Hegel Haus on October 15. Kumazawa along with "some other friends" would ensure that Du Bois saw "the new born country and North China profitably," the Bedford Hills cook wrote. Several Japanese residents awaited Du Bois's arrival in Beijing, and the general secretary of the Japanese YMCA had been asked to assist him in Shanghai. In Kobe, on the Japanese mainland, Hikida's "personal friends," Professor Kodama Kuninoshin and Dr. Toku Noriyoshi would serve as hosts and guides. Kodama, a professor at Kansei Gakuin, Hikida's old school, would "communicate to Tokio [sic] and make immediate connection" as soon as Du Bois reached Shanghai. In Tokyo, another Hikida colleague, Boston University–educated Tagashira Chiyokichi of the Japanese Methodist Church Office, would serve as Du Bois's personal assistant and translator. Speaking engagements in Kobe, Osaka, and Tokyo were still being pinned down, but Du Bois was told to expect lecture invitations from the Buddhist Hoganji University and the Christian Doshisha University, both in Kyoto. Hikida was pleased to forward clippings from "two of the largest influential Japanese daily [sic]," the Tokyo *Asahi* and the Tokyo *Nichi-Nichi* as evidence of mounting interest in Du Bois's impending visit. Hikida announced, moreover, his success in securing the cooperation of Yanagisawa Ken of the semigovernmental Kokusai Bunka Shinkohai (Society for International Cultural Relations), whose president, Prince Konoe Fumimaro, was also president of Japan's upper chamber, the House of Peers. With the promising news that *Souls* was being translated at his own expense, Hikida closed his sheaf of instructions with the promise of another New York sukiyaki party upon Du Bois's return from Asia. And then, with an exciting postscript: news just received that Du Bois would lecture at prestigious Tokyo Imperial University.

"Russia is a world." The voyager was constrained to write in an impressionistic style long on intimation but short on detail." He waxed philosophical in his column about the meaning of what he ardently believed was the greatest chapter in history since the French Revolution. "In any state, a residue of men will sink to the bottom or never rise," his understanding of history told him. "Always an elite of ability, training and spirit will lead." But the residue need not include the majority of humankind. "Russia declares that the majority of mankind can become efficient members of a culture state." Once, Americans believed this, Du Bois continued, but the ideal of equality of opportunity had been gutted by the capture of capital by private power. Russia's rulers had understood that the state must appropriate, "collect and conserve this capital." He applauded the Soviet program, which had made of the working people of the world "a sort of new religion," a form of scientific idealism he posited as being indispensable to progress and dismally diminished in his own United States. Had the Kremlin granted the ten days or so he had wanted for interviews and inspection of cultural institutions, might Du Bois have detected disturbing signs of the inevitable corruption spawned by an exercise of power more absolute than that of the tsars? Another astute observer of political culture, André Gide, had been welcomed as an official guest of the regime six months earlier and vouchsafed an exceptional visit to Stalin's Georgian birthplace. That the Kremlin perceived Du Bois's ranking in the international pantheon of intellectuals as well below that of the premier man of French letters of the period is, of course, obvious. Gide left the Soviet Union persuaded that his privileged scrutiny of high-ranking Communist Party officials revealed the early stages of a totalizing depotism that he soon unmasked in the explosive *Return from the USSR*. Gide's recoil from Soviet contempt for the rights of the individual was a replay of Arthur Koestler's earlier unhappiness over the first purge trials, a reaction that Langston Hughes, on crossing paths with Koestler in Soviet Central Asia in 1933, had regarded as sadly fastidious.

From all that he wrote then and later, very little militates against the inference that, permitted a short sojourn to study Russian minorities, Du Bois would have seen nothing to prevent his sharing Hughes's impatience with critics of the Russian experiment; the Frenchman's apprehensions would have been dismissed as the consequence of overly refined sensibilities. For Du Bois, the dangers the Russian people faced were posed not by Stalin but by Trotsky and the counterrevolutionary International. Radek's performance before the court in a Stalinist rite of inculpation new to modern jurisprudence, his almost enthusiastic admission to plotting with Trotsky and the Nazis against the Soviet state in a January trial observed by FDR's ambassador, Joseph E. Davies (no more credulous than his British counterpart), would have served all the more to convince Du Bois of the real stakes involved in the translation of Marxism into the sweat and tears of a working society. The crucial question, he wrote, was whether, against the determined, massive alliance of capital, "workers and peasants [can] build a nation which will not, like other nations, eventually reconstruct society on the old lines, with perhaps less poverty and distress at bottom, but with the same ruling class at top, whether it is called Nobility, or Middle Classes?"

In his first-class sleeping car aboard the Trans-Siberian "Lux Express," Du Bois was given the leisure to reflect and to write as a palimpsest of endlessly varied images of the startling, the bleak, the dull, and the awe-inspiring played across the window of his compartment. From Moscow to Vladivostok, the express would traverse almost six thousand miles through six time zones with a scribbling Du Bois and his fellow passengers reasonably well attended by the Intourist staff aboard the wagon-lit built by Pullman. The hissing samovar in his sleeper provided a steady flow of tea while he and they dined thrice daily in the dining car, then communed over drinks and discussed life and politics as November gales howled and the lights of the diner reflected against streaming snows. Vyatka, Perm on the Volga, Sverdlovsk in the Urals, then Omsk and Novosibirsk rolled past on the edge of Siberia. On January 23, 1937, describing the epiphany experienced beyond Irkutsk after five days across "a land of essential sameness," Du Bois gave *Courier* subscribers some of the most evocative prose of his travels. Struggling out of a "drug of a dream," he saw the sunrise over Lake Baikal, the planet's deepest continental body of water, 30 miles wide and 395 miles long and holding one-fifth of all the earth's fresh water:

A wide scarf of cloud, poised between earth and heaven, held back the splendor, but beyond lit up the low, serried ranges of snow draped mountains that guarded the lake. On our right rose sheer, great, rough cliffs, bare and gaunt; ever and anon we bowed our heads and plunged through them to the lake that lay calmly curling in wide gray, undulating sheets. Tunnel followed tunnel, until curving, we put the east behind us and drove into the icy winds of the north, with the ghost ranges glittering like silver or piled and broken porcelain. . . . Into this lake a hundred streams hasten with their waters, but only one leaves it. At first it seems bare of man and beast. Then one lone sombre bird flies beside us; then three abreast. Then come little villages here and there. Baikal is a jewel hung

in space at that fateful spot where Europe becomes Asia, and where the
waters part to make Pacific and Atlantic.

According to Du Bois, the express halted at the Russian frontier with Mongolia on the morning of November 17, a Tuesday. Soldiers in full battle gear
manned artillery emplacements in the near distance. In the 4 A.M. mist, he and
the others bleerily followed porters who carried their luggage for minute inspection by Soviet customs officials at Zabaykal'sk. Above the customs house
entrance they could see the appeal that had shaken the century: "Workers of
the World Unite!" Regaining their compartments, they peered into the lifting
darkness as the express moved out of Zabaykal'sk "like a ghost train," recalled
Du Bois, "quietly and slowly into another land." At the Inner Mongolian border
post, he stood respectfully waiting for his baggage to be cleared by customs
officers when someone called his name quietly: " 'Is this Mr. Du Bois?' " A
young man, in the immaculate uniform of the Manchukuo State Railways,
presented his card. Informing Du Bois that a first-class pass across Manchukuo
awaited him, General Director Usami guided his guest to meet the stationmas-
ter. The irony of the situation was duly noted, as Du Bois observed that, under
Jim Crow, the sole courtesy ever extended to colored people by an American
railroad "was the privilege of buying, at top prices, something that nobody else
wanted." Boarding a different train, he steamed due east out of the frontier
checkpoint and soon reached Manchukuo. His first stop was Harbin, Manchukuo's third-largest metropolis. The city was also home to more Russians and
more Russian counterrevolutionaries than any other city outside the Soviet
Union. The hub of rail communications in the Pacific, with spokes to Beijing
and Mukden (Shenyang, today) and to the ports of Vladivostok and Dairen
(Pinyin, today) Harbin had become a powerhouse of commerce and food proc-
essing under the Japanese. At Harbin Central Station, Du Bois transferred to
the south Manchurian line controlled by Manchukuo State Railways and
headed south to the new capital of Manchukuo.

"The whole scene changed as if by magic," Du Bois exulted in his journal.
Speeding from Harbin toward Hsinking (today's Changchun), the new capital
of a new Asian nation, he yielded instantly to the racial romanticism that he
neither always wanted to keep in check nor sometimes could not even when
he wished to do so. "We rode out of the . . . desolation of the northern desert,"
he continued. "We flew easily on a perfect roadbed, ballasted with rock, in
Japanese cars better than Pullmans. The service was perfect." If Russia under
communism had lifted his spirits, Du Bois would herald Manchuria under
Japanese imperialism as marvelous evidence of the beginning of the end of
white world supremacy. He reminded *Courier* readers of the history of that part
of the world, of how the European powers, after nullifying the 1895 Treaty of

Shimonoseki in order to block Japanese expansion on the Chinese mainland, had forced Beijing to cede the Shantung Peninsula to Germany in 1897 and then, the year following, the Liaotung Peninsula to Russia. Manchuria was "the natural mainland of the isles of Japan," he declared. Yet what was Japan to do? The Russians had positioned an army at Harbin and Mukden and encased Port Arthur in fortifications that were supposedly impregnable, while their six-thousand-mile rail link, built with billions of gold francs invested by French bondholders, advanced steadily across Siberia and Mongolia to the Liaotung Peninsula in the Yellow Sea. Outnumbered but superbly equipped (and dispensing with a declaration of war in 1904), Japan's navy had destroyed most of the tsar's Pacific Fleet and reduced Port Arthur. Refusing to accept terms, the Russian government had dispatched its Baltic Fleet eighteen thousand miles around Europe and Africa through the Indian Ocean into the Sea of Japan where, to the amazement of the Great Powers, it was sent to the bottom of Tsushima Straits while, at Mukden, Japan's infantry had routed the tsar's divisions. Four years later, Japan formally annexed Korea. Came next the Manchurian (Mukden) Incident of 1931 (engineered by ultranationalist Japanese army officers), followed by invasion and annexation of Manchuria, then condemnation by the League of Nations. "Gorged with the loot of the world," the *Courier* sneered, Great Britain, France, and the United States "suddenly became highly moral on the subject of annexing other people's land. No! they said, and [so] Japan walked out . . . and took Manchuria."

From Hsinking Du Bois sent a remarkable dispatch captioned with the name of the capital's most important Japanese personage, "Yosuke Matsuoka." Hsinking was headquarters for Manchukuo State Railways, the billion-yen quasi-state corporation that had become Japan's largest business enterprise. The "Mantetsu," as the railway monopoly was familiarly known, had expanded since its creation in 1906 into coal-mining operations, harbor and port facilities, and export of one half of the world's supply of soybeans. Hsinking was to be Manchukuo's Washington, a government center built from the ground up in the old trading town of Changchun. Collected by official automobile from the Hotel Yamato ("a joy"), Du Bois was driven through a city of broad avenues and unfinished buildings, rectangular and monumental in its conception, an ambition in noise, dust, and scaffolding scheduled for completion in 1937. Hsinking already had some one hundred public buildings and nearly eight thousand commercial and residential structures. Although the *Courier* column omitted any reference to the capital, the travel manuscript registered approval: "Clearly, this colonial effort of a colored nation is something to watch." A revealing notation, moreover, for what was the meaning of a "colored nation" that was also a colony? Tokyo had installed the last Chinese emperor, the young Manchu cipher Henry Pu-yi, as emperor of Manchukuo, yet the state railways directorate and the Imperial Army made the major decisions. Somewhat defensively, Du Bois impatiently demurred in the *Courier*, brushing aside as "immaterial the question as to whether Manchukuo is an independent state or a colony of Japan." The real issue, he insisted, was to know what the Japanese were doing for the thirty million Manchurians.

Du Bois decided that an audience with the president of Manchukuo State Railways, Matsuoka Yosuke, largely answered the question. As Du Bois was delighted to explain, Matsuoka was not merely de facto premier or viceroy of Manchukuo but one of imperial Japan's most significant statesmen. It was this tiny, thickly bespectacled figure who had led the dramatic exit of the Japanese delegation from the League of Nations in February 1933. "A quiet man, slow and low of speech," as Du Bois described him, Matsuoka deferred his appointments for a good half hour to discuss large questions with his distinguished American Negro visitor. Believing what he needed to, Du Bois perceived in the little railway president a dark-skinned proconsul whose mission was to prove that "colonial enterprise by a colored nation need not imply the caste, exploitation and subjection . . . always implied in the case of white Europe." The two men ranged over industry, capitalism, and communism, with Matsuoka, fully briefed on Du Bois's socialist writings, observing facilely that "in some ways Japan was the most communistic of modern states" as there had never been as strong a sense of individual property ownership as in the West. Although Japan's formal promulgation of the Great East Asia Co-Prosperity Sphere was four years in the future, as the doctrine's principal formulator, the assumption is risk-free that Matsuoka would have slathered the talk with his visitor with coprosperity rationales. Left unmentioned that morning by Japan's future minister of foreign affairs was that, within days, his country and Nazi Germany would sign the Anti-Comintern Pact against the Soviet Union.

A week in Manchukuo had been sufficient to give Japanese colonialism high marks. Du Bois told his readers that he had seen the borders "north, west and south." He had "walked the streets night and day. . . . talked with officials, visited industries and read reports." He had detected no racial superiority on the part of the occupiers. The separate elementary school systems for Manchurians and Japanese were based solely on language. He found Manchurians to be well represented in the civil service. Law and order was impartially administered, and there was "public control of private capital for the general welfare." He left the puppet state elated at having gazed from the ramparts of Port Arthur — "historic ground," he called it — out to the Yellow Sea, where the Japanese navy had blockaded imperial Russia's Pacific Fleet in 1904. Hikida's contacts had driven him to Port Arthur to a lunch and dinner in his honor attended by Japanese graduates of several American universities, followed by a three-hour lecture and discussion on "Race Segregation." That evening he received a visit from the American consul stationed in Port Arthur. The following morning he was driven a few miles to the great port at Dairen, where he boarded ship. Waving farewell, Du Bois and the other dozen passengers held the ends of the traditional, unwinding colored streamers as friends ashore held the other ends. "We sailed into the Yellow Sea on a perfect day," he wrote. China, roiled by civil war and menaced by invasion from his Japanese hosts, awaited.

The Hikida network welcomed Du Bois to Tientsin (now Tianjin) China's second-largest port city after Shanghai and recently incorporated into the widening sphere of Japanese influence. Some sixty miles southeast of the old imperial capital at Beijing, Tientsin was the site of the humiliating 1860 treaty by which British gunboat diplomacy had forced the legalization of opium upon the Chinese people. Du Bois had made arrangements through the China Institute of America to give lectures in the country before sailing from New York, though he seems to have depended on the Japanese contacts at Tientsin for transportation to his next stop, Beijing, the seat of power of the fallen Manchu dynasty. Parts of Beijing, through which he walked more than ten miles on the first day, somehow reminded him of the Negro sections of New Orleans or Charleston. The noise and smells, the bouillabaisse of classes and occupations in what he described as "this Tartar city" were of an intensity and of a scale that beggared description. "Babies, babies, everywhere," he exclaimed, "and women nowhere, save as mothers, housekeepers, and followers of the world's oldest profession." The Forbidden City lived up to his expectations and evoked the usual rehearsal of cardinal historical facts for his readers. At the Lama Monastery, he remarked that of the eighteen statues of the disciples who brought Buddhism to China two were black. He was carried up the Great Wall, "the only work of man visible from Mars," on the backs of four men for seventy cents. With twenty-three centuries beneath his feet, Du Bois looked through the crenels of the Great Wall into a Manchuria that posed as much a threat in 1936 as it had in the reign of the First Emperor.

China's capital at that moment was at Nanking, 160 miles northwest of Shanghai, where Generalissimo Chiang Kai-shek found himself between the Scylla of Japan and the Charybdis of the People's Liberation Army. The generalissimo had chosen to retreat before the encroaching Japanese in order to contain the Communist forces led by Mao Tse-tung, a strategy many of his fellow generals now believed to be criminally misguided. Du Bois was clearly underwhelmed by the accomplishments of the Kuomintang government, although he did concede that any attempt at reform in China, with all its immensity, diversity, and recent disorders, had to encounter "a rock of opposition and misunderstanding." Never had he experienced such extremes of wealth and poverty, of refinement and degradation—all of it based on an inexaustible supply of cheap labor. "Three things attract white Europe to China," he saw. "Cheap women; cheap child labor; cheap men." One suspects that he gave the Nationalists poor odds for piecemeal transformation of the country in the midst of civil war and foreign incursion. A visit to a girls' school in Beijing where students made silk bulletproof jackets for Kuomintang soldiers fighting a revolt in Mongolia left Du Bois especially depressed. That the Chinese regarded Japan as the prime enemy struck him as being fatally myopic. It was simply too obvious, he warned, that with China and Japan "in rivalry, war and hatred, Europe still continues to rule the world for her own ends."

On Thanksgiving Day, Will sent Nina a telegram from Shanghai that she soon shared with Hikida, who now dropped by the Dunbar regularly enough to give Baby Du Bois piano lessons. The Japanese network had arranged for Du Bois to sail for Japan on December 1. But before leaving China, he intended to speak frankly to the Chinese in a forum of his own choosing about the menace of Europe and the United States. Shanghai could hardly have been a more fitting location, an Asian metropolis in the slavish service of the Occident, London on the Yangtze with yellow people as Helots. By Du Bois's count, 3 million Chinese were lorded over by 19,000 Japanese, 11,000 British, 10,000 Russians, 4,000 Americans, and a thousand other foreigners who not many years ago were subject only to the laws of their own countries. The *Courier* reported that it was no longer the common practice "to kick a coolie or throw a rickshaw's fare on the ground," yet Du Bois was greeted on the first night by such an affront. "A little white boy of perhaps four years order[ed] three Chinese out of his imperial way on the sidewalk. . . . It looked quite like Mississippi." His duty to China was clear. He appeared at the University of Shanghai, occupied a seat on the dais by invitation, listened to a Rockefeller Foundation representative speak about scholarships to the United States, but declined to say even a few words when asked by the university's president. Du Bois proposed instead that he be invited to talk frankly with a representative group of Chinese. The luncheon arranged in his honor at the Chinese Bankers' Club was to be a singular affair. Assembled for the occasion were editors of the Chinese-language newspaper, the secretary general of the Bank of China, the general manager of the China Publishing Company, the director of the city's Chinese schools, and the executive secretary of the China Institute of International Relations. The guest of honor discussed his slave ancestry, advantaged education, extensive travels, and the main outlines of race relations in the United States.

Then, "I plunged in recklessly," Du Bois reported accurately. What did these distinguished men of affairs and arbiters of culture and information intend to do about European hegemony? he asked pointedly. Formal political independence of China was merely a beginning, a false dawn, even, until the sequel of economic independence. "But how do you propose to escape from the domination of European capital? How are your working classes progressing?" he pressed ahead. "Why is it that you hate Japan more than Europe when you have suffered more from England, France, and Germany, than from Japan?" Why had they not grasped the possibility that Europe could be excluded from Asia if China and Japan worked together? Chopsticks were dropped. The silence, Du Bois observed, "was . . . considerable." Some of those present almost certainly had family or friends among the thousands of casualties caused by the Japanese Air Force's savage January 1932 bombardment of Shanghai in retaliation for a mob attack on four Japanese Buddhist priests. Haltingly at first, then in a rising volume of protestations, qualifications, and elucidations, the Chinese acknowledged problems, cited progress, but insisted that Japanese designs hindered the nation's best efforts at economic progress. To the banker, publishers, educators, and journalists in the Bankers' Club that afternoon, their presumptuous guest had turned a blind eye to the bitter paradox that just as China was regaining a modicum of political cohesion and instituted economic reforms, the Japanese had trumped the British as masters of gunboat imperialism. Du Bois would frostily deny the charge, yet he should not have been surprised when the publication *China Weekly Review* made the claim, two years later, that he was a propagandist in the pay of Japan.

As he sailed for Nagasaki, Du Bois offered as a final thought that the fundamental source of Sino-Japanese enmity was in China's "submission to white aggression and Japanese resistance" to it. Something of Du Bois's old, fierce contempt for Bookerite accommodationism under white supremacy in the South was also transferred to China's leaders—Asian Uncle Toms in the grip of the "same spirit that animates the 'white folks' nigger' in the United States," he would snarl somewhat later. Du Bois would not have been long gone, however, when Japanese aggression in China precluded indefinitely and possibility of strategic rapprochement. The rollback of Chiang's forces by the Japanese Kwantung Army as it occupied Beijing and besieged Shanghai in July and August of 1937, and the ensuing mega-atrocities inflicted on the population of Nanking during December and January 1938 ("the Rape of Nanking"), would seal Chinese hatred of Japan in blood and flames. During the four weeks in which the Japanese reduced Nanking to a slaughterhouse, one student of the war crime has estimated that, if the executed prisoners of war and butchered and fatally raped civilians had been stacked on top of one another, the pile would have reached "the height of a seventy-four-story building."

Du Bois's arrival in Nagasaki at noon, December 2, 1936, was an event. News reporters and officials of the Japanese Tourist Bureau met him at the ship's gangplank. He spoke of his abiding admiration of Japanese achievements, of his desire to inform America of what he would see and learn. The next day, representatives of the Japanese Foreign Office and the press accompanied him by train to Kobe, where there were more official exchanges and press interviews, then on to Osaka, once the country's textile capital and now the second center for heavy industry and, together with its sister city, Kobe, of shipbuilding. Du Bois's hosts capped off his immensely satisfying day in Osaka with a sukiyaki party. He awoke, breakfasted in the excellent Osaka Hotel, and was then taken by Hikida's acquaintances to his official reception by the vice-governor of Osaka Prefecture and the mayor of the city. Afterward, he left seven hundred young women students at Kobe College deeply impressed by the life and times of Frederick Douglass and the Kobe faculty charmed by his mannered wit over lunch. Next stop, Kansai University, where Du Bois addressed the faculty on Negro literature and the Harlem Renaissance. That night Du Bois fielded questions from some forty principals and educators after a dinner tendered him by the Board of Education of the prefecture at his hotel. December 5 was devoted to a tour of the city by auto, motor launch, and subway, accompanied by the vice-governor's secretary. Osaka was laid out on a rigid grid, a low, modern, clean city, Du Bois judged—a "beautiful city," all in all, with automobile traffic "rivalling European cities. That evening, introduced by the newspaper's editor-in-chief, Du Bois delivered his "Message to Japan" in the hall of the Osaka *Mainichi*, a daily with a circulation running to several millions. His address, which was also covered by the 5-million-circulation Tokyo *Nichi-Nichi*, praised Japan's political and industrial progress and contemplated the heights to which the nation's disciplined, trained youth could attain. News of his arrival and his address were broadcast over national radio. "Nowhere else in the modern world was there a people so intelligent, so disciplined, so clean and punctual, so instinctively conscious of human good and ill," he rhapsodized in the *Courier*.

These were impressions easily sustained during the next two or three days of travels and lectures in the old and venerated cities of Nara and Kyoto, where he spoke to faculty and students at the Buddhist University and at the Doshisha (Japanese Christian) University of Kyoto. By now, Du Bois was a celebrity whose progress across Japan acquired a large retinue as he sped by train from Kyoto to Tokyo. Once again, the *Courier* carried those vivid descriptions of place of which he was past master, the land cultivated by the square yard, the plots drained and protected by hedge and ditch, the passing cartouche of "tree bamboos, pines and maples, shrines and stone lanterns . . ." the "hills and lakes and everywhere workers with bent backs." The distinguished professor from abroad arrived at the Tokyo terminal on December 10. He seemed much taller than his five feet, five inches in the welcoming crowd, "surrounded by photographers, reporters, and [Hikida's] friends." Rested, after a night in the brooding Imperial Hotel, a low-slung, oblong mass of brick and lava stone that Frank Lloyd Wright insisted was his masterpiece, he was escorted the next morning by the reception committee to the grounds of the Imperial Palace and the Meiji Shrine. Exactly which newspaper he meant when he wrote that he was interviewed by "Shimbun," which ran his biography in installments for three days, is unclear (*shimbun* means "newspaper"), but the Tokyo *Nichi-Nichi* continued to cover his movements. A luncheon was given for him at the Pan-Pacific Club, where he took the opportunity to draw a connection between America's anti-Japanese feelings and the historic mistreatment of its Negro citizens. Indeed, Du Bois explained that the exclusion of Japanese from the United States had resulted from a deal between the South and the West in which the former endorsed the Oriental Exclusion Act of 1924 in exchange for the sacrifice of the Dyer federal antilynching bill.

The affair in his honor at the Imperial Hotel on December 15 was the supreme mark of his hosts' esteem, a dinner sponsored by the Kokusai Bunka Shinkokai. Created soon after Japan's withdrawal from the League of Nations in order to present a more friendly and pacific face to an international community increasingly critical of Japanese expansionism, the Kokusai Bunka Shinkokai resembled a combined Council on Foreign Relations, National Association of Manufacturers, and American Academy of Arts and Letters. The society's presiding officer, Prince Konoe, an aristocrat of ancient lineage, was president of the House of Peers and soon to be appointed as the prime minister who was expected to defuse the government crisis caused by insurgent ultranationalists in the military. Marquis Tokugawa Yorisada, of the clan that had ruled Japan during the Shogunate, was the society's vice-president. Arrangements for the black-tie affair were handled by Hikida's contact at the society, the influential Yanagisawa Ken. If there were extant photographs of the dinner, they might show the guest of honor immaculate in tuxedo, the Liberian Star of Ethiopia at his chest, standing or seated between peers of the realm and executives of the Mitsui and Mitsubishi combines. Du Bois wrote that the presiding nobleman for the evening was a count educated at Amherst with Calvin Coolidge and Dwight Morrow. Another member of the society, Professor K. Miyake of Tokyo Imperial University, who extended himself to make a friendly impression on Du Bois, would come to the United States in the spring of 1938 on a lecture tour to enlighten Americans about Sino-Japanese relations.

The courtesies and distinctions continued during the next week: lunch with the president of Tokyo Imperial University; the Kabuki theater ("a welcome change from [New York] leg shows, and the ever-lasting sight of fifty mortals doing the same thing with machine-like precision and utter disregard to any conceivable meaning"); the extraordinary shrines at Nikko viewed in mist and rain; an engaging chat with the young writer who was translating *Souls* into Japanese. The geisha party given by Foreign Office officials was perfect, he thought. Chaperoned by two elderly ladies, the women danced the traditional steps of the occasion; then the men danced with them until midnight. Du Bois informed his readers that the women were beautiful in their silk kimonos with raven hair piled high. His partner, a "lovely girl with charming manners spoke [English] quite well," he found; and she "especially waited" on him. "Believe it or not, her name was Happy Spring." An almost illegible, penciled paragraph written soon afterward on a loose sheet of paper restates his principles. "I believe in women rights and self assertion," he scribbled, then equivocated. Yet after a lifetime of enduring "the imprudent aggressiveness . . . of American white women, the cast down eyes and modest demeanor of Japanese women was certainly a relief if not an ideal." The new Tokyo PEN Club entertained Du Bois on his last night in the capital. He was pleased to note the presence of three Chinese writers, one of them female. An interesting detail Du Bois saw fit to record was that, as he was settling his bill at the Imperial the next morning, an American woman, "loud-mouthed" and white, demanded immediate service. In the United States, she would have been given instant priority over a brown gentleman. "But not in Tokyo," Du Bois chortled. The clerk carefully finished attending Du Bois "and took time to bow with Japanese politeness and then turned to America."

Du Bois sailed from Yokahoma on the *Tatsuta Maru*, a Japanese liner that, he took vicarious pride in noting, "start[ed] on the dot" on the afternoon of December 17. He pronounced himself overwhelmed.* The sometime recipient of courtesies in cities and countries, never in his life had he received "such a series of attention and evidences of welcome as in Japan," Du Bois informed his readers. This was all the more astonishing "because he had no official status." His reception was in no sense "a personal tribute," he hastened to emphasize, but an unofficial means by which official Japan intended to speak through him to 12 million Americans in whom "she recognized a common brotherhood, a common suffering and a common destiny." Overwhelmed he may have been, but not blinded. Du Bois was perturbed by the conformity of Japanese culture. Shintoism transformed into a modern ethic of emperor-worship yielded impressive results in terms of order, solidarity, and activism, yet he readily discerned the underlying inhospitality to criticism, to deviant ideas, to alien practices. State Shinto hampered "freedom of spirit and expression," he conceded. His journal entry was somewhat more critical: "There is poverty in Japan; there is oppression; there is no democratic freedom." Yet all things have their price. Whatever its serious flaws of conformity and militarism, Japan was for Du Bois that rarest of phenomena in the white imperium, "above all a country of colored people run by colored people for colored people." For the first time in

---

*The *Tatsuta Maru* would serve as the repatriation ship for Japanese nationals after Pearl Harbor, and on which Hikida was a passenger.

his life, he had lived in a country that white people did not control "directly or indirectly," he cheered. "The Japanese run Japan, and that even English and Americans recognize and act accordingly."

In the winter of 1936–37, the political map of the world looked almost unchanged from how it had appeared to Du Bois in 1906 or 1896. Defeated Hohenzollern Germany and Ottoman Turkey had been deprived of extensive African and Middle Eastern real estate under various League of Nations fictions of benefit to Great Britain and France: Iraq and Palestine as British mandates; Syria and Lebanon as French mandates; Libya to Italy. Egypt and India were still British whatever mainly formalistic concessions had been enacted or were promised by Westminister. South Africa belonged to Great Britain. Central Africa was Belgian. North Africa belonged to France. Indo-China belonged to France. Indonesia belonged to Holland. China, like much of Latin America under the protection of the Monroe Doctrine, existed in the iron vise of informal imperialism. The political map of the world, then, colored British red, French green, and even Portuguese yellow, was, in Du Bois's eyes, simply everlastingly white, and the whitest sector of the map was in black Africa. "Africa is prostrate," he had written in the visionary *Atlantic Monthly* essay "The African Roots of the War," some twenty years earlier. Gazing at the receding shore from the deck of the *Tatsuta Maru*, Du Bois could have recalled the essay's anguished interrogation and rejoiced in his present misperceived optimism. "In this great work who can help us?" he had asked. "In the Orient, the awakened Japanese and the awakening leaders of New China," he had answered. Certain now that he had found an answer in the Japanese empire, he would accept with chilling equanimity the Japanese rampage in China and its voracious appetite in the Pacific.

In July 1937, seven months after his return to Atlanta, the Imperial Army stationed in Manchukuo provoked an incident with Chinese troops at the historic Marco Polo Bridge outside Beijing. The Rape of Nanking, in which at least 260,000 Chinese noncombatants were murdered, ensued, followed by the occupation of China. Harry Ward, noted professor at Union Theological Seminary and chairman of the American League Against War and Fascism, naturally anticipated a positive response to his appeal for Du Bois's endorsement of an antiwar congress slated for Pittsburgh in November 1937. He would have no truck with "false friends of China" only intent upon pushing the United States into war against Japan, replied Du Bois by telegram. An intellectual less steeped in the history of European inhumanity to mankind than he, and certainly one lacking Du Bois's belief system, which was now capable of abiding the immoral and inhumane for the sake of ultimate racial and economic justice, must at least have ethically flinched as the terrible news bulletins from China were posted. Yet as the Imperial Army positioned itself for the capture of Nanking,

Du Bois sought to steel the nerves of Japan's many shocked and disenchanted Negro sympathizers in "China and Japan," one of his most disturbing meditations on the higher morality of racialism. "It was Japan's clear cue to persuade, cajole, and convince China," ran the *Courier* homily. "But China sneered and taught her folk that Japanese were devils . . . Whereupon Japan fought China to save China from Europe and fought Europe through China and tried to wade in blood toward Asiatic freedom. Negroes must think straight in this crisis," Du Bois rapped for undivided attention. "Not love for China, but hate for Japan motivates [former Secretary of State Henry] Stimson and the United States; Chamberlain and England." Nor had the Japanese invented or perfected "this killing the unarmed and innocent in order to reach the guilty," he continued with ghastly instances of European conduct drawn from South Africa, the Punjab, and Guernica.

One should be distressed by organized killing, was Du Bois's message, yet resist false sensibilities that obscured praiseworthy designs and liberating results. He would take this message of pro-Japanese understanding to the Negro colleges over the next few months. After declining circulation of the newspaper compelled Vann to suspend "Forum of Fact and Opinion" in December 1937, Du Bois would continue to defend Japan in "As the Crow Flies," in his new column in the *Amsterdam News.* Like Harry Ward, Henry Stimson would be given a stern rebuke when, as its honorary chairman, Stimson at the beginning of 1940 invited Du Bois to join the American Committee for Non-Participation in Japanese Aggression, a group of prominent citizens charged with informing the American public of Japan's threat to peace. "He will not get it," Du Bois announced in Harlem's leading newspaper. Stimson and company wanted "low wages, cheap raw materials and increased private profit" on Asian backs, all of which were being irritatingly countered by Japan's policies. "Moreover," he concluded, "I don't remember Mr. Stimson's protest on Ethiopia." On the other hand, Du Bois remained deeply mindful of what he was certain he had heard and understood among the Japanese about the fate of the world color, having assured his *Courier* readers in late 1937 before suspension of his column that, "without exception," the Japanese with whom he had spoken "classed themselves with the Chinese, Indians and Negroes as folk standing over against the white world." For their part, Hikida confirmed that the Japanese had been deeply impressed by Du Bois's visit, that the Japanese "at large were grateful to [him]," and that friends arriving from Tokyo were planning a sukiyaki reunion with Du Bois in New York. James Weldon Johnson and Channing Tobias were to be invited. A member of the Kokusai Bunka Shinkokai had written Du Bois of his inexpressible pleasure in meeting him: "In a word, it meant the widening of my very narrow horizon — and for that I shall remain grateful."

Some of Du Bois's compatriots were decidedly less grateful for his thoughts and writings. When the *Tatsuta Maru* reached San Francisco in the second week of January, he discovered that segments of the American Jewish community were perplexed and exasperated by his observations written while in the Third Reich. Inquiring where her employer could be intercepted, John Somerville, Du Bois's old Los Angeles friend, had telegraphed Diggs in Atlanta on December 18, 1936, to warn that the local anti-Nazi groups, many of them Jewish, threatened to cancel Du Bois's lectures unless the *Courier* essay were explained. "The German Case Against Jews," appearing in the January 2 edition, understandably distressed and angered many American Jews. While leaving no doubt as to his own detestation of Nazi persecution, Du Bois had recapitulated the confidences shared by a German gentile acquaintance who depicted the "Jewish problem" in terms of the special tensions arising from an alien presence—the arrival "from the East" during the Weimar years of "avaricious elements" having little in common with the assimilated Jews of the Fatherland. "The German people in the depths of their post-war misery felt a bitter jealousy and fear of this foreign element that was usurping power in their own state," Du Bois wrote, in an ambiguous paraphrase. The tribulations in Los Angeles paled beside the consternation in New York after the appearance of an interview on January 29, 1937, in the *Staatszeitung und Herold*, the city's German-language newspaper. Speaking to the reporter in German, Du Bois offered a bizarre interpretation of the Nuremberg Laws in operation. What was occurring in the Third Reich, he said, "occurs in a legal way, and in the open, even if it is cruel and unjust." Consider the contrast between Germany and the United States, he continued. In America, the Negro was secretly "and in flagrant violation of the law, persecuted and neglected." He went on to characterize the similar reactions of both groups to persecution, Jews and Negroes, as both attempted to remain as inconspicuous as possible. Yet such comparisons went only so far, Du Bois concluded, because German Jews and American Negroes were victimized by different histories: one legal, the other unconstitutional. He offered the afterthought that prejudice against people of African descent was inconsequential in Germany, as attested by his reception there.

The American Jewish Committee asked for clarification from Walter White. "Although everything may be all right," but Dr. Leo Stein, the committee's director, was understandably troubled that some of Du Bois's statements "sound[ed] not quite clear." The back-and-forth between them cannot have allayed Stein's concerns, as Du Bois's explanations again distinguished between the "orderly" application of diabilities in Germany and the mob rule and abrogation of laws visited upon people of color in the United States. "But the point I was trying to make," he iterated to Stein, was that the Nazis had made Jewish oppression "legal," rather than the "illegal caste and lynching of Negroes in the United States." Today, inescapably, Du Bois's *Courier* opinions must be read through the burnt lens of the Holocaust, the ocular fixture of the twentieth century that separates humanity's perception of ultimate evil into what was not conceived as morally possible before Kristallnacht and what was revealed to it after the liberation of the death camps. An authority on the American press and the Nazi persecution of the Jews has established, after an exhaustive sampling, that until Kristallnacht, "and even to a small degree thereafter," most of the press "continued to be optimistic regarding Nazism's treatment of the Jews." Unlike Ludwig Lewisohn, one of the few American intellectuals to predict the unthinkable, Du Bois left Germany with no intimation that the Germans were soon to embark on a war of extermination against the Jews — a dragnet of orderly, mechanized, accelerated genocide. "Eliminationist anti-Semitism," that controversial thesis of a historic and virtually congenital German urge to murder Jews, would have been analytically untenable to Du Bois, who never abjured his belief in the Germany of Goethe and Heine. The decision on the Holocaust ratified by the Nazi executive committee, meeting at Wannsee villa, would have been simply inconceivable to him. That he spoke of the German situation with an occasional inflection typical of the WASP of the day was because Du Bois was essentially a brown-skinned New England gentile and, less admirably, because he was willing to score points against his own country for the discrimination against Negroes by recourse to legalistic sophistries about the sufferings of another religious or racial group — sophistries of which he, of all observers, should have been ashamed. Still, he could have pleaded not guilty to any charges of being anti-Semitic as he comported himself in his private and public expressions with none of the Jewish antipathies so pervasive among such prominent contemporaries of his as Mencken, Dreiser, Lippmann, himself Jewish, and even Eleanor Roosevelt.

ATLANTA

THE POLITICS OF KNOWLEDGE

T he trip around the world ended when the *Tatsuta Maru* berthed at San Francisco harbor in the second week of January 1937. Du Bois returned to Atlanta by way of New York at the end of the month. He was a year from turning seventy, yet his intellectual clock seemed to run against time, each minute ticking off some rejuvenating social or scholarship challenge that made him think and act like a man half his age. Thus his moral metabolism imparted an urgency to minister to an imperfect world that was often of such feverish intensity that Du Bois wrote and acted as though an hour's delay or a week's frustration in improving the social contract risked irremediable catastrophe. Just as he had been revolted by Chinese antipathy to modernizing Japan, so he chafed intellectually at what he saw as the timidity and myopia of the Negro American majority in a time of supreme crisis. Dogmatically certain that "we have lived to see the collapse of capitalism," he dismissed as chimerical any New Deal attempt to rehabilitate the rule of finance capital. "We cannot stand still," Du Bois exhorted Africans in America. "We cannot permit ourselves simply to be the victims of exploitation and social exclusion. It is from this paradox that arises the present frustration among American Negroes."

When he had gone off to Europe and Asia in the spring of 1936, Du Bois had believed that two scholarly projects to which he had devoted considerable preparation were well under way, and he counted on both of them to have a critical impact on the theory and practice of economic and civil rights for his race. The first of these, the Bronze Booklets, a series of small volumes to be edited by Alain Locke and published by a new organization called the Associates in Negro Folk Education, was supposed to take a fresh and ranging look at race relations problems in America. The second enterprise, which had been launched five years earlier without even the courtesy of an invitation being sent to Du Bois, was the far more ambitious Phelps-Stokes Fund venture of assembling a definitive, comprehensive body of knowledge about the American Negro: the "Encyclopedia of the Negro." The Associates in Negro Folk Education was in reality a racially separate entity created by the American Association for Adult Education (AAAE). The ten-year-old AAAE in its turn was the creature of the Carnegie Corporation, whose president, Frederick P. Keppel, had been inspired by the educational outreach of the British Workers' Education Association. The impressive pedigree of the Associates in Negro Folk Education and the respectable $200 honorarium persuaded Sterling Brown, Bunche, Harris, Ira Reid, and, among others, even the irascible Woodson, to accept Locke's invitation to write for the series. After a breakfast meeting following an address to a conference at Howard in late April 1935, Du Bois, overcoming his usual skepticism about the philosophy professor's intellectual integrity, had agreed to become a series contributor. Locke had assured him that the Bronze Booklets were intended to be a platform for bold ideas. The following year, within days of his departure for Europe, Du Bois had been elected principal editor at the meeting of the encyclopedia's board on May 16 in Washington. With the board's approval, he had appointed Logan as caretaker of the project until his return from abroad.

Unsettled by well-grounded concerns that Du Bois's booklet "The Negro and Social Reconstruction" was not what the AAAE sponsors of the Associates in Negro Folk Education had in mind, Locke had dithered and demurred until Du Bois sailed. He was not simply editor of the Bronze Booklets series. Locke now enjoyed a special relationship with the Carnegie Corporation because of its president's warm regard for his scholarship and tact. Suavely aligning his views on education and racial uplift to those of the Carnegie head, the middle-aged Rhodes scholar had developed a social friendship with Keppel that Du Bois and Woodson would have been incapable of achieving, let alone sustaining. Keppel's appreciation of Locke's "fertile mind" and reasonable temperament had led to his being designated as the great foundation's "official observer and adviser with reference to Negro adult education experiments." Negro professors, even those with Harvard credentials and Oxford exposure, rarely acquired such derived influence in segregated America. Locke had no intention of risking his unique access by condoning ideas that might lead to problematic tensions between the races. Assuring Du Bois at the end of May that he found himself "in complete agreement" with all but one of its points, Locke had committed the Associates to a timely publication of "The Negro and Social Reconstruction" "substantially as is." But Locke had only been waiting for Du Bois to leave the country before sending notice while Du Bois was in China that the board of the Associates in Negro Folk Education had voted to decline the manuscript. He regretted to inform Du Bois that the trouble, expense, "and extensive revision" required to make "Negro and Social Reconstruction" acceptable were now deemed to be inappropriate.

Du Bois had no way of knowing then that his manuscript had been vetted by a disapproving Lyman Bryson, assigned the role of gatekeeper for the Bronze Booklets by the Carnegie Corporation in his capacity as professor of education at Columbia's Teachers College. Figuratively wringing his hands before Bryson but as yet unwilling to eliminate Du Bois's heterodox treatise from the series, Locke moaned that he had reworked the whole thing, but with "terrible misgivings mainly because of the uncertainty as to whether it was useless work after all." Of course, some of the principal points Bryson made against the manuscript "had been mine also," Locke sighed. The Du Bois Bronze Booklet was not Locke's only headache. Harris appears to have understood early on that it was wiser to withdraw from the series, as his views on the economics of racism were bound to distress the editor. Bunche's contribution, A World View of Race," stippled with such inflections as that "imperialism is an international expression of capitalism," that "paper rights and political privileges have not protected millions of the white [American] population from abject wage-slavery," and that "the race problem throughout the world . . . [is] merely one aspect of the class struggle," had a decidedly Leninist bias that greatly distressed his senior Howard collegue. Bunche had tested the ideological outer limits allowed by Locke's sponsors. Bryson, the white custodian of the Bronze Booklets project, sent word that, although Bunche's manuscript "will do," its Marxist point of view was "wrongheaded," news that Locke received with wheedling relief: "Thanks for your last letter, and the news that the Bunche MSS is safe." "A World View of Race" appeared in late 1936 as Bronze Booklet Number 4, taking its place beside Brown's booklet on Negro drama, Ira Reid's short study of Negro education, and Locke's treatise on art, along with T. Arnold Hill's "The Negro and Economic Reconstruction" (to replace Du Bois), and Eric Williams's "The Negro in the Caribbean," to make a total of nine publications by 1942.

Du Bois's "The Negro and Social Reconstruction" was historically broad in scope and programmatically uncompromising, as its eleven concise chapters traced the history of the black American from 1619 to the eve of the second New Deal and the dawning of a social and economic revolution. The experience of slavery from the colonial era to Reconstruction was brilliantly compressed in the opening chapter, followed by a chapter in which the rise of white supremacy and the hard, bitter, losing struggle to retain civil rights was recounted vividly and with economy. The chapter on the politics of the Atlanta Compromise, the resurgence of civil rights militancy in the Niagara Movement, and the steady advocacy of the NAACP brought the survey to the Depression. With a generosity largely absent from his recent writings about the leadership and program of the association, "The Negro and Social Reconstruction" rather belatedly admitted that the legal-defense approach had a "splendid record of accomplishment, the agitation has made millions listen." But agitation had to be superseded, he stressed, by a program of "inner organization for self-defense." Such a program of planned cooperatives would divert much of the billions of dollars annually expended by 12 million Negroes:

> In fine, by cooperative effort in doing their own laundry, making their own bread, preparing most of their own food, making a considerable part of their clothes, doing their own preparing of all sorts, printing their own papers and books and in hundreds of other ways, the colored people of the United States, if they put their minds to it and secured the proper training could . . . hir[e] themselves at decent wages to perform services which the Negro group needs; and they could do this without antagonism to the white group, without any essential change of law and without a national organization involving army and police.

Social reconstruction meant segregation leavened by socialist agents, voluntary withdrawal from the mainstream's dislocation in order to plan for a robust reentry into the world order of the future. "The Negro and Social Reconstruction" meant nothing less, editor Locke read, than that colored men and women must seize the unique opportunity to organize "the socialistic state within [their] own group by letting [their] farmers feed [their] artisans and [their] technicians guide [their] home industries and [their] thinkers plan this integration of cooperation." As Du Bois would reason in *Dusk of Dawn* somewhat later, since the Negro was now segregated "largely without reason, let us put reason and power beneath this segregation."

Locke had read the Du Bois manuscript with a sinking heart. "It is probably the best we can wangle out of the situation," he wrote Bryson. "The crucial question" was only whether Bryson "consider[ed] the Du Bois mss. as it now stands passable?" Locke had fully expected the negative response that quickly came from Morningside Heights. Unaware that he had failed to make the cut because of the asperity of his economic criticisms and the potential mass appeal of his anticapitalist separatism, Du Bois asked to see the proof sheets for "Social Reconstruction" as soon as he returned from Japan in early January 1937. Finding Locke's November letter in the stack of correspondence awaiting him in Atlanta a week later, he wrote a curt demand for the return of the manuscript on February 4, 1937. "Just who pronounced the veto I do not know," Du Bois would note with a philosophical shrug a few years later. "The Negro and Social Reconstruction" was not to be published until twenty-two years after its author's death, thanks to the dedication of historian Herbert Aptheker. The "Basic American Negro Creed" that had rattled Locke and Bryson appeared much sooner, however, as the concluding portion of the 1940 autobiographical meditation, *Dusk of Dawn*, published by Harcourt, Brace. The main text of the creed, delivered in full Du Boisian orchestra, was dissonant music to Carnegie Corporation ears: the vote must be used to equalize wealth through taxation, "for vesting the ultimate power of the state in the hands of the workers"; twelve million colored people had the capacity to supply their own wants and to establish a cooperative Negro industrial system "in the midst of and in conjunction with the surrounding national industrial organization"; above all was the espousal of the ultimate triumph of "some form of Socialism the world over," defined as the "common ownership and control of the means of production and equality of income." "Not by development of upper classes anxious to exploit the workers, nor by the escape of individual genius into the white world, can we effect the salvation of our group in America." Once again, Du Bois extolled the centrality of the Talented Tenth, charging it to study and scientifically formulate the proper course of racial action "by which the masses may be guided."

As he turned his attention to the Encyclopedia of the Negro," Du Bois had good reason to fear that its status was menaced by a similar combination of forces. Still, he believed that he detected a gradual shift in attitudes about the funding of minority institutions and programs in the boardrooms of the major foundations. The Federal Bureau of Education's 1929 *Survey of Negro Colleges and Universities*, appearing almost contemporaneously with the General Education Board's decision to create and endow the new Atlanta University along with university centers at Nashville and New Orleans, had caused Du Bois, as the Depression decade unfolded, to be cautiously encouraged that it might be feasible to obtain support for a major study of the American race problem under his direction. Such a study had been the first great ambition of his professional career, an imperative he had expounded as a twenty-nine-year-old before the Academy of Political and Social Science meeting in Philadelphia in the winter of 1897. Nothing beyond the bemused compliments of several distinguished participants had come of the spirited discussion Du Bois's paper provoked, however. Just shy of a decade later, he had tried again, writing a personal appeal to Andrew Carnegie in May 1906 for funds to conduct a broad race study. Hearing nothing from the principal benefactor of Tuskegee, Du Bois submitted a remarkable research proposal to the Carnegie Institution of Washington a few weeks later. A model agenda of concision and comprehensiveness, the document proposed a vast exploration and synthesis of virtually every disciplinary aspect of the Negro race. Tenacity personified, he had sent out prospectus and invitations in the spring of 1909 to authorities in the United States, Europe, and Africa to serve on the board of his then named "Encyclopedia Africana," another project far ahead of its time whose inspiration had been commended by the

GEB even as it had regretted the impossibility of assisting Du Bois "in ways more practical."

Du Bois was now determined to assemble and captain a cadre of scholars from three continents whose mandate would be to fill four or more volumes with definitive entries ranging from anthropology to zoology on the Negro in North America, Africa, and the West Indies. For a few outrageous weeks after the launching of the "Encyclopedia of the Negro," however, it had appeared that there would be no place for Du Bois's talents in the Phelps-Stokes Fund enterprise. Anson Phelps Stokes, president of his family's Phelps-Stokes Fund, had invited a stellar group of representative Caucasians and Negroes to the start-up conference of the "Encyclopedia of the Negro" in Carnegie Library at Howard University on November 7, 1931. Embracing the project as the earnest of his beloved aunt's bequest for the education of Negroes, Indians, and poor whites, a sincere but uncertain Stokes, swayed by warnings about the radicalism of the *Crisis* editor and the contrariness of the historian, had condoned the exclusion of Du Bois and Woodson on the advice of Thomas Jesse Jones, the fund's educational director. Jones's antipathy for Du Bois was driven in equal parts by long-simmering personal resentment and the politics of race relations.

In a bald attempt to settle scores with two scholars who had never hesitated to attack the racial motives behind his policies and publications, Jones had struck Du Bois and Woodson from the list and then disingenuously claimed that Monroe Work's *Negro Year Book*, published after a six-year hiatus that year by Tuskegee, had been the inspiration for the fund's encyclopedia plan. His animus against Du Bois was shared by Thomas Woofter of the University of North Carolina and the Commission of Interracial Cooperation (CIC). Woofter, who thought of himself as the voice of southern white liberalism, had been dismayed to see his latest book, *Black Yeomanry: Life on St. Helena Island*, dismissed in *The Crisis* as a "line of so-called sociological research" for which there was "absolutely no need." A younger man than the Chapel Hill professor, Jones's views on civil rights were just as time-warped as Woofter's. Clark Foreman, the well-connected white Atlanta liberal who became the New Deal's expert on race relations, had been surprised when Jones dismissed the argument for equal access to the vote as "a very radical position." As far as Jones was concerned, Du Bois was the definition of radicalism, a brilliant troublemaker bloated with racial pride and devoid of political common sense. Moreover, whatever his personal feelings, Jones's judgment was objectively not unreasonable: namely that Du Bois's association with the encyclopedia project would seriously complicate funding prospects for the $225,000 budget. On the other hand, the Phelps-Stokes Fund officer surely must have known that permanent exclusion of Du Bois from the project was highly untenable, but that by not inviting him to the start-up meeting, Jones and Woofter could count on having a far freer hand in concretizing the project's agenda and personnel.

The hearty, supremely assured whites who assembled in the Moorland Room of the Carnegie Library in response to the call of Caroline Phelps Stokes's nephew, saw little reason to anticipate that the colored gentlemen joining them would depart from the time-honored interracial script for such occasions. They were the lords of largesse and learning, these distinguished white men of Protestant faith and Anglo-Saxon culture, whose names and titles resonated with unmistakable goodness of fit. There was Jackson Davis, Tidewater-bred Virginian and Southern Representative of the General Education Board; James Hardy Dillard, emeritus president of Tulane University and former president of the Jeanes and Slater funds, whose name was to be borne by New Orleans's new Negro university; Charles T. Loram, Sterling Professor of Education at Yale, formerly of South Africa; Robert M. Lester, secretary of the Carnegie Corporation, standing in for Frederick Keppel. The lone woman, Van Kleeck of the Russell Sage Foundation, was detained by other business at the last minute. Will Alexander and Edwin Embree were kept away by the simultaneous meeting of the Rosenwald Fund board. Two of the whites were expected to behave professionally as honorary Negroes: Thomas Elsa Jones, who owed his Fisk presidency to the campus protests sparked by Du Bois; and Arthur Howe, principal of Hampton Institute.

The Negroes were as distinguished in their own separate but equal spheres as the whites: Charles S. Johnson, chairman of the department of sociology at Fisk University, who was, by dint of scholarship and diplomacy, well along to becoming the great foundations' most valued minority consultant; John Hope and Mordecai Johnson, university presidents of Caucasian appearance, who represented their institutions and their racial group with legendary forcefulness; Eugene Kinckle Jones of the National Urban League and Walter White, still battling Du Bois for control of the NAACP; James Weldon Johnson, revivified in his role as Adam K. Spence Professor of Creative Writing at Fisk. Kelly Miller, senior scholar of the Howard faculty, Benjamin Brawley, now of Howard's English department, and Monroe Work, Tuskegee Institute's outstanding sociologist and statistician, rounded out the Talented Tenth component. Robert Moton had been forced to cancel. Distinguished Negroes had long since found it advisable to abide a protocol of deference and decorum in their dealings with the great foundations. To some, like Locke, conforming to the protocol had become second nature. As the final item on the agenda was dispatched, however, White and the aged, but still feisty Kelly Miller raised the most significant consideration unaddressed at the meeting—the illustrious absentees. Readily acknowledging the importance attributed by Jones to Work's annual compendia, they expressed their great disappointment, nevertheless, that the convener of the meeting had seen fit to omit Du Bois and Woodson. Apparently, White made the point with an insistence that brooked no evasion. Openly confronted, the whites quickly agreed that the chastened Anson Stokes should send belated invitations to the premier sociologist of the race and its revered historian, as well as one to Locke, who had, rather surprisingly, also been passed over.

During the month Du Bois took to nurse his wounded ego before answering Stokes, he sought the advice of Embree, Dillard, and Alexander, reminding them, "without false modesty," that, "if any of the persons present at the first meeting knows anything about the American Negro," it was because he, Du Bois, had "initiated the scientific study of the American Negro in the United States and contributed something to it." The three whites, the most liberal in the tight-knit peerage of philanthropy, encouraged him to accept the Stokes invitation. He continued to hesitate, though. Could he be useful to the project as a candid, principled adviser, he wondered, given his strong views about the necessity of a Negro editor? Du Bois felt that he also needed the support of Woodson, to whom he wrote to convey a collegial sense of the unique, potential importance of the Phelps-Stokes venture. But Woodson treated Stokes's apology and invitation with ferocious disdain. Claiming that his organization, the ASNLH, had already expended at least $150,000 since 1922 in amassing data for his (until then undisclosed) Encyclopedia Africana, Woodson advised the Phelps-Stokes Fund to abandon its research agenda for his project. Neither repeated apologies nor generous offers of collaboration by Stokes and Embree or Brawley and Hope succeeded in placating the angry loner who, to the acute discomfort of Stokes, would soon begin broadcasting that the Encyclopedia of the Negro was "being worked out by traducing whites and hired Negroes." With or without Woodson, Du Bois resolved to undermine the designs of Jones and his cautious superior. When he eventually replied to Stokes's awkward attempt to repair the November exclusion, Du Bois minimized the "affront," applauded the overture to Woodson, and agreed to attend the second planning meeting set for January 9, 1932.

"Dr. Du Bois now spoke at length," the minutes of the January meeting state, and in the ensuing animation there occurred in the Moorland Room a highly revealing deployment of positions across the race-relations landscape. "White editors could not possibly express the Negro point of view," Du Bois argued. Would Jews or Catholics permit an encyclopedia about their group experience to be edited, respectively, by a Gentile or a Protestant?" Du Bois thought not. His brief for an Aframerican editor and editorial board moved Brawley to support Du Bois's argument for "spiritual and practical reasons," while Miller strongly dissented for the very practical reason, he said, that Negroes were not yet capable of financially emulating Jews and Catholics. James Weldon Johnson, his diplomatic instincts ever sharp, proposed a Negro editor-in-chief and a racially mixed editorial board and staff. Charles Johnson improved upon Johnson's suggestion by proposing a joint editorship, one black and one white. Moton's solution was a "co-ordinate editorship," whose meaning must have been clear to the participants, although he too could imagine the possibility of a Negro editor-in-chief. Walter White definitely preferred an interracial board headed by a Negro editor-in-chief. Locke reflected on his personal experience as editor of the *New Negro* anthology without expressing a clear preference among the choices on the table. Keppel's representative, Robert Lester, the corporation's secretary, also seems not to have expressed an editorial preference. Back in New York, he complained to Keppel of the meeting's "tense" racial atmosphere and expressed misgivings about the project's feasibility.

To propose during the 1930s a scholarly enterprise run from the top down exclusively by the best-trained men and women of African descent was such a surreal concept that even most distinguished representatives of the race shied away from it as an egregious instance of racial chauvinism. Beyond what he would have regarded as its therapeutic shock value, what Du Bois's largely successful gambit to have a mostly black editorial staff and board had meant to accomplish was simply to shift the point of compromise away from a dominant white outcome. Du Bois himself never truly conceived of a study of the Negro in racially exclusive terms, as an unpublished confidential memorandum to Stokes would forcefully stipulate somewhat later. If Jones had intended to maneuver the appointment of the pliant and wholly predictable Tuskegeean, Monroe Work, as editorial assistant to a prominent and equally predictable white scholar at the November meeting, Du Bois set himself the task of assuring that Jones and Woofter encountered a wall of Negro opposition. What was imperative was that an encyclopedia of the Negro "should be in the hands of those who look upon the Negro race as an integral branch of humanity," Du Bois announced, no mean assumption in the mid-1930s, "and worthy of the same scientific attention and sympathetic study that other branches have received." As he had bluntly reminded Woodson, "the enemy has the money and they are going to use it." The wise choice before them, therefore, was only "how far without great sacrifice of principle, we can keep it from being misused."

But Du Bois's pitch worked better on the doyen of southern white liberalism, Will Alexander, than on the obdurate Woodson. "Dr. Will's" endorsement of a joint editorial board with a Negro editor-in-chief forced Stokes to entertain a vote on the desirability of a white editor-in-chief. Voting down the motion for a white to run the encyclopedia as Du Bois had hoped, the twenty-odd members of the board of directors then proceeded to approve Mordecai Johnson's motion for appointment of an interracial editorial board, this time over Du Bois's and Brawley's objections. The governance of the encyclopedia, as approved, was to be a three-tiered structure consisting of a board of directors ("not to exceed nineteen in number"), an advisory board of two members each selected from thirteen national and international academic institutions and learned societies (viz., American Council of Learned Societies, South African Association for the Advancement of Science, Atlanta University, Tuskegee, International Institute of African Languages and Culture, Social Science Research Council), and an editorial staff to be chosen by the board of directors. Although the board of directors was empowered to select the editors for the project, the conferees decided to vest final approval of all editors in the twenty-six-member advisory board.

When the board of directors reconvened in mid-March, the whites en-countered "an almost unanimous sentiment" for a Negro editor-in-chief on the part of the colored members, with Du Bois as their clearly expressed preference. Will Alexander, joined by a now unambivalent Moton, insisted on such an arrangement. "He could not possibly have done this a few years ago," Moton told the surprised Stokes, but now he supported Du Bois's editorship of the encyclopedia "with great satisfaction." The meeting compromised on a joint editorial arrangement in black and white, unanimously agreeing to Stokes's nomination of Booker Washington's former assistant and ghostwriter, Robert Park, founder of the Chicago school of sociology and legend in the field, as coeditor, subject to the absent Du Bois's acceptance. A troubled Stokes fired off two pages of single-spaced type to the GEB in explanation of the whites' pre-dicament. "Ten years ago, or even five years ago," said the Phelps-Stokes Fund head, "it would not have been possible to consider Dr. Du Bois for this posi-tion in spite of the fact that he is recognized as the outstanding Negro scholar." Perched precariously atop his racial learning curve, the philanthropist detected a definite if gradual shift in the shape of the race-relations landscape. But hadn't Du Bois also changed? Stokes wondered. Although mere mention of Du Bois's name still created a "lack of sympathy in various conservative circles," Stokes assured the GEB that "all who have met him in the last year have been amazed at how much he has mellowed." True enough, the mellower Du Bois was still a well-kept secret in the best Nordic circles, but Stokes was optimistic that the Phelps-Stokes Fund and the GEB could "help to prepare public opin-ion for it."

Accepting the board's offer with "peculiar satisfaction" if not altogether gen-uine surprise at the end of March 1932, Du Bois confessed to Stokes that he had "long ago made up [his] mind that the person who agitates must be perfectly willing to pay the price." A lifetime of advocacy in scholarship and human rights had taught him not to expect "any particular consideration" from the philan-thropies. "That is part of the game," he wrote, but if the times were now truly propitious for funding such an assignment, then he would commit to its execution. Three years earlier, his version of Reconstruction history had been embargoed by the *Encyclopedia Britannica*. Today he was in the enviable position of contemplating the reshaping of the social sciences in the United States. It was an extraordinary opportunity and maybe, after all, too good to be true. Du Bois understood that his watchword must be caution, and that, in what must be the sunset years of his life, he held in his hands a long-denied opportunity to make profound sense of the American race conundrum. He would never have another chance, and he did not doubt for an instant that there was not a single living American more capable than he of achieving this goal. The better to play his part in assuring the success of a twenty-three-year-old aspiration, he promised a much relieved Stokes that he would surrender editorship of *The Crisis* as soon as the large foundations agreed to underwrite the encyclopedia. Editing the "Encyclopedia of the Negro" comported perfectly with a return to academe. Editing a journal of militant propaganda, of course, did not, but both tenure at AU and an endowment for the Phelps-Stokes project had been advanced by those controversial *Crisis* segregation editorials following hard on the Amenia Conference.

Still, as Jones and Woofter had predicted, Du Bois's participation complicated an already controversial initiative. A quarter million foundation dollars for a full-bore study of Americans of African descent and the problems of race unsettled the grey men in the paneled boardrooms of the philanthropies. Stokes had known from the outset that where enthusiasm for his encyclopedia existed there was little money and where there was money there was little enthusiasm among the foundations and learned societies. It was a virtual certainty that the problem of the twentieth century would receive unorthodox treatment with Du Bois guiding the project, an eventuality that more than a few progressive-minded Caucasians genuinely deplored. A perfect case in point was Ernest Hooton, the noted Harvard anthropologist. Hooton declined to lend his name to the project and stated that he seriously doubted the wisdom of devoting an encyclopedia to "any one particular race," although he sympathized with Negroes.

Between the second meeting of the board of directors in early January 1932 and his early June departure for Europe and Asia four years later, Du Bois had assumed de facto direction of the Phelps-Stokes project, simultaneously managing this reponsibility while working to reform the NAACP, to save his magazine, to build a graduate program in sociology at AU, and then to finish his history of Reconstruction. Although he and Robert Park were supposed to be jointly engaged in the editing process, Park's absence in South America, as well as the understanding that the editorial staff was to answer to Du Bois, effectively made Du Bois editor-in-chief, although he remained officially, and awkwardly, designated as "In Charge of Preliminary Correspondence." After some initial

nervousness about further machinations from Jones and some uncertainty as to
the firmness of Stokes's commitment (Moton reassured him that Stokes would
see the project through), he began to cast a widening net of correspondence
over the United States, Europe, and Africa in order to introduce the encyclopedia to the world community of scholars and garner endorsements. Thanks to
the devoted Diggs, dividing her stenographic skills between the *Black Reconstruction* manuscript and the encyclopedia, and the loyal Logan, providing salaried research assistance, areas of investigation were refined, specific subjects
assigned to prospective experts, questionnaires dispatched. After completing
course work for his Harvard dissertation in 1932, Logan had returned to Washington to work as Woodson's research assistant. But in summer of 1933, Hope
had lured him away to the AU history department, where Du Bois immediately
recruited him to work on the encyclopedia. Woodson seldom spoke to Logan
again. By March 1934, with the exception of the SSRC and Woodson's ASNLH,
Stokes could report that the learned societies invited to affiliate with the encyclopedia had officially done so. But the hurdles ahead of Du Bois and Stokes
were formidable in an era when *The New York Times* had but recently agreed
to capitalize "Negro." The very conception of such an encyclopedia—of an
arbitral compendium of knowledge about Negroes—continued to be regarded
as dubious at best by powerful elements in the eleemosynary and scholarly
universes. Too many unanswered questions remained, it was said.

Were Negroes genetically equipped to become full citizens? How significant was the African past to the American future of the Negro? Were Negroes
gradually becoming less Negroid through cultural adaptation and diffusion of
"white" blood? How were the meaningful differences between the races to be
calibrated? Even an encyclopedia booster such as the Columbia psychologist
Otto Klineberg had foreseen a "certain amount of difficulty" because of the
large number of "controversial" issues surrounding the Negro. Instead of becoming a rationale for the research and reflection envisaged by Du Bois, the
encyclopedia was to be hampered by the paradox of a genteel racism in the
philanthropic-intellectual complex that had long wanted to know less rather
than more about the nation's largest minority. Even as it also began to be
troubled enough by the old "scientific" racism and the new National Socialism
to contemplate the possibility of a moderate reassessment of the race perennial,
this genteel racism recoiled from the prospect of learning more about Negroes
from Negroes themselves. And from another corner of the academy, dubious
philanthropoids could solace themselves in the dissenting expertise of contending schools of anthropology—of functionalists (Malinowskians) such as A. R.
Radcliffe-Brown, who sharply discounted the cultural and historical biases of
Du Bois's approach to race, on the one hand; and, on the other, of culturalists
(Boasians) such as Herskovits who, although philosophically in tune with

Du Bois, coveted the encyclopedia's projected budget and whispered that Du Bois's once trailblazing scholarship was now as outdated as Stokes's "uplifter" mentality.

Their first hurdle had not gone at all well. Stokes had presented the Phelps-Stokes Fund proposal to the GEB in the early part of 1934, requesting a subvention of $100,000 as the Rockefeller-backed foundation's portion of the $225,000 budget. Once approved by the GEB, Stokes had intended to ask the Carnegie Corporation to fund the balance. A guarded optimism, based on success in obtaining formal affiliation of all of the learned societies except SSRC, had persuaded him that the prospects for funding were favorable. On June 15, 1934, however, the executive committee of the GEB had rejected the Phelps-Stokes application. Had Stokes been privy to the notes on the board's deliberations, he would have known how correct his surmise was that both Du Bois's involvement and the perception of its inherent complexities would preclude favorable foundation action for an indefinite period. But if Stokes had hoped for a period of quietus, to say nothing of discrete neglect of the "Encyclopedia of the Negro," his timetable was to be frustrated by the cycle of Du Bois's intellectual and professional enthusiasms.

With the editorial and organizational concerns of the NAACP now behind him and the last *Black Reconstruction* corrections on their way to Harcourt, Brace, it had been predictable that a driven Du Bois would turn his questing attention to the venture he had wrenched from the grip of the Joneses and Woofters almost three years before. Du Bois had generated a stellar roster of endorsements that would soon number more than eighty individuals from virtually every discipline in the social sciences and humanities, many of them names that would have a long resonance: both Beards, Charles and Mary; Boas; Margaret Mead; E. Franklin Frazier; Melville Herskovits; Howard Odum; Mencken; Malinowski and his disciple, A. R. Radcliffe-Brown, now at Chicago; Jameson; Lord Hailey; D. Westermann; Roscoe Pound of Harvard Law School; Harold Laski of the London School of Economics; Broadus Mitchell of the Hopkins economics department; and Otto Klineberg of the Columbia psychology department, among others. Mencken thought the encyclopedia ought to be done "as soon as possible." Responding that he hated "like sin" to write encyclopedia articles, Beard offered to make an exception for Du Bois. Mead "enthusiastically" agreed that the time was "ripe for such a project," and Embree surrendered his preference for a fifteen-year postponement after reading Du Bois's eloquent brief. Good-naturedly conceding that Du Bois could state "complex matters more clearly and persuasively" than anyone he knew, Embree rallied to the project, responding that he was "ready to recommend the use of anyone else's money that we can get out hands on." It was all very well for Laski, an acerbic British Fabian, to envisage the encyclopedia as an "armoury against imperialistic anthropology" (a swipe against Malinowski?) or for Mencken, the peerless Baltimore destroyer of humbug, to call for it to be assembled "wholly by Negroes." From long experience, Du Bois knew that the custodians of the great foundations conceived as their special calling in matters of race the detection and exorcism of precisely such subversive notions as those expressed by Mencken and Laski. Although it was never his decision to make, he could have explained to Hopkins economist Mitchell that the latter's preference for "fewer university presidents, etc.," and more men of Du Bois's "training and interest" would have doomed the enterprise from the start. The likes of Bunche, Brown, Harris, and Frazier on the board of directors—a completely far-fetched hypothetical—would have ruffled black establishment figures by their lack of deference almost as much as their perceived intellectual impertinence would have offended vigilant custodians of knowledge.

Rejuvenated by Du Bois's resourcefulness, and delighted with the news that eighty scholars were committed to contribute articles, Stokes had agreed in October 1935 to appropriate 2,500 precious dollars from the Phelps-Stokes reserve fund (including a $500 Du Bois honorarium) in order to supplement the AU salaries of Diggs and Logan and to speed along the research and planning. It must have come as a surprise, however, to receive news a few days later that Du Bois planned to spend six months abroad on an Oberlaender Trust fellowship. The time in Germany might interfere "a little with my work," the de facto editor casually assured Stokes, "but not seriously." In fact, the leading anthropologists, linguists, sociologists, economists, and the like he expected to be able to meet during his travels should prove invaluable to the project, he had explained. What this half year abroad would cost the "Encyclopedia of the Negro" in terms of lead time is susceptible to little more than an educated guess. The likelihood of securing foundation funding might not have been materially improved, even had he declined the Oberlaender fellowship in order to devote optimal attention to the Phelps-Stokes venture. What is certain, though, is that Du Bois was unaware of a decision taken in the fall of 1935 by the Carnegie Corporation at its board meeting on October 24 that would complicate immeasurably the encyclopedia's future.

Newton Baker, erstwhile reform mayor of Cleveland, secretary of war under Woodrow Wilson, corporate boardsman, and a founder of what was to become the National Conference of Christians and Jews, had been distressed by recent unrest and revelations of increasing Negro radicalism. That March, Harlem had exploded for the first time. An incident involving a teenager in a West 125th Street five-and-dime resulted in $2 million worth of damage to white-owned commercial property. The West Virginia son of a Confederate officer, Baker was no racial liberal. He referred with the casualness of a born white southerner to Negroes as an "infant race," assumed that they were biologically inferior, and dabbed his eyes when speaking of the historic nobility of Caucasian Americans. "How many white civilizations could have dared receive so many wild savages, and spread them around over their farms in contact with their own families passes human comprehension," he marveled in a letter to Keppel. On this October Thursday, this conservative Democrat, new chairman of the American Council on Education (ACE), and much troubled Christian trustee proposed that the Carnegie Corporation undertake a broad study of "negro education and negro problems [sic]." Even Negroes deserved a good education, but what that education should be as they moved from farm to town and then north into the great industrial cities cried out for scientific examination and wise prescription, Baker insisted. Drawing on the conclusions of *The Collapse of Cotton Tenancy*, the newly released Rosenwald Fund monograph authored by Alexander, Embree, and Charles Johnson, the transplanted southerner spoke not only of his acute sense of the changes sweeping his birthplace, but of what he now understood to be a national race problem. It would never have occurred to Newton D. Baker to permit himself the thought that the "Encyclopedia of the Negro" might have merited a Carnegie grant in order to provide the answers he called for. Equally significant was Keppel's omission to commend the Stokes–Du Bois project to Baker at that time.

Du Bois's unexpected departure had given special importance to several agenda items for the plenary meeting of the encyclopedia's board of advisers and board of directors on May 16, 1936, three weeks before Du Bois sailed for Europe. There was the shape-shifting matter of Du Bois's title, formally rendered as "In Charge of Preliminary Correspondence," which had continued to alternate, informally, from joint editor to chief editor, just as the role and identity of the white collaborator (Robert Park had never formally assented) still remained vague. The advisability of a third editor to handle the African material also demanded review and a final decision. With a total of six thousand Phelps-Stokes dollars so far invested, the hunt for money had become critical; unexplored possibilities and an expedited resubmission to the GEB had to be discussed. To this crucial May conference, Joel Spingarn would come and Melville Herskovits would not. Professor Otelia Cromwell of the District of Columbia's colored teachers college, the board of directors' secretary and one of two female members, kept correct, dry minutes of these deliberations, but Arthur Schomburg drafted a gossipy, hilarious, and invaluably misinformed account of the daylong meeting in the Carnegie Library. Charles Johnson had sent the Harlem bibliophile as his proxy. Schomburg's attitude toward Du Bois had long been a blend of awe and resentment that his lively, larcenous correspondence took little care to conceal.

After a sumptuous noon meal and a group photo taken on the steps of the library (Spelman's Read holds her own among the rows of manly notables), the two boards had confirmed Du Bois's title as editor-in-chief "in charge of everything from the land to the sky," Schomburg winked through mispellings and misreadings. It now dawned on the ACLS's Leland, who appeared to Schomburg to have been taken somewhat by surprise, that hard questions needed to be put to Du Bois about his plans—"what it was all about. Let me tell you," Schomburg gloated, "Dr. Du Bois was put on the spot. It was a beautiful forensic battle in which Du Bois, through his masterful knowledge of specious pleading, . . . offered [little] and much was said, on his Opus Magnus." Unimpressed by Du Bois's rationale for his world tour, Schomburg mocked that "for the first time, [he] got a true picture of what is going to take place in the present log rolling trip of the Doctor."

Although Schomburg's critique of the encyclopedia's research agenda never went beyond the typos, quaint or confusing nomenclature, and what he deemed the egregious slip of listing the same person twice as Saint Benedict the Moor and Benedict of Palermo, he had correctly divined the cobbled-together nature of the project. But both he and the ACLU's quizzical Leland passed over a fundamental conceptual flaw that Frazier was to identify six months later. In a typically critical response to the wayfaring editor-in-chief's blanket invitation for corrective feedback, Frazier respectfully suggested that "the fundamental weakness of the entire undertaking" was its apriority—the failure to assemble and interrogate the best social-science brains before preparing the encyclopedia's syllabus. The future first Negro president of the American Sociological Association lectured his guru that the syllabus seemed "no more than a confused assortment of almost every conceivable topic and person related to Negro life." A short time later, after a much delayed perusal, Herskovits shared similar reservations, especially with regard to the "tribal terms and classifications" in the syllabus. It is an entirely safe speculation that Du Bois fully appreciated, at least in a general way, the datedness, imprecision, and objectively indicting incompleteness of the work he and his assistants, Diggs and Logan, had scrambled to assemble. But Du Bois had had neither authority nor budget after the 1934 GEB rejection to replicate the empirical social science methodology that had informed the unique Atlanta University Studies. His performance to date had resembled, perforce, the one-man act of a conjurer, a single-handed mounting of an adroit simulacrum, a dazzling light show in which the shapes and images of a globally coordinated enterprise of scholarship temporarily made do for the superior product—for the sake of actualizing the superior product.

DU BOIS'S GENIUS was blessed by good genes and good fortune. In February 1938 he would turn seventy. Clarence Darrow, Henry Hunt, and James Weldon Johnson would pass from the scene that year, Johnson killed in a car crash. Francis Grimké and Henry O. Tanner had died the year before. Hope had been gone two years. Kelly Miller would succumb to the infirmities of his seventy-six years in 1939. Yet Du Bois seemed not to age. The last report from the Life Extension Institute indicated a slight elevation of albumen in his urine, some hearing loss, and a gain in weight. He was informed that he was in robust health otherwise. He had already brought his weight down by 9 pounds to 156 by early January. He was determined not to "fatten up again," he wrote Nina. His single kidney functioned normally, and he needed glasses only to read by. His mental acuity seemed undiminished and his exceptional physical stamina was sustained by abstemious habits and a rigidly self-enforced bedtime retirement at ten. His relationships with exceptional women remained as extensive as ever, and the fortnight before his birthday was an especially active time. Sweeping into Chicago from Detroit for a noontime speaking engagement at the Women's City Club, he had breakfasted with Shirley Graham (she now worked for the Chicago Federal Writers Project and managed the Prince Theater) and had dined with Mildred Jones before taking the eleven o'clock train for Wheeling, West Virginia. The quick stopover left Jones, who wrote that she thought of him "every day," euphoric. Graham would have reason to be even more euphoric six weeks later when she was awarded a Rosenwald fellowship and admitted to graduate study at Yale.

That there were many tens of thousands of women and men whose lives had been enriched by him and who considered themselves honored to be asked to pay him tribute Du Bois discovered on the grandly orchestrated occasion of his seventieth birthday. The nine-person birthday committee, with Reid as chair and Logan as secretary, planned a university convocation (attended by "all institutions with which he has been connected"), a formal banquet, presentation of a personal memento, unveiling of Alexander Portnoff's bust (funds permitting), and the publication of the Du Bois convocation address. Five dollars bought membership in the Friends and Associates, the sponsoring group for the affair. Myron Adams, dean of the old Atlanta University during Du Bois's first tenure there, sent three dollars, the most he could afford as he, like so many others, had to struggle merely to "keep in the middle class," he sighed. Mary Ovington was in more fortunate circumstances than Adams, but her state of mind was far more pessimistic. Along with her five dollars she sent word to Du Bois that her last and only hope now was in communism, such was the hopelessness of persecuted minorities whether in Germany or America. Walter White managed to sound sincere in his message of regret at not being able to pay tribute in person "to the man who has profoundly influenced American and world history, particularly the history of the Negro." Before it was decided that the university would decline the birthday invitation, the secretary to the Harvard Corporation had inquired if the GEB planned to attend. President Raymond B. Fosdick notified Secretary Jerome Greene that, although the board had not received an invitation, it encouraged him to attend both as Harvard's official representative as well as member of the GEB. There was a good reason to do so, Fosdick suggested—"a grand chance to check up" on Du Bois and the "Encyclopedia of the Negro." Fosdick was worried about the "adverse advice from some southern people" contending that the encyclopedia would "accentuate the isolation of the negro race." In the end, the secretary to the corporation begged to excuse the university from sending an official representative, explaining that "it has seemed necessary to confine such appointments to rather narrow limits."

College presidents and administrators, representatives of Greek letter organizations, the NAACP in the person of Joel Spingarn, surrogates of learned societies, teachers, attorneys, and physicians of prominence descended upon the capital of the New South during the brisk February day before the event. White Atlantans heading for trains or passing nearby on Hunter and Piedmont Streets gaped in puzzlement or scowled in resentment as distinguished black and white invitees flowed out of the city's Spanish-style Terminal Station. The Limited from New York and the Express from Chicago disgorged men in homburgs and fedoras whose bearings unmistakably bespoke the habit of command, even if the Negroes were necessarily masters of the etiquette of Jim Crow. As taxi service in Atlanta was segregated and there were few clean, reliable vehicles available to Negro citizens, a fleet of cars belonging to faculty and prosperous colored Atlantans shuttled continuously past the station entrance in order to scoop up arriving dark-skinned celebrants for deposit at the university center. The NAACP and Du Bois had moved on, each becoming more estranged from the other, yet the unitary significance of man and movement was symbolically conveyed by the indispensable presence of Joel Spingarn, association president and Du Bois confidante. Spingarn, gaunt and elegant, arrived with a canister of moving footage taken by Amy of the Amenia Conference that would be shown during the testimonial banquet. Invited almost at the last moment, Nina came, accompanied by Yolande and Baby Du Bois.

Arrayed in doctoral hood and gown (use of the gold tassel was reserved to Harvard's president, he had been informed), Du Bois addressed the capacity audience from the center of the Sisters Chapel dais balanced to his right and left by four eminent, berobed personalities, among them Read and Reid, Johnson and Johnson, Braithwaite and Spingarn. He proposed to review his unique life in a context of universality, choosing, he stated, "to essay this from the aspect of an historical pageant of human kind in which I have been a more or less active spectator, and whose end and meaning I have sought to see." The better to recapture the "elusive unity that may lie therein," the speaker divided his life into ten-year terms to comprise what he described as "A Pageant in Seven Decades: 1868–1938." The address was a tour de force of philosophical summary and biographical compression that began with a somewhat fanciful retelling of his Great Barrington childhood. "A pleasant childhood" it was. He could remember "no poverty although [his] family was certainly poor." It was, he continued "a pleasant and miscellaneous" family: "the father was dead before I can remember; the mother brown and quietly persistent." The real family story had been more complex, checkered by paternal desertion, near destitution, and a bright colored boy's occasional humiliation at the hands of bigots. Still, it had been, as Du Bois remembered, a quintessential New England upbringing with unambiguous notions about wealth and poverty. "Wealth was the result of work and saving and the rich rightly inherited the earth. The poor, on the whole, were to be blamed." There had been definite notions about emotions, too. Less were better. On the streets of his little Berkshire town, "people held themselves in," and Du Bois confessed that he had never been able to outgrow the reserve acquired in those formative years. "Later the habit of repression often returned to plague me," he told the Sisters Chapel audience. Many would continue to believe, though, that Du Bois's aloofness was more a manifestation of arrogance than of awkward reserve.

He sped through the second and third decades of college and graduate school: Fisk, where he underwent editorial teething on the *Herald* and witnessed white supremacy in the raw Tennessee outback; Harvard, where writing improved under the legendary Barrett Wendell, history acumen sharpened with Albert Bushnell Hart, philosophy came alive under Josiah Royce and William James, and his commencement speech on Jefferson Davis received national attention; then to the University of Berlin, where study under Schmoller and Wagner had been financed by the Slater Fund, and where there was bonding with German culture and mastery of empirical social science.

As Du Bois evoked the astonishing *Souls*, rehearsed the David and Goliath scrimmaging of the Niagara Movement, and carried his story across decades five and six (from 1908 to 1928) past the start-up of *The Crisis*, the early legal victories of the NAACP, the bitter miscalculation with Woodrow Wilson, and the launching of the pan-African movement, the hushed chapel audience relived their becoming a modern people, the coming of psychological emancipation within two generations of legal emancipation from the long bondage of chattel slavery. He carried them onward to the rise and fall of Marcus Garvey in a presentation that had none of the bile and thunder that few of his listeners would have forgotten. It seemed, as he told it, to have been an unfortunate misunderstanding between two men of affairs, one of whom was prone to bombast and sloppy accounting methods. Garvey's downfall was regrettable, but had been essentially self-inflicted and owed nothing to his, Du Bois's, opposition.

His seventh decade had brought home the full force of an economic revelation, Du Bois declared. It was his certainty that liberalism was no longer a social philosophy adequate to comprehend the profoundly changed power relationships emerging out of the Great War that had disillusioned him with the program of the NAACP and much else. Much had been accomplished, he noted, but the problem was that twentieth-century liberalism had stood by while corporate wealth throttled democratic government and then collapsed under its own profligacy. Nor had it any effective prescriptions for ending the lengthening Depression. From his reading of Marx, *Crisis* symposia, and world travels he had come to understand better the structural nature of the calamity. In his opinion, neither Russian communism (although theoretically benign) nor Hitlerian fascism were acceptable radical solutions to the world crisis of capitalism as both had been forced "to consolidate their power by assassination and mass propaganda of every sort." Meanwhile, labor and capital had embarked on a desperate economic experiment in the United States, one that Du Bois was certain would be furthered at the expense of black people. Desperately, he had been trying to "spy out in the Universal Gloom a path for the American Negro." One thing was certain, he said. "We could not afford to sit and wait," but had to press forward "actively and intelligently" toward objectives "consistent with the new ways of a world about to be born." His solution — "the advocating of a new segregation in economic lines" — had separated him from the NAACP and impelled a return to academe. Briskly, he mentioned his hopes for the "Encyclopedia of the Negro" and his satisfaction with *Black Reconstruction*.

More honors were in store for the seventy-year-old luminary. AU bestowed an honorary doctorate of laws at its commencement that June. Not to be outdone, Du Bois's first undergraduate college awarded him an honorary doctorate of letters. Fisk's capable President Jones having run the risk of putting a platform at Du Bois's disposal, the unpredictable alumnus returned to campus on June 8 to deliver the seventy-second commencement address. The memory of Du Bois's speech, "The Revelation of St. Orgne the Damned," would be evoked by generations of alumni and faculty on the eve of Fisk commencements as an unforgettable example of the sui generts. The autobiographical indulgence of "Pageant in Seven Decades" carried over into his lengthy, rhetorically ornate, and metaphorically exuberant sermon whose anagrammatical Orgne was, of course, the Negro in the person of St. Du Bois. Above all, St. Orgne excoriated the backwardness of Negro elementary education, notwithstanding a half century of systematic devastation by white southern school budgets and school terms geared to planting and harvesting. "The fault lies with Negroes themselves," he scolded, "for not being willing and eager and untiring" in their determination to build schools that taught the basics. The black church was a culpable. "Instead of building edifices, paying old debts, holding revivals, and staging entertainments," this central institution needed to inculcate citizenship and modern morality, a task for which St. Orgne pronounced "the Hebrew Scriptures and the New Testament canon" to be inadequate.

Never one to rest on his oars, Du Bois returned to finishing a new, much expanded version of his 1915 book, *The Negro*, published by Henry Holt. In the years since its appearance, a world of new material had been unearthed about the African past of the Negro, yet there was no suitable monograph accessible to the general public. He believed that the study of African history and culture was "beginning to spread especially in Negro schools and other schools," or so Du Bois claimed in a letter to Holt. After several unsuccessful attempts to interest the publishing house in the project, Holt had responded positively in late 1937 with a contract for what would become *Black Folk: Then and Now*, virtually a new book. Work on the encyclopedia had continued also, and he and Stokes had allowed themselves to become enthused by the signals emanating from the GEB. A two-hour campus conference with Jackson Davis in mid-October had seemed to be all Du Bois could have wished for, especially after the interim director of AU's School of Education, a white emeritus professor from Columbia's Teachers College, trotted to Du Bois's office to report that Davis was now so impressed as to consider proposing that $130,000 of the GEB's $1.7 million earmarked for the university's endowment be committed to the encyclopedia on a dollar-for-dollar matching basis. It became very quickly clear, though, that the prospect of relocating the encyclopedia from Washington, where it had been incorporated, to Atlanta was neither particularly appealing nor politic, as it evoked agitated objections from Brawley that AU might be favored over Howard.

Everyone knew that Park was now too old for the assistant editor job, and would have to be replaced. Park departed amicably by the first week of January 1938, and Du Bois, after a brief interval of sharp dissent, had agreed to accept Guy Johnson, an urbane young white sociologist from Texas, as associate editor. But even before Park's replacement, a turning-point meeting had taken place at GEB headquarters on November 29, 1937, with Du Bois and Stokes in attendance. Despite the strong undertow of southern white disapproval and the background noise of denigration from a number of authoritative northern whites, Davis, though still equivocal as to its advisability, had become convinced enough of the encyclopedia's legitimacy that he had quietly presented its materials to an informal jury of leading scholars. In conference with Davis and David H. Stevens, director of education for the GEB, on November 29, Du Bois and Stokes had been informed that the southern historian Dumas Malone and the associate editor of the *Encyclopedia of the Social Sciences*, Alvin Johnson, among several others, seconded GEB funding of a portion of what was now a $260,000 enterprise. Now cautiously optimistic, Du Bois and Stokes had held their breaths as they entered upon the last lap of the funding obstacle course.

Even those philanthropoids who were averse to the very concept of a race-specific research enterprise, as well as those who claimed that the American Negro problem and the larger conundrum of race had received sufficient treatment in the *Encyclopedia of the Social Sciences*, were hard-pressed not to concede that the high standard of scholarship deployed in volumes eleven and thirteen by Boas, Herskovits, Hans Kohn, and the superlative "Negro Problem" entry by Abram Harris and Sterling Spero constituted powerful arguments for augmented foundation support of such scholarship. Yale professor John Dollard's *Caste and Class in a Southern Town* and Fisk professor Bertram Doyle's *The Etiquette of Race Relations*, both appearing in 1937, added seminal monographs to the growing bibliography in race relations that included Harold Gosnell's *Negro Politicians* (1935), Charles S. Johnson's *The Shadow of the Plantation* (1934), and Donald Young's *American Minority Peoples* (1932). These books, along with several others, created a race-relations bulge in the decade's midrift. Some, like *The Collapse of Cotton Tenancy* (1935), coauthored by Alexander, Embree, and Johnson, questioned the permanence of the Deep South's racial arrangements and had positive policy consequences in the establishment of the New Deal's Farm Security Administration (FSA) with Alexander as director. *The Shadow of the Plantation*, Johnson's beautifully written study of Macon County, Alabama, supported by the empirical evidence of six hundred family histories, presented a devastatingly critical analysis of a closed southern society rotting inwardly and acutely in need of attention from the nation. Young's *American Minority Peoples* maintained, as had Du Bois in *The Philadelphia Negro*, that the "problems and principles of race relations are remarkably similar, regardless of what groups are involved"—a thesis that was conceptually much too progressive to influence the sociology of contemporary race relations.

The views of Johnson and Young, although they might be respectfully cited the better to be tendentiously interpreted, were departures from a mainstream consensus that had long ago cohered into a binary social-science vision in which latecomer immigrants were lumped into the general category of "ethnics," while blacks were split off as unassimilable others into the category of race. *Alien Americans* (1936), by Bertram Schrieke, a retired Dutch colonial administrator imported by the Rosenwald Fund, was an outstandingly harsh example of the black otherness school which held rigidly to the postulate that relations between the races—between whites and blacks—were so intractable that the social scientist's proper role was uniquely that of the objective observer who obeyed the stricture to do no harm by seldom if ever recommending aggressive solutions. *Alien Americans* appeared just as the concept of "caste" was being introduced into the study of the Negro by W. Lloyd Warner, then at the beginning of his influential career. The analytical utility of the concept of caste (an exotic-sounding euphemism for the dreaded word *race*) became immediately apparent with the release of Dollard's *Caste and Class in a Southern Town*, which threatened to freeze the American race problem into hierarchical immutability just as Du Bois and Stokes were about ready to present their revised project to the foundations. Faithful to the axiom of Yale's William Graham Sumner that stateways were powerless to change folkways, the Warner-Dollard school was to produce community studies of oppressing whites and regressing blacks in what often seemed a timeless symbiosis that collapsed class and even race into the absolute of caste. If Dollard found blacks to be happy in their hopelessness, if Hortense Powdermaker found glimmerings of resentment and resistance in her more discerning and generous *After Freedom* (1939), or Allison Davis and Burleigh and Mary Gardner recorded tremors of change in *Deep South* (1941), the last of the caste monographs, the basic story was still one of almost unstirring stasis. Guy Johnson, the academic now at Chapel Hill who was to replace Park on the encyclopedia, had predicted the appeal of the concept to sociologists and boldly deplored it more than a decade earlier, warning, in Howard Odum's *Social Forces* journal, that "the progress of the Negro since emancipation should be warning enough against the caste method," and that any attempt "to solve the problem by a caste arrangement merely postpones the day when the white man must face the issue squarely." As Du Bois observed in a calculatingly generous review of *Caste and Class*, the value of its matchless insights into the psyches of whites in a small southern community would have been far more illuminating had Dollard's interpretations "been built on a thorough economic foundation." This static schematic of caste Du Bois naturally deplored as but another example of scholarship accommodating itself to the national compromise with the white South, an intellectual justification for evasion in the denial of the Negro's civil liberties.

The encyclopedia project was at a curious crossroads. The more attention paid by the academy and the foundations to the Negro, the more resistance there was to privileging the scholarship of the one authority whose claim to interpret the problem of the century was unexcelled. Two days after the commemoration of his seventieth birthday, Du Bois sent a typed, carefully crafted four-page rebuttal to the eleventh-hour misgivings informally conveyed to Stokes by several GEB trustees. The remaining obstacle was objectivity. "They are only concerned by one thing," Stokes had warned in his letter of February 11, "and that is whether we have thought through ways in which to assure objectivity of our findings." Several GEB trustees were particularly agitated by the opinion of a visiting British anthropologist who had determined that anthropological scholarship in the United States betrayed either a "white or a Negro bias." Stokes had been advised that this distinguished anthropologist appeared to doubt the possibility that there could be "complete objectivity even in historical matters where racial pride on the one hand or racial prejudice on the other was at stake." Interoffice correspondence at 61 Broadway reflected the board's looming dilemma during the months of January through March 1938: whether funding its portion of Du Bois's encyclopedia might not prove unavoidable. The insistence of the highly respected and highly political Charles S. Johnson in mid-March that "interest in [the encyclopedia] is gathering momentum," and that it merited foundation support under Du Bois's direction, was duly noted.

The academic creed of the day proclaimed that objectivity was, if not yet attainable in its purest incarnation, a goal in whose pursuit the disciplined mandarin strove to discard all relativisms except those exactions that were inescapably human. The objective historian, like the objective social scientist, was, in the words of the historian whose work has inimitably captured the fiction, a "neutral or disinterested judge" who "must never degenerate into . . . an advocate or, even worse, propagandist," for the objectivity quest was held to be "at grave risk when history is written for utilitarian purposes." Du Bois's February 1938 memorandum to Stokes, "On the Scientific Objectivity of the Proposed *Encyclopedia of the Negro* and on Safeguards Against the Intrusion of Propaganda," came slightly more than three years after the president of the American Historical Association had touted the detached scholarship of his profession in the ritual of the annual late-December address. Fifty years of undeviating standards and "clear-cut ideal[s]" in the service of an "intellectual assumption" that had been conceived "first in Germany and later accepted everywhere, the ideal of the effort for objective truth," had borne magnificent results, trumpeted Theodore Clarke Smith.

It was a measure of Du Bois's intellectual self-assurance that, German-trained himself, his conception of the imperatives of objectivity was neither reverential nor anarchical. But in submitting to GEB officials through Stokes his forthright reservations concerning the ruling epistemology in academe, Du Bois must have realized that, given the forthrightness of his principles, he faced a dilemma—a trap, really—to which there might be no response that could satisfy the foundation establishment. Emphatic in its rejection of special pleading, his memorandum stated that the object of the encyclopedia would be defeated were it to be written as "a defense of Negroes against attack or as a vehement championship of their possible future development." Just as emphatically, there must not even be an echo of "the old contempt and calumny which used to be so frequent," it declared. Du Bois's memorandum had but boldly articulated a frame of reference in which uncertainty and controversy could be managed and tested with some degree of impartiality, criteria by which constrained bias might yield contingent truth. But as Du Bois knew, his objectivity problem was really a race-relations problem, one in which the objectivity bar was never set higher than when the scholarship to be vetted concerned the study of the American Negro. Finally faced with the imminent prospect of actually having to fund the "Encyclopedia of the Negro," the officers of the GEB and the Carnegie refreshed their understanding of objective social science and began to wonder if its requirements were not so exigent as virtually to prelude the endorsement of any scholar born in the United States for the study of the Negro. Although he was pleased to report that Jackson Davis had been entirely reassured by the "admirable memorandum," Stokes admitted that he fully understood Davis's concerns about other persons to whom, "not unnaturally," Du Bois's tenure as an editor and propagandist "bulk large." Adding Howard Odum or the Englishman Radcliffe-Brown as associate editors would offer more reassurance, Stokes thought, and happily informed Du Bois a few days later of Radcliffe-Brown's willingness to serve in that capacity. There was more good news in a follow-up letter of March 28 in which an almost giddy Stokes exulted that the objectivity qualms had finally been laid to rest. "Well, after I had been with Mr. Stevens and Mr. Davis for an hour, they told me in confidence that they were prepared definitely to recommend the project to their Board at its April meeting."

Du Bois assumed that the thirty-year-old dream was about to materialize, and with it the wherewithal of professional talent and resources sufficient to reformulate the problem of the century. For this encyclopedic venture meant as much to him for the symbol and substance of its interracial collaboration as for what it could produce in the way of old data revised and new findings interpreted about the Negro. For although his seven-decade pageant had filled black America with sound and light, it had been played out largely behind the veil of color, a performance of such exceptional merit and meaning, however, that, despite the enforced invisibility of the most visible national minority, there had been occasions when the condescending white majority had been compelled to notice. He and the country were both the poorer for the racial prejudice that had forced him into a shoestring career as academic, journalist, and man of letters, an existence in the margins where never once during an odds-surmounting half century had there been an offer of a university appointment or learned society affiliation commensurate with his genius. "If we could have at this particular time a conspicuous example of inter-racial fellowship in scientific work," a meld of the leading white social scientists of the United States and Europe and the best and brightest young American Negroes—Bunche, Harris, Frazier, Brown, Carolyn Bond-Day, Logan, Diggs, and Allison Davis— then it would "prove that the foundations and philanthropy are willing to subsidize Negro work when it is segregated, but just as eager to help Negro scientific work of the highest grade and in conjunction with the world's best scientists," he had pleaded in one of his foundation memoranda. Linked arm in arm in this pioneering work, Du Bois saw himself leading the younger generation out of the ghetto of learning onto the broad plain of international scholarship. "Such unusual opportunity for associating with the world's best would be incalculable," he said.

Logan could no longer recall the brand, but he still retained a vivid recollection thirty-six years later of the champagne iced in a bucket in Du Bois's office. The decision of the GEB executive committee to refer the encyclopedia to the full board had already reached Atlanta when Clement, the new AU president, returned from New York with news that the Stokes–Du Bois proposal was slated for approval at a meeting of the GEB trustees on April 6, 1938, a Wednesday. Anticipating Stokes's corroborating telephone call in the late afternoon on Thursday, Du Bois and Logan passed the tension over cigarettes and small talk, as the bottle of excellent champagne nestled in its crib of ice. Logan was one of the few people with whom Du Bois ever descended to mere banter. But as Logan was fond of boasting, "[he] probably knew Du Bois better than anyone else, except, perhaps, his second wife." Even so, not even he really knew Du Bois, he admitted. After any number of furtive and increasingly anxious glances at the clock, it became depressingly obvious as the light went out of the late afternoon that no telephone call would come from Anson Phelps Stokes that day. "Well, I have some disappointing news for you," the fund president wrote a few days later. Putting the best WASP face on the rejection, Stokes complimented Fosdick for being "perfectly fine about the whole matter" and Stevens for fighting for the proposal. "The General Education Board, although not flatly declining our request, has decided that it cannot act favorably upon it." Yet Stokes was clearly disconsolate, ending his letter to Du Bois with a sigh: "You and I may not see this project through, although I hope and believe that we will." His postscript confided that objectivity concerns had continued to nag at certain trustees. Head unbowed, Du Bois replied with stoic brevity that, quite possibly, "the chief impediment to our raising the funds is my own personality." Logan went to his grave convinced that the encyclopedia project had been undermined at both foundations by the machinations of Melville Herskovits. The lesson to be drawn from this mortifying experience, Logan would remind young scholars, was that there was once a time when "the word of one white man could determine whether a project concerning Negroes could be approved or not." The admonition was correct, but Logan blamed the wrong white man. The foundation WASPs were only somewhat less receptive to Du Bois than they were to Herskovits, whose competing, $200,000 proposal for a three-continent study of African peoples had been rejected by the Carnegie Corporation two years earlier.

A conflicted Jackson Davis minced no words about the reasons for the GEB's negative decision in his meeting with Keppel in early May. Stating frankly that Du Bois's activities with the NAACP "oveshadowed his scholarly interests and that more time was necessary to create another impression"—better objectivity, obviously—the sympathetic program officer lobbied the Carnegie Corporation to approve its portion of the Stokes–Du Bois application, despite the action of his own foundation. "Dr. Du Bois is the most influential Negro in the United States," Davis petitioned. "This project would keep him busy for the rest of his productive life." Du Bois had generally found Frank Keppel to be sympathetic. The Carnegie Corporation president had unsuccessfully prodded his trustees to bail out *The Crisis*, twice subventioned publication costs of Du Bois's Reconstruction monograph, and had signaled a noncommittal interest in the "Encyclopedia of the Negro." The problem for Du Bois was not Keppel but the corporation's trustees. Stung by the board's unprecedented rejection of his *Crisis* recommendation, the Carnegie president revealed to one of Du Bois's sponsors that "no fewer than three of the men on the committee had run afoul of him one time or another, and while their adverse vote was quite sincere," Keppel suspected that their vote had "inevitably [been] infuenced by that fact." Yet, as Du Bois knew, Keppel had a reputation for being more receptive to innovation and productive controversy than most of his peers and had been enormously pleased by the considerable academic stir created by *Black Reconstruction*. Corporation trustee Henry James (nephew of Henry James) was wont to remark with qualified admiration, "Keppel loved to try something new." As it was possible to construe the GEB's action as a decision to defer rather than as an outright rejection, there remained the longest of shots that the Carnegie might act favorably on the Stokes–Du Bois request for an appropriation of 60 percent of the $260,000 budget. That he would never receive such an appropriation was to be communicated to Du Bois in a manner that was both indirect and guilt-ridden.

His visitors arrived on campus on the third or fourth day in November 1938 with little advance notice. Putting aside final revisions of *Black Folk: Then and Now*, Du Bois conversed for a half hour or so with Raymond Fosdick, David Stevens, and Jackson Davis. Offering regional business as the ostensible reason for their visit, the real reason was soon evident after some minutes of general discussion of the encyclopedia project. Two young Swedish academics had just arrived in the United States to conduct studies of the Negro under the auspices of the Carnegie Corporation. Their names, Karl Gunnar Myrdal and Richard Sterner, were unfamiliar to Du Bois, but he politely agreed to discuss the encyclopedia project with them when, as Davis informed him, they would come to Atlanta toward the end of the month. Myrdal, a forty-year-old economics professor with a major reputation in Europe, had been Keppel's final choice to conduct the broad-gauge study of the Negro recommended by Newton Baker in the fall of 1935. The astonished University of Stockholm professor and Social Democratic Labor member of the Swedish Parliament had received Keppel's invitation in August 1937. Myrdal and Alva Reimers, his sparkling, university-educated wife, had spent the academic year 1929–30 in the United States on a study grant from the Laura Spelman Rockefeller Memorial Foundation, arriving just as the stock market imploded. The Myrdals had developed decided views about the American economy, but knew almost nothing about Negroes and the race problem. Seven years later, they were being asked by the Carnegie Corporation to return so that Gunnar Myrdal could undertake "a comprehensive study of the Negro in the United States."

The key to the decision to seek a foreign scholar was contained in Keppel's injunction to Myrdal that the Carnegie study must be conducted "in a wholly objective and dispassionate way." The foundation president had become convinced that a congeries of special factors—prejudice, professional jealousies, regional sensitivities—put objectivity beyond the reach of homegrown social science when dealing with the national race problem, notwithstanding what Herskovits and Donald Young had to say to the contrary. In his quest for an ideal European, Keppel had considered and then eliminated two Swiss scholars (an anthropologist and a political scientist), a retired Dutch colonial administrator, a British economist, a South African, the governor of Nigeria, a former headmaster of Rugby, and Bronislaw Malinowski, before deciding that the Swedish economist possessed the mettle to be the Lord Bryce of the American Negro problem. Signaling his acceptance of Keppel's offer, but only after being persuaded by a Rockefeller Foundation friend to withdraw an initial declination, Myrdal concluded, with his wife's concurrence, that the Carnegie option might be the last exciting project before the onset of middle age. "Why not the Negro as well as anything else?" he would recall rather breezily years later. The deal was sealed in the spring of 1938 with a handshake over cocktails at New York's Century Club, where Myrdal was entertained by Keppel and the Carnegie trustees after delivering Harvard's Godkin Lectures and receiving an honorary degree.

Once again, Du Bois put his best face on hard disappointment. He was scrupulously gracious in late November 1938 when Myrdal and Sterner, on a preliminary tour of the South chaperoned by Jackson Davis, paid a courtesy call. Relating in a general way the objectives of his own project and naming experts who could accelerate the two Swedes' learning curve, Du Bois seems to have been impressed in equal parts by Myrdal's energetic brilliance and his unprejudiced ignorance of the Negro. Sharing his mixed estimate with Frazier, he wondered if the ebullient economist hadn't bitten off too large a plug in proposing to study virtually every aspect of the relations between white and black Americans within a two-year time span. It was a rare instance when he and Walter White, who expressed similar skepticism to the publisher of *The Defender* at this time, saw eye to eye. Du Bois's uncustomary delay of three months before sending a critique of Myrdal's January 1939 research agenda may have been due to the newest manuscript deadline, revisions for the *Dusk of Dawn* autobiography. In any case, three pages of concise observations on twenty-three areas identified for investigation showed Du Bois to be favorably impressed (although he urged that the item dealing with Negro population groups be expanded from two to four categories). They arrived just in time for the five days of brainstorming convened by Myrdal and seven key collaborators at Asbury Park, New Jersey, in late April. Above all, Du Bois's critique expressed relief at finding that the research agenda's overarching conception was, as he wrote Myrdal, that "the Negro is an integral part of American civilization and not simply one of America's problems or something extraneous to the main American scene." After reading the confidential, ten-page research agenda developed at Asbury Park, Du Bois offered congratulations on the wonderful assistance committed to the project but stated that he had "no suggestions" to add.

With what seemed a bottomless subvention that would eventually run to 300,000 Carnegie Corporation dollars, Myrdal commanded an empire employing the top tier of American academics in black and white. One by one, the cadre of colored scholars Du Bois had hoped to recruit signed on with what became formally designated as the Carnegie-Myrdal Study: the Young Turks at Howard, Brown, Bunche, Frazier, and Harris; the newest Talented Tenth stars, Allison Davis, Kenneth Clark, St. Clair Drake, G. James Fleming, James Jackson, and Doxey Wilkerson. Wilkerson, tall, imposing, and already regarded as one of the most capable scholars of his generation, would vie with Bunche for the position of most valued staffer until he became one of the project's severest critics after a somewhat mysterious personal dispute with Myrdal. Charles Johnson and T. Arnold Hill, pivotal figures in any race-related undertaking, accepted Myrdal's invitation. Johnson not only had helped formulate the Asbury Park plan, his 1942 *Patterns of Negro Segregation* would be the second of four books spun off by Carnegie-Myrdal, part of which would be reproduced in chapter twenty-nine of *An American Dilemma*. There were at least two white omissions almost as conspicuous as the absence of Du Bois, Locke, and Woodson—the University of North Carolina's Howard Odum and University of Iowa's Edward B. Reuter—but few other leading white sociologists were absent from the Carnegie-Myrdal roster of scholars, which listed Herskovits, Otto Klineberg, Ashley Montagu, Arthur Raper, Arnold Rose, Louis Wirth, Edward Shils, T. J. Woofter, and the encyclopedia's associate editor, Guy Johnson, who nevertheless continued a low-key collaboration with Du Bois.

Du Bois was not yet ready to abandon the encyclopedia; that painful decision would finally come in 1941 with a formal statement that the project was no longer feasible in light of the Carnegie-Myrdal enterprise. Well before then, however—indeed, by the close of 1939—he realized that the inevitable could be only a matter of a year or so. The men who ran the major foundations and guided the national learned societies would never commit their biases to paper, he wrote in 1940, "but after all it would seem to them natural that any such work should be under the domination of white men." And so it had seemed even to two of the most liberal figures in the firmament of learning and philanthropy, Robert Maynard Hutchins, the University of Chicago's innovative president, and Edwin Embree, director of the Rosenwald Fund. "Dear Eddie," Hutchins wrote Embree shortly after the official launching of the Carnegie-Myrdal Study, "[a source] tells me that Keppel has rented the forty-sixth floor of the Chrysler Building and turned it over to a Swede named Gunnar Myrdal to make an elaborate study of Negro education. What is it all about?" Well not exactly, "dear Bob," clarified Embree. "Not Negro education but the whole realm of the Negro in American civilization. . . . My understanding is that they propose to bring out a series of volumes which represent in effect a kind of Encyclopedia of the American Negro and may therefore take the place of the proposed Negro Encyclopedia in which the Phelps-Stokes Fund has been greatly interested. Myrdal is a keen chap," added Embree. "I think he will do a good job." Although mistaken in assuming that Myrdal intended to produce an encyclopedia (a concept he had explicitly rejected at the outset), the Rosenwald director was correct in surmising that Myrdal's project was intended as an answer to two dilemmas: first, to the public relations dilemma caused by Du Bois's refusal to take no for an answer from the foundations; and second, to the satisfactory management of the so-called American dilemma by financing and legitimating a new master theorem of race relations that was interpretively progressive but not socially destabilizing.

Although Keppel had at first suggested that Du Bois be invited to write one of the Carnegie-Myrdal monographs, Myrdal would choose not to do so. Instead, Du Bois's name would be respectfully invoked at critical places in the massive, two-volume investigation whose interpretive impact over some two decades rivaled Tocqueville's Democracy in America. When Anson Phelps Stokes sent the cheery comment, upon the appearance in 1944 of An American Dilemma, that no one "has been quite so often quoted by Myrdal than yourself," Du Bois would decide, partly for strategic reasons, to appear fully reconciled to the Myrdalian interpretation of relations between the races in the United States. Because it gave no quarter to the antidemocratic rationales of the white South, because its "rank order of discrimination" deconstructed and rejected as mostly pathological the miscegenist fears of Caucasians, because it put class back into the analysis of race and poverty within the context of unrelieved discrimination, and because it renounced the fetish of social-science objectivity as a cloak for tolerating and evading societal wrongs, An American Dilemma would genuinely

move Du Bois on first reading. "Never before in American history," he rhapsodized in his review of the book, "has a scholar so completely covered this
field. The work is monumental." In Myrdal's eloquent formulation, racism was
an imperfection in the social order, an incompatible substance the body politic
fights to reject and expel, a moral insult to the nation's founding ideals and thus
a paradox that becomes ever more intolerable to the "American Creed." Myrdal's "Introduction" posited the book's splendid premise in a paragraph of surpassing and unforgettable grandeur:

> The American Negro problem is a problem in the heart of the American.
> It is there that the interracial tension has its focus. It is there that the
> decisive struggle goes on. This is the central viewpoint of this treatise.
> Though our study includes economics, social, and political race relations,
> at bottom our problem is the moral dilemma of the American—the con-
> flict between his moral valuations on various levels of consciousness and
> generality. The "American Dilemma," referred to in the title of this book,
> is the ever-raging conflict between, on the one hand, the valuations pre-
> served on the general plane which we call the "American Creed," where
> the American thinks, talks, and acts under the influence of high national
> and Christian precepts and, on the other hand, the valuations on specific
> planes of individual and group living, where personal and local interests;
> economic, social, and sexual jealousies . . . dominate his outlook.

Impressed as he rightly was by the Myrdalian moral-democratic profession,
it is surely more than a safe conjecture that Du Bois meditated privately on the
full implications of the subtitle to volume one, *An American Dilemma: The
Negro in a White Nation.* For in Myrdal's gendered and raced prose, the Negro
was deprived of agency and rendered a problem that the white man was challenged to solve in *his* country for the sake of *his* shining values, lest the pathologies of oppressed, degraded, though still salvageable people of color pollute
the wellspring of civic virtue. A creed anchored by Judeo-Christian principles
and inspired by the Enlightenment in which the study of racial disabilities was
reduced to pathologies could hardly have satisfied Du Bois. Myrdal announced
that the "economic situation of the Negroes in America [was] pathological,"
whereas Du Bois thought it was economic. As its main economic hypothesis,
An American Dilemma posited a "vicious circle" in which economics, moral
and educational culture, and racial discrimination operated in an interactive
dynamic of equal causation—"no single factor, therefore, is a 'final cause' in a
theoretical sense," Myrdal contended. But to a Du Bois now self-instructed in
Marxism, the book's circular causation would have amounted to the negation
of the primacy of economic factors—to no cause at all. He had envisaged the

"Encyclopedia of the Negro," after all, as a documented record of historic possibilities, triumphs, failures, and deprivations under the regime of white supremacy. If he never publicly questioned the Myrdalian concept of moral tension and its muting of economics, there is ample evidence that, privately, he concurred with the sharp criticisms of *An American Dilemma* made by Marxist scholars such as Herbert Aptheker, Oliver Cox, and Doxey Wilkerson, who largely dismissed Myrdal's *American Creed* as the opiate of the white liberals. Although in his review of the book he confined himself to the neutral observation that Myrdal "rejects the Marxian dogma of economic effort as ever dominant motive," Du Bois could certainly never have been entirely comfortable with a race relations paradigm in which psychology trumped economics, even though he recognized the indisputably positive implications of Gunnar Myrdal's achievement.

ATLANTA

SOLDIERING ON

S tride almost unbroken, Du Bois pressed ahead with other scholarly pursuits even as he faced the reality that the "Encyclopedia of the Negro" project had been all but aborted. Time and again New England stoicism buffered him from deception and disappointment, but there was also the therapy afforded by the next in a never-depleted supply of engrossing projects. *Black Folk: Then and Now, An Essay in the History and Sociology of the Negro Race* appeared in summer of 1939, although last-minute complications involving production costs and libel concerns on the part of the Holt lawyers had threatened to delay the book's release. As he had done with *Black Reconstruction*, Du Bois continued to send his publisher sizable revisions of what should have been final chapter drafts, making changes on galley proofs as late as the last week in February. He incorporated material from the comprehensive *An African Survey*, Lord Hailey's source book for Britain's imperial policy makers and district commissioners, published just as the last pages of *Black Folk: Then and Now* were being written in the winter of 1938. The almost simultaneous appearance of Herskovits's two-volume *Dahomey: An Ancient West African Kingdom*, a marvel of cultural anthropology, set Du Bois to more revisions. He sent eleventh-hour textual alterations to Holt after receiving "illuminating comments" on one of his chapters from Herskovits. A month before the book's scheduled release, the publisher's law firm, apparently disregarding the legal maxim governing reputations of the deceased, opined that Du Bois had libeled Alexander Hamilton and Robert Browning by suggesting that they had Negro ancestry. The law firm was equally concerned that allegations about the role of the Firestone Company in Liberia could result in litigation. In a typical response that settled the issue, Du Bois informed Henry Holt and Company that people were no less human if they were less white, and, in the same breath, dismissed the lawyers's concerns as insufficient to justify "chang[ing] a word."

An ambitious work of synthesis and reinterpretation, accessibly, though not simply, written, Du Bois intended his book to be the popular complement to the stymied "Encyclopedia of the Negro." A sort of world history of black people from the dawn of settled life to the present, the book had forerunners in the scholarship of Diedrich Westerman, Leo Frobenius, Charles G. Seligman, and several other Europeans. Ralph Linton's new book, *The Study of Man*, provided an American antecedent. Yet nothing quite like *Black Folk: Then and Now* had been done before for a broadly educated American readership. If asked to ponder the African past, the great majority of European-Americans would have expressed the view of Hegel in *The Philosophy of History*; some few would even have been able to recall the German philospher's exact words about Africa: "For it is no historical part of the World; it has no movement or development to exhibit." In late-1930s America, the proposition that Africans had been serious contenders in the making of history was scarcely credible. To that end, then, Du Bois committed his genius and vast store of knowledge to contribute an unprecedented "scientific study of mankind in Africa without economic axes to grind, without the necessity of proving race superiority, without religious conversion or compulsion." The universality of the human experience was intended to be the essence of the book, and the human spirit that expanded in Africa Du Bois featured as "the same humanity that all the world knows." Du Bois's narrative introduced readers to iron-smelting in Africa at a time when Europeans made do with stone implements. As the story circled the great lakes of the continent and swept across its grasslands, surprised readers encountered the vast stone enclosure of Great Zimbabwe and the Shona kingdom of Mwanamutapa in the east, then the Mandinka empires of Ghana, Mali, and Songhai in the west, all of them rising before or during the formation of European nation-states. The vaguely familiar in Africa reappeared as "Mulatto" Egypt and Semitic Ethiopia, followed by the unfamiliar and fabulous: Benin and Dahomey; the kingdom of the Kongo; the explosion into southern Africa of the Zulus. With the origin and enveloping devastation of the Atlantic Slave Trade, Du Bois's narrative reached more familiar and profoundly controversial terrain.

On page one, *Black Folk: Then and Now* explicitly denied the biological importance of race. "No scientific definition of race is possible." "Especially is it difficult to say how far race is determined by a group of inherited characteristics and how far by environment and amalgamation," Du Bois stipulated. A scientifically inappropriate construct, the most that could be asserted of race was that "so far as these differences are measurable they fade into one another so insensibly" that only broad, "main divisions" remained. The paradox of *Black Folk*, as Herskovits had immediately perceived in his letter, was that, in its commendable aim of disproving theories of superiority based on race through the panoramic recovery of the cultural and institutional achievements of African

peoples on four continents, the book reintroduced its own model of racial essentialism through the back door. By page three (notwithstanding the specific
caution in Herskovits's letter), references to "ancient Negro blood on the shores
of the Mediterranean" and to Negro blood "as the basis of the blood of all men"
appeared. In agreeing with Du Bois that homo sapiens had most likely origi-
nated in Africa, Herskovits seriously questioned whether the earliest species had
been physically differentiated into categories of Negroid, Mongoloid, and Cau-
casoid. For Du Bois, however, the Negro had to be the original human, the ur-
ancestor from whom descended all others. Inflected by thought patterns dating
back to "The Conservation of Races," parts of *Black Folk* could be likened to
Gobineau's *Inequality of the Human Races* read backward—an anti-Gobineau
applauding the increasing mixture of races and promoting the Negro admixture
as essential. "In all these centers," Du Bois limned, "the Negro race throve,
inspiring and sharing the civilization of Egypt and developing the culture of
Ethiopia." Yet there was a further paradox in that Du Bois intended the book's
racial essentialism to function in the service of racial pluralism, for in validating
an unknown and remarkable Negro past he envisaged a future in which all
races could accept the cultural parity of one another's histories as well as the
interdependence of their destinies.

This was the hope of "The Future of World Democracy," Du Bois's concluding chapter decrying the spiritual cul-de-sac into which the world's poor
and dark-skinned have been herded. "Not only the vast majority of white folk,
but Chinese, Indians and Negroes themselves have been so excited, oppressed,
and suppressed by current white civilization that they think and judge everything
by its terms." The book compensated its rather mild racial essentialism by it-
erating the oneness of humanity and the perniciousness of all doctrines of racial
supremacy—a message never more salient than in a time of spreading fascist
ideologies, Edwin Embree was to remind *Survey Graphic* readers. A similar
balancing of Victorian minuses and Marxist pluses was evident in such Du
Boisian aspersions as that Jamaica's development had been retarded by "lazy
Negro labor," on the one hand, yet, on the other, by the book's superb exposition
of European hegemony in South Africa or of the organic relationship of democracy to racism. Radical reformers learned that they had to take the priggish
solecisms with the socioecomic wisdom in a Du Bois monograph, as when they
read this judgment toward the close of *Black Folk*: "The dream of the new
America came not to be the uplift of labor, but the transmutation of poor white
laborers into rich employers, with the inevitable residue of the poor white and
black eternally at the bottom. In time men became used to the idea that this
submerged mass should form not a tenth, but nine-tenths of all men."

As cutting-edge social science, *Black Folk* was somewhat deficient in its use
of obsolete and misleading terminology, sweeping generalizations, its strains of

racialized romanticism applied to the ancient world and proletarian fantasy imposed on the modern, and in its glaringly superficial treatment of Latin America. Moreover, aside from specialists who found this or that portion of *Black Folk* unsatisfactory, the number of scholars in the United States who possessed Du Bois's continental breadth of knowledge (to say nothing of the educated reading public) could have been contained in a small room. However merited the respectful reviews garnered by the book in *The Nation, The Herald Tribune, The Christian Science Monitor,* and *The New York Times,* one senses that the reviewers were out of their depth and well disposed, as the *Times* critic wrote, to describe it as "one of the most complete essays in the history and sociology of the Negro which has been written in the English language." It would remain for a much later generation of scholars to appreciate *Black Folk: Then and Now* as the point of departure for a line of historical and social-science literature to be variously described as Afrocentric, diasporic, or Black Atlantic. Nearly sixty years before academe was convulsed by Martin Bernal's *Black Athena: The Afroasiatic Roots of Classical Civilization,* Du Bois contended that northern European scholars had gradually foisted upon the historical interaction of Greece and Africa a racist paradigm elevating Aryan culture as the source of ancient civilization. "All history, all science was changed to fit this new condition," he wrote. "Wherever there was history in Africa or civilization, it was of white origins; and the fact that it was civilization proved that it was white."

Asked to review the book for *The New Republic,* Herskovits understandably emphasized the failure of Du Bois to make better use of the latest sources and underscored what he saw as romantic overstatements about the Negro influence upon Egyptian civilization. The second half, dealing with slavery, emancipation, and the modern era, he professed to like much better. Herskovits's critical asperity was more than matched by Carter Woodson, whose *Journal of Negro History* review quipped that there was more *Then* than *Now* to the volume and complained of its rather stale Africa sources. *The Crisis* under Wilkins ignored the book, but the Urban League invited Logan, now professor of history at Howard, to review *Black Folk* for *Opportunity*. Rather unsurprisingly, Logan offered a justification that could have been written by the author: "It should especially be on the study table of all those statesmen who blatantly prate of democracy while forgetting or ignoring the fate of the millions whom those democracies exploit almost as much as the totalitarian States oppress those who dare disagree with their Omnipotent Folly." Reviewing his first Du Bois book in *New Masses,* a young historian named Herbert Aptheker reached a similar, if somewhat more critical, conclusion.

The six-year-old grandchild to whom *Black Folk: Then and Now* was dedicated gave Will and Nina good reason to try living together again. Du Bois Williams—"Baby Du Bois"—had been reared in New York almost exclusively by Nina, every experiment in maternal upbringing having skirted disaster. Although liberated from an abusive marriage and advantaged by a secure teaching position in Baltimore, Yolande, much overweight and prone to transient maladies, remained the despair of her parents and of little consequence in the life of her bubbly daughter. This situation had proved so unsatisfactory by spring of 1937 that Nina reluctantly agreed that she and Baby Du Bois should move to Baltimore. Living conditions in Harlem continued to deteriorate, moreover, and the once-desirable Dunbar had lost many of its Talented Tenth residents; besides, it made more sense to apply the Dunbar rent to a suitable Baltimore homestead. But several trial visits had been more than sufficient to convince Nina that the Baltimore option would be disastrous. Not only had Yolande displayed scant willingness to "try to help us," she complained to Will, but their daughter's lifestyle was simply appalling. She "really felt quite alarmed," Nina reported in gasps, after she *really saw* the situation [Yolande] has allowed herself to drift into there," what with a male lover ten years her junior and much else that was deplorable.

Nina hated the prospect of any move south only somewhat less than Will hoped to avoid the necessity of a prolonged reunion. Necessity became reality soon after the seventieth-birthday celebration, however. The family's short visit to the city had unintentionally served as a successful dress rehearsal for an extended stay by Nina. Despite Nina's almost visceral aversion to Atlanta and Will's decided preference for the convenience of solitary living space, both concluded that their granddaughter's welfare required them to make sacrifices. It was finally decided that she and child would join Du Bois in Atlanta in September 1938. The university accommodated his request for family quarters in the men's wing of the graduate dormitory, a suite for Will and Nina and a separate room for the granddaughter. Baby Du Bois's arrival was the occasion of mild commotion in the AU dormitory during the first week or so when the spunky child would appear unannounced and unaccompanied in the rooms of astonished male students. The youngster's ebullience was and continued to be a constant delight to her grandfather, who divined in her all the brilliance that had skipped one Du Bois generation. As she bore his name, the dedication of *Black Folk* announced, so she must become his flesh-and-blood link to the future. Her bright eyes must "one day see some of the things I dream." In so far as intelligence is destiny, Baby Du Bois was a superb apprentice for the role her grandfather envisaged. She had been a prize student at the Modern School, the prestigious Harlem academy run by Mildred Johnson, austere educator and wife of noted musician Rosamond Johnson. Her score on the Stanford-Binet at age five was a dazzling 144.

Du Bois encouraged his granddaughter at word games, challenged her to debate at the dinner table, checked her homework and gave her books to read, and even brought her along to his lectures. "He was very smart about me, and I was smart about him" was how Du Bois Williams would sum up the relationship. But "Granma made the whole thing work," she also perceived. "Mama was the child, which I wasn't." Granddaughter knew how to please grandfather. Often, when the grown men and women in his classes stumbled over answers, it was Baby Du Bois who supplied them. "He would just say one word which would trigger a whole slew of stuff that I would just sit there and spew out," she could recall long afterward as though it were yesterday. Hers was a precocity that could wreak havoc, and often did, among her classmates at Oglethorpe, AU's laboratory elementary school, where she was daily deposited by Nina or, in inclement weather, from Diggs's Chevrolet coupe. Unimpressed by Oglethorpe's homework requirements, the grandparents arranged for assignments to be mailed from the Modern School along with almost nightly telephone conferences with Mildred Johnson. Baby Du Bois soon came to feel that classes at the laboratory school were a waste of time. Increasingly impatient and fidgety, she was the despair of her earnest teachers, and she recalled that she "simply disrupted the entire school." "I would call out. I would get bored."

Meanwhile, the Atlanta community reached out to Nina. The Twelve and the Chautauqua Circle, the city's most exclusive Negro women's clubs, renewed her membership. She and Will attended lectures and concerts together at the university center's various colleges. Atlanta's rigid segregation ordinances, however, remained as exclusionary as they had been when Nina and Will lived there during the first decade of the century. Whatever the chances the move south might have offered for a semblance of prolonged togetherness, they collapsed by the end of the school year largely because of concerns for Baby Du Bois. If Harlem had become physically dangerous, Atlanta was intellectually and culturally stultifying. Baby Du Bois loathed the place. "The experiment of educating Du Bois [Williams] in Oglethorpe has not been successful," Du Bois notified Clement in early August 1939. The family would remain in New York, where the granddaughter would board by special arrangement at the Modern School. A few weeks later, Du Bois wrote Shivery that Nina would live in the Harlem YWCA until the house he had decided to have built in Baltimore was ready for occupancy.

Nina and Baby Du Bois flowed into the river of his busy life, only to be deposited yet again on the most convenient shore. Du Bois rowed on through eddies of controversy and into and out of ambitious new projects with steady vigor. To close friends, he sometimes spoke of having to husband his strength, and he detected a slight loss of hearing. Infrequently, like the night he slumbered impervious in his armchair as two female faculty members knocked on his apartment door, his age embarrassed him. The next day's note reeked of chagrin. "The champagne had been iced, the squab browned in the oven," but he had awakened only in time to see from his window the young ladies' car leaving. Dashing after them in his dressing gown to Spelman, Du Bois explained that he had been met and turned away from the gate by the campus watchman. Such social pratfalls were far from typical, nonetheless. Much more typical was the courtly stamina on display when Rachel Davis DuBois finally visited him in Atlanta after Nina and Baby Du Bois had gone back to New York. Three years had elapsed since their time together in New York during the 1935 Christmas holidays. Six months later, on her way to New Orleans and Mexico, she had written that a planned stopover in Atlanta was no longer possible and included news that her book, *The Jews in American Life*, was about to appear and another on the Germans was soon to follow.

In addition to the depth of their affective bonds, Du Bois's mentoring role had become increasingly vital to Davis DuBois's professional career after the establishment in 1934 of her Service Bureau for Intercultural Education (SBIE). The Service Bureau provided instructional models for secondary and collegiate courses and served as a clearinghouse for educational propaganda designed to nurture cultural pluralism. That the American melting pot was not only more myth than reality, but that spellbinding bigots such as the radio priest, Father Coughlin, enjoined his 30 million CBS listeners to exclude Jews from the pot, made Davis DuBois's message of ethnic pluralism both controversial and timely. Rebuffed by NBC, where the network's patrician educational counselor and former Yale president, Norman Angell, said that he was ill disposed to "stir up the menagerie just at the moment," Davis DuBois's organization had been able to convince CBS to underwrite *Americans All*, a radio series dramatizing the nation's ethnic groups, which ran for twenty-six weeks during the latter half of 1938. As CBS had contributed significantly to Father Coughlin's alarming popularity, its executives had good reason to recast the network's cultural emphasis in collaboration with the U.S. Office of Education. Fittingly, that November, Paul Robeson would sing "Ballad for Americans" live for the first time on CBS. The song was an expression of melting-pot patriotism that achieved fabulous overnight popularity even as the Negro press reported the sad mockery of its egalitarian lyrics ("Man in white skin can never be free/while his black brother is in slavery") when a Manhattan hotel restaurant refused to serve Robeson lunch immediately after he left the broadcasting studio.

The enormous power of radio for good and evil had impressed Du Bois deeply ever since his tour of the Third Reich. Although the CBS executives had rejected the original title, "Immigrants All—Americans All," as too blunt and instructed scriptwriter Gilbert Seldes to minimize all risk of controversy, Du Bois and Locke, whom Davis DuBois had also asked to serve as an unpaid adviser, were united in their excitement about the unique opportunity to counter popular stereotypes and to evoke the little-known history and achievements of the race. They lobbied for much less Booker Washington and much more Frederick Douglass, as well as the foregrounding of professional achievements by contemporary Negro men and women. As a matter of policy, Seldes had strongly resisted changes to any of his ethnic scripts. Jewish himself, he had received the unsolicited input of *The New York Times's* Sulzbergers and other prominent Jews who strongly advised against a program devoted exclusively to Jewish Americans as potentially inflammatory. In the end, CBS's "Jews in the United States" depicted a religious group composed of various nationalities (persecuted elsewhere but received in America without discrimination) whose myriad contributions to the nation dated from the founding of the republic. Seldes found the NAACP's objections to the revised Negro script only a little less welcome than Mrs. Arthur Hays Sulzberger's. Roy Wilkins deplored too much attention given to slavery and too little to middle-class accomplishments, even though a good portion of Du Bois's suggestions and much of Locke's revisions had been incorporated. The final script for "The Negro" as broadcast by CBS on Sunday, December 18, 1938, omitted, bowdlerized, and backtracked. The CBS orchestra abandoned the African music score in rehearsal. Instead, Jules Bledsoe (a last-minute addition on the curious recommendation of Walter White) bellowed out "Black Boy" in nine interminable minutes of what Locke called a "mammy interpolation." Contemporary achievements of the race were sacrificed to running time. When the much-improved recorded version was released with Bledsoe deleted and the contemporary achievements restored, Du Bois encouraged Davis DuBois with the observation that it wasn't so much "what you actually get in as what you keep out." In that respect, he thought they had been "fairly successful."

In the spring of 1938, one of his Kokusai Bunka Shinkokai aquaintances, a Professor K. Miyake of Tokyo Imperial University, visited Atlanta on a North American speaking circuit arranged by Hikida. Du Bois had continued to play what role he could in fostering the propaganda of imperial Japan as that country's war machine wreaked a swath of devastation across China. Grateful for the opportunity to present "facts" and "truth" to the faculty and students of the Atlanta University Center about Sino-Japanese relations, Miyake wrote Du Bois soon afterward of finding widespread misinformation among the university populations at Charlottesville, Chapel Hill, and elsewhere throughout the South. To a dismayed white supporter of the NAACP's federal antilynching campaign who begged explanation of an editorial in *China Weekly Review* naming him as a paid agent of Japanese propaganda, Du Bois responded with withering candor. It was not that he sympathized with China less, he snapped, but that he hated "white European and American propaganda, theft and insult more." Because "even colored people here do not understand the deeper message of the Japanese struggle." Du Bois used "As the Crow Flies," his new column in the *Amsterdam News,* to tell his side of the story. As the mainstream American press carried horrific news and censorious editorials about Japan's New Order for East Asia and the threat to Hong Kong, Du Bois summoned readers to understand the racial stakes involved in the global game plan as the world tensed for war. Twenty-five years before, he had offered "The African Roots of the War" in profound meditation on the imperialist and racist origins of what was then called the Great War. That prescient *Atlantic Monthly* essay could well have been reissued under the amended title, "The African and Asian Roots of the Second War."

When his fourth *Amsterdam News* column appeared on November 18, 1939, Poland had been occupied by the German army more than eight weeks and warfare had a new term—Blitzkrieg. Less than three months earlier, the geopolitical order of Western Europe and the ideological faith of tens of thousands of Europeans and Americans had been shattered in the diplomatic earthquake of the Nazi-Soviet Nonaggression Pact. Du Bois all but enjoined the Negroes of America to adopt a plague-on-all-houses attitude. Notwithstanding his loathing of Hitler's regime and increasing disenchantment with Stalin's excesses, he was undeceived by what he divined as the real significance of Munich—the plot of western capitalists to redirect Nazi Germany eastward into a good-riddance war between fascism and communism. As the Battle of the Atlantic raged during the winter of 1939–40, Du Bois explained what was at stake to his people. Because he was an expositor of the history of the future—because he was Du Bois—he stated the case for U.S. abstention from the war in accents that brooked no compromise.

Yet there were considerable numbers of noted Americans who were neither dogmatic pacifists nor parochial isolationists of the America First Committee stripe who shared his intellectual opposition. Charles Beard placed his enormous prestige as the nation's greatest historian in the service of nonintervention and increasingly harsh denunciation of Franklin Roosevelt. John L. Lewis could have been reading from the *Amsterdam News* when he delivered his annual Labor Day radio address. "Labor in America wants no war nor any part of war," the CIO president's familiar basso profundo boomed into the microphone. "Labor in America wants the right to work and live—not the privilege of dying by gunshot or poison gas to sustain the mental errors of current statesmen." Serving up the realpolitik of capitalism and racial supremacy in similarly acid doses, Du Bois scorned the counterfeit political morality of the democracies as they inveighed against the Soviet invasion of Poland and Finland. What of the singular restraint of Europe and the United States when Italy invaded Ethiopia in a cloud of poison gas, he asked. Suppose it were Liberia being swallowed up by unprovoked attack instead of Finland, "can you see Hoover trumpeting and bellowing for aid and defense?" Having outmaneuvered the trap set at Munich, the Russians were merely reincorporating territory lost to Finland, Latvia, Estonia, and Lithuania after World War I, lands "designed as jumping off places for Western Europe," according to Du Bois, "when they got ready to smash the Bolsheviki.

> The world is astonished, aghast and angry! But why? France seized her stolen Alsace Lorraine after the World War. England has been seizing land all over the earth for centuries with and without a shadow of rightful claim: India, South Africa, Uganda, Egypt, Nigeria, not to mention Ireland. The United States seized Mexico from a weak and helpless nation in order to bolster slavery; and incidentally, when Italy took Abyssinia she was enabled to do it by means of the oil and supplies which America furnished. . . . This is the sort of world that has grown suddenly righteous in defense of Finland.

On February 24, 1940, the day after his seventy-second birthday, Du Bois apologized for Russia and Japan again in the Harlem newspaper. He still believed in Russia, still believed that Russia "more than any other country in the world is making a frontal attack on the problem of poverty." He had never expected the Russian people to be perfect. They needed more Radeks and fewer Stalins, and they would stumble and retreat many times on the road to socialism. As for Japan in China, he held no brief for war, but he would never permit himself to be misled by the capitalists and missionaries who wanted to keep Asia as the backyard of European commerce and civilization.

Du Bois had achieved an eminence and authority possessed by no other public figure in Negro America on the eve of America's entry into World War II, a stature rivaled, perhaps, by Randolph, Bethune, White, and Bunche in the course of the decade, yet never to be quite surpassed in uniqueness. Since the publication of *The Souls of Black Folk* at the beginning of the twentieth century, a third generation numbering several hundred thousand young people was coming of age in households where Du Bois was admired and sometimes even venerated. The habit of gauging one's thoughts by what Du Bois thought, and the psychic safety-valve effect of doing so, was now deeply engrained — even if the vast majority of black women and men was economically, institutionally, or regionally constrained from giving public voice to many Du Boisian sentiments. At *The Crisis*, he had presumed to speak *as* the NAACP, not *for* it. At Atlanta University, now more than ever, he felt himself unbound by institutional affiliation. Taking the measure of world events with a racial rule made for lively political reading in the *Amsterdam News*, along with a good deal of problematic prophecy. He simultaneously lauded and lectured Marian Anderson in the spring of 1940, after she sang before an interracial audience, separately but equally accommodated, in the Atlanta Municipal Auditorium. Her reception by Atlanta whites "was extraordinary," and "few, if any singers, give me so great satisfaction," he enthused of the matchless contralto whose historic concert at the Lincoln Memorial the previous year had brought a crowd of 75,000 to protest the singer's exclusion from Constitution Hall by the Daughters of the American Revolution. Nevertheless, as an authority on the "Negro sorrow songs," Du Bois felt compelled to deplore Anderson's humorous rendition of one particular spiritual, "There's No Hiding Place." "That song is not funny and it is not meant to be funny and Miss Anderson should not caricature it," he remonstrated.

His political commentary was typically wide-ranging. When Harlem's Ben Davis, whose first fifteen minutes of fame had come in defending the black labor organizer Angelo Herndon, appeared before the U.S. Senate Judiciary Committee in mid-March to urge passage of the Gavagan-Wagner antilynching bill, his testimony baited the southern members into an explosion of vituperation, calls for ejection, and the expunging of a portion of the committee record. In body language reflecting his affluent Atlanta upbringing and verbal repartee with Senators Tom Connally and Warren Austin, the young Harvard-trained lawyer and soon-to-be New York City councilman from Harlem exploded upon the scene as the incarnation of the newest New Negro radical—an Ivy League Bolshevik. Du Bois's response to Davis's performance in Washington was double-barreled. "Amazed and angry," he deplored much of the Negro press for its characterization of Davis's conduct as provocative and impolitic. Davis ought be "applauded for his heroism," in skewering Vice-President John Garner as an "evil old labor-baiter" and denouncing the "Democratic reactionaries and Republican hypocrites," he rapped. Davis's unquestioned right to believe in communism, however, did not mean that Davis's brief for racial advancement was right. Marxism as a theory and communism as a Russian reality had much to commend them, but Du Bois still saw no viable prospect for solving the race problem through interracial class solidarity in the United States.

For all its inequities and deficiencies, then, Du Bois placed more hope for civil rights, economic democracy, and peace in a Roosevelt presidency. Roosevelt's WPA had literally kept a million black people from starving to death, Du Bois calculated. "It is not the part of wisdom to sneer at the hand that feeds you," he upbraided middle-class Negroes who were wont to jibe at the NRA as "Negroes Removed Again" and deride the slender benefits to blacks of the alphabet agencies. Indiana's Wilkie, for all his civil rights blandishments, was still a corporate lawyer and utilities executive who had spent his career making electricity expensive and inaccessible to the poor, Du Bois charged. "The greatest issue in this campaign," readers were reminded, "is the discrimination among men, between the classes of rich and poor, between races and groups," and a servant of finance capital was not to be entrusted with the reconstruction of the national economy. Moreover, wary as he remained of FDR on race, Du Bois genuinely admired the other Roosevelt who had resigned from the DAR and, with Walter White's engineering and Ickes's help, made the uplifting Marian Anderson concert at the Lincoln Memorial possible. He counted on Eleanor Roosevelt to press the cause of civil rights in the administration and celebrated her refusal "to be head housekeeper of the White House and pour tea. She insists on thinking in public. She consorts with Negroes and Communists and says so." Finally, as the 1940 presidential campaign climaxed, Du Bois's assessment of FDR became much more positive. He shuddered at the large influence that John Nance Garner or the "prehistoric" Cordell Hull would have exerted on the Democratic Party had Roosevelt not sought a third term. Whatever the president's mistakes and shortcomings, Du Bois reached a judgment he would hold to permanently that FDR was "the only living man who can lead the United States on the path which will eventually abolish poverty."

A major turning point in American race relations was about to occur between the fall of 1940 and early summer of 1941, although with a speed that must have surprised even Du Bois. Focused and mobilized with unprecedented steadfastness, millions of black women and men spoke out for immediate integration of the military and full participation in the war industry. Giving organizational muscle to generalized feelings, Robert Vann had put considerable resources into the Committee for Participation of Negroes in the National Defense, a lobby formed by World War I army officers in late 1938. His open letter, published at the beginning of the next year, served blunt notice to FDR: "I need not tell you that we are expecting a more dignified place in our armed forces during the next war than we occupied during the World War." It was one of the crusty newspaper publisher's last gestures before dying of adominal cancer in the fall of 1940. Shifting from a decade-long, almost exclusive emphasis on antilynching, Du Bois watched his old organization take up the more energizing issue of the desegregation of the armed services. Addressing the secretary of the army over Roy Wilkins's signature, the NAACP informed Harry Woodring that it knew of "no single issue — except probably lynching — upon which there is a unanimity of opinion among all classes in all sections of the country." When the War Department unveiled its racially retrogressive 1940 Protective Mobilization Plan, restricting the army's nonwhite quota to 5.8 percent and jettisoning any provision for Negro combat units, it became clear that Wilkins had not overstated the gravity of the military service issue. Explaining the General Staff's position to Congress, the secretary of war stated that "mixing colored and white soldiers in closely related units . . . [would] demoralize and weaken" these units.

The administration took notice of the mounting Aframerican fury after White declared in June at the annual convention that the NAACP intended to support any presidential candidate committed to abolishing discrimination in the armed services. "What point is there in fighting and perhaps dying to save democracy if there is no democracy to save?" the secretary shouted to thunderous approval. Race newspapers exhorted readers to press their congressmen on the issue. Highly alarmed by the Baltimore *Afro-American*'s endorsement of Wilkie and other signs of a shift to the GOP, the president asked the first lady and others for advice. With days to go before the November elections, FDR appointed an African-American assistant secretary of war, promoted another to brigadier (the rank denied to Charles Young in the Great War), and appointed a third as adviser to the director of Selective Service. Nor was the new man in the War Department another Emmett Scott. As Secretary of War Henry Stimson would be surprised to discover, William Henry Hastie refused to endorse the status quo of second-class military service. Although the National Negro Congress called on member organizations in 1940 to refuse to fight in a war against the Soviet Union at its April meeting in Chicago, it was a Communist position that none of the major organizations endorsed, nor even its president. Being red was too great a handicap for people already handicapped by being black, Randolph had famously quipped upon resigning from the NNC. Du Bois very likely savored Randolph's political *jeu d'esprit*, but his own conceptions of the peace to come after war instilled within him a skepticism about what would soon be known as the Double-V campaign—victory at home, victory abroad. Who but the author of the memorable "Close Ranks" had more reason to warn the Negro political class of the "dangerous paradox" it faced? "If you love your country, suffer for it; don't bargain. If you hate it for rape, insult and slavery, say so, don't lie." Jingoism was the twin of racism, he declared, and he cheered those who "defend strikes and declare that even communists have rights." Rather than having them bargain for full citizenship, Du Bois seemed to want American Negroes to march out of the Depression into the arsenal of democracy with pan-Africanist principles held high and visions of a new world order inspired by Marx whatever the cost.

On the first day of February 1941, Harlem's leading newspaper carried FDR's inaugural address as rewritten by Du Bois—"what President Roosevelt ought to have said. But he did not say it." America must go to war only for the sake of peace, not to save Great Britain or to punish Hitler and the National Socialist Party, he would have had Roosevelt declare. To the British people was owed the debt of parliamentary democracy, great literature, and technological evolution, he continued. But strict justice also commanded that Britain be blamed for the present world crisis, "for the forcible subjugation of large areas of the world and many millions of people, without giving them voice in their own government." There was also a commensurate debt owed German civilization, as well as the obligation to acknowledge—"and God knows she has suffered"—the suffering imposed on Germany by England, France, and the United States. But no quotient of legitimate grievances could justify the German means to ends that would return Europe to "barbarism and set human culture back a thousand years." The vicarious inaugural address concluded on a high note of Wilsonian idealism: "As a first step toward this Federation of the World," Du Bois imagined FDR demanding "from England and Germany, from Japan and Italy, a cessation from War, and agreement to the principle above enunciated, and an assembly of a World Council with an international police army and navy at the disposal of an elected executive."

Prophecy in the *Amsterdam News* was usually inspired and usually badly belied by the unfolding events of history. Du Boisian predictions might have achieved no better or worse accuracy than those of any practiced seer's, but for their tendency to fly off into the ether of racial romanticism. Abiding affection for the Germans stoked by his roam through the Reich conduced to a surreal indulgence of Hitler and Nazism that Du Bois actually thought was hardheadedly perceptive. There was also the analogous blindness to Japanese militarism, a canker he was given to mitigating by quoting the pacific protestations of prominent Japanese officials. Finally, soaked as he was in the long history of Europe's global vandalism and America's subjugation of Indians and Negroes and Monroe Doctrine interventionism, Du Bois was not at all averse to positing the moral equivalency of totalitarian regimes and western democracies. "If Hitler wins, down with the blacks! If the democracies win, the blacks are already down." Nevertheless, Hitlerian Germany could not, must not, win the war, he insisted repeatedly, because it offered civilization little more than economic efficiency and martial uniformity. Yet, now that Great Britain and the United States had forced Japan into the Axis, Du Bois hypothesized that Germany might prevail if she accommodated her racist ideology to the colored-world imperatives of Japan. Somehow imagining that the objectives in *Mein Kampf* were as negotiable as the campaign pledges of an American political party, he speculated that the ultimate outcome of Nazi-Japanese cooperation might well be "increased freedom and autonomy for the darker world, despite all theoretic race ideology."

A remarkable and now forgotten meditation appearing in the July 1941 *Journal of Negro Education*, "Neuropa: Hitler's New World Order," went even further, stripping National Socialism of its unique, organic malevolence and conceiving it to be another post-laissez-faire ideology along the continuum of increasing industrial rationalization. Nazism, Du Bois decided, was an incomplete version of the economic state planning well under way in the Soviet Union—socialism that had been "held back by the junkers and big business." Pushing up through the debris of capitalism he saw new economic structures of such rational design and egalitarian potential as to render permanently obsolete the old order of unregulated profit and oppressive hierarchy. Du Bois could seriously entertain, therefore, a Europe, conquered and reorganized by Germany, evolving through the "full mobilization of all scientific information and the utilizing of all possible means for one end" into an imperium surpassing the estimable Soviet Union. Among even the select subscribers to Charles Thompson's *Journal of Negro Education* very few participated in Du Bois's wide-angle vision of the world at war. Despite much lingering admiration for the Japanese and popular sentiment holding that more Nazis lived in the South than in Germany, Aframericans were more in tune with Schuyler's position set forth in the *Courier* that, as peace had yielded such few benefits, war would have to be better for the Negro. In the spring of 1941, while Du Bois brooded over deteriorating U.S.-Japanese relations, India's compulsory participation in the war, and the world-historic options confronting the darker races, a coalition of civil rights organizations led by Randolph launched the March on Washington Movement (MOWM).

Randolph's campaign took on evangelical force as thousands of working-class and middle-class black men and women vowed they would "rather die on our feet fighting for Negroes's rights, than live on our knees as . . . semi-citizens, begging for a pittance." The BSCP and NAACP sponsored rallies in large cities in April and May in order to build momentum for a Negro inundation of Washington to force the passage of legislation banning discrimination in defense industries. With little more than Brigadier General Benjamin O. Davis, Sr., and William Hastie, civilian aide to the secretary of war, to show for their protests against segregated armed forces, colored people had been dealt a second body blow when the new Office of Production Management (OPM) made no mention of minority employment in its plans to put the national economy on a war basis. In deference to organized labor, there was an equally enraging silence from the new National Defense Mobilization Board about the exclusion of minorities from the unions. A huge number of signatures was garnered by the manifesto circulated by the interfaith and interracial Committee on Negroes in Defense Industries. Civil rights leaders also counted on the government's alarm that Communist-led labor unions, in obedience to the Nazi-Soviet Pact, would exploit the MOWM in order to slow defense-industry production. The White House mobilized Fiorello LaGuardia, Mrs. Roosevelt, the CIO's Sidney Hillman, and other influentials in a concerted effort to persuade Randolph to call off the crusade. Once before at a critical moment in his career as labor leader and civil rights militant, Randolph had listened to powerful white allies and nearly wrecked the Brotherhood by calling off a strike against the Pullman Corporation. This time, Randolph kept his own counsel. On the eve of the march on Washington and three days after the German invasion of the Soviet Union, FDR folded his poker hand. On June 25, 1941, the president signed the historic Executive Order 8802 banning employment discrimination in defense-related industries. The victory was more than symbolic, even if the new Fair Employment Practices Committee (FEPC) could not enforce but only investigate and issue citations against offending employers, and even though FDR denied Walter White a seat on the committee, which was headed by a white Mississippian.

Operation Barbarossa, the Nazis' lightning attack on their Russian ally on June 22, ended Du Bois's curious equanimity about Germany and Japan with a declaration that war between Russia and Germany "reorientates all our thinking whether we will or no." Until now, he had felt obliged to seek positive possibilities for the world's darker peoples in the standoff between the Axis and the British Empire—to maximize the conceivable by looking well beyond the immediate. If England won, he had wanted to believe that "democracy might grow within her empire by sheer force of logic and despite the past." Similarly, after the National Socialist demonstration that the wealth and health of a nation can be revolutionized without elections, he had desperately hypothesized that, if Germany won, "the very impact of this mighty idea might overflow the faults and limits of class and race." Above all, he had clung to the conviction that as long as Russia survived—"whether England or Germany won"—the slow, ultimate spread of democracy in industry was assured. "Russia was one country which, despite all excess, failure and backsliding, had frankly faced the greatest problem of our day: the problem of poverty." For Du Bois, Operation Barbarossa had irrevocably altered the preferred combatants—but not his suspicions of them; Britain and the United States were still habitual malefactors.

"I do not like the Roosevelt-Churchill manifesto," he complained in late August after the three-day conference aboard ship of the British prime minister and American president in Placentia Bay, Newfoundland. Massive military assistance to Russia and containment of Japan in the Pacific comprised the main business of the two leaders and their staffs, but the release on August 11 of the Atlantic Charter ennobled the Anglo-American cause as a crusade to restore sovereign rights and self-government "to those who have been forcibly deprived of them" and a pledge to seek "no aggrandizement, territorial or other" as a result of the war. It was the old language of the League covenant promulgated over new signatures, pieties belied by unremitting European exploitation, Du Bois warned in the *Amsterdam News.* Who was so naive as to suppose that self-government would be restored to Zululand, Natal, Nigeria, the Dutch

Indies, the Gold Coast, Puerto Rico, "and a hundred other lands of the Blacks?" How, Du Bois asked, quoting the charter, could " 'all men in all lands . . . live out their lives in freedom from fear and want' " when England and America "have been ruling the world for a generation and want and fear has driven this world to war"? Until the goal of the war was to "revise and control and rationalize" the white world's fundamental attitude toward the colored world, Du Bois advised American Negroes to make their patriotism as conditional as the racist democracy they lived under. The test of his advice came fourteen weeks later on a Sunday dawn when 423 Japanese aircraft destroyed the bulk of the U.S. Pacific Fleet in a surprise attack. Good friend Hikida had mistimed his departure from the United States by five days. No longer able to sail from Los Angeles on December 12, he had kept quietly to himself at his West 85th Street address until his arrest and internment one month later on Ellis Island. Bureaucratic confusion, relocation and detention of Japanese nationals in White Sulphur Springs, West Virginia, until June 1942, and belated reassessment of Hikida's importance prevented the FBI from a follow-up and more probing interrogation, despite J. Edgar Hoover's last-minute demand that the State Department delay the bibliophile's departure. As he was already aboard the exchange ship *Gripsholm*, "it was not deemed advisable to permit the interview under these circumstances," Assistant Secretary of State Adolph A. Berle, Jr., informed the FBI director.

Recalling his controversial "Close Ranks" editorial of 1918, it was obvious that Du Bois had no desire to recapture the moment even had it been possible to do so in 1941. He still felt that war with Japan was deeply to be regretted and would state as a fact four years later that "every Negro has been unhappy" over the conflict. One of the very few Negro leaders to put his name to Norman Thomas's open letter condemning Roosevelt's internment of Japanese Americans, Du Bois interpreted Exeuctive Order 9066 as conclusive proof of the racial origins of the Pacific war. In a tone inflected by a quarter-century of world-weariness, then, he uttered a muted call to duty. "We close ranks again, but only, now as then, to fight for democracy not only for white folk but for yellow, brown, and black," he declared. "We fight not in joy but in sorrow with no feeling of uplift; but under the sad weight of duty and in part, as we know to our sorrow, because of the inheritance of a slave psychology which makes it easier for us to submit rather than to rebel. Whatever all our mixed emotions are, we are going to play the game."

AT THE BEGINNING of the year, 1940, Du Bois drove to Louisiana and Texas in the new Buick with Diggs along as his secretary. He lectured at Negro colleges and discussed a still-unfolding plan to resume the Atlanta University Studies with the college presidents. "A very lovely trip" it was, he wrote Nina, who still occupied a room in the 135th Street Harlem Y. She may have been cheered by greetings Will sent her from the Bankses in Prairie View, Texas, and several other families visited along their route. But the "great news," he had shared, was that Harcourt was going to publish the autobiography he called *Dusk of Dawn*. The best news, Nina may have thought, was that she would soon be able to move to their new home in Baltimore. Stoic, in delicate health, and lonely, she was somewhat befriended by another Y resident, vivacious Bobbie Branch, recently arrived from Philadelphia to take a staff position with the NAACP. Branch, who succeeded the stern, aged Richetta Randolph, would rise to assistant office manager and keeper of secrets, institutional and personal. Occasionally, they took tea together, Branch, tall, gregarious, and as white and blue-eyed as Walter White, and Nina, "tiny, and very timid, but sweet," said she. Aside from her hawk-eyed diligence when it came to the welfare of Baby Du Bois, living at the Modern School a few blocks away, Branch believed Nina had little else to live for. Number 2302 Montebello Terrace in Baltimore, ready for occupancy in the spring, would improve the quality of her life and impose a semblance of order in Yolande's life by reuniting the family under the same roof. The house was a two-story brick structure with four bedrooms under a gable roof and nicely sited on a rise in Morgan Park, a faultlessly maintained community of teachers, postal employees, and several affluent Murphies abutting Morgan State College. It made a pleasant foyer for the continuing nurturing of Baby Du Bois, who would be withdrawn the following year from Mildred Johnson's private academy and enrolled in P.S. 103 on Division Street. Although Jim Crow reigned in law and practice in Baltimore, relations between the races were far less raw in this Upper South city than they were in Atlanta.

Du Bois went to Chicago in February 1940 for the Lincoln Day Dinner, an annual affair in which he had often participated. While there, he met Mildred Jones for dinner. He sent precise instructions to present herself at 6:30 at the information desk in Union Station, where he would wait for her "a half hour." She came, lovely and excited, the toll of high school teaching and writing a doctoral dissertation in music theory evident despite her unaffected pleasure at seeing him. A month later, wishing to recapture the mood of the dinner, she would dine alone at the station restaurant, but "I missed you too much to enjoy it," she wrote him, "though the headwaiter noticed it and said something very nice and complimentary about you." While in Chicago, he also attended and enormously enjoyed a lively party thrown by Embree at the Rosenwald Fund offices in honor of several younger Negro writers. It was his first meeting with Richard Wright. *Native Son* was a Book-of-the-Month Club selection and Du Bois admired the novel. Langston Hughes, Arna Bontemps, and the young University of Chicago psychology instructor, Allison Davis, were there. "One feels a certain sense of relief and confidence in meeting such sturdy pillars of the day to come," he wrote in the *Amsterdam News*.

A few days before boarding the Chicago express for the Lincoln Day Dinner and the punctual rendezvous with Jones, Du Bois had written to the young woman whose advancing career meant a great deal to him. Shirley Graham's Rosenwald fellowship for a year of study at Yale Drama School was certainly three parts merit, but it had been virtually guaranteed by Du Bois's recommendation. He apologized for having "neglected [her] shamefully," and promised her a much more attentive future. Her bubbly letter was waiting when he returned. Wright's *Native Son* was horrible, and it made her heart "weep for having borne two sons," she wrote from New Haven. The year had been a great success. Just last month, one of her short plays had been performed in the Yale Theatre, and the Gilpin Players had taken another play for a two-week run in the new theater at Western Reserve University. But she dreaded the day when she would have to leave Yale for the outside world. "I'm afraid of it," this fearless, irrepressible woman pretended. May 1940, departure time arrived, and Graham told Du Bois she was "in blackest despair." The head of the Vassar College Drama School had ruined plans for the Broadway production of another of her plays by dying suddenly. She needed tiding over. Did he think she might land a summer job at AU? "Please, please, put your brilliant mind to some solution," Graham pleaded. His solution—to arrange a stopgap position for her in New York through Lillian Alexander or Arthur Spingarn—failed, he wrote in distress. Graham found her own solution in short order as director of adult activities at the Phillis Wheatley YWCA in Indianapolis, Indiana. Du Bois found her there with her teenage sons, Robert and David, in late October, where the two enjoyed a delicious reunion.

Harcourt had published *Dusk of Dawn* in fall 1940, his ninth nonfiction book, dedicated to Joel Spingarn, "scholar and knight." "Pageant in Seven Decades" provided the skeleton of the manuscript, the incomparable *Souls* and wrathful *Darkwater* the flesh. Subtitled *An Essay Toward an Autobiography of a Race Concept*, Du Bois made large claims for the significance of *Dusk of Dawn*, a work like no other by an American Negro since the appearance of *Life and Times of Frederick Douglass* or James Weldon Johnson's beautifully written *Along This Way*. Douglass had wished his life to be understood as inspirational, instructive, and archetypal, in furtherance of which purpose he filled his autobiography with aphorisms and categorical imperatives in keeping with the hortatory conventions of his day. On the whole, however, Douglass allowed for greater distinction between his life and his times than Du Bois did. For Du Bois, as for Henry Adams, whose *Education* might be said to inform Du Bois's narrative from the cultural right, his life *was* the meaning of his times. Its authorial voice was quintessentially autonomous, spoken through the imperial

first-person characteristic of European witness—a distinctively masculine celebration of self-discovery, presumptuous and solipsistic. The uniqueness of Du
Bois's autobiography was in the extravagant degree to which the descendant of
slaves appropriated a genre reserved to those privileged by color, class, gender,
and race to usurp the voices of social inferiors. As he had in the preface to
Souls, Du Bois feigned dubiety that what he had to say might be worthwhile.
In his experience, "autobiographies have had little lure," he feared. "Repeatedly
they assume too much or too little: too much in dreaming that one's own life
has greatly influenced the world." But that disclaimer had scarcely been penned
than he stipulated that his life was to be understood as the metaphor for the
"central problem of the greatest of the world's democracies and so the Problem
of the future world." He had intended to write not so much the story of his
own life, then, but the autobiography of the twentieth century as it had lived
through him—"the autobiography of a concept of race," he explained, "elucidated and magnified and doubtless distorted in the thoughts and deeds which
were mine. . . . Thus for all time my life is significant for all lives of men."

Du Bois wished to signal by the book's curious title that both he and the
century were passing out of receding darkness into the first light of a new and
far better racial sunrise. He wished it to convey "wider hope," and so infused
Dusk of Dawn with a limpid mellowness usually absent from much of his previous writings as, once again, he chronicled birth by a "golden river" in the
Berkshires and valedictorian progress to Fisk, Harvard, and Berlin. Here and
there, light retouchings of his family's material circumstances are evident. Early
on, he reveals the leitmotif of his life in a paragraph of stunning candor, disclosing that "had it not been for the race problem early thrust upon me and
enveloping me, I should have probably been an unquestioning worshiper at the
shrine of the social order and economic development into which I was born."
His capacious mind had absorbed ever-more-radical conclusions as it studied
the full implications of his and his people's exclusion from American society.
What was wrong, he had thought at first, was that "people like me and thousands
of others who might have my ability and aspiration, were refused permission to
be part of this world." The rub, in other words, was really the refusal to fine
tune racial discrimination so as to admit exemplary people of color to full citizenship. Critics then and later, unmindful or skeptical of its egalitarian evolution, would focus on this espousal of civil rights for the worthy as the essence
of Du Bois's Talented Tenth concept. Then came the frustrations of social-
science research at the old Atlanta University and conflict with Booker Washington's Carnegies and Rockefellers, determined to hammer the Negro
intelligentsia "into conformity," that caused him to realize that the fundamental
question was not why gifted people were discriminated against but why ordinary
black people had so little chance for self-improvement.

The segregating veil of color in *Souls* and other writings was complemented in *Dusk* by an image of the cave as another way of vivifying the "full psychological meaning of caste segregation." Du Bois depicted the invisibility and irrelevance of people of color in the white imperium of interwar America with an implacable verisimilitude, writing that it was as though, "looking out from a dark cave, . . . [one] sees the world passing and speaks to it," imploring it to realize the unjust and spiritually stunting conditions of the cave people. "One talks on evenly and logically in this way, but notices that the passing throng does not even turn its head, or if it does, glances curiously and walks on." More ignored than despised, the segregated clamor to be noticed, to be recognized and respected, with results described in *Dusk* that were to play out in the social-control policies encysting a hundred inner cities in the final quarter of the century:

> Then the people within may become hysterical. They scream and hurl themselves against the barriers, hardly realizing in their bewilderment that they are screaming in a vacuum unheard and that their antics may actually seem funny to those outside looking in. They may even, here and there, break through in blood and disfigurement, and find themselves faced by a horrified, implacable, and quite overwhelming mob of people frightened for their own very existence.

Invisibility, Du Bois emphasized in the sardonic "The White World" (a kinder gentler version of *Darkwater*'s caustic "The Souls of White Folk"), was as much aesthetic as sociopolitical. In his running colloquy with the imaginary Roger Van Dieman (the essay's white straw man), he underscored again the pernicious "discovery of personal whiteness" as the defining feature of northern Europe in the modern age. To Van Dieman's ejaculation of "sheer nonsense and pure balderdash" when Du Bois insists that Negroes are equal in grace and beauty to whites, Du Bois's retort reads like Jefferson's "Notes on Virginia" inverted: "In faces, I hate straight features; needles and razors may be sharp—but beautiful never." Not for Du Bois, then, Van Dieman's ideal of the Venus de Milo or the Belvedere Apollo. As the "child of twilight and night," he celebrates intricately curly hair, black eyes, "full and luscious features." These paragraphs from *Dusk* could not have been more fecund anticipations of the Black Aesthetic twenty-five years in the future than had Du Bois actually written that black is beautiful, which he nearly does in the following passage: "Add to this voices that caress instead of rasp, glances that appeal rather than repel, and a sinuous litheness of movement to replace Anglo-Saxon stalking—there you have my ideal."

The Du Bois of handlebar mustaches, spats, and carved walking sticks re-emerges in *Dusk*, the silk-stocking intellectual whom future left-wing allies would do their best to forget and the pioneering sociologist whose victim-blaming proclivities would cause some future scholars to wince. It may not be biographically presumptuous to suggest that Du Bois would have waved aside such reactions in annoyed dismay. Hadn't his unrivaled oeuvre in history and sociology, to say nothing of three-score years of service to the race, entitled him to the privilege of unflinching analysis without the censure of the politically correct? Didn't profound understanding of his people, together with a little common sense, necessitate the occasional therapy of tough love, he would have retorted? Placed in the social-science context of the early forties, *Dusk* finds an instructive match in Frazier's *The Negro Family in the United States*, one of the seminal books of the era. Published almost contemporaneously with the autobiography, *The Negro Family* acknowledged its debt to Du Bois's *The Negro American Family*, the thirteenth monograph in the Atlanta University Studies. Du Bois, in turn, praised Frazier in a letter to Embree as one of the most brilliant sociologists of his generation. Not only did its elegant formulations of family typologies, its brilliant historicizing of color, class, and mobility, and its prescriptive theorizing about the functionality of matriarchal versus patriarchal structures appeal to Du Bois's intellect, but Frazier's monumental study reso-nated at the deeper level of personal standards. Reading Frazier, although younger than his forerunner by a quarter century, was like reading Du Bois. *The Negro Family* was stippled with censorious terms: "unfettered motherhood"; "promiscuous sexual relations"; "demoralized elements." It was dogmatic in its valuations: the rise of the patriarchal, nuclear household represented an un-qualified advance over the matrifocal or extended family structures coming out of slavery. Puritanical prose and reasoned beliefs that not all social arrangements have equal value would cause Du Bois and Frazier to be temporarily engulfed and distorted in the ideological maelstrom spun off in the sixties by Daniel Patrick Moynihan's black-family pathologies. Du Bois and Frazier, however, merely saw middle-class family values for what they imperfectly were during the ongoing migration of black folk from farm to factory—essential to the progress of the race. With good reason, they assumed that their sociological writings had been pivotal in explaining historic victims of oppression—not in blaming them.

But puritanical prose should not have distracted readers from the core of the autobiography. Of one historic fact, Du Bois was absolutely certain—man-kind had reached the end of an economic era that had seemed "but a few years ago omnipotent and eternal." Capitalism was dying throughout the world. If he couldn't predict the form to be taken by the emerging economic order, he was convinced that among its integral elements would be rational planning and public ownership of the means of production. His was the fateful obligation, therefore, of helping the Talented Tenth choose the correct course for the Aframerican masses to follow into the new political economy. Writing *Dusk* against the backdrop of the 1937 rock-bottom depression that had momentarily caused many economists, Keynes included, to see the New Deal as a failed experiment, Du Bois was certain that capitalism was writing its own obituary. The British Empire was collapsing. Europe, for better and worse, was being reconstructed by German, Italian, and Spanish fascisms. Asia belonged to Japan. American Negroes must not be deceived by an illusory recovery, despite the prosperity looming just ahead as the United States began to convert to a war economy. Instead, Du Bois enjoined them to bide their time, to pull together and smartly develop a parallel economy fueled by group purchasing power and cooperative consumer instruments. He proposed that "into the interstices of this collapse of the industrial machine, the Negro . . . plan for his entrance into the new economic world." At the top of the century, Du Bois had incomparably described double-consciousness as the state of being unique to Negro Americans; forty years later *Dusk* commended to them a unique double economy.

Seer and intellectual, impatient and bitingly contemptuous of what he saw as the fatalism endemic to the colored poor and the timorous parochialism characterizing much of the Talented Tenth, Du Bois sometimes overlooked or minimized those incremental, pragmatic, messy, and corrupt developments that others noticed as hopeful. As he wrote in the autobiography's closing chapter, his leadership "was a leadership solely of ideas." To make things better for the race, it was necessary to think boldly; and because of an almost Sorelian belief in the power of ideas, he was seldom daunted by objections as to their impracticality. In the therapy of an inspired idea he invariably divined an inherent agency sufficient to alter reality. As he reviewed his record of success in setting ideas on the march, Du Bois ended *Dusk of Dawn* on a note of satisfaction that he hoped would not be perceived as boastful: ". . . In the period from 1910 to 1930, I was a main factor in revolutionizing the attitude of the American Negro toward caste. My stinging hammer blows made Negroes aware of themselves, confident in their possibilities and determined in self-assertion. So much so that today common slogans among the Negro people are taken bodily from the words of my mouth." Villard alone, among the large and largely favorable jury, noted what other reviewers left respectfully unsaid, the "very real egotism which shines through these pages in which few others are praised—chiefly those who contributed to [the author's] success." The reviewer for *The New Republic* welcomed Du Bois's autobiography as "proof of the potentialities of the educated Negro, if such proof was ever needed by people of intelligence."

By 1940, a consensus had begun to build among certain educated whites that it was now appropriate to honor Du Bois publicly as a paragon of the

Negro's potential. The theory and praxis of Nazi racism had put well-bred Nordics somewhat on the defensive in the United States. But as one perceptive survey reveals, despite the untiring efforts of Boas and several prominent academics to generate an antiracist movement among social scientists, the retreat of "scientific racism" remained half-hearted, ambivalent, and disengenuous well into the forties. The fall of France and the Battle of Britain had nevertheless quickened the pace of racial liberalism and brought Du Bois speaking requests and membership invitations across the color line that had been out of the question a few years earlier. In February 1939 he had become an incorporating member of the Society of American Historians at the invitation of Allan Nevins, a distinction that followed by several weeks the request from FDR that Du Bois serve on the advisory committee to establish a repository for the president's papers. The editor of *The American Scholar*, Phi Beta Kappa's quarterly journal, invited a Du Bois contribution that appeared in the summer 1939 issue as "The Negro Scientist." Although more a taxonomy than a sociological treatment of the professional marginalizing of able Negro biologists, chemists, physicists, and psychiatrists, his essay introduced a raft of rigorously trained, dedicated scientists whose very existence was so unsuspected by educated whites that, after receiving the final draft, the *Scholar's* associate editor exclaimed by letter, "I take my hat off to you." December brought an invitation from white sociologist Arthur Raper, author of *The Tragedy of Lynching*, to deliver a twenty-minute paper at the annual meeting of the Southern Sociological Society, a request Du Bois immediately accepted. The invitation to chair a session on Negro history at the 1940 annual meeting of the American Historical Association in New York City was so unexpected that it occurred to Du Bois only after agreeing to do so that his membership had long since lapsed. Neither he nor any other person of color had appeared before the principal organization of the profession since 1909, the year in which Du Bois had been complimented after reading his paper on Reconstruction, then studiously ignored thereafter for thirty years.

In the time leading up to the Southern Sociological conference in Knoxville, Tennessee, he pushed himself and those connected with the enterprise to produce the inaugural number of *Phylon*, the new Atlanta University quarterly. *Phylon: The Atlanta University Review of Race and Culture* took its name from the Greek word for "race." It was the first interdisciplinary organ at the service of Negro scholars and their intellectual allies, a journal of history, literature, and the social sciences meant to give voice to the dilplomaed men and women of color to whom the mainstream world of learned-society conferences and refereed publications was, with few exceptions, imperiously deaf. "We seem to see today a new orientation and duty" to study racial groups both from an internal and a comparative perspective, Du Bois prescribed in the opening "Apology." "Here if anywhere the leadership of science is demanded not to obliterate all race and group distinctions, but to know and study them, to see and appreciate them at their true values." The new quarterly was intended to take up where the old Atlanta University Studies ("the beginning in America of applied Sociology and Anthropology to group problems") had left off; but, more than a reprise, the objective was to reinterpret history, education, and sociology "from the ideological and economic point of view." Raper and Reid's lead essay, "The South Adjusts—Downward?" met Du Bois's criteria for applying economics at the grassroots level. "The Negro in France," by the Martinican novelist, René Maran, the second winner of the Prix Goncourt, supplied the international context the editor-in-chief considered to be essential. Although *Phylon* was to become the enduring pride of Atlanta University by completing the triangle of Negro scholarly periodicals of which the *Journal of Negro History* and *Journal of Negro Education* were the first legs, the years leading to the publication's birth had been accompanied by administrative resistance and distaste more typical of an unwanted pregnancy than appropriate to a joyous arrival.

As special custodian of the Rockefeller legacy at Spelman and former officer of the GEB, Florence Read's power in the affairs of the university center, formal and unofficial, had been equal to John Hope's. It was always John Hope II's belief that Read "pretty well deferred to Dad because she admired him and they worked well together" as long as they were teamed. After the AU president's death, her power was unrivaled, and remained so even after the selection in May 1937 of Hope's successor. Her rule over Morehouse would last until the retirement in 1939 of the unremarkable Negro president Samuel Archer. Morris Brown College, a proud but poor Methodist institution, had occupied the buildings of the old Atlanta University after 1932 but remained, as far as Read was concerned, an inconsequential interloper. Many in colored Atlanta speculated — and some even professed to know with certainty — that Hope and Read had transgressed the ultimate taboo of the white South. Circumstantial evidence based on frequent travel together, their marathons in closed conference, Read's jealous displacement of Lugenia Hope as guardian of the president's fragile health (excluding family from visiting the Spelman infirmary during the last weeks of his life), and her anguished return of certain of Hope's personal items to Mrs. Hope only under threat of legal action, were sufficient to convict Hope and Read as lovers in the court of faculty opinion. Fifty years after Hope's death, J. Max Bond, a professor in the school of education, still thought so. Biologist Samuel Nabrit, acting dean of the faculty whose wife served as Hope's secretary, sheepishly commented on these perennial rumors that "theirs was the closest relationship I have ever seen between two people who worked together."

Whatever special appeal she may have exerted on Hope, Read soon discovered that she had almost none for her putative lover's best friend. How could she have so misjudged her own authority and his querulous principles as to bid

Du Bois to offer a prayer at the first faculty assembly of her acting presidency? His curt refusal to do so became legendary in Atlanta and beyond, affixed to and often conflated with another occasion where, asked to pray and muttering toward an amen, he had snapped to a dinner hostess who wished to hear his words, "Madame, I was not speaking to you." Still, Read had reconfirmed Du Bois's flexible teaching agreement with Hope in every detail. Du Bois observed her stewardship of Atlanta, Morehouse, and Spelman (and her visceral distaste for affiliated Morris Brown and Clark College) with a growing impatience he would convey in no uncertain terms to Jackson Davis and Dean Sage at the GEB. He saw pennies accounted for in a university budget that deprived faculty of secretarial assistance. He seethed as Hope's plan to build a fine-arts department shriveled to little more than a salary line for Elizabeth Prophet. "But something, I am not sure what, went wrong," he speculated to Embree about the art department. "I think it had to do with Miss Read of Spelman." In February 1937 he reminded Read that she and the trustees had yet to act on his two-year-old magazine proposal. The magazine matter, he stated, had now become his top priority for the year. Some three months later, Read's letter renewing his faculty position for another year had made a point of thanking Du Bois "for the fine cooperation" extended her, during the acting presidency. A few weeks thereafter, in one of his I-need-hardly-remind-you communiqués, he gravely advised Read of his displeasure should a frustrated Ira Reid go off to a Washington alphabet agency—a "calamity" that would have appalled their beloved Hope, he knowingly added. A month later, Du Bois reported to Read that, after two days of discussions in Nashville, he, Logan, Reid, and Charles Johnson had reached preliminary agreement for an Atlanta-Fisk publication venture. Du Bois's effusive and out of character "We made history" was reciprocated by a rarely effusive Johnson, who wrote back, "It was an unexpectedly long first step."

Having put President Rufus Clement on notice his first month in office about deplorable conditions in the graduate-hall dining room, Du Bois had sharply escalated the unsolicited advice and admonishments in winter of 1938–39. Two pages of single-spaced type about the shortfalls that should "from time to time be considered" read like the report from A to Z of a superconscientious accreditation board. "Culture and creative scholarship" were insufficiently encouraged. There was no faculty senate, but only an amorphous body holding infrequent and perfunctory meetings. It was further noted that while considerable thought had been devoted "to the place and power and dignity of the president" as well as to matters "of student rights and discipline," faculty and clerical staff had been lumped together. On a tear about Morehouse students, Du Bois's memorandum demanded a review of the place of the black men's college in the overall scheme of things. With its lax discipline, indulgence of bad manners, professorial "dead wood," and "very low academic standards,"

Morehouse needed organizational stiffening and an overhaul of its curriculum. But the root of the university center's problems lay with Spelman College. "Spelman is not a good college," it was stated pure and simple. "The traditions of a New England Seminary hang over it." The curriculum was loaded down with Bible subjects, home economics, and other noncollegiate requirements. Its president, although devoted to her task "without rest or play, was lacking in esteem for the Negro race in particular and for humanity in general." Florence Read "need[ed] broad firm guidance." The university needed *Phylon*, the scientific quarterly he had proposed.

In Willette Rutherford Banks, president of Prairie View State College, the Texas land-grant institution for Negroes, Du Bois counted on a former student and dedicated, able ally among the largely white AU trustee board. Banks had played a pivotal part in Clement's candidature and, in addition to a forceful personality, there was the considerable factor of his presidency of the Conference of the Presidents of Negro Land Grant Colleges. Du Bois finally prevailed upon Atlanta University to enhance itself with a learned journal. Meeting on campus in late April 1939, the trustees approved the recommendation of the faculty that a quarterly review be funded. "We have at last succeeded in getting an appropriation," Du Bois wrote Charles S. Johnson, after nearly a year of silence. The chairman of Fisk's department of social science seemed no longer disposed to participate, however. Johnson's motives for never quite finding time to give Du Bois a definite answer remain unclear. Conceivably, Johnson may have been encumbered by resistence from certain Fisk trustees to the *Phylon* overture (Thomas Jesse Jones comes to mind), or, knowing something of the determined Atlanta opposition to Du Bois's scheme, he may well have calculated the chances for success as too slim to justify the effort and risk. Personal animus may have entered the equation; neither man really cared much for the other. Unquestionably, Negro scholarship was the poorer for this missed opportunity.

The venture was off to a shoestring start of two thousand dollars for four issues, thanks, said Du Bois, to the parsimony of Read, who had archly stated that she could afford only to give the magazine money enough to fail. With a GEB subvention of a thousand dollars to run from one to five years, Du Bois thought that he, Reid, Braithwaite (Logan had gone off to Howard in 1938), and several others of the editorial board had a fair chance of succeeding. Speaking after a long silence for the GEB, a sympathetic Jackson Davis, clearly overruled by others at 61 Broadway, declined to be "in any way responsible for [a journal's] publication." With Diggs working round the clock, assisted by Lucy Grigsby, an entering graduate student in literature, *Phylon* debuted on schedule in January 1940. Preparation for the second number, featuring an appreciation of Du Bois's Haitian friend and diplomat, Dantes Bellegarde, began immediately. On signal from Du Bois, President Banks congratulated President Clement on AU's success and observed matter-of-factly that everyone realized "that the modest sum of $2,000 will finally have to be increased." Nine days before Du Bois drove to Knoxville to address his session of the Southern Sociological Society on April 5, the Carnegie Corporation filled the breach left by the GEB's rejection. Against his trustees' advice, Keppel released money from a discretionary account for Du Bois's benefit—a thousand dollars annually for two years. Three weeks after what would turn out to be an aborted experience with the southern white sociologists, an upbeat, grateful Du Bois wrote Keppel that the Carnegie grant would be used to underwrite a *Phylon* institute in the fall. The objective was to assemble a dozen or more experts at AU "for economic study and planning among American Negroes." Somewhat later, Du Bois remembered to inform Clement and Read.

A Negro speaking to a professional organization of whites in the South was extraordinary in 1940; that the Negro was Du Bois mobilized Knoxville's Talented Tenth to turn out in impressive numbers. A senior at Knoxville College who liked to think of himself as having been weaned on *Souls*, Vernon Jarrett piled into a car of excited classmates and headed for the Norris School auditorium, where the address was scheduled for 1:30 P.M. on Friday, April 5. The title of Du Bois's Southern Sociological Society address was "Federal Action Programs and Community Action in the South." The whites, arriving up to an hour late, some proud of breaking with tradition, but many of the locals curious or impertinent, self-segregated themselves in the buzzing auditorium. The blacks, in smaller numbers and almost vibrating with vindication, took seats farther forward than usual. Five minutes, then ten elapsed, and no speaker. "C.P.T" ("colored people's time") rang like a cash register in every colored person's mind as light laughter erupted here and there among the whites. Whether Arthur Raper, Rupert Vance, or another Sociological Society officer was first to notice the paper pinned to the speakers' podium, no one can clearly recall. The nub of the note was to be recapitulated by Du Bois when he responded to Raper's abashed letter blaming the local arrangements committee. "I do not, of course, blame you but I think that if a scientific society advertising a meeting for 1:30 P.M. does not appear upon the scene until an hour later and has neither persons nor placards to explain the delay, that the speaker has a right to assume that his services are not needed."

The Carnegie Corporation president came to Sisters Chapel to give the second annual John Hope Lecture at the end of April. Keppel's presence was a coup for the Spelman president and an occasion during which good feelings flowed between Du Bois and Read. Their mutual comity was fleeting, however, even when it concerned the preserving of Hope's noble legacy of service. Du Bois had tentatively proposed writing Hope's biography when the Rosenwald

Fund invited him to apply for a research grant several months earlier. Lugenia Hope would be entirely supportive, but Read would "be aghast," Du Bois wrote Embree. Unless the fund were willing to indicate a preference, the AU trustees would defer to her wishes to find a well-known popularizer for a substantial sum. Although he was right about Read and the trustees, Du Bois misjudged the caliber of the future biographer. Ridgely Torrence's *The Story of John Hope* was to be a luminous recapturing of the man whom Du Bois described, in a moving review of the 1948 biography, as "probably my closest friend."

But the undeclared war intensified, and, as wars are won one objective at a time, Irene Diggs's salary served as the next objective. To Du Bois, the issue of Diggs's combined salary of eighteen hundred dollars as secretary to the department of sociology and secretary to the *Phylon* quarterly should have posed no complications whatsoever. To Clement, however, academic wages stopped at the end of the nine-month academic calendar year. June through August was a separate budget that Clement and Read expected to be negotiated to the penny. "The University will pay your secretary $1,350, at the rate of $150 for nine months," the president stipulated, but the $450 balance on Diggs's salary was to be drawn from the *Phylon* budget. Minutiae of significance to accountants only, Du Bois would pay Diggs's summer salary for work on the quarterly from whatever monies were available — Phelps-Stokes, Carnegie, *Phylon*, Rosenwald, personal — fully expecting to be reimbursed from AU funds.

Instead, he was to be overwhelmed by Clement's enfilade of questions, objections, dissemblings, and protestations. "I shall pay Miss Diggs the extra $200 from my own funds," Du Bois snorted in June to Banks after another haggle with the president. The dispute over three months' of summer salary would continue until 1943, when Diggs left AU to study anthropology at the University of Havana. Until her departure, every attempt at agreement dissolved in exasperated epistolary salvoes followed by self-righteous complaints about duplicity and bad faith. The last *Phylon* number for the year appeared in October, a success spoiled immediately by the university treasurer's refusal to increase the budget and more questions about Diggs's salary. Du Bois fired his heaviest artillery. On October 26, he spoke to Read in her office. He wished her to know that, after seven years as department chair, three books, a score of articles, and seventy-five major public lectures, he believed that he had fulfilled his part of the bargain, "and that John Hope would say so if he knew." His problems with *Phylon* and with the administration could be traced to a single source: Florence Read. Because of her influence, scholarship was undervalued at AU. Logan had left; Frank Snowden the classicist and three others had followed; Reid had intended to resign. But for "your determined opposition" the plan for a quarterly would have been approved before Hope died. Competent secretarial service was a key to his productivity. Either Read agreed to pay Diggs or he would take the matter to the trustees. "If anyone wished to cripple my future, they could best do it," said Du Bois pointedly, "by depriving me of this secretarial aid." Du Bois gave Clement a similar dressing down when the president came to the meeting of the *Phylon* editorial board. Surprised by Clement's seeming acquiescence, Du Bois enjoyed a few deceived days of victory, crowing to Banks that the president was a "cooing dove. What the devil is the matter with the man I really don't know." Clement's problem was Read, and by early December the Chinese water torture had resumed. Although Dean Sage had ducked his plea to intervene "except as a last resort," Du Bois insisted on presenting his case to the chairman of the board in person in New York. Sage received him at GEB headquarters on Friday afternoon, December 27, 1940, a few hours after Du Bois had presided over a panel at the meeting of the American Historical Association (AHA). "The war is over!" Du Bois exulted to Banks. Clement would have to agree to pay Diggs.

History at a historical association convention is made only very occasionally. As officers of the association, Progressive historians Howard K. Beale and Merle Curti had weighed in against decades of stasis in order to make the 1940 AHA meeting memorable for its attention to the "common man," Negroes, and women. When Du Bois introduced the fourth session, "The Negro in the History of the United States," at 9:30 A.M. on Friday, an expiatory ritual unfolded in the roof garden of Manhattan's McAlpin Hotel. The panel's presenters and discussants were racially balanced. Three Negroes: Charles Wesley; Rayford Logan; and Horace Mann Bond. Three whites: Alex Arnett; A. Ray Newsome; and Vernon Lane Wharton. It seemed afterward to some who were there that the meeting room palpitated with meaning and curiosity. Curti would recall his proud part in having engineered the "first session at which Negro and white historians took part in a discussion of interracial history" when he was elected AHA president fourteen years later. The tribute accorded Du Bois at its 1940 meeting was intended by Beale, Curti, and a caucus of "radicals" as a belated admission by the AHA that, but for racial prejudice, the author of *Black Reconstruction* would long since have enjoyed a place of honor. The symbolism of Du Bois presiding over the Negro panel was unmistakable: a major step in the demarginalizing of the history of one of America's oldest populations. Bond's new monograph, *Negro Education in Alabama: A Study in Cotton and Steel*, and Wharton's article on Mississippi supplied the kind of dense archival substratum that corroborated the biracial corruption claimed in Du Bois's impressionistic Reconstruction tour de force. Henceforth, the Dunning School of historiography would survive only on life support. For Howard University historian Marion Thompson Wright, the lone woman of color present, the session and the "splendid meeting" augured a new regime in the profession. Curti wrote Du Bois immediately to say that his appearance had been "a great compliment to us and we all appreciated it." But Marion Wright's optimism was sadly premature. Another thirty years would pass before black history and black historians burst the Eurocentric bubble encasing the mainstream historical professions.

Forty-nine Aframerican participants (a lone woman, Elsie Lewis, among them) and two whites from thirty-five institutions and organizations spent three days exploring economics and race at Du Bois's *Phylon* institute. Charles Johnson's absence signaled his intention not to play the major collaborative part once envisaged, although Preston Valien's attendance encouraged Du Bois to hope for continued contact between Atlanta and Fisk. Almost half the Negro land-grant colleges were represented at Atlanta, which Du Bois interpreted as propitious for yet another ambitious research initiative he was shortly to unveil. The presence of professors from Hampton and Tuskegee confirmed the declining relevance of the Washington–Du Bois controversy to serious race-relations analysis. Robert Weaver, now with the U.S. Office of Production Management, and the rising young Talented Tenth star William Trent, of the Federal Works Agency, along with an official of the Tennessee Valley Authority, contributed an essential federal cachet to the conference. A late-developing conflict at the Federal Security Agency in Washington where Reid was on special assignment had prevented him from attending, and official duties at Prairie View kept Banks away. "Notwithstanding these three blows," Du Bois put on a game face and claimed publicly that he considered the first *Phylon* institute a success. In raw numbers, attendance had been impressive, but he couldn't hide the obvious from the conferees—that Clement's absence was a vote of no confidence in the enterprise. Clement, who had forcefully expressed displeasure at not having been consulted in advance on the institute's agenda, charged the *Phylon* budget for the use of one hundred folding chairs for the conference. Had *The Nation* agreed to publish Du Bois's recapitulation of the institute's deliberations, the longish article would have broadcast the work in Atlanta to a wide, interested public. Unfortunately, editor Richard H. Rovere found the focus of the piece much too specific even after Du Bois sent in a second version.

Du Bois headed for Baltimore and Montebello Terrace in May, where the three women in his family life now resided, resolved to correct the unsatisfactory domestic regime of the previous summer. Yolande's eating habits and lack of exercise had piled on alarming layers of fat. But her father's correspondence had been especially reproachful about neglect of Baby Du Bois, now seven, and, still worse, Yolande's disposition to "punish her or speak sharply to her when you were impatient or disturbed." This must stop, he ordained, patriarchally conjuring up what he conceived to be the appropriate fix. Yolande must give her daughter a full hour every day of "personal companionship and intercourse." He would "arrange to give her another" himself and Nina a third hour or more. "With these three hours of purposeful contact," Du Bois assured his daughter of his reasonable confidence that they could "easily leave the rest to [Baby] Du Bois herself." His part in the hourly experiment was soon abridged, however.

A trip to Cuba with Diggs at the beginning of June seems to have been planned at the last moment. Although Du Bois informed *Amsterdam News* readers of an interest in the educational system of Cuba's Oriente province, met in Cuba with the undersecretary of communications and a group of government officials, and cited an interview with the superintendent of education ("a colored woman"), the real reason for the week on the island may have been to present Diggs to well-connected Cubans. Diggs had come to AU in 1928, earned the university's first sociology degree under Du Bois's direction five years later, and served him indispensably thereafter, deferring her own professional advancement year after year. Her application for a Rosenwald fellowship in 1939 had been declined, notwithstanding Du Bois's recommendation. Termination of the Phelps-Stokes salary subsidy and the niggardly conduct of Clement and Read were good reasons to begin looking after her own career. Given her decision to enter the University of Havana as a Roosevelt Fellow in the fall of 1943, it seems probable that Diggs went to Cuba with Du Bois as his secretary in summer of 1941 to set in motion a process that would permit her return as a doctoral candidate in anthropology. Their stay in Havana was certainly pleasant, but was less full than Du Bois would have wished. Apparently, plans to meet Nicolas Guillén, the famed mulatto poet who had been enchanted by Langston Hughes ten years earlier, were unrealized. The secretary to the president extended regrets that urgent matters of state precluded an interview. Ordering the Buick and a thermos of lemonade and cracked ice from the Hotel Casa Grande, Du Bois and Diggs left Santiago on June 18 for the ferry back to Key West. Four months later, he would return to Cuba under ACLS sponsorship to attend the Havana conference on intellectual cooperation.

Its budget capped at two thousand dollars, *Phylon* continued to appear. Editor-in-chief Du Bois was the animating mind behind the review, but, in contrast to *The Crisis*, *Phylon* was not the almost single-handed creature of its editor. Du Bois took charge of the "Chronicles of Race Relations" section, a social-science compendium of world developments of synoptic breadth. His imprint on "Books on Race" would generate a rich inventory of much of the best and most of the significant works dealing with the color line. But this time Du Bois was the conductor of a team, not the solo performer. Managing editor Reid, a Du Bois stalwart since Amenia and coconspirator in the campaign to save scholarship from Read and Clement, had returned on the eve of the magazine's debut from a term of postgraduate study at the London School of Economics after publication of *The Negro Immigrant, His Background, Characteristics, and Social Adjustment,* 1899–1937, a monograph solidly establishing his reputation as a major sociologist.

Unappreciated and confounded by his university administration, Du Bois was to be reminded regularly of the esteem he now enjoyed among white scholars. He was pleased to make a point of appearing to take for granted tokens of respect long withheld in obedience to the code of the color line. It was not uncommon, however, that the increasingly ceremonial respect paid by whites interfered with genuine appreciation of Du Bois's phenomenal intellect and experience. Whether or not he would have welcomed an invitation to contribute to *An American Dilemma,* the fact that Gunnar Myrdal, ignoring Keppel's suggestion, had declined to extend the offer, was a slight Du Bois had borne without comment. His relations with Myrdal had remained correct but distant. Until late summer of 1941, his only contact with the Carnegie-Myrdal study had come indirectly — mainly in letters from Ira Reid, who had developed a cordial relationship with the Swedish economist. As he struggled in his tower on the Dartmouth College campus during May and June to shape the enormous and variegated materials generated by a platoon of researchers, Myrdal experienced a bout of depression that alarmed Keppel and his staff. Truly shaken by the ambitiousness of his charge and longing for his wife, who was temporarily prevented from joining him because of the war, he became so depressed that he destroyed his first organizing draft and then succumbed to writer's block. Several weeks after returning from Cuba with Diggs, Du Bois received a letter from Myrdal inquiring about an obscure reference in *Dusk of Dawn* and asking for another opportunity for an extended discussion at a place of Du Bois's choosing. Du Bois's thoughts as he read Myrdal's revealing comment can be safely divined. "In this stage of my work," wrote the anxious scholar, "I think also that I have a better background for benefitting from a frank discussion with you." Unfortunately, for Myrdal, a second opportunity for a frank discussion never happened.

One year after participating in the proceedings of the AHA, Du Bois was denied the opportunity of attending another historical convention. The precedent set by the Negro panel presentation in New York and Du Bois's invitation from the Southern Sociological Society in Knoxville had forced the council of the Southern Historical Association (SHA) to take a position on the exclusion of Negroes at its meeting in Atlanta. Once again, Chapel Hill's Howard Beale led the charge to desegregate, the upshot of which was a compromise scarcely less insulting than the status quo ante. The management of Atlanta's grand Biltmore Hotel agreed to modify its racial ban to apply only to the public restaurants for the duration of the early November convention, but the devil was in the details worked out by the local arrangements committee. Fearful that

Georgia professors employed at state institutions would be dismissed for inter-racial eating by the redneck governor, Eugene Talmadge, the local white SHA membership "begged" Negro members to refrain from attending the associa-tion's luncheon and dinner meetings. Incensed, Beale mounted a symbolic pro-test by inviting Du Bois to breakfast or tea at the Biltmore, and suggested that Du Bois might bring along his junior associates, Clarence Bacote, in the AU history department, and the economist William Dean. Du Bois proposed, in-stead, that Beale and Vernon Wharton join him for tea in his graduate dormitory apartment. "Shall we say at four or four-thirty?" Beale ended up participating in a symbolic bonanza on a Friday afternoon, November 7, 1941. The revision of the Reconstruction era that had commenced with Du Bois in 1909 and that had been endorsed in "On Rewriting Reconstruction History," Beale's year-old *American Historical Review* article, paused importantly for congratulations and refreshments in an integrated space created by Du Bois (for white scholars on a Negro campus) before resuming its progress seven years later with Wharton's *The Negro in Mississippi, 1865–1900.* Du Bois resigned from the SHA three months later.

In spring 1942, Du Bois would deliver lengthy addresses to the student bod-ies of Vassar and Yale on, respectively, "The Future of Africa in America" and "The Future of Europe in Africa." Observing in the *Amsterdam News* that it was "always an adventure . . . to talk to white Students in a Northern institution," he headed for Poughkeepsie and New Haven. As always, there was historical context—the macrohistory of European depredations—to frame an exigent ra-tionale for building a better world. He found the contemporary Vassar much to his liking and took some small credit for having encouraged the admission of students of color. His speech began with signature directness. "One could hardly be born in America, North or South, and not subconsciously regard color and low social status as inevitably connected," Du Bois reminded these mostly wealthy young white women whose institution he had once described as the "leading college of Snobbery in the United States." He left his Vassar audience with more to think about than the usual chapel visitor, warning them that "we are only deceiving ourselves if we try to think that the solution of the problem of these millions of black folk in America is going to cost us nothing."

In New Haven the next day, April 23, he registered silent disapproval of Yale's jumbled Gothic exuberance and vocal pleasure in finding two cases of his own books on display in Sterling Library. He spoke to a class in the morning and put to the men the question asked of him by a Vassar student: "Well, what can I do about it?"—meaning the race problem. After dinner with members of the faculty, he foretold "The Future of Europe in Africa" in the lounge of the graduate school. With Rommel's Afrika Korps driving for Cairo and British defenses in Burma crumbling before the Japanese, Du Bois stated as a certainty that the Allies would "in the end crush and conquer both Germany, Italy, and Japan, especially if Russia continues to cooperate." The question of the hour, then, was not whether the United States and Great Britain would win the war, but what was the "object of the Anglo-Saxon world" in Asia and Africa? To that end, Du Bois enumerated some dozen postwar recommendations of the Committee of Forty, a nongovernmental body of British and American public figures and academics he had recently joined. Highminded and normative, several of them echoed the principles of the Pan-African Congress, stressing cultural interchange, economic development instead of exploitation, and evolving participation of Africans in government.

He left New Haven for New York, where Davis DuBois, emotionally restored after her retreat to Havana, had promised "much of the weekend for you." They saw *Porgy and Bess* Friday night and went to the circus together on Saturday afternoon. Whatever moral judgments it may have deserved, their relationship was continually self-renewing and mutually stimulating. Enjoying himself in Manhattan with Davis DuBois, he was also troubled in the compartment of his mind reserved for Virginia Alexander, who lay near death in Philadelphia. The chronic condition that struck her while earning her master's degree in public health at Yale had been diagnosed as lupus in 1938 at the University of Pennsylvania Medical School. The illness had pounded on her physical constitution repeatedly, leading to several prolonged hospital stays. The worst had struck in late March 1942, when she survived a fourteen-day struggle aggravated by pneumonia, septicemia, and severe anaemia. Du Bois gave Nina a full, disheartened report on her condition.

Always restless, he felt an almost desperate need at this time to find a means of stimulating and guiding long-range thinking about the predicament of the race. "We can only save the world and ourselves," he had written soon after the *Phylon* Institute, "if we use our knowledge, our brains, and our efforts to begin the planning of a new civilization such as will serve the needs rather than the whims of men." Shortly before returning to campus for the fall semester, 1942, Du Bois received an invitation from Morehouse president Benjamin Mays to attend a conference on interracial cooperation in Durham, North Carolina, on October 20. Mays seems to have counted on Du Bois's involvement as a balancing element in what was likely to be a distinctly conservative congregation. The principal conference conveners he identified as Gordon Blaine Hancock of Virginia Union University, P. B. Young, publisher of the Norfolk *Journal and Guide*, and J. M. Ellison, Virginia Union's president. "P. B." (Plummer Bernard) Young was a highly successful Virginia businessman cut from the cloth of Robert Vann. A stern, no-nonsense race leader who placed his *Journal and Guide* at the service of the New Deal in 1936, Young never wavered in his personal conviction that business solutions were best. Sociology professor Hancock was accustomed to being taken seriously in Richmond by the prominent of both races. Articulate and racially conservative, he had espoused a "Hold-Your-Job" campaign during the late 1920s that called for deferring civil rights demands until better times. Jesse Daniel Ames, founder and executive director of the Association of Southern Women for the Prevention of Lynching (ASWPL), publicized her approval of the editorial that the evidence strongly suggests she had suggested to Hancock in the first place. Virginius Dabney of Richmond's *Times-Dispatch* and author of *Liberalism in the South* (a book whose title many Negro progressives thought an oxymoron) found Hancock's a heaven-sent voice in the galimatias of the Ku Klux Klan and the NAACP.

Not quite a month after the Mays invitation, Hancock wrote Du Bois expressing his "deep appreciation of your support." He assured him that the conference intended to rely heavily on Du Bois's wisdom "to help us accomplish something worthwhile." On the other hand, no representation outside the South was thought desirable, wrote Hancock, lest it be said "that our meeting was packed with 'northern radicals.' " For good measure, no one officially connected to the NAACP was invited. *"The main objective,"* as stated in Hancock's italics, *"is for Negroes of the South to set forth . . . what they regard as the essentials of interracial amity and concord in the post-war world."* Du Bois could hardly have been surprised by Hancock's implication that the presence of a founder of the NAACP and the founding editor of *The Crisis* at Durham would be an embarrassment. When the fifty men and seven women gathered in conference on the campus of North Carolina Agricultural and Technical Institute in October, he was predictably absent.

The results were "A Basis for Interracial Cooperation and Development in the South: A Statement by southern Negroes." Released to the public on December 15, the historic document was both highminded and evasive, and elided, at the same time, the cardinal issue of the times—racial segregation. Mays alone had urged a forthright statement calling for the abolition of legal segregation in American society, but the "pragmatic" views of the conveners had easily prevailed. "We recognize the strength and age of these patterns [of segregation]," the preamble conceded.

> We are fundamentally opposed to the principle and practice of compulsory segregation in our American society, whether of races or classes or creeds; however, we regard it as both sensible and timely to address ourselves now to the current problems of racial discrimination and neglect, and to ways in which we may cooperate in the advancement of programs aimed at the sound improvement of race relations within the democratic framework.

The Durham Manifesto posed a problem for Du Bois. Had not his stated reason for leaving the NAACP involved his controversial stance on segregation? Since his dramatic exit almost a decade past, had he not filled innumerable columns of print with the dialectics of separate, cooperatist development? Seldom did he miss an opportunity to challenge his people—faced with dusk-to-dawn reality of Jim Crow—to plan, organize, mobilize, and economize so as to make segregation work for them? Why had the message of Gordon Blaine Hancock and Jessie Daniel Ames failed to satisfy him? And why would the blacks and whites who had sworn to work together over the next months to build an improved race-relations vehicle not find him by their side—in spirit if not in person?

Du Bois offered measured answers. His had been a formula for unremitting opposition to segregation even while optimizing the resources found within American apartheid. In his mind he was utterly clear about the distinction between accommodation and resistance, between a politics of cooptation and one of cooperation. Notwithstanding Mays's dissatisfaction with the final statement and sincere expressions by Johnson, Bond, and others that Durham represented a significant breach in the wall of Jim Crow, Du Bois would announce in *Phylon* two years later that it had created a "new dichotomy in the statement of belief in race relations." The dichotomy was not in the statement itself, however, so much as it was in how it had come about. Without immediately saying so publicly, Du Bois understood Hancock's Durham Manifesto as a well-orchestrated reprise of Washington's Atlanta Compromise. He believed he saw at the drafters' elbows agents of the same class of white paternalists (and at least one maternalist) who had ventriloquized the Great Accommodator a half century earlier. To some of these soi-disant southern liberals, even ultraconservative Gordon Hancock seemed too inclined to forget his race's place. Exceptions noted, their objective was to extend the life of segregation by convincing Negro leaders that the best white folk were finally ready to work with them for the achievement of equality—separately. The silent South's Jessie Daniel Ames, Virginius Dabney, Mark Ethridge, Ralph McGill, and Howard Odum welcomed the moderate spirit of the manifesto and pledged to ratify it when they met as a representative group in Atlanta in April 1943. Ratified in Atlanta, the next carefully scripted step was to be another Richmond meeting in June—this one composed equally of thirty-seven whites and Negroes—from which a new organization of well-meaning whites and blacks would emerge as the Southern Regional Council (SRC) to supplant the stale, tired Commission of Interracial Cooperation.

April 1943 was also the month in which Du Bois hoped to realize a long-planned breakthrough in scholarship at AU By the fall of 1942, he had devised a strategy to overcome opposition in Atlanta through higher-education politics, regional publicity, and a unique source of funding. On several occasions, he had been a guest at the annual convention of the Conference of the Presidents of Negro Land Grant Colleges, an association of seventeen public institutions founded as a result of the Morrill Act of 1862. Telltale alphabetical cabooses identified the colleges as state-supported institutions restricted to Negroes: Florida A&M; North Carolina A&T, Tennessee A&I, and so forth. Affiliated in associate status were the presidents of Hampton, Howard, and Tuskegee and the heads of two vocational academies. In all, they were twenty male college presidents, a compound of ego and testosterone as fissionable as uranium-232. Ensconced and subsidized in houses grand enough yet carefully scaled below the envy-anger thresholds of local white hoi polloi, presiding over generally docile faculties fixed in place by segregation irrespective of ability, sustaining an *in loco parentis* control over students who were mostly neither poor enough nor sufficiently affluent to find rebelliousness appealing, the Dr. Bledsoes of the Tuskhamptons and Fiskadegas answered only to trustees rarely concerned by more than budgets and behavior. College presidents were emperors. Serious cooperation was not their strong suit, but, because Willette Banks of Prairie View College was president of the conference of land-grant presidents, Du Bois had been surprisingly successful in gaining and retaining the attention of these educational generalissimos.

At the 1941 convention in Chicago, where a majority voted his appointment to an exploratory committee, and again, in October 1942, when the committee's report was overwhelmingly approved, Banks and his land-grant colleagues were enkindled by a Du Boisian concept of intellectual self-help. Forty years since the publication of *The Souls of Black Folk*, mere pennies had come from the great foundations for the sophisticated study of the Negro and race relations. The Atlanta University Studies had expired for want of a transfusion. The "Encyclopedia of the Negro" had become another scholar's opportunity. The college presidents had the opportunity to support the social-science research by Negroes about Negroes that the white foundations had shown such chronic reluctance to underwrite. To have succeeded in corralling the land-grant-college presidents to assist in launching a permanent apparatus for the collection, assessment, formulation, and dissemination of knowledge pertaining to all aspects of race in the Americas and abroad represented one of Du Bois's most uncommon triumphs. Their loyalty to him was to prove quite remarkable, strengthened, certainly, by the possibility of increased funding from the federal governent in support of educational outreach programs. But unresolved was the question of the research project's institutional affiliation. As chair of the coordinating committee of five presidents established at the October 1942 meeting, Du Bois reported his success to Clement with the expectation that AU's role as host institution would be duly ratified by the trustees. But Clement had procrastinated, declining to present the matter to the trustees until confronted with the final November 1942 decision of the land-grant presidents. Only then had Du Bois won Clement's promise of a thousand-dollar appropriation and been authorized to plan for the first scholarly conference sponsored by the Negro land-grant presidents, set to meet on April 19–20, 1943.

Du Bois's letter to Jackson Davis on April 14, 1943, narrated blow-by-blow an anguishing struggle to save his research scheme. Eight leading sociologists who had agreed to attend were listed in the letter to Davis: Howard Odum of the University of North Carolina; Charles Johnson of Fisk; T. Lynn Smith of Louisiana State University; William Cole of the University of Tennessee; Donald Young of the Social Science Research Council; E. B. Reuter of the University of Iowa; Edgar Thompson of Duke University; and E. Franklin Frazier of the Library of Congress. But now Du Bois came to the point of the letter. Seventeen days before the conference, Du Bois wrote, "the president of Atlanta University decided that the thousand [dollars] could not be spent except under certain conditions over which I had no control." In response to his frantic appeal, Embree had saved the day, promising by return mail to cover the "modest overhead of this undertaking up to a sum not exceeding $1,000." If ever he had needed the authority and philanthropy of the GEB it was now. As always, Davis thought well of Du Bois's undertaking, although he did wonder whether the "machinery" required to enlist "all of the institutions in a general coordinated plan" might not prove too cumbersome. He invited Du Bois to discuss the scheme when he came to New York after the conference, and expressed regrets that no one from the board was available at such late notice to attend the conference as Du Bois had hoped.

The first scholarly meeting held by the Negro land-grant presidents was officially designated as the twenty-sixth Atlanta University Conference. Thirty-four participants representing thirty-one institutions spent two full days in discussion of papers and reports and in task-force deliberations on the Morehouse campus. Clement, who was in a particularly self-important mood in the wake of the Atlanta meeting of prominent whites to ratify the Durham Manifesto, had raised last-minute objections with Du Bois about the use of the AU library. Putting the president out of his mind, Du Bois savored a triumph. Odum, the South's leading white sociologist, as liberal on race as was compatible with the doctrine of states' rights and separate equality, came to lend his blessings to the land-grant colleges, offering, in his folksy manner, that they had "a fine opportunity to combine the social studies with the physical sciences and to implement them in practical programs." Most of the land-grant presidents experienced these two days of serious intellectual exchange and interracial comity as flatteringly unfamiliar phenomena. They were used to taking themselves seriously, but to be taken seriously by some of the most distinguished contemporary thinkers of both races was evidence of importance sufficient to impress their own trustees. They adjourned, resolved to return the following year, there to address Du Bois's charge: a broad examination of the economic situation of the Negro "during and after the present war. There is going to be increased race friction" and systemic unemployment in the near future, Du Bois stated at the close of the conference. "There will be neither time nor disposition during times of turmoil to initiate new and calm investigation." Six weeks later, an altercation between a policeman and a soldier ignited Harlem, although the death toll of six blacks and loss of some $5 million worth of property paled in comparison to the Detroit riot. Two months later, on June 20, 1943, a fistfight between a black man and a white man served as the excuse for an eruption in Detroit in which twenty-five Negroes and nine Caucasians died after thirty hours of rioting that took six thousand soldiers to quell and left several hundred million dollars' worth of property destroyed in one of the worst racial conflagrations in American history.

In July 1943 Du Bois called at 61 Broadway to make the case for an appropriation and to supplement his occasional critiques of Clement and Read with a forceful warning of possible sabotage of the successfully launched land-grant research operation. Expressing his conviction to Davis that the South had a "great opportunity to lead the world in race relations," Du Bois regretted the necessity of having to work with a president who seemed incapable of appreciating the great opportunity facing the university. Davis said nothing to Du Bois about Clement's complaint two months earlier that Du Bois had become extremely difficult after the trustees declined to fund the land-grant conference. Clement had suggested that Du Bois's age was affecting him and that Ira Reid had long carried the load of the sociology department. "He hopes that Du Bois will retire at the end of next year," Davis minuted. But Clement intended to do more than rest on a hope. Regulations governing rank and tenure at AU had been adopted in 1939 along with a pension program and compulsory retirement at sixty-five. Du Bois's contract had then been renewed for five years by action of the trustees. On November 23, 1943, immediately after an executive committee meeting of the trustees in New York, Clement struck. "In accordance with the tenure and retirement provisions which the board has adopted," the president informed Du Bois that he would be retired "from the active faculty of Atlanta University when your present contract expires on June 30, 1944." A special committee had been appointed to consider "what, if any, financial provisions" would be forthcoming upon his retirement. "The result of this action was disastrous; not merely to me but to the American Negro," Du Bois wrote in *The Autobiography*. "Not only was a great plan of scientific work killed at birth, but my own life was thrown into confusion." There had never been any ambiguity about the special status of his AU tenure, he protested, as he "fought back in despair" against his elimination. He had been sixty-five when he joined

Hope at the university and had come with the understanding that he would work until age or disability required him to stop.

Du Bois counted on a groundswell of public outrage after news of his retirement became widely known, especially as it appeared that he was being turned out to pasture without a dollar from the university. His strategy was to proceed as if Clement's formal notification had never been sent. Christmas week of 1943, one month after Clement's bombshell, Henry Canby, secretary of the National Institute of Arts and Letters, informed Du Bois of his election as a member in the department of literature. It was an accolade of unprecedented mainstream validation. Right on! Ira Reid exclaimed, "you've crashed another barrier for merit and us." After seventy years of solitary struggle, Du Bois remarked to Ridgely Torrence that he might have been tempted to follow in the steps of Upton Sinclair and tread "the rest of the way alone" without the benefit of the Institute of Arts and Letters. "But I am not an individual, I am a group," he decreed, "and the group must say yes very humbly."

As the late April date for the meeting in Atlanta of the full university board approached, the Negro press took notice. Shaping the facts somewhat to meet the predicament, Du Bois informed the concerned and the curious that he had been sacked without a word of warning—"without the chance to prepare a successor, without time to reshape or meet the emergencies," as in a typical explanation written to Shirley Graham. He let it become known that his fifteen-thousand-dollar life-insurance policy had been wiped out in the Depression. He owed three thousand dollars on the Montebello Terrace home, and had five thousand in savings. The former president and the incumbent president of the Atlanta University alumni association joined the chairman of the board of trustees of the AU School of Social Work in a letter to Embree deploring the national "adverse reaction which will come to the University." Louis T. Wright, now chair of the NAACP board of directors, advised trustee Kendall Weisiger of grave repercussions if Du Bois were not given a fair hearing. "On the whole," offered Wright, the retirement decision was a "bizarre mistake." Melville Herskovits expressed keen distress at the apparent lack of charity on the part of the trustees and intimated that the American Association of University Professors (AAUP) ought to launch an inquiry. Yet although there were loud voices raised in protest against the enforced retirement, most of the clamor was caused by the failure to promise Du Bois a pension. Off the record, Du Bois himself had admitted to a friend in Seattle that if he were retired "on a decent pension, I see no hindrance."

The trustees voted his retirement as professor emeritus, effective June 30. Will Alexander and Willette Banks had gone to the meeting determined to lift the stigma of vindictiveness from the institution by providing Du Bois with an adequate pension. The new emeritus professor was awarded a year's salary of

$4,500, annual compensation of $1,800 for five years, and $1,200 thereafter until his demise. The seventy-six-year-old retiree wrote Trevor Arnett, now serving as AU board chairman, in vigorous protest of the statement entered into the minutes of the board that the 1939 contract had been signed with the under-standing that it was not subject to renewal. Arnett's final words were simply to state that as far as he was concerned "the said five-year appointment should be and was to be the final one." The potentially explosive situation had been largely defused, although minor backfires continued. Students at Morehouse, Spelman, Clark, and AU wrote a joint letter of reproach to President Clement for aspersive remarks about Du Bois's teaching that were quoted by the *Afro-American*. "Our regret," said these students, "is that we did not have more courses under him and [that] the students who follow us will not have the opportunity which we have had in absorbing his rich experience and inspiration."

Louise Shivery read Du Bois's adieu to the A.U. alumni association with composed emotion. He had hoped to finish his life at the university, he said through her. "There was no earthly reason why this wish of mine should not have been granted and applauded." The men and women present were, in a sense, "children of my efforts to make straight the Way of the Lord," Shivery continued. He laid on their shoulders the hard duty "of making this institution a real university, which it is not today." A few weeks earlier, a philosophical Arthur Spingarn had done his best to calm a deeply agitated visitor to his office. "He's buried himself in the South too long," the NAACP president told Shirley Graham, "battering his life out against ignorance, bigotry, intolerance and sloth-fulness, projecting ideas nobody but he understands, and raising hopes for change which may be comprehended in a hundred years."

· 14 ·

AGAINST THE GRAIN:

FROM THE NAACP TO THE FAR LEFT

Pensioned at seventy-five, for the first time in his life Du Bois experienced a momentary sensation of uselessness. Not quite two years after the enforced retirement from Atlanta University he would reflect upon the rewards dealt him according to some Gresham's Law governing vision and intellectual integrity. He had, he believed, "launched a program which was destined to settle the Negro problem."

> It was no pat, quick panacea. It called for hard work and time; the work of laboriously and with infinite care searching out the facts of the tangled situation, interpreting them by the most careful methods and then doing the same thing again, decade by decade, century by century. It was an absolutely correct scientific procedure, fool-proof and called simply for time and work. In one respect alone was it vulnerable, and that was whether the world would allow it to be done. . . . I seemed to have inexhaustible strength and eagerness for my task. But I misinterpreted the age in which I lived. I knew that men were selfish, even cruel; thoughtless and lazy. But I assumed that the ruling classes of earth wanted the right and followed the light once they saw it.

Of course, Du Bois had long since known objectively that the last thing "ruling classes" wanted was truth at the price of genuine democracy, but the bitter musings betrayed the nacre of idealism at his core, that hard essence enabling him to believe at the most submerged level of his psyche in the perfectability of the species. For an agonizing fortnight or so, the decision of Atlanta's trustees appeared to extinguish what was left of a productive old age. He saw himself consigned to twilight years of occasional speeches, annual commemorations, grandfatherly dotings in Baltimore, and retouched memoirs. The world, he said, was "tottering beneath [his] feet." Then his bleak mood passed quickly, after all.

Offers from Fisk and Howard were forthcoming. Driving to Baltimore from Atlanta, Du Bois's stopover at the home of the president of North Carolina College For Negroes resulted in a tempting proposal to relocate to Durham. The president had in mind a new research journal backed by the prestige of Du Bois and assisted by a young history professor at nearby St. Augustine College who was writing a Harvard doctoral dissertation. "My appointment was within the hour!" recalled John Hope Franklin of his exhilarating encounter with his idol. But as he piloted the trusty Buick north, another employment offer, unforeseen and exciting, turned over in Du Bois's mind. Nina had been happy to learn that he would "stop off to see us," but he would tarry at Montebello Terrace not quite a month before heading for Harlem and the majestic Hotel Theresa to confer with a specially appointed, five-member NAACP committee.

In the ten years since Du Bois's resignation, the NAACP had grown into a national powerhouse, an organization commanding the loyalty of 325,000 members in 893 branches distributed across the United States and still expanding by the month. The income had quadrupled; the staff had tripled. "The results astonished me," Du Bois admitted, as he informed himself of the state of the organization he had helped to found and which Walter White now commanded with a military efficiency that was becoming famous. Mary Ovington, devoting herself to writing and appearing at 69 Fifth Avenue only occasionally, regretted that board meetings ran like clockwork these days because all the decisions were rubber-stamped. Jovial Arthur Spingarn had relinquished the chairmanship of the Legal Committee to ascend to the honorific of association president after his brother's death in 1939. William Hastie, his successor and now dean of Howard's law school, had presided over the transformation of the old legal committee into the Legal Defense and Educational Fund, the LDF or "Inc. Fund," an unevenly talented team of young lawyers led by hard-driving, hard-drinking, thirty-six-year-old Thurgood Marshall. Although crippled by the Depression, more than enough of Nathan Margold's no-holds-barred plan of attack on *Plessy v. Ferguson* had been salvaged by Charles Houston during his four years as chief association counsel from 1935 to 1939 (with Marshall as apprentice) to confound attorneys general from Maryland to Texas. In April 1944, three months prior to Du Bois's serious negotiations with the special NAACP committee, Marshall and Hastie had prevailed before the U.S. Supreme Court in *Smith v. Allwright*, an historic eight-to-one decision outlawing the "white" Democratic Party primary in Texas.

Du Bois's return to the NAACP was a public-relations coup for Walter White and a fitting gesture of comradeship on the part of Arthur Spingarn and Louis Wright. Wright and Spingarn thought that the old lion was owed a well-salaried repose in his declining years. "They assumed with some others that at seventy-five my life work was done," Du Bois claimed—and that he would settle comfortably into the margins and say "a proper word now and then and give the association and its secretary moral support." Exactly Walter White's reading of the arrangement.

Whether, as he wrote later, Wright and Spingarn had really expected that he would do little more than coast through the remaining years at the association, once installed at 69 Fifth Avenue as director of the Department of Special Research, Du Bois set a pace that would have been envied by the youngest staffer and that astonished the secretary and the board of directors. Age-defying productivity had its secrets, though. Shirley Graham, who resigned from NAACP employment to work for a famous New York novelist and Communist Party member only a few months before Du Bois's return, had taken charge of his domestic affairs. She secured a place for Du Bois on "Sugar Hill" in the most prestigious apartment building in Harlem. Apartment 13-H, a one-bedroom unit atop 409 Edgecombe Avenue, awaited his signature upon arrival. Hugh Smythe, as efficient as Logan and more congenial, was periodically available for research assignments while completing requirements for his sociology doctorate at Northwestern. Diggs, of course, had been constantly at Du Bois's side but for the nine months at the University of Havana. As was his singular style then, he pursued multiple objectives simultaneously, a feat of parallel concentration that differed markedly from the compartmentalized activities typical of the organizational leviathan shaped by Walter White over a fifteen-year period.

Another marked contrast to DuBois's accustomed work environment were the decibel levels acceptable to some of the association officers and staff members.

More than two months after taking up duties and in breach of the employment agreement, he and Diggs were still confined to a single office, eight feet wide, "separated by thin board partition from two of the busiest and noisiest offices in the building," Du Bois complained to White repeatedly. It was soon the common secret of the secretaries on the third floor that Dr. Du Bois suffered his neighbor on the other side of the partition with a stoic forbearance that seemed almost audible in its grim-lipped silence. Thurgood Marshall had his own version of moot court, office manager Bobbie Branch recalled. "He would surround himself with the best minds in the country, and he would throw questions at them." Legal cases were briefed in what often sounded like Saturday night in a cabaret. Telephone conversations intruded word for word, like it or not, and the repercussions from barnyard expletives and raucous laughter ceased only temporarily in response to polite tapping. Du Bois considered Marshall's unbuttoned office manners to be outstandingly bad. Deprived of the use of five of his file cabinets, a thousand of his books still uncrated, and the office partition constantly vibrating.

He delivered an ultimatum. White's response, not a moment too soon, was to surrender his own office to the director of special research until his return from a second trip to the war front as a *New York Post* correspondent.

Du Bois had set about resuscitating the pan-African movement before leaving Atlanta. In the final weeks at A.U., he began to assemble a coalition to sponsor the Fifth Pan-African Congress to be convened in Paris, Dakar, or Liberia six months after the surrender of Japan. One respondent was none other than Amy Jacques Garvey, widow of the UNIA founder. Barred from returning to the United States and convinced that he was too much the world-figure for little Jamaica, Marcus Garvey had emigrated to London, where, his fortunes increasingly dimming, he was to die five years later in obscurity after a second stroke in January 1940. Amy Jacques Garvey expedited one felicitous letter after another enjoining Du Bois to take the lead in framing an African Freedom Charter to complement the Atlantic Charter, to which he responded graciously and with genuine interest. She put him in contact with Harold A. Moody, founding president of the League of Coloured Peoples, a prominent London physician from Jamaica whose series of racial firsts included chairmanship of the Colonial Missionary Society and president of the London Christian Endeavor Federation. Paul Robeson, in his capacity as president of the Council of African Affairs (CAA), along with the versatile Max Yergan, executive director of the council and principal adviser to Robeson, also endorsed the conclave proposal. Mrs. Bethune responded positively on behalf of the National Council of Negro Women (NCNW).

Pan-African Congresses had never quite caught on with the NAACP board of directors when Du Bois had launched them after World War I. A quarter-century later, though, an ethos of internationalism and democratic idealism, albeit broader than it was deep, favored the congress. Pressed to act and to leave him to do the thinking, the board assented to Du Bois's motion to establish a Committee on the Pan-African Congress with gratifying speed. At their well-attended meeting in early October 1944, Justice Charles Toney, Louis Wright, dependable Lillian Alexander, John Hayne Holmes, Chairman Hastie, confrontational Mrs. Lillie May Jackson from Baltimore, and several others were given a wide-ranging tutorial on Africa, colonialism, and the imperatives of the peace by Du Bois. A significant exception to the general enthusiasm, however, was Thurgood Marshall, who kept his own counsel for the time being, despite a conviction that Du Bois's congress was irrelevant to the the battle against segregation—as did Roy Wilkins, who seems to have regarded the former *Crisis* editor as an unaffordable luxury.

The next step had been to bring various representatives of anticolonialist groups together at the Schomburg Library in Harlem for a pan-African workshop on April 6, 1945. Langston Hughes thought the meeting's purpose was "excellent," as did Negro state assemblyman and future Manhattan borough president Hulan Jack, but conflicting schedules would prevent both from attending. Ralph Bunche, on leave from Howard with the State Department's Postwar Planning Unit, found the scheme "very interesting" and suggested several strategic contacts, but wondered about Du Bois's narrow time margin. Harry Emerson Fosdick, the enormously popular and famously liberal pastor emeritus of Manhattan's interdenominational Riverside Church, replied to the invitation with an affected and insulting innocence. "Evidently, the word 'colonies' in your title and in your letter has some special connotation, whose significance I cannot even guess at," the author of *On Being a Real Person* and a half dozen books of moral improvement smirked. Hurrying to chair his ambitiously labeled international colonial conference, Du Bois sent a complete list of colonial possessions so that the celebrity divine might realize that "seven hundred and fifty million people on this earth live in colonies and have rights to which no white nation is bound to respect." Another celebrity man of God was also puzzled by the purpose of pan-Africanism. Invited to contribute to a jubilee edition in honor of the world-famous medical missionary Albert Schweitzer, Du Bois had written a well-considered, severe appreciation of the multitalented Swiss physician, musician, and philosopher, much of whose life had been spent in French Equatorial Africa. "With all this," Du Bois judged that Schweitzer had no "broad grasp of what modern exploitation means, of what imperial colonialism has done to the world. If he had, he probably would have tried to heal the souls of white Europe rather than the bodies of black Africa." From his hospital station in Lambarené, the missionary sent a well-tempered letter regretting that he and Du Bois could not discuss their different visions of African possibilities face-to-face. "What will be the final result of this evolution? What will it contribute to the moral development of the natives and to the development of an organization leading to progress?" Schweitzer confessed he had no clear answer. Du Bois replied: "The great difficulty is that most white men do not believe in the humanity and ability of the black race."

Francis Nkrumah, who would need to reintroduce himself to Du Bois when they met again more than a year later, attended and actively participated in the daylong Schomburg meeting. The conference declaration called for a democratic China, a free Korea, independence for India and Burma, dominion status for the Gold Coast and Nigeria, and the end of exclusive white rule in Kenya and Rhodesia. Italy would surrender its North African conquests and the territory seized from Ethiopia; Japan would cede Formosa to China. For the time being, the "representative" civil rights leaders were on board Du Bois's pan-African express as it picked up considerably more speed throughout the year, although a final vote by the NAACP board was yet to be taken. From London came an enthusiastic pledge of cooperation from Harold Moody's League of Coloured Peoples—with a caveat about the cost of the enterprise. From Manchester, England, an unreckoned compass point, Du Bois received news that the colored leaders of the General Council of the Trades Union Congress (GCTUC) had proposed a September 1945 colonial conference to coincide with the World Trade Union Conference (WTUC) in Paris. The colored labor leaders desired to coordinate their efforts with Du Bois's. But even more unanticipated was the *Defender*'s publication of a "Manifesto to the United Nations," also summoning a meeting of pan-Africanists in Paris to coincide with the WTUC.

George Padmore had become the engine driving this loose assemblage of trade unionists, student radicals, African nationalists, and Caribbean militants. Du Bois remembered the publicized controversy of Padmore's dismissal as head of the American Communist Party's International Trade Union Committee of Negro Workers and expulsion from the party in 1934. One of the CPUSA's most promising intellectuals, Padmore (a.k.a. Malcolm Nurse) had concluded that the shifting priorities of the USSR forced him to choose between conformity to the Comintern and the cause of colonial liberation. His present importance in anti-imperialist circles in the United Kingdom came as a surprise to Du Bois, but was a significant marker also of generational turnover. Reminding the young Trinidadian journalist and lapsed Communist that the pan-African idea had more than forty years of history behind it—much of that history created by himself—Du Bois questioned the logic of Padmore and the coordinating committee's manifesto: "In other words, the definitive statement should come after the congress, and not before." Above all, Paris ought not to be the venue of choice for the congress. "We should meet this time in Africa," Du Bois now insisted. "This seems to me of the greatest importance." Padmore's three-page typewritten response to Du Bois by return mail was intelligently detailed, masterfully deferential, and came just as the head of the Canadian branch of the World Trade Union Conference in Montreal telephoned Du Bois to urge a Paris pan-African meeting. Paris in September it must be after all, Du Bois wrote Padmore, and he fully expected the NAACP to assume "a considerable part of the expense of the meeting."

Through the good offices of Jean de la Roche, director of the French Press and Information Service in New York, prospects for such a meeting seemed promising. As Du Bois informed the French officials, not only would the auspices of France be historically fitting but there were realistic grounds to foresee the pan-African movement gaining political influence under the liberal program of Charles De Gaulle. Had not a black man, Felix Eboué, governor of Equatorial Africa, been the first senior administrator to defy the Vichy regime and rally his people to Free France in the darkest hour of republican defeat? In France reborn, Du Bois declared with calculated overstatement, he divined the "solution for the problem of colonies and the development of black folk in the modern world." It soon became obvious that permission to hold the Pan-African Congress in Paris immediately after the war was less problematic than the complications of a timely return of the delegates to the United States, given the priority transportation accorded several million American fighting men and women once the Germans capitulated. Turning to concentrate on the myriad proposals and resolutions pertaining to the peace generated by what were soon to be known as NGOs (non-governmental organizations), Du Bois decided not to rush into the Paris option. He would depart for California without writing further to Padmore and his coordinating committee until his return.

THE UNITED NATIONS conference in San Francisco was to be the cradle of a new world order. Henry Luce had baptized the coming age the American Century. Although Du Bois would ask the magazine colossus at the end of 1945 for "a little of [his] time" to discuss the relationship of Africa to the post-industrial world, Luce was adamantly uninterested. The two men could not have been more dissimilar, the Great Barrington scholarship prodigy and self-created race leader and the Anglo-Protestant, multimillionaire son of China missionaries. In one crucial respect, however, Du Bois and Luce, although temperamentally and politically antipathetic, were alike. Both were men of Promethean vision who were supremely confident of their ability to divine those rare, irrecoverable intervals during which the speed and direction of history could be altered. Nineteen-forty-five, like 1919, was such an interval, a break in the flow of the past that allowed for the possibility of creating new world-systems. For the Luces of what was to emerge with remarkable speed as the military-industrial-and-communications complex, the goal was the Monroe Doctrine extended to the rest of the planet. For Du Bois, the prospect of the shattered colonial empires of Britain and France being shored up by a North American colossus whose laws abided racial subjugation was almost beyond enduring. "In this war even more than in the last," he contended in *Color and Democracy*, his aptly titled new book, "we face the problem of democracy. How far are we working for a world where the peoples who are ruled are going to have effective voice in their governments?" Wendell Wilkie and Henry Wallace, FDR's abandoned vice president, inspired cautious optimism in the director of special research that men and women of power and prestige could be counted to speak out and to coalesce in numbers large enough to save the peace. The year after *Time* magazine announced the American Century, Wallace had proclaimed in a speech to the Free World Association that the twentieth century would be the "century of the common man."

But the odds were already running against Du Bois that the guarantees of the Atlantic Charter and the imperatives of the Four Freedoms would be formally honored in the parliament of nations about to convene three thousand miles away. A foretaste of white insensitivity appeared in the circular letter released in February 1945 by the influential Commission to Study the Organization of Peace, among whose members were Roger Baldwin, John Foster Dulles, Merle Curti, Max Lerner, Owen Lattimore, Virginia Gildersleve, Philip Jessup, and Claude Pepper. Greatly "disturbed" by its language, Du Bois pleaded by letter with commission executive director Clark Eichelberger to alter the "usual sop to capitalistic investment," to tighten up the distinction between "dependent territories" occupied by the Axis and those of the "great empires," and to amend the proposed "regional commissions" to include "representation . . . of non-governing colonial peoples themselves." The problem with the commission's document (as with most of the well-intentioned world-government formulations involving the rights of subject populations) was that it "combine[d] the interest in colonial peoples with interest in imperial objects and is too strongly weighted on the side of imperialism." He had shared similar concerns in late 1944 with Joseph Proskauer about the American Jewish Committee's "Declaration of Human Rights," a six-point statement that "greatly disappointed" by its failure to mention Africans and Asians "being deprived of rights." How appropriate was it, he asked, to call a document "very easily understood [as a] declaration of Jewish rights [having] apparently no thought of the rights of Negroes, Indians, and South Sea Islanders," a declaration of human rights? Having recently denounced the persecution of European Jewry as the "supertragedy" of European civilization in the *American Journal of Sociology* (after repeatedly addressing it as a scandal in the *Amsterdam News*), Du Bois believed he would be received by American Jewish leadership as a friendly critic.

What he perceived as the myopia of the liberal internationalists and the self-referential concerns of Jewish organizations paled in significance beside the ominous blueprint for the postwar that had been drawn up by the gurus of the foreign services and of the political and technical bureaucracies of the so-called Four Powers at Dumbarton Oaks, Harvard University's center for Byzantine studies. Redacting the "Proposals for the Establishment of a General International Organization" had run to nearly seven weeks of hair-splitting among the American, British, and Russian officials in the grand old mansion located in Washington's Georgetown neighborhood, a venue suggested by the State Department's Alger Hiss. Du Bois had noted the unmistakable significance of the inclusion of the Chinese delegates in the deliberations only after the United States, the USSR, and Great Britain had thrashed out the major issues. Du Bois came away in turmoil from Undersecretary of State Edward Stettinius's special briefing of nearly one hundred organizations in Washington in mid-October of 1944. He acknowledged the historic steps taken at Dumbarton Oaks to guarantee international order and progress, but politely insisted that he spoke for groups who must worry about what had been left unsaid. Du Bois was, he said, "depressed to realize with what consistency the matter of colonies has been passed over."

With Judge Hastie and Mrs. Bethune at his side, he pressed his critique in a hushed State Department auditorium filled with white people, many of them aghast. Du Bois found nowhere in the documents provisions "even to consider the aggression of a nation against its own colonial peoples." Where was the mandates commission that had existed under the League of Nations? Du Bois's deconstruction in the *New Leader* six weeks later of the inchoate United Nations bordered on the pitiless, flatly rejecting an outline for world government in which "at least one-fourth of the inhabitants of the world have no part in it, no democratic rights."

In early March 1945, while Walter White remained overseas covering the war in his special capacity as a journalist for the *New York Post*, the director of special research challenged two assistants of Secretary of Treasury Morgenthau's in Washington during a briefing of more than one hundred organizations on the Bretton Woods Conference convened to restructure the international economic order. With characteristic aplomb (although "uneasy and out of my depth"), he had interrupted the arcane seminar on the embryonic International Monetary Fund (IMF), the gold standard, exchange rates, and investment policy. "Seven hundred fifty millions of people, a third of mankind, live in colonies," he was heard to state crisply. "Cheap colonial labor and materials are basic to postwar industry and finance. Was this matter mentioned in any form at Bretton Woods?" The annoyed responses indicated that Du Bois's interpellation was entirely unwelcome. The north-south problems of extreme economic disparity, of stillborn postcolonial nations doomed to uneven, artificial, contingent development, and to a simulacrum of prosperity at best—the spawn of Bretton Woods and its supra-national money lenders to be reckoned with a half century later—were uncomfortable considerations to be hurried past by treasury officials and international bankers.

As Du Bois framed it, the problem of race was a global one, but as experienced by the great majority of American Negroes the problem was wearyingly personal—an ordeal of the workspace and of the public place. Hence, even the association had paid little more than rhetorical attention to the civil rights implications of the United Nations until Du Bois's return. A one-man committee, he had commenced a chain-reaction of correspondence at the beginning of the year: letters petitioning the State Department for official status as observer or consultant for the NAACP; letters to mainstream organizations devoted to promoting peace and international understanding. Du Bois proposed to Wilkins at the beginning of April that the moment had arrived for the association to start a campaign "to insist that the Department of State give Negro Americans some specific recognition."

Twelve days before Du Bois was scheduled to leave for the United Nations Conference in San Francisco as spokesman for the NAACP, the board voted to amend Du Bois's charge. Walter White had returned unexpectedly from the Pacific. "White without notice appeared on the scene and took back his offices," grumbled Du Bois. Thanks largely to Eleanor Roosevelt's intercession, there was now to be a three-person NAACP delegation appointed to serve with the forty-six non-governmental organizations accredited to the United States delegation. As the budget of the National Council of Negro Women was unable to cover her expenses, Mrs. Bethune's Washington supporters had persuaded White to attach her to the NAACP delegation. To the public, Du Bois praised the arrangement of three consultants extravagantly in his new *Defender* column, "The Winds of Time," as "more than has ever happened before to American Negroes since the Civil War," explaining that the UN consultancy had come about "through temperate but insistent agitation. . . ." He steamed in silence, however, as the secretary engineered his demotion to assistant consultant, reclaimed his office with unconvincing apologies for the unresolved space problem, and manipulated press releases to feature himself. The demotion rankled Du Bois, but he must have appreciated that White's appropriate place was at the head of the delegation. It had been White's twenty-four-hour pipeline into the White House and whirlwind lobbying on Capitol Hill that finally made possible the association's special UN status.

For five weeks in San Francisco, he and White would park their antagonisms under a masquerade of mutual respect. However bitter their coming differences, both men journeyed to the founding conference of the UN determined to entrench FDR's legacy, as they interpreted it, in the new world body. FDR's fatal cerebral hemorrhage nine days before Du Bois, Bethune, and White were due to board the transcontinental express inspired a glowing Du Bois assessment of the president in the *Defender*. The appointment of able persons of color like Hastie and Weaver to high federal office (though endowed "with little power beyond advice") Du Bois cited along with FEPC as evidence of the president's enlightened ideas of race relations. The pragmatic politician and master of balancing acts who made up policy as he went along, and who was simply indifferent to economic orthodoxy rather than motivated in the slightest by radical ideology, was hardly visible in "An Estimate of FDR." In Du Bois's judgment, FDR was a paragon of progressivism, a social democrat committed to the proposition that "work and income [must be] guaranteed the laborer" and that "by determined effort" the wealth and income of the capitalists must be diminished. But the Roosevelt legacy of Soviet-American cooperation was already under attack from a formidable coalition of politicians, journalists, ethnic groups, and religious organizations. Du Bois's old nemesis Oswald Garrison Villard invited him to endorse a letter to *The New York Times* from journalists opposed to the Yalta Agreement permitting the Soviet Union to establish hegemony over much of Eastern Europe. "Never was a moral issue more clearly presented," the letter charged, "than is involved in this abandonment of Poland." Declining Villard's invitation, Du Bois composed his own letter to the *Times* in which he commended the Russians for their fairness in accepting the Curzon Line as the east-west boundary and, for good measure, he lambasted not only the Polish government in exile but the Polish population in the United States as "reactionaries" who spearheaded the burning of Negro public housing in the terrible 1943 Detroit riot.

But if he grasped the potential of the Polish factor to become a domestic lightning rod for those hostile to Russian communism—the National Association of Manufacturers, the Chamber of Commerce, professional elements in the State Department and the military, Catholic labor leaders—Du Bois could hardly have suspected how immediate its impact would be. Even as he sped across the vast expanse of the United States aboard the Pullman "press special" (a devastated Mildred Bryant failed to find him in the crowd when the train halted in Chicago), the Polish question—"that Pandora's Box of infinite troubles," in Cordell Hull's words—served as a decisive element in the deterioration of relations between the United States and the Soviet Union. By the terms of Yalta, Russia was supposed to allow the Polish people to choose a postwar government in a fair election, but those who claimed to know the unstated terms of Yalta would insist that FDR and Churchill had never held realistic expectations of a pro-Western regime coming to power in Poland. The vagaries of an American vice president's role, compounded by Roosevelt's insistence on running foreign policy "out of his pocket," as was said, thrust Harry Truman into the Oval Office as one of the least prepared men in American history to assume the presidency. A small group of powerful Washington and Wall Street insiders—men whose names were to become synonyms of the American Establishment and whose conceptions of power-politics would decisively influence America's postwar foreign policy—gathered at the State Department in order to assist the former Missouri senator. Ambassador Averell Harriman (who flew from Moscow aboard his private bomber to arrange the fateful session), assistant secretary of state Dean Acheson, and State Department liaison to the White House Charles Bohlen administered one of the most momentous presidential foreign policy tutorials in American history. Three days later Harry Truman held his first meeting with Vyacheslav Molotov when the San Francisco–bound Soviet foreign minister stopped in Washington on April 20, 1945. The historic exchange over the Polish question, variously recorded by those present (Harriman, Bohlen, and Edward Stettinius, now secretary of state), dramatically prefigured the onset of the Cold War. When Truman bluntly ordered Molotov to tell Joseph Stalin that he expected Yalta to be faithfully executed, the president's abrupt dismissal of the Soviet foreign minister was met with a flustered protest (translated by Bohlen): "I've never been talked to like that in my life." "Carry out your agreements and you won't get talked to like that," Truman snapped to Molotov.

For Du Bois, White, and Bethune, the story of the United Nations conference centered on Russia, China, and unrecognized India, and on the support received from these delegations for the causes of racial equality and anti-imperialism. These were concerns far removed from the priorities of the superpowers at San Francisco, where sharp disagreement between the United States and Russia over the veto in the Security Council and the admission to the General Assembly of Argentina came within an ace of destroying the conference. Yalta had fudged the complicated issue of the future status of territories conquered by the Axis powers, and did not care to address the sensitive questions of the League of Nations mandates and the rights of peoples under colonial rule. Caught between the Atlantic Charter's Wilsonian high-mindedness renouncing territorial annexation and secret agreements, on the one hand, and the nationalistic, strategic, and economic imperatives unleashed by five years of warfare, Roosevelt, Stalin, and Churchill had settled for a sketchy, three-tiered international trusteeship arrangement for "dependent territories," leaving the details to be worked out within the framework of the United Nations. Beyond symbolism and Eleanor Roosevelt's shrewd calculation that their presence might be "extremely useful" to America's relations with South and Central America as well as the Near East, the doughty NAACP delegation amounted to little more than a gnat among the superpower pachyderms.

No sooner was the grand April 25 opening ceremony of the fifty participating nations concluded in the San Francisco Opera House (Ralph Bunche savored the privilege of being the sole colored American allocated an orchestra seat) than Du Bois, White, and Bethune commenced an intense regime of discussions, dinners, press conferences, and on- and offstage lobbying to generate consensus for the formal acknowledgment in the United Nations Charter of the rights of "dependent peoples" (mainly people of color) to govern themselves. Roy Wilkins's sharp dart from New York about the hiring of three secretaries for the trio was aimed especially at Du Bois, who, in addition to employing local talent, had added transportation and hotel costs to the budget by bringing "Marielle" (Ethel Ray Nance) to San Francisco from Seattle. "I'm ready as fast as I can," this extremely capable intimate of many years had replied by telegram after arranging a furlough from her government job and a trustworthy family to care for her teenage boys.

While Du Bois and his secretarial team produced a steady flow of drafts, memoranda, press releases, and carefully crafted manifestos, White deployed his salesmanship skills. The quick-witted secretary devoted his time to circulating among the delegations, cultivating first-name contacts and fielding invitations to restricted parleys and exclusive social occasions where he made masterful use of ideas supplied by Du Bois. The authentic representatives of India's 400 million were the Congress Party delegates led by Vijaya Pandit, Nehru's sister. Mrs. Pandit captivated Du Bois and White as she did much of the conference and the city of San Francisco. "A charming woman in every way," he enthused in the *Defender* after their first dinner together, "physically beautiful, simple and cordial." She was also recognized in short order as one of the most able diplomats on the international scene. Her suite at the Fairmont Hotel served as the cockpit for information, strategy, and the forming of alliances among Ethiopians, Vietnamese, Egyptians, Liberians, Indonesians, Haitians, and other exploited peoples, many of the ties to be sustained well beyond the San Francisco conference. The Soviet delegation was far less accessible, but Foreign Minister Molotov evoked compliments from Du Bois as positive, though less personal, as those he applied to Mrs. Pandit. Molotov was described as "the one statesman at San Francisco who stood up for human rights and the emancipation of colonies." When the short, square diplomat stated in his address to the international organization that the USSR considered it indispensable to international peace and security that "dependent countries are enabled as soon as possible to take the path of national independence," Du Bois was ecstatic.

The enormous propaganda value to the Russians of their anti-imperialist pronouncements distressed many of the American consultants and observers. They blamed Stettinius for the absence of a clearly articulated policy. Even White's obdurate optimism seemed to give way in an impassioned communiqué to Wilkins about Truman's UN policy. He had been as stunned as Du Bois to hear the secretary of state announce that the United States would neither propose nor support a human rights declaration as an integral part of the charter. "Its timorousness and political mindedness has caused the United States delegation to lose, perhaps beyond regaining, the bold moral leadership which it should have taken," the NAACP secretary wrote Wilkins. "Russia and China have taken the play away . . . on the colonial trusteeship, while the smart boys like Eden appear to have outsmarted our delegation on purely political grounds." In fact, however, the actual U.S. policy called for evasion and ambiguity partly in deference to the British, French, and Dutch, and partly out of concern for the domestic political implications of Palestine. "We all know that the opposition of Great Britain to any international action on the colonial problem has made the United States refrain from this step," Du Bois wrote in his mid-May plea to the American delegation to undertake a more aggressive intervention in the San Francisco proceedings. Counting on Ralph Bunche, one of the strategically positioned members of the United States delegation, to do what he could, Du Bois transmitted precise language that he hoped to see inserted in the UN Charter and that was tantamount to an obituary for the British and French empires. "The colonial system of government, however deeply rooted in history and custom, is today undemocratic, socially dangerous and a main cause of wars," his document intoned. "The United Nations recognizing democracy as the only just way of life for all peoples make it a first statute of international law." He proposed that the charter state: "that at the earliest practical moment no nation or group shall be deprived of effective voice in its own government and enjoyment of the four freedoms." As a press release in the name of the NAACP consultants, Du Bois's proposed language made an arresting document. Its fate in the hands of a delegation headed by Edward Stettinius was entirely predictable.

Du Bois and White hoped that it mattered somewhat that Bunche, who thought that the trusteeship controversy was the "hottest subject" of the conference, fully shared their concerns. Otherwise, Du Bois expected little in the way of leadership, an opinion that Bunche entertained even more firmly based on firsthand observation of the former General Motors vice president and U.S. Steel chairman. An outwardly deferential Bunche, appointed to the U.S. trusteeship committee, would confide to his wife that the secretary of state was "a complete dud, whatever the press may say about him." Bunche had made a meteoric ascent from his Howard University professorship through the OSS into the State Department's elite group of UN planners led by Leo Pasvolsky, a brilliant Russian émigré. Bunche's new standing greatly inhibited his Du Boisian sympathies.

Color and Democracy appeared with almost perfect timing seventeen days after V-E Day and one month into the conference with its unhappy verdict on Dumbarton Oaks and a salient opening sentence memorably proclaiming that "colonies are the slums of the world." Chosen as one of the fifty outstanding books of the year by the American Library Association, Pearl Buck praised it in the *Herald Tribune* for plainspoken truth, concurring fully with the author that the actors at Dumbarton Oaks attempted to design a world organization plan that "put force behind existing systems, ignoring the injustices out of which war will come." Melville Herskovits offered a similar opinion in *The New Republic* and the critic in *The Saturday Review* warned readers that *Color and Democracy* contained "enough dynamite to blow up the whole vicious system whereby we have comforted our white souls and lined the pockets of generations of freebooting capitalists."

The appearance of the book and Du Bois's increasingly critical *Defender* column may have caused some uneasiness to the third member of the trio. Mary McLeod Bethune had been as close a friend of the Roosevelts as had

Walter White. A veteran Washington survivor whose mother wit and standing among millions of women had made her one of the country's most powerful and respected Negro leaders, she fully intended to maintain her welcome at the White House and on Capitol Hill. Little wonder then, that Mary Bethune summoned a National Conference of Negro Leaders in order to formulate a comprehensive position on the proposed charter. "Mrs. Bethune was rather a nuisance, but a harmless one," Du Bois observed off the record, a somewhat condescending view that White shared. To the considerable annoyance of the NAACP leadership, the venerable NCNW president had announced the Washington conference without bothering to discuss her plans with Du Bois or Wilkins, who had taken White's place in San Francisco. Convened on June 23, three days before the United Nations Charter was to be formally adopted, the National Conference of Negro Leaders was attended by fifty persons representing some thirty organizations. The leaders voted to accept the caveat proposed by the absent Du Bois that Article 87 of the Charter be construed as permitting the new Trusteeship Council to receive oral petitions from colonized peoples.

A week to the day after the promulgation of the Charter, as the Senate Foreign Relations Committee commenced hearings on the document, Du Bois asked for fifteen minutes of the committee's time. On Wednesday morning, July 11, 1945, Senator Tom Connally of Texas gaveled the committee to order and asked the "Reverend Dr. Du Bois" to come forward. Du Bois eloquently appealed for the Senate to ratify the Charter with the expression of certain fundamental reservations. Speaking "only officially for [him]self," he underscored the "pressing cries of the 750,000,000 unrepresented [who] were not expressed and even forgotten" at San Francisco. Many of their fellow countrymen and women have come to believe in the universal application of the oldest of American dictum, Du Bois told the senators—that "taxation without representation is tyranny" applies equally to "Latins and Slavs, and the yellow, brown, and black peoples of America, Asia, and Africa." He asked that the Senate validate as a first principle of international law that "at the earliest practical moment no nation or group shall be deprived of effective voice in its own government."

BUSY AS HE had been, Du Bois found opportunity while in San Francisco to write Nina, Yolande, and Du Bois (no longer Baby Du Bois but a clever young girl of thirteen willful years headed for an exclusive academy in Massachusetts). Nina had suffered a bad fall at the beginning of the year and was only just beginning to move about after weeks of painful physical therapy for torn ligaments. Her spirits raised by news of his exciting and important activities, she wrote that Yolande and Du Bois vied with each other for first call on the clippings and other materials he sent them, "as the children and grown-ups all listen and look for some card from you." In a letter to young Du Bois, he described the dinner as Walter White's guest in the company of Vijaya Pandit and the actress, Helen Hayes, at Mardikian's, San Francisco's premier dining experience, a glittering evening when every head turned as the maître d' led the foursome to a center table in a room packed with diplomats, columnists, elected officials, and local society. The word about Yolande was distressing, as Nina wrote that she seemed determined to leave her teaching position and move to New York with little or no prospect of finding work. Nina mentioned the passing of yet another of their close friends. Major Walter Loving was dead in the Philippines, beheaded by a Japanese officer in the last weeks of the war. The news that most surprised Du Bois came the day after his Senate appearance. Virginia Alexander had gotten married. "It happened in Birmingham [Alabama] on June 6, three days before I left there," and she apologized for not having written sooner. His name was William Childs, a Catholic, and Virginia wrote that she was "really very, very happy." She and Bill hoped to see Du Bois soon. She had told Bill that Du Bois was her "dearest friend and advisor in all these years."

Weather conditions at 69 Fifth Avenue began to deteriorate badly soon after San Francisco. Thurgood Marshall's ill will toward the director of special research had been pretty much assured from the outset when White slickly tried to pass Du Bois's salary to the Inc Fund budget. A punctilious Wilkins had laboriously explained the carefully defined duties of the secretarial pool after Du Bois requested the typing of several documents. Pretending not to notice the altering barometer, Du Bois had thanked Wilkins for explaining to Miss Diggs "just the circumstances under which we can hire additional clerical help." For his part, however, there were contractual conditions essential to his research and writing that must be met. He and Diggs had occupied the roving secretary's office from November 1944 until April 1945 while a search for the two private offices promised Du Bois remained in limbo. White's return had triggered an ultimatum on April 10—"something has to be done immediately about office space for my work."

As the San Francisco mission intervened almost immediately, nothing had been done, but in late June, Du Bois rented adequate office space on his own authority, purchased new furniture, and took Diggs, three thousand books, seven filing cabinets, and his antique Dictaphone to 55 West Forty-second Street. Bobbie Branch claimed that she had tried to like Du Bois for the sake of her friend Virginia Alexander, but from her point of view as office manager he was "nothing but trouble, trouble, trouble." Informed that he had exceeded his authority by the secretary, backed by the board, Du Bois was saddled with three months of unreimbursed rent and moving expenses and forced to follow the NAACP into a small office in its new headquarters at 40 Fifth Avenue in November.

His pan-African plans had begun to unravel. The mid-July rebuke administered by the board in connection with the unauthorized move had also instructed the association's Pan-African Committee to vote on the advisability of holding the congress. To Du Bois's astonishment, Rayford Logan had complicated matters by proposing that the name, Pan-African Congress, should be changed to "Dependent Peoples' Congress" on the grounds that the struggle against imperialism was as much Asian as African. Logan's unwelcome suggestion was a decade in advance of the Afro-Asian political solidarity that would coalesce for a heady interval in 1955 at the Bandung Conference in Indonesia. He seems also to have been ahead of his mentor, who may have corrected Logan's suggestion with an excessive sternness because of its appeal to White. We have a "pretty clear right to speak for Africa," Du Bois snapped, but Asians would almost certainly "repudiate such assumptions on our part." A Pan-African Committee meeting in late July at Hastie's Washington home with Channing Tobias and an hour-late Bunche bogged down over Hastie's unhappiness that Du Bois had so far failed to develop a roster of properly titled African invitees and Bunche's unexpected misgivings about the advisability of a pan-African movement. "If there were such a movement, it should be confined to Africans," Du Bois's memorandum reported him as saying.

Displeased by the drift of things, Du Bois had been somewhat cheered after White's meeting with Undersecretary of War Robert Patterson resulted in the conditional promise of military air transportation to the congress if sanctioned by the Secretary of State. Du Bois had urged White to announce an official commitment by the association in order to prevent "radicals" associated with Padmore from hijacking the congress. Not getting the desired response from the secretary, he had distressed the board in early June by publicly announcing the date and place of the congress, with the clear implication of NAACP sponsorship. With grumbles rising over projected costs of the congress and the irritable Marshall's anxieties about the association's legal work being overshadowed, Du Bois reached for the cover of White House commendation on September 12. Assured of the president's keen interest in the "problems [to be] discussed at the forthcoming Pan-African Congress," Truman's appointments secretary nonetheless pleaded urgent matters of state and offered Du Bois acting secretary of state Dean Acheson instead within the week. Acheson and Henry Villard of the Bureau of African Affairs also expressed keen interest in the project in their conference with Du Bois on October 2, 1945, though they feared that the return travel difficulties were formidable.

News from Moody, Peter Milliard of the British section of the Pan-African Federation, Padmore, and others revealed the mounting complications of the Paris site. The latest plan had called for the meeting to be held in London. Suddenly, Padmore informed Du Bois that the Fifth Pan-African Congress had been called for Manchester, England, from October 15 to October 20. The apology for the last-minute communiqué was suspect, as was Padmore's distress that the American delegates from the NAACP, MOWM, and NUL, might have difficulty making travel arrangements. "Delegates must have mandates from organizations," the eleventh-hour letter emphasized. They were to speak not for themselves "but for masses of people, representatives not of the middle-class strata and professionals in the colonies, but of the workers' organizations, the co-operative societies, peasant associations, labour parties and national liberation organizations." The forty-three-year-old Marxian nationalist deeply regretted the NAACP's failure to grant a "plenipotentiary mandate" to Du Bois, but he assured the distinguished civil rights leader that he was welcome "in whatever capacity you come." Provided with a $1,200 appropriation from the board, Du Bois wrangled a passport and visa with less than two weeks to spare. He left from Idlewild Airport in the throes of clashing emotions: elation and sadness. A quarter century after his convoking the first of these congresses in Paris, he was thrilled to fly off to a Pan-African Congress in which the native Africans were going to outnumber the citizens of the United Kingdom, France, and the United States. The sadness was Nina, her left side paraylzed less than a month earlier by a stroke and her prognosis at Manhattan's Montefiore Hospital guarded. Although she had come to New York for the summer, they lived apart, she in a room at the Harlem YWCA, where an attendant monitored her recovery from the fall, and he at 409 Edgecombe Avenue. The arrangement had not at all been to her liking. "I can quite understand that you do not care for company," she had pleaded in vain. She promised not to disturb his way of life if there were a "couch of some sort [she] could use." Nina's stroke came two months later.

The official opening of the Fifth Pan-African Congress on October 15 was delayed until the afternoon so that the Lord Mayor of Manchester could bring the greetings of the city. But there was a warm Monday-morning welcome given by Amy Ashwood Garvey to delegates present at the first session in Chorlton Town Hall. Amy Ashwood, a broad-beamed, dark-skinned woman of forty-eight, and reknowned for her pan-African ubiquity, was the first Mrs. Garvey, a close friend of Padmore and T. R. Makonnen and not to be confused with Amy Jacques Garvey, whose presence at the conference the first Mrs. Garvey had deemed intolerable. On Tuesday morning October 17, Padmore introduced Du Bois to the two hundred delegates as the "father of Pan-Africanism" and the person who epitomized the struggles of 13 million men and women of African descent in the United States. Presenting the gavel to the distinguished scholar, writer, and publicist whose mind was "more alive than many a youth's," Padmore asked Du Bois to chair the session as president of the Congress. Du Bois acknowledged the honor, greeted the delegates in the name of American Negroes, and relinquished the podium to the rapporteur for the session, Francis Nkrumah. A sense of history pervaded the proceedings, though only a clairvoyant could have appreciated the momentous import of the future prime minister of the first nation in black Africa liberated from colonial rule outlining the political trends of the continent in a session presided over by the founder of pan-Africanism.* Now that six years of worldwide carnage had ended, Nkrumah demanded that the victorious democracies commence the unfinished business of dismantling imperialism, "one of the major causes of war." His words tumbling out, the young Gold Coast nationalist excitedly promised the delegates that they would soon see "strong and vigorous action to eradicate [imperialism]."

Nigerians, Togolese, Gambians, the gifted South African writer and publicity secretary for the congress, Peter Abrahams, the fiery Ethiopian intellectual, Ras Makonnen, Barbadians, Trinidadians, Miss Alma La Badie of the Jamaican UNIA—the procession of present and future leaders of Du Bois's darker world stepped forward to be heard over four remarkable days. Gershon Ashie-Nikoi, representing 300,000 West African cocoa farmers, followed Nkrumah to denounce the local government reforms instituted by the British in the Gold Coast as nothing other than a ruse to retard genuine rule by Africans. Wednesday's address by Jomo Kenyatta ranged from Nyasaland to the Rhodesias, six East African territories in all, but the main focus was Kenya, the homeland of the fifty-one-year-old Kikuyu activist. In the forty-odd years since Kamau, son of Ngengi, had evolved from a Christian mission boy to London School of Economics scholar and author of *Facing Mount Kenya* (1938), Jomo ("Burning Spear") Kenyatta, the founder of the Kikuyu Central Association (KCA), had flirted with communism after university studies in the USSR, and taken the full measure of the racist civility of the British when he tried to plead for his people's land. The kindly yet powerful voice told of halcyon days of hunting, planting, and grazing in East Africa, the time before the European occupation. "What is the picture today?" Kenyatta asked rhetorically. "It is quite different. Many of us talk about home, but we have no home, because in order to have a home you must have land on which you can stand your house or hut and say, 'This is my home.'" Du Bois listened intently to these speakers in Chorlton Town Hall and absorbed their discussions at dinner. He thought to himself that many of them were overly optimistic about the new British Labor government. Many of Du Bois's Fabian Society acquaintances were now in the government or very close to those who were—all of whom had given Gershon Ashie-Nikoi the cold shoulder, just as earlier the Conservatives had declined to hear Kenyatta. Du Bois had predicted in writing the resolutions of the Third Pan-African Congress that any possibility of Africa becoming assimilated politically and culturally into Europe would be forfeited by the bad faith of the European rulers. Kwame

---

*A widespread misconception, as the Sudan was the first sub-Saharan nation to become independent in 1955.

Nkrumah and Jomo Kenyatta were the fulfillment of his prediction, Africans exposed under the colonial regime to educational and professional opportunities incapable of bestowing full manhood yet great enough to radicalize and alienate.

"Challenge to the Colonial Powers," the manifesto approved by the delegates, was a virtual farewell to a European tutelage contrived to infantilize its victims in perpetuity. "We are not ashamed to have been an age-long patient people," it proclaimed. But Africans were unwilling to starve any longer "while doing the world's drudgery, in order to support by our poverty and ignorance a false aristocracy and a discredited imperialism." They were determined to be free. They wanted education. "We want the right to earn a decent living; the right to express our thoughts and emotions." The Pan-African Congress ended on a note of insurgency that had been sounded twenty-five years ago as a theoretical probability in *Darkwater*. They believed in peace, the document stressed. "How could it be otherwise when for centuries" Africans had been victimized by violence and slavery? "Yet if the Western world is still determined to rule mankind by force, then Africans, as a last resort, may have to appeal to force in an effort to achieve Freedom, even if force destroys them and the world." Color and democracy were proclaimed to be within the grasp of the continent. The congress resolved to hold a sixth conclave in 1946 on the African continent.

BECAUSE HE WAS presiding that very moment at the Manchester conference, Du Bois missed the thirtieth award ceremony in Manhattan for the NAACP's Spingarn Medal. Seven hundred distinguished people filled the Biltmore Hotel ballroom to honor Paul Robeson, the most famous black man in America and one of the few Americans of any race or creed who was so well known that he could have dropped into a remote village in Uzbekistan or India and been recognized. He and Eslanda ("Essie"), his forceful wife, had preferred to live in England soon after his qualified success in the 1930 London production of *Othello*. The Robesons' several visits to the Soviet Union during their voluntary exile abroad had made a profound impact on their politics. The Comintern scripted their first trip in December 1934 to perfection. Enveloped by adoring crowds and a warmth on the part of the powerful they had experienced nowhere else—with receptions and dinner parties hosted by Maxim Litvinov, Russia's cosmopolitan foreign minister, Sergei Eisenstein, the maestro of cinematography, Mikhail Tukhachevsky, the architect of the new Soviet army—Essie Robeson had written home giddily about passionate testimonials of racial empathy punctuating virtually every champagne and vodka toast. Two years later, the attractive couple returned to Moscow to arrange for the enrollment of their son in the Soviet Model School. Among Paul Jr.'s classmates were to be Stalin's daughter, Svetlana, and Molotov's son. The war had ended the idyll abroad, bringing them home from London in 1939 to what had been Paul Robeson's greatest success as an actor and a singer. His rendition of *Ballad for Americans* over NBC in November of '39 had electrified the nation. His lead in *Othello*, with co-stars Uta Hagen and Jose Ferrer, roused a twenty-minute, opening-night ovation in 1943 and shattered the record for Shakespeare on Broadway with 296 performances. An eloquent advocate of American nonintervention who denounced warmongering bankers and industrialists, Robeson had become an overnight star of the war effort when the Nazis invaded the Soviet Union.

Robeson's Spingarn Medal appearance was considered such a publicity coup for the association that White and Wilkins had almost agreed to import Orson Welles for a huge honorarium from Hollywood to serve as master of ceremonies. As the grand mid-October occasion approached, however, the NAACP leadership became prey to misgivings. Council on African Affairs director and Robeson intermediary Max Yergan had failed to provide the text of the acceptance speech. When Chicago multimillionaire and master of ceremonies, Marshall Field, introduced him, the honoree rose to deliver what White called a straight party line speech. The Spingarn medalist wondered what had happened to the peace and to FDR's ideals. Six months earlier, American and Russian soldiers had celebrated the German defeat together at the Elbe River. A month later, Truman had ordered the cancellation of lend-lease to Russia (temporarily resumed) in a power-play over Poland. In rolling, sonorous cadences, Robeson condemned the emerging hostility toward the Russians as a sign of renascent fascism in the United States and Britain. "Full employment in Russia is a fact and not a myth," he boomed, "and discrimination is nonexistent." But here in the United States, the drift was already away from civil rights reform and toward acquiescence in the maintenance of colonialism. Corinne Wright, Louis Wright's widow, was one of several NAACP insiders who remembered vividly the general consternation caused by Robeson's speech and the apoplexy visible in Walter White's complexion. Du Bois and Robeson were not then close acquaintances; their interaction had amounted mostly to unremarkable official letters pertaining to progressive causes and very little personal contact. But he would heartily concur in the admired celebrity's words that evening.

The Biltmore evening was an omen. But Robeson had been in error to speak of drift. The two superpowers were speeding apart, rather than drifting away, as mistrust and aggressive positioning of forces supplanted cooperation. Had Roosevelt lived, Du Bois and Robeson were among the informed many who believed that, in tone and style, American dealings with the Russians would have been lighter, more flexible, and less pugilistic, even as realpolitik exigencies increasingly, inevitably imposed themselves. These were the counterfactual solaces of American leftists, however. Truman, the gamecock valedictorian of a political machine, had made good his hint at Potsdam in the mushroom clouds rising out of Hiroshima and Nagasaki on August 6 and 9, a triumph of Los Alamos physics and engineering that imparted to the American people and their leaders the conviction that the atomic bomb incommensurably altered the post-war balance of power in their favor. Twenty million Russians had perished in the war, the Ukraine was a wasteland, large portions of Leningrad, Stalingrad, Kiev, Moscow, and other Russian cities lay in rubble. The infrastructure created by Stakhanovite ardor and forced labor under two five-year plans was obliterated. Yet, astonishingly, the Russians (and Du Bois in a *Defender* editorial) refused to accept the terms of atomic power-politics as self-evident. In addition to its eleven million troops and twenty thousand tanks, Russia appeared to have another asset—the real and potential appeal of communism to millions of European minds and bellies amid the measureless devastation of their continent and the suffering that promised to be unrelieved. To save Europeans from themselves, American treasure in prodigious quantities would be needed. Having stiffened the resolve of his island people in their darkest hour, an unemployed Winston Churchill now journeyed to the American heartland to deliver the new political catechism to a victorious people, as yet unware of the global peril facing them. Five months after Du Bois returned from England, Churchill's "iron curtain" speech in Fulton, Missouri, on March 5, 1946, formally inaugurated the Cold War. Churchill's speech was "one of the most discouraging occurrences of modern times," Du Bois would moan.

The legacy of anticommunism within the top leadership of the NAACP was long and strong. Manifest in Walter White's politically correct testimony before Representative Hamilton Fish's anticommunism committee in 1930, it had been set in concrete during the bitter tug-of-war with the CPUSA over the Scottsboro boys three years later. An argument could certainly be made that much of the NAACP's anticommunism was of the strategic variety, rather than animated by the manichaean antipathies of the business and religious communities. Du Bois himself had gone to great analytical lengths to distinguish between what he understood as the ideal under experiment in Russia and the degradation of the dogma at the hands of domestic Communists. Such distinctions made little difference, however, in terms of their practical impact on personalities and policies. In the winter and spring of 1945–46, the secretary, his associate, and several influential board members were in no mood to indulge the theoretical hair-splitting that had been typical of the old *Crisis*. For the second time in a decade, they saw the association and the larger arena of civil rights as dangerously exposed to the blandishments of Communists and their misguided allies. The Robesons, Ben Davises, Max Yergans, William Pattersons, and Doxey Wilkersons were too popular or plausible in their civil rights advocacy to criticize publicly, but the rapidly darkening international picture commended putting a safe distance between the NAACP and these attractive figures and their major organizations—the National Negro Congress, the Council on African Affairs, National Lawyers Guild, and others just being formed under the sponsorship of left-wing labor unions within the CIO. Made nervous by Du Bois's pan-African episode, White and Wilkins found more to upset them in the opinions expressed in the activities report of the director of special research upon his return from England.

From Manchester, Du Bois had gone to London. Once again, as when he and Mrs. Havelock Ellis had called on the famous playwright only to find him away, Du Bois had poor luck in meeting George Bernard Shaw. "The whole American army wants to visit," Shaw scrawled on the bottom of Du Bois's letter. He was unable to entertain any more visitors, "plain or colored, for another year at least." The meeting with H. G. Wells, though, was rewarding, and Du Bois would compose a long obituary a month later in the *Defender* recalling an acquaintanceship spanning more than forty years. Perhaps Wells's *History of the World* might have done better by the Negro, but Du Bois generously made allowances for the state of knowledge of the period. The meeting with Harold Laski in a "poorly lighted and poorly heated" office in the London School of Economics went like old times with talk of race relations in England and the United States, anti-Semitism and Negrophobia, and of Laski's controversial chairmanship of the victorious Labor Party. But it was not encounters with aged Fabians but his meeting with young black American Communists from middle-class backgrounds that was the highlight of his London stay. Thousands of young people had converged on London from Europe, India, China, and the Western Hemisphere for the founding meeting of the World Youth Conference, a rejuvenating experience that brought into Du Bois's life a vivacious young woman of stunning intelligence and poise.

Esther Cooper Jackson, a graduate of Oberlin College who held a master's degree in sociology from Fisk under Charles Johnson, was twenty-seven. Her career path to a doctorate at the University of Chicago had veered suddenly one afternoon when asked to show a handsome, visiting Carnegie-Myrdal researcher around the Fisk campus. In marrying James E. Jackson, Esther Cooper also married the Communist Party. As a Negro Eagle Scout (the first and only one in the South), sixteen-year-old Jim Jackson had stormed out of a public award ceremony in Richmond into the Communist Party after the governor of Virginia tossed his decoration to him in the presence of Jackson's humiliated parents. After college at Virginia Union and a Howard University pharmacy degree to please his prosperous pharmacist father, Jackson worked as a party organizer until his induction into the army. When Sergeant Jackson returned home from duty in Burma to be discharged, he learned that his wife of three years had sailed for the World Youth Conference, after which she would travel to Russia to work as a bricklayer's assistant in the rebuilding of Stalingrad. Many of the

Southern Negro Youth Congress (SNYC) members, executive secretary Esther Jackson among them, idolized Du Bois. He accepted her invitation to meet a small group of representative SNYC-ers at a dinner she cooked for the lot. Although he vaguely remembered an invitation to be keynote speaker at a SNYC convention several years ago, until meeting Jackson Du Bois had known little more about the organization than that it had begun at Howard in 1936 under the auspices of the NNC. They were committed to unity across racial lines and to bringing fundamental economic change to the South, Jackson and her dinner group explained.

Du Bois's report of his English mission spoke of the SNYC as a major social force in the making and of Esther Jackson's organizational aptitude and remarkable political intelligence. Gloster Current, the hardworking executive director of the association's Detroit branch, had attended the World Youth Conference as White's special emissary. The more conservative Current had been selected abruptly to replace Ruby Hurley, the national youth secretary, after new board member Eleanor Roosevelt raised concerns about the large Soviet delegation expected to attend the conclave. Current, a tiny brown man with a pleasant face and an understated manner, had been crushed that his existence at the World Youth Conference went wholly unnoticed in the Du Bois report, but to White and Wilkins the omission was organizationally and politically heinous. Asked to amend his report, Du Bois let his secretary refuse for him. "You know that we suspected at the beginning that this Youth Conference, and particularly the American delegation might be a Communist front group," Wilkins fumed to White. Who had ever heard of this Esther Cooper Jackson, who had been preferred over the expert Gloster Current? Du Bois's glowing appreciation of the SNYC executive secretary unleashed a torrent of denunciations from White about a series of misdeeds. On November 27 and December 21, 1945, the secretary presented Du Bois with a list of grievances and the threat of nonrenewal of his contract. "During the year 1945 certain actions by yourself seriously interfered with the smooth operation of the NAACP as a whole," the secretary charged: a *Defender* editorial claiming that segregated education need not be inferior; the unauthorized rental of office space; insistence that his mail not be opened. But it was Du Bois's appearance before the Senate Foreign Relations Committee "without notifying the association" that rankled as a usurpation of the secretary's prerogatives. Unstated in White's reproach was the patent implication that newsworthy opportunities should be left to the expertly advised secretary.

"Walter White soon undoubtedly set out to get rid of me," Du Bois wrote later, giving an account of their differences that favored himself: the appearance before the Senate committee had come at the invitation of the senators (but only after Du Bois asked to be invited); White had also been invited, "but he did not go" (which was rather beside the point). Du Bois framed the worsening friction with White in terms of the politics of personality. The profile he drew rendered White as an intellectually insecure, egotistical insurance salesman whose basic intelligence, undeniable hard work, and buoyant charm had placed him at the head of the association. The archetypal outer-directed personality, Walter White demanded obsequious fealty from his staff and compliance from a forty-five-member board of directors that was largely ceremonial. It was a "close dictatorship," Du Bois asserted. The obligation of board members "was to accept the report of the committee on administration, which consisted of the secretary, his five assistants whom he appointed, and nine members of the board, only two or three of whom usually attended." Du Bois's depiction of White was so widely shared by the civil rights community that it must be credited — with the caveat, nevertheless, that many found White's civil rights showmanship, bonhomie among the elite, and organizational micromanagement to be admirable (the very attributes Du Bois deplored). In any case, White, with Wilkins, had an organization to run and a program of targeted litigation to advance. Whatever its pan-African parochialisms and top-down rigidity, the NAACP's main goal — the steady dismantling of *Plessy v. Ferguson* — was proceeding right through Oklahoma on *Sipuel v. Oklahoma State Board of Education* and Texas on *Sweatt v. Painter* to the U.S. Supreme Court on briefs that ended the exclusion of Negroes from those states' professional schools. A series of winning suits to force the equalization of salaries between southern black and white public school teachers was under way. After a run of devastating paragraphs in *The Autobiography* on White's stewardship, even Du Bois paused to praise the demonstrated success of the Inc. Fund.

Unloading a civil rights legend was more than a notion. In addition to Spingarn and Wright, Du Bois still had strong backers on the board. Roscoe Dunjee, the fiery publisher of the Kansas *Black Dispatch*; Earl Dickerson, the Chicago lawyer-politician and first Negro member of the FDR-appointed FEPC; John Hammond, maverick great-grandson of William H. Vanderbilt and independent record producer; Hubert Delany, a New York judge; Loren Miller, a California jurist; and Channing Tobias, suave and able international YMCA executive and the first colored president of the Phelps-Stokes Fund (on Du Bois's recommendation) would defend Du Bois's right to differ, if not always his opinions, to the end. And there was Lillian Alexander, still a board member, and as ready as ever to assemble a fire brigade for Du Bois. White devoted five pages of single-spaced typescript at the end of 1945 to calm her charge of a conspiracy " 'to get rid of Dr. Du Bois.' " In declining health, Mary White Ovington devoted her time to writing and to the completion of *The Walls Came Tumbling Down*, an intimate history of the association. Oswald Garrison Villard was astonished to learn that his perennial tenure as a vice president of the association was annulled that year, 1946.

Taking a more cautious measure of the internal and public opinion costs, then, White was disposed to try to live with the problem that Ovington had once described as "our octopus." White and Wilkins vigilantly noted the rightward momentum of national politics, however, and they continued to note, as keenly, Du Bois's favorable pronouncements on the Soviet Union and criticisms of U.S. foreign policy. Meanwhile, Du Bois was already too busy planning another iniative of world import to concern himself with the distress caused to the secretary's brittle ego. Indeed, as far as egoes were concerned, as Du Bois wrote Alphaeus Hunton of the Council on African Affairs, his own had been "greatly embarrassed at developments concerning the Pan-African Congress." While the pan-African movement remained a sidebar, fifteen thousand dollars had been voted to establish an NAACP bureau in Hollywood in order to assist the secretary during his negotiations with studio executives to improve the image of the Negro in the movies. When Padmore, forwarding an autographed copy of his new book, *The World and Africa,* professed puzzlement at the lack of pan-African interest on the part of Negro American organizations, the "father of pan-Africanism" felt obliged to explain. Yes, there was "a great deal of jealousy" among them, and yes, the CAA was narrowly focused on South Africa and probably "financed by the Communists," he went on in an unusually long letter, but the basic problem had simply been his inability to make an official approach to any of the powerful Negro organizations "because of the hesitation of the NAACP."

Ultimately, however, the Pan African Congress petition (received without comment by White) took a back seat to a much more impressive statement that Du Bois prepared for presentation to the United Nations with the association's approval. The five-member team assembled by Du Bois to research and draft the NAACP-authorized document had been working at breakneck speed. Logan, Hugh Smythe (who had replaced Diggs as research assistant), Earl Dickerson, assistant attorney general of Illinois, William Ming, a Howard University law school professor, and Milton Konvitz, a labor relations professor at Cornell University, completed their respective pieces by the first week of December. Bunche and Hastie were to be consulted periodically. The criticism of the preliminary document offered by the association's national legislative counsel, Leslie Perry, impressed Du Bois, who immediately invited the young attorney to compile the statistical matter dealing with employment, wages, comparative literacy, housing, and health. Perry became the team's unofficial sixth member. *An Appeal to the World: A Statement on the Denial of Human Rights to Minorities in the Case of Citizens of Negro Descent in the United States of America and an Appeal to the United Nations for Redress,* ninety-four pages of encyclopedic data, compressed and interpreted, was to be completed in late August of 1947 and submitted to the NAACP board for final approval in September.

An Appeal to the World, as well as the Pan-African UN petition, engaged Du Bois with people and organizations whose politics were uncomfortably far to the left in the nervous estimation of the association secretariat and several long-serving members of the board. In the fall of 1946, national headquarters had become exceedingly worried about any such public impressions. Two months before Du Bois was due to attend the convention of the Southern Negro Youth Conference in South Carolina, Paul Robeson had asked the association to join an anti-lynching crusade sponsored by the NNC. Robeson announced the crusade at a monster rally in Madison Square Garden on the night of September 12. Fifty-six Negroes had been slaughtered, several of them returning soldiers, during the summer in a rampage by the Klan and its ilk to send a message that the war had changed nothing in the relations between the races under Jim Crow. Evoking a thunder of "no's", the great singer called American democracy to account, asking the capacity crowd in a booming voice, "Are we going to give our America over to the Eastlands, Rankins, and Bilbos? If not, then stop the lynchers! What about it, President Truman?" On September 23, the anniversary of the Emancipation Proclamation, Robeson officially launched the American Crusade Against Lynching in the nation's capital. The NAACP had refused its sponsorship, though. Angry internal memoranda and stern telegrams forbidding branches from participating reflected, in almost equal parts, indignation at what was seen as poaching on an historic NAACP monopoly and fastidious aversion to guilt by association. Once again, however, Du Bois had gone his own way, joining with Robeson and the noted white liberal attorney Bartley Crum in the crusade call. He had gladly endorsed the Robeson initiative, the director of special research fired back in response to White's reprimanding memorandum. He had known nothing of the secretary's protest that the association was itself launching a "new anti-lynching movement." Apparently, his, Du Bois's, cooperation had not been required. "The fight against mob law is the monopoly of no one person, no one organization," he snapped. With that, Du Bois went back to his plans for a United Nations petition in the small office at 40 Fifth Avenue assigned by Roy Wilkins. All pretense of the promised two large offices had evaporated. Du Bois and Diggs had gone in quiet protest to the association's new quarters with but a single rebellious gesture: Du Bois had ordered the most expensive furniture he could find and charged it to the NAACP.

On the way to the United Nations with his petition, however, Du Bois made an historic detour to Columbia, South Carolina, one that White, Wilkins, and much of the board viewed with publicly unspoken disfavor. The role of the

Communist Party in the life of twentieth-century America has thus far not lent itself to disinterested, balanced interpretation. The Southern Negro Youth Congress (SNYC), whatever its ties to international communism, was led by native-born Communists idealistically dedicated to bringing a better life to the black and white people of the wretchedly poor South. The organization's honorary president was none other than Frederick Patterson, Moton's successor as president of Tuskegee Institute. Like the majority of the SNYC membership, Fred Patterson was a good Christian of an unideological, practical bent who found more than enough oppression and hypocrisy under Jim Crow to warrant lending his considerable prestige to an activist, progressive organization spearheaded by young Communists. To turn a page or two of Patterson's essay in Logan's anthology, *What the Negro Wants*, was to sense the deep, contemporary civil rights impatience of a man whose distinguished position ten years earlier would have enforced Delphic circumspection. Clark Foreman, president of the Southern Conference on Human Welfare (SCHW), was of the same mind as Patterson. Du Bois had accepted the invitation to deliver the keynote address to the seventh Southeast conference of the SNYC. Langston Hughes had supported the organization from the beginning, writing *Don't You Want to Be Free?*, a one-act agit-prop play, mounted by SNYC units throughout the South. Adam Clayton Powell, Jr., spell-binding pastor of Harlem's Abyssinian Baptist Church and first of his race elected to Congress from the Northeast, was also a supporter of the organization and expected to speak at the 1946 conference. (Powell failed inexplicably to participate.)

Since the dinner meeting in London, Du Bois had become well acquainted with Esther Jackson's husband, James. He, Louis Burnham, a student civil rights militant from City College, and Edward Strong of the American Youth Congress (AYC) were the principal founders of the SNYC. James Jackson's father, a Richmond, Virginia, pharmacist well invested in local real estate, had reared his children on a steady diet of readings from "As the Crow Flies," the young people's section of *The Crisis*. Like many Talented Tenth children, Jackson bore an indelible memory as a ten-year-old of Du Bois's visit to his parents' home on Du Bois Avenue in Frederick Douglass Court, a tree-lined enclave for affluent colored families. Mrs. Jackson had emerged from frenzied preparation of her finest cooking, to be told by the distinguished, perverse guest, "Madam, I will have a slice of cheese on toast and a glass of milk, thank you." Through undergraduate years in Richmond and at Howard as a campus activist and participant in the off-campus Marxist bull sessions at Harrison's Grill, Jackson had followed Du Bois's evolving thought. Discharged from the army in February 1946, he wrote Du Bois for an interview. He remembered four or five sessions, each lasting exactly an hour and forty-five minutes at 409 Edgecombe Avenue. Twenty-two-year-old James Jackson, on orders from the national secretariat, assumed the challenge of bringing W.E.B. Du Bois into the Communist fold. To Jackson's argument that the self-segregation formulation was cousin to the Party's self-determination theses, an amused Du Bois insisted that he was simply a "bourgeois democrat." Engaged by the theoretical bent of Jackson's mind and confirmed in his World Youth Conference estimate of Esther Jackson, and equally impressed now by Louis Burnham and Ed Strong, Du Bois hurried to the South Carolina capital to lend his stature to their "hard work and sacrifice." Paul Robeson and the novelist Howard Fast had spoken the night before. Introduced by a glowing Esther Jackson at the closing mass meeting on the evening of October 20, Du Bois spoke to 850 black and white delegates, joined by several hundred observers, in the crammed chapel of Benedict College. His address, printed as a fifteen-page pamphlet and reproduced in *New Masses*, was to become an instant classic of the left.

"Behold the Land" blended poetry and politics as it endeavored to refocus the struggle of the American Negro from the urban ghettos of the North and Midwest to the cradle of the race. "The future of American Negroes is in the South," he said. "Here they have made their greatest contribution to American culture; and here they have suffered the damnation of slavery, the frustration of reconstruction and the lynching of emancipation." The South was the "firing-line" for the new struggle to emancipate not only American Negroes, Negroes of the West Indies, and Africans of the continent, but the "white slaves of modern capitalistic monopoly." He invited them to envisage the profound trans-formations possible under a new economy—a "new cooperative agriculture on renewed land owned by the state with capital furnished by the state, mechanized and coordinated with city life." The changing world posed a bitter dilemma for the white youth of the region. Saying that there was not a "single great ideal which they can express or aspire to that does not bring them into flat contra-diction with the Negro problem," he offered the optimistic prediction that they would soon turn to the truth in large numbers, "recognizing you as brothers and sisters, as fellow travelers toward the dawn." Du Bois paid the young men and women of the Southern Negro Youth Congress a moving tribute. "Nothing" he had experienced in the past years "has touched me more deeply," he wrote. At 40 Fifth Avenue, Walter White penned a long, offended memorandum when the text of "Behold the Land" reached him. Du Bois's "fellow travelers toward the dawn" were distinctly not to his liking, and he steamed over glowing ref-erences in the *Defender* to "young Negroes with guts" courageously meeting in the heart of the old Confederacy, which ignored the NAACP's unprecedented and bold national convention held in Atlanta in 1920.

His public life had been spent in going against the grain of established belief and practice. Absent overwhelming proof that he had fallen into error, Du Bois did not expect to change his beliefs—and certainly not the unambiguous expression of them — merely because the world was heading in another direction. It seemed to him that well-reasoned contrariness was badly needed in the second year of the Truman administration's foreign policy. "Democracy's Opportunity," in the August number of the *Christian Register*, deplored the Soviet dictatorship but insisted that Russia's was the sole experiment of consequence attacking the problem of poverty endemic to capitalism. The New Deal had been killed by re-action and the mild socialism inaugurated by the British Labour Party did not "ap-ply to the empire." The United States and Great Britain had a perfect right to argue that communism was unworkable. They had no right, Du Bois lectured, "to deny or hinder or slander Russia's pursuit of her own way of life and her economic setup." "Common Objectives," appearing that same month in *Soviet Russia To-day*, was a think piece running straight across the grain of official thinking in Washington. *Soviet Russia Today* had begun as the organ of the Friends of the So-viet Union, but now described itself as an independent entity edited by Jessica Smith, a take-charge Swarthmore graduate who had campaigned for Eugene Debs in 1920, gone to Russia to do famine relief work in 1922, then returned to work for United States recognition of the Soviet Union. Du Bois informed 14 mil-lion American Negroes, "victims of human slavery and the colonial system," they had a special obligation to empathize with the Russians or any people attempting to abolish "race and class discrimination." Providing a bit of personal experience from his Russian travels and his extensive reading of Russian history, the author opined that he was "trained therefore to understand Russia better than most peo-ple." On that basis, then, Du Bois pronounced the Soviet Union the "most hope-ful country on earth."

George Kennan, the son of the Russian scholar cited in the "Common Objectives" article, had a view of the Soviet regime that was diametrically op-posed to that held by Du Bois. As *chargé d'affaires* of the embassy, Kennan dispatched a feverish cablegram to Washington on a Februrary evening in 1946 during Ambassador Harriman's absence that supplied the glossary for the Cold War. In eight thousand words, the "Long Telegram" cast the coming struggle of the two superpowers in terms of an eternal, Mithraic confrontation between the forces of light and darkness that codified containment of Russia as the policy of the postwar era. Proclaiming that, "in the name of Marxism [the Soviets] sacrificed every single ethical value in their methods and tactics," the logic of the Long Telegram reduced all offers of cooperation and compromise to the deceptions of "Oriental secretiveness and conspiracy," congenital qualities anti-thethical to American openness and decency. But one conclusion imposed itself, Kennan exhorted — vigilant containment of the menace. By the time the essen-tials of the Long Telegram appeared in the July 1947 issue of *Foreign Affairs* as the "Mr. X" article (and reprinted in *Life* that same month), the international Cold War had begun to enter its domestic phase. Three months earlier, on

March 25, 1947, President Truman had issued Executive Order 9835, authorizing the FBI to investigate the beliefs and associations of all federal employees. Twelve months before Mr. X's appearance in *Foreign Affairs* and one month before *Soviet Russia Today* carried Du Bois's "Common Objectives," Henry Luce's *Life* magazine published a lengthy piece that instantly became a notable milepost in the domestic Cold War. "The U.S. Communist Party," by Arthur M. Schlesinger, Jr., jolted the entire civil rights establishment. The young Harvard associate professor's detailed piece was designed to inspire unease in readers. Buried in an innuendo-laden text headed by photos of Communist leaders, most of whom looked unkempt and faintly alien, was the assertion that the CPUSA was "sinking tentacles into the National Association for the Advancement of Colored People." As gratuitous and exaggerated, if not wholly unfounded, as the association's angry officers knew the *Life* article to be, Walter White also knew that the NAACP was inherently vulnerable to red baiting. The governor of Michigan lost no time citing the Schlesinger article as proof of his charge that the association was a communist front. Henceforth, caution was to be the NAACP's watchword.

THE WORD WENT unheeded by the director of special research. His sessions with James Jackson at the beginning of 1946 were the prelude to more frequent and politically rewarding associations with men and women on the left. Some of these new relationships came through Shirley Graham, whose friendship with the immensely successful Communist writer Howard Fast had helped pave her way to recognition and modest financial income as a writer of biography and historical fiction. Graham's enthusiastic *Paul Robeson: Citizen of the World* appearing that year would receive the Julian Messner Award. She was already at work on *There Was Once a Slave: The Heroic Story of Frederick Douglass.* "Shirley made wonderful gumbo and she never stopped talking," Fast was fond of saying. Neither could Howard Fast, it was generally agreed, and neither would be libeled by the claim that both possessed outsized egos. They also shared an admiration for Du Bois. *Freedom Road,* Fast's chef d'oeuvre, a fictionalized treatment of Reconstruction, relied on *Black Reconstruction*—"relied heavily" on it, he said proudly. Graham's Communist conversion experience was achingly dramatic, as she recounted it. Her oldest son, Robert, debilitated from pneumonia contracted in army basic training, had come to New York near death. Refused emergency ward treatment by three Manhattan hospitals because of his race, Graham had forced the fourth hospital to admit her boy, only to see him die hours later. What is true is that Robert Graham did die of pneumonia in a New York hospital and his mother did become a Communist. What was also not true at all, contrary to assertions by many of Du Bois's oldest friends, was that Graham pursued the aging legend on orders from the Party. When

Shirley Graham signed on with the CPUSA she had already been in stealthy pursuit of W.E.B. Du Bois for half a lifetime.

As Du Bois began to see more of Shirley Graham, though, he saw less of Rachel Davis DuBois and more of the people in Graham's circle: Fast, Carl Marzani, Paul and Essie Robeson, Frieda Diamond, Abbott Simon, Doxey Wilkerson, and the Jacksons, Max Yergan, Alphaeus Hunton, Marvel Cook—men and women who were acquiring permanent Doppelgängers from the FBI. There were circles within circles, some more red than others, and overlaps with cadre of organizations free of formal CPUSA affiliation but focused on similar causes and sharing common adversaries—the exploitative rich, militarists, and racists. The Party and its allied or sympathetic organizations naturally regarded Du Bois's growing readiness to lend the Du Bois name as a marvelous asset. Du Bois had known Doxey Wilkerson nearly fifteen years. Present at the creation of the National Negro Congress and one of the organization's stalwarts, Wilkerson fit the mold of scholarship combined with activism of which Du Bois was the renowned exemplar. Until his radicalism made his tenure at Howard more problematic than useful (as national vice president of the American Federation of Teachers he tangled continually with the university's authoritarian president), Wilkerson had been assured a stellar Talented Tenth career. A college presidency seemed likely. Tall, courtly, with an easy manner, a distinctly cultured voice, and superlative analytical powers, he had experienced a searing personal tragedy while conducting research for the Carnegie-Myrdal Study. He emerged from it psychologically intact, happily remarried, formally enrolled in the Party, and became a director of the Jefferson School. His essay in Logan's *What the Negro Wants* linking the advance of the Negro to the victory of the Soviet Union and its allies pleased Du Bois. The Wilkersons were among Du Bois's closest young friends. It was a natural enough relationship, genuine for both parties, but also a function of Party objectives. When the time seemed exactly right in Du Bois's fourth year with the NAACP, it would be Doxey Wilkerson in company with Herbert Aptheker who proposed an arrangement sanctioned by the Party hierarchy. Curiously, Wilkerson was unaware of James Jackson's Du Bois mission of friendship and ideological seduction until late in life.

Pleased and challenged by the widening field of associations on the far left, Du Bois's independence of thought, variegated interests, and multiple priorities precluded his being monopolized, as astute acquaintances like Howard Fast understood. "He was very kind, very sweet," Fast recalled, "but there was a wall between him and the rest of the world . . . and there was no way past it." Moreover, even his remarkable capacity for writing and speaking had limits, as he told the editor of the *Daily Worker* in May 1947 and Dashiell Hammett later that year when asked to address a mass meeting of the Civil Rights Congress. This was clearly a period of transition for Du Bois, the begin-

ning of the final phase in the evolution of that divided self immemorially described by him at the beginning of the twentieth century. In *The Souls of Black
Folk*, two souls had warred between identity as a Negro and as an "American."
His ambitious pan-African designs privileged race—the solidarity of people of
color—as the liberating sine qua non from the social and economic ills of this
world: diasporic nationalism. Yet a shift of ideological emphasis was unmistakably evidenced by "Behold the Land" in its program of economic democracy
based on interracial struggle—of unity based on class rather than race. Simply
stated, the central question for the twentieth century was whether economic
empowerment and racial equality were possible under democratic liberalism,
or whether economic egalitarianism was the logical prerequisite for liberal democracy and racial equality. Du Bois was himself in the process of deciding.
The World and Africa, released by Viking Press in January 1947, a large if somewhat composite monograph indebted to *Black Folk Then and Now*, reflected
the divided thought of its author astride the fault line of nationalism and communism. "On the other hand," Du Bois concluded after enumerating the
charges against communism, "if a world of ultimate democracy, reaching across
the color line and abolishing race discrimination, can only be accomplished by
the method laid down by Karl Marx, then that method deserves to be triumphant
no matter what we think." For the present, however, pan-Africa and *An Appeal
to the World* took precedence over Soviet-American friendship meetings and
peace rallies.

The shock and disgust Du Bois felt were acute when he realized that
White's ego stood athwart the timely release of the completed UN petition.
Much time had been invested in clearing a path through the bureaucratic
thicket at Lake Success: a personal note from Gunnar Myrdal to Trygve Lie,
the unspectacular Norwegian UN secretary general (his special adviser explained that "Mr. Lie himself is not in a position to receive such a delegation"); correspondence with John P. Humphrey, director of the UN's Division
of Human Rights; discussions with friendly delegations (including sympathetic appeals on behalf of partition for Palestine); an afternoon with Eleanor
Roosevelt in her capacity as a member of the United States delegation to the
United Nations and member of the Economic and Social Council. Informed
by the Division of Human Rights that only governments were permitted to
present petitions, then told by the U.S. representative to the UN that the
deadline for "new items" had passed, Du Bois had respectfully challenged
Trygve Lie to honor the spirit of the international organization. Finally, on
Thursday, October 20, 1947, the director of the Division of Human Rights received Walter White, Du Bois, and several others in his offices for the noon
presentation of *An Appeal to the World*. *The New York Times* and several major

newspapers reported the ceremony, which brought Du Bois a raft of congratu-lations, among them a hurrah from old nemesis Villard for presenting "the case against the U.S." But as the weeks passed, Du Bois became agitated by an inexplicable delay in the printing of the complete text of the UN petition for distribution to news organizations and to complementary civil rights, human rights, and labor organizations. A memorandum from the secretary explained the mystery. Walter White had recalled *An Appeal to the World* in order to add his own introduction in compliance with his arrangement with a commercial publishing house. White was curtly informed that, the board having voted to print and distribute the document, "I shall not consent to any addition to it." After several weeks more of standoff, the petition was released to the general public in January 1948.

White's vanity, compounding the roadblocks thrown up by the UN secre-tariat at the encouragement of the United States, delayed the circulation of the Du Bois petition until well after the release in late October 1947 of *To Secure These Rights*, the report prepared by the interracial blue-ribbon, fourteen-member President's Committee on Civil Rights. Reifying Myrdal's *An American Dilemma*, the Committee on Civil Rights' report deplored "a kind of moral dry rot" at the heart of American democracy and called for the abolition of the poll tax, anti-lynching legislation, voting rights statutes, a permanent FEPC, an ad-equately staffed civil rights division in the Justice Department, and desegregation of the armed forces. Outside the Deep South, the celebratory response of Amer-icans of all races and creeds to *To Secure These Rights* made *An Appeal to the World* seem almost crankily obsolete. A heartsick Du Bois faced the truth that timing had cost his petition the public attention he believed it so urgently deserved. Walter White, who, with Channing Tobias, had led the six-person delegation of clergy and union officials to Washington to propose the civil rights committee idea to Truman, called *To Secure These Rights* "the most courageous and specific document of its kind in American history." Hyperbole was foreign to Roy Wilkins's nature, but he, too, confessed that the Committee on Civil Rights had recommended "more than [he] had dreamed possible." Two months after the release of the committee's report, Attorney General Tom Clark's Justice Department would file an unprecedented *amicus curiae* brief with the Supreme Court in support of Thurgood Marshall and the Inc. Fund in the restrictive covenants case *Shelly v. Kraemer*. Thereafter, presidential action and the pro-gress of civil rights legislation in Congress would halt completely in the early months of 1948. White Americans were pleased by *To Secure These Rights*, but Gallup polling indicated only 6 percent of them in favor of securing these rights immediately.

Du Bois's petition was an early casualty of the new Cold War civil rights politics. Between September of 1946, when the board had unanimously endorsed the project that produced *An Appeal to the World*, and October 1947, when the director of the UN Division of Human Rights sacrificed his lunch period to receive the entreaty, White, Wilkins, and the board majority were seduced by presidential adviser Clark Clifford's campaign strategy to keep an unpopular and unelected president in the White House. With a supposedly invincible Thomas Dewey to his right and the virtually certain third-party candidacy of Henry Wallace to his left—the public figure widely acclaimed as the last true Rooseveltian—Harry Truman, a worried but canny calculator, bamboozled the NAACP. On June 29, 1947, a glorious Washington Sunday of blue skies and low humidity, the first president of the United States ever to address a national NAACP convention spoke to an audience of ten thousand from the steps of the Lincoln Memorial. Until Harry S. Truman's appearance at the thirty-eighth annual convention of the NAACP, however, no president had spoken publicly, unequivocally on behalf of the constitutional rights of the American Negro. Woodrow Wilson had defaulted on his promise. Harding had muddled his message in Birmingham. FDR left the task to Eleanor, and she was still at that task on Sunday as she preceded Truman at the microphone. "Now is the time," she warbled aristocratically, "for the people of the United States to be as great as their great men." Wearing the expression of a man who had concluded the biggest deal of his life, White applauded vigorously the president's nationally broadcast peroration: "We can no longer afford the luxury of a leisurely attack upon prejudice and discrimination. There is much that state and local governments can do. . . . But we cannot, any longer, await the growth of a will to action in the slowest state or the most backward community. Our national government must show the way."

By the fall of 1947, *An Appeal to the World* had begun to lose its appeal to Walter White and Roy Wilkins. Du Bois perceived that more was involved in the secretary's delaying of the petition than vanity. At the last board meeting in 1947, opinions had diverged on the next best step, with Du Bois forwarding a recommendation for multiple-language translation of the petition for distribution among all delegations attending the conference on the drafting of the UN human rights declaration in Geneva. Channing Tobias had backed the absent Du Bois vigorously with a short speech urging that the NAACP exploit the international embarrassment of America's race relations. "We have to work all the harder to focus our attention on the sore points," he insisted. The secretary's mind, though, was on more pressing developments. The current issue of *Counterattack: The Newsletter of Facts to Combat Communism*, published by three former FBI agents, charged that the association's Philadelphia branch had been infiltrated by Communists. White had gotten telephone calls about the accusation from the *World Telegram* and several other newspapers. Consigning the

UN petition to committee for further study, the board, on White's motion, voted to send instructions to all branches to report suspicious activity promptly to the national office on pain of cancellation "of the charter of any branch" failing to do so.

The secretary brought good and bad news to the first board meeting of the new year, 1948. Once again Du Bois was absent in Baltimore to be with Nina during the holidays and to make arrangements for long-term care now that her eight-month stay in Montefiore Hospital had finally ended. White's good friend the assistant secretary of state had telephoned to ask a favor. "Mr. Acheson said that it was of enormous importance that the association testify" before the House and Senate committees on behalf of the Marshall Plan. Voting to approve White's service to the nation, the directors were deeply upset to learn also that Eleanor Roosevelt had offered to resign to avoid the appearance of a conflict. The Du Bois petition had embarrassed her in her capacity as a member of the United Nations Economic and Social Council and embarrassed the nation, she stated. United States officials in Geneva had needed to maneuver adroitly during the last week in November 1947 (as well as apply direct pressure to a number of delegations) to derail widely publicized Russian and Polish attempts (supported by the Pandit-led Indian delegation) to engineer the reception of *An Appeal to the World* by the UN Human Rights Commission.

The plates under the international order had shifted violently during 1947, with shock waves felt throughout the association. The Walter White who had rushed into print to denounce the House Committee on Un-American Activities attack on the Southern Conference for Human Welfare (SCHW) in the summer of 1947 was moving rapidly through caution to ideological sanctuary. Whatever the realities of Communist Party designs on the NAACP (by White's own careful count, fewer than eight of the NAACP's fifteen hundred branches and chapters harbored Communists), the revving up of the international Cold War in March 1947 obliged Du Bois and Walter White and millions of their countrymen and women to make fateful choices that would shape the balance of the twentieth century. On February 21, the British ambassador had informed Secretary of State George Marshall that the state of Britain's economy compelled the withdrawal of military forces from Greece in six weeks. At the crisis meeting in the White House on February 27, attended by top congressional leaders and the Secretary of State, Marshall's elegant, Anglophile deputy captured the doomsday import of the Greek situation in a simile that shook the group. Soviet penetration of Greece, Dean Acheson pontificated in his ever-so British accent, would be "like apples in a barrel infected by a rotten one. The corruption of Greece would affect Iran and all the east. It would also carry the infection to Africa through Asia Minor and Egypt and to Europe through France and Italy. . . .

We and we alone [are] in a position to break up the play." Senator Arthur Vandenberg, Republican chairman of the Foreign Relations Committee, broke the silence of the Oval Office to say, "Mr. President ... scare the hell out of the country." On March 12, before an emergency joint session of Congress, the president requested $400 million in aid for Greece and Turkey and announced the containment policy that would extend the Monroe Doctrine to the rest of the inhabited planet. His signature on Executive Order 9835 came two weeks after the promulgation of the Truman Doctrine.

"President Truman's plea to arm Greece against Russia," Du Bois had roared in the *Defender*, was the "most stupid and dangerous proposal ever made by the leader of a great modern nation." He scoffed at the administration's claim that it was fighting communism to save civilization, when the aid package to Greece patently was for the benefit of British imperialism "or for the profit of the American oil millionaires." Anticommunism was the last refuge of the rich, the Evangel disseminated by monopoly capital and militarists to prove that any thought "or effort to abolish poverty or break monopoly, or to make unemployment impossible or permit the state to conduct industry, is not only futile but part of a nasty criminal conspiracy." Du Bois's editorial eruptions continued throughout 1947. "That's the ticket; let the Great Truman tell 'em! Down with Stalin. Up with Bilbo and Rankin. $400,000,000 for new wars and not a cent for education." In July, he had denounced the U.S. plan for the international control of atomic energy as a charade mounted by Big Business through the UN speech of the comically vain Bernard Baruch. While the Negro press and most of the political class applauded *To Secure These Rights*, Du Bois had seen much to be discouraged by. "No president has spoken fairer on race discrimination than President Truman," he avowed, "and few presidents have done less to implement their sayings." The entry of the NAACP into the ranks of the Truman administration was to be deplored, and Du Bois took exception to the secretary's request in November for a list of recommendations to send to Eleanor Roosevelt. She was then in Geneva attending the Human Rights Commission conference that would eventually debate the disposition of the Du Bois petition. He notified the flabbergasted White that he could be of no service to Mrs. Roosevelt. She had given only "vague and meager advice" when asked to assist the association at the UN. Had she or the Human Rights Commission "wished our advice or opinion," they had had a year in which to do so. The request was yet another policy charade, he concluded. "Mrs. Roosevelt is following orders."

Du Bois greeted the new year with a request that his readers join him in asking Henry Wallace to run for president on a third-party ticket. There was not, in his view, a single candidate from the two major parties "for whom a

Negro can vote with self-respect." Truman: "What he says today has nothing to do with what he said yesterday." Robert Taft: "He wants an FEPC without teeth." Dewey: "a complete opportunist politician." Du Bois's candidate of choice had been jettisoned by FDR as his vice president at the 1944 Democratic convention. Since his dismissal from the secretaryship of commerce by Harry Truman in 1946, he had been senior editor of the *New Republic* and a powerful critic of Truman administration policies. To his many admirers, Iowa farmer Henry Agard Wallace was Mr. Smith come to Washington, a gangly, hayseed visionary whose independence and honesty evoked American virtues in short supply among elected officials. Harold Ickes and Sidney Hillman spoke of Wallace as the Gideon of a resuscitated New Deal. Colored citizens were intrigued to learn that his earliest instruction in the science of plants had come as a boy in Iowa at the knee of the venerable George Washington Carver.

The day after the president's speech to the joint session of Congress, Wallace had lamented on national radio the Truman Doctrine as a tragic turning point in American history. Like Du Bois, the former vice president (who spoke some Russian) possessed an inflated opinion of his understanding of Russia, having been dispatched by FDR on a fact-finding mission to its outlying regions in the summer of 1944. The famous Madison Square Garden speech that had cost him his cabinet position in September 1946 encapsulated the convictions of several million American progressives and internationalists. "We want peace with Russia," Wallace had shouted on the night of the twelfth, "but we want to be met halfway. We want cooperation." Du Bois deployed his finest imperative phrasing on Wallace's behalf in the *Defender* for January 3, 1948: "In this great crisis of the history of the world, there stands forth in America one man, and one man alone, who is worthy of leadership and of support and that is Henry Wallace." Conceding that the chances of a successful third-party candidacy were "about nil," Du Bois reasoned that it would be "infinitely better for us to throw our votes away upon a great man who stands for real democracy than to shame ourselves, our people, our country. . . ."

For the moment, Du Bois shifted focus to his UN petition. It was intolerable that *An Appeal to the World* should remain any longer in limbo. Senator Warren Austin, head of the U.S. delegation to the United Nations, had won the first round in the Human Rights Commission in Geneva. Du Bois laid the groundwork for a second round in Paris, where the petition would be introduced in debate before the UN General Assembly. Once again, the delegations from India, the USSR, the Eastern Bloc, and Scandinavia went through the motions of endorsement. In a show of sincere empathy and calculated expectation of reciprocity, he and his research assistant, Hugh Smythe, lobbied the resistant

Liberian delegation on behalf of the Palestinian Jews. "The Case for the Jews" in the *Chicago Star* was an almost superheated brief for the establishment of a Jewish state. The centennial suffering of the Jewish people, like the unrelieved afflictions visited on the Negro people, presented "something terribly simple" about the legitimacy of its claim upon the world community. As momentum built up behind the petition, Eleanor Roosevelt communicated her extreme displeasure to Walter White. The great lady summoned Du Bois to an interview in the Park Avenue offices of the U.S. delegation to the UN on June 30, 1948. Mrs. Roosevelt explained that the U.S. Department of State had determined that it was unwise "to put *our* petition" on the agenda of the Assembly for discussion "since no good could come from such a discussion." Du Bois submitted that he felt that the world "ought to know exactly what the situation was in the United States. . . ." They failed to reach an accord, and Du Bois parted with the promise that if any further action were taken to present the petition, she should be notified.

Perhaps he might still influence the course of UN deliberations on the rights of subject peoples when he attended the meeting of the UN General Assembly in Paris, he thought. Suddenly, as in the San Francisco situation in 1945, Du Bois found himself demoted. At its late July meeting, the board voted to have the secretary represent the association in Paris. Du Bois was to remain in New York in an advisory capacity to the secretary. On September 7, 1948, Du Bois informed the secretary and the board of his refusal to comply with White's request for a memorandum "on matters that are likely to come up at the Paris meeting of the United Nations." The memorandum skewered the secretary for having accepted the administration's invitation to serve as special consultant to the U.S. delegation to the UN. This decision was tantamount to collusion, and placed the NAACP in the lap of the United States government, he fumed, a government that had sided with Italy's grab of most of Eritrea, that had "opposed the best interests of India . . . has not defended Indonesia, and is clearly straddling on Israel." He continued: repeated requests for clarification of the policy of nonengagement in "political activities" had gone unanswered. Yet by the actions of the secretary "we are to be loaded on the Truman bandwagon, with no chance for opinion or consultation, [and] we are headed for a tragic mistake." With that, the director of special research signed off. He denied, as he had done in 1934, any role in the leak of the implacable memorandum to *The New York Times* (where irascible George Streator now served as its first Negro correspondent). It was moved by William Hastie and seconded by Hubert Delany in the board meeting on September 13, 1948, that Dr. Du Bois be formally advised that "at the expiration of his present term" his contract will not be renewed.

✳ ✳ ✳

BEFORE THE POINT of no return had come in his relationship with the secretary, Arthur Spingarn and Louis Wright had continued to urge Du Bois to work less and enjoy himself more. Leave the limelight to White. He and they were getting on in years, they had said, and occasionally Du Bois had indeed paused to survey the depopulating scene. Charles Edward Russell, one of the founders of the association, had died. Ernest Just, the first Spingarn medalist, passed away in 1941. In January 1946, Countee Cullen had died. He was forty-three, a dispirited English teacher in the New York public school system and conveniently married to Ida Mae Roberson. Du Bois's obituary was unsentimental and fair. "Cullen's career was not finished. It did not culminate. It had laid fine, beautiful foundations but the shape of the building never emerged." Perhaps American Negroes had failed to give him enough encouragement. It was a great loss. Will had seemed surprised to realize that in May of 1946 he and Nina had passed fifty years together. She was still at Montefiore Hospital, slowly recovering from her stroke, alert and pleading for premature release. He had recaptured with his capable pen the outline and chronology of their loveless but publicly circumspect marital odyssey in a perfectly self-centered piece entitled with Freudian justice, "My Golden Wedding," for *People's Voice*. "I seem in these fifty years always to have been attempting to rear splendid phantasies," he reflected, "but on the wavering foundations of a world which, after moments of fine ballance, moments of high hope, went crazily swaying and dipping." Nina would have certainly nodded yes. "My wife and I have never had the pleasure of meeting Mrs. Du Bois," Anson Phelps Stokes had regretted in his congratulatory note (as did a large number of others) and so addressed the substance of his tribute to the person who had done more "than any other living man to make the world conscious of Negro potentiality and of the necessity of recognizing the Negro's rights to full citizenship in our democracy." That *Inside U.S.A.*, John Gunther's massive best-seller published later that year, quoted his words in conversation and accorded him "a position almost like that of Shaw or Einstein in his field" pleased Du Bois even more than the anniversary messages.

Upon his departure from the NAACP in September 1948, he stood on a pedestal occupied by no other American Negro, the senior intellectual of his race and its unexcelled propagandist—idolized or reviled, depending on the region of the United States and the complexion and education of his audience. The eightieth birthday celebration sponsored by Fisk University and its New York alumni at the Hotel Roosevelt honored him as a national treasure. Arthur Spingarn presided at the occasion with speeches by John Hope Franklin and Mark Van Doren. Greetings came from Nehru and Norman Manley of Jamaica. Regrets sent in response to E. Franklin Frazier's invitations effusively lauded the honoree. Amazed and delighted to see him "carry on," Melville Herskovits thought Du Bois must be deeply satisfied to realize that "slowly but surely, so many of the things that you have been fighting for are being turned into actuality." It was a fragile eminence, nevertheless, hostage not only to the notoriously short attention span of his fellow citizens, but subject to the always special conditions governing racial preferment in America. Implicit in the celebrity or influence accorded people of color was the requirement of a reciprocated gratitude that validated the mythic reality of a land of color-blind opportunity. Although Du Bois had headed the *Negro Digest* list of "The Big Ten Who Run America" and had been equated with Franklin and Jefferson in Henry Steele Commager's 1948 list, "Men Who Make Up Our Minds," three years after exiting the NAACP his reputation would lie in ruins and his freedom to work and walk among his compatriots would hang in the balance of Cold War justice. He would be but one victim among the many accused, censured, and convicted, yet the humiliation to be visited upon him, as with his friend Paul Robeson, was meant as an express warning to his people and their leaders—a message that their long struggle for equality must continue to exemplify commendable patience, conventional patriotism, and indifference to radical economic ideas.

Du Bois had decided by spring of 1948 that the alarming state of domestic and international unrest compelled him to flout the NAACP's prohibition of partisan activity. The attorney general's List of Subversive Organizations had been unveiled at the end of 1947 and the trek of suspect individuals to HUAC sessions and Fifth Amendment obloquy had begun in earnest that spring. Abroad, the snuffing out of Czechoslovakian autonomy and the convenient accidental death of its popular foreign minister, Jan Masaryk, unnerved Western Europeans and outraged American public opinion. Soviet blockading of overland access to Berlin and the narrow defeat of Communists in the Italian elections seemed to confirm Churchill's Iron Curtain prophecy. On March 26, *The New York Times* identified Du Bois, under the caption "Committee to Set Third Party Conclave," as research director of the NAACP among the signatories representing some seven hundred organizations committed to a Wallace run for the presidency. A month earlier, he had shared the stage with Henry Wallace at Harlem's Golden Gate Ballroom and (for an octogenarian whose leadership was "largely one of ideas") delivered a rousing stump speech to five thousand Harlemites. Whether they might lose their jobs or not, Negroes should vote for Wallace, "whether he can win or not," Du Bois urged them, adding an idea that was breathtakingly philosophical even for him—that even if Wallace lost the 1948 election, "there [was] every chance in the world that [his] principles . . . will win in 2048." He carried these convictions to the Progressive Party convention meeting in Philadelphia's Convention Hall in July. Asked by Wallace and campaign manager C. B. Baldwin—irrepressible "Beanie" Baldwin—

to deliver the keynote address, however, Du Bois recalled the NAACP's prohibition, reverted to his role of intellectual, and gratefully demurred.

In "My Fifty Years as an Independent," a lengthy survey of his political frustrations from McKinley to Wallace in *Masses & Mainstream*, Du Bois claimed to believe (with less than three months until the election) that Negroes were going to vote for Wallace or Dewey in November in reaction to Truman's recent silence on civil rights. But nothing had worked for Wallace after February 1948. His mid-May Open Letter to Stalin, proposing a fresh start in U.S.-Soviet relations and responded to positively by the Russian dictator over Radio Moscow, was dismissed out of hand by the administration and savaged as bordering on treason by the Cold War liberals of Americans for Democratic Action (ADA). What ought to have been strong points for the candidate—his internationalism, economic democracy, and civil rights courage—had turned against the naive, principled candidate in a climate of feral hysteria. In June 1948, twelve members of the Communist Party's national committee were arrested and eleven of them indicted under the Smith Act for conspiring to overthrow the government of the United States. A tortured, brilliant *Time* magazine editor with the look of an unmade bed, Whittaker Chambers, had identified a former Communist cell mate, Alger Hiss, an establishment paragon, as one of the Soviet Union's most strategically placed agents—dramatic proof that for paranoiacs there were real enemies in high places of trust. The CIO leadership had deserted Wallace after initial words of encouragement from Sidney Hillman, chairman of the CIO–Political Action Committee. Menaced by provisions of the Taft-Hartley Act requiring union officials to sign noncommunist affidavits on pain of decertification by the National Labor Relations Board (NLRB), and aggressively challenged by Communists within its ranks, the CIO turned upon itself in an orgy of purgation. The November outcome was a rout for the Progressives, a dismal 1,157,172 votes for Wallace—12,000 less than the total amassed by Strom Thurmond's breakaway Dixiecrats. Reflecting on the prominence of Communists among the Progressives, Eleanor Roosevelt feared that "Mr. Wallace was deceived."

Three weeks after the Progressive Party convention, Du Bois traveled to Wilberforce, Ohio, to deliver the annual memorial address to the national convocation of Sigma Pi Phi, the forty-four-year-old association of colored men of professional achievement—the *Boulé*. His topic, as he had duly informed the fraternity's Grand Sire, would be "the Talented Tenth." A half century ago, he had started on his teaching career at Wilberforce University and come near intellectually suffocating in the heat of its suspicious Methodism. He had written disparagingly of the institution down through the years. On the other hand, though, he had found a wife among its students and had come to receive an honorary doctorate in 1940 from Charles Wesley, Wilberforce's president and a

Du Bois disciple. On a warm Thursday afternoon in mid-August, he delivered a surprising text to the well-disposed audience of Sigma Pi Phi in Galloway Hall: 440 doctors, lawyers, college presidents, businessmen, morticians, dentists, and college administrators together with their wives and children—the colored "four hundred" of segregated America. He had come now to abjure the very idea of the Talented Tenth, he told them. "Karl Marx stressed the fact that not merely the upper class but the mass of men were the real people of the world," he began. It had become necessary to refocus the priorities of this leadership class. "My Talented Tenth must be more than talented, and work not simply as individuals," Du Bois continued as questioning side glances among his auditors increased with each paragraph. The passport to leadership was willingness "to sacrifice and plan for such economic revolution in industry and just distribution of wealth, as would make the rise of our group possible." In lieu of the Talented Tenth he proposed the "Guiding Hundredth." Nothing but "congenital laziness" should prevent the *Boulé* from increasing its numbers to three thousand by the next conclave, and to a membership of thirty thousand by 1960—the actual "numerical one-hundredth of our race." It was a speech that would have been much better received by the Progressive Party delegates in Convention Hall. Looking back, the "Talented Tenth Memorial Address" at Wilberforce seems to have marked the beginning of the end of Du Bois's purchase on the political loyalty of the class whose character was synonymous with his name. After the address, *Boulé* members left him sitting alone on a campus bench. The final dispute with Walter White on September 13, 1948, was only a month in the future.

Du Bois felt himself both pushed and pulled further left in the aftermath of Truman's victory and the wreckage of the Progressive Party. The narrowing parameters of patriotism excluded the internationalism of the recent past to such a degree that to advocate disarmament, superpower negotiation, and the existence of legitimate Russian grievances easily solicited a place on the attorney general's list of subversive organizations. Incoming board member and future NAACP chairman Robert Weaver, who admired Du Bois and liked White, praised White and Wilkins for being absolutely clearheaded about two things: "one of them was communism and the other was getting out of being unpatriotic." That Du Bois lost his *Defender* voice in May 1948 was symbolic. The newspaper's owners, the Sengstacke family, uncomfortable with his endorsement of Wallace, terminated the arrangement with Du Bois and dismissed its senior editor, Metz Lochard, one of Du Bois's oldest friends and political sympathizers. Meanwhile, beginning in March 1947, Du Bois also had provided copy to the *People's Voice*. Some of the most informed writing about the history and contemporary politics of the Belgian Congo, South Africa, Kenya, and Ethiopia appeared under his byline in this underfunded, chaotically run newspaper owned by congressman Adam Clayton Powell, Jr., and Harlem city councilman, Ben Davis, soon to be arrested with eleven other leaders of the CPUSA. With the exception of Powell, the circle around the *People's Voice*, comprised of Marvel Cook, Max Yergan, and Doxey Wilkerson, the paper's editor, was enrolled in the Communist Party. Marvel Jackson Cook, once Du Bois's invaluable assistant on *The Crisis* and now the radical newspaper's mainstay, had traveled a surprising ideological distance to become one of the Party's most trusted operatives.

As other leaders of the race made the implementation of *To Secure These Rights* their top priority, Du Bois characteristically looked upon the ultimate value of citizenship for Africans in America with the gravest misgivings if the peoples of Africa and Asia were to become subjects under a *Pax Americana* maintained for the benefit of the military-industrial complex. "Nothing more clearly demonstrates the hysteria of our times than the career of the Council on African Affairs," he judged. The Council on African Affairs was in turmoil when Du Bois was asked to serve on a special committee by Paul Robeson, its president, Hunton, its educational director, and Doxey Wilkerson, a key board member, at the beginning of 1948. An audit disclosed large discrepancies in the expense accounts of Max Yergan, the executive director, as well as in the amounts reported to have been spent on the needs of black South Africans. Frederick Vanderbilt Field, the tall, jolly Vanderbilt heir who had bankrolled the CAA (Field liked to call himself a "striped pants" Communist), concurred with Robeson and several others that Yergan's departure was overdue. Du Bois excepted (George Padmore had revealed distressing details to him about Yergan's South African tenure as YMCA secretary), most people were usually as much impressed by the charismatic Yergan as Field, who called Max "one of the most charming people I have ever met—a wonderful guy to be with." Frederick Field's wife at the time had the same estimate of Yergan, which had been a factor in the Fields' recent separation and divorce.

As chair of the council's special committee, Du Bois was immediately presented with a handwritten blackmail letter sent to Field's wife now in California. Convinced, after comparing the letter with Yergan's handwriting, of the executive director's guilt, Du Bois, Field, and Hunton contacted the Post Office police, whose experts confirmed their suspicions and reported the felony to the Justice Department. What Du Bois, Field, and Hunton had yet to discover, however, was that Yergan had already taken steps to immunize himself from the retributions of the left. Trusted as one of its most effective operatives by the top leadership of the Party, regarded as one of Robeson's closest friends and his principal political adviser, widely admired in civil rights circles for his lobbying and organizing abilities, Max Yergan had decided to walk into FBI headquarters in Manhattan and change creeds. Perhaps, as Lloyd Brown, another

Robeson intimate always believed, Yergan was a clever "hustler who reduced everything to cash," but his career had been a string of firsts, including being the first Negro to teach at City College. In mid-November 1947, a troubled Yergan had met Rayford Logan at Washington's Union Station for lunch. "Max realizes that the feeling against communists is so strong at this time that any individual or organization . . . simply has the cards stacked against it," Logan noted in his diary that night. By December 1948, after fisticuffs between the opposing attorneys, doors padlocked at the 23 West Twenty-sixth Street headquarters, and a hemorrhage of resignations, Robeson, Du Bois, and Hunton inherited the shell of a once vital Council on African Affairs. Max Yergan, by then, had already earned the warm approval of J. Edgar Hoover. FBI documents disclose a connection between the lapse of an FBI investigation into the Field blackmail letter and United States attorney Irving H. Saypol's interest in using Yergan as a witness in a Smith Act trial. The CAA resumed its work but was soon to be "hampered by its proscription by the Attorney General," Du Bois lamented.

The fight for the soul of the Council on African Affairs raged as White, Wilkins, and a majority of the NAACP board raged about Du Bois. Doxey Wilkerson and Herbert Aptheker had a proposition ready as soon as Du Bois resigned or was fired. By 1948, Herbert Aptheker had become indispensable to Du Bois. In January of that year, Du Bois designated him as the "best fitted person" to edit his letters, a decision that would make a comprehensive biography of Du Bois possible. In a sense, their relationship had begun seven years before they actually met when Aptheker, then age twenty-five, wrote an unfavorable review of Dusk of Dawn. Du Bois, of course, knew and admired the young scholar's Negro Slave Revolts and had welcomed his presence at the NAACP as a researcher, a year or so after Major Aptheker returned from artillery service in the U.S. Army. As the years passed, the bond between them would become familial and Du Bois would become like a grandfather to the Apthekers' precocious daughter, Bettina. The two Jefferson School colleagues, Aptheker and Wilkerson, approached Du Bois at some point before September 1948 with an offer. "We can be of help," Wilkerson proposed. "There was no bargaining. He was not asked to do anything, but it was a matter of getting him out from under what he was facing there and facilitating the things that we thought it would be helpful for him to be doing."

The CAA arrangement was certainly welcome. Du Bois's annual income after leaving the association would be somewhat less than $3,000, apart from speeches, and would come from the $1,200 A.U. pension and a similar NAACP annuity. Nina's medical and nursing care came to $3,600 for the year. No sooner had he welcomed the Aptheker-Wilkerson offer than Henry Wallace arranged a meeting in Chicago with Anita McCormick Blaine, the daughter of Cyrus

McCormick and the angel of progressive causes. Anita Blaine's money had underwritten the start-up of the new radical progressive weekly, the *National Guardian*, based in New York and run by the triumvirate of James Aronson, Cedric Belfrage, and John McManus. "The Lady of the Lake," the patrician Belfrage liked to call her—"she didn't understand at all what was going on, of course," he thought. Now, as family members and her attorneys fretted, she was prepared to pledge millions to establish a world peace foundation. Du Bois's requirements were modest. Their conversation in Chicago went extremely well, but Mrs. Blaine would prove to be slightly absentminded. "Your letter was under the door with the check for five thousand dollars which you promised me for the year beginning April first," Du Bois would write her gratefully on June 2, 1949.

The new support network formed up quickly around Du Bois toward the end of 1948. At the invitation of its director, Howard Selsam, Du Bois had delivered a timely speech on freedom in education to the Jefferson School at the beginning of the year. Talented, effusive Annette Rubinstein, who taught literature at the Jefferson School, but would soon leave the Party, possessed a cerebral vivacity and sense of humor that Du Bois found captivating. She discovered that Du Bois was "still, in many ways, [an] aristocratic" Marxist, and this quality delighted Rubinstein. He became active in the National Council of American-Soviet Friendship, headed by the pacifist Presbyterian minister Richard Morford, who was assisted by William Howard Melish, an Episcopal priest in Brooklyn whose radical politics would soon cost him his church.

In September, Aronson, Belfrage, and McManus offered Du Bois the *National Guardian* as an infinitely more appropriate pulpit for his ideas than the *Defender*. The *National Guardian* offer roughly coincided with the final revisions to a lengthy essay to appear in *The Sunday New York Times Magazine* in November. Du Bois's guardedly optimistic "The Negro Since 1900: A Progress Report" predicted that the "goal of democracy" would be within sight if the progress of the last thirty years could be sustained. Arthur Sulzberger would recommend no further pieces from Du Bois after this one. "Africa Today," in the November *National Guardian*, followed by "Africa for the Europeans!" in December, described the colossal schemes for European consolidation of African possessions being seriously discussed in Great Britain. Its best-paid contributor (at fifty dollars an article), Du Bois would appear regularly in the *National Guardian* until 1961, writing some 120 articles. He was a frequent feature at the protest meetings and dinners for the plethora of causes that allowed room for little else on the calendar of the left. "How can we forget," Du Bois wrote when asked by Melish for a Madison Square Garden statement, "that it was the Russian people and their army which saved Western civilization in the Second World War?" Joanne Grant, one of three colored *Guardian* reporters (Louis

Burnham and the Communist hardliner, Eugene Gordon, were the others), was astonished the first time she saw Du Bois rise from his platform chair and quietly exit the hall as speakers droned on interminably. Bed by ten was his commandment.

Invited at the beginning of the year to serve as a member-at-large of the National Council of Arts, Sciences, and Professions (ASP), Du Bois had immediately informed Harvard astronomer Harlow Shapley of his acceptance, although he must have been surprised to see Rufus Clement listed with Linus Pauling, Olin Downes, and John De Boer as one of four regional chairs of the restructured peace organization. Certainly the fight against war should be regarded as "one of the first items in [the] fight against race prejudice," he wrote Shapley on July 2 after attending the large meeting at the Hotel Biltmore summoned by Albert Einstein, but Du Bois frankly doubted that the NAACP would "take any action." By the time of the ASP meeting in late December 1948, the aggravated tensions caused by the Berlin airlift and the retreat of Chiang Kai-shek's nationalist armies made war increasingly likely. Du Bois and Shirley Graham left the meeting early, but not before he had agreed to chair the writers' committee at the ASP-sponsored peace conference to be held in March at the Waldorf-Astoria. Harlow Shapley's call for the international Cultural and Scientific Conference for World Peace was an appeal for sanity as suspect as it was eloquent in the superheated political climate of the United States: "We do not think the question worthy of debate as to whether capitalism and socialism *can* exist together. Both do exist. The only question worth discussing is how to restore the mutual acceptance of that fact . . . which alone can avert World War III." The members of Du Bois's writers' committee were F. O. Matthiessen, a Harvard literature professor, A. A. Fadeyev, secretary-general of the Soviet writers' union, and Norman Mailer, the novelist and Wallaceite.

During three days in late March 1949, the Cultural and Scientific Conference or Waldorf-Astoria Peace Conference convulsed Manhattan's East Side. The Catholic War Veterans picketed. Hundreds of citizens, affiliated and unaffiliated, patrolled the sidewalks hoisting posters bearing a babel of angry messages. Press and radio had given the conference the advance billing reserved for natural disasters. To *Partisan Review* and the ad hoc band of several hundred incensed Cold War liberals calling themselves Americans for Intellectual Freedom, the Waldorf-Astoria Peace Conference was a Communist front whose perniciousness was the more deadly because of the presence of so many of the sincerely misguided. Sidney Hook, Mary McCarthy, and Dwight Macdonald patrolled the corridors and wedged themselves into the panel discussions to combat heresy and Lillian Hellman. Irving Howe, writing for *Partisan Review*, sneered that the Stalinists "could find no 'big name' intellectual—no Dos Passos or Richard Wright or Edmund Wilson—to lead off the conference." Howe made no mention of the fact that the State Department had denied visas to much of Latin America and to all applicants from Western Europe (thereby eliminating Picasso, Paul Éluard, J. D. Bernal, Eugénie Cottin, among others). Seven visas were approved for Russia and four or five each for Poland, Czechoslovakia, and Romania. At Du Bois's writers' session, Howe described Maxim Shostakovich's performance as that of an apparatchik, followed by a reluctant Norman Mailer ("a perfect illustration of a politically inexperienced mind") expressing disillusionment with both superpowers and consigning the world to the terrible prospect of war.

Shirley Graham naturally thought that Du Bois's speech in Madison Square Garden, on March 27, the final night, was the high point. He spoke to the delegates with an intensity that conveyed something of the depth of his revulsion. Centered by spotlight, his clipped diction enhanced by the microphone, Du Bois proclaimed the Cultural and Scientific Conference for World Peace a success. "In a time of hysteria, suspicion, and hate" they had brought together one of the "largest gatherings of creative artists and thinkers the world has seen." They were not now, nor probably ever would be, in agreement on all matters, "but in one vital respect our agreement is complete: *No more war!*" He was there to introduce Harlow Shapley, but he had not yet said enough. When the applause subsided, he continued. "We know and the saner nation knows that we are not traitors nor conspirators; and far from plotting force and violence it is precisely force and violence that we bitterly oppose." He spoke hurriedly of the failure of the League of Nations and now of the United Nations to address the cancers of imperialism and racism. Eighty-one years seemed to fall away as Du Bois delivered his peroration: "I tell you, people of America, the dark world is on the move! It wants and will have Freedom, Autonomy, and Equality. It will not be diverted in these fundamental rights by dialectical splitting of political hairs. . . . Whites may, if they will, arm themselves for suicide, but the vast majority will march over them to freedom!" And still he was not quite finished. Race war was not the answer. "What we all want is a decent world, where a man does not have to have a white skin to be recognized as a man . . . where sickness and death are linked to our industrial system." Then he was done: "Peace is not an end. It is the gateway to full and abundant life." Shirley Graham noted that even some of the policemen in the Garden applauded.

Stirring public addresses became the order of the day. The North Atlantic Treaty Organization (NATO) was heading for approval by the U.S. Senate, the Canadian parliament, and ten European legislatures, a development that Du Bois and the organizers of the Waldorf-Astoria conference regarded as the penultimate step to war. He certainly knew that the Kremlin had called for massive demonstrations to be mounted against the mutual assistance pact by Communist parties and their allies. But Du Bois had no misgivings about the genuine alarm of millions of Europeans and Americans, nor was he at all concerned that by participating with Communists in "peace-loving" demonstrations abroad his internationalist principles would be distorted and impugned. Asked to represent the ASP at the World Congress of the Partisans of Peace in Paris by Shapley, Albert Kahn, and O. John Rogge, who had emerged as one of the most dynamic of the council's leaders, Du Bois readily agreed. He flew to Paris in the third week of April 1949 as head of the small ASP delegation. Shirley Graham arrived two days later. As they entered their second course in the chandeliered dining room of the Hotel Claridge, the orchestra struck up "Old Man River," as Paul Robeson, huge and beaming, headed for their table. He had appeared unexpectedly at the Partisans of Peace conference and was flying off to Norway and Moscow in the morning. Du Bois ticked off the main points of the Waldorf-Astoria conference while Robeson listened with great concentration. "This Paris congress will clear the air," Robeson said forcefully, rising from the table. "Think of it—people of seventy-eight nations joining here to grasp peace in their hands!" He left them in high spirits, none of them having the remotest intimation that the few extemporaneous words spoken that afternoon in the Salle Pleyel by Robeson had ended his career in the United States. Precisely what Robeson had said, what Eslanda Robeson said he said, what the Associated Press wire service distorted, or what he eventually claimed he did say, has finally been largely laid to rest by his careful biographer. It was unthinkable, he asserted, "that American Negroes would go to war on behalf of those who have oppressed us for generations against a country which in one generation has raised our people to the full dignity of mankind."

By the time Du Bois stepped to the bank of microphones in the gigantic stadium on the outskirts of Paris on the morning of April 24, a Sunday, wheels were in motion in the American civil rights community to disavow Paul Robeson. Roy Wilkins called for a meeting of prominent leaders to condemn the performer. Solemn statements of disapproval were uttered by Mrs. Bethune, Adam Clayton Powell, William Hastie, Channing Tobias, Bishop Jacob Walls of the AMEZ Church, and a veritable pantheon of Negro dignitaries. Jackie Robinson, the most representative American Negro of the postwar period, would appear before HUAC hearings on Negro patriotism along with Charles S. Johnson, now president of Fisk, and Lester Granger of the National Urban League. Outside Paris, five hundred thousand French and other Europeans filed through the stadium shouting "Peace, no more war!" Du Bois preceded France's Nobel laureate (held jointly with his wife, Irene Curie), the photogenic physicist, Frederic Joliot-Curie who sat with Louis Aragon, Picasso, Pietro Nenni of Italy, and Konni Zilliacus, the British socialist. He denounced the United States in language that dramatically trumped anything Robeson was alleged to have said. "Let us not be misled," Du Bois cried out. "Leading this new colonial imperialism comes my own native land, built by my father's toil and blood, the United States. . . . Drunk with power, we are leading the world to hell in a new colonialism with the same old human slavery which once ruined us; and to a Third World War which will ruin the world." On April 29, the president of Morgan State College in Baltimore informed Du Bois's office that the failure "to condemn [Robeson's] treasonable statement" made Du Bois unfit to deliver the scheduled commencement address on June 8.

Resting in the French resort town of Hyères in the company of Graham in May, Du Bois began work on *The Ordeal of Mansart*, the first novel in what would become *The Black Flame*, a sprawling historical trilogy commencing in the final year of Reconstruction. He promised Anita Blaine that he would be back on the job of peace at the end of May. His new platform style brought an invitation from Moscow to an all-Soviet Peace Conference scheduled for the end of August 1949. Linus Pauling, Uta Hagen, and O. John Rogge were also invited, but as they were absorbed in the planning of an American Continental Congress for World Peace to be held in Mexico City in September, Du Bois volunteered to represent the ASP council. Shortly before he flew to Moscow, however, he appeared before the House Committee on Foreign Affairs to oppose the Mutual Defense Assistance Act. Helen Gahagan Douglas had no questions for Du Bois. Representative John Kee, Democrat of West Virginia, jousted with Du Bois after his statement that the real enemy was not Russia and communism but "soulless and utterly selfish corporate wealth." In Moscow, Du Bois was the only American in attendance. He spoke to six thousand, presenting a long and unimpeachably Marxist analysis of the United States' role in current world affairs. Returning home via Prague and Warsaw, he forwarded Anita Blaine a lively description of the ruin and rebuilding of these cities. He sent a delighted Czechoslovak female friend nylon stockings and an affectionate thanks for the "few days [they] had together" seeing Prague. The news awaiting him upon his return to New York on September 16 must have brought a flood of thoughts about one of the great romantic friendships of his life. Virginia Alexander had died. The end had come quietly on Sunday, July 24. Their last meeting in early March in Philadelphia had followed from his crisp note: "I shall arrive Saturday at your house about 5:45." Husband Bill had faded away soon after the couple moved from Birmingham to Philadelphia.

On the first day in July 1950, Nina Gomer Du Bois died. Her twilight life had ended in the bedroom of the Montebello Terrace home. "She was never that warm a person," Nurse Matthews thought. Nina lived mostly in the past and still talked occasionally of Burghardt. Elsie Matthews had warned that Nina was failing. "I Bury My Wife," Will's apostrophe, was properly confessional. He had, he said, in effect sacrificed her happiness to his duty to the race. Will took Nina's body to Great Barrington to lie next to Burghardt in Mehaiwe Cemetery.

There was not much time to grieve, however. At the request of Rogge that February, he had taken on the responsibility of chairing the new Peace Information Center (PIC). The charge of the new organization was to publicize the Stockholm Peace Appeal for nuclear disarmament in the United States. The succinct, eloquent document had been drafted and approved by the Partisans of Peace at the Stockholm world peace congress. That it was O. John Rogge's telegram of February 5 inviting Du Bois's participation in a meeting of some thirty persons in his home was to have decisive significance. Oetje John Rogge was the youngest graduate in the history of Harvard Law School. A major force in the Wallace campaign and in the ongoing peace initiatives, the forty-seven-year-old attorney was one of the most respected personalities of the left. The core group involved in the bimonthly meetings in various homes involved a dozen or so individuals: McManus, Rogge, Robeson, Graham, C. B. Baldwin, Albert Kahn, Johannes Steel of the *New York Post*, Gene Weltfish of the Congress of Women, Leon Straus, with Einstein sending encouraging statements from time to time.

The principals of the impressive-sounding Peace Information Center, located in the Chelsea Hotel in the beginning, were Du Bois, chairman; Abbott Simon, business manager; Kyrle Elkin, treasurer; Sylvia Soloff, secretary; and Elizabeth Moos, an educator and the oldest member of the group after Du Bois. "They were all straightforward people, unencumbered by personal ambitions or petty idiosyncrasies," said Du Bois. "They simply saw a job worth doing." Elkin, a successful hardware manufacturer with a large social conscience had been uninvolved in organized political activity until the Wallace campaign. He was never quite comfortable with any of his associates, particularly Elizabeth Moos, one of his "unfavorite people," he said, a grand dame who "fluttered around all the time. And she adored Du Bois." Elkin assumed Abbott Simon represented the CPUSA and reported regularly and directly to Joseph Starobin, the *Daily Worker*'s foreign editor. Abbott Simon had blazed into City College at fifteen, dropped out of Harvard Law School and into the Party, but remained at heart a gifted musician with training by Arnold Schoenberg. Simon was a well-groomed thirty-seven-year-old, polished, soft-spoken, but electrifying as a public speaker when denouncing the class enemy. His manner, keen mind, and prowess as an organizer were noticed by Eleanor Roosevelt and earned him White House access during his service in Washington as field director for the American Youth's Congress (AYC). Simon's admiration for "the Doctor" was filial and, in time, won Du Bois's deep affection. Sylvia Soloff prided herself on being an excellent secretary.

On July 13, 1950, nineteen days into the Korean War, the Peace Information Center issued a *Peacegram* stating that the Stockholm Appeal had received 1.5 million signatures from forty states. By Abbott Simon's count, two Nobel laureates, five Protestant bishops, and Duke Ellington (an error) had signed the petition. Overseas endorsements included Shaw, Thomas Mann, Madame Sun Yat-Sen, Edouard Herriot, the cardinals and archbishops of France, and a raft of prominent writers and educators. The goal of 2 million names was predicted to be but six weeks away. The *Peacegram* announced plans under way for a rally in New York on the scale of the Paris, Warsaw, and Stockholm peace congresses. On July 12, Dean Acheson, now secretary of state, had released a statement headlined across the nation. The Stockholm petition should be recognized for what it is, warned Acheson, "a propaganda trick in the spurious 'peace offensive' of the Soviet Union." Five days later, Du Bois's rejoinder was published by *The New York Times*: "Dr. Du Bois Calls on Acheson to Promise U.S. Will 'Never Be First to Use Bomb.'" And so Du Bois did, upbraiding the secretary's statement as devoid of all "intimation of a desire for peace, or a realization of the horror of another world war or of sympathy with the crippled, impoverished and dead who pay for [the] fighting." On August 11, William Foley, chief of the Foreign Agents Registration Section in the Justice Department informed Du Bois that he was required immediately to register the PIC "as an agent of a foreign principal within the United States." The foreign agents registration act had rarely been invoked before in American history. In the back-and-forth between the PIC and the Justice Department, Du Bois and the PIC's attorney, Gloria Agrin (of future Rosenberg case prominence), realized that all appeals for meetings and objections in law were irrelevant.

Du Bois had answered the call to yet another peace conference during the height of the non-negotiations with the Justice Department. Frankly, as he would admit later, he had simply been unable to take the demands of the Justice Department "too seriously." He flew to Prague to address the World Youth Conference in mid-August. His motives for the Czechoslovakian junket were clearly as much personal as organizational. Du Bois Williams, his attractive, willful granddaughter, had gone to Prague with the American youth delegation and promptly fallen in love with a young Czech film technician. She would soon decide that her ardent suitor "was really looking for a way out," but in the summer of 1950 she declared that Lubar Marek would be the love of her life. Philosophical reproaches by her grandfather were met with tearstained letters written in scalding language. In the midst of the family drama came an intercepting telegram from Abbott Simon underscoring the gravity of the Justice Department's registration demands. Du Bois arrived home to face the PIC dilemma in earnest and to give a final answer to the pressing request from the American Labor Party of New York that he accept its candidature for the U.S. Senate. His response to the latter, after weeks of amused indecision, was affirmative. On October 12, 1950, in a manuever that was thought to moot the issue, the PIC board voted to disband the organization.

Comedy and tragedy exchanged places rapidly. Du Bois was informed on February 2, 1951, that dissolution was unacceptable. The now-nonexistent Peace Information Center was again ordered to register as an organization representing, in effect, a foreign power. One week later, a grand jury in Washington handed down indictments against Du Bois and the officers of the peace center. Arraignment of the five was set for February 16 in the nation's capital. "Dear," she said, "this changes our plans. We must be married right away." Du Bois and Graham had originally planned to wed in a quiet ceremony in Graham's St. Albans, New York, home on February 27. "By morning I had a plan worked out," Graham recalled. A somewhat shaken W.E.B. Du Bois accompanied Shirley McCants Graham to the home of Reverend Edward McGowan on the evening of February 14. The unannounced ceremony was witnessed by Graham's surviving son, David. The following morning, a Thursday, the newlyweds flew to Washington for the federal ceremony set to unfold on the sixteenth. Simon, Elkin, and Soloff departed by train. Elizabeth Moos remained in Europe for the present, her plea of speaking engagements and travel complications having been acceded to by the court. A white and black battery of lawyers awaited them: Gloria Agrin, a thin, impatient woman feeling the strain of the Rosenberg defense; even-tempered Stanley Faulkner, a civil-liberties specialist without ties to the Party and retained by Elkin; Bernard Jaffe, already a veteran of Party battles despite his age and a good friend of Simon's. As the white attorneys were not members of the District of Columbia bar, representation of the PIC case by two local colored law firms was both mandatory and racially astute. George Parker of Parker and Parker was what Washington called a "cave dweller," a tall, patrician man whose family had resided in the city for generations. Attorney James A. Cobb of Cobb, Howard, and Hayes was of similar family background. As the defendants and their attorneys assembled for introductions and preliminary briefings, they realized that they faced the practical problem of accommodations in the segregated capital. The knowledgeable Du Boises had reservations in the Dunbar Hotel, the city's single habitable hostelry available to people of color. The New York attorneys and three of the defendants had arrived at the Dunbar not yet realizing the full Jim Crow implications of an extended stay in Washington. To continue the battle for peace and justice from two separate and unequal locations would have amounted to a preposterous mockery of principles. In violation of local ordinances, then, the Dunbar management agreed to house the interracial defendants. "We didn't know [that] it also accommodated later at night people drinking socially and people shooting craps in the lobby," but Soloff made the best of the ordeal. Du Bois's comments are unrecorded.

A group photo exists of the defendants in *U.S. v. Peace Information Center*. Shirley Graham Du Bois stands with them on the sidewalk. The federal courthouse provides the backdrop. Du Bois is at the center in homburg and gloves, and they appear to be mildly amused by a remark he has just made. The mood of the group would alter as the day wore on. Agrin only narrowly succeeded in getting the overtly hostile Judge Dickinson Letts of the U.S. District Court for the District of Columbia to postpone the trial date. A federal marshal led the defendants down a narrow hall and into a small basement room. As they were fingerprinted, Du Bois was ordered to remove his coat, empty his pockets, and answer details about his life. He was carefully examined for concealed weapons and then handcuffed to Elkin before being taken to the bail hearing. Du Bois recalled that "a stir and a murmur rose sharply from beyond the grated partition where the public could look through and see what was happening. . . . The marshal grumbled, looked disconcerted, but finally unlocked our handcuffs." Perry Howard's patronage days as GOP national committeeman from Mississippi had ended with the New Deal, but he still had the carriage and presence of his former influence in Washington, and it was his voice that rattled the marshal. Released on bail of one thousand dollars, Agrin understood how profoundly Du Bois "really felt debased by the whole process." His statement released immediately after the proceedings was appropriate. "It is a curious thing," it read, "that today I am called upon to defend myself against criminal charges for openly advocating the one thing all people want—peace."

Du Bois would reach his eighty-third year in eight days. Much planning had been invested in the birthday testimonial banquet to be held at the exclusive Essex House in Manhattan on the twenty-third. On February 19, the hotel informed banquet chairman E. Franklin Frazier that it would not honor its commitment. Notices of withdrawal and for-the-record declinations poured in from Mordecai Johnson, Rabbi Abba Hillel Silver of Cleveland, President Charlotte Hawkins Brown of Palmer Memorial Institute, and many more. Arthur Spingarn washed his hands of the event. Great as was her admiration for the Du Bois of the past, Margaret Mead refused "in any way to have my name associated with [the occasion]." Reminding Frazier of Du Bois's sharp public attack while his negotiations in Palestine were at a critical point, Ralph Bunche stated that it would be "sheer hypocrisy" to attend the testimonial. He could stand a good deal, Du Bois told himself, "but this experience was rather more than I felt like bearing." The desperate improvisation at Small's Paradise Restaurant in Harlem turned out to be a splendid solution. "You people always come down to see me when you're in trouble," the amused owner observed. "It was a mad house—if you could get a seat," Louise Patterson remembered. More than seven hundred people pressed into the famous nightspot. Frazier presided with gusto. The national head of Alpha Phi Alpha, Belford Lawson, roused the audience with a fighting speech on Du Bois's behalf. Paul Robeson spoke with great emotion. Greetings were read from Charles S. Johnson, Leonard Bernstein, Shostakovich, Langston Hughes, Mary Bethune, and the Partisans of Peace luminaries. Four days later, Du Bois and Graham Du Bois flew to the Bahamas for a three-week honeymoon. Shirley Graham Du Bois would make a point of telling friends that it had been a "real honeymoon" when they returned home. Du Bois sent roughly identical letters to Mildred Bryant Jones, Eileen Diggs, Ethel Ray Nance, and Georgia Douglas Johnson explaining the logic behind his decision to remarry. With the proceeds from the sale of her St. Albans home, Graham Du Bois negotiated the purchase of an imposing Brooklyn town house at 31 Grace Court belonging to the playwright Arthur Miller. Its formal parlor and French windows made an ideal setting for the replica of the *Winged Victory of Samothrace* and the vaguely Biedermeler furnishings that appealed to her husband. Du Bois protested the venture's extravagance but very quickly succumbed.

"The response of Negroes in general was at first slow and not united," Du Bois observed stoically in *In Battle for Peace*, his memoir of the trial. He perceived a reaction to his situation that revealed a sharpening class division. His own Talented Tenth hesitated, cogitated, and then decided in the main to keep a safe distance—notwithstanding notable exceptions. "This dichotomy in the Negro group, this development of class structure, was to be expected," the first sociologist of the race observed. The dichotomy would become more manifest in the future "as discrimination against Negroes as such decreases," Du Bois forecast. Walter White quietly let it be known in the right places of personal assurances to him from the attorney general that the evidence in the case was conclusive. For the sake of public appearance, however, the board, after voting down a sympathetic resolution, released a statement of august neutrality in late March. A statement drafted by the National Committee to Defend Dr. Du Bois for circulation among prominent lay and religious leaders in the Negro community failed to obtain enough signatures to be effective.

If representative Negroes were in short supply for the Du Bois cause, those who did not fit the classic Talented Tenth profile began to show their support. On a circuit of the Midwest and the Pacific Coast during June and part of July 1951, Du Bois gave fifteen speeches and Shirley twenty. The response in Chicago was exceptional. Joining with the left, blacks and whites, labor, students, and church people united in their support of Du Bois, the epitome of the Talented Tenth, Truman K. Gibson, Sr., president of Supreme Life Insurance Company, chairing the meeting in the coliseum. The National Committee to Defend Dr. Du Bois event in Los Angeles was an impressive success—"the largest meeting since the Dean of Canterbury was there," Du Bois was told. In San Francisco, two thousand filled the Civic Auditorium and a comparable number a large hall in Oakland, where Vincent Hallinan, the defender of Harry Bridges, fired the people up to make defense fund contributions. The support of the United Electrical Workers, the International Fur and Leather Workers, and a number of red CIO unions helped fill auditoriums and churches along the defense fund route. An encounter with a third-year history major at Berkeley must have gratified the Du Boises. Curious to know the history currently being taught in a great university, Du Bois arranged to meet one of the best students after a speaking engagement in a local Unitarian church. "Impressed and astonished," he learned from Leon Litwack and Professor Kenneth Stampp's teaching assistant that he, Du Bois, was being taught in the classroom at Berkeley.

Gloria Agrin's vexing petitions to the court caused the date of the trial to recede—April 2, May 14, October 3. Her strategy was at all costs to remove the case from Judge Alexander Holtzoff's calendar, the jurist who had sentenced Howard Fast to prison for refusing to reveal the membership of the Joint Anti-Fascist Committee. She was certain that her clients would be given severe sentences if found guilty, as was highly likely with Holtzoff presiding. To ascertain the veracity of the evidence of the government's alleged connection between the Peace Information Center and "foreign principals," Agrin demanded Holtzoff's authorization of several weeks of discovery proceedings among peace groups in Paris. The defense and prosecuting attorneys left together for France. "There was not a legitimate legal excuse for doing it," Agrin revealed. "The government lawyers were clowns," completely out of place in the French capital. While the strategic charade continued in Paris, Du Bois persevered in a vain quest for the support or endorsement of civil liberation and professional organizations. Arthur Garfield Hays of the American Civil Liberties Union replied to him that he personally regretted his board's decision not to take up the matter "until *after* the trial." The secretary of the Institute of Arts and Letters made a similar determination in the matter. Liberal circles in New York City showed extreme skittishness whenever secretary Alice Citron sought to involve them in Defense Fund events.

In the end, the trial of the Peace Information Center defendants was a judicial misfire by the Truman administration's Department of Justice. Although most colored Americans separated themselves from the main defendant's views as they knew them, they had expressed a determination to save the symbolic Du Bois by the time the parties faced Judge Matthew F. McGuire on the morning of November 8, 1951. The significance of Albert Einstein's agreement to testify on behalf of the accused was duly noted by the Justice Department. Lawrence Reddick, now librarian of Atlanta University, had given a powerful speech in New York's Town Hall in late September. The senior bishop of the AME Church sat with Corliss Lamont on the platform. The Chicago *Defender* published "The Accusers' Names Nobody Will Remember, But History Records Du Bois," a well-crafted piece by Langston Hughes (accompanied by a disclaimer) distributed in thousands of barbershops and beauty parlors by the Du Bois defense committee.

Hughes had proclaimed that "if W.E.B. Du Bois goes to jail a wave of wonder will sweep around the world." There were millions of Americans of all races, nevertheless, who thought it would be a wonder if Du Bois were acquitted.

Ex-congressman Vito Marcantonio's final two-hour argument for the defense was both theatrical and lucid. Marcantonio had been the tribune of the far left on Capitol Hill for seven consecutive terms, representing his Italian and Puerto Rican constituents of East Harlem and the radical politics of the American Labor Party (ALP) until his 1950 defeat in what he called the "gang-up" by a coalition of New York Democratic, Republican, and Liberal party leaders. His lone vote against United States entry into the Korean War had been a significant factor in the loss of his seat. Du Bois's decision the previous year to oppose Herbert Lehman for the Senate had been part of a desparate gambit to trim liberal votes from the Democrats for the ALP ticket. Senatorial candidate Du Bois ran a vigorous campaign, making seven radio broadcasts and ten public appearances across the state, starting off at Harlem's Golden Gate Ballroom and climaxing in a powerful delivery on behalf of peace and civil rights in Madison Square Garden on the night of October 24, 1950. "On the whole I enjoyed this unique excursion," Du Bois decided, astonishing himself by winning 4 percent of the New York vote and 15 percent of Harlem's for a total of 205,729 ballots—impressive totals for Du Bois, but insufficient to benefit Marcantonio. The defense of Du Bois and the peace center officers was Marcantonio's return of the favor.

The ex-congressman rolled over the government's almost suspiciously mediocre attorneys ("pinheads," Marcantonio called them) and demolished O. John Rogge, the government's surprise witness and the person whose February 1950 telegram to Du Bois had led to the PIC's creation. The prosecution's argument was one of "parallelism," a variation on the walking-talking-looking-like-a-duck thesis. It contended that similarities in the behavior of known European communists were sufficient to establish a subversive connection to the peace center defendants. Winding down from his ridicule and anger, Marcantonio put the nub of the case to the court: "Unless connection has been shown, there is no relationship of agency and principal." The case was that simple. The jury of eight Negroes and four whites was not permitted to render a verdict. To hand the decision to the jurors would be to "permit them to speculate on a speculation," stated Judge McGuire, and, in so saying, *US v. Peace Information Center* was dismissed on November 13. It was a rare courtroom victory in this Red Scare era, and the defendants, their attorneys, some two hundred supporters, and a good representation of the capital's Negro press corps celebrated that evening in the Hilton, racially desegregated but a few months earlier. Du Bois would be generous in his appraisal of the reasons behind Judge McGuire's decision, but Simon and Elkin felt sure that the White House and the State Department had reevaluated the political and public relations stakes involved in a conviction. The unexpected ruling precluded the public relations coup of Einstein's expected appearance as a character witness for the principal defendant. The acquittal also deprived the defendants of an opportunity to register memorable words in open court, but Du Bois could hardly have improved on the pith and appropriateness of remarks he penned several years after the acquittal. "I would have been hailed with approval if I had died at fifty," he ironized. "At seventy-five my death was practically requested."

EXEUNT

Du Bois would spend the next eight years without a passport, and he would remain deeply wounded because, with a few notable exceptions, the Talented Tenth that he had summoned into being had run for cover during his indictment and prosecution, even as large numbers of working-class black men and women attended Du Bois rallies, along with thousands of politically progressive white Americans. "It was a bitter experience," he admitted, "and I bowed before the storm. But I did not break." Comforted and assisted by Shirley Graham, and friends on the left—Esther and James Jackson, Abbott and Priscilla Simon, Doxey and Yolande Wilkerson, Herbert and Faye Aptheker, Anna Louise Strong, Howard Fast, Louis Burnham, George Murphy—Du Bois continued speaking, writing, scolding, and infuriating from his book-lined study in Grace Court and from his third-floor Manhattan office on Twenty-sixth Street. Henry Miller, the novelist, never forgot the experience of hearing the proud pariah speak one evening in a Newark, New Jersey, meeting hall. "The very majesty of the man silenced any would-be demonstration," he wrote afterward. "There was nothing of the rabble-rouser in this leonine figure—such tactics were beneath him. His words, however, were like cold dynamite."

"The Hard-Bit Man in the Loud Shirts," Du Bois's *National Guardian* farewell to Truman, was savage: "He ranks with Adolf Hitler as one of the greatest killers of our day." "Anything but Truman—even Eisenhower," he demanded. But what Du Bois and the nation got was Eisenhower's indulgence of Joe McCarthy, John Foster Dulles's policy of massive nuclear retaliation, the rearming of Germany, and the CIA-orchestrated overthrow of the governments of Iran and Guatemala. He protested Luce's American Century over and again. "These interests want war," he thundered in the *National Guardian*. "Only by war can China, Africa, Southeast Asia, and the Middle East be kept in their control." He liked Cedric Belfrage's description of the United States as a "frightened giant," and he grieved as he observed the frightened responses of Negro leaders to the auto-da-fe of McCarthyism. He became an embarrassment in the ultra-correct purlieus of representative Negroes and an unperson to the NAACP. His predicament was increasingly explained away as the result of age, ego, bitterness, and communist handlers, not least of whom was said to be Shirley Graham Du Bois.

Du Bois's opposition to the Marshall Plan, NATO, the Point Four program for the developing world, and the Korean War as instruments of capitalist imperialism were heresies that most of the spokespersons for the race deemed to be evidence of unreality bordering on the certifiable, an opinion Walter White allowed to be attributed to him over the Voice of America. His causes were not theirs—unrelated, dangerous civil liberties issues that brought guilt by association: endorsing *We Charge Genocide*, the Civil Rights Congress's 1951 petition that Robeson and William Patterson carried to the United Nations; defending the Rosenbergs with Aronson and Belfrage; serving as character witness in the Smith Act trial of Ben Gold, the former Furriers Union head who had provided funding for the National Committee to Defend Dr. Du Bois; testifying on behalf of James Jackson and Alexander Trachtenberg, the publisher, in the second round of Smith Act trials of CPUSA functionaries. On an October evening in 1952 as bleak as the prospects of the two convicted traitors, Du Bois spoke from a tightly woven text at a "Save the Rosenbergs" rally sponsored by the Civil Rights Congress at Central Plaza. The arguments he rehearsed to the packed meeting hall would be developed in his *amicus curiae* brief submitted (and denied) to the U.S. Supreme Court on behalf of the Rosenbergs. He thought it was highly relevant to note, as others had, that "at the time the alleged deed was perpetrated, we were friends and allies of the Soviet Union." But his next point—the suggestion that the world would have been a more fortunate place if "at the time the Rosenbergs were accused we had in fact freely given to the Soviet Union and to the whole world the secret of the atom bomb"—was decidedly a minority opinion on the left. Beyond the tragic fate of Ethel and Julius Rosenberg, he decried the larger tragic fate of a nation that does "unbelievable things . . . in the midst of war and fear." From his and Shirley's home in Grace Court, Michael and Robert Rosenberg departed after a children's party on Christmas Day with Anne and Abel Meeropol, the couple who were to be the boys' new parents.

In an utterly self-defeating gesture of contempt for capitalist justice that gave credence to the foreign-agents presumptions of a majority of Americans, Jim Jackson had followed a number of Party leaders in flight while on bail in 1951. He alone eluded the FBI dragnet for five years before turning himself in to be tried with Trachtenberg and several other prominent Party figures at Foley Square in an eleven-month show trial. Du Bois found himself derided as a character witness by the presiding judge and repeatedly challenged by the federal prosecutor to avow his membership in the Communist Party. Significantly, under oath, he stated flatly that he was not a Communist, but Judge Alexander Bix jibed that the witness was "a fella who would decide who and what was a Communist for himself." While Du Bois's editorials, speeches, and Smith Act testimonials were featured in the *Guardian, Daily Worker,* and *Masses and Mainstream,* the Negro civil rights establishment played out the hand dealt it by the national security state—uncritical patriotism in return for incremental race-relations progress. The NAACP secretary's "Time for a Progress Report" in *The Saturday Review of Literature* for September 22, 1951, was pure Dr. Pangloss. Du Bois knew that Mary McLeod Bethune was considerably less sanguine about the republic than White. She awaited news from Carl Murphy at that moment about his success in gaining Eleanor Roosevelt's help in removing her name from the attorney general's list of subversive individuals. A year later, in March 1953, Du Bois watched Langston Hughes perform an act of obscene obeisance before Senator McCarthy's senate subcommittee on investigations. The author of the poem "Good Morning Revolution" and the play *Scottsboro Limited* groveled before Joe McCarthy and Roy Cohn, agreeing with a smile that any of his works tainted by communism ought be removed from the overseas libraries of the United States Information Service. He was even "amazed to hear" that they hadn't already been purged, said the indignant Hughes. Serving as his own censor, Harlem's most popular man of letters deleted Du Bois and Robeson from the new editions of *Famous American Negroes* and *Famous Negro Music Makers.* "Much time and thought of misguided intellectuals has been devoted to helping deprive American Negroes of natural leadership or to scaring them into silence," Du Bois observed a month after Hughes's appearance before the McCarthy committee.

Thus, because he believed that the enemies of his enemies were his friends in Africa and Asia, neither communism's doctrinal rigidities nor the Soviet Union's 1956 rampages in Eastern Europe would shake Du Bois's commitment to world socialism. The axiom he now embraced was, he proclaimed, that, just as Africans in the United States "under the corporate rule of monopolized wealth . . . will be confined to the lowest wage group," so the peoples of the developing world faced subordination in the global scheme of things capitalist. Du Bois concluded that, for the sake of underdeveloped peoples everywhere, all tactics that contained American capitalism were fair. As a battle to the death had been joined between the two superpowers, he saw himself being compelled by the logic of his racial and economic priorities to espouse the cause of opponents of Wall Street and the Pentagon, even when such advocacy corrupted other ideals of intellectual honesty and humanism. "On Stalin" was an apostrophe to the dead dictator in the *National Guardian* that would have flattered the memory of Abraham Lincoln. It was of a piece with "Russia and America," the large manuscript that Harcourt, Brace rendered Du Bois's legacy a favor by declining to publish. The venom and plain bad taste of passages in "Russia and America" dealing with Leon Trotsky were at variance with the studied dignity of the Du Boisian polemical style and even beggared the exceptional, outrageous savaging expended on Marcus Garvey twenty years earlier. Khrushchev's Twentieth Party Congress revelations in February 1956 of Stalin's crimes left him publicly unmoved. In contrast to Robeson, who found the exposure of Stalinist horrors, whose enormity he had tried not to know, psychologically devastating, Du Bois adjusted the Russian casualty tables in light of the Atlantic slave trade, the scramble for Africa, the needless First World War, Nazi death camps, and the color-coded poverty and wage-slavery raging within and beyond North America. To Du Bois, the degradation of the communist ideal in Soviet Russia was philosophically irrelevant to the expiation of the sins of American democracy, whose very possibility he now deeply doubted.

His opposition to the Korean War had terminated the special rapport with Henry Wallace, and now close friendships began to fray and dissolve into embarrassed acrimony in the wake of the Kremlin revelations. Howard Fast, who had brought *The Souls of Black Folk* back into print, left the Party under a hailstorm of abuse the following year, severing one of Shirley Graham's closest ties. The publisher Albert Kahn withdrew into a troubled silence. Many of those who kept the political faith in their circle of friends and acquaintances had been made to pay with their freedom: Ben Davis, Cedric Belfrage, Alphaeus Hunton, James Jackson, Carl Marzani, Howard Melish, William Patterson, Henry Winston. Some, like F. O. Matthiessen, paid with their lives. Yet, out of this hollow American decade of terror and complacency came *Brown v. Board of Education*, and the old warrior was elated. "I have seen the impossible happen. It did happen on May 14, 1954." But the *Brown* decision also proved illusory, for Du Bois concluded the following year that freedom on the basis of "all deliberate speed" was an oxymoron. Heartsick, he watched as the Eisenhower administration encouraged by silence and indifference the white South's most intransigent and violent elements, thereby delaying the dismantling of legal segregation by a decade. The appearance of Martin Luther King, Jr., and the Montgomery bus boycott were something of a puzzle for Du Bois. He observed somewhere that he had expected to live to see anything but a militant Baptist preacher. In the Indian journal *Gandhi Marg*, Du Bois drew obvious parallels between Gandhi's liberation of India and King's success in Alabama and went on to speculate that the gifted, committed preacher might be the American Gandhi. King wrote a grateful note in response to the Du Boises' letter supporting the Montgomery boycott. But nonviolent passive resistance devoid of an economic agenda increasingly disappointed Du Bois, and he finally decided in late 1959 that King was not Gandhi: "Gandhi submitted," Du Bois asserted, "but he also followed a positive [economic] program to offset his negative refusal to use violence."

An eloquent grumpiness seemed to overtake him more often than not as the fifties ran down, a rutted readiness to pontificate apocalyptically that was less due to advanced age than to ideological predilections in need of updating and fine tuning. Just as the long-blocked evolution in the nation's race relations was about to undergo its most momentous transformation in a century, the great contrarian foretold a dismal future for American Negroes. Minority incomes were rising as jobs in industry and membership in organized labor made unprecedented increases. The augmentation of the black middle class by G. I. Bill–educated professionals was a striking social feature of the Eisenhower years—the rise of an ostentatiously successful black bourgeoisie sadly lacking in social conscience who provided E. Franklin Frazier with the material to write an American classic. But while the cadres of the NAACP and the Urban League and the subscribers to *Ebony* magazine rejoiced at what they understood as indisputable vectors of progress, Du Bois remained skeptical and often depressed. "I myself long stressed Negro private business enterprise," he allowed, but now he knew that "the one hope of American Negroes is socialism." His American Negroes, once the vanguard of the darker world, were now imprisoned in a militant capitalism cutting them off from the progressive trends of the day. "Whither now do we go?" he implored. "We American Negroes can no longer lead the colored peoples of the world because they far better than we understand what is happening in the world today. But we can try to catch up with them."

In April 1958, he came to Howard University's Rankin Chapel to speak to seven hundred students hungry to hear the legend. "Today, the United States is fighting world progress," Du Bois told the students and faculty, "progress which must be towards socialism and against colonialism." His appearance on the Howard campus and induction several weeks later as an alumni member of Fisk University's chapter of Phi Beta Kappa were significant indications of the abating red scare, as had been the evening of tributes and unveiling of the famous Zorach bust at the Schomburg Collection the year before (authorized by nervous trustees of the New York Public Library). Van Wyck Brooks had brought greetings from his Connecticut neighbor Helen Keller, who remembered as a twelve-year-old the day William James and Du Bois had come to speak with her at Boston's Perkins Institute for the Blind. Brooks avouched that the evening's guest of honor was the first to see that "the darker people of the world would overthrow the world unless they got their share of democracy."

Ninety years old, Du Bois's birthday was celebrated by a thousand people at New York City's Roosevelt Hotel on the evening of March 2, 1958. Gruff Angus Cameron, ousted for his progressive politics from Little, Brown where, as senior editor, he had given C. Vann Woodward his *Reunion and Reaction* title, co-chaired the grand anniversary dinner with Essie Robeson. Hubert Delany and Essie Robeson spoke, Paul sang, followed by John Hope Franklin, now chairman of the Brooklyn College history department (a racial first) and a Brooklyn Heights neighbor of the Du Boises. Arthur Edward McFarlane II seated in his mother's lap on the dais was two months old and kept his bright-eyed counsel throughout the long evening. "He has kindly consented to permit me to read to you a bit of advice," proud great-grandfather Du Bois announced, as Yolande Du Bois Williams, Du Bois Williams McFarlane, and the thousand guests listened to the distinguished preceptor enjoin the well-behaved infant, "Make this choice then, my son. Never hesitate, never falter." Salutes arrived from the humble and the prominent, from the presidents of Fisk, Morehouse, Morris Brown, Spelman (Florence Read had retired), and Tuskeegee. The *Courier* and the *Defender* issued special biographical supplements. Corliss Lamont, soon to seek his advice about a symbolic U.S. senate run for himself, spoke through Carl Marzani to praise Du Bois's exceptional contribution to the "great democratic and human contributions of our time."

Still, Franklin noted that neither Fisk University nor the NAACP sponsored the occasion and that "numerous so-called respectable people steered clear of [Du Bois] as though he were tainted by the rantings of the McCarthyites and the cold war hawks." "Respectable" folk in the academic mainstream were prone to condescension when not distinctly hostile. Two historians whose biographies of Du Bois appeared only months after the Roosevelt Hotel occasion agreed, as one of them wrote in *The Progressive*, that Du Bois was "a lonely and tragic Negro. Once a national audience, black and white, heard his plea for Negro equality. Now few listen, and fewer still heed him." Readers of the *Nation* must have expected a similar verdict from the author of "W.E.B. Du Bois: Prophet in Limbo." But the biographer Truman Nelson delivered a judicious message rather different from that suggested by the title imposed upon his essay. His theme was the redemption of the unappreciated prophet, "arrested — as Thoreau was arrested, and Theodore Parker and Garrison, Phillips, Samuel Gridley Howe, Frank Sanborn, Ezra Heywood, Sacco and Vanzetti." And Nelson wagered against the present: "Someday the people in this country will demand that their own records be set straight, and alongside the political accidents, the Presidents and Senators, will go the enduring and usable truths of the American Prophets. Among these Prophets will be W.E.B. Du Bois."

The month after the birthday celebration, the Supreme Court, in a five-to-four decision in the Rockwell Kent and Walter Briehl cases, finally handed down an opinion consonant with the First Amendment. The State Department's denial of passports on political grounds was ruled unconstitutional. His passport restored, Du Bois and Shirley Graham Du Bois sailed away in August 1958 to red-carpet receptions in Eastern Europe, the Soviet Union, and China, mooring in London for a replenishing four weeks in Paul and Essie Robeson's London town house before resuming their triumphant progress. He appeared on BBC television, gave several lectures, then crossed over to Holland, where Paul Bremen, an energetic young one-worlder, arranged a lecture and a television interview. Czechoslovakia's Charles University, the oldest in Central Europe, bestowed its honorary doctorate of the science of history *honoris causa* upon the erect nonagenarian in a six-hundred-year-old ceremony accompanied by the playing of the "Star-Spangled Banner" in the ancient Carolinium. In recognition of his politics and his scholarship, Humboldt University (the former Kaiser Friedrich Wilhelm University of Berlin) fulfilled an old dream by bestowing the honorary degree of Doctor of Economics, the degree he had "coveted . . . sixty-five years before . . . to the strains of Bach in the great hall" where, Du Bois observed with satisfaction, "women students [were] now common but in 1892 never admitted."

But where was Uzbekistan and what was his role to be there? In any case, it was politically evident that Du Bois was expected to accept the invitation to attend the African and Asian Writers Conference in Tashkhent. The Du Boises bore up under one week of bad films, badly dubbed, and badly written literature, better left untranslated, until the Soviet Writers Union flew them out of Central Asia to Moscow. They were in nonstop motion from September to December, with Shirley Graham peeling off for ten days to represent her somewhat flagging husband in Accra, Ghana, at the All-Africa Conference organized by George Padmore. The message she read to the conference was a compendium of Du Boisian imperatives that owed perhaps as much to Ben Franklin as to Lenin. "My Brothers . . . You are not compelled to buy all they offer now. You can wait," he exhorted through her. "You can starve a while longer rather than sell your great heritage for a mass of western pottage."

In Moscow, they were given places of honor in Red Square from which to watch the world's longest stage show on November 7. Alla Bobricheva, the Du Boises' excellent young interpeter from the Soviet Peace Committee, faltered for an eternal few seconds as she captured in the Russian language Du Bois's nuanced remarks when the American guest and the Soviet premier stood face to face in the Kremlin receiving line. "But Du Bois did not speak simply" and Nikita Khrushchev "had bloodshot eyes from the vodka people drank to keep warm during the long parade," and she remembered vividly the premier's annoyed stare as she recovered her fluency. The second encounter went splendidly, just the four of them in the premier's private office in the Kremlin with talk of novels and Russian geography. "Nikita impressed me greatly this time," said this attractive, stylish woman who would become indispensable to the running of Georgi Arbatov's Canadian-American Institute, as Du Bois explained the need for the creation of an institute of African studies in the Soviet Academy of Sciences with a learned clarity that was equally impressive. At the end of the two hours, Khrushchev announced that the African institute would be authorized immediately under the direction of Russia's outstanding Africanist, Ivan Potekhin.

"By this time, however, nature had caught up with me," Du Bois wrote George Murphy, the red scion of the Baltimore newspaper dynasty, and Abbott and Priscilla Simon. Alla Bobricheva and her husband, Ovid Gorchakov, a writer of historical fiction and formerly Stalin's English language interpreter, bundled Du Bois off to Barveekha, the exclusive enclave and spa for the Communist Party aristocracy—"a beautiful place—fifty miles outside Moscow with tall pines and birches and snow," Du Bois wrote to friends in the United States. A decorated veteran of the Great Patriotic War, as all Russians of his generation called it, Gorchakov had spent his teens in Brooklyn and lost his only sister in the gulag. "Absolutely amazed by the breadth of his culture, his grasp of events, his vast erudition," Gorchakov wanted to impress Du Bois with his own worldliness. On long walks through the snows of Barveekha, he occasionally spoke his mind about the abuses, petty and terrible, of the calcified regime. But Gorchakov soon realized that, like Stafford Cripps, Du Bois "excused Stalin's terror" and that he was not at all disposed to discuss (wisely enough) the continuing imperfections of the Soviet system. After Shirley's return from Africa the friendship between the Du Boises and the Gorchakovs deepened. They were genuinely distressed by the spell of sickness that placed the durable nonagenarian in the Barveekha clinic, and their relief was delightfully tweaked by his first words upon being released. "Well, now," Du Bois told Ovid, "no sheets changed, no underwear, no nurses to come to you. I see why medical care is free of charge in your country." Some defects in the workers' paradise deserved criticism, after all.

Fully recovered, Du Bois went back to work preparing the text of his John Brown biography for publication in Russian. Du Bois's own autobiography that Angus Cameron had failed to persuade him to update was to be turned over to the writers' union translator, Vasily Kuznetsov, in Leningrad. *Vospominanya—The Autobiography of W.E.B. Du Bois*—would appear in the Soviet Union in Russian, six years before the English-language original would be published in the United States. Another Russian-language monograph, the thin book *Africa: Toward a History of the Continent*, saw life in the USSR and remains unavailable in English. Moscow State University awarded him an honorary degree and Russian television introduced him to the *nomenklatura* who had somehow never heard of *The Souls of Black Folk*. Meanwhile, Du Bois observed, read, and inquired in this nation that had grown up, he would suggest, under his care. He claimed to believe that in Khrushchev's Russia "the overwhelming power of the working class as representing the nation is always decisive." Yet his old reflex concept of the Talented Tenth melded with the dictatorship of the proletariat, for "as the workingman is today neither skilled nor intelligent to any such extent as his responsibilities demand," Du Bois applauded the role of the Party in "directing the proletariat toward their future duties."

The Kremlin New Year's Eve party offered for a magic moment a cinematic tableau of such poignant significance that even cynical KGB generals were momentarily affected. In a powerful tribute to Paul Robeson appearing in the *National Guardian* not long before sailing for Europe, Du Bois had written four short, coruscant sentences that he believed applied equally to himself: "In America he was a 'nigger'; in Britain he was tolerated; in France he was cheered; in the Soviet Union he was loved for the great artist that he is." The pariah years had annealed an unbreakable emotional bond from their respect for each other. Paul and Essie Robeson had arrived in the capital only a few hours before the Kremlin party. The festivities were already under way when they entered the vast, colonnaded hall by a side door and, as inconspicuously as possible for the giant Robeson, began to make their way among the long tables to sit with the elect of the International who were arrayed in bemedaled uniforms and Italian suits and gowns. Shirley Graham Du Bois captured the sequel:

> Both men rose simultaneously and began threading their way though the maze of tables toward each other. The going was a bit difficult; chairs were pushed out of the way and waiters with loaded trays had to sidestep them. But the two seemed unaware of the commotion they were causing. When finally they did meet, big Paul and small Du Bois threw their arms around each other in a bear hug and Mr. Khrushchev rose to his feet applauding. Then everybody in the hall was up, applauding and shouting their names.

China had been "lost," bawled Senator Joe McCarthy, because of a "conspiracy so immense and an infamy so black as to dwarf any previous such venture in the history of man." Hence, the United States denied the existence of Mao Tse-tung's People's Republic and forbade its citizens traveling to mainland China. The Du Boises' plane touched down in Beijing in early February 1959. Notwithstanding the Sino-Soviet split much in the world news, Du Bois had accepted the invitation of the Chinese Peace Committee without a second thought. Minister of Culture Kuo Mo-Jo headed the reception committee awaiting his descent from the plane that included the minister of health, Madame Li-Te'ch'uan, and the executive secretary of the Chinese Peace Committee. "Tall, slender, with dancing eyes," the Peace Committee secretary reminded Shirley Graham Du Bois of the colored executive secretary of the Urban League. Over tea in the terminal, China's minister of culture politely inquired whether the Du Boises wished to have their visit pass without publicity. "So far as we are concerned," Du Bois answered emphatically, "you can tell the whole world!" Twenty-three years earlier, his few days in Beijing had imparted a jumble of impressions: age-old monuments, an amorphous mass of people, and the "helpless, undefended welter of misery and toil." His mind must have filled with a flood of memories of cooperative Japanese officials in Manchuria, of the European-owned succubus of Shanghai and of an extraordinary luncheon tendered him in that city at which he spoke to the Chinese with brutal frankness. The Du Boises would spend nearly the entire month of February in the capital in a considerately paced, but full, itinerary of cultural events, interviews, press, and television appearances. To Du Bois's eyes, Mao Tse-tung's China had been transformed almost beyond recognition.

As they moved about Beijing in their ceremonial cocoon, Du Bois and Graham Du Bois knew absolutely nothing of the catastrophe inflicted upon the Chinese people by their omnipotent ruler. The combined disasters of Lysenkoism in agriculture, the metallurgical voodoo of millions of backyard furnaces, and the Pharonic great works projects across the land had so dislocated the labor force that by the time Du Bois arrived nearly ten million people had perished in the famine of the Great Leap Forward. For the first time in Chinese history, "every corner of this huge country experienced hunger" wrote one authority whose research has withstood challenge. The calamity of the unharvested grain from the new communes had shaken party cadres all the way to the top of the pyramid of communist power, although not party chairman Mao. "With the approach of the new year, 1959," the great leader's personal physician noted in his diary, "Beijing was in panic." The scenes to which the Du Boises were exposed presented a fable of disciplined bees working in revolutionary unison. Cataloging the public places, restaurants, homes of officials, factories, and schools visited, Du Bois assured himself that "always I saw happy people with faith that needs no church or priest," people who "laugh gaily when the Monkey King overthrows the angels." On the evening before Du Bois's ninety-first year, Premier Chou En-lai hosted a birthday party in his home that evoked superlatives from Shirley Graham Du Bois. The government officially observed February 23, and Du Bois was driven to Beijing University to deliver an address to be broadcast to Africa. "When Du Bois alighted from the car, a great shout of welcome went up," to his and Graham Du Bois's astonishment, she wrote, because the regime had assembled students and faculty from all of the academic institutions in the city. Enjoying the moment enormously and with an unfailing sense of occasion, the father of Pan-Africanism embraced this opportunity to speak to his ancestral people and their future. He had "no authority, no assumption of age nor rank." He held no position and had no wealth, the firm voice carried from a land of six hundred million people to a continent of three hundred million. "One thing alone I own and that is my own soul. Ownership of that I have even while in my own country for near a century I have been nothing but a 'nigger.' On this basis alone," he dared to speak. "Speak, China, and tell your truth to Africa and to the world. What people have been despised as you have? Who more than you have been rejected of men? . . . Tell this to Africa, for today Africa stands on new feet, with new eyesight, with new brains and asks: 'Where am I and why?' "

Taken by special train to Wuhan on the Yangtze, Du Bois astonished his hosts by climbing to the top of a platform to watch molten steel being poured from a monster furnace at the giant Wuhan Steel Works. A few days later, the Du Boises' greatest wish was accommodated—an audience with the Chairman at his Wuhan villa. Du Bois discussed world politics with Mao Tse-tung in the latter's garden with Anna Louise Strong present and barely pausing for breath as she volunteered firm opinions about Russia and America. Mao's remark that he would like to be able to visit the dying John Foster Dulles in the hospital made Du Bois shake with laughter. Mao added that he would "talk no politics," if such a visit were possible. But when the Chairman presumed to explain at some length the "diseased psychology" affecting the American Negro, Du Bois interjected to say that Negroes and the working people of his country were not afflicted by a psychological condition but by their lack of income, an observation that led Mao and Du Bois to debate the primacy of economics and psychology among evolving groups. In the course of answering a barrage of questions about the United States, Du Bois expressed regret about several notable failures in his fight for equality. Graham Du Bois, uncharacteristically quiet on this occasion, recorded Mao's animated correction in her notebook. Shaking his head, he told Du Bois that a man's only mistake is to lie down and let the enemy walk over him. "This, I gather, you have never done. You have continued the struggle for your people, for all the decent people of America." The couple traveled about the country—around "the vast miracle of China today," as Du Bois despatched to the *Guardian*—until the end of March. (Three years later, in the autumn of 1962, he would carry his ninety-four years of still vibrant curiosity back to China for a final visit.) The Gorchakovs welcomed them at Moscow's Sheremetyevo Airport on April 6, 1959. The Du Boises returned home on the *Liberté* just in time to celebrate the Fourth of July in their Grace Court garden after a stay in Sweden to attend the World Peace Council in Stockholm and a few days in Stratford on Avon to see Robeson in *Othello*. The Soviets had awarded Du Bois the Lenin Peace Prize, but he had asked that it be formally bestowed at the Russian embassy in Washington.

Mansart Builds a School, the second volume of the historical trilogy Du Bois had continued to construct during the years of internal exile, appeared from Aptheker's *Masses & Mainstream* press in the fall of 1959. Almost imme-

diately after their return, he composed an addendum to *The Autobiography* —
the confessional "Postlude" — in which he admitted to being "a little puzzled
now about the ordering of [his] life." Du Bois wrote that several times in the
past he had prepared for death, but "death has not come." But each day, he
prepared his calendar of duties and plans, as he had since high school days in
Great Barrington. He had lived a "good and full life," he continued. He had
tasted delights and known pain, suffering, and despair. But now he was tired.
"I am through," he declared. Let Arthur McFarlane II accomplish the work that
remained to be done. Carter Woodson was dead; so were Mary McLeod Bethune and Walter White in the same year, followed one year later in the summer
of 1956 by Charles S. Johnson. Du Bois began to growl at Shirley that "the
doctor can't cure old age!" Shortly before his ninety-second birthday, the two
of them enjoyed a month's vacation in the Virgin Islands. Du Bois took high
dives from the hotel diving board and swam across the lagoon.

Then, notwithstanding the *Weltschmerz* of the "Postlude," he and Graham
Du Bois boarded a plane on July 1, 1960, for the long flight to Accra to attend
the ceremonies establishing the Republic of Ghana. His refusal to sign the State
Department's non-communist affidavit had prevented him from celebrating
Ghana's independence in person three years ago, even though the Ghanaian
government had publicly requested the State Department to allow Du Bois to
attend. Cedric Belfrage, who covered the 1957 Ghana independence ceremonies
for the *National Guardian*, had reported the consternation among all classes of
Ghanaians at the bizarre policy that sent Vice President Richard Nixon to Accra
and refused Du Bois a passport. In the intervening years, and during his 1958
state visit to the United States, Prime Minister Kwame Nkrumah had continued
to urge Du Bois to come to Ghana, where he would put government research
resources at his disposal. Thirty-four years after first feeling the Liberian earth
of Africa under his feet, Du Bois had returned to the continent not as the
honorific token of an almighty United States of America to a debt-burdened
simulacrum of a nation, but as the honored and greatly moved guest of a virile
black republic headed by a disciple. George Padmore, a rival pan-African
visionary Du Bois had come to appreciate affectionately, had died in Accra only
a few weeks too soon to enjoy the historic moment with Du Bois. There was
opportunity, however, for only one or two discussions with Nkrumah during the
six-week sojourn in the new republic. Ghana was sending its crack British-
trained infantry regiments to the former Belgian Congo, and Nkrumah huddled
with Patrice Lumumba in Flagstaff House attempting to plot a survival course
for the overwhelmed Congolese prime minister. Du Bois spoke insistently
when his hour with Nkrumah came, as he had in Moscow, of the need for a
well-endowed social science apparatus dedicated to African problems. He and
Nkrumah reached an agreement in principle that Du Bois should initiate plans

for the creation of a secretariat for the *Encyclopedia Africana* and commence correspondence with learned societies and noted experts throughout the world.

The Du Boises had not long unpacked their suitcases in Brooklyn Heights when the invitation arrived calling them to the November 16, 1960, installation of their friend, Nnamdi Azikiwe, as the first African governor-general and commander in chief of the federation of Nigeria. Their reception in Lagos was inspirational, but also tornadic, which probably contributed to a frighteningly memorable few hours of drama during their brief London stopover. Responding to Shirley Graham's almost hysterical phone call, physician Josephine Martin, Cedric Belfrage's wife at that time, found Du Bois lying on a couch, his speech slurred and his right arm and leg exhibiting a slight weakness. Martin insisted that they take the earliest possible flight to New York, but Du Bois, willing himself upright, politely but firmly rejected her advice. "Well, I can't do that," she was amazed to hear him say. "I have an appointment with my tailor."

On February 15, 1961, a few days shy of his ninety-third birthday, Du Bois received a cable from President Nkrumah informing him that the *Encyclopedia Africana* project had been "accepted and endorsed by the Ghana Academy of Learning. Substantial financial support has been voted." Nkrumah had answered the puzzle of the "Postlude." The Du Boises began preparations for relocation to Africa before the end of the year, but in the meantime they collaborated with Esther Jackson, Ernest Kaiser, Jack O'Dell of the Southern Christian Leadership Conference, and Lorraine Hansberry to launch *Freedomways*, a journal of radical politics and culture. Yolande's death from a coronary attack the following month devastated him. He repeated over and over to Mae Miller Sullivan during the funeral services in Baltimore that death should have taken him instead. But as always, there was work that must be done, and now it was work for black folk not only in the United States but also for the peoples of Africa. The student sit-in upheaval cheered Du Bois. "Students at last to the rescue, even in the West," he enthused, and admitted that he had lost faith in them as he looked "into their blank faces" during the McCarthy nightmare. But he remained witheringly cynical about their elders, "despite all the declarations of the johnnie-come-latelies frantically scrambling aboard the bandwagon." Du Bois's vision—delusion, some would say—carried him past the desegregation of lunch counters and high schools and beyond the "cruel dilemma" of giving thanks "for partial equality" to a better world trying to be born outside the folds of rapacious capitalism. That world he and his partner and wife were now resolved to join in order to make what contributions they could. In one of his last jeremiads before exiling himself to Ghana, Du Bois called for the restoration of democracy in America. "Make it again possible for the people to express their will," he implored. "Today the rich and the powerful rulers of America divide themselves into Republican and Democats in order to raise ten million dollars to buy the next election and prevent you from having a third party to vote for, or to stop war, theft and murder by your votes."

On April 26, 1961, he sent Alex Kwapong, the acting secretary of the Ghana Academy of Learning, the penultimate activities report for twenty-eight weeks of work on the encyclopedia project. Du Bois projected an additional eight weeks for a total expenditure of three thousand dollars. "I think it fair to say that our project has been received favorably almost everywhere in the world," he concluded with satisfaction. As if to corroborate Du Bois's agonized skepticism about the corruption of the nation's institutions, the Supreme Court upheld the constitutionality of the McCarran Act, sending him into a rage. Probably the greatest legislative insult to the constitution in the twentieth century, the 1950 McCarran Internal Security Act, passed over Truman's veto, authorized the Subversive Activities Control Board (SACB), whose purpose was to force the registration of "Communist-action," "Communist-front," or "Communist-infiltrated organizations." Failure to register entailed imprisonment and massive fines. Aliens whose writings "displayed" communist doctrines were to be barred from the United States, the sanction that had been imposed on his friend Cedric Belfrage in 1952. In 1934, Du Bois had made his exit from the NAACP after carefully formulating a civil rights position that dumbfounded, scandalized, and infuriated millions of black people. The Supreme Court's McCarran opinion decided him upon a similar course of action in the final weeks of 1961—a therapeutic apostasy for his countrywomen and men of all races and creeds, he might have called it.

On October 1, 1961, at ninety-three, Du Bois applied for membership in the Communist Party of the USA and then departed immediately with Shirley Graham for Nkrumah's Ghana. There was an element of satisfying Homeric nose-thumbing in his decision to join a political organization whose membership, FBI agents included, was well under ten thousand. His letter to CPUSA chairman Gus Hall stated, "Today, I have reached a firm conclusion. Capitalism cannot reform itself; it is doomed to self-destruction." Ghana received the Du Boises with a warmth and material support that surpassed their expectations. The republic of twelve million with its high rate of literacy and reasonably competent bureaucracy was the lodestar of a continent appearing to be on its way to prosperity in unity at the time of his and Shirley's expatriation. "We come to witness the last act (or the first?) of a great world drama," Du Bois mused in "Pan-Africa: The Story of a Dream," a memoir begun after only a month in the country. A large home in Accra's most exclusive neighborhood was placed at their disposal, along with Khrushchev's gift of a Russian Chaika limousine. The Du Bois residence became a place of pilgrimage instantly, drawing Mohammed Ben Bella, the head of the Algerian Front de Libération Nationale, to Cantonments Road in a votive train of third world figures, international peace partisans, would-be revolutionaries, black Americans, and an endless procession of students from the University of Ghana and abroad. The CIA chief of station in Ghana noted the attention China's ambassador, Wong Wa, paid the Du Boises, but finally concluded that the encyclopedia business was devoid of intelligence value and was merely a way for Nkrumah to play the old man "for a sucker." Alphaeus and Dorothy Hunton's arrival in March 1962 from Guinea (a *lycée* teaching post in Conakry had been the only work available to the Smith Act victim) provided the encyclopedia some assurance of continuity after Du Bois's demise. With Hunton as his assistant and Ghana's first Rhodes Scholar, Fifi Hesse, assigned to the staff, Du Bois was officially designated director of the *Encyclopedia Africana* secretariat in May.

Adu Boahen, a Ghanaian aristocrat and one of Africa's leading historians, was always unpersuaded of the goodness of fit of Du Bois and Kwame Nkrumah. Boahen believed that Nkrumah's real spiritual mentor was not W.E.B. Du Bois but Marcus Garvey, that the Ghanaian president "reached out for Du Bois out of reverence and because he was the lone survivor—but Garvey was the source." One need only register the significance of the red, black, and green colors of the national flag, centered by a black star, to realize the powerful influence of Garvey, suggested Boahen. The chemistry of the two men, of the African sage and the continental liberator, never fully mixed. Insecure, unevenly educated, increasingly autocratic, criticized as too favorable to expatriate black Americans by his own advisers, and engulfed by a ubiquitous corruption he soon altogether ceased trying to contain, the Osagyefo (redeemer) was inwardly never entirely comfortable with his incorruptible, imported icon. A visiting American professor of constitutional law and consultant to governments in Africa and Latin America felt obliged to call Du Bois's attention to the regime's spreading rot as Shirley Graham Du Bois sat tight-lipped in the living room. "He just listened, but he said that communism must succeed," said Albert Blaustein. But there was one person to whom Du Bois confided his unease about Ghana. Anna Livia Cordero, an exceptionally beautiful Puerto Rican physician in the National Institute of Medical Health and Research, became a friend as well as a clinician Du Bois could consult for reliable second opinions. Cordero's husband, Julian Mayfield, the American novelist, actor, journalist, and radical black nationalist, served as Nkrumah's speech writer and aide. "He wasn't happy," Du Bois told her. "He knew things weren't right, and he complained all the time to me that he was isolated." Cordero served as as his sounding board.

Du Bois discharged his role as oracle and symbol consummately until the end came, encouraging the regime with generalities, presiding over an international conference of scholars at the Legon campus of the University of Ghana, granting audiences in Cantonments Road between afternoon naps and early dinners interspersed with diverting rides about the city and countryside in the

Chaika with Cordero, and fairly regular attendance until 1963 at the weekly veranda gatherings hosted by Vice Chancellor Conor Cruise O'Brien. "He would sit there in a winged chair, very sparing of utterance," O'Brien remembered, "but he listened very carefully to the students." On one veranda occasion when the exuberant vice chancellor raved on about his Congolese nemesis, Moise Tshombe, leader of the breakaway province of Katanga, a student volunteered that Tshombe was another Booker T. Washington. O'Brien never forgot Du Bois's response, recapturing the moment vividly: "The old man stirred like a tortoise putting its head out of its shell. 'Don't say that. I used to talk like that,'" Du Bois insisted and recalled the chastening words of an aunt to such sentiments. "'Don't you forget that that man, unlike you, bears the mark of the lash on his back. He has come out of slavery. . . . You are fighting for the rights here in the North. It's tough, but it's nothing like as tough as what he had to face in his time and in his place.'" The journalists came to Cantonments Road, among them young Cameron Duodo, a local reporter who revered Du Bois, and the *Atlanta Constitution*'s Ralph McGill, who called shortly before the curtain descended. "Mark Lewis [of USIA] and I said good-bye. There was a feeling of having emerged from a place far back in time as we came out of the high-ceilinged house," McGill would write. "There was a lot of history in the slender, sick, and slowly dying man."

And he was dying, slowly but lucidly. Improper medical treatment in Ghana had caused an infection to his prostate gland in 1962, a condition Du Bois insisted on having surgically addressed in Bucharest, Rumania, after the specialists in Moscow declined to undertake the risk of operating. The Rumanian operation was unsuccessful, however, and so Du Bois risked a second operation in London to have the prostate removed. His neighbors and friends Robert and Sarah Lee, a black American dentist couple who had expatriated to Ghana in the early fifties, could see the toll taken on Du Bois's constitution when he and Shirley Graham returned. Anna Livia Cordero knew he was fading away. Respectful of his feeble condition and the couple's privacy, anxious members of the capital's large black American expatriate community—Preston King, the noted political scientist; Vickie Garvin, his treasurer at the Council on African Affairs; Maya Angelou; and many others—phoned their concerns to Shirley Graham Du Bois and asked to be called on if needed. Abbott Simon, to whom Du Bois had entrusted his precious plaster of Paris *Winged Victory*, brought news of the New Frontier, updates about their resilient friends, and a reason to take restorative walks in Aburi Gardens in the hills above Accra. On his ninety-fifth birthday, Du Bois became a citizen of Ghana, another symbolic decision taken largely because the American embassy refused to renew his passport. The University of Ghana conferred an honorary degree to mark the birthday, and the Nkrumahs came to Cantonments Road for a birthday dinner. As Nkrumah

stood to leave, Du Bois reached for his hand and held it tightly. He thanked
Kwame Nkrumah for making it possible for him to finish his life in Africa. He
had but one regret, he said solemnly. "I failed you — my strength gave out before
I could carry out our plans for the encylopedia. Forgive an old man." Nkrumah
protested, but Du Bois persisted. He had wanted to do much more, he said
quietly. Silence hung over the room and then Du Bois smiled and said goodbye. The first president of the Republic of Ghana took his leave in tears.

Du Bois followed the limited news about the impending March on Washington filtered by Ghana Radio and the polemical *Ghanaian Times* during the
last week of August 1963. Cordero brought news of plans for a large contingent
of black Americans to march on the American embassy on the evening of the
twenty-seventh. Nurse Christine Debrah informed Dr. Sanago, the attending
physician, that Du Bois was unusually languid on the day of the announced
embassy demonstration. He died in his sleep at 11:40 that night. In Washington,
250,000 of his countrymen and women began assembling along the great reflecting pool in front of the Lincoln Memorial. As far as can be known, W.E.B.
Du Bois said nothing in his last hours. But it had all been said.

WITH RUSSIA NOW ravaged by a phase of toxic capitalism that would repel
Jay Gould and communism seemingly headed for history's curiosity shop of
failed religions, Du Bois's pronouncements may ring so oddly as to cause doubt
as to his standing as one of the twentieth century's intellectual heavyweights.
Few would commend the ideological and geographical resting places of his
final years. What has befallen his beloved continent of Africa would dismay Du
Bois, although it would probably not disillusion him. It should be understood
that it is by far the significance of Du Bois's protest and of his gradual alienation,
rather than the solutions he proposed, that are instructive. For he was an intellectual in the purest sense of the word — a thinker whose obligation was to be
dissatisfied continually with his own thoughts and those of others. No doubt he
was precipitous in totally writing off the market economy. Even so, it may be
suggested that Du Bois was right to insist that to leave the solution of systemic
social problems exclusively to the market is an agenda guaranteeing obscene
economic inequality in the short run and irresoluble political calamity in the
long run. In one of his most prescient essays, "Negroes and the Crisis of Capitalism in the United States," written ten years before his death, he left a diag-
nostic of the contemporary, omnivorous turbo-capitalism that now assails the
planet, admonishing that

> the organized effort of American industry to usurp government surpasses
> anything in modern history. . . . From the use of psychology to spread truth
> has come the use of organized gathering of news to guide public opinion,

then deliberately to mislead it by scientific advertising and propaganda. . . . Mass capitalistic control of books and periodicals, news gathering and distribution, radio, cinema, and television has made the throttling of democracy possible and the distortion of education and failure of justice widespread.

In the course of his long, turbulent career, then, W.E.B. Du Bois attempted virtually every possible solution to the problem of twentieth-century racism — scholarship, propaganda, integration, cultural and economic separatism, politics, international communism, expatriation, third-world solidarity. First had come culture and education for the elites; then the ballot for the masses; then economic democracy; and finally all these solutions in the service of global racial parity and economic justice. An extraordinary mind of color in a racialized century, Du Bois was possessed of a principled impatience with what he saw as the egregious failings of American democracy that drove him, decade by decade, to the paradox of defending totalitarianism in the service of a global ideal of economic and social justice. The enduring Calvinist temper of that mind was never so well disclosed as in Du Bois's first published work, *The Suppression of the African Slave Trade*:

> A certain hard common sense in facing the complicated phenomena of political life must be expected over every progressive people. In some respects we as a nation seem to lack this; we have the somewhat inchoate idea that we are not destined to be harassed with great social questions, and that even if we are, and fail to answer them, the fault is with the question and not with us. Consequently we often congratulate ourselves more on getting rid of a problem than on solving it. Such an attitude is dangerous; we have and shall have, as other peoples have had, critical, momentous, and pressing questions to answer. The riddle of the Sphinx may be postponed, it may be evasively answered now; sometime it must be fully answered.

PERSONS INTERVIEWED

ADAMS, Kathleen

AGRIN, Gloria (Josephson)

ALEXANDER, Adele

ANGELOU, Maya

APTHEKER, Herbert

ARONSON, Grams

ARONSON, James

BANKS, Kathryn

BELFRAGE, Cedric

BELFRAGE, Mary

BELL, Emma

BLAUSTEIN, Albert

BOAHEN, Adu

BOND, Julia (Mrs. Horace Mann)

BOND, J. Max and Ruth

BRANCH, Bobbie

BROWN, Lloyd

BURNHAM, Dorothy

CAMERON, Angus

CAMMER, Harold

CAREY, Mrs. Johnnie Davis

CARTER, Lisle

CATLETT, Elizabeth

CAYTON, Revels & Louise

CHILDRESS, Alice

CITRON, Alice

CLARK, John Henrik

COBB, Montague

COOK, Marvel

CORDERO, Anna Louise

CROCKETT, George

CURRENT, Gloster

DARR, John

DAVIS, Chester

DAVIS, Mrs. Eugene

DAVIS, William B.

DAWSON, William L.

DEBRAH, Christine

DIAMOND, Frieda

DICKENS, Helen

DRAKE, St. Clair

DUBERMAN, Martin

DUBOIS, David

DU BOIS, Rachel Davis

DUODO, Cameron

DUNBAR, Carl L.

DUNCAN, Charles

EDGECOMB, Gabrielle

FAST, Howard

FAULKNER, Stanley

FIELD, Frederick Vanderbilt

FLEMING, G. James

FLORY, Ishmael

FRANKLIN, John Hope

FREEMAN, Robert

GARVIN, Vickie

GOLDEN, Lili

GORCHAKOV, Alla (Bobricheva)

GORCHAKOV, Ovid

GRAHAM, Lorenz

GRANT, Joanne

GRECHURKIN, Alla & Alexei

GREENLEA, Pete

GRIGSBY, Lucy

GUZMAN, Jessie

HALLINANS, Vivian & Vincent

HAMILTON, Grace

HAMMOND, John

HEALEY, Dorothy

HELLUM, Mrs. J. C.

HESSE, Fifi

HOPE II, John

HUNTON, Dorothy

HUTSON, Jean

IVANOV, Rhobert

JACKSON, Esther & James

JAFFE, Bernard

JAMES, C. L. R.

JOHNSON, Howard "Stretch"

JONES, Madison

KAISER, Ernest

KATANIAN, Vasily and Wife

KATZMAN, Lillian Hyman

KAUFMANN, Mary

LAZARUS, Julius

LAZARUS, Ruth

LEE, Robert and Sarah

LOCHARD, Mrs. Metz

LOVE, Josephine

LURIE, Frieda

MARTIN, Josephine

MARTIN, Louis

MARZANI, Carl

MATTHEWS, Elsie

MEAD, Homer

MEEROPOL, Robert and Michael

MEIER, August

MELISH, Mary

MERRIAM, Eve

MURPHY, Henry

NABRIT, Samuel

NANCE, Ethel Ray

NEWMAN, Thelma

NKETSIA, Nana

O'BRIEN, Connor Cruise

PANKE, Kay

PARRISH, Lila

PATTERSON, Louise

PAULING, Linus

PECK, Theodora

PERLMUTTER, Morris

PITTMAN, John

QUARLES, Benjamin

RAMSAY, Alan

REID, Mrs. Ira (Anne Cook)

ROBESON, JR., Paul

ROBERTSON, Frank

RUBINSTEIN, Annette

SCHAPPES, Morris

SHIVERY, Veoria

SIMON, Abbott

SIMMONS, Ruth

SMYTHE, Mabel

SOLOFF-SIMON-JAFFE

SPINGARN, Edward

SULLIVAN, Mae Miller

SUTHERLAND, Efua

SUTHERLAND, Essie

TANNENBAUM, Gerald

THEURMER, Angus

USHER, Bazolene

VALIEN, Bonita & Preston

VANDERPUYE, Jacob

WEAVER, Robert

WILKERSON, Doxey

WILLIAMS, Arnette

WILLIAMS, Dennise

WILLIAMS, Du Bois

WILLIAMS, Franklin

YOUNG, Pauline

ZAND, H. H.

NOTES

Chapter 1: *The Reason Why*

1. "... THIS TYPE OF PHOTO.": Picture editor, *Chicago Tribune* to W.E.B. Du Bois, October 21, 1919, The Papers of W.E.B. Du Bois, Special Collections, W.E.B. Du Bois Library, University of Massachusetts at Amherst (hereafter, Du Bois Papers/UMass). ON RED SUMMER: Florette Henri, *Black Migration: Movement North, 1900–1920* (Garden City, N.Y.: Anchor Books, 1976), 318–322; John Higham, *Strangers in the Land: Patterns of American Nativism* (New York: Atheneum, 1963); David Levering Lewis, *When Harlem Was in Vogue* (New York: Penguin Books, 1997; originally published by Alfred A. Knopf, Inc., 1981), 17–20; William Leuchtenburg, *The Perils of Prosperity, 1914–1932* (Chicago: University of Chicago Press, 1958), 78; Robert K. Murray, *Red Scare: A Study of National Hysteria* (Minneapolis: University of Minnesota Press, 1955); Arthur I. Waskow, *From Race Riot to Sit-in: 1919 and the 1960s* (Garden City, N.Y.: Anchor Books, 1966), ch. 2.

2. "... OR KNOW THE REASON WHY.": Du Bois, "Returning Soldiers," *The Crisis* (July 1918), cited in David Levering Lewis, ed., *W.E.B. Du Bois: A Reader* (New York: Henry Holt and Company, 1995), 697. Also, David Levering Lewis, *W.E.B. Du Bois: Biography of a Race, 1868–1919* (New York: Henry Holt and Company, 1993), 578. "... PROBABLY REACH $72, 000.": "The Crisis," *The Crisis* (September 1919), 235. "... SOMETHING ABOUT MY OWN RACE.": Petruchio E. Moore to W.E.B. Du Bois, October 23, 1919, Du Bois Papers/UMass, also cited in Herbert Aptheker, ed., *The Correspondence of W.E.B. Du Bois* (Amherst: University of Massachusetts Press, 1973), 3 vols, I, 235. See Dianne Johnson-Feelings, ed., with an introduction by Marian Wright Edelman, *The Best of the Brownies' Book* (New York: Oxford University Press, 1996). On comparative circulation figures of *Nation, New Republic, Liberator:* John Tebbel and Mary Ellen Zuckerman, *The Magazine in America, 1741–1990* (New York: Oxford University Press, 1991), 203–207, 217–218.

3. "... SEPARATE RACIAL EQUALITY.": Du Bois, "The Social Equality of Whites and Blacks," *The Crisis* (November 1920): 16–18. "... SUCH A PREPOSTEROUS IDEA": Charles Young to Du Bois, August 22, 1919, Du Bois Papers/UMass. "... THE FIRST TIME IN TWO YEARS": Du Bois, "Report of the Director of Publications and Research, August 1919" in Du Bois Papers/UMass; Du Bois, "The Crisis," *The Crisis* (September 1919), 235.

4. "... NUDE FEMALE PUBLIC SCHOOL TEACHERS.": The murky affair involving a visiting Dutch anthropologist, Herman M. B. Moens, who photographed public school teachers nude for "scientific" purposes, implicated several prominent Washingtonians, resulted in U.S. Senate hearings, and left rumors and innuendoes for many years afterward: Du Bois, "Hysteria," *The Crisis* (June 1919), 61–62; Du Bois Papers/UMass contain a curious Du Bois document, "The Washington Public Schools Situation," and extracts from Hearings before the Senate Select Committee of the United States Senate (Resolution 310) about the case. Montague Cobb, professor emeritus of medicine at Howard University, remembered the Moens case vividly, and produced for my benefit a copy of the Moens book filled with graphic nude photos of females. According to Professor Cobb, a murder and a suicide resulted

from the scandal. Superintendent of the colored schools, Roscoe Conkling Bruce, lost his position as a result of the uproar. Lewis interview with Montague Cobb, August 31, 1988. " . . . NEGRO TROOPS.": Du Bois, "An Essay Toward the History of the Black Man in the Great War," *The Crisis* (June 1919): 59; A. E. Patterson (Office of the Division of Judge Advocate, HQ, 92nd Division, U.S. Army) to Du Bois, April 7, 1919; Du Bois to Maj. A. E. Patterson, April 1919, Du Bois Papers/UMass. Lewis, *When Harlem Was in Vogue*, 24; see William Colson, "The New Negro Patriotism," *Messenger* (August 1919), in Theodore G. Vincent, ed., *Voices of a Black Nation* (Trenton, N.J.: Africa World Press, n.d.; orig. pub. Ramparts Press, 1973), 67. " . . . BUT FIGHTING BACK.": Claude McKay, "If We Must Die," in David Levering Lewis, ed., *The Portable Harlem Renaissance Reader* (New York: Penguin Books, 1995), 290.

4. BOLSHEVIK REVOLUTION": Du Bois, "IWW," *The Crisis* (June 1919): 60. Charles Kellogg, *NAACP: A History of the National Association for the Advancement of Colored People, 1909–1920* (Baltimore: John Hopkins University Press, 1967, 1973), 287; Du Bois, "Opinion," *The Crisis* (June 1919): 59–62, 60. Patrick S. Washburn, *Question of Sedition: The Federal Government's Investigation of the Black Press during World War II* (New York: Oxford University Press, 1986), 21–22.

4. " . . . AND NOT BY MURDER.": Du Bois, "The Class Struggle," *The Crisis* (June 1921): 55–56; also in Aptheker, ed., *Crisis Selections*, I, 303–4. Du Bois, "Radicals," *The Crisis* (December 1919): 46; also in Aptheker, ed., *Crisis Selections*, I, 247. Washburn, *Sedition*, 21–62.

5. AFTERWAR SOCIAL UNREST AND ITS EFFECT IN THE USA: David M. Kennedy, *Over Here: The First World War and American Society* (New York: Oxford University Press, 1980), esp. 278–84; Melvin Dubofsky and Warren Van Tine, *John L. Lewis: A Biography* (Urbana: University of Illinois Press, 1986), esp. 35–47; Edward P. Johanningsmeier, *Forging American Communism: The Life of William Z. Forster* (Princeton, N.J.: Princeton University Press, 1994). COMMUNISM: Theodore Draper, *The Roots of American Communism* (Chicago: Ivan R. Dee, Inc., 1989; orig. pub. 1957), esp. ch. 11; Theodore Kornweibel, Jr., *Seeing Red: Federal Campaigns Against Black Militancy* (Bloomington, Ind.: Indiana University Press, 1998), esp. 107–10, 157–59; Murray, *op. cit.*, esp. 49–53, 193–203; David H. Bennett, *The Party of Fear: From Nativist Movements to the New Right in American History* (Chapel Hill: University of North Carolina Press, 1988), esp. 190–98; Fraser M. Ottanelli, *The Communist Party of the United States from the Depression to the New* World War II (New Brunswick, N.J.: Rutgers University Press, 1991), 2–11; Richard Gid Powers, *Not Without Honor: The History of American Anticommunism* (New York: The Free Press, 1995), esp. ch. 2. " . . . SUCH WHOLESALE VIOLATION OF CIVIL LIBERTIES.": William Leuchtenburg, *op. cit.*, 78.

5–6. " . . . EVIDENCE OF SEDITION.": On April 10, soon after returning from France, Du Bois had lectured a keenly attentive interracial audience in Boston's historic Tremont Temple, that the economics of racism was creating global conditions inimical to democracy and certain to "prepare future wars," a speech reported as "Negro at Paris," in Rochester, N.Y., *Democrat and Chronicle*, May 4, 1919, 3. J. EDGAR HOOVER ON RACE MATTERS: Washburn, *op. cit.*, pp. 26–27. Du Bois, "The Tenth Anniversary," *The Crisis* (August 1919); 189–93; also, Kellogg, *op. cit.*, p. 288.

6. " . . . FUTURE SECRETARY OF STATE.": Du Bois, "Byrnes," *The Crisis* (October 1919): 284–285; also in Aptheker, ed., *Crisis Selections*, I, 245. " . . . WHITE PEOPLE WISHED TO GIVE THEM.": Du Bois, "Causes of Discontent," *New York Sun* (October 12, 1919), 5, 7, also in Aptheker, ed., *Writings by W.E.B. Du Bois in Periodicals Edited by Others* (Millwood, N.Y.: Kraus-Thomson, 1982), 4 vols., II, 130–36, 130, 135.

7–8. ON LOVING: see Lewis, *Du Bois: Biography of a Race*, 559–60; Loving to Director of Military Intelligence, Washington, D.C., August 6, 1919, Subject: "Final Report on Negro Subversion," Walter H. Loving Papers, Moorland-Spingarn Research Center, Howard University (hereafter M-S/HU). I surmise that J. Edgar Hoover profited professionally from Loving's report, as the similarity of his to Loving's antecedent document seems much more than coincidence. WASHINGTON AND CHICAGO RIOTS: see Waskow, *op. cit.*, ch. 2, 3; Constance McLaughlin Green, *The Secret City: A History of Race Relations in the Nation's Capital* (Princeton, N.J.: Princeton University Press, 1967), 190–93; Green, *Washington: A History of the Capital* (Princeton, N.J.: Princeton University Press, 1962), 266–67; St. Clair Drake and Horace R. Cayton, *Black Metropolis: A Study of Negro Life in a Northern City* (New York: Harper and Row, 1962; orig. pub. by Harcourt, Brace and Co., 1945), 2 vols, I., ch. 4; James R. Grossman, *Land of Hope: Chicago, Black Southerners and the Great Migration* (Chicago: University of Chicago Press, 1989); Allan Spear, *Black Chicago: The Making of a Negro Ghetto* (Chicago: University of Chicago Press, 1967); William M. Tuttle, *Race Riot: Chicago in the Red Summer of 1919* (New York: Atheneum, 1970), 25–29; Graham Taylor and Charles S. Johnson, *The Negro in Chicago: A Study of Race Relations and a Race Riot in 1919* (New York: Arno Press, 1968; orig. pub. 1922). On these riots, see Du Bois, "Causes of Discontent," *loc. cit.*, 132–34.

8–9.   ON THE ARKANSAS POGROMS: Henri, *op. cit.*, 321–22; Waskow, *op. cit.*, 135. ". . . TO DISPUTE WHITE SUPREMACY.": Du Bois, "The Arkansas Riots," New York *World*, November 28, 1919; Walter White, *The Lynchings of May, 1918, in Brooks and Lowndes Counties, Georgia. An Investigation Made and Published by the NAACP, September 1918*, M 343.3 in M-S/HU. See also W. Fitzhugh Brundage, *Lynchings in the New South: Georgia and Virginia, 1880–1930* (Urbana, Ill.: University of Illinois Press, 1993), 35. HALF MOONS ANECDOTE: A part of the lore of the White family related to me. White, "'Massacring Whites' in Arkansas," *The Nation* (December 6, 1919) 715–16.

9–10.   ". . . LEGAL DEFENSE FUND.": "Funds needed to Fight Arkansas Cases" (December 1920) 65–66; "Delinquent Branches" (December 1920): 67–68; "Arkansas Justice" (February 1921): 163–65, all in *The Crisis*. ". . . WE ARE DEPENDING ON OURSELVES.": Du Bois, "Opinion," *The Crisis* (November 1920): 5. ". . . A MOST FAR-REACHING EFFECT.": Du Bois, "Funds Needed", *loc. cit.*, p. 67. Cost of victory in Arkansas cases discussed: Walter White to Joel Spingarn, February 27, 1923, Box 12 V-Z, Joel Spingarn Papers, Special Collections, New York Public Library (hereafter JSP/NYPL). ". . . A COMPLETE VICTORY FOR THE NAACP.": Du Bois, "Arkansas Cases," *The Crisis* (April 1925): 272–73; Richard Kluger, *Simple Justice: The History of Brown v. Board of Education, the Epochal Supreme Court Decision that Outlawed Segregation, and of Black America's Century-Long Struggle for Equality Under Law* (New York: Random House, 1977; orig. pub. by Alfred A. Knopf, Inc., 1976), 114.

11.   ON THE FRIENDSHIP OF DU BOIS AND JOEL SPINGARN: see Lewis, *Du Bois: Biography of a Race*, 475–76. ". . . [HIS LIFE] HAD PASSED.": Du Bois, *The Autobiography of W.E.B. Du Bois. A Soliloquy on Viewing My Life from the Last Decade of Its First Century* (International Publishers, Inc., 1968), 13. ". . . DEDICATED BOOK TO NINA.": On writing and publication of *Darkwater*, see Aptheker, ed., "Introduction," *Darkwater: Voices from Within the Veil* (Millwood, N.Y.: Kraus-Thomson, 1975, orig. pub. by Harcourt Brace and Howe, 1921), 8.

11–12.   ". . . PERSISTENT INSULTING": *Darkwater*, 172. ". . . FREE WOMANHOOD MUST PASS": *ibid.*, 164. On Du Bois and Anna Julia Cooper and white feminists: Margaret Sanger to Du Bois, February 7, and Du Bois to Margaret Sanger, February 14, 1925, Du Bois Papers/UMass, also in Aptheker, ed., *Du Bois Correspondence*, I, 301–2; *Darkwater*, 181; Kevin K. Gaines, *Uplifting the Race: Black Leadership, Politics, and Culture in the Twentieth Century* (Chapel Hill: University of North Carolina Press, 1996), 132–33; Ellen Chester, *A Woman of Valor: Margaret Sanger and the Birth Control Movement in America* (New York: Simon and Schuster, 1992), 296, 388.

12–13.   INTERSECTION OF THE DOMESTIC AND PUBLIC LIFE: "Feeling some better than when you left. . . . We went to see *Heartbreak House* by Shaw. It was a queer play, left me all up in the air. . . . The snow is piled high in our street," Nina Du Bois to Will Du Bois, February 23, 1921; "I am some rested. The neck still aches badly" and Yolande has an abcessed tooth, Nina Du Bois to Will Du Bois, August 30, 1921; ". . . most of the day in bed," Nina to Will, March 5, 1923, all in Du Bois Papers/ UMass. ". . . THE DAMNATION OF WOMEN": *Darkwater*, 164; *ibid.*, 180.

19–20.   "THE SOULS OF WHITE FOLK,": *Darkwater*, 34; and *The Independent*, 69 (August 18, 1910): 339–42, also in Aptheker, ed., *Periodical Literature*, II, 25–29. "WHITENESS . . . FOREVER AND EVER, AMEN!": "Souls of White Folk," *loc. cit.*, 26.

14.   ". . . WHITE MAN BY ELIMINATION OR ABSORPTION": Lothrop Stoddard, *The Rising Tide of Color* (1920), excerpted in Russell Jacoby and Naomi Glauberman, eds., *The Bell Curve: History, Documents, Opinions* (New York: Times Books, 1995), 553–60, 556; on background for Grant and Stoddard, see Thomas F. Gossett, *Race: The History of an Idea in America* (New York: Oxford University Press, 1997; orig. pub. 1963), 353–64, 390–98 et passim.; John Sedgwick, "Inside the Pioneer Fund," *Bell Curve*, 144–61; Elazar Barkan, *The Retreat of Scientific Racism: Changing Concepts of Race in Britain and the United States Between the World Wars* (London: Cambridge University Press, 1992), 67–70; Pat Shipman, *The Evolution of Racism: Human Differences and the Abuse of Science* (New York: Simon and Schuster, 1994), 123–25. ON DU BOIS–STODDARD DEBATE, Report of *Debate Conducted by the Chicago Forum* (Chicago Forum, 1929), in Aptheker, ed., *Pamphlets and Leaflets by W.E.B. Du Bois* (White Plains, N.Y.: Kraus-Thomson, 1986): 222–29.

14–15.   ". . . BARBARISM AND MURDER": *Darkwater*, p. 33. ". . . YELLOW PEOPLE ARE CONCERNED": *ibid.*, 50. ". . . EXPLOITING DARKER RACES": *ibid.*, 49. ". . . STRIPPED AND VISIBLE TODAY": *ibid.*, 39. ". . . NOT ONE MOMENT LONGER": *ibid.*, 49.

15. "... AND TO THE LABORERS": *Darkwater*, 43. "... ENDEAVOR BY ASIA AND AFRICA": *ibid.*, p. 17. "... UNIVERSAL STRUGGLES OF ALL MANKIND": *ibid.*, 40. "... SATISFACTORY HUMAN READING": *ibid.*, 136. "... SPECIAL TALENTS AND GENIUS": *ibid.*, 208.

16. "... WRATH AGAINST WHITE RACISM.": "I hate the oh!/ I hate them well,/ I hate them, Christ!/ As I hate hell!/ If I were God,/ I'd sound their knell/ This day!", in "The Riddle of the Sphinx," *Darkwater*, 54. "... CALL ME MISBIRTH": *ibid.*, 29. "... BUT BE BRAVE!": *ibid.*, 30. "... POSSESSED SPECIAL POWERS OF INSIGHT.": *The Souls of Black Folk* (Millwood, N.Y.: Kraus-Thomson, 1973; orig. pub. 1903), 3. "... OR CAPITALIST OF ARTISAN": *Darkwater*, 29. Arnold Rampersad makes the cogent observation that Du Bois "virtually declared that he was singular and outside both races": Rampersad, *The Art and Imagination of W.E.B. Du Bois* (Cambridge: Harvard University Press, 1976), 173.

17–18. "SUSTAIN ... TRIALS AHEAD": *Darkwater*, 20. "... A HARVARD SCHOLARSHIP": *ibid.*, 17. "... ITS OWN FUTURE AND FAITH": *ibid.*, 202. "... SOULS LAY NAKED TO THE NIGHT": *ibid.*, 270.

18. "THE SERVANT IN THE HOUSE.": *Darkwater*, 115. "OF WORK AND WEALTH.": *ibid.*, 99; and see Du Bois, "Labor Omnia Vincit," *The Crisis* (September 1919): 231–32.

19. THE TORTURED PLOT of "The Princess of the Hither Isles," *Darkwater*, 75–80: Courted by a young king who represents in cold arrogance and will-to-power the archetypal Blond Beast, the Princess accepts a marriage proposal. Together they ascend to "Yonder Kingdom," where the king promises there is even more gold just beneath the sun. Trailing behind them is the shambling, ragged figure of a dark beggar, whose "formless black and burning face" startles the princess as she glimpses its "glad gleam of utter understanding." Du Bois's description of the trio's ascent manages to be at once fabulous and historical in a melodramatic paragraph of allusive compression that recaptures chattel and wage slavery, women subjugated cynically upon an idolatrous pedestal, and the wedge politics of race and gender perfected under capitalism by white patriarchy. The Princess of the Hither Isles realizes that it is her historic protector—the patriarchal white man—who is determined to prevent communion between two groups whose social fate as dominated sex and exploited race has long been similar. Turning back to "offer her bleeding heart" to the despised race, she is stopped and punished. " 'It's a Negro!' " the young king snarls; " 'and it may not be.' The woman quivered. 'It's a nigger!' he repeated fiercely."[*ibid.*, p. 79] Suddenly horrified, the Princess refuses the cruel, sterile riches offered by the Blond Beast, as she grasps the full significance of the black beggar's humanity. Du Bois closes with a parody of the literary and cinematic convention in which suicide is the exit of choice for white women whose virginity was at risk from racial inferiors. To save herself from life on a pedestal in a realm founded on exploitation, the Princess leaps to her death.

19. ON RELIGIOUS INFLECTIONS: see Rampersad, *Art and Imagination*, 104; "The Call," 161–62; "Jesus Christ in Texas," 123–33; "The Second Coming," 105–8, all in *Darkwater*.

19–22. REVIEWS: Royalties check for $280.00, Harcourt, Brace and Howe, Inc., to Du Bois, March 22, 1920, Du Bois Papers/UMass. A useful survey of critical reactions to *Darkwater*, Aptheker, ed., "Introduction"; *The Times Literary Supplement*, November 4, 1920, 712; *The Spectator*, August 21, 1920, 124; *Atlantic Monthly*; *The Nation*, May 29, 1920, 726–27; New York *Herald*, September 6, 1920; *The New York Times Book Review*, August 8, 1920, 19–20; *Outlook*, December 15, 1920, 690; *The New Republic*, April 7, 1920, 189–90; *The Crisis* (May 1920):34–36; *The Messenger*, April–May 1920, 10–11; Raleigh *Independent*, May 21, 1920; Harold Laski to Oliver Wendell Holmes, November 20, 1920, in Mark DeWolfe Howe, ed., *Holmes-Laski Letters* (Cambridge: Harvard University Press, 1953), 298. Remember that Franz Boas declined to review *Darkwater* for the New York *Evening Post* when asked by William Rose Benet. Boas said the "book is so much an emotional literary product."—in Boas Papers, March 22, 1920.

22–23. "... SALES.": Sales figures for *Darkwater* and *Souls*: Aptheker introductions to both books, 26 and 34. "I NEED THAT BOOK.": Aptheker, Introduction, *Darkwater*, 24. Du Bois, "Mississippi," *The Crisis* (June 1920): 69–71.

22–23. "... OF BEAUTY AND DEATH.": *Darkwater*, 229. "... EACH MONTH, EACH YEAR": *ibid.*, 223. "... A FULLER REALIZATION OF LIFE": "Intro," *ibid.*, 24.

23–24. "HAD NEVER BEFORE BEEN HELD.": Du Bois, "Atlanta," *The Crisis* (May 1920): 5–8; Kellogg, *op. cit.*, 230.

24. "... SAVAGELY BEATEN.": Du Bois, "Opinion [Shillady]," *loc. cit.* (October 1919): 283–87; Du Bois, "The Task," *loc. cit.* (August 1920): 165–66; Kellogg, *op. cit.*, 240.

24–25. "... A VISIBLE EMPIRE IN AFRICA": Du Bois, quoted in Lewis, *Biography of a Race*, 135. "... FOR A FRENCH PERIODICAL.": The Comte J. de Voilement to Du Bois, March 3, June 30.

"...ATTITUDE TOWARD THE NEXT ELECTION": Du Bois to Comte de Voilemont, July 15, 1920, Du Bois Papers/UMass. On Voilemont (Esterhazy, Charles Marie Ferdinand [Walsin]) identity, see David Levering Lewis, *Prisoners of Honor: The Dreyfus Affair* (New York: Henry Holt and Company, 1994, orig. pub. by William Morrow, 1973), ch. 4; Du Bois, "The Republicans and the Black Voter," *The Nation* (June 5, 1920): 757–58, also in Aptheker, ed., *Periodical Lit.*, II, 139–43. "...HENRY FORD.": Henry Ford and the *Protocols of the Elders of Zion*, in "American Christians," cited in "Chronology," *W.E.B. Du Bois* (New York: The Library of America, 1986), 1294.

25–26.   ON NAACP RECRUITMENT OF JAMES WELDON JOHNSON, see Du Bois, "The New Secretary," *The Crisis* (December 1920): 68; Lewis, *Du Bois: Biography of a Race*, 523–24; Kellogg, *op. cit.*, 113–14; August Meier and Elliott Rudwick, "The Rise of the Black Secretariat," in *Along the Color Line: Explorations in the Black Experience* (Urbana: University of Illinois Press, 1976), 94–127. On Walter White (who awaits his biography by Kenneth Janken), see *ibid.*, 110, 112; Kluger, *op. cit.*, 138–50; Lewis, *Vogue*, ch. 5; B. Joyce Ross, *J. E. Spingarn and the Rise of the NAACP, 1911–1939* (New York: Athenuem, 1972); Walter White, *A Man Called White: The Autobiography of Walter White* (Athens: University of Georgia Press, 1995; orig. pub. 1948).

26.   "...HAITI": James Weldon Johnson, *Self-Determining Haiti* [collection of four *Nation* articles] Minutes for September 13, 1920, NAACP Board Minutes, Series A, Board of Directors File: Minutes 1909–1959, NAACP Papers, Library of Congress (hereafter BRDMINS/LC). An excellent account of James Weldon Johnson's trip and the sequel to Haitian politics is found in Brenda Gayle Plummer, "The Afro-American Response to the Occupation of Haiti, 1915–1934," *Phylon* (Vol. XLIII): 125–43, esp. 132–34.

27.   "FLORIDA'S HOMICIDAL ELECTION.": White, "Election Day in Florida," *The Crisis* (January 1921): 106–9; interesting to note that Madeline Allison's byline is beginning to run regularly in *The Crisis*, *viz.*, Allison, "The Lynching Industry, 1920" (February 1921): 160–62; as well, she composes section titled "The Horizon." "Disfranchisement in Congress," *The Crisis* (February 1921): 165. ON CONGRESSIONAL REPRESENTATION: Du Bois, "Opinion," *The Crisis* (February 1921): 149–52, and also, Aptheker, ed., *Crisis Selections*, I, 292–93; and Du Bois to John D. Wray, May 26, 1921 ("I appreciate Dr. Moton's character and good intentions, but I am continually astonished at his lack of courage"), Du Bois Papers/ UMass.

28.   "...CONSIDERABLE NUMBER OF NEGRO VOTES": Du Bois, "Republicans and the Black Voter," *loc. cit.*, 141. "...TO FEEL SCOOPED.": Advertisement for Kelly Miller's *Authentic History of the Negro in the World War, The Crisis* (February 1921): 192; Emmett Scott, *Official History of the American Negro in the World War* (Chicago: Homewood Press, 1919).

29.   THE WAR HISTORY: Wellington Willard to Du Bois, May 6, 1919; S. D. Redmond to Du Bois, June 10, 1919; Elmer A. Carter to Du Bois, May 7, 1919, all in Du Bois Papers/UMass; for the fascinating career of Eugene Bullard, see Bernard C. Nalty, *Strength for the Fight: A History of Black Americans in the Military* (New York: The Free Press, 1986), 123–24; Du Bois, "Report of the Director of Publications and Research, December 1, 1918–April 1, 1919," April 8, 1919, Du Bois Papers/UMass.

29.   MANEUVERING FOR THE SECOND PAN-AFRICAN CONGRESS: E. Butler Ceruti to Du Bois, November 13, 1920; Paul Otlet to Du Bois, December 17, 1920, Du Bois Papers/UMass. "...A PERMANENT SELF-SUPPORTING BODY.": Du Bois, "Opinion," *The Crisis* (January 1921): 101–4, 101 [news that NAACP is severing official connection with the Pan African Congress]. "...ANYTHING OF THE SORT": Du Bois, *Dusk of Dawn: An Essay Toward an Autobiography of a Race Concept* (Millwood, N.Y.: Kraus-Thomson, 1975; orig. pub. by Harcourt, Brace and Company, 1940), 275; John H. Harris, Anti-Slavery and Aborigines Protection Society, to Du Bois, May 6, 1921; Du Bois to J. L. Dube, May 27, 1921; Du Bois to Rene Chaparade, Geneva, April 7, 1921; Albert Thomas to Du Bois [n.d.] 1921, all in Du Bois Papers/UMass.

30.   "...DO NOT GET DISCOURAGED": Du Bois to Rayford Logan, July 12, 1921; and Du Bois to Logan, May 13; Logan to Du Bois, June 4, 1921, Du Bois Papers/UMass. On Rayford Whittingham Logan, see Kenneth R. Janken, *Rayford W. Logan and the Dilemma of the African-American Intellectual* (Amherst: University of Massachusetts Press, 1993) and August Meier and Elliott Rudwick, *Black History and the Historical Profession, 1915–1980* (Urbana: University of Illinois Press, 1986), 89–92 *et passim*. "...IT IS SHEER TYRANNY": Du Bois to Dr. William Felter, Principal of Girls' High School, April 14; and Felter to Du Bois, April 13, 1920, Du Bois Papers/UMass. "...DECLARED NET INCOME": Individual Income Tax Returns—1920, Du Bois Papers/UMass.

31–32.   MORE FAMILY MATTERS: Yolande Du Bois to Nina Du Bois, February 20; Yolande Du Bois to Du Bois, March 16; Nina to Will, August 30; Yolande to Du Bois, November 16; Du Bois to Yolande, November 25, 1921, all in Du Bois Papers/UMass.

32–33. "... NOTHING ABOUT HIS OWN RACE": Du Bois, "Opinion," *The Crisis* (October 1919): 283–87. "... DECEPTION, AND SELF-DISTRUST": *ibid.*, 204. "... MUST CEASE TO BE.": Johnson-Feelings, *op. cit.*, 347.

33–34. BROWNIES': "... WRITE YOU ABOUT IT.": Alice Martin, quoted, in Johnson-Feelings, *op. cit.* 26; "... MORE STORIES LIKE THAT.": Pocahontas Foster, quoted in *ibid.*, 54; "... WE DEDICATE THE BROWNIES' BOOK.": Jessie Fauset, quoted in *ibid.*, 25; "ALL OUR PROBLEMS CENTER IN THE CHILD. ALL OUR HOPES, OUR DREAMS ARE FOR OUR CHILDREN.": Du Bois, *Darkwater*, 213.

34–35. "... INCREASE IN THE PRICE.": "Report of the Director of Publications and Research— August 1919," and "Report of the Dir. of Pub. and Research for Month of April 1921," in Du Bois Papers/UMass. "... AGENTS ... FEELING THE INDUSTRIAL DEPRESSION": "Report of the Dir. of Pub. and Research for November 1921," Du Bois Papers/UMass; Minutes for July 11, 1921, BRDMINS/LC. "... THE CLOTHES ON THEIR BACKS.": "Tulsa Riots," *The Crisis* (July 1921): 114–16. ON TULSA: see Scott Ellsworth, *Death in a Promised Land: The Tulsa Race Riot of 1921* (Baton Rouge: Louisiana State University Press, 1982), 47–66; and John Hope Franklin, *Race and History: Selected Essays, 1938–1988* (Baton Rouge: Louisiana State University Press, 1989), 279.

35–36. "... MERIT NO FURTHER CONSIDERATION": "Memorandum to the Treasurer on Mr. Holmes's Examination" [1921], Du Bois Papers/UMass; Minutes for February 14, 1921, BRDMINS/LC. CRISIS OF CONFIDENCE: "Miss Madeline Allison Shopper" [full-page ad, business address given as 70 5th Avenue], *The Crisis* (February 1921): 184; "... [POWER] OVER WHITE PEOPLE": remarks gleaned from the following sources—John Haynes Holmes to Mary White Ovington, November 19, 1920, Arthur B. Spingarn Papers, Library of Congress/ "Memorandum for Friday conference between Mr. Holmes and Dr. D. B." [July 29, 1921], A. B. Spingarn Papers, LC; M. W. Ovington to Mother, March 12, 22, 1921, M.W.O. Papers, Box 8, Wayne State University (hereafter WSU); M.W.O. to A. B. Spingarn, April 2, July 24, 1921, M.W.O. Papers, WSU. I was greatly assisted in unraveling this controversy by Carolyn Wedin, professor emerita of University of Wisconsin–Whitewater. I relied heavily on Professor Wedin's unpublished manuscript, "Portraits in Color—and Black and White: W.E.B. Du Bois; James Weldon Johnson—and Mary White Ovington" (not included in her biography of Ovington). Also, Carolyn Wedin, *Inheritors of the Spirit: Mary White Ovington and the Founding of the NAACP* (New York: John Wiley and Sons, Inc., 1998).

Chapter 2: Du Bois and Garvey: Two "Pan-Africas"

37. "... HIS NOBLE HEAD." "... NONCHALANTLY DOWN THE PLATFORM": Lewis, taped interview with Rayford Logan, October 1974, Voices of the Harlem Renaissance, Special Collections, Schomburg Center for Research in Black Culture (hereafter SCRBC); also, Kenneth R. Janken, *Rayford W. Logan and the Dilemma of the African-American Intellectual* (Amherst: University of Massachusetts Press, 1993), 50–51.

38. PAN-AFRICAN ARRANGEMENTS AND CORRESPONDENCE: Paul Otlet to Du Bois, December 17, 1920; Du Bois to Rayford Logan, May 13; Du Bois to Logan, July 12; Rayford Logan to Du Bois, June 4; Logan to Du Bois, August 9, 1921; Logan to Du Bois [midnight 1921?]; Robert Broadhurst, Sec'y. of the African Progress Union, to Du Bois, June 29; Du Bois to Robert Broadhurst, July 11; Du Bois to Broadhurst, August 4; Du Bois to Blaise Diagne, April 13; Du Bois to Blaise Diagne [n.d. August?, 1921]; Du Bois to John H. Harris, Anti-slavery and Aboriginese Protection Society, May 6—all in the Papers of W.E.B. Du Bois, Special Collections, W.E.B. Du Bois Library, University of Massachusetts at Amherst (hereafter, Du Bois Papers/UMass). *The Second Pan-African Congress, Bulletin 2, May 1921*; obsigned by Diagne and Du Bois, in Herbert Aptheker, ed., *Pamphlets and Leaflets by W.E.B. Du Bois* (White Plains, N.Y.: Kraus-Thomson Organization Limited, 1986), 190–91, 191.

38. DIFFICULTIES WITH BLAISE DIAGNE: Du Bois to Diagne [n.d.], Du Bois Papers/UMass; Du Bois, "A Second Journey to Pan-Africa," *New Republic* (December 7, 1921): 39–42, in Aptheker, *Periodical Literature*, II, 158–62, 159; Lewis, interview with Rayford Logan, October 1974, VOHR/SCRBC; Kenneth Janken informs me that Logan's negotiations with Diagne were assisted by William Stuart Nelson, a young Howard University–trained theologian studying at the Sorbonne; Janken, *Rayford Logan*, 52; see also, for insightful profile of Diagne, Janet G. Vaillant, *Black, French, and African: A Life of Leopold Sedar Senghor* (Cambridge, Mass.: Harvard University Press, 1990), esp. 45–48.

39. JUSTIFICATION FOR PAN-AFRICAN CONGRESS: ". . . GREATEST EVENT IN MODERN NEGRO HISTORY": *Second Pan-African Congress*, 191; Du Bois, *Dusk of Dawn: An Essay Toward an Autobiography of a Race Concept* (New York: Harcourt, Brace and Company, 1940), 274–78; Du Bois, "Pan-African Congress Defended by Du Bois" [letter], New York *Age*, May 28, 1921; Du Bois, *The World and Africa* (Millwood, N.Y.: Kraus-Thomson, 1976; orig. pub. 1947), 237. To those who conceded the visionary significance but questioned the timing, as well as to outright skeptics, the editor replied with stirring arguments and dogged organizing. The "feeling of the necessity for understanding" among Africans throughout the world justified the Congress, he claimed, a feeling manifested in the recent National Congress of British West Africa, in the increasing agitation for Egyptian independence, in the activities in South Africa of the African Political Organization, and in like-minded movements in the Canal Zone and the West Indies ["Pan-Africa," *Crisis* (March 1921): 198–99]. Garvey's Universal Negro Improvement Association (UNIA) went unmentioned. ON DEBATE WITHIN THE NAACP: NAACP Board Minutes, Group 1, Series A/LC, July 11, 1921.

Not yet a century old in 1921, the pan-African idea was religious and secular, African and European, and less a comprehensive belief-system than an eclectic group aspiration [*cf.*, Immanuel Geiss, *The Pan-African Movement: A History of Pan-Africansim in America, Europe and Africa* (New York: Holmes and Meier, 1974; orig. pub 1968), esp. 114–51, and J. Ayodele Langley, *Pan-Africanism and Nationalism in West Africa, 1900–1945* (Oxford: Clarendon Press, 1973), esp. 2]. Among its notable African exponents were James Africanus Horton of Sierra Leone, J. E. Casely-Hayford of the Gold Coast, and Duse Muhammad Ali of Egypt. "Africa for the Africans!" Duse Muhammad's *African Times and Orient Review* catechized its far-flung readership. But the chief aspirants, those who elaborated the pan-African idea most fully, were educated men and women of color born outside Africa, those in what came to be called the Diaspora. Henry Garnett, Wilmot Blyden, Alexander Crummell, James Holly, and Bishop Henry Turner were men of God who divined in the Old Testament prophecy, "Ethiopia shall soon stretch forth her hands unto God," a messianic agenda of Negro ethical perfection and cultural triumph aptly characterized today as "ethiopianism" [*cf.*, Kevin Gaines, *Uplifting the Race: Black Leadership, Politics, and Culture in the Twentieth Century* (Chapel Hill: University of North Carolina Press, 1996), esp. ch. 4; David Levering Lewis, W.E.B. Du Bois: Biography of a Race, 1868–1919 (New York: Henry Holt and Company, 1993), 162–64; and Wilson J. Moses, *The Golden Age of Black Nationalism, 1850–1925 (New York*: Oxford University Press, 1989)]. In a secular vein, David Walker's 1829 *Appeal* and Martin Delany's *The Condition, Elevation, Emigration and Destiny of the Colored People*, twenty-three years later, foretold destruction of white rule and black nation-building, as did the hefty 1913 book, *The African Abroad*, by the brilliant eccentric William Ferris. Alternating between integration and emigration, along with being patriarchal, moralizing, and elitist—Victorians, in a word—their writings were imprinted with the pan-isms of their European century: Greek, Hungarian, German, Italian, Irish, and Slav.

39–40. PAN-AFRICAN CONTINGENTS: List of delegates grouped by nationality, Du Bois Papers/UMass; *Le Matin*, September 6, 1921; *La Petite Parisienne*, September 5, 1921; "Session Ends in Uproar," *Times* of London, September 3, 1921; Jessie Fauset, "What Europe Thought of the Pan-African Congress," *The Crisis* (December 1921): 60–68—all in Du Bois Papers/UMass. Ho Chi Minh's participation is highly likely, given his attendance at the Congress of Tours in December of the previous year, *cf.*, Robert Wohl, *French Communism in the Making, 1914–1924* (Stanford, Calif.: Stanford University Press, 1966), 197. See also William R. Scott, *Sons of Sheba* (Bloomington: Indiana University Press, 1993), 12–23; Langley, *Pan-Africanism and Nationalism in West Africa*, 74–75.

40. ON SAILING AND PAC LONDON AND PARIS ARRANGEMENTS OF WHITE, LOGAN, HUNT: Walter White to James Weldon Johnson, August 13, and White to Mary White Ovington, September 15 1921, regarding White's meeting with H. G. Wells at the Reform Club in Walter White Correspondence, NAACP Papers/Library of Congress; Ida Gibbs Hunt to Du Bois, June 17, 1921, Du Bois Papers/UMass. FRANCOPHONE NEGOTIATIONS: Ida Gibbs Hunt to Du Bois, August 28, 1921, Du Bois Papers/UMass; Lewis interview with Rayford Logan, October 1974, VOHR/SCRBC; White, *A Man Called White*, ch. 8 (somewhat unreliable); Janken, *Logan*, 52.

40. "WE RECEIVED ONLY EVASIONS": White, *ibid.*, 61; but Kenneth Janken informs me that White makes no mention of MacDonald being present in his formal report to the NAACP board of directors. Du Bois, "A Second Journey to Pan-Africa," *loc. cit.*, makes no mention of MacDonald meeting. ". . . MAIN ASPIRATIONS . . . PLAIN SENSE": Fauset, "What Europe Thought of the Pan-African Congress," *loc. cit.*, 67.

40–41. ". . . ALL ONE FAMILY IN LONDON": Jessie Fauset, "Impressions of the Second Pan-African Congress," *The Crisis* (November 1921): 5–11. ". . . LACKED . . . EDUCATION AND COHESION": London *Times*, August 29, 1921. ". . . WRITTEN IN THE STARS": quotes in Du Bois, *To the World (Manifesto of the Second Pan-African Congress)*, *The Crisis* (November 1921): 6–10, also in Aptheker, ed., *Pamphlets and Leaflets*, 195–99, 198, 197. Equally imperative was the demand of the sixth resolution that the "ancient common" land rights of original inhabitants be guaranteed against the unrestrained greed of "invested capital,": *ibid.*, 198. Du Bois, *Dusk of Dawn*, 276; Du Bois, *World and Africa*, 238–40. See Langley, *Pan-Africanism and Nationalism in West Africa*, 75–76.

41. PRESS COVERAGE: London *Challenge*; *Punch*—in Fauset, "What Europe Thought," *loc. cit.*, 67; Du Bois, *World and Africa*, 239–40.

42. BRUSSELS: ". . . WHITE SEPULCHRE": Joseph Conrad, *Heart of Darkness* (New York.: Penguin Books, 1999; orig. pub. 1903), 13. Fauset, "Impressions of the Second Pan-African Congress," *loc. cit.*, 13–14; two of Belgium's most distinguished public figures, Senator La Fontaine and Paul Otlet (referred to by Du Bois as the "father of the League"), served as co-sponsors of the occasion. Otlet and La Fontaine saw to it that the delegates were accorded red-carpet treatment, including a lavish reception at the fifteenth-century Hôtel de Ville, Brussels's huge, distinctively spired city hall in the historic Grand-Place. General and Mrs. Luis Sorelas of Spain, participants in the Congress, hosted the delegation in their temporary residence with convivial flair. Belgian officialdom took the Congress more seriously than had the British, and it quickly dawned on Fauset why. "Their interest was deeper, more immediately significant than that of the white people we had found elsewhere."

42. ". . . CARRIED INTO THE CONGO?": Fauset, "Impressions," *loc, cit.*, p. 13. On the role of Paul Panda, see Du Bois, "Worlds of Colors," *Foreign Affairs* (April 1925): 423–44, also in Aptheker, ed., *Periodical Lit.*, II., 241–56, 243–44; and Joseph Harris, ed., *Global Dimensions of the African Diaspora* (Washington, DC: Howard University Press, 1994), chapters 14 & 15. ". . . EXQUISITE BEAUTY OF ART": Du Bois, "A Second Visit to Pan-Africa," *New Republic* (December 7, 1921): 39–42, also in Aptheker, ed., *Periodical lit.*, II, 158–62, 159. ". . . FURNISH A PROTOTYPE"; ". . . AMERICANS ARE TOO CLEVER"; ". . . THE BELGIAN EAR LISTENED"—quotes in Fauset, "Impressions," 14.

43–44. BRUSSELS DELIBERATIONS: Du Bois, "A Second Journey to Pan-Africa," *loc. cit.*, 159. ". . . THE BANKS AND GREAT CORPORATIONS": Du Bois, *To the World*, *loc. cit.*, 197. ". . . ABSOLUMENT INADMISSIBLE!": "Session Ends in Uproar," London *Times*, September 3, 1921; Du Bois, "A Second Journey," *loc. cit.*, 159–60; Fauset, "Impressions," 14; and, Janken, *op. cit.*, 53.

44. ". . . RATHER, IT FULFILLS IT": Du Bois, *To the World*, *loc. cit.*, 195. Du Bois, *World and Africa*, 237–39; ". . . REAL MASTERS OF THE SITUATION": Fauset, "Impressions," 14. ". . . DEVOTION TO THE BLACK RACE": *Echo de la Bourse*, cited in Fauset, "What Europe Thought," 67. ". . . THOUGHTFUL AND PUZZLED MOOD.": Fauset, "Impressions," 15.

45. TALENTED TENTH ADMIRATION FOR FRANCE AND PORTUGAL: Du Bois, "Vive La France!", *The Crisis* (March 1919): 215–16, also in Aptheker, ed., *Crisis Selections*, I, 215–16; Du Bois, "Pan-African Ideals," *Nation* (September 28, 1921): 357–58, also in Aptheker, *Periodical Lit.*, II, 153–57; White, *A Man Called White*, 63. ON FRENCH AND PORTUGUESE ASSIMILATIONIST POLICIES: Hubert Deschamps, "France in Black Africa and Madagascar between 1920 and 1945," 226–85, and James Duffy, "Portuguese Africa," 171–93, in L. H. Gann and Peter Duignan, eds., *The History and Politics of Colonialism* (New York: Cambridge University Press, 1970), 2 vols., II; and Vaillant, *Leopold Senghor*, ch. 2.

45–46. ". . . INTELLECTUAL EFFLORESCENCE OF THE NEGRO RACE": Fauset, "What Europe Thought," 231; Janken, *op. cit.*, 54. PARIS DELIBERATIONS: ". . . victims of a revolution."—*Le Matin*, quoted by Fauset, "What Europe Thought," 231; ". . . ASSASSINATION OF A RACE . . .": Diagne, in Du Bois, "A Second Journey to Pan-Africa," 160; Henry Ossawa Tanner to Du Bois, April 24, 1921, Du Bois papers/UMass; Isaac Beton to Jessie Fauset, January 26, 1922, Du Bois Papers/UMass.

46–47. EUROPE: White, *op. cit.*, 62; Fauset, "Impressions"; Fauset, "What Europe Thought"; Du Bois, "A Second Journey," 161; Janken, *op. cit.*, 54; ". . . ACCEPTED WITH THEIR SOULS.": Fauset, "Impressions," 16.

47. ". . . DESTINED TO REMAIN SO FOREVER": *Humanité*, quoted by Fauset, "What Europe Thought," 63. The *Humanité* reporter also noticed the presence at the congress of "that charming young woman who was the first colored aviatrix of America," undoubtedly a reference to Bessie Coleman, who was at that time taking flight instructions near Paris (*cf.*, "Coleman, Bessie," *Black Women in America: An Historical Encyclopedia*, edited by Darlene Clark Hine [New York: Carlson Publishing, Inc., 1993], 2 vols., I, 262–63). ". . . INTERNATIONAL INSTITUTE": Du Bois, "Manifesto to

the League of Nations," *The Crisis* (November 1921): 18, also in Aptheker, ed., *Crisis Selections*, I, 322–23; Du Bois, *Dusk*, 276. ". . . PROVED THE OPEN SESAME": Fauset, "Impressions," 16.

47.   Du Bois and Smuts compared in *Echo de la Bourse*, cited by Fauset, "What Europe Thought," 67.

47–48.   ". . . GENEVA.": Assisted by Bellegarde, Spiller, and Thomas in Geneva: Fauset, "Impressions," 17. ". . . '[PAN-AFRICAN MOVEMENT] IMPOSSIBLE AT THE TIME": Du Bois, *Dusk*, 277.

49.   ". . . GOING RATHER SLOWLY NOW": Nina to Will, August 30. "YOU WILL BE COMING HOME PRETTY SOON, WON'T YOU?": Nina to Will, September 22, 1921, Du Bois Papers/UMass. Fauset, "La Vie, C'est la Vie" ["And there's a man whose lightest word/Can set my chilly blood afire;/Fulfillment of his least behest/Defines my life's desire. . . . The world is full of jets like these.—/ I wish that I were dead."], *The Crisis*, July 1922, also in David Levering Lewis, ed., *The Portable Harlem Renaissance Reader* (New York: Penguin Books, 1994), 254–55. ". . . BEAUTY AND HURT OF ITS JOY!": Du Bois, "Chamonix," *The Crisis* (December 1921): 56–58, 58.

50.   "MARCUS GARVEY.": Although no comprehensive biography exists, the literature on Marcus Garvey is extensive: see the well-researched but tendentious study by Tony Martin, *Race First: The Ideological and Organizational Struggles of Marcus Garvey and the Universal Negro Improvement Association* (Westport, Conn.: Greenwood Press, 1976); an excellent history of the intellectual sources, Rupert Lewis, *Marcus Garvey: Anti-Colonial Champion* (Trenton, N.J.: Africa World Press, Inc., 1988); formidably researched and brilliantly partisan, Winston James's *Holding Aloft the Banner of Ethiopia: Caribbean Radicalism in Early Twentieth-Century America* (New York: Verso, 1998), esp. ch. 5; Judith Stein's indispensable institutional study, *The World of Marcus Garvey: Race and Class in Modern Society* (Baton Rouge: Louisiana State University Press, 1986); the still useful biography by E. David Cronon, *Black Moses: The Story of Marcus Garvey and the Universal Negro Improvement Association* (Madison: University of Wisconsin Press, 1955); the indispensable collection edited by John Henrik Clarke with the assistance of Amy Jacques Garvey, *Marcus Garvey and the Vision of Africa* (New York: Vintage Books, 1974); and a fortiori, Robert Hill's splendid edition, *The Marcus Garvey and Universal Negro Improvement Association Papers* (Berkeley: University of California Press, 1983–2000), 9 vols. (hereafter, *Garvey Papers*). Du Bois, "An Amazing Island," *The Crisis* (June 1915): 80–81, also in Aptheker, ed., *Crisis Selections*, I, 100–101; Lewis, *W.E.B. Du Bois*, 456. ". . . FIASCO . . . EVER SEEN": "Account by W. A. Domingo of Marcus Garvey's St. Mark's Church Hall Lecture [n.d.]," Hill, *Garvey Papers*, I, 190. TROTTER SATIRIZING BOOKER T. WASHINGTON: see, Stephen R. Fox, *The Guardian of Boston: William Monroe Trotter* (New York: Atheneum, 1970), 39.

51.   ". . . INSTITUTION FOR NEGROES IN JAMAICA": Du Bois, "Item," *The Crisis* (May 1916), cited in Hill, *Garvey Papers*, I, 194. ". . . UNABLE TO TELL . . . A WHITE OFFICE OR THAT OF THE NAACP": Garvey, "Editorial letter," *The Negro World*, September 8, 1923, *ibid.*, V, p. 438; in fact, Garvey left his calling card and followed up with a cordial message to Du Bois soon after his visit to NAACP headquarters.

52.   ". . . EXPANSIVE CHAIN IN SCATTERED ETHIOPIA": Garvey, "West Indies in the Mirror of Truth," *Champion Magazine* (January 1917): 197–201, *ibid.*, I, p. 198. MAROON ANCESTRY: Robert Hill negates Garvey's maroons claim in a letter to the author, dated November 30, 1998, stating that "this is pure fable, probably started by Garvey's second wife, Amy Jacques Garvey, in her *Garvey and Garveyism*. . . . There were NO maroon communities or settlements anywhere in the parish of St. Ann, where Garvey was born." ". . . SEPARATE AND DISTINCT SOCIAL LIFE": Garvey, "The Negroes' Greatest Enemy," *Current History* (September 1923), cited in Hill, *Garvey Papers*, I, 3–12, 4.

52–53.   WORK AND EARLY INFLUENCES: Hill, *op. cit.*, I, 23–29; Martin, *Race First*, 4–5; Rupert Lewis, *Marcus Garvey*, 21–34. ". . . WITHOUT GETTING RACE CONSCIOUSNESS": *ibid.*, 25. Lewis, *ibid.*, 34–37, credits a shadowy influence on Garvey of Alexander Bedward, Baptist preacher and ardent black nationalist, whom the British authorities arrested for sedition and judged insane in 1891. Released, Bedward roamed the island denouncing the British and their mulatto subalterns as godless until 1921, when he was permanently incarcerated in an asylum after leading a protest march on Kingston. Bedward's mystical appeal to the island's dark-skinned masses of peasants and urban poor was the seedbed of the Rastafarian movement of a later decade. Robert Hill, however, discounts the Bedward influence (November 30, 1998): "The alleged linkage between Bedward and Garvey was first raised by Claude McKay and repeated by others thereafter, but the association is spurious and lacking substance." ON SINN FEIN: *ibid.*, 42–44; and Hill, *op cit.*, I, lxxii.

53.   Rupert Lewis, *op. cit.*, 45, accepts Amy Jacques Garvey's claim that Marcus Garvey visited Ecuador, Chile, and Peru, but Robert Hill asserts (November 30, 1998, letter to David Lewis) that this

was impossible in view of the time available. GARVEY'S EXPERIENCES IN EUROPE: Martin, *op. cit.*, 4–5; Rupert Lewis, *op. cit.*, 45–47. "... PURPOSE OF ALL BLACK HUMANITY": various versions of this epiphany exist. I have taken the liberty of combining them. See Garvey, "A Journey of Self-Discovery," *Current History* (September 1923), in Clarke, *Marcus Garvey*, 71–76, 73.

54. "... SO MUCH COLOR PREJUDICE IN JAMAICA": Garvey, "A Journey of Self-Discovery," *Current History* (September 1923), in Clarke, *Marcus Garvey*, 71–82, 74.

54. HUBERT HARRISON: In default of a Hubert Harrison biography, see Gaines, *Uplifting the Race*, ch. 9; James, *Banner of Ethiopia*, ch. 5; Stein, *World of Marcus Garvey*, 43–44; "Harrison, Hubert H.," *Dictionary of American Negro Biography*, edited by Rayford W. Logan and Michael R. Winston (New York: W. W. Norton and Co., 1982), 292–93 (hereafter, *DANB*); and "Harrison, Hubert H.," *Encyclopedia of the American Left*, edited by Mari Jo Buhle, Paul Buhle, and Dan Georgakas (Urbana: University of Illinois Press, 1992), 292–94.

55. WEST INDIAN IMMIGRATION AND INTRA-RACIAL FRICTION: see Irma Watkins-Owens, *Blood Relations: Caribbean Immigrants and the Harlem Community, 1900–1930* (Bloomington: Indiana University Press, 1996) 1–5, 121–32; James, *op. cit.*, ch. 1 and 3; McKay incident, in Watkins-Owens, *op. cit.*, 5; especially revealing is George Edmund Haynes, "Confidential—Impressions from a Preliminary Study of Negroes of Harlem, Borough of Manhattan, New York City, 1921," in George Edmund Haynes Papers, Box 1, SCRBC/NYPL; "... JEWS ARE SMART": Lewis taped interview with G. James Fleming, June 1976; and Lewis taped interview with George Schuyler, September 1974, VOHR/SCRBC.

56. "... A LITTLE DIFFICULT TO CHARACTERIZE": Du Bois, "Marcus Garvey," *The Crisis* (December 1920): 58–60 and (January 1921): 112–15, in Aptheker, *Crisis Selections*, I, 284; Mary Church Terrell: "Among the Negroes of Harlem," *Home News*, October 3, 1917, in Hill, *Garvey Papers*, I, 223–24. NICHOLAS MURRAY BUTLER: Butler to Garvey, December 21, 1917, *ibid.*, 231. "... CARRYING OUT OF ALL COMMANDS": *Constitution and Book of Laws, July 1918—Preamble, Constitution, Articles, ibid.*, 259–62. DU BOIS INVITED TO UNIA: Garvey to Du Bois, July 14; Du Bois to Garvey, July 22, 1920, *ibid.*, II, 426, 432.

56–57. "... MADE PERFECT SENSE": Du Bois, "Close Ranks," *The Crisis* (July 1918), in Lewis, *Du Bois Reader*, 697; and Lewis, *Du Bois*, 555–57. "... BUT YOU KNOW EVERYTHING": "Du Bois Heckled," *The Crusader* (June 1919), in *The Crusader: A Facsimile of the Periodical, Edited with a New Introduction and Index by Robert A. Hill* (New York: Garland Publishing, Inc., 1987), 3 vols., I, 352; see eyewitness account in W. Burghardt Turner and Joyce Moore Turner, eds., *Richard B. Moore, Caribbean Militant in Harlem, Collected Writings, 1920–1972* (Bloomington: University of Indiana Press, 1988), 30. "WHO MAKE COMPROMISE WITH SIN": "Digest," *Crusader* (October 1918), in Hill, *Crusader*, I, 51–52, 52.

57. *NEGRO WORLD* CHEERED THE BOLSHEVIKS: "NEGRO AGITATION," *New York Times*, August 29, 1919, cited in Hill, *Garvey Papers*, II, 7 ("... the Negro has no cause against Bolshevism"); see Jervis Anderson, *A. Philip Randolph: A Biographical Portrait* (New York: Harcourt Brace Jovanovich, 1972), ch. 3; Paula E. Pfeffer, *A. Philip Randolph, Pioneer in the Civil Rights Movement* (Baton Rouge: Louisiana State University Press, 1990), 15–18; Stein, *op. cit.*, 62; also Sterling D. Spero and Abram Harris, *The Black Worker: The Negro and the Labor Movement* (New York: Columbia University Press, 1931), 389–97.

57. "... ANGRY BLOND NEGRO": quoted in Hill, "Introduction," *The Crusader*, vi. ON FORMATION, IDEOLOGICAL FARRAGO, AND FOUNDING PERSONALITIES OF THE AFRICAN BLOOD BROTHERHOOD AND HAMITIC LEAGUE: see *ibid.*, vi–xxx; Hill, *Garvey Papers* [introductory essays], I, II; William J. Maxwell, *New Negro, Old Left: African-American Writing and Communism Between the Wars* (New York: Columbia University Press, 1999), esp. 31–36; Stein, *op. cit.*, 53–62; and, invaluably, Cedric J. Robinson, *Black Marxism: The Making of the Black Radical Tradition* (Chapel Hill: University of North Carolina Press, 2000; orig. pub. 1983), 215–18, for a credible explanation of the relationship between the racialist, Omaha, Nebraska-based Hamitic League of George Wells Parker and the nationalist and increasingly Leninist, New York–based ABB of Cyril Briggs; also, "The Crusader," Buhle and Buhle, *Encyclopedia of the Left*, 169–171; and Theodore Draper, *American Communism and Soviet Russia* (New York: Viking, 1960), esp. 320–25. Agreement as to details and ideological evolution of these two organizations is wanting in Hill (November 30, 1998), Robinson, and Buhles. I find Robinson's account most persuasive. ON PERSONALITIES: Martin, *op. cit.*, 238; Turner and Turner, *op. cit.*, 30–32; Stein, *op. cit.*, 50–53; Watkins-Owens, *op. cit.*, 103–4; Buhle and Buhle, *loc. cit.* "LOST ALL THE OTHERS ...": "The Lost leader," *Crusader* (September 1918), in Hill, *Crusader*, I, 15–16. "... REAL FOUNDER OF HUMAN CIVI-

LIZATION": George Wells Parker, "The Children of the Son," quoted, *ibid.*, xx. IRISH INFLUENCES: R. Lewis, *op. cit.*, 95; Martin, *op. cit.*, ??; Stein, *op. cit.*, 53; Hill, *Garvey Papers*, I, 95.

58. ON "NEW NEGRO" PUBLICATIONS: Du Bois, "The Class Struggle," *The Crisis* (June 1921): 55–56, also in Aptheker, ed., *Selections*, I, 303–4; Hill, "Intro," *Crusader*; Theodore Vincent, *Voices of a Black Nation.* "AFTER THE WAR WE WERE DEPRIVED OF ALL THE DEMOCRACY WE FOUGHT FOR": Garvey, quoted in Hill, *Garvey Papers*, I, 95. ". . . NULL AND VOID . . . NEGRO IS CONCERNED. ": *ibid.*, 96. VARIOUS UNIA SUPPORTERS: "Bureau of Investigation Reports—December 5, 1918," *ibid.*, 305–6; Martin, *op. cit.*, 11; Watkins–Owens, *op. cit.*, 113. ". . . AID OF JAPAN . . . WIN SUCH A WAR": Garvey quoted, *ibid.*, 306.

58–59. Martin, *op. cit.*, 11–12; Stein, *op. cit.*, 49–50. ". . . NEW ERA OF FREEDOM EVERYWHERE": Stein, *ibid.*, 52. MADAME C. J. WALKER: "Walker, Madame C. J. (Sarah Breedlove)," in Hine, *Black Women in America (BWIA)*, 1209–14; Stein, *op. cit.*, 50. ". . . [CADET'S] ALREADY DIFFICULT DUTIES": Garvey, quoted in Hill, *Garvey Papers*, I, 392. Cadet's specific charge that Du Bois had somehow "defeated his articles in the French newspapers" was widely repeated until it became accepted as fact even among many sophisticated African-Americans.

60. UNIA ATTACKS: "Dr. W.E.B. Du Bois Characterized As Reactionary Under Pay of White Men," *Negro World*, April 5, 1919, in Hill, *Garvey Papers*, I, 394–99; "Du Bois Heckled," *Crusader* (June 1919), Hill, *loc. cit.*

61. ". . . THIS GREAT CONVENTION ASSEMBLED": Garvey, "Editorial Letter," *Negro World*, June 22, 1920, in Hill, *Garvey Papers*, II, 390–92, 391.

61. ". . . THOUSANDS OF OUR MEN AND WOMEN": Garvey, "Editorial Letter," [Newspaper source obliterated], September 25, 1919, reprinted from *Garvey v. United States*, in Hill, *Garvey Papers*, II, 26–27, 27. LIBERTY HALL: *ibid.*, I, lxxii. ". . . THE UNIVERSAL OPPRESSOR": Du Bois, "Bleeding Ireland," *The Crisis* (March 1921): 200. YARMOUTH: Garvey, "Editorial Letter," September 25, 1919, Hill, *Garvey Papers*, II, 26; Hugh Mulzac, *A Star to Steer By* (New York: International Publishers, 1963), excerpted in Clarke, *op. cit.*, 127–38; Martin, *op. cit.*, 73.

62–63. ". . . ITS METHODS AS FRAUDULENT": Du Bois to James Burghardt, August 27, 1919, Du Bois Papers/UMass and Hill, *Garvey Papers*, II, 3; Du Bois to H. L. Stone, July 24, 1920, and Truman K. Gibson to Du Bois, July 24, 1920, both in Du Bois Papers/UMass, and Hill, *loc. cit.*; C. Dodd to Du Bois, August 19, 1920, both in Du Bois Papers/UMass; "Weekly Comment," *Chicago Defender*, September 6, 1919, cited in Hill, *Garvey Papers*, II, 14; "Wins First Case Against *Chicago Defender* That Published Libel," *Negro World*, June 19, 1920, *ibid.*, 349–50. ". . . AFRICA FOR THE AFRICANS": Du Bois, "The Rise of the West Indian," *The Crisis* (September 1920): 214–15, also in Aptheker, ed., *Crisis Selections*, I, 273; Du Bois to Garvey, July 22, 1920, Du Bois Papers/UMass and *Garvey Papers*, II, 431–32 (". . . I beg to say that I thank you for the suggestion but under no circumstances can I allow my name to be presented."). "I DO NOT BELIEVE THAT MARCUS GARVEY IS SINCERE. I THINK THAT HE IS A DEMAGOGUE, AND THAT HIS MOVEMENT WILL COLLAPSE IN A SHORT TIME. HIS FOLLOWERS ARE THE LOWEST TYPE OF NEGROES, MOSTLY FROM THE WEST INDIES. IT CANNOT BE CONSIDERED AN AMERICAN MOVEMENT IN ANY SENSE OF THE WORD.": Du Bois quoted, "Interview with W.E.B. Du Bois by Charles Mowbray White," in *Garvey Papers*, II, 620–21. Similar opinions expressed by Frederick Moore (publisher of New York *Age* and of West Indian origins)—"Absolutely we believe him to be a mountebank, a money grabber and a discredited cunning schemer. His financial record in Jamaica, Panama, and everywhere he has been, including the United States, is bad."—*ibid.*, 622. ". . . SHAN'T RAISE A HAND TO STOP IT.": Charles Mowbray White interview with Du Bois, *ibid.*, 620. ". . . FREE TO BREAK WITH THEM NOW": Garvey quoted, "Interview with Marcus Garvey by Charles Mowbray White," *ibid.*, p. 603.

63. ". . . FOOL OR A ROGUE": Owen and Randolph quoted, "Interview with Chandler Owen and A. Philip Randolph by Charles Mowbray White," August 20, 1920, *Garvey Papers*, II, 609–12, 609. Stein, *op. cit.*, 62–63.

63. ON GARVEY'S EVOLVING REACTIONISM: Summoned to assistant district attorney Edwin P. Kilroe's office on August 5, 1920, Garvey squirmed under tough grilling about Wobblies, anarchists, Reds, and the Washington, D.C., race riot. Kilroe informed Garvey that several sources within the UNIA claimed that bombs had been sent through the mails from Liberty Hall to unspecified persons. Once again, the assistant district attorney served notice to the shaken leader of the risk of prosecution for mail fraud in connection with the public solicitations of money for Black Star Line ships

and his Negro Factories Corporation. "... WITH PRO-NEGRO POLITICS.": Garvey quoted, 13; Hill, "Retreat from Radicalism," *Garvey Papers*, I, lxxviii–lxxx; and see Watkins-Owens, *op. cit.*, 118; Martin, *op. cit.*, 183; Cedric Robinson, *Black Marxism*, 316–18; Stein, *op. cit.*, 62–68. Garvey was and would always remain far more fascinated by the success stories of captains of industry and finance than by schemes for the socialization of wealth. Garvey's speeches often revealed a Social Darwinian edge sharper and more racialist than the Wizard's, as when spelling out the imperative of an African Zion. "The weaker and unprepared group is bound to go under," he would predict in "The Negro's Greatest Enemy" [*Current History* (September 1923), *Garvey Papers*, I, 3–12.]. "That is why, visionaries as we are ... , we are fighting for the founding of a Negro nation in Africa, so that there will be no clash between black and white and that each race will have a separate existence and civilization all its own without ... rivalry within the borders of the same country" [11]. "... HE CHOSE NOT TO UNDERSTAND. ...": McKay, *Liberator* (April 1922): 8–9; and McKay, on Garvey, in *A Long Way from Home* (New York: Harcourt, Brace & World, 1970; orig. pub. 1937), 109, and "Marcus Aurelius Garvey," in *Harlem: Negro Metropolis* (New York: Harcourt, Brace & World, 1968; orig. pub. 1940); Hill, "Surrender to Racial Purity," *Garvey Papers*, lxxx–lxxxiv; Stein, *op. cit.*, p. 63. The attempt on Garvey's life by a former officer of the UNIA two months after his interrogation by assistant D. A. Kilroe must have been unnerving, and may well have been a factor in his radical backpedaling. George Tyler fired at point-blank range in the Provisional President's office, inflicting two flesh wounds before being subdued. [Martin, *op. cit.*, 12.] By curious coincidence, Kilroe was suing Garvey for libel at that time and intending to summon Tyler as a witness in the case; by even more curious circumstance, would-be assassin Tyler committed suicide while in the custody of the police. [Lewis, *Vogue*, 43].

63–64. "... TAKEN ADVANTAGE OF THE WORLD": Garvey quoted, in Moses, *Golden Age of Black Nationalism*, 243. By the end of 1919, Garvey claimed two million of them (Du Bois estimated eighteen thousand [*Garvey Papers*, I, 10; Du Bois, "The UNIA," *The Crisis* (January 1923): 120–22, *Selections*, I, 350–53, 352]. "... IN A DISTANT, BEAUTIFUL LAND": Mary White Ovington, *Portraits in Color* (New York: Viking, 1927), 24. "You might think I have money," an inspired Panamanian wrote Garvey, enclosing another small contribution, "but the truth, as I have stated before, is that I have no money now. But if I'm to die of hunger it will be all right because I'm determined to do all that's in my power to better the conditions of my race": cited in Cronon, *Black Moses*, 56. *The Negro World* would reach 75,000 readers by the middle of 1921, netting more than a thousand dollars monthly to the UNIA treasury ["Intro," *Garvey Papers*, III, xxxiii–xxxvii, xxxiv]. LIBERIAN CONSTRUCTION LOAN: *ibid.*, xxxiv. Small wonder that Du Bois, in an unsuccessful bid to enhance the popular presence of the NAACP, would soon urge fellow board members to consider moving the national headquarters from Fifth Avenue to Harlem: Minutes for December 12, 1921, BRDMINS/LC.

65. INTERNATIONAL CONVENTION: Robed in white, a choir of two hundred women sang wondrously, while Provisional President Garvey, the Honorable Gabriel Johnson, mayor of Liberia's capital, the UNIA chancellor, William Ferris, the forceful "international organizer," Henrietta Vinton Davis, the able chaplain-general, Reverend J. W. H. Eason, and other grand officers gazed benevolently upon the enthusiastic congregation. "For over three hundred years we who are citizens and denizens of this Western Hemisphere have been held in slavery," Garvey proclaimed, as he rose to welcome the delegates. "For that period we have been separated from our brothers and sisters in the great continent of Africa. ..." His emotions plainly visible on his expressive face, Garvey sounded chords of manhood, solidarity, enterprise, and destiny, deeply moving the vast assembly as he concluded that they had come that day, "the representatives of 400,000,000 of Negroes. ... We are here because we recognize ourselves as men, and we desire to be free men." See "Opening of UNIA Convention," August 1, 1920, *Garvey Papers*, II, 476–87, 476, 478. "... GREATEST DEMONSTRATION": "Report on UNIA Convention," *ibid.*, 490–94, 493; Lewis, *Vogue*, 39.

66. "... FIGHT FOR A FREE IRELAND": Garvey quoted, in "Report of a Madison Square Garden meeting," *Garvey Papers*, II, 497–99, 499. These opening words and gestures augured well for a politics of a nationalistic collaboration, for transracial alliances based on comparable historical experiences. There was no hint of Garvey's anti-Semitism or of the leprosy theory he would concoct to explain white people [*cf.*, Garvey, "Poetic Meditations of Marcus Garvey," 1927, and note 27 in "General Intro," *Garvey Papers*, I, xxxv–xc, xliii]. The purpose of the convention was to frame a "Declaration of Rights of the Negro Peoples of the World," to mobilize an abused race for the challenges ahead. He bore the white race no ill will, but if Europe and Canada were reserved for the whites, Garvey

continued to rolling applause, "then, in the name of God, Africa shall be for the black peoples of the world" [*Garvey Papers*, II, 501]. By the time the final tumultuous session of the convention adjourned in Liberty Hall on September 1, Garvey would be elected Provisional President General of Africa. The Monrovia mayor, Gabriel Johnson, would have been elected Supreme Potentate of the UNIA along with Eason, an independent-minded North Carolina preacher, who assumed the dignity of Leader of the Fifteen Million Negroes of the United States. There would be two Leaders of the Negroes of the West Indies ("eastern and western provinces") [Garvey, "Editorial Letter," *Negro World*, September 11, 1920, *ibid.*, III, 3]. Princely annual salaries ranging from five to twenty thousand dollars were allocated, while the payroll at national headquarters in 135th Street daily grew longer. ". . . IF [DU BOIS] HAD HEARD IT": Lewis interview with Charles Harris Wesley, April, 1975, VOHR/SCRBC.

66. ". . . IS OF A HIGH PLANE": Du Bois, "Marcus Garvey," *The Crisis* (December 1920): 58–60, 285; Du Bois to Lloyd's Register, November 6, Du Bois to North American Shipping Corporation, November 6, 1920, in *Garvey Papers*, III, 72–7. ON FERRIS'S SEEING DU BOIS: Garvey, "Evening Session," August 3, 1920, *ibid.*, II, 525–26, 525; Robert Hill (November 30, 1998) dismisses the possibility of Du Bois's presence at Madison Square Garden; I believe that Ferris's claim, even though relayed by Garvey, cannot be ignored and that it may be true given the lengths to which Du Bois went to obtain accurate information about Garvey and the UNIA (*cf.*, Du Bois, "Rise of the West Indian," *Selections*, 273. Noting the trebling of Harlem's West Indian population to more than 100,000 in the past decade, he had written that it was "increasingly necessary for us to understand this new ally in the fight for black democracy.")

67. ". . . PUNISH THE MAN WHO ATTEMPTS TO ESTABLISH IT": Du Bois, "Marcus Garvey," *loc. cit.*, 288; ". . . TUSKEGEE PEOPLE IS LIKE THAT.": quoted in Eric J. Sundquist, *To Wake the Nations: Race in the Making of American Literature* (Cambridge, Mass.: Belknap Press, 1993), ". . . WHERE HE FINDS ASYLUM AND SYMPATHY?": Du Bois, "Marcus Garvey," 288.

67. BLACK STAR LINE: There was no characterization to apply to the Black Star Line operation other than "sinister," Du Bois believed: $289,066.27 in advertising fees in order to raise $472,706.72 — "in other words, it has cost nearly $300,000 to collect a capital of less than half a million." — "Marcus Garvey," *loc. cit.*, 286. THE FIASCO OF THE SHIPS: Tied up in Cuba by a month-long longshoremen's strike, the Black Star Line flagship had sailed with a single passenger and no cargo to Jamaica for boiler repair. The arrival at Bocas del Toro had occasioned such joy and pride that the United Fruit Company gave its workers a holiday. An incredulous Mulzac watched as thousands of jubilant peasants "seized the hawsers as they came out of the water and literally breasted us alongside the dock" — Mulzac, in Clarke, *op. cit.*, 134. But the cargo of Jamaican coconuts had mostly rotted by the time Captain Cockburn (ordered to stop at Philadelphia and Boston by Garvey) dropped anchor in New York Harbor just in time for the convention. *Cf.*, also, Mulzac, "Why the Black Star Line Failed," *Cleveland Gazette*, November 3, 1923, 6–27, in Aptheker, ed., *Garvey Papers*, V, 472–78; Du Bois, "The Black Star Line," *The Crisis* (September 1922): 210–14, in Aptheker, ed., *Selections*, I., 335–40; Stein, *op. cit.*, 90–9.

68. ". . . OF THE MODERN NEGRO WORLD": Du Bois, "Marcus Garvey," *loc. cit.*, 289. The mistaken description in the *Crisis* of the *Yarmouth* as an unseaworthy "wooden vessel" had given Arthur Spingarn almost as much concern about liability as Du Bois expressed about Garvey. With the editor balking at issuing an immediate retraction and UNIA attorneys readying court petitions for large damages, the board sternly ordered two corrections printed in the monthly. See A. Spingarn to Wilford H. Smith re. Black Star Line, Inc., February 10, 1921, Du Bois Papers/UMass and *Garvey Papers*, III, 172; and NAACP Board Minutes, Group I, Series A, February 14, 1921. ON HOOVER AND GARVEY: For the moment, Garvey had not gone quite far enough to be prosecuted, but Hoover reassured his superiors that there was likely soon to be "some proceeding against him for fraud in connection with his Black Star Line propaganda." — Martin, *op. cit.*, 178. ". . . ENGLISH, FRENCH, OR GERMANS": "Reports by Special Agent P-138," *Garvey Papers*, III, 5. NEW ORLEANS UNIA BRANCH: Martin, *op. cit.*, 74. "British Military Intelligence Report," *Garvey Papers*, II, 205–13. UNIA IN SOUTH AFRICA: Hill, ed., *Africa for the Africans, 1913–1921*, volume VIII of the *Garvey Papers* (as yet unpublished and courtesy of Robert Hill); also, Tony Martin, *The Pan-African Connection: From Slavery to Garvey and Beyond* (Dover, Mass.: The Majority Press, 1983), 134. NEGRO WORLD FOREIGN LANGUAGE EDITIONS: Hill, *Garvey Papers*, V, xxxv.

69. NEGRO WORLD SUPPRESSED: *Garvey Papers*; and *Africa for the Africans, 1913–1921* (Berkeley: University of California Press, 1997), esp. volume VIII of *Garvey Papers*; also, Alphonso Pinckney, *Red, Black, and Green: Black Nationalism in the United States* (New York: Cambridge University Press,

1976), 52. "... FORCE NOR REVOLUTION IN ITS PROGRAM": Du Bois to Hon. Charles [Evans] Hughes, June 23, 1921, Du Bois Papers/UMass, also in Aptheker, ed., *Correspondence*, I, 250–51, 251. Du Bois sent a number of letters to Pan-African Congress supporters, like the one to the Anglo-African, W. A. Aldridge, in which he sought to scotch any enthusiasm for the Pan-Africanism of the UNIA and "a wild and irresponsible agitator whose work cannot possibly be permanent" [Du Bois to W. A. Aldridge, June 20, 1921, Du Bois Papers/UMass]. So far, such misgivings were expressed privately and only to a select number of persons. With Garvey's popularity among ordinary men and women of color exceeding anything ever seen before in the United States, Du Bois was still unprepared to write him off publicly. The influential mainstream magazine, *World's Work*, ran a complimentary two-part story about Garvey and his organization [*Garvey Papers*, III, xxxvii]. Hard-hitting "Bruce Grit" (John E. Bruce), one of African America's most respected journalists, had signed on with the *Negro World* in May 1921, joining Ferris, its able literary editor. For a noisy moment in the fall of 1921 it had even seemed that William Pickens, the new field secretary and only the second Negro inducted into Phi Beta Kappa at Yale, was about to quit the NAACP for a larger salary with the UNIA. Then, too, there were more than a few letters to *The Crisis* reproaching the editor's decidedly unenthusiastic two-part "Marcus Garvey," running in the December 1920-January 1921 issues. She felt safe in saying, one anonymous but regular reader complained, "that the greater part of our race would have you speak differently of any man who has made such an effort to bring from under bondage our people who so much need it." [Anonymous to Du Bois, January 16, 1921, Du Bois Papers/UMass]. The editorial treatment meted out to Trotter a few years back (silence alternating with equivocal scrutiny), Du Bois found not to work so well with the UNIA founder.

69–70. Du Bois, "The Tulsa Riots," *The Crisis* (July 1921): 114–16. ON UNIA-NAACP-DYER: NAACP Board Minutes, September 13, 1920, BRD MINS/LC; Martin, *op. cit.*, 278. ON LIBERIA: *Garvey Papers*, III, xxxiii. Garvey to Du Bois, November 5, 1921, Du Bois Papers/UMass. "Marcus Garvey's Farewell Speech," February 22, 1921, *Garvey Papers*, III, 224–33, 229. "... WHAT EUROPEAN CHILDREN ARE TAUGHT": Jones according to Norman Leys, in Kenneth James King, *Pan-Africanism and Education: A Study of Race Philanthropy and Education in the Southern States of America and East Africa* (Oxford: Clarendon Press, 1971), 134. "... GREAT FAITH IN [JONES'S] DECISIONS": Du Bois, "Thomas Jesse Jones," *The Crisis* (October 1921): 252–56, also in Aptheker, ed., *Selections*, I, 311–16, 314; King, *op. cit.*, 56–57. "... TO ACCEPT THEIR 'FRIENDLY' PROTECTION": Garvey quote, *ibid.*, 135–36.

70. "... TO ASSOCIATE WITH ONE'S FELLOW MEN": Du Bois, "The Social Equality of Whites and Blacks," *The Crisis* (November 1920): 16–18, also in Aptheker, ed., *Selections*, I, 280–82, 280. "... EVERY SUGGESTION OF SOCIAL EQUALITY": Harding quote, *ibid.*, 326; and see Kenneth O'Reilly, *Nixon's Piano: Presidents and Racial Politics from Washington to Clinton* (New York: The Free Press, 1995), 96. The widespread belief among African Americans that Harding had African ancestry compounded the distress with which the Birmingham speech was received. See comment on Harding by Henry Lincoln Johnson, in Gloria T. Hull, ed., *The Diary of Alice Dunbar-Nelson* (New York : W.W. Norton, 1986 orig. pub. by Penguin Books), 87. ON THE NAACP AND HARDING'S HAITIAN GAMBIT: *cf.*, James Weldon Johnson, *Along This Way: The Autobiography of James Weldon Johnson* (New York: Viking Press, 1933, 1961), 345–59.

71. "... LIBERTY HALL ROARED WITH LAUGHTER": "Speech By Marcus Garvey," October 30, 1921, *Garvey Papers*, IV, 141–51, 144. "... PHASES OF NATIONAL ACTIVITY": James Weldon Johnson, "A Crime Against Nature," New York Age, September 24, 1921, *Garvey Papers*, IV, 79–81, 80. See also the somewhat derisory article by Herbert J. Seligmann (the new director of NAACP publicity, "Negro Conquest," *World Magazine* December 4, 1921), *Garvey Papers*, IV, 239–44; although the almost simultaneous publication of field secretary Pickens's flattering "Africa for the Africans" in *The Nation* (December 28, 1921), *ibid.*, 527 [note 1], sent mixed signals to the Association's members. Also Martin, *op. cit.*, 278.

72. "... FOR LESS THAN THE WHITE WORKER": Garvey quoted, Amy Jacques-Garvey, ed., *Philosophy and Opinions of Marcus Garvey* (New York: Atheneum, 1969), "... LOYAL TO ALL FLAGS": EXPULSION OF ABB AND CRUSADER ELEMENTS: "Twenty-First Day," August 26, 1921, *Garvey Papers*, III, 690–92; After Tulsa's African-American community had been almost wiped out at the beginning of June 1921, the Briggs cadre rapidly moved away from emigrationist schemes for Africa and South America and concluded that membership in the American Communist Party (and then the Workers [Communist] Party) was the only meaningful revolutionary option available to them. See, *Encyclopedia of the Left*, 169–171; and Robinson, *op. cit.*, 216–18.

73. "... BECAUSE WE ARE NOT RADICAL": Convention Speech by Rose Pastor Stokes with remarks by Garvey, August 19, 1921, in Hill, *Garvey Papers*, III, 675–82, 676; on Stokes and *Theses on the Negro Question*, see Robinson, *op. cit.*, 221–22. "... EXPLOITING NEGROES FOR THEIR OWN SUBSERVIENT ENDS.": Garvey, "Bolshevism in Flight," *ibid.*, 691–692; "Mr. Garvey and the ABB," ca. September 23, 1921, *ibid.*, IV, 74–77 ("Is Mr. Garvey really in earnest when he talks about the liberation of Africa? ... Or is he too busy Resurrecting Medieval Systems and Titles and making of the Glorious UNIA Movement a Tinsel Show and a Laughing stock to give Time to Real Efforts ... ?[p. 75]). Communism was alien to the Negro, Garvey asserted, a "white man's creation to solve his own political and economic problems" [Robert Hill and Barbara Bair, eds., *Marcus Garvey: Life and Lessons* (Berkeley: University of California Press, 1987, p. 296]. Yet consider "Speech by Marcus Garvey," January 27, 1924, *Garvey Papers*, V, 548–56: After lavishing praise on Lenin, Garvey states, "I believe, in time, that the whole world will take on the social democratic system of government now existing in Russia. It is only a question of time ... I also regard Trotsky with great respect, with great reverence" [pp. 552–53].

73. "... HIS WIDE POWERS AND INFLUENCE": Du Bois, "Marcus Garvey," *loc. cit.*, 115. "... HIS FAILURE WOULD BE THEIRS": *ibid.*, 115; "Reports by Bureau Agent H. J. Lenon," September 27, 1920, *Garvey Papers*, III, 30–33 ("... at princely salaries of from $5,000 to $20,000 yearly, for doing practically nothing ... "[31]); Fred D. Powell, "Black Star Line Needs Big Change," New York *News*, March 11, 1920, *Garvey Papers*, II, 239–41; Du Bois, "Pan-Africa," *The Crisis* (March 1921): 198–99, also in Aptheker, ed., *Crisis Selections*, I, 296–97; W. A. Domingo, "Figures Never Lie, But Liars Do Figure," *Crusader* (October 1921): 13, in Hill, *Crusader*, 1247, and *Garvey Papers*, IV, 153–56. BRIGGS V. GARVEY: "Intro," *ibid.*, xxxi–xxxv, xxxii; "Confidential Informant 800 to George F. Ruch," October 18, 1921, *ibid.*, IV, 125; and Mulzac, "Why the Black Star Line Failed!" *Garvey Papers*, V, 472–78, 473.; Du Bois, "The Black Star Line," *loc. cit.*, 335–40. In Washington, Hoover fretted as he followed the eleventh-hour maneuverings of Garvey's attorney, Henry Lincoln Johnson, who apparently hoped to persuade Postmaster General Hays to drop the case for a $20,000 consideration [J. Edgar Hoover to William J. Burns, January 12, 1922, *Garvey Papers*, IV, 373].

74–75. "... FIGURES NEVER LIE": By early 1922, Du Bois knew enough about the shaky finances of Garvey's multiple operations to be certain that the UNIA edifice was bound to collapse in noisy, humiliating failure. Reverend J. D. Brooks, member of the Executive Council and one of Garvey's most trusted American associates, had been arrested on charges of grand larceny at the end of November 1921. Months earlier, the crew of the expired *Kanawha* had been brought home courtesy of the United States government [Du Bois, "The Black Star Line," *loc. cit.*, 336]. The excursion boat *Shadyside*, after a few trips up the Hudson in summer 1920, now lay capsized on the beach near 175th Street [*ibid.*, 337]. S.S. ORION: Hill, "Intro," *Garvey Papers*, IV, xxxi–xxxv, xxxi. ARRESTED OFFICIALS: Cronon, *op. cit.*, 101. "... BY WEST INDIANS OR AMERICAN NEGROES": Du Bois, "Africa for the Africans," *The Crisis* (February 1922): 154–55, also in Aptheker, ed., *Crisis Selections*, I, 331.

75. "... TELEGRAPHED IT ALL OVER THE WORLD": Du Bois, "Back to Africa," *Century Magazine* (February 1923): 539–48, in Aptheker, ed., *Periodical Literature*, II, 173–82, 178. LIBERIAN CONSTRUCTION LOAN: Elie Garcia to President C. D. B. King, June 8, 1920, *Garvey Papers*, II, 345–47. ON LIBERIAN POLITICAL ECONOMY: A. Adu Boahen, *Africa under Colonial Domination, 1880–1935* (London: James Currey Ltd., 1985), 120–21; and Peter Duignan and L. H. Gann, *The United States and Africa: A History* (London: Cambridge University Press, 1984), 201–6; "... AGRICULTURE AND BUSINESS PROSPECTS": Edwin Barclay to Elie Garcia, June 14, 1920, 347; "$2,000,000 Convention Fund for Great Race Movement," *Negro World*, June 19, 1920, *Garvey Papers*, II, 374–77.

75–76. UNIA DELEGATION TO LIBERIA: Also others, especially Supreme Deputy Potentate, George O. Marke, a Sierra Leonian educated in Scotland and soon bitterly at odds with Cyril Crichlow [Garvey to Gabriel M. Johnson, January 18, 1922, *Garvey Papers*, III, 135–36]. The Liberians would discover sometime later that Secretary Garcia, after a brief visit in the summer of 1920, had prepared an assessment of their government that was so negative that Garvey had sealed and filed it away [Cronon, *op. cit.*, 124]. The UNIA leadership would be slow to appreciate the extent to which no understanding with the Liberians was ever more than tentative, contingent, or free of unscrupulousness. "... WHAT ... THEY LIKE TO HEAR": Barclay quoted, in Martin, *op. cit.*, 124. Left unsaid was the obvious implication that the UNIA would receive the same treatment, as in fact it would a few months later, when Barclay informed the British consul general in Monrovia that Garvey's "movements and activities are, however, of no practical interest to this government. ..." [*ibid.*, 125].

77. "... CONSPIRACY AGAINST OTHER SOVEREIGN STATES": C. D. B. King to Du Bois, April 13, 1921,

Du Bois Papers/UMass; Du Bois to C. D. B. King, April 7, 1921, *ibid.*, and *Garvey Papers*, III, 342; "An Open Letter from the President of Liberia," *The Crisis* (June 1921): 53. Cyril A. Crichlow to the UNIA Executive Council, June 19, 1922, *Garvey Papers*, III, 478; (*African World*) Martin, *op.cit.*, 127. ". . . TRYING TO WRECK [THE UNIA]": Ida May Reynolds to Du Bois, July 5, 1923, Du Bois Papers/UMass, also in Aptheker, ed., *Correspondence*, I, 271–72. ". . . THEN BURST AND DISAPPEAR": Du Bois, "Demagog," *The Crisis* (April 1922): 333.

78. ". . . MOST GROUPS OF TWELVE MILLIONS": *ibid.*, 333.

78. ". . . WATERS THE PENNIES OF THE POOR": *ibid.*, 333. ". . . WEST INDIAN . . . PROUD OF THE FACT": Du Bois to W. A. Domingo, January 18, 1923, Du Bois Papers/UMass, also in Aptheker, ed., *Correspondence*, I, 263–64; Martin, *op. cit.*, 331; and see a recent, cogent revisiting of African-American intra-group intellectual dissonances, in James, "Postscript," *Holding Aloft the Banner of Ethiopia*, 261–91; also, Watkins-Owens, *op. cit.*, 56–125.

78–79. ". . . PUNISH HIM AT HIS JUDGMENT?": Garvey quote, Du Bois, "Black Star Line," *loc. cit.*, 339. ". . . SYSTEM TO HIS DISHONESTY": Garvey quote, Clarke, *op. cit.*, 141. UNIA MEMBERSHIP: Du Bois, "UNIA," *The Crisis* (January 1923): 120–22, also in Aptheker, ed., *Selections*, I, 350–53, 350. "MARCUS GARVEY MUST GO": "2,000 Negroes Hear Garvey Denounced," New York *Times*, August 21, 1922, *Garvey Papers*, IV, 932–33.

80–81. ". . . GIVE ME THE KLAN": Garvey quotes, Martin, *op. cit.*, 344, 277; and Garvey, "An Appeal to the Soul of White America," October 2, 1923, *Garvey Papers*, V, 464–68. ". . . THE 'BLUE VEIN' ARISTOCRACY": Garvey quote, Amy Jacques-Garvey, *op. cit.*, 57; and *Garvey Papers*, V, 226. ". . . AS MUCH AN AMERICAN AS ANYONE": James Weldon Johnson quote, in Lewis, *Vogue*, 42. TELEGRAM TO THE ATTORNEY GENERAL: James Weldon Johnson to Judge Julian W. Mack, May 17, 1923, *Garvey Papers*, V, 305 ("[NAACP] had nothing whatever to do with the document addressed to Attorney General Daugherty."); Carl Murphy, editor, Baltimore *Afro-American*, to Harry M. Daugherty, February 16, 1923, *ibid.*, 245; Martin, *op. cit.*, 325.

81–82. MUSSOLINI AND MURDER: "Intro," *Garvey Papers*, V, xxxv, and xxxiii–xxxiv; Martin, *op. cit.*, 59–62. ". . . WHAT DID IT ALL MEAN?": Du Bois, "Back to Africa," *loc. cit.*, 173. In eight fast-moving, packed paragraphs Du Bois developed his version of the rise of mulatto power and the evolution of demeaning, dark-skinned peasant deference in the West Indies. In this hegemony of the near-whites, black labor was exploited and then proletarianized and black talent and success, where they emerged, were intimidated or co-opted. Then came the labor demands of the Panama Canal, of insatiable cartels like United Fruit, and the opportunities of the Great War attracting peasant labor like metal shavings throughout Latin America and to the United States, paying them "something like decent wages" and allowing them to travel and to aspire as never before. Garvey, wrote Du Bois, was a product of these new currents coursing through the Antillean peasantry, "a facile speaker, able to express himself in grammatical and forceful English." The pity was, however, that this gifted Jamaican was "inordinately vain and egotistic, jealous of his power, impatient of details, a poor judge of human nature, and had the common weakness of untrained devotees that no dependence could be put upon his statements of fact" [*ibid.*, 175]. Breaking upon the Negro world with a startling doctrine of African immigration and liberation, he donned the mantle of leader without bothering to take account "of the American Negro problem," Du Bois charged; "he knew nothing about it." His attempt to foist a West Indian conception of the color-line in the United States was so bitterly resented and vigorously opposed, said Du Bois, that Garvey eventually realized something of the enormity of his error and protested that the UNIA was proud to be a rainbow coalition. Still, he never quite got it right. "Thus with one voice he denounced Booker T. Washington and Frederick Douglass as bastards, and with the next named his boarding-house and first steamship after these same men!" [*ibid.*, 176].

ON BACK TO AFRICA: "Back to Africa" recounted the balance sheet and maritime fiascoes detailed in the two *Crisis* articles, the grandiosity and paranoia impervious to advice and incapable of reform, the obdurate and even comic gymnastics to sustain a crumbling empire. Garvey knew he had missed the "key to some dark arcanum," the editor declared with exquisite schadenfreude. "Beaten and overwhelmed with loss and disappointment, he will not yet surrender. . . . He is today a little puppet, serio-comic, funny, yet swept with a great veil of tragedy; meaning in himself little more than a passing agitation, moving darkly and uncertainly from a little island of the sea to the panting, half-submerged millions of the first world-state" [*ibid.*, 179]. Striding into his thesis that inexorable forces were working to bring about global unity among peoples, Du Bois grandly determined that Garvey's movement ran against the grain of history. "Here is a world that for a thousand years, from the First Crusade to the Great War, had been breaking down the barriers between nations and races in order to build a world-wide economic unity and cultural solidarity." Du Bois indulged a gross exaggeration and glided knowingly over the economic pitfalls of capitalist exploitation in order to score a debater's point. In the "squat and dirty old 'Liberty Hall'" Garvey could be heard screaming his propaganda, and "yelling to life, from the black side, a race consciousness which leaps to meet Madison Grant and Lothrop Stoddard and other worshippers of the great white race." By contrast, yesterday, today, and tomorrow, the "super-diplomacy of race politics" demanded policies that transmuted interdependence into "cultural sympathy, spiritual tolerance, and human freedom" [*ibid.*, 180].

82–83. ". . . AND FIGHT THE WHITE WORLD": Du Bois, "Back to Africa," *loc. cit.* 180. DU BOIS–GARVEY ENCOUNTER RECALLED: Charles Wesley (April 1975), George Schuyler (September 1974), Arthur P. Davis (March 1977) taped interviews with Lewis, VOHR/SCRBC.; *cf.*, Martin, *op. cit.*, 305. ". . . ALL THAT IS WHITE IS BEAUTIFUL": "Editorial Letter by Marcus Garvey," *Negro World*, February 17, 1923, *Garvey Papers*, 232–41, 233.

84. Du Bois to P. B. Young, August 8, 1925, Du Bois Papers/UMass, *Selections*, I, 317–18. ". . . LITTLE WONDER IT FAILED": "Garvey found Guilty," Pittsburgh *Courier*, June 23, 1923, *Garvey Papers*, V, 376–77; *United States against Marcus Garvey, Elie Garcia, George Tobias and Orlando M. Thompson, Defendants, ibid.*, 302–5; "Closing Address to the Jury by Marcus Garvey," June 15, 1923, *ibid.*, 330–59; W. H. Ferris to William Pickens, June 12, 1923, Du Bois Papers/UMass; William J. Burns to W. W. Husband, Commissioner of Immigration, June 28, 1923, *Garvey Papers*, V, 384; Martin, *op. cit.*, 192. ANTI-SEMITISM: "Intro," *ibid.*, lviii–lix.

84. ". . . HIS PERSONALITY AND HIS PROGRAM": Du Bois, "Back to Africa," *loc. cit.*, 179. [Garvey, "The Negro's Greatest Enemy," *loc. cit.*]

Chapter 3: On Being Crazy and Somewhat Devious

85. "On Being Crazy," *The Crisis* (June 1923): 56–57, in Herbert Aptheker, ed., *Creative Writings by W.E.B. Du Bois: A Pageant, Poems, Short Stories, and Playlets* (White Plains, N.Y.: Kraus-Thomson Organization Ltd., 1985), 126–27.

86. EMPLOYMENT DATA: Florette Henri, *Black Migration: Movement North, 1900–1920* (Garden City, N.Y.: Anchor Books), 148–49.

86–87. ". . . EXACTLY WHAT LYNCHING IS": Du Bois, "A University Course in Lynching," *The Crisis* (June 1923): 55, also in Aptheker, ed., *Selections from "The Crisis"* (Millwood, N.Y.: Kraus-Thomson, 1983), 2 vols., I, 357. ON THE BIRTH OF A NATION FIGHT: Du Bois, "The Birth of a Nation," *The Crisis* (March 1923): 218–20; David Levering Lewis, *W.E.B. Du Bois: Biography of a Race, 1868–1919* (New York: Henry Holt and Co., 1993), 506–9; Thomas Cripps, *Slow Fade to Black*, John Hope Franklin, "*The Birth of a Nation*: Propaganda as History," *Race and History: Selected Essays, 1938–1988* (Baton Rouge: Louisiana State University Press, 1989).

87. INSUFFICIENT GUARANTEE OF DUE PROCESS: "Lawyers Hail Arkansas Decision," *The Crisis* (May 1923): 24, "Victory," *ibid.* (August 1923): 151; Henri, *op. cit.*, 321–22; Richard Kluger, *Simple Justice: The History of Brown v. Board of Education, the Epochal Supreme Court Decision that Outlawed Segregation, and of Black America's Century-Long Struggle for Equality under Law* (New York: Random House, 1975), 112–14; Robert L. Zangrando, *The NAACP Crusade Against Lynching, 1909–1950* (Philadelphia: Temple University Press, 1980), 85–86. DYER BILL: Du Bois, "Dyer Bill," *The Crisis* (April 1922): 25; Du Bois, "Dyer Bill," *ibid.* (January 1923): 103–4; Zangrando, *op. cit.*, 43–45. ". . . WHAT A TRUMPET BLAST.": Joel Spingarn to Du Bois, December 6, 1922, W.E.B. Du Bois Papers, Special Collections, Du Bois Library, University of Massachusetts at Amherst (hereafter Du Bois Papers/UMass).

87–88. HARVARD: For the family oral history of Harvard Jim Crow and for contemporary news clippings, I am indebted to Spencer Jourdain, son of Edwin (class of 1921). See Werner Sollors, Caldwell Titcomb, and Thomas A. Underwood, eds., *Blacks at Harvard: A Documentary History of African-American Experience at Harvard and Radcliffe* (New York: New York University Press, 1993), esp. 197–98; Du Bois, "Fair (!) Harvard," *The Crisis* (August 1922): 178–79. ". . . I DON'T RESPECT IT,": Edwin Jourdain quote, in Spencer Jourdain to David Levering Lewis, September 8, 1993, letter based on Spencer Jourdain's interview with "two of the three principal players in the event," William J. Knox and Edwin B. Jourdain; Edwin B. Jourdain, "Harvard Spirit of Fair Play Knows Not Color or Creed," New Bedford (Mass.) *Evening Standard*, June 18, 1922, 1.

89. "... THE OLD NEW ENGLAND STOCK": President Lawrence Lowell, quoted in *Literary Digest*, 78 (August 16, 1922): 28–29; also Sollors, Titcomb, *op. cit.*, 197. "... OUTCASTS AND VICTIMS OF EUROPE": Du Bois, "Brothers Come North," *The Crisis* (January 1920): 105–6. "... THAN TEN MERE JEWISH SCHOLARS": Sollors, Titcomb, *op. cit.*, 197; and *cf.*, President John Grier Hibben of Princeton to L. S. Gannett, April 8, 1922, on "fortunate" under-enrollment of Jews, Lewis Stiles Gannett Papers, Houghton Library, Harvard University. "... INFILTRATING CHERISHED ORGANIZATIONS": Leonard Dinnerstein, *Anti-Semitism in America* (New York: Oxford University Press, 1994), 79 and esp. 5; E. Digby Baltzell, *The Protestant Establishment: Aristocracy and Caste in America* (New York: Random House, 1964), 65–93, 202–11; John Higham, *Strangers in the Land: Patterns of American Nativism, 1860–1925* (New Brunswick, N.J.: Rutgers University Press, 1988; orig. pub. 1995), 278; and David Levering Lewis, "Parallels and Divergences: Assimilationist Strategies of Afro-American and Jewish Elites from 1910 to the Early Thirties," *Journal of American History* 71 (December 1984): 543–67.

89–90. Stephen R. Fox, *The Guardian of Boston: William Monroe Trotter* (New York: Atheneum, 1970), 261–63. Series of letters re Harvard racial policies—1922, reel 11, frame 206 ... "... OF LIMITATION [JEWISH] ENROLLMENT": Gannett quote, Sollors, Titcomb, *op. cit.*, 198; Du Bois, "Fair (!) Harvard," *loc. cit.*; Raymond Pace Alexander, "Voices from Harvard's Own Negroes," *Opportunity* (March 1923): 29, and Sollors, Titcomb, *op. cit.*, 199; Ernest Gruening to O. G. Villard, June 2, 1922, Villard Papers, Houghton/Harvard. "... RULE OF NORDIC WHITE THROUGH BRUTE FORCE": Du Bois, "Americanization," *The Crisis* (August 1922): 154, also in Aptheker, ed., *Crisis Selections*, I, 334.

90. *Ibid.*, 334; Ernest Gruening to O. G. Villard, April 7, 1922, Villard Papers, Houghton/Harvard; Sollors, Titcomb, *op. cit.*, 198. "... FIERCE FIGHT": Moorfield Storey to L. S. Gannett, February 9, 1923, Gannett Papers, Houghton/Harvard; Sollors, Titcomb, 201; L. S. Gannett to Du Bois, March 3, 1922; Du Bois to L. S. Gannett, March 9, 1922; and see, formal letter of protest—"To some of us it has seemed that the establishment of the color line at Harvard was a shameful abandonment of a long and honorable tradition. From the days when Robert Gould Shaw, '60, led the 54th Massachusetts Infantry at Fort Wagner, Harvard has given the Negro fair and equal treatment. Most of us recall Negroes in the Harvard dormitories and dining-halls, and so far as we know there was never any protest against their presence," in Du Bois Papers/UMass.

91. V.A. HOSPITAL CONTROVERSY: Du Bois, "The Tuskegee Hospital," *The Crisis* (July 1923): 106–7, 106, also in *W.E.B. Du Bois: Writings* (New York: The Library of America, 1986), 1202–1204. Pete Daniel, "Black Power in the 1920s: The Case of Tuskegee Veterans Hospital," *The Journal of Southern History* (August 1970): 368–88. "... COMMAND A NEGRO 'NURSE-MAID.' ": Du Bois, "The Tuskegee Hospital," *loc. cit.*, 106. "... MORE STRAIGHTFORWARD TYPE": Du Bois, "The Dilemma of the Negro," *American Mercury* (October 1924): 179–85, in Aptheker, ed., *Periodical Lit.*, I, 222–29, 225. "... SOLDIERS WOUNDED IN SOUL AND BODY": Du Bois, "Tuskegee Hospital," *loc. cit.* 107.

92–93. "... IN THIS ASTONISHING GENERATION": "Fear of Efficiency," *loc. cit.*, 358. Albon Holsey to Du Bois, July 14, 1923, Du Bois Papers/UMass—"On the afternoon of July 3d, Miss Phelps borrowed from the store-room at the hospital ten new sheets." Du Bois, "Tuskegee Hospital," *loc cit.*; Annie H. Howe to Du Bois, July 27, 1923, Du Bois to Mrs. John H. Howe, August 1, 1923, Du Bois Papers/UMass, also in Aptheker, ed., *Correspondence*, I, 273–75.

94–95. "... OR GOVERNMENT INTERESTS WERE INVOLVED": NAACP Board Minutes, July 9, 1923; and Secretary's Report to the Board for the September 1923 meeting, NAACP Board Minutes, Group I, Series A/Library of Congress "... CUPIDITY GONE STARK MAD!:" Du Bois, "Tuskegee Hospital," *loc. cit.*, 107.

95. Ernest Peixotte to Miss Ernestine Rose, April 23, 1923; and J. M. Hewlett to Du Bois, May 29, 1923, Du Bois Papers/UMass. For profile of Augusta Savage, see Darlene Clark Hine, ed., *Black Women in America* (New York: Carlson Publishing Inc., 1993), 2 vols., II, 1010. "... AND HER CONDUCT IRREPROACHABLE": Du Bois, "The Technique of Race Prejudice," *The Crisis* (August 1923): 152–54, in *Du Bois Writings*, 1204–1208, 1204; Du Bois, "Fear of Efficiency," *loc. cit.*

95. "... LOST THROUGH BEING OVEREDUCATED": Malcolm Cowley, *Exile's Return: A Narrative of Ideas* (New York: W. W. Norton and Co., 1934), 230. "COOL AND CAUTIOUS NEW ENGLAND REASON": Du Bois, *The Gift of Black Folk: The Negro in the Making of America* (Millwood, N.Y.: Kraus-Thomson, 1975; orig. pub. 1924), 320, 287, iv., 339. ON THE AMBIGUOUS IMPLICATIONS OF RACIALIZED CHARACTERISTICS: see James Weldon Johnson, "Preface," *The Book of American Negro Poetry* (New

York: Harcourt, Brace, 1921); Frederick J. Hoffman, *Freudianism and the Literary Mind* (Baton Rouge: Louisiana State University Press, 1945); Van Wyck Brooks, *The Confident Years, 1885–1915* (New York: E. P. Dutton, 1952), 41; Marianna Torgovnick, *Gone Primitive: Savage Intellects, Modern Lives* (Chicago: University of Chicago Press, 1990), ch. 1; Ann Douglas, *Terrible Honesty: Mongrel Manhattan in the 1920s* (New York: Farrar, Straus and Giroux, 1995), esp. ch. 2, 8, is an extreme example of a trend to minimize racism in the cultural interaction of whites and blacks in the twenties.

95–96.   Prominent cultural pluralists: "Transnationalists" fought a losing battle against conservative Americanizationists. Bourne's *War and the Intellectuals*, ed. by Carl Resek (New York: Harper Torchback, 1964); Waldo Frank, *Our America* (New York: Boni and Liveright, 1919); Horace Kallen, *Culture and Democracy in the United States* (New York: Boni and Liveright, 1924), appearing, significantly, simultaneously with Du Bois's *Gift of Black Folk*; Josiah Royce, *Race Questions, Provincialism and Other American Problems*; also, Edward Abrahams, *The Lyrical Left: Randolph Bourne, Alfred Stieglitz and the Origins of Cultural Radicalism in America* (Charlottesville: University of Virginia Press, 1986); Casey Nelson Blake, *Beloved Community: The Cultural Criticism of Randolph Bourne, Van Wyck Brooks, Waldo Frank, and Lewis Mumford* (Chapel Hill: University of North Carolina Press, 1990); and Robert B. Westbrook, *John Dewey and American Democracy* (Ithaca, N.Y.: Cornell University Press, 1991); Bruce Kuklick, *The Rise of American Philosophy: Cambridge, Massachusetts, 1860–1930* (New Haven: Yale University Press, 1977).

97.   NATIVISM, RACE, AND GENDER: William Graham Sumner, *On Liberty, Society, and Politics: The Essential Essays of William Graham Sumner*, ed. by Robert C. Bannister (Indianapolis: Liberty Fund, 1992), esp. ch.4; Jacoby and Glauberman, eds., *op. cit.* esp. ch. 4 and 7; Reflective of the top tier of organized labor's anti-alien bias is the 1923 declaration by the National Industrial Conference Board that immigration was "essentially a race question—a question of the kind of citizenship and national life we desire to develop in the United States" [quoted in David Montgomery, *The Fall of the House of Labor: The Workplace, the State, and American Labor Activism, 1865–1925* (New York: Cambridge University Press, 1987), 464]. FOR NATIVIST EXTREMISM: David H. Bennett, *The Party of Fear: From Nativist Movements to the New Right in American History* (Chapel Hill: University of North Carolina Press, 1988); David M. Chalmers, *Hooded Americanism* (Chicago: Quadrangle Books, 1968); Thomas F. Gossett, *Race: The History of an Idea in America* (New York: Oxford University Press, 1997), chap. XV; Richard Hofstadter, *Social Darwinism in American Thought* (Boston: Beacon Press, 1992; orig. pub. 1944), esp. ch. 9; Higham, *Strangers in the Land*, esp. ch. 7, 8, 9; David Lanier Lewis, *The Public Image of Henry Ford: An American Folk Hero and His Company* (Detroit: Wayne State University Press, 1976); William E. Leuchtenburg, *The Perils of Prosperity, 1914–32* (Chicago: University of Chicago Press, 1958), 10; and Michael E. Parrish, *Anxious Decades: America in Prosperity and Depression, 1920–1941* (New York: W. W. Norton, 1992), part 1. ". . . TOLERANCE FOR OPPOSITION AND HATRED": Du Bois, *Gift of Black Folk*, 12. THE CONQUERING IDEOLOGY OF "WHITENESS": Du Bois, *Darkwater: Voices from Within the Veil* (New York: Kraus-Thomson, 1975; orig. pub. 1920), 29. ON AMERICA WHITENING: see Theodore Allen, *The Invention of the White Race* (London: Verso, 1994); Neal Gabler, *An Empire of Their Own: How the Jews Invented Hollywood* (New York: Crown Publishers, Inc., 1988); Matthew Guterl, *Investing in Color: A Cultural History of Race in Modern America, 1900–1940* (Cambridge, Mass.: Harvard University Press, forthcoming); Noel Ignatiev, *How the Irish Became White* (New York: Routledge, 1995); Matthew Frye Jacobson, *Whiteness of a Different Color: European Immigrants and the Alchemy of Race* (Cambridge, Mass.: Harvard University Press, 1998); Eric Lott, *Love and Theft: Blackface Minstrelsy and the American Working Class* (New York: Oxford University Press, 1993); Toni Morrison, *Playing in the Dark: Whiteness and the Literary Imagination* (Cambridge, Mass.: Harvard University Press, 1992); David Roediger, *The Wages of Whiteness: Race and the Making of the American Working Class* (London: Verso, 1991); Michael Rogin, *Blackface, White Noise: Jewish Immigrants in the Hollywood Melting Pot* (Berkeley: University of California Press, 1996), esp. ch. 5. "DEMOCRACY!": Du Bois, *Darkwater*, 120.

97–98.   ". . . DID HE KNOW?": Du Bois, "Rhinelander Case," *The Crisis* (January 1926): 112–13, 112. For the details of the case, I was materially assisted by Elizabeth Smith's forthcoming dissertation, "Passing and the Anxious Decade: The Rhinelander Case and the 1920s" (Ph.D. diss., Rutgers University, 2001), an early portion of which was provided by the author. Court cases dealing with racial-identity claims seem to have been decided mainly on the basis of "common sense"—i.e., the appearance and personal history of the party in question. *Cf.*, Peggy Pascoe, "Miscegenation Law, Court Cases, and Ideologies of 'Race' in Twentieth-Century America," *The Journal of American History*,

83 (June 1996): 44–69, an article called to my attention by Matthew Guterl, now of Washington State University.

98. "... MAY WE NOT LIVE SOMEWHERE?": "The Challenge of Detroit," *The Crisis* (November 1925): 7–10, and Du Bois, "Now or Never," *The Crisis* (December 1925): 59–60, both in Aptheker, ed., *Selections*, I, 428–30, 429, and 431. Headline accounts, heavily biased in favor of the assailants: "200 Police Guard Scene as 1 Is Slain and 1 Shot by Negroes," *Detroit Free Press*, September 10, 1925, 1; and "Prosecutor's Aide Doubts They Will Free Accused in View of Warrants," *Detroit Free Press*, September 11, 1925, 1; also objective coverage in "Accusers Lied in Sweet Case, Darrow Says," *Herald Tribune*, November 25, 1925, 19. A seven-hour defense by Darrow resulted in the acquittal of Henry Sweet, Ossian's brother, who admitted firing the fatal shot. Ossian Sweet's life was tragically affected by the arrest and trial. His wife's eighty-four-day incarceration and hunger strike left her weakened and vulnerable to tuberculosis. She died in Arizona less than two years after the final trial. Her young daughter contracted her mother's illness and died with her, as did Henry Sweet somewhat later. Ossian Sweet became reclusive, socialized with his working-class patients, and committed suicide in 1960, according to an obituary. "Detroit's Last Angry Man," *Jet* (April 7, 1960), 24–27.

99. "... KEEP DOWN PRIVILEGE": Du Bois, *Gift of Black Folk*, 5. "... PASSED" OVER INTO THE WHITE RACE: inescapably speculative, but see "The Vanishing Mulatto," *Opportunity* (October 1925): 291, cites from the 1910 and 1920 census 2,050,686 mulattoes and 1,600,554, respectively.

99. On reactions to Jack Johnson: Du Bois, "As to Pugilism," *The Crisis* (April 1923): 247–51; Du Bois, "Opinion," *The Crisis* (August 1923): 151–54; Al-Tony Gilmore, *Bad Nigger! The National Impact of Jack Johnson* (Port Washington, N.Y.: Kennikat Press, 1975); and Jeffrey T. Sammons, *Beyond the Ring: The Role of Boxing in American Society* (Urbana: University of Illinois Press, 1988), 34–44. "... WAS EAGERLY DESIRED": Du Bois, "Fear of Efficiency," *loc. cit.*, 358.

99–100. "... THOUGHT OR FEELING": Du Bois, "Technique of Race Prejudice," *loc. cit.*, 1206. "... LEADERS OF WHITE CIVILIZATION": *ibid.*, 1207. "... WHITE WORLD RECENTLY": Du Bois, "Fear of Efficiency," 358. "... ONE SUNDAY AFTERNOON": Richard R. Wright to Du Bois, January 4, 1923, Du Bois Papers/UMass.

100–101. Du Bois, "Charles Young," *The Crisis* (February 1922), in *Library of America*, 1195–1196. DU BOIS AND YOUNG EXCHANGES: Charles Young to Du Bois, April 30, 1919, Young telegram to Du Bois, October 31, 1919, Du Bois Papers/UMass. Across bottom of telegram Du Bois pencils, "Believe that if you refuse Liberia, New York position would open." YOUNG'S DEATH: Du Bois to Madame Loulouse Chapoteau, December 16, 1922, Du Bois Papers/UMass. YOUNG BIOGRAPHY: "Young, Charles," *BODANB*, 677–79. NEWS ACCOUNTS OF OBSEQUIES: "Metropolis Salutes Col. Chas. Young," and "Color Did Not Bar Col. Young," in *New York Amsterdam News*, May 30, 1923; "Funeral Orators Clash Over Body of Negro Officer," *New York World*, May 28, 1923, 1; "Homage to Negro Officer," *New York Times*, May 28, 1923.

101–2. "... WOULD YOU LIKE TO BE A NIGGER?": Young quoted, in Rayford Logan Diaries, 1940–51, entry for April 23, 1950, Manuscript Division, Library of Congress. "... OVERLAID WITH LIES": Du Bois tribute, in "Charles Young," *The Crisis* (July 1923): 104–6, 106; this is the second apostrophe, accompanied by a full-page photograph captioned, "The Funeral of Charles Young," 106.

102. Fauset, "The Prize Story Competition," *The Crisis* (June 1923): 57–58, 58; Langston Hughes, "The Negro Speaks of Rivers," in Lewis, *When Harlem Was in Vogue* (New York: Penguin Books, 1997, orig. pub. 1981), 79; Jean Toomer, "Song of the Son," *The Crisis* (April 1922): 261; Lewis, *Vogue*, 67–68. "... TO STARVE COLORED ARTISTS": "Art for Nothing," *The Crisis* (May 1922): 8–9, in Daniel Walden, ed., *W.E.B. Du Bois: The Crisis Writings* (Fawcett World Library, 19??), 278–79, 278.

103. LOS ANGELES AND SAN DIEGO: Du Bois, "Wayfaring," *The Crisis* (May 1923): 7–11. "... CARE OF [HER] NECK": Nina to Will, March 5, 1923, Du Bois Papers/UMass.

103. ON LOUISE THOMPSON: "... PROUD TO BE BLACK": David Levering Lewis interview (taped) with Louise Thompson, June 29, 1987; "Patterson, Louise Thompson," in Hine, *BWIA*, II, 911; Lewis, *Vogue*.

104–5. Du Bois to Anita Thompson, May 3, 1923; "... MORE OR LESS A HUM DRUM MATTER": Du Bois to Anita Thompson, June 16, 1923; "... PERHAPS? HA HA." "... LOVE YOU FOREVER FOR IT": Anita Thompson to Du Bois, June 2, 1923; "... 'PROPERLY WATCHED,' HA, HA": Anita Thompson to Du Bois, July 4, 1923; "... WHY I HAVEN'T WRITTEN?" Thompson to Du Bois, [n.d. 1923?], Du Bois Papers/UMass.

106. CORRESPONDENCE ABOUT 606 ST. NICHOLAS AVENUE: Jacob Breen to Nina G. Du Bois, January 4, 1923; John Nail to Du Bois, January 15, 1923; Nina to Will, May 6, 1923; Will to Nina, May 9, 1923; Nina to Will, March 7, 1923; Nail to Du Bois, April 16, 1923, all in Du Bois Papers/UMass. YOLANDE HOSPITALIZED: Louis T. Wright to Dr. F. A. Stewart, October 22, 1922; Du Bois to Madame Loulouse Chapoteau, December 16, 1922, both in Du Bois Papers/UMass. "... BE AT YOUR TOILET": Du Bois to Yolande Du Bois, February 13, 1923. "... YOU AND YOUR MOTHER": Du Bois to Yolande, February 13, 1923; Nina to Will, May 6, 1923; Will to Nina, May 9 and 11, 1923; "... IN THE CINCINNATI DEPOT": Du Bois to Nina, May 11, 1923, Du Bois Papers/UMass.

107–8. The Decagynians, *The Crisis* (March 1923): 69. "... TICKED WITH MYSELF": Yolande to Nina and Will, March 4, 1923, Du Bois Papers/UMass. ON JIMMY LUNCEFORD: see Hugues Panassie, "Jimmy Lunceford and His Orchestra," *Le Jazz Hot*, 1st series, no. 21 [1937]: 3–17, 10; David Schiff, "In the 30's Black Swing Was Golden," Arts and Leisure, *New York Times*, July 28, 1991; John S. Wilson, "Celebrating Jimmie Lunceford, a Big-Band Master," *New York Times*, December 14, 1989; and "Lunceford, James Melvin 'Jimmie,' " in Jack Salzman et al., eds., *Encyclopedia of African-American Culture and History* (New York: Simon and Schuster, 1996) 5 vols., III, 1666–1667 (hereafter, EAACH). John Aveni, former member of my dissertation seminar, called my attention to Lunceford materials in the Rutgers University Jazz Institute. "... IF THEY HAD MARRIED.": Lewis interview with Du Bois Williams, June 28, 1987; and various confidences from interviews with Harlem Renaissance principals during the 1970s (VOHR/SCRBC). I'm told Lunceford married 'Chris,' Yolande's Fisk roommate: Lewis interview with Mae Wright Peck Williams, September 12, 1988. "... SHOULD HAVE BEEN MINE": Lunceford quote, Lewis interview with Du Bois Williams. "... TRYING TO LIVE ON LOVE": Du Bois to Yolande, March 30, 1923, Du Bois Papers/UMass.

108. HARVARD'S EXCLUSIONARY POLICIES: Sollors and Titcomb, *op. cit.*, 224. "... VINDICATED FOR ONCE": Du Bois, "Tuskegee and Moton," *The Crisis* (September 1924): 199–203.

108. Du Bois to the Countess de Robilant of the Italian-American Society, April 20, 1926, Du Bois Papers/UMass; *cf.*, "Savage, Augusta," in *BWIA*, II, 1010–1013.

109–10. "... UNEXPECTED DEVELOPMENTS": "Third Pan-African Congress," Du Bois Papers/UMass; "Pan-African Congress," in Aptheker, ed., *Pamphlets and Leaflets by W.E.B. Du Bois* (White Plains, N.Y.: Kraus-Thomson, 1986), 204–5. "... SEEMED ABOUT TO FAIL.": "Third Pan-African Congress"; Du Bois to Miss Ira Aldridge, September 11, 1923; Du Bois to Messrs. Beton and Magalhaes, August 13, 1923, both in Du Bois Papers/UMass. "... CANNOT POSTPONE ... A CONGRESS": Du Bois to Logan, August 24, 1923, Du Bois Papers/UMass. "... AS APART FROM FRENCH DEVELOPMENT": Du Bois, "Worlds of Color," *Foreign Affairs* (April 1923): 423–44, 248. "... LA BONNE NOUVELLE": Isaac Beton to Du Bois, September 27, 1922, Du Bois Papers/UMass. "... L'AMOUR SEUL QUI DOIT DECIDER": Beton to Fauset, n.d., 1923, Beton to Du Bois, December 21, 1992, Du Bois Papers/UMass. ... TO MAKE THE CONGRESS A SUCCESS: Logan to Du Bois, September 6, 1923, Du Bois Papers/UMass.

110. "... BUSINESSLIKE WAY OF WRITING HIM": *ibid.*; Du Bois to T. A. Marryshaw, September 11, 1923, Du Bois Papers/UMass. "... WITH YOU AND YOUR FRIENDS": Magalhaes to Du Bois, November 7, 1923, Du Bois Papers/UMass; Du Bois, "High Ideal of Pan-Africanism," *African World*, October 6, 1923, 1352, 1367, also in Aptheker, ed., *Writ. Periodical Lit.*, II, 213–14. Principal funding actually came from the Circle for Peace and Foreign Relations—comprised of women like Addie Hunton, Dorothy Peterson, Bouttee, Lillian Alexander, et al.: Du Bois to Ida Gibbs Hunt, September 27; Annie Dingle to Du Bois, March 3, 1927; and Annie Dingle and Eunice Hunton Carter to Du Bois, March 1927, all in Du Bois Papers/UMass. "... ADDING LONDON TO LISBON": Du Bois to C. Hallinan, September 6, 1923, Du Bois Papers/UMass; Logan to Jessie Fauset, September 19, 1923, Du Bois Papers/UMass.

111. "... REPRESENT EGYPT AND THE SUDAN?": Du Bois to P. A. Hamilton, September 1923; Du Bois to Mrs. Casely Hayford, September 11, 1923; Norman Leys to Du Bois, September 4, 1923; Du Bois to Ramsay MacDonald, September 6, 1923; Ramsay MacDonald to Du Bois, September 24, 1923; H. G. Wells to Du Bois, June 12, 1923; Woodson to Du Bois, October 1, 1923; Du Bois to Carter Woodson, October 4, 1923, all in Du Bois Papers/UMass.

112–13. GOING TO LIBERIA: Du Bois to William H. Lewis, September 20, 1923 ("... Would it not be a graceful thing if the United States Government could make me their special representative on that occasion? ... I understand that you have the privilege of calling Coolidge by his first name and I therefore write to you for your advice."); William H. Lewis to Du Bois, October 4, 1923, Du Bois Papers/UMass; Lewis, William Henry, see Logan, *DANB*, 396–97; Du Bois, memo to James Weldon

Johnson and Walter White, September 20, 1923, Du Bois Papers/UMass. "... GREAT AND GOOD FRIEND ... MINISTER PLENIPOTENTIARY": Calvin Coolidge to Charles D. B. King, December 26, 1923, Du Bois Papers/UMass. "... WHITE SUNSHINE OF PROMISE": Du Bois, "Sketches from Abroad," *The Crisis* (March 1924): 203–5, in Aptheker, ed., *Crisis Selections*, I, 381–84, 381. "... FIFTY MILLION BLACK AFRICANS": "Worlds of Color," *loc. cit.*, 252–53. Roster of participants in Du Bois Papers/UMass. According to Rayford Logan, Ruth Anna Fisher was very much in evidence at the Third Pan-African Congress; Lewis interview with Ruth Anna Fisher, VOHR/SCRBC.

113. LONDON MEETING: Du Bois with Logan and B. F. Seldon, "History of the Pan-African Movement," week of November 4, 1923, Du Bois Papers/UMass; "The Pan-African Congress (Third Biennial Sessions)" [2-page leaflet], Aptheker, ed., *Pamphlets and Leaflets*, 204–5; and see, "Dr. Du Bois Sketches a History of the Pan-African Congress," *West Africa*, November 10, 1923, 1352, 1367, 1368. "... THE BLACK MAN'S FREEDOM": Sidney Olivier quoted, Du Bois, "The Negro Takes Stock," *New Repubic*, January 2, 1924, 143–45, in Aptheker, ed., *Periodical Lit.*, II, 218–21, 218. "... APPEAL OF UGANDAN AFRICANS": *ibid.*, 219. CLOSING REMARKS: *ibid.*, 219; Isaac Kramnick and Barry Sheerman, *Harold Laski: A Life on the Left* (New York: Allen Lane The Penguin Press, 1993), 222–23; Du Bois to Fauset, November 9, 1923, Du Bois Papers/UMass. "... IRREDUCIBLE NEEDS OF OUR PEOPLE": Du Bois, "The Negro Takes Stock," *loc. cit.*, 220–21; Brenda Gayle Plummer, *Rising Wind: Black Americans and U.S. Foreign Policy, 1935–1960* (Chapel Hill: University of North Carolina Press, 1996), 21; Edgar S. Efrat, "Incipient Pan-Africanism: W.E.B. Du Bois and the Early Days," *The Australian Journal of Politics and History* (December 1967): 382–93, 391.

114. "... THAT THEIR DEVELOPMENT PERMITS": Du Bois, "To the World" [2-page pamphlet], in Aptheker, ed., *Pamphlets and Leaflets*, 195–99, 198; Du Bois, "Negro Takes Stock," *loc. cit.*, 220; Brenda Plummer, *Rising Wind*, 1. "... PERMANENTLY RULED BY THE FORWARD": "High Ideals of Pan-Africanism," *loc. cit.*, 214.

114. "... THEY DARE NOT PROMOTE HIM": Du Bois, "Sketches from Abroad," *loc, cit.*, 381–82; Du Bois, "Pan-Africa in Portugal," *The Crisis* (February 1924), in Aptheker, ed., *Crisis Selections*, I, 374–75; Hunt, William Henry Alexander, see Logan, *DANB*, 334–36. CARCASSONNE TO LISBON: "... SIMPLY A MAN.": Du Bois, "Sketches from Abroad," 383; Du Bois, "The Primitive Black Man," *The Nation* (December 17, 1924), 675–76, in Aptheker, ed., *Writ. Periodical Lit.*, II, 230–32, 230; Du Bois, "Sketches from Abroad," 384; Du Bois to C. Kamba-Simango, July 10, 1924, Du Bois Papers/UMass.

116. ON MAGALHAES: Du Bois, "Pan-Africa in Portugal," *loc. cit.*, 374; and Du Bois, "Worlds of Color," *loc. cit.*, 241–42. LOGAN IN LISBON: Logan to Du Bois, September 26, 1923, Du Bois Papers/UMass; Du Bois, "The Third Pan-African Congress," *The Crisis* (January 1924): 120–22. Du Bois to Arthur Spingarn, December 2, 1923, Du Bois Papers/UMass. "... SO MUCH ANCIENT BLACK BLOOD": Du Bois, *Worlds of Color*, 242, 243.

117. "... STRONG FINANCIAL MEANS": Isaac Beton to Du Bois, December 10, 1923, DuBois Papers/UMass. "... GARVEY WALKED INTO THE SCENE": Du Bois, *Dusk of Dawn*, 277.

117. "... THE AFRICAN SECTION OF GREAT BRITAIN": Randolph and Owen quoted, Martin, *Race First*, 301.

Chapter 4: Rearranging Ethiopia Abroad and at Home

118. Du Bois sent a wire via Dakar to President King: "Arrive Saturday, Henner—Du Bois." TELEGRAM: See Du Bois, "Africa," *The Crisis* (April 1924): 247–54, also in Herbert Aptheker, ed., *Selections from the Crisis* (Millwood, N.Y.: Kraus-Thomson, 1983), 2 vols., II, 386. "... I TURN MY FACE TOWARDS AFRICA": Du Bois, "Pan Africa in Portugal," *The Crisis* (February 1924): 170. Du Bois, "Africa," *op. cit.*, 385. GREAT BARRINGTON CHILDHOOD : David Levering Lewis, *W.E.B. Du Bois: Biography of a Race, 1868–1919* (New York: Henry Holt and Company, 1993), 14.

118–19. LONGBOAT: Du Bois, "Africa," *op. cit.*, 387. Lillie Mae Hubbard to W.E.B. Du Bois, February 16, 1924, The Papers of W.E.B. Du Bois, Special Collections, W.E.B. Du Bois Library, University of Massachusetts at Amherst (hereafter Du Bois Papers/UMass). Elliot Skinner, *African Americans and U.S. Policy Towards Africa, 1850–1925* (Washington, D.C.: Howard University Press, 1992), 446.

119. AMERICO LIBERIANS: Some ten thousand Americo-Liberians governed sixteen or more indigenous ethnic groups numbering almost 2 million with a rapacity that would eventually require the

attention of a League of Nations commission. See I. K. Sundiata, *Black Scandal: Americans and the Liberian Labor Crisis, 1926–1936* (Philadelphia: Institute for the Study of Human Issues, 1980), 7–11.
119. "... THE BEAUTIFUL BLACK SKIN OF THEIR NECKS":Du Bois, "Africa," *op. cit.*, 388; Du Bois, *ibid.*, 391. "... GLIDE OF DARK SNAKE": Du Bois, "Little Portraits of Africa," *The Crisis* (April 1924): 273–74; also in Aptheker, ed., *Selections*, I, 391. The photo of Du Bois can be found under the heading "In the African Bush" in *The Crisis* (June 1924): 57. "... MYSTERY AND WIDE-RANGING INFLUENCE": Du Bois, *The Negro* (Millwood, N.Y.: Kraus-Thomson, 1975; orig. pub. 1915), 9.
120. "... THE FIRST OF ALL WESTERNERS": Alain Locke, "Apropos of Africa," *Opportunity* (February 1924): 37–40; "... A LITTLE THING": Du Bois, "Africa," *op. cit.*, 389.
120. Du Bois, "Africa," *op. cit.*, 389; Skinner, *African Americans and U.S. Policy*, 497; Memorandum for William R. Castle, Jr., Esq., from De la Rue—office of the General Receiver, Monrovia, January 26, 1924, "Subject: Report on W.E.B. Du Bois, Minister Extraordinary, etc., specially appointed for the inauguration of the President of Liberia, January 7, 1924," RG 59, National Archives, 6: 882.00/739–882.00/743. DU BOIS'S INTERPRETATION OF SILENT CAL: Skinner, *op. cit.*, 513.
121. "... THE LIGHTER ELEMENTS AGAINST THE DARKER ONES": Marcus Garvey to President C. D. B. King of Liberia, December 5, 1923, in Robert A. Hill, ed., *The Marcus Garvey and Universal Negro Improvement Association Papers* (Berkeley: University of California Press, 1983–2000), 9 vols., V, 508, 509 (hereafter *Garvey Papers*). UNIA MISSION: Tony Martin, *Race First: The Ideological and Organizational Struggles of Marcus Garvey and the Universal Negro Improvement Association* (Dover, Mass.: The Majority Press, 1976), 127; Hill, editorial note, *Garvey Papers*, III, 694; Hill, editorial note, *Garvey Papers*, V, 510; Skinner, *op. cit.*, 498–99.
122. EXPORT BUSINESS: Du Bois to Lillie Mae Hubbard, April 4, 1924, and Hubbard to Du Bois, April 5, 1924, both in Du Bois Papers/UMass. "... MY DEAR LILLIE MAE": Du Bois to Lillie Mae Hubbard, May 1, 1924, Du Bois Papers/UMass. HUGHES: Du Bois to Charles Hughes, January 5, 1923, in Du Bois Papers/UMass, also in Herbert Aptheker, ed., *The Correspondence of W.E.B. Du Bois* (Amherst: University of Massachusetts Press, 1973), 3 vols., I, 260–61.
122–23. DU BOIS'S RECOMMENDATIONS: Du Bois to C. D. B King, January 21, 1924; C. D. B. King to Du Bois, June 30, 1924; C. D. B. King to Du Bois, June 30, 1924; and Du Bois to C. D. B. King, July 29, 1924, all in Du Bois Papers/UMass. "W.E.B. Du Bois to the Honorable Charles Evans Hughes, the Secretary of State, March 24, 1924," RG 59, National Archives, 6:882.00/739. For reactions in Washington to Du Bois's Liberian mission: Hon. Solomon Porter Hood to the Secretary of State, Feb 17,1924, enclosures to letter—address of the American Minister Resident presenting Du Bois to President of Liberia; (2) DuBois address at the inauguration of the Liberian President; (3) Liberian President's response to Du Bois adress; also, letters, telegrams and memoranda regarding Du Bois's appointment as envoy extraordinaire and Minister Plenipotentiary to represent the President of the United States at the inauguration of President King of Liberia, Record group 59, Records of the Department of State, Decimal Files 1910–1929. Microfilm publication M613, reels 6, 7.
124. RUBBER: Sundiata, *Black Scandal*, 34–35; Du Bois, "Liberia and Rubber," *New Republic* (November 18, 1925), 326, also in Aptheker, ed., *Writings by W.E.B. Du Bois in Periodicals Edited by Others* (Millwood, N.Y.: Kraus-Thomson, 1982), 3 vols., II, 272. DU BOIS, HOOD, AND FIRESTONE: Solomon Porter Hood to Du Bois, November 16, 1925, Du Bois Papers/UMass; Du Bois to Harvey Firestone, October 26, 1925, Du Bois Papers/UMass, and also in Aptheker, ed., *Correspondence*, I, 320–23.
124. DU BOIS ON ANGOLA AND SIERRA LEONE: Du Bois, "Britain's Negro Problem in Sierra Leone," *Current History* (February 1925): 690–700, also in Aptheker, ed., *Writings in Periodicals*, II, 233–40; Du Bois, "Worlds of Color," *Foreign Affairs* (April 1925), 423–44, also in Aptheker, ed., *Writings in Periodicals*, II, 241–56. Du Bois had originally proposed to write four separate articles, with one devoted entirely to the Liberian situation [Du Bois to Archibald C. Coolidge, October 23, 1924, Du Bois Papers/UMass]. LIBERIA AS LODESTAR: Du Bois, "Liberia and Rubber," 273; Sundiata, *op. cit.*, 150.
125. "... TO TREAT LIBERIA FAIRLY": Du Bois to C. D. B. King, July 29, 1924, Du Bois Papers/UMass. "... A PURELY COMMERCIAL PROJECT": W. D. Hines to Du Bois, November 10, 1925, in Du Bois Papers/UMass, and also in Aptheker, ed., *Correspondence*, I, 323. "... THE ATTITUDE OF WHITE CAPITAL": Du Bois, "Liberia and Rubber," 276, 272; Sundiata, *op. cit.*, 34. PRESIDENT KING'S RECOMMENDATIONS: C. D. B. King to Du Bois, June 30, 1924, Du Bois Papers/UMass; Sundiata, *op. cit.*, 40–46.
125. THE LIBERIAN GAMBIT: Sundiata, *op. cit.*, 40, 175; Du Bois, "Liberia and Rubber," 276; Du Bois

to Bruce Bliven, October 15, 1925, Du Bois Papers/UMass. ON HAYFORD: David Kimble, *A Political History of Ghana, 1850–1928* (Oxford: Clarendon Press, 1963), 375–84; Casely Hayford, *Ethiopia Unbound: Studies in Race Emancipation* (London: Frank Case, 1969; orig. pub. 1911), viii; Martin, *Race First*, 301.

126–27. "... WATCH HIM": Martin, *Race First*, 136; Kimble, *Political History of Ghana*, 399–400; Bruce Grit to Marcus Garvey, January 2, 1924, in *Garvey Papers*, V, 513. DU BOIS IN SIERRA LEONE: Lillie Mae Hubbard to Du Bois, February 16, 1924, Du Bois Papers/UMass; Sierra Leone *Weekly News*, April 5, 1924. "... THE PRIMITIVE BLACK MAN": Du Bois, "The Primitive Black Man," *The Nation* (December 17, 1924), 675–76, also in Aptheker, ed, *Writings in Periodicals*, II, 231.

127–28. "... THE FAITH OF THE GULLIBLE": Skinner, *op. cit.*, 498; Du Bois to C. D. B. King, January 21, 1924, Du Bois Papers/UMass; Du Bois to the Editor of the *Daily Worker*, August 28, 1924. THE UNIA COMMUNE: Martin, *Race First*, 127; Hill, editorial note, *Garvey Papers*, V, 571.

128. ON THE RUCKUS AT THE NAACP CONVENTION: Du Bois to James Weldon Johnson, April 15, 1924, Du Bois Papers/UMass, also in Aptheker, ed., *Correspondence*, I, 286–87. The slate of articles includes Du Bois, "Pan Africa in Portugal"; Du Bois "The Primitive Black Man"; Du Bois, "Britain's Negro Problem in Sierra Leone"; Du Bois, "Worlds of Color"; Du Bois, "Liberia and Rubber"; and Du Bois, "The Negro Takes Stock," *New Republic* (January 2, 1924), 143–45, also in Aptheker, ed., *Writings in Periodicals*, II, 218–21. "... WE ARE GRADUALLY GAINING GROUND": Moorfield Storey to Du Bois, April 2, 1924, Du Bois Papers/UMass.

128–29. REGRETS: Joel Spingarn to Du Bois, April 12, 1924; Moorfield Storey to Du Bois Dinner Committee, April 5, 1924, both in Du Bois Papers/UMass. Arthur Spingarn to J. E. Spingarn, April 6, 1924, Joel E. Spingarn Papers, New York Public Library. "... AN ASTONISHING OCCASION": Du Bois to Joel Spingarn, April 16, 1924, Du Bois Papers/UMass. Du Bois, "On Being Dined," *The Crisis* (June 1924), 55–56, also in Aptheker, ed., *Crisis Selections*, I, 403. Jessie Fauset wrote to Joel Spingarn and indicated that Du Bois had been quite moved by the dinner—see Fauset to Joel Spingarn, May 9, 1924, Du Bois Papers/UMass.

129. "... THE SHADOW OF DEATH": Lewis, *Du Bois*, 524. "... A PRIVATE HEALTH CLINIC": Life Extension Institute Report, dated May 17, 1923, and Du Bois to Life Extension Institute, August 14, 1923, both in Du Bois Papers/UMass.

130. SPAT WITH JOHNSON: Du Bois to James Weldon Johnson, April 15, 1924, Du Bois Papers/UMass, also in Aptheker, ed., *Correspondence*, I, 286–87; James Weldon Johnson to Du Bois, April 17, 1924, Du Bois Papers/UMass, also in Aptheker, ed., *Correspondence*, I, 288, 287; Joel Spingarn to Du Bois, October 24, 1919, Du Bois Papers/UMass, also in Aptheker, ed., *Correspondence*, I, 200–202.

131. THE WOUNDED WORLD: Du Bois, "The Black Man and the Wounded World: A History of the Negro Race in the World War and After," *The Crisis* (January 1924): 110–114, also in Aptheker, ed., *Selections*, I, 366–71. "... CLAMORING FOR THEIR RETURN": Major A. E. Patterson to Du Bois, May 15, 1923; Du Bois to Patterson, May 22, 1923; Du Bois to Patterson, July 6, 1925; Du Bois to Patterson, July 22, 1925, all in Du Bois Papers/UMass. Nor was ex-Major Patterson alone in being so shabbily treated. One James W. Johnson, a lawyer and ex-officer, asked for return of his artillery maps, loaned in 1920. Du Bois continued to evade Johnson's requests for a year, see Johnson to Du Bois, May 28, 1927, and Du Bois [letter signed "Secretary"] to Johnson, September 23, 1927, Du Bois Papers/UMass.

132. "... MERELY A HISTORY": Carter Woodson to Du Bois, April 28, 1924, Du Bois Papers/UMass.

132–33. AN INVITATION TO FISK: Fisk Alumni Association to Du Bois, February 13, 1924, Du Bois to Yolande, April 24, 1924, and Yolande's Grade Transcript, dated March 14, 1924, all in Du Bois Papers/UMass. "... SUPERIOR LIBERAL ARTS EDUCATION": Joe Martin Richardson, *A History of Fisk University, 1865–1946* (Tuscaloosa: University of Alabama Press, 1980), 81; Raymond Wolters, *The New Negro on Campus: Black College Rebellions of the 1920s* (Princeton: Princeton University Press, 1975), 30.

133. MCKENZIE: Wolters, *New Negro on Campus*, 30–37; "Statement of Grievances Against Fayette A. McKenzie," and M. V. Boutté to Du Bois, May 19, 1924, both in Du Bois Papers/UMass.

133. "THE LAST BEST HOPE ON EARTH": Wolters, *op. cit.*, 30–32, 34; Richardson, *History of Fisk*, 81. "... COURTING NASHVILLE": Du Bois, *Diuturni Silenti* (pamphlet), Du Bois Papers/UMass; Wolters, *op. cit.*, 37–38. "... THE ONLY SOLUTION": David Levering Lewis, *When Harlem Was in Vogue* (New York: Alfred A. Knopf, 1981), 159. "... THE MOST NOTED AND NOTABLE COLLEGE FOR NEGROES": Richardson, *op. cit.*, 82; Boutté to Du Bois, May 19, 1924, in Du Bois Papers/UMass.

134. "... UNPLEASANT DUTY": Du Bois, *Seven Critiques of Negro Education, 1906–1938* (Atlanta: Atlanta University Press, 1940), 34. "... THIS DAY BRINGS AN END": Du Bois, *Diuturni Silenti*, 1.

"...AT HARVARD BUT NOT OF IT": Du Bois, *Dusk of Dawn* (Millwood, N.J.: Kraus-Thomson, 1975; orig. pub. 1940), 37; Du Bois, *The Autobiography of W.E.B. Du Bois* (New York: International Publishers Co., Inc., 1968), 136. "...TWENTY YEARS AFTER": Du Bois, "Careers Open to College-Bred Negroes," in *W.E.B. Du Bois: Writings* (New York: Library of America, 1985), 827–41.

134. "...OF ALL THE ESSENTIALS": Du Bois, *Diuturni Silenti*, 3.

135. THE SCANDAL INVOLVING MCKENZIE: Maurice Weinberger to *The American Mercury*, November 7, 1924, in Du Bois Papers/UMass; Wolters, *op. cit.*, 38. "...I AM TOLD.": Du Bois, *Diuturni Silenti*, 10. "...NO PRESIDENT.": Fayette McKenzie to Paul Cravath, n.d., 1924, Du Bois Papers/UMass.

136. "...A NATIONAL UNIVERSITY": *Opportunity* (August 1924). "...I INTEND TO PUBLISH": *Fisk Herald*, vol. 33, No. 1 (1925), also in Wolters, *op. cit.*, 40; Du Bois, "Opinion," *The Crisis* (September 1924): 199–203.

136. "...THE ONLY HOPE FOR NEGRO EDUCATION": "Gifts and Education," *The Crisis* (February 1925): 151–52, also in Aptheker, ed., *Selections*, I, 416.

137. "...ATLANTA UNIVERSITY IS STARVING TODAY.": Du Bois, "The Dilemma of the Negro," *American Mercury* (October 1924), 179–85, also in Aptheker, ed., *Writings in Periodicals*, II, 226, 227, 228.

137. "...WOULD BE CALAMITOUS": Du Bois, "Dilemma of the Negro," 228, 229

138. ON WESLEY AND HARRIS: see "Wesley, Charles Harris," in Jack Salzman, et. al., eds., *Encyclopedia of African-American Culture and History* (New York: Macmillan, 1996), 5 vols., V, 2802 (hereafter *EAACH*), and "Harris, Abram Lincoln, Jr.," in Salzman, et. al., eds., *EAACH*, III, 1226. "...NEED FOR ACTION": Charles H. Wesley to Du Bois, December 7, 1924, Du Bois Papers/UMass; Abram Harris to Du Bois, November 21, 1925, Du Bois Papers/UMass. "...A COLORED MAN AS HEAD OF THE INSTITUTION": Dillard to Du Bois, November 24, 1924, Du Bois Papers/UMass. "...OLD CONFIDENCE AND TRUST": Chicago Fisk Club Statement, February 13, 1925, Du Bois Papers/UMass. FEDERATED FISK CLUB: Mamie Turner, December 3, 1924, Du Bois Papers/UMass; Wolters, *op. cit.*, 40. "...PUBLISHED OCCASIONALLY": Du Bois, *Diuturni Silenti*, 1.

138–39. "...I WANT THE PRESS ASSOCIATION": Du Bois to N. B. D. Brascher, November 17, 1924, Du Bois Papers/UMass, also in Aptheker, ed., *Correspondence*, I, 299. "...INSIDER INFORMATION": Alphonse D. Philipps, "Analysis of Fisk University," Du Bois Papers/UMass; "Slowe, Lucy Diggs," in Darlene Clark Hine, ed., *Black Women in America: An Historical Encyclopedia* (Brooklyn, N.Y.: Carlson Publishing Co., 1993), 2 vols., II, 1071 (herafter *BWIA*). One woman wrote encouragingly that "[w]hat hurt most of all was to see professors afraid to say one word in defense of their race"—Miss Eunice C. H. Baker to Du Bois, March 16, 1925, Du Bois Papers/UMass. ON STREATOR: See the obituary for Streator in *The New York Times*, July 29, 1955.

139. STREATOR'S INTELLIGENCE GATHERING: McKenzie to Cravath, no date, 1924, Du Bois Papers/UMass; Wolters, *op. cit.*, 38–43. "...TO ITS KNEES": George Streator to Alphonse D. Phillipe, November 28, 1924, Du Bois Papers/UMass. "HIS COLLEGE": Du Bois, "Fisk," *The Crisis* (October 1924), 251–52. FOOTBALL: Wolters, *op. cit.*, 45. "...AWAY WITH THE CZAR!": Wolters, *op. cit.*, 48–49; letter from a student to Du Bois, November 11, 1924, Du Bois Papers/UMass.

140. "...MAKE THE SEPARATED RACES LESS UNEQUAL": Wolters, *op. cit.*, 34–35. "...A NOTE FROM ME": Du Bois to L. Hollingsworth Wood and William H. Baldwin, September 9, 1924, Du Bois Papers/UMass. THE ROAST: Du Bois to Elizabeth Ross Hodges, October 8, 1924, Du Bois Papers/UMass; Wolters, *op. cit.*, 47; Wood to Du Bois, September 22, 1924, Du Bois to Wood, September 23, 1924, both in Du Bois Papers/UMass.

140. "...HE IN NO WAY DESERVES IT": Mrs. B. T. Washington to Du Bois, December 12, 1924. THE BOULE: Du Bois to Dr. A. F. Boyer, November 12, 1924, and Henry Pace to Du Bois, November 20, 1924, both in Du Bois Papers/UMass; Hobart Sidney Jarrett, *The History of Sigma Pi Phi: First of the African-American Greek-Letter Fraternities* (Philadelphia: Quantum Leap, 1985). "...FISK'S DIRTY LINEN:" Dr. Allen A. Wesley to Du Bois, December 22, 1924, Du Bois Papers/UMass. "...DUCKED HIS REQUEST": Du Bois to Alpha Phi Alpha, undated, 1925, Du Bois Papers/UMass. "...THE BEST THING FOR DAUGHTERS": Wolters, *op. cit.*, 51.

140. "...ALMOST HUMAN": John Hope to Du Bois, November 15, 1924, Du Bois Papers/UMass, also in Aptheker, ed., *Correspondence*, I, 298. OVINGTON: Memorandum from Ovington to Du Bois, March 4, 1925, NAACP Papers, Library of Congress, Group I, Series A, Board of Directors Files (hereafter BRD MINS/LC). "...A DEAF EAR:" Wolters, *op. cit.*, 36. "...A DIKTAT": Wolters, *op. cit.*, 47.

141. THE RIOT AT FISK: Mrs. Jessie E. Proctor to Du Bois, March 5, 1925, Du Bois Papers/UMass; Wolters, *op. cit.*, 49–50. "...MCKENZIE, YOU'RE THROUGH:" Wolters, *op. cit.*, 49.

141. "... EQUALITY OF RIGHTS": Wolters, *op. cit.*, 53, 59. "... I KNEW NOTHING OF YOUR PLANS.":
Du Bois to George Streator, March 13, 1925, Du Bois Papers/UMass; Du Bois, "Fisk," *The Crisis* (April
1925), 247–51, also in Aptheker, ed., *Crisis Selections*, I, 411–12.

142. "... ON THE SAME TERMS AS THE CLAIMS OF WHITE MEN.": Du Bois, "Memorandum of Representatives of Fisk Alumni to the Board of Trustees," August 10, 1925, Du Bois Papers/UMass; Wolters,
op. cit., 43; NEW FISK FACULTY: Wolters, *op. cit.*, 113.

143. "... COMPULSORY CHAPEL SERVICES": Lewis, interview with Mae Miller Sullivan, Voices of the
Harlem Renaissance, Schomburg Center for Research in Black Culture, New York Public Library
(hereafter VOHR/SCRBC). "... POPULAR SONGS, PLANTATION MELODIES": Quoted in Rayford W.
Logan, *Howard University: The First Hundred Years, 1867–1967* (New York: New York University Press,
1969), 220. TINY MAE AND KELLY MILLER: "Miller, May (Sullivan)," in Hine, ed., *BWIA*, II, 797;
"Miller, Kelly," in Rayford Logan, et. al., eds., *Dictionary of American Negro Biography* (New York:
W. W. Norton, 1982), 435–38. "... WE USED TO RESPOND CHEERFULLY": Interview with Zora Neale
Hurston.

144. "... LUCKY": Du Bois, "Opinion," *The Crisis* (August 1925), 163–65; also see Du Bois, "Opinion,"
The Crisis (September 1925), 215–20; Wolters, *New Negro on Campus*, 98. "... BLACK DOG": Du Bois
to Locke, August 5, 1925; Locke to Du Bois, August 9, 1925; Thomas W. Turner to Du Bois, September
17, 1925, all in Du Bois Papers/UMass. "... HONORABLE SETTLEMENT": Kelly Miller to Du Bois, August
11, 1925; Du Bois to Miller, August 11, 1925, both in Du Bois Papers/UMass. "CONTEMPTIBLE PUPPY":
Du Bois, "Opinion," *The Crisis* (October 1925), 267–72.

144. ATLANTIC CITY: George Frazier Miller to Du Bois, August 19, 1925, Du Bois Papers/UMass.
"... AS THE FACTS WARRANT": Freda Kirchwey to Du Bois, November 20, 1925, Du Bois Papers/UMass.
"LACK OF SOCIAL CONTACT ... STARVING TO DEATH": Du Bois, "Negroes in College," *The Nation*
(March 3, 1926), 228–30, also in Aptheker, ed., *Writings in Periodicals*, 278, 279.

145. "... A SUBORDINATE CASTE?": Du Bois, "Negroes in College," 281. LOCKE: Locke to Du Bois,
June 28, 1927, Du Bois Papers/UMass.

146. "... WE REFUSED": Letter to Du Bois, signed "A Loyal Hamptonian," October 10, 1927, in Du
Bois Papers/UMass, also in Aptheker, ed., *Correspondence*, I, 360. HAMPTON STRIKE: Du Bois, "The
Hampton Strikes," *The Crisis* (December 1927), 347–48; "... THE FUTURE OF THE NEGRO RACE":
Letter to Du Bois, signed "A Loyal Hamptonian," 360, Du Bois Papers/UMass.

146–47. TUSKEGEE: In the fall of the following year, Du Bois would deliver a public address at
Tuskegee on the occasion of his first visit to the campus in twenty-five years. The event would fairly
leap from the pages of *The Crisis* as the editor was shown standing with Moton before the founder's
tomb with its famous statue equivocally depicting a slave either rising from or descending into bondage.
In other days, Tuskegee had been a "silent marching regiment," Du Bois would remind readers, but
seeing it after a quarter century he would be favorably impressed. "The marching is [still] overdone,
and yet, the grade of students, their intelligence, their civilization, has greatly increased." [Du Bois,
"A Pilgrimage to the Negro Schools," *The Crisis* (February 1929), 43–44, 65–69.] "... GENERAL BACK-
WARDNESS ... JUSTICE IN THE STUDENT'S STAND": Louise Thompson to Du Bois, May 2, 1928, Du
Bois Papers/UMass.

147. "... THEIR OWN CHILDREN": White parents, Du Bois argued, would never allow their sons and
daughters to be subjected to "silly insistence upon dumb, unthinking obedience" against their legitimate, outraged will, he continued in a rage, yet black parents lamented the children's lack of independence, on the one hand, yet, as some did at Fisk and Hampton, turned upon their own children
"like wild beasts, ready to beat them into submission; insisting that even if the school authorities are
wrong, it was the business of black boys and girls to submit." Du Bois, "The Hampton Strike," 347–
48. "... STRICT MILITARY DISCIPLINE": Du Bois, "The Hampton Strike," *The Nation* (November 2,
1927), 471–72, also in Aptheker, ed., *Writings in Periodicals*, II, 291–93.

148. GARVEY: Special Agent Frank C. Higgins to Robert S. Sharp, March 18, 1924, in Hill, *Garvey
Papers*, 8 vols., V, 571, 568. "... THE PUBLIC REAPPEARANCE OF MARCUS GARVEY:" *New York World*,
March 17, 1924, also in *Garvey Papers*, V, 572. "AFRICA FOR THE AFRICANS": Editorial note, *Garvey
Papers*, V, 573.

148. "... GREAT RESPECT FOR MEMBERS OF THE KU KLUX KLAN": Speech by Marcus Garvey, January
6, 1924, in *Garvey Papers*, V, 515. "... TO THE HORROR OF *THE CRISIS*": James Weldon Johnson to
John Mitchell, Jr., editor, *Richmond Planet*, April 3, 1924, in *Garvey Papers*, V, 578; Tony Martin, *Race*

First: The Ideological and Organizational Struggles of Marcus Garvey and the Universal Negro Improve-
ment Association (Westport, Conn.: Greenwood Press, 1976), 302. "... WEAKER PEOPLES OF THE
WORLD": Speech by Marcus Garvey, January 27, 1924, in *Garvey Papers*, V, 551. "... LET EDISON TURN
OFF HIS ELECTRIC LIGHT": Speech by Marcus Garvey, January 20, 1924, in *Garvey Papers*, V, 537–38.
"... TO HAVE OURS IN AFRICA": Speech by Marcus Garvey, January 15, 1924, in *Garvey Papers*, V, 531.
149. "LET'S PUT IT OVER": *Negro World* (May 1924), reprinted in *Garvey Papers*, V, 581. The editor
thought that his language had been stern yet impersonal, his probing analyses studiedly objective. Until
now, as he said, *"The Crisis* has almost leaned backward." In spite of Garvey's "monumental and
persistent lying," only the "larger and truer aspects of his propaganda" had been subjected to scrutiny.
When he landed in New York, he had been astounded to learn that friends of his had actually felt
compelled to secure police protection at the dock. The mails had brought letters "of such unbelievable
filth that they were absolutely unprintable." He had been advised to take the assassination threats
seriously. See Du Bois, "A Lunatic or a Traitor," *The Crisis* (May 1924), 8–9, also in David Levering
Lewis, ed., *W.E.B. Du Bois: A Reader* (New York: Henry Holt, 1995), 340, 341. "... THIS VICIOUS
MOVEMENT": Martin, *Race First*, 327; Robert Bagnall, "The Madness of Marcus Garvey," *The Mes-*
senger (March 1923), 638–48.
149. Du Bois, "A LUNATIC OR A TRAITOR." The NAACP struck an official position that was almost
as censorious as Du Bois's editorial, although without calling for imprisonment or deportation. Rebutting charges in the *Richmond Planet*, a black newspaper, that the association "set out to attack"
Garvey, Johnson pointed out that the NAACP "felt itself in duty bound not to 'let Marcus Garvey
alone'" in view of the racially divisive tactics employed by the UNIA head. "Lunatic or a Traitor"
amounted to a declaration of unconditional warfare with the big guns lined up behind the editor. See
Richmond Planet, May 3, 1924; James Weldon Johnson to John Mitchell, Jr., editor, *Richmond Planet*,
April 3, 1924, in *Garvey Papers*, V, 578.
150. "... VERY PLEASED ABOUT IT": Leo Weinthal to Du Bois, September 3, 1924, Du Bois Papers/
UMass. "... NO PERSONS": Ernest Lyon to Du Bois, July 10, 1924, Du Bois Papers/UMass; Du Bois,
"Garvey and Liberia," *The Crisis* (August 1924), 154–55. More UNIA officials arrived on July 30, only
to meet the fate of the previous party. Just as immigration officers were dispatching these half dozen
Garveyites, a UNIA shipment of heavy equipment weighed anchor for Liberia. THE CARGO: Martin,
Race First, 128–35. "... UNMITIGATED LIE": Du Bois to the editor of the *Daily Worker*, August 28, 1924,
Du Bois Papers/UMass. Whatever the pros and cons of Minor's accusation, Randolph and Owen
decided, after "A Lunatic or a Traitor," that Du Bois was an intellectual giant, notwithstanding the
Messenger's previous harsh verdicts on the editor's bourgeois politics. Garvey, on the other hand, was
simply a "low-grade moron." See Martin, *Race First*, 332.
150. RESPONSE TO DU BOIS: Tim Fortune had blasted Du Bois in the *Negro World* as the real menace
to the advancement of the Negro, and the newspaper's associate editor, Norton Thomas, penned a
malicious parody, "With Apologies to Shakespeare," in which Johnson, Pickens, and Du Bois were
wittily depicted as Cassius, Casca, and Brutus plotting Garvey's overthrow: Why, man, he doth bestride
the world of Negroes / Like a Colossus; and we petty men / Walk under his huge legs, and peep about
/ To find ourselves honorable graves. . . . / Du Bois had rather be a Nordic, / Than to repute himself
a son of Ham / Under these hard conditions as this time / Is like to lay upon us. See Martin, *Race
First*, 304.
    Garvey's own retort had come dripping with sarcasm: "Du Bois is speculating as to whether
Garvey is a lunatic or a traitor. Garvey has no such speculation about Du Bois" because he, Garvey,
knew for a certainty that the real traitor was Du Bois. What this "cross-breed, Dutch-French-Negro
editor" needed was a "good horsewhipping." See David Levering Lewis, *When Harlem Was in Vogue*
(New York: Alfred A. Knopf, 1981), 42; Martin, *Race First*, 273. Garvey's chance to act upon his words
had come soon after Du Bois's last editorial assault, when a chance meeting brought the two titans
face-to-face. Waiting in a lobby for an elevator to carry them to a banquet, the editor and his good
friend Wendell Dabney, the Cincinnati newspaper publisher, had been startled by an apparition—the
President General of Africa, attired in the full majesty of his decorations, stepped out, accompanied
by several ladies of his court. " 'Twas Garvey," gasped Dabney in his account of the moment. "He saw
me, a smile of recognition, then a glance at Du Bois. His eyes flew wide open. Stepping aside, he
stared; turning around, he stared, while Du Bois, looking straight forward, head uplifted, nostrils quivering, marched into the elevator." More than fifty years afterward, Charles Wesley, George Schuyler,

Arthur Davis, and several others would say, when asked about his quivering nose, that Du Bois icily attributed its flaring to odors emanating from the banquet. See Lewis, interviews with Wesley, Schuyler, and Davis, VOHR/SCRBC; Martin, *Race First*, 305. "... PRETERNATURAL FORESIGHT": "Report on the UNIA Convention," *Garvey Papers*, V, 616; "Religious Ceremony at Liberty Hall That Corrects Mistake of Centuries and Braces the Negro," *Garvey Papers*, V, 831. "... THE MOST CARELESS AND INDIFFERENT PEOPLE": "Speech by Marcus Garvey," *Garvey Papers*, V, 631. "... BLESSINGS": Joel Williamson, *Crucible of Race: Black-White Relations in the American South Since Emancipation* (New York: Oxford University Press, 1984). "... FACE THE WORLD": "Speech by Marcus Garvey," August 1, 1924, *Garvey Papers*, V, 632. "... FABULOUS PROSPECTS": "Editorial Letter by Marcus Garvey," August 19, 1924, *Garvey Papers*, V, 756.

151–52.   TOVALOU-HOUENOU: Du Bois to Prince Kojo Tovalou-Houenou, August 29, 1924, Du Bois Papers/UMass. Garvey's formal ban on joint membership of UNIA members in the NAACP on pain of expulsion left Du Bois and Walter White no choice, but the prince's well-intentioned evenhandedness also seemed justified. See Convention Report, August 29, 1924, *Garvey Papers*, V, 814. The final session of the convention was held at Carnegie Hall on August 31. In closing, the President General dispatched a committee of seven to Washington, D.C., bearing a petition representing "the four million members of the Universal Negro Improvement Association." The petition asked the president and Congress of the United States to support American Negroes in their plans for the "establishment of a nation of their own in Africa." See Convention Reports, August 31, 1924, *Garvey Papers*, V, 823. "... SCOUNDREL AND A THIEF": Rene Maron to Du Bois, August 15, 1924, and Du Bois to Rene Maron, August 25, 1924, both in Du Bois Papers/UMass; Convention Reports, August 31, 1924, *Garvey Papers*, V, 823.

152.   "... SIMPLY PHENOMENAL": Lewis interview with Charles Wesley, VOHR/SCRBC. "... THERE IS A DIFFERENCE:" Lewis, *When Harlem Was in Vogue*, 42.

Chapter 5: Civil Rights by Copyright

153.   DEMISE OF BLACK ZIONISM: "A Lunatic or a Traitor" ran in the May 1924 issue of *The Crisis* and coincided with the end of what had given every appearance of being a remarkable comeback from self-inflicted disaster for the President General of Africa. That same month the National Urban League's *Opportunity* carried "The Debut of the Younger School of Negro Writers," an editorial by Charles S. Johnson, the magazine's director of research and investigations. *Opportunity*, (May 1924), p. 143. The coincidence could hardly have been more significant. Johnson's editorial was significant, because, at the very moment *The Crisis* called for the demise of Garveyism, *Opportunity* unveiled with considerable fanfare the beginnings of a Talented Tenth program of racial uplift that was every whit as visionary as the Black Zionism it was intended to supplant.

204.   JESSIE FAUSET PUBLISHED HUGHES AND TOOMER ...: David Levering Lewis, *When Harlem Was in Vogue* (New York: Knopf, 1981), 79; Jessie Fauset begged Hughes to dedicate a poem to W.E.B. He told Hughes, "I should be honored to have a poem of yours dedicated to me." Arnold Rampersad, *The Life of Langston Hughes: I, Too, Sing America, I, 1922–1941* (New York: Oxford University Press, 1986), p. 116. She recognized the talents of Hughes and Jean Toomer before anyone else did. Lewis, *op. cit*; Fauset, "As to Books," *The Crisis* (June 1922), 66. "SPREAD THE GLAD TIDINGS": Du Bois, "The Younger Literary Movement," *The Crisis*, (February 1924), 161–3.

205.   THE MAGAZINE NOW IN THE ASCENDENT IS *OPPORTUNITY*: "Ovington on the State of Crisis," a report dated May 12, 1924, The Papers of W.E.B. Du Bois, Special Collections, W.E.B. Du Bois Library, University of Massachusetts at Amherst (hereafter Du Bois Papers/UMass).

206.   SUBJECTS COMPATIBLE WITH THE SOCIAL SCIENCE OBJECTIVES: Lewis, *When Harlem Was in Vogue*, 95. "We shall try to set down interestingly but without sugar-coating or generalizations the findings of careful scientific survey and the facts gathered from research," a solemn Eugene Kinckle Jones, the League's director, emphasized. Fare for the earliest subscribers to the magazine had included a pathbreaking analysis of the racial results of wartime Army intelligence testing, a broad discussion of Negro education, statistical data on racial variations in physiognomy, and studies on the urban and rural effects of migration.

156.   ON CHARLES S. JOHNSON: Lewis, *When Harlem Was in Vogue*, 45–49.

157.   ... DISTINGUISHED ROSTER OF THE TALENTED TENTH: "The Debut of the Younger School of Negro Writers," *Opportunity* (May 1924), 143. "... GEORGIA DOUGLAS JOHNSON": See "Johnson,

Georgia Douglas," in Darlene Clark Hine, ed., *Black Women in America: An Historical Encyclopedia* (Brooklyn: Carlson Publishing, 1993), 2 vols, I, 640. . . . THE FOCUS OF THE EVENING WAS ALLOWED TO DRIFT: "Opinion," *Crisis* (August 1923), 151–4. THAT DINNER GIVEN AT THE CIVIC CLUB: Lewis, *When Harlem Was in Vogue*, 93, 274. . . . BEST FRIEND AND SEVEREST CRITIC: "The Debut of the Younger School of Negro Writers," 143.

158.   . . . CHOICE OF SUBJECT BLOCKED BY RACIAL CONVENTIONS: "The Debut of the Younger School of Negro Writers," 143. ". . . THE YOUNG WASHINGTON WRITER JEAN TOOMER": Du Bois, "The Younger Literary Movement" *The Crisis* (February 1924), 161–2, also in Herbert Aptheker, ed., *Selections from The Crisis*, I, 372. ". . . INVALUABLE ENCOURAGEMENT TO THE WORK OF THIS YOUNGER GROUP": Lewis, *When Harlem Was in Vogue*, 93. ". . . ALBERT BARNES, THE PHILADELPHIA PHARMACEUTICAL TYCOON": Barnes had opened his home to the planners of the gala and (Locke and Johnson eagerly anticipated) potentially his checkbook to the movement. Alain Locke, ed., *The New Negro* (New York: Atheneum, 1992), 20. Barnes's Picassos, Modiglianis, Derains, and Soutines, along with dozens of other canvases and Lipschitz statues alien to Main Line aesthetics, had caused a scandal when exhibited at the musty Pennsylvania Academy of the Fine Arts the year before. Alain Locke–Albert Barnes correspondence, February 1924, see Alain Locke Papers, Howard University.

His improbable involvement with African Americans was a deeply emotional one with a long history. He had begun when he was eight years old, Barnes was fond of recalling. Taken by his parents to a black camp-meeting in Mechanicsville, New Jersey, Barnes had been swept up in the intensity of the experience to such a degree that he often confessed that it had "influenced my whole life." OTHER SPEAKERS: Only a few months away from being a published novelist himself, the NAACP's irrepressible secretary offered advice about the pitfalls of outmoded literary stereotypes and a plug for his *The Fire in the Flint*. Knowing more about his subject than White did, his drama professor, Thomas Montgomery Gregory, one of Howard's most accomplished faculty members, sketched the virtually unknown history of Africans in the theater, beginning with the early nineteenth-century tragedian Ira Aldrich. "The Debut of the Younger School of Negro Writers," 143.

158.   "IF THE NEGROES ARE NOT IN A POSITION TO CONTRIBUTE THESE ITEMS": "The Debut of the Younger School of Negro Writers," 143.

158.   "TO MAKE A POET BLACK AND BID HIM SING!": "The Debut of the Younger School of Negro Writers," 143. ". . . THEN HE WOULD BE A POET AND NOT A NEGRO POET": Gerald Early, ed., *My Soul's High Song* (New York, Anchor Books, 1991), 23. "HE SEEMED 'SO YOUNG' AND SHE 'LIKE TO HEAR HIM TALK' ": Letter from Yolande Du Bois to Harold Jackman, August 6, 1923, Harold Jackman Papers, unprocessed collection Clark—Atlanta University.

159.   "DU BOIS HAD LEFT THE CIVIC CLUB ELATED": "The Negro in Literature and Art," Herbert Aptheker, ed., *Writings in Periodical Literature*, II, 88–91. "THE FINAL MEASURE OF THE GREATNESS OF ALL PEOPLES": Lewis, *When Harlem Was in Vogue*, 149. NANCE: "A big plug was bitten off. Now it's a question of living up to the reputation," a euphoric Johnson wrote to Ethel Ray, a young Minnesota woman he wanted to come to New York to be his secretary. Lewis, *When Harlem Was in Vogue*, 95. Locke was persuaded a few days later to accept the charge of assembling materials for a special "Negro" issue of *The Survey*. ". . . THE MOST EFFICACIOUS MEANS OF ESTABLISHING THE RIGHT OF THE BLACK RACE TO 'UNIVERSAL RECOGNITION' ": Du Bois, *The Crisis* (May 1922), 8–9. ". . . THE FIRST TO CALL WHAT WAS HAPPENING A 'NEGRO RENAISSANCE' ": Lewis, *op cit.*, 116. ". . . THE YOUNG SCHOLAR HORACE MANN BOND.": "Opinion," *The Crisis* (November 1925), 7.

160.   ". . . URBAN LEAGUES UNEXPECTED ANNOUNCEMENT . . . FOR ITS OWN PRIZE COMPETITION.": "Editorial," *Opportunity* (September 1924), 258. Lewis, *When Harlem Was in Vogue*, 97. ". . . INTELLECTUALS COULD HAVE PREDICTED": David Levering Lewis, *Portable Harlem Renaissance Reader* (New York: Viking Press, 1994), xix. ". . . BOARD OF DIRECTORS AUTHORIZED DU BOIS IN LATE SEPTEMBER TO OFFER CRISIS PRIZES": Du Bois, *The Crisis* (September 1924), 259. Deadline for entries was set for April 15, 1925. What the Spingarns sensed and Du Bois moved cautiously to promote was a mainstream development in race relations that was complicated, deeply paradoxical, and motivated by designs, conscious and unconscious, that simultaneously validated and devalorized black people as deserving, capable participants in the commonwealths of knowledge, business, and government. The afterwar release from tensions during the early twenties made this latest "rediscovery" of Africans in America first a precondition of and then a constitutive element in the coming Jazz Age. ". . . AVATARS OF WHAT A LATER GENERATION WOULD CALL MODERNISM": Norman F. Cantor, *The American Century: Varieties of Cultures in Modern Times* (New York: Harper Collins, 1997).

161. "... FREUD THROUGH PSYCHIC RELEASE, MARX THROUGH POLITICAL REVOLUTION": Bergson through a mixture of zoology and mysticism called creative evolution, and Weber through the reordering power of ideal types. Hence, from his temporary job in Wall Street, the muckraking novelist Matthew Josephson loudly denounced the social system, the Great War it had made necessary, and the soul-dead order created in its aftermath, while the cruelly deformed Bourne, driven from the *New Republic* to *Seven Arts* magazine because of his uncompromising pacifism, hurled one of the memorable apothegms of the period—"War is the health of the State"—before dying of influenza in the epidemic of 1918. Waldo Frank, Jean Toomer's mentor and, briefly, homoerotic soulmate, resisted the revolutionary option for America but fervently believed, nevertheless, that somehow, "out of our terrifying welter of steel and scarlet, a design must come." That coming design must spring from "literature alone," Van Wyck Brooks declared in the 1916 inaugural issue of *Seven Arts*.

161. "... INVITATION TO JUDGE THE FIRST *OPPORTUNITY* CONTEST": Edna Underwood, in Lewis, *When Harlem Was in Vogue*, 115. When Eastman wrote the introduction to McKay's hugely acclaimed *Harlem Shadows* (1922), he characterized McKay, his close friend and *Liberator* editor, in a manner altogether typical of the best white liberals, progressives, and socialists of the day, as a wonderful post sprung "from this most alien race among us" (Lewis, *ibid.*, 51).

162. "THEY STIR, THEY MOVE, THEY ARE MORE THAN PHYSICALLY ACTIVE.": Alain Locke, "Harlem," *The Survey Graphic*, 6:6 (March 1925), 630. See also Lewis, *When Harlem Was in Vogue*, 18; "The New Negro," *The Crisis* (January, 1926), 140–41; In Herbert Aptheker, ed., *Book Reviews by W.E.B. Du Bois* (Millwood, N.Y.: Kraus-Thomson, 1977), 78.

162. "... THE BLACK MAN BRINGS HIS GIFTS": *The Survey* (New York) (March 1, 1925): 655–57, 710. Also in Herbert Aptheker, ed., *Creative Writings by W.E.B. Du Bois* (White Plains, N.Y.: Kraus-Thomson, 1985), 139.

163. "I AM CONVINCED THAT SOMETHING BY MISS FAUSET SHOULD APPEAR IN THE BOOK": Du Bois to Alain Locke, May 15, 1925, Du Bois Papers/UMass. "LOCKE HAS SHOWN A NASTY ATTITUDE TOWARD *THE CRISIS*": Du Bois to Roscoe Conkling Bruce, December 11, 1925, Du Bois Papers/UMass.

163. "THE HIGHEST INTELLECTUAL DUTY IS THE DUTY TO BE CULTURED.": Lewis, *When Harlem Was in Vogue*, 149. "MERCER COOK REVEALED THAT MANY A FRESHMAN'S HEAD WAS TURNED.": Lewis interview with Mercer Cook, VOHR/SC. "TO CATCH THE PASSING FANCY OF THE REALLY UNIMPORTANT CRITICS AND PUBLISHERS.": Du Bois, *The Crisis* (January 1926), 140–41, in Aptheker, ed., *Book Reviews by W.E.B. Du Bois*, 79.

163–64. "... THE NEGRO IS BECOMING TRANSFORMED.": Alain Locke, "The New Negro," in Alain Locke, ed., *The New Negro* (New York: Atheneum, 1992), 6–7. "... BLACK MIGHT BE WHITE ... BUT IT COULDN'T BE THAT WHITE.": Lewis, *When Harlem Was in Vogue*, 34. Charles S. Johnson, "The New Frontage on American Life," in Locke, ed., *The New Negro*, 287. "THE MIGRATION OF THE TALENTED TENTH:" Carter G. Woodson, "The Migration of the Talented Tenth," in Lewis, ed., *The Portable Harlem Renaissance Reader* (New York: Viking, 1994), 6–9. "COME NORTH! NOT IN A RUSH": "Brothers Come North," *The Crisis* (January 1920), 105–06, in Herbert Aptheker, ed., *Selections from The Crisis*, (Millwood, NY: Kraus-Thomson, 1983), I, 48. "... V.F. CALVERTON'S TWO-YEAR-OLD *MODERN QUARTERLY*" Abram Harris to Du Bois, October 29, 1924, Du Bois Papers/UMass, introduces Calverton to Du Bois and mentions George Goetz as a young man who wishes to contact Du Bois and Du Bois mentioned he had never heard of Goetz. BY 'A CERTAIN GROUP COMPULSION' ": Du Bois, "The Social Origins of American Negro Art," *Modern Quarterly* 3 (October-December 1925): 53–56, in Aptheker, *Writings by W.E.B. Du Bois in Periodicals*, II, 269–71. "... PRECLUDE FOR GENERATIONS 'THE MERE STYLIST AND DILETTANTE.": Aptheker, ed., *Selections from The Crisis*, I, 270.

165. "THE BOLL-WEEVIL NOR THE KU KLUX KLAN IS A BASIC FACTOR.": Locke, *op. cit.*, 6. "... THE BUOYANCE FROM WITHIN": Locke, ibid., p. 4. Through a fusing of sentiment and experience, what Locke called "a great race-welding," African Americans were becoming a nation within the nation— but not *apart from* the nation, he hastened to emphasize. "The Negro mind reaches out as yet to nothing but American wants, American ideas." " 'UNIQUE SOCIAL EXPERIMENT' WHOSE ULTIMATE OBJECTIVE WAS TO BECOME MORE AMERICAN BY BECOMING MORE NEGRO": Locke, ibid., 12. "ONE EVER FEELS HIS TWO-NESS—AN AMERICAN, A NEGRO": Du Bois, *Souls of Black Folk* (Millwood, NY: Kraus-Thomson, 1973), p. 3. "... PRECEDE OR ACCOMPANY ANY CONSIDERABLE FURTHER BETTERMENT OF RACE RELATIONSHIPS.": Locke, ibid., 15. "HARLEM HAS THE SAME ROLE TO PLAY FOR THE NEW NEGRO AS DUBLIN HAS HAD FOR THE NEW IRELAND.": Locke, ibid., 7. All in all, Locke's introduction to *The New Negro* was a brilliant encapsulation of the social ambitions of a minuscule class

of educated professionals, primarily located in the urban North, almost all of whom had imbibed Du Bois's notions of racial identity and civil rights militancy with their mothers' milk or on their fathers' knee. "The New Negro" essay was a manifesto, as had been the promotion of American cultural independence from Great Britain almost a hundred years earlier. See Ralph Waldo Emerson, "The American Scholar," lecture, 1837.

There was another model, however, closer in time, for Locke's essay—"The Conservation of Races," that powerful, deeply problematic effusion of Du Bois at twenty-nine. Neither Du Bois nor Locke ever alluded to a conceptual link between "The Conservation of Races" and "The New Negro," but, text for text, they bear such striking similarities that, whether Locke consciously borrowed or not, the form and content of the latter indubitably reveal the primordial persistence of the former. Just as Locke's "talented group" comprised the vanguard of the New Negroes, "The Conservation of Races" had anointed eight million black Americans as the "advance guard of the Negro people" throughout the world. The beat of the prose and the grandiosity of metaphor of the 1897 manifesto plainly informed the Ur-text of the Harlem Renaissance. Du Bois, "The Conservation of Races," in Herbert Aptheker, ed., *Pamphlets and Leaflets by W.E.B. Du Bois* (White Plains, N.Y.: Kraus-Thomson, 1986), 4.

166. ". . . HE MANEUVERED PEOPLE LIKE CHESS ON A BOARD.": Lewis, *When Harlem Was in Vogue*, 126.

166. ". . . BETTER TO BE A DISHWASHER IN NEW YORK": Lewis, *When Harlem Was in Vogue*, 96; also Amy Helene Kirschke, *Aaron Douglas; Art, Race, and the Harlem Renaissance* (Jackson, Miss.: University Press of Mississippi, 1995). ". . . A SORT OF RENAISSANCE USO": Lewis, *When Harlem Was in Vogue*, 127. ". . . UNEXPECTED VACANCY IN THE *CRISIS* STOCKROOM": Du Bois to Douglas, November 18, 1925, Du Bois Paper/UMass. "FOLLOW RIGHT INTO [REISS'S] OWN FOOTSTEPS.": Lewis interview with Aaron Douglas, VOHR/SC. ". . . I WAS CALLED UPON TO PREPARE COVER DESIGNS AND DRAWINGS AND SKETCHES": Kirschke, *Aaron Douglas*, 12. ". . . HARLEM RENAISSANCE ACQUIRED ITS 'OFFICIAL ILLUSTRATOR": Lewis interview with Aaron Douglas, VOHR/SCRBC.

167. "HE CRIED THAT ANYONE SO BRILLIANT SHOULD HAVE TO BE SO BLACK.": Lewis interview with Bruce Nugent, VOHR/SCRBC ". . . [NUGENT] PACKED HIS SUITCASE AND BOUGHT A TICKET FOR NEW YORK CITY.": Lewis, *When Harlem Was in Vogue*, 96. ". . . HURSTON, WITH JOHNSON'S INTERCESSION, A FULL SCHOLARSHIP TO BARNARD.": "Georgia Douglas Johnson," in Hine, ed., *BWIA*, I, 598. "THE WRITER MOST IN TOUCH WITH THE SOULS OF THOSE BLACK FOLK": Lewis, ed., *Renaissance Reader.*, 690; Also Bruce Kellner, ed., *The Harlem Renaissance: A Historical Dictionary for the Era* (Westport, Conn.: Greenwood Press, 1984), 180; Also Robert E. Hemenway, *Zora Neale Hurston: A Literary Biography* (Urbana, Ill.: University of Illinois Press, 1980).

168. "THE SIGNIFICANCE OF EUGENE O'NEILL BY ONE OF THE MOVEMENT'S PRIZE RECRUITS": Paul Robeson, "Reflections on O'Neill's Plays," in Lewis, ed., *The Portable Harlem Renaissance Reader*, 58–60.

168. ROBESON HAD PRUDENTLY RETIRED WHATEVER ACTING ASPIRATIONS HE MAY HAVE HAD": Martin Duberman, *Paul Robeson: A Biography*. (New York: The New Press, 1989), 53. ". . . INTERESTING AND MUCH NEEDED ADDITION TO THE DRAMA OF AMERICA": Lewis, ed., *Renaissance Reader*, 60. ". . . PRESIDENT COOLIDGE HAD SAID A GOOD WORD FOR *APPEARANCES*.": Kellner, *The Harlem Renaissance*, 14. "EXCELLENT PLAY.": Du Bois, "Garland Anderson," *The Crisis* (January 1926), 112. ". . . UPLIFTING RACIAL PROPAGANDA.": James Weldon Johnson to Edwin Embree, January 23, 1929, James Weldon Johnson Memorial Collection, Beinecke Library, Yale University.

169. COUNTEE CULLEN'S GREAT POEM 'THE SHROUD OF COLOR.' ": Du Bois, "A Negro Art Renaissance," *Los Angeles Times* (June 14, 1925): pt. 3, 26–27, in Herbert Aptheker, ed., *Writings by W.E.B. Du Bois in Periodicals, II* (Millwood, N.Y.: Kraus-Thomson, 1982), 259. ". . . CULLEN'S LONG AND SOMBER MEDITATIONS ON THE BURDEN OF RACE AND THE DIVIDED SELF.": Early, ed., *My Soul's High Song*, 102. In addition to 'Shroud' and 'Heritage' (dedicated to Jackman), *Color* also contained "Yet Do I Marvel," the poem that Du Bois might have praised as the hallmark of the Renaissance, along with "Incident" (dedicated to Walrond) and "For a Lady I Know," two of the most effective pieces of propaganda of the New Negro Movement: "She even thinks that up in heaven/Her class lies late and snores./While poor black cherubs rise at seven/to do celestial chores." Early, *op. cit.*, 111. With Carl Van Vechten's help, Hughes gained access to *Vanity Fair* that September, marking the first time his poetry had appeared in a mainstream publication, another achievement *The* Crisis noted with pride. ". . . THE POET HAD BEEN A BUNDLE OF NERVES.": Rampersad, *The Life of Langston Hughes*, 53. "AN EXCELLENT BRAIN AND IMPRESSIVE TALENTED TENTH FAMILY PEDIGREE": The Editor saw

these qualities and more reflected in *The Weary Blues*, "the fine qualities of force, passion, directness and sensitive perception." Aptheker, ed., *Book Reviews by W.E.B. Du Bois*, 93. See also Rayford Logan and Michael R. Winston, *Dictionary of American Negro Biography* (New York: W. W. Norton, 1982), 31. Du Bois ordered the race to buy the book. It diminished in no way his admiration for Cullen's exquisitely polished craft that Du Bois instantly recognized in the Hughes volume a breakthrough in the genre, an uncanny distilling of the soul of ordinary black men and women struggling to make their way in the cities. When had the melancholy fatalism of the migrant ever been more faithfully evoked than in the title poem? "Droning a drowsy syncopated tune,/Rocking back and forth to a mellow croon,/ I heard a Negro play . . . /Swaying to and fro on his rickety stool/He played that sad raggy tune like a musical fool./Sweet Blues!/Coming from a black man's soul./O Blues." Langston Hughes, "The Weary Blues," in Lewis, ed., *Renaissance Reader*, 260. See also "The Book Shelf," *The Crisis* (March 1926), 239.

170. ". . . THE PUSHKIN PRIZE": For biographical information on Caspar Holstein, see J. Saunders Redding, "Playing the Numbers," *North American Review*, 238 (December 1934): 533–42; Bruce Kellner, ed., *Harlem Renaissance*, 171–72; Lewis, *When Harlem Was in Vogue*, 129–30; Claude McKay, *Harlem: Negro Metropolis* (New York: Harcourt, Brace and World, 1968, orig. pub. 1940), 114–16; Lewis, 179. "*TROPIC DEATH* . . . HARD READING AND DIFFICULT TO UNDERSTAND IN PARTS": Du Bois, "Book Review," *The Crisis* (January 1927), 152–53, in Aptheker, ed., *Book Reviews by W.E.B. Du Bois*, 92." . . . REDISCOVERED THE DESCENDANTS OF THEIR ANCESTORS' SLAVE WITH AN EMPATHY.": North Carolinian Paul Green's expressionist plays about ordinary black folk had just begun to garner the attention that would win the Pulitzer Prize in 1927 for *In Abraham's Bosom*. Du Bois thought Peterkin's 1924 novel, *Green Thursday*, was excellent, but he would find *Black April* a "disappointing" conjure tale. "All the characters are ignorant," he sniffed, "almost none can read and write; they have no ambition or outlook." They were simply not Du Bois's kind of Negroes. See Aptheker, ed., *Book Reviews*, 96.

Heyward's slender novel about poor black people in Charleston evoked hyperbole. Published at the beginning of 1926, *Porgy* was an instant rave north and south. "A beautiful piece of work," Du Bois called it, "the Iliad of a small black beggar in the underworld of labor and crime, surrounded by whiskey and lust and sanctified with music." Du Bois, "'Porgy,' by DuBose Heyward," *The Crisis* (March 1926), in *W.E.B. Du Bois: Writings* (Library of America, 1986), 1215.

COUNTEE CULLEN: Du Bois's favorite young poet managed not only to begin writing "The Dark Tower" column in 1926, a monthly literary feature for *Opportunity*, but to assemble *Caroling Dusk*, the first Negro poetry anthology since Johnson's five year-old *The Book of American Negro Poetry*, as well as offering *Copper Sun*, a second volume of his own poetry, released by Harper's in 1927. Early, *op. cit.*, "Introduction," 3–73. See also Jean Wagner, *Black Poets of the United States from Paul Laurence Dunbar to Langston Hughes* (Urbana: University of Illinois Press, 1973). VAN VECHTEN: Ubiquitous in Harlem during this period and rendering services high and low to its residents, Van Vechten persuaded Knopf to republish *The Autobiography of an Ex-Colored Man*, James Weldon Johnson's quasi-autobiographical, proto-existentialist novel, published anonymously in 1912. Johnson's *God's Trombones: Seven Sermons in Verse*, published by Knopf in the same year, 1927, was a huge popular success.

170–71. ". . . BOSTONIANS LAUNCHED THE *SATURDAY EVENING QUILL*.": Lewis, *When Harlem was in Vogue*, 157.

171. ". . . HARMON FOUNDATION DECIDED TO SHIFT ITS PHILANTHROPY.": Kellner, *Harlem Renaissance*, 157. ". . . EIGHTH PRIZE OF FIVE HUNDRED DOLLARS RESERVED FOR A DISTINGUISHED AMERICAN OF ANY RACE.": Lewis, *When Harlem Was in Vogue*, 179. ". . . SECOND GENERATION OF THE TALENTED TENTH": Edwin R. Embree and Julia Waxman, *Investment in People: The Story of Julius Rosenwald* (New York: Harper and Row, 1949).

171. ". . . A COMMON PLATFORM UPON WHICH MOST PEOPLE ARE WILLING TO STAND.": Sondra Kathryn Wilson, *The Selected Writings of James Weldon Johnson: Social, Political and Literary Essays* (New York: Oxford University Press, 1995), 398. ". . . OUR DEVELOPMENT ALONG THE HIGHER LINES.": Lewis, ed., *Renaissance Reader*, xxi.

172–73. ". . . THERE WILL NEVER BE ANOTHER CONCERT LIKE THAT FIRST ONE AT TOWN HALL.": Lewis, *When Harlem Was in Vogue*, 163. ". . . WROTE AN EQUIVOCAL REVIEW.": David Belasco to Du Bois, March 23, 1926, Du Bois Papers/UMass. See also Du Bois, "Lulu Belle," *The Crisis* (May 1926),

34. ". . . VIRTUALLY JUMPSTARTED THE RUSH OF SIGHTSEEING CAUCASIANS TO THOSE PARTS OF HARLEM.": "Lulu Belle," *The Crisis*, 4:40 (April 1926): 134. ". . . TALL, TAN AND TERRIFIC.": Lewis, *When Harlem Was in Vogue*, 209; Also Lewis interview with Gerri Majors. *VOHR/SCRBC*. ". . . HARLEM'S OWN SOCIETY FOLK LIKE RUDOLPH FISHER'S SISTER.": Lewis interview with Pearl and Jane Fisher, VOHR/SCRBC.

174. ". . . P&J's WAS FAVORED BY. . . . TALLULAH BANKHEAD AND HER HARLEM BEAU GEORGE.": Lewis, *When Harlem Was in Vogue*, 209.

174. ". . . YOU GO SORT OF PRIMITIVE UP THERE.": Lewis, *op. cit.*, 208.

175. "HE WARNED THAT *THE CRISIS* WOULD BECOME 'MORE FRANKLY CRITICAL OF THE NEGRO GROUP' ": Du Bois, "The New Crisis," *The Crisis* (May 1925), 7–9.

175–76. ". . . ALL ART IS PROPAGANDA.": Du Bois, "The Chicago Conference," *The Crisis* (May 1926): 23. "I DO NOT GIVE A DAMN FOR ANY ART THAT IS NOT USED FOR PROPAGANDA.": Du Bois, "Criteria of Negro Art," *The Crisis* (October 1926): 290–297; also in Aptheker, ed., *Crisis Selections*, II, 444. Lewis, ed., *Harlem Renaissance Reader*, 103. Daniel Walden, ed., *W.E.B. Du Bois: The Crisis Writings* (New York: Fawcett, 1975), 280. ". . . THE STREAM OF NOVEL ABOUT THE DEBAUCHED TENTH": "Opinions," *The Crisis* (February 1926), 165. ". . . DU BOIS'S SOCIAL AND ETHICAL CONCERNS ABOUT THE 'CREATIVE SPIRIT' WERE MISPLACED.": "The Negro in Art," *The Crisis* (April 1926), 281. ". . . TURN THE TABLES.": "The Negro in Art—a Symposium," *The Crisis* (March 1926), 220. ". . . WHILE WHITE WRITERS WERE RUNNING AWAY WITH A WEALTH OF . . . MATERIAL.": "The Negro in Art," *The Crisis* (March 1926), 219. "REGRETTING THAT, AT THE VERY MOMENT WHEN THEY WERE BEGINNING TO BE READ.": "The Negro in Art," *The Crisis* (April 1, 1926), 279.

177–78. "THERE SHOULD ARISE A DIVISION OF OPINION.": "The Negro in Art," *The Crisis* (April 1926): 280. Walter White was writing a *Pittsburgh Courier* column to encourage reading of Harlem Renaissance literature. ". . . THE TRUE LITERARY ARTIST IS GOING TO WRITE ABOUT WHAT HE CHOOSES ANYWAY REGARDLESS OF OUTSIDE OPINION.": "The Negro in Art," *The Crisis* (April 1926), 278.

179. "NEGROES HAD NOT QUITE YET A SUFFICIENT CORPUS OF 'SOUND, HEALTHY RACE LITERATURE'.": "Negro in Art," *The Crisis* (August 1926) 193. HE WOULD NEVER GENUFLECT AWAY FROM TRUE ART.": See Cullen's comments on Hughes's poetry for being folksy and Hughes's rejoinder, in Early, ed., *High Song*, 43–49. ". . . BLACK READERS TO 'SHRINK AND CRITICIZE.": Du Bois, "The Younger Literary Set," *The Crisis* (February 1924), 161–163, in Aptheker, ed., *Book Reviews*, 69. ". . . WHY THEY HAD BEEN SO LONG ASHAMED AND APOLOGETIC FOR A PAST.": Du Bois, "Criteria of Negro Art," *The Crisis* (October 1926), 290–97, in Aptheker, ed., *Crisis Selections*, II, 446. "DU BOIS INVEIGHED AGAINST THE CULTURAL TABOOS OF SEX, COLOR": Du Bois, "Black Folk and Birth Control," *Birth Control Review* 16 (June 1932): 166–176. "HE RELISHED BRITISH NOVELIST RONALD FIRBANK'S PRANCING NIGGER.": Du Bois, *The Crisis* (September 1924), 24, in Aptheker, ed., *Book Reviews*, 70.

"AS A DEEPLY DISTURBING MANIFESTATION OF ANARCHY.": Gerald Early, ed., *My Soul's High Song*, 49. ". . . THE SCRIBLINGS OF OCTAVUS ROY COHEN HUGH WILEY.": George S. Schuyler, "Negro Art Hokum," in Lewis, ed., *Harlem Renaissance Reader*, 97. ". . . I WANT TO WRITE LIKE A WHITE POET.": Langston Hughes, "Negro Artist and the Racial Mountain," in Lewis, ed., *Harlem Renaissance Reader*, 91.

179–80. "WE YOUNGER NEGRO ARTISTS": Langston Hughes, "The Negro Artists and the Racial Mountain," in Lewis, ed., *Harlem Renaissance Reader*, 95.

180. "YOU CAN REDEEM MR. VAN VECHTEN BY WRITING SOMETHING TO COUNTERACT WHAT HE HAS DONE.": Lewis, *When Harlem Was in Vogue*, 180. "*NIGGER HEAVEN* WAS A 'BLOW IN THE FACE' ": Critiques of Carl Van Vechten's *Nigger Heaven* in Lewis, ed., *Harlem Renaissance Reader*, 106. Also in Du Bois, "Books," *The Crisis* (December 1926), 81; Charles W. Chesnutt to Du Bois, October 27, 1926, Du Bois Papers/UMass. Also, Kelly Miller sharply reviews *Nigger Heaven*, Kelly Miller, "Where is the Negro's Heaven?" *Opportunity* (December 1926), 370–373.] HUGHES AND THURMAN JOINTLY AUTHORED THE FREE-FORM VERSE GIVING THE GOAL OF THE QUARTERLY *FIRE*!: Lewis, *When Harlem Was in Vogue*, 194.

181. ONE-LINE NOTICE OF THE MAGAZINE'S APPEARANCE: Lewis, *Vogue*, 197. MASTER OF CEREMONIES AT AWARDS CEREMONY AT INTERNATIONAL HOUSE: "Krigwa," *The Crisis* (December 1926), 70–71. MUCH OF THE 1927 PRIZE MONEY WAS EARMARKED FOR TOPICS DEALING WITH BUSINESS AND EDUCATION: Du Bois to G. W. Buckner, October 27, 1927, Du Bois Papers/UMass. "SEVEN ANONYMOUS DONORS TO FUND HONORARIUM NAMED FOR CHARLES CHESNUTT: "Krigwas 1927," *The Crisis*

(February 1927), 191. JESSIE FAUSET RELINQUISHED POSITION OF LITERARY EDITOR: Du Bois, "Miss Jessie Fauset," *The Crisis* (May 1926), 7. KRIGWA FOR 1928: Krigwa Prizes announcement for 1928 with donors and categories, "Krigwa announcement-Krigwa 1928," in Du Bois Papers/UMass.
181. "THE EFFLORESCENCE OF NOVELS AND PAINTING AND POETRY DID NOT MEAN THAT BLACK PEOPLE HAD GAINED FIRM CONTROL OF THEIR CREATIVE ENERGIES.": Du Bois, "Criteria of Negro Art," *The Crisis* (October 1926), 290–297, also in Aptheker, ed., *Crisis Selections*, II, 447.

Chapter 6: Bolsheviks and Dark Princesses

183. ". . . I SHALL KISS YOU": Du Bois to Georgia Douglas Johnson Sept. 17, 1926. This letter, in the possession of the author, was retrieved from the long-vacated Washington, DC, home of Johnson at 1461 S Street, NW, by Professor Claudia Tate, English Department, Princeton University, and provided to the author in 1988. ". . . THE GOD OF DAY": Georgia Douglas Johnson, "A Sonnet to Dr. W.E.B. Du Bois," The Papers of W.E.B. Du Bois, Special Collections, W.E.B. Du Bois Library, University of Massachusetts at Amherst (hereafter, Du Bois Papers/UMass).
184. ". . . THE HEART OF A WOMAN": Johnson, "The Heart of a Woman," in David Levering Lewis, ed., *The Portable Harlem Renaissance Reader* (New York: Viking, 1994), 274. On Johnson, see "Johnson, Georgia Douglas," in Darlene Clark Hine, ed., *Black Women in America* (Brooklyn, N.Y.: Carlson Publishing, 1993), 2 vols., I, 640–42 (hereafter BWIA). ". . . AWAY!": Johnson, "Let Me Not Lose My Dream," in Lewis, ed., *Renaissance Reader*, 273.
184. GEORGIA AND DU BOIS: Upon reading "An Autumn Idyll," Alice Dunbar-Nelson would suspect an affair between Johnson and Du Bois. See Gloria Hull, ed., *Give Us Each Day: The Diary of Alice Dunbar-Nelson* (New York: W.W. Norton, 1984), 88. ON THE SATURDAY NIGHTERS: Glenn Carrington, "The Harlem Renaissance — Personal Memoir," *Freedomways* (Summer 1963), 307–11. Waldo Frank's attendance at one of Johnson's Saturday-night sessions is discussed in David Levering Lewis, *When Harlem Was in Vogue* (New York: Alfred A. Knopf, 1981), 67. ". . . SUNDAY DINNER": Du Bois to Georgia Douglas Johnson, February 13, 1923, Du Bois Papers/UMass. ". . . IF YOU SAY SO": Johnson to Du Bois, January 16, 1924, Du Bois Papers/UMass.
185–86. ". . . BLAZING AN ORBIT": Johnson, "A Sonnet to Dr. W.E.B. Du Bois." ". . . TO LOSE FRIENDS": Georgia Douglas Johnson to Du Bois, October 15, 1926, Du Bois Papers/UMass. ". . . A POORLY KEPT SECRET": Lewis, interview with Mae Miller Sullivan, February 16, 1987. ". . . HE NEVER MADE ME FEEL INFERIOR": Lewis, interview with Anne Cook. ". . . WELL HUNG": Lewis, interview with Mabel Smythe, March 13, 1988.
186–87. ". . . THE MALE RACE": John H. Britton, interview with Arthur Spingarn, The Civil Rights Documentation Project, Moorland-Spingarn Research Center, Howard University. ". . . MARVEL'S MOTHER": "How pretty she was," he ruminated, "with the crimson flooding the old ivory of her cheeks and her gracious plumpness!" He met and walked home with her "in the thrilling shadows, to an old village home I knew well"—in Du Bois, *Darkwater: Voices from Within the Veil* (Millwood, N.Y.: Kraus-Thomson, 1975, orig. pub. 1921), 118. ". . . IMMOBILIZED": Lewis, interview with Marvel Jackson Cook. Also, see the newspaper, *Madre Speaks* (May-June, 1986). Du Bois would take Jackson to see the grand parade celebrating the return of a triumphant Charles Lindbergh in 1927: Lewis interview w. Marvel Jackson Cooke, August 1988. ". . . I WAS SO IN AWE OF HIM": Lewis, interview with Marvel Jackson Cooke, August 1988.
187. ". . . THAT OLD MAN": Lewis, interview with Wilhelmina Adams, Voices of the Harlem Renaissance/Schomburg Center for Research in Black Culture (hereafter VOHR/SCRBC). On the evolving sexual mores of the decade, see Ann Douglas, *Terrible Honesty: Mongrel Manhattan in the 1920s* (New York: Farrar, Straus, Giroux, 1995); George Chauncey, *Gay New York: Gender, Urban Culture, and the Making of a Gay Male World, 1890–1940* (New York: Basic Books, 1994). ". . . MOST OTHER THINGS": Lewis, interview with Robert Weaver.
188. ". . . HIS DOMESTIC SITUATION": Lewis, interview with Marvel Jackson Cook, August 1988. ON FAUSET'S PROBLEMS: Even before the year began, there had been the disorienting snub from Arthur Spingarn's wife, a stinging rap of Fauset's racial-etiquette knuckles after she blithely phoned a second time to suggest a rendezvous in response to what she now realized was "only a social pleasantry" on the Spingarns' part. For Fauset, to whom status and breeding signified a state of grace, her gaffe in appearing "importunate"—"No one in the world hates more than I to seem importunate"—and her

"stupidity" in assuming a casual equality outside the NAACP's formal social structure scalded like a massive gastric reflux. "Chagrined and humiliated," she gave Mrs. Spingarn a piece of her well-bred mind in a long, rebuking letter ending with instructions that the recipient need not "make some special arrangement to see me." See Jessie Fauset to Mrs. Arthur Spingarn, December 5, 1925, Arthur Spingarn Papers, Moorland Spingarn Research Center, Howard University (hereafter ASP/HU). ". . . BEHAVING BADLY": Jessie Fauset to Joel Spingarn, January 17, 1926, Joel Spingarn Papers, New York Public Library, Box 4: Folder 3. ". . . BORROWING AGAINST HIS INSURANCE POLICY": Du Bois to Herman Perry of Standard Life, September 17, 1924, Du Bois Papers/UMass.

189.   ". . . DU BOIS'S GROSS INCOME": Du Bois to J. E. Spingarn, February 1, 1926, Du Bois Papers/UMass; Nail and Parker financial statements, 1923–1931, W.E.B. Du Bois Collection, Fisk University (hereafter WEB/FU). ". . . JUST IN FRONT OF OUR HOUSE": Nina to Will, August 18, 1926, and Henry L. Shaad to Du Bois, November 11, 1927, both in Du Bois Papers/UMass. ". . . THEIR FEET OUT OF THE FRONT WINDOWS": Du Bois to Mrs. Turner, June 17, 1927, Du Bois Papers/UMass. ". . . KIND OF PEOPLE": "Du Bois to John Nail, September 19, 1928, and John Nail to Du Bois, October 26, 1928—both in Du Bois Papers/UMass.

189.   ". . . VERY GENEROUS AND KIND MAN": Jessie Fauset to Joel Spingarn, June 8, 1926, Joel Spingarn Papers, NYPL. ". . . WITH COLD CORRECTNESS": Du Bois to A. L. Sutton, March 6, 1926, and John Asbury to Du Bois, March 22, 1926—both in Du Bois Papers. DUBOIS: Lewis, interview with Ethel Ray Nance, March 17, 1989; Cleveland Call Post, March 1, 1990; Du Bois to Nance, March 11, 1926, Du Bois to Rachel Davis DuBois, April 26, 1926, and Du Bois to Rachel Davis DuBois—all in Du Bois Papers/UMass.

189–90.   ". . . I HOPE I MAY RUN ACROSS YOU": Du Bois to Nance, February 5, 1926, Du Bois Papers/UMass. ". . . THE REPAYMENT": Du Bois to Fauset, March 29, 1926, and Du Bois to Helen H. Lanning, January 7, 1926, both in Du Bois Papers/UMass. ". . . NO OPERATION WAS NEEDED" Jessie Fauset to Joel Spingarn, April 14, 1926, Joel Spingarn Papers, NYPL. ". . . LA VIE": Fauset, "La Vie, C'est la Vie," in Lewis, ed., Portable Harlem Renaissance, 254. ". . . CONTRIBUTING EDITOR": Du Bois, "Onions", The Crisis (May 1926), 7–11. ". . . LOVE IS LOST": See Carolyn W. Sylvander, Jessie Redman Fauset: Black American Writer (Troy, N.Y.: Whitston, 1981). ". . . THE REDESIGN OF A MAGAZINE": See The Crisis for November of 1926.

191.   ". . . THE STUDY DECREED": Du Bois, "Education in Africa," The Crisis (June 1926), 86–89, also in Aptheker, ed., Book Reviews by W.E.B. Du Bois (Millwood, N.Y.: Kraus-Thomson, 1977), 89. ". . . AFRICA SAFE FOR WHITE FOLKS": Du Bois, ibid., 91: L. A. Roy to Du Bois, May 15, 1925, Du Bois Papers/UMass.

191.   ". . . THIS SORT OF IMPOSITION": Du Bois to Aaron Phelps Stokes, December [3], 1924, Du Bois Papers/UMass. ". . . YOU HAVE INJURED YOURSELF AND YOUR CAUSE": L. A. Roy to Carter G. Woodson, April 18, 1924, Phelps-Stokes Fund Archives, Schomburg Center for Research in Black Culture, New York Public Library (hereafter PSF). Roy was writing in response to Woodson's own attacks on the Phelps-Stokes Fund in Carter G. Woodson, The History of the Negro Church (Washington, D.C.: Associated Negro Publishers, 1945; orig. pub. 1921), 310.

192.   ". . . FOR THAT TIME": James W. Johnson to Du Bois, May 28, 1927, Du Bois Papers/UMass. In response to Johnson's letter, Du Bois sought out Arthur Spingarn's opinion as to the bothersome legal question behind his continued possession of these materials. Spingarn urged Du Bois to return the materials. See Du Bois to Arthur Spingarn, June 6, 1928, and Arthur Spingarn to Du Bois, June 6, 1928, both in Du Bois Papers/UMass. Soon, Du Bois would have been turned down by the Garland Fund for a book on the Great War, would have failed to get anything from the Rosenwald Fund, and would have tried (unsuccessfully) to get May Childs Nerney to intercede with members of the Ford family. See Scott Nearing to Du Bois, May 1, 1929, Du Bois to Mae Childs Nerney, August 11, 1928, and William G. Graves to Du Bois, January 25, 1927—all in Du Bois Papers/UMass.

192.   ". . . DILLARD'S OFFER": Du Bois to J. H. Dillard, June 14, 1927; Dillard to Du Bois, June 25, 1927; Du Bois to Dillard, July 8, 1927; Dillard to Du Bois, September 17, 1927—all in Du Bois Papers/UMass ". . . TO WRITE FOSDICK HIMSELF": Dillard to Du Bois, September 17, 1927, Du Bois Papers/UMass. ". . . UNDER SEVERE CRITICISM": Du Bois to Raymond B. Fosdick, November 18, 1927, Du Bois Papers/UMass. ". . . NO LACK OF SYMPATHY": Du Bois to Fosdick, November 18, 1927; Thomas Appleget to Du Bois, November 28, 1927—both in Du Bois Papers/UMass, also in Aptheker, ed.,

Correspondence, I, 367–368. "... IT IS MY DUTY TO COMPLETE": Du Bois to Henry Allen Moe, August 11, 1928, Du Bois Papers/UMass. "... A GRANT": Executive Office, American Philosophical Society to Du Bois, April 2, 1937.

192–93. "... TO CAPITALIZE NEGRO": Du Bois to Editor, *New York Times*, November 7, 1925, Du Bois Papers/UMass. "... THIRTY FOUR NEGROES": "Opinion", *The Crisis* (February 1924), 179–83. "... NO RACE IN THE HISTORY OF THE WORLD": William E. Borah to Du Bois, July 15, 1926, Du Bois Papers/UMass. Also see William Borah, "Negro Suffrage," *The Crisis* (January 1927), 132–33; Eugene Levy, *James Weldon Johnson: Black Leader, Black Voice* (Chicago: University of Chicago Press, 1973), 251. "... ONE OF THE FINEST ILLUSTRATIONS": Borah to Du Bois, July 17, 1926, Du Bois Papers/UMass.

195–94. "... THREE FAMILY MEMBERS": The mob was displeased with the state supreme court's annulment of the victim's murder convictions. Also see "Aiken," *The Crisis* (January 1927), 141–42. Their actions floodlighted by the press, South Carolina's solons tinkered with due process, appropriated a forty-five-thousand-dollar reward, assigned a special investigator to the case, and the attorney general went through the motions of accepting the lame-duck governor's request that evidence be presented to the grand jury. "... DESPATCHES FROM AIKEN": "Aiken Grand Jury will Get Lynching Cases Next Month," *New York World*, December 1, 1926; "Lynching Inquiry Steps Aside for Football Game," *New York World*, November 14, 1926. "... WHAT THE KKK SAYS AND DOES": Du Bois, "The Shape of Fear," *North American Review* (June 1926), 291–304, also in Aptheker, ed., *Writings*, II, 289. "Go into any Western town," Du Bois would write, "from Pittsburgh to Kansas City: 'The Klan? Silly—but!—You see these Catholics, rich, powerful, silent, organized. Got all the foreigners corralled—I don't know. And Jews—Jews own the country. They are trying to rule the world. They are too smart, pushing, impudent. And niggers! And that isn't all. Dagoes, Japs; and then Russia! I tell you, we gotta do something. The Klan?—silly, of course, but—"

194. "... TO VISIT THE SOVIET UNION": Lincoln Steffens, *The Autobiography of Lincoln Steffens* (New York: Harcourt, Brace, and Co., 1931), 741–746; Justin Kaplan, *Lincoln Steffens: A Biography* (New York: Simon and Schuster, 1974), 250. "... BRITISH FABIANS": David C. Smith, *H. G. Wells: Desperately Mortal* (New Haven, Conn.: Yale University Press, 1986), 270–72. "... LESS LIBERTY IN RUSSIA": Richard Pipes, *Russia Under the Bolshevik Regime* (New York: Alfred A. Knopf, 1993), 317, 320. HARLEM, MCKAY, AND HUISWOOD: Lewis, *Vogue*, 57–58; Richard B. Moore, "Radical Politics," in W. Burghardt Turner, et. al., eds., *Richard B. Moore: Caribbean Militant in Harlem—Collected Writings, 1920–1972* (Bloomington: Indiana University Press, 1988), 46–47. "... SUPERFICIAL OMNISCIENCE": Du Bois, "The Negro and Radical Thought," in David Levering Lewis, ed., *W.E.B. Du Bois: A Reader* (New York: Henry Holt, 1995), 532.

195. "THE TOILERS OF THE WORLD": Du Bois, "The Negro and Radical Thought," *The Crisis* (July 1921), also in Lewis, ed., *Du Bois Reader*, 532. "... PHYSICAL OPPRESSION": Du Bois, "The Class Struggle," in Lewis, ed., *Du Bois: A Reader*, 555. "... A CLEARNESS OF THOUGHT ... THE [WHITE] WORKING CLASSES": Du Bois, op. cit., also in Lewis, ed., *Du Bois Reader*, 533, 534, 535.

196. "... ALLOWED THEMSELVES TO BE MANIPULATED": Du Bois, "The Negro and Radical Thought," *The Crisis* (July 1921), also in Lewis, *Du Bois Reader*, 531. "... INEXTRICABLY BOUND UP WITH": Frank W. Crosswaith, "Toward the Home Stretch," *Messenger* (July 1926), 196. Also see Du Bois, "Pullman Porters," *The Crisis* (January 1926), 113; "The Black Man and Labor" in "Opinion," *The Crisis* (December 1925), 59–62. Randolph had asked Du Bois to "address the men," but Du Bois claimed a prior engagement. See Randolph to Du Bois, September 10, 1925, and Du Bois to Randolph, September 14, 1925—both in Du Bois Papers/UMass. "... WITH OPEN MIND AND LISTENING EARS": "The Black Man and Labor," 59–62.

197. "... WE ARE RAPIDLY APPROACHING THE DAY": Du Bois, *Darkwater: Voices from Within the Veil* (Millwood, N.Y.: Kraus-Thomson, 1974; orig. pub. 1920), 100. "... A GREAT AND WONDERFUL THING": Du Bois to Elizabeth Gurley Flynn, December 25, 1929, Du Bois Papers/UMass. ABRAM HARRIS: Harris to Du Bois, November 21, 1925, Du Bois Papers/UMass. "... NO CONFIDENCE": See the letters about a Northern center for black education: Harris to Du Bois, November 21, 1925, and Du Bois to Harris, December 15, 1925—both Du Bois Papers/UMass, also in Aptheker, ed., *Correspondence*, I, 327–328. On Harris more generally, see "Harris, Abram Lincoln," in Rayford Logan and Michael R. Winston, eds., *Dictionary of American Negro Biography* (New York: W. W. Norton, 1982), 291–292 (hereafter DANB).

197–98. "... DUBIOUS DECLARATION": George Schuyler, "Dubious Declaration of Dr. Du Bois,"

Messenger (June 1925), 262. GEORGE GOETZ: Abram Harris to Du Bois, October 28, 1924; Du Bois to Abram Harris, November 3, 1924—both in Du Bois Papers/UMass. "... ADVANCED IDEAS TO THE COMMON MAN AND WOMAN": V. F. Calverton to Du Bois, September 15, 1928, and Du Bois to Calverton, September 18, 1928—both in Du Bois Papers/UMass, also in Aptheker, ed., *Correspondence*, I, 377–78.

198. "... THREE VISITORS": Du Bois, *Dusk of Dawn* (Millwood, N.Y.: Kraus-Thomson, 1975; orig. pub. 1941), 285. "... SAT AT THEIR FEET": Du Bois, *Dusk of Dawn*, 289. "... THE MOST MOMENTOUS CHANGES": Du Bois, *Dusk of Dawn*, 286. In the December 1926 *Crisis*, Du Bois indicated that it was "an American citizen of Russian descent" who made the offer. See Du Bois, "Travel," *The Crisis* (December 1926), 63. Significantly, in the same piece, Du Bois praises Walker Manufacturing Co. for its "brilliant" travel grants to African Americans.

198–99. JOHN PRESTON DAVIS: Hilmar F. Jensen, "The Rise of an African American Left," unpublished manuscript, 73, 64, 65. "... FROM MY POINT OF VIEW": Du Bois to Oswald Garrison Villard, July 15, 1926, Du Bois Papers/UMass. "... COL. W.E.B. DU BOIS": Du Bois, "Opinion," *The Crisis* (October 1926), 283–288; Passport materials in Du Bois Papers/UMass.

199. "... WE'VE SPOKEN EUROPEAN": H.A.L. Fisher, *A History of Europe*, II (London: Willmer Bros. & Haram, 1962; orig. pub. 1935), 1302.

199–200. "... UNFORGETTABLE IMPRESSION": Du Bois, *Dusk of Dawn*, 287. "... WHEELBARROWS FILLED WITH MARKS": Du Bois does write that Berlin the "giant city" had become "one of the few centers of the world." See Du Bois, "My Recent Journey," *The Crisis* (December 1926), 66.

200. "... TO KNOW MARX AND LENIN": Du Bois, *Dusk of Dawn*, 287. "... WERE AS GHOSTS": Du Bois, "Russia and America," Du Bois Papers/UMass.

201. "... RUSSIA IS AT WORK": Du Bois, "Russia and America," Du Bois Papers/UMass. "... OFFICIALS AND TEACHERS WITH QUESTIONS": Du Bois, "Russia, 1926," in Lewis, *Du Bois Reader*, 581. "... ALL THESE THINGS": Du Bois, *Dusk of Dawn*, 287; Du Bois, *The Autobiography of W.E.B. Du Bois: A Soliloquy on Viewing My Life from the Last Decade of Its First Century* (U.S.A.: International Publishers, 1968), 29. "... HERE WAS A PEOPLE ... NOT SWIFTLY, BUT SURELY": Du Bois, *Autobiography*, 29.

201. "... PEASANTS AND LABORERS": Du Bois, "Russia, 1926," Lewis, ed., *Du Bois Reader*, 582. LUNARCHARSKY AND RADEK: On Lunarcharsky and his assistant, see Du Bois, "Russia and America," 37. In his autobiography, Du Bois indicates that he met Radek. See Du Bois, *Autobiography*, 290. He was also impressed with the quality of the Russian people: "Never before have I seen so many among a suppressed mass of poor, working people—people as ignorant, poor, superstitious and cowed as my own American Negroes—so lifted in hope and starry-eyed with new determination, as the peasants and workers of Russia." See Du Bois, *Autobiography*, 290. "... NEW SOVIET MAN AND WOMAN": Pipes, *Russia Under the Bolshevik Regime*, 331–34. "... TELL SELIGMAN": Memo, Du Bois to James Weldon Johnson, NAACP Board Minutes, Series A; Board of Directors file, Minutes 1909–1959, NAACP Papers, Library of Congress (hereafter BRDMINS/LC).

202. "... ALONE AND UNACCOMPANIED": Du Bois, "Russia, 1926," in Lewis, ed., *Du Bois Reader*, 582. "... NOT SEEN SINCE 1913": Martin Malia, *The Soviet Tragedy: A History of Socialism in Russia, 1917–1991* (New York: Free Press, 1994), 162–63.

203. "... REAL RUSSIA LIES OUTSIDE": Du Bois, "My Recent Journey," *The Crisis* (December 1926), 64–65. This later account of friends in Russia is inconsistent with his statement that he walked unaccompanied for miles. He seems to be anticipating questions about his language ability. See Du Bois, "Russia, 1926," ibid., 581–82. "... THE SPIRIT OF ITS LIFE AND PEOPLE": Du Bois, "Russia, 1926," 582. "... SWEEP THE WORLD": Christopher Phelps, *Young Sidney Hook, Marxist and Pragmatist* (Ithaca: Cornell Univ. Press, 1997), 48–49. "... I AM A BOLSHEVIK": Du Bois, *Autobiography*, 290.

203. BEGINS *DARK PRINCESS*: I surmise this based on the limited time in which he had to finish the novel and also the showy references to *Dark Princess* in Soviet literature. Sailing from Naples, Du Bois met the members of the Matthews family, who would endow the Du Bois Literary Prize, and who would also become close friends with the editor. Du Bois argued that he was booked in first class by his Italian agent, who simply assumed that even a poor Negro American would have to go first class. See "The Annual Du Bois Literary Prize of One Thousand Dollars," *The Crisis* (April 1931), 137–38; "The Donor of the Du Bois Literary Prize," *The Crisis* (May 1931), 157. "... TO CRUSH RUSSIA": Du

Bois, "The Wide Wide World," *The Crisis* (March 1927), 3. ". . . THE HELPLESS TOOL OF MODERN INDUSTRIAL IMPERIALISM": Du Bois, "My Recent Journey," *The Crisis* (December 1926), 64–65. ". . . CAUSE FOR CONCERN": Du Bois, "Postscript," *The Crisis* (March 1927), 33–34.

204. ". . . OUR JEWISH FRIENDS": Augustus Dill to Du Bois, December 4, 1926, Du Bois Papers/UMass.: ". . . NEW AND UNDREAMED OF ASPECT OF SEX": Du Bois, *Autobiography*, 283; Du Bois to Dill, December 29, 1927, Du Bois Papers/UMass.

205. ". . . THE UNHINGED BUSINESS MANAGER": Du Bois, "Augustus G. Dill," *The Crisis* (February 1928), 96. ". . . NOT FIT FOR THE WORK": Du Bois to Mary Dill Broaddus, November 14, 1927, Du Bois Papers/UMass. ". . . CREDITED TO FRANKE HORNE": Georgia Douglas Johnson to Du Bois, April 20, 1927, in Du Bois Papers/UMass. ". . . YOUNG JOHN DAVIS": Hilman L. Jensen, "Rise of an African American Left," in *John P. Davis and the Negro Congress*, 2 vols. Unpublished monograph, 1997, 116; Du Bois to Thomas E. Jones, March 9, 1927, Du Bois Papers/UMass. ". . . INCREASINGLY ON AUTO-PILOT": Annie Dingle to Marvel Jackson Cooke, February 14, 1927, Du Bois Papers/UMass.

206. THE GARLAND FUND: Garland Fund Minutes, May 6, 1925, Lewis Stiles Gannett Papers (bMS AM 1888.3), Houghton Library, Harvard University ". . . TO OFFER FRAZIER": Du Bois to E. Franklin Frazier, [April], 1925; Du Bois to Frazier, January 21, 1927; Du Bois to Julius Rosenwald, January 21, 1927 — all in Du Bois Papers/UMass. ". . . THE ANNOYING UPSHOT": Du Bois to Bond, October 18, 1926, Du Bois Papers/UMass.

206–7. ". . . USE YOUR OWN JUDGEMENT": Du Bois to Dr. and Mrs. J. A. Somerville, January 10, 1927, Du Bois Papers/UMass. ". . . RATIONALIZATION OF THE SOUTHERN POSITION": Anthony M. Platt, *E. Franklin Frazier Reconsidered* (New Brunswick, N.J.: Rutgers Univ. Press, 1991), 60, 71. ". . . FISK SOURCES REPORTED": E. Franklin Frazier to Du Bois, March 27, [n.d.], Du Bois Papers/UMass; Frazier to Du Bois, January 18, 1927, E. Franklin Frazier Papers, Moorland-Spingarn Research Center, Howard University. ". . . JUST THE MAN WE NEED": Thomas E. Jones to Du Bois, March 26, 1927, and Du Bois to Jones, March 30, 1927 — both in Frazier Papers/Moorland-Spingarn.

207–8. "A PURSE IN CHESNUTT'S HONOR": Charles Chesnutt to Du Bois, January 11, 1927, Du Bois Papers/UMass. MAGGIE LENA WALKER: "Walker, Maggie Lena," in Darlene Clark Hine, eds., *Black Women in America: An Historical Encyclopedia* (Brooklyn, N.Y.: Carlson Publishing, 1993), 2 vols., II, 1214–1219 (hereafter BWIA). CHARLES CLINTON SPAULDING: See "Spaulding, Charles Clinton", in Logan, et. al., eds., *Dictionary of American Negro Biography*, 567–68. ". . . MY DEAR MADAME": Du Bois to Mrs. Edith S. D. Butler, September 28, 1927, Du Bois Papers/UMass. ". . . PARAMOUNT IMPOR-TANCE OF BUSINESS": Du Bois to Maggie Lena Walker, October 27, 1927, Du Bois Papers/UMass. Also, very helpfully, L. M. Collins compiled a detailed list of all prizes and judges and categories for Krigwa and Opportunity prizes between 1925 and 1927. Business prizes amounted to $725. For another concerned letter about business disinterest, see Du Bois to G. W. Buckner, October 27, 1927, Du Bois Papers/UMass. ". . . I HAVE LONG BEEN A SOCIALIST": Du Bois to Helen Tufts Bailie, June 14, 1928 ". . . OUR ECONOMIC FUTURE": Du Bois, "Our Economic Future," *The Crisis* (April 1928), 169–70.

208. ". . . A VENUE IN THE WEST INDIES": Du Bois to E. Franklin Frazier, September 16, 1925, Frazier Papers/Moorland-Spingarn; C. M. King to Du Bois, March 11, 1925, Du Bois Papers/UMass. ". . . A LEGEND AMONG FEMINISTS AND CIVIL RIGHTS LEADERS": "Hunton, Addie Watts," in Hine, ed., *BWIA*, I, 596–97. On the generous support for the Pan-African Congresses by clubwomen, see Du Bois, "The Pan African Congresses," *The Crisis* (October 1927), 263–64, also in Aptheker, ed., *Crisis Selections*, II, 480–84. As late as March of 1926, Du Bois was considering Philadelphia as a possible venue for the Congress. John C. Asbury to Du Bois, March 22, 1926, Du Bois Papers/UMass. ". . . CONSERVATIVE AND REACTIONARY": Du Bois to Mrs. Annie Dingle, February 8, 1927, Du Bois Papers/UMass.

208–9. ". . . BY OUR NATIONAL ORIGINS": Ferdinand Q. Morton to Du Bois, January 28, 1927, Du Bois Papers/UMass. ". . . OUR DUTY LAY IN GETTING MONEY": Addie Hunton to Du Bois, July 27, 1927, Du Bois Papers/UMass. ". . . SHE IS INCOMPETENT:" Du Bois to Dantes Bellegarde, July 18, 1928, Du Bois Papers/UMass. ". . . NEWSPAPER": *Amsterdam News*, August 23, 1927; *The World*, August 22, 1927; *New York Times*, August 22, 1927; *New York Times*, August 25, 1927; *The Worker*, August 23, 1927; Seattle *Record*, August 29, 1927. ". . . PARADED THROUGH HARLEM ON OPENING DAY": *Amsterdam News*, August 23, 1927.

209. ". . . THE STATUS OF THE NEGRO": *New York Times*, August 14, 1927. ". . . DELEGATES REPRE-SENTING": Du Bois, "The Pan-African Congress," *The Crisis* (October 1927), 263–64, also in Aptheker, ed., *Crisis Selections*, 480. ". . . VISION OF BROTHERHOOD OF THE DARKER RACES": *Amsterdam News*, August 22, 1927; *Amsterdam News*, August 23, 1927; *Amsterdam News*, August 24, 1927.

209–10. "... ALMOST TO GASP": *Amsterdam News*, August 22, 1927. "... SCHOOLED CONVERT TO MARXISM": *The Worker*, August 23, 1927. "... URGES PROLETARIAN UNITY": *New York Herald Tribune*, August 22, 1927. "... SEEMINGLY UNMINDFUL": *Amsterdam News*, August 24, 1927.

210. HANSBERRY: "Hansberry, William Leo", in Logan, et. al., eds., *DANB*, 284–86. THE CLOSING SESSION: Among those attending the Pan-African Congress was Chief Amoah III of the Gold Coast, described by Du Bois as "small, black, and earnest, a descendant of ancient rulers of the Gold Coast, never enslaved." Du Bois, "The Negro Takes Stock," *New Republic* (January 2, 1924), 143–145, also in Aptheker, ed., *Writ. Periodical Lit.*, II, 218. "... NOT MERELY FOR THE PROFIT OF EUROPEANS": Du Bois, "The Pan-African Congresses," 481. "... CIVILIZATION AND SPIRITUAL UPLIFT": Du Bois, "The Pan-African Congresses," 482.

211. "... ASK DU BOIS": Ida Gibbs Hunt to Addie Hunton, September [?], 1927, Du Bois Papers/ UMass. "... ALGIERS, TUNIS": Du Bois to Gratian Candace, October 24, 1928, Du Bois Papers/ UMass. "... WILLING TO DO ANYTHING": Du Bois to Dantes Bellegarde, July 18, 1928, Du Bois Papers/UMass.

211. "... YOLANDE'S THREE-MONTH STUDY ABROAD": Du Bois to Mrs. Calman-Levy, January 4, 1927. A series of didactic letters would follow Yolande to Grenoble, the typical one of July 27 cautioning her eating habits and promising, "You have no idea how much you are going to learn in a short time if you persist in speaking French." Du Bois to Yolande, July 27, 1927, Du Bois Papers/UMass. "... HAD BECOME UNTENABLE": Du Bois to John Nail, February 29, 1929, W.E.B. Du Bois Collection, Fisk University. Nail's understanding response was a revealing document in the urban history of Black America. "There is no block in Harlem where the kind of people you and I feel should live but that in most part the so-called underworld people are the people in control of the housing situation," he sighed. John E. Nail to Du Bois, October 26, 1928, Du Bois Papers/UMass.

212. "... HOME FOR FLASHY, PROSPERING FAMILIES": Ten of its tenants declared themselves un-skilled laborers and fifty-eight others were listed as domestics, but the critical mass of the Dunbar's co-owners—those who set the tone of the place—was to be middle and upper class. A passage by an historian of the period records the Dunbars' roster of notables: "The Dunbar became home for ... E. Simms Campbell (illustrator and cartoonist for *Colliers*, *Esquire*, *Life*, and *Saturday Evening Post*), Rudolph Fisher (briefly, before moving to Jamaica, New York), ... Fletcher Henderson (at the pinnacle of bandleader fame), Asa and Lucille Randolph (Lucille entertained a great deal), Paul and Essie Robeson (briefly), Leigh Whipper (stage and film character actor), and Clarence and Cameron White (noted violinist composer)." David Levering Lewis, *When Harlem Was in Vogue* (New York: Alfred A. Knopf, 1981), 218. "... REALLY TOO SMALL FOR US": Du Bois to Roscoe Conkling Bruce, October 18, 1927, Du Bois Papers/UMass. Also see Bruce to Du Bois, October 24, 1927; Bruce to Du Bois, December 7, 1927, both in Du Bois Papers/UMass.

212. ON VANN: "Vann, Robert Lee," in Logan, et. al., eds., *DANB*, 614–16; Nancy Weiss, *Farewell to the Party of Lincoln: Black Politics in the Age of FDR* (Princeton: Princeton Univ. Press, 1983), 13–14.

212. "... PALATIAL OFFICES ON FIFTH AVENUE": Andrew Buni, *Robert L. Vann of the Pittsburgh Courier: Politics and Black Journalism* (Pittsburgh: Univ. of Pittsburgh Press, 1974), 149. "... AN URGENT APPEAL TO RECONSIDER": Buni, *Robert L. Vann*, 150–51.

213. "... A THIEF": Du Bois to Allen Wesley, June 15, 1927. "... WITHOUT MUCH ADO": Wesley to Du Bois, June 19, 1927, Du Bois Papers/UMass. "... A FOLLOW UP LETTER": Wesley to Du Bois, June 27, 1927, Du Bois Papers/UMass. "... I HAVE WAITED PATIENTLY": Du Bois to W. C. McNeill, September 20, 1927, Du Bois Papers/UMass. "... BOTH PARTIES HAD ERRED": W. C. McNeill to Du Bois, October 6, 1927, Du Bois Papers/UMass. "... A RETRACTION": "Postscript," *The Crisis* (November 1929), 386–88; Du Bois to Robert L. Vann, August 23, 1929, with enclosure dated August 15, 1929, Du Bois Papers/UMass.

214. Du Bois, review of Claude McKay, *Home to Harlem*, *The Crisis* (June 1928): 211; in Herbert Aptheker, ed., *Book Reviews by W.E.B. Du Bois* (Millwood, N.Y.: Kraus-Thomson, 1977), 113. McKay's heated response: McKay to Du Bois, June 18, 1928, Du Bois Papers/UMass. "... WHAT IT THINKS IT WANTS TO HEAR": Du Bois to Amy Spingarn, January 19, 1928, Joel and Amy Spingarn Collection, Schomburg Center for Research in Black Culture, New York Public Library (hereafter J&ASC/SCRBC). Kelly Miller had composed his own indignant review of *Home to Harlem*: Miller, "Where is the Negro's Heaven?" *Opportunity* (December 1928), 370–73. "... INVITING SPINGARN'S SUGGESTIONS": In a letter to Du Bois, Amy Spingarn decided to discontinue supporting prizes: Amy Spingarn to Du Bois, June 17, 1928, Du Bois Papers/UMass. "... BACK ON THE RIGHT TRACK": Du

Bois wrote to Joel Spingarn in early September that he had finished his novel and would like to offer it to Harcourt: Du Bois to Joel Spingarn, September 8, 1927, Du Bois Papers/UMass.

214. *"COMÉDIE HUMAINE"*: Du Bois to Alfred Harcourt, October 25, 1928, Du Bois Papers/UMass.

215. Ovington, cited in Aptheker, "Introduction" in Du Bois, *Dark Princess: A Romance* (Millwood, N.Y.:" Kraus-Thomson, 1974; orig. pub. 1928), 8. Reading Ovington's response, the old *roue* Wendell Dabney wrote Du Bois wickedly that he would bet that a "white princess would have been nearer the mark." See Wendell Dabney to Du Bois, May 24, 1928, Du Bois Papers/UMass. ". . . NO HUMAN BEING": Du Bois, *Autobiography*, 108. ". . . DEAREST MATTHEW": Du Bois *Dark Princess,,* 277.

215–16. ". . . BURNED AWAY": *ibid.* 12. ". . . AND SHE WAS COLORED": Du Bois, *Dark Princess*, 8. ". . . WE REPRESENT": *ibid.*, 16. ". . . THE DEEPER QUESTION": *ibid.*, 21.

216–17. ". . . HE SURRENDERS ALL": *ibid.*, 18. ". . . BUT A KING": *ibid.*, 308.

217. John Bassett, *Harlem in Review: Critical Reactions to Black American Writers, 1917–1939* (London and Toronto: Susquehanna Univ. Press, 1992), 99. ". . . MESSENGER AND MESSIAH": Du Bois, *Dark Princess*, 311.

218. ". . . COULD HE GO THERE FOR MEALS": Wendell Dabney to Du Bois, October 10, 1927, Du Bois Papers/UMass; Du Bois to Adelbert H. Roberts, October 11, 1927, Du Bois Papers/UMass. OSCAR DEPRIEST: Sammy Scott is modeled on Oscar De Priest before the latter's election to the House.

218. ". . . THE PALE MASTERS OF TODAY": Du Bois, *Dark Princess*, 279. ". . . THE INTELLECTUAL CONNECTIONS": Arnold Rampersad, "Du Bois's Passage to India: Dark Princess," unpublished essay. Also, see Du Bois to the Editor of Lahore *People*, January 10, 1929, in Du Bois Papers/UMass, also in Aptheker, ed., *Correspondence*, I, 386. Du Bois's review of *Unhappy India, The Crisis* (May 1929): 175, can be found in Aptheker, ed., *Book Reviews*, pp. 129–131.

219–20. ". . . FAVORITE BOOK": Du Bois, *Dusk of Dawn: An Essay Towards an Autobiography of a Race Concept* (Millwood, N.Y.: Kraus-Thomson, 1975; orig. pub. 1940), 270; Du Bois, *Dark Princess*, 19. LOCKE: Claudia Tate, "Introduction", in Du Bois, *Dark Princess*, (Jackson: University of Mississippi Press, 1995) ". . . AS NO OTHER BOOK": George Schuyler to Du Bois, October 11, 1928, Du Bois Papers/UMass, also in Aptheker, ed., *Correspondence*, I, 382. GRIGGS AND HOPKINS: "Griggs, Sutton E[lbert]", in Logan et. al., eds., *DANB*, 271; "Hopkins, Pauline Elizabeth," in Hine, et. al., eds., *BWIA*, II, 577–79; Dickson D. Bruce, *Black Writing from the Nadir* (Baton Rouge: Louisiana State Univ. Press, 1989), 191–263. ". . . DARK PRINCESS WOULD DISAPPEAR": Aptheker, "Introduction," in Du Bois, *Dark Princess*, 20. ". . . A PECULIAR DU BOISIAN WAY": Du Bois intended his sprawling creation to be a *Bildungsroman* encapsulating and advancing the Pan-African Movement and the ideals of the 1911 Congress of Races — a blend of "Credo," his eloquent secular doxology, and of his pageant of humankind, as was suggested many decades later by literary scholar Claudia Tate. Yet even this interpretation was obscured for some readers who found the paramount role ceded to an upper class Hindu not at all to their tastes, if not demeaning to the accomplishments and leadership pretensions of people of African descent.

It was not unreasonable to suspect that Du Bois was speaking for himself when the Princess explains to Towns: "Democracy is not an end; it is a method of aristocracy" [Du Bois, *Dark Princess*, 225]. However inflated its sense of class and inclined to equate racial progress with opportunities for itself, the Talented Tenth was inherently committed to the promise of democratic forms. India was a race relations model, therefore, that seemed almost as implausible as the antebellum South.

220. ". . . AMBITIOUS SELF-SEEKERS OF ALL RACES": Quoted in Aptheker, "Introduction," in Du Bois, *Dark Princess*, 19. ". . . EVERY SHAPE AND KIND AND HUE": Du Bois, *ibid.*, 227.

221. ". . . AS EASY TO PROVIDE AS CLAWHAMMERS": Du Bois to Countee Cullen, January 31, 1928, Du Bois Papers/UMass. THE WEDDING DATE: Du Bois to Cullen, February 17, 1920, Du Bois Papers/UMass. ". . . AS TO BE VULGAR . . . TO FEEL WEAK": Du Bois to Yolande, January 13, 1928, Du Bois Papers/UMass. ". . . THE CULLEN AND DU BOIS CLANS": In his *Crisis* account of the wedding, Du Bois would count nearly three thousand at the wedding, but in a letter to Mildred Bryant Jones he would cite a figure one half as large. See "So the Girl Marries," *The Crisis* (June 1928), 192–93, 207–9, also in Aptheker, ed., *Crisis Selections*, II, 514; Du Bois to Mildred Bryant Jones, April 13, 1928, Du Bois Papers/UMass.

222. ". . . ALONG WITH MUCH OF THE NATIONAL BLACK PRESS": Curiously, there was no report of the wedding in *New York Age*, *New York Times*, the *World*, the *New York Post*, or the *New York Tribune*. [". . . CHILLY EASTER MONDAY MORNING": weather report, *New York Times*, April 9, 1928.] It rained on Tuesday. The distinguished procession comprised among others the James Weldon Johnsons, the Eugene Kinkle Joneses, Mary White Ovington, the two Spingarn families, the Charles Johnsons,

and the Walter Whites. Sixteen-year-old Katherine Bell, whose mother and physician father were among the Du Boises' first New York friends, was too old to be a ring bearer and too young for a bridesmaid, but her disappointment was overcome as she watched the tuxedoed young men who ushered guests to their seats—Lewis, interview with Katherine Bell Banks, April 1997. For the wedding lineup, see Du Bois, "So the Girl Marries," *The Crisis* (June 1928), with a two-page photo spread. Also see Lewis, *Vogue*, 202; Arnold Rampersad, *The Life of Langston Hughes: I, Too, Sing America, Volume One: 1902–1941* (New York: Oxford Univ. Press, 1986), 162.

222. "... A NEW RACE": Du Bois, "So the Girl Marries," *The Crisis* (June 1928), 514. "... LESS EXPENSIVELY MOUNTED": On March 29, Du Bois wrote to Walker Studios that since 400 had been invited, he would have to cancel the contract. Du Bois to Mrs. Price Patton, March 29, 1928; Du Bois to Rev. Cullen, April 14, 1928—both in Du Bois Papers/UMass. Du Bois, "... SO THE GIRL MARRIES": "So the Girl Marries," *The Crisis* (June 1928), 515.

222–23. "... GENES WERE DESTINY": Lewis, interview with Montague Cobb, August 31, 1988. "... THE WORLD LOVED HIM": Du Bois, *Souls of Black Folk*, 211.

223–24. "... HOME AND FREE AT LAST": Du Bois to Mildred Bryant Jones, April 13, 1928, Du Bois Papers/UMass. "... YOUR ENDORSEMENT OF MY APPLICATION": Countee Cullen to Du Bois, March 27, 1928, Du Bois Papers/UMass. "... THE ACLU'S BROADER CIVIL LIBERTIES CONCERNS": Roger Baldwin to Du Bois, May 9, 1928, Du Bois Papers/UMass. "... TOO ILL THE NIGHT OF THE WEDDING": Charles Cullen to Countee Cullen, Countee Cullen Papers, Amistad Research Center, Tulane University (hereafter CCP/ARC) "... TIS TRUE!": Willie Barlour to Cullen, May 9, 1928, CCP/ARC. "... A WHOLE CROWD OF RATHER NICE": Quoted in George Chauncey, *Gay New York: Gender, Urban Culture, and the Making of the Gay Male World, 1890–1940* (New York: Basic Books, 1994), 264. Also see Kevin Mumford, *Interzones: Black/White Sex Districts in Chicago and New York in the Early Twentieth Century* (New York: Columbia Univ. Press, 1997); Chauncey, *Gay New York*, pp. 257–264.

224. REVERED POWELL: See Chauncey, *Gay New York*, 254. "... BECAUSE OF THEIR SEXUAL PREFERENCES": Lewis, interview with Gerri Major, May 1977, Voices of the Harlem Renaissance/Schomburg Center for Research in Black Culture, New York Public Library (hereafter VOHR/SCRBC) ON JACKMAN: Lewis, interview with Harold Ivy Jackman, VOHR/SCRBC.

225. "... ABSURD": Lewis, interview with Marvel Jackson Cooke, August 1988. Jackson also claimed that Du Bois told her a few days after the wedding that it would not last—"he had a very hurt look on his face."

225. "... A FEW PLACES OF IMPORTANCE": Countee Cullen to Du Bois, May 11, 1928, Du Bois Papers/UMass. "... DU BOIS SENT A SHORT LETTER": Du Bois to Cullen, June 30, 1928, Du Bois Papers/UMass. "... TO WRITE HIM REGULARLY": Du Bois to Cullen, June 30, 1928, Du Bois Papers/UMass.

226. "... I REALLY DON'T": Lewis, interview with Robert Weaver, March 17, 1989. COBB: Lewis, interview with William Montague Cobb August 31, 1988.

226. "... GET OUT OF THE CENTER OF THE PICTURE": Du Bois to Yolande, September 7, 1928, Du Bois Papers/UMass. "... PHYSICAL AND PSYCHOLOGICAL": Du Bois to Countee Cullen, September 11, 1928, CCP/ARC.

227. "... NOT STANDING FOR ALL THAT FOOLISHNESS": Lewis, *When Harlem Was in Vogue*, 203. "... TRY AGAIN": Du Bois to Cullen, CCP/ARC.

227. "... WE ARE ALL OF US": Quoted in Peter Gay, *The Bourgeois Experience: Victoria to Freud* (New York: Oxford Univ. Press, 1984), 109. "... THE MAIN THING": Du Bois to Cullen, October 11, 1928, CCP/ARC.

227–28. VICTORIAN BLACK AND WHITE SEXUAL MORALITIES: Carol Smith-Rosenberg, *Disorderly Conduct: Visions of Gender in Victorian America* (New York: Alfred A. Knopf, 1985); Bram Dijkstra, *Evil Sisters: The Threat of Female Sexuality and the Cult of Manhood* (New York: Alfred A. Knopf, 1996); Kevin K. Gaines, *Uplifting the Race: Black Leadership, Politics, and Culture in the Twentieth Century* (Chapel Hill: Univ. of North Carolina Press, 1996). "... HER POSITION AS AN ADJUNCT": Quoted in Dijkstra, *Evil Sisters*, 41.

Chapter 7: The Possibility of Democracy in America

229. "... LESS THAN 25,000.": Board minutes July 14, 1930, NAACP Papers, Library of Congress, Group I; Series A, Board of Directors file, (hereafter NAACP BRD MIN); Du Bois gave higher cir-

culation figure, in Du Bois to Thomas J. Calloway, April 24, 1929, The Papers of W.E.B. Du Bois, Special Collections, W.E.B. Du Bois Library, University of Massachusetts at Amherst (hereafter Du Bois Papers/UMass). ". . . TESTIMONIAL FUND ORGANIZED": Mrs. Bethune gave $100, Clarence Darrow, Jane Adams, Ovington, et al. Arthur Spingarn to Du Bois, December 15, 1928; Du Bois to Louise Oliver, February 28, 1928; Du Bois to J. McArthur Vance, April 17, 1928; Du Bois to Vance, April 23, 1928; Vance to Du Bois, June 7, 1928; Du Bois to Vance, June 12, 1928, Du Bois Papers/UMass. In fact, exactly 56 persons contributed a total sum of $3,038.41 of which $2,105.24 remained for restoration of the property after its purchase. Du Bois obviously used the restoration money to take care of other expenses. Relevant document: "To the Contributors of the Du Bois Testimonial," dated June 12, 1929, Arthur Spingarn Papers, Moorland-Spingarn Research Center, Howard University (hereafter ASP/HU). 296–297. ". . . PASS FROM THE SCENE": Du Bois to Mrs. Clement G. Morgan, June 6, 1929, Du Bois Papers/UMass. Untitled and unsigned tribute to the late Moorfield Storey by Du Bois appears beneath a photograph of him, The Crisis (Dec. 1929), 404; Robert L. Vann objects to Joel Spingarn succeeding Storey as NAACP president: Robert Vann to Du Bois, December 26, 1930, in Herbert Aptheker, ed., The Correspondence of W.E.B. Du Bois (Amherst, Mass.: University of Massachusetts Press, 1973), 3 vols. I., 430; David Levering Lewis, When Harlem Was in Vogue (New York: Alfred A. Knopf, 1982), 248; Du Bois to Mrs. M. V. Boutte, August 18, 1927, Du Bois Papers/UMass; John W. Vandercook, Black Majesty: The Life of Christophe, King of Haiti (New York: Harper & Bros, 1928), 196. 298. ". . . TO MUCH VIOLENCE": J. Max Barber to William Pickens, June 18, 1930, Du Bois Papers/ UMass. ". . . WEDDING INVITATION LIST": Du Bois to James C. Thomas, May 1, 1928, Du Bois Papers/ UMass.

231. ". . . ONE OF DU BOIS'S MOST ACERBIC CRITICS": Neval H. Thomas to James Weldon Johnson, July 25, 1928, Du Bois Papers/UMass; Thomas to NAACP Board of Directors, December 3, 1928, Du Bois Papers/UMass; Du Bois to Charles E. Russell, December 12, 1929, Du Bois Papers/UMass; For biographical information on Thomas see Kenneth Janken, Rayford W. Logan and the Dilemma of the African-American Intellectual (Amherst, Mass.: University of Massachusetts Press, 1993), p. 21. 232. ". . . SO INDUBITABLY SOMEBODY": "Wings for God's Chillun', The Story of Burghardt Du Bois" in World Tomorrow (August 1929): 333–36. 299–300. ". . . THE POSSIBILITY OF DEMOCRACY": Leonard C. Cartwright to Du Bois, September 28, 1928, Aptheker, ed., Correspondence of W.E.B. Du Bois, I, 380; Du Bois to Cartwright, October 4, 1928, Du Bois Papers/UMass. 232. ". . . ENCYCLOPEDIA BRITANNICA": Du Bois to Mrs. Worth T. Hedden, November 27, 1927; Du Bois to Hedden, December 20, 1927; Du Bois to Joel Spingarn, February 25, 1929; William Albert Robinson to Du Bois, March 16, 1929, Du Bois Papers/UMass. For biographical information on Robinson see Who's Who in Colored America (New York: Who's Who in Colored America Corp., 1927), 173; Robinson to L. P. Dudley, Feb. 18, 1929 [letter forwarded to Du Bois with galleys of Robinson's essay], Du Bois Papers/UMass; Walter B. Pitkin to Du Bois, May 13, 1928; Du Bois to Pitkin, June 6, 1928, Du Bois Papers/UMass. 233. ". . . CORPORATE UPHEAVAL": Between mid-February 1929 and early March 1929 the successor to Mrs. Worth T. Hedden, Franklin Henry Hooper and his editorial assistant L. P. Dudley, engaged in a heated exchange with Du Bois over substantive changes they made to his article. Embree's substitute article would serve as the Negro entry until the 14th edition was revised in 1973. See Du Bois to Joel Spingarn, March 2, 1929; Franklin H. Hooper to Du Bois, March 8, 1929; Hooper to Du Bois, June 18, 1929, Du Bois Papers/UMass, also in Aptheker, ed., Du Bois Correspondence, I, 391–99. 235. ". . . DU BOIS/STODDARD DEBATE": Du Bois to Paul Kennaday, March 14, 1929; E. C. Aswell to Du Bois, September 27, 1927, Du Bois Papers/UMass. See profile of Lothrop Stoddard in Thomas F. Gossett, Race: The History of an Idea in America (New York: Oxford University Press, 1963, 1997), 390–98; A debate on equality between Alain Locke, "The High Cost of Prejudice (500–510) and Stoddard, "Impasse at the Color Line" was carried in the October 1927 issue of The Forum; The Stoddard/Du Bois debate and Du Bois's "gripping" remarks were widely reported by the black press and 4,000 or 5,000 people attended with thousands more outside, Report of a Debate by the Chicago Forum: Shall the Negro Be Encouraged to Seek Cultural Equality? March 17, 1929 (Chicago: Chicago Forum Council, 1929), see also Herbert Aptheker, ed. Pamphlets and Leaflets by W.E.B. Du Bois (White Plains, N.Y.: Kraus-Thomson, 1986), 226–29; "Du Bois Shatters Stoddard's Cultural Theories" in Defender, March 23, 1929, 1–3; Du Bois, "Postscript" in The Crisis (May 1929), 167–68. 237. Du Bois's statement on Thomas: Du Bois to Walter Frank, October 10, 1929, Du Bois Papers/

UMass, Reel 26 (T-0616). "... SOCIALIST IDEALS": Du Bois to Algernon Lee, February 15, 1929, Lee to Du Bois, February 19, 1929, both in Aptheker, ed., *Correspondence*, I, 388–89.

237. "... COLORED SOCIALISTS": Harvey Sitkoff, *A New Deal for Blacks: the Emergence of Civil Rights as a National Issue* (New York: Oxford University Press, 1978), 161–62.

238. "... OPPORTUNIST LINE OF REASONING": Michael Parrish, *Anxious Decade: America in Prosperity and Depression, 1920–1941* (New York: W. W. Norton, 1992), 159; Du Bois to Walter Frank, October 10, 1929/UMass; Harry Laidler to Du Bois, October 10, 1929, both in Du Bois Papers/UMass. "... DEPRIEST'S ELECTION": Margaret Deland to Du Bois, December 3, 1928, also in Aptheker, ed., *Correspondence*, I, 383, Du Bois Papers/UMass; Du Bois, "Ideals" in *The Crisis* (October 1929), 349, also in Aptheker, ed., *Crisis Selections*, II, 561; Du Bois, "Postscript", in *The Crisis* (December 1929), 418; Du Bois to Margaret Deland, December 12, 1928, Aptheker, ed., *Correspondence*, I, 383–84.

238. "... BIG CITY MACHINES": Du Bois, "The Negro Politician," in *The Crisis* (May 1928), 168. "... DEFIANCE AND DESPAIR": Du Bois, "Lynchings" in *The Crisis* (August 1927), 203, also in Aptheker, ed., *Crisis Selections*, I, 472; Du Bois, "Mob Tactics" in *The Crisis* (August 1927), 204, also in Aptheker, ed., *Crisis Selections*, I, 474; Du Bois, "Wallace Battle, the Episcopal Church and Mississippi: A Story of Suppressed Truth" in *The Crisis* (Oct. 1927), 262–63, 282–83, also in Aptheker, ed., *Crisis Selections*, I, 475; Du Bois, "The Possibility of Democracy in America," *The Crisis* (September and October 1928), 295–96, 314–15, 336, 353–55, also in Aptheker, ed., *Crisis Selections*, I, 520; Du Bois "The Shape of Fear" in *North American Review* (June 1926), 291–304, also in Herbert Aptheker, ed., *Writ. Periodical Lit.*, II, 282–90; Du Bois, "The Negro Politician," in *The Crisis* (May 1928), 168, also in Aptheker, ed., *Crisis Selections*, II, 503–4.

239. "... TAMMANY HALL": Ira Katznelson, *Black Men, White Cities: Race, Politics, and Immigration in the United States, 1900–30, and Britain, 1948–68* (London: Oxford University Press, 1973), 167; Gilbert Osofsky, *Harlem: the Making of a Ghetto, Negro New York, 1890–1930* (New York: Harper & Row, 1971), 2nd ed., 130.

239. "... BARELY EVER HIRED": Nancy J. Weiss, *The National Urban League, 1910–1940* (New York: Oxford University Press, 1974), 22; Jessie Fauset to Du Bois, June 4, 1929, Du Bois Papers/UMass; Lewis, *Vogue*, 129 (Lewis called the apartment shared by Regina Andrews and Ethel Ray Nance at 580 St. Nicholas a "sort of Renaissance U.S.O.," 127). "... NEW YORK PUBLIC LIBRARY": For material on Rose, Anderson (nee Andrews), Lattimer, and the NYPL as well as anti-Semitism see Du Bois to Ernestine Rose, March 1, 1930, Regina Andrews Papers/Schomburg Center (hereafter RAP/SCRBC); Du Bois to Virginia Powell-Florence, September 35, 1931, Powell-Florence to Du Bois, October 28, 1931, Du Bois to Lloyd Imes, December 8. 1931, all in Du Bois Papers/UMass; Du Bois to Ferdinand Q. Morton, February 18, 1930, in Aptheker, ed., *Correspondence*, I., 416–17. "... CHICAGO": Douglas Bukowski, *Big Bill Thompson, Chicago, and the Politics of Image* (Urbana: University of Illinois Press, 1998).

241. "... NATIONAL ELECTIONS": Kenneth O'Reilly, *Nixon's Piano: Presidents and Radical Politics from Washington to Clinton* (New York: The Free Press, 1995), 97–100; Parrish, *Anxious Decades*, 117; Du Bois wrote two *Crisis* editorials in 1924 on the Progressive Party and KKK: the first, "LaFollette" (August 1924), 154, deplores LaFollette and the second, "How Shall We Vote?" (Nov. 1924), 13, praises him, both also in, Aptheker, ed., *Crisis Selections*, I., 410, 413.

241. "... PROGRESSIVE POLITICS": Edward P. Johanningsmeier, *Forging American Communism: the Life of William Z. Foster* (Princeton, N.J.: Princeton University Press, 1994), 208; Nick Salvatore, *Eugene V. Debs: Citizen and Socialist* (Urbana: University of Illinois Press, 1982), 334–35; Mary Jo Buhle, et. al., eds., *Encyclopedia of the American Left* (Urbana: University of Illinois Press, 1992), 408. "... NEGRO VOTES": Du Bois, "LaFollette" (August 1924), 154, also in Aptheker, ed., *Crisis Selections*, I, 410; Du Bois, "The Election" in *The Crisis* (Dec. 1924), 55–56, also in Aptheker, ed., *Crisis Selections*, I, 414; Du Bois, "The Negro Voter" (August 1928), 203, also in Aptheker, ed., *Crisis Selections*, II, 519; *The World Almanac and Book of Facts 1990* (New York: World Almanac, 1990), 550.

242. "... MISSISSIPPI FLOOD": John M. Barry, *Rising Tide: the Great Mississippi Flood of 1927 and How It Changed America* (New York: Simon & Schuster, 1997); Donald J. Lisio, *Blacks and Lily Whites: a Study of Southern Strategies* (Durham, N.C.: University of North Carolina Press, 1985), 4; Walter White, *A Man Called White: the Autobiography of Walter White* (Athens, Ga.: University of Georgia Press, 1948, 1995), 80–81; White, "The Negro and the Flood" in *The Nation* (June 24, 1927), 688–90; Du Bois, "Flood" in *The Crisis* (July 1927), 168, also in Aptheker, ed., *Crisis Selections*, II, 471; Du Bois, "Is Al Smith Afraid of the South?" in *The Nation* (October 17, 1928), 392–94, also in Aptheker,

ed., *Writ. Periodical Lit.*, II, 296–301; Du Bois, "The Flood, the Red Cross, and the National Guard" in *The Crisis* (February 1928), 41–43, 64; NAACP Board meeting minutes for Oct. 9, 1933, reveal that wages of flood control workers were increased thanks to money provided to the NAACP by Sisters of the Blessed Sacrament, NAACP BRDMINS; also in Robert L. Zangrando, *The NAACP Crusade Against Lynching, 1909–1950* (Philadelphia: Temple University Press, 1980); Biographies of Howard, McDonald, Davis, and Church in Rayford W. Logan and Michael R. Winston, eds., *Dictionary of American Negro Biography* (New York: W. W. Norton, 1982); Jack Salzman, et. al., eds., *Encyclopedia of African-American Culture and History* (New York: Simon & Schuster Macmillan, 1996); and Lisio, op. cit.

245. "... SOUTHERN STRATEGY": O'Reilly, *op. cit.*, 28; Du Bois, "Hoover and the South" in *The Crisis* (May 1929), 167, also in Aptheker, ed., *Crisis Selections*, II., 546–47; Lisio, *op. cit.*, 136.

245. "... BLACK PATRONAGE": Du Bois, "Opinion" in *The Crisis* (January 1925), 103–6; Du Bois, "Opinion" in *The Crisis* (February 1923), 151–54; Du Bois, "Every Four Years" in *The Crisis* (April 1920), 297; Du Bois, "Opinion" (January 1923), 103–7, all articles also in Aptheker, ed., *Crisis Selections*, I/II; Lisio, *op. cit.*, 42.

245. "... AL SMITH": Henry Lewis Suggs, *P. B. Young Newspaperman: Race, Politics, and Journalism in the New South 1910–1962* (Charlottesville: University Press of Virginia, 1988 (especially ch. 5). Du Bois, "Is Al Smith Afraid of the South?", *The Nation* (October 17, 1928), 392–94, also in Aptheker, ed., *Writ. Periodical Lit.*, II, 297; Lewis, *Vogue*, op. cit., 206.

247. "... NO SOLUTION TO THE DILEMMAS": Lisio, *op. cit.*, 92. Lewis, *Vogue*, 206; Du Bois, "Race Relations in the United States" in *Annals of the American Academy of Political and Social Sciences* (November, 1928), 6–10, also in Aptheker, ed., *Writ. Periodical Lit.*, II, 304; Du Bois, "The Possibility of Democracy in America" (September and October 1928), 295–96, 314–315, 336, 353–355, also in Aptheker, ed., *Crisis Selections*, I, 528.

248. "... NONVOTERS": "The Possibility of Democracy in America" (September and October 1928), 295–96, 314–15, 336, 353–55, also in Aptheker, ed., *Crisis Selections*, I, 520, 526: Du Bois "A Third Party" in *The Crisis* (November 1928), 381; also in Aptheker, ed., *Crisis Selections*, I, 531–32.

249. "... CONSTITUTIONAL LAPSES": Du Bois, "Race Relations in the United States" in *Annals of the American Academy of Political and Social Science*, 6–10, also in Aptheker, ed., *Writ. Periodical Lit.*, II, 304, 305; Du Bois "A Third Party" in *The Crisis* (November 1928), 381, also in Aptheker, ed., *Crisis Selections*, II, 531–32.

250. "... SACCO AND VANZETTI": Du Bois, "As the Crow Flies" (December 1928), 401; Du Bois, "The Terrible Truth" in *The Crisis* (October 1927), 276, also in Aptheker, ed., *Crisis Selections*, II, 485; Vivid accounts of the S-V case appear in Parrish, *op. cit*, 200–203. and John P. Diggins, *The Rise and Fall of the American Left* (New York: W. W. Norton, 1975, 1992), 143–44. "... UNIONS": Du Bois, "Unions" in *The Crisis* (January 1927), 131, also in Aptheker, ed., *Crisis Selections*, II, 456; Du Bois, "To the American Federation of Labor" in *The Crisis* (August 1924), 153–54, also in Aptheker, ed., *Crisis Selections*, II, 409. Weiss, *op. cit.*, 213.

251. "... SUPREME COURT": Richard Kluger, *Simple Justice: the History of 'Brown v. Board of Education, the Epochal Supreme Court Decision that Outlawed Segregation, and of Black America's Century-Long Struggle for Equality under Law* (New York: Vintage Books, 1975), 144; *Roy Wilkins, Standing Fast: the Autobiography of Roy Wilkins* (New York: Da Capo Press, 1994), 91; Du Bois, "The Defeat of Judge Parker" in *The Crisis* (July 1930), 225–27, 248, also in Aptheker, ed., *Crisis Selections*, II, 581–89. Lisio, *op. cit.*, 204. Kluger, *op. cit.*, 141, 144.

252. "... LEAGUE FOR INDEPENDENT POLITICAL ACTION (LIPA)": Robert B. Westbrook, *John Dewey and American Democracy* (Ithaca, N.Y.: Cornell University Press, 1991), 446; Charles Kellogg, *History of the NAACP* (Baltimore: Johns Hopkins University Press, 1967), 20, 45; See Lewis, *Vogue*, op. cit. for discussion of Dewey and Barnes during the Harlem Renaissance; Lillian Alexander to Du Bois, November 6, 1933, Du Bois Papers/UMass. Du Bois to Devere Allen, June 24, 1929, Du Bois Papers/UMass, also in Aptheker, ed., *Correspondence*, I, 405–6. "... LIPA PLATFORM": "Liberals Here Plan an Opposition Party, Prof. Dewey Heads National Organizing Group" *New York Times* (September 9, 1929); Du Bois, a vice president along with Paul Douglas, Zona Gale, and Jim Maurer. The platform included public ownership of public utilities; unemployment, health, and old age pensions; free-trade for farm economy; high progressive income taxes; abolition of injunction in labor disputes; abolition of yellow dog contracts; independence of the Philippines; non-restriction of Negro and immigrant labor voting rights; elimination of war, see Westbrook, *op. cit.*, 146; Rhoda F. Levine, *Class Struggle*

and the New Deal: Industrial Labor, Industrial Capital, and the State (Lawrence: University of Kansas Press, 1988), 59; Westbrook, *op. cit.*, 156. "... DEWEY'S ANTI-SOCIALIST ... BIASES": John Dewey sends message to the 1932 NAACP convention meeting in Washington, DC, *The Crisis* (July 1932), 219. "... MUSTE'S *demarche*": A. J. Muste to Du Bois, December 1, 1930, Du Bois Papers/UMass; For biographical information on A. J. Muste see Buhle, *op. cit.*, 498–500.

253. "... DU BOIS PROFILE": Devere Allen to Du Bois, July 25, 1929, Du Bois Papers/UMass, also in Aptheker, ed., *Correspondence* I, 407. "... WW I RESPONSIBILITY": Du Bois to Kirby Page, June 24, 1930, Aptheker, ed., *Correspondence* I, 425.

254. "... A NEW PARTY": Du Bois, "A New Party," *The Crisis* (August 1930), 282. "... NO CLEAR ROLE": John Patrick Diggins. *The Rise and Fall of the American Left*, 134.

254. "... SHARP LETTER TO PAUL DOUGLAS": Du Bois to Paul H. Douglas, February 21, 1930, Aptheker, ed., *Correspondence* I, 419. "... ROTTEN BOROUGH VOTE SYSTEM": *Ibid*, 419 "... THE ISSUE AT HEART": Paul H. Douglas to Du Bois, February 28, 1930, in Aptheker, ed., *Correspondence* I, 419; But in the October 1930 issue of *The Crisis*, 353–354, Du Bois calls attention approvingly to a LIPA pamphlet by Henry R. Mussey. Norman Thomas had spoken to the membership though *The Crisis* (February 1931), 45, soliciting its vote more directly than ever before for the Socialist Party. Thomas had even called in the debts he claimed were owed his party, asserting that "Socialists have earned a degree of Negro support they have not received." In the same issue featuring "The Future of 'The Black Vote,'" Congressman Oscar De Priest offered the kind of nonpartisan advice that was becoming conventional wisdom among sophisticated black voters, even from a GOP officeholder: "support men and measures; principles and policies; rather than a bland adherence to any one party for local office." "... DARKNESS RATHER THAN LIGHT": Du Bois "Race Relations in the United States" in *Annals of the American Academy of Political and Social Science* 140 (November 1928) 6–10, also in Aptheker, ed. *Writ. Periodical Lit.*, II, 304–8.

256. "... NEGRO SOVIETS IN THE DEEP SOUTH": "Communists Boring into Negro Labor" *New York Times* (January 17, 1926), sect. 2, 1–2; Du Bois "The Black Man and Labor" in *The Crisis* (December 1925), 59–62, also in Aptheker, ed., *Crisis Selections* I, 432; Du Bois "Postscript" in *The Crisis* (April 1930), 137–138; Buhle *op. cit.*, 27. "NATIONAL ORGANIZER/ANLC": Lovett Fort-Whiteman to Du Bois, April 9, 1928, Du Bois Papers/UMass; Allison Blakeley, *Russia and the Negro: Blacks in Russian History and Thought* (Washington, D.C.: Howard University, 1986), 78, 96, 100, 108. "... TO ATTRACT COLORED MEMBERS": Blakeley, *ibid.*, 108.

256. "... PRESS CHARGES": Dan T. Carter, *Scottsboro: A Tragedy of the American South* (Baton Rouge: Louisiana State University Press, 1969), 4; James Goodman, *Stories of Scottsboro*. (New York: Pantheon, 1994).

257. "... JURY CONTAMINATION": Carter, *op. cit.*, 60. "... UNWRITTEN PENALTY": Du Bois "Scottsboro" in *The Crisis* (July 1931), 247, also in Aptheker, ed., *Crisis Selections*, II, 627. "... MURDERED SWIFTLY": Du Bois "Blunders" in *The Crisis* (February 1932), 58, also in Aptheker, ed., *Crisis Selections*, II, 647; Du Bois "Scottsboro" in *The Crisis* (January 1934), 21, also in Aptheker, ed., *Crisis Selections*, II, 730.

258. "... PICKENS' PRAISE": Carter, *op. cit.*, 60. "... NAME CHANGE": "... ROADSHOW": Foner and Schapiro, *op. cit.*, xx. Goodman, *op. cit.*, 68.

258. "... ATTACK ON NAACP": *The Liberator* (July 29, 1933), 1. "... ANYTHING BUT SLAVERY." Foner and Schapiro, *op. cit.* xvii; Carter, *op. cit.*, 69. "... CONFLICTING STATEMENTS": Carter, *op. cit.*, 72.

259. "... THEY WILL DIE": Lewis, *Vogue, op. cit.* 272. "... NOT ONE PERSON": *ibid*. "... COMMUNIST MOVEMENT": Du Bois "The Negro and Communism" in *The Crisis* (September 1931), 313, also in Aptheker, ed., *Crisis Selections*, II, 634.

261. "... TRIUMPHANT PROLETARIAT": John W. Van Zanten "Communist Theory and the American Negro Question" in *Review of Politics* (October 1967), 435–56; Philip Foner and Herbert Schapiro, *American Communism and Black Americans.*, xiii. "... SELF-DETERMINATION FOR NEGROES": Foner and Schapiro, *op. cit.*; Fraser M. Ottanelli, *The Communist Party of the United States: From the Depression to World War II* (New Brunswick, N.J.: Rutgers University Press, 1991); Theodore Draper, *The Roots of American Communism* (Chicago: Ivan R. Dee, 1989); James E. Jackson, *The Communist Position on the Negro Question*, an undated CPUSA pamphlet given to David Levering Lewis by the author. "... BEWILDERED JANITOR": *New York Times*, March 1, 1931, 38. For March 1930 demonstrations see also Rhoda Levine, *Class Struggles and the New Deal, op. cit.*, 53–54 and Cyril Briggs, "The Decline of the Garvey Movement" in *Communist* (June 1931), 547.

261. "... WELCOMED COMMUNIST LEADERSHIP": Robin D. G. Kelley, *Hammer and Hoe: Alabama Communists During the Great Depression* (Chapel Hill, N.C.: University of North Carolina Press, 1990), 40. "... NEGRO REDS": Kelley, *ibid.*, 41; Foner and Schapiro, *op. cit.*, 202. "... TOO DESPICABLE FOR WORDS": Du Bois "The Negro and Communism" in *The Crisis* (September 1931), 313, also in Aptheker, ed., *Crisis Selections*, II, 635.

262. "... CAMP HILL": But Du Bois took a much more reasoned view on the CPUSA in *The Crisis* (February 1933), 44–46, but see Foner and Schapiro, *op. cit.*, 216–19. "... YOUNG JACKASSES": Du Bois "The Negro and Communism" in *The Crisis* (September 1931), 313, also in Aptheker, ed., *Crisis Selections*, II, 637. "... WHITE'S SIGNATURE": Foner and Schapiro, *op. cit.*, 287. "... THE DIE WAS CAST": Du Bois "The Negro and Communism" in *The Crisis* (September 1931), 313, also in Aptheker, ed., *Crisis Selections*, II, 633.

263. "... GIVE COMMUNISM A HEARING": Du Bois to Rachel Davis Dubois, May 13, 1931, Du Bois Papers/UMass. "... BUSINESS POINTS THE WAY": Albon Holsey "Business Points the Way" in *The Crisis* (July 1931), 225–26; Will Herberg "Shall the Negro Worker Turn to Labor or to Capital?" in *The Crisis* (July 1931), 227–28. "... STRIKES AND AGITATION": Du Bois "The Negro and Communism" in *The Crisis* (September 1931), also in Aptheker, eds. *Crisis Selections*, II, 638. "... NORMAN THOMAS": *Ibid.* "... BARRAGE": Eugene Gordon "Camp Hill" in *Daily Worker* (July 28, 1931); Foner and Schapiro, *op. cit.*, 214–16.

263–64. "... LITERARY LIONS": Carter, *op. cit.*, 146; Walter White "The Negro and the Communists" in *Harper's Magazine* (December 1931); Foner and Schapiro, *op. cit.*, 274–88. "... GROSSEST OF LI-BELS": Du Bois "The Negro and Communism" in *The Crisis* (September 1931), also in Aptheker, ed. *Crisis Selections*, II, 635–36. "... GROUP OF LEADERS": Du Bois "The Negro Bourgeoisie" in *The Crisis* (September 1931), also in Aptheker, ed., *Crisis Selections*, II, 635–37. "... DARROW": Du Bois "Scottsboro" in *The Crisis* (March 1932), 81. "... INTELLIGENCE OF THE NAACP": Du Bois "The Scottsboro Cases" in The Crisis (September 1931), also in Aptheker, ed., *Crisis Selections*, II, 634–35. "... COM-MUNISTS ... BUNGLED": Du Bois, *Dusk of Dawn* (Millwood, N.Y.: Kraus-Thomson, 1940, 1975), 298.

265. "... WHITE ALABAMA ... WORKERS": Du Bois, "White Labor" in *The Crisis* (September 1931), also in Aptheker, ed., *Crisis Selections*, II, 637–38; Buhle, op. cit. 435; "... DIFFERENCE BETWEEN": Du Bois to Will Herberg, September 23, 1931, Du Bois Papers/UMass.

265. "... SHOCK TROOPS": Du Bois "Communists and the Color Line" in *The Crisis* (September 1931), also in Aptheker, ed., *Crisis Selections*, II, 638–39. "... HATE NEGROES LESS": Du Bois "The Right to Work" in W.E.B. *Du Bois: Writings* (New York: Library of America, 1986), 1235–1238.

Chapter 8: Holding On, Amorously and Angrily

266. YOLANDE'S DIVORCE: Jean Beauvais to Du Bois, January 9, 1930, February 13, 1930, The Papers of W.E.B. Du Bois, Special Collections, W.E.B. Du Bois Library, Univ. of Massachusetts at Amherst (hereafter Du Bois Papers/UMass). "... HIS MOMENTARY SON-IN-LAW": Du Bois to Countee Cullen, February 18, 1930, Countee Cullen Papers, Amistad Research Center, Tulane University (hereafter CCP/ARC). "... MAKE YOURSELF COMFORTABLE": Will to Nina, May 5, 1929; Will to Nina, April 11, 1929—both in Du Bois Papers/UMass.

267. "... WHEN HE HAD TO SAVE FACE": Lewis, interview with Gerri Major, Voices of the Harlem Renaissance, Schomburg Center for Research in Black Culture, New York Public Library (hereafter VOHR/SCRBC). "... A REAL LADY": Lewis, interview with Katherine Bell Banks, April 1997. "... AS FULLY COMPLETE BEINGS": Maud Cuney-Hare, for one, was still anticipating visits from the editor in the 1930s. See Maud Cuney-Hare to Du Bois, May 6, 1931, Du Bois Papers/UMass; Du Bois, *The Autobiography of W.E.B. Du Bois* (U.S.A.: International Publishers, 1968), 138. On Cuney-Hare, see "Cuney-Hare, Maud," in Rayford Logan and Michael R. Winston, eds., *Dictionary of American Negro Biography* (New York: W. W. Norton, 1982), 152 (hereafter *DANB*). The actual one-sidedness of these relationships could emerge with striking clarity. To Maud Cuney-Hare, upset that Du Bois failed to contact her when traveling, Du Bois would write dismissively: "I am afraid you are getting dippy ... I did not even remember your aunt's name, much less her address or telephone number, and there was no way for me to inquire." Du Bois to Cuney-Hare, July 5, 1929, Du Bois Papers/UMass. Still, Du Bois could also be explicitly manipulative as well: "I was rather scared the night after you went to the physician," he would write in a letter to Mildred Bryant Jones, July 19, 1920, Du Bois Papers/UMass.

267–68. MILDRED BRYANT JONES: Du Bois, "Dr. Mildred Bryant Jones," *The Crisis* (November 1928), 378. "... HER SOUTHSIDE HOME": Du Bois to Mildred Bryant Jones, December 21, 1933; Du Bois to Jones, March 30, 1928; Du Bois Papers/UMass. "... OH, OH!": Jones to Du Bois, March 24, 1932, Du Bois Paper/UMass. "... I MISS SEEING YOU, MR. MAN": Jones to Du Bois, August 15, 1932, Du Bois Papers/UMass.

268. ETHEL RAY: Upon her return to Minnesota, Ethel became the first black policewoman in Duluth, Minnesota, in 1928 for four years. Lewis, interview with Ethel Ray Nance, May 17, 1987. "... MY DEAR ETHEL": Du Bois to Ethel Ray, July 17, 1929, Du Bois Papers/UMass. "... THOUGHTS OF THE SEA": Ray to Du Bois, October 7, 1929, Du Bois Papers/UMass. "... EIGHT YEARS": Lewis, interview with Ethel Ray Nance, May 17, 1987.

268–69. ELIZABETH PROPHET: "Prophet, Nancy Elizabeth," in Darlene Clark Hine, ed., *Black Women in America: An Historical Encyclopedia* (Brooklyn: Carlson Publishing, 1993), 2 Vols., II, 947–48 (hereafter *BWIA*). "... THE FIERCELY DEDICATED PROPHET": Augusta Savage would write to Du Bois of Prophet's monastic temperament—Savage to Du Bois, Sept. 22, 1929, Du Bois Papers/UMass. "... NEITHER FRIENDS NOR MONEY TO AID ME": Elizabeth Prophet to Du Bois, September 12, 1929, Du Bois Papers/UMass. "... NO LONGER BELIEVE IN ANY OF THEM": Prophet to Du Bois, January 22, 1931, Du Bois Papers/UMass.

269–70. "... A PART OF THE GLORY": Du Bois to Prophet, May 18, 1931, Du Bois Papers/UMass. "... TOO SAD, TOO SERIOUS": Prophet to Du Bois, May 11, 1931, Du Bois Papers/UMass. "... I CAN NEVER FORGET YOU": Prophet to Du Bois, November 14, 1931, Du Bois Papers/UMass.

270. RACHEL DAVIS DUBOIS: See Rachel Davis Du Bois, *All This and Something More: Pioneering in Intercultural Education* (Bryn Mawr: Dorrance & Co., 1984); "Rachel D. Du Bois, 101, Educator Who Promoted Value of Diversity," *New York Times*, April 2, 1993. Also, see Barbara Dianne Savage, *Broadcasting Freedom: Radio, War, and the Politics of Race, 1938–1948* (Chapel Hill: Univ. of North Carolina, 1999), 21–62. "... EARNEST WHITE LIFE": Davis DuBois, *All This and More*, 30. "... THE CELLS OF MY SKIN": *ibid.*, 36. "... DEEPLY INFLUENCED ... AND DISTURBED": Du Bois's article was mis-remembered by Davis DuBois in her autobiography as "Race and War"—*ibid.*, 35.

271. "... QUICKLY ENDEARED HERSELF": Davis DuBois, *ibid.*, 51. "... HER WOODBURY PLAN": See the excited telegram about Davis DuBois's program from Will Alexander to Edwin Embree, July 11, 1930, Julius Rosenwald Fund Archives, Fisk University (hereafter RSWLD), "... RELATED BY MARRIAGE": Davis Du Bois, *ibid.*, 69. "... SUBTLE OF HUMOR": Davis Du Bois, *ibid.*, "... A HIGH SCHOOL LESSON PLAN": Rachel Davis Du Bois to Du Bois, December 30, 1925, Du Bois Papers/UMass.

271–72. "... SURPRISE ON THEIR FACES": Davis Du Bois, *All This and More*, 69. "... VERY, VERY LOVING": Lewis, interview with Rachel Davis Du Bois. "... TO VALUE HER OPINIONS": See Du Bois to Abram Harris, April 9, 1931, Du Bois Papers/UMass. "... I AM HOME AGAIN": Du Bois to Rachel Davis DuBois, March 25, 1931. "... THE REMAINDER OF THE WEEK": Davis DuBois to Du Bois, June 1, 1931, Du Bois Papers/UMass. "... DROP UP TO NEW YORK": Du Bois to Davis DuBois, July 14, 1931, Du Bois Papers/UMass. "... I AM TIED UP": Du Bois to Nora Waring, October 15, 1929, Du Bois Papers/UMass.

272. "... THE LIBERAL CLUB OF BRYN MAWR": A. V. Grant to Du Bois, March 19, 1931, Du Bois Papers/UMass. VIRGINIA MARGARET ALEXANDER: I am extremely grateful to Vanessa Gamble of the University of Wisconsin at Madison for her very useful paper, "Taking a History: The Life of Dr. Virginia Alexander," the Fielding H. Garrison Lecture, the American Association for the History of Medicine, Toronto, Canada, May 8, 1998. RAYMOND PACE ALEXANDER: "Alexander, Raymond Pace," in Jack Salzman, et. al., eds., *Encyclopedia of African-American Culture and History* (New York: Macmillan, 1996), 94–95 (hereafter *EAACH*). "... REBUKING PRESIDENT LOWELL": Werner Sollars, et. al., eds., *Blacks at Harvard: A Documentary History of African-American Experience at Harvard and Radcliffe* (New York: New York Univ. Press, 1993), 199.

273. SADIE TANNER MOSSELL: "Alexander, Sadie Tanner Mossell," in Hine, et. al. eds., *BWIA*, I, 17–19. "... FIRST IN A THOUSAND APPLICANTS": Gamble, "Taking a History" "... THAT ANY CREATURE": One male professor particularly enjoyed telling his class "every discreditable, dirty and insulting story" about African Americans that came to mind. The three black students (one would soon withdraw) were trying to "get above their people," he said, and whatever their accomplishments they would always be nothing more than "Negroes." See Gamble, "Taking a History."

273–74. "... FOUR-BED BIRTH CONTROL CLINIC": Her Aspiranto Health Home in Philadelphia was a four-bed clinic largely devoted to caring for women and children, but, as the name implied, all types of persons were treated in the three-story Jefferson Street house in which she lived with her infirm father. One account says that the facility only had three bedrooms, but I prefer to take Helen Dickens's figure, given to me in interview, July 15, 1993. ". . . PROPRIETARY PRIDE": Margaret Sanger to Du Bois, November 11, 1930; Du Bois to Margaret Sanger, [n.d.]—both in Du Bois Papers/UMass; Gamble, "Taking a History." ". . . THE JOKE OF HER FRIENDS": Du Bois, "Can a Colored Woman be a Physician?" *The Crisis* (February 1933), 33–34.

274–75. ". . . INSEPARABLE AND HORRIBLY OBVIOUS": Gloria T. Hull, ed., *Give us Each Day: The Diary of Alice Dunbar-Nelson* (New York: W. W. Norton, 1984), 426. ". . . TO BE IN THEIR COMPANY": Lewis, interview with Julia Bond, January 11, 1987. ". . . THE *CRISIS* TRADEMARK": Department of Commerce to NAACP, January 30, 1929, Du Bois Papers/UMass. ". . . OF EQUAL CAPACITY TO THE EDITOR": Paul Kennedy to Du Bois, May 8, 1929, Du Bois Papers/UMass.

275–76. ". . . FAULTY BUSINESS MANAGEMENT": Minutes for July 14, 1930, NAACP Board Minutes, Series A, Board of Directors file, Minutes 1909–1959, NAACP Papers, Library of Congress (hereafter BRDMINS/LC). ". . . WE MUST CARRY ON": Du Bois to Pierce Thompson, May 10, 1929, Du Bois Papers/UMass. In a long letter to Roy Wilkins, Du Bois blamed Thompson for failing to pay debts. See Du Bois to Wilkins, April 24, 1930, Du Bois Papers/UMass. ". . . A HELL OF A TIME": Du Bois to James Weldon Johnson, April 17, 1929, James Weldon Johnson Memorial Collection, Beinecke Library, Yale University (hereafter JWJMC/YU), Folder 136: "Du Bois, W.E.B." ". . . FOUR PERSON CRISIS FINANCE COMMITTEE": Board minutes for September 8, 1930, NAACP.

276. ". . . THE POSITION OF BUSINESS MANAGER": Du Bois to Thomas Junius Calloway, May 3, 1929, Du Bois Papers/UMass. LAKE MINNETONKA: David Levering Lewis, *W.E.B. Du Bois: Biography of a Race, 1868–1919* (New York: Henry Holt & Co., 1993), 247. ". . . AT ALL POINTS": T. J. Calloway to Du Bois, October 15, 1929, Du Bois Papers/UMass.

277. ". . . RELATIVELY UPBEAT NEWS": "To the Crisis Finance Committee," October 24, 1929, Du Bois Papers/UMass. ". . . WITHIN THE YEAR": T. J. Calloway to Du Bois, December 1, 1929. MALVAN: Du Bois to Arthur Spingarn, December 9, 1930, Du Bois Papers/UMass; also see the *The Crisis* of November, 1930, for the announcement of her tenure as business manager. ". . . BLACK TUESDAY": John Garraty, *The Great Depression: An Inquiry into the Causes, Course, and Consequences of the Worldwide Depression of the Nineteen-Thirties as Seen by Contemporaries in the Light of History* (New York: Harcourt, Brace, Jovanovich, 1986). ROY WILKINS: Lewis, interview with Marvel Jackson Cook, August 1988; "Wilkins, Roy Ottoway," in Jack Salzman, ed., *EAACH*, V, 2835–2837.

277. ". . . A CHARTER MEMBER OF THE ST. PAUL BRANCH": Roy Wilkins (with Tom Matthews), *Standing Fast: the Autobiography of Roy Wilkins* (New York: Da Capo Press, 1982), 36. ". . . TO BE AN ENGINEER": Wilkins, *Standing Fast*, 39. ". . . FROM LIGHT POLES": Wilkins, *Standing Fast*, 41–43. ". . . HE HAD SEEN A GREAT LEADER": Wilkins, *Standing Fast*, 53.

277–78. ". . . AN ENERGIZING ROLE": Wilkins, *Standing Fast*, 53. ". . . OPPORTUNIST BENT": Lewis, interview with Marvel Jackson Cook. ". . . THE SPECIAL CONNECTION": Nancy J. Weiss, "Long Distance Runners of the Civil Rights Movement: The Contribution of Jews to the NAACP and the National Urban League in the Early Twentieth Century," in Jack Salzman and Cornel West, eds., *Struggles in the Promised Land: Toward a History of Black-Jewish Relations in the United States* (New York: Oxford University Press, 1997), 136. ". . . DISCUSSION AND PROJECTION": Mary White Ovington to Du Bois, January 3, 1930, Du Bois Papers/UMass.

278. ". . . EXCEPT AS A CHEERER ON": August Meier and Elliot Rudwick, "The Rise of the Black Secretariat in the NAACP," in Meier and Rudwick, eds., *Along the Color Line: Explorations in the Black Experience* (Urbana and Chicago: University of Illinois, 1976), 114. ". . . TO GO A BIT SLOWER": Du Bois to James Weldon Johnson, October 15, 1930, JWJMC/YU, Folder 136: "Du Bois, W.E.B." ". . . HOW HE CAN TALK ABOUT HIMSELF": Lewis, *When Harlem Was in Vogue*, 245.

278. ". . . NO TIME TO APPLY IT": It is interesting that even as he was composing his note to Johnson, a typical name-dropping memo from White arrived on Du Bois's desk ("Some days ago while in the office of Dr. Keppel of the Carnegie Foundation . . .") sunnily suggesting a story about the American Library Association and the new Atlanta University. In response, Du Bois fairly snarled that he was "just now Editor, Business Manager, and Shipping Clerk of *The Crisis*," and hadn't a single minute to spare. See the memo from Du Bois to White, January 31, 1930, Du Bois Papers/UMass. ". . . WHITE'S AUTHORITY": No doubt the deaths of both Louis Marshall and Moorfield Storey in 1929

influenced the decision of the Garland Fund to vote for this permanent legal department. See August Meier and Elliot Rudwick, "Attorneys Black and White: A Case Study of Race Relations within the NAACP," in Meier and Rudwick, eds., *Along the Color Line*, 128–73; Richard Kluger, *Simple Justice: The History of Brown v. Board of Education, the Epochal Supreme Court Decision that Outlawed Segregation, and of Black America's Century-Long Struggle for Equality Under Law* (New York: Vintage Books, 1975), 132–33. "... BEEN ESPECIALLY PROMINENT": Du Bois, "Postscript," *The Crisis* (November 1929), 386–88. "... A FEW MONTHS BEFORE DYING": Kluger, *Simple Justice*, 122. "... TROUBLE EVER SINCE": "Louis Marshall Addresses Meeting," *The Crisis* (February 1929), 210–13; Nancy J. Weiss, "Long Distance Runners of the Civil Rights Movement", 134.

279. "... SHARE WHOLEHEARTEDLY": Spingarn to Du Bois, April 26, 1930. "... DEFICITS AND PO-TENTIALITIES": Wilkins to Du Bois, April 12, 1930, Du Bois Papers/UMass. "... TO MAKE THE MAG-AZINE POPULAR": Du Bois to Wilkins, June 11, 1930, Du Bois Papers/UMass. "... KNOWLEDGE AND COURAGE": Du Bois to Wilkins, April 24, 1930, Du Bois Papers/UMass. "... STRONGLY URGED ACCEPTANCE": Wilkins, *Standing Fast*, 97. "... TO REMAIN IN KANSAS CITY": Wilkins to Du Bois, July 9, 1930, Du Bois Papers/UMass, also in Herbert Aptheker, ed., *Correspondence of W.E.B Du Bois* (Amherst: Univ. of Massachusetts Press, 1973), 2 Vols., I, 426–27.

280. "... IN THE EAST OR IN THE SOUTH": Bunche to Du Bois, May 11, 1927, Du Bois Papers/UMass. "... HIS FIRST PUBLICATION": Ben Nnamdi Azikiwi to Du Bois, February 18, 1930, in Du Bois Papers, also in Aptheker, ed., *Correspondence*, I, 415–16. "... CHECKERED ACADEMIC PERFORMANCE": St. Clair Drake to Du Bois, August 10, 1930, Du Bois Papers/UMass, also in Aptheker, ed., *Correspondence*, I, 429 "... LARGER GROWTH AND LARGER REMUNERATION": Wilkins to Du Bois, June 14, 1930, Du Bois Papers/UMass.

281. "... A BIT IMPERTINENT": Wilkins, *Standing Fast*, 96. "... TO MAKE HIS LIFE MISERABLE": Wil-kins, *Standing Fast*, 93–94.

281. "... EDUCATIONAL PUBLICITY": Du Bois to Arthur Spingarn, December 9, 1930; J. E. Shepard to Du Bois, June 14, 1929 — both in Du Bois Papers/UMass. Du Bois to R. R. Moton, December 2, 1929; Du Bois, "Memorandum to the Finance Committee," March 26, 1930; Du Bois to Edwin Em-bree, June 3, 1930 — all in Du Bois Papers/UMass. MRS. JACOB SCHIFF: Du Bois to G. F. Peabody, November 25, 1930; Du Bois to Mrs. Jacob Schiff, October 22, 1930 — both in Du Bois Papers/UMass. "... THE WORK OF THE FIELD SECRETARIES": G. W. Crawford to Walter White, July 12, 1930, Du Bois Papers/UMass.

281. "... INTENSE DELIBERATIONS ... BY THE BOARD OF DIRECTORS": Minutes for July 14, 1930, NAACP, Group I; Series A; Board of Directors Files: Box "A10."

282. "... IT CANNOT BELONG TO YOU": Mary White Ovington to Du Bois, December 20, 1930, Du Bois Papers/UMass, also in Aptheker, ed., *Correspondence*, I, 430.

283. "... OR IT IS NOT": Du Bois to Ovington, December 24, 1930, Du Bois Papers/UMass, also in Aptheker, ed., *Correspondence*, I, 431. "... DOWNTOWN": Jackman quoted, Lewis, *When Harlem Was in Vogue*, 245. "... A WELCOMING SMILE": "On James Weldon Johnson," *Journal of Negro History* 52 (July 1926), 224–27, also in Aptheker, ed., *Writings in Periodical Literature* (Millwood, N.Y.: Kraus Thomson, 1982), 4 Vol., II, 309–10. "... THE HONORARY TITLE": Johnson's own speech at the testi-monial dinner can be found in Sondra Kathryn Wilson, ed., *The Selected Writings of James Weldon Johnson* (New York: Oxford Univ. Press, 1995), 2 Vols., II, 123–28.

283. "... FUZZY": See the impression of the young Walter White in Du Bois, *Autobiography*, 293. "... MOST OF THE CREDIT": Lewis, interview with Robert Weaver, March 17, 1988.

284. "... FAITHFUL WORKERS AT THESE PLACES FOR YEARS": Joe William Trotter, Jr., *From a Raw Deal to a New Deal?* (New York: Oxford Univ. Press, 1995), 21. "... A CHRONIC STATE OF BEING FOR NEGRO AMERICANS": As early as 1927, some employers were dismissing blacks and hiring whites — Nancy Weiss, *The National Urban League* (New York: Oxford University, 1974), 238. Also see Harvard Sitkoff, *A New Deal for Blacks: the Emergence of Civil Rights as a National Issue — the Depression Decade* (New York: Oxford University Press, 1978), 35–36, et. passim. "... FOUR PERCENT OF THE CITY'S POPULATION": Weiss, *National Urban League*, 239. "... IN DETROIT, FORTY": Sitkoff, *New Deal for Blacks*, 36. "... AT NO TIME IN HISTORY": *ibid.*, 35.

285. "... BY THE END OF 1930.": Donald J. Lisio, *Hoover, Blacks, and Lily Whites: A Study in Southern Strategies* (Chapel Hill: Univ. of North Carolina Press, 1985), 15.

. "... WHAT YOUR ENEMIES MOST WISH YOU TO SAY": Charles Edward Russell to Walter White,

December 27, 1930, Du Bois Papers/UMass. ". . . WHITE IS IMPOSSIBLE": Du Bois to Abram Harris, January 27, 1931, Du Bois Papers/UMass. ". . . TO PLACE DAVIS DUBOIS IN THE POSITION INSTEAD": Du Bois to Abram Harris, April 9, 1931, Du Bois Papers/UMass.

286.   ". . . BETTER EDUCATION, AND HIGHER EDUCATION": Du Bois, "The General Education Board", *The Crisis* (July 1930), 229–30. According to John Stanfield, a 1927 special report by Jackson Davis on black higher education led to more GEB emphasis on higher education—see John H. Stanfield, *Philanthropy and Jim Crow in American Social Science* (Westport, Conn.: Greenwood, 1985), 80. SAVING *THE CRISIS*: Du Bois had tried to stem the decline in subscriptions month after month, fully cognizant of his weakening purchase on the board's willingness to continue underwriting the magazine. Statements praising the value of *The Crisis* had come from Gandhi and Rabindranath Tagore, the Indian Nobel literary laureate, several months before the stock market crash. Although the magazine had become thinner during the summer of 1930, there was no loss of self-confidence. "Not to read *The Crisis* is not to be thoroughly intelligent in matters on which you must be intelligent, if you would live completely," the November issue would challenge subscribers. The covers for March and April featured the sultry motion picture actresses Nina Mae McKinney and Victoria Spivey, respectively. McKinney, so white of complexion that the studio insisted on darkening her appearance, had achieved the star-crossed distinction of being dubbed the "Black Garbo" for her role in King Vidor's box-office success, *Hallelujah*. See "McKinney, Nina Mae," in Hine, et. al. eds., *BWIA*, II, 772–73. In May, Chesnutt departed from his disheartened reticence to allow Du Bois to publish "Concerning Father", a polished short story. See Charles Chesnutt, "Concerning Father," *The Crisis* (May 1930), 153–55, 175. The July special August education numbers for 1930 were a mixture of controversy, significant analysis, and race achievement that might have hiked the circulation curve in earlier days. Henry Hunt, principal of the Fort Valley High and Industrial School and sixteenth Spingarn medalist, was profiled, followed by "The Negro College Student," a skeptical assessment by Arthur P. Davis of the scholastic caliber of the contemporary college generation. Davis, a future master teacher of literature at Howard, was identified as a Phi Beta Kappa graduate of Columbia and instructor at Virginia Union University. See "The Negro College Student", *The Crisis* (August 1930), 270–71. ". . . ALWAYS TO BE HAPPY": Du Bois, "General Education Board" ". . . TEN-FOLD INCREASE OVER 1919": "Annual Report of the General Education Board, 1930–1931," Rockefeller Foundation Archives. ". . . THE LAST THREE YEARS": Du Bois, "The General Education Board." In *The Crisis* of August 1931, the number of African Americans in college (white and black schools) was listed at 18,500 (with 2,500 in white schools)—see "The Year in Negro Education," *The Crisis* (August 1931), 261–62. The drop in numbers between GEB figures and those of *The Crisis* may be due to Depression. ". . . A SPECIAL REASON FOR REJOICING": Du Bois, "Postscript", *The Crisis* (June 1929), 203–4, 212–14.

287.   ". . . THE MAGAZINE'S SERIOUS EMPHASIS": In the fall of 1931, in response to Du Bois's invitation, a penetrating sociological reply came from Alfred Einstein, who, "overburdened with work," regretted that he was unable to send a fuller statement. The great physicist observed that the gravest consequence of the prejudice against minorities was the tendency of minorities to "acquiesce in this prejudiced estimate" of themselves. Einstein commended "every recognition and assistance" to black Americans for their determination to emancipate themselves spiritually. See Alfred Einstein to Du Bois, October 29, 1931, Du Bois Papers/UMass, also in Aptheker, ed., *Correspondence*, I, 444–45. The aged philanthropist George Foster Peabody praised the magazine and deplored any possibility that might cause the world to be deprived of its "brilliant writing and comment," though he declined to advance the five-thousand-dollar loan suggested by the Editor. See Peabody to Du Bois, December 10, 1931, Du Bois Papers/UMass. Among those from whom Du Bois failed to secure endorsements were ex-Kaiser Wilhelm II and (until the eleventh hour) Paul Robeson, whose failure to acknowledge repeated requests evoked a tinge of Du Boisian exasperation—"I have about given up . . . this is a sort of last appeal." See Du Bois to Paul Robeson, April 17, 1931, Du Bois/UMass. Robeson's powerful image as Othello in the London production of the Shakespeare tragedy had been deployed across a full page of the annual October children's number for 1930, with British actress Peggy Ashcroft on the recto page, followed by a photo of the mature Paul Robeson, Jr. See "Paul Robeson's Presentation of 'Othello' in London", *The Crisis* (October 1930), 332. ". . . MATTERS OF THEIR GROUP LIFE": Du Bois, "Memorandum on the Present and Future Editorial Program of *The Crisis*", 1931, Du Bois Papers/UMass.

287.   JESSIE BINGA: "Binga, Jessie," in Logan, ed., *DANB*, 45. ". . . A GREAT CALAMITY": Du Bois, "Binga", *The Crisis* (December 1930), 425–26. ANTHONY OVERTON: "Overton, Anthony," in Salzman, et. al. eds., *EAACH*, V, 2070–2071. ". . . CLOSED!": "Work—Waste—Wealth," *The Crisis* (July 1932),

228. ". . . THE AMOUNT OF INDEBTEDNESS": Lewis, *When Harlem Was in Vogue*, 265; "Work—Waste—Wealth", 227. ". . . LOAN TO HIS BROTHER IN LAW": Lewis, *When Harlem Was in Vogue*, 241.

288. ". . . HIS FORMER SON-IN-LAW": Du Bois to Cullen, February 18, 1930; Du Bois to Cullen, June 28, 1930—both in CCP/ARC; also see Lewis, *When Harlem Was in Vogue*, 241. ". . . FULL CHARGE OF OUR BUSINESS": Du Bois to Augustus Dill, January 5, 1929, Du Bois Papers/UMass. ". . . THERE IS NO REASON IN THE WORLD": Du Bois to Mrs. Mary Dill, October 6, 1930, Du Bois Papers/UMass. "HIS MIND IS GIVING WAY": Du Bois to Spingarn, September 30, 1930, Arthur Spingarn Papers, Moorland-Spingarn Papers, Howard University (hereafter ASP/HU). "YOUR ACTIONS ARE DISTRESSING AND HU-MILIATING": Du Bois to Dill, September 10, 1931, Du Bois Papers/UMass.

288. ". . . CONSERVATIVELY $25,000": Joel Spingarn to Arthur Spingarn, October 21, 1930, ASP/HU. ". . . PRESSURES OF CRISIS WORK": Du Bois to John Nail, December 16, 1930, W.E.B. Du Bois Collection, Fisk University.

289. ". . . 1301 MADISON AVENUE IN BALTIMORE": Nina to Will, October 31, 1931, Du Bois Papers/UMass. ". . . HAD FELT SO FATIGUED": Du Bois to Mr. Mason A. Hawkins, June 3, 1931, Du Bois Papers/UMass. ". . . ANOTHER INTEREST": Elizabeth Prophet to Du Bois, November 14, 1931, Du Bois Papers/UMass. ". . . HAVE HIM WRITE": Lewis, interview with Arnette Williams, September 12, 1993; Du Bois to Yolande, September 24, 1931, Du Bois Papers/UMass.

289. ". . . FACING THE FINANCIAL CRISIS": Joel Spingarn to Du Bois, December 18, 1930, Du Bois Papers/UMass. ". . . FIGHTING RACE PREJUDICE": Du Bois, "Memorandum on the Present and Future Editorial Program of *The Crisis*."

290. ". . . MONOPOLIZE THE SPEECHMAKING": Du Bois quoted, in Carolyn Wedin, *Inheritors of the Spirit: Mary White Ovington and the Founding of the NAACP* (New York: John Wiley & Sons, 1998), 248–49. LOUIS WRIGHT: "Wright, Louis Tompkins," in Logan, ed., *DANB*, 670–71.

291. ". . . WRIGHT RAISED THE ISSUE": Wright first raised this issue on October 13, 1930 in an NAACP board meeting—see the Minutes for October 13, 1930, NAACP, "Board Minutes for 1930". ". . . TO MODERNIZE PROVIDENT HOSPITAL": Minutes from the Annual Meeting of the Trustees of the Julius Rosenwald Fund, Julius Rosenwald Papers, University of Chicago (hereafter JRF/UC), Addenda I: Box III. In July of 1930, the Executive Committee of the Rosenwald Fund approved a request from Flint-Goodridge Hospital (New Orleans) to cover the salaries of "white physicians" who would act as "clinical teachers for the negro medical staff, chiefly in the outpatient department of the Hospital." See Minutes for July 1, 1930, "Meeting of the Executive Committee," JRF/UC, Addenda I: Box III. ". . . GIFTED AND THOROUGHLY UNSELFISH": Du Bois, *Dusk of Dawn: An Essay Towards the Autobiography of a Race Concept* (Millwood, N.Y.: Kraus-Thomson, 1975; orig. pub. 1940), 308. ". . . WITHOUT DISCRIM-INATION": "A Proposed Resolution" [1931], Du Bois Papers/UMass, also in the Minutes of March 9, 1931, NAACP, "Board Minutes for 1930." ". . . ADVOCATED THE SEGREGATION OF JEWISH STUDENTS": Lewis, *When Harlem Was in Vogue*, 256.

291. ". . . AN UNPARDONABLE MISINTERPRETATION": Du Bois to Philadelphia *Tribune*, [n.d.], 1924, Du Bois Papers/UMass. ". . . WHAT DU BOIS HAD ACTUALLY SAID": Du Bois, "The Tragedy of Jim Crow," *The Crisis* (August 1923), 169–72. ". . . A FINE LINE": James Weldon Johnson to Du Bois, October 21, 1924, Du Bois Papers/UMass. ". . . ONE OF THE MOST EXPLOSIVE EDITORIALS": "Segregation", *The Crisis* (January 1934), 20. ". . . I WAS HEART AND SOUL WITH THE ROSENWALD FUND": Du Bois, *Dusk of Dawn*, 309. Interestingly, Mary White Ovington disagreed with White and Wright about the Rosenwald hospital funding. See Mary White Ovington to Walter White, April 6, and June 14, 1932—both in Walter White Correspondence, NAACP Papers, Library of Congress.

292. ". . . MERIT AND PRINCIPLE": H. J. Pinkett, in a letter to Du Bois, would write that "New York is not the United States," in support of Du Bois's call for an overhaul of the NAACP's organizational structure. See H. J. Pinkett to Du Bois, May 5, 1931, Du Bois Papers/UMass. At the same time that the Editor backed Wright's agenda, he presented the board with a proposal to overhaul the governance of the Association. He found the board's resolution of May 1929 subjecting all officers salaried by the NAACP to the authority of the secretary onerous, especially so, as his own salary had been assumed by the Association in July of the previous year. Times had changed since those early days when power needed to be concentrated in a few hands for the sake of fidelity and efficiency, the Editor reasoned. Black Americans had come overwhelmingly to endorse the mission of the NAACP. Its methods, Pinkett wrote, were "so clear and fixed and backed by such widespread public opinion" that the leadership "must give heed to the continual criticism that the Association is run by a small, self-perpetuating clique." Although Johnson's successor had been voted a robust annual salary of $5,500 and invested

with the powers of his office on March 9, 1931, White's hold on the board was still insecure. Even though he had become popular with the heads of some of the largest branches, his assertive personality was a source of frequent resentment among the membership. See the Minutes of March 9, 1931, NAACP, "Board Minutes for 1930." Not only would the new permanent secretary find his control of staff salaries limited by Du Bois's success in getting the 1929 resolution on salaries repealed, Du Bois floated a scheme for the radical overhaul of the Association. He proposed in mid-May that the board of directors should be comprised of "a certain number of candidates" nominated by the annual conferences, that the large municipal branches should also be empowered to elect a single board representative, and that the state and regional branch organizations have the right to elect "certain members" of the board. There was more. In furtherance of that board democracy to which the NAACP was consecrated, the governance of the NAACP was to be vested in the board of directors as an upper chamber and an assembly of delegates chosen by the branches. Objectively, Du Bois's proposed restructuring had much to commend it—personalities aside. The widely held belief that the NAACP had gradually evolved along corporate lines into a highly centralized command structure monopolized by well-intentioned elitists was accurate, as was the Editor's premise that, whatever the gains in efficiency and coherence, a high price had been paid in the loss of rejuvenating contact with many of the issues vital to the membership. Arguably, Du Bois's scheme, modified and duly adopted, might have laid the foundations for a more broadly based Association, more varied in its class, generational, and geographical compositions and energized by them. ". . . DU BOIS HIMSELF": Minutes of April 13, BRDMINS/LC ". . . AGAINST JUDGE PARKER": Wilkins, *Standing Fast*, 91. ". . . HOPELESSLY INEPT": Wilkins, *Standing Fast*, 117. ". . . THICKER THAN SMOG IN LOS ANGELES": Wilkins, *Standing Fast*, 116.
293. ". . . UNBEARABLE": Du Bois, *Autobiography of W.E.B. Du Bois*, 294. ". . . WE MUST HAVE THIS MONEY": Du Bois, "Memorandum to Miss Ovington from Dr. Du Bois," October 6, 1931, Du Bois Papers/UMass. ". . . HARLEM'S DUNBAR BANK": Du Bois to William Pickens, August 10, 1931, Du Bois Papers/UMass. ". . . $1,200.": Du Bois, "Memorandum to Mr. J. E. Spingarn and Mr. Arthur Spingarn," November 28, 1932, ASP/HU. ". . . THE EXPECTED ROSENWALD SUBSIDY": The big debate over the money from the Rosenwald Fund took place in 1930—Walter White wanted it all for himself; J. E. Spingarn ordered that it be shared. See B. Joyce Ross, *J. E. Spingarn and the Rise of the NAACP, 1911–1939* (New York: Atheneum, 1972), 144. Mary White Ovington disagreed with White and Spingarn, suggesting that Du Bois should get half of the grant. See Ovington to White, April 6, 1932, Walter White Correspondence, NAACP Papers, Library of Congress. ". . . AT THE PRESENT TIME": Walter White, "Memorandum from Mr. White to Dr. Du Bois," Du Bois Papers/UMass.
294. ". . . THE WHOLE STAFF": Du Bois, *Autobiography of W.E.B. Du Bois*, 294. ". . . JUST TO OTHERS": Wedin, *Inheritors of the Spirit*, 253. ". . . STAGING AN OPEN REVOLT": Wedin, *Inheritors of the Spirit*, 252. ". . . NULLIFYING MALVAN'S POSITION": The action on *The Crisis* was ruled illegal on a technicality with the Board met on January 4, 1932—see Minutes for January 4, 1932, BRDMINS/LC. ". . . IT IS OUR SOLEMN AND CAREFULLY CONSIDERED OPINION": "To the Board of Directors," signed by Du Bois, Herbert Seligmann, William Pickens, R. W. Bagnall, and Roy Wilkins, in the William Pickens Papers, Schomburg Center for Research in Black Culture, New York Public Library. Wedin's chronology for these two meetings is helpful, but her interpretation is strongly hostile to Du Bois and highly favorable to Ovington and White. See Wedin, *Inheritors of the Spirit*, 254–55.
294. ". . . THE ASSOCIATION'S HANDLING OF THE SCOTTSBORO CASE": Lewis, *When Harlem Was in Vogue*, 272; Dan T. Carter, *Scottsboro: A Tragedy of the American South* (Baton Rouge: Louisiana State University Press, 1969), 89–91; James T. Goodman, *Stories of Scottsboro* (New York: Vintage Books, 1994). ". . . TO DEFEND THE NAACP": See Du Bois, "The Negro and Communism," *The Crisis* (September 1931), 313–315, 318, 320, also in Herbert Aptheker, ed.,: *Crisis Selections* (Millwood, N.Y.: Kraus-Thomson, 1983), 2 Vols., II, 634. ". . . TERRIFIED TERRIER": Du Bois, *Autobiography*, 294. OVINGTON AND SPINGARN: Meier and Rudwick, "The Rise of the Black Secretariat in the NAACP," 117–19; Wedin, *Inheritors of the Spirit*, 254–55; Ross, *J. E. Spingarn*, 141–42. ". . . I DID NOT TRUST WALTER WHITE": Du Bois, *Autobiography*, 294. J. E. Spingarn wrote to Du Bois about the mutiny, "I hope you will do the manly thing, and make a complete retraction," quoted in Wedin, *Inheritors of the Spirit*, 257. As the months passed, the quieter, gentler reign of the dissembling secretary acquired an almost unassailable dominion over the organization that Du Bois had helped found and define. "Any employee who opposed him soon lost his job. Everyone who signed the protest, except Wilkins, lost his position," contended the Editor, "and Wilkins yielded to White in every request."—See Du Bois, *Autobiography*,

294. Bagnall, relieved of duty by the board at the beginning of 1932, was just shy of fifty and worn down by constant travels. Herbert Seligmann had chafed under White's regime and needed little encouragement from the board before deciding to seek a more secure salary source in the business world at the beginning of 1933. Even though Pickens survived White's animosity, serving as director of branches for a total of twenty-two years, his preacherly *modus operandi* increasingly clashed with the corporate culture imposed upon the Association after 1932, and his influence was soon reduced to a bare minimum. Where the Editor saw only machinations and retaliation behind White's motives, room has to be allowed for decisions driven by the prioritizing of resources and the aging out of personnel. The secretary's orchestration of press attacks upon vulnerable politicians, his coordination of branch assaults on unlawful segregation, launching of the embryonic anti-lynching initiative and identifying of targets for the skeletal legal department—all these kept the board busy and the shrinking budget depleted.

295. "... DR. WILL": John Egerton, *Speak Now Against the Day: The Generation before the Civil Rights Movement in the South* (Chapel Hill: Univ. of North Carolina Press, 1994), 47–50. For Rosenwald support of Dillard University, see the Minutes of the Meeting of the Executive Committee, Julius Rosenwald Fund, September 24, 1930, JRF/UC "... SOCIAL FRIEND OF BLACK FOLK": Du Bois, "Dillard University," *The Crisis* (January 1932), 467. "... BEGINS WITH NEGROES": Du Bois, "The Negro College," *The Crisis* (August 1933), 175–77, also in Daniel Walden, ed., *W.E.B. Du Bois: The Crisis Writings* (Greenwich, Conn.: Fawcett, 1972), 176–86. "... THE PASSING OF JULIUS ROSENWALD": Du Bois, "Postscript", *The Crisis* (February 1932), 58–59.

296. "... HARLAN COUNTY": Du Bois, "Miners," *The Crisis* (March 1932), 94, 101, also in Aptheker, ed., *Crisis Selections*, II, 659. Also see Robert Cohen, *When the Old Left Was Young: Student Radical and America's First Mass Student Movement, 1929–1941* (New York: Oxford Univ. Press, 1993), 44–46.

297. "... ARKANSAS SHARECROPPERS": Milton Meltzer, *Brother, Can You Spare a Dime? The Great Depression, 1929–1933* (New York: Facts on File, 1991), 37–38. "... ON PUBLIC RELIEF": Weiss, *National Urban League*, 240. "... THE MACHINE HAS GONE TO PIECES": Du Bois, "Buying and Selling," *The Crisis* (November 1931), 393, also in Aptheker, ed., *Crisis Selections*, II, 643–44.

297. "... EVERY MONTH OF THE YEAR": Du Bois, "Lynchings," *The Crisis* (February 1932), 58, also in Aptheker, ed., *Crisis Selections*, II, 648. Also see, Sitkoff, A New Deal for Blacks, 221.

297. "DERRICOTTE DEATH": Ethel Bedient Gilbert to Miss Leslie Blanchard, Executive National Student Council, YWCA, November 10, 1931, 11-page account. "... UGLY, BAREFOOTED WOMAN": Du Bois, "Dalton, Georgia," *The Crisis* (March 1932), 85–87, also in Aptheker, ed., *Crisis Selections*, II, 651. "... TO LIE THERE AND SUFFER": Du Bois, "Dalton, Georgia," 651. "... NOT ONLY WARDS BUT PRIVATE ROOMS": Du Bois, "Dalton, Georgia," 652.

298. "... DIED IN THE EARLY MORNING OF NOVEMBER 7": Victor Schuster, M.D., of Einstein Medical Center, and Eugene White, M.D., of Case Western Reserve University Hospital, opine that Derricotte had a thyroid condition, a heart condition, and probable internal injuries—this last fact deduced from the symptom of the dried tongue. Could she have been saved, I asked? Schuster, at least, is agnostic. "... I SHALL ALWAYS HAVE TO COMPARE": Gilbert quoted, in Du Bois, "Dalton, Georgia," 653.

299. "... NEGRO EDITORS ON COMMUNISM": Du Bois, "Negro Editors on Communism," *The Crisis* (June 1932), 190–91, also in Aptheker, ed., *Crisis Selections*, II, 660–61, but under the heading of "Colored Editors on Communism." On CPUSA activism on behalf of black Americans, see Rhonda Levine, *Class Struggle in the New Deal: Industrial Labor, Industrial Capital, and the State* (Lawrence, Kans.: Univ. of Kansas Press, 1988), 53–59; Sitkoff, *New Deal for Blacks*, 159. The role of the ILD in Scottsboro, the expulsion from the CPUSA of the hapless August Yokinen, and the Party's rent-strike campaigns in Chicago and New York earned communists a good deal of solid respect among "respectable" African Americans like NAACP board member Murphy. See Du Bois, "Negro Editors on Communism", 661. The opposition ranged from the Atlanta *Daily World's* editor, who warned that associating with communists was too dangerous, to the *Courier's* Vann, whose faith in capitalism was as unshaken as his cynicism about the portability of the ideals of a foreign political system. "If communism ever comes into power at all," Vann huffed, "it will treat the Negro just as the Negro is now treated by the Republicans and the Democrats"—a position not dissimilar to Du Bois's. For that was the other critical unknown of concern to all of the newsmen, emphasized the Editor, whatever they thought of the theory and practice of communism in the Soviet Union—their grave doubts "as to

whether the mass of the working class in America [was] ever going to be brought to accept the equality of colored workers." See "Negro Editors on Communism," in the April and May editions of *The Crisis* for 1932.

300. ". . . THE CONSCIENCE OF A NATION": Du Bois, "Postscript," *The Crisis* (June 1931), 207–8. FLORENCE KELLEY: Du Bois, "Postscript," *The Crisis* (April 1932), 131–32; Du Bois, "Florence Kelly," *Social Work* (October 1966), 99–100, reprinted in Aptheker, ed., *Writings in Periodical Literature*, II, 317–19. ". . . THE EMOLUMENTS OF OFFICE": John Dewey quoted, in Du Bois, "The 23rd Conference of the NAACP," *The Crisis* (July 1932), 219.

300. ". . . WELCOMING OF YOUTH": "The 23rd NAACP Conference," 218. ". . . VOICE THEMSELVES THROUGH IT": "The 23rd NAACP Conference," 18. ". . . HE HAD ALWAYS EXPECTED AS MUCH": Du Bois to Lillian Alexander, June 23, 1933, Du Bois Papers/UMass. In a July 12 memorandum to Wilkins, he expressed his incredulity. He had supposed that a list of persons to be invited had been made up long ago. "If the invitations [went] out before July 15," Du Bois thought it just possible "to get some worthwhile persons to attend a meeting scheduled for the week of August 21." See Du Bois, "Memorandum to Mr. Wilkins from Dr. Du Bois," July 12, 1932, Du Bois Papers/UMass. The Editor appended a *crème de la crème* list to his memorandum of younger generation Talented Tenth that included Arthur Fauset, Allison Davis, Abram Harris, and Frank Horne, Forrester Washington, Hubert Delany, Houston, Schuyler, and Wesley. He had offered, he informed Lillian Alexander, to help when Spingarn proposed the conference, "but Walter did nothing. Therefore, I did nothing." Du Bois to Lillian Alexander, June 23, 1933, Du Bois Papers/UMass. The minutes reveal that the board gave formal consideration to planning Amenia II only on September 12, 1932, but that White and Wilkins did so largely as a concession to Spingarn rather than from any favorable convictions about the proposal. See "Minutes of the Meeting of the Board of Directors," September 12, 1932, Du Bois Papers/UMass. Clearly disappointed, the NAACP president pressed the matter in the final days of December, strongly suggesting that the secretary and the Editor recommence planning a conference for the following summer to which about twenty-five persons ought be invited, he thought. Joel Spingarn, "Memorandum to Mr. White and Dr. Du Bois," December 22, 1932, Du Bois Papers/UMass. *The Crisis* meanwhile continued to ignore Russell's advice about lighter fare, with one indicative exception — Wilkins's debut in July with "Radio Rhythm Makers," a profile of the popular singing quartet known as the Southernaires. See Roy Wilkins, "Radio Rhythm Makers," *The Crisis* (July 1932), 217, 236. An editorial on Hitler's installation as chancellor of the Weimar Republic sarcastically observed that the Western democracies were "at last happy . . . [to] have forced Germany from Socialism to Fascism." See Du Bois, "As the Crow Flies," *The Crisis* (July 1932), 214. In the same column, the position of the two American presidential candidates on racial discrimination was derided: "Mr. Roosevelt's record on the Negro problem is clear. He hasn't any. Mr. Hoover's record on the Negro problem is not clear and in that respect it resembles his record on everything else." Du Bois's antipathy to Roosevelt and his southern running mate was shared by two-thirds of blacks who would vote in the elections that November. See Sitkoff, *New Deal for Blacks*, 41; Du Bois, "As the Crow Flies," 214.

301. ". . . EQUAL SHARES": Du Bois to Edwin Embree, September 15, 1932, Du Bois Papers/UMass. ". . . TO STRIKE AND SUSPEND *CRISIS* OPERATION": Du Bois to Lillian Alexander, November 17, 1932, Du Bois Papers/UMass. On the draconian cuts at *The Crisis*, see Du Bois, "Memorandum to Mr. J. E. Spingarn and Mr. Arthur Spingarn," ASP/HU. These cuts are the context for the firing of Malvan. ". . . MALVAN'S INSUBORDINATION AND FINAL TERMINATION": See "Mr. Menken's Suggestions Regarding the Crisis," March 10, 1932; Du Bois, "Memorandum to Mr. White and Mr. Seligmann" [n.d.]; "Memorandum to Dr. Du Bois from Mr. Wilkins and Mr. Seligman" [n.d.] — all in *Crisis* File, NAACP Papers, Library of Congress. ". . . THE DAY OF THE FATEFUL MEETING": John Hope to Du Bois, July 20, 1932, Du Bois Papers/UMass. Du Bois's darkening mood during this period may have been somewhat ameliorated by a splendid "Literary Dinner" held at the new Harlem YWCA in mid-August, the first in a series of such occasions to be sponsored by *The Crisis* to benefit authors and the magazine. Three hundred persons came to hear Brawley, James Weldon Johnson, Fisher, and White, together with ten other writers, discuss their works under the ceremonial guidance of columnist Heywood Broun. See "A Literary Dinner," *The Crisis* (October 1932), 331. Elizabeth Prophet was in the city for the summer, residing with the Du Boises at the Dunbar. It was her first visit since departing for Paris. See "Woman Artist," *The Crisis* (August 1932), 259. Prophet required attention, but Du Bois's major project was the writing of the first chapters of his book on the reconstruction era, under contract to Harcourt Brace and Company since late October of 1931. A significant feature in the August number

was the large photograph of thirty-six-year-old, Oberlin College graduate student Shirley Graham. Many years later, this wide-eyed musicologist was to become the second Mrs. Du Bois. See "Shirley Graham," *The Crisis* (August 1932), 258.

Chapter 9: A New Racial Philosophy

302. "... EVEN GOOD FRIENDS": W.E.B. Du Bois to Helen Bryan, November 19, 1931, The Papers of W.E.B. Du Bois, Special Collections, W.E.B. Du Bois Library, University of Massachusetts at Amherst (hereafter DuBois Papers/UMass). "... MALVAN HAD BEEN SACKED": Curious letter about Malvan being in hospital with abdominal hemorrhaging; Hazel Brown to Du Bois, March 29, 1933, Du Bois Papers/UMass. "... CIRCULATION RANGE OF ABOUT THIRTEEN THOUSAND": Du Bois to Joel Spingarn and Arthur Spingarn, November 28, 1932, Arthur Spingarn Papers, Moorland-Spingarn Research Center, Howard University, Box 94-20, Folder 446 (hereafter ASP/HU).

302. "... THE ARRIVAL OF HOPE'S": Du Bois to John Hope, January 5, 1931, Hope to Du Bois, December 11, 1932, December 28, 1932, all in Du Bois Papers/UMass. "... A CHANGE OF WORK": W.E.B. Du Bois, *The Autobiography of W.E.B. Du Bois* (New York: International Publishers, 1968).

302. "... AN EARLIER VISITING": Du Bois to John Hope, January 15, 1931, Du Bois Papers/UMass. "... WE COULD DO SO MUCH TOGETHER": John Hope to Du Bois, April 24, 1932, Hope to Du Bois, June 2, 1929, both in Du Bois Papers/UMass. "... DU BOIS TRANSITION": John Hope to Du Bois, December 28, 1932, Du Bois Papers/UMass. "... A.U. PROPOSITION": John Hope to Du Bois, December 28, 1932, Du Bois Papers/UMass.

303. "... RESIGNATION THREAT": Du Bois to Joel Spingarn and Arthur Spingarn, November 28, 1932, Memorandum Box 94-20, Folder 446, ASC/HU. Du Bois to Joel Spingarn, December 14, 1933, Folder 11, James Weldon Johnson Memorial Collection/Collection of American Literature (Small Collection): Beinecke Rare Book and Manuscript Library, Yale University (hereafter JWJMC/YU). BRANCH AND BURTON: Du Bois to Hazel Branch, February 6, 1933, Du Bois Papers/UMass. "... EVOKED GRATITUDE BORDERING": Du Bois to Hazel Branch, April 20, 1933, Du Bois Papers/UMass.

303. "... ANOTHER OF OUR PERIODICAL FIGHTS": Du Bois to Rachel Davis Du Bois, January 3, 1933, Du Bois Papers/UMass. Text of Du Bois's resignation and brief letter to Arthur Spingarn, January 2, 1933, on the withdrawal of the resignation in Countee Cullen Papers: Amistad Research Center, Tulane University (hereafter CCP/ARC). See also Du Bois Memo to NAACP Board detailing terms of his leave at Atlanta University, Minutes for January 20, 1933, BRDMINS/LC. January 20, 1933, NAACP Papers at Library of Congress, Board minutes, January 20, 1933.

303. "... WILLIS SEDAN": Nina to Will, January 31, 1934, Du Bois Papers/UMass. "... POOR GEORGIA JOHNSON": Georgia Douglas Johnson to Du Bois, February 21, 1931, Johnson to Du Bois, June 26, 1933, Du Bois Papers/UMass.

303. "... MEETING FLORENCE READ": Florence Read to Du Bois, December 4, 1928, Du Bois Papers/UMass. "... READ AT THE CLOSE": Read to Du Bois, May 25, 1932, Du Bois to Read [undated], Read to Du Bois, October 8, 1932, all in Du Bois Papers/UMass; Read became President of Spelman College in 1927, succeeding Lucy Tapley. For further information see Florence Matilda Read, *The Story of Spelman College* (Atlanta: 1961). Author is indebted to Virginia Hannon (attended Spelman soon after Read's installation) for a physical description and character typology of Florence Read, telephone interview in NYC, December 23, 1998.

304. "... ELISABETH PROPHET": Nina to Will, n.d. 1933, Du Bois Papers/UMass. "... LIFE AT SPELMAN": Will to Nina, February 6, 1933—an unusually long and warm letter to his wife, Du Bois Papers/UMass. "... BABY DU BOIS": Nina to Will, February 20, 1933, Du Bois Papers/UMass. "... BEGIN TO WORRY": Will to Nina, May 19, 1933, Du Bois Papers/UMass. "... HE PLUNGED INTO HIS TWO COURSES": Du Bois "Marxism and the Negro Problem" in *The Crisis* (May 1833) 103–4, 118, also in Herbert Aptheker, ed., *Crisis Selections*, 2 vols. (Millwood, N.Y.: Kraus-Thomson, 1983), II, 695–99; Du Bois "Our Class Struggle" (July 1933), 164–65, also in Aptheker, ed., *Crisis Selections*, 711–13; David Brighouse, "In Battle for Scholarship: W.E.B. Du Bois and the Return to Atlanta University: 1834–1944" (New Brunswick, N.J.: Unpublished Henry Rutgers University Honors Thesis, May 1998), 14.; For further information see Herbert Aptheker, ed., *Correspondence of W.E.B. Du Bois*, 2 vols. (Amherst: University of Massachusetts Press, 1973/1976), 465.

304. "... INSPIRING": Du Bois to Matthew Boutte, March 13, 1933, Du Bois to Arthur Spingarn, February 27, 1933, Du Bois to Rachel Davis DuBois, March 27, 1933, all in Du Bois Papers/UMass.

". . . STUDENTS AND TEACHING": Du Bois, *Autobiography*, 205. ". . . ONE OF THE INTELLIGENT: Du Bois to Mrs. Louie Shivery, March 29, 1933, Du Bois to Mr. Whittaker [Registrar], April 4, 1933, both in Smith/Shivery Family Papers, Schomburg Center (hereafter SSFP/SCRBC); Lewis, Interview with Veoria Shivery, February 16, 1988. ". . . GODFATHER": Du Bois to Henrietta Shivery [goddaughter], September 1, 1933, SSFP/SCRBC.

305. "ON IRENE DIGGS": Lewis, Interview with James G. Fleming, February 6, 1986; For information on Irene Diggs see Darlene Clark Hine, ed., *Black Women in America*. 2 vols. (Brooklyn, NY: Carlson Publishing, 1993), I., 338.

306. ". . . MARXIST LIBRARY": Du Bois, *Autobiography*, 308. ". . . IT WAS TO BE MARX": David Levering Lewis, *W.E.B. Du Bois: A Reader* (New York: Henry Holt, 1995), 543; Du Bois "Marxism and the Negro Problem" in *The Crisis* (May 1933), 103–4, 118, also in Aptheker, ed., *Crisis Selections*, 695–99. ". . . NEW RACIAL PHILOSOPHY": Du Bois "Toward a New Racial Philosophy" in *The Crisis* (January 1933), 20–21, also in Aptheker, ed., *Crisis Selections*, 683.

306. ". . . ECONOMIC FOUNDATION": Du Bois, *Autobiography*, 290. ". . . NEGRO CHURCH": W.E.B. Du Bois, *The Gift of Black Folk* (Millwood, N.Y.: Kraus-Thomson. 1975), 320.

307. ". . . NO PROOF OF AN INTELLIGENT DEITY": Du Bois to E. Pina Moreno, November 15, 1948, Aptheker, ed., *Correspondence*, III, 223. THE GREAT POLITICAL PHILOSOPHER: Du Bois "Karl Marx and the Negro" in *The Crisis* (March 1933), 55–56, also in Aptheker, ed., *Crisis Selections*, 689; Will Herberg to Du Bois, March 3, 1933, Du Bois to Herberg, March 9, 1933, Herberg to Du Bois, March 3, 1933, Du Bois Papers/UMass. ". . . SIDNEY HOOK": Christopher Phelps, *Young Sidney Hook* (Ithaca, N.Y.: Cornell University Press, 1997), 78. Hook, a thirty-year-old professor advantaged by fourteen weeks of Russian residency and superlative training in philosophy, would end his long, distinguished career celebrated on the political right as an anti-communist socialist par excellence who even refused to allow the reprinting of his brilliant book. In the spring of 1933, however, New York University's first Jewish faculty member predicted that the "dominant attitudes and values of Western and Oriental cultures" were to be supplanted by a social order "avowedly Marxist in inspiration," a prognostication widely regarded as a sure bet in progressive circles. See Sidney Hook, *Towards the Understanding of Karl Marx: A Revolutionary Interpretation* (New York: John Day, 1933). Such was the political temper of many Depression-era intellectuals that, as has been so often recounted, some of the best brains of the hard right began life in the Old Left. See Ella Winter, *Red Virtue: Human Relationships in the New Russia* (New York: Harcourt, Brace, and Company, 1933); ". . . 'YOUNG TURKS' ": African American intellectuals were swept up in Marxist interpretation, e.g., at Howard University, the triumvirate of "Young Turks"—Bunche, Franklin, and Harris, with Sterling Brown and Charlie Houston in close collaboration—generated enough controversy that Charles Thompson, chairman of the education department, and even Locke occasionally dropped by Harrison's "Red Top" Grill, the off-campus cafe where they held forth Saturday nights to sample the polemical excitement. Bunche's mildly Marxist "A Critical Analysis of the Traits and Programs of Minority Groups," appearing in Thompson's *Journal of Negro Education*, was tested in debate at the "red topics round table" on Florida Avenue—See William Darity, Jr., "Soundings and Silences on Race and Social Change: Abram Harris, Jr., and the Great Depression" (courtesy of the author). By the time Doxey Wilkerson, the brilliant education specialist and future CPUSA official, joined the Howard faculty in 1935, the circle of Marxist dilettantes would have taken on a more serious tone. "The whole thing began to broaden more and more," recalled Wilkerson shortly before his death in 1993. Literature professor William Alphaeus Hunton, pharmacy student James Jackson, medical student Henry Callis all thought of themselves as forming an intellectual vanguard seriously committed to the overhaul of the national economy.

307. REVISING MARX: Lewis, *Du Bois Reader*, 538. Daniel Yergain and Joseph Stanislaw, *The Commanding Heights: The Battle Between Government and Market Place that is Remaking the Modern World* (New York: Simon & Schuster, 1998), 12. At its core, Du Bois still conceived of the good society in the virtuous terms described thirty years earlier when he had inveighed against the displacement of idealism by creeping vulgarization and commodification—lamenting in *Souls* the disappearance "of the strife for another and a juster world, the vague dream of righteousness, the mystery of knowing," all of which, he saw "suddenly sink[ing] to a question of cash and a lust for gold." See W.E.B. Du Bois, *Souls of Black Folk* (Millwood, N.Y.: Kraus-Thomson. 1973), 80; Unregulated capitalism offended him by its cultural banality, its cruel and capricious wasting of human and material resources, its manipulative ordering of classes, races, and genders. How then, could he not subscribe to the prophetic science of this "colossal genius . . . with a mind of extraordinary logical keenness and grasp." See Lewis,

Du Bois Reader, 538; if the details of humanity's future might not be exactly as Marx predicted, Du Bois countered that a social revolution was inescapable in which public control of the means of production promoted the equitable distribution of wealth. "It will come by the action of the great majority of men who compose the wage-earning proletariat," the readers of *The Crisis* were assured, "and it will result in the common ownership of all capital, the disappearance of capitalistic exploitaion, and the division of the products and services of industry according to human needs, and not according to the will of the owners of capital." See Lewis, *Du Bois Reader*, 540.

308.   . . . PHANTOM CLASSES: Lewis, *Du Bois Reader*, 542.

308.   ". . . CAPITALISTIC SYSTEM": Lewis, *Du Bois Reader*, 541. "COLORED LABOR HAS NO COMMON GROUND": Lewis, *Du Bois Reader*, 542, 541.

309.   ". . . WORKING-CLASS ARISTOCRACY": Du Bois not only saw this new aristocracy as forming a layer between "the older proletariat and the absentee owners of capital," but he seems to have confused this so-called working-class aristocracy with another relatively new phenomenon, "a new class of technical engineers and managers"—the emergent managerial class featured in the forthcoming works of young Keynesean economists Adolph Berle and John Kenneth Galbraith. Galbraith, *American Capitalism* (Boston: Houghton Mifflin, 1952) coined the term "countervailing powers." "We can only say, as it seems to me, that the Marxian philosophy is a true diagnosis of the situation in Europe in the middle of the 19th century despite some of its logical difficulties. Lewis, *Du Bois Reader*, 543.

310.   ". . . EXPLOIT COLORED LABOR": Lewis, Du Bois, "Marxism and the Negro Problem," *Du Bois Reader*, 542.

310.   "IRON LAW OF WHITENESS": Conceding that this line of reasoning left the Aframerican in a terrible bind—pretty much "where he was before the Russian Revolution," as he had previously written—"Marxism and the Negro Problem" proposed the "only defense" available against exploiting capital and exclusionary labor: "such internal organization as will protect him from both parties, and such practical economic insight as will prevent inside the race group any large development of capitalistic exploitation." Du Bois, "Marxism and the Negro Problem," Lewis, *Du Bois Reader*, 592, 543.

310.   ". . . IMPORTED RUSSIAN COMMUNISM": W.E.B. Du Bois, *Dusk of Dawn* (Millwood, N.Y.: Kraus-Thomson, 1940, 1975), 205. In "Marxism and the Negro Problem" (*The Crisis* May 1933), Du Bois reached a position of Marxian affirmation that bore a curious parallelism, although for different reasons, to the Marxism of the New York anti-Stalinist Marxists about to gather around *Partisan Review*. On the one hand, he would iterate, as would they, an abiding respect for the explanatory potency of scientific socialism. On the other, he would continue to denounce the CPUSA, as would they, though for the opposite reasons that while he deplored the American Party but admired the Soviet regime, the New York intellectuals, Hook, MacDonald, William Phillips, and Phillip Rahv, distanced themselves from the CPUSA because of their hatred of Stalinism. Perhaps a case of the reactions to anti-Semitism by one and to white supremacy by the other. See Alan M. Wald, *The New York Intellectual: the Rise and Decline of the Anti-Stalinist Left from the 1930s to the 1980s* (Chapel Hill: University of North Carolina, 1987). Also note that Will Herberg wrote a piece in Nancy Cunard's *Negro*, "Marxism and the American Negro."

310.   "A MINORITY GROUP LIKE NEGROES": Du Bois, *Autobiography*, 291; Du Bois, "Postscript, The Strategy of the Negro Vote" in *The Crisis* (June 1933), 140–42. "PETTY BOURGEOIS NATIONALISTS": Harry Haywood, "The Struggle for the Feminist Position on the Negro Question in th U.S.A.," in Philip Foner and Herbert Shapiro, eds., *American Communism*, 93–107, 107.

311.   The reactions of African Americans to the Marxist lessons in *The Crisis* are inescapably speculative, although many subscribers must have been provoked by their revelations and implications. Walter White was ecstatic, calling "Marxism and the Negro Problem" "superb" and by long odds "the most sane and important analysis yet written." Walter White to Du Bois, May 1933, Du Bois Papers/ UMass. Only a few months were to pass, however, before White would find himself disconcerted by the full implications of Du Bois's thinking.

311.   ". . . 'U.S. WILL COME TO COMMUNISM' ": "U.S. Will Come to Communism, Du Bois Tells Conference," full-text appeared in Baltimore *Afro-American*. May 20, 1933; "Sees Nation's Gain in Negro Welfare" reported in *New York Times*, Sunday, May 14, 1933; The Economic Status of the Negro Conference represented a galaxy of civil rights, academic, federal, and philanthropic notables: economists Broadus Mitchell and Paul Douglas of Hopkins and Chicago universities, respectively; sociologists Frazier and Johnson; university presidents Hope, Moton, Thomas Elsa Jones, and Mordecai Johnson of Atlanta, Tuskegee, Fisk, and Howard, respectively; the Urban League's Jones, Hill, and Ira

Reid; Tobias of the YMCA; Alexander of the CIC; Mary Anderson, director of the Labor Department's Women's Bureau; Embree and Alfred K. Stern of the Rosenwald Fund. Although none of the major players in the federal government's alphabet agencies addressed the meeting, it was broadly understood that the conference was meant to serve as an opportunity to communicate to the New Deal establishment the pressing concerns of black Americans. ". . . MAGNIFICENT ADDRESS": Herman Feldman to Du Bois, May 25, 1933, Du Bois Papers/UMass; Unsigned evaluation of "The Rosenwald Conference," in *The Crisis* (July 1933), 156–57.

314. ". . . TODAY, A FAMINE IS ON": Hazel Branch to Du Bois, March 30, 1933, Du Bois Papers/UMass. ". . . IF HOPE INVITED HIM"; HE WAS SIMPLY STUNNED": Will to Nina, March 17, 1933, Du Bois Papers/UMass. ". . . DU BOIS HAD COUNSELED": Du Bois to Joel Spingarn, Memo dated December 9, 1932, Joel Spingarn's Collection: Manuscript Division, New York Public Library (hereafter JSC/NYPL); NAACP Board Minutes of March 14, 1933, include Joel Spingarn's resignation as well as Arthur Spingarn's proposal for a second Amenia conference and organizing committee consisting of Du Bois, Walter White, and Joel Spingarn; ". . . DU BOIS WAS PROMISED": Du Bois to Joel E. Spingarn, March 17, 1933, Du Bois Papers/UMass.

315. "THWARTED BY THE SECRETARY": Joel Spingarn to Mary Ovington, March 28, 1933, JSC/NYPL; Spingarn to James Weldon Johnson, April 4, 1933, JWJMC/YU; Spingarn has been called an "economic liberal" by his biographer, an important qualification to any assessment of his disaffection from the NAACP and of the apparent radicalism motivating it. See B. Joyce Ross, *Joel E. Spingarn and the Rise of the NAACP: 1909–1939* (New York: Atheneum, 1972), 13; If he and Du Bois shared the cosmopolitan culture of men of letters, their prescriptions for economic recovery could hardly have been more dissimilar. Du Bois was already headed down the quixotic path to Marxism and ethnic solidarity. Spingarn, the racial progressive, though shaken and troubled in the aftermath of the 1929 crash, would continue to put his trust in enlightened capitalism.

315. ". . . NEITHER THE SECRETARY": Du Bois to Joel Spingarn, March 14, 1933, JSC/HU"; ". . . WHITE NOW MADE A CONVINCING SHOW"; ". . . HE SETTLED ON THIRTY-TWO": Joel Spingarn to Du Bois, April 7, 1933, Walter White to Du Bois, April 8, 1933, both in Du Bois Papers/UMass.

316. ". . . SLIGHTEST HURT TO INTELLIGENT DISCUSSION": Du Bois to Joel Spingarn, April 10, 1933, JSC/HU. ". . . IT MIGHT BE WELL TO CONSIDER AN APPOINTMENT": Dean Sage to Trevor Arnett, February 19, 1932, General Education Board, Rockefeller Archives; Jackson Davis to Trevor Arnett, July 23, 1930, Atlanta University, Rockefeller Archive: See also NY *Times* obituary for Arnett, "Trevor Arnett, Finance Expert" (April 1, 1955). Obituary cites his interest in Negro education and identification with the Atlanta University Center. ". . . REORGANIZATION OF NAACP": Du Bois, "Memorandum to John Hope," April 10, 1933, Du Bois Papers/UMass. CRAWFORD RESIGNATION: Du Bois to Henry Crawford, April 20, 1933, Du Bois Papers/UMass.

316. "TINKERING WITH OUR PRESENT ORGANIZATION": The full text of Du Bois's reorganization program is in Group I, Subject File: Amenia, NAACP/LC. ". . . A THREE-DAY PLENARY BOARD MEETING": Joel Spingarn to Du Bois, April 21, 1933, Du Bois Papers/UMass. BEFORE THE DECEMBER RESIGNATION DEADLINE": ". . . ENLIST THE SUPPORT OF COLORED PEOPLE": Joel Spingarn to Du Bois, April 26, 1933, "We are both of the opinion that your proposals are neither feasible nor advisable and that they would inevitably result in the disruption of the organization," Du Bois Papers/UMass.

317. ". . . ABOUT HIS NEXT STEP": Lillian Alexander to Du Bois, April 25, 1933, Du Bois to Alexander, May 18, 1933, both in Du Bois Papers/UMass. "TREND OF THE NAACP": Du Bois to Walter White, June 16, 1933, Du Bois Papers/UMass. ". . . JOB WITH PRESIDENT ROOSEVELT": Du Bois to Davis DuBois, March 27, 1933, Du Bois Papers/UMass. ". . . A BLISTERING ACCOUNT": Hamilton Fish Armstrong to Du Bois, March 14, 1933, Du Bois to Hamilton Fish Armstrong, April 3, 1933, both in Du Bois Papers/UMass.

317. "LIBERIA": White asked Du Bois to represent the NAACP regarding Liberia in Washington, D.C., in July 1933; Walter White to Du Bois, July 22, 1933; Du Bois went to Washington, D.C. to see the Secretary of State about Liberia, Du Bois to Robert L. Vann, August, 31, 1933, all in Du Bois Papers/UMass. Dramatic developments at the end of 1932 had caused Washington to impose a de facto suspension of Liberia's sovereignty. The unit price of rubber had dropped from 75 cents to five on the world market in the wake of the Depression, a calamity ferociously impacting Liberian workers whose daily wages were cut from a shilling to six pence by the American company. Saddled with extortionate interest payments on the 1926 Firestone loan along with the burden of salaries for a bloated corps of

American financial advisers that, combined together, consumed one-third of the country's total revenues, the Liberian government had finally balked at meeting its foreign obligations until the League of Nations fulfilled its commitment as mediator. Matters stalemated with the United States refusing to recognize the new government of President Edwin Barclay and the arrival in Monrovia of an American major general to take virtual control of the country. The NAACP had lodged a formal protest of American highhandedness with the new Roosevelt administration. Supplied with a cache of League of Nations documents sent from Geneva by Anna Graves, another tireless officer of the Women's International Circle for Peace and a loyal pan-Africanist, Du Bois produced an exposé of corporate avarice and high-level Washington legerdemain that almost evoked the horrors perpetrated in the Belgian Congo. True, he had played his own naive and not insignificant part in the Liberian travesty. But he had not then "lost faith in the capitalistic system," and had believed that Firestone was headed by a "man of vision," Herbert Aptheker, ed., W.E.B. *Du Bois: Writings in Periodical Literature* (Millwood, N.Y.: Kraus-Thomson, 1982), 333. It was also true that the West African country was inefficient, gullible, and corrupt, Du Bois admitted, although his *Foreign Affairs* article greatly underplayed the government's slave labor practices and spendthrift self-victimization. Neither honesty nor efficiency would have altered the exploitative outcome, however, concluded Du Bois. Liberia's chief crime, as she fought against Goliath odds to defer her debt payments and keep her independence, "[was] to be black and poor in a rich, white World; and in precisely that portion of the world where color is ruthlessly exploited as a foundation for American and European wealth." His *Foreign Affairs* article attracted considerable notice in the black press and was commented on in government and diplomatic circles, although the attention it generated would have little more than ceremonial influence on the State Department interview accorded the Editor several weeks later, Du Bois "Liberia, the League and the United States" in *Foreign Affairs* (July 1933), 682–95, also in Aptheker, ed., *Writings in Periodical Literature*, 332.

318. "... UNDER THE GENERAL DIRECTION OF THE EDITOR": Du Bois to Arthur Spingarn, January 2, 1933, ASC/HU. "... THE CANDIDATE DU BOIS HAD IN MIND": Joel Spingarn to Du Bois, June 5, 1933, Du Bois Papers/UMass. "... ORGAN OF THE MASSES": Expressing a desire to work for the magazine in letters written during the winter and spring of 1933, the young college teacher seemed indifferent to the financial risks; George Streator to Du Bois, January 11, 1932, January 31, 1932, February 18, 1932, February 26, 1932, May 28, 1933, all in Du Bois Papers/UMass; With six years of print-shop apprenticeship under his belt, a year of selling life insurance, and recent experience preparing school catalogues and designing ads, Streator was optimism personified. At a time when subscribers were falling away like dying leaves, Streator and his wife, Olive (daughter of future Brigadier General Benjamin O. Davis, Sr.), had dipped into their modest resources in the spring of 1932 in order to send a small monetary contribution for the work of the magazine. "*The Crisis* must not die," the couple exclaimed by letter, George Streator to Du Bois, April 11, 1933, August 25, 1933, both in Du Bois Papers/UMass. DESPERATE EFFORT TO FINISH: Du Bois to Mary White Ovington, September 26, 1933, Du Bois Papers/UMass.

318. AMENIA CONFERENCE: Du Bois, *Dusk*, 301, 302. The Amenia organizing committee consisted of conference host Joel Spingarn, in whose name (rather than the Association's) invitations were issued.: NAACP Secretary White was "delighted . . . to attend," Walter White to Joel Spingarn, April 26, 1933, JSC/HU. The shuttling of paper between Troutbeck, 69 Fifth Avenue, and Rockefeller Hall during mid-April produced two lists from which forty-three names were eventually culled to receive invitations to the conference. A delighted Virginia Alexander suggested in her acceptance letter that the conferees be given reading assignments. "One, two or three books," she thought, along with magazine articles and commencement addresses—"(Dr. Du Bois's on 'Education and Work', for instance, at Howard University)," Virginia Alexander to Joel Spingarn, May 24, 1933, JSC/HU. As her presence at Amenia was to be that of a senior observer, Du Bois stalwart Lillian Alexander was careful not to appear "to meddle" when she urged Joel Spingarn not to forget the ladies. She noted that Anna Arnold (Hedgeman), the dynamic young director of the Harlem YWCA, and Wenonah Bond, two of the most "advanced and most level headed thinkers and leaders of young women," had somehow been overlooked, Virginia Alexander to Joel Spingarn, June 26, 1933, JSC/HU. Arnold and Bond received their Amenia invitations. Eleven of the thirty-two invitees were women. A dimming light from a literary era that already felt oddly remote, Jessie Fauset seems never to have been considered, even though her last novel gamely appeared earlier that year. Nor was Zora Hurston, whose outre manners and maverick mind must have been regarded as ill-suited to the high-toned gravity of the occasion.

319. ". . . FOUR OF THE ELDER STATESMEN": Du Bois, *Dusk*, 300. HOWARD THURMAN": Jack Salzman, et al, eds., *Encyclopedia of African American Culture and History* (NY: Simon & Schuster, 1996), V, 7 (hereafter EAACH).

319. ". . . BEDROCK SURVEY": Benjamin Mays, *The Negro Church*. On Mays, see Salzman, et al. eds., *EAACH*, III, 1727. JOINT COMMITTEE ON NATIONAL RECOVERY: See Hilmar Jensen, "The Rise of the African American Left: John P. Davis and the National Negro Congress" (Unpublished manuscript in author's possession); Harvard Sitkoff, *The New Deal and Blacks* (New York: Oxford University Press, 1978), 47. Allison Davis was invited but did not reply. Curiously, Du Bois wrote that he barely knew Davis. "Mr. Davis and his friends [Joint Committee on Negro Recovery] should be treated as individuals of intelligence and not as the representatives of any mass movement." See Du Bois to Myra Colson Callis, August 28, 1933, Du Bois Papers/Mass.

320. ". . . A WEALTHY SAN FRANCISCO PATRON": Langston Hughes to Joel Spingarn, August 1933, Joel Spingarn Papers: Moorland-Spingarn Research Center, Howard University (hereafter JSP/HU). ". . . WILLIAM HASTIE HAD HOPED": Rayford Logan to Joel Spingarn, August 12, 1933, JSP/HU.

320. ". . . A NUMBER HAD ADVANCED DEGREES": Wenonah Bond gives the number of BAs as 14, MAs as 8 and Ph.Ds as 3. FRAZIER: Du Bois to Joel Spingarn, October 16, 1933, JSP/HU. . . . STERLING BROWN: Sterling Brown to Joel Spingarn, August 9, 1933. JSP/HU. ". . . NEGRO INTELLIGENTSIA": Ben Keppel, *The World of Democracy: Ralph Bunche, Kenneth B. Clark, Lorraine Hansberry, and the Cultural Politics of Race* (Cambridge: Harvard University Press, 1995), 47.

320. ". . . THE THINKERS AND DRINKERS FACULTY GROUP": Anthony M. Platt, *E. Franklin Frazier Reconsidered* (New Brunswick, N.J.: Rutgers University Press, 1991), 105; Peter Novik, *That Noble Dream: The 'Objectivity Question' and the American Historical Profession* (New York: Cambridge University Press, 1988), 245.

320. YOUNG TURKS: For information on the "Young Turks" see Wayne J. Urban, *Black Scholar: Horace Mann Bond, 1904–1972* (Athens: University of Georgia Press, 1992); Ralph Bunche, *A World View of Race* (Washington, D.C.: Associates in Negro Folk Education, 1934); Ben Keppel, *op. cit.*; Walter Jackson, *op. cit.*; Platt, *op. cit.* ". . . HOUSTON'S POSITION AS VICE DEAN": B. Joyce Ross, *J. E. Spingarn and the Rise of the NAACP: 1911–1939*, (New York: Atheneum, 1972), 228; Robert Zangrando, *NAACP Crusade Against Lynching*, (Philadelphia: Temple University Press, 1980), 130.

320. ". . . POLITICAL STATUS AND CONDITION OF THE NEGRO RACE": Du Bois to John Hope, January 5, 1931, Du Bois Papers/UMass. "PROGRAMS, IDEOLOGIES, TACTICS AND ACHIEVEMENTS": An earlier version of this 1940 essay appeared in the July 1935 issue of the *Journal of Negro Education*.

321. ALL SHADES . . . CONSERVATIVE: Frazier, in Anthony M. Platt, *E. Franklin Frazier Reconsidered*, (New Brunswick, N.J.: Rutgers University Press, 1991), 186. ". . . THE HOWARD GROUP": On Ralph Bunche see Walter A. Jackson, *Gunnar Myrdal and America's Conscience: Social Engineering and Racial Liberalism, 1938–1987* (Chapel Hill: University of North Carolina Press, 1990) on unpublished Bunche ms, "Conceptions and Ideologies of the Negro Problem," 429 and his work on the Carnegie/Myrdal Study, 395–96; see also Gunnar Myrdal, *An American Dilemma*, 2 vols. (New York: McGraw-Hill, 1944, 1964), chapters 22, 37, and especially chapter 39, 833 [note a]. ON STERLING BROWN: see Jean Wagner, *Black Poets of the United States: From Paul Laurence Dunbar to Langston Hughes* (Urbana: University of Illinois Press, 1973). See also David Levering Lewis, ed., *Harlem Renaissance Reader* (New York: Viking, 1994), 227; Salzman, eds. *op. cit.*, 456; Platt, *op. cit.*

322. ". . . SATURDAY MORNING BELONGED TO THE RADICALS": B. Joyce Ross, *op. cit.*, 179–80. ". . . IMPORT OF THE YOUNG TURKS' ARGUMENT": The resolutions that had just been voted at the twenty-fourth annual NAACP convention that July might have encouraged the radicals at Amenia. The delegates meeting in Chicago had approved a document demanding redistribution of wealth through progressive taxation of large incomes, the "conduct of industry and government for the benefit of the many and not the few," and the enactment of old age, sickness, and unemployment insurance."

322. THE BLACK WORKER: Abram Harris and Sterling Spero, *The Black Worker: The Negro and the Labor Movement*, (New York: Columbia University Press, 1931). Harris revered the editor, but kept his independence, writing Du Bois soon after Amenia that in spite of "fundamental disagreement there is hardly a single living man for whom I have greater affection and genuine admiration." See Keith P. Griffler, *What Price Alliance? Black Radicals Confront White Labor, 1918–1938* (New York: Garland Publishing, 1995), 124; Du Bois, *Dusk*, 300. Frazier, the thirty-nine year-old Chicago-trained sociologist insisted that he was not advocating some form of bourgeois separatism or "Negro ghetto, stratified according to bourgeois society," but what he called "revolutionary nationalism." As he expanded upon

it, Frazier's idea of developing racial solidarity "as a cohesive force among people who were exploited by the white master class" sounded curiously like the separatist thesis Du Bois was to advance in less than a year. Platt, *op. cit.*, 188.

322. "... A STRONG FOUNDATION FOR SELF-SUPPORT": Du Bois, *Dusk*, 301. "... DID NOT APPRECI-ATE THE JOKE": Du Bois, *Dusk*, 302. "... FATHER FELT THAT THIS WAS A TRAGIC MISTAKE": David Levering Lewis interview with Edward Spingarn, March 4, 1989. "... CONSENSUS FOR CHANGE": On the range of reactions to Amenia, see Du Bois to Joel Spingarn, March 14, 1933, William Hastie to Spingarn, August 9, 1933, Charles H. Houston to Spingarn, August 30, 1933, Langston Hughes to Spingarn, August 1933, Rayford Logan to Spingarn, August 12, 1933, all in JSC/HU.

323. "... WELFARE AND SOCIAL UPLIFT": Du Bois, *Dusk*, 300. "... CONTINUATION COMMITTEE": Jensen, *op. cit.*, 245. Zangrando, *op. cit.*, 109; Abram Harris would reproach Joel Spingarn about Amenia and revising the NAACP: Harris to Spingarn, July 27, 1934, JSP/NYPL. For what was actu-ally accomplished at Amenia, see text (undated 1933), "From the Publicity Committee, Second Amenia Conference" in Du Bois Papers/UMass. "... THE EDITOR REVEALED HIS CAUTIOUS OPTI-MISM": Du Bois to Joel Spingarn, JSC/HU. "... THE END OF IT ALL": Du Bois, *Dusk*, 302; Du Bois, "Youth and Age at Amenia," in *The Crisis* (October, 1933), 226–27. Du Bois, "Memorandum to the President of Atlanta University," August 3, 1933, Du Bois Papers/UMass. Minutes for November 13, 1933, BRDMINS/LC. "... ASSOCIATION GUARANTEED SEVEN THOUSAND DOLLARS": Du Bois, "Memo-randum to Board of Directors of the NAACP," September 8, 1933, ASC/HU, Du Bois to Walter White, August 4, 1933.

324. "... DAISY WILSON, DU BOIS'S SECRETARY": Du Bois, "To the Board of Directors of the Crisis Publishing Company," September 28, 1933, in BRDMINS/LC. "... HOPE AND FLORENCE READ AP-PROVED": Du Bois to Florence Read, August 16, 1933, C. T. Crocker to Du Bois, September 14, 1933, both in Du Bois Papers/UMass. "... WILL'S PLANS FOR NINA": Nina to Will, June 27, 1933, Du Bois Papers/UMass. "... LOVE TO THE WHOLE FAMILY": Will to Nina, March 17, 1933; Will to Nina, May 19, 1933, both in Du Bois Papers/UMass.

325. "... SUCH EDITORIALS AS HE MAY WISH TO CONTRIBUTE"; Board Minutes for November 13, 1933, BRDMINS/LC.

325. "... TELLING YOU THIS IN STRICT CONFIDENCE"; Joel Spingarn to Du Bois, August 24, 1933, Du Bois Papers/UMass. On Henry Morganthau, see William O'Neill, *A Better World: The Great Schism, Stalinism and the American Intellectual* (New York: Simon & Schuster, 1982), 58; Doris Kearns Goodwin, *No Ordinary Time: Franklin and Eleanor Roosevelt: The Home Front in World War II*, (New York: Simon & Schuster, 1994), passim.

326. "... MORGENTHAU CHOOSE HUNT": Henry Hunt to Du Bois, November 22, 1933, Du Bois to Joel Spingarn, September 27, 1933, both in Du Bois Papers/UMass. "... PORKBARRELENSIS AFRI-CANUS": John Hope Franklin, *Slavery to Freedom: A History of American Negroes* (New York: Alfred Knopf, 1947), 392. "... DISMAL CONSEQUENCES OF AAA": Sitkoff, *op. cit.*, 54.

326. NRA: For alphabet discrimination data, see Sitkoff, *op. cit.*; Nancy J. Weiss, *The National Urban League, 1910–1940* (New York: Oxford University Press, 1974); Kenneth O'Reilly, *Nixon's Piano: Pres-idents and Racial Politics from Washington to Clinton* (New York: The Free Press, 1995), 113–15. For explication of New Deal corporatism and the NIRA philosophy, see John Garraty, *The Great Depres-sion: An Inquiry into the Causes, Course, and Consequences of the Worldwide Depression of the Ninteen-Thirties* (New York: Harcourt Brace Jovanovich, 1986). "... QUIXOTIC DUO": Jensen, *op. cit.*; Keith P. Griffler, *What Price Alliance? Black Radicals Confront White Labor, 1918–1938* (New York: Garland Pub., 1995), 134.

327. "... HAROLD ICKES WAS RECOVERING": The 2-tier arrangement prevailed. Davis had only a moral victory, see Jensen, *op. cit.*, 251, 253; Griffler, *op. cit.*, 140. "... MAKING NO MENTION OF DAVIS": On Du Bois's resistent attitude toward John Davis, see George Streator to Du Bois, October 5, 1933, Du Bois Papers/UMass. See also Aptheker, ed., *Crisis Selections*, II, 718. Jensen, *op. cit.*, 237. "... CRISIS FOR OCTOBER 1933 ROARED": Du Bois "Postscript" in *The Crisis* (October, 1933), 236–37. "... FORT VALLEY'S HUNT AT FCA": Federal service biographies were gleaned from *DANB, EAACH*, Darity, Jensen, Sitkoff, and O'Reilly. Mary McCloud Bethune arrived at NYA in 1935. BEATEN INTO SUBMISSION: Du Bois, "On Being Ashamed of Oneself: An Essay on Race Pride" in *The Crisis* (Sep-tember 1933), 199–200, also in Aptheker, ed., *Crisis Selections*, 717.

329. "... KNOWING LESS ABOUT NEGROES THAN ESKIMOS": On race and Eleanor Roosevelt, see Goodwyn, *op. cit.* and Blanche Wiesen Cook, *Eleanor Roosevelt, 1933–1938* (New York: Viking, 1999).

On the 4-hour meeting, see Jensen, *op. cit.*, 256; O'Reilly, *op. cit.*, 115; Walter White, *op. cit.*, 168. "... OUR ANXIOUS COLORED BRETHREN": O'Reilly, *op. cit.*, 114. Du Bois was, however, gratified when FDR spoke against lynching in a fireside chat, see Du Bois "Roosevelt" in *The Crisis* (January 1934), 20–21, also in Aptheker, ed., *Crisis Selections*, II, 729; O'Reilly, *op. cit.*, 114; White, *op. cit.*, 169.

330. "... THE MAILED FIST HAS GOT TO BE CLENCHED": Du Bois "William Monroe Trotter," in *The Crisis* (May 1934), 134, also in Aptheker, ed., *Crisis Selections*, II, 753. "... HE IS OF NEGRO DESCENT": Du Bois, "On Being Ashamed of Oneself: An Essay on Race Pride," in *The Crisis* (September 1933), 199–200; also in Aptheker, ed., *Crisis Selections*, II, 714–17. "... ASSIMILATION HAD BEEN REDUCED TO A MIRAGE": Du Bois, *ibid.*, 714: The assimilation process was going to be slower on account of the badge of color; but then, after all, it was not so much the matter of physical assimilation as of spiritual and psychic amalgamation with the American people.

331. "... YEARS OF COMPLAINT": A. Clement MacNeal, former editor of the spikey Chicago *Whip* and the new NAACP branch president, had infused a self-assured impatience into what had long been a cozy, top-down relationship between the city's black leadership and the white power structure. "... WOMEN FOUND IT ESPECIALLY GALLING": Beth T. Bates, "A New Crowd Challenges Agenda of the Old Guard in the NAACP, 1933–1941" in *American Historical Review* (date unknown).

332. "... WILKINS'S SALARY": Rosenwald's brother, Lessing, chairman of the Sears board, had not even thought it "worth the trouble" to answer MacNeal's letter "as it was couched in so unpleasant a tone," wrote William Rosenwald. Despite the rift with the NACW, which adopted the boycott, and the awkwardness it caused Field Secretary Daisy Lampkin, a candidate for the NACW presidency, national headquarters informed its Chicago branch that a nationwide boycott of Sears was untimely.

Another controversy played out in the black press during this period and did much to spread the belief that policy and politics were hand in glove at national headquarters. The association's investigation of conditions at Harlem Hospital resulted in a positive report concerning treatment and promotion of African American nurses, the preparation of interns, and optimal use of physicians' skills. The *Amsterdam News* and the CPUSA joined together in shrilly denouncing the report as a "whitewash" by the NAACP's special hospital committee (on which Du Bois served), the newspaper howling that in protecting Louis Wright and his friends "Walter White and the NAACP have done that race a disservice that cannot be forgiven." Although he calmed the jittery Secretary with an assurance that the fracas would soon blow over, the editor may not have regretted seeing how much distress the blistering community censure caused the public-relations-minded White. See Bates, "A New Crowd".

332. CRAWFORD CASE: White, *op. cit.*, 154.

333. "... WE GLADLY WOULD HAVE SUPPLIED YOU": Walter White to Du Bois, June 23, 1933, Du Bois Papers/UMass. Walter White, "George Crawford — Symbol" in *The Crisis* (January 1934), 15. In fact, Streator withdrew Crawford editorial, and explained why. Du Bois to George Streator, April 11, 1934, Du Bois Papers/UMass.: "... DON'T FAIL ME OR THE ASSOCIATION NOW": Joel Spingarn to Du Bois, October 10, 1933. Du Bois Papers/UMass.

334. "... THERE WERE TWO ALTERNATIVES": Du Bois, *Dusk*, 312. ... HARRIS WAS KNOWN FOR HIS INDEPENDENT INTELLECT: Du Bois to Joel Spingarn, October 16, 1933, Du Bois Papers/UMass. Du Bois, in a letter to George Streator, wrote favorably of Martha Gruening, October 16, 1933, Du Bois Papers/UMass. "... THESE PEOPLE STOOD IN THE WAY": Abram Harris to Du Bois, January 6, 1934. Du Bois Papers/UMass, also in Aptheker, ed., *Correspondence*, I, 473. A MILD HEART ATTACK: Du Bois to Lillian Alexander, November 11, 1933, Du Bois Papers/UMass.

335. "THE EDITOR STILL SMOLDERED": Du Bois to Joel Spingarn, January 27, 1933, Du Bois Papers/UMass. The Chairman was less sure of the reforming course of action he had encouraged so recently in a moment of frustration. He was frankly weary of the whole business, weary and increasingly disengaged as Harcourt, Brace and Company, the publishing house in which Spingarn was a founding partner, absorbed his energies. Then, too, he was finding Du Bois's co-operatist and reorganizational notions increasingly outre. Meanwhile, White and Wilkins steadily consolidated their influence with Francis Grimke, Carl Murphy, Louis Wright, and several other powerful Board members who were now much more concerned about organizational solvency than with bold new departures. See Carl Murphy to NAACP Board of Directors, September 9, 1933, Du Bois Papers/UMass.

335. Du Bois, "The Right to Work," *The Crisis* (April 1933), also in *W.E.B. Du Bois Writings* (New York: Library of America, 1986), 1235. "... THE THOUGHT SURELY SUGGESTED": Du Bois, "Pan-Africa and New Racial Philosophy" in *The Crisis* (November 1933), 247, 262, also in Aptheker, ed., *Crisis Selections*, II, 721–23, 721. Du Bois, "Segregation," *The Crisis* (May 1934), also in Aptheker, ed., *Crisis*

Selections, II, 755. ". . . VERY REAL DANGER FROM USE OF YOUR NAME": Walter White Telegram to Du Bois, November 24, 1933, Du Bois Papers/UMass. Clarence Pickett to Du Bois, November 22, 1933, Clark Foreman to Du Bois, December 5, 1933, both in Du Bois Papers/UMass. ". . . OPPOSITION TO SEGREGATION": Du Bois, "Segregation" in *The Crisis* (January 1934), 20, also in Aptheker, ed. *Crisis Selections*, II 727. ". . . WITHOUT CONSULTING THE EDITOR IN CHIEF": For details of the December 11, Board coup, see Du Bois to Joel Spingarn, December 14, 1933, Du Bois Papers/UMass; see also Minutes for December 11, 1933, BRDMINS/LC.

Du Bois's November memorandum reiterating his September threat to resign on January 1, unless the magazine received a five thousand-dollar subsidy the following year, had provoked several last-straw expressions of exasperation from the Board. W.E.B. Du Bois to Board of Directors of the NAACP, November 11, 1933, ASC/HU.

336. JOEL SPINGARN EXPLAINS: Joel Spingarn to Du Bois, December 12, 1933. Du Bois Papers/UMass. Du Bois to Hazel Branch, December 14, 1933, Du Bois Papers/UMass. STREATOR'S EDITORIAL AUTHORITY AND SALARY: "Memorandum from Dr. Du Bois to Mr. Spingarn," December 13, 1933, Folder 447, ASC/HU. For correspondence on this Board decision between the Spingarns, Du Bois and Streator, see Du Bois to Arthur Spingarn, December 15, George Streator to Joel Spingarn, December 16, 1933, Joel Spingarn to Du Bois, December 16, Du Bois to George Streator, December 16, Du Bois Papers/UMass, Du Bois to Joel Spingarn, May 22, 1933, NAACP/LC ". . . PLEASE DO YOUR WORST": Hazel Branch to Du Bois, December 12, 1933, Joel Spingarn to Du Bois, December 16, 1933, Du Bois Papers/UMass.

337. ". . . THE WHOLE MOVEMENT MIGHT AS WELL FOLD UP": George Streator to Joel Spingarn, December 16, 1933; Du Bois to Chairman of Board of Directors of NAACP, December 27, 1933. Du Bois Papers/UMass. SEGREGATION COULD BE POSITIVE: Du Bois, "Segregation," *The Crisis*. (January 1934), 20. Also in Aptheker, ed., *Crisis Selections*, II, 727. "SEGREGATION" HAD COME INSTEAD: See, Du Bois's explanatory letter to Harry Davis about the attempts to oust him and Spingarn's reversal of *Crisis* policy. Du Bois to Harry Davis, January 16, 1934, in Du Bois Papers/UMass. Also in Aptheker, ed., *The Correspondence of W.E.B. Du Bois*, University of Massachusetts, 1973, 474. See also the text of December 27, 1933, Du Bois resignation letter sent to Joel Spingarn, in ASC/HU.

338. ". . . ACCOMPLISHED THE GREATEST ADVANCE": Du Bois, "Segregation," 20. "OH, MR. DU BOIS! HOW COULD YOU": William Henry Hastie, *Washington Afro-American*, January 25, 1934. WHITE OBJECTS: Clark Forman to Du Bois, December 5, 1933, Du Bois Papers/UMass. ". . . MEETING MRS. ROOSEVELT AT THE WHITE HOUSE": Walter White to Du Bois, February 8, 1934, Du Bois Papers/ UMass.

338. BUDGED IN ITS OPPOSITION TO SEGREGATION: White to Du Bois, January 17, 1934, Du Bois Papers/UMass. Also in Aptheker, ed., *Correspondence*, 476. For the full texts of exchanges over Eleanor Roosevelt, the Arthurdale, West Virginia settlement and segregation, see in Walter White Letters— HR/NAACP folder. HE RETURNED WHITE'S LETTER: Du Bois to White, January 17, 1934, Du Bois Papers/UMass. Also Aptheker, ed., *Correspondence*, 475. SEGREGATION SYMPOSIUM: Du Bois to Walter White, January 11, 1934, Du Bois Papers/UMass. HE'S NEITHER STRAIGHT NOR HONEST: Du Bois to Lillian Alexander, December 15, 1933, Du Bois Papers/UMass PERSONALLY, HE LIKED THE MAN: Robert Vann to Du Bois, December 26, 1930. Du Bois Papers/UMass. Also in Aptheker, ed., *Correspondence*, 432. AS WHITE MEN WHO WERE JEWS: If he assumed that the Chairman would feed him to the integrationist lions, Du Bois must have been pleased when Joel Spingarn shared the substance of his confidential memorandum to White on the explosive subject. "I told him," Spingarn revealed, that the record would show that the Association had "never 'defined' its attitude on segregation, but had merely authorized concrete acts." Joel Spingarn to Du Bois, January 16, 1934, Du Bois Papers/ UMass. Spingarn had reminded White of the Amenia Conference's vote in favor of "cultural nationalism for the American Negro." It was akin to the concept of cultural and political separation espoused, he said, by Ludwig Lewisohn and "certain advanced groups of Jews" who were opposed to all forms of "assimilation," Joel Spingarn to Walter White, January 10, 1934, NAACP/LC. Like it or not, Spingarn predicted, Zionism and "self-imposed 'segregation' " were part of a "strong contemporary trend."

White's irate memo: After twenty years of believing that he was fighting for integration, he was "frankly not interested in the Association unless that is the policy," he declared. Cultural nationalism or "racialism" was a vastly different thing, in the Secretary's opinion, "from acceptance of segregation without protest from the United States government or the states." Walter White to Joel Spingarn, January 15, 1934. Du Bois Papers/UMass.

339. SEGREGATION WAS A FACT OF LIFE: Du Bois, "A Free Forum," *Crisis*. (February 1934), Also in Aptheker, ed., *Crisis Selections*, II, 732. OPEN LETTER TO CARL MURPHY: January 5, 1934, Walter White Papers, NAACP/LC. EXASPERATION OF THE EDITOR: See Walter White to Martha Gruening, January 10, 1934, NAACP/LC.

Old friends like both Alexanders, Dabney, and Crawford, Georgia Johnson, and others either generally remained silent or gave Du Bois the benefit of further elaboration. Further elaboration came with "The NAACP and Race Segregation" in the February 1934 *Crisis* announcing next month's open forum. The public, still unsure of the full implications of the thesis, responded guardedly.

340. ". . . SOMETHING LIKE THE CULTURAL NATIONALISM OF ZIONISTS": Joel Spingarn, in "Segregation: A Symposium," *The Crisis* (March 1934), 79, 82. See also, Du Bois, *Dusk of Dawn*, 307.

David H. Pierce, a symposium contributor from Cleveland, Ohio, had no tolerance for such theorizing, flatly reproving a position that involved "too great a retreat." Furthermore, the present order was not, as Du Bois seemed to believe, "the permanently established order," objected Pierce, *ibid.*, 80. Kelly Miller and George Schuyler contended that segregation in the North was gradually receding before more effective civil rights strategies. Both saw heartening evidence of merit overcoming prejudice. LAMENTING THAT DU BOIS WAS "SLIPPING": Manning Marable, *W.E.B. Du Bois: Black Radical Democrat* (Boston: Twayne Publishing, 1986), 141. ALARMED BOARD MEMBERS: Walter White Correspondence, March 1934, NAACP/LC. "The Board of Directors on Segregation," *The Crisis* (May 1934), 149. Also in Aptheker, ed., *Crisis Selections*, II, 761. ON BOOKER WASHINGTON: College students, August Meier and Elliot Rudwick, eds., *Along the Color Line: Explorations in the Black Experience*, University of Illinois, 1976, 115. A WISE GENERAL: Meier and Rudwick, eds., *Along the Color Line*, 115–116.

341. HE GOES WHERE HE WILL IN NEW YORK CITY: W.E.B. Du Bois, "Segregation in the North," *Crisis*, (April 1934) 115–17. Also in Aptheker, ed., *Crisis Selections*, 746, 745.

341. SPINGARN QUOTED HIM AS SAYING: Joel Spingarn to Amy Spingarn, November 22, 1926. JSC/HU. Significantly, Joel Spingarn warned Walter White not to tangle with Du Bois over segregation because he was vulnerable to charge of being white, Joel Spingarn to Walter White, January 10, 1934, NAACP/LC. ". . . THE DEBATE IS ONE OF DU BOIS VERSUS WHITE": Meier and Rudwick, eds., *Along the Color Line*, 115. ". . . DEEPLY PAINED, JOEL SPINGARN": Joel Spingarn to Du Bois, March 27, 1934, Du Bois Papers/UMass. ". . . SCHUYLER, EMBITTERED BY DU BOIS": Meier and Rudwick, eds., *Along the Color Line*, 279. See also, George Schuyler to Du Bois, January 27, 1932, Du Bois Papers/UMass.

342. ". . . THE CHIEF CHAMPION OF EQUAL RIGHTS FOR BLACK"; Frances W. Grimke, "Dr. Grimke on Segregation," *The Crisis* (June 1934), 174. Also in Aptheker, ed., *Crisis Selections*, II, 762. "THE UPPER CLASS COLORED WORLD": Du Bois, *Dusk of Dawn*, 313.

342. ". . . THE EDITOR'S IDEOLOGY": Making the most of his injuries, White humbly appealed to James Weldon Johnson and other Association elders. Claiming to be at a loss to comprehend the Editor's ingratitude and malice, White whined to the sympathetic Johnson that it was "somewhat disheartening when we have cut our force and salaries, gone practically without literature, which has hurt the Association, to pay over to *The Crisis* during the last four years more than thirty thousand dollars from funds of the Association and then on top of all this to be accused of trying to 'oust' him." Walter White to James Weldon Johnson, February 24, 1934, JWJ/Yale. More accurately, however, Du Bois would oust himself, with the full cooperation of the Secretary. Because his was a leadership "solely of ideas," as he said by way of justification later, he could never compromise those ideas. "The question of leaving was only a matter of time," he sighed. Du Bois, *Dusk of Dawn*, 312 And so, with the icy rectitude of a leader who knew that he "never was, nor ever will be, personally popular," Du Bois forced the Board to make the only choice consonant with its conservative character. Du Bois, *Dusk of Dawn*, 303.

343. "THE END OF PACIFISM": Stephen Wise, "Parallel Between Hitlerism and the Persecution of Negroes," *Crisis*. (May 1934), 127–29. See also, Tracy B. Strong and Herbert Aysoar, *Right in her Soul: The Life of Anna Louise Strong*, London, 1983. ". . . BUT NEGRO POVERTY AND IDLENESS": Du Bois, "Segregation," *Crisis*, (May 1934), 147. Also in Aptheker, ed., *Crisis Selections*, II, 755.

343. IS THE BOARD OF THE NAACP AFRAID: "The Board of Directors on Segregation" *Crisis*. (May 1934), 149. Also in Aptheker, ed., *Crisis Selections*, II, 762. NO SALARIED OFFICER OF THE ASSOCIATION: Minutes of Board of Directors, April 23 and May 14, 1933, NAACP/LC. See also, Bruce Kellner, ed., *The Harlem Renaissance Dictionary*, Westport, Conn.: Greenwood Press, 98. HE ENCLOSED HIS IMMEDIATE RESIGNATION: Du Bois to the Board of Directors of the NAACP, May 21, 1934, Du Bois

Papers/UMass. Also in Aptheker, ed., *Correspondence*, I, 478. DU BOIS AGREED TO STAY PENDING: Board Minutes, May 14, 1933, NAACP/LC, Also in Aptheker, ed., *Correspondence*, I, 473. "GAVE UP MY CONNECTION WITH THE ASSOCIATION": Du Bois, *Dusk of Dawn*, 313.

344. "WE ARE CAST BACK UPON OURSELVES": Du Bois, "Counsels of Despair," "The Conservation of Races," *The Crisis* (June 1934), 182–84. Also in Aptheker, ed., *Crisis Selections*, II, 765–69.

345. "SOMEDAY SMASH ALL RACE SEPARATION": Du Bois, *The Crisis.* (June 1934), 182–84. Also in, Aptheker, *Crisis Selections*, II, 768. FIRM RESPONSE HAD BEEN: W.E.B. Du Bois, "Westward Ho!", *The Crisis.* (May 1934), 149. Also in Aptheker, ed., *Crisis Selections*, II, 759. ON THE WHOLE I AM RATHER PLEASED: Du Bois, *The Crisis.* (June 1934), 182–84. Also in Aptheker, ed., *Crisis Selections*, II, 767. LOVEJOY, HOWEVER, WAS WHITE: Owen Lovejoy to Du Bois, June 18, 1934, Du Bois Papers/UMass. Also in Aptheker, ed., *Correspondence*, I, 481.

346. "JEWS ACCEPT THEIR FATE": J. B. Watson, "Du Bois and Segregation." Francis Grimke also had an article in (June 1934), *The Crisis* — 'Segregation'. Also, Jacob Weinstein, 'The Jew and the Negro' in same issue." *The Crisis*, (August 1934), 243–44. ". . . HE INFORMED THE BOARD": Du Bois to the Board of Directors, June 16, 1934, Du Bois Papers/UMass. Also in Aptheker, ed., *Correspondence*, I, 479. ". . . FURTHER TEMPORIZING": Walter White to Joel Spingarn, June 12, 1934, Carl Murphy to Walter White, June 9, 1934, Irving C. Mollison to Board of Directors, June 3, 1934, Walter White Collection, NAACP/LC.

347. DEPARTURE WAS ACCEPTED: E. Franklin Frazier to Walter White, May 17, 1934, Walter White to E. Franklin Frazier, May 21 1934 in E. Franklin Frazier Papers, Moorland-Spingarn Center, Howard University [hereafter EFF/MSCHU] It seems clear that on the day after his resignation letter, dated, June 26, 1934, Du Bois left for Chicago and Mildred Jones — they attended the World's Fair. Du Bois to Mildred Jones, July 2, 1934. Du Bois Papers/UMass. ". . . NOW WE ARE RID OF OUR OCTOPUS": Mary White Ovington to Oswald Garrison Villard, July 22, 1934; Oswald Garrison Villard Papers, Houghton Library, Harvard University. MY DEMAND FOR A CHANGE: "Dr. Du Bois Resigns," *The Crisis*, (August 1934), 245–46. Also in Aptheker, ed., *Crisis Selections*, II, 771.

348. SIMPLY TAKING THE NEGRO RACE TO ANOTHER PLACE: On his resignation, see Virginia Alexander to Du Bois, July 10, 1934, Du Bois Papers/UMass; and Shirley Graham in Aptheker, ed., *Correspondence*, I. ". . . I AM SIMPLY CHANGING": Quoted from, Du Bois to Carrie W. Clifford, July 19, 1934, Du Bois Papers/UMass.

Chapter 10: Atlanta: Black Reconstruction *and Casanova Unbound*

349. ". . . NAACP": Lillian Alexander to Du Bois, December 1934; Du Bois Papers/UMass; Robert L. Zangrando, The NAACP Crusade Against Lynching, 1909–1950 (Philadelphia: Temple University Press, 1980); Ibid, 130.

350. ". . . ROSENWALD FUND": Reports vary as to exact figures and details. See Edwin Embree to DuBois, January 9, 1931; Embree to Du Bois, January 17, 1931; Embree to Du Bois, February 16, 1931, all in Julius Rosenwald Fund Arcives, Fisk University (hereafter RosFund Archiv/FU); Du Bois to NAACP Board of Directors, May 9, 1931, Du Bois Papers/UMass. See also Herbert Aptheker's Introduction to W.E.B. Du Bois, *Black Reconstruction* (Millwood, N.Y.: Kraus-Thomson, 1963), 11.

350. ". . . HARCOURT": Alfred Harcourt to Du Bois, September 11, 1931; Du Bois to Harcourt, September, 23, 1931; Du Bois to Harcourt, October 21, 1931; Harcourt to Du Bois, October 22, 1931; Du Bois to Harcourt, October 28, 1931, Du Bois Papers/UMass. Also in Herbert Aptheker, ed., *The Correspondence of W.E.B. Du Bois*, 3 vols. (Amherst, MA: University of Massachusetts, 1973), I., 442–44. ". . . AMERICAN HISTORICAL ASSOCIATION": Du Bois to Edwin Embree, December 19, 1930; Du Bois, "Reconstruction and the Benefits" in *American Historical Review* (July 1910), 781–99, also in Herbert Aptheker, ed., *Writings by W.E.B. Du Bois in Periodicals Edited by Others*, 4 vols. (Millwood, N.Y.: Kraus-Thomson, 1982), II., 5–22; For information on U. B. Phillips see August Meier and Elliot Rudwick, Black History and the Historical Profession, 1915–1980 (Urbana: University of Illinois Press, 1986); see also Merton L. Dillon, *Ulrich Bushnell Phillips: Historian of the Old South* (Baton Rouge: Louisiana State University, 1985); For information on William A. Dunning see Herbert Aptheker's Introduction to W.E.B. Du Bois, *Black Reconstruction, op. cit.*, 7.; Du Bois, "A Negro Nation within the Nation" in Current History (June 1935), 265–70, also in Aptheker, ed., *Writings in Periodical Literature*, III, 1–6.

351. ". . . SOUTHERN HISTORIOGRAPHY": James Ford Rhodes, *History of the United States from the*

Compromise of 1850 to the McKinley-Bryan Campaign of 1896, 8 vols. (Port Washington, N.Y.: Kennikatt Press, 1967), VI, 2; Claude G. Bowers, *The Tragic Era: the Revolution after Lincoln* (Cambridge, Mass.: The Literary Guild of America, 1929), 56.

352. "... RADICAL RECONSTRUCTION": John Hope Franklin, *Reconstruction After the Civil War* (Chicago: University of Chicago, 1960), 42; James S. Pike, *The Prostate State, South Carolina under Negro Government* (New York: Loring & Mussey, 1935), 17. "... THE NEGRO IS INFERIOR": Peter Novick, *That Noble Dream: the 'Objectivity Question' and the American Historical Profession* (New York: Cambridge University Press, 1988); Albert Bushnell Hart, The Southern South (New York: D. Appleton & Co., 1910); *Woodrow Wilson, Division and Reunion, 1829–1909* (New York: Longsman, Green & Co., 1920). "... NOT ALL SHAM": Rhodes, *op. cit.*, 201; Hans L. Trefousse, *Reconstruction: America's First Effort at Racial Democracy* (Malabar, Fla: Krieger, 1999); Howard Rabinowitz, ed., *Southern Black Leaders of the Reconstruction Era* (Urbana: University of Illinois Press, 1982).

352. "... WILLIAM ARCHIBALD DUNNING": Du Bois, *Black Reconstruction, op. cit.*, 717; Novick, *op. cit.*, 84; Rhodes, *op. cit.*; Rudwick and Meier, *op. cit.*, 96; William A. Dunning, *Essays on the Civil War and Reconstruction*, introduced by David Herbert Donald (New York: Harper, 1965), viii; Rabinowitz, *op. cit.*; Du Bois, *Black Reconstruction*, 719; Novick, *op. cit.*, 77.

354. "... DUNNING'S BEST STUDENTS": Dunning, *Essays on the Civil War and Reconstruction*, introduced by David Herbert Donald; Novick, *op. cit.*, 228, reports on C. Vann Woodward grinding his teeth in J. G. D'Rouilhac Hamilton's racist lectures while a doctoral candidate at the University of North Carolina. Meier and Rudwick, *op. cit.*, 111–12; John Hope Franklin, *Reconstruction After the Civil War* (Chicago: University of Chicago Press, 1960), 236. "... 'SPOILED' THROUGH CONTACT WITH CARPETBAGGERS": Ibid., 102, 135. "... FREEDMEN'S BUREAU": Walter L. Fleming, *Civil War and Reconstruction in Alabama* (New York: Columbia University Press, 1905), 627. "... THE SOUTHERN VIEW": Novick, op cit., 77.

356. "CURRENTS IN AMERICAN HISTORY": Works on influence of Progressive historians: Richard Hofstadter, *The Progressive Historians: James, Beard, Parrington* (Chicago: University of Chicago Press, 1968, 1979); Gerald N. Grob and George Athan Billias, eds., *Interpretations of American History: Patterns and Perspectives*, vol. I: to 1877, 5th ed. (New York: The Free Press, 1987), 218; Novick, *op. cit.*, 92–97. Also, see John Mack Faragher, *Rereading Frederick Jackson Turner: The Significance of the Frontier in American History and Other Essays* (New York: Henry Holt and Co., 1994), 27–77. "... NO STRIKING DEVELOPMENTS IN INTELLIGENCE": Charles and Mary Beard, *Rise of American Civilization* (New York: Macmillan Co., 1927, 1956), 116. "... STEAL OR KILL": Du Bois, *Black Reconstruction*, 725; see "Cuney, Norris Wright," in Rayford W. Logan and Michael R. Winston, eds., *Dictionary of American Negro Biography* (New York: W. W. Norton & Co., 1982), 151 (hereafter *DANB*). "... REMARKABLE JOHN R. LYNCH": See "John Roy Lynch," in *DANB*, 407–9. "... TEXTBOOK SUITABLE FOR NEGRO HISTORY COURSES": Meier and Rudwick, *op. cit.*, 8; ON BLACK HISTORIANS, see Meier and Rudwick, *op. cit.*; and Novick, *op. cit.*, 231–2.

357. "... NEGRO IS THE CENTRAL THREAD": W.E.B. Du Bois, *The Gift of Black Folk* (Millwood, N.Y.: Kraus-Thomson, 1924, 1975), 15. "... I AM WHITE": W.E.B. Du Bois, *Darkwater Voices From Within the Veil* (Millwood, N.Y.: Kraus-Thomson, 1921, 1975), 34. "... THEORY OF HUMAN CULTURE": Du Bois, *Darkwater*, 44. "... HAD NEVER SEEN A NIGGER": Novick, *op cit.*, 75. "... PHILLIP'S PROBLEMATIC MASTERPIECE": Meier and Rudwick, *op cit.*, 4.

358. ON REVIEWS OF *AMERICAN NEGRO SLAVERY*: see Merton L. Dillion, Ulrich Bonnell Phillips: *Histories of the Old South* (Baton Rouge: Louisiana State University, 1985), 111–112. "... USAGES OF THE PLANTATION-BORN UNIVERSITY OF MICHIGAN PROFESSOR": Herbert Aptheker, ed., *Book Reviews by W.E.B. Du Bois* (Millwood, N.Y.: Kraus-Thomson, 1975), 58. "... SLAVERY INVOLVED ORDINARY HUMAN LABOR PROBLEMS": Aptheker, ed., *Book Revs.*, 59. "... A MODEL OF CRITICISM": David Levering Lewis, *W.E.B. Du Bois: Biography of a Race, 1868–1919* (New York: Henry Holt, 1993), 112. "... A CONDEMNATION UNANSWERED BY MR. PHILLIPS": Aptheker, ed., *Book Revs.*, 60.

359. "... NO ONE WAS MORE CAPABLE": Aptheker's Introduction to W.E.B. Du Bois, *Black Reconstruction*, 7; "... RECEIVING A FINISHED MANUSCRIPT": Alfred Harcourt to Du Bois, December 18, 1933, Du Bois Papers/UMass.; "... CRACKS IN THE SOLID SOUTH": Novick, *op cit.*, 462. "... SHOWING US THE TORTURE CHAMBERS": Claude G. Bowers, *The Tragic Era: The Revolution After Lincoln* (Literary Guild of America, 1929), vi; "... ECONOMIC STATUS OF THE RACES": Bowers, *op cit.*, 60.

360. "... 'THOU ART THE MAN!'": Aptheker's Introduction to Du Bois, *Black Reconstruction*, 9. "... NEGRO'S SIDE OF THE STORY": Ibid., 9.

361. "... THE AUTHOR READILY ASSENTED": Original work titled W.E.B. Du Bois, *Black Reconstruction of Democracy in America: An Essay Toward a History of the Part Which Black Folk Played in the Attempt to Reconstruct Democracy in America, 1860–1880*, in Aptheker's Introduction to W.E.B. Du Bois, *Black Reconstruction*, 12; "... 'WILL WRITE MORE LATER' ": Mildred B. Jones to Du Bois, April 20, 1933, Du Bois Papers/UMass; "... A STATE STUDY OF RECONSTRUCTION": Du Bois to Rachel Davis Du Bois, March 27, 1933, Du Bois Papers/UMass; "... MOST UNREALISTIC SCHEDULES": Du Bois to Charles Pearce (of Harcourt, Brace), March 23, 1933, Du Bois Papers/UMass; "... 'TOO MANY FIG-URES' ": Aptheker's Introduction to W.E.B. Du Bois, *Black Reconstruction*, 13.; "... 'NOTHING FOR ME TO DO' ": Aptheker's Introduction to W.E.B. Du Bois, *Black Reconstruction*, 14.

362. "... 'NO VACATION' ": Du Bois to John Hope, September 14, 1933, Du Bois Papers/UMass; EVENTS AND CONVERSATIONS WITH SARELLA SHOOK: Sarella Shook to Du Bois, September 14, 1933, Du Bois Papers/UMass, Sarella Shook to Du Bois, June 20, 1933, Du Bois Papers/UMass. "... WRITE NINA." Du Bois to Nina, October 4, 1933, Du Bois Papers/UMass.

362. "... 'FINISHED ON DECEMBER 1' ": Du Bois to Mildred Jones, December 21, 1933, Du Bois Papers/UMass. "... 'A VERY DIFFICULT JOB' ": Aptheker's Introduction to W.E.B. Du Bois, *Black Reconstruction*, 14; "... ONE THOUSAND DOLLAR GRANT": Frederick P. Keppel to Du Bois, March 10, 1934, Du Bois Papers/UMass; ON RESEARCHERS AND READERS OF *Black Reconstruction*, see Emmet E. Dorsey (Howard University History Dept.) to Du Bois, n.d. 1931, Du Bois Papers/UMass; Du Bois to Mrs. Lewis Chandler, September 22, 1934, Du Bois Papers/UMass; Aptheker's Introduction to W.E.B. Du Bois, *Black Reconstruction*, 20, Herbert Aptheker, ed., *The Correspondence of W.E.B. Du Bois*, II (Amherst, University of Massachusetts Press, 1976), 22. "... ON E. FRANKLIN FRAZIER WORKING FOR DU BOIS". Du Bois to E. Franklin Frazier, October 13, 1933, E. Franklin Frazier Papers/ Moorland-Spingarn Center, Howard Univeristy (hereafter EFF/MSCHU). GOOD EXAMPLE OF RAYFORD LOGAN ASSISTING: Du Bois to Rayford Logan, November 1, 1934, Du Bois Papers/UMass.

363. ON NAMING CHAPTER 10 of *Black Reconstruction*: Aptheker's Introduction to W.E.B. Du Bois, *Black Reconstruction*, 41. "... USE OF THE TERM PROLETARIAT": Aptheker's Introduction to W.E.B. Du Bois, *Black Reconstruction*, 41. "... REDUCE HIS COURSE LOAD": Du Bois to John Hope, June 18, 1934, Du Bois Papers/UMass. "... WITHDRAWAL OF DEPARTMENTAL SECRETARY": Du Bois to Ira Reid, April 23, 1934, Du Bois Papers/UMass. "... RELIEVED TO GET FIRST 160 PAGES": Aptheker, ed., *Correspondence*, II, 15.

364. DISCUSSIONS WITH HARCOURT: Aptheker, ed., *Correspondence*, II, 18; *Ibid.*, 17. "... CUPBOARD WAS PRETTY BARE": Aptheker's Introduction to W.E.B. Du Bois, *Black Reconstruction*, 19. "... PUBLICATION DATE": David Levering Lewis's Introduction to W.E.B. Du Bois, *Black Reconstruction in America, 1860–1880* (New York: Atheneum, 1935, 1992), xi. Translation rendered by Jack Cargill and John Lenaghen.

364. "... DENIGRATION PREVAILING IN UPPER MIDDLE-BROW PUBLICATIONS": Aptheker's Introduction to W.E.B. Du Bois, *Black Reconstruction*, 22. " '... WHITE PROLETARIAT FREE": Jonathan Daniels, Book Review of *Black Reconstruction* by W.E.B. Du Bois, *Book-of-the-Month Club News* (July 1935). "... HEARTS DAILIES": *Ibid.*, 22.

365. " '... IF ANYTHING FINER HAS BEEN WRITTEN.' ": Lewis Gannett, "Books & Things," *New York Herald Tribune*, June 13, 1935. *NEW YORK SUN* REVIEW: Aptheker's Introduction to W.E.B. Du Bois, *Black Reconstruction*, 24. "... SPLENDIDLY RECAPTURED": *Ibid.*, 28. "... SUGGESTIVE AS IT WAS SUS-PECT": Lewis's Introduction to W.E.B. Du Bois, *Black Reconstruction*, xii. "... TIMES REVIEW": *Ibid.*, xii.

366. " '... GET THE PRESIDENT TO READ IT": Aphtheker, ed., *Correspondence*, II, 25. " '... SMEAR THE NEGRO'S PART": *Correspondence*, II, 24.

367. ON CORRUPTION AND LIMITED BLACK CONTROL OF RECONSTRUCTION POLITICS: Eric Foner, *Reconstruction: America's Unfinished Revolution, 1863–1877* (New York: Harper & Row, 1988), 352; A. A. Taylor, *The Negro in South Carolina During Reconstruction* (Washington, D.C.: Association for the Study of Negro Life and History, 1924), 123. "... NEGRO LEGISLATORS": Foner, *op. cit.*, 354. "... GEARING UP TO WRITE": Francis Butler Simkins and Robert Hilliard Woody, *South Carolina During Reconstruction* (Chapel Hill: University of North Carolina Press, 1932). " '... DEMOCRATIC INSTRUMENT OF GOVERNMENT' ": A. A. Taylor, *The Negro in the Reconstruction of Virginia* (Washington, D.C.: Association for Study of Negro Life and History, 1926), 262. " '... PROTECT THE POLIT-ICAL RIGHTS' ": Simkins and Woody, *op. cit.*, 547.

368. " '... FREE, FREE, FREE' ": Du Bois, *Black Reconstruction*, 124. " '... EVERYTHING BLACK WAS

HIDEOUS' ": *Ibid.*, 125. ". . . SONATA BUILDS": *Ibid.*, 124. " '. . . PROVOCATIVE.": John R. Selby, Book Review of W.E.B. Du Bois, *Black Reconstruction*, in *Richmond Times Dispatch*, June 1935.

369. ". . . FULCRUM OF INDUSTRIAL REVOLUTION": Du Bois, *Black Reconstruction*, 5. ". . . TEN MILLION": The actual number of slaves imported into USA is given as 10 million by Du Bois in *Gift of Black Folk*, based on a 60 million total. On page 147, Du Bois wrote, "It cost Negro Africa perhaps 60 million souls to land ten million slaves in America." Also, see David Eltis, *Economic Growth and the Ending of the Transatlantic Slave Trade* (New York: Oxford University Press, 1987), 35. ". . . TRIANGULAR TRADE": Eric Williams, *Capitalism and Slavery* (Chapel Hill: University of North Carolina Press, 1944, 1994); Eltis, *op. cit.*, 4, *et passim*. After the Asiento as part of Treaty of Utrecht [1713] ending War of the Spanish Succession, UK became world's leading slave trader [Williams, 40]. Du Bois Papers Inventory indicates four letters—first in 1945. In one letter to Ruth Anna Fisher, Du Bois spells out capitalism-slavery thesis completely: "I look upon the development of the African slave trade through chartered companies as the beginning of modern international capitalism and imperialism." Du Bois to Ruth Anna Fisher, December 3, 1934, Du Bois Papers, UMass.

370. ". . . THOMAS CARLYLE'S WITTICISM": Du Bois, *Black Reconstruction*, 85. " '. . . HIDDEN BENEATH A DIFFERENT COLOR OF SKIN": Du Bois, *Black Reconstruction*, 88.

371. " '. . . RACE RELATIONS IN THE LOWER SOUTH' ": Joel Williamson, *New People: Miscegenation and Mulattoes in the United States* (Baton Rouge: Louisiana State University Press, 1995), 25, 2. " '. . . KEEPING THE WHITE MAN SUPERIOR' ": Du Bois, *Black Reconstruction*, 80. ". . . CITIZEN POLICE.": John Hope Franklin called my attention to this antebellum constabulary role. See John Hope Franklin and Loren Schweninger, *Runaway Slaves: Rebels on the Plantation* (New York: Oxford University Press, 1999). ". . . SOUTHERN WHITE LABORERS": Du Bois, *Black Reconstruction*, 680. ". . . HYSTERICAL ONE-DROP RULE": See "whiteness" literature: David Roediger, *Wages of Whiteness: Race and the Making of the American Working Class* (London: Verso, 1991); Matthew Frye Jacobson, *Whiteness of a Different Color: European Immigrants and the Alchemy of Race* (Cambridge: Harvard University Press, 1998); Matthew P. Guterl, *Investing in Color: A Cultural History of Race, 1900–1940* (Cambridge: Harvard University Press, forthcoming). ". . . COLORFUL HISTORY OF ALABAMA": Walter Fleming, *Civil War and Reconstruction in Alabama* (New York: Columbia University, 1905), 207; For a history on the subservience of the Negro to the Confederate States of America, see James Ford Rhodes, *History of the United States from the Compromise of 1850 to the McKinley-Bryan Campaign of 1896*, vol. 6. (Port Washington, N.Y.: 1906), 45. ". . . CATEGORICAL REPUDIATION":Sterling D. Spero, "The Negro's Role," Book Review of W.E.B. Du Bois, *Black Reconstruction*, *The Nation*, July 24, 1935.

371–72. " '. . . GENERAL STRIKE": Dan Georgakas, "General Strike," in *Encyclopedia of the American Left*, edited by Mary Jo Buhle, Paul Buhle, and Dan Georgakas (Urbana: University of Illinois Press, 1992), 266. ". . . SELF PRESERVATION": See Bell I. Wiley, *Southern Negroes 1861–1865* 2nd ed. (1953), on widespread 'disloyalty' of slaves if given a chance to flee. ". . . WHOLESALE EVACUATION": Du Bois, *Black Reconstruction*, 67.

". . . NEGRO TROOPS": Joseph T. Glatthaar, *Forged in Battle: The Civil War Alliance of Black Soldiers and White Officers* (New York: Free Press, 1990), 71. " '. . . RETURN FUGITIVE SLAVES' ": Du Bois, *Black Reconstruction*, 57. ". . . POSTWAR LAMENT": Kenneth M. Stampp, *The Era of Reconstruction, 1865–1877* (New York: Vintage, 1965), 121. ". . . CRUCIAL COMPONENT IN NORTH'S VICTORY": *Ibid.*, 121; Foner, *Reconstruction*, xvii.

372. " '. . . AMERICAN ASSUMPTION' ": The historians' debate during 1860's as to whether the political economy of the Cotton Kingdom was 'precapitalist' certainly owed something to Du Bois, even though Eugene Genovese attributed his thesis to Max Weber and U. B. Phillips. See what Du Bois wrote in Chapter 1, "The Black Worker": "[The planter] could not use higher wages to induce better work or a larger supply of labor. He could not allow his labor to become intelligent." " '. . . GREAT WAIL OF DESPAIR' ": Du Bois, *Black Reconstruction*, 183. " '. . . NORTHERN INDUSTRY' ": Du Bois, *Black Reconstruction*, 185; See also Du Bois, *Black Reconstruction*, 40, and Eugene D. Genovese, *Political Economy of Slavery: Studies in the Economy and Society of the Slave South* (New York: Vintage Books, 1961, 1965), 17. ". . . FREEDMEN'S BUREAU'S SUCCESS": On the implications of Du Bois's "American Assumption," see Foner, *Reconstruction*, 71, for Field Order 15—"a blueprint for the transformation of Southern society." Also, Foner's take on Radical Reconstruction being a "civic ideology" (233). See also Eric Anderson and Alfred A. Moss, Jr., eds., *The Facts of Reconstruction, Essays in Honor of John Hope Franklin* (Baton Rouge: Louisiana State University, 1991), 35: on land redistribution—"never truly viable options in an America with such a strong ethic of laissez-faire."

373. "'. . . VICTORIOUS INDUSTRIAL CAPITAL": Spero, *op. cit.* ". . . LAND REDISTRIBUTION": Foner, *Reconstruction*, 117; Du Bois, *Black Reconstruction*, 367–68. ". . . IGNORE THE CONTRADICTION": *Ibid.*, 378.

374. "'. . . SHALL THEY USE THE TORCH AND DYNAMITE'": Du Bois, *Black Reconstruction*, 703. ". . . CURE FOR THE RACE PROBLEM": W.E.B. Du Bois, *The Autobiography of W.E.B. Du Bois: A Soliloquy on Viewing My Life from the Last Decade of Its First Century* (International Publishers Co., 1968, 1983), 197.

480–481. "'. . . TO PREJUDICE OR BUTTRESS A LIFE'": Du Bois, *Black Reconstruction*, 725. ". . . THEY DESCENDED INTO HELL": *Ibid.*, 727. ". . . FLAMES OF JEALOUS MURDER": *Ibid.*, 728.

481–482. ". . . BUNCHE'S INVITATION": Aptheker, ed., *Correspondence*, II, 114. ". . . RESIGNATION IN FRUSTRATION": B. Joyce Ross, *J. E. Spingarn and The Rise of the NAACP, 1911–1939* (New York: Atheneum, 1972), 241; Abram Harris to Du Bois, July 11, 1934, Du Bois Papers/UMass. ". . . SHOW-PIECE CRITIQUE": Aptheker, ed., Correspondence, I, 473. HARRIS' REACTION TO BLACK RECONSTRUCTION: Lewis, *Introduction to Black Reconstruction*, xv. "'. . . READ [THE BOOK] WITH DUE CAUTION": Ralph J. Bunche, "Reconstruction Reinterpreted," Book Review of W.E.B. Du Bois, *Black Reconstruction, Journal of Negro Education* 4 (October 1935), 570. "'. . . LIMITED BOURGEOIS DEMOCRACY": See, for example, a typical letter congratulating Du Bois on *Black Reconstruction* from Horace Cayton, but violently objecting to separation thesis, Horace Cayton, to Du Bois, September 14, 1935, Du Bois Papers/UMass. Curiously, Martha Gruening wrote Du Bois that she was assigned *Black Reconstruction* by *New Republic*—but Harris got it: Martha Gruening to Du Bois, October 4, 1934, Du Bois Papers/UMass. Miller accompanied Langston Hughes on the ill-fated Russian film project, see David Levering Lewis, *When Harlem Was in Vogue* (New York: Alfred A. Knopf, 1984), 288–90.

376. C. VANN WOODWARD INTERVIEWED DU BOIS: Meier and Rudwick, *op. cit.*, 111. ". . . DUNNINGITE LECTURES": Novick, 228. ". . . ACKNOWLEDGING WOODWARD": C. Vann Woodward to Du Bois, April 3, 1938, Du Bois Papers/UMass. ". . . RICH HISTORY OF THE AMERICAN HISTORICAL PROFESSION": Novick, 234.

377. ". . . STOLBERG'S DISMISSIVE": "The Browsing Reader," *The Crisis*, 37:9 (September, 1930), 313, 321. "'. . . RACIAL PREJUDICES OF WHITE LABOR": Lewis, Introduction to W.E.B. Du Bois, *Black Reconstruction*, xv. "'. . . COURAGE TO FIGHT ON'": Bernice Hereford to Du Bois, March 31, 1937, Du Bois Papers.

378. "'. . . NICE TO SEE YOU'": Will to Nina, January 15, 1936, Du Bois Papers/UMass. ". . . INDIANA AVENUE HOME": Du Bois to Mildred Jones, June 27, 1934, Du Bois Papers/UMass. ". . . FINANCIAL RUIN": Du Bois to Arthur Spingarn, June 5, 1933, Du Bois Papers/UMass. ". . . EVENTUAL REMITTAL": On property woe—and Nail and Spingarn—see Arthur Spingarn to Du Bois, May 1 1933, May 22, 1933, June 2, 1933, Du Bois Papers/UMass; Du Bois to Arthur Spingarn, June 5, 1933, June 6, 1933, Du Bois Papers/UMass.

378. "'. . . FELT THE PINCH SEVERELY'": Will to Nina, March 6, 1935, Du Bois Papers/UMass. ". . . EXTENDING RELIEF": Harvard Sitkoff, *A New Deal for Blacks, The Emergence of Civil Rights as a National Issue: The Depression Decade* (New York: Oxford University Press, 1978, 1981). ". . . YOLANDE'S LIMITED CAPABILITIES": Will to Nina, April 20, 1933, May 19, 1933, Du Bois Papers/UMass.

379. ". . . PLACE WITH A GARDEN": Will to Nina, May 19, 1933, Du Bois Papers/UMass. ". . . SUNDAY WASHINGS": Will to Nina, April 20, 1933, Du Bois Papers/UMass. ". . . NINA'S MOVE": Will to Nina, April 10, 1935, Du Bois Papers/UMass. ". . . COLORED PEOPLE ARE UNWELCOME": Nina to Will, April 24, 1935, Du Bois Papers/UMass.

380. "'MUST DO LESS WORK'": Will to Nina, October 24, 1935, Du Bois Papers/UMass. "'. . . APART-MENT ROOMS'": Nina to Will, October 20, 1935, Du Bois Papers/UMass. ". . . PLAYS DIRECTED BY YOLANDE": Lewis Interview with Arnett Williams, September 12, 1993. ". . . STUDIES AT LINCOLN": Arnett Williams to Du Bois, March 8, 1933, Du Bois Papers/UMass. "'. . . ONE LETTER A MONTH'": Arnett Williams to Du Bois, January 15, 1933, Du Bois Papers/UMass. "'. . . IMPROVE HIS ENGLISH": Du Bois to Arnett Williams, February 28, 1933, Du Bois Papers/UMass. "'. . . EXCEEDINGLY SELFISH": Du Bois to Yolande, August 30, 1933, Du Bois Papers/UMass.

381. ". . . UNBEARABLE MARITAL CONDITIONS": Nina to Will, January 24, 1936, Du Bois Papers/UMass. SADIE ALEXANDER: Darlene Clark Hine, ed., *Black Women in America: An Historical Encyclopedia* (Brooklyn N.Y.: Carlson, 1993), 18. "'. . . DRINKING TO EXCESS'": Du Bois to Arnett Williams, February 4, 1936, Du Bois Papers/UMass. "'. . . ATTENTION OF YOUR EMPLOYERS'": Du Bois to Arnett

Williams, February 4, 1936, Du Bois Papers/UMass. ". . . PROTRACTED DIVORCE PROCEEDINGS": Lewis Interview with Arnett Williams, September 12, 1993.

382. ". . . WHISPERED-ABOUT CONFRONTATION": Ross, *op. cit. //.* " ' . . . INSIGNIFICANT WIDOW' ": Ann Rucker to Arthur Schomburg, November 27, 1934, AASP/SCRBC. ". . . PRIZE GRADUATE STU-DENT": Will to Nina, September 21, 1934, Du Bois Papers/UMass.

382. MOVIES AND WINE: Du Bois to Louie Shivery, July 11, 1934, Smith/Shivery Family Papers/SCRBC. ". . . THEY ARGUED A GOOD DEAL": Du Bois to Louie Shivery, March 4, 12, 1936, Smith/Shivery Papers/SCRBC. ". . . REBUFFED": Du Bois to Louie Shivery, undated, 1937, Smith/Shivery Papers/SCRBC. " ' . . . NEVER WORK AFTER MIDNIGHT' ": Du Bois to Louie Shivery, undated, 1935, Smith/Shivery Papers/SCRBC. ". . . GRADUATE HISTORY COURSES": Mildred B. Jones to Du Bois, June 29, 1935, Du Bois Papers/UMass. " ' . . . VERY DISCRIMINATING' ": Rachel Davis Du Bois to Du Bois, April 1935, Du Bois Papers/UMass. ". . . SHIVERY'S MASTER'S THESIS": See Du Bois letters to Louie Shivery about academic work, Du Bois to Louie Shivery, December 10, 1935, January 23, 1936, Du Bois Papers/UMass. Also, see Ira Reid to Louie Shivery, April 8, 1936, Du Bois Papers/UMass. ". . . DUE TO SAIL FOR EUROPE": Jack Salzman et al., *Encyclopedia of African-American Culture and History,* I (New York: Simon & Schuster, 1996), 216 (hereafter EAACH). ". . . FRENZIED REVISIONS": Du Bois to Louie Shivery, January 23, 1936, Du Bois Papers/UMass. ". . . PIONEERING SCHOLARSHIP": Jacqueline Anne Rouse, *Lugenia Burns Hope: Black Southern Reformer* (Atlanta: University of Georgia, Athens and London, 1989).

383. ". . . IRENE DIGGS AND ELIZABETH PROPHET": Will to Nina, June 26, 1936, Du Bois Papers/UMass. ". . . SPECIAL RESEARCH ASSISTANT": Lewis conversation with Irene Diggs, spring 1969. ". . . SECOND MRS. DU BOIS": Lewis conversation with Diggs. ". . . RESIDENCY AT THE UNIVERSITY CENTER": Elizabeth Prophet to Du Bois, April 1, 1934, Du Bois Papers/UMass. ". . . MEMORABLE NIGHT": Lewis conversation with Diggs. ". . . MAGNANIMOUS TO A FAULT" Leroy Davis, *A Clashing of the Soul: John Hope and The Dilemma of African American Leadership and Black Higher Education in the Early Twentieth Century* (Atlanta: University of Georgia, 1998), 338. ". . . LINGERING BETWEEN LIFE AND DEATH": Davis, *op. cit.,* 320. " ' . . . WORRIES' ": Du Bois to R. R. Moton, November 11, 1933, Du Bois Papers/UMass. ". . . MAYO CLINIC": Davis, *op. cit.,* 307–9.

384. " ' . . . TERRIBLE LOSS' ": Du Bois to Virginia Alexander, February 21, 1936, Du Bois Papers/UMass. " ' . . . MY CLOSEST FRIEND' ": Du Bois, *Autobiography,* 287. ". . . HOPE'S QUIET INSPIRATION": Du Bois, *Autobiography,* 308; Du Bois, *Dusk of Dawn,* 315. Du Bois's farewell to Charles W. Chesnutt, W.E.B. Du Bois, *Writings* (New York: Library of America, 1986), 1234–5. JOHN HOPE'S MEMORIAL SERVICE: Mordecai Johnson spoke forever, Davis, *op. cit.,* 310; Du Bois's obituary to John Hope in the *Pittsburgh Courier,* March 28, 1936, is oddly bloodless: Aptheker, ed., *Newspaper Columns,* I (White Plains, N.Y.: Kraus-Thomson, 1986), 50.

385. " ' . . . I'M DYING HERE' ": Shirley Graham to Du Bois, April 6, 1936, Du Bois Papers/UMass. " ' . . . FIND A PLACE' ": On the Nashville-Louisville arrangements, Du Bois to Shirley Graham, April 8, 1936, Du Bois Papers/UMass " ' . . . SECRET' ": Shirley Graham to Du Bois, April 10, 1936, Du Bois Papers/UMass. ". . . MAVERICK GRANDSON": Salzman et al., EAACH *op. cit.,* 509. ". . . LEWIS AND CLARK HIGH SCHOOL": Shirley Graham Du Bois, *His Day Is Marching On: A Memoir of W.E.B. Du Bois* (Philadelphia: J. B. Lippincott, 1971); Interview with Shirley Graham Du Bois, February 26, 1991, Hatch-Billops Collection. " ' . . . QUIETLY ELEGANT AND TWINKLING' ": Shirley Graham Du Bois, *op. cit.,* 43.

386. ". . . FAMILY PARSONAGE": Shirley Graham Du Bois, *Ibid.,* 36. ". . . BORN AS LOLA GRAHAM": Interview with Graham, Hatch-Billops Collection. ". . . COMMOTION": Lewis Interview with Lorenz Graham, June 1, 1989. " ' . . . NOSY LITTLE THING' ": Shirley Graham Du Bois, *op. cit.,* 17. " ' . . . LOLA MORPHED INTO SHIRLEY GRAHAM McCANTS.' ": David Du Bois told the author that his father was alive long after divorce. They wrote to each other, but he died before David could meet him. David Du Bois says father owned a black Seattle newspaper, *Northwest Herald*: Interview with David Du Bois, September 19, 1988. Details of Shirley's life are vague, see Gerald Horne, *Shirley Graham Du Bois* (New York: New York University Press, 2000), read in manuscript form thanks to the author. ". . . ENDED QUICKLY IN DIVORCE": Interview with Shirley Graham Du Bois, Hatch-Billops Collection.

386–87. ". . . BURLEIGH ON THE ORGAN": Interview with Shirley Graham Du Bois, Hatch-Billops Collection. ". . . AFRICANISMS": *Ibid.* ". . . GRAHAM'S ESSAY": Du Bois to Shirley Graham, March 27, 1933, Du Bois Papers/UMass. ". . . IRREPRESSIBLE STYLE": Shirley Graham to Du Bois, August 7, 1933, Du Bois Papers/UMass. ". . . PROFESSIONAL OPTIONS": Graham to Du Bois, October 30, 1935, Du Bois

Papers/UMass; Aptheker, ed., *Correspondence*, II, 34–36. "'... CONSUMING FIRE OF LONELINESS'":
Aptheker, ed., *Correspondence*, I, 481. "... ALPHA PHI ALPHA": It is interesting that Du Bois was Alpha's
first honorary member, indicated at behest of Henry A. Callis, one of Alpha's founders at Cornell.
Callis was a D.C. physician of progressive inclinations. "'... TO PART IS TO DIE A LITTLE'": Shirley
Graham to Du Bois, undated, 1935, Du Bois Papers/UMass. "'... NOT GOING TO THINK ABOUT IT'":
Virginia Alexander to Du Bois, May 27, 1936, Du Bois Papers/UMass.

Chapter 11: *Dictatorships Compared: Germany, Russia, China, Japan*

388. "... OBERLAENDER TRUST.": Du Bois to Wilbur K. Thomas, May 3, 1935, The Papers of W.E.B.
Du Bois, Special Collections, W.E.B. Du Bois Library, University of Massachusetts at Amherst (hereafter Du Bois Papers/UMass), also in Herbert Aptheker, ed., *The Correspondence of W.E.B. Du Bois*,
Selections (Amherst: University of Massachusetts Press, 1976), 2 Vols., II., pp. 57–58, Du Bois to Tho-
mas, January 17, 1935, February 7, 1935, Thomas to Du Bois, April 17, 1935, (research agenda), May 3,
1935, Thomas to Du Bois ($1,600 one-year grant), June 12, 1935, Thomas to Du Bois, Thomas to Du
Bois ($1,600 six-months grant), November 23, 1935, all in Du Bois Papers/UMass. "... FRANK TAN-
NENBAUM." Frank Tannerbaum to Wilbur K. Thomas, March 11, 1935, Aptheker, ed., *Correspondence*,
II, p. 56. It is quite curious that on April 24, 1931 Du Bois had proposed studying colonial policy with
a view to assessing Germany as "superior to that of the English and equal perhaps to the French," Du
Bois to Thomas, July 15, 1931, Du Bois Papers/UMass.
389. "... ENCYCLOPEDIA.": The Social Science Research Council (SSRC) awarded Du Bois a small
grant for "completion of your history of the Negro troops in the World War" in the same month as
the Philadelphia philanthropy approved its stipend, Donald Young to Du Bois, March 20, 1935, Du
Bois Papers/UMass. "... EDUCATION AND WORK.": Du Bois "Education and Work", *The Crisis* (August
1930), p. 280, also in Daniel Walden, *W.E.B. Du Bois: The Crisis Writings* (Greenwich, CT: Fawcett,
1972), p. 175. "... SEARCH FOR DEMOCRACY.": Du Bois to Alfred Harcourt, February 11, 1937, in Aptheker, ed., *Correspondence*, II., pp. 137–138.
390. "... MONTHLY SALARY.": Correspondence between Du Bois and Robert L. Vann, January 4, 13,
16, 21, 23, 27, 1936, Du Bois Papers/UMass; Du Bois also wrote to Malcolm Cowley at the *New Republic*
suggesting he write travel articles, May 15, 1936, Du Bois Papers/UMass; "... AN AMERICAN ACQUAIN-
TANCE IN MOSCOW.": William A. Burroughs, an African-American writer for the Moscow *Daily News*
(and possibly Mrs. Burroughs), to Du Bois, July 27, 1936, Burroughs to Du Bois, August 7, 1936, October
18, 1936, all in Du Bois Papers/UMass; Du Bois, "Russia and America," [1950], p. 102, Du Bois Papers/
UMass. "... YOUNG JAPANESE STUDENT.": Ibid., p. 127, further biographical details about Hikida are
in the William Pickens Record Group/Special Collections: Schomburg Center for Research in Black
Culture, New York Public Library, Box 2 (hereafter WPRG/SCRBC), see Percival Prattis, *Pittsburgh
Courier* editor, to William Pickens, April 26, 1934, WPRG/SCRBC; Rayford Logan was certain that
Hikida was an operative of the Japanese empire, and so informed a contact in the OSS. Logan Diaries,
entry for June 14, 1942, Rayford Logan Diaries, LC. Biographical information on Yasuichi Hikida, FBI
File No. 65-29505, FOIPA; FBI (New York City), File No. 100-704 MFK; Internal Security (J), Alien
Enemy Control, 6-24-42/7-1-42, FOIAPA; Hikida, Yasuichi, Record Group 59, 894. 20211, State De-
partment Documents, National Archives; and especially, J. Edgar Hoover to Adolph A. Berle, assistant
secretary of state, "personal and confidential by special messenger," June 10, 1942; Adolph Berle to J.
Edgar Hoover, July 1, 1942, "personal and confidential," State Department, Rec. Grp. 59, 20211; also,
Reginald Kearney, *Afro-American Views of the Japanese, 1900-1945: Solidarity or Sedition?* (Albany, N.Y.:
SUNY Press, 1998); Ernest Allen, Jr., "Satokata Takahashi and the Flowering of Black Messianic
Nationalism," *The Black Scholar*, Vol. 24 (winter 1994): pp. 23–45.
390. "... SOMETHING VAGUELY MORE SIGNIFICANT.": Reginald Kearney, *African American Views of
the Japanese: Solidarity or Sedition?* (Albany, N.Y.: SUNY Press, 1998), p. 83. "... SCHOMBURG'S SPON-
SORSHIP.": Hikida to Arthur A. Schomburg, March 27, 1933, Arthur A. Schomburg Papers/Special
Collections: Schomburg Center for Research in Black Culture, New York Public Library (hereafter
AASP/SCRBC). "... NEGROES AND JAPAN.": Lewis, *Vogue*, p. 302.
391. "... NEGROES AND JAPAN.": Hikida Yasuichi to James Weldon Johnson, October 11, 1935, Du
Bois Papers/UMass; For information on Claude Barnett and the Associated Negro Press, see Jack
Salzman et. al., eds., *Encyclopedia of African-American Culture and History* (N.Y.: Macmillan, 1996),
p. 266 (hereafter *EAACH*); William Pickens to Percival Prattis, January 30, 1934, WPRG/SCRBC.

"... RUSSO-JAPANESE WAR." Jacques Chastenet, *La Republique Triomphante 1893–1906* (Paris: Librairie Hachette, 1955); Du Bois, "Coming of the Lesser Folk," in *New York Post* (August 19, 1911), pp. 1–2, also in Herbert Aptheker, ed., *Writings in Periodical Literature* (Millwood, N.Y.: Kraus-Thomson, 1982), 4 Vols., II., p. 45; Du Bois, "The African Roots of the War," in *Atlantic Monthly* (May 1915), pp. 707–714, also in Aptheker, ed., *Writings in Periodical Literature*, II., p. 99; Percival Prattis to William Pickens, April 27, 1934, WPRG/SCRBC. "... ADWA.": David Levering Lewis, *The Race to Fashoda: European Colonialism and African Resistance in the Scramble for Africa* (New York: Weidenfeld & Nicholson, 1987); "... ASIATIC BY FORCE.": Du Bois, "Japan and China," *The Crisis* (March 1932), p. 93, also in Herbert Aptheker, ed., *Selections from the Crisis* (Millwood, N.Y.: Kraus Thomson, 1983), 2 Vols., II, p. 655; Philadelphia *Tribune*, October 22, 1931. More generally, see Reginald Kearney, *African-American Views of the Japanese: Solidarity or Sedition?* (Albany, N.Y.: SUNY Press, 1998). "... NATURAL AND MORAL.": Kearney, *African-American Views of the Japanese,* p. 61.
392. "... RACIAL EQUALITY AMENDMENT.": Walter LeFeber, *The Clash: U.S.—Japanese Relations throughout History* (New York: W. W. Norton, 1997), p. 124; Earnest Allen, Jr., "Satokata Takahashi and the Flowering of Black Messianic Nationalism", *Black Scholar* 24 (Winter 1994), pp. 23–46. Also see Akira Iriye, ed., *Mutual Images: Essays in American-Japanese Relations* (Cambridge: Harvard University Press, 1975). "... CHERRY TREES.": Lewis, *When Harlem was in Vogue*, p. 302. "... THE RIGHTS OF DARK SKINNED PEOPLE.": Kearney, *African-American Views of the Japanese*, p. 78. "... TO SERVE IMPERIALIST PURPOSES.": Percival Prattis to William Pickens, March 8, 1934, WPRG/SCRBC.
392. "... THE JAPANESE EDITION OF 'LIFT EV'RY VOICE AND SING'.": Walter White to Y. Hikida, September 17, 1935, Walter White Correspondence, NAACP Papers, Library of Congress (hereafter, WWC-NAACP/LC). "... AMATEUR SOCIOLOGIST'S MANUSCRIPT.": James Weldon Johnson to Hikida, September 27, 1935; Hikida to Johnson, October 11, 1935; White to Hikida, September 27, 1935—all in WWC-NAACP/LC. "... GREAT PLEASURE.": Hikida to Du Bois, [n.d.], 1935, Du Bois Papers/UMass. ON HIKIDA'S INTEREST IN DU BOIS: Hikida to Du Bois, June 1, 1935, Du Bois Papers/UMass. For the regrets of the Japanese ambassador, see Y: Iseki to Du Bois, December 23, 1935, Du Bois Papers/UMass. "... BLACK RECONSTRUCTION.": Hikida to Du Bois, November 6, 1935, Du Bois Papers/UMass. "... HIS JAPANESE FRIEND'S EMBOSSED CARDS.": Hikida to Du Bois, October 15, 1936, Du Bois Papers/UMass.
393. "... THE S.S. ST. LOUIS.": Du Bois to Mildred Bryant Jones, April 2, 1936, Du Bois Papers/UMass. The S.S. *St. Louis* was the "ship of fools" whose Jewish passengers were denied entry in Cuba in June of 1939. "... A KEY TO THE BRITISH MUSEUM.": [Quote from Cooney document that needs identifying] "... BELOVED CHIEF.": Ruth Anna Fisher in Ruth Anna Fisher and William Lloyd Fox, eds., *J. Franklin Jameson: A Tribute* (Washington D.C.: Catholic University of America, 1965), p. 1–8. On Fisher more generally, see Darlene Clark Hine et. al., eds., *Black Women in America: An Historical Encyclopedia* (Brooklyn N.Y.: Carlson Publishing, 1993), 2 Vols., I, p. 434; August Meier and Elliot Rudwick, *Black History and the Historical Profession* (Urbana: University of Illinois Press, 1986), pp. 27–28.
394. "... DEAR BURGHARDT.": Ruth Anna Fisher to Du Bois, November 11, 1934, Du Bois Papers/UMass. "... REBUILT AND REORIENTED THE MODERN WORLD.": Du Bois to Fisher, December 3, 1934, Du Bois Papers/UMass. MALINOWSKI: Bruno Malinowski to Du Bois, March 2, 1937, Du Bois Papers/UMass. WELLS: Du Bois to P. S. Anson, June 29, 1936, Du Bois Papers/UMass. On Du Bois's schedule and notes, see "London Memorandum", 1936; Du Bois to Anson, June 29, 1936—both in Du Bois Papers/UMass. There were stops at the League of Coloured Peoples on Monday and at the International Institute of African Languages and Culture on Tuesday, important institutions for Du Bois's *Encyclopedia of the Negro*. He missed Julian Huxley, the biologist grandson of Thomas Huxley, but had drinks and a good chat on Wednesday at the Athenaeum Club with Reinhold Niebuhr and his old British Pan African collaborator, J. H. Oldham. There was a brief meeting with Lord Hailey. Afterwards, he took in Chekhov's *Seagull*, starring Edith Evans and John Gielgud, at the open-air theater in Regents Park that evening.
394. LEOPOLD: Adam Hochschild, *King Leopold's Ghost: A Story of Greed, Terror and Heroism in Colonial Africa* (Boston: Houghton Mifflin, 1998). Lewis, *Fashoda*. Du Bois recalled in the *Courier* his conversations before and after the Great War with Emile Vandervelde, the dean of Belgian socialists and former Minister of Foreign Affairs. If the workers were in a "sorry plight," Du Bois charged, it was because, when the socialists ruled the country, they had failed to understand that the "cause of the black slave in the Congo was one with that of his white fellow in Belgium." Du Bois, "Forum of

Fact and Opinion," Pittsburgh *Courier*, August 29, 1936. ". . . FOR TWO RACES IN TWO LANGUAGES.":
Pittsburgh *Courier*, August 29, 1936.
395–96. ". . . ITALY'S INVASION.": With press and radio coverage at top volume, demonstrations in
Harlem, earnest if mediocre relief efforts (Defense of Ethiopia, Friends of Ethiopia, American Aid for
Ethiopia), a Negro delegation to Geneva sponsored by the Defense of Ethiopia, and the arrival in
Addis Ababa of the "Black Eagle" (Hubert Julian) and the "Brown Condor" (John Robinson), Afro-
america's premier air aces [see Joseph Harris, *African-American Reactions to War in Ethiopia, 1936–
1941* (Baton Rouge: Louisiana State University Press, 1994), 54], the *Courier* column running two weeks
before Du Bois sailed had vented considerable passion on the "incalculable and unending" harm done
by Mussolini's rape of the African kingdom. Du Bois despaired that the Duce had smashed the League
of Nations—"the noblest dream of a united humanity in a federation of the world since the Holy
Roman Empire." Du Bois, "Forum of Fact and Opinion," Pittsburgh *Courier*, May 23, 1936; Du Bois,
"Inter-Racial Implications of the Ethiopian Crisis: A Negro View," *Foreign Affairs* 14 (October 1935),
pp. 83–92, also in Aptheker, ed., *Writings in Periodical Literature*, III, pp. 15–23. More generally, see
Joseph Harris, *African-American Reactions to War in Ethiopia, 1936–1941* (Baton Rouge: Louisiana State
University Press, 1994). Millions of Italian-Americans disagreed, however, and cheered General Pietro
Badoglio's avenging of Adwa. JOE LOUIS: "Louis, Joe," in Salzman et. al., cds., *EAACH*, III, pp. 1651–
1654.
396. ". . . ACCUMULATED KNOWLEDGE.": Du Bois to Boas, May 5, 1936; Franz Boas to Du Bois,
April 22, 1936—both in Du Bois Papers/UMass, both also in Aptheker, ed., *Correspondence*, II, p. 135–
136. ". . . POTEMKIN.": Boas to Du Bois, May 11, 1936, also in Aptheker, ed., *Correspondence*, II, p. 136.
". . . TWELVE MILLION PEOPLE.": Du Bois to Victor Lindeman, March 31, 1936, Du Bois Papers/UMass.
The reservations of Boas and Lindeman about the value of his educational research project definitely
should have concerned him, however. In a country where a former Brown Shirt *Obergruppenfuhrer*
now served as the Minister of Science, Education and Popular Culture, a sharp decline in the quality
of arts and sciences preparation was inescapable. At the University of Berlin where Du Bois had studied
economics and sociology in the 1890s, the new rector had instituted twenty-five courses in *Rassenkunde*
(National Socialist race science). See William Shirer, *The Rise and Fall of the Third Reich: A History
of Nazi Germany* (New York: Fawcett, 1959), p. 345.
396–97. On Jews in Nazi Germany, see Shirer, *Rise and Fall of the Third Reich*; Daniel Jonah
Goldhagen, *Hitler's Willing Executioners: Ordinary Germans and the Holocaust* (New York: Random
House, 1996); Norman G. Finklestein and Ruth Bettina Burns, *A Nation on Trial: The Goldhagen
Thesis and Historical Truth* (New York: Henry Holt, 1998); Marian Kaplan, *Between Dignity and
Despair: Jewish Life in Nazi Germany* (New York Oxford Univ. Press, 1998); Victor Klemperer, *I Will
Bear Witness: A Diary of the Nazi Years* (New York: Random House, 1998). ". . . FROM ONWARD.":
Michael R. Marrus, *The Holocaust in History* (New York: Meridian, 1987).
398. ". . . DON'T USE THAT NAME.": Memorandum, 1936, Du Bois Papers/UMass. ". . . THE JEWISH
DREAM.": Klemperer, *I Will Bear Witness*, p. 154.
398. ". . . SEEN MUCH.": Du Bois, "Forum of Fact and Opinion," Pittsburgh *Courier*, December 12,
1936, also in Aptheker, ed., *News Columns*, I, p. 143. ". . . GOOD GERMANS.": ". . . BACKED BY CHILD
TEACHING . . . CONVENTIONAL WORD": Du Bois, "Forum of Fact and Opinion," Pittsburgh *Courier*,
December 19, 1936, also in Aptheker, ed., *New Columns*, I, p. 148. ". . . AT HARVARD?": Du Bois,
"Forum of Fact and Opinion," Pittsburgh *Courier*, January 9, 1937, also in Aptheker, ed., *News Columns*, I, p. 159.
398. ". . . RECORD A SINGLE INSTANCE.": Du Bois, "Forum of Fact and Opinion," Pittsburgh *Courier*,
December 5, 1936, also in Aptheker, ed., *News Columns*, I, p. 142–144. HOUSTON STEWART CHAMBER-
LAIN: Thomas F. Gossett, *Race: the History of an Idea in America* (New York: Oxford Univ. Press,
1963, 1997), pp. 347–353 ". . . THAN ONE JEW.": Quoted in Charles Bracelen Flood, *Hitler: The Path
to Power* (Boston: Houghton Mifflin, 1989), p. 162.
399. ". . . NEARER [TO] BEING INSTINCTIVE . . . THE OBSTRUCTION OF WORLD TRADE.": "Forum of
Fact and Opinion," Pittsburgh *Courier*, December 19, 1936, also in Aptheker, I, ed., *News Columns*,
pp. 148–150. ". . . THE OFFICIAL REPRESSION UNLEASHED BY THE HITLER REGIME.": Deborah E. Lipstadt, *Beyond Belief: The American Press and the Coming of the Holocaust* (New York: Free Press,
1986), pp. 42–45. ". . . HIS RACE NONSENSE WOULD FIT BEAUTIFULLY.": Du Bois, "As the Crow Flies,"
The Crisis (September 1933), p. 197. Susan E. Tifft and Alex S. Jones, "The Sulzbergers, the Jews, and
America's Premier Newspaper," *New Yorker*, April 19, 1999, pp. 44–52.

400. "... SET CIVILIZATION BACK A HUNDRED YEARS.": Du Bois, "Forum of Fact and Opinion," Pittsburgh *Courier*, December 19, 1936, in Aptheker, ed., *News Columns*, I, p. 149. "... BEST CIGARET [SIC] I EVER TASTED ... BETTERMENT WILL SLOWLY FOLLOW IN TIME.": Du Bois, "Forum of Fact and Opinion," Pittsburgh *Courier*, January 2, 1937, also in Aptheker, ed., *News Columns*, I, pp. 154, 156. "... MUCH OF THE AMERICAN PRESS.": See Lipstadt, *Beyond Belief*.

400. "... THE PROBLEM OF UNEMPLOYMENT HAD BEEN LICKED.": Shirer, *Rise and Fall of the Third Reich*, p. 321. "... PUBLIC ORDER IS PERFECT.": Du Bois, "Forum of Fact and Opinion," Pittsburgh *Courier*, December 12, 1936, also in Aptheker, ed., *News Columns*, I, p. 142.

401. "... DU BOIS WAS NOT ENTIRELY IMMUNE.": Shirer, *Rise and Fall of Nazi Germany*, p. 322; A. Scott Berg, *Lindbergh* (New York: G. P. Putnam's Sons, 1998), p. 362. "... TO PUT THE STATE IN ORDER.": Du Bois, "Forum of Fact and Opinion," Pittsburgh *Courier*, December 12, 1936, also in Aptheker, ed., *News Columns*, I, p. 146. "... 40,000 SONS OF THIS CITY.": Du Bois, "Forum of Fact and Opinion," Pittsburgh *Courier*, December 5, 1936, also in Aptheker, ed., *News Columns*, I, p. 143. "... ALL EXCUSE FOR BEING.": Quote from Du Bois, "Forum of Fact and Opinion," Pittsburgh *Courier*, December 26, 1936, also in Aptheker, ed., *News Columns*, p. 153. In "Russia and America," an unpublished work, Du Bois argued that "[t]he longer I looked at Hitler's Germany the more I realized that it was a socialistic state. It was copying the Soviet Union in innumerable ways." Du Bois, "Russia and America," Du Bois Papers/UMass.

402. "... I SUMMON THE YOUTH OF THE WORLD.": Richard D. Mandell, *The Nazi Olympics* (New York: Ballantine, 1971), pp. 142–3, 162–63.

403. THOMAS WOLFE: William J. Baker : *Jesse Owens: An American Life* (New York: Free Press, 1986), p. 101. "... RIVALS FOR POPULARITY.": Mandell, *Nazi Olympics*, p. 258.

403. "... DU BOIS'S TWO OLYMPICS PIECES.": Du Bois, "Forum of Fact and Opinion," *Pittsburgh Courier*, October 24, 1936, also in Aptheker, ed., *News Columns*, I, pp. 127–128; Du Bois, "Forum of Fact and Opinion," Pittsburgh *Courier*, September 19, 1936, also in Aptheker, ed., *News Columns*, I, pp. 114–116. "... STAGED.": *Der Angriff*, on feigning civility, wrote that "[w]e must be more charming than the Parisians, more easygoing than the Viennese, more vivacious than the Romans, more cosmopolitan than London, and more practical than New York." Quoted in Mandell, *Nazi Olympics*, p. 156. "... NO NEGRO OPPRESSION.": Du Bois, "Forum of Fact and Opinion," Pittsburgh *Courier*, December 19, 1936, also in Aptheker, ed., *News columns*, I, p. 149. "... NOT ONLY IN SPORTS, BUT IN SCIENCE.": Du Bois, "Forum of Fact and Opinion," Pittsburgh *Courier*, October 24, 1936, also in Aptheker, ed., *News Columns*, I, p. 127. "... FOUR INCHES HIGHER THAN ALL THE REST.": Klemperer, *I Will Bear Witness*, p. 182.

404. "... BLACK MEN AS FRENCHMEN.": Du Bois, "Forum of Fact and Opinion," Pittsburgh *Courier*, October 24, 1936, also in Aptheker, ed., *News Columns*, I, p. 127. Elizabeth Prophet may have been the unidentified friend Du Bois quoted as often remarking that she liked Paris "because she could start out without wondering where she could get lunch." See Du Bois, "Forum of Fact and Opinion," Pittsburgh *Courier*, December 19, 1936, also in Aptheker, ed., *News Columns*, I, p. 148. Nina, in what seems to have become the sad role of facilitator, had written that Prophet and Diggs would arrive on July 20th, having sailed together from New York. He noted once again, interestingly, that mail from home had been opened by the authorities. See Du Bois, "Forum of Fact and Opinion," Pittsburgh *Courier*, December 5, 1936, also in Aptheker, ed., *News Columns*, I, p. 142. To share expenses, the ladies traveled from Atlanta to Paris where both eagerly planned to await their roving scholar. See Nina to Will, July 19, 1936, Du Bois Papers/UMass. Du Bois would have been a great comfort to Prophet as she knew that her life as a Parisian was over. She had come back to close her studio in the Rue Broca and to arrange for the shipment of its contents to Atlanta. He also devoted attention to Diggs. Ultimately, however, this *menage a trois* proved less than satisfactory. Diggs and Prophet had come to Paris together as friends, but, as the gossip in the Atlanta University community disclosed, they were no longer on speaking terms when they returned. See Lewis, interview with John Hope and Elise Oliver, January 21, 1988; Nina to Will, October 5, 1936, Du Bois Papers/UMass. "... WITH DIEDRICH WESTERMANN.": Westermann to Rayford Logan, September 11, 1936, Du Bois Papers/UMass. Du Bois also interviewed with Egon von Eichstedt and Dominick Josef Woelful—see Irene Diggs to Du Bois, November 19, 1936, Du Bois Papers/UMass. "... THE END OF AUGUST.": Du Bois, "Forum of Fact and Opinion," Pittsburgh *Courier*, November 7, 1936, also in Aptheker, ed., *News Columns*, I, p. 132. "... OF BEER.": Du Bois, "Forum of Fact and Opinion," Pittsburgh *Courier*, November 14, 1936, also in Aptheker, ed., *News Columns*, I, p. 135.

404. ". . . WHERE THEY CAN RENEW THEIR STRENGTH.": Du Bois, "Forum of Fact and Opinion," Pittsburgh *Courier*, October 17, 1936, also in Aptheker, ed., *News Columns*, I, p. 124. ". . . MY IMPERFECT EDUCATION IN LIFE.": Du Bois, "Forum of Fact and Opinion," Pittsburgh *Courier*, October 31, 1936, also in Aptheker, ed., *News Columns*, I, p. 131. ". . . *FREUDIG GEFUERT, ZIEHET DAHIN.*": Du Bois, "Forum of Fact and Opinion," Pittsburgh *Courier*, October 31, 1936, also in Aptheker, ed., *News Columns*, I, p. 130.

405. ". . . MUST UNDERSTAND WAGNER.": Quoted in Shirer, *Rise and Fall of the Third Reich*, p. 147. On Hitler and *Die Walkure*, see Frederic Spotts, *Bayreuth: A History of the Wagner Festival* (New Haven: Yale University Press, 1994), p. 167. See also Robert W. Gutman, *Richard Wagner: The Man, His Mind, and His Music* (San Diego: Harcourt Brace Jovanovich, 1990; orig. pub. 1968). DU BOIS AND WAGNER: The delicacy of the beer was incomparable, and Du Bois regretted that his American readers might never know its wonders, but more wondrous yet was the musical education he shared in two elevated essays. At Munich, he was enthralled by his first performance of *Die Meistersinger*. He pressed on to Bayreuth, the Bavarian town consecrated to Richard Wagner's music and memory, where summer festivals drew thousands from all corners of Europe as well as a good representation of Americans. *Courier* readers, having been denied a first hand description of the Olympic games, were now subjected to Wagnerian raptures entitled, "Bayreuth" and "Opera and the Negro Problem." Well might Du Bois have anticipated "a certain type of not unthoughtful American Negro" asking what Wagnerian opera had to do with Arkansas tenant farmers or college graduates "searching New York for a job?" [Du Bois, "Forum of Fact and Opinion," Pittsburgh *Courier*, October 31, 1936, also in Aptheker, ed., *News Columns*, I, p. 129] His answer—that Wagner's life exemplified the triumph of genius over adversity—may not have satisfied every reader, especially any who may have known of the Nazis' affinity for the composer and his music. By his own admission, Du Bois was a Wagnerian neophyte, familiar only with the early opera *Lohengrin* whose music he had described in *Souls* as "strangely more beautiful than anything he had ever known," yet he felt compelled to expatiate on the liberating meaning of Wagner's *oeuvre*, which Du Bois interpreted as the ennoblement of the common people. [Du Bois, *Souls of Black Folks* (Millwood, N.Y.: Kraus Thomson, 1903, 1983), p. 236.] "Real hatred of poverty and fear of ignorance" were its essential meaning, he proclaimed. "That is what Richard Wagner lived to teach." [Du Bois, "Forum of Fact and Opinion," Pittsburgh *Courier*, October 17, 1936, also in Aptheker, ed., *News Columns*, I, p. 126.]

405. ". . . ITS PARISIAN FLAVOR STILL LIVES. . . . INTO THE PROSE OF THE TWENTIETH CENTURY.": Du Bois, "Forum of Fact and Opinion," Pittsburgh *Courier*, January 9, 1937, also in Aptheker, ed., *News Columns*, I, p. 158.

406. ". . . IT WILL BE QUITE IMPOSSIBLE.": William Burroughs to Du Bois, October 18, 1936, Du Bois Papers/UMass; Robert Tucker, *Stalin in Power: Revolution from Above, 1929–1941* (New York: W. W. Norton, 1990). ". . . TIMETABLES AND POINTS OF INTEREST.": Y. Kumazawa to Du Bois, September 9, 1936, Du Bois Papers/UMass. Also see the earlier introductory letter from Kumazawa/WEB-July 29, 1936, Du Bois Papers/UMass. ". . . EVERYTHING WAS ALL RIGHT FOR YOU.": Nina to Will, September 12, 1936, Du Bois Papers/UMass.

407. ". . . PRESTIGIOUS TOKYO IMPERIAL UNIVERSITY.": Hikida to Du Bois, October 15, 1936, Du Bois Papers/UMass.

407. ". . . RUSSIA IS A WORLD.": Du Bois, "Forum of Fact and Opinion," Pittsburgh *Courier*, January 23, 1937, also in Aptheker, ed., *News Columns*, I, p. 160, 163. Also see Du Bois, "Russia and America," unpublished manuscript, Du Bois Papers/UMass; Du Bois, "Forum of Fact and Opinion," Pittsburgh *Courier*, January 23, 1937, also in Aptheker, ed., *News Columns*, I, p. 164. ". . . COLLECT AND CONSERVE THIS CAPITAL.": Du Bois, "Forum of Fact and Opinion," Pittsburgh *Courier*, January 23, 1937, also in Aptheker, ed., *News Columns*, I, p. 163. Du Bois's route through the Urals and across the western edge of Siberia would be a moving showcase of industrial centers created seemingly overnight or sprung out of retrofitted cities by the dynamo of the second Five-Year Plan as it racked up its ambitious final quotas. There was much talk of the draft of the new Constitution of the USSR containing an inspiring bill of rights and the declaration that socialism had been achieved in Russia. Du Bois would conclude that the Russian people supported the policies of the regime "because they vote in huge numbers," an observation he did not bother to recall having made about the Germans. ". . . GIDE LEFT THE SOVIET UNION.": Tucker, *Stalin in Power*, p. 336. ON LANGSTON HUGHES: Lewis, *When Harlem Was in Vogue*, p. 291.

408. ". . . WITH THE SAME RULING CLASS AT TOP.": Du Bois, "Forum on Fact and Opinion," Pittsburgh *Courier*, January 23, 1937, also in Aptheker, ed., *News Columns*, I, p. 162. On the trial of Radek, and on George Kennan and Joseph Davies observing the purge trials, see Tucker, *Stalin in Power*, Walter Issacson and Evan Thomas, *The Wise Men: Six Friends and the World They Made* (New York: Simon and Shuster, 1986); Joseph Davies, *Mission to Moscow* (New York: Simon & Schuster, 1941).

408. ". . . FROM MOSCOW TO VLADIVOSTOK." : Du Bois, "Russia and America," 130. ". . . A LAND OF ESSENTIAL SAMENESS.": Du Bois, "A Forum of Fact and Opinion," Pittsburgh *Courier*, January 23, 1937, also in Aptheker, ed., *News Columns*, I, p. 161.

409. ". . . LIKE A GHOST TRAIN . . . THE PRIVILEGE OF BUYING.": Du Bois, "Russia and America," p. 128. Also see Louise Young, *Japan's Total Empire: Manchuria and the Culture of Wartime Imperialism* (Berkeley: University of California Press, 1998). By the Treaty of Portsmouth, Japan got the South Manchurian railroad, the Liaotung Peninsula, half of Sakhalin Island, and a Russian surrender of claims on Korea.

409. ". . . OUT OF THE DESOLATION OF THE NORTHERN DESERT.": Du Bois, "Russia and America," p. 130. ". . . THE NATURAL MAINLAND OF THE ISLES OF JAPAN.": Du Bois, "Forum of Fact and Opinion," Pittsburgh *Courier*, February 13, 1937, also in Aptheker, ed., *News Columns*, I, p. 166. ". . . REFUSING THE ACCEPT TERMS.": See LaFeber, *The Clash: U.S.-Japanese Relations Throughout History* (New York: W. W. Norton, 1997), pp. 82–86. ". . . AND TOOK MANCHURIA.": Du Bois, "Forum of Fact and Opinion," Pittsburgh *Courier*, February 13, 1937, also in Aptheker, ed., *News Columns*, I, p. 166.

410. ". . . THE MANTETSU . . . HSINKING.": Young, *Japan's Total Empire*, p., 4. ". . . THIS COLONIAL EFFORT OF A COLORED NATION.": Du Bois, "Russia and America," p. 130. ". . . COLONY OF JAPAN.": Du Bois, "Forum of Fact and Opinion," Pittsburgh *Courier*, February 13, 1937, also in Aptheker, ed., *News Columns*, I, p. 166.

411. ". . . SLOW AND LOW OF SPEECH . . . THE CASE OF WHITE EUROPE": Du Bois, "Forum of Fact and Opinion," Pittsburgh *Courier*, February 13, 1937, also in Aptheker, ed., *News Columns*, I, p. 166. ". . . WITH CO-PROSPERITY RATIONALES.": Edwin O. Reischauer, *Japan: The Story of a Nation* (New York: McGraw Hill, 1990), p. 712; LaFeber, *The Clash*, pp. 186–192.

411. ". . . WALKED THE STREETS NIGHT AND DAY . . . FOR THE GENERAL WELFARE": Du Bois, "Forum of Fact and Opinion," Pittsburgh *Courier*, February 13, 1937, also in Aptheker, ed., *News Columns*, I, p. 167. ". . . HISTORIC GROUND.": Du Bois, "Forum of Fact and Opinion," Pittsburgh *Courier*, February 13, 1937, also in Aptheker, ed., *News Columns*, I, p. 167. ". . . THE AMERICAN CONSUL.": Du Bois, "Forum of Fact and Opinion," Pittsburgh *Courier*, February 13, 1937, also in Aptheker, ed., *News Columns*, I, p. 168. ". . . ON A PERFECT DAY.": Du Bois, "Forum of Fact and Opinion," Pittsburgh *Courier*, February 20, 1937, also in Aptheker, ed., *News Columns*, I, p. 169.

412. ". . . THROUGH THE CHINA INSTITUTE OF AMERICA.": C. Meng to Du Bois, September 10, 1936, Du Bois Papers/UMass. ". . . VISIBLE FROM MARS.": Du Bois, "Forum of Fact and Opinion," Pittsburgh *Courier*, February 20, 1937, also in Aptheker, ed., *News Columns*, I, p. 170; Du Bois, *Autobiography*, p. 44.

413. ". . . CHEAP WOMEN; CHEAP CHILD LABOR; CHEAP MEN . . . ESPECIALLY DEPRESSED": Du Bois, "Forum of Fact and Opinion," Pittsburgh *Courier*, March 6, 1937, also in Aptheker , ed., *News Columns*, I, p. 176. ". . . IN RIVALRY, WAR AND HATRED.": Du Bois, "Forum of Fact and Opinion," Pittsburgh *Courier*, February 27, 1937, also in Aptheker, ed., *News Columns*, I, p. 174. Also see Du Bois, "Forum of Fact and Opinion," Pittsburgh *Courier*, March 6, 1937, also in Aptheker, ed., *News Columns*, I, p. 177.

413. ". . . WITH HIKIDA.": Nina to Will, September 12, 1936, Du Bois Papers/UMass. Lewis, interview with Du Bois Williams, June 28, 1987. ". . . THE JAPANESE NETWORK.": See the folder marked "Travel — 1936 — Japan", W.E.B. Du Bois Collection, Fisk University. ". . . IT LOOKED LIKE MISSISSIPPI.": Du Bois, "Forum of Fact and Opinion," Pittsburgh *Courier*, February 27, 1937, also in Aptheker, ed., *News Columns*, I, p. 172.

414. ". . . YOU HATE JAPAN MORE THAN EUROPE.": Du Bois, "Forum of Fact and Opinion," Pittsburgh *Courier*, February 27, 1937, also in Aptheker, ed., *News Columns*, I, p. 174. ". . . SAVAGE BOMBARDMENT OF SHANGHAI.": Iris Chang, *The Rape of Nanking: the Forgotten Holocaust of World War II* (New York: Basic Books, 1997), p. 27; LaFeber, *The Clash*, p. 171. ". . . A PROPAGANDIST IN THE PAY OF JAPAN.": Du Bois to Walter McNutt, February 25, 1939, Du Bois Papers/UMass.

414. ". . . WHITE AGGRESSION AND JAPANESE RESISTANCE.": Du Bois, "Forum of Fact and Opinion," Pittsburgh *Courier*, February 27, 1937, also in Aptheker, ed., *News Columns*, I, p. 174. ". . . THE WHITE

FOLKS' NIGGER IN THE UNITED STATES.": Du Bois, "Forum of Fact and Opinion," Pittsburgh *Courier*, October 23, 1937, also in Aptheker, ed., *News Columns*, I, p. 245. ON THE RAPE OF NANKING: Chang, *Rape of Nanking*, p. 37; LaFeber, *The Clash*, p. 187.

414–15. "... AN EVENT.": C. J. Tagashira to Du Bois, November 21, 1936, Du Bois Papers/UMass. "... CHARMED BY HIS MANNERED WIT.": folder marked "Travel—1936—Japan", W.E.B. Du Bois Collection, Fisk University. "... ADDRESSED THE FACULTY ON NEGRO LITERATURE.": Du Bois, "Forum of Fact and Opinion," Pittsburgh *Courier*, February 20, 1937, also in Aptheker, ed., *News Columns*, I, p. 170. For somewhat jumbled details of arrival and movements, see Du Bois, "Russia and America," pp. 142–144; the folder marked "Travel—1936—Japan", W.E.B. Du Bois Collection, Fisk University; Du Bois, "Forum of Fact and Opinion," Pittsburgh *Courier*, March 13, 1937, also in Aptheker, ed., *News Columns*, I, p. 179. Also see Reginald Kearney, "The Pro-Japanese Utterances of W.E.B. Du Bois," unpublished paper in author's possession; Kearney, *African-American Views of the Japanese*. And Hikida to Du Bois, October 15, 1936, Du Bois Papers/UMass. JAPANESE PRESS COVERAGE: "For the Youth of Japan," Osaka *Mainichi*, Dec. 2, 1936, which announced Du Bois's lecture for December 5; "The Father of the American Indian Dr. Du Bois Visits Japan," Tokyo *Nichinichi*, Dec. 3, 1936, which quotes Du Bois as saying aboard ship that he had "just finished my inspection of Manchuria, and China seems an interesting country.... I'm quite interested in Ainu people, and this is a good chance for me to study them."; "The Father of American Black People," Osaka *Mainichi*, Dec. 4, 1936, which quotes Du Bois as saying that he "had a feeling that we can't avoid war any more. We twelve million black Americans support President Roosevelt because he is having a sympathetic policy toward blacks."; Osaka *Mainichi*, Dec. 5, 1936, which recounts Du Bois's presentation at the Osaka *Mainichi* auditorium, where he read excerpts fom the *Souls of Black Folk*; "Japanese Youth Are the World's leaders," Osaka *Mainichi*, Dec. 6, 1936, which quoted Du Bois as saying that "when Japan demanded the abolition of racial discrimination at the Versailles meeting, the question of reconstructing the world appeared before us and that the future of the world should not be ruled by white people but by colored people, who are actually the majority. He said he believes that the day will come when Asia will become the leader of the world, and that the happiness of the common people in Asia and Africa will mean the happiness of the world." I am immensely grateful to my former student, Professor Kiyofumi Tsubaki of Tuda College's English department, Tokyo, for tracking down and translating Japanese press accounts of Du Bois's visit. "... RIVALING EUROPEAN CITIES.": Du Bois, "Russia and America," p. 145. "... MESSAGE TO JAPAN.": Kearney, "The Pro-Japanese Utterances of W.E.B. Du Bois." "... A PEOPLE SO INTELLIGENT, SO DISCIPLINED.": Du Bois, quoted in Kearney, *African-American Views of the Japanese*, p. 90.

415. "... SURROUNDED BY PHOTOGRAPHERS.": Du Bois, "Forum of Fact and Opinion," Pittsburgh *Courier*, March 13, 1937, also in Aptheker, ed., *News Columns*, I, 180. "... A NIGHT IN THE BROODING IMPERIAL HOTEL.": Folder marked "Travel—1936—Japan," W.E.B. Du Bois Collection, Fisk University; Neil Levine, *The Architecture of Frank Lloyd Wright* (Princeton: Princeton University Press, 1996), p. 123. "... TO COVER HIS MOVEMENTS.": Kearney, "The Pro-Japanese Utterances of W.E.B. Du Bois"; Du Bois, "Forum of Fact and Opinion," Pittsburgh *Courier*, March 13, 1937, also in Aptheker, ed., *News Columns*, I, 180. For Du Bois on Dyer and Japanese immigration, see Du Bois, "Forum of Fact and Opinion," Pittsburgh *Courier*, March 13, 1937, also in Aptheker, ed., *News Columns*, I, p. 180. On Japanese immigration restriction as part of the 1924 Johnson Act, see David M. Reimers, *Still the Golden Door: The Third World Comes to America* (New York: Columbia University Press, 1985), p. 6; Ronald Takaki, *Strangers from a Different Shore* (New York: W. W. Norton, 1989).

416. ON DU BOIS'S SCHEDULE: See the travel itinerary dated November 26, 1936, in the folder marked "Travel—1936—Japan," W.E.B. Du Bois Collection, Fisk University. "... KOKUSAI BUNKA SHINKO-KAI.": On Kokusai Bunka Shinkokai, see the pamphlet entitled *The Society for International Cultural Relations: Its Prospectus and Scheme* (n.p., Tokyo, April, 1934). For the date of the dinner, see Tagashira to Du Bois, November 21, 1936, Du Bois Papers/UMass. "... ULTRA-NATIONALISTS IN THE MILITARY.": Reischauer, *Japan*, p. 103. "... THE INFLUENTIAL YANAGISAWA KEN.: Hikida to Du Bois, October 15, 1936, Du Bois Papers/UMass. "... THE PRESIDING NOBLEMAN.": Du Bois, "Forum of Fact and Opinion," Pittsburgh *Courier*, March 20, 1937, also in Aptheker, ed., *News Columns*, I, p. 182. "... PROFESSOR K. MIYAKE.": Miyake to Du Bois, March 15, 1938, Du Bois Papers/UMass.

416–17. "... TRANSLATING *SOULS* ... HAPPY SPRING.": Du Bois, "Forum of Fact and Opinion," Pittsburgh *Courier*, March 20, 1937, also in Aptheker, ed., *News Columns*, I, p. 181–182. "... MODEST DEMEANOR OF JAPANESE WOMEN.": folder marked "Travel—1936—Japan," W.E.B. Du Bois Collection,

Fisk University. ". . . BUT NOT IN TOKYO.": Du Bois, "Forum of Fact and Opinion," Pittsburgh *Courier*, March 13, 1937, Aptheker, ed., *News Columns*, I, p. 179.

417. *"TATSUTA MARU."*: The *Tatsuta Maru* would serve as the repatriation ship for Japanese nationals after Pearl Harbor, and on which Hikida was a passenger. See Johann Porodos, *Combined Fleet Decoded: The Secret History of American Intelligence* (New York: Random House, 1995), p. 159. ". . . ON THE DOT.": Du Bois, "Forum of Fact and Opinion," Pittsburgh *Courier*, March 13, 1937, Aptheker, ed., *News Columns*, I, p. 183. ". . . NO OFFICIAL STATUS.": Du Bois, "Forum of Fact and Opinion," Pittsburgh *Courier*, March 13, 1937, also in Aptheker, ed., *News Columns*, I, p. 178. ". . . COMMON SUFFERING AND A COMMON DESTINY.": Du Bois, "Forum of Fact and Opinion," Pittsburgh *Courier*, March 13, 1937, Aptheker, ed., *News Columns*, I, p. 182. ". . . FREEDOM OF SPIRIT AND EXPRESSION.": Du Bois, "Forum of Fact and Opinion," Pittsburgh *Courier*, March 13, 1937, also in Aptheker, ed., *News Columns*, I, p. 178. ". . . A COUNTRY OF COLORED PEOPLE RUN BY COLORED PEOPLE . . . THE JAPANESE RUN JAPAN.": Du Bois, "Forum of Fact and Opinion," Pittsburgh *Courier*, March 13, 1937, Aptheker, ed., *News Columns*, I, p. 182.

418. ". . . AFRICA IS PROSTRATE.": Du Bois, "The African Roots of the War," *Atlantic Monthly* (May 1915), 707–714, also in Herbert Aptheker, ed., *Writings in Periodical Literature* (New York: Kraus Thomson, 1982), 4 Vols., II, p. 99 ". . . THE AWAKENING LEADERS OF NEW CHINA.": Du Bois, "African Roots of the War," p. 104.

418. ". . . FALSE FRIENDS OF CHINA.": Du Bois to Harry F. Ward, October 7, 1937, Du Bois Papers/ UMass, also in Aptheker, ed., *Correspondence*, II, p. 147. ". . . NOT LOVE FOR CHINA.": Du Bois, "Forum and Fact and Opinion," Pittsburgh *Courier*, October 23, 1937, also in Aptheker, ed., *News Columns* I, p. 246. On Stimson and Du Bois, see Stimson to Du Bois, January 24, 1940, Du Bois Papers/UMass, also in Aptheker, ed., *Correspondence*, II, pp. 205–206. ". . . KILLING THE UNARMED AND INNOCENT.": Du Bois, "Forum and Fact and Opinion," Pittsburgh *Courier*, October 23, 1937, also in Aptheker, ed., *News Columns* I, p. 246.

419. ". . . AS THE CROW FLIES.": Robert L. Vann to Du Bois, December 1, 1937, Du Bois Papers/ UMass. ". . . STERN REBUKE.": Du Bois, "As the Crow Flies," *Amsterdam News*, February 24, 1940, also in Aptheker, ed., *News Columns*, I, p. 286. Stimson's invitation can be found as Stimson to Du Bois, January 24, 1940, Du Bois Papers/UMass, also in Aptheker, ed., *Correspondence*, II, pp. 205–206. ". . . STANDING OVER AGAINST THE WHITE WORLD.": Du Bois, "Forum of Fact and Opinion," Pittsburgh *Courier*, March 13, 1937, Aptheker, ed., *News Columns*, I, p. 182. ". . . GRATEFUL TO [HIM].": Hikida to Du Bois, March 3, 1937, Du Bois Papers/UMass. ". . . THE WIDENING OF MY VERY NARROW HORIZON.": Shigeyoshi Sakake to Du Bois, December 28, 1936.

420. ". . . TO CANCEL DU BOIS'S LECTURES.": J. A. Somerville to Irene Diggs, December 18, 1936, Du Bois Papers/UMass. ". . . FEAR OF THIS FOREIGN ELEMENT.": Du Bois, "Forum of Fact and Opinion," Pittsburgh *Courier*, January 2, 1937, also in Aptheker, ed., *News Columns*, I, p. 154.

420. ". . . SOUNDED NOT QUITE CLEAR.": Leo Stein to Du Bois, February 16, 1937, Du Bois Papers/ UMass. ". . . 'ORDERLY' APPLICATION OF DISABILITIES . . . THE POINT I WAS TRYING TO MAKE.": Du Bois to Leo Stein, May 10, 1937, Du Bois Papers/UMass. ". . . NAZISM'S TREATMENT OF THE JEWS.": Lipstadt, *Beyond Belief*, p. 53. ". . . ELIMINATIONIST ANTI-SEMITISM.": Goldhagen, *Hitler's Willing Executioners*.

Chapter 12: Atlanta: The Politics of Knowledge

422. ". . . IMPARTED AN URGENCY.": W.E.B. Du Bois, *Dusk of Dawn* (Millwood, N.Y.: Kraus-Thomson, 1975. orig. pub. 1941), pp. 192, 198.

423. ". . . TEN-YEAR-OLD AAAE.": Ellen Condliffe Lagemann, *The Politics of Knowledge: The Carnegie Corporation, Philanthropy, and Public Policy* (Chicago and London: Univ. of Chicago, 1989), 104–106. ". . . THE BRONZE BOOKLETS.": Du Bois to Alain Locke, April 26, 1935; Locke to Du Bois, April 29, 1935; Du Bois to Locke, May 16, 1935; Du Bois to Locke, May 28, 1935; Locke to Du Bois, June 4, 1935; Du Bois to Locke, February 27, 1936; Locke to Du Bois, [date unknown, early March 1936] Locke to Du Bois, March 6, 1936; Memorandum from Du Bois to Locke, May 22, 1935; Locke to Du Bois, May 30, 1936; Locke to Du Bois, November 30, 1936; all in the Papers of W.E.B. Du Bois, Special Collections, W.E.B. Du Bois Library, Univ. of Massachusetts at Amherst (hereafter Du Bois Papers/UMass). Also in Herbert Aptheker, ed., *The Correspondence of W.E.B. Du Bois* (Amherst: University of Massachusetts Press, 1976), 3 vols., II, 80–85. See also, Du Bois to Locke, March 6, 1935; Du

Bois to Locke, March 23, 1935; Du Bois to Locke, May 16, 1935; Du Bois to Locke, September 10, 1935; Locke to Du Bois, October 8, 1935; Du Bois to Locke, May 22, 1936; all in Alain Leroy Locke Papers, Moorland-Spingarn Research Center, Howard University (hereafter ALLP/HU). See also, correspondence between Locke and Morse Cartwright of American Association of Adult Education, Cartwright to Locke, March 28, 1934; Cartwright to Locke, May 28, 1934; Cartwright to Locke, June 21, 1934; Cartwright to Locke, January 23, 1935; Locke to Cartwright, March 6, 1935; all in ALLP/HU. ". . . HE HAD APPOINTED LOGAN.": Du Bois to Anson Phelps Stokes, March 19, 1936 and "Board of Directors Meeting," May 16, 1936, both in Phelps-Stokes Fund Archives, *Encyclopedia of the Negro* Correspondence, 1931–1946, Special Collections: Schomburg Center for Research in Black Culture, New York Public Library [hereafter PSF]; Du Bois had called his contribution "The Negro and Social Reconstruction," intending it to reflect his most developed thinking about the racial challenge and response to the collapse of the national economy, a " "fair and pretty exhaustive study of the Negro from 1932 to 1936," he thought. (Du Bois, *Dusk*, p. 319) The issue in contention was an eleven-point addendum Du Bois called the "Basic American Negro Creed," a credo devised, he said, after conferring with "a number of the younger Negro scholars." (*Dusk*, p. 319).

423. ". . . LOCKE'S 'FERTILE MIND' ": Lagemann, *Politics of Knowledge*, p. 130. ". . . IN COMPLETE AGREEMENT": Locke to Du Bois, May 30, 1936, in Du Bois Papers/UMass, and Aptheker, ed., *Correspondence*, p. 84–85. ". . . HAD VOTED TO DECLINE": Locke to Du Bois, November 30, 1936, ALLP/ HU. ". . . AND EXTENSIVE REVISION": Locke to Du Bois, November 30, 1936, Du Bois/UMass, and Aptheker, ed., *Correspondence*, II, p. 85.

424. ". . . TERRIBLE MISGIVINGS": Locke to Lyman Bryson, June 8, 1936, ALLP/HU. ". . . IMPERIALISM IS AN INTERNATIONAL EXPRESSION": Ralph Bunche, *A World View of Race*. Bronze Booklet No. 4 (Association of Negro Folk Ed., 1936), pp. 40, 86, 89. ". . . MARXIST POINT OF VIEW": Bryson to Locke, June 23, 1936; Locke to Bryson, June 25, 1936, both in ALLP/HU. ". . . TAKING ITS PLACE BESIDE": see editor's note in Aptheker, ed., *Correspondence*, p. 80.

425. ". . . SPLENDID RECORD": Du Bois, "The Negro and Social Reconstruction" (1936), in Herbert Aptheker, ed., *Against Racism: Unpublished Essays, Papers, Addresses, 1887–1961* (Amherst: University of Massachusetts Press, 1985), p. 146. ". . . BY COOPERATIVE EFFORT": Ibid., p. 148.

425. ". . . THE SOCIALISTIC STATE": Du Bois, "The Negro and Social Reconstruction," in Aptheker, ed., *Against Racism*, p. 149. ". . . DU BOIS WOULD REASON": Du Bois, *Dusk*, p. 215. ". . . THE CRUCIAL QUESTION": Locke to Bryson, May 31, 1936, ALL/HU. See also, Cartwright to Locke, November 30, 1936, ALLP/HU. ". . . A CURT DEMAND": Du Bois to Locke, January 27, 1937; Du Bois to Locke, February 4, 1937, both in ALL/HU. "JUST WHO PRONOUNCED . . .": Du Bois, *Dusk*, p. 322.

426. ". . . EFFECT THE SALVATION": Du Bois, *Dusk*, p. 320. ". . . SOME FORM OF SOCIALISM": DuBois, *Dusk*, p. 321.

426. ". . . A MAJOR STUDY": On the creation and endowment of the new Atlanta University, see Eric Anderson and Alfred A. Moss, *Dangerous Donations: Northern Philanthropy and Southern Black Education, 1902–1930* (Columbia: University of Missouri Press, 1999), pp. 169–170, 171, 199. On the Federal Bureau of Education's 1929 *Survey of Negro Colleges and Universities*, see Anderson and Moss, *Dangerous Donations* pp. 211–212.

426–27. ". . . NO SUCH OPPORTUNITY": David Levering Lewis, *W.E.B. Du Bois: Biography of a Race, 1868–1919* (New York: Henry Holt, 1993), 194. "A MODEL AGENDA . . .": The indirect response he got for his pains came in the form of an invitation from Alfred Holt Stone, a white amateur sociologist, to assist in the Mississippi planter's own Carnegie-funded researches. See Lewis, *W.E.B. Du Bois*, 367. ". . . IN WAYS MORE PRACTICAL": Ibid., 380. ". . . NOW DETERMINED TO ASSEMBLE": Stokes to Robert T. Crane, December 4, 1931; Thomas Jesse Jones to Crane, November 23, 1931, both in PSF.

427. ". . . ADVICE OF THOMAS JESSE JONES": Personally Stokes had wanted to invite Du Bois, he confided to Jackson Davis, a GEB official who would loom large in Du Bois's encyclopedia aspirations, "but owing to strong opposition from a certain source which I will not name," explained Stokes, "this was not done." Anson Phelps Stokes to Jackson Davis, March 31, 1932, General Education Board Records, Rockefeller Archives [hereafter GEB]. Also, it is important to note that Thomas Jesse Jones rejected the idea that Negroes were ready for more civil rights. See Patricia Sullivan, citing Clark Foreman, in *Days of Hope: Race and Democracy in the New Deal Era* (Chapel Hill: University of North Carolina, 1996), 35. See also, Stokes' first letter concerning the possible preparation and publication of an "Encyclopedia of the Negro," October 19, 1931, and Howard University, "Conference on the Advisability of Publishing an Encyclopedia of the Negro," November 7, 1931, both in PSF.

". . . HAD STRUCK DU BOIS AND WOODSON FROM THE LIST": Stokes to Jackson Davis, March 31, 1932, GEB. On Monroe Work's *Negro Year Book* influence, see T. J. Jones to Crane, November 23, 1931, PSF. On the publication of the work after a six-year hiatus, see W.E.B. Du Bois, review of Monroe N. Work, ed., *The Negro Year Book: An American Encyclopedia of the Negro, 1931–32* (Tuskegee: Tuskegee Institute, 1932), in *The Crisis* (February 1932), pp. 67–69, also in Herbert Aptheker, ed., *Book Reviews by W.E.B. Du Bois* (Millwood, N.Y.: KTO Press, 1977), 160–162. Also, Linda O. McMurry, *Recorder of the Black Experience: A Biography of Monroe Nathan Work* (Baton Rouge and London: Louisiana State University Press, 1985), pp. 74–77. ". . . SO-CALLED SOCIOLOGICAL RESEARCH": Aptheker, ed., *Book Reviews*, p. 151. ". . . A VERY RADICAL POSITION": Quoted in Sullivan, *Days of Hope*, p. 35, and Kenneth James King, *Pan-Africanism and Education: A Study of Race Philanthropy in the Southern United States of America and East Africa* (Oxford: Clarendon Press, 1971), pp. 26, 29.

427. ". . . SERIOUSLY COMPLICATE FUNDING": Stokes to Edwin Embree, April 12, 1935, Embree to Stokes, April 17, 1935; PSF.

427. ". . . DETAINED BY OTHER BUSINESS": "Encyclopedia of the Negro" proceedings supplied to the author by Adelaide Cromwell Hill, Reprint of March 1936, p. 3, in author's possession.

429. ". . . INITIATED THE SCIENTIFIC STUDY": Du Bois to Embree, December 2, 1931, PSF; Du Bois to James H. Dillard, November 30, 1931, Du Bois Papers/UMass, also in Aptheker, ed., *Correspondence*, I, p. 447. ". . . THE SUPPORT OF WOODSON": Du Bois to Carter G. Woodson, January 29, 1932, Du Bois Papers/UMass, also in Aptheker, ed., *Correspondence*, I, pp. 448–449.

429. ". . . WOODSON ADVISED": Woodson to Benjamin Brawley, November 28, 1931; Woodson to Phelps-Stokes Fund, October 22, 1932, both in PSF.

429. ". . . BEING WORKED OUT BY": Stokes to Woodson, February 12, 1934; Dillard to Stokes, July 13, 1936, both in PSF. ". . . AGREED TO ATTEND": Du Bois to Stokes, December 9, 1932, Du Bois Papers/UMass. ". . . DU BOIS NOW SPOKE AT LENGTH": Minutes for "Second Conference on 'Encyclopedia of the Negro,'" January 9, 1932, PSF. ". . . WHITE EDITORS": Minutes for "Second Conference on 'Encyclopedia of the Negro,'" January 9, 1932, PSF. ". . . MILLER STRONGLY DISSENTED": In agreeing with Miller, John Hope underscored the benefits of an all-too-rare collaboration between influentials of both races as an even more compelling reason. Responding more or less to Hope, Thomas Jesse Jones remarked that it would be lamentable if the principal rationale for interracialism was that Negroes were unable to carry through the project alone. ". . . PROPOSED A NEGRO EDITOR-IN-CHIEF": Minutes for "Second Conference on 'Encyclopedia of the Negro,'" January 9, 1932, PSF. ". . . PROPOSING A JOINT EDITORSHIP": *Ibid.* ". . . HE COMPLAINED TO KEPPEL": Lester, quoted in Walter A. Jackson, *Gunnar Myrdal and America's Conscience: Social Engineering and Racial Liberalism, 1938–1987* (Chapel Hill: University of North Carolina Press, 1990), pp. 25–26.

430. ". . . WORTHY OF THE SAME": Du Bois, "Confidential Memorandum Regarding the Significance of the Proposed *Encyclopedia of the Negro*," in Aptheker, ed., *Against Racism*, p. 161. ". . . ENEMY HAS THE MONEY": Du Bois to Woodson, January 29, 1932, Du Bois Papers/UMass, and Aptheker, ed., *Correspondence*, 1, p. 448–449. ". . . MORDECAI JOHNSON'S MOTION": Minutes for "Second conference on 'Encyclopedia of the Negro,'" January 9, 1932, PSF.

431. ". . . THE CONFEREES DECIDED": The original members of the board of directors and their formal affiliations, elected by the Conference on January 9, 1932, included the following: W. W. Alexander, President of the Commission on Interracial Cooperation, and President of Dillard University; Professor Franz Boas, Professor of Anthropology, Emeritus, Columbia University; Professor Benjamin Brawley, Professor of English, Howard University; Otelia Cromwell, Professor of English, Miner Teacher's College, Washington, D.C.; James H. Dillard, Ex-President of the Jeanes and Slater Funds; W.E.B. Du Bois, Director of Publications and Research, National Association for the Advancement of Colored People; Leo Favrot, Field Representative of the General Education Board, and member of the President's Commission to Haiti; John Hope, President of Atlanta University; J. Franklin Jameson, Chief of the Division of Manuscripts, Library of Congress; Charles S. Johnson, Professor of Sociology, Fisk Universisty; Professor James Weldon Johnson, Professor of Creative Literature, Fisk University; President Mordecai Johnson, Howard University; Dr. C. T. Loram, Sterling Professor of Education, Yale University; Robert Russa Moton, Principal of Tuskegee Institute, and Vice-President of the National Urban League; President Florence Read, Spelman College, Atlanta University; Anson Phelps Stokes, President, Phelps-Stokes Fund; Monroe N. Work, Director of Research and Records, Tuskegee Institute. Boas, Favrot, and Jameson were ultimately unable to serve on the board; they were replaced by Professor A. R. Radcliffe Brown, Department of Anthropology, University of Chicago; Dr. Waldo

G. Leland, Permanent Secretary of the American Council of Learned Societies, Washington, D.C.; and Joel E. Spingarn, President of the National Association for the Advancement of Colored People, and former Professor of Comparative Literature at Columbia University. "Encyclopedia of the Negro" proceedings supplied to the author by Adelaide Cromwell Hill, Reprint of minutes of March 1936, p. 10–11, in author's possession. The Advisory Board, proposed by the board of directors, was to be drawn from the following organizations: the American Council of Learned Societies, the Social Science Research Council, the American Council on Education, the National Research Council, the International Institute of African Languages and Culture, the South African Association for the Advancement of Science, Howard University, Fisk University, Atlanta University, Hampton University, Tuskegee Institute, the Commission on Interracial Cooperation, and the Association of Negro Life and History. Only the Social Science Research Council and the Association of Negro Life and History declined membership. "Encyclopedia of the Negro" proceedings supplied to the author by Adelaide Cromwell Hill, Reprint of March 1936, p. 12, in author's possession.

431. ". . . WITH GREAT SATISFACTION": Ibid. ". . . DU BOIS'S ACCEPTANCE": Du Bois to Anson Phelps Stokes, December 17, 1931; Stokes to Du Bois, March 19, 1932, both in PSF. "TEN YEARS AGO . . .": Strokes to Jackson Davis, March 31, 1932, GEB.

431. ". . . PECULIAR SATISFACTION": Du Bois to Stokes, March 25, 1932, PSF. See also, Dillard to Stokes, February 5, 1932, PSF, in which Dillard recommends James Weldon Johnson, instead of Du Bois, as editor.

432. ". . . SURRENDER EDITORSHIP": Anson Phelps Stokes to Jackson Davis, March 31, 1932, GEB. ". . . ANY ONE PARTICULAR RACE": Ernest Q. Hooton to Phelps-Stokes Fund, March 23, 1932, PSF. Elazar Barkan's *The Retreat of Scientific Racism. Changing Concepts of Race in Britain and the United States Between the World Wars* (New York: Cambridge University Press, 1992) has excellent material on Hooton and his kind. Hooton's doubts were typical of a broad sweep of aversions whose common denominator was a conviction that the best solution to the race problem was to ignore the Negro race. Racial "progressives" of the Hooton stripe prided themselves on never noticing that some Americans were not white — or that some whites were less "white" than others. For similar reasons, the Social Science Research Council (SSRC) was similarly disinclined to foot a portion of the bill to study the problem, even though its director agreed with Stokes that the American Negro was "the most important problem in the future of our national life." (See Robert T. Crane to Stokes, December 4, 1931, PSF.) If the reluctance of the SSRC was partly due to its funding of the costly, fifteen-volume *Encyclopedia of the Social Sciences*, racial considerations were by no means irrelevant. At the Rosenwald Fund where the value of assets had dropped by more than forty percent, Embree approved of the Phelps-Stokes plan in principle but frankly doubted that current economic conditions or the attitude of the general American public favored the project (see Embree to Du Bois, December 4, 1931, PSF). The gregarious Waldo Leland of the American Council of Learned Societies (ACLS), an early proponent of Stokes's plan, had been somewhat more encouraging about eventual funding (see Stokes to Crane, February 9, 1934, PSF). In his report to the board of directors in late May 1932, Stokes had to acknowledge that "conditions favorable to securing the large amount of money" probably would be delayed for at least another year. Whereupon he sailed for Africa five days later on Phelps-Stokes Fund business. PSF, "Encyclopedia of the Negro," Correspondence General and Special, 1931–1946.

433. ". . . CAST A WIDENING NET": Du Bois to R. R. Moton, September 26, 1933, Du Bois Papers/UMass.

433. "WOODSON SELDOM SPOKE . . .": August Meier and Elliot Rudwick, eds., *Black History and the Historical Profession, 1915–1980* (Urbana: University of Illinois Press, 1986), 91. ". . . INVITED TO AFFILIATE": Stokes to Crane, February 9, 1934, PSF. "CERTAIN AMOUNT OF DIFFICULTY": Otto Klineberg to Du Bois, February 9, 1936, Du Bois/UMass, and Aptheker, ed., *Correspondence*, II, p. 70.

434. ". . . TRAILBLAZING SCHOLARSHIP": On the discussion of anthropological schools of race at the time, see Jack Salzman et. al., eds., *Encyclopedia of African-American Culture and History*, 5 vols., I, (New York: Simon & Schuster, 1996), 141–147. On Herskovits and *Encyclopedia of the Negro*, see Jackson, *Gunnar Myrdal*, pp. 25–27, and on Stokes as "uplifter," p. 25.

434. ". . . WRENCHED FROM THE GRIP": "It is a great idea," wrote Du Bois to Stokes, focusing again on their joint encyclopedia project, "and it ought to go through." (Du Bois to Stokes, February 2, 1935, PSF.) Almost simultaneously, Du Bois had pursued a similar course with what seemed, for a suspenseful two summer months in 1935, strong prospects for success as Ira Reid in Washington personally lobbied the Federal Works Project's (FWP) assistant director for a commitment. (Reid to Du Bois,

September 12, 1935, Du Bois Papers/UMass.) A chance encounter at New York's Pennsylvania Station with Robert Weaver led to submission to the New York FWP of another encyclopedia proposal as part of the unit's "History of the Colored Person in New York." (Stokes to Du Bois, January 17, 1936; Du Bois to Stokes, Jan 15, 1936, both in PSF.) Once again, budget limitations had followed initial expressions of interest. (Du Bois to Stokes, August 29, 1935; Stokes to Du Bois, September 7, 1935; Ira Reid to Du Bois, September 12, 1935, all in PSF.) Howard University had been in no position to take on the project because of its delicate congressional relations. (Stokes to Du Bois, October 8, 1935, PSF.) After one-hundred-fifty-six letters to a who's who in scholarship and philanthropy, Du Bois had espied a possible breakthrough: support from the Library of Congress. At the last minute, though, the September appointment with Jameson, the chief of manuscripts, had had to be cancelled. (Du Bois to Stokes, October 2, 1935, PSF.) Jameson had been happy to reschedule the appointment but warned that he had little in the way of practical assistance to offer, Du Bois informed Stokes (Du Bois to Stokes, October 11, 1935, PSF).

434. "...A STELLAR ROSTER": Du Bois to Stokes, October 24, 1935, PSF; Frank Porter Graham to Du Bois, November 26, 1935; Du Bois to Bronislaw Malinowski, February 17, 1937; Malinowski to Du Bois, March 2, 1937, all in Du Bois Papers/UMass; Stokes to Du Bois, February 11, 1938, PSF.

434. "...BEARD OFFERED": Du Bois to Stokes, October 11, 1935, PSF. "...READY TO RECOMMEND": Embree to Du Bois, April 30, 1935, Du Bois Paper/UMass, also in Aptheker, ed., *Correspondence*, II, p. 66. "...WHOLLY BY NEGROES": H. L. Mencken to Du Bois, October 15, 1935, Du Bois Paper/UMass, and Aptheker, *Correspondence*, II, p. 69. "...THE LATTER'S PREFERENCE": Broadus Mitchell to DuBois, July 29, 1936, Du Bois Papers/UMass, also in Aptheker, ed., *Correspondence*, II, pp. 70–71. "REJUVENATED BY...": Stokes to Du Bois, October 15, 1935, PSF. "...TIME IN GERMANY": Du Bois to Stokes, October 24, 1935, PSF.

435. "NEWTON BAKER": For biographical information on Newton Baker, see Jackson, *Gunnar Myrdal*, pp. 16–21. See also, David W. Southern, *Gunnar Myrdal and Black-White Relations: The Use and Abuse of 'An American Dilemma,' " 1944–1969* (Baton Rouge: Louisiana State University, 1987), pp. 2–3. Valuable specifics about Baker's racialism can be found in Lagemann, *The Politics of Knowledge*, esp. pp. 127–128. Oswald Villard and Ira Reid had spoken passionately at the conference of Christians and Jews of the causes of the Harlem riot and of the impoverishment and compounding alienation of colored Americans. "...A BROAD STUDY": Lagemann, p. 127. "...THE TRANSPLANTED SOUTHERNER": Southern, *The Politics of Knowledge, Gunnar Myrdal*, p. 2–3.

436. "...UNEXPECTED DEPARTURE": In fact, May 16, 1936, was the first meeting of the advisory board. "...THE WHITE COLLABORATOR": DuBois to Stokes, June 29, 1936, PSF. "SCHOMBURG'S ATTITUDE...": Arthur Schomburg to Charles S. Johnson [n.d., 1935], Arthur A. Schomburg Papers/ Special Collections: Schomburg Center for Research in Black Culture, New York Public Library [hereafter AASP], 561–562 "...IN CHARGE OF EVERYTHING": Arthur Schomburg to Charles S. Johnson. "...WHAT WAS IT ALL ABOUT": Arthur Schomburg to Charles S. Johnson [n.d., 1935], AASP.

437. "...THE FUNDAMENTAL WEAKNESS": E. Franklin Frazier to Du Bois, November 7, 1936, Du Bois Papers/UMass, also in Aptheker, ed., *Correspondence*, II, p. 71–72. "...SIMILAR RESERVATIONS": Herskovits to Du Bois, September 28, 1936, Du Bois Papers/UMass. See also, the letter from the editor of the *American Sociological Review* to Rayford W. Logan, November 6, 1936, Du Bois Papers/UMass. "...JOHNSON KILLED": Du Bois to Mrs. James Weldon Johnson, September 21, 1938, Du Bois Papers/ UMass. "...MILLER WOULD SUCCUMB": "Miller, Kelly," in Rayford Logan and Michael R. Winston, eds., *Dictionary of American Negro Biography* (New York: W.W. Norton, 1982), pp. 435–439.

438. "...THE LAST REPORT.": Life Extension Institute Report, October 6, 1933, Will to Nina, February 3, 1938, both in Du Bois Papers/UMass. "...ROSENWALD FELLOWSHIP.": Shirley Graham to Du Bois, December 16, 1937, Graham to Du Bois, April 27, 1938, both in Du Bois Papers/UMass. "...A FORMAL BANQUET.": Rayford Logan to William Pickens, January 4, 1938, WPRG/SCRBC; Lewis interview with Logan, October 1974, Voices of the Harlem Renaissance/Schomburg Center for Research in Black Culture, New York Public Library (hereafter VOHR/SCRBC). "...FIVE DOLLARS BOUGHT MEMBERSHIP.": Myron Adams to Rayford Logan, January 29, 1938, Du Bois Papers/UMass. "...HOPELESSNESS OF PERSECUTED MINORITIES.": Mary White Ovington to Logan, March 11, 1938, Du Bois Papers/UMass.

438. "...MESSAGE OF REGRET.": Walter White to Rayford Logan, February 23, 1938, Du Bois Papers/ UMass. "...ENCYCLOPEDIA OF THE NEGRO.": Raymond B. Fosdick to Jerome Greene, February 4,

1938, Greene to Rufus Clement, February 10, 1938, Rockefeller Archives; GEB. ". . . AT THE LAST MOMENT.": Will to Nina, February 3, 1938, Du Bois Papers/UMass. ". . . TEN-YEAR TERMS.": Du Bois, "A Pageant in Seven Decades: 1868–1938" in Herbert Aptheker, ed., *Pamphlets and Leaflets by W.E.B. Du Bois* (White Plains, N.Y.: Kraus-Thomson, 1986), pp. 244–274.

440. ". . . WERE TO BE BLAMED.": Du Bois, "A Pageant in Seven Decades," p. 245.

441. ". . . A WORLD ABOUT TO BE BORN.": DuBois, "A Pageant in Seven Decades," 270.

441. ". . . HAVING RUN THE RISK.": Du Bois to Thomas E. Jones, April 22, 1938, Du Bois Papers/ UMass.

442. ". . . VIRTUALLY A NEW BOOK.": Du Bois, *Black Folk Then and Now* (Millwood, N.Y.: Kraus Thomson, 1975, orig. pub. 1939). ". . . TWO HOUR CAMPUS CONFERENCE.": Program for the National Conference under the Auspices of the Joint Committee of National Recovery, Social Science Division of Howard University, May 18–20, 1935, Du Bois Papers/UMass. ". . . THAT AU MIGHT BE FAVORED OVER HOWARD.": Benjamin Brawley to Stokes, February 25, 1937, PSF.

442. ". . . AS RECENTLY AS MID APRIL.": Fosdick to Du Bois, April 15, 1937, PSF. ". . . HE SEEMED INTERESTED.": Anson Phelps Stokes to Du Bois, October 27, 1937, Du Bois Papers/UMass, also in Aptheker, ed., *Correspondence*, II, p. 151. On the selection of Guy Johnson, see Jackson, *Gunnar Myrdal*, pp. 109–110. Du Bois himself preferred Arthur Raper. On Park, see D. H. Stevens to Jackson Davis, January 6, 1938, GEB. ". . . $260,000 ENTERPRISE.": Staff "interview" by Jackson Davis and D. H. Stevens with Anson Phelps Stokes and W.E.B. Du Bois, November 29, 1937, GEB.

443. ". . . THE HIGH STANDARD OF SCHOLARSHIP.": Franz Boas, "Race," in Edwin R. A. Seligman and Alvin Johnson, eds., *Encyclopedia of the Social Sciences* (New York: Macmillan, 1935), XIII, pp. 25–34 (hereafter ESS); Melville Herskovitz, "Race Conflict," in Seligman and Johnson, eds., ESS, XIII, pp. 36–43; Abram Harris and Sterling Spero, "Negro Problem," in Seligman and Johnson, eds., ESS, XI, pp. 335–355. ". . . COLLAPSE OF THE COTTON TENANCY.": Jackson, *Gunnar Myrdal*, p. 24. ". . . IN NEED OF ATTENTION FROM THE NATION.": Charles S. Johnson, *Shadow of the Plantation* (Chicago: University of Chicago Press, 1934). Also see James B. McKee, *Sociology and the Negro Problem: The Failure of a Perspective* (Urbana: University of Illinois, 1993), p. 130.

443. ON SCHRIEKE: See the editor's note on Schrieke in Herbert Aptheker, ed., *Book Reviews by W.E.B. Du Bois* (Millwood, N.Y.: Kraus Thomson, 1977), p. 208. "JUST AS THE CONCEPT OF 'CASTE'.": McKee, *Sociology and the Negro Problem*, p. 153. ". . . AGAINST THE CASTE METHOD.": Guy Johnson, quoted in *Ibid.*, p. 146. ". . . ON A THOROUGH ECONOMIC FOUNDATION.": Du Bois, review of Dollard, *Caste and Class in a Southern Town*, in Aptheker, ed., *Book Reviews*, p. 176. Also see E. Franklin Frazier on Dollard in Anthony M. Platt, *E. Franklin Frazier Reconsidered* (New Brunswick, N.J.: Rutgers University Press, 1991), p. 167. Walter Jackson has emphasized that Dollard used more Freud than Sumner—Jackson, *Gunnar Myrdal*, p. 104. ". . . NATIONAL COMPROMISE WITH THE WHITE SOUTH.": See Jackson, *Gunnar Myrdal*; McKee, *Sociology and the Negro Problem*; Fred H. Matthews, *Quest for an American Sociology: Robert H. Park and the Chicago School* (Montreal and London: Queens University Press, 1977); Thomas F. Pettigrew, *The Sociology of Race Relations: Reflection and Reform* (New York: Free Press, 1980).

444. ". . . A CURIOUS CROSSROADS.": The Encyclopedia still had expert critics in Donald Young at the Social Science Research Council, in John Dollard's younger brother, Charles, on the Carnegie staff, who took a personal dislike to Du Bois, and in Herskovitz, who continued to snipe at the project from Northwestern. However, the international roster of prospective contributors Du Bois and Stokes had assembled by winter of 1937 appeared to counter concerns about the project's catholicity of expertise. A pledge of collaboration had just come to Stokes from Seligman, France's expert on Africa, with further pledges arriving weekly. See Anson Phelps Stokes to Du Bois, April 4, 1938, PSF. ". . . OBJECTIVITY OF OUR FINDINGS.": Phelps Stokes to Du Bois, February 11, 1938, PSF. ". . . RACIAL PRIDE ON THE ONE HAND AND RACIAL PREJUDICE ON THE OTHER.": Phelps Stokes to Du Bois, February 11, 1938, PSF. ". . . GATHERING MOMENTUM.": Staff "interview" with Dr. Charles S. Johnson, March 16, 1938, GEB.

445. ". . . THE OBJECTIVITY QUEST.": Peter Novick, *That Noble Dream: The 'Objectivity Question' and the American Historical Profession* (New York: Cambridge University Press, 1988), p. 2. Du Bois, reviewing Lamarr Middleton's *The Rape of Africa* (1938), wrote—of modern historians—that "they seek the aloofness and imperturbability of the biologist who dissects bugs or the geologist who hammers stones" [in Aptheker, ed., *Book Reviews*, p. 174]. ". . . DU BOIS'S FEBRUARY 1938 MEMORANDUM.": Du

Bois, "On the Scientific Objectivity of the Proposed *Encyclopedia of the Negro* and on the Safeguards Against the Intrusion of Propaganda," in Aptheker, ed., *Against Racism*, pp. 164–168. "... THE IDEAL OF THE EFFORT FOR OBJECTIVE TRUTH.": Novick, *That Noble Dream*, p. 269.

445. "... THE OBJECTIVITY BAR.": The model for "objective" scholarship was E. B. Reuter who was later to attack Myrdal's *American Dilemma* as a disgrace to social science. See Jackson, *Gunnar Myrdal*, p. 254. "... EDITOR AN PROPAGANDIST.": Phelps Stokes to Du Bois, March 22, 1938, PSF. "... MORE REASSURANCE.": Anson Phelps Stokes to Du Bois, March 22, 1938, PSF. "... MORE GOOD NEWS.": Phelps Stokes to Du Bois, March 28, 1938, PSF. For the General Education Board's terms, see Phelps Stokes to Du Bois, April 10, 1938, PSF. On the final appointment of Guy Johnson as associate editor of the *Encyclopedia of the Negro*, see Dollard to Phelps Stokes, August 11, 1938, PSF. Stokes emerged from a long conference with Stevens and Davis in which the two officers had stipulated nine essential prerequisites in order for the GEB to underwrite its portion of the $260,000 budget: among them, a smaller advisory board to include Dumas Malone and Charles S. Johnson; a white southerner or two added to the advisory board; Guy Johnson as indispensable assistant editor; strengthening of the expertise on Africa; and no budget overruns. "... TO RECOMMEND THE PROJECT.": Phelps Stokes to Du Bois, March 28, 1938, PSF.

446. "... FOUNDATION MEMORANDA.": Du Bois, "On the Scientific Objectivity of the Proposed *Encyclopedia of the Negro*," in Aptheker, ed., *Against Racism*, p. 163.

447. "... SLATED FOR APPROVAL.": Lewis, interview with Rayford Logan, Voices of the Harlem Renaissance, Schomburg Center for Research in Black Culture (hereafter VOHR/SCRBC). "... HE PROBABLY KNEW DU BOIS BETTER THAN ANYONE ELSE.": Lewis, interview with Rayford Logan, VOHR/SCRBC. "... IT CANNOT ACT FAVORABLY UPON YOUR REQUEST.": Phelps Stokes to Du Bois, April 10, 1938, PSF. "... YOU AND I MAY NOT SEE THIS PROJECT THROUGH.": Phelps Stokes to Du Bois, April 10, 1938, PSF. "... MY OWN PERSONALITY.": Du Bois to Phelps Stokes, April 18, 1938, PSF. "... THE WORD OF ONE WHITE MAN.": Lewis, interview with Rayford Logan, VOHR/SCRBC. Logan claimed that years later Herskovits, over lunch at the Northwestern Faculty Club, said, "I killed the 'Encyclopedia of the Negro' project." On Herskovits' Carnegie application, see Jackson, *Gunnar Myrdal*, pp. 26–27.

448. "... THE MOST INFLUENTIAL NEGRO IN THE UNITED STATES.": Jackson Davis to Robert M. Lester, May 5, 1938, GEB. "... INFLUENCED BY THAT FACT.": Quoted in Jackson, *Gunnar Myrdal*, p. 25. "... KEPPEL LOVED TO TRY SOMETHING NEW.": *Appreciations of Frederick Paul Keppel by Some of his Friends* (New York: Columbia University Press. 1951), p. 53.

449. "... A COMPREHENSIVE STUDY OF THE NEGRO.": Frederick Keppel to Gunnar Myrdal, August 12 [13?], 1937, Carnegie Corporation — Myrdal Study, Correspondence, Schomburg Center for Research in Black Culture (hereafter C-MS).

449. "... IN A WHOLLY OBJECTIVE AND DISPASSIONATE WAY.": Southern, *Gunnar Myrdal and Black-White Relations*, p. 5. "... THE LORD BRYCE OF THE AMERICAN NEGRO PROBLEM.": See Jackson, *Gunnar Myrdal*, pp. 29–31. "... WHY NOT THE NEGRO?": Jackson, *Gunnar Myrdal*, p. 86. "... A HANDSHAKE OVER COCKTAILS.": Southern, *Gunnar Myrdal and Black-White Relations*, p. 7.

449. "... A COURTESY CALL.": Gunnar Myrdal to Du Bois, November 26, 1938, Du Bois Papers/UMass. Also see Jackson, *Gunnar Myrdal*, p. 8. "... EYE TO EYE.": Southern, *Gunnar Myrdal and Black-White Relations*, p. 9. "... THE NEGRO AS AN INTEGRAL PART OF AMERICAN CIVILIZATION.": Du Bois to Myrdal, April 13, 1939, Du Bois Papers/UMass. A copy of the 10-page report prepared by Myrdal is in the Du Bois Papers/UMass.

450. ON CHARLES JOHNSON: See the review of *Patterns of Negro Segregation* in "Books and Race," *Phylon* 4.2 (1943), pp. 181–182, 187–191. The roster of scholars is taken from Gunnar Myrdal, *An American Dilemma* (New York: Harper & Row, 1944), 2 vols., I, iii.

451. "... UNDER THE DOMINATION OF WHITE MEN.": Du Bois, *Dusk*, p. 323. "... I THINK HE WILL DO A GOOD JOB.": Robert Maynard Hutchins to Edwin Embree, September 27, 1939, and Embree to Hutchins, September 29, 1939, both in Julius Rosenwald Fund Archives, Fisk University.

451–52. "... INTERPRETIVE IMPACT.": Jackson, *Gunnar Myrdal*, p. 112. "... WOULD GENUINELY MOVE DU BOIS.": Du Bois, "An American Dilemma" in *Phylon* 5.2 (1944), pp. 118–124. For other views, see E. Franklin Frazier's review of Myrdal in *The American Journal of Sociology* (May 1945), pp. 555–557 and Ralph Ellison in *The Collected Works of Ralph Ellison* (New York: Modern Library, 1995), pp. 328–340. "... WORK IS MONUMENTAL.": Du Bois, "An American Dilemma" in *Phylon* 5.2 (1944), p. 123. On leftist Myrdal critics, see Jackson, *Gunnar Myrdal*, p. 258.

452. "... DOMINATES HIS OUTLOOK.": Myrdal, *An American Dilemma*, p. lxxi. "... NO SINGLE FAC-TOR.": Ibid., p. 208. "... OPIATE OF THE WHITE LIBERALS.": Jackson, *Gunnar Myrdal*, p. 258.

Chapter 13: Atlanta: Soldiering On

454. "... LORD HAILEY'S SOURCE BOOK": Herbert Aptheker, Introduction in W.E.B. Du Bois, *Black Folk Then and Now* (Millwood, N.Y.: Kraus-Thomson, 1939, 1975), p. 8. "... TEXTUAL ALTERATIONS ": Herskovits to Du Bois, December 2, 1930, Du Bois to Herskovits, December 10, 1930, Melville J. Herskovits Collection, Northwestern University [hereafter MJH/NW]. Herskovits seriously questioned what he regarded as the racial essentialism running throughout the book. "... DU BOIS INFORMED HENRY HOLT: Aptheker, ed., Introduction in Du Bois, *Black Folk Here*, p. 10.

455. "... AN AMBITIOUS WORK": Du Bois, *Black Folk Then and Now*, viii. A SORT OF WORLD HISTORY OF BLACK PEOPLE: For importance of C. G. Seligman in British anthropology and his book, *Races of Africa* (1930), see E. Barkan, *Retreat of Scientific Racism* (New York: Cambridge University Press, 1992), pp. 30–31. "... IF ASKED TO PONDER.:" Georg Wilhelm Friedrich Hegel, *Philosophy of History*. (New York: Willey, 1900).

455. "... NO SCIENTIFIC DEFINITION OF RACE IS POSSIBLE.": Du Bois, *Black Folk Then and Now*, i. BY PAGE THREE: For quotes regarding Negro blood, see *Black Folk Then and Now*, 3–4. Also, Herskovits to Du Bois, January 9, 1939. MJH/NW. "... IN ALL THESE CENTERS.": On Gobineau's thought see Michael Biddiss, ed., *Selected Political Writings* (New York: Harper & Row, 1970), and see Du Bois, *Black Folk Then and Now*, 220. On African origins, cf Christopher Stringer and Robin McKie, *African Exodus: The Origins of Modern Humanity* (New York: Henry Holt, 1997), and see "... NOT ONLY THE VAST MAJORITY OF WHITE FOLK.": Du Bois, *Black Folk Then and Now*, 368.

456. "... EDWIN EMBREE WAS TO REMIND.": Aptheker, ed., Introduction, in Du Bois, *Black Folks Then and Now*, 13. "... ORGANIC RELATIONSHIP OF DEMOCRACY TO RACISM.": On democracy and racism, Du Bois, *Black Folk Then and Now*, p. 370. On slavery and capitalism, p. 369. On South Africa, see chapter. P. 186 for aspersive Jamaican remarks. "... NOT A TENTH BUT NINE-TENTHS OF ALL MEN.": Du Bois, *Black Folk Then and Now*, 370. "... ONE OF THE MOST COMPLETE ESSAYS IN THE HISTORY.": Aptheker, ed., Introduction, in Du Bois, *Black Folk Then and Now*, 12.

457. "... WHEREVER THERE WAS HISTORY IN AFRICA.": On democracy and racism, see Du Bois, *Black Folk Then and Now*, 221. See Martin Bernal, *Black Athena*, Introduction, esp. p. 31. "... HER-SKOVITS CRITICAL ASPERITY.": Evaluating the book in *The Saturday Review*, Herbert Seligmann, the NAACP's former public relations officer who was now a capable amateur sociologist and author of a just released book on race, judged Du Bois's book flawed in some of its details but successful in the larger significance of being an "effective assault upon the parochialism of the historic and sociological writing which neglects the darker groups." Rayford Logan review in Aptheker, ed., Introduction, Du Bois, *Black Folk Then and Now*, 12. Du Bois received an admiring letter from Charlie Scudder, a retired surgeon and a friend from Great Barrington. Scudder to Du Bois, June 29, 1939, Du Bois Papers/UMass. "... STATES OPPRESS THOSE WHO DARE DISAGREE.": Aptheker, ed., Introduction, in Du Bois, *Black Folk Then and Now*, 15.

458. "... REALLY FELT QUITE ALARMED.": Nina to Will, February 13, 1937, Du Bois Papers/UMass. "... NINA HATED THE PROSPECT OF ANY MOVE.": Du Bois to Yolande, April 24, 1939, Du Bois Papers/UMass. "... IT WAS FINALLY DECIDED.": Memorandum to President Clement, June 23, 1938, Du Bois Papers/UMass. "... A SUITE FOR WILL AND NINA.": Du Bois to Ira De A. Reid, February 11, 1938, Du Bois Papers/UMass. Lewis interview with J. Max Bond, October 5, 1991, regarding Diggs spending nights with Du Bois, also Lewis interview with Samuel Nabrit, June 13, 1987. "... HER SCORE ON THE STANFORD-BINET.": Mildred Johnson to Du Bois, May 30, 1938, Du Bois Papers/UMass.

459. "... MAMA WAS THE CHILD, I WASN'T;": Lewis, interview with Du Bois Williams, June 28, 1987. "... THE FAMILY WOULD REMAIN.": Du Bois to Rufus Clement, August 7, 1939, Du Bois Papers/UMass. "... NINA WOULD LIVE IN HARLEM.": See, Bobbie Branch, who observed the lonely Nina in the YWCA, Lewis interview June 3, 1988. Also, Du Bois to Louie Shivery, August 24, 1939, Du Bois Papers/UMass.

460. "... DASHING AFTER THEM IN HIS DRESSING GOWN.": Du Bois to Anne Cooke and Billie Geter, November 1, 1935, Du Bois Papers/UMass. "... SUCH SOCIAL PRATFALLS.": Du Bois to Ra-chel Davis DuBois, April 12, 1940. "... THREE YEARS HAD ELAPSED, *THE JEWS IN AMERICAN LIFE*.": Du Bois to Rachel Davis DuBois, January 3, 1936, Rachel Davis DuBois to W.E.B. Du Bois, June 3, 1936, both in Du Bois Papers/UMass. "... FATHER COUGHLIN ENJOINED HIS THIRTY MILLION.":

Although many old stock Americans regarded the subject of immigration and ethnicity as inherently divisive, the New Deal administration, shaken by the 1937 economic recession and supported by influential elements of the business sector, had signaled approval of a campaign to counter the hate mongers and reactionaries. On CBS motives, see Barbara Savage, *Broadcasting Freedom: Radio, War and the Politics of Race, 1938–1948* (Chapel Hill: University of North Carolina Press, 1998), 22, for Davis Du Bois, CBS, and quote from James Angell. On nativist upsurge see, Michael E. Parrish, *Anxious Decades, America in Prosperity and Depression, 1920–1941* (New York: W. W. Norton, 1992), pp. 325–7; also Alan Brinkley, *End of Reform* (New York: Knopf, 1995), 24–25, for New Deal panic after 1937 recession.

460. ". . . RESTAURANT REFUSED TO SERVE ROBESON LUNCH.": Barbara Savage, *Broadcasting Freedom: Radio, War, and the Politics of Race, 1938–1948* (Chapel Hill: University of North Carolina Press, 1999), 62. ". . . THE ENORMOUS POWER OF RADIO.": W.E.B. Du Bois, "As The Crow Flies," *Amsterdam News*, November 4, 1939. Also in Aptheker, ed., *Newspaper Columns of W.E.B. Du Bois*, I, 267. ". . . ALTHOUGH THE CBS EXECUTIVES.": In a lively study of the politics of race and radio, historian Barbara Savage has followed the back and forth of the CBS script between Seldes at CBS, Davis Du Bois, Locke in Washington and Du Bois. "Carry Me Back to Ol' Virginia" was dropped after Du Bois recommended music by William Grant Still and the Johnson Brothers. Locke rewrote entire sections of the script. Cf. Savage, *Broadcasting Freedom*, chapter 1. ". . . THEY LOBBIED FOR MUCH LESS BOOKER WASHINGTON.": Savage, *Broadcasting Freedom*, 38–9.

461. ". . . THE FINAL SCRIPT FOR 'THE NEGRO' ": Savage, *Broadcasting Freedom*; 47. ". . . THOUGH THEY HAD BEEN FAIRLY SUCCESSFUL.": Regarding the script for the Negro Program and the disastrous results, see Davis DuBois to Du Bois, December 5, 1938, Du Bois Papers/UMass. The Du Bois Reconstruction segment was safely garbled. Mention of enforced second-class citizenship and economic disabilities was so muted as to pass virtually unnoticed by the white South. Davis DuBois insisted, along with a large number of Talent Tenth influentuals, that Commissioner Studebaker required CBS to re-record "The Negro" before public distribution of the program as a phonograph record by the Office of Education. ". . . GRATEFUL FOR THE OPPORTUNITY TO PRESENT FACTS.": K. Miyake to Du Bois, March 15, 1938, Du Bois Papers/UMass.

461–62. ". . . HATED WHITE EUROPEAN AND AMERICAN PROPAGANDA.": Du Bois to Waldo McNutt, February 25, 1939, Du Bois Papers/UMass. Du Bois to Hikida, January 3, 1939, Du Bois Papers/UMass.

462. ". . . WHEN HIS FOURTH.": See Peter Young, ed., *World Almanac Book of World War II*, 39–40. ". . . IT WAS NOT A SECOND WORLD WAR.": Du Bois, "As the Crow Flies," *Amsterdam News*, November 18, 1939. Also in Aptheker, ed., *Newspapers*, 272.

462. ". . . LABOR IN AMERICA": For John L. Lewis quote, see Melvyn Dubofsky and Warren Van, *John L. Lewis: A Biography* (Urbana: University of Illinois Press, 1986), 245. ". . . SUPPOSE IT WERE LIBERIA BEING SWALLOWED.": Du Bois, "As the Crow Flies," *Amsterdam News*, January 6, 1940. Also in Aptheker, ed., *Newspaper Columns*, I, 282.

463. ". . . THE WORLD IS ASTONISHED, AGHAST, AND ANGRY.": Du Bois, "As the Crow Flies," *Amsterdam News*, December 23, 1939, January 6, 1940. Also in Aptheker, ed., *Newspaper Columns*, I, 277, 282. ". . . THEY NEEDED MORE RADEKS AND FEWER STALINS.": Du Bois, "As the Crow Flies," *Amsterdam News*, February 24, 1940. Also in Aptheker, ed., *Newspaper Columns*, I, 287, 311.

464. ". . . HER RECEPTION BY ATLANTA WHITES.": Darlene Clark Hine et al, eds. *Black Women in America* (Brooklyn, N.Y.: Carlson Publishing), 33 (hereafter BWIA). ". . . NEVERTHELESS, AS AN AUTHORITY.": Du Bois, "As the Crow Flies," *Amsterdam News*, May 4, 1940. Also in Aptheker, ed., *Newspaper Columns*, I, 295. Ironically, on the anniversary of his fiftieth Harvard class reunion, he mused about the poignancy of sitting under the elms of the Yard again and the thrill of a twenty-year-old student upon seeing James, Royce, Shaler, and Hart "in the flesh." Those 150 returning classmates Du Bois found to be cordial and interesting in their concerns for the fate of the British Empire. "They represented the power of the white world and with it much of beauty and grace." With pleasure, he shook the hand of Harvard's "curiously young" President James Conant. "Yet much was amiss," he felt, "something wrong lay here, something of the continuing arrogance of wealth and chance of birth." But then he had also been heartened by the "saving grace of Harvard democracy" evident in the number of Japanese, Chinese, Jews, and Negroes moving through the Yard.

Eulogies were plentiful and usually poignant. John R. Lynch of the Reconstruction Era and Heywood Broun of radio and newspaper celebrity died within months of each other. Du Bois, "As the Crow Flies," *Amsterdam News*, November 18, 1939, Aptheker, ed., *Newspaper Columns*, 271, 284. John

Hardy Dillard and Robert Russa Moton followed soon afterward. Du Bois, "As the Crow Flies," *Amsterdam News*, June 8, 1940, October 19, 1940, Aptheker, ed., *Newspaper Columns*, 305, 334. Placing their sometimes stormy differences in perspective, Du Bois professed an affectionate, latter-day respect for Moton, a man whose professional position had required him to walk adeptly over hot coals. Du Bois had discovered only years later that it was not the Tuskegee principal who said that Negroes should refrain from first-class travel after Mrs. Moton was ejected from a Pullman coach but, rather, a white trustee who volunteered to approach the offending railway company. Recalling his arch comments at that time, Du Bois gently observed that Washington's successor had faced a characteristic dilemma of either calling a white man a liar "or keeping still." Du Bois, "As the Crow Flies," *Amsterdam News*, June 8, 1940, Aptheker, ed., *Newspaper Columns*, 306.

464–65. "... MARXISM AS A THEORY.": On Du Bois and Ben Davis: Du Bois, "As the Crow Flies," *Amsterdam News*, March 23, 1940, also in Aptheker, ed., *Newspapers Columns*, 290. On Davis's Judiciary performance, see Gerald Horne, *Black Liberation/Red Scare: Ben Davis and the Communist Party* (Newark, Del.: University of Delaware Press, 1994), 83–84. "American workers had more sympathy with capital than with uplift of labor," he preached again. "They are so torn by race and group prejudice that the white workers of the South would rather submit to disfranchisement and starvation than be put on an equality with black labor." "... 'NEGROES REMOVED AGAIN'.": Du Bois, "As the Crow Flies," *Amsterdam News*, December 2, 1939, also in Aptheker, ed., *News. Columns*, p. 274. "... ELEANOR ROOSEVELT.": Du Bois, "As the Crow Flies," *Amsterdam News*, December 30, 1939, also in Aptheker, ed., *News. Columns*, p. 280. "... THE GREATEST ISSUE IN THIS CAMPAIGN.": Du Bois, "As the Crow Flies," *Amsterdam News*, August 3, 1940, also in Aptheker, ed., *News. Columns*, p. 317. "... CORDELL HULL WOULD HAVE EXERTED.": Du Bois, "As the Crow Flies," *Amsterdam News*, November 23, 1940, also in Aptheker, ed., *News. Columns*, p. 343. "... DU BOIS REACHED A JUDGEMENT.": Du Bois, "As The Crow Flies," *Amsterdam News*, December 21, 1940, see also Aptheker, ed., *News. Columns*, p. 349. On FDR, Du Bois, "As the Crow Flies," *Amsterdam News*, November 23, 1940; On the Solid South reasons for Wilkie's rout by FDR without a campaign, Du Bois, "As the Flow Flies," *Amsterdam News*, December 7, 1940, both also in Aptheker, ed., *News. Columns*, pp. 344, 346. "... DU BOIS HAD FEARED.": Du Bois, "As the Crow Flies," *Amsterdam News*, February 1, 1941, see slso, Aptheker, ed., *News. Columns*, p. 356.

465. "... A MAJOR TURNING POINT.": The NAACP and its allies lost the fight to prevent the Selective Training and Service Act from being shorn of New York Senator Robert Wagner's amendment barring rejection of any volunteer for military service on account of race. On the Selective Service Act, the law read that anyone could volunteer "provided he is acceptable to the land or naval forces for such training." Quick reaction by the Committee for the Participation of Negroes in the National Defense led to an amendment to the Act to Expedite the Strengthening of the National Defense by Democratic senators Minton of Indiana and Schwartz of Wyoming. It explicitly barred color and race discrimination in all branches of the military establishment. "... NO DEMOCRACY TO SAVE?" NAACP/LC, reel 10, June 23, 1940. Also, Horace Cayton, "Negro Morale" in *Opportunity* (December 1941).

466. "... NATIONAL NEGRO CONGRESS.": Ira Reid to Du Bois, May 9, 1939, Du Bois Papers/UMass, from the London School of Economics, where he is studying, writes that Paul Robeson is agitated and is returning to the U.S. to keep colored people out of the war.

469. "... EXECUTIVE ORDER 8802.": Finally noticing the furious opposition of civil rights groups to segregated armed forces, FDR expressed concern in a cabinet meeting in mid-September 1940 about the War Department's restriction of African Americans to labor and service battalions. A long-sought Oval Office meeting was held on September 17, 1940. Walter White of the NAACP, T. Arnold Hill of the National Youth Administration, and A. Philip Randolph of the Brotherhood of Sleeping Car Porters attended. The apparently sympathetic President was handed a memorandum urging an end to "all segregation of Negroes as individuals throughout the services." On October 9, the White House released what Press Secretary Early claimed was the text of an understanding reached between FDR and the civil rights leaders. African Americans would serve in the Army in proportion to their percentage of the national population, it stated encouragingly. Then the stunned leaders read: "The policy of the War Department is not to intermingle colored and white enlisted personnel in the same regimental organizations." Eleanor Roosevelt and Walter White had lost to corporation lawyer Henry Stimson, the new Secretary of War. "[My credibility] is seriously impaired," White telegraphed the White House.

469.   ". . . HABITUAL MALEFACTORS.": Mary Ovington to Du Bois, March 11, 1938, Du Bois Papers/
UMass.
470.   ". . . GOOD FRIEND ' HIKIDA.": Hikida to Du Bois, December [nd], 1941, Christmas and New
Year's greetings; Du Bois to Hikida, February 3, 1941, Du Bois papers/UMass; ". . . HIKIDA'S DEPOR-
TATION.": "Yasuichi Hikida, with aliases," N.Y. File 100-704, prepared by P. E. Pettybone, 8-20-42,
Internal Security, Alien Enemy Control, NY FBI Office, 4-page document. "Yasuichi Hikida," File
No. 65-29505, declassified 9-22-97, FBI/FOIPA. Hon. J. Edgar Hoover to Adolf A. Berle, Jr., assistant
secretary of state ("by special messenger"), June 10, 1942; Adolf A. Berle, Jr., to J. Edgar Hoover, July
1, 1942, in Record Group 59, State Department Decimal Files, 1940–1944, case number 894-2211/
National Archives. Assistant Secretary of State to Mrs. Bethune, Sept. 10, 1940, R.G. 59, State Dept.
Decimal Files, 1940–1944, Nat. Archives: ". . . the activities of this man are anything but favorable."
470.   ". . . PLAY THE GAME.": Du Bois, "As the Crow Flies," Amsterdam News, March 14, 1942, Ap-
theker, ed. News. Columns, I, p. 415; ". . . DUSK OF DAWN.": Will to Nina, January 31, 1940, Du Bois
Papers/UMass; ". . . LITTLE ELSE TO LIVE FOR.": Lewis interview with Bobbie Branch, June 3, 1988.
472.   ". . . SUCH STURDY PILLARS.": Amsterdam News, March 9, 1940, Aptheker, ed., News. Columns,
I, p. 288; ". . . SHIRLEY GRAHAM'S ROSENWALD.": Shirley Graham to Du Bois, September 20, 1939, Du
Bois Papers/UMass; ". . . SOME SOLUTION.": Shirley Graham to Du Bois, May 23, 1940, Du Bois Papers/
UMass; ". . . MISSED YOU TOO MUCH.": Mildred Jones to Du Bois, May 26, 1940, Du Bois Papers/
UMass; Ten months later Jones would collapse from exhaustion. Du Bois raged at her "perfectly
idiotic" work regime, but wrote that her dissertation was "a magnificent piece of work." He promised
to publish it in his new magazine, Du Bois to Mildred Jones, December 13, 1940, Du Bois Papers/
UMass.
472.   ". . . SHIRLEY GRAHAM'S ROSENWALD FELLOWSHIP.": Shirley Graham to Du Bois, September
20, 1939, Du Bois Papers/UMass.
472.   ". . . A DELICIOUS REUNION.": Shirley Graham to Du Bois, November 7, 1940, Du Bois Papers/
UMass.
473.   AUTOBIOGRAPHY: For a suggestive linking of Henry Adams and Du Bois, see Albert E. Stone,
Autobiographical Occasions and Original Acts: Versions of American Identity from Henry Adams to Nate
Shaw (Philadelphia: University of Pennsylvania, 1982). Arthur Spingarn also compared it to Adams'
Education of Henry Adams, in the Herald Tribune, September 8, 1940. For a lively discussion of western
autobiography, see Anne McClintock, Imperial Leather: Race Gender and Sexuality in the Colonial
Conquest (New York: Routledge, 1995), pp. 313–314. ". . . MY ABILITY AND ASPIRATION.": Du Bois, Dusk,
p. 27.
473–75.   ". . . LITTLE CHANCE FOR SELF-IMPROVEMENT.": Du Bois, Dusk, p. 74. ". . . MOB OF PEO-
PLE.": Du Bois, Dusk, p. 131. ". . . FULL AND LUSCIOUS FEATURES: Du Bois, Dusk, p. 142. ". . . LAST
OF THE DUNNINGITE HISTORIANS.": E. Merton Coulter to Du Bois, January 24, 1941, W.E.B. Du Bois
Collection/Fisk University. That Coulter, one of the last of the Dunningite historians, could write Du
Bois that he found his autobiography "tremendously interesting and revealing" is revealing, as is, on
the one hand, Herbert Aptheker's acute displeasure in New Masses (October 8, 1940) at the author's
"vulgarization" of Marxism. On Du Bois's critique of Marx, see Dusk, pp. 320–321, 205. In many ways,
Dusk was Du Bois's most conflicted book since The Philadelphia Negro, and for much the same reason
that he was writing in intellectual mid-passage. The Philadelphia monograph had commenced an
evolution beyond Victorian moralizing; the 1940 autobiography was a major marker in the transition
from Talented Tenth radicalism to Talented Tenth Marxism by way of parallel economic development.
It was in Dusk that Du Bois deployed his illuminating critique of Marx's underappreciation of the
power of racial solidarity to trump class solidarity, and there that he unveiled his "Basic American
Negro Creed," the manifesto that had driven Locke with its prediction of the "ultimate triumph of
some form of Socialism the world over." Yet, the "Basic American Negro Creed" maintained the
hegemony of Du Bois's favorite elite as uniquely fitted "by education and character to think and do
. . . for racial action and the method by which the masses may be guided . . . That those masses were
desperately in need of guidance by their betters Du Bois made clear in "The Colored World Within,"
a condescending arraignment of Negro deficiencies that could have been lifted from the forty-year-old
Philadelphia Negro. ". . . LOW SOCIAL CONDITION.": Dusk, pp. 180, 181. Some plain speaking about the
"low social condition of the majority of Negroes" was in order, he felt. Slavery, labor exploitation, and
contemporary discrimination were but part of the problem. However one "rationalized and explained"
the historic guilt and chronic racism of white people, black people had work to do among themselves

to ameliorate their poverty, ignorance, "bad manners, disease, and crime," he remonstrated, "no matter what the true reasons are, or where the blame lies. Progress has been made. Illiteracy had fallen. The death rate was now below that of most South American countries, Italy, and even of Japan. A gain of yards, there were miles yet to travel. Consider the crime rate." Although badly skewed by racism and fostered by appalling poverty, crime among blacks was a scandal, Du Bois sniffed, ticking off their common malefactions: "disorder of all sorts, theft and burglary, fighting, breaking the gambling and liquor laws and especialy fighting with and killing each other."

475. "... FRAZIER'S *THE NEGRO FAMILY*.": Du Bois is given credit in the book, as well in a letter which accompanied an autographed copy of *The Negro Family in the United States* (Chicago: University of Chicago, 1939). E. Franklin Frazier to Du Bois, August 2, 1939 ("In fact, my feeling in regard to the work which some of us are doing has been that we are building upon a tradition inaugurated by you in the Atlanta studies"), Du Bois Papers/UMass; useful telephone conversation with Professor George Bond on Frazier.

475. "... MOYNIHAN.": See James B. McKee, *Sociology and the Race Problem: The Failure of a Perspective* (Urbana: University of Illinois Press, 1993), esp. pp. 200–201; Anthony M. Platt, *E. Franklin Frazier Reconsidered* (New Brunswick, NJ: Rutgers University Press, 1991), pp. 111–120. "OMNIPOTENT": DuBois, *Dusk*, p. 198;

476. "... NEW ECONOMIC WORLD": Du Bois, *Dusk*, p. 298; "... LEADERSHIP": Ibid. p. 303; "... SCIENTIFIC RACISM": See Elazar Barkin, *The Retreat of Scientific Racism: Changing Concepts of Race in Britain and the United States between the World Wars* (New York: Cambridge University Press, 1992), esp. pp. 310–318. As in the case of the *Encyclopedia of the Negro*, Harvard's distinguished anthropologist and author of the popular *Up from the Ape*, Ernest Hooton, exemplified the staying power of genteel racism in the academy, giving qualified public endorsement of the Boasians yet privately fretting over the "small infiltration of Negro blood into the White group" and seconding, off the record, Madison Grant's opposition "to the flooding of this country with alien scum." Dispite the Hootons and the Davenports, though, a change of attitude was underway.

477. "... HAT OFF": Ruth Campbell to Du Bois, April 13, 1939, Du Bois Papers/UMass; "The Negro Scientist," *American Scholar* (Summer 1939), pp. 309–320; also in Aptheker, ed., *Writ. Periodical Lit.*, III, pp. 88–95; "... INVITATIONS": Du Bois to Arthur Raper, December 7, 1939; Du Bois to Mary Williams, February 20, 1940, both in Du Bois Papers/UMass.

477. "... PHYLON.": Du Bois to Elmer Carter, December 4, 1939, Du Bois Papers/UMass.

478. "... FLORENCE READ.": Author's interview with Mr. and Mrs. John Hope, January 21, 1988; "... READ'S POWER": Du Bois to Read, February 1, 1937, Du Bois Papers/UMass.

478. "HOPE AND READ": Author's interviews with Samuel M. Nabrit, June 13, 1987; with Mr. and Mrs. John Hope, January 21, 1988; with J. Max and Ruth Bond, October 5, 1991; "... NOT SPEAKING TO YOU": Author's interviews with Bonita Valien, February 12, 1988; with Josephine Love, ... 19..; with Mrs. John Hope, January 21, 1988. "... FINE ARTS DEPARTMENT": Du Bois to Edwin R. Embree, October 3, 1938, Du Bois Papers/UMass. "... MAGAZINE TOP PRIORITY": Du Bois to Florence Read, February 1, 1937, Du Bois Papers/UMass; "... ACTING PRESIDENCY": Read to Du Bois, May 27, 1937, Du Bois Papers/UMass; "IRA DE REID": Du Bois to Read, June 22, 1937, Du Bois Papers/UMass.

479. "... LONG FIRST STEP.": Charles S. Johnson to Du Bois, May 18, 1937, Du Bois Papers/UMass; for full text of "On the Roots of *Phylon*," see Herbert Aptheker, ed., *Against Racism: Unpublished Essays, Papers, Addresses, 1887–1961* (Amherst, University of Massachusetts Press, 1985), pp. 168–170.

479. "... DINING ROOM": Du Bois to Rufus Clement, September 24, 1937 (unclear if actually sent), Du Bois Papers/UMass; "... MEETING WITH CLEMENT": Du Bois to Ira De A. Reid, April 14, 1939, in Aptheker, ed., *Correspondence*, II, p. 188. See also Du Bois's elegant statement on Braithwaite's return to A.U., Du Bois to Clement, June 13, 1938, Du Bois Papers/UMass.

480. "... BANKS": Information on W. Rutherford Banks is in *Who's Who in Colored America* (New York, 1927), p. 9; "... CONFERENCE.": Du Bois to W. R. Banks, April 19, 1939, Du Bois Papers/UMass; Du Bois was convinced that all the best people were at risk, a concern he had intimated to Embree six months earlier when recommending Elizabeth Prophet for a Rosenwald fellowship, Du Bois to Embree, October 3, 1938, Du Bois Papers/UMass. The Valiens' investigative innovations were a critical factor in Fisk's remarkable postwar ascendancy as a sociological research center second to none in the South; "... PERSONAL ANIMUS.": Du Bois had little respect for C. S. Johnson's scholarship, author's interview with Bonita Valien, February 12, 1988; Once before, when Du Bois was about to announce his *Crisis* literary prizes, he had been scooped by a competing project of Johnson's. Fisk's Institute of

Race Relations was not far in the future. "... *PHYLON'S DEBUT*": Correspondence between Du Bois and Charles S. Johnson, May-June 1939, Du Bois Papers/UMass, and Jackson Davis to Du Bois, December 2, 1939, GEB/Rockefeller Archives.

481. "... MODEST SUM": W. R. Banks to Rufus C. Clement, April 15, 1940; Frederick Keppel to Du Bois, April 17, 1940, Du Bois Papers/UMass.

481. "... SOUTHERN SOCIOLOGICAL SOCIETY.": The text of the address is in Aptheker, ed., *Correspondence* III, pp. 126–131. "... ABASHED REPLY": Du Bois to Arthur Raper, April 11, 1940, Du Bois Papers/UMass; Read between the lines, Raper's apology divulged the determination of some of Knoxville's leading white citizens (including some of the very sociologists who had invited Du Bois) to dawdle over dinner and drink in order to make a racial point through insulting procrastination. Author is indebted to telephone conversation on March 17, 2000, with Vernon Jarrett who was present at Norris High School that evening. Jarrett is positive that Ira Reid was there, but author believes Reid was still in the UK.

481–82. "... HOPE'S BIOGRAPHY.": Du Bois to Edwin Embree, October 17, 1939, Du Bois Papers/UMass; "... BOOK REVIEW.": Aptheker, ed., *Book Revs.*, pp. 233–235; also in *The Crisis*, September 1948, pp. 270–271. "... ANOTHER HAGGLE.": Du Bois to W. R. Banks, June 28, 1940, Du Bois Papers/UMass. "... DUPLICITY AND BAD FAITH.": Rufus Clement to Du Bois, June 19, 1940, Du Bois Papers/UMass. Waiting until Du Bois had left campus for the summer, Clement revisited the Diggs salary terms in fine detail, amended them downward after concluding that the quarterly "certainly does not require a full-time secretary," then wished Du Bois "a pleasant vacation."

482. "... CLEMENT AND READ PROBLEM.": Du Bois to W. R. Banks, November 14, 1940, Du Bois Papers/UMass; Du Bois to W. R. Banks, December 16, 1940, Du Bois Papers, UMass.

483. "... 1940 AHA MEETING.": Wesley—"The Negro in the Organization of Abolition, 1831–1837," Logan—"Some New Interpretations of the Negro Colonization Movement," Wharton—"The Race Issue in the Overthrow of Reconstruction in Mississippi." To his great regret, John Hope Franklin, a Ph.D. candidate in Harvard's history department, was unable to attend. Logan's diary gives the flavor of the occasion and names the African Americans (Harcourt Tynes, Lorenzo Greene, Marian Thompson Wright, Lawrence D. Reddick, Hugo Johnston, a cousin of Wesley's) and quotes Du Bois's presiding remarks. Diary entry, January 13, 1941, Rayford Logan Papers, unprocessed, Diaries, 1940–1951, Library of Congress, Manuscript Division.

483. "... BIRACIAL CORRUPTION.": Horace Mann Bond, *Negro Education in Alabama: A Study in Cotton and Steel* (New York: Athenaeum, 1969); "... SPLENDID MEETING": August Meier and Elliot Rudwick, *Black History and the Historical Profession, 1915–1980* (Urbana: University of Illinois Press, 1986) p. 114; Du Bois praised Bond's book for filling in the missing data for him; see Wayne J. Urban, *Black Scholar: Horace Mann Bond, 1940–1972* (Athens: University of Georgia Press, 1992), p. 84. "... GREAT COMPLIMENT": Merle Curti to Du Bois, December 31, 1940, DuBois Papers/UMass.

484. "... PHYLON INSTITUTE": Du Bois to W. R. Banks, April 18, 1941, Du Bois Papers/UMass; Florence Read invited Du Bois to dinner and he declined, Read to Du Bois, February 27, 1941, Du Bois Papers/UMass; "I thought I was doing awfully well to invite you more than 24 hours ahead of time." "... CONTACT BETWEEN ATLANTA AND FISK.": Within three years, Johnson's department of social science would have obtained generous foundation support for an institute of race relations, an annual three-week, interracial symposium at Fisk that would become almost mandatory for scholars and policymakers; "... HAMPTON AND TUSKEGEE.": Du Bois, "Moton of Hampton and Tuskegee," *Phylon* (4th Quarter, 1940), pp. 344–351, also in Aptheker, ed., *Selections from Phylon* (Millwood, N.Y.: Kraus-Thompson, 1980), p. 341–348.

484. "... INSTITUTE A SUCCESS.": Du Bois to W. R. Banks, April 11, 1941, Du Bois Papers/UMass; "... REID AT FEDERAL SECURITY AGENCY": Ira Reid to Du Bois, March 4, 1941, Du Bois Papers/UMass; "... CLEMENT'S ABSENCE": Rufus Clement to Du Bois, April 12, 1941, Du Bois Papers/UMass; "... THE NATION.": Letters between Du Bois and Richard Rovere, February 15, March 13, April 23, May 16, May 29, 1941, and Keith Hutchinson to Du Bois, June 17, 1941, all in Du Bois Papers/UMass. "... BABY DU BOIS, NOW SEVEN.": Du Bois to Yolande, September 28, 1940, Du Bois Papers/UMass.

485. "... TO CUBA WITH DIGGS.": Hotel bill from Santiago, June 18, 1941, W.E.B. Du Bois Collection, Fisk University; Du Bois to Senorita Causse, Superintendent of Schools in Oriente, July 7, 1941, Du Bois to Dr. Ramon Garcia, Governor of Oriente Province, July 7, 1941; Dr. Miguel Angel Cespedes, Undersecretary of Communications, to Du Bois, June 7, June 25, July 7, 1941, all in Du Bois Papers/UMass. "... DIGGS.": Du Bois correspondence from December 1942 indicates Diggs's residency at

Clark College; see also Darlene Hine, *Black Women in America* (New York: Carlson, 1993), pp. 337–338; "... GUILLEN.": See Arnold Rampersad, *The Life of Langston Hughes* (New York: Oxford University Press, 1986), vol. I, pp. 179–180; see also Nestor R. Ortiz Oderigo, "A Note on Nicholas Guillen," *Phylon*, vol. 13, pp. 284–285. "... URGENT MATTERS OF STATE.": Miguel Angel Cespedes to Du Bois, July 7, 1941, Du Bois Papers/UMass; "... LEMONADE AND CRACKED ICE.": Du Bois to hotel manager, June 18, 1941, Du Bois Papers/Fisk Univ.; "... ACLS.": Rufus Clement to Du Bois, November 10, 1941, Du Bois Papers/UMass. "I am happy to note that the American Council of Learned Societies has invited you as one of a group of representatives to attend the Havana Conference beginning November 23."
485. "... CHRONICLES OF RACE RELATIONS.": See Herbert Aptheker, ed. *Selections from Phylon.*
486. DU BOIS AND MYRDAL.: Ira De A. Reid to Du Bois, February 3, 1939, Du Bois Papers/UMass. "... MYRDAL, DU BOIS AND POSSIBLE MEETING.": Gunnar Myrdal to Du Bois, August 15, 1941. Du Bois Papers/UMass. "... MYRDAL BREAKDOWN.": David Southern, *Gunnar Myrdal and Black-White Relations: the Use and Abuse of "An American Dilemma"* (Baton Rouge: Louisiana State University Press, 1987), pp. 37–38.
486–87. "... SOUTHERN HISTORICAL ASSOCIATION AND NEGROES.": Meier and Rudwick, op. cit., p. 114. "... DU BOIS RESIGNS FROM THE SOUTHERN HISTORICAL ASSOCIATION.": Du Bois to The Southern Historical Association, January 14, 1942, Du Bois Papers/UMass.
487. "... AN ADVENTURE TALKING TO NORTHERN STUDENTS AND THE CONNECTION.": Du Bois, "As the Crow Flies," *Amsterdam News*, May 16, 1942. Also in Herbert Aptheker, ed., *Newspaper Columns*, I, p. 433.
487. "... COLOR AND LOW SOCIAL STATUS,": Du Bois, "The Future of Africa in America" (April 1942) in Herbert Aptheker, ed., *Against Racism: Unpublished Essays, Papers, Addresses.* (Amherst: University of Massachusetts Press, 1985), pp. 173–184. "... DU BOIS'S ANSWER TO "WHAT CAN I DO ABOUT IT? [THE RACE PROBLEM].": Du Bois, "As the Crow Flies," *Amsterdam News.* May 16. 1942. Also in Aptheker, ed., *News Columns*, p. 434. "... IT WAS A CERTAINTY THAT THE ALLIES WOULD CONQUER GERMANY.": Du Bois, "The Future of Europe in Africa," in Aptheker, ed., *Against Racism*, p. 190. "... COMMITTEE OF FORTY POSTWAR RECOMMENDATIONS.": Du Bois, "The Future of Europe in Africa," in Aptheker, ed., *Against Racism*, p. 197.
488. "... WE CAN ONLY SAVE THE WORLD AND OURSELVES.": Du Bois, "As the Crow Flies," *Amsterdam News*, May 10, 1941. Also in Aptheker, ed., *Newspaper Columns*, I, p. 371.
488. GORDON BLAINE HANCOCK.: His most recent pronouncements had been widely syndicated through the Associated Negro Press as an editorial "Interracial Hypertension." To the immense satisfaction of those white southerners who were neither arch conservatives nor Negrophobes, Hancock's editorial deplored the extremists of both races and warned of "disastrous consequences" unless the "better class whites and Negroes" combined to face the reality that race relations were in a "state of hypertension and rupture" in the South; see Benjamin E. Mays, *Born to Rebel: An Autobiography* (Athens: University of Georgia Press, 1987), p. 217.
489. "... TO HELP US ACCOMPLISH SOMETHING WORTHWHILE.": Gordon Blaine Hancock to Du Bois, September 12, 1942, Du Bois Papers/UMass, in Aptheker, ed., *Correspondence*, II, pp. 342–45, p 243. On the Hancock-Durham Manifesto history and whites, cf., John Egerton, *Speak Now Against the Day: The Generation Before the Civl Rights Movement in the South* (New York: Knopf, 1994), p. 302; Kenneth Janken, *Rayford Logan*, p. 149; Benjamin Mays, *Born to Rebel: An Autobiography*, p. 214; Jacquelyn Dowd Hall, *Revolt Against Chivalry: Jessie Daniel Ames and the Women's Campaign Against Lynching* (New York: Columbia University Press, 1993, rev. ed.), p. 258–59; Henry Lewis Suggs, *P. B. Young, Newspaperman: Race, Politics and Journalism in the New South, 1910–62* (Charlottesville: University of Virginia Press, 1988), p. 82.
489. "... NO ONE CONNECTED TO THE NAACP WAS INVITED.": Six categories for discussion in Durham had been agreed upon by a small group in Richmond—"civic, educational, economic, industrial, social welfare, and domestic." More than seventy questionnaires had yielded a treasure of recommendations that were to be reduced by Charles Johnson to a policy agenda for consideration at Durham.
489–90. "... WE ARE FUNDAMENTALLY OPPOSED TO THE PRINCIPLE AND PRACTICE OF SEGREGATION.": Benjamin E. Mays, *Born to Rebel*, p. 217. "... DURHAM REPRESENTED A SIGNIFICANT BREACH IN THE WALL OF JIM CROW.": Du Bois, "A Chronicle of Race Relations," in Aptheker, ed., *Selections from Phylon*, p. 323.
490. "... NEW DICHOTOMY IN THE STATEMENT OF BELIEF IN RACE RELATIONS.": Du Bois, "A Chronicle of Race Relations," *Phylon: The Atlanta University Review of Race and Culture* (Second

quarter 1944), 165–188, in Aptheker, ed., *Selections from Phylon*, p. 323. On the upshot of the Durham Manifesto: cf., John Egerton, *op. cit.*, pp. 301–12; and Jacquelyn Dowd Hall, *op. cit.*, pp. 259–260.

491. PRESIDENTS OF NEGRO LAND GRANT COLLEGES CONFERENCE.: Announcement of Conference, Du Bois Papers/UMass.

491. "... SCHOLAR'S OPPORTUNITY.": Although the *Encyclopedia of the Negro* was a scholar's opportunity, another research application had recently been rejected by the Boston's Filene Good Will Fund, See Percy S. Brown (Filene Good Will Fund) to Du Bois, Jan 10, 1942, "... LAND GRANT COLLEGES AND THE LAUNCHING OF A PERMANENT APPARATUS FOR COLLECTION OF KNOWLEDGE OF THE RACE.": W.E.B. Du Bois, *The Autobiography of W.E.B. Du Bois* (International Press, 1968), p. 312. "... DU BOIS REPORTED HIS SUCCESS TO CLEMENT.": Outlines the composition of forthcoming Land-Grant Conference, Du Bois to Rufus Clement, April 23, 1943, Unprocessed Rufus Clement Papers, Special Collections, Woodruff Library, Clark Atlanta University. "... CONCERNED BY MORE THAN BUDGETS AND BEHAVIOR.": On the culture of the historically black college and university, see these fictional and monographic treatments—J. Saunders Redding, *Stranger and Alone* (New York: Harcourt, Brace, and Co., 1950); Nella Larsen, *Quicksand* (New York: Knopf, 1928); Ralph Ellison, *Invisible Man* (New York: Random House, 1952); James D. Anderson, *The Education of Blacks in the South, 1860–1935* (Chapel Hill: University of North Carolina Press, 1988), Henry Allen Bullock, *A History of Negro Education in the South: From 1619 to the Present* (New York: Praeger, 1967); and "The Future of Black Colleges," *Daedalus: Journal of the American Academy of Arts and Sciences* (summer 1971).

492. STRUGGLE TO SAVE RESEARCH SCHEME.: Du Bois, *Autobiography*, p. 320.

492. "... CLEMENT RAISES OBJECTION TO USING A.U. LIBRARY FOR CONFERENCE.": Clement memorandum to Du Bois, April 5, 1944, Du Bois Papers/UMass "... ODUM LENT HIS BLESSING TO LAND GRANT COLLEGES.": Du Bois, *Autobiography*,. 320. "... LAND GRANT PRESIDENTS ADDRESS DU BOIS'S CHARGE.": Du Bois, *Autobiography*, p. 321. "... HARLEM AND DETROIT IGNITE.": See Thomas J. Sugrue, *The Origins of the Urban Crisis* (Princeton: Princeton University Press, 1996), pp. 33–55. See also Cheryl Lynn Greenberg, *Or Does It Explode: Black Harlem in the Great Depression* (New York: Oxford University Press), pp. 211–214, 219.

493. "... [CLEMENT] HOPES THAT DU BOIS WILL RETIRE.": Interview, Jackson Davis, May 12, 1943, Rockefeller Archives. "... A.U. RULES ON TENURE AND PENSION.": Clarence A. Bacote, *The Story of Atlanta University, A Century of Service, 1865–1965* (Atlanta: Atlanta University, 1969), pp. 372–373. "RESULT OF THIS ACTION IS DISASTROUS.": Du Bois, *Autobiography*, p. 323. "... MY OWN LIFE WAS THROWN INTO CONFUSION.": Arnold Rampersad, *The Art and Imagination of W.E.B. Du Bois* (Cambridge: Harvard University, 1976), p. 222.

494. "... HENRY CANBY INFORMS DU BOIS OF ELECTION TO ACADEMY OF ARTS AND LETTERS DEPARTMENT OF LITERATURE.": Henry S. Canby to Du Bois, in Small Collections, American Academy and Institute of Arts and Letters Archives.

494. "... NEGRO PRESS TOOK NOTICE.": Shirley Graham Du Bois, *His Day Is Marching On: A Memoir of W.E.B. Du Bois* (Philadelphia, J. Lippincott, 1971), p. 77. "OWED THREE THOUSAND DOLLARS ON MONTEBELLO TERRACE.": Manning Marable, *W.E.B. Du Bois: Black Radical Democrat* (Boston: Twayne Publication, 1986), p. 162. "... ADVERSE REACTION TO THE UNIVERSITY.": Austin T. Walden to Du Bois, May 1, 1944, Du Bois Papers/UMass. Also joint letter signed by A. T. Walden, E. M. Martin, Thomas H. Slater, M. D., among others. "... AWARD SALARY AND ANNUAL COMPENSATION.": Du Bois, "A Farewell Message to the Alumni of Atlanta University" (Summer 1944), in Aptheker, ed., *Against Racism*, p. 226.

495. "... LOUIE SHIVERY READ DU BOIS'S ADIEU.": Du Bois, "A Farewell Message," in Aptheker, ed., *Against Racism*, p. 227. "... HE'S BURIED HIMSELF IN THE SOUTH TOO LONG.": Arthur Spingarn, in Shirley Graham Du Bois, *His Day Is Marching On*, p. 71.

Chapter 14: Against the Grain: From the NAACP to the Far Left

496. "... TO SETTLE THE NEGRO PROBLEM.": Du Bois, "The Winds of Change," in *Chicago Defender* (January 6, 1945), also in Herbert Aptheker, ed., *Newspaper Columns by W.E.B. Du Bois*, 2 vols. (White Plains, N.Y.: Kraus-Thomson, 1986), II, 615.

497. ". . . TOTTERING BENEATH [HIS] FEET.": W.E.B. Du Bois, *The Autobiography* ([New York]: International Publishers, 1968), 323. ". . . OFFERS.": Charles Johnson successfully sought President Jones's agreement to offer Du Bois a research professorship at Fisk. From Howard University came Frazier's news that President Johnson only awaited Du Bois's terms before making a formal offer. Had Du Bois decided for Howard, the prospects for a permanent land-grant research program in collaboration with Frazier would have been greatly enhanced. See Charles S. Johnson to Du Bois, April 19, 1944, E. Franklin Frazier to Du Bois, May 11, 1944, both in the Papers of W.E.B. Du Bois, Special Collections, W.E.B. Du Bois Library, University of Massachusetts at Amherst (hereafter Du Bois Papers/UMass). ". . . TEMPTING PROPOSAL TO RELOCATE TO DURHAM.": John Hope Franklin, "W.E.B. Du Bois: A Personal Memoir," p. 11, an unpublished document made available to the author by Dr. Du Bois Williams. ". . . STOP OFF TO SEE US.": Nina to Will, April 1944, Du Bois Papers/UMass. ". . . FIVE-MEMBER NAACP COMMITTEE.": Walter White to William Hastie, April 21, 1944, Du Bois to Walter White, June 26, 1944, both in Du Bois Papers/UMass; Board Minutes for June 12, 1944, and June 14, 1944, NAACP Board Minutes, Series A, Board of Directors File, Minutes, 1909–1959, NAACP Papers, Library of Congress (hereafter BRD MINS/LC).

497. ". . . RESULTS ASTONISHED ME.": Du Bois, *Autobiography*, 328. On the new NAACP, see Elliott Rudwick and August Meier, "The Rise of the Black Secretariat in the NAACP, 1909–1935," 94–127 and Meier and Rudwick, "Attorneys Black and White: A Case Study of Race Relations within the NAACP," 128–73, in Meier and Rudwick, eds., *Along the Color Line: Explorations in the Black Experience* (Urbana: University of Illinois Press, 1976); "National Association for the Advancement of Colored People," in Jack Salzman et. al., eds., *Encyclopedia of African-American Culture and History*, 5 vols. (New York: Simon and Schuster, 1996), IV, 1923–1951. On legal victories: *Hocutt v. Wilson*, the 1933 challenge to the University of North Carolina's Jim Crow School of Pharmacy, had been a near-disaster in the superior court of Durham County, but in *Murray v. Maryland* (or Pearson) in 1936 and *Missouri ex rel. Gaines v. Canada* in 1938, Houston and Marshall had finally breached the ramparts of legal discrimination in higher education. Henceforth, the South faced the dilemma of either admitting its colored citizens to "white" law, medical, dental, and pharmacy schools or of expending scarce tax dollars to build parallel university systems offering the full range of professional degrees. *Grovey v. Townsend*, 1936, was a judicial rout. In a unanimous opinion that defied logic and the Fifteenth Amendment, the U.S. Supreme Court held that the Democratic Party of Texas, as a private organization having little connection to the state, could exclude Negroes from its primary. See Richard Kluger, *Simple Justice: The History of Brown v. Board of Education and Black America's Struggle for Equality* (New York: Vintage Books, 1975), esp. chs. 8 and 9; Loren Miller, *The Petitioners: The Story of the Supreme Court of the United States and the Negro* (Cleveland: World Publishing, 1966); and Harvard Sitkoff, *New Deal for Blacks, The Emergence of Civil Rights as a National Issue: The Depression Decade* (New York: Oxford University Press, 1978), 222–28.

498. ". . . SETTLE COMFORTABLY INTO THE MARGINS.": Du Bois, *Autobiography*, 327; Little time was wasted in agreeing to his terms; $5,000 in annual salary; $2,500 for a research assistant; a small expense account; an appropriate office and space for files and two thousand books, Du Bois to Walter White, August 1, 1944, Memorandum of the Board for July 14, 1944, both in BRD MINS/LC. Expected to start his new position on September 1, Du Bois took a detour through Haiti on the way to Fifth Avenue, much to White's displeasure. With second-nature imperiousness, Du Bois insisted upon the broad relevance of his two-week trip, flatly rejected the salary readjustment threatened by White, and flew to a round of conferences, official white-dinner-jacket receptions, and addresses tendered into classic French by Du Bois's junior A.U. colleague, Mercer Cook, on special assignment to the Haitian ministry of education, Will to Nina, Yolande, and [Baby] Du Bois, September 12, 1944. The official purpose of the sojourn in the island republic with Irene Diggs (back from Havana) was to give lectures to a teachers' conference, an assignment arranged by Rayford Logan through the Haitian ambassador and promptly approved on a per diem basis as good Atlantic Charter policy by the State Department, Herschel Brickell to Du Bois, August 10, 1944, Du Bois Papers/UMass; Rayford Logan Diary entry, November 23, 1944, Logan Papers Manuscripts Division, Library of Congress.

498. ". . . WHITE'S READING OF THE ARRANGEMENT.": White, having become a Washington fixture on first-name basis with senators, cabinet officers and, above all, Eleanor Roosevelt, worked with ebullient charm and skill to position the NAACP and himself to speak for the people of color whose rights had been acknowledged in the Atlantic Charter. He needed Du Bois's knowledge to boost these

efforts. In one remarkable effervescence in spring of 1942, White deluded himself that private discussions with Lord Halifax, the British ambassador to the United States and former viceroy of India, might eventuate in an Anglo-American announcement encouraging Indian independence in order to mobilize British subjects in the Far East, Africa, and the West Indies behind the war effort. "... 409 EDGECOMBE AVENUE.": Will to Nina, November 27, 1944, Du Bois Papers/UMass.

498–99. "... THE BEST MINDS IN THE COUNTRY.": Author's interview with Bobbie Branch, June 3, 1988; Lewis interview with Gloster Current, April 28, 1987. "... SURRENDER HIS OWN OFFICE.": Despite his limited quarters, Du Bois maintained a productive work schedule. On the last day in November 1944, he mailed a brief sentence outline of the book for which he had just signed a contract with Harcourt, Brace and Company, his usual publisher. Conceived as an uncharacteristically short work, *Color and Democracy: Colonies and Peace* (Millwood, N.Y.: Kraus-Thomson, 1975) was characteristically ambitious in its compass: "the problem of colonies and their peoples; the problem of foreign investments for profit; the question of the expansion of democratic governments for the mass of men; the future role of Russia and her ideologies in the world; and the possibility of world governments through mandates and missions," in W.E.B. Du Bois, *Color and Democracy: Colonies and Peace* (Millwood, N.Y.: Kraus-Thomson, 1975; orig. pub. 1945), 6. "Winds of Time," his new column in the *Chicago Defender*, would begin running the first week of January 1945. "... SECOND TRIP TO THE WAR FRONT.": To speak with greater authority about the imperatives of the peacetime world, White had flown off to the European and North African theater of operations for several months during winter and spring of 1943–44 as special correspondent for the *New York Post*. Despite the grumbling of several board members about his prolonged absence, White insisted on leaving for the Pacific war front almost immediately after the national elections in November. *A Rising Wind*, to be released by Doubleday in 1945, would kaleidoscope the ending phase of World War II, with General Eisenhower receiving the author's advice, with Negro troop morale being lifted by White's lightning visits, with the U.S. military's export of Jim Crow to England and North Africa exposed, and with White's moderate message of colonial liberation iterated. See Walter White, *A Rising Wind* (New York: Doubleday, 1945); Board Minutes for May 8, 1944, BRD MINS/LC; Janken, "From Colonial Liberation to Cold War Liberalism," *Ethnic and Racial Studies* 21 (November 1998): 1074–1093. "... COALITION TO SPONSOR.": Du Bois to Harold A. Moody, February 15, 1945, Du Bois Papers/UMass. "... MARCUS GARVEY HAD EMIGRATED.": Rayford W. Logan and Michael R. Winston, eds., *Dictionary of American Negro Biography* (New York: W. W. Norton, 1982), 256.

499. "... AMY JACQUES GARVEY.": For Du Bois/Amy Jacques Garvey correspondence, see Aptheker, ed., *The Correspondence of W.E.B. Du Bois*, II, 375–77. Du Bois had expressed a desire to head a research unit to collect and disseminate data on the politics and culture of Africa, to study African-descended groups throughout the world, and to continue the research generated by the *Encyclopedia of the Negro*. "... ENDORSED THE CONCLAVE PROPOSAL.": Du Bois to Max Yergan, December 12, 1944, Du Bois Papers/UMass. "... WE ARE CONCERNED.": The widely circulated "Declaration by Negro Voters" sponsored by the NAACP and the National Negro Congress and subscribed to by twenty-seven Aframerican representatives of sororities and fraternities, trade unions, and professional organizations at the end of 1943 reflected the evolved mentality. "We are concerned that this war bring an end to imperialism and colonial exploitation," declared the signatories in the full spirit of the Four Freedoms. "We believe that political and economic democracy must displace the present system of exploitation in Africa, the West Indies, India, and other colonial areas." Aptheker, Introduction to Du Bois, *Color and Democracy*, 9; John Hope Franklin and Alfred A. Moss, Jr., *From Slavery to Freedom: A History of African Americans*, Seventh Ed. (New York: McGraw-Hill, 1994), 455.

499. "... AN UNAFFORDABLE LUXURY.": Board Meeting for November 13, 1944, BRD MINS/LC; Roy Wilkins to Walter White, November 23, 1945, Roy Wilkins Papers, Manuscript Division, Library of Congress (hereafter RWP/LC).

499–500. "... A PAN-AFRICAN WORKSHOP.": Langston Hughes to Du Bois, January 27, 1945; Ralph Bunche to Du Bois, January 31, 1945, Du Bois Papers/UMass. "... THE CELEBRITY DIVINE MIGHT REALIZE.": Harry Emerson Fosdick to Du Bois, January 11, 1945, Du Bois to Fosdick, January 17, 1945, Du Bois Papers/UMass.

500. "... WORLD-FAMOUS MEDICAL MISSIONARY, ALBERT SCHWEITZER.": Albert Schweitzer to Du Bois, December 5, 1945, Du Bois to Schweitzer, July 31, 1946, both in Du Bois Papers/UMass, also in Aptheker, ed., *Correspondence*, III, 51–54; Du Bois, "The Black Man and Albert Schweitzer," in A. A.

Roback, ed., *The Albert Schweitzer Jubilee Book* (Cambridge, Mass.: Sci-Art Publishers, n.d.), also in Herbert Aptheker, ed., *Writings by W.E.B. Du Bois in Non-Periodical Literature Edited by Others* (Millwood, N.Y.: Kraus-Thomson, 1982), 253–57.

500. ". . . DAYLONG SCHOMBURG MEETING.": The colonial conference explored the present and future conditions of exploited peoples in a daylong deliberation whose participants included Logan, representing Alpha Phi Alpha, the leading Negro college fraternity; Alphaeus Hunton from the C.A.A.; P. B. Young, representing the Committee of Negro Editors; Lawrence Reddick, historian and Schomburg chief librarian; two Indian nationalists recommended by Mrs. Vijaya Lakshmi Pandit, diplomat sister of Jawaharlal Nehru; a Burmese, a Puerto Rican, and a Jamaican nationalist, Richard B. Moore of the West Indian National Council; and a fiery Lincoln University student from the Gold Coast, Francis Nkrumah. On the Schomburg conference, see Gerald Horne, *Black and Red: W.E.B. Du Bois and the Afro-American Response to the Cold War, 1944–1963* (Albany: State University of New York Press, 1986), 29; Aptheker Introduction to Du Bois, *Color and Democracy*, 9

[Aptheker gives wrong year for conference]; list of conference speakers, Du Bois Papers/UMass; Du Bois to Jean de la Roche, director of the French Press and Information Bureau, March 28, 1945, Du Bois Papers/UMass; ". . . LEAGUE OF COLORED PEOPLES.": Harold Moody to Du Bois, April 28, 1945, Du Bois Papers/UMass. ". . . COORDINATE THEIR EFFORTS.": Harold Moody to Du Bois, March 23, 1945, Du Bois Papers/UMass. ". . . 'MANIFESTO TO THE UNITED NATION.' ": Described as the product of a pan-African "co-ordinating committee" comprised of officials of the colored members of the G.C.T.U.C., the West African Student Union (WASU), the International African Service Bureau (I.A.S.B.) run by the Ethiopian expatriate Ras Makonnen and the Sierra Leonian labor organizer I.T.A. Wallace-Johnson; West Indian activists, and others. The name of one of the Manifesto signers, George Padmore, was immediately familiar to Du Bois. For detailed discussion of these British-based organizations and George Padmore's role, see J. Ayodele Langley, *Pan-Africanism and Nationalism in West Africa, 1900–1945* (Oxford: The Clarendon Press, 1973), esp. ch. 9; and James R. Hooker, *Black Revolutionary: George Padmore's Path from Communism to Pan-Africanism* (New York: Praeger, 1970), esp. ch. 2. ". . . CPUSA'S MOST PROMISING INTELLECTUALS.": Mark Naison, *Communists in Harlem during the Depression* (Urbana: University of Illinois Press, 1983), 131.

501. ". . . MEET THIS TIME IN AFRICA.": Du Bois to George Padmore, March 22, 1945, Du Bois Papers/UMass. ". . . PARIS IN SEPTEMBER.": Du Bois to Padmore, April 11, 1945, Du Bois Papers/UMass; William L. Patterson, *The Man Who Cried Genocide: An Autobiography* (New York: International Publishers, 1971). ". . . MEETING SEEMED PROMISING.": On proposed P.A.C. meeting in Paris, see exchanges between Du Bois and Jean de la Roche, March 28, April 11, May 7, July 30, August 1, and September 1, 1945, Du Bois Papers/UMass. ". . . PRIORITY TRANSPORTATION.": Du Bois to Harold Moody, July 20, 1945, Du Bois Papers/UMass.

502. ". . . LUCE WAS ADAMANTLY DISINTERESTED.": Du Bois to Henry Luce, December 17, 1945, Du Bois Papers/UMass, also Aptheker, ed., *Correspondence*, III, 94–95; Townsend Hoopes and Douglas Brinkley, *FDR and the Creation of the UN* (New Haven: Yale University Press, 1997), 57. ". . . EFFECTIVE VOICE IN GOVERNMENT": Du Bois, *Color and Democracy*, 73.

503. ". . . COMMISSION TO STUDY THE ORGANIZATION OF PEACE.": Hoopes and Brinkley, op. cit., 18–19; Horne, op. cit., 35. ". . . PLEADED WITH COMMISSION EXECUTIVE DIRECTOR.": Du Bois to Clark M. Eichelberger, March 8, 1945, Du Bois Papers/UMass. ". . . WEIGHTED ON THE SIDE OF IMPERIALISM.": Hoopes and Brinkley, *op. cit.*; Horne, *op. cit.* ". . . NO THOUGHTS OF THE RIGHTS OF NEGROES.": Du Bois to Joseph M. Proskauer, November 14, 1944, Du Bois Papers/UMass.

503. ". . . AMERICAN JEWISH LEADERSHIP.": Du Bois, "As the Crow Flies: An Example of "Civilization," in *Amsterdam News*, January 16, 1943, also in Aptheker, ed., *Newspaper Columns*, I, 494; Du Bois, "Prospect of a World without Race Conflict," in *American Journal of Sociology* (March 1944), 450–56; reprinted in condensed form in *Negro Digest* (August 1944), 44–47. Also in Aptheker, ed., *Writings by W.E.B. Du Bois in Periodical Literature*, III, 184–92. ". . . CHINESE DELEGATION.": Hoopes and Brinkley, op. cit., 134–35. ". . . DUMBARTON OAKS.": Du Bois report to NAACP Board, November 13, 1944, W.E.B. Du Bois Collection/Special Collections: Fisk University (hereafter WEB/FU. ". . . COLONIES HAVE BEEN PASSED OVER.": Du Bois, *Color and Democracy*, 15. ". . . MANY OF THEM AGHAST.": Ibid., 15.

504. ". . . NO DEMOCRATIC RIGHTS.": Du Bois "Imperialism, United Nations, Colonial Peoples," in *New Leader* (December 30, 1944), 5, also in Aptheker, ed., *Writ. Periodical Lit.* III, 225. ". . . BRETTON

WOODS.": Du Bois, "Winds of Time: The Meaning of Bretton Woods," in *Chicago Defender* (March 17, 1945), also in Aptheker, ed., *News. Columns*, II, 624. ". . . PEACE AND INTERNATIONAL UNDERSTANDING.": Du Bois's circular letter inviting statements and suggestions from a broad range of Negro organizations—National Baptist Convention, National Negro Insurance Association, National Bar Association, National Association of Ministers' Wives, Alpha Phi Alpha, and others—had mainly yielded pledges of support for his UN mission. He may have been somewhat surprised to learn from Randolph that the MOWM had not "as yet drafted any resolution on the subject [of the UN]," nor that, as yet, had Lester Granger's National Urban League, A. Phillip Randolph telephone call to Du Bois, April 24, 1945; Lester Granger to Walter White, April 20, 1945, both in Du Bois Papers/UMass; See also Horne, *op. cit.*, 35; For a complete list of organizations represented at San Francisco by the NAACP, see Aptheker, ed., *News. Columns*, II, 640–41. ". . . SOME SPECIFIC RECOGNITION.": Du Bois to Roy Wilkins, April 4, 1945, Du Bois Papers/UMass.

505. ". . . THE BOARD VOTED.": Board Minutes for April 9, 1945, BRD MINS/LC. ". . . TOOK BACK HIS OFFICE.": Du Bois, *Autobiography*, 329. ". . . THREE-PERSON NAACP DELEGATION.": Brian Urquhart, *Ralph Bunche: An American Life* (New York: W. W. Norton, 1993), 116. ". . . MRS. BETHUNE'S WASHINGTON SUPPORTERS.": Board Minutes for June 11, 1945, BRD MINS/LC. THROUGH TEMPERATE BUT INSISTENT AGITATION.": Du Bois, "The Winds of Time: Recognition at Frisco," in *Chicago Defender* (April 28, 1945), also in Aptheker, ed., *News. Columns*, II, 633.

505. ". . . 'AN ESTIMATE OF FDR.' ": Du Bois, "The Winds of Change," in *Chicago Defender* (May 5, 1945), also in Aptheker, ed., *News. Columns*, II, 635. ". . . DECLINING VILLARD'S INVITATION.": Osward Garrison Villard to Du Bois, April 5, 1945 and Du Bois to Villard, April 10, 1945, Du Bois Papers/UMass; Du Bois, "The Winds of Time: Poles Despised Negroes," in *Chicago Defender* (April 7, 1945), also in Aptheker, ed., *News. Columns*, II, 627. ". . . POLISH FACTOR.": Du Bois was not shy about making acid statements to American delegates at the UN: "We have allowed ourselves in this conference to be estranged from Russia by the plight of a dozen reactionary and Jew-baiting Polish landlords, and have no comment and taken no action on the great words spoken by Molotov." See Horne, op. cit., 36. ". . . PANDORA'S BOX.": Mildred Bryant Jones to Du Bois, April 26, 1945, Du Bois Papers/UMass.

506. ". . . ONE OF THE LEAST PREPARED MEN.": Walter Isaacson and Evan Thomas, *The Wise Men, Six Friends and the World They Made: Acheson, Bohlen, Harriman, Kennan, Lovett, McCloy* (New York: Simon and Schuster, 1986), 255. ". . . TRUMAN SNAPPED TO MOLOTOV.": Truman chose not only to disregard the cautious advice of secretary of war Henry Stimson and Army chief of staff George Marshall, by tone, if not altogether in substance, he exceeded the counsel of the hard-liners for whom Harriman, ambassador to the USSR and head of Brown Brothers Harriman, spoke with unimpeachable authority; *Ibid.*, 267; see Alonzo L. Hamby, *Man of the People: A Life of Harry S. Truman* (New York: Oxford University Press, 1995), 316. ". . . RACIAL EQUALITY AND ANTI-IMPERIALISM.": The Chinese negotiator had unsuccessfully pressed for a racial equality clause at Dumbarton Oaks, and the eloquent appeals of Mohandas Gandhi for justice for all colored peoples received banner notice in the Negro press, Sudarshan Kapur, *Raising Up a Prophet: The African-American Encounter with Gandhi* (Boston: Beacon, 1992). ". . . AN ACE OF DESTROYING THE CONFERENCE.": Hoopes and Brinkley, op. cit., 189–201.

507. ". . . INTERNATIONAL TRUSTEESHIP ARRANGEMENT.": Charles P. Henry, *Ralph Bunche: Model Negro or American Other?* (New York: New York University Press, 1999), 136; Walter LaFeber, *American Russia and the Cold War, 1945–1990* (New York: McGraw-Hill, 1991), 12. ". . . GNAT AMONG THE SUPERPOWER PACHYDERMS.": Urquhart, *op. cit.*, 116. ". . . RIGHTS OF DEPENDENT PEOPLE.": Du Bois, "The Winds of Change," in *Chicago Defender* (May 19, 1945), also in Aptheker, ed., *News. Columns*, II, 641. ". . . 'MARIELLE.' ": Ethel Ray Nance to Du Bois, June 8, 1945, Du Bois Papers/UMass; Lewis interview of Ethel Ray Nance, March 17, 1988.

508. ". . . USE OF IDEAS SUPPLIED BY DU BOIS.": Janken, *loc. cit.*, 1080–1081; Du Bois, "Is It Democracy for Whites to Rule Dark Majorities," in *New York Post* (May 15, 1945), 8, also in Aptheker, ed., *Writ, Periodical Lit.*, IV, 4–5; In one curious instance, Lochard's newspaper and several others published a story about a nonstory. Caught exiting their hotel together by a *Courier* photographer, Du Bois and White had paused for the camera, only to realize that the photographer wanted to make a group snapshot by including three approaching Indian delegates. "These three men were the stooges of the British Empire," Du Bois would explain after he and the secretary had suddenly taken to their heels, Du Bois, "The Winds of Time: India and British Imperialism," in *Chicago Defender* (May 12,

1945), also in Aptheker, ed., *News. Columns*, II, 637. Gandhi's denunciation of Great Britain's unilateral selection of Indians eligible for observer status at the conference had been reported throughout the world. Du Bois to Du Bois Williams, May 9, 1945, Du Bois Papers/UMass. ". . . WHO STOOD UP FOR HUMAN RIGHTS.": Du Bois, "The Winds of Time," in *Chicago Defender* (June 23, 1945), also in Aptheker, ed., *News. Columns*, II, 645.

508. ". . . DU BOIS WAS ECSTATIC.": Du Bois, "The Winds of Time: Molotov at the United Nations," in *Chicago Defender* (May 26, 1945), also in Aptheker, ed., *News. Columns*, II, 642. ". . . A HUMAN RIGHTS DECLARATION.": Walter White, *A Man Called White: The Autobiography of Walter White* (New York: Viking, 1948), 295. ". . . RUSSIA AND CHINA HAVE TAKEN THE PLAY AWAY.": On White at the UN, see Horne, *op. cit.*, 36; White, *A Man Called White*, 295–98. Restricted from formulating a detailed position on the colonial and dependent territories question, Stassen and Bunche felt some satisfaction that the Australian delegation had agreed to counter Great Britain's almost meaningless proposal for an international trusteeship system with one modeled on the stronger American draft, Urquhart, *op. cit.*; Henry, *op. cit.* ". . . IMPLICATIONS OF PALESTINE.": Urquhart, *op. cit.*; Kapur, *op. cit.*, 120. ". . . PLEA TO THE AMERICAN DELEGATION.": Walter White to Board of the NAACP, May 9, 1944, BRD MINS/LC.

509. ". . . EDWARD STETTINIUS WAS ENTIRELY PREDICTABLE.": Du Bois to Edward Stettinius, [n.d.] 1945, Du Bois Papers/UMass. Du Bois received a reply citing the May 18, 1945, official U.S. statement endorsing the "social advancement of the trust territories and their inhabitants and their progressive development toward self-government," Stettinius to Du Bois, June 7, 1945, Du Bois Papers/UMass. ". . . SECRETARY OF STATE WAS A COMPLETE DUD.": Urquhart, *op. cit.*, 118; Henry, *op. cit.*, 138.

509. ". . . SLUMS OF THE WORLD.": Du Bois, *Color and Democracy, op. cit.*, 17. ". . . IGNORING THE INJUSTICES.": Aptheker, Introduction to *Color and Democracy, op. cit.*, 12, 13. ". . . MRS. BETHUNE WAS RATHER A NUISANCE.": Horne, *op. cit.*, 37. ". . . ANNOUNCED THE WASHINGTON CONFERENCE.": White to Roy Wilkins, May 24, 1945, BRD MINS/LC.

510. ". . . TO RECEIVE ORAL PETITIONS.": Henry, *op. cit.*, 138. ". . . PROCESS OF DECOLONIZATION.": Full text of UN Charter in Hoopes and Brinkley, *op. cit.*, 242. The Charter stated the duty of the trusteeships as follows: b. to promote the political, economic, social, and educational advances of the inhabitants . . . and their progressive development towards self-government or independence as may be appropriate to the particular circumstances of each territory and its peoples concerned, and as may be provided by the terms of each trusteeship agreement; c. to encourage respect for human rights and for fundamental freedoms for all without distinction as to race, sex, or religion, and to encourage recognition of the interdependence of the people of the world. Ralph Bunche expressed qualified satisfaction with the trusteeship results in the following manner: "We have a Trusteeship Chapter in this Charter, though many thought it could never be pulled off," Bunche told his wife with understandable pride in his handiwork. "It is not as good as I would like it to be, but better than any of us expected it could get." See Urquhart, op. cit., 121. Later, Du Bois offered a more moderate assessment of the Charter in an article, "The Colonies at San Francisco," published in *Trek* (Johannesburg) (April 5, 1946), 12, also in Aptheker, ed., *Newspaper Columns*, II, 6–8. ". . . FIFTEEN MINUTES OF THE COMMITTEE'S TIME.": Du Bois to Senator Tom Connally, July 2, 1945, Du Bois Papers/UMass, also in Herbert Aptheker, ed., *Contributions by W.E.B. Du Bois in Government Publications and Proceedings* (Millwood, N.Y.: Kraus-Thomson, 1980), 383. ". . . NO NATION OR GROUP SHALL BE DEPRIVED.": Ralph Bunche to Walter White, August 1, 1945, includes file copy of Du Bois's speech to Senate hearings on the UN Charter, BRD MINS/LC.

510–11. ". . . NINA HAD SUFFERED A BAD FALL.": Nina to Will, March [n.d.] 1945, Du Bois Papers/UMass. ". . . ALL LISTEN AND LOOK FOR SOME CARD FROM YOU.": Nina to Will, May 4, 1945, Du Bois Papers/UMass. ". . . A CENTER TABLE IN A ROOM PACKED WITH DIPLOMATS.": Du Bois to Du Bois Williams, May 9, 1945, Du Bois Papers/UMass. ". . . MAJOR WALTER LOVING WAS DEAD.": Will to Nina, May 12, 1945, Du Bois Papers/UMass. ". . . VIRGINIA ALEXANDER HAS GOTTEN MARRIED.": Virginia Alexander Childs to Du Bois, July 9, 1945, Du Bois Papers/UMass. ". . . DU BOIS SALARY TO THE INC. FUND BUDGET.": Walter White to Thurgood Marshall, September 28, 1944, Marshall to White, October 2, 1944, both in BRD MINS/LC.

511. ". . . OFFICE SPACE FOR MY WORK.": Du Bois to Walter White, April 10, 1945, BRD MINS/LC. ". . . RENTED ADEQUATE OFFICE SPACE ON HIS OWN.": Walter White to Du Bois, July 17, 1945, BRD MINS/LC. ". . . NOTHING BUT TROUBLE.": Lewis interview with Bobbie Branch, [n.d.]. ". . . SMALL OFFICE IN NEW HEADQUARTERS.": Du Bois, "My Relations with the NAACP," October 1945, Du Bois

Papers/UMass. ". . . ADVISABILITY OF HOLDING THE CONGRESS.": Walter White to Du Bois, July 12, 1945, BRD MINS/LC. ". . . LOGAN'S UNWELCOME SUGGESTION.": Rayford Logan to Walter White, June 30, 1945, Du Bois Papers/UMass. "ASIANS.": Du Bois to Rayford Logan, July 3, 1945, Du Bois Papers/UMass.

512. ". . . SHOULD BE CONFINED TO AFRICANS.": Du Bois to Walter White, July 20, 1945; William Hastie to White, July 17, 1945, both in BRD MINS/LC. ". . . MILITARY AIR TRANSPORTATION.": Walter White to Du Bois, July 31, 1945, BRD MINS/LC. ". . . DEAN ACHESON INSTEAD.": Du Bois to President of the United States, September 12, 1945; Mathew J. Connolly to Du Bois, September 19, 1945, both in Du Bois Papers/UMass. ". . . TRAVEL DIFFICULTIES WERE FORMIDABLE.": Once again, Du Bois found his esteem for Bunche badly shaken. Henry Villard had heard nothing from Ralph Bunche, a member of the Pan-African Congress committee and senior member of Villard's own staff, about a conference sponsored by the NAACP involving Negro delegates bound for Europe; Du Bois to Henry Villard, October 3, 1945, Du Bois Papers/UMass.

512. ". . . TO BE HELD IN LONDON.": For PAC correspondence between Du Bois and George Padmore, see Aptheker, ed., *Correspondence*, III, 81–83. ". . . MANCHESTER, ENGLAND.": Du Bois to George Padmore, March 22; Du Bois to Padmore, April 11; Padmore to Du Bois, April 12; Du Bois to Padmore, July 9; Padmore to Du Bois, August 17; Du Bois memorandum to Secretary and the Pan-African Committee, September 4, 1945, all in Du Bois Papers/UMass. See also Hooker, *op. cit.*, ch. 6. ". . . REPRESENTATIVES NOT OF THE MIDDLE CLASS STRATA.": George Padmore to Du Bois, September 18, 1945 in Aptheker, ed., *Correspondence*, III, 88. ". . . DU BOIS WRANGLED A PASSPORT AND VISA.": NAACP Board Minutes for September 10, 1945, in Du Bois Papers/FU. Significantly, the board at this meeting appropriated a maximum sum of fifteen thousand dollars to establish a Hollywood office. ". . . A STROKE AND HER PROGNOSIS . . . GUARDED.": Du Bois to Associated Hospital Service, April 25, 1947, Du Bois Papers/UMass. Puts in an insurance claim giving Nina's medical history; Walter White telegram to Du Bois, September 21, 1945, BRD MINS/LC. ". . . PROMISED NOT TO DISTURB HIS WAY OF LIFE.": Nina to Will, July 7, 1945, Du Bois Papers/UMass.

513. ". . . MRS. GARVEY.": Darlene Clark Hine, et al. eds., *Black Women in America*, 2 vols. (Brooklyn, N.Y.: Carlson, 1991), 481–83. ". . . NKRUMAH DEMANDED.": Langley, *op. cit.*, ch. 9. ". . . FUTURE LEADERS OF DU BOIS'S DARKER WORLD.": *ibid, ch.* 9.

514. ". . . 300,000 WEST AFRICAN COCOA FARMERS.": W.E.B. Du Bois, *The World and Africa: An Inquiry into the Part Which Africa Has Played in World History* (New York: Viking, 1947), 245. An invaluable source is George Padmore, ed., *History of the Pan-African Congress: Colonial and Coloured Unity, a Programme of Action* (Manchester: Pan-African Federation, 1945), courtesy of Paul Breman. ". . . PLEAD FOR HIS PEOPLE'S LAND.": On Jomo Kenyatta, see Wunyari O. Maloba, *Kenya and Mau Mau* (Bloomington: Indiana University Press, 1998) and Carolyn Martin Shaw, *Colonial Inscriptions: Race, Sex and Class in Kenya* (Minneapolis: University of Minnesota Press, 1995). On Kwame Nkrumah, see David Birmingham, *Kwame Nkrumah: The Father of African Nationalism* (Athens: Ohio University, 1998); Marika Sherwood, *Kwame Nkrumah: The Years Abroad, 1935–1947* (Accra, Ghana: Freedom Publications, 1996). ". . . KENYATTA ASKED.": Padmore, *History of the Pan-African Congress*, 49. ". . . CONSERVATIVES HAD DECLINED.": Du Bois, *The World and Africa*, 245.

515. ". . . EVEN IF FORCE.": Padmore, *History of the Pan-African Congress*, 5. ". . . SIXTH CONCLAVE IN LIBERIA." Hooker, *op. cit.*, 97.

515. ". . . OTHELLO.": Jeffrey C. Stewart, ed., *Paul Robeson: Artist and Citizen* (New Brunswick, N.J.: Rutgers University Press, 1998), 217; Martin Bauml Duberman, *Paul Robeson* (New York: Knopf, 1988), p. 302, "The Spingarn Medal," pamphlet published by the NAACP, 1978. ". . . IN A POWER-PLAY OVER POLAND.": The three-power Potsdam Conference running from mid-July to August 2 had strained relations between the allies. Stalin had flatly rejected Truman's insistence upon free elections in the countries liberated by the Russian army and had forced the redrawing of Poland's boundaries. Truman had hinted to Stalin (who already knew) of the existence of a secret weapon of mass destruction in the American arsenal, and his cocky, tough attitude reflected confidence that the Pacific war would end quickly without the help of the Soviet army and the horrendous American casualties predicted in an assault on Japan itself. See LaFeber, *op. cit.*, ch. 2; Martin J. Sherwin, *A World Destroyed: The Atomic Bomb and the Grand Alliance* (New York: Vintage Books, 1977), chs. 3, 4; Martin Walker, *The Cold War: A History* (New York: Henry Holt), 1993), ch. 1; Bernard A. Weisberger, *Cold War, Cold Peace: The United States and Russia since 1945* (New York: American Heritage, 1985), chs. 1, 2.

516. ". . . MAINTENANCE OF COLONIALISM.": Duberman, *op. cit.*, 300. ". . . VISIBLE IN WALTER

WHITE'S COMPLEXION.": Lewis interview with Corinne Wright, May 1977, Voices of the Harlem Renaissance: Schomburg Center for Research in Black Culture, New York Public Library (hereafter VOHR/SCRBC).

517. "... ATOMIC POWER-POLITICS.": From somewhat different reasoning, Du Bois also believed that his country's military supremacy was more apparent than real. Two considerations militate against this "easy assumption," he declared in the *Defender*. "First, can white nations trust each other?" he asked. "Can we hope to see them now calmly do the lion and the lamb act just because of the atom bomb?" Second, he doubted that the secret of the atom could remain "a monopoly of white folk." Du Bois, "Atom Bomb and the Colored World," *Defender* (January 12, 1946), also in Aptheker, ed., *Newspaper*, II, 670–71. For an extreme view of the foreign policy use and abuse of the atomic bomb, see Gar Alperovitz, *The Decision to Use the Atomic Bomb and the Architecture of an American Myth* (New York: Knopf, 1995). "... CHURCHILL'S SPEECH.": *ibid.*, 680. "... WHITE'S POLITICALLY CORRECT TESTIMONY.": Press release, "Lynching and Oppression of Negroes Best Communist Propaganda Says White," September 28, 1930, BRD MINS/LC.

518. "... DU BOIS ... TO LONDON.": Hooker, *op. cit.*, 97, says Padmore acted as toastmaster for a party for Du Bois in a London Chinese restaurant; they then escorted Du Bois to his plane. "... PLAIN OR COLORED.": George Bernard Shaw to Du Bois, November 9, 1945, Du Bois Papers/UMass. "... MEETING WITH HAROLD LASKI.": Du Bois, "Laski Talks Color and Class," *Defender* (December 15, 1945), also in Aptheker, ed., *Newspapers*, II, 666.

518. "ESTHER COOPER JACKSON.": Lewis interview of Esther and James Jackson, February 5, 1995. "... PRESENCE OF JACKSON'S HUMILIATED PARENTS.": Lewis interview with James Jackson, February 2, 1995; also, "Getting Blacks Into Scouting Took Some Work," *Richmond Times-Despatch*, August 11, 1997, p. 1. "... BRICKLAYER'S ASSISTANT.": Jackson interviews. "... SOUTHERN NEGRO YOUTH CONGRESS.": Mari Jo Buhle et al., eds. *Encyclopedia of the American Left* (Urbana: University of Illinois Press, 1992), 739; Robert Cohen, *When the Old Left Was Young: Student Radicals and America's First Mass Student Movement, 1929–1941* (New York: Oxford University Press, 1993), 220.

519. "... ELEANOR ROOSEVELT.": Mrs. Roosevelt was formally presented to the NAACP board at its October 8, 1945 meeting: Minutes of the Board, in Du Bois Papers/FU. "... AMEND HIS REPORT.": Lewis interview with George W. Crockett, June 4, 1988. "... GLOSTER CURRENT.": Roy Wilkins to Walter White, memorandum, December 6, 1945, BRD MINS/LC. "... USURPATION OF THE SECRETARY'S PREROGATIVES.": Walter White to Du Bois, November 27, 1945, Du Bois to Senator Tom Connally, July 2, 1945, both in Du Bois Papers/UMass. "... WALTER WHITE.": Du Bois, *Autobiography*, p. 331.

520. "... BOARD OF DIRECTORS LARGELY CEREMONIAL.": Du Bois, *ibid.*, p. 330. "... NAACP'S MAIN GOAL.": Kluger, op. cit., pp. 250–270; Louis R. Harlan, *Separate and Unequal: School Campaigns and Racism in Southern Seaboard States, 1901–1915* (Chapel Hill: University of North Carolina, 1958). "... WINNING SUITS.": On the NAACP litigation to equalize salaries and integrate professional schools, see Du Bois, "Little Rock," *Defender* (June 14, 1947), also in Aptheker, ed., *Newspaper Columns* II, p. 717; Du Bois writes about John Henry Lewis, Sr., principal of Little Rock's Dunbar High School who, though not identified by name, was key to the Arkansas teachers' salary litigation. See also, Eric Anderson and Alfred A. Moss, *The Facts of Reconstruction: Essays in Honor of John Hope Franklin* (Baton Rouge: Louisiana State University Press, 1991); Harlan, *op. cit.* "... STRONG BACKERS.": For biographical information on Dungee, Dickerson, Tobias, see *Encyclopedia of African American Culture and History*; on Miller, W. Augustus Low and Virgil A. Clift, eds., *Encyclopedia of Black America* (New York: McGraw-Hill, 1981); on Hammond, Kenneth T. Jackson, *The Encyclopedia of New York* (New Haven: Yale University Press, 1995). Further biographical information is in letters from Earl B. Dickerson to Du Bois, October 7 and 21, 1946, Du Bois Papers/UMass. "... LILLIAN ALEXANDER.": Walter White to Lillian Alexander, November 29, 1945, BRD MINS/LC.

520. "... HISTORY OF THE ASSOCIATION.": Carolyn Wedin, Ovington Manuscript, ch. 4, "Volunteer Transplant, Social Researcher to Activist, 1904–1908" [read June 1991, courtesy of Esme Bahn, Moorland-Spingarn Collection, Howard University]. "... WAS ANNULLED THAT YEAR, 1946.": Aptheker, ed., *Correspondence* III, p. 107; Board Minutes, March 1, 1946, in Du Bois Papers/FU. "... PAN-AFRICAN CONGRESS.": Du Bois to Alphaeus Hunton, May 10, 1946, Du Bois Papers/UMass. "... NEGRO IN THE MOVIES.": Board Minutes for September 10, 1945, October 15, 1946, BRD MINS/LC. "... HESITATION OF THE NAACP.": Du Bois to George Padmore, July 12; Padmore to Du Bois August 9, 1946, both in Du Bois Papers/UMass, also in Aptheker, ed., *Correspondence*, III, pp. 141–148. A memorandum to the

secretary in late March 1946 proposed three initiatives for the association. With the collaboration of the Council on African Affairs in mind, Du Bois recommended a media attack on South Africa for its repressive policies in its South West Africa mandate (Namibia) as well as that nation's systematic denial of rights to the majority of its people. He proposed further that the NAACP formally petition the United nations for the right to "speak for the [. . .] interests" of African peoples being denied their rights under the mandates. White's generally positive response encouraged Du Bois to propose an even bolder initiative four months later. The National Negro Congress had circulated a petition drafted by the Marxist historian Herbert Aptheker that it intended to present to the UN General Assembly, see Aptheker. ed., *Correspondence*, III, p. 163. Du Bois thought the petition calling for international attention to the condition of American Negroes well done "but too short and not sufficiently documented." Pointing out that Palestinian Jews, Indonesians, South African Indians, and several other claimants to the right of self-determination or sovereignty would file petitions, he called for an analogous NAACP document, something of no less than one hundred "and not more than two hundred printed pages."

Operating on parallel tracks as he often did, as international president of the Pan-African Congress, Du Bois had already drafted a petition he intended to submit for endorsement at the Schomburg Library meeting of some twenty-five professional, religious, fraternal and sororal organizations at the beginning of September. This "Pan-African Movement" document, although identical in intent to the UN presentation authorized by the NAACP, was only several pages long. Approved by the Schomburg conferees, he circulated the Pan-African petition to a broader array of organizations. Robeson and Yergan committed the CAA to the project. The concurrence of Randolph's March on Washington Movement may well have influenced the endorsement of AFL President William Green, see Aptheker, ed., *Correspondence*, III, p. 156. From Nigeria, Nnamdi Azikiwe telegraphed the "support and cooperation" of the Nigerian National Council for the petition, see Aptheker, ed., *Correspondence*, III, p. 155. Nkrumah telegraphed unanimous approval of his London-based West African National Secretariat. Oswald Villard signed on, as did John Haynes Holmes, another founder of the association. UN Secretary General Trygve Lie was dutifully informed on September 4, 1946, of the Pan-American Congress's intention to lay the document before the General Assembly, see Aptheker, ed., *Correspondence*, III, p. 153. ". . . THE FIVE-MEMBER TEAM.": Hugh H. Smythe to Earl B. Dickerson, October 20, 1947, Hugh Smythe Papers/Schomburg Center for Research in Black Culture (hereafter HSP/SCRBC).
521. ". . . LESLIE PERRY.": Aptheker, ed., *Correspondence*, III, p. 178. ". . . AN APPEAL . . .": Du Bois, *Autobiography*, p. 333; Board Minutes for September 8, 1947, WEB/FU. ". . . STOP THE LYNCHERS.": Duberman, *op. cit.*, p. 305. ". . . FASTIDIOUS AVERSION.": Alfred Baker Lewis to White, October 18, 1946, BRD MINS/LC.
522. ". . . MONOPOLY OF NO ONE ORGANIZATION.": Du Bois, "My Relations with the NAACP," October 1948, Du Bois Papers/UMass; Duberman, *op. cit.*, p. 306. ". . . SNYC.": On the SNYC, see Cohen, *op. cit.*, 220–24; Buhle, ed., *op. cit.*
523–24. ". . . JAMES JACKSON.": Lewis interview with Esther and James Jackson, October 8, 1994; Du Bois, *Autobiography*, p. 332. ". . . A BOURGEOIS DEMOCRAT.": Du Bois quoted, David Levering Lewis interview with James E. Jackson, October 8, 1994. ". . . AN INSTANT CLASSIC OF THE LEFT.": Du Bois, "Behold the Land," *New Masses* (January 14, 1947), 18–20; and David Levering Lewis, ed., *W.E.B. Du Bois: A Reader* (New York: Holt, 1995), 545–50; see also Du Bois, *Autobiography*, 332.

Listed in the SNYC program for the Columbia convention are Osceola McKaine, John H. McCray, publisher of the *Lighthouse and Informer*, Thomas Richardson, executive vice president of the United Public Works of America, Kenneth C. Kennedy, National Commander of United Negro and Allied Veterans of America, Louis Burnham, Rose Mae Catchings, President of the SNYC, in *Souvenir Journal, Southern Youth Legislature, Columbia, South Carolina, October 18–20, 1946.* I am grateful to my student, Peter Lau, for the use of his excellent unpublished work on the SNYC: Peter Lau, "Race, Rights and the Transformation of Class Politics: The Southern Negro Youth Congress and the 1964 Columbia, South Carolina, Youth Legislature" (May 2000). ". . . LYNCHING OF EMAN-CIPATION." Du Bois, *Autobiography*, p. 332; Lewis, ed., *Du Bois Reader*, op. cit. ". . . NOTHING . . . HAS TOUCHED ME MORE DEEPLY.": Du Bois, "The Winds of Time: A Book of Remembrance," in *Defender* (November 16, 1946), also in Aptheker, ed., *News. Columns*, II, p. 699. ". . . YOUNG NEGROES WITH GUTS.": Du Bois, "The Winds of Time: The Firing Line," in *Defender* (November 16, 1946), also in Aptheker, ed., *News. Columns*, II, p. 698. For text of White's *Defender* piece contesting Du Bois's statements about the SNYC Conference, see "Du Bois and White," November 21, 1946, Rec. Group

II, NAACP General Office Files, LC. Although Du Bois had been careful to state that he was participating in the SNYC conclave on his own account, White and Wilkins were troubled by the inescap-
able public impression of NAACP endorsement of SNYC activities.
525. "... RUSSIA'S PURSUIT OF HER OWN WAY OF LIFE.": Du Bois, "Democracy's Opportunity" in
Christian Register (August 1946), also in Aptheker, ed., *Writ. Periodical Lit.*, IV, p. 12. "... EDITED BY
JESSICA SMITH.": John J. Abt, *Advocate and Activist: Memoirs of an American Communist Lawyer*
(Urbana: University Of Illinois Press), pp. 53–54. "... DU BOIS INFORMED FOURTEEN MILLION AMER-
ICAN NEGROES.": Du Bois, "Common Objectives" in *Soviet Russia Today* (August 1946), p. 15. "...
MOST HOPEFUL COUNTRY ON EARTH.": *Ibid.*, p. 16; also in Aptheker, ed., *Writ. Periodical Lit.*, III,
p. 225.
525. "... GLOSSARY FOR THE COLD WAR.": On the personality and importance of George Kennan,
see George F. Kennan, *Around the Cragged Hill: A Personal and Political Philosophy* (New York:
W. W. Norton, 1993); Walter Isaacson and Evan Thomas, *op. cit.* "... THE 'LONG TELEGRAM.' ": Joel
Kovel, *Red Hunting in the Promised Land: Anticommunism and the Making of America* (New York:
Basic Books, 1994), pp. 44–47; LaFeber, *op. cit.*, 63–64; Isaacson and Thomas, *op. cit.*, 353–54. For a
trenchant summary of the force of the containment paradigm, see Michael J. Hogan, *A Cross of Iron:
Harry S. Truman and the Origins of the National Security State, 1945–1954* (Cambridge: Cambridge
University Press, 1998), esp. 10–19. "... EXECUTIVE ORDER 9835.": Explaining what he saw as the
sensible politics of preemption behind the momentous decree, Truman told civil rights lawyer Clifford
Durr that the loyalty boards and the attorney general's subversive organizations index were designed
"mainly to take the ball away from the House committee on Un-American Activities (HUAC) under
its ... reactionary [New Jersey GOP] chairman, J. Parnell Thomas." See Griffin Fariello, *Red Scare:
Memories of the American Inquisition, An Oral History* (New York: Avon, 1996), 36; David Caute, *The
Great Fear: Anti-Communist Purge under Truman and Eisenhower* (New York: Simon & Schuster,
1978), 27.
526. "... SINKING TENTACLES INTO.": Arthur M. Schlesinger, Jr., "The Communist Party," *Life*, July
29, 1946, pp. 84–96, 90. For a useful survey of changing American opinion on Russia, see Ralph B.
Levering, *American Opinion and the Russian Alliance, 1939–1945* (Chapel Hill: University of North
Carolina Press, 1976), esp. 157–96. "... ASSOCIATION WAS A COMMUNIST FRONT.": On CIO-NAACP
labor union activity in Detroit, see August Meier and Elliot Rudwick, *Black Detroit and the Rise of
the UAW* (New York: Oxford University Press, 1979), and Horne, op. cit. " ' ... WONDERFUL
GUMBO.' ": Lewis interview with Howard Fast, November 19, 1990. "... FICTIONALIZED TREATMENT
OF RECONSTRUCTION.": Lewis interview with Howard Fast, "... REFUSED EMERGENCY WARD TREAT-
MENT.": Graham's story about her dying son: Lewis interview with Howard Fast, Lewis interview with
Lorenz Graham, June 1, 1988; Hatch-Billops interview with Shirley Graham Du Bois (Hatch-Billops
Collection); Gerald Horne, *Shirley Graham Du Bois* (New York: New York University Press, 2000);
Howard Fast, *Being Red: A Memoir* (Boston: Houghton Mifflin, 1990), 156.
527. "... STEALTHY PURSUIT.": Opinions about Shirley Graham, Du Bois, and the CPUSA: "... There
were times when I felt that Shirley had been assigned from the Party to take ... to grab him," Lewis
Interview with Kyrle Elkin, February 14, 1987; "... She was the one who turned him towards com-
munism ... I think he turned because everything else was finished," Lewis interview with Rachel Davis
Du Bois, 1989.
527. ON DOXEY WILKERSON'S CAREER, see "Doxey Alphonso Wilkerson," *EAACH*, V, p. 2834. WILK-
ERSON AND APTHEKER: Lewis interview with Doxey Wilkerson, September 9, 1988.
527. " 'THERE WAS A WALL BETWEEN HIM AND THE REST OF THE WORLD.' ": Lewis interview with
Howard Fast, November 19, 1990. "... REMARKABLE CAPACITY FOR WRITING AND SPEAKING.": Dashiell
Hammett to Du Bois, September 24, 1947, Du Bois to Hammett, September 26, 1942, both in Du Bois
Papers/UMass. "... METHOD LAID DOWN BY KARL MARX.": W.E.B. Du Bois, *Worlds of Color*
(New York: Mainstream Publishers, 1961), p. 258. "... AFTERNOON WITH ELEANOR ROOSEVELT.": Du
Bois to Eleanor Roosevelt, September 19, September 22, and October 14, 1947, Du Bois Papers/UMass.
"... DRUMMING UP SUPPORT FOR THE UN PETITION.": The cooperation of Roger Baldwin and Clark
Eichelberger of the American Association for the United Nations, Inc., was useful, Roger Baldwin and
Clark Eichelberger circular letter, Jan. 17, 1947, Rec. Group II, NAACP General Office Files, LC; Du
Bois to Eleanor Roosevelt, July 17, 1946, Du Bois Papers/UMass; Du Bois to Oswald Garrison Villard,
July 24, 1947 and July 19, 1947, Du Bois Papers/UMass; Adam Clayton Powell, Jr. to Du Bois, August

10, 1946, Du Bois Papers/UMass; also in Aptheker, ed., *Correspondence*, III, pp. 149–52. "... TRYGVE LIE.": Du Bois to Trygve Lie, October 14, 1947, Du Bois Papers/UMass. " 'THE CASE AGAINST THE U.S.' " Shirley Graham Du Bois claimed that White forbade press coverage of the ceremony in order not to offend some of the association's backers. However, the presentation of the petition did receive newspaper coverage. Shirley Graham Du Bois, *His Day Is Marching On: A Memoir of W.E.B. Du Bois* (Philadelphia: J.B. Lippincott Co., 1971), p. 95; Oswald Garrison Villard to Du Bois, November 6, 1947, Du Bois Papers/UMass.; George Streator, "U.N. Gets Charges of Wide Discrimination," *New York Times* (October 24, 1947). The *Times* states that the Du Bois petition was in the form of 155 mimeographed pages. "... CONSENT TO ANY ADDITION TO IT.": Du Bois, "My Relations with the NAACP," p. 7; Printing of UN Petition: Memorandum of White to Du Bois, December 15, 1947, Rec. Group II, NAACP General Office Files, LC; Minutes of the Board, January 5, 1948, WEB/FU.

529. " '... MORAL DRY ROT.": Hamby, *op. cit.*, p. 433. "... A HEARTSICK DU BOIS.": Du Bois, *Autobiography*, p. 33. " '... MORE THAN [HE] DREAMED POSSIBLE.": Roy Wilkins with Tom Matthews, *Standing Fast: The Autobiography of Roy Wilkins* (New York: Da Capo Press, 1983, 1994):, p. 200. "... SHELLY V. KRAMER.": White leads a delegation to see President Truman, see White, *A Man Called White*, p. 333, Kluger, *op. cit.*, pp. 248–51; Hamby, *op. cit.*, p. 435. "... WHITE AMERICANS WERE PLEASED.": Hamby, *ibid.*, p. 435.

530. " '... AS GREAT AS THEIR GREAT MEN.' ": Wilkins, *op. cit.*, p. 198. "... GOVERNMENT MUST SHOW THE WAY.": Harry S. Truman, quoted in *Highlights of NAACP History, 1909–1983* (NAACP Pamphlet, July 1984), p. 30; White, *A Man Called White*, p. 348; Wilkins, *op cit.*, p. 198; Hamby, *op. cit.*, p. 433. On Clark Clifford's advice to Truman, see Norman D. Markowitz, *The Rise and Fall of the People's Century: Henry Wallace and American Liberalism, 1941–1948* (New York: The Free Press, 1973), 257.

530. " '... FOCUS OUR ATTENTION ON THE SORE POINTS.' ": Minutes of the Board, December 8, 1947, in Du Bois Papers/FU. "... REPORT SUSPICIOUS ACTIVITY.": Ibid.; Fariello, op. cit. p. 315.

531. ON THE MARSHALL PLAN AND PRINTING THE UN PETITION: Minutes of the Board, January 5, 1948, NAACP Board Minutes, in Du Bois Papers/FU ". . . IDEOLOGICAL SANCTUARY.": White increasingly spoke the hardline language of the board's most influential anticommunist, the white insurance executive, Alfred Baker Lewis. Alfred Baker Lewis to Walter White, October 18, 1946, Rec. Group II, NAACP General Office Files, LC: "It is plain that the communists are out to get us and to get our organization either to win control of it or to tear it down by building up the National Negro Congress in opposition to us." "... BALANCE OF THE TWENTIETH CENTURY.": Horne, *Black and Red*, p. 66. " '... LIKE APPLES IN A BARREL.' ": For various versions of the White House crisis meeting and what was said, see Thomas and Isaacson, *op. cit.*, p. 395; Weisberger, *op. cit.*, pp. 51–61; LaFeber, *op. cit.*, 51; Kovel, *op. cit.*, 59.

532. " '... AMERICAN OIL MILLIONAIRES.": Du Bois, "The Winds of Time: Stupid and Dangerous," *Defender* (April 19, 1947), also in Aptheker, ed., *Newspapers*, II, p. 711. " '... CRIMINAL CONSPIRACY.' ": Du Bois, "The Winds of Time: An Attack on Civilization," *Defender* (April 19, 1947), also in Aptheker, ed., *Newspapers* II, p. 711. " '... NOT A CENT FOR EDUCATION.' ": Du Bois, "The Winds of Time: In Complete Control," *Defender* (April 26, 1947), also in Aptheker, ed., *Newspapers*, II, p. 713. "... COMICALLY VAIN BERNARD BARUCH.": Du Bois, "The Winds of Time: War," *Defender* (July 5, 1947), also in Aptheker, ed., *Newspapers*, II, p. 723. " '... TO IMPLEMENT THEIR SAYINGS.' ": Du Bois, "The Winds of Time: Truman on Discrimination," *Defender* (February 7, 1948), also in Aptheker, ed., *Newspapers*, II, p. 760. " '... MRS. ROOSEVELT IS FOLLOWING ORDERS' ": Du Bois to Walter White, November 24, 1947, Rec. Group II, NAACP General Office Files, LC.

533. " '... A COMPLETE OPPORTUNIST POLITICIAN.' ": Du Bois, "The Winds of Time: Candidates," *Defender* (January 3, 1948), also in Aptheker, ed., *Newspapers*, II, p. 752. "... IOWA FARMER HENRY AGARD WALLACE.": Graham White and John Maze, *Wallace: Henry A. Wallace, His Search for a New World Order* (Chapel Hill: University of North Carolina Press, 1995); John C. Culver and John Hyde, *American Dreamer: A Life of Henry A. Wallace* (New York: W. W. Norton & Co., 2000); and Curtis D. MacDougal, *Gideon's Army*, 3 vols. (New York: Marzoni & Muncell, 1965). "... KNEE OF THE VENERABLE GEORGE WASHINGTON CARVER.": *Ibid.*, I, 92. To his many detractors, the sixty-year-old former New Deal secretary of agriculture was a political misfit whose loopy idealism and arrogance beneath the aw-shucks manner made him a danger to the Republic. GOP Congresswoman Clare Boothe Luce, delivering her 1946 maiden address in a House of Representatives just captured by her

party, zinged Wallace with an unforgettable neologism—"globaloney." See also White and Maze, *op. cit.*, Culver and Hyde, op. cit.

533. "... FACT FINDING MISSION.": White and Maze, *op. cit.*, I, 190, 194. "'... WE WANT COOP-ERATION.'": MacDougal, *op. cit.*, I, viii. "'... OUR PEOPLE, OUR COUNTRY.'": Du Bois, "The Winds of Time: Third Party," *Defender* (January 3, 1948), also in Aptheker, ed., *Newspaper*, II p. 753. EX-EMPTED FROM THE MUZZLING 1944 RESOLUTION: Executive Session of the Board, March 8, 1948, BRD MINS/LC. Du Bois's reaction to a board resolution of March 1948 reaffirming the 1944 rule barring paid executives of the association from partisan political activity was to ignore it. Proposing a modifying motion, he stated his assumption that the board could not "possibly have meant to forbid any individual, in his capacity as a private citizen" from expressing his political convictions publicly." Earl Dickerson, Hubert Delany, and John Hammond were among the dwindling liberals supporting Du Bois's failed motion to be exempted from the muzzling 1944 resolution. "... CLAIM UPON THE WORLD COMMUNITY.": Du Bois, "The Case of the Jews," *Chicago Star*, May 8, 1948, also in Aptheker, ed., *Writ. Periodical Lit.*, IV, p. 56.

534. "... REPRESENT THE ASSOCIATION IN PARIS.": Lewis interview with Gloster Current, April 28, 1989. "... IN AN ADVISORY CAPACITY TO THE SECRETARY.": Board Minutes for July 26, 1948; minutes for the July 26, 1948 meeting of the board are not to be found in the NAACP papers at the Library of Congress. "... IS CLEARLY STRADDLING ON ISRAEL.": Memorandum to the Secretary and the Board of Directors of the NAACP from W.E.B. Du Bois, September 7, 1948, BRD MINS/LC. Actions re-ported in minutes for September 13, 1948, BRD MINS/LC. "... EXPIRATION OF HIS PRESENT TERM.": Text of the motion dismissing W.E.B. Du Bois from the NAACP: Motion passed by NAACP Board of Directors at the regular meeting, September 13, 1948—"That in view of Dr. Du Bois's written refusal to cooperate with the NAACP executive staff of which he is a member in preparation for representation at the forthcoming meeting of the General Assembly of the UN, in view of his distribution of his memorandum of September 7, addressed to this Board, before its consideration by this Board, it is the conclusion of this Board that it will not be in the best interest of the association to continue the employment of Dr. Du Bois as a staff member beyond the term of his present contract; that formal notice of this decision be transmitted to Dr. Du Bois." On September 13, 1948, as Walter White was sailing for France, he sent a memorandum of his own—Memorandum to Dr. Du Bois from Mr. White, September 13, 1948—"I wish first to comment on your patent annoyance that someone else other than yourself was sent to represent the NAACP at the UN General Assembly in Paris . . . In my memorandum of July 13, I stated, 'It is the Secretary's position that Dr. Du Bois would be the best person to represent the NAACP.' For what the committee on Administration considered good and sufficient reasons, my recommendation was not agreed to and I was instructed to go the Paris." For a typical at-large skepticism about the purity of White's motives, see Louis Lautier, "In the Nation's Capital", *Call & Post*, August 25, 1948—"No one who really knows Walter White . . . will doubt for a moment that he maneuvered to get himself appointed as a consultant to the United Nations General Assembly to satiate his vanity and to enable him to get material for his newspaper column and for his magazine article."

535. "... LEAVE THE LIMELIGHT TO WHITE.": Du Bois, *Autobiography*, p. 335. "... COUNTEE CUL-LEN HAD DIED.": in Bruce Kellner, ed., *The Harlem Renaissance: A Historical Dictionary for the Era* (Westport, CT: Greenwood Press, 1984), pp. 88–89. "... THE SHAPE OF THE BUILDING NEVER EMERGED." : Chicago *Defender*, January 26, 1946. "... PLEADING FOR PREMATURE RELEASE.": Du Bois to Caroline Bond Day, March 18, 1946, Du Bois Papers/UMass. "... CRAZILY SWAYING AND DIPPING.": Du Bois, "My Golden Wedding", *People's Voice*, June 29, 1946, p. S-2, also in Aptheker, ed., *Writ. Periodical Lit.*, IV, pp. 9–10. "... JOHN GUNTHER'S MASSIVE BEST SELLER.": John Gunther, *Inside U.S.A.* (New York: Harper & Brothers, 1951), p. 681. For congratulatory messages to Nina and Will, see Edwin Embree to Du Bois and Nina, May 12, 1946; Amy Spingarn to Du Bois, May 11, 1946, both in Du Bois Papers/UMass.

536. "... TURNED INTO ACTUALITY.": Melville Herskovits to Du Bois, February 20, 1948, Du Bois Papers/UMass. "... HANG IN THE BALANCE OF COLD WAR JUSTICE.": Roi Ottley, "The Big Ten Who Run America," *Negro Digest*, May 1948—others on the list were Charles S. Johnson, Walter White, Robeson, Bethune, and Mordecai Johnson; Henry Steele Commager's 1948 list in the magazine 48 contained sixty-one names. Du Bois was number sixty-one.

536. "... CHURCHILL'S IRON CURTAIN PROPHECY.": M. J. Heale, *American Anticommunism: Combating the Enemy Within, 1830–1970* (Baltimore: Johns Hopkins University Press, 1990), p. 142;

Weisberger, op. cit., p. 81. "... COMMITTED TO A WALLACE RUN FOR THE PRESIDENCY.": Du Bois plausibly explained that, although a vice-president of the Progressive Citizens Association, he did not sign the Wallace third party call, but that organizers assumed that he would have. See Walter White to Du Bois, March 29, 1948; Du Bois to Arthur Spingarn, April 2, 1948, both in Du Bois Papers/UMass, and also in Aptheker, ed., *Correspondence*, III, pp. 239–241. "... SHARED THE STAGE WITH HENRY WALLACE.": Henry Wallace to Du Bois, November 29, 1948, Du Bois Papers/UMass. "... WILL WIN IN 1948.": Du Bois, "Winds of Time," *Defender*, February 21, 1948, also in Aptheker, ed., *Newspaper Columns*, II, p. 764. PROGRESSIVE PARTY CONVENTION: Culver and Hyde, *op. cit.*, p. 484. "... ASKED ... TO DELIVER THE KEYNOTE ADDRESS.": *Ibid.*, p. 486. The keynote was given by Charles P. Howard, a successful Negro businessman and a Republican who demanded that Truman immediately integrate the armed services.

537. "... NEGROES WERE GOING TO VOTE FOR WALLACE.": Du Bois, "From McKinley to Wallace: My Fifty Years as an Independent", *Masses & Mainstream* (August 1948), 3–14, also in Aptheker, ed., *Writ. Periodical Lit.*, IV, p. 65. "... COLD WAR LIBERALS OF AMERICANS FOR DEMOCRATIC ACTION.": See MacDougall, op. cit.; Culver and Hyde, *op. cit.* Wallace sent a copy of the Stalin letter to Du Bois, who praised its contents, see Wallace to Du Bois, May 17, 1948; Du Bois to Wallace, May 24, 1948, both in Du Bois Papers/UMass. "... OVERTHROW THE GOVERNMENT OF THE UNITED STATES.": Victor Navasky, *Naming Names* (New York: Penguin Books, 1980), p. 4; Heale, —op. cit., p. 142. "... THE LOOK OF AN UNMADE BED.": See Sam Tanenhaus, *Whittaker Chambers: A Biography* (New York: Random House, 1997). "... THE CIO TURNED UPON ITSELF.": Heale, *op. cit.*, p. 138. "... A ROUT FOR THE PROGRESSIVES.": *World Almanac and Book of Facts 2000* (Mahwah, N.J.: Primedia Reference, 2000), p. 502.

538. "... THE REAL PEOPLE OF THE WORLD.": Lewis, ed., *Du Bois Reader*, op. cit., p. 349. "... 'NUMERICAL ONE HUNDREDTH OF OUR RACE'." : Du Bois, "The Talented Tenth: Memorial Address", pp. 347–353, from *Boulé Journal*, 15 (October 1948) also in Aptheker, ed., *Writ. Periodical Lit.*, IV, pp. 78–88; abridged text in Lewis, ed., *Du Bois Reader, op. cit.*, pp. 345–353; see also Howard Sidney Jarrett, *The History of Sigma Pi Phi: First of the African-American Greek-Letter Fraternities* (Philadelphia: Quantum Publishers, 1995), pp. 249–250. After the "Talented Tenth Memorial Address," Du Bois sat alone on a shaded campus bench where he was approached by very few of the members of his fraternity as the day ran down, according to Charles Wesley; see Charles H. Wesley, "W.E.B. Du Bois, the Talented Tenth and Sigma Pi Phi," *Boulé Journal* 37 (winter 1973–spring 1974), 8–12: "the address was received coolly and almost shoved aside. Leaving the auditorium after perfunctory greetings, he went and sat alone on a campus seat. My wife, Louise, seeing him from the front porch of our residence, went across to him and asked him to come to our porch and have a cup of tea, to which he readily agreed."

538. "... GETTING OUT OF BEING UNPATRIOTIC.": Lewis interview with Robert Weaver, March 17, 1988. "... ONE OF THE PARTY'S MOST TRUSTED OPERATIVES.": For reasons neither she nor her attorney, Victor Rabinowitz, could fathom, Marvel Jackson Cook would be the first witness called to testify in the Army-McCarthy hearings. Her sharp humor, which Du Bois remembered from *Crisis* days and savored occasionally as the Cooks' neighbor at 409 Edgecombe, would serve her well when she amused the senate hearing room in answer to Senator Everett Dirksen's opening question: She replied that she was born "across the St. Croix River from where Senator McCarthy is from, but we're not all the same out that way." "... CAREER OF THE COUNCIL ON AFRICAN AFFAIRS.": *EAACH*, II, pp. 666–667. "... YERGAN'S DEPARTURE WAS OVERDUE.": Hugh H. Smythe to Du Bois, February 17; Du Bois to Paul Robeson, February 9; Shelton Hale Bishop to Du Bois, February 13; Alphaeus Hunton to Du Bois, February 20; Du Bois to Max Yergan, March 5; CAA Minutes, March 5; Du Bois to Smythe, March 7; Du Bois to Robeson, March 8; Smythe to Hunton, March 12; Du Bois to Hunton, March 26, 1948, all in Du Bois Papers/UMass.

539. "... A WONDERFUL GUY TO BE WITH.": Lewis interview with Frederick Vanderbilt Field, September 1, 1987; see Frederick V. Field, *From Right to Left: An Autobiography* (Westport, CT: Laurence Hill, 1983); Max Yergan's papers are housed at Howard University's Moorland-Spingarn Research Center. Regrettably, his heirs refuse all requests for access to these papers, despite continual entreaties by the Howard archivists. There is a well-researched unpublished biography of Max Yergan, courtesy of its author: David Henry Anthony, III, "A Pan-African Enigma: The Life and Times of Max Yergan, 1892–1975" (Work in progress. Limited circulation. Copyright 1994. David Henry Anthony, III). For George Padmore's opinion of Yergan in South Africa, see George Padmore to Du Bois, August 9,

1946, Du Bois Papers/UMass, also in Aptheker, ed., *Correspondence*, III., pp. 146–147. ". . . FIRST NEGRO TO TEACH AT CITY COLLEGE.": Lewis interview with Lloyd Brown, October 26, 1995, and with Maurice Schappes, February 2, 1995, 'on demonstration against Yergan at New York's City College. ". . . SIMPLY HAS THE CARDS STACKED AGAINST IT.": For Yergan's views as expressed by Logan, see Rayford Logan Diaries, November 16, 1947, Manuscript Division, Library of Congress. ". . . A WITNESS IN A SMITH ACT TRIAL.": See FBI Memorandum marked "Confidential, December 6, 1948, Director, FBI, Attention FBI Laboratory, re: Communist Party, USA—Brief, Internal Security—C. Dr. Max Yergan, File No. 100-210026, Vol. 12, serials 225–270, FOIA;" Harold Cammer acted as attorney for the Hunton-Robeson group and provided a vivid account of the dispute, Lewis interview with Harold Cammer, September 7, 1989. ". . . PROSCRIPTION BY THE ATTORNEY GENERAL.": Du Bois, *Autobiography*, 345; FBI records reveal that the Bureau closed its files on Du Bois on April 27, 1943: "Case placed in closed status inasmuch as extensive investigation has failed to reveal any subversive activities." Du Bois's file was reactivated at some point in 1948: FBI document, August 26, 1948. WEB Du Bois File No. 100-99729 Vol. 1, serials 1–30.

FBI surveillance of Shirley Graham commenced surprisingly late. J. Edgar Hoover ordered an "appropriate investigation of this subject in order to determine if her name should be included in the Security Index." Graham HQ 100-370965, Section 1. October 3, 1950.

FBI surveillance of Max Yergan was ongoing and intensive. His telephone conversations were electronically recorded and transcribed. As Yergan spoke frequently with the CPUSA top leadership, the FBI considered him "a prize source of information": Max Yergan File, Vol. 2, Serials 49–73.

William Alphaeus Hunton was also placed on the Security Index and as late as April 1966 categorized as "potentially dangerous" because of his background; membership or participation in Communist movement; or he "has been under active investigation as member of other group or organization inimical to U.S.": Bureau File No. 100-30762; NY 100-52572.

540. ". . . BIOGRAPHY OF DU BOIS POSSIBLE.": Du Bois to Herbert Aptheker, January 8, 1948, Du Bois Papers/UMass, also in Aptheker, ed., *Correspondence*, III, pp. 177. ". . . UNFAVORABLE REVIEW OF *DUSK OF DAWN*.": Lewis interview with Herbert Aptheker, March 19, 1986. ". . . MAJOR APTHEKER RETURNED.": Mari Jo Buhle, et al., eds., *op. cit.*, p. 52; Aptheker and Du Bois never quite developed the deep warmth that Du Bois felt for Louis Burnham or Hugh Smythe, whose future appointment to New York's City College faculty and ambassadorship to Syria were to be surprisingly unaffected by his association with Du Bois. Thelma Ostrow Newman, C.B. Baldwin's secretary, says that Du Bois surprised her by revealing that "his friendship with Herbert was a professional one; it wasn't a social one. He entrusted me with that." Lewis interview with Thelma Newman, May 3, 1987. ". . . HELPFUL FOR HIM TO BE DOING.": Lewis interview with Doxey Wilkerson; Lloyd Brown assumed that most everyone on the left understood that Du Bois "would not take leadership from anybody. So that he would go along with you if he agreed with where you were going." Lewis interview with Lloyd Brown, October 26, 1995.

540. ". . . A.U. PENSION AND A SIMILAR NAACP ANNUITY.": Du Bois to Anita Blaine, December 14, 1948, Papers of Anita Blaine, Wisconsin Historical Society; also in Du Bois Papers/UMass and Aptheker, ed., *Correspondence*, III, pp. 230–232. ". . . ANITA MCCORMICK BLAINE.": Henry Wallace to Du Bois, November 29, 1948, Du Bois Papers/UMass. ". . . THE PATRICIAN BELFRAGE.": Lewis interview with Cedric Belfrage, July 2 1987. A British citizen, it was Belfrage's article in the *NATIONAL GUARDIAN* on the Rosenbergs that led to his imprisonment and deportation. Eventually taking refuge in Cuba with his American wife Mary Bernick, Belfrage settled 1963 in Cuernavaca, Mexico, as a writer/translator, and proprietor with Mary of a successful hostelry. ". . . SLIGHTLY ABSENT-MINDED.": Du Bois to Anita Blaine, June 2, 1949, Du Bois Papers/UMass. On Du Bois's arrangement with Blaine, see Aptheker, ed., *Correspondence*, III, pp. 230–236.

541. ". . . THE JEFFERSON SCHOOL.": Howard Selsam to Du Bois, January 28; Du Bois to Selsam, February 4; Selsam to Du Bois, February 17, 1948, all in Du Bois Papers/UMass. ". . . EFFUSIVE ANNETTE RUBINSTEIN.": Lewis interview with Annette Rubinstein, October 16, 19[?]. ". . . WOULD SOON COST HIM HIS CHURCH.": Lewis interview with William Howard Melish, March 10, 1988. Richard Morford to Du Bois, June 6, 1946, Du Bois Papers/UMass. ". . . OFFERED DU BOIS THE *NATIONAL GUARDIAN*.": Cedric Belfrage to Du Bois, September 24; Belfrage to Du Bois, October 2; Du Bois to Belfrage, October 7; Belfrage to Du Bois, November 10, 1948, all in Du Bois Papers/UMass. ". . . 'THE NEGRO SINCE 1900: A PROGRESS REPORT'.": On the *New York Times* article, see Du Bois to Arthur Sulzberger, July 12; Lester Markel to Du Bois, July 15; Du Bois to Markel, August 2; Du Bois to Editor

of the *Times*, August 3; Daniel Schwartz to Du Bois, August 6; Du Bois to Schwartz, August 9; Schwartz to Du Bois, September 2; Du Bois to Schwartz, September 10; Schwartz to Du Bois. October 21, 1948, all in Du Bois Papers/UMass. For "The Negro Since 1900" report which finally appeared in the *Times*, November 21, 1948, see Aptheker, ed., *Writ. Periodical Lit.*, IV, pp. 90–96. ". . . CONSOLIDATION OF AFRICAN POSSESSIONS.": Du Bois, "Africa Today," in *National Guardian* (November 29, 1948); "Africa for the Europeans," in *National Guardian* (December 6, 1948), both in Aptheker, ed., *Writ. Periodical Lit.*, IV, pp. 855, 858. ". . . WRITING SOME ARTICLES.": Author interview with Jim Aronson, undated. ". . . SAVED WESTERN CIVILIZATION IN THE SECOND WORLD WAR.": William Howard Melish to Du Bois, November 14, 1946; Du Bois to Melish, November 16, 1946, both in Du Bois Papers/UMass.
542. ". . . MADE WAR INCREASINGLY LIKELY.": Hannah Dorner to Du Bois, December 16, 1948; Muriel Alexander for Dorner to Du Bois, December 29, 1948, both in Du Bois Papers/UMass. ". . . WHICH ALONE CAN AVERT WAR.": Shirley Graham Du Bois, *His Day Is Marching On: A Memoir of W.E.B. Du Bois* (Philadelphia: J. B. Lippincott, 1971), p. 106.
543. ". . . TO THE TERRIBLE PROSPECT OF WAR.": Irving Howe, "The Culture Conference," in *Partisan Review* (May 1949), pp. 505–511; William Barrett, "Culture Conference at the Waldorf: The Artful Dove," in *Commentary* (May 1949), pp. 487–493. See also the account of the conference by one of its principal architects, Howard Fast, op. cit., 199.
543. ". . . EVEN SOME OF THE POLICEMEN IN THE GARDEN.": Graham Du Bois, *His Day Is Marching On*, p. 350. Du Bois wrote a detailed account of the conference for Nina—see Will to Nina, March 30, 1949, Du Bois Papers/UMass, also in Aptheker, ed., *Correspondence*, III, pp. 260–261.
544. ". . . HEAD OF THE SMALL ASP DELEGATION.": See the moving footage taken by Julius Lazarus of Du Bois in flight with the delegates in the Paul Robeson Papers, MSRC/Howard University. ". . . TWO DAYS LATER.": Graham Du Bois, *His Day Is Marching On*, p. 116. ". . . PEOPLE OF SEVENTY-EIGHT NATIONS.": Ibid., p. 118. ". . . PRECISELY WHAT ROBESON HAD SAID.": Duberman, op. cit., p. 342. ". . . CIVIL RIGHTS COMMUNITY.": Ibid., p. 344; Arnold Rampersad, *Jackie Robinson: A Biography* (New York: Knopf, 1997), 213–14.
545. ". . . LEADING THE WORLD TO HELL.": Du Bois, *Autobiography*, p. 350. ". . . TREASONABLE STATEMENT.": Martin D. Jenkins to Du Bois, April 29, 1949; Lillian Murphy to Jenkins, May 4, 1949—both in Du Bois Papers/UMass, and also in Aptheker, ed., *Correspondence*, III, p. 259.
545. ". . . BACK ON THE JOB OF PEACE AT THE END OF MAY.": Du Bois to Anita Blaine, May 6, 1949, Anita Blaine Papers, Wisconsin Historical Society, also in Du Bois Papers/UMass. Du Bois also wrote Ethel Ray Nance of his activities—"Dear Marielle: Here I am on the Riviera facing the Mediterranean and writing a novel. I've been here ten days until I finish in two weeks." Du Bois to Ethel Ray Nance, May 22, 1949, Ethel Ray Nance Correspondence, in the possession of the Nance family. This letter and others were read by me into a tape recorder in the presence of Mrs. Nance on March 17, 1987. For another more detailed summary of his peace activities during this time, see Du Bois, *In Battle for Peace* (New York: Masses & Mainstream, 1952). ". . . UTTERLY SELFISH CORPORATE WEALTH.": See U.S. Congress, Committee on Foreign Affairs, *Mutual Defense Assistance Act of 1949: Hearings on H.R. 5748 and 5895*, 81st Congress, 1st session, July 28–29 and August 1–2, 5 and 8, 1949, pp. 261–270, also in Aptheker, ed., *Contributions by W.E.B. Du Bois in Government Publications and Proceedings* (Millwood, N.Y.: Kraus Thompson, 1980), p. 395. ". . . IN MOSCOW.": Du Bois, *Autobiography*, 352. No doubt mischievously, Du Bois wrote to Henry Luce about his forthcoming Moscow trip asking if Luce would be interested in having articles written. See Du Bois to Luce, August 17, 1949, Du Bois Papers/UMass; Memorandum to Mr. Luce from J. S. Billings, August 18, 1949—"We want nothing from this negro commie—an all around trouble maker. He sponsors all Red meetings in the US . . . do you want me to write him NO for you?" Luce writes beneath Billings' signature, "No—the best answer is none!", John Shaw Billings Papers, the South Carolina Library. I am most grateful to Mr. Miles S. Richards of Columbia, SC, for the Luce background. ". . . RETURNING HOME VIA PRAGUE AND WARSAW.": Du Bois to Anita Blaine, September 27, 1949, Du Bois Papers/UMass, also in Aptheker, ed., *Correspondence*, III, p. 268. ". . . AND AFFECTIONATE THANKS.": Du Bois to Ruzena Mrstikovia, September 21, 1949, Du Bois Papers/UMass. ". . . I SHALL ARRIVE SATURDAY.": Du Bois to Virginia Alexander, March 10, 1949, Du Bois Papers/UMass.
545–46. ". . . HAD WARNED THAT NINA WAS FAILING.": Lewis interview with Elsie Matthews, 1990. ". . . I BURY MY WIFE.": "I was not, on the whole, what one would describe as a good husband." Du Bois, "I Bury My Wife," in *Chicago Globe* (July 15, 1950) and *Negro Digest* (October 1950), 37–39. ". . . ONE OF THE MOST RESPECTED.": Oetje John Rogge to Du Bois, February 5, 1949, Du Bois Papers/

UMass. For O. John Rogge's precocious career, see Michael R. Belknap, ed., *American Political Trials* (Westport, CT: Greenwood Press, 1981), ch. 9. "... EINSTEIN SENDING ENCOURAGING STATEMENTS FROM TIME TO TIME.": Einstein to Du Bois, May 5, 1949, Du Bois, Du Bois Papers/UMass.

546. "... PEACE INFORMATION CENTER.": Lewis, interview with Bernard Jaffe, Abbott Simon, and Sylvia Soloff, October 25, 1994. "... A JOB WORTH DOING.": Du Bois, *In Battle for Peace*, p. 36. "... SHE ADORED DU BOIS.": Lewis, interview with Kyrle Elkin, February 14, 1987.

547. "... THE SPURIOUS 'PEACE OFFENSIVE' OF THE SOVIET UNION.": Acheson's comment in the *New York Times*, July 17, 1950. "... SYMPATHY WITH THE CRIPPLED, IMPOVERISHED AND DEAD.": Du Bois to Acheson, July 14, 1950, Du Bois Papers/UMass, also in Aptheker, ed., *Correspondence*, III, pp. 303–304. "... AN AGENT OF A FOREIGN PRINCIPAL.": William Foley to Du Bois, August 11, 1950, Du Bois Papers/UMass, also in Aptheker, ed., *Correspondence*, III, p. 306.

547. "... A YOUNG CZECH FILM TECHNICIAN.": Du Bois Williams appears to have undergone considerable changes in appearance in a short time. A fellow student who sailed with Williams to the 1950 World Youth Congress in Prague describes her as "a very attractive young lady." But seeing her later, he was struck that she "was a whole different person from the person I had met just six years before." See Lewis, interview with Chester Davis, July 26, 1989. "... THE LOVE OF HER LIFE.": Lewis, interview with Du Bois Williams, June 28, 1987. "... TEAR-STAINED LETTERS.": Du Bois to Du Bois Williams, n.d.; Elizabeth Moos to Du Bois, October 31, 1950—both in Du Bois Papers/UMass. "... TO DISBAND THE ORGANIZATION.": Du Bois to William E. Foley, n.d., Du Bois Papers/UMass, also in Aptheker, ed., *Correspondence*, III, pp. 308–309.

548. "... INDICTMENTS.": Du Bois, *In Battle for Peace*, p. 55. "... WE MUST BE MARRIED RIGHT AWAY.": Du Bois, *In Battle for Peace*, p. 58; Shirley Graham Du Bois, *His Day Is Marching On*, p. 139. "... THE UNANNOUNCED CEREMONY.": Du Bois, *In Battle for Peace*, p. 59.

548. "... THE FEDERAL CEREMONY." See *United States of America v. Peace Information Center, William Edward B. Du Bois, Kyrle Elkin, Elizabeth Moos, Abbott Simon, Sylvia Soloff. Points and Authorities in Opposition to the Defendants' Motion to Dismiss the Indictment and for Other Relief. Criminal No. 178–51.* "... SEPARATE AND UNEQUAL LOCATIONS.": Du Bois, *Battle for Peace*, p. 60.

548–49. "... A GROUP PHOTO.": The photograph is reproduced in Shirley Graham Du Bois, *Du Bois: A Pictorial Biography* (Chicago: Johnson Publishing Co., 1978), p. 87. "... UNLOCKED OUT HAND-CUFFS.": Arraignment proceedings before Judge F. Dickenson Letts, District Judge of the U.S. District Court for the District of Columbia, Criminal No. 178–51, February 16, 1951; Du Bois, *In Battle for Peace*, p. 71. The long run of Democratic administrations had finally ended Perry Howard's reign as GOP national committeeman and a dispenser of federal patronage, but the Howards were still one of the most influential Negro families in Washington. Perry Howard's explosion that afternoon—"Take off those handcuffs"—had disconcerted the federal marshal. See Graham Du Bois, *His Day Is Marching On*, p. 143. "... DEGRADED BY THE WHOLE PROCESS.": Lewis interview with Gloria Agrin, September 25, 1984. "... THE ONE THING ALL PEOPLE WANT—PEACE.": Du Bois, quoted in Aptheker, ed., *Correspondence*, III, 310–11. Kyrle Elkin claims that this statement was actually composed by himself and Abbott Simon, a claim that is corroborated by Simon, who adds that David Graham was also present at the Dunbar Hotel for the drafting of the statement. For another description of the arraignment by a participant, I am indebted to Kyrle Elkin for his "W.E.B. Du Bois, The Last Years—A Memoir" (typescript in my possession); also, Lewis interview with Kyrle Elkin.

549. "... WASHED HIS HANDS OF THE EVENT.": Horne, *Black and Red*, p. 164. "... TO HAVE MY NAME ASSOCIATED.": Margaret Mead to E. Franklin Frazier, February 8, 1951, Du Bois Papers/UMass. "... SHEER HYPOCRISY.": Ralph Bunche to E. Franklin Frazier, January 29, 1951, Du Bois Papers/UMass. Du Bois would apologize in Madison Square Garden to Jewish Americans for Bunche, described as a disgrace to his race for his perceived lack of sympathy for the Jewish position in Palestine. Texts of congratulatory telegrams are in appendix to Du Bois: *In Battle for Peace*, 186–90. See Charles Henry, *Ralph Bunche: Model Negro of American Other?* (New York: New York University Press, 1999), pp. 242–243; Urquhart, op. cit., p. 198. "... IT WAS A MAD HOUSE.": Lewis interview with Louise Patterson, June 29, 1987. "... ROBESON SPOKE WITH GREAT EMOTION.": Du Bois, *Autobiography*, p. 369; Graham Du Bois, *His Day Is Marching On*, pp. 225–226; Horne, *Black and Red*, pp. 158–160. "... REAL HONEYMOON.": "... A REAL HONEYMOON.": Lewis interview with Abbott Simon, September 17, 1988, and Vivian Hallinan, June 2, 1993. "... ROUGHLY IDENTICAL LETTERS.": Du Bois to Ethel Ray Nance, January 8, 1951: "Dear Marielle: I am going to marry Shirley Graham in February. No, I'm not crazy, but lonesome and so is she, although she has plenty of time being only forty-six. But we

have work in common and it seems to us a good idea. You'll always be our good friend," Du Bois Papers/UMass. "... THE PURCHASE OF AN IMPOSING BROOKLYN TOWNHOUSE.": Graham Du Bois to Du Bois, September 1, 1950, Du Bois Papers/UMass.

550. "... THIS DICHOTOMY IN THE NEGRO GROUP.": Du Bois, *In Battle for Peace*, pp. 76, 74. "... A STATEMENT OF AUGUST NEUTRALITY.": Du Bois, Ibid., p. 90. At its national convention in July, the NAACP membership voted a strong resolution in support of Du Bois. See Du Bois, Ibid., p. 90. It is interesting to note that the FBI determined after several years of observation that its file on Du Bois should be closed in 1943: "Case placed in closed status inasmuch as extensive investigation has failed to reveal any subversive activities," FBI Document, August 26, 1943. Six years later, the FBI remained unsure of Du Bois: "report on Du Bois's speech in Prague, Paris, and Moscow, stated that 'it had very little political significance,' FBI Document, September 20, 1949. The bureau's interest in Du Bois became more intense the following year: J. Edgar Hoover to Special Agent in charge of Atlanta ordering an updating of files and forwarding of them to the New York FBI office, FBI Document, June 12, 1950, all in William Edward B. Du Bois File, No. 100-99729, Vol. 1, Serials 1-30, FOIPA/Justice Department. "... FAILED TO OBTAIN ENOUGH SIGNATURES.": Du Bois, *Battle for Peace*, p. 72.

550. "... SINCE THE DEAN OF CANTERBURY WAS THERE.": Du Bois to Cedric Dover, July 10, 1951, Du Bois Papers/UMass. "... ALONG THE DEFENSE FUND ROUTE.": An effective propaganda document that was widely distributed by the National Committee to Defend Dr. Du Bois was Albert E. Kahn's *Agent of Peace*, a five-cent pamphlet printed by the Hour Publishers in 1951. "... BEING TAUGHT IN THE CLASSROOM AT BERKELEY.": Leon Litwack to David Levering Lewis, July [undated] 1986. Professor Litwack's 1996 Organization of American Historians (OAH) presidential address also references his meeting with Du Bois. For the McCarthy-era impact on Berkeley and Du Bois, I have benefited from the recollections of a Berkeley student who heard Du Bois speak off campus in 1953 at the local Unitarian church. Rule 17 forbade radical speakers from appearing on campus. David Levering Lewis interview with Ruth Simmons, Rutgers University special collections librarian, February 20, 1987.

551. HOLTZOFF: Judge Alexander Holtzoff was extremely conservative and had manifested hostility to the defendants at the arraignment in February. On May 11, 1951, Agrin petitioned the court to take depositions in France—"Transcript of the Proceedings," *U.S. v. Peace Information Center*, May 11, 1951, Criminal No. 178–51: "Order for Commission to Take Deposition of Jean LaFitte in Paris, Republic of France," filed. Holtzoff. Transcript of Trial preliminaries provided through the Freedom of Information Act, United States Department of Justice, CRM-941166F, and includes the deposition of Jean LaFitte, general secretary of the Councils of the Partisans of Peace. Also see the arraignment proceedings before Judge F. Dickenson Letts, District Judge of the U.S. District Court for the District of Columbia, Criminal No. 178–51, February 16, 1951; also "Statement by Dr. W.E.B. Du Bois," April 27, 1951 (undelivered). Du Bois Papers/UMass. "... THE GOVERNMENT LAWYERS WERE CLOWNS.": Lewis interview with Gloria Agrin, September 25, 1986. "... UNTIL *AFTER* THE TRIAL.": Arthur Garfield Hays to Du Bois, April 26, 1951, Du Bois Papers/UMass. "... THE INSTITUTE OF ARTS AND LETTERS.": Felicia Geffen to Mark Van Doren, February 16, 1951, Archives of the American Academy and Institute of Arts and Letters.

551. "... TO SAVE THE SYMBOLIC DU BOIS.": Du Bois, *In Battle for Peace*, p. 85. "... A WAVE OF WONDER.": Langston Hughes, "The Accusers' Names Nobody Will Remember, But History Records Du Bois," Chicago *Defender*, October 6, 1951. "... A POWERFUL SPEECH.": *Ibid.*

552. "... FINAL TWO-HOUR ARGUMENT.": Lewis interview with Gloria Agrin, September 25, 1986. "... GANG UP.": Gerald Meyer, *Vito Marcantonio: Radical Politician, 1902–1954* (Albany: State University of New York Press, 1989). "... ON THE PLATFORM.": *Ibid.* For a profile of Marcantonio, see Buhle, *op. cit.*, 447–48; Vito Marcantonio, *I Vote My Conscience: Debates, Speeches and Writings, 1935–1950*, selected and edited by Annette T. Rubinstein and Associates (New York: The Vito Marcantonio Memorial, 1956). "... IMPRESSIVE TOTALS FOR DU BOIS.": Du Bois, *In Battle for Peace*, pp. 43–50; Du Bois, *Autobiography*, p. 363; Du Bois's campaign manager for the senate run was George Murphy, maverick member of the *Afro-American* newspaper family, assisted by Ewart Guinier, the first director of the Black Studies program at Harvard University. The George Murphy Papers (unprocessed, when examined by the author), M-H/HU, are posterior to the 1950 ALP campaign, but contain much of interest on Du Bois and his circle during the mid-1950s and later. "... THE POLITICAL AND PUBLIC RELATIONS STAKES.": Lewis interview with Abbott Simon, September 17, 1988; Lewis interview with Kyrle Elkin, February 14, 1987. It appears certain that the government offered Du Bois a deal, as Du Bois stated, "I have refused too many offers to sell out in America to be bribed in my old age"—Du

Bois to Judge James A. Cobb, April 10, 1951, provided by Stanley Faulkner to the author, and also in Du Bois Papers/UMass, and Aptheker, ed., *Correspondence*, III, pp. 313–314. The volume of petitions addressed to the President asking that the indictment against Du Bois be dismissed was quite high. See "Petitions," General File, Papers of Harry S. Truman, Harry S. Truman Library. Text of Vito Marcantonio's summation in *I Vote My Conscience*, 441–45. On Du Bois's generous reading of McGuire, see *In Battle*; and less generous interpretations by Joffe, Elkin, and Simon in Lewis interviews. ". . . TO SPECULATE ON SPECULATIONS.": on the dismissal of the case, see "Du Bois, 4 Others Acquitted, Judge Rejects Gov't Frameup," *Daily Worker*, November 21, 1951; "Selection Takes Most of Day; Trial Recessed to Tuesday," Washington *Afro-American*, November 10, 1951.

553. ". . . MY DEATH WAS PRACTICALLY REQUESTED.": Du Bois, *Autobiography*, 414. I am indebted to the surviving participants for the drama of the trial and the victory celebration, Lewis group interview with Bernard Jaffe, Abbott Simon, and Sylvia Soloff, October 25, 1994.

Chapter 15: Exeunt

554. ". . . WERE LIKE COLD DYNAMITE.": Henry Miller, *The Rosy Crucifixion, Book Two: Plexus* New York: Grove Press, 1963), p. 562. ". . . EVEN EISENHOWER.": Du Bois, "The Hard-Bit Man in the Loud Shirts," *National Guardian*, Jan. 22, 1953, also in Aptheker, *Newspapers*, II., pp. 905–6, p. 905. . . . Only by war can China . . . : Du Bois, "There Must Come a Vast Social Change in the United States," *National Guardian*, July 11, 1951, also in Lewis, *Reader*, pp. 619–21. On the escalation of the Cold War and at the close of the Truman and *commencement of the Eisenhower administrations, cf.,* Stephen Ambrose, *Eisenhower: The President and Elder Statesman, 1952–69* (New York: Simon & Schuster, 1984), chaps. 1, 2; Douglas Brinkley, *Dean Acheson, The Cold War Years, 1953–71* (New Haven: Yale University Press, 1992), pp. 8–20; Hamby, op. cit., Chap. 30; Townsend Hoopes. *The Devil and John Foster Dulles* (Boston: Atlantic-Little Brown, 1973); Kovel, *op. cit.*, chaps 4, 5. LaFeber, *op. cit.*, pp. 109–85.

555. ". . . WE CHARGE GENOCIDE.": See, William L. Patterson Papers, MSRC/HU: William L. Patterson *The Man Who Cried Genocide: An Autobiography* (New York: International Publishers, 1971). "THE ROSENBERG CONVICTION—IS THIS THE DREYFUS CASE OF COLD WAR AMERICA?" *National Guardian*, August 15, 1951; cited in Ronald Radoch and Joyce Milton, *The Rosenberg File* (New Haven: Yale University Press, 1997; orig. pub. 1983), p. 324.

555. ". . . IN THE MIDST OF WAR AND FEAR."; Du Bois, "Speech of Dr. W.E.B. Du Bois at a Save the Rosenbergs rally under the auspices of the Civil Rights Congress, on Thursday, Oct. 23, 8 P.M. at Central Plaza"; and Re: *Rosenberg v. United States*. No. 111, *Sobell v. United States*, No. 112. Motion of Dr. W.E.B. Du Bois and others for leave to file brief as *amici curiae*, with service, filed November 7, 1952. Oct. Term, 1952, Du Bois Papers/UMass; also, Du Bois, "The Rosenbergs, Ethel and Michael, Robert and Julius", *Masses & Mainstream*, 6 (July 1953): 10–12, also, in Lewis, *Reader*, pp. 793–95. The legalisms of the Rosenberg case are accessibly discussed in Michael E. Parrish, "Cold War Justice: The Supreme Court and the Rosenbergs." *American Historical Review*, 82 (October 1977): 805–42; see, also, David M. Oshinsky, "A Story with No Heroes: The Rosenbergs Revisited," *The New Leader*, Oct. 17, 1983, pp. 5–21; and the two antagonistic but complementary exhaustive Rosenberg monographs: Walter and Miriam Schneir, *Invitation to an Inquest* (New York: Pantheon Books, 1965) and Ronald Radosh and Joyce Milton, *The Rosenberg File: A Search for the Truth* (New York: Holt, Rinehart and Winston, 1983); for a legacy, Robert and Michael Meeropol, *We Are Your Sons: The Legacy of Ethel and Julius Rosenberg* (Urbana: University of Illinois Press, 1986; orig. pub. 1975). The declassification of the Venona intercepts, the project of U.S. intelligence to decode Soviet-ciphered communications, appears to resolve the debate about the intentions, if not the significance, of Julius Rosenberg's transmittal of classified atomic information. See, John Earl Haynes and Harvey Klehr, *Venona: Decoding Soviet Espionage in America* (New Haven: Yale University Press, 1999); also, Michael Dobbs, "The Man Who Picked the Lock," *Washington Post*, Oct. 19, 1996, p. 1.

555. ". . . JACKSON TRIAL.": At one point, asked if he saw any communists in the court room, Du Bois gave Jackson's principal attorney, Charles Duncan of Howard Law School, a jolt when he replied that he thought he did not: David Levering Lewis interview with Charles Duncan, Nov. 4, 1988, David Levering Lewis interview with James and Esther Jackson, October 8, 1994, Joseph R. Starobin, *American Communism in Crisis, 1943–1957* (Cambridge: Harvard University Press, 1972), pp. 220–21. *United States of America vs. Alexander Trachtenberg et al.* Criminal 136–7. New York, June 29, 1956. Stenographer's

minutes. Mary Kauffamann, one of the defense attorneys in Trachtenberg, says Du Bois was shamefully treated at the trial—"the ugliest that you could possible imagine"—but Du Bois was "terrific": David Levering Lewis interview with Mary Kaufmann, October 22, 1987.

556. "... UNCRITICAL PATRIOTISM.": Du Bois, "Negroes and the Crisis of Capitalism in the United States," *Monthly Review*, 4 (April 1953): 478–85, in Lewis, *Reader*, pp. 622–25, p. 625. "... WAS PURE DR. PANGLOSS": White, "Time for a Progress Report," *Saturday Review of Literature*, Sept. 22, 1951, pp. 9–10, 38–41.; and Kenneth Janken, "From Colonial Liberation to Cold War Liberalism: Walter White, the NAACP, and Foreign Affairs, 1941–1955." *Journal of Ethnic and Racial Studies*, 21 (November 1998): 1074–95. "... BETHUNE'S NAME FROM THE ATTORNEY GENERAL'S LIST ...": Carl Murphy to Eleanor Roosevelt [telegram], April 25, 1952, and Carl Murphy to Mary McLeod Bethune, May 14, 1952, in Carl Murphy Letters, MSR/HU "... SAID THE INDIGNANT HUGHES": Hughes, quoted in, Arnold Rampersad, *The Life of Langston Hughes*, II, p. 218, and p. 259; according to James Aronson, Du Bois was so angered by Hughes's perfidy that it was necessary to return his initial *Guardian* opinion piece because of its vituperation. "THE DOCTOR" WAS RESPECTFULLY REQUESTED TO SOFTEN THE TEXT.: David Levering Lewis interview with James Aronson.

556. "... GLOBAL SCHEME OF THINGS CAPITALIST.": Du Bois, "Negroes and Socialism", *National Guardian*, April 29, 1957, in Aptheker, *Newspapers*, II., pp. 988–89.

557. Du Bois, "Russia and America: An Interpretation" [draft mss, dedicated to Shirley Graham. n.d. 1940's?], Du Bois Papers/UMass; Robert Giroux, editor, Harcourt, Brace and Co, to Du Bois, Oct. 17, 1949; Robert Giroux to Du Bois, July 13, 1950, Du Bois Papers/UMass. Gerald Horne quotes Herbert Aptheker's critical appraisal of the manuscript which he found grossly deficient in Communist orthodoxy. Horne, *op. cit.*, pp. 267–68. Du Bois, "On Stalin", *National Guardian*, Mar. 16, 1953, in Aptheker, *Newspapers*, II., p. 910, and in Lewis, *Reader*, pp. 796–97. Interestingly, "Russia and America" was declined by Jessica Smith of *Soviet Russia Today* because of concerns for accuracy: Jessica Smith to Du Bois, June 29, 1950, Du Bois Papers/UMass.

557. "... WAGE SLAVERY AND RAGING BEYOND NORTH AMERICA.": A curious exchange between Du Bois and Ovid Gorchakov (writer, translator, and influential Party member), assigned to the care and feeding of the Du Boises while in Russia (resting at the exclusive spa for the nomenklatura at Barveekha) was related to me by Gorchakov. Venturing to criticize Party abuses, he found Du Bois wholly unmoved: David Levering Lewis interview with Ovid Gorchakov, Dec. 3, 1998; and see the essay implicitly reproving Krushchev for exposing Stalin: Du Bois, "Socialism and Democracy," *American Socialist* (Jan. 1957): 6–9, in Aptheker, *Periodical Lit.*, IV., pp. 278–83.

557. "... ONE OF SHIRLEY GRAHAM'S CLOSEST TIES.": Interview with Annette Rubinstein, October 16, 1988; Fast, *Being Red*, pp. 354–58. ... WHOSE VERY POSSIBILITY HE NOW DEEPLY DOUBTED: Du Bois, "Cold War Hysteria," *National Guardian*, June 11, 1956, in Aptheker, *Newspapers*, II., pp. 968–69. "... ON THE BLUE HERON EDITION OF SOULS.": After acquiring the plates to the original (1903) edition of *Souls* from A. C. McClurg & Co., of Chicago in 1946, Du Bois agreed in 1953 to have Howard Fast's Blue Heron Press publish a new edition. In October 1953, Blue Heron released the new edition. Herbert Aptheker enumerates "seven substantitive changes" to the 1903 text, all having to do with references to Jews. Du Bois was urged to agree to these changes in order to eliminate any possibility of anti-Semitic interpretation. Du Bois himself refers in a February 27, 1953, letter to Jacob Schiff's much earlier observation along these lines. I found my interviews with Aptheker and Morris Schappes informative on this point: David Levering Lewis interview with Herbert Aptheker, March 19, 1986, and David Levering Lewis interview with Maurice Schappes, February 2, 1995.

557. ... PAID WITH THEIR LIVES: for a sampling of assessments of the personal and institutional costs of the Red Scare useful to the author, cf, Noam Chomsky et al., *The Cold War and the University* (New York: The New Press, 1997); Griffin Pariella, op. cit.; Harvey Klehr and Ronald Radosh, *The Amerasia Spy Case: Prelude to McCarthyism* (Chapel Hill: University of North Carolina Press, 1996); Joel Kovel, *op. cit.*, Harvey Matusow, *False Witness* (New York: Cameron & Kahn, 1955); Gary May, *Un-American Activities: The Trials of William Remington* (New York: Oxford, 1994); Roger Morris, *Richard Milhous Nixon: The Rise of an American Politician* (New York: Henry Holt and Co., 1990): David M. Oshinsky, *A Conspiracy So Immense: The World of Joe McCarthy* (New York: Free Press, 1983); Edward Pessen, *Losing Our Souls: The American Experience in the Cold War* (Chicago: Ivan R. Dee, 1993); Richrd H. Rovere, *Senator Joe McCarthy* (Berkeley: Univ. of California Press, 1996; orig. pub. 1956); Ellen Schrecker, *No Ivory Tower: McCarthyism and the Universities* (New York: Oxford,

1986); Ellen Schrecker, *Many Are the Crimes: McCarthyism in America* (Boston: Little, Brown and Co., 1998).
557.   ". . . DISMANTLING OF LEGAL SEGREGATION.": Du Bois, "What Is the Meaning of 'All Deliberate Speed'?" *National Guardian*, Nov. 4, 1957, also in Aptheker, *Newspapers*, II., pp. 999–1002. Du Bois, "The School Desegregation Decision". *National Guardian*, May 31, 1954, in Aptheker, *Newspapers*, II., pp. 930–31.
558.   ". . . NEGATIVE REFUSAL TO USE VIOLENCE.": Du Bois, "Crusader Without Violence," *National Guardian*, Nov. 9, 1959, in Aptheker, *Newspapers*, II, p. 1017, and Lewis, *Reader*, pp. 361–62. Martin Luther King Jr., to W.E.B. Du Bois, March 19, 1956, Du Bois Papers/UMass; also Aptheker, *Correspondence*, III, pp. 399–400; Du Bois, "Gandhi and the American Negroes", *Gandhi Marg* (Bombay), (July 1957): 1–4; also in Aptheker, *Periodical Lit.*, IV., pp. 286–88; and Horne, *op. cit.*, pp. 240, 250. ". . . HOPE OF AMERICAN NEGROES IS SOCIALISM.": Du Bois, "Negroes and Socialism". *National Guardian*, April 29, 1959, also in Aptheker, *Newspapers*, II., p. 988.
558.   ". . . TRY TO CATCH UP WITH THEM.": Du Bois, *The American Negro and the Darker World*, [six-page pamphlet] (New York: National Committee to Defend Negro Leadership, 1957), in Aptheker, ed., *Pamphlets and Leaflets*, pp. 329–33.
558.   ". . . TOWARDS SOCIALISM AND AGAINST COLONIALISM.": "Du Bois Addresses H. U. Body", *Hill Top*, April 14, 1958] On the Schomburg Collection event, at which Van Wyck Brooks, E. Franklin Frazier spoke and a paper from Judge Jane Bolin was read by Regina Anderson, see, Graham Du Bois, *op. cit.*, pp. 224–26; "NYPL Schomburg Collection, 1953–57," Folders 1 and 2, Manuscripts, NYPL.
559.   ". . . NEVER HESITATE, NEVER FALTER.": Du Bois, "To an American Born Last Christmas Day," *National Guardian*, March 10, 1958, in Aptheker, *Newspapers*. II., pp. 1006–1007, p. 1007.
559.   ". . . THESE PROPHETS WILL BE W.E.B. DU BOIS.": Truman Nelson, "W.E.B. Du Bois: Prophet in Limbo", *The Nation*, Jan. 25, 1958, pp. 76–79; Du Bois, "To an American Born Last Christmas Day," *National Guardian*, March 10, 1958, also in Aptheker, *Newspapers*, II., pp. 1006–1007, p. 1006 run of congratulatory birthday letters, in Aptheker, *Correspondence*, III., pp. 426–29; Francis Broderick quote, in Graham Du Bois, *His Day*, pp. 27–33; John Hope Franklin, "W.E.B. Du Bois: A Memoir," pp. 26–27; Francis L. Broderick, *W.E.B. Du Bois: Negro Leader in Time of Crisis* (Stanford: Stanford University Press, 1959); Elliott M. Rudwick, W.E.B. *Du Bois, A Study in Minority Group Leadership* (Philadelphia: University of Pennsylvanian Press, 1960); a telegram over the signature of Chicago Mayor Richard J. Daley applauded the recognition to be accorded "a renowned leader whose life span . . . encompassed much of the most significant and stirring history of our nation": Richard J. Daley to Truman Gibson, 5 May 1958, Du Bois Papers/UMass, also in Aptheker, *Correspondence*, III, p. 426.
560.   ". . . BUT IN 1892 NEVER ADMITTED.": Du Bois, *Autobiography*, p. 23; and, especially, the detailed letter, Du Bois to George Murphy, pp. 432–34, Du Bois Papers/UMass; also Aptheker, *Correspondence*, III., pp. 432–34.
560.   ". . . A MASS OF WESTERN POTTAGE.": The complete text of the Accra speech is found in Du Bois, *Autobiography*, p. 403.
560.   ". . . NIKITA IMPRESSED [HER] GREATLY THIS TIME.": David Levering Lewis interview with Alla Bobricheva (Gorchakov), Dec. 11, 1988: Du Bois, *Autobiography*, pp. 33, 34.
561.   . . . WORKERS' PARADISE DESERVED CRITICISM, AFTER ALL: David Levering Lewis interview with Ovid Gorchakov, Dec. 3, 1988. On Barveekha, Du Bois to George Murphy, December 26, 1958, Du BoisPapers/UMass, in Aptheker, *Correspondence*, III, pp. 432–34, p. 433.
561.   *Vospominanva* [*The Autobiography*] differs in a number of ways from the English original. At my request, Edward Belaiev of Columbia University's Harriman Institute prepared a concordance of the Russian- and English-language texts. The Russian text deletes passages of Du Bois's early personal life that would make him appear to have been privileged. Also, his notorious elitism is much softened in the Russian text. Angus Cameron who founded with Albert Kahn the progressive publishing house of Cameron & Kahn, had been excited by Du Bois's autobiography, but then had second thoughts about the dated quality of portions. He and Shirley Graham urged Du Bois, unsuccessfully, to add new material. David Levering Lewis interview with Angus Cameron, May 18, 1993.
562.   ". . . PROLETARIAT TOWARD THEIR FUTURE DUTIES.": Du Bois, *Autobiography*, p. 38.
562.   ". . . IN AMERICA HE WAS A 'NIGGER.' ": Du Bois, "The Real Reason Behind Robeson's Persecution," *National Guardian*, April 7, 1958, also in Lewis, *Reader*, pp. 798–800, p. 799 ". . . AND SHOUTING THEIR NAMES.": Graham Du Bois, *His Day*, p. 270; also, see Duberman, *op. cit.*, p. 473.

562. "... A CONSPIRACY SO IMMENSE ...": Joseph McCarthy in, David Oshinsky, *A Conspiracy So Immense* "... TELL THE WHOLE WORLD.": Graham Du Bois, *His Day*, p. 277; and, pp. 266–67, for her airport observations.

563. "... ON THE FAMINE.": Cf., Jasper Becker, *Hungry Ghosts: Man's Secret Famine* (New York: The Free Press, 1996), pp. 99 and 270. "... BEIJING WAS IN PANIC.": Dr. Li Zhisui, *The Private Life of Chairman Mao* (New York: Random House, 1994), p. 288.

564. "... WHERE AM I AND WHY?": Du Bois's message to Africa, Du Bois, *Autobiography*, pp. 405–08.

564. " ... THE PRIMACY OF ECONOMICS AND PSYCHOLOGY ... ": The exchange between Mao Tse-tung and Du Bois is related by Strong, in Tracy B. Strong and Helene Keyssar, *Right in her Soul: The Life of Anna Louise Strong* (New York: Random House. 1983), pp. 300–301; and cf., Anna Louise Strong, *I Change Worlds, The Remaking of an American* (New York: Henry Holt and Co., 1935). "... FOR ALL THE DECENT PEOPLE OF AMERICA.": Graham Du Bois, *His Day* ... p. 285.

564. "... THE VAST MIRACLE OF CHINA TODAY.": Du Bois, "The Vast Miracle of China Today," *National Guardian*, June 8, 1959, p. 6, also, Lewis, *Reader*, pp. 626–30.

565. "... I AM THROUGH.": Du Bois, *Autobiography*, p. 413 "... THE DOCTOR CAN'T CURE OLD AGE!": Graham Du Bois, *His Day*, p. 301.

565. "... RESEARCH RESOURCES AT HIS DISPOSAL.": Kwame Nkrumah to Du Bois, April 4, 1957: February 5, 1958; Du Bois to Nkrumah, February 15, 1958; Nkrumah to Du Bois, June 18, 1960, Du Bois Papers/UMass; and Horne, *op. cit.*, p. 216. "I gathered that they are quite sympathetic about the whole thing," Nkrumah wrote, "but that they have to stand by their rules and regulations and the long and short of it is—No Affidavit—No Passport!" (Nkrumah to Du Bois, Feb. 5, 1958). "So far as I am concerned, I am not a member of the Communist Party and I never have been," Du Bois replied. "I still stand on my decision that the Secretary of State has no business to ask me as a prerequisite to travel to make any statement as to my political or religions beliefs." (Du Bois to Nkrumah, Feb. 2, 1958).

565. " ... REPUBLIC HEADED BY A DISCIPLE.": Du Bois, "I Never Dreamed I Would See This Miracle," *National Guardian*. September 19, 1960, in Aptheker, *Newspapers*, II., pp. 1033–1036.

566. "... AN APPOINTMENT WITH MY TAILOR.": David Levering Lewis interview with Josephine Martin, November 10, 1986. Du Bois's New York physician Morris Pearlmutter confirms Martin's stroke diagnosis and Du Bois's recovery: David Levering Lewis interview with Morris Pearlmutter, December 3, 1986.

566. "... SUBSTANTIAL SUPPORT HAS BEEN VOTED.": Kwame Nkrumah to Du Bois, cablegram, Feb. 15, 1961. Du Bois Papers/UMass, in Aptheker, *Correspondence*, III, pp. 448. "... NKRUMAH ON RELOCATION.": See, run of letters between Nkrumah and Du Bois, in Aptheker, *Correspondence*, III., pp. 443–459.

566. " ... SHOULD HAVE TAKEN HIM INSTEAD.": Interview with Mae Miller Sullivan, April 1977. "... ON FREEDOMWAYS.": See Esther Cooper Jackson and Constance Pohl, eds., *Freedomways Reader: Prophets in Their Own Country* (Boulder: Westview Press, 2000); and Buhle and Buhle, eds., *Encyclopedia of the Left*, pp. 244–45.

566. "... SCRAMBLING ABOARD THE BANDWAGON.": Du Bois, "A Program of Reason, Right and Justice for Today", *National Guardian*, May 23, 1960, in Aptheker, *Newspapers*, II., pp. 1025–28, p. 1025.

567. "... THEFT AND MURDER BY YOUR VOTES.": Du Bois, "Let Us have Freedom In America," *Worker*, March 6, 1960, also, Aptheker, *Periodical Lit.*, IV., pp. 315–19, p. 318.

567. "... IT IS DOOMED TO SELF-DESTRUCTION.": Du Bois to Gus Hall, October 1, 1961, Du Bois Papers/UMass, and Aptheker, *Correspondence* III., pp. 439–40, p. 440.

567. "... PLACED AT DU BOIS'S DISPOSAL.": According to Donald Stewart, then a young Ford Foundation officer in Nigeria, the house provided to the Du Boises by the Ghana government belonged to the Ford Foundation. Stewart was sent to Accra to explain to the Du Boises that the property would have to be repossessed. Invited to lunch, Stewart was overwhelmed by the Du Bois presence and charmed by Shirley Graham Du Bois. He abandoned his mission and returned to Lagos: David Levering Lewis interview with Donald M. Stewart, n.d., 1995. "... AFTER ONLY A MONTH IN THE COUNTRY.": Du Bois, "Pan Africa: The Story of a Dream" [eleven-page draft], 1961, Du Bois Papers/UMass. Ghana during the Nkrumah years, 1956–1966, was the African American Camelot, drawing hundreds of black Americans to Accra and Kumasi, many enrolling at the national university of obtaining teaching positions in it, with some intending to remain in Ghana indefinitely. Others considered themselves obligated to visit. Cf., David Levering Lewis, "Ghana: A Memoir," *The American Scholar* (winter 1999):

39–60; Maya Angelou, *All God's Children Need Traveling Shoes* (New York: Random House, 1986); and Leslie Laccy, *The Rise and Fall of a Proper Negro: An Autobiography* (New York: Macmillan, 1970).

568.   "... FOR A SUCKER.": David Levering Lewis interview with Angus Theurmer, August 15, 1991.

568.   "... BUT GARVEY WAS THE SOURCE.": David Levering Lewis interview with Adu Boahen, August 20, 1986.

568.   "... HE JUST LISTENED. ...": David Levering Lewis interview with Albert Blaustein, n.d. 1986.

568.   "... HE KNEW THINGS WEREN'T RIGHT ...": David Levering Lewis interview with Anna Livia Cordero, May 30, 1989.

569.   "... SICK, AND SLOWLY DYING MAN.": Ralph McGill, "W.E.B, Du Bois." *Atlantic Monthly*, November 1965.

569.   "... REFUSED TO RENEW HIS PASSPORT.": A somewhat complicated story. The Du Boises left the U.S. embassy indignant at the refusal of officials to renew their passports. Du Bois announced his intention to renounce U.S. citizenship. In fact, however, no action was taken either by the embassy in Accra or the State Department when Du Bois accepted Ghanaian citizenship, the result being that Du Bois, unintentionally, retained his U.S. citizenship and became also a Ghanaian. I am indebted to William B. Wharton, retired general counsel in the Passport Division of the U.S. State Department for researching this information.

570.   "... TOOK HIS LEAVE IN TEARS.": Graham Du Bois, *His Day*, p. 366–67.

571.   "... DISTORTION OF EDUCATION AND FAILURE OF JUSTICE WIDESPREAD.": Du Bois, "Negroes and the Crisis of Capitalism in the United States," *Monthly Review* 4 (April 1958): 478–85, in Lewis, *Reader*, pp. 622–25, p. 623.

571.   "... SOMETIME IT MUST BE FULLY ANSWERED.": Du Bois, *The Suppression of the African Slave Trade to the United States of America, 1638–1870* (Millwood, N.Y.: Kraus-Thomson Ltd., 1973; orig. pub. 1896), p. 199.

INDEX